THE DOCTRINE OF
THE WORD OF GOD

CHURCH DOGMATICS

BY

KARL BARTH

VOLUME I

THE DOCTRINE OF THE WORD OF GOD

SECOND HALF-VOLUME

EDITORS

REV. G. W. BROMILEY, PH.D., D.LITT.

REV. PROF. T. F. TORRANCE, D.D., D.THEOL.

EDINBURGH : T. & T. CLARK, 38 GEORGE STREET

THE DOCTRINE OF
THE WORD OF GOD

(Prolegomena to Church Dogmatics, being Vol. I, 2)

BY

KARL BARTH, Dr.Theol., D.D., LL.D.

TRANSLATORS

Rev. Prof. G. T. THOMSON, D.D.
Rev. HAROLD KNIGHT, D.Phil.

Edinburgh: T. & T. CLARK, 38 George Street

Authorised English Translation from
DIE KIRCHLICHE DOGMATIK, I :
Die Lehre vom Worte Gottes, 2

Published by

EVANGELISCHER VERLAG A.G.
ZOLLIKON—ZÜRICH

PRINTED IN GREAT BRITAIN BY
MORRISON AND GIBB LIMITED

FOR

T. & T. CLARK, EDINBURGH

NEW YORK: CHARLES SCRIBNER'S SONS

FIRST PRINTED · · · · · · 1956
LATEST IMPRESSION · · · · · 1963

EDITORS' PREFACE

Twenty-one years have now passed since the first half-volume of Karl Barth's *Kirchliche Dogmatik, Die Lehre vom Worte Gottes*, was translated by Prof. G. T. Thomson and published in English under the title *Church Dogmatics, The Doctrine of the Word of God.* The second world war interrupted the programme of work upon the succeeding volumes, and its effects upon the printing industry have made the production of such massive books an even more formidable and costly enterprise. Work was further delayed through the declining health of Prof. Thomson, who was able to offer only a draft translation of sections 13–20 of the second half-volume of *The Doctrine of the Word of God.* Since then, with the encouragement and unfailing support and courtesy of the publishers, T. & T. Clark of Edinburgh, a team of scholars and theologians has been engaged on the subsequent nine volumes which have appeared to date. Most of these have now been translated, and although the work of editorial revision and printing is slow and exacting, it is hoped that two part-volumes may now appear each year, the immediate successors of the present volume being IV, 1, *The Doctrine of the Atonement*, and II, 1, *The Doctrine of God.*

The translation of Barth's *Kirchliche Dogmatik* is far from being an easy task, not only because of the difficulty of his German style, but particularly because of the sustained scientific intention of his dogmatic procedure. By directing relentless questions to the subject of inquiry Barth seeks to let the truth declare itself clearly and positively, and then he seeks to express the truth in its own wholeness without breaking it up into parts and thus dissolving its essential nature by unreal distinctions. It is this disciplined purpose which governs his style throughout and greatly lengthens the exposition. At every point he probes ruthlessly into the subject from all angles to make it declare itself, and then in long balanced sentences he sets the truth forth surrounded with careful clarifications and exact delimitations in subordinate clauses, and yet in such a way that by means of these *Abgrenzungen*, as he calls them, the whole truth is made to appear in its own manifoldness and in its native force.

This makes it very difficult for the reader until he realises that even the style is subordinated to the scientific intention of the dogmatic procedure. But once he gets used to it and follows the method of exposition, in which Barth goes round and round the same point with a different series of questions, he discovers that, though he does not grasp it at first, the spiral method of procedure brings him face to face with different aspects of it until the truth comes home to him with great force and clarity. On the other hand, this makes it very difficult for the translator who wishes to turn the text into good English. To break up the long and carefully balanced sentences into short clear-cut statements would often destroy the scientific intention and dissolve the theological content into scholastic *distinctiones*, the very thing which Barth seeks to avoid. The English translation, therefore, while working with shorter sentences, must be as faithful as possible to the style of Barth in so far as that is dictated by his deliberate procedure. Often this can be done only by transposing the order and repeating the subordinate clauses lest they should be cut off from the main subject as independent items of truth. At the same time, it is desirable to erase from the English text those many particles, emphases and exclamatory nuances which are very characteristic of Barth's vigorous and humorous personality but which have no real equivalents and can hardly be retained if the translation is to read like English. If in the following out of these principles something characteristic of Barth has been omitted from this translation, it is only in order that his own thought may be more clearly accessible to the English reader.

The publication of this half-volume completes the English version of Barth's Prolegomena to Church Dogmatics. In these two half-volumes, which are the foundation for all that follows, Barth has sought to work out in thoroughgoing fashion a critical and truly scientific understanding of the relation between faith and reason. He insists that reason is unconditionally bound to its object and determined by it, and that the nature of the object must prescribe the specific mode of its activity. Faith is this reason directed to the knowledge of God, and it involves a way of knowing that answers to the nature of the unique and incomparable object—the living God; that refuses to prescribe arbitrarily to the object how it is to be known; and that humbly tries to be obedient to the divine revelation in Jesus Christ alone as given to us in the Holy Scriptures. Dogmatic theology is thus understood as the discipline which we must undertake within the bounds of the Church where the Word of God is heard in the preaching of the Gospel, where we are face to face with the mystery of Christ as true God and true Man, and where we are given, through the outpouring of the Holy Spirit, to participate in Him, in His life, death and resurrection. Thus the great heart of Barth's theology is the doctrine of Jesus Christ. In theology as in faith we give ourselves to the obedience of Christ, and let all our thinking be taken captive by Him. That is why the doctrine of the person and work of Christ forms the centre and core of all Christian theology and determines all our thinking in the Christian Church.

Although Barth seeks to expound this in all the wealth of our modern inheritance in language and thought, he does so by carrying on a discussion with the whole history of Christian theology, and above all by grounding his exposition on the exhaustive exegesis of the Holy Scriptures through which we hear the Word of God speaking to us in the Church. Thus instead of binding theology to the philosophy of one age, like an Aquinas or a Schleiermacher, Barth has sought to give theology such an expression in our thought that the living Truth becomes the master of our thinking, and not thinking the master of the Truth.

In the present half-volume the translation of pp. 1–660 has been done by Prof. G. T. Thomson, and of pp. 661–884 by Dr. Harold Knight. The whole translation has been carefully scrutinised and extensively revised to give it a homogeneous character—the main burden in this respect being borne by Dr. G. W. Bromiley. The editors wish to record their gratitude to Prof. J. K. S. Reid and the Rev. T. H. L. Parker as assistant editors, to the former for his assistance in the revision and the reading of the proofs, and to the latter for many valuable corrections and suggestions at the proof stage. They also wish to pay tribute to the printers for their patience and meticulous care with very difficult manuscripts.

In this and all succeeding volumes, the biblical quotations are always given in the Authorised Version, except where a different rendering is specifically demanded by the German original.

EDINBURGH, *Christmas* 1955.

IN PLACE OF A FOREWORD

It is not we who can sustain the Church, nor was it our forefathers, nor will it be our descendants. It was and is and will be the One who says: " I am with you alway, even unto the end of the world." As it says in Heb. 13 : " Jesus Christ, *heri, et hodie, et in secula.*" And in Rev. 1 : " Which was, and is, and is to come." Verily He is that One, and none other is or can be.

For you and I were not alive thousands of years ago, but the Church was preserved without us, and it was done by the One of whom it says, *Qui erat,* and *Heri.*

Again, we do not do it in our life-time, for the Church is not upheld by us. For we could not resist the devil in the Papacy and the sects and other wicked folk. For us, the Church would perish before our very eyes, and we with it (as we daily prove), were it not for that other Man who manifestly upholds the Church and us. This we can lay hold of and feel, even though we are loth to believe it, and we must needs give ourselves to the One of whom it is said, *Qui est,* and *Hodie.*

Again, we can do nothing to sustain the Church when we are dead. But He will do it of whom it is said, *Qui venturus est* and *in secula.* And what we must needs say of ourselves in this regard is what our forefathers had also to say before us, as the Psalms and other Scriptures testify, and what our descendents will also experience after us, when with us and the whole Church they sing in Psalm 124 : " If the Lord himself had not been on our side, when men rose up against us," and Psalm 60 : " O be thou our help in trouble, for vain is the help of man."

. . . May Christ our dear God and the Bishop of our souls, which He has bought with His own precious blood, sustain His little flock by the might of His own Word, that it may increase and grow in grace and knowledge and faith in Him. May He comfort and strengthen it, that it may be firm and steadfast against all the crafts and assaults of Satan and this wicked world, and may He hear its hearty groaning and anxious waiting and longing for the joyful day of His glorious and blessed coming and appearing. May there be an end of this murderous pricking and biting of the heel, of horrible poisonous serpents. And may there come finally the revelation of the glorious liberty and blessedness of the children of God, for which they wait and hope in patience. To which all those who love the appearing of Christ our life will say from the heart, Amen, Amen.

LUTHER (W.A. 54, 470 and 474 f.).

CONTENTS

CHAPTER II

THE REVELATION OF GOD

PART II. THE INCARNATION OF THE WORD

PART III. THE OUTPOURING OF THE HOLY SPIRIT

CHAPTER III

HOLY SCRIPTURE

CHAPTER IV

THE PROCLAMATION OF THE CHURCH

CHAPTER II
THE REVELATION OF GOD

PART II
THE INCARNATION OF THE WORD

CHAPTER II

PART II

THE INCARNATION OF THE WORD

§ 13

GOD'S FREEDOM FOR MAN

According to Holy Scripture God's revelation takes place in th fact that God's Word became a man and that this man has becom God's Word. The incarnation of the eternal Word, Jesus Christ is God's revelation. In the reality of this event God proves that He is free to be our God.

1. JESUS CHRIST THE OBJECTIVE REALITY OF REVELATION

The doctrine of God's three-in-oneness gives the answer to the question about the subject of the revelation attested in Holy Scripture. This answer may be summarised by saying that the revelation attested in Holy Scripture is the revelation of the God who, as the Lord, is the Father from whom it proceeds, the Son who fulfils it objectively (for us), and the Holy Spirit who fulfils it subjectively (in us). He is the One God in each of these modes of being and action, which are quite distinct and never to be identified with each other. God is the constant Subject of revelation. Neither in His Son in whom He becomes manifest to us, nor in His Holy Spirit in whom He is manifest to us, does He become the predicate or object of our existence or action. He becomes and He is manifest to us. But this very becoming and being is and remains a determination of His existence. It is His act, His work.

It is with this becoming and being, this twofold objective and subjective fulfilment of revelation that we are concerned now. That means, we have to deal, in the first place, with the incarnation of the Word, with Jesus Christ as God's revelation for us, and after that with the outpouring of the Holy Spirit as God's revelation in us.

In considering this we must not for a moment lose sight of the previous answer we gave to the question about the subject of revelation, namely, the doctrine of the Trinity. On the contrary, it is

inevitable that in the light of that discussion we give the same decisive answer to these further questions about the nature of revelation. Every question about the objective and subjective reality of revelation must likewise lead us to the lordship and glory of the one God. Otherwise we should be passing by the evidence of Holy Scripture in search of a different revelation.

But the answer to the question about the subject of revelation authorises, nay compels us to ask further questions here also. We could not allow the first question to be put to us or the first answer to be given to us, without actually having before us the further questions about what God does for us, and what God does in us, in His revelation, and the answers they require regarding the incarnation of the Word and the outpouring of the Holy Spirit. Likewise the doctrine of the Trinity itself, so far as it teaches not only the divinity of God the Father, but also the divinity of the Son and of the Holy Spirit in their special modes of being and action, demands that we evaluate the proper work of revelation on its objective and subjective sides, and thus grasp in its totality the concept of the divine revelation.

In these second and third elements in the concept of revelation we are concerned with two questions intimately related to each other and complementary to each other. It is both possible and right to formulate them from different standpoints. We may, for example, ask how and with what object the event of revelation actually takes place. We may also ask what is taking place and what is the power, significance and effect of revelation. We may ask about God's self-manifestation and His manifestation to us, in the sense of the objective and the subjective reality of His revelation. We might wish to regard revelation in the first case as the movement proceeding from God to man, in the second as that proceeding from man to God. With a view to a thorough clarification or revision of the concepts, we might also inquire into divine spontaneity and human receptivity in revelation. But a better way of putting the question is to ask, (1) how far God in His revelation is free for us, i.e., free to reveal Himself to us, free to be our God without at the same time ceasing to be God the Lord ; and (2) how far God in His revelation is also free in us, i.e., free to deal with us as His own, who belong to Him and obey Him, although we are but men, and sinful men at that. This second question at once includes and answers the other question : how far in God's revelation we become free for Him, so that He can be manifest to us. This question about the freedom of God for man and in man is the one which points most comprehensively and decisively to the two answers which we have to take up here. God is not prevented either by His own deity or by our humanity and sinfulness from being our God and having intercourse with us as with His own. On the contrary, He is free for us and in us. That is the central content of the doctrine of Christ and of the doctrine of the Holy Spirit.

Christology and Pneumatology are one in being the knowledge and praise of the grace of God. But the grace of God is just His freedom, unhindered either by Himself or by us.

The object to which we first turn in continuing the analysis of the concept of revelation, which we began by developing the doctrine of the Trinity, is the doctrine of the incarnation of the Word of God made flesh. We are concerned here with the first basic part of Christology, the part which answers the question : How does the encounter of His revelation with man become real in the freedom of God? The doctrine of the person and work of Christ has its own necessary place within the doctrine of reconciliation, with which we are not yet directly concerned. The first part of Christology, specially called the doctrine of the incarnation, belongs to the doctrine of the Word of God, and so to prolegomena, to the basis of Church Dogmatics.

If we turn our attention now to the question *how the encounter of His revelation with man is real in the freedom of God*, then the very first point to be made is that this question is and must be the primary one. For there is also a second question regarding the incarnation of the Word of God. It concerns the possibility of revelation : How is the encounter of His revelation with man possible in the freedom of God ? This second question, too, has its propriety and its necessity. It is the question of interpretation, the question of exegesis, which must certainly follow the question of fact, the question of the text. But it can only follow it. It must not claim to precede it.

It would be fruitless at this point to begin considering what conditions must be fulfilled in God and in ourselves to enable this revelation to encounter us—in order subsequently to look round and see whether revelation actually encounters us in accordance with these conditions. Even in the most searching consideration and determination of such conditions, even in the most believing acknowledgment that a fact of revelation corresponds with these conditions, there lurks a fallacy. In such considerations we put ourselves, so to speak, midway between God and man, with a twofold illusion and assumption, the claim to know what God can and must do, to know what is necessary and appropriate to us men so that revelation between Him and us can become an event. This illusion and assumption will certainly betray itself when the second element, our claim to know our own needs and possibilities, is openly or secretly put forward as the compass and measure of the first, our claim to know the divine possibilities or necessities. In such circumstances, it is inevitable that even the most conscientious theology will prescribe for God what His revelation must be and how it must be handled, if He is to count upon our recognition of it as such. But the revelation of God cannot be circumvented in this way. And even if in spite of that we are prepared to acknowledge, perhaps very willingly and very piously, a fact of revelation corresponding to our conditions, yet even in this acknowledgment there lurks the same fallacy. For once more we plant ourselves mid-way, this time between the supposedly God-given fact on the one side, and the result of our own deliberations on the other. When our alleged faith is brought face to face with this fact, it is seen to repose only upon the cunning conclusion that God has made out His case in accordance with our well-founded convictions. Even the most positive result of this process, perhaps squaring exactly in vocabulary with the Bible and with every traditional dogma, will make no difference to the fact that it is certainly not God's revelation that we have recognised in this way. The point midway between God and man and the point midway between the conviction gained there and the God-created fact, are not the points from which the man thinks and speaks whose thought and speech really have God's revelation as their object. Such a man must inevitably be deprived of this midway position. He neither imagines that he can use what he himself holds to be appropriate to God and beneficial to man as a standard with which to measure God, nor does he affirm the God-created fact on the ground that it corresponds to the conviction he has gained with the help of that same standard.

It may be asserted very definitely that no matter whether a theology claims to be liberal or orthodox, it is not a theology of revelation in so far as it rests openly or secretly upon this reversal, in so far as it asks first what is possible in God's freedom, in order afterwards to investigate God's real freedom. In the middle position which it takes—and in the measure in which this middle position is really its point of view—it will of necessity be completely blind to the fact of God's revelation. Whatever it regards and proclaims as this fact is one of those constructs of memory or imagination in which even the blind can indulge. This will become apparent sooner or later when it finds that it cannot deal with this fact with any more confidence and assurance than it can deal with a construct of memory or imagination. This reversal is the great temptation of all theology. We shall therefore not be surprised to meet traces of it here and there as early as the Apologists of the second century of the Church, and thereafter in every subsequent development. In the Protestant theology which has prevailed since about 1700, it has actually become a fundamental presupposition. The basic difference between this theology and the theology of older Protestantism is that from some source or other, some general knowledge of God and man, it is known beforehand, known *a priori*, what revelation must be, may be, and ought to be. In these conditions and by using such a standard of measurement, a definite attitude to the reality of revelation can be taken up *a posteriori*. That need not necessarily mean criticism or even negation of this reality. Pious, even inspired recognition of this reality is perfectly possible. It should be noted that theological Neo-Protestantism in its beginnings (J. F. Buddeus and C. M. Pfaff among the Lutherans ; S. Werenfels, J. F. Osterwald, J. A. Turrettini among the Reformed, and in C. Wolff and the theologians of his school, also in its later forms) could deal with the Bible and dogma in a thoroughly conservative way. Nevertheless even in these conservative forms it means misconstruction, nay, denial of revelation. Only by happy inconsistencies, only by occasional abandonment of the basic presupposition, only by contradicting itself, can it ever be anything else.

If God's freedom is that which a man thinks he ought to hold on the ground of his own knowledge of God and man, then he is by no means speaking of what is possible in God's freedom. And if he grounds his recognition of the fact created by God's freedom, upon the conviction gained by this roundabout procedure, then what he recognises has nothing to do with a fact created through God's freedom—not even if this conviction of his coincides in form with the statements of the Bible and of dogma. In that case it may equally well take another form at any moment. In virtue of the very authority by which he now says Yes, he may also say No. The same judge who is satisfied with God to-day may no longer be so to-morrow. It is not the incidence of this dissatisfaction that is so bad, not the outbreak of a partial or complete denial of biblical or dogmatic statements, although mere affirmation of them is not much good either. On the contrary, we might almost say " Thank God," if on occasion revolt at least admits openly that it is revolt. The bad thing, and that is revolt indeed, is the denial that barely conceals the illusion and presumption that we have either power or right to say Yes or No to God's revelation, merely because we are satisfied or dissatisfied with it. Where a man becomes so arbitrary, where he has assumed this role of judge, whatever his verdict may be, he has nothing to do with God or with the God-created fact of revelation. His verdict is an empty delusion, it is objectless, no matter if it be given in positive or in negative terms.

The position to be maintained against this is, simply, that theological judgments and convictions can only be reached when what a man acknowledges and confesses to be appropriate to God and salutary for himself is that which God has previously determined and revealed to be appropriate to Himself and salutary for man. Divine determination and revelation, and not man's approval, are the criterion of what is appropriate to God and salutary for us. It is not for our human approval to precede the divine approval, but to follow it up. The God-created fact of revelation is the manifestation of this divine approval. And therefore it is the judge of our convictions and not *vice versa*. Moreover, this Judge may utter a Yes or a No. God's revelation may mean for us illumination or blinding, and the human attitude indicated thereby may mean faith or unbelief. From this standpoint even the thought and language of unbelief may have its own serious and weighty objectivity. The thought and language of faith at all events will possess objectivity not by preceding but by following up God's revelation, by desiring to understand but not to prove it. In relation to revelation it will not be free, i.e., free to exercise authority or power over it from some superior vantage point, but will be altogether bound to it, so as to do nothing but reflect the thought and language of revelation.

If we are asked how we arrive at this position and what justification we have for rejecting so definitely the alternative assumption which sets man up as the judge of God's possibilities and realisations, we answer that, so far as the confrontation and relationship of God and man, of divine acts and human reactions spoken of in Holy Scripture attest God's revelation to us, they cannot betoken for theology the kind of object which it can calmly docket along with other objects. On the contrary, if theology is really to correspond to the witness of Holy Scripture, they must give theology its essential forms and they must also determine its methods, for without these it could not be theology. That is to say, unless it takes account of these, theology could not even perceive its object, not to speak of classifying it with ease or excitement. The very definite order of being which Holy Scripture makes manifest, when in its witness to God's revelation it confronts and relates God and man, divine facts and human attitudes, enforces an order of knowing corresponding to it. It does not enforce faith. It does not even exclude unbelief. But where it finds faith, it does enforce a basically obedient thought and language. And where it finds faith, it excludes free thought, i.e., thinking which openly or secretly hurries ahead of the previously given object, acts critically toward it by way of selection and distinction, patronising it with its applause or reproach. Correspondingly, it excludes sovereign language, which in the last resort appeals against itself to man's responsibility. It excludes an arbitrary theology. If there is anything sure in biblical exegesis it is this, that where according to the Bible God's revelation to man was an event, there is none of that anticipatory thinking or that sovereign language, none of that *a priori* theology. The prophets and apostles thought and spoke merely as hearers, as hearers of a God who is bound only to His own law and in no sense to any presupposition of man.

The inner necessity of the theological method employed in Holy Scripture and demanded by it can be made clear by following out the contrary method to its consequences. To characterise the latter in terms of the arbitrariness by which man takes liberties with God is hardly sufficient. This arbitrariness is itself obviously just a symptom of a very peculiar opinion which man has formed about himself, about God and about his own attitude to God. In the usual critical way, he thinks that he can set himself over against God as partner and opposite number. He therefore thinks that God and His revelation belong to the sphere of his own capacity, since by revealing Himself God does something which man can foresee and anticipate in its content as well as in its form. To a certain extent God is doing His duty in revealing Himself to man ; and, moreover, it is His duty to reveal Himself to man precisely in a way which the latter can foresee and anticipate, and on the basis of such foresight and anticipation understand and appreciate. It belongs to man that God is and is free for him, and so becomes manifest to him. Thus that arbitrariness of his is quite in order. Because of his self-awareness he is also aware of what it must mean if God reveals Himself to him. He should and must measure the so-called revelations that meet him—so many encounter him claiming to be revelation—by the measure of himself, of his thoughts about what is appropriate to God and salutary for man. If this view is valid, that God is originally as bound to man as man is to God, the view that God is not the free Lord, His revelation not free mercy, the fact of His revelation not the presupposition, freely created by Him, of all our thought and language about it—if all this is valid, then arbitrariness must have its place, and the objection that such arbitrariness is illegitimate will be quite incomprehensible. Then will it not rather be praised as a fine gift of God Himself and used with the appropriate assurance ? But behind this view does there not still lurk something quite different ? In the speculative, *apriori-aposteriori*, critical thought and language about God and man, as it reached predominance in Protestant theology in the period of Leibniz, should there really be only a relation of parity between God and man ? Should we not rather posit here a relation of superiority in favour of man ? Such thought and language may of course be embellished and justified by the edifying reflection that, to enable man to know Him, God has permanently planted Himself in man's heart. Yet we are bound to agree with L. Feuerbach in his objection to theology, that the essence of such thought and language consists practically in man creating God for himself after his own image. No doubt this also may be interpreted as a work of serious, sincere piety. But in that case piety must mean a profound meditation by man on himself, a discovery of his inmost agreement with his own most intimate and essential being, a disclosure, affirmation and realisation of the entelechy of his I-ness, which constantly asserts itself in natural and historical form, in joy and sorrow, in good and evil, in guilt and reconciliation, in truth and error, and which ought to be addressed as a divine being. The contrast between the conditioning of man by God and that of God by man now becomes secondary, colourless and unimportant. Are the two not the same thing ? Is not the objection brought against the arbitrariness of man quite futile ? Have we not control of God, because we have control of ourselves, control of ourselves because we have control of God ? Can the second view be avoided, once we have admitted the first ?

It is not necessary to pursue these conclusions to their full limit, if the significance and basis of the other method is to become equally manifest. It is not necessary to go so far as to deny the objective reality of revelation, which is apparently the ultimate goal of this other method. It is a long way to Feuerbach from the " reasonable " or " mild " orthodoxy, which consciously and systematically used this method for the first time two hundred years ago. But the continuity of the way cannot be disputed. That must open our eyes to the fact, should we fail to see it otherwise, that the way of the prophets and apostles right from the start is quite a different way.

The method prescribed for us by Holy Scripture not only assumes that the entelechy of man's I-ness is not divine in nature but, on the contrary, is in contradiction to the divine nature. It also assumes that God is in no way bound to man, that His revelation is thus an act of His freedom, contradicting man's contradiction. That is why the language of the prophets and apostles about God's revelation is not a free, selective and decisive treatment of well-found convictions, but—which is something different—witness. That is, it is an answer to what is spoken to them, and an account of what is heard by them. That is why their order of knowing corresponds to the order of being in which God is the Lord but in which man is God's creature and servant. That is why their thought and language follow the fact of God's revelation, freely created and provided by Him. That is also why their interpretation of it is a following after, in which any revolt of man on the ground of any categories of understanding which he brings along with him is out of the question. That is why their conception of what is possible with God is guided absolutely by their conception of what God has really willed and done, and not *vice versa*.

If the aim of theology is to understand the revelation attested in the Bible, theology as distinguished from all philosophical and historical science of religion will have to adhere to this method quite rigidly. It is not thereby decided whether its thought and language is a thought and language based on faith or on unbelief. No one will deny that even the devil can quote the Bible, that unbelief too can imitate and adopt the method of Scripture and faith. But the decision whether the thought and language in a theology are based on faith or on unbelief is not a scientific, still less a human, decision. It belongs to the hidden judgment of God that sooner or later it unmasks a dead orthodoxy for what it is. But that cannot and ought not to hinder us from inquiring about the thought and language enjoined upon faith, or from deciding for this method because of its objectivity and against the other method because it lacks objectivity.

We have to remind ourselves of the need for this decision, if we are to think and speak correctly about " The Incarnation of the Word of God." As the approach to the doctrine of the Trinity is affected by the realisation that in order to perceive God's revelation at all we must follow the order of being in Holy Scripture and first ask about God as the Subject of revelation, so the approach to Christology is affected by the realisation that first we have to put the question of fact, and then the question of interpretation. Or (because interpretation is involved in the question of fact, and nothing but fact is involved in the question of interpretation) we must first understand the reality of Jesus Christ as such, and then by reading from the tablet of this reality, understand the possibility involved in it, the freedom of God, established and maintained in it, to reveal Himself in precisely this reality and not otherwise, and so the unique possibility which we have to respect as divine necessity.

In looking back on this consideration of method it remains for us to make the following points.

1. The definiteness with which we refused to speak first of the possibility (in the sense of " necessity ") of revelation, and only then of its reality, does not imply a negative verdict upon all attempts in the history of theology which have been undertaken in this order of sequence. I am not thinking now only of the fact that in the theological conceptions which follow this method—I would have the reader think throughout of the characteristic conceptions of Neo-Protestantism—even where the arrangement is obviously perverted, an element of right knowledge of things may always accompany them, and in practice does, thanks to their happy lack of logic, an element which may actually snatch them from complete futility, like a brand from the burning, in spite of their dubious character. It would go ill with the Church, particularly with the Evangelical Church, were this not actually and generally the case, even in modern times. In earlier times, however, it happened that the *apriori-aposteriori* procedure here rejected was applied in a thoroughly correct manner, harmless in arrangement, in meaning and purpose, at least at that time ; so that in spite of every objection to this procedure, in spite of the fallacy which its use already involved, it would be out of place to raise subsequent objection to what then took place. The first classical example of which I am here thinking is the *Cur Deus homo ?* of Anselm of Canterbury. In it Anselm wished *intelligere, rationabiliter* (and that *sola ratione, remoto Christo, sine scripturae auctoritate*) *demonstrare* the possibility or necessity of Christ's becoming man and of His reconciling death. In view of this programme he has often enough been accused of the " rationalism " which we have just rejected. But in this the important point is missed. It is undoubtedly in keeping with Anselm's peculiar method, which is applied in all his writings, that in *Cur Deus homo ?* he did not assume the truth of the incarnation because of the authority of the divine revelation, but first treated it as a question and then proved its truth. Yet his method cannot be called rationalistic, because of all the decisive elements by which he proves that the incarnation is possible (i.e., necessary) and so intelligible and true—his conceptions of God's purpose with humanity, of man's duty of obedience to God, of sin as an infinite guilt, of the necessary wrath of God, of man's incapacity to redeem himself, of God's glory as the Creator—not one is a general truth. They are all derived from revelation, which for merely incidental reasons arising from the special purpose of this work is not regarded as authority. And at the climax of his exposition even this " dogmatic rationalism " (if we may so speak) is expressly broken through with the declaration that *si vis omnium quae* (Christus) *fecit et quae passus est veram scire necessitatem, scito omnia ex necessitate fuisse, quia ipse voluit. Voluntatem vero eius nulla praecessit necessitas* (*C.d.h.* II 17). What else does this mean than that Anselm also did not think of the reality on the basis of an arbitrarily constructed possibility, but thought of its possibility on the basis of its reality ? Questions 12–19 of the *Heidelberg Catechism* are the other classical example calling for mention here. The important pronouncement upon Christ as the Mediator and Redeemer is there reached in the following way. God being righteous, grace exists for us who have become indebted to God only if, either by ourselves or through another, we pay for our sins. We cannot pay for ourselves, for we ourselves can but increase our guilt daily. But neither can any

other creature intervene on our behalf; for man is guilty; he is the debtor, not some other creature. Furthermore no creature is able to bear the burden of the wrath of God and to redeem another creature from it. On the one hand, therefore, the Mediator and Redeemer must be a true man, and on the other He must be stronger than all creatures, i.e., true God. True man; because man must do the paying, and for that he would have to be sinless. True God; because in the power of His divinity He has to bear the wrath of God and must restore righteousness and life to us. And now Q. 18 may lead us to the point. Who is that same Mediator who is at once true God and a true, righteous man? Ans.—Our Lord Jesus Christ, who is given to us for perfect redemption and righteousness. And Q. 19—Whence knowest thou that? Ans.—From the Holy Gospel. . . . That even the *Heidelberg Catechism* here takes the path from possibility (or necessity) to reality, and not, as was required, the other way round, we cannot fail to acknowledge. But let us not overlook the fact that here also all decisive elements in the course of proof, as the Scripture passages attached to the questions and answers show, must, in the authors' opinion, themselves be grounds based on revelation, and certainly not on interpretation. And, above all, let us not fail to note, that long before this weighing of the possibility (or necessity) of a Mediator and Redeemer, i.e., right in Q. 1 of the Catechism, the assumption of the reality of Jesus Christ is already made in extremely comprehensive fashion. Hence we may say of Anselm as of the authors of the *Heidelberg Catechism*, in spite of the way in which they present their position, that in point of fact they have not deduced revelation *a priori*, only to find it subsequently, *a posteriori*, fulfilled in Christ. If actually—and this must be our purpose also—they have asked about the rationality of faith, i.e., about the interpretation of revelation, still they were not thinking of any other rationality than that proper and appropriate to revelation itself. To that the noetic-dogmatic-scientific rationality of their deductions was actually meant to conform, to be adapted, and to be related to it as the yielding wax to the seal stamped upon it. The result of their deductions was as a matter of fact the same as their starting point. In this sense, *credo ut intelligam* means that in view of the fact that in faith God's objective truth has met and mastered me, I am determined under the instruction of this truth alone to give an account of the encounter in thought and speech. That for their purpose they have chosen the way from possibility to reality cannot in our eyes be any ground for disapproval. Of the estimation of man as the measure of all things, about which we have just been speaking, they have not actually made themselves guilty.

2. That does not mean, however, that we may and should take the same way to-day, even if, thanks to a happy lack of logic, it need not be altogether wrong for us either. No doubt it is still possible, in theory and in principle, to take this way quite harmlessly after the fashion of Anselm and the *Heidelberg Catechism*. Nevertheless it must be recognised that, if at that time it was at least liable to be misunderstood, yet now, because of the manner in which it has been trodden for the last two hundred years, it has become so compromising, so tempting and seductive, that in actual fact it has been made impossible for us. Consciously or unconsciously, the Neo-Protestant tradition, in which Lessing, Kant and Schleiermacher sought access to Christ along a road that could not lead to Him, is still far too active amongst us. It is extremely probable, therefore, that if we wished to take the same road we would involve ourselves in the fallacy of proving knowledge of Christ by a systematics of our own. And if we were sure that this would not be the case, we should very definitely have to face the possibility of being misunderstood on all sides. I speak as one who has tried it out. In connection with Anselm and the *Heidelberg Catechism* in particular, I tried as early as 1927, at the point of my Prolegomena corresponding to our section (p. 214 ff.), under the heading, "The Objective Possibility of Revelation," to prove that if the triune God wished to reveal Himself to man He would have to

become man, because only as man could He be at once hidden and manifest. I took care to guard myself against the interpretation that I wished to give a sketch of its possibility in advance of the fact of revelation. But if that had been clear, perhaps I should not have felt the need to make such a fuss about it. At all events, I was immediately misunderstood, in spite of precautions I had taken. To-day I think it better to begin and proceed in such a way as to avoid the need for any preliminary precautions against misunderstanding. It would be out of place, to-day, to say the least, to try to repeat what Anselm and the authors of the *Heidelberg Catechism* did. (In any exposition of Questions 12–19 of the *Heidelberg Catechism*, we must lay all the stress upon the Scripture passages and upon the background of Q. 1 if we are to avoid confusion.)

If we now question Holy Scripture about the reality of God's revelation, to which it claims to bear witness, and if we obtain from it the answer that Jesus Christ is this reality, it would be well to realise above all, that this answer, in spite of the problems in which it is presented to us, even in the plainest form in which we can hear and grasp it, points to a reality that is utterly simple, as simple as anything else in the world, as simple as only God is.

The answer of the New Testament to our question about the reality of God's revelation is to be found in the constant reiteration in all its pages of the name Jesus Christ. This name is God's revelation, or to be more exact, the definition of revelation arising out of revelation itself, taken from it and answering to it (cf. for what follows *Church Dogmatics* I 1 p. 363 ff. E.T.). In this name, says Peter, Ac. 4[10], the lame man of the Beautiful Gate of the Temple stands whole before all eyes. In this and in none other name is there salvation. The words Κύριος Ἰησοῦς Χριστός (Phil. 2[11]; 1 Cor. 12[3]; Rom. 10[9]) also are to be interpreted not synthetically but analytically—the name Jesus Christ is as such the name of the Lord. It is the first and at the same time the decisive and all-inclusive fact in which men should and can conceive revelation—exactly as in the Old Testament the name Yahweh is the revelation of Yahweh, the first and the last fact between Him and His people (cf. Oskar Grether, *Name und Wort Gottes im Alten Testament* 1934). That is precisely why we say that by the answer of the New Testament is meant the simple reality of God. The real fact, the fact meant, namely Jesus Christ and, earlier, Yahweh, did not admit of utterance, just because in both cases it was the simple reality of God. Any utterance of it by the witnesses could only hint, and was only meant to hint, that the One indicated by this name is the Self-Utterer, the Word. That is why all further utterances of biblical witness first point back to this name. In so doing, of course, they point past the name to the bearer of it, whom man can no longer express, because He wills to express or utter Himself in the power of the truth (ἀλήθεια) which He Himself is. But the utterance as utterance has the name for its content. What is ascribed to it in the way of attributes and values can only be an utterance about God's revelation, by being ascribed to this name and to no other. Imagine for a moment the relative clause in 1 Cor. 1[30], ὃς ἐγενήθη σοφία ἡμῖν ἀπὸ θεοῦ, δικαιοσύνη τε καὶ ἁγιασμὸς καὶ ἀπολύτρωσις, without the Subject Jesus Christ on which it depends, dependent upon some other subject. For the writers of the New Testament it would have become a totally meaningless statement in spite of the high content of its predicates. For them wisdom, righteousness, sanctification, redemption are not relevant conceptions in themselves, but only as predicates of the subject Jesus. And so one can never say of a single part of the narrative, doctrine and proclamation of the New Testament, that in itself it is original or important or the object of the witness intended. Neither the ethics of the Sermon on the Mount nor the eschatology of Mk. 13 and parallels, nor the healing of the blind, lame and possessed, nor the battle with the Pharisees and the Cleansing of the Temple, nor the statements of Pauline and Johannine metaphysics and mysticism (so far as there are any), nor love to God nor love to neighbour, nor the passion and death of Christ, nor the miraculous raising from the dead—nothing of all that has any value, inner importance or abstract significance of its own in the New Testament, apart from Jesus Christ being the Subject of it all. His is the name in which it is all true and real, living and moving, by which, therefore, everything must be attested. He is the μνστήριον τοῦ θεοῦ, ἐν ᾧ εἰσιν πάντες οἱ θησαυροὶ τῆς σοφίας καὶ γνώσεως ἀπόκρυφοι (Col. 2³).

It was always a serious misinterpretation of the New Testament as well as of the Old Testament, to think of discovering its content (after the manner of all legalism) in certain principles. It makes no difference whether it was the principle of sonship to God, or perhaps the principle of the struggle of true religion with the Church, or *vice versa* the principle of the Church as the place of the true transmission of salvation and adoration of God, or a definite moral principle (say that of action on conviction or that of unconditioned love), or the principle of a life-or-death metaphysics, or the principle of this or that mystical or social theory and practice which was to be preferred and presented as the essence of the matter. It is at once tragic and amusing to see the many points of view that have arisen in the course of time, and how without fail, from the standpoint of one of them, all the rest have been judged and discredited or else neglected as incidental and of secondary importance, as time-conditioned or even as later accretions. And then without fail there has come, not unneeded to be sure, a reaction against " over-emphases " and " one-sidednesses," one or more of the other principles had to be played off against the one and presumably only principle, until in turn the one-sidedness of the newly erected principle became too obvious for it to conceal its essentially relative character. And yet not every principle which good-will can discover in the New Testament has been thus extracted and held up to view. Notwithstanding, more recent historical research might permit itself the assertion that apart from the name Jesus Christ almost everything in the New Testament, everything that could at a pinch be worked up into a principle, has its more or less exact parallel outside the Bible, and so certainly cannot be the very essence of the matter. However, we would do well to realise that in the sense of the New Testament writers themselves, literally everything they say would be but marginal and incidental and transient, if interpreted as the proclamation of a principle, idea or general truth—but that literally everything is central and fundamental and eternal, the moment it is interpreted as the predicate in an utterance about Jesus Christ. Jesus Christ is not one element in the New Testament witness alongside of others, but as it were the mathematical point toward which all the elements of New Testament witness are directed. Ultimately only the name Jesus Christ, in what would appear to be its utter emptiness as a mere name, which by itself can express no content, principle, idea or truth, but is only the symbol for a person—this eternally inexpressible name, known and still to be made known, alone represents the object which they all signify and to which they all point. As such the name Jesus Christ, which stands for the reality of revelation itself, is found, as it were, midway between Jesus Christ and the witness of the New Testament to Him. It is given along with Jesus Christ to men, and yet in distinction from Him, given as really the first, decisive and comprehensive fact in their hearts and on their lips. As such it is also the last, decisive and comprehensive thing they have to say about Him, so that it even throws its importance and significance as the last and ultimate fact upon what is said before. The fact that this first and last thing according to the New Testament is precisely the name of Jesus, reminds us that the reality in which the New Testament sees God's revelation taking place is utterly *simple*, the simple reality of God.

This simple reality, however, is also a reality absolutely once-for-all. But we must add immediately, as once-for-all as God is once-for-all. (We have yet to speak particularly about " Revelation and Time," but here a few of the most essential points may now be laid down.) The simplicity of revealed reality is not that of a repeated or general event, like that of an event formulated in the law of causality. It is the simplicity of a definite, temporally limited, un-repeated and quite unrepeatable event. According to the prophecy and recollection of Holy Scripture, there is an authentic witness and a legitimate proclamation of this event. In this way other, earlier or later, times are given to participation in this event. Finally, this event is to be understood both in principle and in fact as future, as the end of all time. In other words, Jesus Christ who has come is also the One who is yet to come. But there is no anticipation or repetition of this event. The reality of revelation is not a determina-tion of all history or of a part or section of the whole of history. It is history, this very definite history, which has not happened before and will never happen again, which happened once for all, not once in every age or once in many, but quite literally once for all. Before Christ there was an age of prophecy about Him, and after Christ an age of witness about Him, but that *before* and *after* are governed by relation to the name of Jesus as the midpoint of time. Thus the real temporal pre-existence of Jesus Christ in prophecy and His real temporal post-existence in witness are identical with this once-for-all existence of His as the midpoint of time. The midpoint of time—which, after all, belongs to time—is the fulfilment of time. That is what distinguishes it from all other times. That is what it has in common with the end (and, from this point of view, with the beginning) of all time.

The name of Jesus Christ is thus not to be regarded in any sense, open or secret, as a name for man. Neither is it to be regarded as a name for the men who stand in a definite historical connection with Jesus Christ, as forerunners or followers. There are χριστοί, anointed prophets, priests and kings in the Old Testament, χριστιανοί in the New Testament, but only depending upon and pro-ceeding from the fact that there is a unique Χριστός, the Lord of the covenant attested in the Old and New Testaments. Before Him and after Him there is no one to be compared to Him. He is utterly different from all others, the proper Χριστός, of whom they are but types.
It was a disastrous misunderstanding when liberal theologians like A. E. Biedermann, R. A. Lipsius, H. Lüdemann and even A. Ritschl (in the applica-tion of a method which became predominant about 1700) thought they could interpret the reality revealed in Jesus Christ simply as the revelation of the deepest and final reality of man. But it was not essentially better when the so-called " positive " theologians of the 19th century, with a certain mythologising clarity, separated off the special historical context before and after Christ as the so-called *Heilsgeschichte*, yet within this *Heilsgeschichte* asserted the once-for-allness of Jesus Christ over against all others, with rather more force than clarity. No wonder they were unable to carry the position in their fight with the liberal counter movement, and that in their last representatives (think of R.

Seeberg and his school) all difference between them was lost, i.e., the only difference left concerned certain questions of judgment and taste.

When Peter, in the passage already cited, Ac. 4$^{10\text{ff.}}$, rules out as the source of σωτηρία any other name given to men under heaven, he gives the name Jesus Christ a significance of once-for-allness incapable of being modified either in a more general or a more particular sense. Note how in 1 Tim. 2^5 it is immediately related to the once-for-allness of God—εἷς γὰρ θεός, εἷς καὶ μεσίτης θεοῦ καὶ ἀνθρώπων, ἄνθρωπος Ἰησοῦς Χριστός. Note that in Phil. 2$^{9\text{ff.}}$ the name Jesus Christ is called " the name that is above every name," the name at which the knees of all shall bow. But above all note the ἅπαξ or ἐφάπαξ often so impressively added when Jesus Christ's work of redemption is mentioned, especially in Hebrews. In Heb. 7^{27} ; 9^{12}; 9$^{26-28}$; 10^{10}, it characterises the once-for-allness of Jesus Christ, compared with the manifold preparation for it in time under the old covenant. Note here in particular Heb. 9^{27}, where it is compared with the death of every man once for all. In Rom. 6^{10} ; 1 Pet. 3^{18}, it is true, the word rather emphasises the difference between Christ and the Christians reconciled through it. But from the passages Heb. 6^4 ; 10$^{2, 10}$; Jude 3, we gather that this is the once-for-allness which also belongs to what makes the Christians into Christians, i.e., to their illumination, sanctification, etc. ; and Heb. 12$^{26f.}$ assures us that even Christ's second coming does not call in question the once-for-allness of His revelation, but that precisely in its once-for-allness His revelation is also the end of all things. " This word ἅπαξ signifieth the removing of those things that are shaken, as of things that are made, that those things which cannot be shaken may remain," Heb. 12^{27}. In conclusion, reference should be made in the same sense to the chronological attempts made at the beginning of the Gospels according to Matthew and Luke. It is part of their purpose and effect to point out Christ as this simple fact, when they point to His position in the history of Israel (Matthew) and of the world (Luke) as precisely the individual who exists here alone and nowhere else, either before or afterwards.

We come now, on the basis of the New Testament witness, to speak more specifically of this simple, once-for-all reality of Jesus Christ. The Word or Son of God became a Man and was called Jesus of Nazareth ; therefore this Man Jesus of Nazareth was God's Word or God's Son. Before attempting to understand the content of this statement we have also, in view of its place and significance, to make the following points clear.

1. In regard to the exegetical question, it must be said that this twofold statement, whether as such or in its two constituent parts, is not very often found in so many words in the New Testament. As a rule, only one of its two parts appears at certain solemn climaxes in the New Testament witness, where it is manifestly the writer's business to gather up what has been said before coming to the ultimate fact, i.e., before coming to the name Jesus Christ itself. But this confession does not seem to come easily from their lips. Nor is it frequent. On the whole they prefer other ways of laying bare its truth to explicit articulation. There is, moreover, no single passage in which this confession is formulated with the dogmatic exactitude which we might like, or in which it is actually formulated at a later period. The christological dogma, like that of the Trinity, is obviously not the text but the commentary on the text. Nowhere in the Bible is it to be found word for word. It must also be noted that this

confession simply does not appear at every point at which its appearance
might be expected. There are important passages in the New Testament witness where it is even lacking.

I refer to the beginning of Mark, ἀρχὴ τοῦ εὐαγγελίου 'Ιησοῦ Χριστοῦ, where the
addition υἱοῦ θεοῦ is of course not genuine ; so that in its original form the Gospel
should only be described as the Gospel about the bearer of this name, or simply
as the Gospel about this name. But in the passages in Acts as well, which reproduce the apostolic *kerygma*, the confession occurs only once in so many words,
namely in Ac. 10³⁶ᶠ·, though there it is set most impressively at the very beginning. It is lacking in Ac. 2²²ᶠ· ; 3¹³ᶠ· ; 13²³ᶠ· It appears indeed at the climax
of the Johannine Easter narrative (Jn. 20²⁸), but not in the Synoptic parallels.

As a rule it is to be found between the lines and inferred by the
reader or hearer from what is otherwise said directly or indirectly
about the name Jesus Christ. It awaits, as it were, the reader's or
hearer's own confession. These facts might weigh heavily upon a
dogmatics especially eager for as clear, comprehensive and precise an
answer to its questions as possible. They cannot surprise us. The
New Testament is the instrument of proclamation and witness ; it
is neither a historical exposition nor a systematic treatise. The modest
task of dogmatics it has left to the Church, to us. But it is possible
that by the very reserve with which it handles the confession at
this central point, it might direct us more forcibly to the twofold
statement as being well-nigh the final import of its utterances.

2. In regard to the substance of the matter we must say that the
statements about the divinity and humanity of Jesus Christ which
the New Testament gives us (sometimes directly and explicitly, sometimes, quite often in fact, indirectly and implicitly), belong unquestionably to those elements in New Testament witness to be described as
secondary in relation to the name Jesus Christ itself. Thus, however
central the importance of the matter, we ought not to say that the
incarnation is the proper content of the New Testament. It is as
little so as man's sonship to God or eschatological redemption or any
other of these elements, i.e., as a principle or revealed truth in abstraction from the name Jesus Christ. As an idea, even the incarnation
is admittedly not peculiar to the New Testament, but is also represented in the myths and speculation of every other possible religious
area. We cannot, then, from the standpoint of a previously clarified
conception of God, or of a previously clarified anthropology, understand what it means when in the New Testament the Son of God is
called Jesus of Nazareth, and Jesus of Nazareth the Son of God ;
nor yet from the standpoint of a previously clarified general conception
of incarnation, nor in the light of some general truth regarding a paradoxical unity of God and man. No general idea has any relevance
here. The incarnation of which Holy Scripture speaks can be understood only from the standpoint of Holy Scripture, i.e., of the name
Jesus Christ, or of the simple, once-for-all reality indicated by this

name. It is thus a mark of the lofty concreteness of the New Testament writers, that they make such scanty use of the conception of the God-manhood of Christ, which is of such decisive importance for understanding the nature of revelation. Undoubtedly they make a solemn use of this conception—a fact which makes it right for us and compels us to give it special consideration—but not more frequent use than of the other forms of confession which bring out only indirectly the truth in question. Thus they remind us that everything, even the most important things they say, have a special reference. Even man's sonship to God is not in itself the content of the New Testament. The content of the New Testament is solely the name Jesus Christ, which, of course, also and above all involves the truth of His God-manhood. Quite by itself this name signifies the objective reality of revelation. Even the truth of the God-manhood of Christ can do no more than point to this name, and so to the truth of revelation, though it does that indirectly, even when it is directly expressed. Thus, when we single out this truth for particular attention (in any discussion of the conception of revelation), we are called upon to look in the direction in which all truths attested in the New Testament point, i.e., to look at what is intended and attested, even where the God-manhood is not directly and explicitly mentioned. Strictly speaking, to reach a real understanding of the truth of Christ's God-manhood, we should discuss the entire realm of New Testament witness, and let it force us to look in the direction in which all the apparently scattered arrows of narrative and teaching in the New Testament point. But, even so, really to see what there is to see there, and so to gain a real understanding of Christ's God-manhood, does not rest upon our choice or goodwill, for the decision concerning whether it is reached or not depends not upon us, but upon the object whose reality is here to be seen and understood.

We now turn to the twofold statement, that God's Son is called Jesus of Nazareth, and that Jesus of Nazareth is God's Son. In doing so we indicate as briefly as possible the twofold course of christological confession in the New Testament (cf. *Church Dogmatics* I 1, p. 482 f. E.T.).

That the name Jesus Christ is really the primary fact and that the christological confession is but secondary (for it can only point to this name and the reality which this name denotes) is shown at once by the twofold character of this confession. In it the one original light is already refracted, and although it bears witness to that light, it makes no statement about it. Only the name Jesus Christ can bear witness to it as such. But does not this name already point to a twofold statement? Clearly we have to choose between two things: either to debar ourselves from thinking or speaking at all, or to adopt for ourselves the thoughts and words of the New Testament, i.e., the already refracted light of its christological confession. On the whole, there are two questions and two answers which appear to determine the statements of the New Testament about Jesus Christ. The discovery made by the New Testament witnesses about the reality of Jesus Christ or about this name, or rather the illumination which they received from Jesus Christ, consists either in the knowledge that God's Son or God's Word is identical with a man, with this man, whose name is Jesus of Nazareth, or in the knowledge that a man, this man, Jesus of Nazareth is identical with the Son or Word of God.

In the New Testament it is not the rule, as in our dogmatic procedure, for the two to be mentioned at the same time or in juxtaposition. On the contrary the christological pronouncements are to be expounded and understood as the expression of either the one or the other of these two insights. Strictly speaking, they cannot be separated and allotted to the various groups of New Testament witness. Nevertheless two types of christological pronouncement do arise from this in the New Testament. And of the Johannine writings at least it can definitely be said that their Christology as a whole pertains to the first type, of the Synoptics that their Christology as a whole pertains to the second ; whereas in St. Paul, if I am right, the two types are equally represented. At the same time there are three passages where the two pronouncements are immediately related in the same way in which we have put them together. In 1 Jn. 1¹ we find set side by side in two simple relative clauses as the object of the apostolic witness, (1) that which is from the beginning, and (2) that which we (the apostles) have seen, heard, beheld, handled. And that is repeated in vv. 2–3 : (1) the life that was with the Father was manifested and we have seen, attested and proclaimed it ; (2) that which we have seen and heard we proclaim unto you. In the same order Phil. 2⁶ᶠ· ascribes to Jesus Christ (1) the divine mode of existence, equality with God, (2) equality with men, (3) a second, and this time a fuller, equality with God, the name of Lord. A parallel, in the reverse order from Phil. 2⁸⁻⁹, is offered in Eph. 4¹⁰—" He that descended (from above ' into the lowest parts of the earth ') is the same also that ascended up far above all heavens "—where apparently the humanity of the Son of God, Jesus Christ, is indicated by the one, while the divinity of the man Jesus Christ is indicated by the other.

The ascertaining of the first fact, that the Son of God is this man, that the Christ is Jesus, is not to be conceived of as though those who thus thought and spoke had first a definite conception of God or of a Son or Word of God, of a Christ, and then found this conception confirmed and fulfilled in Jesus. That would be an arbitrary Christology, docetic in its estimate and in its conclusions, on the basis of which there can be no serious recognition of the divinity of Christ. An object which is really God only so far as man sees in it the confirmation and fulfilment of his own imported conception of God and therefore clothes it with the character of God, God's Word or God's Son—such an object is God only in a quite frivolous sense ; it remains fundamentally what it is, an object. Although and just because docetic Christology clothes its object, the man Jesus of Nazareth, with that character (and this is where it gives itself away), in the last resort in His objectivity, as a man, Jesus is a matter of indifference. It is not concerned with Jesus but only with Christ, i.e., with its presupposed and imported conception of a Christ or Logos or Mediator.

It can upon occasion abandon Jesus, the historical existence ot Jesus of Nazareth, and yet retain Christ, i.e., its Christ. It can regard this very paradox as a peculiar triumph of a strong faith. (About 1910—the time of A. Drews' Christ myth—when a theological stripling, I was of that opinion myself). Even if it does not push matters so far, it will see in the man Jesus a " vehicle " or " symbol," and if it speaks of His divinity will mean the divinity of the idea incorporated and realised in Him, and so will have difficulty in conceding that the divinity is incorporated and realised only in Him and perfectly in Him. On the contrary, it will see in Jesus one vehicle, one symbol alongside of others, and it will see in Him only a vehicle or symbol, i.e., a revelation of divinity imperfect in principle and in fact.

. In identifying with divinity a humanly conceived idea, one, that is, already belonging to man prior to, or even apart from, any revelation, it may set store by the man Jesus, but it may also do without Him. It may strip Him of His mantle of divinity, just as it cast it over Him.

It would then be misleading in the extreme to interpret the New Testament statement that the Son of God is this man, that the Christ is called Jesus, in terms of such a docetic Christology. On the contrary, we understand this statement only when we realise that it implies a direct and express contradiction of this Christology. Those who gave thought and expression to this statement did not come to Jesus armed with an idea of the Christ or the Logos or the Son of God in order to find the fulfilment of this idea of theirs in Him. But they believed and recognised in Jesus first and foremost what they had nowhere believed or recognised before, namely " the life which was with the Father," the reality of divine sending and divine work as the real presence of God Himself, i.e., the Word or the Son of God. They thus derived their conception of the Son or Word of God from no other source than Jesus Himself. And this was their faith and their knowledge, this was the discovery they made about Jesus, that they found in Him the fulfilment of the conception of the Son of God, and in so doing, and only in so doing, they found the conception itself. Nothing more alien could be read into their thought and language about the life manifested in Jesus, than a belated recognition of His divinity arbitrarily acquired on the basis of an imported precognition of it. The recognition of His divinity, or rather His divinity itself, and therefore its unreserved recognition was, on the contrary, the element of fact from which they started, and apart from which their whole procedure would have been impossible. Only in a very different procedure is there really to be found the conviction that the man Jesus as such might be less important or actually indifferent or even troublesome, as compared with a Christ who could be distinguished and separated from Him. So far as the statement that " the Christ is named Jesus " had a polemical point, it was directed straight against this early outcrop of docetic indifference to the man Jesus. They were, of course, acquainted with the distinction, but they were not aware of any separation ; on the contrary they were only aware of the distinction in the removal of it, only aware of the Christ in the event of His essential oneness with Jesus. They had no interest in an idea that had to be applied for the first time to Jesus, not to speak of having identified it with divinity, or of having weighed Jesus in this scale and found Him to be too light as a mere vehicle and symbol—one among others. Their very confession contradicted all that. Their statement made the definite claim that in Him alone, for the first time, and fully, they had found the Godhead. How then could this statement be explained in a docetic sense ?

It is οὗτος, this man, who in the beginning was with God, as we read in Jn. 1². Who is this man ? The Logos who became flesh, whose glory we beheld because He tabernacled among us (Jn. 1¹⁴). Then in Jn. 1¹⁷ for the first time the Name is mentioned, in direct contrast to those of Moses and the Baptist, the witnesses. This is he !, says John the Baptist repeatedly (Jn. 1¹⁵· ²⁹· ³⁵f·). That is why in the same Gospel Jesus Himself says ἐγώ εἰμι, I am the bread of life (6³⁵), the light of the world (8¹²), the door for the sheep (10⁷), the good shepherd (10¹¹), the resurrection and the life (11²⁵), the way, the truth and the life (14⁶), the true vine (15¹). And Nathanael says, Thou art the Son of God ; thou art the king of Israel (1⁴⁹). And Martha of Bethany says, Thou art the Christ, the Son of God, that cometh into the world (11²⁷). And Peter says, Whither shall we go ? Thou hast the words of eternal life. And we have believed and known that thou art the holy one of God (6⁶⁸f·). It is significant that even Pilate says, Art thou the king of the Jews ? (18³³) and, Behold the man ! (19⁵). Thomas had to see the hands of the Risen One with the nailprints of the Crucified and put his own hands in His side and so become " believing and not unbelieving," in this very identification confessing, My Lord and my God (20²⁷f·). To the other disciples also Jesus had shown His hands and His side, and thereupon they rejoice ἰδόντες τὸν κύριον (20²⁰). Hence in Jn. 6⁵²f· the " hard saying " about eating the flesh and drinking the blood of Jesus, whereupon many of His disciples ἀπῆλθον εἰς τὰ ὀπίσω (6⁶⁶). In accordance with all this, the entire meaning of the Gospel is summarised in 20³¹, " This is written, that ye may believe that Jesus is the Christ, the Son of God." The Fourth Gospel is distinctively the Jesus-Gospel, so far as it aims at the definite assertion that Jesus is the Christ. So and only so does it follow that it is naturally also the Christ-Gospel. In the Johannine Epistles this statement acquires the polemical note even more clearly. With a reference to the fact that that which was from the beginning, namely the life, was manifested, seen, heard and handled by the apostles, and therefore and thereupon proclaimed by them (1 Jn. 1²), the theme of Jn. 1¹⁻¹⁸ is taken up. The spirits are divided, according to 1 Jn. 4²f·, into those who confess Jesus as ἐν σαρκὶ ἐληλυθότα, and those who do not confess Him in this sense, i.e., it is Antichrist who confesses Him in another, in a docetic sense. The meaning here (and in 2 Jn. 7) is sharp and unmistakable. But 1 Tim. 3¹⁶, without making this antithesis visible and in order to describe the Christian mystery, also insists in the first place that ἐφανερώθη ἐν σαρκί. Behind that stands Rom. 8³ : Because the law is weak in the flesh (in man, or in the world of the flesh), and in order to condemn sin in the flesh, God sent His son ἐν ὁμοιώματι σαρκὸς ἁμαρτίας ; Gal. 4⁴ : When the fulness of the time was come, God sent His son, born of a woman, made under the law ; and Phil. 2⁶f· : Who being in a divine mode of existence humbled Himself by assuming a servant's mode of existence, had His being in likeness to men, was seen in human form (σχήματι εὑρεθεὶς ὡς ἄνθρωπος), and right up to death, the death of the cross, maintained this obedience of a servant. Therefore—that is, in His actual treading of this path and because He trod it, in the concreteness of His humanity—God exalted Him and gave Him the name of Lord. The name Jesus as such is the name of the Lord (1 Cor. 12³ ; Rom. 10⁹). In distinction from and in contrast with the Jews who demand a sign, and the Greeks who hanker after wisdom, we preach Christ crucified (1 Cor. 1²³). Because the children whom God has given Him have part in flesh and blood, He is not ashamed to call them brethren and so in like wise to have part in flesh and blood. He thus adopts not the status of the angels but the status of Abraham's race ; He had to be equal with His brethren in every respect, in order to show them mercy, and at the same time be their righteous High Priest before God (Heb. 2¹⁴ᶠ·). In Him we have such a High Priest as can sympathise with our weaknesses, who in everything was tempted like as we are. Consequently we come with confidence to the throne of His grace (Heb. 4¹⁵ᶠ·). All along the line these christological pronouncements are directed to the fact that God's Son became and is man ; that event is the reality of revelation ; in it God has preserved His freedom to be our God. Thus to believe in and know God's revelation means to believe in and know this man in His identity with the presence and action of God. The *kerygma* here is the message about Jesus, proceeding from the discovery of salvation, forgiveness, life, lordship, the eternal Word, the Son of God in Him and in no one else, consisting therefore in the proclamation that Jesus possesses and is all that. Such a starting point for the confession safeguards it from devotion to and suspicion of historism, false realism, deification of the creature, all of them characteristics of ebionite Christology, of which we shall have to speak later. Moreover, such a starting-point renders intelligible the frequently emphasised and unusual transparence of the Johannine picture of Christ and the dominant position, at first so striking in view of 1 Cor. 1²³, of the risen Christ in the Pauline message. Neither must in any way be brought into connexion with Docetism. Wherever the incarnation becomes the subject of discussion or assertion, then demonstration consists in the exposition of the Logos as seen and heard in the flesh ; wherever the Crucified is the theme, its exposition will have to be completed in the proclamation of the Risen One. How should the statement, " Jesus is the Christ " be proved otherwise than by indicating that Jesus is the Word, the Light, the Life, the Way, the Truth ? For the actual purpose of this proof no abstractly historical knowledge of the man Jesus or any becoming acquainted with Him as such could be contemplated (2 Cor. 5¹⁶). Precisely in relation to Jn. 6 we shall also be able and bound to take warning that ἡ σὰρξ οὐκ ὠφελεῖ οὐδέν (Jn. 6⁶³). The unfolding of the witness of the concrete man Jesus has its fitting place where the witness is meant primarily to be a Christ-message, where the evidence is to be adduced that Jesus is the Messiah. On the other hand, where it is meant to be a Jesus-message, where the anti-docetic evidence is to be adduced, the emphasis must be laid directly upon the Messiahship, the divinity of the person and work of Christ. That anyone should deliberately and frequently mention John and Paul in the same breath with the idea of Docetism because of their undoubtedly spiritual view of the human life of Jesus, belongs to the very worst kind of misunderstandings of the New Testament. Docetism cannot be countered adequately in any other way than that used by the Fourth Evangelist and Paul.

2. In distinction from this first piece of knowledge about Jesus Christ, there is in the New Testament a second, which is apparently the direct opposite of it. The content of it is that this man is the Son of God, that Jesus is the Christ. This, too, we best understand by guarding against a similar misunderstanding. In this statement it is not a question of idealising or deifying a man. There was and is a counterpart and extension of Docetism in the shape of an equally arbitrary Christology of Ebionitism. On the ground of this, too, a

serious recognition of the divinity of Christ is impossible. As Docetism starts from a human conception to which it logically returns in due course, so does Ebionitism start from a human experience and impression of the heroic personality of Jesus of Nazareth. On the basis of this impression and experience, divinity is ascribed to this man.

If in relation to docetic Christology we can think to-day of the older theological Liberalism influenced by Kant, Fichte and Hegel, and including A. Ritschl, then the structure of " ebionite " Christology—represented in almost greater than life size in the early Church by Paul of Samosata—is once more typically recognisable in the peculiar Jesus-theology which, after the victory of philosophical positivism in a spiritual world, which thought it could live on the alternative to pure empiricism, and deriving from influences emanating from Thomas Carlyle and P. de Lagarde, flourished for a while about the turn of the 19th and 20th centuries, under the leadership of A. von Harnack.

By the divinity ascribed to Jesus is here meant the strong, perhaps very strong, inner emotion into which man feels himself transported by Him. Here, too, we have to do with an arbitrary undertaking, so far as here also man obviously takes too seriously his authority to deal with this predicate according to his own judgment. And here, too, the statement about the divinity of Jesus is by no means serious—and is almost bound to be less and less serious, because the mere assertion, built upon an uncontrollable inner experience, must from the very first be less credible for him who expresses it, not to mention his hearer or reader, than its rival, which can at least claim for itself the relative clarity and superiority of the idea. If there must be enthusiasm—so one might interject here—then at least let it be the genuine Platonic article, not this thin historicising enthusiasm of a hero-cult. The weakness underlying this assertion will become evident soon enough in the feeling that the title assigned to this man is too ponderous and says too much—mere feelings have a habit not only of rising but of falling away again—so that openly or secretly it has to be explained in a sense which weakens its wording. And actually it can be so explained, for ebionite Christology is not concerned with the conception of God, God's Son or God's Word—words are but husk and smoke, as so often happens when a man's words have no " heavenly fire " or are only vague enough to act as a smokescreen. Rather is it concerned with the stimulating man Jesus, with this historical creaturely reality as such and with the effects proceeding from it. Therefore—in which case it may well take some pride in its " integrity " and " honesty "—as gladly as it first adopted them, and without suffering any loss in actual content, it will drop the unduly lofty descriptions of Jesus as a divine being practically identical with God, descriptions which fundamentally do not quite correspond with the actual degree of human enthusiasm. What is really meant can be stated in another way, and perhaps still better than by means of those epithets. As the true humanity of Christ is ultimately

dispensable for Docetism, so is the true divinity of Jesus for Ebionitism
—in fact, in the last resort it is a nuisance. However one may word the
conception which ought to give expression to the experience, so it
will be argued, the experience itself, the event and impression of
which it consists, is susceptible of various forms and degrees (which
the liability of conceptions to change makes inevitable), but in its
factuality and in the value which it has for man in every case, it
stands upon its own feet, and can neither be established nor impaired
by the conception, by the dogmatic formula, as we are so fond of
saying in mockery. It may be handled quite freely. It may be used,
or for various reasons—above all, reasons of honesty—it may not be
used. It is easily done without, and in the last resort gladly done
without. It should not require to be said that the New Testament
statement that the man Jesus is the Christ has also nothing to do
with this Christology, and is not implicated in its inevitable dialectic.
On the contrary, it too can only be understood when thought out
and expressed in direct contradiction to this Christology. Those who
thought it out and expressed it did not intend to say : We have met a
hero or sage or saint, for the adequate description of whom we, in
our highest rapture, are left only with provisional terms such as the
word God or God's Son. But here, too, preceding all experiences
and possible raptures, knowledge of the divinity of Jesus Christ was
the beginning of the way. Even if the New Testament witnesses also
find in Jesus heroic or saintly traits, or the characteristics of a sage,
a " great man," even if He actually made that impression upon them,
yet that does not mean that we can go on to say that this was the
line along which is to be sought the distinctive and original thing to
be found in Jesus and to be said about Him. On the contrary all
that—so far as traces of it are to be found in the New Testament—
is nothing but the stammering, inadequate expression of their initial
and basic awareness : we have met God, we have heard His Word—
that is the original and ultimate fact. The movement of thought here
is not from below upwards but from above downwards. From above,
however, does not mean from the conception or idea as in Docetism,
for God's " aboveness " is to be sought (or rather discloses itself) from
beyond the opposition of idea and experience. It was this " aboveness " of God and so not a human " belowness," however important
and relevant, that entered their experience in the man Jesus. He was
not simply a " great man." That does not mean that the humanity
of Jesus was of no importance for them, since it was actually in it that
His divinity was encountered. For that reason they could not be
indifferent to His divinity, because it was the divinity that met them in
His humanity. It could never have occurred to them to make light of
the conception and formula of their faith or knowledge of Jesus, as
men in recent times have falsely attributed to them. On the contrary,
the conception of the Messiahship or divine Sonship of Jesus was the

absolutely decisive fact they had to think and to say of Him. If they had an experience—and, of course, they had—it was the experience of the presence of God's Son or God's Word. In all their witness to Him that experience was taken for granted. For them therefore there could be no talk of ecstatic apotheosis of a man and of the inevitable disillusionment that follows it. On their lips the statement " Jesus is God's Son " is entirely a self-authenticating statement as much as its counterpart : the Word became flesh. On their lips both of these are analytic, not synthetic statements.

In this sense the Synoptics, as distinguished from the Johannine Gospel of Jesus, are meant to be regarded as Gospels about Christ. Inwardly and essentially they start from the fact that the man Jesus of Nazareth, " the carpenter's son " (Mk. 6³), shows Himself in His resurrection from the dead to be the Messiah and the Son of God. In that light they look back and understand all His words and actions. The revelation of this man as God and Lord that takes place in His resurrection is the very thing they wish to say and attest. But that means that externally they must start from His humanity, from His life before the resurrection. According to John, the great mystery is that God assumed humanity in Jesus. That in this man divinity appeared among us, the divinity of Christ, is the same mystery according to the Synoptists. According to them the voice from heaven at Jesus' baptism (Mt. 3¹⁷ and par.) and at the Transfiguration on the mount (Mt. 17⁵ and par.) says : " This is," or (in distinction from all the others who came to Jordan to be baptised, in distinction even from the Baptist himself) " Thou art my beloved Son, in thee I am well pleased," or, " hear ye him." This pointing out, or discovery, or revelation, of the Son of God in the Jèsus of Nazareth who appears first as one man with all other men, is the decisive presupposition from which the Evangelists (as witnesses of the resurrection) always start. It is the ultimate solution which they always wish to attest and proclaim. Their entire exposition is therefore a continual propounding and solving of problems. The problem before them is the humanity of Jesus Christ—although it is no longer a problem for them and is only to be offered to their readers complete with the solution. The solution is the divinity of Christ, but it has to be achieved again and again. Too much cannot be heard of its achievement, and even to the readers it is offered only in process of achievement. This is the manifest mystery which begins with the conception and pregnancy of Mary in the pre-history of Matthew and Luke, namely that she is the fulfilment of the prophecy (Is. 7¹⁴) of the virgin who should bear a son, whose name (the solution of the problem) should be called Immanuel, i.e., God with us (Mt. 1²³). According to Mt. 4¹ᶠ· and par. this is the mystery which is only too plain to the devil. According to Mk. 1²⁴, 5⁷ even the demons discover it and cry out about it. Even the scribes, according to Mk. 2⁷, unwittingly lay their finger upon it, at least externally. According to Mt. 20³⁰ it breaks forth from the cry for help of the two blind men of Jericho. According to Mt. 21¹⁵ᶠ· it is shouted out by the children in the Temple : " Hosanna to the Son of David." According to Mk. 15³⁹, the heathen centurion had solemnly to confess at the foot of the cross : " Truly this man was the Son of God." To this also naturally belongs the Baptist's question in Mt. 11³ : " Art thou he that should come, or do we look for another ? " the indirect answer to which is without doubt essentially one with the content of the confession just given. In the Synoptic Gospels the christological climax is reached in the question : " Whom do men say that I the Son of man am ? " John the Baptist, Elias, Jeremiah, one of the prophets, men say—such is the answer. But to the question : " Whom say ye that I am ? " there follows the confession (made by Peter, we must say, as the Confession of the Church) : " Thou art the Christ, the

Son of the living God " (Mt. 16¹³ᶠ·). We see here with special clearness the juxtaposition and contraposition of problem and solution. The view that Jesus' designation of Himself as the "Son of man," so frequent in the Synoptics, is to be regarded as a declaration of dignity, a standing confession of His Messiahship by Himself (still advanced by G. Kittel in *R.G.G.*², art. "Menschensohn "), seems to me very unsatisfactory. Without being able to adduce proof of this, I would prefer to think of this designation in relation to the name *Messiah* as that of a pseudonym to the correct name, at least as an element of veiling and not of unveiling. On the other hand, it is essentially in line with the exclamations at the mystery of the Messiah that in Ac. 10³⁶ the *kerygma* is at once opened with the assertion, οὗτός ἐστιν πάντων κύριος. Very much in line with this is also the important passage from Paul's Epistle to the Romans (1³ᶠ·), where, quite in the manner of the Synoptists, there is set against Christ's being born of the seed of David according to the flesh, the declaration of Him as the Son of God with power according to the Holy Ghost by the resurrection from the dead. In this answer to the problem, He is the υἱὸς θεοῦ, and so the κύριος ἡμῶν. We must remember here the sequence of Christ's humiliation and exaltation (Phil. 2⁸⁻⁹) ; and Heb. 12² where " he endured the cross, despising the shame, and is set down at the right hand upon the throne of God " ; and Ac. 8³³, where " in his humiliation his judgment was taken away " ; but also the saying in Jn. 12²⁴ about the corn of wheat falling into the ground before it can bring forth fruit. The content of this New Testament witness is the message of the resurrection and ascension which runs through all the Gospels and Epistles and is the mainstay of everything. He who died on the cross and thereby clearly showed Himself to be a man, He who completed His incarnation on the cross and was thereby veiled in His divinity, rose again the third day from the dead, and sits on the right hand of the Father—was exalted from the earth, went to the Father, as the Fourth Gospel puts it—that is the solution of the problem of Jesus, to which even the miracles could only point as Messianic signs. It belongs to the incarnation itself as a mighty counterpart to it—the decisive contradiction to any ebionite Christology. The same is true of Jesus Christ in another respect as the child with the name "God with us," as the man who is at the right hand of God. Here we are concerned with knowledge of the reality of revelation, with knowing that God is active and present in this man. Certainly the *kerygma* here is the message about Jesus, but if so, it is also the message about Christ. For that very reason it differs from John and Paul in the way it " fills up " the *kerygma*, or unfolds the witness of Jesus' life as a man before and apart from His resurrection. What is indicated and attested is the divine Sonship, the risen Christ. In the nature of the case no proof can be offered except in the form of an exposition of Jesus of Nazareth the Crucified, who in His humanity is at the same time the authentic witness to His divinity. Here the concretely historical outlook must come first, the spiritual second. Here, too, an exposition like that of Luke, so akin to a biography that paints in the hues of history and psychology, is possible and in its own way necessary. Yet Luke should as little be reproached with ebionite historicism as Paul with Docetism. His attention to the historical and psychological is of direct service to the anti-ebionite thesis of the God-man. To think of contrasting the Synoptists at all as historians with John and Paul, whether in praise or blame, is surely a part of the secular misunderstanding of the New Testament. Real ebionite historicism cannot be countered in any other way, or in any better way than in the extremely logical way adopted by the Synoptists themselves, each in his own fashion.

To sum up : that God's Son or Word is the man Jesus of Nazareth is the one christological thesis of the New Testament ; that the man Jesus of Nazareth is God's Son or Word is the other. Is there a synthesis of the two ? To this question we must roundly answer, No.

Of course there is a place where these two theses are not two but a single one. The New Testament witnesses obviously have this place in view, for it determines their thinking and speaking. And obviously they wish to challenge their readers to look in this direction, and so to recognise for themselves the truth of what they are telling them. In the variety of their language about the reality of revelation, when they call the true God man and the true man God, they are uttering only their penultimate word, not their ultimate. When they are uttering their ultimate word, they say the same thing. This ultimate word, however, is not a further thesis, not a synthesis, but just the name Jesus Christ. By naming Him, they want to let Him who is so named have the final word.

Thus we can as little speak of an antithesis within the New Testament as of a synthesis. It may be the case that the Synoptic Gospels arose out of a certain opposition to Paul, and that the Fourth Gospel arose out of opposition to the Synoptics. But at once the extraordinary criss-cross relations between the theses and their proof will not allow us to regard this opposition as polemical in the proper sense. There is no Jesus-Gospel proclaimed here which is not also a Christ-Gospel, nor is there a Christ-Gospel in the New Testament which is not as such a Jesus-Gospel. On the contrary, as we have seen, their relations are so interlocked, that if we are to understand one we must first do justice to the other and *vice versa*. That Paul and John could be reproached with Docetism and the Synoptists with Ebionitism is indeed testimony to the mutual interrelation of the two theses.

We are dealing with testimonies to one reality, which, though contrary to one another, do not dispute or negate each other. That must be remembered when we are compelled to adopt a position towards the antitheses which repeat the same variety in Church history, namely between the Christologies of Alexandria and of Antioch, of Luther and of Calvin. It is in the succession of the Johannine type that we have obviously to see Eutyches' and later Luther's interpretation of Christ, in the succession of the Synoptic type that of Nestorius and of Calvin. The unity of the twin points of view has not remained so clear in the later forms of antithesis as in the New Testament. In the former we shall be faced with handling the possibility of heretical or hereticising antitheses. Even with the best will in the world to do justice to both sides, we shall in the end have to make our choice. However, if we would have a wise and just attitude towards the antitheses (at any rate of the 16th century), we would do well to remember that in their original New Testament form the antitheses are not solved. Rather do they mutually supplement and explain each other and to that extent remain on peaceful terms. From the standpoint of the New Testament the christological antitheses among the Reformers may be and are very significant and no doubt call for a decision between them ; but they are not the Church-splitting antitheses of a theological school. In adopting an attitude to and amid these later antitheses it is well to note that in the New Testament the name Jesus Christ is the beginning, middle and end, on which the various pointers to the reality of revelation converge. By reference to it every attitude will have to be oriented and gauged.

Because the name Jesus Christ is the last word we hear in the New Testament, we need not expect that in regard to pronouncements upon the reality of revelation we will have yet another unity placed in our hands, namely a systematic unity or principle. What we hear about the name Jesus Christ is witness about God's Son who became a man, about the man who was God's Son, one related to the other, but not in such a way that the first ceases to be the first or the second to be the second, nor in such a way that the first and second dissolve into a higher third. Our task is to hear the second in the first, the first in the second, and, therefore, in a process of thinking and not in a system, to hear the one in both. Of a Christology related to the Christology of the New Testament, that is, aiming at understanding and understanding only what is attested for us in the New Testament as the reality of the revelation of God, it will have to be said in anticipation, that in all its results it can be nothing more than an attempt. It will constantly keep in view the fact that it is not chance but necessity that retains the penultimate sayings, the statements about God and man, about Jesus and Christ, in their position of relative antithesis in the New Testament and in this very position makes them point beyond themselves to the ultimate Word, Jesus Christ, which as such can only be explained in terms of the reality thereby indicated and by nothing else. The realm of grace in which God deals with sinful men would have to be dissolved by the realm of glory if it were to be otherwise, if a Christology of the third conclusive Word were to be possible, beyond the antithesis of divinity and humanity. In obedience to Scripture as the witness to God's revelation we shall not only renounce that third Word ; we shall also be aware why we have to renounce it, aware that we have, not too little, but enough and more than enough on our hands in listening to the Name and then to the two penultimate words, very God and very Man.

2. JESUS CHRIST THE OBJECTIVE POSSIBILITY OF REVELATION

God's freedom for us men is a fact in Jesus Christ, according to the witness of Holy Scripture. The first and the last thing to be said about the bearer of this name is that He is very God and very Man. In this unity He is the objective reality of divine revelation. His existence is God's freedom for man. Or *vice versa* God's freedom for man is the existence of Jesus Christ. And now we continue by saying that in this objective reality of the divine revelation there is presupposed and grounded and brought within our knowledge its objective possibility.

It is the tablet from which we have to read off, if we would also understand, what we have heard and simply adopted as it was told us. The way we have thereby gone and are still going has its parallels in the experience of two Reformed theologians of the 17th century, F. Burmann, *Syn. Theol.* 1678 V c. 5 f., and F. Turrettini, *Instit. Theol. el.* 1682 XIII *qu.* 1 f., who have likewise tried first to show from Scripture, (1) that the Messiah has appeared, (2) that Jesus is the Messiah ; in order next on the basis of this fact to press on to the interpretation of it, i.e., to the explanation of the conception of the incarnation.

By visualising the possibility presupposed and made available to knowledge in the reality of the revelation of God, we regard the reality as the answer to a question which we must put. In the light of our previous discussion it is clear that we cannot regard this as a general question, a question of theological anthropology which can be raised independently and then applied, as it were, from without to the reality of Jesus Christ. It is, of course, the question aroused in us by the reality of Jesus Christ, thrust at us by it, so to speak, and rendered meaningful and necessary by its own relation to the question, i.e., the question how far the existence of Jesus Christ is identical with God's freedom for man. We cannot, and so should not, do more than let ourselves be told quite simply that this is the case. We can and really ought to do that. We do that, however, only if we hear it as an answer embedded in the question which the thing itself puts to us, and if at the same time we hear it as the answer to this question. It would not be a genuine interpretation of the reality that is there, if it did not at the same time throw light upon its possibility as well. We have not genuinely let ourselves be told, if we cannot also as a result tell ourselves what has been told us—tell ourselves, not arbitrarily, but obediently. It would not be a serious awareness of this reality, were it not immediately to turn to understanding also. That would not be a *credere*, which did not force its way through to an *intelligere*. It is with God's revelation that we are concerned in this reality, that is, with God's relation to us, with His reality as it concerns us. If we would or could merely be aware without wanting to understand, merely let ourselves be told without also telling ourselves what had been told, merely have faith without knowledge, it certainly would not be God's revelation with which we had to do. If it were, such a refusal on our part would only reveal our disobedience, or our unwillingness to be involved in it. Obedience to revelation must invariably mean to let oneself be involved. To be involved must then mean to be questioned, in such a way that the question to which revelation is the answer becomes our own question, and so revelation, as the answer acquires a direct relation to ourselves. We said that the question of fact must precede the question of interpretation of the fact. There is a reason for that. But just as definitely we must now state that the question of interpretation must follow the question of fact. The question of fact would certainly have been put and answered wrongly, did the question of interpretation not follow it. The indolence and futility, the lack of participation in which we would then remain in face of the reality of revelation, must never be confused with humility and awe towards it. And, on the other hand, the attempt to question ourselves and to receive what is told us as the answer to our own question must never be decried as rationalism, if it comes within its limits and its meaning, i.e., if it is undertaken with regard to the reality of revelation which precedes all questioning and answering and does not claim precedence over this reality. Whether the first and not the second is the case (be it openly or secretly), is a question that must always be raised in each instance and very carefully considered. The uncertainty always to be found here cannot in principle be set aside—for in the act of understanding, where does obedience cease, and where does illegitimate prognostication begin ? In the last resort it will be not a matter of technical assurance, but of divine decision, whether in our desire to understand, we find ourselves on the first and good or on the second and bad way. But that does not alter the fact that at least there is a good way in this matter and that we cannot grant ourselves a dispensation from looking for it and treading it to the best of our knowledge and conscience.

It would be wholly and utterly childish to permit a primitive desire for understanding that worked first with the best popular categories and arguments, and then, when thought penetrated to some deep hinterland and even precipitous region, to turn round and brand it as rationalistic ("intellectualistic"). Many a man thinks in very popular terms and in doing so is actually very intellectualistic. And one may think very scientifically, and in doing so be in profound conformity with revelation. One thing is certain, that if here by the reality of God's revelation we are actually faced with the demand for thought, then we shall never give the matter the attention and respect it deserves, even when we have exerted ourselves to the utmost in strict, orderly thinking.

My name for the question aroused in us by the reality of revelation and which we now have to take up is the question as to the possibility, in our context the objective possibility, of revelation. We formulate the question in a manner parallel to the one first put, namely : How in God's freedom is it possible for His revelation to encounter man ? How far can the reality of Jesus Christ, i.e., the unity of God and man indicated by this Name, be God's revelation to man ? We assume, i.e., we let ourselves be told by Holy Scripture, that it actually is so. But we should like to know how far it is so, so as to tell ourselves that it is so. Thus we are not asking about a possibility superior to revelation, which would first be the ground of its reality, from an insight into which our knowledge of this reality would first become a grounded knowledge. But we are asking about the actual possibility presupposed and grounded in revelation and through revelation, and only to be known from and in it. We might formulate the question thus : How far is the reality of Jesus Christ (about which we let ourselves be told that it is identical with the reality of the revelation of God) an adequate ground for the fact that God's revelation encounters men, and for its effective operation ? How far has the reality Jesus Christ the power (*potestas, virtus,* δύναμις) to be the reality of revelation ? How far, therefore, has such identity validity ? Our question is not whether it has it. We assume that we have been told it has. Nor is our question where it gets it from, how it comes to have it, etc.

We assume that we have been told that it has it in itself and not from any other source. But our question is : Wherein does it have it ? In what does it consist ? What is its suitability for this specific work and for this specific effect ? How far does it require this same reality for this work and for this effect ?

It can be shown that this question is not purely arbitrary and self-willed, but that it is prescribed for us. The reality of revelation as such answers a question. It tells us what is required in order that the work of God's revelation may take place and in order that it may achieve this effect, namely a manifestness of God for man. How should we understand it, if we were not to regard it as the answer to this question ? But if we let ourselves be told that this answer is called Jesus Christ, i.e., God's Son who became Man, the Man who was God's Son, and if therefore this existence of Jesus Christ is itself the objective possibility of revelation consisting in God's freedom, then obviously we are faced with the task of understanding the existence of Jesus Christ as the objective possibility of revelation. Obviously, what it needs with regard to the fact and effect of revelation is precisely that which Jesus Christ is. Our question as to this need thus does not proceed from a previously conceived general concept of revelation, but is prescribed for us by what we find fulfilled and realised in the revelation attested in Holy Scripture. But it is this fulfilled and realised revelation that we regard—how else should we regard it ?— as the fulfilment and realisation of a need, as the answering of a question. Our task, therefore, if we wish to understand revelation, is to understand this question as such in its relation to the answer given, and this answer itself in relation to the question answered in it.

How are this question and answer reached ? To discern this we must start with the fact that, so far as it is attested for us in Holy Scripture as the reality of God's revelation, the reality of Jesus Christ has also a strictly critical significance. When we are told in it that God is free for us here, we are also told restrictively that He is not free for us elsewhere. It limits the freedom of God for us to itself. It tells us that only here, in this man-ness of God, in the God-ness of this Man, is God free for us. It stamps itself—we shall still have to speak specially about this—as a mystery and in token thereof as a miracle, i.e., as an exception from the rule of the cosmos of realities that otherwise encounter man, it claims to be attested and known in this exceptional way corresponding to its exceptional character. Viewed apart from itself, it makes God a God hidden from men, and it makes man a man blind to God. To that extent the very reality of revelation in which God shows His freedom for us, also tells us that God is not free for us, not for us to attain or to have. It is not the sceptic or atheist who is aware of this. The God whose existence or manifestness they doubt or deny is not God at all. And so too His absence, as they think they should assert it, is not God's absence at all. In order to be aware of God's absence they would first of all have to know God and therefore God's revelation. All general intellectual difficulties and impossibilities respecting knowledge of so-called supernatural things assert nothing at all in face of the negation of all other know-ability of God which is achieved by God's revelation itself. God does not belong to those supernatural things which may be believed and asserted to-day, doubted and denied to-morrow. And so the diffi-culties and impossibilities respecting knowledge of these things, which the sceptic and atheist fancy they should take so very seriously, have nothing whatever to do with the hiddenness of God for man or with man's blindness for God. The seriousness of the fact that God is not free for us, not to be possessed, first begins with the revelation which delimits this fact, yet also illumines and confirms it in its factuality.

We have to remember here that both the inconceivability of God and also the darkening of man's reason regarding Him are not general truths but the truth of revelation and faith. The Psalmists are aware of God's real absence (cf. e.g., Pss. 22, 28, 38, 39, 42, 44, 69, 74, 77, 80, 83, 85, 88, 89, 130, 139, 142, 143) not although, but precisely because, they are in a position to confess and to glorify His presence. On the contrary, all the denials of His presence, all the assertions of which we are masters respecting the hiddenness of God and our own incapacity to know Him without the Gospel, are only exercises (not to say prevarications) of no consequence compared to the limit really drawn between God and man. By their means we can but deceive ourselves as to the real position of things between Him and us.

Revelation itself is needed for knowing that God is hidden and man blind. Revelation and it alone really and finally separates God and man by bringing them together. For by bringing them together it informs man about God and about himself, it reveals God as the Lord of eternity, as the Creator, Reconciler and Redeemer, and char-acterises man as a creature, as a sinner, as one devoted to death. It does that by telling him that God is free for us, that God has created and sustains him, that He forgives his sin, that He saves him from death. But it tells him that this God (no other) is free for this man (no other). If that is heard, then and not till then the boundary between God and man becomes really visible, of which the most radical sceptic and atheist cannot even dream, for all his doubts and negations. Since the boundary is visible, revelation, which crosses this boundary, is also visible as a mystery, a miracle, an exception. The man who listens here, sees himself standing at the boundary where all is at an end. Whichever way I look, God is hidden for me and I am blind to Him. The revelation that crosses this boundary, and the together-ness of God and man which takes place in revelation in spite of this boundary, make the boundary visible to him in an unprecedented way. No longer need he yield to deceptions regarding the cosmos of realities that otherwise encounter him. This cosmos will lose the power to prepare for him either illusions or disillusionments. He knows all about it. Not because he has supplied himself with information

about it by intuitive or analytico-synthetic means, but because
he has been informed about it. But this information is, that among
the realities of this cosmos there is not one in which God would be
free for man. In this cosmos God is hidden and man blind. Once
more, it is God's revelation which gives him this information. That
it does so is its critical significance. By that very fact, however, the
further question is thrust at us : how far is God free for us in His
revelation ? No less than everything, i.e., no less than the whole of
man's cosmos, seems to speak against this possibility taking place.
Even if it is ever so great and rich, as it actually is, how could one
of its realities have the power to be God's revelation to man ? Once
again, man would have to leave the real revelation of God out of
account ; he would have to forget that he is informed about God and
about himself, if he is to assert boldly the presence of such a power
as one of the realities of his cosmos.

To such bold forgetfulness or forgetful boldness much is, of course, possible
and also much is to be forgiven. Who has not daily caught himself thus evading
the real revelation with which he ought to be content when once he has heard
it ? Who does not daily need pardon here ? Who, then, need be amazed and
indignant if talk about the possibility of a revelation alongside revelation or
about a twofold revelation crops up continually like weeds in a newly weeded
garden, even in the best theological society ? But if we are constantly to be
asking pardon for ourselves and therefore constantly to be pardoning others,
it is still the case that this talk is a scandal which can proceed only from a
permanent, or passing, but always radical, incompetence with regard to the
whole business. If a man cannot rest content with such information as we
receive through revelation, if in addition to it, he can still go on, or go back
to speak uncritically of the possibility of a second and perhaps a third or fourth
revelation alongside of the one, he at once betrays the fact that, permanently
or temporarily, the reality of it has ceased to be present to him. He is no longer
aware of what he is speaking when he speaks about revelation. If he were
looking steadily at the cross and the resurrection of Jesus Christ, he could not
look in any other direction, neither could he any longer allow talk about such
possibilities to pass his lips or to flow from his pen. If and so far as he is capable
of that, he cannot be expert in his understanding of matters of revelation.

If, then, it is fixed that from the side of revelation itself absolutely
everything speaks against the possibility of revelation becoming an
event, then the question arises respecting the reality in which miraculously and exceptionally it is nevertheless an event. How can it
become an event here ? That it is, and therefore can be, an event,
is not self-evident for the very reason that we let ourselves be told so.
To understand, then, must mean to hear an answer to the question
necessarily raised by the critical significance of revelation itself. But
the thing to do here is to listen to the reality of revelation itself, and
not to bypass it. No other possibility can be the possibility that calls
for interrogation here ; otherwise it would be identical with the possibility miraculously and exceptionally realised and fulfilled in revelation. If we remember that we have been informed and how we have
been informed, no other possibility than this can be considered along-

side of this one. Consideration of any other possibility is already cut off by this information. Therefore, to the question how far the reality of Jesus Christ can be God's revelation for us, the only fundamental answer is : As far as the reality of Jesus Christ requires for the revelation of God to us. What we need, what is necessary for this, follows from what Jesus Christ can do. He can do exactly what we need. And what He can do is all that we need. The possibility of revelation is actually to be read off from its reality in Jesus Christ. Therefore at bottom the individual explanation to which we now proceed can be only a reading and exegesis of this reality.

1. We infer from the reality of Jesus Christ that God is free for us in the sense that revelation on His side becomes possible in such a way that He is God not only in Himself but also in and among us, in our cosmos, as one of the realities that meet us. The reality of Jesus Christ, consisting in the fact that God is this Man and this Man is God, invariably asserts that God can cross the boundary between Himself and us ; or expressed in general terms, between His own existence and the existence of that which is not identical with Himself. However strictly this boundary line may be drawn and remain drawn —and we do not find it easy to think strictly enough about it—it is no obstacle to Him in the act of His revelation. His nature as God compared with our nature as men, His nature as Lord, Creator, Reconciler and Redeemer compared with ours as creatures and sinners doomed to die, does not limit Him in such a way that, in spite of all, He cannot be God within the sphere indicated by this nature of ours. His majesty is so great that even in the lowliness of this God-existence of His in our sphere, even when identical with one of the realities of our cosmos which meet us, and precisely in the midst of this lowliness, it can still be majesty, indeed in that very way it can show itself to be majesty. Not only what is impossible with us men, but also what must rightly appear to us impossible with God Himself, is possible with God. So it becomes possible in His freedom that He should be our God.

'Η δὲ πρὸς τὸ ταπεινὸν κάθοδος περιουσία τίς ἐστι τῆς δυνάμεως οὐδὲν ἐν τοῖς πάρα φύσιν κωλυωμένης. There is nothing surprising in a flame shooting upwards and not downwards ; on the contrary, it corresponds with its nature. But the fact that the flame is bound to its own nature is the very sign of its creatureliness. It corresponds with the greatness of God, however, not to be tied down and limited by His own nature. Therefore more than in the greatness of the heavens corresponding with their nature, more than in the brightness of the stars, more than in the ordering and control of the universe, the " divine transcendent power " in the act of its ἐπὶ τὸ ἀσθενὲς τῆς φύσεως ἡμῶν συγκατάβασις, is proved by the fact, that that which is high, without descending from its height, bows down to that which is lowly and itself appears in lowliness, in that Deity becomes human and yet remains divine (Gregory of Nyssa, *Or. cat.* 24).

The majesty of God in His condescension to the creature—that is the most general truth always told us by the reality of Jesus Christ.

If, then, we cannot conceive of His God-ness according to its nature either in its pure majesty or in its condescension to earth, but can only recognise and worship it in its actuality in virtue of its revelation, yet this much we can understand, that clearly we are always in need of the very fact that God showed us His condescension, in order that He might be free for us. As we reflect on the way that He has actually opened up, we can say that if He wished to reveal Himself, if He wished to be free for us, this very miracle had to take place, namely, that without ceasing to be Himself He entered our sphere, assumed our nature. He had to if He wished to impart Himself to us, to become the Mediator of Himself to us. That is what we mean when we say that He is God, not only in Himself but also in us and among us. In that case we are saying that He becomes a Mediator, God in Himself, but also a reality in our cosmos. That He can be both and that this possibility of His as such is the possibility of His revelation, is the most general meaning of the incarnation of the Word of God, of the name Jesus Christ, of His God-ness and His man-ness.

Therefore is *Christus homo et Deus ex utroque concretus, ut mediator esse inter nos et patrem posset* (Cyprian, *Ad. Quir.* II 10). *Non mediator homo praeter deitatem, non mediator Deus praeter humanitatem. Ecce mediator : divinitas sine humanitate non est mediatrix ; humanitas sine divinitate non est mediatrix ; sed inter divinitatem solam et humanitatem solam mediatrix est humana divinitas et divina humanitas Christi* (Augustine, *Sermo* 47, 12, 2). Christ is the way, and as God the *via quo itur,* the way in its direction to the goal—as Man the *via qua itur,* the way as the stretch leading to this goal (*De civ. Dei* XI 2). " Christ is the light of men through His humanity . . . through which His divinity shineth as through a mirror or a coloured glass, or as the sun through a light cloud ; for the light is ascribed to the divinity not to the humanity ; yet the humanity is not despised, since it is there as the cloud and curtain of this light " (Luther, *Pred. über Jn.* 1^(ff.), *Kirchenpostille* 1522 *W.A.* 10^I p. 223 l. 21).

We must know what we mean when we say that God " had to " become His own Mediator, and therefore " had to " become man, in order to become manifest to us, and that by so becoming He " was able " to become manifest to us. Derived from general conceptions of God, man and revelation, this statement would be wrong. Even in this connexion, apart from the reality of revelation itself, there is no discoverable necessity compelling us to say of God that He had to do one thing and could not do something else.

Augustine (*De Trin.* XIII 10) and Thomas Aquinas (*S. theol.* III *qu.* 1 *art.* 2c) rightly call attention to the fact that the freedom of God's almightiness must be respected here under all circumstances. " To make any one of His revelations unconditionally necessary is to make Him dependent upon creatures " (F. Diekamp, *Kath. Dogm.*^6 vol. 2 1930 p. 187).

But the statement in question can also be read off from the reality of revelation. The words " had to " and " was able " may explain the necessity of this reality as posited and determined thus and not otherwise in God's freedom, as the reality meets us in His revelation.

In this case the question whether God had to, whether He could not do otherwise, can be met by pointing to what is in accordance with His good pleasure according to Holy Scripture.

We can then appeal with a good conscience to the ἔπρεπεν in Heb. 2¹⁰ and the ὤφειλεν in Heb. 2¹⁷. *Nec putandum, nos hoc statuendo limites ponere velle omnipotentiae Dei, vel quid summo jure possit in creaturam definire. Sed tantum ostendimus ex scriptura quid possit vel non possit Deus iuxta potentiam ordinatam* (F. Turrettini, *Instit. Theol. el.* 1682 XIII *qu.* 3, 18).

2. We infer from the reality of Jesus Christ that God is free for us, in the sense that He reveals Himself to us in such a way that His Word or His Son becomes a man—not God the Father, and not God the Holy Spirit. If we try to understand this also, we have first of all to remember that the distinctions of God the Father, Son and Holy Spirit do not signify a partition in God's nature and activity. As Father, Son and Holy Spirit He is in His nature the one God completely and not partially. The statement that it is the Word or the Son of God who became man therefore asserts without reserve that in spite of His distinction as Son from the Father and the Holy Spirit, God in His entire divinity became man.

It was, of course, not merely a statement of the early Lutheran, but also a statement of the early Reformed theology, that *tota quidem natura divina bene dicitur incarnata . . . quia personae Filii Dei nihil deest quoad perfectionem divinae naturae* (F. Turrettini, *Instit. Theol. el.* 1682 XIII *qu.* 4, 7).

But it is not the one nature of God as such with whose operation we have to do here. It is the one nature of God in the mode of existence of the Son, which became Man.

The Word which is God became Man, but not the Deity as such (John of Damascus, *Ekdos.* 3, 11). *Persona Filii, non natura quae tribus personis communis, proprie loquendo incarnata est, nisi naturam consideremus qua Filii est* (*Syn. pur. Theol.* Leiden 1624 *Disp.* 25, 9).

In view of the unity of God's nature, which is not disputed but confirmed by the threeness of His modes of existence as Father, Son and Spirit, and in view of the mutual inner unity of these three modes of God's existence, it has to be said further that the Word or the Son does not become Man without the Father or without the Holy Spirit, but that the Word's becoming Man, like all the works of God, has to be regarded as the common work of the Father, the Son and the Holy Spirit.

Omnia simul Pater et Filius et amborum Spiritus pariter et concorditer operantur. And so also : *ipsam carnis assumptionem trinitas operata est* (Petr. Lomb. *Sent.* III *dist.* 1D).

In the work of becoming Man, common to the Father, the Son and the Holy Spirit, the order as in the Trinity is generally that the Father represents, as it were, the divine *Who*, the Son the divine *What*, and the Holy Spirit the divine *How*. Therefore, in spite of

2

and in the mutuality of this work, we must not say of the Father or
of the Holy Spirit but only of the Son, that He assumed humanity.

*Trinitas enim nos sibi reconciliavit per hoc quod solum Verbum carnem ipsa
trinitas fecit. Trinitas ergo carnis assumptionem fecit, sed Verbo, non Patri vel
Spiritui sancto* (Petr. Lomb., *op. cit. sup.*). The *actus assumentis* in the becoming
man is the common work of the Father, the Son and the Spirit, the *terminus
assumptionis* on the other hand is the Son alone ; *tres enim personae fecerunt, ut
humana natura uniretur uni personae Filii* (Thomas Aquinas, *S. theol.* III qu. 3
art. 4, c). The becoming man is *inchoative* (as divine action) a *commune opus*
of the whole Trinity, *terminative* on the other hand (as the divine determination
achieved through this action) it is the *opus proprium Filii* (A. Polanus, *Synt.
Theol. christ.* 1609 p. 2347). The early theologians (e.g., A. Polanus, *op. cit. sup.*
and A. Quenstedt, *Theol. did. pol.* 1685 III *c.* 3 *memb.* I *sect.* 1 *thes.* 24) liked to make
the event clear to themselves by the picture of two persons helping a third to put
on a cloak, so that we can just as well say of the third that (together with the
other two) he clothed himself, as that he was only clothed in the operation.

Even here, where we see what has actually happened in His Son,
there can be no question of understanding *how* the condescension of
God acts. We can only know and worship its actuality. But here
we can understand that what the Scripture attested for us as having
taken place in God's revelation was needed in order that God might
become free for us, that is, become manifest to us. Because God in
His one nature is not solitary but different in His modes of existence,
because He is the Father who has an only-begotten Son, therefore the
fact that He can be free for others, that He can be free for a reality
different from Himself, is eternally grounded within God Himself.
There is—amid the complete dissimilarity of divine and non-divine—
a similarity between the eternal Word of God and the world created
by this Word, but also and still more a similarity between the eternal,
natural, only-begotten Son and those who are through Him God's
adopted sons, who by grace are His children. In this similarity
between Him and us we recognise the possibility of the revelation of
God.

The two points were both made by Thomas Aquinas (*S. theol.* III qu. 3
art 8c), that the Second Person of the Trinity is a *similitudo exemplaris totius
creationis* and a *similitudo filiationis per adoptionem.* It can also be summarised
in this way : δι' οὗ ταύτην (κτίσιν) ἐδημιούργησεν ὁ πατήρ, ἐν αὐτῷ καὶ τὴν ταύτης
σωτηρίαν εἰργάσατο (Athanasius, *De incarn.* 1, 2). Or, *eius fuit ἀνακτίζειν, recreare,
cuius fuit creare, ut Verbum, per quod omnia facta sunt in prima creatione, reformaret
nos ad sui imaginem in secunda* (F. Turrettini, *op. cit. sup.* XIII 4, 6). In this
connexion we should recall the passage Jn. 1[11], according to which by entering
the world the Logos came to His own.

It is in this mode of being as the Word or the Son that God is
able to become manifest to us. We needed Him, God the Word or
the Son, in order that God might become manifest to us. In that
way He had to become manifest to us. Why ? Because already from
eternity, already in Himself, before we or the world existed, He was
ready and open for us, He was confederated with us in His Word or

Son. God in His Word or Son is identical with God who reveals Himself, who is able to be free for us.

We shall do well, however, to put in brackets all our talk about "needing" and "being able" and "must," and so all our inquiry after understanding. The trinitarian theology in which we have been engaging does not allow us to assert that God absolutely could not become manifest to us except in this way. The doctrine of the Trinity is not itself a text of revelation but only a commentary upon it. From the standpoint of the trinitarian theology it must be remembered that it is indeed a legitimate, genuine and necessary "appropriation" because taken from Holy Scripture, but it is no more than an appropriation, when we say actually of God the Son, as distinguished from the Father and the Holy Spirit, that He assumed humanity. There can be no talk of an absolute necessity in this statement or of an absolute understanding of its content. Let us be satisfied with understanding it at least relatively from the standpoints adduced—relatively to the factual reality of revelation as attested for us in Holy Scripture.

For this reason Thomas Aquinas' thesis is not *Necessarium* . . . but *Convenientissimum fuit personam Filii incarnari* (*op. cit. sup. art.* 8c), and (like Peter Lombard *op. cit. sup.*) he grants in principle that speaking absolutely, it might just as well have been otherwise, namely that *Pater vel Spiritus sanctus potuit carnem assumere sicut et Filius* (*op. cit. sup. art.* 5c). But absolute speaking can never be the subject matter of theology. The first *ratio* for the Son of God becoming man which F. Turrettini (*op. cit. sup. qu.* 4, 4) adduces, is in fact also the last, namely *quia scriptura hoc Filio soli tribuit, non Patri aut Spiritui sancto.* It is this and this alone that makes talk about "being able" or "having to" effective in this connexion.

We understand that the incarnation of the Son of God could be revelation, that for the purpose of God's revelation it was God's Son who had to become man—we may speak with a clear conscience of "can" and "having to"—because we take our stand not above but beneath the reality of revelation, and assign necessity to it and not to our grounds, not even to our grounds in trinitarian theology. All that our grounds can do is to show us the need for this reality. If we wanted or were able to speak absolutely we should only betray the fact that we have lost our theme.

3. We conclude from the reality Jesus Christ that God reveals Himself, that He is free for us, in such a way that God's Son or Word assumes a form at least known to us, such that He can become cognisable by us by analogy with other forms known to us. His humanity is the covering which He puts on, and therefore the means of His revelation. We return at once to the fact that it is humanity. But as such it is a form of being belonging to the cosmos, whose reality is also known to us in another way. God could have revealed Himself immediately, in His invisible glory. Or in order to be manifest to us, the Word might have assumed the form of a being previously

and otherwise wholly foreign to us, a being belonging to some other cosmos of reality. But that is not the case. As a mystery, revelation does not anywhere infringe the nature and history of our cosmos as we know them. Although with signs and wonders, things happen as they have always and everywhere happened since this cosmos began to exist. That is to say, at a definite point in space and time there lives and dies a human being like us all. In this human being God's Word is revealed to us.

Jesus Christ can be " placarded " before the eyes of men (Gal. 3¹). In the *Epistle to Diognetus* (7 2 f.) the fact is stressed that in His revelation God has not acted tyrannically, by surprise or terrifyingly, but ἐν ἐπιεικείᾳ καὶ πραΰτητι, by sending Christ, One like Himself, to men as one like themselves, ὡς καλῶν οὐ διώκων, ὡς ἀγαπῶν, οὐ κρίνων. Βία γὰρ οὐ πρόσεστι τῷ θεῷ. The same gentleness of God is also indicated by Ignatius of Antioch (*Ad Eph.* 7²) when he describes Jesus Christ in His unity of flesh and Spirit, of begottenness and unbegottenness, who came in the flesh and was alive in death, son of Mary and Son of God, sufferer and above all suffering, as a physician because of this condescension to our estate. And Irenaeus, in his description of the incarnation, writes : *Homo verbum Dei factum est, semetipsum homini et hominem semetipsi assimilans, ut per eam quae est ad Filium similitudinem, pretiosus homo fiat Patri* (*C.o.h.* V 16, 2). And Augustine : *Oportebat ut haberet aliquid simile Deo, aliquid simile hominibus* (*Conf.* X 42, 67). And Luther : " Let us thank the Father that He hath so ordered it, and hath put between us one who is God and is like God, and is man and is like men. For we are men and He is God ; if they are to encounter each other, the man must go to pieces. Therefore hath God tempered it, in that He hath set one to be the means who is God and man, by whom we must come to the Father. . . ." (*Pred über Joh.* 3¹⁶ᶠ, 1522 *W.A.* 10ᴵᴵᴵ p. 161 l. 21).

Through this likeness, then, God can become accessible to us because—in the broadest sense of the word—visible to us. A man we can see, physically or spiritually or both at once. Jesus Christ can reveal God because He is visible to us men as a man. His actual entry into this visibility signifies, let us remember, the entry of the eternal Word of God into veiling, into *kenosis* and passion. But this very veiling, *kenosis* and passion of the Logos, has to take place in order that it may lead to His unveiling and exaltation and so to the completion of revelation. God's revelation without this veiling or in the form of an unknown being from another world would not be revelation but our death. It would be the end of all things, because it would mean the abolition of the conditions of our existence.

In that case revelation would obviously be the act of violence, of which the Epistle to Diognetus says that it would not have been worthy of God. Εἰ γὰρ μὴ ἦλθεν ἐν σαρκί, οὐδ᾽ ἂν πως ἄνθρωποι ἐσώθησαν βλέποντες αὐτόν, they who are unable for one moment to gaze into the beams of the created sun (Ep. of Barnabas, 5¹⁰). But : *Per incarnati Verbi mysterium nova mentis nostrae oculis lux tuae claritatis infulsit : ut, dum visibiliter Deum cognoscimus, per hunc in invisibilium amorem rapiamur* (*Missale Rom., Praef.* to Christmastide).

God bends down to us as it were, by assuming this form familiar to us. His love is already announced to us in the fact that even in

His veiling—in which He has first to be unveiled as God, to be believed in as God—He yet does not meet us as a stranger.

Qui propter immensam suam dilectionem factus est quod nos sumus (Irenaeus, *C.o.h.* V *praef.*).   He is *Deus homo* and as such *indicium divinae in nos dilectionis* (Augustine, *De cat. rud.* 4, 8).

But if we conclude from this that God was able and had to reveal Himself to us in this familiar form, that it was the very thing we needed—we must not forget that we can say so only in thankful retrospect upon what God has really done—not on the ground of an *analogia entis* already visible to us beforehand, of an affinity and aptitude for God's revelation, belonging to the world since creation, familiar to us and recognisable in it despite the Fall, as if God were now utterly bound to it.   What happens to the familiar cosmic reality now that the human nature in Christ is adopted and taken up into this unity with the Son of God, is substantially a restoration and confirmation of its original connexion with God.   But—because this connexion was broken and lost—it is not a linking up with a condition which it already possessed and with which we could already be familiar, but a free and undeserved distinction, based only upon grace and not at all upon nature, a distinction which happens to "nature."   Of that which is worthy of God we cannot speak on the basis of a previous understanding, but only on the basis of a subsequent understanding, whereby we do not express any judgment as to what was necessary for God, but only acknowledge what He obviously regarded as necessary.   God could also reveal Himself in His invisible glory.   He could also do so in the form of a being unknown to us and so at the end of all things, which that would necessarily involve.   When we say that He had to act otherwise, we honour the actual will of God visible in the event of His revelation, as the source and inner concept of all necessity. We are thus repeating what was previously told us.   By such repetition we shall and must acknowledge the necessity of His actual manifest will, His *potentia ordinata*.

4. From the reality of Jesus Christ we gather that revelation is possible on God's side, that God is free for us, in such a way that His Word by becoming Man at the same time is and remains what He is, the true and eternal God, the same as He is in Himself at the Father's right hand for ever and ever.   The *kenosis*, passion, humiliation which He takes upon Himself by becoming man, signifies no loss in divine majesty but, considered in the light of its goal, actually its triumph. We may and must, of course, speak of a veiling of the divine majesty. By becoming flesh the Word enters the hiddenness, the "servant form," which in respect of the knowability of God undoubtedly signifies an "externalisation" (*kenosis*) compared with the "divine form" in which God knows Himself, in which the Father knows the Son and the Son the Father.   It is in this veiling—which after all is a veiling

in a form familiar to man—that the Majesty can meet men and so far make knowledge of itself possible through men. But it may also fail of recognition in this its " servant form." Its actual exposure to this failure to be recognised is the " externalisation " which the Word allows to befall itself in becoming flesh. Knowledge of it becomes real to men only in virtue of a special unveiling through Jesus' resurrection from the dead, or through all the sayings and acts of His life so far as they were signs of His resurrection. Thus God's becoming man means undoubtedly in the first instance that His divinity becomes latent.

Ἐπειδὴ τὸ τῆς θεότητος πρόσωπον οὐδεὶς ἠδύνατο ἰδεῖν ζῶν, ἀνέλαβε τὸ τῆς ἀνθρωπότητος πρόσωπον, ἵνα τοῦτο ἰδόντες ζήσωμεν (Cyril of Jerusalem, *Cat.* 10, 7).

> " In our poor flesh and blood
> Is clad th' eternal Good." (Luther.)

Humilitate contentus, carnis velamine suam divinitatem abscondi passus est. . . . Quid enim hoc sibi vult, figura repertum fuisse tanquam hominem, nisi quia ad tempus non resplenduit divina gloria, sed tantum in vili et abiecta conditione apparuit humana species ? (Calvin, *Instit.* II 13, 2). *Paulisper interea delitescebat eius divinitas, hoc est vim suam non exserebat (Cat. Genev.* 1545 in K. Müller p. 123, 17).

But the succession of veiling and unveiling, incarnation and resurrection (John and the Synoptists) suggests that in the veiling, in the incarnation, we do not have to do with a lessening in the divinity of the eternal Word. That it is only veiling, not abandonment nor yet lessening of His divinity, is shown by the unveiling, which is not only the result but from the start—it is revelation we are concerned with—its goal. He who the third day rose from the dead was no less true God in the manger than on the cross. By becoming flesh the Word is no less true and entire God than He was previously in eternity in Himself. Incarnation of the Word means neither wholly nor in part any changing of the Word into something else, but the becoming flesh of the Word that remains the Word, the Word-ness and the flesh-ness of the Word simultaneously.

Τοῦτο γίνεται, καὶ ἐκεῖνο ἔστιν (Gregory of Nyssa, *Or. cat.* 24). *Descendit a Patre, qui nunquam desiit esse cum Patre . . . nec amisit, quod erat, sed coepit esse, quod non erat, ita tamen ut perfectus in suis sit et verus in nostris* (" *Fides Damasi,*" end of 4th cent. ? Denz. No. 16). *Manens quidem in divinitate sua et non recedens a Patre nec in aliquo mutatus, assumendo tamen hominem et in carne mortali hominibus apparendo venit ad homines* (Augustine, *De cat. rud.* 26, 52). The Incarnation takes place *non conversione divinitatis in carnem sed assumptione humanitatis in Deum (Quicunque vult). Incarnationis mysterium non est impletum per hoc quod Deus sit aliquo modo a suo statu immutatus, in quo ab aeterno fuit : sed per hoc novo modo creaturae sibi univit vel potius eam sibi* (Thomas Aquinas, *S. theol.* III qu. 1 art. 1 ad. 1). *Virgo, Dei genetrix, quem totus non capit orbis in tua se clausit viscera factus homo (Miss. Rom., Graduale* for the Feast of Mary's Birth).

> Whom all the world could ne'er contain
> He lies in Mary's lap ;
> Who all things doth alone sustain
> Hath ta'en an infant's hap. (Luther.)

Idem ille, qui antehac Verbum, qui vita, qui lux erat, idem caro iam factus est. Quod prius fuerat, id esse non desiit et factus est quod non fuerat prius (J. A. Bengel, on Jn. 1[14] in the *Gnomon N.T.*).

Again we have to say that we cannot conceive *how* this actually took place. How could the breaking through of the rule of the conceivable, with which we are here concerned, succeed in becoming conceivable ? But we can understand that this very breaking through was needed, in order that revelation in its genuine, proper sense might become an event. In this way God is able to reveal Himself ; in this way it has to be, if He wishes to reveal Himself. As a transformation of the Word into a reality different from God, the incarnation of the Word obviously could not be God's revelation, any more than if in its place an immediate appearance of the invisible glory of God had become an event. It can be God's revelation as the presence of the Word, undiminished though veiled in its God-ness, in the fleshly reality different from God. In this way God may be present to us, but present precisely as God.

Neque enim alius poterat enarrare nobis, quae sunt Patris nisi proprium ipsius Verbum (Irenaeus, *C.o.h.* V 1, 1). *Ut homo fidentius ambularet ad veritatem, ipsa veritas, Dei Filius, homine assumpto, constituit atque fundavit fidem* (Augustine, *De civ. Dei* XI 2).

All these are conclusions from the reality in which it was God's actual good pleasure to reveal Himself, but they are not assumptions —where should we get these ?—with which we could control this reality. We speak of " needing " and " being able " and " having to," because we acknowledge that it has pleased God to reveal Himself to us through the unrestrictedly true presence of His divinity in the man Jesus of Nazareth. We acknowledge this reality to be necessary. But we cannot deny that it might have pleased God to reveal Himself in another way as well.

Here we must venture the dangerous statement that it might have pleased Him to reveal Himself after the fashion posited by the theory of ancient and modern Docetism or Ebionitism, which does not do justice to the witness of the New Testament, i.e., by some sort of abandonment or diminution of His divinity. Were that so, were the New Testament witness to run otherwise than it now does, then we should just have to regard as necessary a reality corresponding to such a witness in the New Testament and indeed to one of the above theories.

But once more it would be senseless to allow the possibility of a reality not actually given (which can come up for consideration only if we deviate from the witness of Holy Scripture) to become a rival, so to speak, of the possibility realised in the actually given reality. On the contrary, by holding to the latter, we say (under the proviso that we were not already aware of it beforehand, that we were only repeating it) that it is the possibility, the necessary form, of revelation.

5. Finally, we conclude from the reality of Jesus Christ, that God's revelation becomes possible in such a way that God's Son or Word

becomes Man. He does not become any kind of natural being. He becomes what we ourselves are.

It is not for us to know in advance what we are on the ground of a general anthropology. We are what the Word of God tells us we are. We are flesh. And that is what God's Word Himself becomes in His revelation. Right in the decisive passage Jn. 1¹⁴, it does not say generally " man," but concretely " flesh." Flesh, of course, signifies man, humanity or man-ness, but not in such a way that by this designation a fuller content is added to a conception of man already familiar or to a conception which can be acquired from other sources. In a fundamental, final and exclusive sense, the concept of man ought to be that he is " flesh," because it is this which fundamentally, finally and exclusively distinguishes man as he stands before God. That alone determines the true conception of man : the way he stands before God. But that is an assertion that man's interpretation of himself as " flesh " is not one to be gained in advance, but only to be derived from the revealed Word and verdict of God. To regard ourselves as " flesh " means to adopt this verdict of God in faith. The Word of God tells us that we are created by God out of nothing and held up by Him over nothing. We are exposed to His just judgment and wrath, and if we are not lost but saved, that is not our work and merit but God's free grace. We are liable to die, and if nevertheless we live in the midst of death, it is because here and now we are already encountering an eternal redemption through Him. This is the meaning of being flesh. This is the tenor of the Word and verdict of God upon us. This is how we stand before God. This is the real meaning of being a man.

It is this humanity that the Son of God has assumed. The act of the triune God in the reality of Jesus Christ is that in this reality He was not only what He is in Himself in eternity. He was also with us and among us. He was also what we are. He was also flesh. Of course, as His humanity, it became a different thing from ours, for sin, man's strife with God, could not find any place in Him. Yet apart from this single characteristic it is our own familiar humanity out and out, namely, not only with its natural problems, but with the guilt lying upon it of which it has to repent, with the judgment of God hanging over it, with the death to which it is liable. The Son of God could not sin—how could God be untrue to Himself ? But all of this, the entire curse of sin, which is what Holy Scripture means when it calls men flesh, this curse the Son of God has taken upon Himself and borne by becoming a man. And to that very extent He became a real, genuine, true man, man placed before God.

And now, once more, we cannot conceive how this can actually take place, as in fact it really has taken place in Jesus Christ. How can the grace that becomes visible at this particular point be conceivable by us ? Yet here too we can understand that this inconceivable thing had to become an event in order that God's revelation might become possible. The Word of God a man, a man the Word of God—this is the objective possibility of revelation. We can understand that it is so—because it is a reality. God wills to veil Himself by becoming a man, in order by breaking out of the veiling to unveil Himself as a man. He wills to be silent and yet also to speak. His humanity must be a barrier, yet also a door that opens. It must be a problem to us, yet also the solution of the problems. He would die as a true man, only to rise from the dead the third day as the same true man. It is always in the act of moving from the one point to the other, in the decision by which the second springs from the first, that God's revelation is accomplished in the reality of Jesus Christ. It was by revealing Himself as a man that He was able to do both. Man—that is, not in the sense of an anthropology, but man whose understanding of himself is stamped by the verdict of God, man as he is faced with God, man who is flesh—man is able to do both the things in question here. He takes his place in this divine decision. We can understand that God is able to veil and to unveil Himself in flesh. Pointedly put : (1) we can understand that we can fail to understand man who is flesh, fail to understand him more radically than we can with anything else in the world; (2) we can understand that we can understand man who is flesh, so understand him as we can understand nothing else in the world. Thus—putting the two together—we can understand that God can reveal Himself in man who is flesh, i.e. can, veil and unveil Himself. But this requires a brief elucidation.

On the one hand, there is nothing stranger, nothing more puzzling to a man than a fellow-man. All other relationships in which we live may become plain to us ; we can finally and ultimately dissolve them into relationships to ourselves.

Our ability to do so is shown in the theoretical field by the possibility of an idealist theory of knowledge ; by which we need not think straight away of its culmination in J. G. Fichte, or of its reversal in Max Stirner. In practice this solubility of the non-human non-ego becomes most evident when we think of what man can be in relation to the beast, which of all non-human things stands, as is said, nearest to him. And man has only to be relatively a little lonely in the non-human cosmos (forest, ocean, mountains)—and the more so, the more overpowering, the more Indian the profusion of visions—to be impelled to attempt to regard it all as " his " world, as a reflection of his ego, as the veil of Maya. It is possible to regard it as that.

This astonishing power in man and in his fellow-man in the historical world has its limits, often unnoticed or forgotten, yet perfectly definite and always returning to the field of vision. What proclaims itself to us in other men is objectivity. And if there is anything like a really hard, impervious objectivity, it is in other men that it succeeds in making itself known to us..

Ludwig Feuerbach regards God as a projection of human self-consciousness, but, unlike M. Stirner, he not only recognises this but interprets it to mean that it is first of all from the objectivity of our neighbour that we are able, that we are bound to have any acquaintance with objectivity at all. " An object, a real object is given me only where I am given a being that acts upon me, where my self-activity . . . finds its limits—finds resistance—in the activity of another being. The concept of object is originally nothing else than the concept of another ego . . . hence the concept of an object in general is mediated by the concept of a Thou, of an objective ego " (*Philos. d. Zukunft* 1843 § 32). " The first stone of stumbling upon which the pride of egoism breaks is the Thou, the other ego. . . . A completely self-existent man would lose himself without self or distinction in the ocean of nature ; he would neither apprehend himself as man nor nature as nature. The first object of man is man " (*Das Wesen des Christentums*, 1841, *Recl.* p. 155). Now in this matter Feuerbach must have been brought up upon a surviving scrap of Christian insight, the origin of which he had ceased to be aware of. That the pride of the ego does not, as a rule, secretly shatter itself upon another ego, that although we do not exist alone we may very well get lost in the ocean of nature, that we are quite capable of dodging a Thou, since with Fichte we let it get swallowed up in the huge mass of non-ego—rather proves that man in general does not possess the property of objectivity over against his fellow. Man who is flesh, man the creature, the sinner liable to death, has these qualities. To behold this man is to behold what is alien, puzzling, insoluble, that which is not yet transparent, that which stands over against us as object (*Gegen-Stand*). If Feuerbach meant what the Bible calls " our neighbour," then we must agree with him.

If we are aware of what we are by God's verdict, and thence aware also of what a fellow-man is, then he becomes for us a real other, an object, a closed door. The encounter with man who is flesh is the encounter by which we exist. And in that case we will understand that his existence can cover up and conceal something, make a mystery of it, as nothing else in the world can. It may therefore become the means of divine revelation which is always a veiling as well.

On the other hand, there is nothing nearer or more familiar to man than just man. Nothing else comes closer to us, is so constitutive for ourselves, as the other man in all his strangeness and obscurity. To live as a man means to be related to man, to differ from him and to agree with him, to come from man and depend on man.

It was an exaggeration to think of defining human existence as " man that comes from man." We do not exist for our fellow-man, we exist for God. Nor is our existence for God dependent on our existence for our fellow-man. We are always dependent on our fellows, and we are ourselves and are mixed up with one another because we depend upon fellows. As a matter of fact we never are what we are except as we depend upon others, and depend upon them in a way that we are not dependent upon anything else in the world.

To see and hear is to see and hear men. The words that come to us, without which we ourselves would have no language, are human words. The place in the cosmos in which objectivity is announced to us, in which we can no longer say It, and therefore no longer I, but only Thou, and in which alone we can ultimately recognise ourselves in this particular way, is the human countenance. What is announced to us precisely in our neighbour is also something very near, extremely familiar and most intimately belonging to us. And if in an ultimate sense there is a disclosure, an impartation, a communication which comes to us, where else will it announce itself than as it does, in the same neighbour, who can stand for us as the essence of objectivity ?

But we cannot say even this about man in general, if we remember how problematic communication between men actually is—so far as we face up to ourselves as men in general. For who knows whom ? The man who might really open up and impart himself to us, the man whom we might really see and hear, whose words were bound to reach us, would have to be the man of the Bible who is flesh, man the creature, the sinner, doomed to death.

Once more it all comes down to our knowing what we are ourselves by God's verdict, with a view to knowing what our neighbour is too, so that he may be to us not only a closed door but also an open one. And then we will understand that his existence can make something hidden visible, can speak, can reveal—and this in a way that nothing else in the world can. His existence can thus become the means to divine revelation which is not only veiling but always unveiling as well.

To sum up : If God's revelation is the way from veiling of the eternal Word to His unveiling, from crib and cross to resurrection and ascension, how can it possibly be anything else than God's becoming man, His becoming flesh ? As the incarnation of the Word it can be revelation. To be revelation it had to be an incarnation. Incarnation was needed in order that God might become manifest to us, that He might be free for us.

But it will be appropriate if we put this last argument of ours in specially strong brackets. Let us first be clear that it has nothing to do with the attempt to prove a special property in man as such to be a bearer of the revelation of God. It might, of course, be said that man, too, belongs to the world which God has made very good, that this original goodness of man is certainly to be sought in his capacity for being the instrument of divine revelation, and that revelation in the shape of becoming man is the confirmation and restoration of this original goodness in man. But this line of thought is not adapted to prove the presence of an *analogia entis* by which we can measure God's action in revelation and by means of which we can understand His revelation in advance. It is not adapted to prove that man has a special capacity for revealing God. The fact that, and the extent to which, our humanity as such or man in general is in God's wisdom and goodness as Creator a useful means for God's revelation, is completely hidden from us (i.e., hidden in ourselves and in the world we know and in the way we know it). In revelation, in the reality of Jesus Christ, it is, of course, discernible by us. But how can we possibly draw inferences from the reality of Jesus Christ as to revelatory powers in our humanity as such, in man in general ? In the reality of Jesus Christ we do not find that the Word of God has become man in general but flesh. Thus, even if it were possible, the argument

just mentioned would not prove what has to be proved. It is certainly
not in its general humanity, in its intelligence, etc., but in its fleshliness
that man's nature has been chosen by the Word and made His temple
and tool. And it is not of man in general but of man who is flesh that
we have shown an ability to veil and to unveil, and thus to be a means
to God's revelation. But man who is flesh is man who faces God and
so already in himself man in spiritual reality, man whom God's revelation encounters. We are not saying too much when we say that really
and originally only Jesus Christ is man who is flesh, and then deriva-
tively and secondarily those who in faith are one flesh with Him.
Really and originally, therefore, flesh as the possibility of the revelation of God is entirely and emphatically the possibility of Jesus Christ
Himself. And only with Him in view can we say generally (with the
limited generality apposite in such a case) that the Word had to
become flesh, in order that thus and not otherwise God's revelation
might become objectively possible. Regarded generally, man as flesh
can only veil and unveil, because the Word became flesh, because it
pleased God to elect his fleshness and to make it the means to this
in the humanity of Jesus Christ. Far from being founded upon any
sort of general anthropology, our proof is absolutely related to Christology. The latter it only proves, so far as it already assumes it as the
means of proof.

Let us summarise. We set out to understand how far the reality
Jesus Christ is God's revelation. We let ourselves be summoned by
the abolition, brought about by revelation itself, of any other possibility of revelation, to ask precisely how far God's revelation is possible,
as it meets us in the reality of Jesus Christ. And then we discovered
this possibility of revelation (1) in the condescension whereby God in
Jesus Christ becomes identical with a reality different from Himself,
(2) in the fact that Jesus Christ is identical with God's Son or Word,
(3) in Jesus Christ's belonging actually to the cosmos of reality familiar
to us, (4) in Jesus Christ's belonging without diminution to God Himself, (5) in the man-ness, i.e., the flesh-ness of Jesus Christ. We have
thus spoken of the possibility of revelation, and of that only, which
is to be read off from its reality. Essentially this is the (only possible)
answer to the question : *Cur Deus homo ?* and the only legitimate
fulfilment of the programme : *Credo ut intelligam.*

THE TIME OF REVELATION

God's revelation in the event of the presence of Jesus Christ is God's time for us. It is fulfilled time in this event itself. But as the Old Testament time of expectation and as the New Testament time of recollection it is also the time of witness to this event.

1. GOD'S TIME AND OUR TIME

If by the statement, " God reveals Himself " is meant the revelation attested in Holy Scripture, it is a statement about the occurrence of an event. That means it also includes an assertion about a time proper to revelation. If stated with reference to this, it is equivalent to the statement, " God has time for us." The time God has for us is just this time of His revelation, the time that is real in His revelation, revelation time. Moreover in the interpretation of the concept of this time, which is now our task, we shall not have to take as a basis any time concept gained independently of revelation itself. If our consideration of the question as to the time of revelation is serious, we shall at once be aware (1) that we have no other time than the time God has for us, and (2) that God has no other time for us than the time of His revelation. Thus we must let ourselves be told what time is by revelation itself, and only then, and with that reference, form our idea of the time of revelation as such.

The sufficient reason for rejecting the possibility of working here with a time concept gained elsewhere, is contained in the basic subordination of the investigation here instituted to the revelation attested in Holy Scripture. Theologically the only sensible way of putting and answering the question as to the time of this revelation is to assume the special concept of this special time. But incidentally and without prejudice we may also indicate that time concepts gained otherwise are unsatisfactory, if our concern is to understand the time of revelation. I illustrate this with two very authoritative examples. (Cf. for what follows H. Barth, *Das Sein in der Zeit* 1933).

Augustine (*Conf.* XI 14 f.) regarded time as *quaedam distentio* (23), the subject of which is the human *animus* (26). This *distentio* is fulfilled in the act of measuring movement in the external world : *In te, anime meus, tempora metior* (27). In virtue of this measuring, the past becomes for us the object of recollection, *memoria*, the future the object of expectation, *exspectatio* (26, 28). If recollection and expectation mean representation of past and future (20), they also mean that past and future, as what has ceased to exist and what does not yet exist, are contrasted with what properly does exist (14). But what is the present ? My own present, my measurement as such of times : *Ecce distentio est vita mea* (29).

According to M. Heidegger (*Sein und Zeit*, vol. I 1929, § 65) " original time " is to be regarded as temporality, i.e., as the possibility of existence in virtue of which there may be " anxiety," i.e., in virtue of which one may " ecstatic-ally," by a " preliminary resolve " to achieve one's " very own and distinct possibility of existence," attain to oneself, i.e., to one's guilty past, and so in this past possess a present. Time is not, but existence is—by " bringing to a head " its own future, its own past, its own present.

Both these time concepts, so different in spite of their intimate relationship, would for two reasons be unsuitable presuppositions for interpreting the concept of revelation time.

1. Augustine, like Heidegger, regards time definitively and unequivocally as a self-determination of man's existence as a creature. Man possesses time by taking it for himself, in fact by creating it. That his time may be the time which God has for him, which God gives to him, is quite an alien idea on the ground either of the classical or of the modern time concept. In the case of Heidegger, in whose system God and His revelation are not provided for at all, nor indeed can be, this needs no proof ; time is just " brought to a head " in a " preliminary resolve " by a future indistinguishable from existence, i.e., from man himself. That there should be for us anything like God's time might in the framework of Heidegger's thought be little more than a quite superfluous metaphor. But the case with Augustine is not a whit different. Elsewhere (*De civ. Dei* XI 6, cf. XII 25) he does call God the *creator et ordinator temporum*. But in the great passage on time in the *Confessions* this statement is lacking ; and if it says there that past, present and future are in the soul and nowhere else (*et alibi ea non video, Conf.* XI 20), if times only originate in my own measure-ment (27) . . . *quia in animo, qui illud agit, tria sunt* (28), it is also difficult to see what independent content the statement just quoted can have for Augustine. Obviously it might be omitted altogether without there being any change in his time concept. Difficulties about a time which originates in the act of man's spirit, difficulties due to the consideration that this time which we think we "possess" might be a "lost" time, seem never to have come within his purview. For him as for Heidegger man possesses time—and he possesses it undisturbed (Heidegger gets rid of the "anxiety" by the device of transferring it to the existence which as such constitutes time) through realising himself. But if we are to understand the time of God's revelation, then our possession of time must be made compre-hensible as God's possession of it for us, overcoming the difficulties of our possession of it. A time concept which cannot rise to that can be of no service to us.

2. Augustine, like Heidegger, regards time definitively and conclusively as a conditioned reality, conditioned by being a determination, indeed a self-determination of man's existence as a creature. Reality lies with this exist-ence, with the act of man's *animus*, with " temporality " as the possibility of existence, but not with time as such. And we possess no other time than this, which in the last resort is only improperly real, which we ourselves posit by existing. This impropriety is not to be altered by Augustine's statement (natur-ally impossible to Heidegger) about God being the creator and ordainer of time. God creates time only so far as He creates man's existence, which as a *distentio* on its own account is the creator of time. On the lines of Augustine's thought, considering the impropriety of its reality, it would be an intolerable anthropo-morphism for God Himself to have to possess time and have time for us, by time becoming a determination of Himself in His revelation. But if we are to understand revelation time, time cannot be regarded merely as the product of man's existence interpreted as a *distentio* ; it must be regarded as a proper reality, as accessible to God as is human existence. A time concept which denies this cannot be of service to us.

There must be no appeal to God's creation of the world, and there-fore of time also, to justify taking over a time concept gained elsewhere as the precondition of investigating the concept of revelation time. Of course God is the Creator of time also. But the time we think we know and possess, " our " time, is by no means the time God created. Between our time and God-created time as between our existence and the existence created by God there lies the Fall. " Our " time, as Augustine and Heidegger in their own ways quite correctly inform us, is the time produced by us, i.e., by fallen man. If on the basis of God's Word being in this time of ours we believe that God created time, this belief does not sidetrack our time ; yet we cannot in any way identify our time with the time created by God. Our time, the time we know and possess, is and remains lost time, even when we believe that God is the Creator of time. God-created time remains a time hidden and withdrawn from us. If God's revelation has a time also, if God has time for us, if we really (really, in a theologically relevant sense) know and possess time, it must be a different time, a third time, created alongside of our time and the time originally created by God.

Cf. for the following K. Heim, " Zeit und Ewigkeit " (in *Glauben und Leben* 1928 p. 539 f.), E. Brunner, " Das Einmalige und der Existenzcharacter " (*Blätter für deutsche Philosophie* 1929 p. 265 f.), W. Vischer, " Das Alte Testament und die Geschichte " (*Z.d.Z.* 1932 p. 22 f., esp. p. 29).

In Jer. 33[20f. 25f.] we read of a " covenant " which Yahweh made with day and night, " that they should be in their season." This " covenant," as it were, guaranteeing time, is not simply identical with the creation of time as indicated in Gen. 1[14], on the occasion of the creation of the heavenly bodies. Time after the Fall is a different, a new time. It too consists in the alternation of day and night and in the continuance of this alteration. But the occurrence and continuance of this alternation cease to be on an obvious level with the created state of man and his world. After he ate of the tree of the knowledge of good and evil man was cut off from the tree of life (Gen. 3[23f.]). Moreover, " when the Lord saw that the wickedness of men grew great in the earth, and that every imagination and thought of their heart was only evil continually, it repented the Lord that He had made man upon the earth, and it grieved Him at His heart. And the Lord said, I will pluck the men whom I have created away from the earth . . . for it repenteth me that I have made them " (Gen. 6[5f.]). Even if the outcome is not the fulfilment of this judgment but on the contrary—after He had proclaimed clearly in the Flood how serious He was—an " everlasting covenant between God and every living creature of all flesh that is upon the earth " (Gen. 9[16]), man's existence continues to be a fallen one, and fundamentally guilty. It is an existence continuously dependent on divine patience and on hope, an existence grounded not on itself but upon the Word which God directs toward man, and by which God, while not restoring man to the tree of life, proclaims the covenant of grace. Human existence no longer possesses its time as that which is to be taken for granted in its created state. Its possession of time— " while earth remaineth, seedtime and harvest, cold and heat, summer and winter, day and night shall not cease " (Gen. 8[22])—has now become the object of a special promise, a work of special divine goodness.

How hidden and withdrawn from us is that first real time which God created, and how problematic the time actually is which we think we know and possess, may be illustrated—once more incidentally and without prejudice—by the three great difficulties in the common concept of time, which continue to be questions even when contrasted with the time concept of an Augustine or a Heidegger.

1. What is meant by the present, the present by whose measurement past is supposed to be past and future future, in and out of which time is supposed to arise ? Is the present really a third such thing and, as Augustine asserts, an original thing ? Is it not always, by our very desire to fix it, already relegated to the past or else transferred to the future ? Has it no place of its own, from the standpoint of which there is properly a past and a future and therefore time ? And is it supposed to exist, if the present is not a third thing but the one and entire thing, with past and future as mere *modi* of the present ? What do we know of time, if we have to admit that we know nothing of the present, which is apparently its so manifest medium, and which, so they say, is supposed to be its ground as well ?

2. Is time without beginning and end or has it a beginning and an end ?— the famous first antinomy of the antithetic of pure reason in Kant. It appears to be without beginning or end. Would not every beginning in time itself in turn be the end of a past time, and every end in time itself in turn the beginning of a future time ? Though separate time series may begin and end, time as such cannot. But would time be time without the moment in the present from the standpoint of which past is past and future is future ? And does this moment not continually change, does not the present move steadily forwards ? Must not this move forward mean, as Augustine (*Conf.* XI 28) already perceived, an increase in past time, a decrease in future ? Must not this move forward be an illusion, would not the present have to be stationary, if time before and after it were endless ? If this move forward were an illusion, and the present therefore stationary—at what point would it be stationary and how far would past and future, and therefore time, be recognisable ? But if this move forward is not an illusion, if the present is therefore not stationary, is not time in that case an endless quantum, capable of increase here, decrease there, because here it starts from a beginning, there it goes towards an end ? But the very fact that time has a beginning and an end we have had to regard as an impossibility. What then do we know about time, if we are equally unable to regard it as coming to an end and as without an end ?

3. What is the relation between time and eternity ? Has time its goal and therefore its purpose in eternity, or possibly just its nature and therefore its meaning ? Do we in the forward-moving present proceed from it in order to go and meet it ? Or are we in this move forward, to echo Schleiermacher, " eternal every moment " ? What a venture—what an illusion, we shall perhaps have to say plainly—to transfer eternity to the beginning and end of time, and thus to make time out to be increasingly remote from it and approximate to it —and then merely an increasing remoteness from it and approximation to it. But likewise what a venture and perhaps what an illusion, to explain it as the hidden content of all time, and therefore all time as a vessel—and then only a vessel—of eternity. Who will stand sponsor for the one thesis, who for the other ? For the belief in evolution or the expectation of catastrophe with which we have to seek eternity in the one case, or the flight of time with which we have to seek it in the other ? It is not easy at this point to see how far this responsibility is lightened, if with Augustine and Heidegger we strip time of its objectivity, in order to regard it as the way in which human existence exists. Am I who exist in time one who merely issues from eternity and goes to meet it, or one who already possesses it ? Can this question be evaded or left open ? And if not, who here is of opinion that he knows the first or knows the second, and can represent his case right to its ethical conclusions ? But what have we said, if we say " time " without being able to say something clear about its relation to eternity ?

All these *aporiae* do not mean that we know what we are saying, when in view of " our time," or in appealing to the first article of the *Credo* regarding the time created by God, we speak of a time which is known and belongs to us apart from and prior to God's revelation. And if anyone, by identifying both, asserts that his cataract has been removed by Christ, so that he can now, unlike the unbeliever, recognise the world once more as God's creation, and so " our time " as God-created time, let him prove it by answering the three questions. If " our " time is not a lost time, if God-created time is not permanently hidden and withdrawn, were these two times really identical or at least identical for a believer, these three questions will be answerable. Their unanswerability shows that we can only believe in the creation of time by God, as we believe in the creation itself, but cannot know it. And " our " time, the time we have and know, is preserved as " our " time obviously because all along the line it regards us as fools. The denial of the reality of time, as it was often enough attempted with more or less logicality and openness in pre-Christian as also in post-Christian philosophy, is nearly enough achieved where in solving the time problem account is taken only of the two times, the God-created and " our " time. To assert the reality of time in face of and in spite of these difficulties without the desire or the ability to set them aside, or even without letting oneself be worried by them, is perhaps in practice only possible for theology when it is revelation theology, and as such in a position to reckon not only with these two times, but in addition, with a quite different time.

But this different time is the new, the third time, which arises and has its place because God reveals Himself, because He is free for us, because He is with us and amongst us, because in short, without ceasing to be what He is, He also becomes what we are. God's revelation is the event of Jesus Christ. We do not understand it as God's revelation, if we do not state unreservedly that it took place in " our " time. But, conversely, if we understand it as God's revelation, we have to say that this event had its own time ; in this event it happened that whereas we had our own time for ourselves as always, God had time for us, His own time for us—time, in the most positive sense, i.e. present with past and future, fulfilled time with expectation and recollection of its fulfilment, revelation time and the time of the Old Testament and New Testament witness to revelation—but withal, His own time, God's time ; and therefore real time.

K. Heim writes (*op. cit. sup.* p. 560) : " If God is the highest reality upon which all existence rests, then this fact carries with it a negative judgment upon the time form. For in the latter God is invisible. The highest reality can only be expressed indirectly in the time form by denying temporality. God cannot be objectified in time." These statements may be approved only with the reservation that from our standpoint God is invisible in the time form, cannot be directly " expressed " in it by us, cannot be objectified in it by us—but that it has pleased Him to make Himself visible in the time form, to express, to objectify Himself and thereby to create a " time form," not liable to a negative judgment. What would have been the meaning of " revelation," how could it have become an event in Jesus Christ, if He had not done so ? In revelation a negative judgment is given upon our time, which we are so fain to identify with God-created time. As lost, fallen, condemned time, as time that some day will cease to be, it is described—and " with a great voice, as a lion roareth, and when he cried, the seven thunders uttered their voices "—by the angel with the book which John had later to swallow (Rev. 10³), saying, χρόνος (note the God of the world and time, *Chronos*), οὐκέτι ἔσται (Rev. 10⁶). Revelation would have to explain that some day it itself would cease to exist, if by that time was to be meant its own time also, God's time, the time He has for us, the time of Jesus

Christ. But according to Is. 40⁸ the Word of our God " abideth for ever."
And according to Jn. 1¹⁴ this Word became flesh. And according to the entire
New Testament witness, it remained flesh even in His resurrection. It is still
flesh even in His glory at the right of God the Father. Therefore eternity (the
eternity of the God who has revealed Himself according to the witness of Holy
Scripture) is not apart from time. So the time God has for us, as distinguished
from our time that comes into being and passes away, is to be regarded as eternal
time.

The time God has for us is constituted by His becoming present to
us in Jesus Christ, i.e., *Deus praesens*. If we say Jesus Christ, we also
assert a human and therefore temporal presence. Every moment of
the event of Jesus Christ is also a temporal moment, i.e., a present with
a past behind it and a future in front of it, like the temporal moments
in the sequence of which we exist ourselves. " The Word became
flesh " also means " the Word became time." The reality of the
revelation of Jesus Christ is also what we call the lifetime of a man.
It is also a section of what we call " historical time " or world-history
and its prehistorical time. It is not only that, but it is also that.
The same is true of its reality in Old Testament expectation witness
and in New Testament recollection witness. Revelation in the sense
of Holy Scripture—this is quite unambiguous in its proper form in
the event of Jesus Christ as well as in the twofold witness—is an
eternal, but not therefore a timeless reality. It is also a temporal
reality. So it is not a sort of ideal, yet in itself timeless content of
all or some times. It does not remain transcendent over time, it does
not merely meet it at a point, but it enters time ; nay, it assumes
time ; nay, it creates time for itself.

I should like at this stage to utter an express warning against certain passages
and contexts in my commentary on Romans, where play was made and even
work occasionally done with the idea of a revelation permanently transcending
time, merely bounding time and determining it from without. Then, in face of
the prevailing historism and psychologism which had ceased to be aware at all
of any revelation other than an inner mundane one within common time, the
book had a definite, antiseptic task and significance. Readers of it to-day will
not fail to appreciate that in it Jn. 1¹⁴ does not have justice done to it.

Revelation will never be discovered by anyone who undertakes to
arrive at a kind of timeless core by abstracting from all times or
from specific times, or who attempts to rise from the human to the
divine. It will never be understood by one to whom its temporality
is a worry, who thinks it his duty and within his power to pass by its
temporality and interrogate and grasp its nature as something trans-
cendently timeless. Revelation has its time, and only in and along
with its time is it revelation. How otherwise can it be revelation
to and for us who are ourselves temporal to the core ?

At this point we recall once more the extraordinary significance of chronology
in the Old and New Testaments. The whole of the patriarchal ages in Genesis,
the rise of the prophets, the various historical co-ordinates of the place of Jesus

Christ at the beginning of the Gospels according to Matthew and Luke are presented with a rare exactitude. In this, use may have been made of antiquated Oriental number-symbolics or number-mysticism, whereby arithmetical errors, whimsies and impossibilities may have crept in. But the wonderful thing to be noted here in the Bible is not the correctness or incorrectness in content of the temporal figures, but their thoroughgoing importance as time data, which is but underlined by incidental number-mysticism and other liberties. There is not a suggestion that revelation and its attestation might have been localised just as well elsewhere or anywhere in historical space. How important it was for the early church, too, to be able to date the incarnation of the Word, is shown by the *passus sub Pontio Pilato*, already in the oldest forms of confession. Revelation is thus and not otherwise localised. In the event of Jesus Christ, as in the various events in anticipation and recollection, it is as genuinely temporal and therefore as temporally determined and limited as any other real events in this space of ours. It is also—think for a moment of the story of creation—described as temporally real, where according to the measurements of modern history this description can only be " saga " or " legend." The Bible also says the same where it transmits parables in the Old and New Testaments. Myths, on the contrary, i.e., narrative expositions of general spiritual or natural truths, narratives which although savouring perhaps of saga do not claim to be narratives, but are to be understood only when stripped of their narrative character, so that the eternal core is liberated from the temporal shell—myths do not occur in the Bible, although mythical material may often be employed in its language (*Church Dogmatics* I 1 p. 373 f.). The dialogue between God and Satan at the beginning of the book of Job " took place on a day " (1⁶) corresponding to the day on which subsequently the earthly misfortune burst upon Job. Also Job's question of God (10⁴) : " Hast thou eyes of flesh, or seest thou as man seeth ? Are thy days as the days of men, or thy years as a man's years ?", is in the sense of the text certainly not to be answered with a simple negative. In view of the time concept we must not try to avoid the way of Holy Scripture's " privileged anthropomorphism " (J. G. Hamann, *Schriften*, ed. F. Roth, vol. 4 p, 9). Year, day, hour—these are concepts which cannot possibly be separated from the Biblical witness to God's revelation, which in the exposition of it cannot be treated as trifles, if we are not to turn it into a quite different witness to a quite different revelation.

Having said that, we must, of course, go on to say that the time we mean when we say Jesus Christ is not to be confused with any other time. Just as man's existence became something new and different altogether, because God's Son assumed it and took it over into unity with his God-existence, just as by the eternal Word becoming flesh the flesh could not repeat Adam's sin, so time, by becoming the time of Jesus Christ, although it belonged to our time, the lost time, became a different, a new time.

In Lev. 25⁸ᶠ· there is prescribed for Israel the interval of one year of freedom or jubilee every seven times seven years, beginning with the Day of Atonement in the last of these forty-nine years, and announced by trumpet blasts in the whole land, a year in which there was to be neither sowing nor harvesting, in which every man by means of redemptions adjusted on easy terms was to return again to his own property which he had lost by sale in the course of the forty-nine years. The author of Is. 61² already saw typified in this year the " acceptable year of the Lord," i.e., the time of Messiah's redemption, and actually this utterly extraordinary year is according to Lk. 4¹⁹ᶠ (σήμερον πεπλήρωται ἡ γραφὴ αὕτη ἐν τοῖς ὠσὶν ὑμῶν, v. 21) the time of Jesus Christ. True, this time is a time in the series of times, as the fiftieth year was a year in the series of years, but now, exactly on the analogy of that year, it is the time of festival, of rest, of release and restoration, that is, to say, in relation to previous and to coming times the real, the normal time. Similarly Heb. 4¹⁻⁸ shows how the Old Testament Sabbath, as the day of God's rest and of the rest also promised to His people, is fulfilled " after so long a time " in the day of Jesus. Moreover, alongside of the six days of the working week, with which it nevertheless stands in series, and which, unlike the Sabbath, have no name of their own but are only numbered, the Sabbath is, so to speak, the day, the normal day. And everywhere in the New Testament where we meet the words ἄρτι, νῦν, τὰ νῦν, ὁ νῦν καιρός, ὥρα, σήμερον, ἡμέρα, we must at least take into account that not only a definite calendar or clock time is supposed to be indicated, but in, with and under a definite calendar or clock time the time of Jesus Christ, remarkable also as a time because of its content. For the pregnant use of νῦν let us emphasise among many Pauline and Johannine passages 2 Cor. 6² : ἰδοὺ νῦν καιρὸς εὐπρόσδεκτος, ἰδοὺ νῦν ἡμέρα σωτηρίας. For ὥρα, 1 Jn. 2¹⁸ : παιδία, ἐσχάτη ὥρα ἐστίν. For σήμερον, Lk. 19⁹ : " To-day is σωτηρία come to this house," Lk. 2¹¹ : " Unto you this day is born the σωτήρ," and from Hebrews : " This day have I begotten you " (1⁵, 5⁵), and so : " To-day if ye hear his voice, harden not your hearts " (3⁷ᶠ· ¹⁵, 4⁷)—ἄχρις οὗ τὸ σήμερον καλεῖται (3¹³).

But the special thing about the time of Jesus Christ is that it is the time of the Lord of time. Compared with our time it is mastered time and for that very reason real, fulfilled time. Here the dilemma does not arise, between a present that disappears midway between past and future, and a past and future that dissolve for their part into a present. Here there is a genuine present—and not now in spite of it but just because of it, a genuine past and future. The Word of God is. It is never " not yet " or " no longer." It is not exposed to any becoming or, therefore, to any passing away, or, therefore, to any change. The same holds also of the Word of God become flesh and therefore time. In every moment of His temporal existence, and also at every point previous or subsequent to His temporal existence, in which He becomes manifest as true God and true man and finds faith and witness, Jesus Christ is the same. The Word spoken from eternity raises the time into which it is uttered (without dissolving it as time), up into His own eternity as now His own time, and gives it part in the existence of God which is alone real, self-moved, self-dependent, self-sufficient. It is spoken by God, a perfect without peer (not in our time, but in God's time created by the Word in the flesh, there is a genuine, proper, indissoluble, primal perfect), and for that reason there is coming into the world a future without peer (for not in our time but rather in this God's time created by the Word in the flesh there is a genuine, proper, indissoluble, primal future). And so it is a present that is not a present without also being a genuine perfect ; and a perfect and a future, the mean of which constitutes a genuine, indestructible present. Yet it is not any present, hopelessly collapsing into a " not yet " or a " no longer " like every present in our time. It is *Deus praesens*, who always was and will always be and for that very reason has a genuine before and after ; in other words, the active Lord of time, who in His action creates and sustains His own time out of the wretched span of this lost time of ours, the Lord before whom time can have no legality of its own, before whom the longest time is the shortest and the shortest the longest, before whom the irreversibility of time is not for one moment in an indestructible position. This mastered, this fulfilled time is the time of revelation, the time of Jesus Christ. No doubt after its kind this is not a different time from the time, so hidden and withdrawn from us, which was created by God in the beginning. But freshly posited in and with revelation, it is likewise by its very hiddenness and withdrawnness set apart from it as a new, third time. Since here God has real time for us, we in the midst of our time, lost time, must believe that He made time, and that like all His works, without our having any possible knowledge of it, it was " very good."

In Tit. 1³ we read that God revealed His Word καιροῖς ἰδίοις, " in his own seasons." According to Mk. 1¹⁵ the first statement of the " Gospel of God " proclaimed by Jesus Himself is πεπλήρωται ὁ καιρός. In the same way in Gal. 4³ Paul tells of the condition we children were in and how we were enslaved under the στοιχεῖα τοῦ κόσμου, continuing in v. 4 thus : ὅτε δὲ ἦλθεν τὸ πλήρωμα τοῦ χρόνου, ἐξαπέστειλεν ὁ θεὸς τὸν υἱὸν αὐτοῦ, γενόμενον ἐκ γυναικός. *Pleroma* is that which fulfils (fills full) a vessel, plan, concept or form. It is, therefore, the content, the meaning, the reality proclaimed as a possibility in this form. " Fulness of time " cannot, therefore, be regarded otherwise than as " real time." In and with the incarnation of the Word, in and with the approach of the kingdom of God—we should perhaps say as its precursor or its concomitant—it also happens that real time breaks in as new time, as the now and to-day of the Saviour. Thus in Eph. 1⁹ᶠ· " God made known to us the mystery of His will, according to His good pleasure to renew (or—and it seems to mean the same thing—to sum up) all things in heaven and on earth εἰς οἰκονομίαν τοῦ πληρώματος τῶν καιρῶν, for the orderly bringing about of the fulness of the times (i.e., in order that by the renewal time also might be fulfilled, become real time).

As everyone knows, the name of God in the Old Testament according to Ex. 3¹³ᶠ· is " I am that I am." Whatever the further interpretation of it be, the author of the New Testament Apocalypse at least regarded it as bearing a reference to the relation of God to time, in that God is described as unchangeable because in His nature He is the Living One : " I am He who re-presents myself to myself, who am present through myself." He has therefore characteristically expanded it to " I am ὁ ὢν καὶ ὁ ἦν καὶ ὁ ἐρχόμενος," with the pregnant addition ὁ παντοκράτωρ (Rev. 1⁸ ; cf. 1⁴). In a sequence at first more illuminating but less significant, Rev. 4⁸ speaks of ὁ ἦν καὶ ὁ ὢν καὶ ὁ ἐρχόμενος. And then 1¹⁷, obviously in exposition of this formula : " I am ὁ πρῶτος καὶ ὁ ἔσχατος καὶ (once more so pregnant) ὁ ζῶν, and 21⁶ (cf. 1⁸, 22¹³) in double parts (the I is now as such the designation of being present) : " I am Alpha and Omega, the beginning and the end, the first and the last.' From the fact that God is He who exists and therefore is the Living One in the supreme sense and therefore the Almighty, it follows that He is not only this, but, as this, also He who was *and* He who cometh, Alpha *and* Omega, the beginning *and* the end, the first *and* the last. And *vice versa*, by the fact that He is the first and the last, it is indicated that He is truly He who is, the Living One, the Almighty. If the name of God, Ex. 3¹⁴ is to be translated " I shall be that I shall be," or " I shall exist as I shall exist," a particular emphasis will be given the relation present-future, and the extension of the utterance to the past in the Apocalypse will in that case have to be regarded as a distinctly New Testament interpretation of the famous text ; i.e., it will expressly declare that now, after the fulfilled time, *recollection* is added to *expectation* as a category not yet belonging to the Old Testament or at least not yet customary. With that the saying in Heb. 13⁸ will then agree : Ἰησοῦς Χριστὸς ἐχθὲς καὶ σήμερον ὁ αὐτὸς καὶ εἰς τοὺς αἰῶνας, in which the emphasis according to the context is clearly upon the yesterday and therefore upon the relation present-past. But the fact that the formula " I am the first and the last " already occurs in Is. 41⁴, 44⁶, 48¹² should be taken as a warning against holding that a two-dimensional view of God's time is exclusively a New Testament matter. Be that as it may, what is known about the fulfilment of time in the present of Jesus Christ is shown in the New Testament by no means only in an unusual consciousness of the present, but also in an extremely accentuated awareness, inherent in this particular consciousness of the present, of past as past, of future as future, an awareness for which the two of them are not merely different times but, as different times, emphatically different worlds, a pair of " æons " ranged under utterly opposed signs—one an essentially past æon, yet even as such still to-day an extremely real æon in the light of the present ; and one an essentially future æon, but precisely as such still to-day likewise an extremely real æon in the light of the present. What is more significant about this consciousness of the present than this, that it is so serious about the past on the one hand and about the future on the other, each in its own way and after its own fashion ? that it tears open the gulf between the two as profoundly as possible ? and yet, conversely, that it holds together in its own to-day, as in iron brackets, two such separated things as the old æon that is passing away and the new one that is coming in, i.e., that it does not just let them coalesce into one, but holds them together in separation ? Think of all the contrasts. As in Ac. 17³⁰f. : " The times of ignorance God overlooked, but now τὰ νῦν, he commandeth all men everywhere that they should repent, inasmuch as he hath appointed a day, ἔστησεν ἡμέραν (the day of Jesus Christ), in the which he will judge the world in righteousness." Or Col. 1²¹ : " Ye too were in time past alienated and enemies in your mind by your evil works—but now, νυνὶ δέ, hath he reconciled you in the body of his flesh through death." Or 1 Pet. 2¹⁰ : " which in time past were no people, but now, νῦν δέ, are the people of God, which had not obtained mercy, but now, νῦν δέ, have obtained mercy." Or Eph. 5⁸ : " for ye were once darkness, but now, νῦν δέ, are light in the Lord." Or Col. 1²⁶ : " Once was the Word of God, the mystery, hidden from all times and generations ; but now, νῦν δέ, hath it been manifested to his saints " (cf. Rom. 16²⁶ ; 2 Tim. 1¹⁰). Note that the relation between the two æons is the relation of a decision. The decision is made ; that is the present ; that is the proper content of the New Testament witness. Τὰ ἀρχαῖα παρῆλθεν (2 Cor. 5¹⁷). But that does not mean that the past disappears ; it remains present in its παρέρχεσθαι, just because and since it is so definitely recognised as the past, i.e., it is precisely a genuine past, as surely as it is made a past by the death of Christ. And that is also why the Old Testament does not disappear in the New Testament but continues to live on every page of the New Testament, as witness to the time of the old æon as well which was fulfilled in the cross of Christ. In the Old Testament the genuine past continues its existence in the form of expecting the time fulfilled in the death of Christ. But neither is the future a thing that has ceased to exist ; as the future it is already present. Ἰδοὺ γέγονεν καινά (2 Cor. 5¹⁷)— just because it is so definitely recognised as the future, as the breaking in of a new world, it is a genuine future. For it opens with the resurrection of Christ. And that is why the Old Testament cannot now stand alone. That is why the apostles had to come alongside of the prophets. For the future can be proclaimed only in the form of recollecting the resurrection of Christ. It is in the form of recollection that the future is actually proclaimed here.

Now we can understand the equation with which we started. "God reveals Himself" means "God has time for us." God's revelation is God's inconceivable freeness and so His existence for us. But this very freeness and existence consist in His having time for us. The entire fulness of the benefit of God's revelation and of the reconciliation accomplished in it lies in the fact that God has time for us, a time which is right, genuine and real.

In this context we might well pause to think of the fact that to have time for another, although in the abstract this says little, is in reality to manifest in essence all the benefits which one man can show to another. When I really give anyone my time, I thereby give him the last and most personal thing that I have to give at all, namely myself. If I do not give him my time, I certainly continue to be his debtor in everything, even though in other ways I give him ever so much. The difference at once to be noticed between our having time for others and God's having time for us is twofold, that if God gives us time, He who deals with us is He who alone has genuine, real time to give, and that He gives us this time not just partially, not with all sorts of reservations and qualifications, such as are habitual with us when giving to others, but entirely. The fulfilment of time that took place in Jesus is not just an alms from the divine riches ; if, according to Gal. 4⁴, Jesus Christ is the "*pleroma* of the time," we have to remember that, according to Col. 2⁹, "in him dwelleth all the *pleroma* of the Godhead bodily."

In revelation God stands in for us entirely. And so also the time He creates for Himself in revelation, the genuine present, past and future of which we have been speaking, is presented to us entirely. It should, it can, it will become our time, since He directs His Word to us ; we are to become contemporary with this time of His. His genuine time takes the place of the problematic, improper time we know and have. It replaces it in that, amid the years and ages of this time of ours, the time of Jesus Christ takes the place of our time, coming to us as a glad message presented to us as a promise, and to be seized and lived in by us. Just as a light in an otherwise dark space is a light for its own little area and has light for the whole space, so far, that is, as it is a bright open light and so far as there are eyes in the space, and open eyes, to behold it as a light, so is the Gospel.

Huc omnia quae praecesserunt tempora, ut ad faustum et felix suum centrum spectant et omnia posteriora hinc ut a fonte in finem saeculi decurrunt (F. Turrettini, *Instit. Theol. el.* 1682 XIII *qu.* 10, 1). "There is but one single covenant between God and man, the covenant of grace, and the mediator of that covenant is the man Christ Jesus. The right way to regard the Gospel story—the proclamation of the birth, death and resurrection of Christ—will accordingly be to recognise in it the temporal execution of an eternal counsel, so that its facts are eternal facts, the truth and effect of which forwards and backwards are extended over all periods. Here on earth God was robbed of His glory by man, and sin and death entered the world ; therefore here also upon earth all things had to be restored by a man. That this did happen is the Gospel already attested in Paradise to our first parents, and this Gospel has been confirmed and clarified, has been proclaimed beforehand with growing plainness and definition down to its smallest details ; that these promises are fulfilled, that what is to happen did happen, is the message of the evangelists and apostles" (J. Wichelhaus, *Die Lehre der heiligen Schrift*³, 1892 p. 242–43).

Let us first attempt to make plain the sense in which we are to say that there, at that point of general time, the light of the special new time is to be seen. It is the problem which has played a large part in more recent theology under the title of " Revelation and History." At this point we must emphasise the fact that God has time for us because—and this is a fact, an act (and an incomparable act at that) of which God Himself and He alone is the Subject—He reveals Himself, i.e., proceeds out of a veiling and unveils Himself. If we mean to use revelation in the Bible sense, we must think of the two as the two elements, as the *terminus a quo* and the *terminus ad quem* of the event of Jesus Christ, namely the veiledness of the Word of God in Him and the breaking through of this veil in virtue of His self-unveiling. The veil of which we must speak in this context is general time, the old time, our time, so far as He assumes it in order to make it—and this is the unveiling—His own time, the new time. As we said before when expounding some New Testament texts, neither the old nor the new time exists abstractly and solely as such ; they exist because the new time which already exists triumphs over the old which therefore still exists also. This triumph, this act of victory in which the victor already exists and the vanquished likewise still exist, this transition from the Old Testament to the New Testament, from the old æon that ends with the cross of Christ to the new one that begins with His resurrection—this transition is revelation, is the light of fulfilled time.

Again, that is why the Old Testament and the New Testament are so indissolubly linked together. That is why, in both, the revelation of the divine judgment and the revelation of the divine grace are nowhere to be abstracted from each other. That is why in the Gospels everything runs to meet the passion story, yet also why everything in the passion story runs to meet the resurrection story and why nothing can be understood except from these two, or better, from the turning-point between these two.

The modern problem of " revelation and history," i.e., the question whether and how far man's time may be regarded at any definite point as the time of God's revelation, rests upon a portentous failure to appreciate the nature of revelation.

We must speak separately of at least three major errors which have been committed and go on being committed in this respect.

1. There has been a failure to see that in answering this question we cannot start with the general phenomenon of time, or, as it is preferably called, history. We cannot assume that we know its normal structure on the basis of comparative observation, and then go on to ask whether and how far the phenomenon of revelation discloses itself, perhaps, to the said comparative observation at a specific point. On this it is to be said that the general phenomenon of time or history in its manifold state is certainly not the text in perusing which we will ever come directly or indirectly upon the phenomenon of revelation. This general phenomenon of time as such is by no means what in the New Testament itself is called the old æon that passes away in view of the new one coming. To a man, therefore, who actually stands in front of this phenomenon as in

front of a wall and is unable to perceive anything of revelation at all (e.g., with
P. Althaus, *Grundr. d. Dogm.*, I, 1929 p. 17, or G. Kittel, " Der historische Jesus,"
Myst. Christi, 1930, p. 45), it may well be said it is the historical as such in
its universality and relativity which is the necessary " offence " to revelation.
" Offence " itself, of course, is already a very serious theological concept, denoting
an event which already presupposes both the event and the knowledge of revelation. John the Baptist is " offended " in Christ (Mt. 11²ᶠ·) but not the average
historian who declares he cannot perceive revelation in the story. And similarly
the Isaianic-Pauline " servant form " of the Son of God (P. Althaus, *op. cit.
sup.*, G. Kittel, *op. cit. sup.* p. 57) is really quite different from the generally
admitted and obvious " questionableness and uncertainty of history." If with
Isaiah or Paul a man really sees this servant form, he will see that the cross
of Christ was the end of the old æon. He will then also be aware of the new
one and therefore of the turning-point from old to new, and therefore of God's
revelation. If he begins to think in terms of general time, he will have to stop
thinking in terms of it too, if he is honest. Neither by direct ascertainment
nor by indirect dialectics will he ever find his way through to the problem of
the special time of revelation. He can be asked only upon what dogmatic
ground he regarded this particular beginning as particularly important and
" genuine." Theologians who, with an excess of solemnity, help the historian
with talk of " offence " and of " servant form " must be told that they are not
doing him a good service.

2. There has been failure to see that the event of Jesus Christ as God's
revelation can be found only when sought as such, i.e., when we are seeking what
we have already found. This rule which apparently—but really only apparently
—grossly contradicts all honest investigation of truth, is the inevitable result
of the nature of the question before us here. God's revelation in Christ, in the
way in which Holy Scripture declares that it has taken place, is not something
problematic, which is perhaps (but perhaps not) hidden behind the wall of
another sort of reality, so that this other sort of reality is the non-problematic,
nay the axiomatic thing, to which we are unconditionally bound, in the light of
which we have to take into account a thousand considerations of genuineness,
starting from which we will some time perhaps (but perhaps not) push through
with extreme caution and reserve to the mystery. On the contrary, we have
to recognise that in the matter in question everything is pretty much the other
way round. The problematic element here is precisely the different effect the
old æon has, in that even at best, even if the name of its representative is
John the Baptist, it must always be waiting for the Messiah, must always be
failing to grasp that He has come. On the other hand, there are no problems
in the axiomatic *Deus dixit*, that " the blind see and the lame walk, the lepers
are cleansed and the deaf hear, the dead are raised and the poor have the Gospel
preached to them " (Mt. 11⁵). To this even the passing æon in the person of
the Baptist has to give its witness : " Behold the Lamb of God, that taketh away
the sin of the world " (Jn 1²⁹), along with the witness of the apostle of the new
æon : " who was delivered up for our offences and was raised for our justification "
(Rom. 4²⁵). If a man does not have this turning-point, this transition before
him as a text, if he has not noticed, or if for some reason he refuses to accept the
fact that in the New Testament, and also in the Old Testament from the standpoint of the New Testament, everything speaks constantly and exclusively of
this turning-point of the times and so of God's time, how can he have an intelligent
part in the whole question of revelation and time ? Whatever negative or positive
results he may reach, will not all that he says inevitably be beside the point ?
" Everything so far has been just abstraction," explains G. Kittel on the second
last page of his above-mentioned essay. And at the end, in a few sentences
which are not very convincing at this stage, he finishes up at the point at which
he should have started. As a matter of fact there can be nothing but abstraction

here unless we are really ready, in an honest investigation of truth, to start where the New Testament itself starts.

3. There has been a failure to see that if revelation is revelation, we cannot speak of it as though it can be discovered, dug up, worked out as worked out as the deeper ground and content of human history. If the sentence " God reveals Himself " has anything even remotely in common with interpretation, hypothesis, assertion, with appraising and valuing, with an arbitrary fixing, extracting, or excising of a definite bit of human history out of its context, if anything like " absolutising " a reality relative to itself is even remotely the meaning of the sentence in question, then it will be better omitted altogether, especially if it is perhaps to be general, as expressing a very profound and congenial historical intuition. If general human time and history are taken seriously as the veil concealing revelation from us, then they are regarded precisely as the vanquished old æon—vanquished not by us but by the Word of God—as the time of the Fall. To break through and abolish this time cannot be a matter of our skill and effectiveness. It is first recognised in its frightfulness and inscrutability in the crucifixion of Christ, when we are aware that there is nothing in it to interpret and nothing in it to appraise, that it can only be set and is only set, before our eyes, as it was set long ago, by virtue of the unveiling in revelation itself, i.e., in Christ's resurrection. The " eye of faith " (*oculus fidei*), to which the older Protestant orthodoxy referred so readily is better admitted to be blind, unless it is stipulated that this eye is a seeing eye only in virtue of the unveiling in revelation itself. Even with the better representatives of the usual solution of our problem in modern days, we cannot say that it has been stipulated. Otherwise, there would not have been so much suspicious labour to render revelation somehow generally intelligible as the ultimate, deepest content and meaning of history. The very terminology stamps it as a predicate, admittedly a special one, but nevertheless a predicate of history. Writers have called it " redemption history " (like the earlier Erlangen school), or " superhistory " (like M. Kähler, *Wissensch. d. chr. Lehre*[2] 1893 p. 12 f., and, after him, P. Althaus), or " prime-history " or " qualified history " (as I did myself, unfortunately, in reference to F. Overbeck, in the first edition of this book, p. 230 f.). *Revelation is not a predicate of history, but history is a predicate of revelation.* Of course, we can and must speak of revelation first of all in the principal statement, in order subsequently to speak of history by way of explanation. But we may not first of all speak of history in order subsequently or by epithet to speak with force and emphasis about revelation. When the latter happens, we betray the fact that we have gone our own way in interpreting, valuing, absolutising. We have not gone the only possible way, the way of obedience.

If we regard the presence of Jesus Christ as the fulfilment of time, if we therefore say that His time is the light of new time in the midst of old time and for the whole of old time, that cannot mean that we are in a position to see through and regard any part of this old time as new, fulfilled time. To put it quite concretely, the statement " God reveals Himself " must signify that the fulfilled time is the time of the years 1–30. But it must not signify that the time of the years 1–30 is the fulfilled time. It must signify that revelation becomes history, but not that history becomes revelation. Only those interpretations of the statement " God reveals Himself " can be legitimate, in which, as in the statement itself, God is and remains the Subject. The moment another subject is intruded here, the moment it is made the form of an utterance about time as such (even if it were the time 1–30), or about history as such, or about definite contents of history as such (e.g., about the " historical Jesus " as such), it loses its meaning, at all events the meaning that alone can be proper to it in view of the revelation attested in Holy Scripture.

Let us then attempt to unravel the " proper meaning " of this statement about the revelation attested in Holy Scripture.

1. " God reveals Himself "—if this is said in the light of the revelation attested in Holy Scripture, it is said in view of a factual act of lordship which has already become an event, from which the person making the statement cannot withdraw. Time, and, with the time of revelation itself, the time also of the person making the statement, has found its Master ; it has become mastered time. He who makes this statement has ceased to have any other time as such which is limited and determined by fulfilled time. In his own time he is aware of this fulfilled time, and in this awareness he has become contemporary with it, a partner in this time and so a time-partner or contemporary of Jesus Christ, of the prophets and apostles. Hence, too, he has now no outlook upon an event, upon history, which is not limited and determined by the history of fulfilled time. Between his, between our time and fulfilled time, there now exists for him a strict and irreversible order. What are we to say about his time, the time, that is, which we call " our " time, the highly questionable time of our calendar and clocks ? If we are contemporaries of Christ because of His act of lordship in revelation, then as contemporaries of His apostles in recollection of Him we can only look back upon this time of ours as the lost, i.e., already essentially past time of the old æon, real only in its passing. Nevertheless, so far as it continues as such still to be our time, what else can our business be in this time than with the prophets to await Him ? This order of rank between the time of revelation and our time, is not, however, of our devising. We need have no anxiety about its meaning and status. It is withdrawn from our anxiety. We do not need to defend it. It speaks for itself. We cannot prove it. We ought not to want to prove it, because with every attempt to prove it we would be denying it. God's act of lordship in the fulfilment of time, the institution of this order of rank between His and our time, is not the fulfilment of a general form, of which man already has previous cognisance, so that he has power to measure the fulfilment as such, to prove the reality of its fulfilment on the ground of his previous acquaintance with the form to be fulfilled. With the peculiar reality of revelation there does not correspond, as with other peculiarities, a general possibility, a truth, an idea, an acquaintance with a value, it may be an extremely high value of life generally in historical time, from knowledge of which man can subsequently judge of revelation and form an opinion upon it. Revelation is not a matter that also occurred and was known in a definite place elsewhere, so that by comparing historically the various revelations the most genuine and valuable can be established as the

authentic and real revelation. This is impossible because the means for deciding what is genuine and non-genuine, what is valuable and less valuable in revelation, are not in our possession. Revelation would not be revelation if it belonged to those matters which can occur elsewhere in a different place and if there is a vantage point from which we might judge its genuineness and its value. Because it is temporal, historical revelation, that does not abolish its freedom. But precisely in its temporality and historicity it is free and so not the object of man's interpretation and appraisement. The statement, "God reveals Himself," can only express recognition of what it has actually pleased God to do in His freedom in time and history. It regards revelation as necessary against the background of God's and not a human *a priori* in time and history. It therefore regards "fulfilled time" from the standpoint of the fulfilment, not of the time. Time in fulfilled time is what it is entirely and altogether in virtue of its fulfilment. In other words, history is what it is, entirely and altogether in virtue of the Subject who acts here.

In the *Shepherd of Hermas* (*Mand.* XI 4 f.) the distinction between true and false prophets is very instructive as to what was known as early as the 2nd century about the nature of revelation. For instance, the spirit of the false prophet is known by the fact that it answers to what is demanded by men ; the God-given spirit of the true prophet on the contrary by the fact that it does not answer to anything but speaks on its own, if and whatever it is commanded to speak. Thus the former has no power—just as a stone or a drop of water hurled at the sky certainly will not reach the sky, whereas a hailstone or a drop of water falling from the sky will reach the earth. Similarly in the *Epistle to Diognetus* 7[1] the peculiarity of Christian knowledge and doctrine is described thus : Οὐ γὰρ ἐπίγειον εὕρημα τοῦτ' αὐτοῖς παρεδόθη, οὐδὲ θνητὴν ἐπίνοιαν φυλάσσειν οὕτως ἀξιοῦσιν ἐπιμελῶς, οὐδὲ ἀνθρωπίνων οἰκονομίαν μυστηρίων πεπίστευνται ἀλλ' αὐτὸς ἀληθῶς παντο-κράτωρ καὶ παντοκτίστης καὶ ἀόρατος θεός, αὐτὸς ἀπ' οὐρανῶν τὴν ἀλήθειαν καὶ τὸν λόγον τὸν ἅγιον καὶ ἀπερινόητον ἀνθρώποις ἐνίδρυσε καὶ ἐγκατεστήριξε ταῖς καρδίαις αὐτῶν. "There-fore the Gospel and its understanding is a wholly supernatural preaching and light which pointeth to Christ alone. This is indicated first of all herein, that not one man told another, but an angel from heaven came and proclaimed this birth of Christ to the shepherds, for no man knew ought thereof. Secondly also the mid-night indicateth it, on which Christ was born, whereby it sheweth that all the world is dark in its future and hath no reason wherewith to recognise Christ. It must be manifested from heaven. Thirdly the light sheweth it which shone about the shepherds, to teach that here must be a quite other light than any reason, and St. Luke saith here that the *gloria dei*, the glory of God hath shone about them, and calleth the same light a *gloria*, or honour of God. Why so ? To touch the mystery and to point to the way of the Gospel. For since the Gospel is a light from heaven which teacheth no more than Christ, in which God's grace is given us and our thing rejected, it setteth God's glory up, that none hence-forth can glory in his own ability but must give God the honour and leave the glorifying to Him, that it is His pure love and goodness that we through Christ are blest. Lo, the divine glory, the divine honour is the light in the Gospel which shines around us from heaven through the apostles and their followers who preach the Gospel ; for the angel was in place of all preachers of the Gospel, and the shepherds in place of all hearers, as we shall see. Therefore the Gospel can suffer no other doctrine beside itself ; for man's doctrine is earthly light, is likewise men's glory, likewise setteth up praise and glorying for men, maketh souls daring about their own work, which the Gospel teacheth should be daring about Christ, God's grace and goodness, should boast and be defiant about Christ." (Luther, *Pred. üb. Luk.* 2¹⁻⁴, *Kirchenpost.* 1522 *W.A.* 10ᴵᴵᴵ 76, 15.)

2. " God reveals Himself "—if this is said of the revelation attested in Holy Scripture, it is said in view of the equally factual resistance of man to the divine act of lordship, a resistance in which he who makes this statement will be aware that he participates, and shares in its guilt. Of course, the limitation and determination of our time is completed, the order of rank between God's time and our time is instituted. The man who does not know this does not know what he is saying when he repeats the statement in question. But again he does not know what he is saying if he does not know, too, that our time, i.e., that we ourselves are far removed from acquiescing in this limit and order of rank of our own inclination and capacity, that on the contrary we seek to defend ourselves against them in downright earnest. The old æon which passes away in revelation and yet in passing away is still present, stands to the new one that comes in revelation by no means in the neutral relation of any time to any other time following upon it. The old æon is rather God's time confronting men who boast of their own power and in that very fact are sinful and fallen ; and in these men we recognise ourselves, if we really recognise God's revelation—ourselves as God's enemies. In this encounter with us as His enemies God's revelation is a reality. On its reality in this encounter is grounded its hiddenness.

As the Son who accomplishes the revelation Jesus Christ is He " who endured such gainsaying (τοιαύτην ἀντιλογίαν) of sinners against himself " (Heb. 12³). His light " shineth in the darkness " (Jn. 1⁵). It was when the lord of the vineyard sent his beloved son that the vine-dressers' rebellion first became fundamental and final : " This is the heir, let us kill him, so the inheritance will be ours " (Mk. 12⁷).

In respect of the irruption of the new æon, over against Jesus Christ, the old æon, Adam's sin, comes to its true proportions. Revelation and only revelation brings it to its true proportions, draws it into the light in its totality, in which it now confronts and resists revelation, so that now nothing can be more hidden than revelation. It is just this revelation that the whole man resists. It is against the new fulfilled time that every time necessarily fights, and indeed " our " time also, because even we ourselves fight against it. It is primarily only at revelation that one can—and inevitably must—be " offended." " God in time," " God in history "—that is the offending thing in revelation. God in Himself is not offending. Time in itself is also not offending. But God in time is offending because the order of rank mentioned is thereby set up, because we are thereby gripped by God, as it were, in our very own sphere, namely in the delusion that we possessed time. Fulfilled time in our midst is the enemy who has forced himself in, the centre of confusion which, driven by necessity, we want to destroy or at least render innocuous or conceal from our sight. What becomes of our time if it is really limited and determined by a " fulfilled time," described as an æon already past, thrown as it were wholesale upon the scrap heap ? What a menace ! And—for us as members and citizens of our own time—what a challenge !

The crucifixion of Jesus, in which the old æon said its last word, was by no means a specially shameful act when seen in this context, but an act of very primitive self-preservation and self-defence. Far from being an act that can be laid to the charge of the people of Israel particularly, it was an act in which they behaved and proved themselves as the representatives and accredited agents of all nations as never before or since. Thus it was not of the Jerusalem Sanhedrin as such, but of the ἄρχοντες τοῦ αἰῶνος τούτου that Paul said that they had crucified the Lord of glory (1 Cor. 2⁸). It is difficult to conceive how anyone can speak of this matter as does E. Brunner (" Zur Judenfrage," *Neue Schweizer Rundschau* 1935 p. 385 f.), as though it were a case of a kind of deep-rooted Jewish preference for their own national religion which they could just as well have abandoned in the end, with the result that the entire history of the Church and the world might have taken a different and a happier course. " Blessed is he who shall not be offended in me " (Mt. 11⁶). But who is not offended, when John the Baptist himself was ? Ἀνάγκη γὰρ ἐλθεῖν τὰ σκάνδαλα (Mt. 18⁷). Ἀνένδεκτόν ἐστιν τοῦ τὰ σκάνδαλα μὴ ἐλθεῖν (Lk. 17¹). Πάντες ὑμεῖς σκανδαλισθήσεσθε ἐν ἐμοὶ ἐν τῇ νυκτὶ ταύτῃ (Mt. 26³¹). And the very man who regarded himself as an exception here had to submit to being told : " Thou shalt deny me thrice " (Mt. 26³⁴)—Peter, the same upon whom Christ was to build His Church.

Because it is inevitable that offence should be taken at revelation, at " God in time," the form of revelation is necessarily the Isaianic-Pauline " form of a servant," the unapparent and unknown form in which it is true that the " fulfilled time " is the time of the years 1–30. It has nothing to do with the relative hiddenness of every fact of history which has become past. It also has nothing to do with the absolute hiddenness of the invisible Creator from the corporeal and spiritual eye of His creatures. It is not a natural hiddenness but a hiddenness contrary to nature. It is because we are seekers of self and resist God, that we take offence at revelation. It is because we take offence at it, that we contradict and resist it. Amid this contradiction and resistance arises the " form of a servant," i.e., the amazing existence of revelation before our eyes, as though it were not revelation at all. This existence Israel prepared by crucifying their manifested Messiah. It was a drastic attempt to get clear of the offence of revelation, to make God's time the same as our time, to abolish and to level up that order of rank between these times which was becoming visible. This was an utterly singular attempt, because God's revelation, because the manifestation of the Messiah and therefore His rejection also, was a purely Israelite matter. But as by this very rejection the revelation of God became a universal matter, so now there is also a universal participation in the particular sin, perpetrated by Israel, of rejecting revelation. This rejection takes place whenever we wish to regard the reality of revelation in the scheme of a possibility, a truth, an idea, a value concept. This would mean that before revelation and even apart from it we are already informed, and are thereby able through judgment, valuation and proof, we suppose, even to dispose of revelation. By such means in fact we set aside (or fancy we can set aside) the offence of revelation, and so (if our attitude to it has to be a positive one) prepare the way for its existence, as though it were not revelation, the servant-form, the form of the unknown. So there arises the singular, indestructible, importunate picture of a single, almighty world-time and world-reality. Surprisingly, it reckons its time according to the years before and after Christ's birth. But in reality it is without Christ, without revelation, a hard surface of secularity, smooth as a mirror. It covers the years 1–30 like all others. It is a world history in which, along with history of culture, history of nations, history of war, history of art, there is also a history of religion and the Church. But there is certainly nothing that we can seriously call a history of " God's mighty acts." In it the time of Christ's manifestation does not constitute an epoch, but, as the time of the " rise of Christianity," even in its singularity it is ultimately a time like any other.

In a manner distinguished by clear deduction from many partial insights, and not without a certain notable awareness of what, to some extent, the reality of revelation might signify, Otto Petras (*Post Christum*, 1935) has shown how the one, single, almighty world-time and world-reality present themselves. While naturally making it clear what laboured historical combinations are necessary for the attempt, he asserts his real desire consciously and completely to avoid the riddle of the years 1–30.

This hiddenness, completely contrary to nature as it is, is a necessary determination of revelation, and not a chance difficulty in understanding it that might perhaps be got over. We shall have to think ourselves away, ourselves in the rebellion in which we confront God, even in His revelation in Christ, if revelation is not to be hidden for us. We shall also have to think God's special action away, if it is meant to be otherwise. For it is just the profundity of divine revelation, that God does not refuse Himself to this man that rebels against Him, but adopts the hiddenness prepared for him because of this rebellion ; that it pleased Him to be present to us in just this way and with just this reality.

3. " God reveals Himself "—if the statement is made in respect of the revelation attested in Holy Scripture, it is made in view of the actually *miraculous event*, the special new direct act of God in the breaking in of new time into the midst of the old.

In the Bible a miracle is not some event that is hard to conceive, nor yet one that is simply inconceivable, but one that is highly conceivable, but conceivable only as the exponent of the special new direct act of God in time and in history. In the form in which it acquires temporal historical actuality, biblically attested revelation is always a miracle, and therefore the witness to it, whether direct or indirect in its course, is a narrative of miracles that happened. Miracle is thus an attribute of revelation. As it were, it marks off the limits of revelation time from all other time. Our existence, our time and history are non-miraculous, just as they are also without offence. God's existence in itself is also not a miracle, just as it is also without offence. But what is an offence and what becomes manifest as a miracle is the fact that God's existence is present to our existence, that He has time for us, that there is a divine time in the midst of our time.

That revelation can be understood only in the form of miracle is the result of its being, according to the witness of the New Testament, revelation in the resurrection of Jesus Christ from the dead. We can understand this by means of our first two findings. If revelation is (1) a divine act of lordship and (2) a divine act of lordship upon man, who must face it as God's enemy, who is the darkness that did not and also cannot comprehend the light—it follows that if revelation nevertheless takes place it can only take place in the form of a miracle. And if it is nevertheless to be an event, which a man confesses by saying " God reveals Himself," it can only be the confession of a miracle that has happened, but not the expression of an insight into a content, which he can also explain otherwise than by the special direct new act of God. Otherwise he again abolishes and levels up the order of rank, created by the divine act of lordship, between God's time and our time. Otherwise he again deludes himself as to the hiddenness of revelation created by his own resistance. For that reason all attempts at weakening or conjuring away the miraculous character of revelation are to be rejected on principle.

The so-called historico-critical method of handling Holy Scripture ceases to be theologically possible or worth considering, the moment it conceives it as its task to work out from the testimonies of Holy Scripture (which does ascribe to revelation throughout the character of miracle), and to present as the real intention, a reality which lacks this character, which has to be regarded as reality otherwise than on the basis of God's free, special and direct act. This must be said particularly of the gigantic attempt (still as gigantic as ever) of the " Life of Jesus research," i.e., the attempt, made in every style from mildest conservatism to the most imaginative or else most unimaginative, " hypercriticism," to uncover out of the New Testament, by means of a series of combinations, restorations and also and particularly deletions, the figure of the mere man Jesus, the so-called " historical Jesus," as he might have lived in the years 1–30. In this way he might be presented as an enthusiast well-nigh deluded, perhaps even as a lofty religious and moral personality, or perhaps also as a superman equipped with extraordinary, nay unique, gifts, but withal fundamentally as a man, one of our own time. It is an abiding merit of Martin Kähler, which cannot be over-praised, that in his work *Der sogenannte historische Jesus und der geschichtliche biblische Christus*, 1892—at a time when it cost something to say so—he called the whole " Life of Jesus movement " in plain language a " wrong way." He grounded his assertion historically on the simple fact that we possess no sources for a life of Jesus which a historian could accept as reliable or adequate, because the Gospels are testimonies not sources—and on the equally simple exegetico-dogmatic fact that the real historical Christ is no other than the biblical Christ attested by the New Testament passages, i.e., the incarnate Word, the risen and exalted One, God manifest in His redeeming action as He is the object of His disciples' faith. There is no reason why historico-critical Bible research should not contribute to the investigation and exposition of this historical Christ of the New Testament, instead of—a proceeding every whit as arbitrary, whether the science is history or theology—chasing the ghost of an historical Jesus in the vacuum behind the New Testament. It did not in the very least require the wooden sword of a non-miraculous revelation to gain its end or to make itself guilty of criminal assault upon revelation. It might just as well have been ready to extend aid to as exact and discriminating an understanding as possible of the New Testament witness as such, i.e., to the attestation of the θαυμαστὸν φῶς into which God hath called us out of darkness (1 Pet. 2⁹).

The fact that the statement " God reveals Himself " is the confession of a miracle that has happened certainly does not imply a blind credence in all the miracle stories related in the Bible. If we confess the miracle, we may very well, at least partially and by degrees, accept additional light from the miracles as necessary signs of the miracle. But even if we confess the miracle, why should we not constantly find this or that one of the miracles obscure, why should we not constantly be taken aback by them ? It is really not laid upon us to take everything in the Bible as true *in globo*, but it is laid upon us to listen to its testimony when we actually hear it. A man might even credit all miracles and for that reason not confess *the* miracle. What it means is to confess revelation as a miracle that has happened ; in other words, it means that the statement " God reveals Himself " must be a statement of utter thankfulness, a statement of pure amazement, in which is repeated the amazement of the disciples at meeting the risen One—but in no wise at all the statement of a self-conscious, superior acquisition and possession, comprehension and awareness. The contemporaneousness of a confessor with the first disciples of Christ, which is expressed in this statement, is simply not one of the possibilities that belong to man.

Man's own possibilities all point in quite a different direction. *Tota natura hominis Evangelium legit et audit extra Christum velatum tamquam historiam civilem et miraculis ornatam* (B. Aretius, *Probl. Theol.* II, 1575, p. 734 f.). We are continually confronted by revelation in history like the camel by the needle's eye, i.e., " With men it is impossible . . ." (Mt. 19²⁴ᶠ·). *Verbum enim caro factum est et sapientia incarnata ac per hoc abscondita nec nisi intellectu attingibilis, sicut Christus non nisi revelatione cognoscibilis* (Luther, *Schol.* on Rom. 3¹¹ *Fi.* II 75, 15).

" But with God all things are possible." Therefore even the hiddenness, the servant-form, the offence, which impenetrably surrounds His revelation, is not an obstacle for Him. When revelation takes place, it never does so by means of our insight and skill, but in the freedom of God to be free for us and to free us from ourselves, that is to say, to let His light shine in our darkness, which as such does not comprehend His light. In this miracle, which we can only acknowledge as having occurred, which we can only receive from the hand of God as it takes place by His hand, His kingdom comes for us, and this world passes for us. It is in this coming and passing that there takes place for us the movement which Holy Scripture calls revelation.

3

We have still to sketch briefly what it means for our time that there is a fulfilled time, that God's revelation is history. That this fulfilled time is the time of God's time for us is the point from which we started. We frequently touched upon this side of the problem, when we said that our time was the time limited and determined by fulfilled time. Our time lies, so to speak, in the neighbourhood, it stands under the sign and shadow, of this quite different time. This time is God's time. Our time, on the contrary, is improper time ruined by the Fall. Even when we say time, we can only imagine it as time, without knowing it or possessing it. Therefore our time is, as it were, overtopped and completely dominated by this, the fulfilled time. It is so overtopped and dominated by it that in practice the remotest past and the remotest future times are in its neighbourhood. But this means that the gap of centuries and millenia cannot prevent the days of Cain and Abel and our days too from being limited and determined by fulfilled time in the same sense and with the same force as the days of the apostle Peter.

Fulfilled time must not be compared with a very high mountain, or even the highest mountain rising up from the plain of the rest of time, at one point visibly, but at some distance less visibly, and finally at a still greater distance invisibly. On the contrary, every spatial metaphor goes to pieces here; for in fulfilled time the earth is one with the heavens which are arched over the whole earth. This is the point at which to recall the famous saying of the Psalm : " A thousand years in thy sight are but as yesterday when it is past and as a watch in the night " (Ps. 90⁴). The God thus addressed is, of course, the eternal God, but not the timeless God of the Greeks ; He is the covenant God of Israel, revealing Himself in time. Not in the sight of God the Timeless, but in the sight of Him, the very temporally Revealed, are a thousand years as a day ; or as Luther once put it, " . . . what we regard and measure as a very long drawn-out measuring line, He seeth it all as wound together upon one clew. And so the two of them, the last man and the first, death and life, are to Him no more than a moment is " (*Pred. üb. Matth.* 9¹⁸ᶠ. *Conc. Somm. Post. W.A.* 22 p. 402, 17). This is also the proper place for the Evangelists' interpretation of the name of God : " The God of Abraham and the God of Isaac and the God of Jacob . . . is not the God of the dead but of the living ; πάντες γὰρ αὐτῷ ζῶσιν " (Lk. 20³⁷ᶠ.).

We may break up the meaning of the determination and limitation of our time by fulfilled time into four concepts :

1. Fulfilled time takes the place of our non-genuine and improper time as genuine, proper time. What we mean when we say " time " is real there. We thus have our real time not here but there. It is therefore not an edifying trick of thought, but the assimilation of nourishment absolutely indispensable to our life, when Holy Scripture and the proclamation of its message call and transpose us from our own time away into that time, namely, into the time of Jesus Christ. There and only there, in contemporaneousness with Christ mediated to the Church by the witness of the prophets and apostles, do we really possess time. That time, its presence in the coming of the Kingdom and in

the passing away of this world, is in truth our time, really presented to us in God's revelation.

> The words: " A day in thy courts is better than a thousand " (Ps. 84¹⁰) may be applied appropriately here.

2. The fulfilment of time by revelation means—once more we are not in any sense speaking metaphorically but absolutely really—that our own time, the thing we suppose we know and possess as time, is taken from us. No philosophical scepticism, no discovery of *aporiae* in the concept of time is going to force us to find and recognise that we do not know at all what we are saying when we say " time," that it is just this most obvious thing among the things we suppose ourselves to possess, namely time, that we do not in reality possess at all. Revelation destroys this appearance, it unveils it as an untruth, and to that extent it takes our time away from us. Precisely as the time of grace that breaks upon us, it is the crisis that breaks into general time. This is where the offence of revelation arises. We are quite right to be shocked to death when revelation confronts us ; for it is actually the end of our time, and also of everything that is real in our time, and it announces itself as immediately imminent.

> " Ye cannot serve God and Mammon " (Mt. 6²⁴). Why not ? In itself we could do so perfectly well. But because we cease to have any time for Mammon along with the revealed God, because God in His revelation is He " who changeth the time and the season " (Dan. 2²¹)—that is why we cannot. In the translation of Ps. 31¹⁴ᶠ·, " But I hope in thee, O Lord, and say, Thou art my God. My time is in thy hands," the last expression is not properly a saying of Scripture but of Luther. But why should we not treasure it for itself, as a sufficiently apt formulation of what we are dealing with here ? In this translation Luther has not said anything different from what is really also to be found in Ps. 139¹⁶ in the original, that all my days " were written in thy book . . . when as yet there was none of them." Or the same thing put negatively, Ps. 102³ : " My days are consumed like smoke." Even in such sayings, provided that we are quite clear that the writers of them were Israelites and not Greeks, we shall not find abstract speculations about time, but the hard, concrete finding that the disposal of our days is taken from us by the revealed God, that our time is really in His hands.

3. The fulfilment of time by revelation does not so far mean, of course, the completion, but it means only the announcement, the immediate imminence of the taking away of our time. It is true, with the full seriousness and weight of divine truth. It appears and meets us in revelation as really as is possible. But still it is meeting us, still it is limiting and determining our time, this puzzling Somewhat of ours which we always merely suppose we know and possess, but of which we are told by revelation that we neither know it nor really possess it. This Somewhat still accompanies or confronts fulfilled time. In the circle of it, the latter is the centre. We are still " in possession " of time. Some portion of the time still remains, of which we are already deprived in principle. This *still* means that it limits

and determines our time and also that it so to speak limits and determines itself. The course of things is inevitable in itself, but it is held up in face of the end of our time. At least it is not yet accomplished.

The concept which comes in here is that of the patience, or long-suffering, of God, though it occurs comparatively rarely in Holy Scripture in so many words. Note the passages Ex. 34[6]; Joel 2[13]; Pss. 86[15], 103[8], 145[8], in which the attribute " long-suffering " comes in formally as the third alongside the typical attributes of the covenant God, " merciful " and " gracious." Note Rom. 2[4], 3[25], 9[22], where the time which man has alongside of and apart from divine revelation is described as the time of the divine μακροθυμία or ἀνοχή, and 1 Tim. 1[16], where in the same sense Paul describes himself as the object of Christ's long-suffering. Note for its special interest in this connection the passage on the long-suffering of the Lord, 2 Pet. 3[9, 15]. And above all note once again the end of the Noah story, Gen. 8[20]–9[29] (cf. on it W. Vischer, " Der noachitische Bund," *Z.d.Z.*, 1933, p. 10 f.).

So far as revelation is not yet redemption, not yet the breaking in, but (Mk. 1[15]) only the " at-handness " of the Kingdom of God itself, our time is actually conserved. The fact that Christ has not yet come " in the glory of his Father " (Mt. 16[27]), the fact that God's new time is not yet the only time, that this very revelation involves in its self-restraint a delay, or holding up of the end of all things, means that a parallelism is maintained between fulfilled time and general time. Accordingly God's time is really the time God has for us, in the sense that by it our improper, fallen time—which is indeed our present time—is conserved, and continually made possible in all its exposed impossibility. To that extent we may say that the whole history of the world has happened, happens and will happen, because the revelation in Jesus Christ has happened in the way in which it actually did happen, not, that is, as the completed end of time and all things, but as the announcement of the end of all things in time itself. The grace and mercy of God, which become effective in that He has time for us, i.e., His own time for us, answer to the long-suffering of God whereby He leaves us time, and our time at that, to adopt an attitude to this condescension, time, that is, to believe and repent. Is it necessary to say that in this very relation between revelation and other history, between God's time and our time, rests the whole immense tension which revelation of necessity imports into every consciousness of history ? How do we take up this position, if we have that same fulfilment of time to thank for it, by which all time is taken away from us, if some portion of our time still remains, if we can only understand our existence in the light of revelation, as an existence under God's long-suffering ?

4. If time is fulfilled in Jesus Christ, we can no longer regard our time, the time we still possess because of God's long-suffering, as endless. It is finite time, and therefore its flow from one conjectural present to another is merely a course *from* its end *to* its end ; from its end—that is, so far as the end is already announced to it ; to its

end—so far as it belongs to the concept of God's long-suffering that it (and with it our time) must once for all really come to an end. The myth of infinite or endless time is shattered by revelation. In revelation time has discovered its origin and its aim. Infinite time (and in this infinite time all infinite, absolute values and magnitudes) exists only for a time-consciousness which is unaware of or forgetful of revelation. A time-consciousness aware of it and mindful of it will quite certainly not be a consciousness void of time, but full of time and congruous with it. In the presence of the Word of revelation, its time is marked by the irresistible dissolution of what we call time and the equally irresistible advent of God's time. In time thus determined and in accordance with the law corresponding to it, it will be an historical, cosmic, ethical, political consciousness. It exists in this time and in no other, because here and now it has really ceased to possess any time other than this time of God's long-suffering in respect of fulfilled time.

In the Old Testament this consciousness of time is shown perhaps most finely in Eccles. 3$^{1-11}$: " To everything there is a season, and a time to every purpose under the heaven : a time to be born, and a time to die ; a time to plant, and a time to pluck up that which is planted ; a time to kill, and a time to heal ; a time to break down and a time to build up ; a time to weep, and a time to laugh ; a time to mourn, and a time to dance ; a time to cast away stones, and a time to gather stones together ; a time to embrace, and a time to refrain from embracing ; a time to seek, and a time to lose ; a time to keep, and a time to cast away ; a time to rend, and a time to sew ; a time to keep silence, and a time to speak ; a time to love, and a time to hate ; a time for war, and a time for peace. What profit hath he that worketh in that wherein he laboureth ? I have seen the travail which God hath given to the sons of men to be exercised therewith. He hath made everything beautiful in its time : also he hath set eternity in their heart, yet so that man cannot find out the work that God hath done from the beginning even unto the end." That all man's action has its time, its own time, and therefore has nothing to answer to the eternity which God has set in his heart, and therefore no eternal work, but is circumscribed by the incomparable work which God Himself alone does in His time—such is the character of this time-consciousness. And if in the sequel we find it expressed as follows : " I know that there is nothing better for them than to rejoice and to do good so long as they live. And also that every man should eat and drink and enjoy good in all his labour, is the gift of God "—let us not fail to realise, that read in the context of Ecclesiastes and the rest of the Old Testament and New Testament, and in the context of the Old Testament with the New Testament, this confession which impinges upon the confines of Epicureanism is intended and is to be understood as the sharpest expression of a consciousness of time and life really shattered by the presence of God. In the New Testament we find the description of the same time-consciousness compressed on the one hand into the concept of endurance (ὑπομονή ; Luther translates it *Geduld*, patience or long-suffering), on the other hand in the concept of being awake (γρηγορεῖν or ἀγρυπνεῖν). These two concepts together constitute an adequate correspondence to the long-suffering of God (μακροθυμία or ἀνοχή). Endurance is unflinching continuance in the time concluded in principle in Christ, but still allowed us with all its oppressive and treacherous content, in face of which we must be confident of the end, in face of which the end demands our loyalty and steadfastness. Contrariwise watching or wakefulness is constant attention to the fact that or time is still allowed us, but that in principle it is already concluded in Christ, and therefore every moment must actually reach its end, so that our existence in it must of necessity continue to be a recurrent readiness to answer before the Judge. The Church of the New Testament lives in this time-consciousness ; that is, it is the Church of those who " wait " and " hasten " (2 Pet. 3¹²). The meaning of the *kerygma*, baptism, the Lord's supper, exhortation, sanctification, faith and justification in this waiting Church, what an " apostle " is, who the " saints " are, the nature of the gifts of the Holy Spirit, the reason why the concepts " miracle " and " sign " belong to each other : all these (and even more) have to be explained and admit of explanation from the standpoint of the New Testament consciousness of time.

2. THE TIME OF EXPECTATION

Fulfilled time has a quite definite pre-time co-ordinated with it. We speak of the time *ante Christum natum*. But it is not this time as such that is the pre-time to fulfilled time, but a time within this time, namely, the time of a definite history that takes place in it. The time of this history is the pre-time to revelation. For revelation itself is nothing else than the ultimate continuation, the peak and the goal of this history. Its time is the time of the fulfilling of this historical time. As the time of its *fulfilment*, as the time of the unique occurrence of the one revelation of God, it is quite different from the other. But, again, as the time of its fulfilment it is entirely related to it and bound up with it. This pre-time is the time of the Old Testament or the time of the witness to the expectation of revelation. This pre-time belongs to the time of fulfilment. It is co-ordinated with it, although it is a quite different time. We cannot speak of the time of revelation without also speaking of its pre-time. It, too, is revelation-time, although in the sense of the time of expecting revelation. Genuine expectation of revelation does not exist without the latter ; as expected, revelation is also present to it. Where expectation is genuine, " previously ". does not mean " not yet " ; just as, where recollection is genuine, " subsequently " does not mean " no longer." Genuine expectation and genuine recollection are testimonies to revelation, mutually as different as expectation and recollection are different, but one in their content, in their object, in the thing attested, and also one in that for them this thing attested is neither merely future nor merely past ; as " future " and as " past " it is present.

The Old Testament is the witness to the genuine expectation of revelation. This raises its time (from the standpoint of revelation or in view of revelation) high above the other times in the time area *ante Christum natum*. What is in question here is not the independent significance belonging to the history as such which is attested in the Old Testament. The historical uniqueness of Israel, particularly the

originality of its religious history, is another matter. On that ground
we could speak only improperly and with reservation of a revelation
of God in the Old Testament. For that involves making an historical
value-judgment, whether it is in place to recognise revelation of God
in the Old Testament, and not in the Babylonian or the Persian or
even the early German tradition. But what we purport to recognise
as revelation in such circumstances is not revelation at all. Revelation is not a predicate which may be attributed or not attributed
to this or that historical reality. If we are speaking of revelation
in the Old Testament, by that cannot be meant this or that attribute
supposed to belong as such and in itself to the Old Testament or to
the stories attested in the Old Testament. The history of Israel has
such attributes, as the history of any nation has. But it is not
because of such attributes that we see in the time of the Old Testament a time which has prominence in relation to the other times
in the time area *ante Christum natum*. Revelation in the Old Testament is really the expectation of revelation or expected revelation.
Revelation itself takes place from beyond the peculiar context and
content of the Old Testament. It breaks into the peculiar context
and content of the Old Testament, from an exalted height which
has not the slightest connexion with a peak point in the history
of early oriental religion or the like. Even in the most significant
context and content of the Old Testament as measured by general
historical standards we shall only recognise revelation, in so far as
the significance of the Old Testament is actually aligned to this revelation. Apart from this revelation breaking in from without or from
above, or apart from this alignment to revelation, we cannot speak
of revelation in the Old Testament. In that case it is much better
not to ascribe singularity to the Old Testament in the strict sense,
not to use theological emphasis, but to content ourselves with regarding it as one remarkable phenomenon among others within the world
of piety in the ancient East. Exactly the same will also have to
be said later about the time of the New Testament and about the
New Testament itself. The real singularity of the Old Testament
consists sufficiently in the sole fact that in it expectation of revelation
takes place and is attested. It can thus be seen and asserted only
from the side of revelation or in view of revelation.

But what is meant by " from the side of revelation " or " in view
of revelation " ? We must recall all that was said about the hiddenness of historical revelation itself, and about the miracle which we
indicate, when we dare to employ this concept at all or to take it
upon our lips. Revelation is not a standpoint from which, or an end
towards which, all we need to do is to draw a circle with a pair of
compasses, in order to make it plain that at such and such points
there is genuine expectation of revelation. Like revelation itself,
genuine expectation of it is also surrounded by hiddenness. And here

also revelation itself alone can and will break through this hiddenness. As it makes the decision about itself, so it does also about the witness to itself. It makes it its witness and it attests it as such. So in confirmation of the statement that revelation, i.e., genuine expectation of revelation, is to be found in the Old Testament, we cannot ultimately and in principle point to any other authority than to revelation itself, i.e., to Jesus Christ Himself. His death on the cross proves the truth of the statement, and it proves it by the power of His resurrection. If the statement is true, it is so because Jesus Christ is manifest in the Old Testament as the expected One. All attempts to show how far He is can claim only to be explanations of this fact, which is confirmed in itself because it confirms itself. But if they are really theological explanations, they will not claim to be proved or independently demonstrated.

This fact, which is confirmed in itself because it confirms itself, the fact that Jesus Christ is also manifest in the Old Testament as the expected One, we cannot bring forward as being ourselves witnesses; but, with reference to this ultimately sole witness and so the axiomatic character of the statement, we can bring up the counterproof, by addressing the question about Jesus Christ in the Old Testament to the New Testament, in which we have before us the witness to recollection of Christ. But in this respect we are, above all, brought up against the fact that the unity of the revelation of Christ with the history of the expectation of it in the Old Testament is not an item that occurs in His proclamation, doctrine and narrative with a certain frequency alongside other items; it is taken for granted as their universal and uniform presupposition. Remember what that means in view of the fact that historically speaking the New Testament as we have it before us is altogether a collection of documents about a Hellenistic spiritual movement, for which Judaism and its antecedents might just as well have been one connecting point among others, and a connecting point validated by its various representatives only more or less or even not at all. But the New Testament writers are utterly unanimous in seeing, not in Judaism—not one of them was concerned with that—but in the history of Israel attested in the Old Testament Canon the connecting point for their proclamation, doctrine and narrative of Christ; and *vice versa*, in seeing in their proclamation, doctrine and narrative of Christ the truth of the history of Israel, the fulfilment of the Holy Scripture read in the synagogue.

There are New Testament documents such as the Gospel according to Matthew, the Epistle of James and, above all, Hebrews (so pre-eminent within the New Testament for its Greek style), of which it must be said that the identity of the revelation of Christ attested by them with the revelation expected in the Old Testament constitutes not only the presupposition, but—in each of the three, although in a different way—the very theme and substance of their special witness, so that to illustrate it properly one would, strictly speaking, have to quote almost verse for verse. But we must be sure to realise that the assertion of the connexion even in the supposedly or actually very " Greek " Gospel according to John takes up a much more central position than might well appear at first glance. It is according to John that the disciples discovered in Jesus the Messiah of Israel, of whom Moses wrote in the Law and the prophets (1⁴¹· ⁴⁵). It is here that Jesus says with almost explicit offence : " Salvation is of the Jews" (4²²) ; yet He also claims Scripture as the witness about Him and for Himself (5³⁹) ; He describes Moses as the prosecutor of the Jews who resist Him : " If ye believed Moses, ye would believe me ; for he wrote of me. But if ye believe not his γράμματα, how shall ye believe my ῥήματα ? " (5⁴⁵⁻⁴⁷). And it is according to John that Jesus says of Abraham, ἠγαλλιάσατο, ἵνα ἴδῃ τὴν ἡμέραν τὴν ἐμὴν καὶ εἶδεν καὶ ἐχάρη (8⁵⁶). In 12³⁷⁻⁴¹ the Evangelist himself, to throw light upon the unbelief of the Jews, adduced the passages Is. 53¹ on the hiddenness of the revelation, and Is. 6⁹ᶠ· on the hardening, in order (incalculably) to make the comment on the passage, ταῦτα εἶπεν 'Ησαίας ὅτι εἶδεν τὴν δόξαν αὐτοῦ καὶ ἐλάλησεν περὶ αὐτοῦ. And above all we have to note in John the figure of John the Baptist which distinguishes, nay dominates the entire beginning of his Gospel and in which he finds the completion and exposition of an, as it were, systematic co-ordination of the word and work of Jesus Himself on the one hand, and on the other hand of the New Testament apostolic witness about Him, with the witness of the Old Testament. Again, actually in Luke (Marcion's favourite writer), we have as a summary of the Gospel these words in Mary's hymn of thanksgiving : " He hath holpen his servant Israel and remembered his mercy, as he spake to our fathers, to Abraham and to his seed for ever " (1⁵⁴ᶠ·, cf. ⁷²) ; further the saying about the many prophets and kings who, without seeing or hearing, desired to see and to hear what the disciples were seeing and hearing (10²⁴) ; and above all the story of the Emmaus disciples (24¹³ᶠ·), whose recognition of the risen One attains its height of concreteness when the Unknown who attached Himself to them summons them out of their foolishness and slowness of heart " to believe all that the prophets have spoken " (24²⁵), " opening up unto them the Scripture " (24³²), that is, " beginning from Moses and from all the prophets he interpreted (διηρμήνευσεν 24²⁷) to them in all the Scriptures τὰ περὶ αὐτοῦ," and finally (this sign belongs to this word) He broke bread for them 24³⁰). In consequence they are now told that " it behoved the Christ to suffer these things and to enter into his glory " (24²⁶). When He tells them this, Jesus Himself is their resurrection witness. But according to Luke's Acts, too, all the prophets bear witness that everyone who believes on Jesus receives forgiveness of sins (10⁴³). The eunuch of Queen Candace is reading ch. 53 of Isaiah but does not understand what he is reading, and in expounding the passage Philip tells him the glad message about Jesus (8¹⁶ᶠ·). Paul declares to King Agrippa that he is " saying nothing but what the prophets and Moses did say should come " (26²²). The people of Beroea searched in the Scripture daily, " whether these things were so " (17¹¹). And according to the particularly remarkable passage in Peter's speech on Pentecost there are, in addition to the days of Jesus Christ's life, the coming " times of refreshment," beginning with the Second Coming. These are to complete the announced redemption, and so from the standpoint of revelation are still outstanding, the χρόνοι ἀποκαταστάσεως πάντων ὧν ἐλάλησεν ὁ θεὸς διὰ στόματος τῶν ἁγίων ἀπ' αἰῶνος αὐτοῦ προφητῶν (3²⁰ᶠ·). Among the New Testament writers Paul is the man who as an Hellenistic Jew disputed most sharply with the Jews of the synagogue. And yet his doctrine is that God had His Gospel " proclaimed beforehand " (προεπηγγείλατο) by the prophets (Rom. 1²). The revelation of the δικαιοσύνη θεοῦ χωρὶς νόμου, which constitutes the proper content of this Gospel, is " witnessed by the law and the prophets " (Rom. 3²¹). In amazing correspondence with Mt. 5¹⁷ᶠ·, it therefore holds for Paul, too, that " we do not abolish the law by faith, we establish it " (Rom. 3³¹). It is held up against the Jews, zealous in their lack of understanding about God, seeking their own righteousness, not subjecting themselves to the righteousness of God, that the end, purpose and meaning of their own Law is simply Christ (Rom. 10⁴ᶠ·). The Law is nothing else than " our tutor to bring us to Christ " (Gal. 3²⁴). That they, the people of the Law, do not realise this is their lack of understanding. According to 2 Cor. 3¹⁴ᶠ· at the reading of the " old covenant " in the synagogue there lies a veil upon the hearts of the Jews, which will lie there so long as Christ Himself does not take it away, so long as they do not turn to Him. " Christ hath been made a minister of the circumcision for the truth of God, that he might confirm the promises given to the fathers " (Rom. 15⁸). The fact that, according to Paul,

His promise in the Old Testament already signifies His real presence in the pre-time is shown by 1 Cor. 10$^{1-4}$, which speaks about baptism and the Father's gift of spiritual meat and drink in the desert, and which says expressly of the rock from which they drank, ἡ πέτρα δὲ ἦν ὁ Χριστός. Luther's comment on this passage is exegetically sound, that no " allegory or spiritual interpretation " must be admitted : " for 'twas not a figure but a plain seriousness, God's Word, that maketh alive and the right faith was there, thus it befell them in no appear-ance, but 'tis the fact itself was there " (*Pred. üb. Ex.* 14.1525 *W.A.* 16, 275) In conclusion I mention the particularly rich and moving passage 1 Pet. 1$^{10-12}$, where in a way resembling Ac. 3$^{20f.}$ it says of the σωτηρία to come, which is now joyfully believed in the Church, that concerning it the prophets had searched and sought diligently ; they had prophesied the grace laid up for the Church, they had searched what time (καιρός) or what manner of time the Spirit of Christ revealed to them, when it attested beforehand the sufferings of Christ and the glories which should follow them. They received revelation not for themselves but for the Church, the same revelation which now through the preachers of the Gospel is being preached in the power of the Holy Ghost sent forth from heaven.

To indicate the axiomatic character of the statement that Christ was mani-fested as the Expected One even in the time of the Old Testament, we may make the further point that this statement was one which was taken for granted by the whole of the early Church from the 2nd century up to and including the Reformation and the orthodoxy of the 17th century determined by the Reforma-tion, in spite of all the changes in the interpretation and evaluation of the Old Testament. Marcion in the 2nd century and the Socinians in the 16th were already in the eyes of the Church of their time regarded as opponents of the Old Testament, theologians with whom one could not discuss, against whom one could only dispute as against heretics—in fact in the last resort could not dispute at all, because in abandoning the Old Testament they had abandoned not something but everything, namely the New Testament itself as well, and the whole New Testament at that. *Nemo potest vetus testamentum vel tollere vel elevare quin et novum testamentum convellat, cum novum identidem ad vetus provocat, ut per se constat* (Quenstedt, *Theol. did. pol.* 1685 I *c.* 4 *sect.* 2 *qu.* 5 *beb. obs.* 5). So obvious to the Early Church was the recognition that Christ is also manifest in the Old Testament. A. v. Harnack, who admittedly had no desire that this recognition should prevail, in his spirited way propounded the thesis that " to reject the Old Testament in the 2nd century was an error which the great Church rightly rejected ; to cling to it in the 16th century was a destiny from which the Reformation could not yet withdraw ; but still to preserve it after the 19th century as a canonical source in Protestantism is the result of a religious and ecclesiastical paralysis. . . . To make a clean sweep at this point and honour the truth in confession and instruction is the mighty act—already almost too late—required to-day of Protestantism " (*Marcion*, 2nd Edn. 1924 pp. 217, 222). Upon which the simple comment to be made is that by this " mighty act " the Evangelical Church would lose her identity with the Church of the first sixteen centuries. " The Gospels are ' the flesh of Christ ' and the apostles the priest-hood of the Church," writes Ignatius of Antioch ; " but leave us also the dear prophets, because their proclamation also aims at the Gospel, because they too hope for and expect Him, are saved by faith in Him, ἐν ἑνότητι Ἰησοῦ Χριστοῦ ὄντες . . . ὑπὸ Ἰησοῦ Χριστοῦ μεμαρτυρημένοι καὶ συνηριθμημένοι (*Ad Philad.* 5, 2). They lived κατὰ Χριστόν Ἰησοῦν, in spirit they were His disciples and were expecting Him as their Teacher ; they were persecuted for His sake and were moved by His grace (*Ad Magn.* 8, 2 ; 9, 1).

One of the most outspoken representatives of recognition of the essential identity of Old Testament and New Testament, i.e., of the revelation of Jesus Christ in the Old Testament also, is Irenaeus, who especially in the fourth book of his chief work is never tired of speaking as follows. He says that the new

2. *The Time of Expectation* 75

thing which Christ brought in His incarnation was, of course, the greatest *novitas*, i.e., here and here only did He bring Himself forward as the One previously announced (*C.o.h.* IV 34, 1). Here and here only does the *muneratio gratiae* take place. But the *commutatio agnitionis* (11, 3) was by no means introduced thereby, according to Irenaeus. Christ came *non propter eos solos qui temporibus Tiberii Caesaris crediderunt . . . nec propter eos qui nunc sunt homines . . .* (22, 2). But from the beginning there were those who recognised God and prophesied the coming of Christ, and if they did so, it was because they *revelationem acceperunt ab ipso Filio* (7, 2). Them as well as us He forgave their sins (27, 2). The relation between the fathers and us ought to be, *uti et qui seminat et qui metit, simul gaudeat in Christi regno, qui omnibus adest, de quibus ab initio bene sensit Deus, attribuens adesse eis Verbum suum* (25, 3). Abraham's rejoicing (Jn. 8⁵⁶), so to speak, descended to his posterity, who really saw Christ and believed in Him— but again the rejoicing ascended to Abraham, who once desired to see the day of Christ (7¹).

Among the great theologians the next to be named here is Augustine. He declared that the *res ipsa quae nunc religio christiana nuncupatur* was from the beginning of the world simply absent (*Retract.* 1, 13). The Israelite *res publica* was a *prophetatio et praenuntiatio* of the City of God to be gathered out of all nations (*De civ. Dei*, X, 32). A part of the body of Christ or of the Church in the patriarchs and prophets preceded their Head as regards manifestation (*De cat. rud.* 3), as at a birth the child's hand appears first, depending upon him, the head, so that we cannot speak of an independent worth and significance in these forerunners (*Ib.* 19). There was already grace before Christ, although veiled and hidden ; but there it was also not outside the *fides Christi* (*Enchir.* 118). *Per fidem futurae passionis* the fathers were blessed, as we *per fidem praeteritae passionis* (*Conf.* X 43). None must lack salvation who was worthy of it, and those must lack it who were not worthy of it (*De praedest.* 9). In short, the same Church that bore Abel, Enoch, Noah, Abraham also bore Moses and the prophets, also bore *post adventum Domini* the apostles and the martyrs and all good Christians (*De bapt.* I 16). And the relation between the Old Testament and the New Testament was such that the Old Testament is the *occultatio novi*, the New Testament the *veteris revelatio* (*De cat. rud.* 4). Or *in veteri novum latet, in novo vetus patet* (*ib.* 5). And we shall have to say of the unconverted Synagogue that *codicem portat Judaeus unde credat Christianus. Librarii nostri facti sunt. . . .* (*Enarr. in Ps.* 56⁹).

In the Reformation period it was particularly Calvin who emphatically expressed in words what the Early Church thus took for granted. God, he said, gave Himself to be known to the fathers *eadem imagine* as to us. *Nihil ad bene sperandi certitudinem defuit*. The same only-begotten Son of God in whom we recognise the Father was also manifest in Israel (*Instit.* II, 9, 1). The revelation in Christ Himself is the *clara mysterii manifestatio*, the *veritas promissionum* (9, 2). John the Baptist proclaims two things, promise and fulfilment, and thus is at once Old Testament prophet and New Testament witness (9, 5). The fathers were *eiusdem nobiscum hereditatis consortes et eiusdem mediatoris gratia communem salutem speraverunt* (10, 1). God's covenant with them is *substantia et re ipsa* not different from God's covenant with us but identical with it ; we must not speak of *similitudo* only between them but of *unitas* ; for both cases are concerned with the hope of eternity, with the covenant of grace between God and His own, and with the one Mediator, Christ (10, 2). Christ is manifest in the Old Testament, not only in virtue of His eternal Godhead, but in virtue of His special significance as the revealed Word (10, 4), in the real sacramental presence in which He is present to us also. The fathers, too, received the Holy Spirit, not only as the general breath of life—He is present as that in all created beings—but as the special gift *qua piorum animae et illuminantur in Dei notitiam et illi quodammodo copulantur*, as the *illuminatio verbi* which includes a *solida Dei participatio* in all parts (10, 7). The Old Testament promise " I will be your God, and ye shall be my people " is a promise of unlimited content (10, 8). *Constituamus ergo secure, quod nec ullis diaboli machinis revelli queat : vetus testamentum seu foedus, quod cum israelitico populo percussit Dominus . . . spiritualis aeternaeque vitae promissionem continuisse ; cuius expectationem omnium animis impressam opportuit, qui in foedus vere consentiebant* (10, 23). The difference between Old Testament and New Testament is a difference of *administratio* not of *substantia* (11, 1) ; the promise in the Old Testament has a sensible, figurative, legal, literal, particular form, which later falls away in the New Testament (11, 1–12). But its content in the time of the New Testament is not a different one, but *in eo elucet Dei constantia, quod eandem omnibus saeculis doctrinam tradidit* (11, 13). In the same sense we have the language of the *Heidelberg Catechism, Qu.* 19, about " the Holy Gospel which God Himself revealed at the beginning in Paradise, next preached by the holy patriarchs and prophets and continued by the sacrifices and other ceremonies of the Law, but finally fulfilled by His beloved Son."

But it would be a sorry delusion to think that in this matter, because of his well-known and pointed doctrine about the Law and Gospel, and because of the tone of belittlement with which in this connexion the name of Moses in particular is incidentally mentioned by him, Luther is bound to look in a different direction from Calvin. In expounding what is said in Rom. 13[11] (" for now is our salvation nearer than when we first believed ") Luther explains it as follows. The words " when we first believed " should be related to faith in the promise to Abraham, " in thy name shall all the nations in the earth be blessed." " This promise of God was accordingly pretty well urged and spread abroad by the prophets, and all of them have written of the coming of Christ, of His grace and Gospel, as St. Peter saith in Ac. 4 ; for in the same divine promise did all saints have faith for Christ's birth, and so in and by the Christ who was to come persisted and were blest with such faith, that even Christ calleth the same promise Abraham's bosom, Lk. 16, wherein all saints are gathered in unto Abraham until Christ. Such is St. Paul's meaning here, that he saith, ' our salvation is now nearer than when we believed,' as though he should say God's promise made to Abraham is now no more to be awaited in the future, it is fulfilled. . . . Therewith the apostle described the spiritual day, whereof he later speaks, which is really the rise and shining of the Gospel. . . . But thereby is faith not done away but rather stablished, for like as they believed beforehand in the promise of God, that it would be fulfilled, so we believe in the same promise, that it is fulfilled now, as promise and fulfilment follow each other ; for they both depend on the seed of Abraham, i.e., on Christ, some before, the others after His coming. . . . Of the twain faiths saith Paul, Rom. 1 : ' in the Gospel is revealed the righteousness given by God from faith to faith ' : what is ' from faith to faith ' ? No other than just that as faith is all one, the fathers' and ours, which believeth in the coming and appeared Christ, so the Gospel leadeth from the former to the latter faith, which is to believe God not alone for the promise but alike for the fulfilment achieved, in which Abraham and the ancients did not have to believe, although they had the same Christ which we have. One faith, one Spirit, one Christ, one communion of all saints, apart from them preceding and us coming after Christ. Thus have we (i.e., the fathers with us in like common faith in one Christ) believed and do still also believe in Him, but in a different fashion. And as we for the common faith's and Christ's sake say, We have believed, still were we not alive at the time but the fathers believed it. So in turn do they act and say they would or shall hear, see and believe in Christ, though they are not at our time, but we do the same" (*Adv. Post.* 1522 *Pred. üb. Rom.* 13[11t.] *W.A.* 10[12] 4, 27). According to Luther, " 'tis all apostles' and evangelists' idea in the whole New Testament, that they hunt and pursue us into the Old Testament, which alone they also call Holy Writ ; for the New Testament should really be only the living Word corporeally, and not Scripture . . ." (*ib., Pred. üb. Matth.* 21[lt.] *W.A.* 10[12] 34, 27 ; *ib.* p. 60). According to Luther we have " to know that all the apostles taught and wrote they drew from the Old Testament ; for in the same is all proclaimed that was to befall in Christ coming and to be preached, as St. Paul in Rom. 1 saith, that God promised the Gospel of His Son Christ through the prophets in Holy Writ : therefore base they also all their preaching on the Old Testament, and there is no word in the New Testament that looketh not behind itself into the Old, in which 'twas proclaimed previously . . . for the New Testament is not more than a revelation of the Old, just as when a man had first a closed letter and afterwards broke it open. So the Old Testament is a testament epistle of Christ, which after His death He opened and caused to be read through the Gospel and proclaimed everywhere, as it is shown in Rev. 5 by the Lamb of God which alone openeth the book with the seven seals, which otherwise none could open, or in heaven or in earth or under the earth " (*Kirchen-post.* 1522 *Pred. üb. Jn.* 1[lt.] *W.A.* 10[11] 181, 15). Luther sees in the little cloth into which the infant of Bethlehem was wrapped " Holy Writ wherein Christian truth lies wrapped, where we find faith described. For the whole Old Testament hath naught else in it save Christ as He is preached by the Gospel." Luther is convinced " that also the law and the prophets are not rightly preached or known, save we see Christ wrapped up in them " (*Pred. üb. Lk.* 2[lt.] *W.A.* 10[11] 80, 4 ; 81, 8). According to Luther " the God-fearing Jews' belief for the coming of Christ was not that they were blest by the law or circumcision. But that they were directed by circumcision to the Messiah who would bring a new laver and doctrine, and all were born and died, yea entered bliss upon the Christ to come, and believed on Him, though He was not yet born into the world, they built not upon their own righteousness, but what He would teach, therein believed they even before His coming " (*Ausl. des dritten and vierten Cap. Joh.* 1539 *W.A.* 47, 12, 9). " Therefore Moses' law, baptism, sacrifice, kingship and priest-hood was not ordained to last, but only to be for a time. How long then ? Till the seed of the woman should come. And all who understood it so became blest, like the Patriarchs. As then we also still preach, teach, baptise and bear rule, all of which is instituted, not that it should remain so, but that we wait and hope upon Christ who did come in a body. Therefore they are but arousers which remind and exhort us. So then Christ remaineth our Saviour future and present. The children who go before Christ sing Hosanna like the Patriarchs. But we follow with the whole world and it is all the one song, so we have it from Christ, only they precede and we follow after. So what is ordained is ordained upon Christ " (*ib. W.A.* 47, 163, 15). And so in view of Gen. 3[15] (" the same shall bruise thy head " . . .) Luther can preach that " it is a strong claim that smites all to the ground that is preached otherwise. It is already resolved we must despair and renounce, and depend alone upon the Seed which alone doeth it. . . . Therefore behold how boldly the Old Testament speaketh of matters. There it standeth that Adam was already a Christian so long before Christ was born, for he had precisely the faith in Christ which we have, for time maketh none difference to faith, Faith is the same from the beginning of the world to the end, Therefore he did receive by his faith that which I have received, Christ he saw not with his eyes any more than we did, but he had Him in the Word, so we have Him also in the Word. The sole difference is that then it should happen, now it has happened. The faith is all the same, so all the fathers just like ourselves were justified by the Word and faith and also died therein " (*Pred. üb. 1. Buch Mose* 1527 *W.A.* 24, 99, 26). " Thus read we likewise in Acts 17, How Paul preached the faith to the Thessalonians, led them to Scripture and expounded it to them. And how daily they returned to Scripture and searched whether it was so as Paul had taught them. Therefore we should also act, as to run through it and learn to ground the New Testament out of the Old. Therein shall we see the promise of Christ. . . . Therefore ought we to let useless fanatics skip, that despise the Old Testament and say that 'tis no longer of use. Nay, of it alone must we take the ground of our faith. For God did send the prophets to the Jews, that they should give witness to the coming Christ" (*Ep. S. Petri* 1523 *W.A.* 12, 274, 24).

This idea was and also remained, at least in essentials, the basic idea of Lutheran orthodoxy. It, too, declared emphatically that in the Old Testament and New Testament there was but one way of salvation, but one promise, but one covenant and that accomplished in Christ, but one faith, that the revelation of Christ was also proclaimed in the time of the Old Testament, and that the fathers entered bliss solely by the grace of Jesus Christ. When the Lutheran theologians of the 17th century (cf. J. Gerhard, *Loci theol.* 1610 *L.* XIV 123 f. and A. Quenstedt, *Theol. did. pol.* 1685 IV *c.* 7 *sect.* 2 *qu.* 3) disputed the statement of Calvin and the Reformed theologians, as to the identity in substance of Old Testament and New Testament, this was admittedly because they were afraid of a Reformed inference from the statement, that the sacraments of the New Testament were to be regarded on the analogy of the Old Testament as *quaedam per externa et visibilia signa repraesentatio* (Quenstedt). In view of the community in fundamentals just cited, what they adduced in support of their assertion of a difference in substance between Old Testament and New Testament could not reach beyond the difference in *administratio* or *dispensatio* stressed also by Calvin and the Reformed theologians, namely, that *libri veteris testamenti . . . futurum ac suo tempore complendum pronuntiant et praefigurant illud, quod in novo testamento annuntiatur completum* (J. Gerhard, *op. cit.* I 1, 55). And in conclusion, even the Lutheran Hollaz (*Ex. theol. acroam.* 1707 *Prol.* 2 *qu.* 9) could say of the *religio Israelitarum in veteri et christianorum in novo testamento*, that it is *una quoad substantiam*. To a more than formal difference between the Old Testament and the New Testament (say in the contrast between them from the standpoint of Law and Gospel), no one within the sphere of early Protestantism ever actually gave serious thought.

We will now try to explain in detail the statement that Jesus Christ was already manifest as the expected One in the time of the Old Testament. The explanation does not affect the actual thing itself (which is certain in itself and which can only explain itself), but only our statement about this thing, or our way of regarding it. Again, we are quite simply called upon to follow up in thought and expression the truth which we have previously thought out and expressed in the particular way in which the New Testament material justified us in so doing.

This task is not made easier because the eyes and methods with which we seek to read and understand the texts of the Old Testament to-day have been changed by the host of textual, literary, historical and in particular religio-historical problems, or because our interpretations of these texts have become more fluid, varied, and concrete and much more conservative than those of all the Early Church. In itself, perhaps, this betokens an enrichment and deepening of our biblical knowledge. In the sphere of the New Testament, and here too after a long and painful history of manifold errors and confusions, it may be said to-day that the same modern method of interpretation is fitted at long last to render the content and the force of the relations in which these New Testament texts stand, not obscurer, but clearer ; that is, the Church should now completely surmount the times when she had rightly to lament an obscuring of these relations or a merely negative criticism on the part of scientific theology. That is not the case in the sphere of the Old Testament. Research in the Old Testament texts from the theological standpoint appropriate to these very texts has not remotely kept pace with the multiplication, so promising in itself, of material serviceable to such research, material linguistic, literary and historical. A. v. Harnack (*Marcion*[2] 1924 p. 215 f.) summed up his verdict upon the Old Testament by saying, as Luther once said of the Apocrypha, that because of certain edifying sections it might stand at the head of the books that are " good and useful for reading," but had no place in the Canon of Holy Scripture in the Christian Church, " because the essentially Christian element cannot be found in it " (p. 223), at least it cannot be held to be contradicted by the sum total of achievement in Old Testament science from the 18th century down to the present. That one must speak of God's revelation in the Old Testament in a different sense from any book good and useful for reading, cannot be proved by the fact that after recovering from the almost purely destructive attitude of the Neology period towards the Old Testament, along the lines indicated by Herder (as represented in the sphere of Old Testament research by the name of W. M. L. De Wette at the beginning and by the name of H. Gunkel at the end of the 19th century), we can now show the peculiarity of Old Testament piety to be historically unique. For this uniqueness is only of a relative kind and can be described as revelation only in an improper sense of the concept. However brilliantly and happily conceived, the " history of Israelite religion " is not the " biblical theology of the Old Testament." Nor has there yet been proved what needs to be proved, namely, the nature of this Old Testament piety as the historical adumbration and basis of the piety of the New Testament, its kinship and homogeneity with the latter. No real attempt has been made to give this prominence, although it has, of course, always been valued by the wing of Old Testament science which pointed in a positive church direction, and it was not neglected by J. Welhausen and his school (B. Stade). That was and is merely carrying out the programme which Schleiermacher had evolved in relation to the Old Testament. According to him the Old Testament is to be studied and valued as " the most universal literary aid to the understanding of the New Testament " (*Kurze Darst.* § 141), because " Christianity " stands in a " special historical connexion " with " Judaism " ; which does not exclude Christianity, in respect of its nature, from standing in just as neutral an attitude to Judaism as to heathendom (*The Christian Faith*, Eng. tr. § 12) : " that the Jewish codex does not contain a normal exposition of peculiarly Christian statements of faith will soon be generally acknowledged " (*Kurze Darst.* § 115). Even to meet this doctrine of Schleiermacher's and his already clearly expressed wish to see the Old Testament removed from the Canon of the Christian Church, a sound objection can scarcely be made, so long as it is not realised that the whole concern is neither " Judaism " nor " Christianity," neither Old Testament nor New Testament piety, but Jesus Christ as the object of the Old Testament and the New Testament witness. Therefore it is not a matter of an historical relation between two religions, nor yet of one that can be described by the concepts of " kinship " or of " homogeneity," but of unity of revelation in both cases which connects the two so-called religions. The cognition or recognition of this unity as it was alive in the whole Early Church, still confronts modern Old Testament science as its chief task. The case is indeed as put by W. Eichrodt (*Theol. d.A.T. Bd.* 1 1933 p. 4), " that all the ever so brilliant results of historical research cannot seriously offer any substitute for a grasp of the essential connexion between the Old Testament and the New Testament." As regards the attitude to the Old Testament the proclamation of the Church, and with it dogmatics, can in a much less degree than as regards its attitude to the New Testament stand by the results achieved by the important representatives of the relevant scientific discipline, but for good or ill sees itself compelled to seek its way itself, conscious of the dangers therein involved. The unconcern with which the layman must proceed is the parlous result of the unconcern shown by Old Testament experts for the last 200 years or so to their main theological task. For what follows I

am glad to refer to the work just mentioned of W. Eichrodt, whose theological
purpose, to be sure, I should be pleased to see carried out more fundamentally
and radically than it has been ; above all to W. Vischer, " Das Alte Testament
und die Verkündigung," *Theol. Bl.* 1931 p. 1 f., and " Das Alte Testament und
die Geschichte," *Z.d.Z.*, 1932, p. 22 f., as well as to his book which already has
a clear grip of the problem in its title, *Das Christuszeugnis des Alten Testaments*
1 Bd. 1934. In reading this, one should add the review by G. v. Rad, *Theol. Bl.*
1935 p. 248 f., as not unprofitable (a fruitful criticism of Vischer can, of course,
be delivered only by one who is in a position to perform the same task better).
I also refer specifically to the books of Israelite contemporaries like Martin
Buber, *Königtum Gottes*, 1932, H. J. Schoeps, *Jüdischer Glaube in dieser Zeit*,
1932, and *Jüdisch-christliches Religionsgespräch*, 1937, E. B. Cohn, *Aufruf zum
Judentum*, 1934, who, just because they are " pure " students of the Old Testament, are instructive to listen to on our question, both in what they say as
earnest Jews, and in what they cannot say as unconverted Jews.

In our context there can be no question of more than a cross-
sectional indication of the state of matters in the Old Testament
witness. There are three lines along which the unity of Old Testament
with New Testament revelation in the relation of expectation to
fulfilment appears to me to become recognisable.

1. The Old Testament like the New Testament is the witness to
revelation, which is decidedly to be regarded as a free, utterly once-
for-all, concrete action of God. All along the line it has to fight against
deviations from this attitude. But in itself the line is clear : when
it speaks of the togetherness of God and man, the Old Testament is
thinking neither of an objectively nor of an ideally grounded manifest
state of God. It is thinking of revelation. It is therefore neither
thinking of a givenness of God in and with the present of the spatio-
natural cosmos, nor of a knownness of God in the form of a doctrine
of transcendental truth known once for all or to be co-opted into
knowledge. It holds that God's presence is not bound up with the
national existence, unity and peculiarity of the people Israel, nor yet
with the individuality of this or that religious personality. But God's
revelation in the Old Testament is throughout a self-relation of God
which posits itself from time to time in the sovereign freedom of divine
action : a self-relation to a nation, but to a nation which from time to
time concretely confronts Him in certain individual men and on which
from time to time He acts through these individual men; a self-
relation to definite individual men, who can concretely confront and
serve Him only as examples, only as representatives of this nation ;
a self-relation which relativises and leaves behind it the contrast
between nature and history as supremely as it does that of individual
and community; a self-relation of the one, only God out of His own
untrammelled initiative in the sheer Now of His decision. This Now
of the divine decision and hence the revelation of God is the *berith*,
the covenant, carried out in the flight from Egypt, introduced, made
possible and led by God, proclaimed in the once-for-all lawgiving,
sealed in the equally once-for-all covenant sacrifice at Sinai. This

does not discover Israel already existing as such. It creates Israel as a national unit. And only in view of this covenant does the Old Testament witness have an interest in this nation, and this nation in particular.

Israel is first a *qahal* (assembly) and an *edah* (congregation). Only then and as such (emphatically not as independent and not as its own end) is it a nation. The covenant does not admit of being translated back into the dogma of a national religion, in which God can achieve only the role of a personification of national genius and self-consciousness, or of the natural force which mysteriously lies at the roots of national blood and soil. On the contrary, the observation of the covenant demanded by God consists in a repudiation of this backward translation.

The covenant is a sanctification, a claiming, a commandeering, an arrest of man for God, not of God for man. The Torah, the cultic and moral law, is not, therefore, an instrument put into man's hands, by means of which he can get control of God and dispose of His goodness and succour. It is the instrument of the divine compassion. It is this in a twofold sense. It *achieves*, as it were existentially, the liberating " thou art Mine " upon man. It also distinguishes it as a divine utterance, before any " thou art mine " which in attempted self-help man may arbitrarily say to himself in order to circumvent the gods of the land. As law, the covenant is grace, exactly as *qua* grace it is law. The covenant is grace ; i.e., it does not compel God, but for God it is dissoluble any moment : it may work itself out in God's wrath and judgment, as well as in His goodness and succour. It is God's free faithfulness if He does not dissolve the covenant, and it is God's mercy if He punishes sins and forgives sins, if after having punished He always likewise blesses again. If the nation on its side is faithful, if it keeps His commandments, if it honours His name, if it brings Him sacrifices, it does nothing out of the way. It merely acknowledges that the decision has been made, that God has adopted His own, that from Him it may from time to time receive forgiveness and help. Sacrifice is possible only on the basis of the covenant, not *vice versa*. The presentation of man to God by the agency of the priest can only typify what God in reality does for man. As always, all man's obedience can be only a copy, a repetition, a confirmation of what with incomparable majesty God does for man. But the covenant is also law. A man of God is always a servant of God. And it is because it is a nation claimed, totally demanded by its God with a view to the obedience which—whatever may be the case with its realisation—is the unalterable will of God, that it is this nation, His nation. The existence of the covenant is the constantly self-renewing command of God.

This covenant attested in the Old Testament is God's revelation, because it is expectation of the revelation of Jesus Christ. It is expectation of the revelation of Jesus Christ once for all in its strict genuine historicity. As freely, as concretely, as uniquely as in the Old Testament *berith*, God in Jesus Christ becomes history, and with the same mercy and strictness man in Christ is adopted by God. To that extent, therefore, Jesus Christ is already the content and theme of this prehistory, of the Old Testament covenant. As prehistory, as revelation in expectation, the Old Testament covenant is character-ised by its division into several covenants side by side, equipped with the same marks, even with the marks of the same uniqueness. Before the Sinaitic covenant we admittedly find the covenant with Abraham underlying the election of Israel, and again, before the Abrahamic covenant, the covenant with Noah, in which the particular covenant with Israel, even before it became an event, is already carried beyond its particularity and raised to universality. So, although it is already a reality from that early beginning, Israel's election is a present reality. In Deuteronomy we find that the covenant is to some extent a lasting ordinance, under which the Israel of the present stands, although it is still based upon the free love and lordship of God. In the prophets Jeremiah, Ezekiel and Deutero-Isaiah it appears, on the contrary, as an actuality which is regarded with increasing strictness and depth as future, as existing prior to all time, and only in that way as present to all time, but again extending universally into the world of the nations. In addition to all this, and in special relation to the future covenant of the time of salvation, should we not remember the special covenant with the house of David, not to mention the covenant with Levi, the priestly tribe ? What shall we say then ? Which of these covenants is *the* covenant intended by the Old Testament, and meant to be understood and attested as the original, central and true covenant? An answer in terms of the Old Testament texts themselves can only be to the effect that each one is in its own place and in its own way. For it is always the one covenant with the same direction and order. But—and in this context this is the Old Testament element in the Old Testament—in each of its forms it is rendered problematic, because it still possesses such wholly different subsidiary forms. *The* covenant seems to be none of these forms—neither the covenant with Noah nor the covenant with Abraham, neither the Deuteronomic time of salva-tion nor the one to come, nor yet the covenant of Sinai, so central historically. Or rather the covenant seems to lie outwith any of these forms ; it seems in each of them to be a promise, and so and only so to be present in each of these forms. Many a genuine " Now," many a genuine " once-for-allness " in this region is awaiting the confirma-tion of its genuineness, the " once-for-all-times " which is, of course, always intended in it but is also never attained. To that extent, in regard to the reality of the Old Testament covenant we may speak of an expectation, but only of an expectation, of the revelation of Jesus Christ as the covenant between God and man.

But the relation of the Old Testament covenant to Jesus Christ (or rather the relation of Jesus Christ to the Old Testament covenant) is still closer and more direct. It is characteristic of the Old Testament covenant, as already stated at the outset, not to be founded and renewed, maintained and fostered, proclaimed and defended without human " instruments." *A priori* it is not being properly viewed, if it is viewed in the, so to speak, bare relation of " God-Nation." For it, the existence of the third mediating, portent-bearing factor of the God-Man is not secondarily but primarily essential. At the decisive place as proclaimer of the Torah, as led leader of the nation out of Egypt into the borders of Canaan, his name is Moses. But he may also be called Abraham as " our father." Once upon a time in the dawn of time Abraham was the first and only human partner in the covenant with God, a covenant already concluded beforehand with all the yet unborn generations of his successors. But he may also be called David as the vehicle of victory, or Solomon as the vehicle of glory ; in both of whom is reflected the blessing of the covenant. And he may be the unnamed " servant of God " of the last days in Deutero-Isaiah, who proclaims the counsel of God no longer in victory and glory, but in lowliness and suffering. Between these great individual Mediator-forms and their portent-bearing functions stand the smaller folk, regularly called, as it were, significant as types, the judges and later the *kings*, whose leadership in the external history of the nation does not bear the character of politics, but in the strictest sense the character of sacramental administration, so far as they represent God as the sole King of Israel, by setting up in the sphere of human law and human might the standard of the law and might of the sole sovereignty of God. Along with them are the priests, who alone are set apart and authorised to consummate the sacrifice which only the male of the nation may offer, obviously to show that God alone is the Subject of the event which the sacrifice pictures. Finally the prophets are the prominent guardians of the covenant, as well as the disturbers of the people's tranquillity. By their accusations, threats and consolations they see to it that the question of the covenant is continually raised, that the covenant is always brought before men's mind, that in short it is made visible in the supreme sense as the future reality of Israel. They, too, are representatives of God, in that by their human speech and action they set up the standard of the creative and ruling Word of God.

The Old Testament covenant is the revelation of God as thus specially defined, in so far as, being so defined, it is expectation of the revelation of Jesus Christ. Humanly God will be made manifest, when He is made manifest in Jesus Christ. Man will have to do with one Man as God's representative, as the upholder and proclaimer of the covenant ; he will have to do with a prophet, priest and king. An office of revelation will be set up and exercised. Of this the Old Testament is aware, and so it must also be said in this respect that

Jesus Christ is its content and theme. That its revelation is only
the expectation of revelation is shown from this aspect, not only in
the confusing number and variety of its mediating forms, which
already in their parallelism and succession (like the various forms of
the covenant itself) point beyond themselves, but still more in the
limitation under which they are all manifestly what they are, in the
thoroughgoing portent-bearing nature of their functions, in the impropriety of their office as God's representatives. The kings of Israel
did not indeed (as the usual idea of "theocracy" leads us to believe)
carry out the law of Yahweh in their law, or exercise the might of
Yahweh in their might, but Yahweh reserved His law and His power
for Himself, and did so precisely in face of them. The priests did not
forgive sins or create reconciliation between God and the nation, when
they offered the sacrifices for the nation. With their human actions
as priests they could only hint at this divine action. The prophets,
too, did in all actuality receive and transmit the Word of the Lord.
But they only received and transmitted it. They did not utter it of
themselves, or as their own word. That the Word of God became this
man himself and therefore flesh, the Old Testament does not venture
to assert even of its greatest prophets. The almighty representation
of God among men—the representation in which as a man God Himself
is His own representative among men—is only announced in Abraham,
Moses and David and the kings, priests and prophets of the Old
Testament. They are all of them only instruments of divine action,
not themselves or of themselves divinely active. Obviously they all
signify the divine Agent, i.e., God Himself humanly present, God's own
Son. They do really signify Him. To that extent He is also manifest
in them, and to that extent men may already be called in the Old
Testament "sons of God," even incidentally "gods." But they signify
Him in terms of the infinite distance that lies between the one who
signifies and the One who is signified. They all have to point beyond
themselves, and with them we have to look beyond themselves, in
order to see the One who is signified. Or rather we must regard them
from the standpoint of the One who is signified in order to realise that
they do really signify Him. The covenant of God with His people
through the incarnation is in truth the mysterium, the true mysterium,
the mystery of the Old Testament.

We can summarise all that concerns the reality and the preliminary nature
of Old Testament revelation, its unity with that of the New Testament, and its
variety in this unity, in the introductory words to the Epistle to the Hebrews :
πολυμερῶς καὶ πολυτρόπως πάλαι ὁ θεὸς λαλήσας τοῖς πατράσιν ἐν τοῖς προφήταις . . .
(Heb 1¹).

2. The Old Testament like the New Testament is the witness to
the revelation in which God remains a hidden God, indeed declares
Himself to be the hidden God by revealing Himself. In and with this
attested revelation a judgment is pronounced upon the whole world

surrounding it, since God—here and now actually present—declares
the whole world surrounding His revelation to be godless, irrespective
of what it apparently believed itself to possess in the way of divine
presence. And by this judgment this entire surrounding world is as
such destined to die off, to pass away. If it has a hope, it is not to
be found in itself, but only in connexion with the divine presence
which breaks out fresh in revelation, and is the only real presence.
But in the first instance it has no hope. It must first of all pass
away. The nations settled in Palestine, which were in certain respects
highly civilised nations, were struck with surprise and horror at the
nomad nation that broke in from the desert with their first and second
commandments, although it was really questionable how far even
they understood and followed these commandments themselves. The
revelation which was the origin of this nation was the revelation
of the one, only God, to be acknowledged without analogy and to be
worshipped without image. What invaded Palestine was the radical
dedivinisation of nature, history and culture—a remorseless denial
of any other divine presence save the one in the event of drawing
up the covenant. If there were any pious Canaanites—and why
should there not have been such ?—the God of Israel must have
appeared to them as death incarnate, and the faith of Israel as irreligion
itself. But admittedly no time was left them for such reflections. In
remembering this hiddenness of the Old Testament covenant-God,
we also understand that the question, as it was obviously put to Israel
in the time of Joshua and the Judges down to and including Samuel,
consisted in the frightful dilemma : either God's presence, guidance
and help and therefore fidelity and obedience to the covenant on the
nation's side, or peaceful assimilation into the nature, history and
culture of the country, i.e., a common human life with its inhabitants.
Or the question put the opposite way : either surrender of the covenant
with consequent loss of the presence and help of God, or a complete
break with any supposed presence of God in the nature, history or
culture of the country, even involving the physical elimination of its
inhabitants. The whole inexorable sharpness of the difference between
Yahweh and the *baalim*, between the prophets on the one hand and the
nation and the kings and the " false " prophets on the other, which
constituted the theme of the history of Israel down to the Deuteronomic
reform and beyond, is understandable in the light of the typical
either/or, which according to tradition, constituted the end of the
wandering in the wilderness and the beginning of the history of Israel
in the country of their fathers (or, rather, in the country of Yahweh).
Was it nationalistic narrow-mindedness, religious fanaticism, hatred
of men and lust for blood that commanded this people to take such
a stand and to act upon it ? According to the unanimous testimony
of the Old Testament, it is rather driven, against its will and amid
numerous attempts to carry out its own opposite will, along this hard,

inhuman way. It would have been very like them to become one civilised Canaanite nation among others, and to be religiously open and pliable or at least tolerant. King Saul, whom Samuel had to withstand, and later King Ahab, whom Elijah had to withstand, must in their way have been outstanding representatives of this naturally human Israel. But Israel could not do as it wished. Wherever the voice of its prophets thundered and was heard, the abyss reopened between the gods and men of the country, and the holy nation, the natural, human Israel was accused, it was called back to the offensive attitude of unconditional resistance. It is not its religious and natural peculiarity that is the resistant here—it would never have been so unconditional in its resistance—but its God, who cannot become manifest without at the same time becoming hidden. The country belongs to Him. It cannot therefore belong to the *baalim* also or even at all. No other loyalty is compatible with loyalty to Him. Since by its own existence Israel pointed out God's revelation to the world around it, it had to deny their gods, i.e., their very deepest, best and most vital thing, the supposedly absolute relations in which they thought they stood. Israel had to point out to this world the end, the judgment coming upon them. That Yahweh's exclusiveness is fundamental, that His revelation really points out the judgment coming upon the world, is to be seen in the fact that the prophetic accusations and threats, which apart from Israel are in Amos still directed only against the nearest nations, reach over in the later prophets to the great world nations on the Euphrates and the Nile. From this later message of judgment we shall have to read off the meaning and trend of the earlier one.

The revelation of God in Jesus Christ is actually the end and judgment, the revelation of the hidden God which the Old Testament indicates. In the cross of Christ God is really and finally to become hidden from the world, from this æon. And thereby judgment will be passed upon this æon. The old will have passed away in the incarnate Word of God. The history of Israel runs to meet this Word and so this passing away. It only runs to meet it. But it does run to meet it. It signifies the proclamation of world judgment in fulfilled time. It is the time for expecting it. But because it is the time for expecting it, it is itself revelation-time.

As the bearer of the revelation imparted to it, Israel only too clearly means catastrophe for the surrounding world. But even more clearly Israel itself as the recipient of revelation has to suffer in this world. It encounters in its history incomparably much more evil than good. According to the account in the historical books of the Old Testament, the brief periods of victory and expansion serve only as a foil, as a silver edge, to emphasise what is really happening, namely the trouble and distress in which this nation constantly has to live ; the blows which it receives on all sides ; and finally the downfall which with a certain inevitability is its end. In terms of world history the existence of this people as a nation and state midway between Egypt and Asshur-Babylon might even be regarded as only a limited interlude. Its covenant with God does not in any sense guarantee that things go well with it. Health, prosperity or security, the political unity and strength which enable a nation to conquer and maintain a place for itself in the world's history, were contemplated neither by the Law nor by the prophets of this nation. Of the prophets it must in fact be said that on the contrary they actually worked against any striving for these things. The prophets' desire was not for Israel to be a nation, but for it at any price, even at the literal cost of its natural nationhood, to be God's nation. Politically, it was quite normal for the kings to be afraid of the prophets, to reject, to combat them. They could never hear from them what as statesmen they desired to hear. Only false prophets could seek to advocate the cause of Yahweh and the cause of the nation at the same time. The true prophets advocated exclusively the cause of Yahweh, His concern for this nation. This nation as such had undoubtedly to suffer at the hands of its God. It did not suffer primarily from the unfavour-ableness of external circumstances, from its smallness or weakness, from the violence of foreign nations—and never from the fact that its God did not have the power to overcome these difficulties. This is the power that Israel's God constantly manifests, and because of it the prophets are men who challenge the nation politically to courage and trust. But Israel suffers primarily from the resistance with which God Himself opposes it, namely, with an unwavering : " Except ye believe, ye shall not abide." What is the severity with which this nation had to confront other nations in the typical action of the time of the Judges compared with the continual severity with which Israel's own God confronts it, and which finally destroys Jerusalem and its palace and temple ? The story of this nation is only too much a repetition of the story of its tribal ancestor, who has to wrestle not only with man but with God, and though disabled by God never-theless wrestles with this One till dawning : " I will not let thee go except thou bless me." This nation's decline and fall seems to be God's own triumph, and this nation's salvation seems to lie exclusively in the fact that, like a drowning man, it must clutch constantly at the hand, must constantly be saved by the hand, that smites it so frightfully. Between the covenant and its fulfilment there is suffering and death for those in whom it ought to be fulfilled. This sequence is repeated in detail more or less clearly in the cases of God's special emissaries in the Old Testament. They can none of them be understood in terms of a genius, a hero, a great man who grasps his calling as his dearest and highest, who produces a successful work, who sheds a glory which also falls back upon himself. They, too, seem to be grasped by a hard fist and put in their place, to be used, and to be used up, by the

will and for the glory of another, without consideration for their own
well-being or glory, often, in fact, in such a way that they have to
prove by their personal suffering what God's counsel is for His people.
Moses may see from afar, but not attain, the goal for which he has lived.
And the name of Jeremiah is typical here of all other true prophets.
To none of them is it permitted, in fulfilment of their commission, to
walk even outwardly or inwardly upon the high places of life. Unlike
Jacob, they are not all blessed—least of all the " servant of God " of
the last days in Deutero-Isaiah : " When we see him, there is no
beauty that we should desire him." This is true of the figure of every
true prophet. Since, according to the comprehensive picture which
the New Testament has of them, they are all persecuted, stoned and
done to death, they are not only an accusation against the unbelief
and disobedience of the nation, but rather are they above all a personal
exposition of the unsearchableness of God's ways. They are themselves
the first to have to suffer, and they are themselves the ones who have
to suffer most, for the truth of their proclamation, for the fact that the
God who has ever loved Israel is such a hidden God. And the same
order is repeated again in the figure of the single righteous man, who,
without special office, simply lives concretely the existence of Israel
before his God. We meet this figure in the Psalms or most impressively
in the Book of Job, but also in quite a different fashion in the Preacher
Solomon.

Cf. on this W. Vischer, " Der Gottesknecht," *Jahrb. d. theol. Schule Bethel,*
1930, p. 59 ff. ; " Hiob ein Zeuge Jesu Christi," *Z.d.Z.,* 1933, p. 386 ff. ; *Der
Prediger Salomo,* 1926.

According to Job and Ecclesiastes particularly, the righteous man
of the Old Testament sees himself unmercifully faced with the question,
whether it is not really quite futile to fear and to serve God, whether
all that mortal man can do is not in vain even in the best and wisest
and most obedient life. But he is also just as unmercifully faced
with the answer, that to this question we have literally no possible
answer to give, that the force and comfort of all man's answers suffer
shipwreck on the fact that they are man's answers, and not the answers
of Him who exclusively is good and who exclusively can say or will
say what is good. Even to His truest friends, and because they are
so, the God of Israel is the hidden God, hidden in a work which from
their own standpoint they can and perhaps will describe as unright-
ousness and unreason, hidden in the work of their wickedest enemy.
It must be that they think of Him and seek after Him ; that asking
naught of heaven or earth they nevertheless abide by Him, clinging
fast to Him. It must be that they love Him because they have heard
Him, and have heard Him because He Himself has spoken to them.
It must be that He Himself has constantly loved them and so drawn
them to Himself and so addressed them, in order to justify them and
at the same time to justify Himself as their Friend. Only because of

His free goodness made known in the event of His Word is it not in vain to fear Him. That is the reason why everything is not futile, why it is not futile to know and to fear Him. Thus the end of the world, or the judgment of the world, is seen above all in Israel. To it especially God is a hidden God. It especially, the beloved, chosen, sanctified nation, the house of God, must be the place where the old æon begins to pass in face of the coming of God and His new work.

Now suffering Israel, the suffering prophet, the suffering righteous man, is not Christ. The old has not passed away because the nation has been led by its strangely hard way, because Jacob, Jeremiah or Job had to be so mortally sick at God's hand. The revelation of God will become reality, where His Word, His Son has become flesh Himself, and has taken to Himself and upon Himself this whole illimitable burden of the flesh. God will really be the hidden God and be manifest in this very hiddenness, where God Himself has hidden Himself, in the way He was hidden here for Israel and for all these men of Israel, i.e., in the way of " My God, my God, why hast thou forsaken me ? " But we obviously have to repeat our assertion, that Jacob, Jeremiah and Job, the whole obscure happening in and to Israel, points towards this real hiddenness of God and so towards His real revelation, that the whole figure of " the servant " in Is. 53—and Is. 53 is only a re-capitulation of what is to be found in almost every chapter of the Old Testament—typifies the suffering and crucified Christ. So far as the Old Testament is not only a problem but a solved problem, so far as Yahweh really acts mercifully, shows rivers of eternal gentle-ness to this nation, so far as these poor souls are nevertheless all comforted by the real and infinitely comforting nearness of God in spite of His hiddenness and in it, so far as God does not let them suffer in vain and they are not faithful to God in vain : to that extent Christ was indeed suffering Israel, the suffering prophet, the suffering righteous man. Not an idea of Christ, but the real, historical Christ *qui passus est sub Pontio Pilato*. As such, the Old Testament does not say that its problem is solved, or how. As such, the Old Testa-ment does not know the God who is really hidden. It does not know, therefore, the God who is really manifest. But as such, and in and for itself, the Old Testament of which this must be said is not a reality at all, but a Jewish abstraction.

Only theological dilettantism (the dilettantism of the average Old Testament scholar), for which the abysses of the Old Testament are concealed to its own salvation, or, of course, a genuine unconverted Judaism, can be capable of such an abstraction. Some idea of what genuine unconverted Judaism is, of the grim unredeemedness and yet want of ultimate seriousness with which at this point the Old Testament abstractly read and interpreted points straight into the void, may be had from Richard Beer-Hoffmann's drama *Jaakobs Traum*, 1920.

The real Old Testament is not such an abstraction. The real Old Testament attests the strict,. entire mystery of God's judgments (a

mystery also manifested in that very way as grace), and so not only
the miseries of men involved in this judgment, but the suffering of
God Himself who has Himself assumed and borne this judgment. It
attests the expectation of Jesus Christ. It attests not any sort of
hiddenness of God, but that which points forward to the hiddenness
of God in the stable at Bethlehem and on the cross on Golgotha.
Therefore and to that extent it attests revelation in the full sense of
the concept.

But in relation to the hiddenness and the judgment of God in the
witness of the Old Testament we must give our attention to still a
third point. It is not an absurdity or a whim, nor yet is it a metaphysical necessity, which is at the root of the fact that God is hidden
in this way in the history attested in the Old Testament, and that this
history is thus subject to the order of the dissolution of man and his
world and must therefore point to the cross of Christ. There is no
gnosis or mysticism underlying this order. It holds true in strict, clear
relation to the fact that in the covenant, in his meeting with God,
man proves himself to be sinful man, striving with God, turning aside
from the way of God. The history of Israel in its covenant with God
is not only the story of its sickness, of its suffering shipwreck upon
the Lord by whom it is chosen and loved, but also the story of its
continual misunderstanding, its continual self-will, its continual rebellion. And the two things correspond and mutually condition each
other. As we see, for instance, in the story of the setting up and
worship of the golden calf, the rebellion occurs in connexion with the
strict lordship of the hidden God; i.e., it arises not from some chance
and therefore incomprehensible weakness or wickedness, but from a
very revealing protest against the *opus alienum* by which God keeps
faith with His own and shows them love. And *vice versa* the *opus
alienum*, the punishment, is the only way God can keep faith with
and show love to this nation, which is a wicked, stiffnecked, obdurate
nation. Israel's sin is, so to speak, the human side of God's hiddenness. It is not with pure, good, moral men that God makes and keeps
covenant, but with transgressors, and incorrigible transgressors at that.
In the historical picture given in the Old Testament even the greatest
heroes, even a Moses or a David, are obviously not excluded from this
category. Even the prophets do not except themselves. The " righteous man " in the third section of the Old Testament writings was
the very last person not to submit to this rule. It is not just that
he confesses himself a sinner (so that the matter can be regarded
as a literary question), but he acts in such a way that it is quite
evident that he really is a sinner. The God of the Old Testament
cannot be approached, least of all by way of the human excellences of
those whom He calls His own. Again, Israel's sin is not something
" wicked "; it is not " vice " or " immorality." In the Old Testament it is evident that God often punishes in a very striking way,

where according to ethical judgments there is no sin at all or else the very opposite of sin. On the other hand, God frequently does not punish or punishes extraordinarily lightly, in cases where from an ethical point of view there really is serious sin. In neither case does the different nature of ancient oriental ethics offer more than a partial explanation. So then the God of the Old Testament cannot even be reached by way of the obvious righteousness of His punishments—because sin in the Old Testament is itself a mystery, the mystery of the breaking of the covenant. But that means that sin is committed within the radius of the covenant itself; by being committed it is brought into relation with the economy of the divine will and action. This neither lightens nor excuses it, let alone justifies it. On the contrary, it is real, serious, deadly sin for that very reason, such as Philistines or Moabites in all their superstition and unbelief could never commit. But while sin is committed God is also the Lord over Israel's sin, (1) in so far as it is against Him and Him only that sin can be committed; (2) in so far as His reaction to it, punishment, the hiding of His face from His covenant partner, is an act of His own faithfulness to the covenant and not a dissolution of it; (3) in so far as the two, sin and punishment, take place within the bounds, and so also with the meaning and aim, which He sets them. The statement may be ventured, perilous though it may sound, that man is necessarily a sinner. Jacob, the elect of God before His brother Esau, had to be the thoroughly problematic figure he is depicted as being in Genesis. The people led by God out of Egypt amid signs and wonders had to behave in the wilderness as unbecomingly as they did. The kings entrusted with the proclamation of the sole rule of God had to fail as did Saul, Jeroboam and Ahab, and also in their way David, Hezekiah and Josiah. An Isaiah had to be a man of " unclean lips," and Jonah had first to behave like a righteous rebel against the service of his God, only to try very comically to vie with Him in impatience over Nineveh. It had to be that in the temple at Jerusalem the " liberal " declension into Canaanitism and the over-confident but at root no less secular " positive " churchiness of many Deuteronomists and their later spiritual kindred, are the only two possibilities to be considered. The prophets sent to this people had to be persecuted, stoned and done to death. Even the " righteous " in this nation, and all because they were righteous, had to be exposed to God's accusation and judgment. Job had to go to extremes in revolt and the Preacher likewise in scepticism. Had to ? Yes, he had to, they all had to, because and so far as here, in the covenant on the basis of which it all takes place, God is really God, and therefore man, too, is really man. In this encounter God meets man in the way in which for the sake of His own truth and the truth of His creation He must meet him, man the faithless in his inmost, deepest and most intimate heart, man turned away from Him. That is to say, God confronts man with Himself in His hiddenness and holiness, whose thoughts are as exalted over those of men as heaven is higher than earth. And in this encounter, precisely because God in unapproachableness is so close to man, he is challenged to be and to show himself as he is ; in this encounter he is cited to appear as what in truth he is, i.e., simply as a sinner. This does not happen anywhere. How can it happen on the Nile or the Euphrates or amid the forests of Germany ? Only upon the basis of the covenant can this happen. But there it *must* happen. This necessity is conditioned by the basis of the covenant—between the real God and real man judgment *must* become an event. Therefore, these two things, God's hiddenness and man's resistance to it, or to put it the other way round, man's resistance to God and the divine hiddenness in the form of punishment which is the answer to it, are caught up into God's over-ruling design. We cannot, of course, penetrate into that design and must not therefore think of trying to explain it in terms of a synthesis of sin and punishment. On the contrary, it is as unsearchable as God Himself (not as a concept, but in His real lordship). It is as unsearchable as He who in the very assertion of His real lordship manifests Himself in such a way as to make that judgment a necessity, and as He who, because He is God in the assertion of His real lordship, will not let His hiddenness be the last word—that makes it all the more impossible for man in his rebellion to retain the last word. It must be so because there must be Christmas, because reconciliation must take place in the event of God's real lordship.

Nevertheless we have not said the decisive thing that is to be said in connexion with this Old Testament necessity, namely, that on the basis of the covenant Jesus Christ had to be crucified. If, when the Word was made flesh, anything else could have happened upon the ancient critical stage of Galilee and Jerusalem than actually did happen, then a different God and a different man would at once have had to confront each other upon that stage. If God did not become another, if, therefore, man did not become another in the event when God asserted His real lordship, if, on the contrary, this event was the fulfilment of time, the fulfilment of the covenant, how could its content be other than the real hiddenness of God and so the suffering and dying servant of God ? And likewise on the side of man, how could it be other than rebellion and desertion really and finally consummated ? Jesus had to go up to Jerusalem. But the high priests, too, and the scribes and the people, had to do as they did in the only too genuine succession of tradition. The disciples had to leave Him, Peter had to deny Him, Judas had to betray Him. Not even here does this necessity imply the slightest excuse. Man unveils himself here as really and finally guilty. But that this did happen, that man really and finally revealed himself as guilty before God by killing God, had to happen thus and not otherwise in the event in which God asserted His real lordship. Of course this necessity can be expressed only in retrospect of this event, i.e., in retrospect of Easter to Good Friday ; we might also say, in prospect of Christmas to Good Friday. " Our chastisement was upon him, that we might have peace." If that is true, if the encounter of God and man here is really reconciliation, then it may be said that Christ had to be crucified, that God had to meet man here as the Hidden, and that man had to meet God here as a rebel. And if reconciliation is the truth about God's action on Good Friday, and is recognised as the truth, in virtue of the revelation at Easter or Christmas, then this " had to " must also hold for the Old Testament, and the events in the Old Testament are to be regarded as expectation, as prophecy of the revelation in Jesus Christ. Then the truth of God's hiddenness in the Old Testament and the truth of Israel's sin is seen to be the forgiveness of sins. So, in view of the terrible encounter of God and man in the Old Testament, we shall have to say that here, too, we already have the communion of saints, the forgiveness of sins, the resurrection of the flesh and the life everlasting. To expect Christ in this full and complete way, as was the case here, means to have Christ and to have Him fully. The fathers had Christ, the complete Christ. Here, too, naturally, not an idea of Christ, but the incarnate Word, the Christ of history. Such a statement is allowable only from the standpoint of a Good Friday illumined by Christmas and Easter. To this day the Synagogue cannot make it. To this day the Synagogue repeats what it did when it crucified Christ, and at the same time exactly what Israel has always been doing. The Synagogue is corporately, so to speak, the Old Testament *per se* and *in abstracto* stiffened into petrifaction. To that extent it is quite in order for it to claim the Old Testament for itself as an unfulfilled Old Testament, an Old Testament without reconciliation. Apart from the event of real divine lordship in Jesus Christ, apart from Christmas and Easter, as a possession of the Synagogue, the Old Testament is bound to be such an abstraction. But in that case it is not revelation. For how can this unfulfilled encounter between the Holy God and unholy man be revelation ? God's hiddenness which is genuine and man's rebellion against Him which is genuine will not be found attested in the Old Testament, if the crucifixion of Jesus is adjudged to be an episode not completely explained on every side.

Who possesses, who reads the real Old Testament ? Who understands it according to its tenor and as it claims itself to be understood ? To this day the question stands between Church and Synagogue. For the witnesses of the New Testament it was not an historical or a scientific question, but the burning, vital question of faith and revelation. They recognised and believed in Jesus Christ, not *in vacuo* but as the One attested in the Law and the prophets, the expected One of the fathers. The necessity with which He became their Lord was inevitably the very same necessity which imposed upon them the Word of God in the Old Testament. Without the Word of God in the

Old Testament the Church would be believing in a different Christ
from the New Testament witnesses. The New Testament Christ is the
fulfilment of Old Testament expectation. Thus the question outstanding between Church and Synagogue is always being decided for
the Church in that this New Testament Christ is revealed and believed
in it. If this is what happens, there can be no debate as to the real
Old Testament. And in that case the Church will be no less glad of
the witness to His coming in the Old Testament, than it is of the
witness to His having come in the New Testament.

3. The Old Testament like the New Testament is the witness of
the revelation in which God is present to man as the coming God.
Present and *coming* are both to be stressed. In this way we describe
the side of the Old Testament witness, according to which it is now
explicitly witness to expectation ; from the New Testament standpoint
we say, expectation of Jesus Christ, according to which it is prophecy.
It is this implicitly, as we have seen, even as a witness of God's covenant
and God's hiddenness.

In the Early Church theology was too onesidedly occupied only with explicit
prophecy in the Old Testament. The same cannot be said, of course, of Luther
and Calvin. And a closer inspection will show that it applies only to a limited
extent to the usual caricature of Old Testament interpretation in the age of
orthodoxy, as though at that time the chief occupation in this field was to hunt
up in a more or less imaginative way all manner of Messianic prophecies and to
produce an unnaturally exact Christology of the Old Testament. In this respect
we have only to recall the labours of the so-called federal theologians of the
school of J. Coccejus, which achieved supremacy in the Reformed Church in
the second half of the 17th century, and soon enough spread over into Lutheranism. Their attempts to show the unity of Old Testament with New Testament
were, like those of Calvin, discreet and comprehensive, in spite of the very
questionable nature of the historical viewpoints and methods. If any objection
can be raised against them, it is the irruption of a philosophy of history into
their thinking, which obscured theological clarity. But there is no truth in the
wholesale criticism of their age, that, without paying any attention to the concrete historical contexts, they searched and found " mechanically " in the Old
Testament prophecies and types of the person and work of Christ. And it is
even less in accord with historical truth to think of passing a judgment of this
kind upon the labours say of J. C. Konrad v. Hofmann of Erlangen on " Prophecy and Fulfilment." Against his conception (not to speak of historical questions) theological doubts of the severest kind may certainly be raised. We
must be careful, however, to appreciate the fact, that it was one of the basic
ideas of these theologians that Old Testament prophecies of Christ were not to
be sought in this or that isolated passage of direct prophecy, but in the concrete
historical contexts of the Old Testament, and the passages in question were to
be studied only within these special contexts. As a matter of fact, there have
been theologies earlier and more recently which have not considered this at all.
Even with the best intentions, the result can only be a dreary emptying of the
Old Testament. The characteristic witness to revelation in the early period
claimed to be heard as a whole, not only where expectation is explicitly mentioned, but where it is factually presented. To emphasise this I have put into
the foreground that which is recognisable factually (i.e., apart from formal
" prophecy ") as expectation in the Old Testament witness to God's covenant
and to God's hiddenness.

Moreover the existence in the Old Testament of a complete thread of explicit witness to expectation should serve to confirm us in thinking that in what has preceded we have not, at bottom, yielded to an illusion or been guilty of an unwarranted assumption—at least in principle. There is an eschatological thread in the Old Testament in line with which, as the Old Testament recognises and explicitly states, the covenant of God with man comes to be realised, and the hiddenness and revelation of God beyond the actual event attested in the Old Testament is primarily future event. The eschatological character of the divine reconciliation and revelation does not mean any negation of its presence, either here or in the New Testament. If a man presents himself to me or knocks at my door, he is present as one who is " future " to me, that is, as one " who comes to me." I am still alone, but I expect to see him beside me. I have still time, but only to make it clear to myself that I shall soon have no more time. Now, is not God's future the most intensive presence, incomparably more intensive than anything we regard as present ? We have seen with what intensity God's covenant and hiddenness in the Old Testament point to God's coming. In this very intensity they are already present, and Abraham, Moses and the prophets are recipients of revelation in the full sense of the term. But we still have to put it in this way, that they receive the revelation of Yahweh as those who wait for it and hasten toward it. The bearers of the Old Testament revelation, however, do not go to meet the fulfilment that comes, and is already at the door, as those who are actually unconscious of the incompleteness of their situation and its need for fulfilment. They go to meet it because they see it before them. So far as they are conscious of seeing it before them, there is an eschatological thread in the Old Testament. It does not stand side by side with the rest of its witness ; it grows out of it by a most inward necessity ; it is an " integral factor in Israelite faith in God " (Eichrodt, *op. cit.*, p. 255). But within this whole it stands apart as a special factor.

The point is this. Of a whole series of ideas which have decisive significance for the world of the Old Testament, we may safely say that to understand them correctly in the sense of the texts, we have to know them from two aspects, like the winged altars of the Middle Ages. In front there is presented to us a definite aspect of the covenant and of the hiddenness of God in a definite present of historical time. But from behind there is presented to us at the same time, in terms of the same or related concepts, the corresponding aspect of fulfilled time, the finished work of God to come. We might also speak of a two-dimensional picture when, when we look at it, miraculously acquires depth and becomes plastic. If, as readers and commentators, it is our duty everywhere to estimate the first form of these conceptions, we must take care not to miss their second form, which is always there for observant eyes.

When, for example, the Old Testament speaks of the " people " or of " Israel " or of " Judah ", the primary meaning is, of course, the sum-total of the descendants of the sons of Jacob, with whom as such the covenant was made at Sinai. But at once the separation of the ten northern tribes from the two southern suggests that this primary idea of " people " will not carry all that is meant in the Old Testament by God's people, the chosen people. A people within the people, as it were, is the people which is meant in the divine covenant and participates in its fulfilment. But we are still involved only with the primary idea if we regard Judah-Benjamin as this people, compared with whom North Israel finally disappears from history. For Judah-Benjamin is not this people, but as their own prophets say, a converted " holy remnant," spared in the judgment. Who belongs to this remnant ? Who are now God's people ? The adherents of a prophetic community of disciples ? A community of the faithful congregating about the temple ? The few righteous who walk in the way of Yahweh's commandments ? Yes and No. Yes, because actually such a people is discernible in the foreground ; No, because prophetic exhortation and hope do not remain with this people, because later prophets like Jeremiah and Deutero-Isaiah speak again of a " people," of Jerusalem, even of Israel as a whole. The people within the people, the genuine Israel, is obviously not identical either with the sum-total of Jacob's descendants or with any section of this sum. But the genuine Israel, elect, called and finally blessed by Yahweh, is merely typified in both, and remains a goal beyond the history of either. In the strictest sense this people is ahead of itself in time. It has still to be seen what this people really is.

When the Old Testament speaks of the " land " promised and then given to this people, the primary meaning, of course, simply is the land of Canaan commended to the fathers by God. But, again, whatever the qualities of this geographical entity may have been at that time, as such they are wholly unsuited to exhaust the full meaning that lies in the conception of the promised land. When we look beyond the conception of a land " flowing with milk and honey," to the promises associated with it (particularly when things were really not going well in this land), our gaze is necessarily directed to the paradise lost and restored which is to be the dwelling-place of this people, to the miraculously renewed earth upon which this people will some day live amid the other happily and peaceably united peoples. Thus the " land " is certainly Palestine, but with equal certainty, in and along with this land, there is meant the quite different land which is not actually visible in the history of Israel, because it is its goal, because it is therefore outside it. The one land is waiting for the other.

When the Old Testament speaks of the " temple," by that is assuredly meant the house in Jerusalem which David wished to build for the Lord and which Solomon did build for Him as His abode, and therefore as a place of prayer and sacrifice for this people. But this temple could be destroyed and rebuilt and destroyed again, without losing anything of the intensity of its significance. What it is and is not in the foreground is governed by the temple of the future in the background, which, built according to Isaiah not by men but by God Himself, will stand and shine upon some quite other mount of God, to which some day not only Israel but the nations will make pilgrimage. It is from the standpoint of its future that the temple at Jerusalem is what it is.

What does " lordship of God " mean in the Old Testament ? First, of course, the present fact, as such apparently of infinite significance, that this people belongs to Yahweh, is ruled, punished and rewarded in its destinies by Yahweh, has therefore as a whole and in all its members to obey Yahweh's instructions and commands. Can there be anything more here, a supreme background ? Yes, here particularly, and it is quite understandable that attempts have been made to concentrate in the idea of the " complete lordship of God " the entire eschatology of the Old Testament. For at this very point everything present is to be regarded from the standpoint of its own future. Is it not at present bounded on all sides by what is before our eyes, the fact that this people belongs to Yahweh, that He exercises power over them, that they have to listen to Him ? Does not the hope necessarily arise of the Kingdom without end ? Not only does this hope actually arise, but it clearly gives power and possibility to faith in God's lordship even in this very present moment. It is by future accomplishment that God's people lives even in the imperfection of its present situation and government. And it never sees its fulfilment. Its presence seems, on the contrary, to grow more imperfect on every side. At all events, the political equivalent of the Kingdom of God in the external power and position of this people grows more and more insignificant. But in the same proportion it seems to be the more definitely aware of that which is the goal and boundary of His ways, namely, that God shall put all His enemies under His feet. His lordship is to be established as much over the innermost heart of His people as over the whole world.

What is the meaning of " judgment " in the Old Testament ? In the first instance judgment is executed quite concretely and with disturbing frequency in the form of great national disasters, from the plague of serpents in the wilderness to the destruction of Jerusalem. This is the dreadful picture in the foreground, from which according to the Old Testament very few generations of this people were entirely spared. But apart from the very real picture of slaughtered and burned towns and villages, of fields full of slain, of long processions of exiles—apart from all this there is no knowledge of what " judgment " means in the Old Testament. And yet the Old Testament thought of

4

judgment does not derive its seriousness and gravity from this source. For something far more dreadful is at the back of it all, the end of God's love, the rejection of Israel, and over and above, the burning wrath of God upon all nations, the judgment of the world. This is not present ; strictly speaking, it is future. But it is a matter of this future in the present. The prophets look beyond the flames which, kindled by hostile men, destroy Samaria and Jerusalem, but also in the end Nineveh and Babylon, to see this quite different, unquenchable flame. And they were speaking of it, of this background, of this future judgment, when they referred so threateningly and definitely to the foreground.

The most important of the ideas we have to mention is that of the " king." The king is in the first instance and as such the autocrat who rules at a given time in Jerusalem, one of the smaller or smallest among the many of his kind in the Near East of that day. But we have already been told that the king is at the same time one of the outstanding instruments of the divine covenant. If any figure stands strikingly in the shadow of the divine hiddenness, it is that of the king. That is to say, this figure, too, points beyond itself. It is probably an old tradition that David already conceived of himself as the type of the righteous man, one " that ruleth over men, that ruleth in the fear of God, and is as the light of the morning when the sun riseth, a morning without clouds, when the grass springeth out of the earth through the clear shining after the rain " (2 Sam. 23$^{1\text{-}7}$). This righteous king, who is at once threatened and promised in the future by the existence of the present king, is the Messiah, the king of Israel, nay the world king " at the end of the days." Once more selection is effected as in the case of the " people " ; for the kings of Samaria do not share in this hope, but only those of Jerusalem. Even here the lineage of David seems often enough to be broken as regards this preparation for the coming king ; the king for the moment, even if counted among the " good " kings, frequently seems to be little more than a symbol of this lineage of David. The political titles of *melek* and also *masshiah* are avoided by the prophets when they speak of the coming prince of peace. But even so, the political conception of kingship is the main form their expectation takes so far as it comes to be personalised. In the extension of this political idea lies the picture of the human helper, comforter and lord sent by God, who some day, at the approaching end of time, will realise the promise of the covenant for this people. And so even this political idea as such can never remain or become wholly secular. When the king is called God's son, when to him is ascribed the wisdom of an angel, when to him is ascribed not only sacred inviolability because of his anointing but also the power of the Spirit because of special endow-ment, when in the songs sung at his enthroning, at the New Year festival, or at his marriage, a highly coloured picture is given of him as a godlike ruler, saviour and benefactor, when his struggles and victories are solemnised in the royal Psalms as if they were so many theophanies introducing the consummated Kingdom of God itself— then as far as the linguistic and pictorial material is concerned, all that is no doubt borrowed from the palatial style of the ancient East, particularly the Babylonian ; but the very fact that the petty kingdom of Judah—in times, naturally, in which its king in the political sense was actually nothing more than a shadow king—adopted the linguistic and pictorial material suitable for glorifying real world rulers like those of Babylon, shows that here was an idea operating which had nothing to do with this palatial style or the mythology behind it (Eichrodt, p. 258 f., 271). What is involved in Messianic expectation is not an intensifying but a sheer transcending of present political experience. It comes to this, that the conception of the king in particular can be described as the central form of Messianic expectation, but as such it is clearly too narrow to express all that is to be said of the expected bringer of salvation. The " servant " in Deutero-Isaiah is much less a king than a prophet, and the son of David in Ps. 110 and the *tsemach* in Zech. 6 is priest and king at once. The " son of man " appearing in the clouds of heaven in Dan. 7 shows all the characteristics of a ruler, but, naturally, the ruler who makes an end of the world powers and of world power as such. If the interpretation of the Book of Enoch is applicable, he is no less than the first man returning in glory—first also in a supreme sense even as compared with Adam. And the functions of the expected One, namely, a victory which is not preceded by a struggle (the Messiah does not Himself take part in the Messianic woes which precede Him, but when they are finished He appears), a rule of peace without end, the rooting out of sin, the judgment of the world, supreme sway not only over human spirits but also over a renewed world of nature—all these can be summed up under the concept of rule, but only in such a way that the functions of an earthly king obviously fall very far behind, having really become a mere parable. Against this background the king of Judah is what he is in the foreground. It is only indirectly the case that the eschatology of the Old Testament is exhausted in the Messianic expectation. But indirectly it is the case. We have seen that along with the idea of the king there are other ideas with which Old Testament expectation is linked ; nation, land, temple, the lordship of God, judgment. At the same time it cannot be denied that all these other ideas, or the expectations linked up with them, culminate and become concrete in this one, the idea and expectation of the king of the end of time. The Messiah is already " the hope of Israel," so far as all Israel's hopes point to an historical event on earth, an event altogether introduced by God, breaking into all other history from above, but actually within history, a real historical event. The analogy between present type and coming reality does not break down, because the reality to come will also be a man ruling in the name of God—ruling, of course, in quite a different way. And with his appearance all that is now expected will be quite different, the true Israel, the land of promise, the temple on the mount of God, the Kingdom without end, the judgment of the world.

This, then, is the explicit expectation of the Old Testament. It must be held together with what is said about the covenant concluded but not fulfilled and about the revealed but not realised hiddenness of God in the Old Testament. And what was said about the covenant and about the hiddenness of God receives confirmation from the presence of this explicit expectation. It is only *ex eventu*, however, from the recollection of fulfilled time, from the New Testament point of view, that we can say that in respect of this expectation the Old Testament is the witness to divine revelation, so that its expectation is no illusion, but the kind of expectation when the expected One has already knocked at the door and is already there, though still outside. Mere expectation, therefore, or abstract expectation, an autonomous time of preparation, is excluded. Is there fulfilled time and expectation ? Has the Messiah appeared ? Later Judaism, the documents of which were not adopted into the Old Testament Canon, more than once thought so, and every time the end was a bitter disillusionment. And when Jesus Christ arose in Galilee and Jerusalem, the same later Judaism, represented by the authorised experts in the canonical Old Testament and the official bearers of the sacred tradition, looked right past Him, in fact rejected Him outright and smote Him on the cross. If He was the Messiah to come, if He was the revelation attested by the Old Testament in expectation, as the Christian Church confesses it, then we can only say that it had to be so, that rejection was possible in spite of the fact that Holy Scripture of the Old Testament lay open straight in front of these men's eyes and was read by them with genuine industry and attention. Revelation does not speak directly even in its most definite testimonies—i.e., not by way of a demonstration that can be carried out by experiment and logic. The expectation of revelation in the Old Testament is prophecy, not prediction to be controlled experimentally by logic. That is why it was and is possible to look past it. That is why it could and can be rejected. How could it be otherwise ? It is self-attested by the fact that this expected revelation is really revelation, that the Old Testament present participates in a future which is really God's future. That is, one may be offended by it ; it can only be believed in ; it speaks only in the way revelation speaks. To this day the Synagogue waits for the fulfilment of prophecy. Is it really waiting ? Is it waiting as the fathers waited ? The fathers' waiting was no mere abstract, infinite waiting, but a waiting which already participated in fulfilled time. Ought it not to have been in this knowledge that the Synagogue closed the Canon as the document of this waiting ? Did it not thereby

confess that there is a time for waiting but that waiting has only its
own time ?   Could the Canon be closed and Christ yet be rejected ?
Can the closed Canon of witness to expected revelation be read with
meaning apart from the counter-canon of revelation that happened ?
Is an infinite waiting, such as is the result of an abstracted Old Testament faith, a real waiting and not rather an eternal unrest ?   Is revelation that is only awaited real revelation ?   We have already denied
this and can only repeat the denial.   The Synagogue of the time after
Christ is the more than tragic, uncannily pitiful figure with bandaged
eyes and broken lance, as depicted on the Minster at Strasbourg.   We
must remember, however, that revelation, especially in the Church
which believes in it as revelation that happens, which believes in Jesus
Christ, only speaks as revelation speaks.   Knowledge of it in either
case, whether related to witness to it in the Old Testament or in the
New Testament, is decision.   The Church may also be a figure with
bandaged eyes and a broken lance, even though the New Testament is
in her hands, the Canon of the witness to the revelation that happened.
And if the Church is not this, if it recognises revelation and lives by
revelation, that is unmerited grace, as Paul says in Rom. 11[20f.]   The
mystery of revelation, which is the mystery of free, unmerited grace,
includes the Church of the New Testament inseparably with the people
whose blessing is attested for us in the Old Testament as expectation
of Jesus Christ.   And this very mystery acts not only as a barrier but
as a bond between Church and Synagogue which, like the impenitent
sister with seeing eyes, refuses to see that the people of the Old Testament really expected Jesus Christ and in this expectation was graciously
blessed.

3. THE TIME OF RECOLLECTION

Fulfilled time is followed by a very definite time that is bound up
with it.   This definite subsequent time as little coincides with the time
post Christum natum as preceding time does with the time *ante Christum
natum*.   We are concerned here with the time of a definite history
taking place in this new era of time.   This is history which is derived
from the revelation that has happened in the same individual and
unique way as the pre-history we spoke of runs to meet it.   Like
that pre-history, it is quite different from fulfilled time, but like it,
too, it is wholly related to fulfilled time and bound up with it.   This
subsequent time is the time of the New Testament, or the time of the
witness to recollection of revelation.   It belongs to the time of fulfilment.   It is bound up with it.   We cannot speak of the time of revelation without also speaking of it.   That there is this subsequent time and
a witness to the recollection of revelation, that Christ as the recollected
One was also manifest in the time of the New Testament and is recognisable in the witness of the New Testament, seems more illuminating

and comprehensible than the corresponding statements which we had
earlier to draw up and ponder regarding the preceding time of the
Old Testament. But this opinion does not rest upon insight. The
connection between Jesus Christ and the New Testament is only understood, when it is realised that in principle it is just as hard and just
as easy to understand as that between Jesus Christ and the Old Testament. For the connexion between Jesus Christ and the New Testament, and the origin of New Testament history in revelation, have
nothing to do with the relation of historical cause and effect. That
New Testament history, the history of the proclamation, of the Evangelists and apostles, takes its rise in revelation, is no less a miracle than
that the Old Testament finds its goal in the same revelation. In both
cases there is the possibility of offence. In both cases it may be that
revelation (expected or recollected revelation) will not be noticed or
will be rejected as such, so that we will never get the length of the
existence of witnesses and testimonies. In both cases it is due to the
power of revelation, it depends upon election, whether there are witnesses and testimonies to revelation at all, and in both cases it may
be that the witness available, which in the one case speaks of revelation as the goal, in the other of revelation as the start, will not be
recognised or accepted as such. If it is otherwise, if the witness finds
real hearers, in either case it is due to the power of revelation, it
happens by grace. Thus the connexion under discussion can as little
rest upon the illuminating historical relation, say, between New Testament religion and its founder, as previously upon the relation between
Old Testament religion and the original religious personality of Jesus
as rooted in it. And even less can we see this connexion by seeking
the revelation of Jesus Christ, say, in this New Testament religion as it
is related to Jesus Christ, in early Christian piety and conduct as such.
Of course, speaking in the manner of secular history, it may be said
that this religion is related to that original religious personality as
rooted in Old Testament religion, and, of course, even apart from that,
it displays remarkable characteristics. But if all this is the case, the
question arises for the New Testament as well, by what right these
particular monuments of a religious past among so many others will
have to be regarded as documents of the revelation of God. And
here, too, one can only revert to an historical judgment of value and
taste, which is to proclaim that the New Testament's claim to reveal
had not yet been understood at all. For this claim does not mean
that we will decide to single out New Testament religion above all
other religions on the ground of our judgments of value and taste,
and so make our own its special relation to its founder. The New
Testament makes no claim at all in favour of the religion documented
in it, but it does claim to be heard as witness, as witness to the recollection of a revelation which is just as much beyond the factual
condition and content of the New Testament as it was beyond the

condition and content of the Old Testament, but with this difference that the completed event of revelation does not lie before but behind the witness to it. In the New Testament, too, revelation breaks in from above, from an altitude which is not that of a so-called historical peak. Moreover, the condition and content of the New Testament are to be understood in terms of their own peculiar alignment, their formation on the basis of revelation, and only in view of this formation or alignment, not in view of itself can we speak sensibly of revelation in the New Testament. Along with the New Testament itself we must stand within the perspective of revelation in order to achieve the act of recollecting the revelation that happened, which its witness demands of us. And this understanding from the perspective of revelation, which constitutes the genuine act of recollection, and which is the prerequisite for anyone reading the New Testament in the right way, i.e., participating in this genuine act of recollection, lies in no one's power, but only in the power of revelation itself. It must not only speak itself, it must also fashion our hearing, the obedience of faith. In other words, even in relation to the New Testament's claim to revelation, we are pointed to Jesus Christ Himself, to the act of lordship in which He gives the Holy Spirit of hearing and obedience to whom He will. The Evangelists and apostles are only servants of His Word; they cannot substitute their word for it. The truth of His revelation is grounded and proved solely by Himself. Here, too, theological explanation cannot take the place of this basis. Here, too, it can only think of offering a subsequent description.

In this theological explanation we shall also have to show to what extent the recollection attested in the New Testament really corresponds with the expectation attested in the Old Testament. Since Old Testament and New Testament mutually witness to each other, they jointly witness to the one Jesus Christ. We need not point out the fact but only the manner of this mutual witness. We must respect a mystery which claims to speak for itself. In the New Testament we have the witness of recollection, and it tells us itself that its object is identical with the object of expectation in the Old Testament. Therefore, now that we have tried to be clear how far expectation in the Old Testament is actually expectation in respect of this object, we can also try to see how far recollection in the New Testament can be related to the same object. Obviously what we need here is not an exhaustive exposition but merely an indication of the content in question. We have to understand how the three lines of Old Testament expectation which we sought to indicate are continued beyond the time fulfilled in Jesus Christ in New Testament recollection, in the complete change conditioned by the accomplished fulfilment, and yet also in that unity of recollection with expectation which is conditioned by the common medium.

1. The New Testament, like the Old Testament, is the witness to a togetherness of God and man, based on and consisting in a free self-relating of God to man. What in the Old Testament, in the expectation, was God's covenant with man, is here, in the fulfilment, God's becoming man. To the protest of the Synagogue we can and must

reply unreservedly that God's becoming man is the goal of the Old Testament. Man's sanctification by God as the Lord of the covenant through grace and law, his adoption by God in utter mercy yet utter strictness—such a programme only God Himself can carry through, namely, God Himself Who has become man. The New Testament does not only think that this event has taken place in the light of the existence of Jesus Christ to which it looks back. This is not merely an explanation or interpretation of His life. It is not proclaimed as the result of subsequent consideration and reflection. But it is as such the object of its recollection, it is already the subject of the sentence which proclaims it. Every statement in the New Testament originates in the fact that the Word was made flesh. God's covenant with man, the covenant which God made with Abraham, with Moses and David, finds its reality solely, but completely and finally, in the fact that God was made man, in order that as man He might do what man as such never does, what even Israel never did, appropriate God's grace and fulfil God's law. This is what God did Himself as man in Jesus Christ. For that very reason in Jesus Christ the Kingdom of God is at hand, as nigh as it can get while time has not yet become eternity. So the New Testament declares. It declares nothing else, it declares, broadly speaking, nothing more than the Old Testament. But it declares it in a different way, because it is looking back at the fulfilment. The form now has a content which corresponds to it exactly. The question has now achieved its precise answer.

This is shown chiefly in the fact that recollection as compared with expectation points back, not only implicitly and not merely with the ambiguous explicitness of the Messianic hope in the Old Testament, but with such explicitness that now everything can be expressed by a particular name, the name Jesus Christ, circumscribed by particular space and particular time. Thus recollection points back to one centre at which God's free, utterly unique, concrete action has taken place. In the Old Testament God's action is history, in the New Testament it is just one history. God's covenant in the Old Testament is not datable, it is repeated; from time to time it has to be renewed. The Old Testament, too, has, of course, one covenant in mind. But it only prophesies it by witnessing to many covenants. The New Testament knows only one covenant. The Old Testament knows many real Nows, but not a Now which does not wait for an indisputable Now. The New Testament knows only one Now, which is not in any sense or in any way disputable. For though the New Testament is the witness to hope (which it is, of course, absolutely), it must be said that the object of its hope is none other than just this one Now, Jesus Christ very God and very Man, to whom it looks back, only, at the same time, to wait for Him as the aim and end of all things. There is no question of repeating the covenant. For Peter, for John, for Paul, for the churches in Corinth and Rome, it was concluded in

Christ. It was quite unthinkable that it should have to or could be concluded anew with Peter or John or Paul or the Corinthians or Romans. There can be no question of anything but their inclusion in the one covenant. They are called and converted to the one Mediator Christ, and thereby and in that way to God. So, of course, it was quite unthinkable that there should be any talk of an incarnation of God in them. The point, and the sole point, for them was that Christ should dwell in them. For this reason there ceases to exist in the New Testament the manifold and multiform office of men of God, the instruments of the covenant. At most, the Evangelists and apostles can be called men of God only indirectly, in the sense of witnesses to Christ. The one and only real man of God is He Himself and He alone, who is so without reserve or limitation. Unless we are to say, which would, of course, be correct, that all the functions of the Old Testament men of God, the kings, priests and prophets, have passed as such to Christ's community, from which alone they can proceed again because of the special gifts of the Holy Spirit entrusted to it ; but not in the form of a hierarchy, only in the form of service in special offices, which neither know of precedence among themselves, nor signify a precedence in their holders over the community members not in office, because in principle there is no other mediator, because the mediators have found their fulfilment in the Mediator of the New Testament and can never again acquire an independent significance.

We will, therefore, if we sink to the level of the Jewish attitude to the Old Testament, again regard Christ as a mere sign or symbol, a mere witness to the real togetherness of God and man. There are signs and witnesses, because there is a thing signified. If there is no thing signified, the signs and witnesses do not exist as such. If we reject the thing signified, we certainly reject, too, the signs and witnesses, just as Israel confirmed by anticipation its rejection of Christ by rejecting more or less clearly all its men of God. Just because the signs and witnesses of the Old Testament point to the real togetherness of God and men, unlike the symbols and symbol-bearers of heathendom, they do not point to the empty space of metaphysical ideal truth, but to coming history. And it is to this history as history achieved that the signs and witnesses of the New Testament point back. But the common object of the two testimonies does not point anywhere but says : *I am the way, the truth and the life.* In a way different from Israel's kings He exercises with His right the right of God, with His power the power of God. In a way different from Israel's priests He forgives sins and creates reconciliation between God and men. In a way different from Israel's prophets He is not there to receive and transmit the Word of the Lord, but He speaks Himself, in fact He is this Word. He accomplishes a plenipotentiary representation of God in which God Himself is the witness for man before Himself and the witness in man for Himself. He is not an instrument of divine action. He acts Himself divinely and therefore as a true Mediator. This is the tenor of the witness of recollection in the New Testament, the sole intention of which is exclusively to confirm the Old Testament witness of expectation.

We cannot recall sufficiently or realise sufficiently the significance of the facts. This witness was given directly in face of the sharpest protest from the Synagogue as the guardian and official expositor of the Old Testament Canon, and yet this witness was not in the least given in an anti-Judaic sense. Of the Evangelists and apostles of the New Testament not one even dreamed of acceding to this protest, in the sense of abandoning the relation of their recollection to Old Testament expectation ; not one of them regarded Jesus otherwise than as the Messiah of Israel. This being the case, what iron links they must have seen fixed between the old time and the new, between Israel and the Church ! How inevitably it must have impressed itself upon their recollection that in its object it was coincident with the earlier expectation ! The very rejection of Christ by Israel completely established the fact for them that this *is* He that should come ; His very crucifixion is the event in which both the new time is established and the old fulfilled. This is and remains a problem. And we may say that to this problem of New Testament thought and language there is no answer. On the contrary, it is understandable that to this problem the witnesses of the New Testament could themselves give no other answer than that which belongs decisively to their recollection, that He was crucified and rose again.

2. The New Testament, like the Old Testament, is the witness to the revelation of the hidden God. The conclusive proof of this is the circumstance just touched upon, that it sees revelation, the revelation expected by the whole of the Old Testament, at the very point at which one might well have seen the contradiction and annihilation of it, in the rejection and crucifixion of the Son of God by His chosen people. Here, too, essentially, the New Testament asserts nothing that differs from the Old Testament. On the contrary, we shall have to show that it is in the New Testament that the hiddenness of God in the Old Testament is first disclosed in all its completeness.

The judgment of God, which Christ's community sees visited upon the world about it, as upon a wicked world ordained to dissolution, is no less severe than that which finds expression in the exclusiveness of Israel compared with the Gentiles and their gods. The bloody wars of Yahweh against Baal have now, of course, ceased ; not because the radical nature of the rejection of the " form of this world " (Rom. 12²) has been mitigated, but because now it has become so utterly inward and basic. This æon has been overcome in Christ with all its principalities and powers. Christ took it in His body to the cross and bore it to the grave. Therefore now the form of the struggle in the Old Testament which it still presupposes, can and must fall to the

rear. As such it is pointless. It has become a sign which can be
dispensed with as such and even disappear, now that the thing itself
has been brought to the fore in Christ's triumph over all His enemies
(Col. 2$^{14f.}$). The secularisation of nature, history and civilisation now
ceases to present a problem as we look back upon the cross of Christ.
The programme of the Old Testament has been carried through to a
finish. For that reason, and not because of the increase in humanity,
toleration or joy in living, the Church's attitude to the world is so
utterly different, so much calmer and so much more superior than
Israel's of old. If the old æon has been done away, as is the case
according to the New Testament *kerygma*, we no longer need to fight
against it. Or rather, the armour in which it is combated has now
become the purely spiritual kind described in Eph. 6.

So, too, the suffering of the people of God, of the prophet, of the
righteous man, does not cease in the New Testament, not even in
the sense of having perhaps acquired a less central significance for the
existence of man in covenant with God. On the contrary. How
could it be otherwise ? The life-story of Jesus cannot be unfolded in
the four Evangelists, because obviously the narrators have no other
interest but to show how *a priori* this life struggled to its own passion
and death, the portrayal of which then assumes such proportions,
that there can be no doubt that in what befell on Good Friday they
saw the Christ-event proper as the meaning of the whole life-period
of Jesus. With this also corresponds the picture of those who hear
the Word of Christ. They are blessed as the poor, i.e., as the oppressed
righteous, who are so " in spirit," who are therefore persecuted for
Christ's sake. The address to the disciples in Matt. 10 is one single
indication as to the attitude in persecution. Similarly, in the Epistles
the picture repeatedly emerges of the threatened apostle, partaking
in the sufferings of Christ and in the end prepared to sacrifice his
life, and the picture ,too, of the oppressed, persecuted, suffering community. The menace of martyrdom and readiness to face it belong,
as it were, to the obvious factors to which the New Testament has
to bear witness in respect of the situation of the man called and converted to Christ. They are not in any way unusual, but are annexed
to membership of Christ. They have to take place, just because
Christ is the crucified Son of God. This is the total change, as compared with the Old Testament, even in the total unity which exists
at this particular point. That it is a matter of Jacob's conflict with
God is succinctly indicated in the passion story of Jesus, namely, in
the story of Gethsemane and in the cry of Jesus on the cross : " My
God, my God, why hast thou forsaken me ? " It is indicated in such
a way that we cannot fail to see that we have here the answer to the
insoluble question of Job and the Psalmists. But this question as
such does not figure greatly in the life and teaching of Jesus, and in
the suffering of His followers generally it has ceased to play any part.

The doubts, complaints and protests, even the prayers of sufferers in the Old Testament seem silenced in Paul and John, and the other New Testament writers, as though there never had been anything of the kind. Recollection of it, as in Rom. 7^{24}, may just crop up, only to disappear again at once. Yet suffering itself is not only not lacking, but is emphasised in quite a different way from the Old Testament. Obviously the reason for this change is not that a more harmonious, more optimistic, more joyous attitude to life holds the field, or that the Evangelists and apostles have ceased to be aware of the depths of forsakenness, even God-forsakenness, out of which man must cry to God. Job, the Preacher and the Psalmists are in place in the midst of the New Testament with their bitter, nay embittered questions, but not now as independent figures, not as those who still have to discuss a problem, and not in such a way that their bitterness or embitterment must have a further outlet. For now their problem has ceased to be a problem. We must know their problem, the problem of man's suffering at the hand of God, in order to understand the New Testament. But with the New Testament we must know it as a problem solved, if our knowledge of it is to be real. All those who are led by so strange a way find here their journey's end. And how strange the way was, the fact that it was a way through complete and trackless darkness, that on this way they really had no comfort save God alone and Him only as the hard master, to whom they had to cling in a hope against hope—it is only here that all this becomes unambiguously clear. Only here, because here God Himself goes right into this darkness in which man has to stand and move before Him, and He does not let the extreme bitterness of His wrath and of death touch sinful man, but—and this is the mystery of the New Testament—experiences and bears it Himself. In this way and in this fact the hiddenness of God, which includes all that the Old Testament attests concerning the suffering of the righteous, becomes an event. And that is why now there can be no further continuation of the series of prophets and servants of God, or of desperate crying and protest and unbelief, but only the strict matter-of-factness of those who are challenged to bear their cross and follow Christ. The fact that Christ's disciples and also His communities must suffer is important only in connexion with Christ, but in itself it is actually a trifle. There is a mysteriously effective restraint in the circumstance that apart from the one account of Stephen, the exception that proves the rule, not one martyrdom is described in the New Testament, neither Paul's nor Peter's nor John's. The Acts of the Martyrs in succeeding centuries continued the Old Testament or rather the Synagogue tradition, not that of the New Testament. By this they prove themselves to be apocryphal testimonies, which without exception can only falsify the real testimony of the New Testament if they are restored to a place of honour.

The New Testament answer to the problem of suffering—and it alone is the answer to the sharply put query of the Old Testament—is to the effect that *One has died for all*.

And in this way the Old Testament hiddenness of God extends its existence into the New Testament in the twofold reality of sin and punishment. It can even be said that one part of the Old Testament finds its direct continuation, so to speak, in certain New Testament settings, namely, where it speaks of men who have wilfully excluded themselves from the revelation in Christ, e.g., King Herod and his death, Judas Iscariot and his suicide, Ananias and Sapphira in Acts 4. These are still genuinely Old Testament scenes. To a certain extent the same can be said of the account of Zacharias in Luke 1, or even of the conversion of Saul. And above all, every passage is in this category which is related directly or indirectly to the event which, as it were, constitutes the historical horizon of New Testament witness in a forward direction, namely, to the destruction of Jerusalem. It need not be underlined that the problem of the punishment of sin is constantly to the fore elsewhere too, even in the speeches and parables of Jesus, in the instructional and hortative developments of the *kerygma*, in the epistolary literature, and in the Apocalypse. In the same way even the disciples and the Christian communities constantly stand in the shadow of it, a shadow which for darkness has increased rather than decreased in comparison with the Old Testament parallels. How can it be otherwise, in view of the New Testament's central view of the cross of Christ, in which the early Christian community saw involved the mystery of man's sin against God and the mystery of the execution of God's punishment upon sinful man—and saw involved in both mysteries the hiddenness of God in its completed reality? Now for the first time and from this standpoint the accusation against man becomes fundamental and comprehensive. Now for the first time and at this point the threat of judgment becomes the threat of eternal judgment. Now for the first time and from this standpoint the meeting of a holy God with sinful man, to which the Old Testament bears witness, ceases to have the appearance of a rather unsatisfactory attempt at pædagogy, and acquires instead an ultimate seriousness and, in its whole mysterious course, an inner necessity—since Golgotha was a direct sin against God and since that is the very spot where God Himself bears the punishment of sin. Small wonder if the connexions between existence and sin, existence and death, are now emphasised with the inexorable stringency which is the case in New Testament proclamation. Certainly they are also to be found in Old Testament proclamation; but only when they have been seen in that clarity which takes its rise in the place to which the New Testament points back. Certainly the whole problem of the Old Testament can and must be regarded as compressed into the twofold question as to why it goes so ill with this people, and why it is so evil. These two questions belong inseparably together—not in the sense that the one can be answered by the other and their inseparability can be clearly understood, but that they cohere in the single hiddenness of God. We cannot but bow humbly before the inseparability of these two questions, because at their point of contact we are concerned, not with a human, but with a divine mystery. Where that is known, it is knowledge of Jesus Christ, " who was delivered up for our trespasses, and was raised for our justification." And now that the entire gravity of the accusation and of the threat of judgment becomes visible, there also becomes visible the second thing which the Old Testament, abstractly considered, allows us at best to suspect, namely, that the accusation and threat are directed against all men. " Through one man sin entered into the world and death through sin ; and so death passed unto all men, for that all sinned " (Rom. 5¹²). The co-operation of Jews and heathen at the crucifixion of Jesus is naturally not accidental, different though their respective shares in it are. In much the same way they also stand side by side in the first two chapters of Romans as concluded under the same judgment. It has now been made clear that the problem of the punishment of sin is not a peculiarity of Israel. Nor was it because of any special wickedness or any special destiny in this people. Nor did the gravity with which it was put at the very heart of this people bring any advantage to it as a people, compared with the somewhat less serious situation of other peoples. In Israel's crucifixion of its Messiah it becomes clear that the sinful and punished people of God does not coincide with the people Israel, that Israel as a people was acting only in a representative capacity for the future Church of sinners. " God hath concluded all under disobedience " (Rom. 11³²).

This is the point at which attention must be drawn to what does not distinguish but separates New Testament from Old Testament witness to God's hiddenness. The fearful statement that " God hath concluded all under disobedience " derives its importance and gravity from its sequel, " that he might have mercy upon all." In the New Testament the hiddenness of God is recognised to be so profound and comprehensive, because here it does not stand alone but has a perfectly direct, concrete Beyond, because here it is limited, yet in this very limitation is also illumined and verified by God's revelation. As regards the great centre of New Testament witness we must now emphasise the moment, without the consideration of which it cannot· be regarded either as the centre or as anything else. This centre is the passion, the suffering, the crucifixion and death of Christ. But the New Testament never speaks abstractly about the passion of Christ. It always appears limited, illumined and verified by the reality of His resurrection—and that is what makes it central. Obviously in the New Testament the resurrection of Jesus, the aspect of Easter, does not play the part of a second aspect alongside Good Friday, or a final aspect following the many other aspects of the rest of the preceding life of Jesus. True, its special place in the history is at the end, as the limit of the story of Jesus' life and death. But its function extends further, namely, to cover all that precedes it. Our reading of the Gospels from the beginning is only right if they are read from the standpoint of this place ultimately reached in their narrative. And because this whole story culminates in the passion, the function of the resurrection is related directly and comprehensively to the fact that the rejected One of Israel and the crucified One of Pilate rose again from the dead. But the function of the resurrection is to make the passion of Christ, in which the incarnation of the Word of God was consummated, clearly and unmistakably revelation, the realisation of the covenant between God and man, God's act for us, as reconciliation. The occurrence of the resurrection is not a second and further stage, but the manifestation of this second dimension of the Christ event. The resurrection is meant when it says in Jn. 1^{14}: " We saw his glory." The resurrection is the event of the revelation of the Incarnate, the Humiliated, the Crucified. Wherever He gives Himself to be known as the person He is, He speaks as the risen Christ. The resurrection can give nothing new to Him who is the eternal Word of the Father ; but it makes visible what is proper to Him, His glory. It is in the limitation, illumination and verification of this event and not otherwise that the New Testament views the passion of Christ. That is why in the passion it sees so powerfully the hiddenness of God. That is why it speaks so inexorably of the passing of this æon. That is why it is so naturally aware of the necessity of the sufferings of this time. That is why above all it binds man so strictly and universally under the divine accusation and the divine threat. The power of revelation is the power of God's hiddenness attested by Him in this way. Therefore it is not just the passion and energy of a protesting, critical, resigned human No to man and his world that is operative here. It is really the passion of Christ. And it is the passion of Christ lit up and made articulate, made a real " word of the cross " (1 Cor. 1^{18}) by the supremely wonderful story in the background, which passes all comprehension and imagination, that " Christ is from His agony arisen, whereof we must all be glad ; Christ will be our comfort." In what the New Testament says of the world, of suffering, of sin and punishment, we do not find ourselves on a level at which man's joy in creation or love of life, however genuinely human or even justified in its place, can make good its relative affirmation against a too one-sided denial of what is this-worldly. This No is a No which cannot be ignored or contradicted, a divine No which reposes upon the divine Yes of revelation, because, in virtue of what happened at Easter, the passion in which it takes its rise is the passion of the only-begotten Son of God, full of grace and truth. It is because all things **are** become new, and for no other reason, that the old is done away. It is only because Jesus lives that His cross is the sign under which His Church marches. It is only because He is the Lamb of God that victoriously bears and bears away the sins of the world that God has concluded all under unbelief. The No of the New Testament, its witness to the hiddenness of God, is no less than the demonstration of the manifest glory of the Son of God. If the same is also said of the No of the Old Testament—as it can and must be said—it is because we are taught to say it by the New Testament. As distinct from the apostles, the prophets were not " witnesses of the resurrection " (Ac. 1²²). But the resurrection was their final meaning.

From the altitude of revelation that has actually taken place, the New Testament witness to God's hiddenness acquires in content, too, a meaning and importance which we have still to point out. The view is to be rejected that this witness is less grave and dark in the New Testament than in the Old Testament. But correctly understood, it is not in any sense an oppressive witness in the New Testament. Here in its utter gravity and its utter darkness it is outspokenly the Gospel, glad tidings. World contempt or world agony is not deducible from it, nor can lamentation for sin or fear of God as its avenger be the last word to be heard from the New Testament witness. For these things have all become objectless in the passion of Christ as, illumined by Easter Day, it spoke to the New Testament witnesses and speaks from their witness to us. Against the whole unending burden, which witness to God's hiddenness necessarily signifies in itself, stand the words : " It is finished." The decisive factor that turns the scales is that the man who hears this witness is told that this burden no longer lies upon him, that he does not require to deal with it, and that therefore he cannot succumb to it. The man who has to fight and despise the world is the one to whom it still means something, whom it can still tempt and attack. This could, of course, apply particularly and acutely to the man who hears the New Testament witness. Nevertheless he is not summoned to battle with, or contempt for, the world, but to belief and awareness that this world is a past world in the death of Christ, and that its gods and idols have ceased to wield any power. If Christ really fought the fight with the old world and if man already lives with Him in faith in the new, his only business, his only fight is to acknowledge and confirm that the fight in question has already been fought. Even oppression at the inevitable suffering of the world, even world agony can, properly speaking, only be found where man still poses as the master of himself, capable of fighting against the suffering or succumbing to it like a hero. Good care will be taken that we always discover ourselves to be this man. But even from this discovery the New Testament witness will rescue us. As distinguished from stoicism, it takes no account of this man, it takes no account of man at all, but of Christ as Him who has already fought this fight victoriously, so that neither as victors nor as vanquished are we left with any independent case to undertake. We are left only with the acknowledgment and confirmation of the " agony and pain " which is not ours but that of the Son of God, and as such adapted to snatch us out of those agonies of ours which, strictly speaking, have become anachronistic. And so, finally, the divine accusation and threat can be a burden to man only if he thinks he can or ought to take up God's case with himself and his own case with God. Clearly both ideas constantly recur. In the arrogance of life resulting from this attitude we are sinners against God and His punishment falls on us. If we assume that the Gospel can create in us the hearing ear to counter this attitude of ours, this means that both troubles will be removed, because in the word of the Gospel Christ takes our place, really undertaking and conducting God's case with us and our case with God. It was His conducting of God's case with us sinners that brought Him to the cross, and His conducting of our sinners' case with God is the eternal effect, the victorious result of His suffering and death. If it is true that this did happen and was consummated through Him who could actually do it, if it is true that as true God and true man He intercedes for God with us and for us with God, then we are in fact no longer the object of the divine accusation and threat. It is then the burden which is taken from us by God Himself and is laid entirely upon Christ. But for us remains life in a freedom for which we have to thank the compassion that became event in Christ. This whole alteration in the witness to God's hiddenness takes place in so far as it is the witness of recollection to revelation which has happened, and is therefore New Testament witness. But, of course, the hearer of this witness will have to say at once that in this alteration there is disclosed only what, rightly understood, had already been said by the Old Testament witness.

3. The New Testament, like the Old Testament, is the witness to the revelation in which God is present to man as the coming God. In this statement, in the real agreement which it expresses in spite of every difference, the full circle of our deliberations is closed in a most extraordinary way. We had no right to expect it, yet the fact remains that the New Testament, the explicit witness of recollection, is also itself witness to the coming God. And that is really much too jejune a statement of the reality. We speak of an expectation explicitly unfolding itself in the Old Testament, of a specific eschatological line in the Old Testament. As regards the New Testament that would be much too mild a statement. Where in the New Testament is the eschatological line simply one line parallel to others ? Which of the New Testament pronouncements, because they are the pronouncements of a definite recollection, are not implicitly or explicitly eschatological ?

A big exception must, of course, be made here, an exception which proves the rule. I mean the Easter narratives of the four Gospels, together with that of Paul in 1 Cor. 15. In the slender series of New Testament accounts of the disciples' meetings with the risen Lord we are dealing with the attestation of the pure presence of God. Obviously, the previous narrative of the life of Jesus is still pure expectation, even according to Jesus' own words. Even the miracles of this life purport only to be signs of the presence of God. Only the transfiguration on the mount, in face of which Peter immediately wants to build tabernacles, seems formally to prepare for the great exception. And the sequel to Easter, the birth of the Church of Christ, is again the clearest and most consistent possible expectation—again perhaps with the exception of Christ's appearance at the conversion of Saul. But the Easter story (with, if you like, the story of the transfiguration and the story of the conversion of Saul as prologue and epilogue respectively) actually speaks of a present without any future, of an eternal presence of God in time. So it does not speak eschatologically. The Easter story, Christ truly, corporeally risen, and as such appearing to His disciples, talking with them, acting in their midst—this is, of course, the recollection upon which all New Testament recollections hang, to which they are all related, for the sake of which there is a New Testament recollection at all. This very exception, then, deals with something of the utmost importance.

We could do so only *cum grano salis*, but if we were to press the question, which was fulfilled time between Old Testament expectation and New Testament recollection, we would have to reply, the forty days in which Jesus let Himself be seen in this way (Ac. 1³). It is from the recollection of these forty days that light is thrown by the New Testament witnesses upon recollection of the death of Christ and therefore upon His life. Moreover, if we ask concretely what was the object of their testimony, they are the " witnesses of his resurrection " (Ac. 1²²ᶠ·, cf. 1⁸, 4³³ ; Lk. 24⁴⁸ ; 1 Cor. 15¹⁴ᶠ·).

Why does this particular story receive this central place ? We recall its direct relation to the passion, how it is the resurrection of Jesus that makes His passion manifest as the saving happening from God's side, how in virtue of the resurrection the glory of the incarnate Word was seen by His followers. But how far does this resurrection possess this power to reveal ? Because in the recollection of these witnesses the fact that Christ had risen actually points to a time, a real part of human time amid so many other portions of time, which, as it cannot become past, neither needs any future, a time purely present because of the pure presence of God among men. In this way the Easter story—which is quite indispensable to the whole, impossible to think away, the subject whose predicate is all the other narratives— signifies the event which is the proper object of all other narratives and teachings in the New Testament. The whole historical difficulty occasioned by the Easter story itself has its foundation in the fact that in it the New Testament witness touches the point at which as witness, i.e., as human language about and concerning Christ, it comes up against its true object, against the point where everything else depends upon this object, which in itself contains the Word of revelation. Little wonder human language begins to stammer at this point even in the New Testament.

The Easter story is not for nothing the story whose most illuminating moment according to the account of Mark's Gospel consists in the inconceivable fact of an empty sepulchre, a fact which (in producing a τρόμος καὶ ἔκστασις) lays hold of the three woman disciples and reduces them to complete silence ; for they told no one of it, ἐφοβοῦντο γάρ (Mk. 16⁸). Everything else related by this story can be heard and believed in the very literalness in which it stands, but can really only be believed, because it drops out of all categories and so out of all conceivability. It cannot be sufficiently observed that in the most artless possible way all the New Testament Easter narratives fail to supply the very thing most eagerly expected in the interests of clearness, namely an account of the resurrection itself.

How could it be otherwise ? Recollection of the pure presence of God, recollection of a time which cannot be the past and has no future before it, recollection of eternal time, as this recollection obviously purports it to be—what sort of recollection is this ? This fact, that the New Testament witnesses have this very recollection, and not just incidentally, but as the recollection which underlies and holds together all others—this fact is the amazing circumstance which can never be overlooked or denied in these texts, nor directly or indirectly overlooked anywhere else in the New Testament. The difficulty of grasping how this recollection of theirs was created, a difficulty which manifestly goes back to the fact that the New Testament witnesses themselves scarcely found language (and did not find it at all at the critical point) to transmit this recollection—this difficulty reflects the uniqueness of that to which their recollection is related, that which they manifestly had to say, and which manifestly had to be heard. We must, of course, regard the riddle which is posed here from another side as well. The witness to the resurrection of Jesus, however hard it may be to understand it as such, offers itself in every form as the recollection of an event that occurred at a definite time in the past. Now in all other cases such recollection is the mental repetition of this happening as of a fact belonging to the past. But the resurrection of Jesus is not a fact belonging to the past. What happened here according to the witness of the New Testament cannot, by its nature, cease to be, any more than it cannot yet exist. This witness has in view a being immune from dissolution and above the need of coming into being. And yet this being is the object of recollection. Once again, what sort of recollection is this ? If we adhere to it that the meaning of the New Testament in this context is practically speaking recollection of a definite, datable time (yet as fulfilled time and as such not merely past time, as it is also not primarily future, but purely present time), we must add to the uniqueness of the object of this recollection the further finding, that this recollection as such possesses an absolute uniqueness. Both this recollection and its object fall into the same category, the category of the single event of God's revelation. God's revelation is the one thing that makes possible both the Easter story and the Easter message. This is the point from which we can realise that the exception of the Easter message proves the rule, namely, that the New Testament witness, this uniformly outspoken witness to recollection of the Messiah who has come—like the Old Testament, though even more outspoken than it, more Old Testament than the Old Testament, we might almost say—is witness to the expectation of the coming Christ. The recollection found in the New Testament cannot be mere recollection, a mere backward look at a once for all happening. If it is, it will inevitably be, like all other recollection, merely recollection of a past event. But the Easter story, though it is a happening that once became an event in datable time, does not merely belong to the past. Easter cannot just be regarded in retrospect. Recollection of Easter cannot be merely the repetitive reflection, which is all that any other kind of recollection is, even the most living and realistic. Of course, recollection of Easter is also this repetitive reflection. Its only object is that unique happening, and therefore the content of the forty days. That the Messiah has come, is the unmistakable statement of the New Testament. This perfect tense must not be disturbed if New Testament Christology is not to be hopelessly dissolved into a docetic philosophy. And all Christian proclamation is relentlessly gauged by this perfect. The New Testament is really the witness to recollection of revelation. But because it is the witness to recollection of *revelation*, the recollection attested by it is thereby extended. Recollection of eternal time, which is what recollection of the risen One is, is necessarily recollection of a time which overarches our time, and which therefore cannot be confined to the datable time with which it is in the first instance related. Recollection of this time must also be expectation of this same time. If it is true that God once had time for us, our whole time must be bounded by the reality of this time of God; i.e., if God really had time for us, then He will also have it. In other words, we have His revelation not only behind us; because we have it behind us, we also have it in front of us. When we hear what did happen in Christ on our behalf, what is going to happen to us in the future cannot be indeterminate, nor can it possibly be determined by our own estimation or capacity. But in that moment we also hear what is to happen to us through Christ. We hear, then, that what is to happen to us is not left to chance or to ourselves but to Christ Himself as our Lord. Therefore just because the New Testament looks back at history, its message leaves the Old Testament far behind it and becomes a message completely eschatological in direction and intention. This God, who is revealed, believed in and confessed in His pure presence, is *per se* also the coming God. In speaking of Christ as come, the New Testament says it of Him who " shall come again, to judge the quick and the dead." Its faith, being directed strictly to what happened on Good Friday, is hope in what is to be and to obtain at the end of all. Since this faith accepts the justification which took place once for all before the gates of Jerusalem about the year A.D. 30, it also expects this justification at the judgment of God upon whose decision all our decisions converge. When here and now we love the brethren because Christ commanded it, or do not love them although He commanded it, it is revealed what we shall or shall not be in the final future of our existence. If according to 1 Jn. 3² we are now children of God because Jesus Christ the Son of God has had mercy on us and adopted us, we know that in His revelation to come our own being will be revealed. If we confess that Christ is risen and risen bodily, we must also confess to our own future resurrection. If for any reason we wish not to confess it, according to 1 Cor. 15¹³ this is tantamount to denying His resurrection also. If in the New Testament the matter ends with a mere recollection, if recollection does not actually become expectation, if for it the First from whom its witness proceeds is not also the Last, the *Eschatos*, if it is not this with the same seriousness, the seriousness of a knowledge of the First, the New Testament is simply a bit of ebionite tradition. It is often enough regarded as such. But the real New Testament says clearly that He who came is also **He that** comes. Not a line of the real New Testament can be properly understood unless it is read as the witness to finally achieved divine revelation and grace and therefore as the witness to hope. Aligned upon the Archimedean point of the story and message of Easter, which have no eschatological intention, it is in the rest of its constitution and content completely eschatological in intention. In this respect it takes its place naturally alongside of the Old Testament. It is only the sharpened and clarified message of the expectation in which Israel was already living. From this standpoint it is particularly easy to see why the Church of Christ had straightway to recognise itself as the lawful heir of the Synagogue. The adoption of the Old Testament into the Canon of the Church really meant far more than a welcome confirmation of Christ as the fulfilment of ancient expectation and prophecy. It was because on the basis of Christ's manifestation expectation and prophecy constituted the very element by which His Church lived, that it naturally had to claim and to read as its own the book of expectation and prophecy.

Everything depends upon understanding the eschatological trend of New Testament faith, if we are to understand this faith itself.

In the Reformation period it was M. Servetus who represented the view that Christ and His Gospel and belief in it were the fulfilment of the promise in such a way that by the pure presence of grace vouchsafed to us in Christ the promise as such and therefore the need for hope were abolished (cf. Servetus' Letters to Calvin, *C.R.* 36, 649 f., esp. *Epp.* 10 and 14). Against him Calvin (*Instit.* II 9, 3) rightly proved that this meant abolishing the remaining difference between us and Christ. True, in Christ the fulness of all salvation was present, but in Christ Himself, not as already mediated to us, not as proper to us in any other way than in the act of His giving. On the contrary, for us it was (Col. 3³) *abscondita in spe.* True, faith was a continual *transire a morte in vitam,* but for that very reason (1 Jn. 3²) not yet an attainment of the goal. *Quamvis ergo praesentem spiritualium bonorum plenitudinem nobis in evangelio Christus offerat, fruitio tamen sub custodia spei semper latet, donec corruptibili carne exuti, transfiguremur in eius qui nos praecedit gloriam. Interea in promissiones recumbere nos iubet Spiritus sanctus.* To be sealed with the " Spirit of promise " (Eph. 1¹³) was now the *summa felicitatis,* beside which there was none other, no *fruitio Christi, nisi quatenus eum amplectimur promissionibus suis vestitum. Quo fit ut habitet ipse quidem in cordibus nostris, et tamen ab ipso peregrinemur: quia per fidem ambulamus et non per aspectum* (2 Cor. 5⁷). In the same way Luther had rejected the view that Old Testament expectation was abolished by recollection of Christ. *Cum enim nullus sit in hac vita, in quo impleta sit omnis plenitudo novi testamenti, nullus quoque invenietur, in quo non sit aliqua pars veteris testamenti reliqua. Transitus enim est et phase quoddam haec vita de lege ad gratiam, de peccato ad justitiam, de Mose ad Christum, consummatio autem futurae resurrectionis est* (*Op. in Pss.* 1518 f.: on *Ps.* 2, 7 *W.A.* 5, 61, 19). As compared with Abraham we know Christ *exhibitus et praesens,* yet with Abraham we also expect Him. *Diversa tempora non mutant fidem, Spiritum sanctum, dona; eadem semper voluntas et cogitatio fuit et est de Christo, in praeteritis patribus et praesentibus filiis. Sic et nos aeque habemus futurum Christum et credimus in eum ac patres veteris testamenti. Expectamus enim eum in extremo die venturum cum gloria ad iudicandos vivos et mortuos, quem iam credimus venisse ad salutem nostram* (*Comm. Gal.* 3⁷ *W.A.* 40¹ 378, 15).

New Testament faith is constantly characterised by the distinction in unity between Christ and ourselves. It is not a continuation of Christ's faith and still less a kind of prolongation of the existence of Christ Himself, but it is faith in Christ. The forty days and the apostolic age, fulfilled time and the time of recollection, are two different things. There is no word of the apostles and their communities after Pentecost thinking that they were living directly in the eternal presence of God in the days of Easter. Revelation remains revelation and does not become a revealed state. Revelation remains identical with Christ and Christ remains the object of Christian faith, even though He lives in Christians and they in Him. Its gravity and its liberating power depend upon the fact that the believer is not alone by himself, not even in a supreme ecstasy of union with his Lord, but that in faith he really has a Lord, in the form of another different from himself, confronting him. What Christ is in us, that He is for us and therefore in His difference from us. This is what is assured by the eschatological trend of New Testament faith. Indeed this difference could not be more strongly emphasised, or at the same time explained in its true significance, than by the fact that this faith regards and expounds itself as hope in Christ. Faith has Christ as it hopes in Him. So in hope in Christ it has the calling which is its foundation, it has justification, it has sanctification, it has the Spirit as the surety for its hidden sonship to God, it has peace with God

amid the pressure and temptation of the present. All that is included
in Christ, intended for and offered to us, but included in Christ, proper
to us in faith in Christ and therefore in hope in Him. Yet Christ is
always He who stands at the door and knocks, and faith is always the
decision in which a man opens to Him that He may enter, and as this
decision is made, the man has Christ and all that He is and brings.
It is thus and not otherwise. The time of recollection is not fulfilled
time. But as the time of recollecting the risen One it is of necessity
the time of expecting Him, and so it partakes in fulfilled time. We
say, of course, that New Testament faith has Christ as it hopes in
Him ; we do not say, because it hopes in Him. Hope describes the
manner or mode of faith. If we wish to ask about its foundation,
we shall have to answer that it has Christ because it has *Him*. Moreover, it can only hope in Him because it has Him, i.e., because it looks
back to Him, because it recognises that all that had to happen has
already happened and been completed, i.e., that God has revealed
Himself, has reconciled the world to Himself ; the believer is called,
is already justified, is already sanctified, is already God's child, has
peace with God. But this very backward look cannot be cast in such
knowledge of faith without the look forwards, without grasping the
promise : " Behold, I come quickly ! " without the prayer : " Amen,
come, Lord Jesus ! " (Rev. 22[20]). Upon the foundation that is laid,
beside which there is no other (I Cor. 3[11]), building cannot take place
except in the manner or mode of hope. The man really gripped by
Christ has no other choice than that of stretching forward to the things
which are before (Phil. 3[13f.]). It is in this way that the Christian
present from time to time participates in the fulfilled time which it
recollects, that it stands under the Word of Christ—it all comes to
this, that it makes itself really apprehensible as the Word of Christ,
and that it is heard as such. " Lo, I am with you alway, even unto
the end of the world ! " (Matt. 28[20]).

With regard to expectation in the New Testament the change that
has taken place as compared with the Old Testament consists in the
fact, and only in the fact, that the coming Christ of whom New Testament witness speaks is now the object of recollection as He that has
come. This cannot be said of the Messiah expected in the Old Testament, although Old Testament expectation refers only to Him that
came according to the New Testament witness. As distinguished from
Old Testament expectation, New Testament expectation knows concretely and explicitly who it is that is expected. It is simply recollection turned at an angle of 180°, the recollection of the Word come in
the flesh, whose glory the New Testament witnesses have seen. Similarly, the Christ it expects is none other than He whom it already
knows as very God and very man, from whom also it is already derived.
His coming is in fact only His second coming. Of course, this means
a change. But the change is not a weakening of the alignment of

this witness. What it means, rather, is that because of the concreteness and explicitness proper to the latter the Old Testament hope is also related to that of the New Testament as the question correctly put is to the answer correctly given. He who makes both question and answer correct by the fact that He comes, as the prophets hoped with the apostles and the apostles with the prophets, is the Lord to whom both testify as His servants.

It is fitting to close these paragraphs with a hint at the biblical figure which (apart from Christ Himself) is perhaps the most remarkable of all as to its place and role from the actual standpoint of the time-problem—John the Baptist. The account of his preaching constitutes the beginning of all four Gospels and thus the beginning of the whole New Testament. But apart from his being a contemporary of Jesus, it is not at all clear at first sight how far he really belongs to the New Testament. According to the Synoptists, at any rate, his function is almost wholly Old Testament. He arraigns, he preaches repentance, he proclaims the nearness of judgment. He comes ἐν ὁδῷ δικαιοσύνης, as it says so significantly in Mt. 21³². He promises the coming of the Messiah, from whom he knows how to distinguish himself in the strictest subordination (Mk. 1⁷ᶠ· Par. ; Jn. 1⁶ᶠ·, 15 f., 19 f.). He is therefore rightly regarded as a prophet (Mt. 21²⁶). Jesus Himself calls him the greatest that has arisen among men (Mt. 11¹¹). Also purely Old Testament is the last thing we hear in the Synoptics about his attitude to Jesus, the question, " Art thou the ἐρχόμενος or ought we to expect another ? " (Mt. 11³). Moreover he also dies the typical death of a prophet. The Evangelists call him unanimously the messenger or even the voice of him that crieth, who goes before the Lord, to prepare the way for Him (Mk. 1²ᶠ· Par.). But this line of exposition is strangely intersected by another. Jesus calls him more than a prophet (Mt. 11⁹). And according to Jn. 1²⁰ᶠ· not only does he not claim to be the Christ, but not even to belong to the independent order of the forerunners of the Messiah : " I am not Elias nor the prophet ! " But what then ? He is the " voice of one crying," the " witness," obviously in a definite sense but in quite another than the Old Testament sense. According to Mt. 3¹³ᶠ· he refuses to baptise Jesus, but wants to be baptised by Him. According to Jn. 1³² he witnesses the descent of the Spirit upon Jesus. Therefore he is clearly singled out from those who are merely waiting for the Messiah. It is especially the Fourth Gospel which has so very emphatically stressed this line. Here, too, the Baptist is the one who points to the future : " He that cometh after me is preferred before me ; for he is more than I " (Jn. 1¹⁵· ²⁷· ³⁰). He himself says here most emphatically : " I knew him not " (Jn. 1³¹· ³³). But the same Baptist actually does know Christ, though obviously not by his own powers of knowledge. He points to Him as Him that had come : " Behold the Lamb of God " (Jn. 1²⁹· ³⁶). According to Jn. 1¹⁵ᶠ· the same Baptist speaks very like one of those who already saw the glory of the Word made flesh. In Jn. 3²⁷ᶠ·, he contrasts with Nicodemus, the " teacher in Israel," almost as though he himself were already an apostle. The recurrent (Jn. 1⁸, 1²⁰ᶠ·, 3²⁸, 5³⁶) emphasis on the limitations of his mission does not so much mark off the prophet from the apostle, as both together from the object of their witness, Christ. Why is it that the very first chapter of the Fourth Gospel takes so long to make it clear that by " John " it means John the Baptist and not its own author ? And finally, does not this extremely Old Testament John administer the same sacrament of water baptism that is also the permanent sacrament of the Church ? True, he cannot baptise with the Holy Ghost ; but neither can the apostles. Only One can do that. The difference between the witnesses before and after is very clearly discernible in the person of John, but all the same it seems neutralised. *Inter legem et Evangelium interpositus fuit Joannes, qui medium obtinuit munu·*

et utrique affine (Calvin, *Institut.* II, 9, 5). The preparedness of the prophets becomes in John the thanks of the apostles, so that necessarily the thanks of the apostles is recognisable in the preparedness of the prophet. " Hence John is also put midway between Old Testament and New Testament to bring the people to heaven and take away hell. For his voice made the letter live, and brought the Spirit to Scripture, and led Law and Gospel together. For the two preachings of John are these ; the first that depresseth, the second that exalteth ; the one that leadeth to hell, the one that leadeth to heaven ; the one that killeth, the other that maketh alive ; the one that woundeth, the other that maketh whole. For he preacheth both, Law and Gospel, death and bliss, letter and Spirit, sin and righteousness " (Luther, *E.A.* 15, 352, *Pred. üb. Luk.* 1[57-80]). Apart from anything else, this figure in particular would have to be eliminated from the New Testament witness if the intention was to separate the object of its recollection from the object of Old Testament expectation, i.e., to make a cleavage between recollection and expectation, instead of explaining the one by the other from the standpoint of this their object.

§ 15

THE MYSTERY OF REVELATION

The mystery of the revelation of God in Jesus Christ consists in the fact that the eternal Word of God chose, sanctified and assumed human nature and existence into oneness with Himself, in order thus, as very God and very man, to become the Word of reconciliation spoken by God to man. The sign of this mystery revealed in the resurrection of Jesus Christ is the miracle of His birth, that He was conceived by the Holy Ghost, born of the Virgin Mary.

1. THE PROBLEM OF CHRISTOLOGY

In § 13 we answered the question as to the objective possibility of revelation (or the question as to the freedom of God for man) by pointing out its reality. And in § 14 we held this reality to be the object of Old Testament expectation and of New Testament recollection, to be fulfilled time in the midst of the times. In a strict and proper sense this reality, and so fulfilled time in the midst of the times, is the Easter story and the Easter message. It is the revelation of the Word of God, with which Holy Scripture and with it the proclamation of the Christian Church are connected. With it they stand and with it they fall. With it also all church dogmatics obviously stands or falls. From the Easter story the passion story is of course inseparable. In it takes place the hidden work of Jesus Christ which is subsequently revealed and believed in His resurrection. And to the passion story belongs the story of the whole life of Jesus prior to it, although that life is not without signs and anticipatory revelations of the Kingdom at hand, not without announcements of His resurrection. What happens in this life and passion of Christ is thus the concrete content of the revelation which takes place in the event of Easter.

We now have to inquire into the presuppositions of this work and event, hidden in the life and passion of Christ and revealed in His resurrection. What is the power of the resurrection, and so of this work and event? How can it be the Word of reconciliation, spoken by God to men, at once divinely true and humanly real and effective? Who is the subject of it? Who is Jesus Christ? We have already in the most varied contexts underlined emphatically the answer to be given here, that Jesus Christ is very God and very Man. From this fact and from this standpoint the work and event in question, and so the revelation of it, derives its force and significance. From this standpoint we have already answered the question as to the objective possibility of revelation. From it we have obtained a view of the unity of times in fulfilled time, or the time God has for us. But just because everything else depends upon this " standpoint," it now claims special investigation for its own sake. At this point we are entering the problematic sphere of Christology, in the special sense of this concept. A church dogmatics must, of course, be christologically determined as a whole and in all its parts, as surely as the revealed Word of God, attested by Holy Scripture and proclaimed by the Church, is its one and only criterion, and as surely as this revealed Word is identical with Jesus Christ. If dogmatics cannot regard itself and cause itself to be regarded as fundamentally Christology, it has assuredly succumbed to some alien sway and is already on the verge of losing its character as church dogmatics.

The collapse of church dogmatics in modern times under the devastating inrush of natural theology would not have been possible had the way not been already paved for it in the age of orthodoxy (and even to some extent in mediæval Scholasticism and among the fathers), because the necessary connexion of all theological statements with that of Jn. 1^{14} did not receive the obvious attention required at this point, if the construction of sub-centres alien to its content was to be avoided. Too frequently in the older and early periods Christology had already acquired the character of a special structure of statements, parallel to which all sorts of other structures also appeared to have an importance of their own. In time, therefore, it inevitably came to be thought superfluous, while the other parts of dogmatics ran the risk of degeneration ; and dogmatics itself as a whole was forced to ask whether it had anything at all to say of its own that had anything to do with the Christian Church. And when in due course in the 19th century a reaction, sound in itself, arose in the direction of a christocentric theology, first in Schleiermacher and subsequently and still more outspokenly in A. Ritschl and his school, it was then too late. In the interval, due to the decentralisation in question (especially in the form of general epistemology and moral philosophy), so much natural theology had been incorporated that men were no longer in a position to regard Jn. 1^{14} as genuine. One cannot subsequently speak christologically, if Christology has not already been presupposed at the outset, and in its stead other presuppositions have claimed one's attention. On the contrary, one must have the experience of Mt. 6^{24}, of either hating the one or loving the other, or of cleaving to the one and despising the other. And so Schleiermacher's romantic conception of history and Ritschl's Kantian metaphysics on the one hand, and their christocentric efforts on the other, could only render each other unworthy of credence.

As a whole, i.e., in the basic statements of a church dogmatics, Christology must either be dominant and perceptible, or else it is not Christology.

That is precisely why there has to be a special Christology, an express doctrine of the person of Jesus Christ. Here we shall invade the sphere of it only so far as it is absolutely necessary for a complete answer to our question about revelation, especially about its objective reality. The first essential to a complete grasp of this matter is a statement about the content of the incarnation, about God and man becoming one (the so-called " two natures ") in Jesus Christ, in which the mystery of revelation must be brought to its definite expression. This must be accompanied and followed by a statement about its form, about the miracle of Christmas, i.e., about Jesus being born of the Virgin Mary.

In the past these two mutually complementary statements have not been included among the basic doctrines or prolegomena of church dogmatics. They have not, then, had validity and effectiveness as a presupposition of the whole. Like the doctrine of the Trinity itself, they have been treated as individual statements among others. I regard this, if not as an error, at least as a lurking source of error in earlier Christian doctrine. As such, it has had a disastrous effect, and it is our present task to overcome it. After all that has befallen it, church dogmatics will not become "church" again, i.e., free from the alien dominion of general truths and free for Christian truth, until it summons up sufficient courage to restore what is specifically Christian knowledge, that of the Trinity and of Christology, to its place at the head of its pronouncements, and to regard and treat it as the foundation of all its other pronouncements.

Everything else that belongs to a complete doctrine of the person of Christ we must put back to the much later context of the doctrine of God the Reconciler. But a few fundamental clarifications are required before we approach our twofold theme.

Our crucial first statement, " that the eternal Word of God chose, sanctified and assumed human nature and existence into oneness with Himself, in order thus, as very God and very man, to become the Word of reconciliation spoken by God to man," signifies the mystery of the revelation of God in Jesus Christ. That is to say, in this statement we describe absolutely the sole point in which New Testament witness originates, and therefore, also, the sole point from which a doctrine of revelation congruous with this witness can originate. We do not look for some higher vantage point from which our statement can derive its meaning, but we start from this point itself. This, of course, we cannot do by our own authority and discretion. We can only make it clear from the Evangelists and apostles what it will mean to start from this point, and then try to make clear what our own starting-point is. But we cannot get " behind " this point. Therefore we cannot derive or prove the statement, in which this point is to be described, from a higher discernment. We can only describe it as a starting-point. Whatever we think or say about it can only be with the aim of describing it again and again as a mystery, i.e., as a starting-point. If revelation is to be taken seriously as the revelation of God, and not just as an emphatic expression for a discovery which man has made in himself or in his cosmos by his own powers, then in any doctrine of revelation we must deal expressly with the point that constitutes the mystery of revelation, the starting-point of all thought and language about it. At all costs we must make it clear that an ultimate mystery is involved here. It can be contemplated, acknowledged, worshipped and confessed as such, but it cannot be solved, or transformed into a non-mystery. Upon no consideration must it be treated in such a way that the mystery is resolved away. In Christology the limits as well as the goal must be fixed as they are seen to be fixed already in the Evangelists and apostles themselves; i.e., the goal of thought and language must be determined entirely by the unique object in question. But this same object in its uniqueness must also signify for us the boundary beyond which we are not to think or speak. Christology has to consider and to state who Jesus Christ is, who in revelation exercises God's power over man. But it must avoid doing so in such a way as to presuppose that man may now exercise a power over God. It must state definitely what cannot be stated definitely enough. But even so it must observe its own limits, i.e. the limits of man who has seriously to do with God's revelation.

This condition under which alone Christology is possible takes visible form in the main picture on the altar at Isenheim by M. Grünewald. Its subject is the incarnation. There are three things to be seen in the picture, and it is difficult to say where the observer should begin. In the background upon the heights of heaven, beyond earth's highest mountains, surrounded by innumerable angels, there is God the Father in His glory. In the foreground to the left there is the sanctuary of the old covenant. It also is filled with and surrounded by angels, but inexorably separated from the background by an immensely high, gloomy partition. But towards the right a curtain is drawn back, affording a view. And at this point, at the head of the whole world of Advent looking to see the Messiah, stands Mary as the recipient of grace, the representative of all the rest, in adoration before what she sees happening on the right side. Over there, but quite lonely, the child Jesus lies in His mother's arms, surrounded with unmistakable signs reminding us that He is a child of earth like all the rest. Only the little child, not the mother, sees what is to be seen there, the Father. He alone, the Father, sees right into the eyes of this child. On the same side as the first Mary appears the Church, facing at a distance. It has open access on this side, it adores, it magnifies and praises, therefore it sees what is indeed the glory of the only-begotten of His Father, full of grace and truth. But it sees only indirectly. What it sees directly is only the little child in His humanity; it sees the Father only in the light that falls upon the Son, and the Son only in this light from the Father. This is the way, in fact, that the Church believes in and recognises God in Christ. It cannot run over to the right side, where the glory of God can be seen directly. It can only look out of the darkness in the direction in which a human being is to be seen in a light, the source of which it cannot see itself. Because of this light streaming down from above, it worships before this human being as before God Himself, although to all visual appearance He is literally nothing but a human being. John the Baptist too, in Grünewald's Crucifixion, can only point—and here everything is bolder and more abrupt, because here all indication of the revelation of the Godhead is lacking—point to a wretched, crucified, dead man. This is the place of Christology. It faces the mystery. It does not stand within the mystery. It can and must adore with Mary and point with the Baptist. It cannot and must not do more than this. But it can and must do this.

The central statement of the Christology of the early Church is that God becomes one with man : Jesus Christ " very God and very man." And it describes this event in the *conceptus de Spiritu sancto, natus ex Maria virgine.* The merit of the statement is that it denotes the mystery without resolving it away. In all the (apparently or really) complicated explanations which are indispensable to the understanding of this statement of primitive Christology, we must be quite clear from the very start that (with the descriptive statement about the miracle of Christmas) it speaks not only simply and clearly, but with real humility and relevance about the very mystery of revelation.

Primitive Christology (for what follows cf. the attractive exposition by Arnold Gilg, " Weg und Bedeutung der altkirchlichen Christologie," in *Jesus Christus im Zeugnis der Heiligen Schrift und der Kirche*, 1936 pp. 91–178) did not intend to solve the mystery of revelation with its formula about the two natures of Christ, which was clarified at the Council of Chalcedon in 451. It began and ended with the realisation that this was simply impossible. Its purpose in this formula was to fix the fact regarding the subject active in revelation. Its purpose was not to explain this fact. Neither by the formula itself, nor by narrower explanation of what it meant, nor by its pronouncement upon the miracle of Christmas, did it in any sense pretend to have mastered the mystery of revelation. The purpose of this formula and of its narrower explanations and of its pronouncements upon the miracle of Christmas was simply to state that (even in his thinking) man has no power over this reality. At this point he can only begin to think, and only describe the beginning of his thinking. As early as 1 Tim. 3¹⁶ the revelation of Christ in the flesh is not only actually but confessionally (ὁμολογουμένως) the " great mystery of godliness " (μέγα τὸ τῆς εὐσεβείας μυστήριον). Gregory of Nyssa expressed himself quite clearly on the point. We can have no insight (συνιδεῖν) into the mode (τρόπος) of the unity (ἀνάκρασις) of the divine and human in Christ. Its being an event (its γεγενῆσθαι) is beyond question for us. Its How (τὸ δὲ πῶς) we refuse to investigate as being beyond our understanding. Much in the same way as we leave the mode of creation undiscussed as being altogether inexpressible and inexplicable (ὡς ἄρρητον παντάπασιν ὄντα καὶ ἀνερμήνευτον—*Or. cat.* 11). So too the *Syn. pur. Theol. Leiden* 1624 *Disp.* 25, 2 f. calls the unity of the divine and human nature in Christ the profoundest mystery after that of the Trinity. . . . *Quare etiam humana ratione doceri et accipi non potest*: *quod nullum eius in tota natura, perfectum et omnino respondens, exstet exemplum. . . . Verum divinitus e scriptura doceri et probari oculisque fidei accipi debet.*

What are we to say to the reproach of intellectualism so often brought against primitive Christology ? We will allow J. G. Herder to speak for many others. He once gave expression to it as follows : " The desire was to define in monkish language what no human reason . . . will ever be able to define, namely, the union of the two natures of Christ, and the result was to obscure the healthy picture of His whole life, as given to us by the Evangelists without any such verbal definitions. Our Protestant Church has nothing to do with this monkish delusion of the Greeks. . . . A divine phantom that walks on earth I can neither imitate nor follow, and since Paul, since all Evangelists say that Christ was a man like us . . . since all apostles make it our duty to follow Him upon the way of virtue in the severest struggle of imitation, therefore for every Christian, every Christian theologian, the Christ is not a picture in the clouds to be wondered at, but a type on earth for imitation and instruction. Every writing which historically develops and ethically expounds this type, the figure of the purest man on earth, is an evangelical book. All scholastic hair-splitting, on the other hand, which turns Him into an ex-human illusion, is directly contrary to the Scriptures of the New Testament and pernicious " (*Br. d. Stud. d. Theol. betr.* 1780, ed. Suphan, vol. 10, 238 f). The core of this somewhat headstrong language is twofold, namely a formal and a material reproach, and in these two forms we must visualise it, as we now think not only of Herder, but of his many followers in the 19th and 20th centuries.

The formal objection is quite simply aimed at the unmistakable meticulousness with which the fathers, the scholastics and the post-Reformation orthodox theologians pursued the task of explaining, of defining more precisely, and guarding against misunderstandings, the cardinal statement *vere homo vere Deus*. It is aimed at the polemical zeal that developed on all sides, at the systematic precision which sought as far as possible to make sure that no problem should be left unexamined. That, we are told, is (rabbinic, trifling, contentious, unreal) intellectualism, " monkish language," " scholastic hair-splitting." Who can deny this ? But, on the other hand, what importance can this reproach have for one who has himself taken a single glance at the question put by New Testament witness, at the mystery of revelation ? Even if this reproach does more or less incriminate all the historical individuals in question, it is impossible to deny that the alleged meticulousness with which the Early Church and its theology went to work is anything else than an expression of the force with which it felt itself challenged by the question as to who Christ is. Later, as a matter of fact, people learned to answer this question with much less exertion, dispute or precision, much " more simply," than the early thinkers did. Yet this was only possible because secretly the question had already been simplified, i.e., because by various means and methods people had learned to circumvent the riddle set by the New Testament. For instance, if one regards the biography of the so-called historical Jesus as the original and proper content of the New Testament, it will be easy to get on in Christology without meticulousness or polemics, without monkish language or scholastic hair-splitting. But such a person will also have to face the question whether his simple answer is not there from the outset, itself simplifying, therefore, the question put by the New Testament. If unperturbed by docetic or ebionite prejudice he begins his reading of the New Testament at the point at which, as we saw, Paul and John with their statement that Jesus is the Christ, and the Synoptics with their statement that the Christ is Jesus, make contact, if he acknowledges that Christology involves the task of giving an account of the one reality described by these two statements, the reality which is at once the object of Old Testament expectation and the object of New Testament recollection—then he will at least understand that the Church's Christology may become an involved task, and necessarily so in face of the errors that actually preoccupy the Church in every century. And then he has only to participate a little himself in working at this task— here as everywhere onlookers find it easy to criticise, but the result can be nothing more than onlookers' criticism—to realise that here are burdens to be moved which he may, of course, leave lying, but which he cannot move without at once being involved in the difficulties evident in the very profound discussions undertaken at this point by the early workers. In itself there is really neither shame nor disgrace if as theologians we are forced by the christological task along difficult and impassable paths of thought and language. The only decisive question is this : whether on this path we are really trying to do real justice to this task. To make sure of this we must always take heed to the warning against " intellectualism." But if this warning is meant to put an end to our task or to forbid us taking pains over it, it is sheer folly.

More substantial (or apparently so) is the *material* reproach which is perhaps brought against primitive Christology in the above passage. Herder's complaint was that it turned Christ into a " divine phantom " walking on earth, whom we " can neither imitate nor follow." Later, this reproach, especially in A. Ritschl and the historians of his school, chiefly A. v. Harnack, received the concrete form that the Christ of primitive Christology was, as their basic ideas of divine and human " nature " showed, the construction of a metaphysics essentially not religious, because its interest was not ethical but physical. (Cf. for what follows, E. Brunner, *Der Mittler*, 1927, p. 206 f., 219 f.) According to the presuppositions of Greek perception and thinking, this Christ-picture rested upon a naturalistic, mystico-magico-mechanical conception of salvation as a miraculous transformation of man's physical mode of existence into the immortal mode of existence of the deity, a salvation imparted to man in a manner essentially physico-mechanical, by way of a sacrament with an effect like that of a medicine. In the same way, in the incarnation of the Logos as the uniting of the immortal divine nature with the mortal human nature to form the person of Christ, salvation is procured for man in an essentially physico-mechanical way. The reproach of " intellectualism " is therefore brought against primitive Christology for this reason, that conceptually the physico-mechanical event which is its content can be only the object of a theoretical faith, which is really to be described as speculative vision. Christ " a picture in the clouds to be wondered at ! " " A monkish delusion of the Greeks ! " We cannot regard this reproach as well-founded either. Because it is our prime task to think and speak correctly of Christ, it was right for primitive Christology to deal most seriously with the fact that the mystery of revelation can be, not solved, but recognised, and must be recognised if it is to be known at all. It is true that the desire of this Christology was not that of Herder or that of Ritschl, to expound Christ as " the form of the purest man on earth," as an actual type answering to the pattern of a so-called healthy ethics. Nor was it interested in Christ in an ethical way only. It is correct that its conception of salvation included man's physical nature and its hope, the resurrection of the flesh. Even when it spoke of God, it did not primarily, far less exclusively, think of Him as the giver and guarantor of the moral law, but in fact it thought also of His unchangeableness and immortality. Even when it spoke of man, it thought of the inward *and* the outward, of his existence as body and soul, of the ethical and the physical question. It had, therefore, above all a richer view of God and divine salvation than its modern critics. The decisive fact, however, is that its interest was primarily neither ethical like its modern critics, nor physical as the latter accused it of thinking. Beyond these interests it had the supreme, comprehensive and therefore simple desire to regard Christ in the way in which it found Him attested in the New Testament as Lord of the complete man, as bringer of life to both sides of his existence, as the Reconciler of man's being. It was this being of man in its unity and in its totality that was meant when it spoke of the " human nature " in Christ ; and, on the other hand, the divine being in its unity and in its totality, when it spoke of the " divine nature " in Christ. These two basic concepts have therefore nothing to do with the narrower concept of " nature," of which the modernist Protestant thinks when he hears this word. " Nature " for the modernist Protestant is " the sum of everything that is corporeal, that goes back to what is elementary, in its variously divided appearance, in which all that we denote by it is mutually conditioned. Over against what is divided and conditioned in this way, we posit God as the unconditional and absolutely simple " (Schleiermacher, *Der chr. Glaube*, § 96, 1). But what he calls " nature " in this sense is contained in the concept of early dogmatics, θεῖα φύσις, *natura divina*, only so far as God, because He is God, is also Lord over the *physis* in this narrower sense. And what he calls " nature " is contained in the concept of ἀνθρωπίνη φύσις, *natura humana*, in the sense of early dogmatics, only so far as man (because he is man) is not only soul or spirit but body too, because he exists not only spiritually and morally, but corporeally also. Quite simply, then, it was an optical illusion, when modern theologians, themselves interested only in the spiritual and moral, thought they could catch out the primitive theologians (who were admittedly *also* interested in the physical) in an exclusive interest in the physical. It must not be contested that in the Christology and the general theology of the Early Church there was always the possibility of a lapse back to the " natural," in the narrower sense, and therefore the mystico-magico-mechanical. And it did actually happen. But strangely enough—A. v. Harnack himself has drawn sufficient attention to this—there were clear and definite lapses in the direction of spiritualism and moralism as well. Moreover, there were not wanting in the Early Church powerful tendencies in the direction of the type-Christology so successfully demanded by Herder in the new period. If both are wrong, yet in this double fault there is revealed (if only negatively) the original superiority of primitive Christology, for only from the altitude of its comprehensive concept of God, man and salvation, was this twofold lapse possible. Modern theology, on the other hand, following in the steps of Herder, has succeeded miraculously in freeing itself from all magic, from all sacramental mysticism, from all naturalism. Without this counter-weight, without its danger but also without the warning element of truth which it involved, modern theology has made a onesided surrender (apart from a soft sad echo of soul-mysticism) to the Christology of moral example. Even in the perils and faults of the theology of the Early Church we can still recognise that it had to do with the Christ of the New Testament. It spoke of Him as the most high Lord. It meant God Himself, the Creator of heaven and earth. In spite of its dangers and faults it was sound. And that is why the reproach of intellectualism brought against it is not appropriate. Neither God nor man, neither Christ nor the salvation created through Him, were for it natural entities, in the sense that they might actually have been for it merely the object of a theoretical faith. Its faith, of course, rested entirely upon recognition of its object. Its object had being. It was, therefore, a realistic faith. But it would have been an optical illusion if it had for that reason been called a mere intellectual assent, related to gnosis. Whatever the errors to which this Christology might be exposed on the right and the left, there can be no doubt that it did perceive and respect the mystery of revelation.

But the same cannot be said of the doctrine of its modern opponents. The pathos of the reproach of "intellectualism" in its two forms reaches out to something more than the reproach actually expresses. It means something quite different. It is directed against the offence of revelation which was, of course, very abruptly formulated in the two-nature doctrine of the Early Church. Right from the outset, modern Christology aims at a very different statement from that of the Early Church. Hence the repugnance to its meticulousness, hence the subjection of it to the reproach of naturalism. For what it refuses to say is that Christ is the datum upon which we can reflect and speak as upon the beginning of all Christian thought. It refuses, at bottom, to say what was once said in the formula *vere Deus vere homo*. But it is ready to say of Christ, *either* that it regards Him as the highest instance of what elsewhere it claims to know as good, reasonable, moral and to that extent divine, *or* that it will value Him empirically as a bit of specially impressive reality. In either case the meaning is that the beginning of Christian thought and language is by no means in Christ Himself but in our own powers of judgment and our own capacity for experience.

It is now clear how the formal reproach arises against primitive Christology. In either of these ways—we call them the docetic and the ebionite—there may, of course, be all sorts of strong and lofty statements about Christ. But it is also obvious that in neither of these ways can we allow our language to go too far or even to become too definite. We cannot commit ourselves to fundamental statements or venture precise assertions. On the contrary, we may well feel, not without justification, that all statements about Christ or christological teaching are just so much sound and fury. There is, therefore, no point in entering into a serious discussion here. It cannot be a discussion between truth and falsehood. At best, it can only be the free rivalry of various expressions for the same thing. For ultimately they all mean the same. In this context we are right to use the simple formula " very God and very man " with considerable reserve, for it has too important and substantial a significance for what is really intended in such assertions. Similarly, there is the formal justification for the weakness and tolerance shown towards all these statements, for they are

5

mere statements grounded upon the self-sufficiency with which man confronts God, even in face of the open New Testament. By the possession of God which he already has in his mind or conscience or feeling, man reaches a definite " value-judgment " or " value-perception " concerning the Christ of Holy Scripture, and then on the ground of this value-judgment or value-perception he gives Him this or that predicate. Even if they are the very highest of predicates, he can never forget that in the long run they are grounded only upon himself as the man who feels and judges and speaks, upon his own control over God. As a matter of fact, why should he presume to too definite a knowledge or too definite a manner of speech ? Why should he commit himself so much to his own assertions ? Why should he not realise the relativity of all human expression ? How could he ever envisage the possibility of hard theological thinking or serious theological debate ? It is, indeed, impossible to descend to scholastic hair-splitting on this view. We can only look back with a forgiving spirit and some head shaking to the disputes of the 5th and also the 16th and 17th centuries, in sincere amazement to see how stubbornly theologians of those days defended their views, how keen they were to clear matters up to the last detail. Serious opposition is offered only to the suggestion that it is worth while to pay serious attention to the questions at issue, or to push them to clear decisions. Ever since the 18th century it has been almost a dogma in the widest theological and non-theological circles, that this attitude, which is the logical outcome of the presuppositions of modern Christology, is the attitude of true Christian humility, and is infinitely to be preferred to the contentious rigidity of a (" dead ") ortho-doxy which thinks it knows what no one can possibly know.

But we can also see from the material reproach against primitive Christology how people come by this alleged humility. We have already seen that modern as distinct from early Christology is exposed not to two dangers but to one. It is not really guilty of a physical interpretation of salvation, of sacramental mysticism or magical objectivism, but only of the opposite error of a spiritualistic moralism. This is what shows that its criticism of early Christology is materially neither justifiable nor apposite. For it does not arise from a superior knowledge of Christ, but from the same arbitrary moralism that existed in the Early Church, except that in this case it lacks the contrary emphasis which always acted as a certain corrective in the early Church. The absence of what was a source of danger to the " Greeks " is certainly not an asset in modern Christology. It has a horror of *physis*, of externality, of corporeality ; it cannot take breath save in the thin air of moral judgment and of powers of psychic experience. It does not know what to make of what the New Testament calls σῶμα, σάρξ, θάνατος, ζωή, ἀνάστασις and the like. Biblical miracles are painful to it, apart from any-thing else because every one of them is extremely " natural." What is it to say to Jesus' bodily resurrection, or to *natus ex virgine* ? Horror of this means a strange impoverishment, but that is not of decisive importance here. What is important is that in all this there lurks a horror of the being of God in His revelation. The polemic against the concept of the two " natures " in Christ does not rest only upon a misunderstanding of terms. Rather, in refusing to acknowledge a " natural " element in revelation, it refused to acknowledge an ontological element. It was opposed to the realism of the biblical message of revelation. It wanted to accept it only so far as it proved to be " historical " —and by that was meant a similar assertion of moral judgment and religious experience to that which was fathered by the wish. But there was no desire to accept it as the supreme Word of the Lord, who is the Lord before we have experienced or adjudged Him as such by our own glory. Because objection was raised at this point, the New Testament had to be worked over, partly by inter-pretation, partly by literary, partly by religious-historical criticism, until nothing more was said of this Lord, until realism was completely stripped away. And what was more natural than to cease to derive any commands from a New

Testament thus purged, to feel no need to face the mystery of its witness to Christ, or to maintain any connexion between its own Christology and this witness to Christ ? What was more natural than to feel that even the New Testament gives us liberty to use this or that language or to make this or that assertion about Christ ? From this point of view it is very understandable that they could and had to arrive at the humility which renounces beforehand all serious and responsible inquiry for the truth and every attempt to respond obediently to it. For such humility there is rather an incalculable wealth of possibilities, all equally good and acceptable in themselves and in their respective places, but not such as to give rise to serious debate. Let us be quite plain. This humility may be ever so straightforward and admirable. In many an instance, from the standpoint of human morality, it may actually stand out from that of so many of the orthodox zealots as the better attitude. But we must roundly contend that it is not Christian humility, i.e., not the humility that is faced with the mystery of God's revelation. On the contrary, however high our praises of it in other respects, it rests upon a fundamental circumvention and conjuring away of this mystery, and upon a consciousness of human control over God, which necessarily has to be described as pride rather than humility.

We have, then, no cause to give ear to the charge of intellectualism urged against primitive Christology. In its formal as in its material shape its root and upshot are the same, a half-bold, half-puzzled failure to see what the New Testament actually says and what is actually heard in the Church and by the Church. Whatever may be alleged against primitive Christology, it was not guilty of this failure, and therefore, in spite of the reproach in question, at every decisive point we have good reason to take our stand on its side and not on that of its accusers.

At this point there is no particular need to unfold again the content of the " problem of Christology " as such, i.e., all that leads up to the statement that " Jesus Christ is very God and very Man." We recall the entire content of §§ 11 and 13, which brought us to the point we have now reached. Only one thing should be insisted upon here under the title of " the problem of Christology," namely, that if we have let ourselves be led to Jesus Christ along the only sensible, legitimate path for the Church, i.e., by the prophetic and apostolic witness to revelation, then the statement, " Jesus Christ is very God and very Man," is the assumption upon which all further reflection must proceed. We could have reached a different assumption only by a different path. But this assumption is a genuine and proper assumption, in so far as it cannot be over-topped by any other, and therefore suspended on, and even disputed by, a higher assumption. Christology deals with the revelation of God as a mystery. It must first of all be aware of this mystery and then acknowledge it as such. It must assume its position at the place where the curtain of the Old Testament is drawn back and the presence of the Son of God in the flesh is visible and is seen as an event ; yet visible and seen as the event in which, in the midst of the times, in the simple datable happening of the existence of Jesus, a " man like as we are," God the Lord was directly and once for all the acting Subject. At this point He was Man : God without reserve and man without reserve. Scripture leads us to the place confronting this event. This is the place Christology has to occupy with its question : Who is Jesus Christ ? From this place it cannot fail to see or forget the mystery as such. It cannot, therefore, take further account of the possibility of denying it. Nor can it reckon with the possibility of transmuting it into something devoid of mystery. It has to stand by it and to stand by it as a mystery. It is, so to speak, fixed upon this object with this as its particular character. It can do otherwise only by dropping its problem. This is what modern Christology has done. And in so doing it has been guilty of an unpardonable error, an error which renders impossible any understanding, in fact in the long run any discussion at all, between itself and a Christology which refuses to commit this error. Primitive Christology did not commit this error. It did not drop the problem, but stuck to it. It saw the mystery and, on the whole, was able to preserve it, whatever other faults it may have been guilty of in detail. All its efforts were directed towards preserving the mystery. In this respect it was always relevant. And for this reason we must emphatically take its side both at the outset and in principle.

2. VERY GOD AND VERY MAN

We understand this statement as the answer to the question : Who is Jesus Christ ? and we understand it as a description of the central New Testament statement, Jn. 1^{14} : " The Word was made flesh." Therefore this New Testament verse must guide us in our discussion of the dogmatic statement that Jesus Christ is very God and very man.

I

For what follows cf. Heinrich Vogel, *Das Wort ward Fleisch : Ein Kapitel aus der Christologie*, 1936.

'Ο λόγος, the " Word " spoken of in Jn. 1^{14}, is the divine, creative, reconciling, redeeming Word which participates without restriction in the divine nature and existence, the eternal Son of God.

According to the whole context of Jn. 1^{1-12}, what is meant by Jn. 1^{14} is the Word that was in the beginning, that was with God and was indeed God Himself, by whom all things were made, the sum total of the life which shines as the light of revelation in man's darkness. His name is not John, but He is the object of John's witness. He begets children for God among men, not of their will or power, but completely and solely by His own might, whose glory is that of the only-begotten, of whose fulness His witnesses can only receive grace. The Logos is He who proclaims God, who is invisible for all other. He alone can proclaim Him, because He is Himself the only-begotten, in the bosom of His Father.

For that reason, the Word, and therefore the Jesus Christ who is identified with the Word according to Jn. 1^{1-18}, is " very God." And " very God " means the one, only, true, eternal God. It is not deity in itself and as such that was made flesh. For deity does not exist at all in itself and as such, but only in the modes of existence of the Father, the Son and the Holy Spirit. It is the Son or Word of God that was made flesh. But He was made flesh in the entire fulness of deity, which is also that of the Father and of the Holy Spirit. Here we make contact at once with the mystery of revelation, which is the real object of Christology, namely, the source and root of all the various problems and their solutions which are to engage us from now on. If we wish to state who Jesus Christ is, in every separate statement we must also state, or at least make clear—and inexorably so—that we are speaking of the Lord of heaven and earth, who neither has nor did have any need of heaven or earth or man, who created them out of free love and according to His very own good pleasure, who adopts man, not according to the latter's merit, but according to His own mercy, not in virtue of the latter's capacity, but in virtue of His own miraculous power. He is the Lord who in all His action is always Himself entirely and unalterably, in a manner free of all complications or ties, who in His works in the world and on man never ceases in the very slightest to be God, who does not give His glory to another. In this, as Creator, Reconciler and Redeemer, He is a truly loving, serving God. He is the King of all kings just when He enters into the profoundest hiddenness in " meekness of heart." This has to be said in every statement we make about Jesus Christ. It must never be obscured or denied. Every statement about Jesus Christ that contradicts it is thereby at once unmasked as a false, heretical statement.

The reason why orthodox Christology has become such a sharply defined, complicated and polemical structure is because it was concerned to express, unfold and set forth the truth of this statement that " Jesus Christ is very God." It was concerned to guard and maintain it with the utmost zeal against all open and covert weakenings and denials. Anyone who has once realised its position at this point cannot but be surprised at the intense surprise of the moderns at this Christology. In itself its position is perfectly simple, perfectly childlike, perfectly peaceable. Its one concern in every direction, on every question that arises, is to deal seriously with the fact that this man, οὗτος, Jesus Christ, was in the beginning with God (Jn. 1^2), in the clear sense which this utterance possesses once for all in Jn. 1^{1-18}.

The importance of this truth and its recognition extends not only over the whole of Christian proclamation but also over the whole of Church dogmatics. It is not to be circumvented, forgotten, or disdained in any quarter where there is a duty to speak correctly about God and about man. If Christology in particular insists upon this truth and its recognition, it thereby describes as it were an inner circle surrounded by a host of other concentric circles in each of which it is repeated, and in which its truth and recognition must be maintained and expounded. This inner circle can come fully into view only if we read the text right to the end, " the Word was made flesh." We will begin at once by making a number of affirmations which ought to clarify and establish this prime fact, that the Word which was made flesh is really the eternal Word of the eternal Father.

1. In the statement, " the Word was made flesh," the Word is the Subject. Nothing befalls Him ; but in the becoming asserted of Him He acts. The becoming asserted of Him is not, therefore, to be regarded as an element in the world process as such. It rests upon no inner necessity of human history, nor is it to be understood as having its source in any such necessity. There is no condition of the world or man which can form the basis of a claim or capacity whereby this becoming can have been predicted. This becoming cannot be brought into connexion with creation. It cannot be regarded as one of its evolutionary possibilities. No such idea is tolerable even if this becoming is not the divine reaction to the Fall. A higher evolution of the world created by God, to the extent of bringing forth His own Word as one of the elements in its own substance, is also a quite impossible idea even apart from the Fall. God's Word becoming a creature must be regarded as a new creation. How much more so, since man and man's history are stamped and hallmarked by the Fall. How could Christ ever become possible as the product of an immanent world evolution ? No, the Word's becoming flesh is not a movement of the creature's own. Like creation itself, it is a sovereign divine act, and it is an act of lordship different from creation.

It was Schleiermacher who, after the example of many a Gnostic in the 2nd century, after the example of John Scotus Erigena and of Duns Scotus, taught that the appearance of Jesus Christ was to be regarded as " the creation (in Schleiermacher equivalent to ' preservation ') of human nature now completed for the first time "—so far, i.e., as there is to be found in it the preservation " of the receptivity implanted in human nature from the beginning and continuously evolving, a receptivity which enables it to take up into itself such an absolute potency of the God-consciousness " (*The Christian Faith*, Eng. tr., § 89, 3). Schleiermacher can say this, because sin, against which, in his thought also, the appearance of Christ as Redeemer reacts, consists for him merely in the " insuperable lack of potency in God-consciousness " (i.e., the God-consciousness of the natural man). It is not understood as the enmity of man towards God, an enmity to which God's wrath is the answer and which involves a real and fundamental darkening of this natural man before God. According to Schleiermacher, the communion of man with God established by creation is not seriously compromised by sin. Therefore neither need the work of Christ consist in dead man being made alive again, nor need the unity of God and man in Christ be a new creation. For him Christ means simply the continuation and completion of the development initiated by the creation of man in the direction of an energising of his God-consciousness, within which sin, of course, being the supporting element in the imperfection which still provisionally encumbers the whole, is a reality, in which, however, Christ's function is simply to expound and assert the continuity of human nature, which was originally good and unbroken in its God-consciousness. It is clear that if we assume a different conception of sin, the relation of Jesus Christ to man's original creation will have to be described differently, namely, as the creation of a new man. To put the matter the other way round, by regarding Jesus Christ as the new man we abolish Schleiermacher's assumption about sin, i.e., about early man's capacity to develop from the angels. For the proper and primary objection to Schleiermacher's conception must be to the effect that what he calls redemption through Jesus Christ is not a free, divine act of lordship. The Word of God is not seriously regarded by him as the Subject of the redeeming act, but as one of the factors in the world-process.

2. When it says that the Word became flesh, this becoming took place in the divine freedom of the Word. As it is not to be explained in terms of the world-process, so it does not rest upon any necessity in the divine nature or upon the relation between Father, Son and Spirit, that God becomes man. We can certainly say that we see the love of God to man originally grounded upon the eternal relation of God, Father and Son. But as this love is already free and unconstrained in God Himself, so, too, and only then rightly, is it free in its realisation towards man. That is, in His Word becoming flesh, God acts with inward freedom and not in fulfilment of a law to which He is supposedly subject. His Word will still be His Word apart from this becoming, just as Father, Son and Holy Spirit would be none the less eternal God, if no world had been created. The miracle of this becoming does not follow of necessity from this or that attribute of God. Further, it does not follow either from creation, in the sense that God was in duty bound to it or to Himself to command a halt to its destruction through sin by a fresh creation. If He has actually done this, we have to recognise His free good will in doing so, and nothing else.

It may be asked whether Athanasius has sufficiently thought out the matter when (*De incarn.* 6) he writes that the actual victory of death in consequence of sin would have been ἄτοπον ὁμοῦ καὶ ἀπρεπές, that the extinction of an intelligent being participating in the Logos would have been unseemly, that the destruction of this creation would have been incompatible with the goodness of God, that the undoing of the divine work of art would have been τῶν ἀπρεπεστάτων. Since such an undoing of reality threatened to take place, τί τὸν θεὸν ἔδει ποιεῖν ἀγαθὸν ὄντα ; . . . Οὐκοῦν ἔδει τοὺς ἀνθρώπους μὴ ἀφιέναι φέρεσθαι τῇ φθορᾷ διὰ τὸ ἀπρεπὲς καὶ ἀνάξιον εἶναι τοῦτο τῆς τοῦ θεοῦ ἀγαθότητος. And the same question may be put when Anselm of Canterbury deduces the necessity (*necessitas*) for the incarnation (1) from the infinite injury done by sin to God's glory, which demanded a corresponding satisfaction (*Cur Deus homo* I 11, 13, 15), (2) from the impossibility that man as God's finest work should become extinct (*ib.* I 4, II 4), (3) from the need to restore the totality of the heavenly order destroyed by the Fall of Lucifer and the wicked angels, for which a corresponding number of redeemed men was required (*ib.* I 16-19). There is a wrong note in all this, as everyone must admit. But in the particular case of Anselm it can be shown that the intention was not so wrong as it sounds. For him *necessitas* is not a last word either noetically (in the recognition of an object of faith) or ontically (in this object's existence prior to faith's recognition). But the last word is had by and is *veritas* itself, God, for whom and over whose will there is no necessity. *Deus nihil facit necessitate quia nullo modo cogitur aut prohibetur facere aliquid.* (II 5). *Omnis necessitas . . . eius subiacet voluntati. Quippe quod vult, necesse est esse* (*Medit.* 11). *Voluntatem vero eius nulla praecessit necessitas* (*Cur Deus homo* II 17). From the whole tenor of the Early Church's thought on this matter the Athanasius passage can be understood only in this context. This tenor may be summarised in the words of Epiphanius, Ἀναίτιος ὁ δημιουργὸς θεὸς λόγος . . . ἐνανθρώπησε . . . δι' ὑπερβολὴν φιλανθρωπίας, οὐ μετὰ ἀνάγκης, ἀλλ' ἑκουσίᾳ γνώμῃ (*Adv. haer. pan.* 69, 52).

So we say that when the Word becomes flesh, we are concerned with a miracle, an act of God's mercy. There takes place in the created world the unforeseen, that which could not be constructed or postulated from the side either of the world or of God, the work of the love of God to a world distinct, nay divided from Him, to a creature which He does not need, which has nothing to offer Him, to which He owes nothing, which rather is permanently indebted to Him for every-thing, which has forfeited its existence in His eyes.

3. When it is said that the Word became flesh, even in this state of becoming and of having become, the Word is still the free, sovereign Word of God. Strictly speaking, the Logos can never become predicate or object in a sentence the subject of which is different from God. The statement " very God and very man " signifies an equation. But strictly speaking, this equation is irreversible. If it is reversed and Jesus is called not only very God who is very man, but also very man who is very God, in the second statement we must not neglect to add that it is so because it has pleased very God to be very man. The Word became flesh, and it is only in virtue of this becoming, which was quite freely and exclusively the becoming of the Word, that the flesh became Word. The Word speaks, the Word acts, the Word prevails, the Word reveals, the Word reconciles. True enough, He is the incarnate Word, i.e., the Word not without flesh, but the Word in the flesh and through the flesh—but nevertheless the Word and not the flesh. The Word is what He is even before and apart from His being flesh. Even as incarnate He derives His being to all eternity from the Father and from Himself, and not from the flesh. On the other hand, the flesh not only could not be the flesh apart from the Word, but apart from the Word it would have no being at all, far less be able to speak, act, prevail, reveal or reconcile. Finally, in becoming flesh the Word never ceases to be the Word. The equation " very God and very man " must always be regarded as an equalising of the unequal. As we have made it plain earlier, the incarnation of the Logos is not a change from His own nature or His own mode of being as the divine Word into the nature and mode of being of a creature, nor yet the rise of a third thing between God and man. Here, and perhaps here alone, the use of the word " and " is legitimate and theological, and it must be maintained and under-stood with absolute strictness.

Epiphanius remarked upon the irreversibility of the statement " the Word became flesh," and he continued by stating that in the text as it stands there is expressed the primacy of the Logos from heaven who gave reality to the flesh in Him, the Logos Himself, and so bound the whole incarnation to Himself (εἰς ἑαυτόν, *Adv. haer. pan.* 77, 29).

Likewise from this point there results the inevitable rejection of any abstract Jesus-worship, i.e., any Christology or christological doctrine or practice which aims at making the human nature, the historical and psychological manifestation of Jesus as such, its object. Of course, the manifestation can be considered in this way. Revelation is certainly history and only as such is it revelation and only as such can it be recognised and believed. The "flesh" of Christ may and must be eaten, as explained in Jn. 6. But only upon the basis that God acts in history is history revelation and so the object of faith. History abstractly considered is assuredly not revelation. Jn. 6⁶³ should be pondered here, τὸ πνεῦμά ἐστιν τὸ ζωοποιοῦν, ἡ σάρξ οὐκ ὠφελεῖ οὐδέν. Not of its own activity but in virtue of the Word united with it did the flesh of the Lord do what was divine ; by the same means the Word proved His own divineness. Red-hot iron burns, not because by its nature it possesses burning activity, but because it has acquired the latter through its union with the fire. The flesh is mortal on its own account, and quickening because of its hypostatic union with the Word (John of Damascus, *Ekd.* 3, 7). *Regnum divinitatis traditur Christo homini non propter humanitatem sed divinitatem. Sola enim divinitas creavit omnia, humanitate nihil cooperante. Sicut neque peccatum et mortem humanitas vicit, sed hamus qui latebat sub vermiculo, in quem diabolus impegit, vicit et devoravit diabolum, qui erat devoraturus vermiculum. Itaque sola humanitas nihil effecisset, sed divinitas humanitati coniuncta sola fecit et humanitas propter divinitatem* (Luther, *Komm. z. Gal.* 3, 10, 1535, *W.A.* 40¹, 417, 29). The revealing power of the predicate "flesh" stands or falls with the free action of the Subject Logos. The Word is Jesus Christ. With this the "historical Jesus" of modern Protestantism falls to the ground as the object of faith and proclamation. It was purposely discovered, or invented, in order to indicate an approach to Jesus Christ which circumvents His divinity, the approach to a revelation which is generally understandable and possible in the form of human judgment and experience. If Erasmus is disregarded, it is probably in the preaching of Zinzendorf, with its peculiar interest in the creaturely sufferings of Christ, that we shall find one of the most significant sources of this undertaking. For in spite of the obvious differences, we have here the precursor in method of the rationalistic portraits of Jesus later in the century. In the decades before and after the turn of the century it exhausted its last possibilities in the Life-of-Jesus movement, and the books on Jesus by P. Wernle 1916 and *Maurice Goguel* (*La Vie de Jésus*, English trans. by Olive Wyon 1933) are its last noteworthy achievements.

This undertaking finds its exact material and historical parallel in the Heart of Jesus cult which (on the basis of a vision of Maria Margareta Alacoque in 1675) arose and spread in the Roman Catholic Church of the same period with the special co-operation of the order of Jesuits. On all sides efforts were made to guard against any connexion between these two phenomena, but it makes no difference to the reality of it. In the Heart of Jesus cult, too, it is blatantly a matter of finding a generally illuminating access to Jesus Christ which evades the divinity of the Word. The "material object" of this cult, according to Catholic theologians, is, of course, a whole Christ. But we must distinguish from this material object the "objects of manifestation," namely, the humanity of Christ and the parts of it in which the divine perfections are specially expressed. Among these, special mention is to be made of the stigmata and of the Heart of Jesus itself. "To these objects of manifestation, then, adoration is rendered, but the reason for it is the infinite love of God which has redeemed us and is revealed in and through them" (B. Bartmann, *Lehrb. d. Dogm.*⁷, vol. 1, 1928, p. 358 f.). By the "Heart of Jesus" is meant "the heart in the true and proper, though extended, sense of the corporeal heart in connexion with the entire inner life of the God-man, whose most attractive organ it is" (F. Diekamp, *Kath. Dogm.*⁶, vol. 2, 1930, p. 262). "This heart is the physical sounding-board of the redemptive acts and sufferings ; it is the psychological fountainhead of every holy affection in the love of God and man ; it is also the short, symbolical expression for all that Christ intended and achieved in His redemptive activity" (B. Bartmann, *op. cit.*). No *separatio vel praecisio a divinitate* is supposed to take place in the worship of it according to a declaration of Pius VI (1794, *Denz.* No. 1563). *Cor Jesu, Verbo Dei substantialiter unitum*—such is the express statement in the " Litany of the most sacred Heart of Jesus " in the *Miss. Rom.*   In fact, the objection is not to the *separatio vel praecisio a divinitate*—there can be no justification for bringing such a charge against Zinzendorf or the Neo-Protestant Life-of-Jesus movement.   The objection is that by direct glorification of Christ's humanity as such the divine Word is evaded and camouflaged.   For when we are speaking of Jesus Christ, this Word does not possess its human-ness as an " object of manifestation " alongside Itself.   It is God's revelation to us in Its human-ness : inseparable from it, but in such a way that this human-ness is not only inseparably linked with the Word on its own account, but also receives its character as revelation and its power to reveal solely from the Word and therefore certainly cannot in itself, abstractly and directly, be the object of faith and worship.   Where it is made such an object, recollection of the really intended " material object " is a belated reservation void of force.   Therefore both Neo-Protestant faith in the religious hero Jesus and Catholic devotion to the Heart of Jesus are to be rejected as a deification of the creature.

4. To a certain extent it amounts to a test of the proper understanding of the incarnation of the Word, that as Christians and theologians we do not reject the description of Mary as the " mother of God," but in spite of its being overloaded by the so-called Mariology of the Roman Catholic Church, we affirm and approve of it as a legitimate expression of christological truth.   We must not omit to defend it against the misuse made of the knowledge expressed in this description.   But the knowledge in question and so the description as well must not for that reason be suppressed.

'Εξαπέστειλεν ὁ θεὸς τὸν υἱὸν αὐτοῦ, γενόμενον ἐκ γυναικός (Gal. 4[4]).   In Lk. 1[43] Mary is addressed as the μήτηρ τοῦ κυρίου μου, cf. Lk. 1[31f. 35].   Just because the Gospels throughout assume and attest the divinity of Christ, in the last resort we have to remember at this point all the passages where Mary is described as the mother of this Jesus.   The description of Mary as the " mother of God " was and is sensible, permissible and necessary as an auxiliary christological proposition. It makes a twofold assertion.   1. It explains ἐγένετο in the sense that in the incarnation of the Word we are not concerned with a creation out of nothing, but that through His mother Jesus Christ really belongs to the unity of the human race.   " God's child who links Himself with human blood," says P. Gerhardt. Christ's human being is one of the many, not infinitely but limitedly many, possibilities of historical humanity.   One of these possibilities, to wit this one, Mary's son, is God's eternal Son Himself.   The statement thus explains and deepens the *vere homo* from this side and asserts that ἐγένετο means quite simply " born."   2. But the statement says secondly and above all that He whom Mary bore was not something else, some second thing, in addition to His being God's Son.   He who was here born in time is the very same who in eternity is born of the Father.   In this case human being has an existence identical with the existence of the eternal Son of God.   On this side, then, the statement illumines and strengthens the *vere Deus* in its unity with the *vere homo*, and says that revelation, and therefore the Word of God, and therefore God Himself is not to be sought anywhere else save in Him who was born of the Virgin Mary, and again, that in Him who was born of the Virgin Mary nothing else is to be sought than revelation, God's Word and therefore God Himself.   The second and third century emphasis on Christ's birth of Mary had, of course, its main source (in opposition to docetic *gnosis*) in the first of these two motifs.   Ὁ γὰρ θεὸς ἡμῶν Ἰησοῦς ὁ

Χριστὸς ἐκυοφορήθη ὑπὸ Μαρίας (Ignatius of Antioch, *ad. Eph.* 18), and the *natus ex Maria virgine* of the creeds calls attention not only to the virgin birth but above all to the *vere homo*. But it was the second motif, the identity of Him born of Mary with Him born of the Father in eternity (in opposition to the nestorian distinction of a twofold Christ) that led to the subsequent dogmatising of the formula θεοτόκος, *Dei genitrix*, at the Council of Ephesus in 431. Εἴ τις οὐχ ὁμολογεῖ θεὸν εἶναι κατὰ ἀλήθειαν τὸν ᾿Εμμανουήλ, καὶ διὰ τοῦτο θεοτόκον τὴν ἁγίαν παρθένον (γεγέννηκε γὰρ σαρκικῶς σάρκα γεγονότα τὸν ἐκ θεοῦ λόγον) ἀνάθεμα ἔστω (*Anathema* of Cyril, *can.* 1, *Denz.* No. 113, confirmed by the Council of Chalcedon in 451, *Denz.* No. 148). What is expressed by θεοτόκος cannot be better described than in Luther's words : *Peperit (Maria) non separatum hominem, quasi seorsim ipsa haberet filium et seorsim Deus suum Filium. Sed eundem quem ab aeterno Deus genuit, peperit ipsa in tempore* (*Enarr.* 53 cap. *Esaiae*, 1550 *E.A. ex. op. lat.* 23, 476). Luther himself, therefore, had no hesitation in using this description of Mary ; not only in his exposition of the Magnificat (1521) but also in his sermons we continually find incidental use of " mother of God." Zwingli, too (*Christ. fidei expos.* 1536), declares expressly : (*virginem*) *deiparam θεοτόκον appellari iusto vocabulo et iudicamus et probamus*. It is different with Calvin who, so far as I see, rejects Nestorianism and insists that in Lk. 1[43] *virgo ipsa mater Domini nostri appellatur* (*Institut.* II 14, 4), but even in his explanations of this passage (*C.R.* 73, 35 ; 74, 106 f.) avoids, if he does not contest the θεοτόκος or any similar expression about Mary. Lutheran and Reformed Orthodoxy took sides with Luther and Zwingli and in spite of obvious difficulties in confessional tactics expressly validated the use of θεοτόκος to express the *duplex nativitas* in question.

The statement has a biblical foundation, and is very instructive in the christological context. But its use as the basis of an independent Mariology (as it is called) was and is one of those characteristically Roman Catholic enterprises against which there has to be an Evangelical protest not only for their arbitrariness in form but also for the precariousness of their content. The content of the biblical attestation of revelation does not give us any cause to acknowledge that the person of Mary in the event of revelation possesses relatively even such an independent and emphatic position as to render it necessary or justifiable to make it the object of a theological doctrine that goes beyond the one statement made, or even of a mariological dogma. Nor can we conclude otherwise from the most earnest interpretations of the dogma which have arisen than that in this case we are dealing essentially, not with an illumination, but with an obscuring of revealed truth, in other words, with a false doctrine. Mariology is an excrescence, i.e., a diseased construct of theological thought. Excrescences must be excised.

The New Testament, like the Councils of Ephesus and Chalcedon, takes a christological and only a christological interest in the person of Mary. This is particularly true even of the Christmas story and its pre-history. A. Schlatter's dictum is exegetically incontrovertible, that in them she is merely the " subsidiary figure of a servant " (*Marienreden*, 1927, p. 95). Neither can we gather from the scene between the angel Gabriel and the Virgin (Lk. 1[26-38]) a single statement that does not point away from Mary to Christ. In this category is to be put the well-known κεχαριτωμένη of Lk. 1[23], which, translated *gratia plena*, has given rise to so many mariological speculations, against which it ought to have constituted a serious warning. In the same Gospel (Lk. 11²⁷ᶠ·) we read of the woman who lifted up her voice and (far too mariologically, one might say) said to Jesus : " Blessed is the womb that bare thee, and the breasts which thou didst suck ! " She received the unmistakable answer : " Yea rather, blessed are they that hear the word of God and keep it ! " We should also remember here the repudiation : " Who is my mother and who are my brethren ? ", and the declaration that these my disciples are " my mother and my brethren. For whosoever shall do the will of my Father which is in heaven, he is my brother, and sister, and mother " (Matt. 12⁴⁸ᶠ·). As Luther understood it in his perfectly correct exegesis of the Magnificat, the greatness of the New Testament figure of Mary consists in the fact that all the interest is directed away from herself to the Lord. It is her " low estate " (ταπείνωσις, Lk. 1⁴⁸), and the glory of God which encounters her, not her own person, which can properly be made the object of a special consideration, doctrine and veneration. Along with John the Baptist Mary is at once the personal climax of the Old Testament penetrating to the New Testament, and the first man of the New Testament : " Behold the handmaid of the Lord ; be it unto me according to thy word " (Lk. 1³⁸). She is simply man to whom the miracle of revelation happens. This man may, perhaps, be the holder of an office like the apostles, and so this office in its relation to the office of Christ may become the object of a doctrine. But it is the office, not the person of Paul, Peter or John. How much less is it the person of Mary who has no such office, but who, in conceiving the Lord, can only represent man (both Old Testament and New Testament man alike) in his reception of God. Such a one need not remain nameless or unnoticed. In her very lack of emphasis, in the infinite significance of her reserve, just because she is only important as the one who receives and is blessed, the figure of Mary is an indispensable factor in Bible proclamation. But every word that makes her person the object of special attention, which ascribes to her what is even a relatively independent part in the drama of salvation, is an attack upon the miracle of revelation, because it is, after all, an attempt to illumine and to substantiate this miracle from the side of man or of his receptivity. What happens in the New Testament is the very opposite. What are we to say when M. J. Scheeben (*Handb. d. kath. Dogm.*, vol. 3, 1882, new edn. 1925, p. 458) ventures to interpret what is exegetically so unambiguous as follows : " That Christ and the apostles do not expressly stress and celebrate Mary's glory is abundantly explained by the fact that to begin with the whole attention of believers had to be turned upon Christ Himself. His divine glory together with His personal exaltation above His mother had first to be established, before anything could be said of the glory redounding to His mother from this source. Moreover, it is obvious that during Mary's lifetime her modesty had to be spared, respected and preserved." In reply, it must be affirmed that the New Testament is utterly unaware of any such glory " redounding " to the one who receives and is blessed in this way. In this respect it observes a rule which is understood quite non-dialectically (2 Cor. 10¹⁷) : " he that glorieth, let him glory in the Lord." This is the point that must have been very impressive to the first four centuries A.D. *Ac ne quis hoc derivet ad Mariam virginem ; Maria erat templum Dei, non Deus templi. Et ideo ille solus adorandus, qui operabatur in templo* (Ambrose, *De. Spir. s.* III 11, 80). Mary is spoken of partly for the sake of Christ's true humanity, partly for the sake of His true divinity, but not for her own sake. When perpetual virginity was ascribed to her, as was, of course, the case even at an early date, even this was still done in a christological, not in a specifically mariological interest. The early parallel between Eve and Mary (Justin, *Dial. c. Tryph.* 100 ; Irenaeus, *C.o.h.* III 22, 4 ; V, 19, 1 ; Tertullian, *De carne Christi*, 17) was one of the not always too happy discoveries of the same type which were made at that time in the Old Testament. If these particular parallels are to be insisted upon, it must be noted that at least according to the New Testament interpretation of Gen. 3, Eve does not play an independent part alongside of Adam in the story of the Fall. Even 1 Tim. 2¹³ᶠ· cannot be appealed to here. For if it says there that it was not Adam but Eve who was deceived—that she " introduced transgression " is only to be found in Luther's text—this occurs in the context of an argument to prove that the position appropriate to women is that of ἡσυχία and cannot be one of αὐθεντεῖν. This can be applied even more appropriately to the relation between Christ and Mary. In the characteristic form of the hymn : " *O gloriosa virginum* " from the *Off. B. Mariae Virg.* in the *Brev. Rom.* :

> *Quod Heva tristis abstulit*
> *Tu reddis almo germine,*

the parallel is utterly arbitrary. It is admitted that the first four centuries do not know either the later dogma of Mary or the later worship of Mary. " During the first four centuries, alike in the doctrine and in the worship of the Church, the person of Mary as such " stands " even further in the background " (Scheeben, *op. cit.* p. 474 f.). Even the θεοτόκος of the Council of Ephesus attributed to Mary absolutely no " co-operation in the work of redemption " (against F. Heiler, *R.G.G.*², III, 2015).

But all that changed. What had been an annexe to Christology (for that is how the θεοτόκος must be conceived) became the chief proposition of an ever-expanding special " Mariology " and the dogmatic justification of a luxuriantly unfolding liturgical and ascetic practice with legendary accretions. And there is no doubt that the change meant a twisting both of the New Testament witness and of the sound christological tradition of the first four centuries. However we interpret it, in increasing measure men began to listen to the voice of a stranger, not to the voice of the Word of God, the founder of the Church. (For what follows, cf. M. J. Scheeben, *op. cit.* p. 455 ff. ; F. Diekamp, *Kath. Dogma*⁶. vol. 2, 1930, p. 347 ff. ; B. Bartmann, *Lehrb. d. Dogm.*⁷ vol. 1, 1928, p. 419 ff. ; R. Grosche, " Fünf Thesen zur Mariologie," *Catholica*, 1933, p. 25 ff.)

Over and above the doctrine of the divine motherhood, which is so incontestable in its christological context, over and above the fine statement which occurs so often in the Roman Missal and Breviary : *Ex te ortus est sol justitiae Christus,* there developed a doctrine of the so-called privileges of the mother of God. The first to be regarded as such was the *virginitas et post partum,* and this was made a dogma at the first Lateran Council in 649. To this there was naturally added the doctrine of the *immaculata conceptio,* that although naturally begotten, Mary is by prevenient grace set free from all taint of original sin, and has entered upon existence in a state of sanctifying grace. A feast of St. Anna first solemnised in England seems to have given the impulse in the West to this doctrinal construction. Among the doctors of the Middle Ages, together with many others, Anselm of Canterbury, Bernard of Clairvaux, Thomas Aquinas and Bonaventura seem to have adopted an attitude of reserve towards it, though not of rejection. It was Duns Scotus who led it to victory in the field of theology. But it was not till 1854 that it was raised to a dogma by Pius IX (Bull " *Ineffabilis Deus,*" *Denz.* No. 1641). From this statement it may further be concluded (and on the basis of an incidental remark in the decrees of Trent (*Sess.* VI *can.* 23, *Denz.* No. 833) it also accepted as a doctrine of the Church that Mary in addition never actually sinned. Other positive graces, advantages and titles (information about the nature and extent of these can be got from the so-called Laurentian Litany in the *Miss. Rom.*) are all in accord with this. The corporal ascension of Mary to heaven was not a dogma when this was first written, but it was celebrated as early as the 7th century, rather like the *immaculata conceptio* and even a little earlier. It has been generally regarded as a *sententia pia et probabilissima* and its final definition as a dogma was almost inevitable. It stands " at the logical terminus of the main Marianic dogma " (Bartmann, *op. cit.* p. 444). According to Thomas Aquinas, the basis of all these privileges is that because of her motherhood, the dignity of Mary, as that of the first to be redeemed by her divine Son, is like that of the humanity of Christ, infinite and surpassing that of all other creatures (*S. Theol.* I *qu.* 25 *art.* 6 *ad.* 4). To her, too, according to Thomas, there belongs a *specialis affinitas ad Deum* (*S. Theol.* II 2 *qu.* 103, *art.* 4 *ad.* 2). *Regina coeli*, and whatever other predicates of being may be ascribed to her in mariological language, cannot possibly now be only lofty expressions. From this dignity, and the privileges derived from it, it follows further and pre-eminently that, as the mother of the Saviour, Mary is the mediator, the *mediatrix* of our salvation : i.e., as mediatrix of the Mediator she is herself the *mater gratiae*. Investigation is still in process as to whether she should not be called outright *corredemptrix* (Bartmann p. 441 f., as opposed to Scheeben, is in favour). There is agreement, however, as to the concept *coadjutrix*, which is explained by saying that what is involved is a *cooperatio ministerialis*, or that Mary obtains for us (*promeret*) *de congruo* what Christ Himself obtains for us *de condigno* (so Pius X, Encycl. " *Ad diem*," 1904, *Denz.* No. 3034). One of the last Papal utterances on this matter is to the following effect : *Per arcanam cum Christo conjunctionem eiusdemque gratiam omnino singularem Reparatrix* (="Mediatrix of our reconciliation with God ") *item exsistit pieque appellatur. Cuius nos confisi apud Christum deprecatione, qui . . . suam sibi Matrem adsciscere voluit peccatorum advocatam gratiaeque ministram ac mediatricem* (Pius XI, Encycl. " *Miserentissimus Redemptor*," 1928, cited from Bartmann, *op. cit.* p. 443). At all events the practical issue is that : *de . . . gratiae thesauro, quem attulit Dominus . . . nihil nobis, nisi per Mariam Deo sic volente impertiri, ut, quomodo ad summum Patrem nisi per Filium nemo potest accedere, ita fere nisi per Matrem accedere nemo possit ad Christum* (Leo XIII, Encycl. *Octobri mense*, 1891, *Denz.* No. 3033). " The mother of God permeates Catholic humanity as an intercessory omnipotence, and it is already manifest to us in clear conscious-ness that not a pulse-beat makes its way from the Redeemer's heart, of which His mother is not aware, that as she is the mother of the Redeemer, she is also the mother of all His graces " (K. Adam, *Das Wesen des Katholizismus*[4], 1927, p. 132 f.). As we may read in numerous mariological passages in the *Missale* and *Breviarium Rom.*, Mary is the subject of an independent *intercessio* of her own. Since this is so, there accrues to her " a veneration essentially less than the worship of God, but outreaching the veneration of all saints and angels " (Diekamp, *op. cit.* p. 392), not a λατρεία, nor yet the simple δουλεία bestowed upon the saints and angels, but a ὑπερδουλεία, as the *potissima species* of δουλεία in general (Thomas Aquinas, *S. theol.* III *qu.* 25 *art.* 5c). " For what binds us to God and leads us heavenwards is, along with Christ and in subordination to Him, the most blessed Virgin. It therefore involves an upsetting of the ordinance made by God and a dissolution of true Christianity, if Mary is separated from Christ in worship, and it is therefore a mark of the true Church of Christ that she venerates Mary ; where Mary is not venerated, there the Church of Christ is not " (Diekamp, *op. cit.* p. 395). For this reason it can be said in the famous " *Stabat mater dolorosa*,"

> *Christe, cum sit hinc exire,*
> *Da per matrem me venire*
> *Ad palmam victoriae !*

Or again, in the Graduale to the Scapular Feast : *Per te, Dei genitrix, nobis est vita perdita data.* Or again, in the *Oratio* of the Feast of Mary's Ascension : *Domine, delictis ignosce ; ut qui tibi placere de actibus nostris non valemus, genitricis Filii tui, Domini nostri, intercessione salvemur.* Or again, in the Offertory of the Feast of the Rosary Mary is made to say of herself : *In me gratia omnis viae et veritatis, in me omnis spes vitae et virtutis ; ego quasi rosa plantata super rivos aquarum fructificavi.* Or again, it can be said in the hymn " *Ave, maris stella* " (*Commune festorum B. Mariae V.,* in *I vesperis Brev. Rom.*) :

> *Salve vincla reis*
> *Profer lumen caecis*
> *Mala nostra pelle*
> *Bona cuncta posce*
> *Monstra te esse ·matrem*
> *Sumat per te preces*
> *Qui pro nobis natus*
> *Tulit esse tuus.*

Or again, in the *Praefatio* of the Feast of Mary it can be said of Mary : *lumen aeternum mundo effudit.*

We can only confront Diekamp's declaration with the equally definite Evangelical declaration that where Mary is " venerated," where this whole doctrine with its corresponding devotions is current, there the Church of Christ is not.

It is not to be recommended that we should base our repudiation on the assertion that there has taken place here an irruption from the heathen sphere, an adoption of the idea, current in many non-Christian religions, of a more or less central and original female or mother deity. In dogmatics you can establish everything and nothing with parallels from the history of religions. The biblical witness to revelation itself worked with " heathen " ideas and germs of ideas ; indeed it had to do so, as the world in which it aimed at getting a hearing was a " heathen " world. The assertion may be ever so correct in itself : but leave your Catholic opponent at peace in this respect. Such an assertion cannot possibly be a statement of Evangelical belief. It cannot, therefore, be a serious question for Catholicism.

We reject Mariology, (1) because it is an arbitrary innovation in the face of Scripture and the early Church, and (2) because this innovation consists essentially in a falsification of Christian truth. We must now touch briefly on these points. Our best procedure is to take the actual explanation of Marian dogma attempted by Catholic theology and let it speak for, i.e., against, itself. Scheeben *op. cit.* p. 456 quotes with approval the antiphon from the third nocturn in the *Commune festorum B. Mariae V.* in the *Brev. Rom.*, an anonymous saying of the 8th century, in which Mary is addressed thus : *Cunctas haereses sola interemisti in universo mundo.* However this may have been intended at the time, if it is a satisfactory expression of Roman Catholic systematics (and we have reason to believe that this is the case), it means that Marian dogma is neither more nor less than the critical, central dogma of the Roman Catholic Church, the dogma from the standpoint of which all their important positions are to be regarded and by which they stand or fall. It is a profoundly based fact that for the popular consciousness, Catholic or Protestant, there is probably no Reformed position which has proved so illuminating even to a child as the simple No uttered from the standpoint of Reformed knowledge in answer to the whole doctrine and worship of Mary, an answer which in every circumstance must be uttered inexorably. In the doctrine and worship of Mary there is disclosed the one heresy of the Roman Catholic Church which explains all the rest. The " mother of God " of Roman Catholic Marian dogma is quite simply the principle, type and essence of the human creature co-operating servantlike (*ministerialiter*) in its own redemption on the basis of prevenient grace, and to that extent the principle, type and essence of the Church.

Roman Catholic dogmatics has every reason to insist with Thomas Aquinas (*S. theol.* III *qu.* 25 *art.* 5 *sed contra*) that *mater Dei est pura creatura.* Not only its delimitation against heathen parallels, but everything else that it can say positively in Mariology, depends upon the fact that in spite of her infinite dignity, in spite of her incomparable privileges, and in spite, nay because of her co-operation in redemption, Mary is not a goddess and does not belong to the sphere of being of the triune God, but, compared with Him, belongs wholly to the creaturely, indeed to the earthly, human sphere. It is as a creature that her dignity, her privileges, her work of co-operation, and with it the central, systematic place and function mentioned above, are attributed to her. The decisive act by which she acquires her dignity and her privileges, and on the basis of which she is capable of the co-operation, is not merely that physically she is the mother of God, but that there is a bridal relation to God which accompanies the mother-hood, expressed in the words : *Ecce ancilla Domini, fiat mihi secundum verbum tuum.* In this believing acquiescence in the promise made to her she proves that she is disposed to possess the grace of the motherhood in question. She desires the positive receptivity required (Scheeben, *op. cit.* p. 489 ff.). *Beata Virgo dicitur meruisse portare Dominum omnium non quia meruit ipsum incarnari, sed quia meruit ex gratia sibi data illum puritatis et sanctitatis gradum, ut congrue possit esse mater Dei* (Thomas Aquinas, *S. theol.* III *qu.* 2 *art.* 11 *ad.* 3). But this definition of Mary's *meritum* fairly describes the way in which according to Roman Catholic doctrine the human creature in general may acquire a *meritum*, and what this consists of. Man is capable, by prevenient grace, of preparing himself for genuine sanctifying grace, by uttering this *fiat.* The creature blessed in virtue of its acquiescence is the proper object of Mariology. Therefore accord-ing to Thomas Aquinas it was appropriate that the *annunciato* preceded the *conceptio* : *Per annuntiationem expectabatur consensus Virginis loco totius humanae naturae* (*S. theol.* III *qu.* 30 *art.* 1c). " By her ' Be it so ' in the name of all man-kind, Mary entered into co-operation in redemption " (Grosche *op. cit.* p. 38). According to Catholic ideas Mary represents " living, passive and active recep-tivity to regenerating grace " (Scheeben, *op. cit.* p. 456). She appears " next to Christ as the noblest and most outstanding member of humanity (or rather as one who reaches a higher rank), by whom and in whom the latter (humanity) is kept in mystical communion with Christ and God " (*ib.* p. 510). It was neces-sary for " a person belonging to the mankind which was to be redeemed, and therefore partaking passively in the redemption, to enter actively in the name of all other men into the carrying out of redemption, in order by preparation of the same, and by participation in the redeeming sacrifice, to perfect in every way the appropriation of the redemptive act and its effects upon men " (*ib.* p. 598 f.). Scheeben has a speculative substructure for this. The entire content of the passages on the wisdom of God in Prov. 8 (the lesson for the feast of the Immaculate Conception), Eccles. 24 (the lesson for the Feast of Mary's Ascension) and Wisd. 7 is applied by him to Mary and interpreted as follows : Wisdom in these passages is portrayed " as a person that has gone out from God, is in close relation to the world, exists and acts in the world outside and along with or even under God." It is " in the form of a female person that has proceeded from God, i.e., such a person as in virtue of her proceeding from God and her relationship to God stands by God's side in a manner similar to that of a daughter by her father, and exercises over the world an influence similar to that which a mother exerts in a father's house—i.e., as a principle which has proceeded from God, is similar to Him, and is the seat, vessel and instrument of God for His consummating, quickening and illuminating impact upon the world " (*ib.* p. 465). What is the meaning of this *sophia* proceeding from God, like God, yet immanent in the world ? E. Przywara purports to give us final clarity in the matter when he writes that there are contained " in the Catholic doctrine of the *analogia entis* the possibilities of a true incarnational cosmos, including body and soul, com-munity and individual, because in their totality . . . they are ' open ' to God. From the standpoint of the Catholic doctrine of the *analogia entis* creation in its totality is the vision, mounting from likeness to likeness, of the God who is beyond every likeness. It is, therefore, a receptive readiness for Him. In its final essence it is, as it were, already Mary's ' Behold, the handmaid of the

Lord. Be it unto me according to Thy word ' " (*Religionsphil. Kath. Theol.*
1926, p. 53). But again, in the warm, modern rhetoric of K. Adam this means :
" God is a God of life and love. So great, so exuberant is this love, that it not
only exalts men by the natural endowment of free intellectual will in the image
of His own Creative power, but it also calls these beings, rendered self-reliant
in this way by the precious gift of sanctifying grace, to an incomparable participation in the divine nature and its powers of blessing, to a kind of creative
co-operation in the work of God, to a saving initiative in the building of God's
Kingdom. The profoundest meaning, the greatest richness of redemption, is
that it raises the creature endowed with reason from the infinite remoteness
of its natural impotence, and from the abysmal forlornness of sin, into the living
divine tide, and thereby enables it, while preserving its essential creaturely
condition, to co-operate in the work of redemption. . . . Thus in a certain measure
all redeemed humanity enters the sphere of the living divine powers. To that
extent it is not merely an object, but also a subject of the divine redemptive
activity " (*op. cit.* p. 121 f.). Along the same lines Gertrud von le Fort has
expressed herself unambiguously (*Die ewige Frau*, 1934) : " The dogma of the
Immaculata means the proclaiming of what man was as a creature not yet fallen.
It means the unpolluted face of the creature, the divine image in man " (p. 14).
It means " the creature's co-operation in redemption " (p. 25). " On the humble
fiat with which she (Mary) answers the angel hangs the whole mystery of redemption on the side of creation. . . . Mary is . . . the religious element by which
God is honoured, the world's power of submission in the form of a bridal woman "
(p. 15, cf. 33). Mary is the original type of a " tremendous hierarchy of sub-
missions." As such she is unique and infinitely supreme. Only brokenly can
others after and before enter into the same experience. (p. 17). " As the Sybil
precedes Mary, the Saint follows her " (p. 19). But " wherever the creature
participates with final sincerity, there too appears the *mater creatoris*, the *mater
boni consilii* ; wherever the creature is delivered from itself, there the *mater
amabilis*, the ' mother of fair love,' comforts an anguished world ; wherever
the nations are of a good will, there the *regina pacis* prays for them " (p. 27).
" Co-operating creation is the daughter of the Eternal Lady, the splendid bearer
of the *fiat mihi* " (p. 141). " Invariably fulfilment in Christ is preceded by the
annunciation to Mary, manifestation by what is hidden, redemption by humble
readiness, the initiative of heaven by the Yes of the creature " (p. 157). And,
finally, the accordance of all this in principle with the early days of Roman
Catholicism may be shown from Gregory the Great, who in his exposition of
1 Ki. 1 says of Mary : *Mons quippe fuit, quae omnem electae creaturae altitudinem,
electionis suae dignitate transcendit. An non mons sublimis Maria, quae ut ad
conceptionem aeterni Verbi pertingeret, meritorum verticem supra omnes angelorum
choros usque ad solium Deitatis erexit ?* This is what is meant by Mariology :
Mary affirming grace on the basis of grace *loco totius humanitatis* ; in this Mary,
therefore, the divine *Sophia* dwelling in the world apart from the incarnation
of the Logos ; this *Sophia* in the sense of the creature's openness or readiness
for its God ; this readiness in the sense of the *vertex meritorum*, i.e. the creature
which is " also the subject of the divine redemptive activity." All this is what
Mariology means. For it is to the creature creatively co-operating in the work
of God that there really applies the irresistible ascription to Mary of that dignity,
of those privileges, of those assertions about her *co-operatio* in our salvation,
which involve a relative rivalry with Christ.

The exact equivalent of this creature is the Roman Catholic concept of the
Church (cf. for what follows E. Wolf, " Der Mensch und die Kirche im kath.
Denken," *Z.d.Z.* 1933, p. 34 ff.). *Mater ecclesiae* is one of the honorific titles
ascribed to Mary by Catholic dogmatics. This does not only mean what is
obvious because of her mediation of grace, the fact that she is " the mother of
all believers " (cf. for this Grosche, *op. cit.* p. 35 f.). It does not only mean that

Mary is the heart of Christ's mystical body (Scheeben, *op. cit.* p. 514). But it means the relation—Scheeben (*op. cit.* p. 618) speaks of a *perichoresis*—between her motherhood and the motherhood of the Church. It means an " inner link and resemblance " between the two, so great " that either of the two can be known perfectly only in and with the other." As we must speak of a motherhood of Mary to the redeemed, so, in relation to the eucharistic Christ, we must speak of a motherhood of the Church to Christ. To that extent it holds quite generally and strictly that in Mary " the Church is pictured as the mediatorial principle for applying redemptive grace in respect of her dignity, power and efficacy " (p. 455), " and it is altogether to the point when a Protestant scholar opined that in Mary Catholics glorified and maintained their mystical conception of the Church as the mother and mediatrix of grace " (p. 456). Here, too, the *tertium comparationis* is clear. Like Mary (and like the pardoned human creature in general) the Church also possesses a relatively independent place and function in the redemptive process. It, too, vies with Christ, in the infinite distance, it is true, between creature and Creator, yet in such a way that not only is it born of Christ but, particularly in the eucharistic centre of its life, Christ is also born of it. Not only does it need Christ, but in all seriousness Christ also needs it. As Mary inevitably co-operates in man's redemption as an " intercessory power," so does the Church in consummating the sacraments. As, therefore, Mary acquires the dignity that distinguishes her from all other creatures, as her existence from her procreation to her death is inevitably an only slightly weaker parallel to the existence of Christ Himself, so, too, within the creaturely limit there may be ascribed to the Church a dignity, authority and omnipotence, whose independence is only too insufficiently relative. Utterly logical was the connexion in the life-work of Pius IX between the proclamation of the *immaculata conceptio* in 1854 and that of papal infallibility in 1870 (and the canonisation of natural theology in Thomas's sense, achieved at the same Vatican Council). The Church in which Mary is venerated is bound to regard itself as it has done in the Vatican decree ; just as the same Church must be the Church of the man who co-operates with grace on the basis of grace.

The Evangelical statement of faith which we must set against Marian dogma is thus the very same as must be maintained against the Roman Catholic doctrine of grace and the Church. Jesus Christ, the Word of God, exists, reigns and rules in as sovereign a way within the created world as He does from eternity with the Father, no doubt over and in man, no doubt in His Church and by it, but in such a way that at every point He is always Himself the Lord, and man, like the Church, can give honour only to Him and never, however indirectly, to himself as well. There can be no thought of any reciprocity or mutual efficacy even with the most careful precautions. Faith in particular is not an act of reciprocity, but the act of renouncing all reciprocity, the act of acknowledging the one Mediator, beside whom there is no other. Revelation and reconciliation are irreversibly, indivisibly and exclusively God's work. Thus the problem to which the Roman Catholic doctrine of grace and the Church, to which Mariology in particular is the so-called answer, i.e., the problem of creaturely co-operation in God's revelation and reconciliation, is at once a spurious problem, the sole answer to which can be false doctrines. *Quid est creaturam loco creatoris ponere, si hoc non est ?* With this question of early Protestant polemic (F. Turrettini, *De necessaria secessione nostra ab ecclesia Romana*, 1678, *Disp.* 2, 16) we too must protest against Mariology as such.

But in honesty it must be said that Protestant resistance to Marian doctrine and worship will on its side be non-genuine so long as Protestantism is still enmeshed in that spurious problem, and therefore still maintains the false doctrine of a partial grace and the false doctrine of the Church's leadership. Indeed, it is only the basically non-classical character of this Protestantism which so fa has prevented it from constructing a kind of Mariology of its own.

II

1. That the Word was made "flesh" means first and generally that He became man, true and real man, participating in the same human essence and existence, the same human nature and form, the same historicity that we have. God's revelation to us takes place in such a way that everything ascribable to man, his creaturely existence as an individually unique unity of body and soul in the time between birth and death, can now be predicated of God's eternal Son as well. According to the witness of the Evangelists and apostles everything miraculous about His being as a man derives its meaning and force from the fact that it concerns the true man Jesus Christ as a man like ourselves. This is true especially of the Easter story, the *evangelium quadraginta dierum*, as the supreme event of revelation. It is true of the sign of His birth of the Virgin at the beginning, and the sign of the empty tomb at the end of His historical existence. It is true of the signs and wonders already manifested between this beginning and end, which proclaim the Kingdom of God in its relation to the event of Easter. What in fact makes revelation revelation and miracle miracle is that the Word of God did actually become a real man and that therefore the life of this real man was the object and theatre of the acts of God, the light of revelation entering the world.

Hence Paul in particular emphasises that Christ is γενόμενος ἐκ γυναικός (Gal. 4⁴), γενόμενος ἐκ σπέρματος Δαυίδ κατὰ σάρκα (Rom. 1³), ἐν ὁμοιώματι ἀνθρώπων γενόμενος καὶ σχήματι εὑρεθεὶς ὡς ἄνθρωπος (Phil. 2⁷). "Since then children in the world are sharers in flesh and blood (κεκοινώνηκεν αἵματος καὶ σαρκός), he also himself in like manner partook of the same, that through death he might bring to nought him that had the power of death, that is the devil ; and might reconcile all them who through fear of death were all their life-time subject to bondage. For verily he taketh not on him the nature of angels, but he taketh on him the seed of Abraham. Ὅθεν ὤφειλεν κατὰ πάντα τοῖς ἀδελφοῖς ὁμοιωθῆναι ἵνα ἐλεήμων γένηται" (Heb. 2¹⁴ᶠ·). In the early creeds, the whole series of pronouncements between the *conceptus de Spiritu sancto* and the *resurrexit tertia die*, namely *natus ex virgine, passus sub Pontio Pilato, crucifixus, mortuis, sepultus*, all have, in addition to their own meanings, the significance of emphasising the *vere homo*. We must stop our ears, declares Ignatius of Antioch, if anyone does not speak of the Jesus Christ who came of the tribe of David, of Mary, was really (ἀληθῶς) born, ate and drank, really suffered under Pontius Pilate, was really crucified and died before the eyes of all in heaven, on earth and under the earth, and so was also really raised from the dead (*Ad Trall.* 9, 1). The fathers insist that He is γεγονὼς πάντα ὅσα ἐστὶν ἄνθρωπος (Hippolytus, *C. Haer. Noeti* 17). His σῶμα was ἀληθινόν, ἐπεὶ ταὐτὸν ἦν τῷ ἡμετέρῳ (Athanasius, *Ep. ad Epict.*). *Non enim alterius naturae caro nostra et caro illius, nec alterius naturae anima nostra et anima illius. Hanc suscepit naturam, quam salvandam esse indicavit* (Augustine, *Sermo* 174, 2, 2). *Nullus homo est, fuit vel erit, cuius natura in illo assumpta non est* (*Conc. Carisiac.* I 853 c. 4, *Denz.* No. 319). For if the human nature ruled by death was one and that assumed by the Lord another, death would not have ceased to do its work, the sufferings of the σὰρξ θεοφόρος would have profited us nothing, He would not have slain sin in the flesh ; and we who died in Adam would not have been made alive in Christ (Basilius, *Ep. ad Sozopolitanos* 2). The Reconciler had to be of Adam's race, *ut satisfaciens idem sit qui peccator aut eiusdem generis. Aliter namque nec Adam nec genus eius satisfaciet pro se* (Anselm of Canterbury, *C.d.h.* II, 8).

In this way " God was in Christ " (2 Cor. 5¹⁹); He was the true light that cometh into the world (Jn. 1⁹) : ἐφανερώθη ἐν σαρκί (1 Tim. 3¹⁶) ; He was ἐρχόμενος ἐν σαρκί (1 Jn. 4² ; 2 Jn. 7). According to 2 Jn. 7, to deny this is to be " the deceiver and the antichrist." What the Bible calls revelation stands or falls with this " coming in the flesh." Any reservation, whether against God's Word being actively present in person, or against the active presence of God in person being here in the flesh in the likeness of man, makes revelation and reconciliation incomprehensible. And *vice versa*, the more definitely the two are seen to be one, the Word of God—flesh, or God Himself in person—in the likeness of man, the better is our realisation of what the Bible calls revelation.

The humanity of Christ alone is the revelation of the eternal Word, that tabernacle of the Logos of Jn. 1¹⁴ in which His glory is seen . . . *ut quae (anima) Deum in secreto maiestatis fulgentem videre non poteras, Deum in homine apparentem aspiceres, aspiciendo agnosceres, agnoscendo diligeres, diligens summo studio ad eius gloriam pervenire satageres* (Anselm of Canterbury, *Medit.* 8). *Longe dulcius est memoriae diligentis te, videre te ex matre virgine in tempora natum, quam in splendoribus ante luciferum a Patre genitum. . . . Quis mihi aufert locum in regno, ubi is omnipotens est, qui frater et caro mea est ? . . . Secura certa per omnem modum et in nullo temeraria praesumptio, quam formavit in mente consideratio humanitatis in Christo (Medit.* 12). . . . " Whether I will or not, when I listen to Christ, there is sketched in my heart a picture of a man hanging on a cross, just as my countenance is naturally sketched upon the water, when I look therein . . ." (Luther, *Wider die himml. Proph.* 1525, *W.A.* 18, 83, 9). *Humanitas enim illa sancta scala est nostra, per quam ascendimus ad Deum cognoscendum. . . . Igitur qui vult salubriter ascendere ad amorem et cognitionem Dei, dimittat regulas humanas et metaphysicas de divinitate cognoscenda et in Christi humanitate se ipsum primo exerceat. Impiissima enim temeritas est, ubi Deus ipse se humiliavit, ut fieret cognoscibilis, quod homo aliam sibi viam quaerat proprii ingenii consiliis usus (Hebr.-Br.* 1517–18 on Hebr. 1, 2, *Fi. Schol.* p. 2, 25). " For 'tis surely true that if we reckon apart from Christ how far God and man are apart from each other, we find that they are further apart than heaven and earth. But if we reckon in Christ, true God and man, we find that they are much more intimate than two brothers are to one another ; for God the Creator of heaven and the earth became true natural man, the eternal Father's Son became the temporal Virgin's son " (*Pred. üb. Jes.* 9, 1 f., 1532, *E.A.* 6, 42). " For where we believe firmly and would know naught better than that God was born of the Virgin Mary, sucked His mother's milk, did eat from her hands, received of her watchful care as any child is wont to do, and where such is our highest skill and wisdom, there followeth the benefit of Himself, and we draw this comfort from it, that we grasp, feel, and grope for the line, to wit, that God is not against us men. For were God thus hostile to the whole human race, He had not truly taken upon Himself poor, wretched, human nature. But now not only hath He created human nature, He also becometh Himself such a creature as is called and is true man. Because He doth this, so is there not merely wrath and displeasure with Him. For were He so hostile to the whole human race . . . He would have taken on Himself angelic nature, which is nearer God than human nature, and not been a man but an angel. . . . He could, of course, have assumed an angel's nature, or have created a nature that would have been neither God nor man and assumed that. But He would not do so, but assumed human nature and became man as I and thou art men, sucked His mother's the virgin Mary's milk, as I and thou did suck when we were put to our mother's breast. Every Christian who believeth such must rejoice at such knowledge" (*ib.* p. 40). "The Evangelist will not deal with the divine, almighty, eternal word of God nor speak of it, except in terms of the flesh and blood that walked on earth. He will not have us search all through the creation made by Him, so as to pursue, seek or speculate upon Him there as do the Platonists. But he will gather us from these same far-flying wandering thoughts into Christ . . ." (*Kirchenpostille* 1522, *Pred. üb. Joh.* 1[1t.] *W.A.* 10[1] 202, 9). "The deeper we can fetch Christ into the flesh, tne better it is" (*Pred. üb. Luc.* 2[22f.], 1531 *E.A.* 6, 155). "But here do we see that God so closely becometh the Friend of us men, that of no creature hath He so closely become the Friend as of us ; and again with no creature are we men made friends so closely as with God. Sun and moon do not come so near us as God does, for He hath come in our flesh and blood. God not alone ruleth over us, not alone moreover dwelleth in us, but hath likewise wished to become personally man" (*Pred. üb. Luc.* 1[26f.], 1552, *E.A.* 6, 201). "That is why He is also called Emmanuel, God with us : not alone because He is around us and with us and dwelleth among us, which were enough ; but because He also became what we are" (*ib.* p. 200).

2. That the Word became flesh means, indeed, that He became a man. But we have to be careful about the sense in which alone this can be said. If we ask what the Word became when in His incarnation, without ceasing to be the Word, He nevertheless ceased to be only the Word, and if we allow ourselves to say that He became flesh, we must note that primarily and of itself "flesh" does not imply a man, but human essence and existence, human kind and nature, humanity, *humanitas*, that which makes a man man as opposed to God, angel or animal.

Natura humana Christi est essentia seu substantia humana, qua Christus nobis hominibus coessentialis est (Polanus, *Synt. Theol. chr.* 1609, p. 2336).

"The Word became flesh" means primarily and of itself, then, that the Word became participant in human nature and existence. Human essence and existence became His. Now since this cannot be real except in the concrete reality of one man, it must at once be said that He became a man. But precisely this concrete reality of a man, this man, is itself the work of the Word, not His presupposition. It is not (in the adoptianist sense) as if first of all there had been a man there, and then the Son of God had become that man. What was there over against the Son of God, and as the presupposition of His work, was simply the potentiality of being in the flesh, being as a man. This is the possibility of every man. And here—for the individuality and uniqueness of human existence belong to the concept of human essence and existence—it is the one specific possibility of the first son of Mary. The Word appropriated this possibility to Himself as His own, and He realised it as such when He became Jesus. In so doing He did not cease to be what He was before, but He became what He was not before, a man, this man.

Christus non hominem, sed humanitatem, non personam sed naturam assumit (J. Wolleb, *Chr. Theol. comp.* 1626, I, c. 16 *can.* 3, 1). On good grounds appeal is made for this statement to Phil. 2[7], which with, it is true, a certain conscious reserve, speaks of the μορφὴ δούλου, of the ὁμοίωμα ἀνθρώπων, of being εὑρεθεὶς σχήματι ὡς ἄνθρωπος. On which be it noted that it is *naturam non ἐν ἰδέᾳ, non ἐν ψιλῇ θεωρίᾳ*, and not *naturam, ut est in omnibus individuis eiusdem speciei*, but *naturam ἐν ἀτόμῳ singulariter in uno certo individuo consideratam* (Polanus, *op. cit.* p. 2406).

As the Son of God made His own this one specific possibility of human essence and existence and made it a reality, this Man came into being, and He, the Son of God, became this Man. This Man was thus never a reality by Himself, and therefore, since the Son of God became this Man, He is not another or second being in Jesus Christ alongside of the Son of God.

Of Christ's *natura humana* we must therefore say *quae nunquam per se et sua propria subsistentia extra personam Filii Dei substiterit, sed eodem momento quo creata est, statim in persona Filii Dei in qua exempta fuit, exsistere coeperit : sic ut ne cogitandum quidem sit, humanam Christi naturam vel per unicum momentum antea substitisse quo assumpta est a λόγῳ* (Polanus, *op. cit.*).

" Jesus Christ very God and very Man " does not mean that in Jesus Christ God and a man were really side by side, but it means that Jesus Christ, the Son of God and thus Himself true God, is also a true Man. But this Man exists inasmuch as the Son of God is this Man—not otherwise. He exists because the Son of God appropriated and actualised His special possibility as a Man. The appropriation of human essence and existence in this special possibility by the Son of God, or the adoption and assumption of this special possibility of human essence and existence as that of the Son of God and the actualisation of it by Him and in Him—this is the creation and preservation, this is the sole ground of existence, of this Man, and therefore of Christ's flesh.

We must return to this again when explaining ἐγένετο. But even now we may take a look back from this point at our exposition in I, 3. The fact that the Word of God is and must remain the Subject in the sentence, " the Word became flesh," we there proved from the standpoint of His divinity. We have the same result now from the side of His humanity. It has no independent existence alongside of the Word. It exists only in the Man who as the creature of the Word is the Word Himself. What is added to the Word in His incarnation is not a second reality alongside of Him, but His own work upon Himself, which actually consists in this, that He assumed human existence. In this closer definition of the concept of the flesh or human nature of Christ, Augustine was able to make it beautifully clear how the incarnation of the Word is so to speak the prototype of justifying grace ; the Word of God is related to the human nature, as grace is related to sinful man. *Quid enim natura humana in homine Christo meruit, ut in unitatem personae unici filii Dei singulariter esset assumpta ? Quae bona voluntas, cuius boni propositi studium, quae bona opera praecesserunt quibus mereretur iste homo una fieri persona cum Deo ? Nunquid antea fuit homo et hoc ei singulare beneficium praestitum est cum singulariter promereretur Deum ? Nempe ex quo esse homo coepit, non aliud coepit esse homo quam Dei Filius. . . . Unde naturae humanae tanta gloria, nullis praecedentibus meritis sine dubitatione gratuita, nisi quia magna hic et sola Dei gratia fideliter et sobrie considerantibus evidenter ostenditur, ut intelligant homines per eandem se justificari a peccatis, per quam* *factus est ut homo Christus nullum habere posset peccatum ? . . . Veritas quippe ipsa, unigenitus Dei Filius (non gratia sed natura) gratia suscepit hominem tanta unitate personae, ut idem ipse esset etiam hominis filius (Enchir.* 36). *Ipse namque unus Christus et Dei Filius semper natura et hominis filius qui ex tempore assumptus est gratia. Nec sic assumptus est, ut prius creatus post assumeretur, sed ut ipsa assumptione crearetur (C. serm. Arian.* 8).*

Thus the reality of Jesus Christ is that God Himself in person is actively present in the flesh. God Himself in person is the Subject of a real human being and acting. And just because God is the Subject of it, this being and acting are real. They are a genuinely and truly human being and acting. Jesus Christ is not a demigod. He is not an angel. Nor is He an ideal man. He is a man as we are, equal to us as a creature, as a human individual, but also equal to us in the state and condition into which our disobedience has brought us. And in being what we are He is God's Word. Thus as one of us, yet the one of us who is Himself God's Word in person, He represents God to us and He represents us to God. In this way He is God's revelation to us and our reconciliation with God.

3. So far we have looked upon σάρξ as a description of neutral human nature. This fact, too, that the Word became flesh, we have had to establish in its generality. But what the New Testament calls σάρξ includes not only the concept of man in general but also, assuming and including this general concept, the narrower concept of the man who is liable to the judgment and verdict of God, who having become incapable of knowing and loving God must incur the wrath of God, whose existence has become one exposed to death because he has sinned against God. Flesh is the concrete form of human nature marked by Adam's fall, the concrete form of that entire world which, when seen in the light of Christ's death on the cross, must be regarded as the old world already past and gone, the form of the destroyed nature and existence of man as they have to be reconciled with God.

" The Word became flesh " in this narrower sense means that the divine Word puts Himself on the side of His own adversary. His relation to the world which inconceivably resists Him as its Creator is, of course, one of opposition (Jn. 1⁵), but not merely one of opposition. The opposition created on the one hand by the inconceivable presence of His divinity as the light of revelation and on the other by the world's inconceivable darkness, its unwillingness to receive Him, is already overcome—which is more inconceivable than either—by the presence of the Logos exactly where men are. He came to His own (Jn. 1¹¹) and His own—His own lieth in darkness—received Him not ; nevertheless He came to His own. The true Light came into the world (Jn. 1⁹), and it shineth in the darkness (Jn. 1⁵). So to real men living in the world and in darkness there can be given power (ἐξουσία), which they do not possess of themselves, to be children of God (Jn. 1¹²f.).

The Word is not only the eternal Word of God but " flesh " as well, i.e., all that we are and exactly like us even in our opposition to Him. It is because of this that He makes contact with us and is accessible for us. In this way, and only in this way, is He God's revelation to us. He would not be revelation if He were not man. And He would not be man if He were not "flesh" in this definite sense. That the Word became "flesh" in this definite sense, this consummation of God's condescension, this inconceivability which is greater than the inconceivability of the divine majesty and the inconceivability of human darkness put together : this is the revelation of the Word of God.

Calvin is right in the following comment on Jn. 1¹⁴. *Ostendere voluit, ad quam vilem et abiectam conditionem Dei Filius nostra causa ex caelestis suae gloriae celsitudine descenderit. Scriptura, quum de homine contemptim loquitur, carnem appellat. Quum autem tanta sit distantia inter spiritualem sermonis Dei gloriam et putidas carnis nostrae sordes, eousque se Filius Dei submisit, ut carnem istam tot miseriis obnoxiam, susciperet* (C.R. 47, 13). *Pro immensa gratia ad sordidos et ignobiles se aggregat Christus* (Instit. II 13, 2 : cf. M. Dominicé, *L'humanité de Jésus d'après Calvin*, 1933 p. 121 f.). *In summa, sub nomine carnis non modo verus integer et perfectus homo intelligitur, nobis* ὁμοούσιος, *sed etiam humilis, misera ac prima hominis conditio . . . comprehenditur* (Syn. pur. Theol., Leiden 1624, Disp. 25, 14). In fact, " he thought it not robbery to be equal with God, but ἑαυτὸν ἐκένωσεν μορφὴν δούλου λαβών (Phil. 2⁷). God sent his Son ἐν ὁμοιώματι σαρκὸς ἁμαρτίας, to condemn sin in the flesh (Rom. 8³). Him who knew no sin he hath made to be sin for us, it may even be said (2 Cor. 5²¹). And what do the Evangelists fail to record of Him ? " He is beside himself " (Mk. 3²¹). " He hath Beelzebub " (Mk. 3²²). " A man gluttonous and a wine-bibber, a friend of publicans and sinners " (Mt. 11¹⁹). " He deceiveth the people " (Jn. 7¹²). " He blasphemeth " (Mt. 9³ ; cf. 26⁶⁵). They are not afraid to speak of the suspicion already attaching to His parentage (Mt. 1¹⁹). At the beginning of His life they let Him " fulfil all righteousness," that is, take upon Himself the baptism of repentance (Mt. 3¹⁵). They let Him be crucified between twc malefactors (Mt. 27³⁸). He bears away the sin of the world, but He does bear it (Jn. 1²⁹). It can all be summarised in the terrible saying of Gal. 3¹³, γενόμενος ὑπὲρ ἡμῶν κατάρα.. That He was innocent of it, without sin of His own, that the whole accusation does not touch Him but us, and Him only in our stead : that is another question which will require separate treatment. But He became a curse for us. He was not a sinful man. But inwardly and outwardly His situation was that of a sinful man. He did nothing that Adam did. But He lived life in the form it must take on the basis and assumption of Adam's act. He bore innocently what Adam and all of us in Adam have been guilty of. Freely He entered into solidarity and necessary association with our lost existence. Only in this way " could " God's revelation to us, our reconciliation with Him, manifestly become an event in Him and by Him. " In that he suffered and himself was tempted, he is able (δύναται) to succour them that are tempted " (Heb. 2¹⁸). " We have not an high priest which cannot be touched with the feeling (συμπαθῆσαι μὴ δυνάμενον) of our infirmities, but was tempted in all things like as we are (κατὰ πάντα καθ' ὁμοιότητα), yet without sin " (Heb. 4¹⁵), who " can have compassion " (μετριοπαθεῖν δυνάμενος) on the ignorant and them that are out of the way, for that he himself also is compassed with infirmity, and by reason thereof he ought (δι' αὐτὴν ὀφείλει), as for the people, so also for himself, to offer for sins " (Heb. 5²ᶠ·).

Note : it is here that we find ourselves at the point at which the biblical doctrine of the incarnation of the Word and the familiar parallels in the history of religions part company. There are also incarnations of Isis and Osiris ; there is an incarnation in Buddha and in Zoroaster. But it is only the New Testament that says " he hath made him to be sin " and " he became a curse for us." Only here do we have so strict a concept of Emmanuel, of revelation and reconciliation.

We must pay all the more attention to the fact that the New Testament does say this, that it speaks of this divine solidarity and necessary association with man. To deviate from this, to try to make God's becoming flesh merely a becoming man or even a hero, is to descend to the level of the religions : they can all do this.

The Early Church and its theology often went too far in its well-intentioned effort to equate these statements with those about the sinlessness of Jesus. But there must be no weakening or obscuring of the saving truth that the nature which God assumed in Christ is identical with our nature as we see it in the light of the Fall. If it were otherwise, how could Christ be really like us ? What concern would we have with Him ? We stand before God characterised by the Fall. God's Son not only assumed our nature but He entered the concrete form of our nature, under which we stand before God as men damned and lost. He did not produce and establish this form differently from all of us ; though innocent, He became guilty ; though without sin He was made to be sin. But these things must not cause us to detract from His complete solidarity with us and in that way to remove Him to a distance from us. We must not agree with Gregory of Nyssa (*Or. cat.* 15 f.), when he bases his statement that the incarnation is not unworthy of God upon the intrinsic goodness of human nature itself, upon the fact that birth and death in themselves do not involve suffering in the strict and proper sense. Our comment must be that our nature is not a human nature good in itself. We cannot agree with Honorius I when in the monothelite controversy he declared : *A divinitate assumpta est nostra natura, non culpa, illa (natura) profecto, quae ante peccatum creata est, non quae post praevaricationem vitiata* (*Denz.* No. 251). We can only comment that our nature is now *natura vitiata*. On the other hand, we cannot agree when he strangely weakened his already quoted comment on Jn. 1¹⁴ by this addition: *Caeterum " caro " minime hic pro corrupta natura accipitur (ut saepe apud Paulum) sed pro homine mortali.* How far, then, was it a *vilis et abjecta conditio* to which the Son of God condescended ? Why does Scripture always speak *contemptim* of the flesh unless *natura corrupta* is really meant ? The weakening involved, if any other assertion is made, emerges clearly in the proof given on the point by the *Syn. pur. theol.* Leiden 1624 *Disp.* 25, 18 : *Non enim conveniebat humanam naturam peccato obnoxiam Filio Dei uniri. Non conveniebat ?* If that is true, then precisely in the critical definition of our nature Christ is not a man like us, and so He has not really come to us and represented us. In this *non conveniebat*, by which God's honour is obviously being protected against any smirch, does there not lurk a secret denial of the miracle of His condescension and thereby of God's honour itself, which according to Scripture celebrates its loftiest triumph in its very condescension ? But, of course, this weakening is also involved in Luther's refusal to realise the application of the words of Is. 52¹⁴ and 53² to the personal form of Christ : *quia fuit integer, sanissimi corporis, mundissimae carnis, sine peccato conceptus* (*Enarr.* 53 *cap. Iesaiae* 1544 *E.A. ex. op. lat.* 23, 457). So, too, on the basis of passages like Ps. 45³ and Col. 1¹⁸, Lutheran dogmaticians thought to ascribe specifically to Christ's human nature a *singularis animae et corporis excellentia ac* ἐξοχή *qua reliquos homines superavit,* supreme health (*summam bonam et aequabilem corporis temperiem seu habitudinem*), immortality, and *summam formae elegentiam ac venustatem* (Quenstedt, *Theol. did. pol.* 1685 III *c.* 3 *m.* 1, *sect.* 1, *thes.* 14 and 16). Hollaz even claims to know (*Ex. theol. acroam.* 1706 III *sect.* I *c.* 3, *qu.* 12) that to these perfections there belongs the fact that Christ never laughed (*a risu abstinuit*). We cannot but seriously ask whether and how far in this whole method serious account is being taken of the reality of Christ's humanity and so of revelation.

All earlier theology, up to and including the Reformers and their successors, exercised at this point a very understandable reserve, calculated to dilute the offence, but also to weaken the high positive meaning of passages like 2 Cor. 5²¹,

Gal. 3¹³. In virtue of its distinctive moralism, modern theology as a whole is obviously unable to change this. But we have to admit that at the very heart of it certain sorties have actually been made in this direction. Above all, mention must here be made of Gottfried Menken, who " dismissing all the definitions of human doctrine on the person of Christ " concluded from Rom. 8³ that " the Son of God when He came into the world did not then assume a human nature such as this nature was when it came forth from God's hand, before the Fall, before it had in Adam . . . become sinful and mortal. On the contrary, it was a human nature such as was in Adam after the Fall and is in all his successors " (*Homilie üb Hebr.* 9¹³ᵗ·, Works, vol. 3, p. 332 f. ; cf. " *Über die eherne Schlange* " 1812, Works, vol. 6, p. 391 f.). The same doctrine was delivered about 1827 by the Scottish theologian Edward Irving and it led to his excommunication : " This point of issue is simply this, whether Christ's flesh had the grace of sinlessness and incorruption from its own nature or from the indwelling of the Holy Ghost ; I say the latter. . . . It was manhood fallen which He took up into His Divine person, in order to prove the grace and the might of Godhead in redeeming it." So the humanity was without guilt but with everything else that belongs to man, and was " held like a fortress in immaculate purity by the Godhead within." " Christ was holy in spite of the law of the flesh working in Him as in another man ; but never in Him prevailing " (cited by H. R. Mackintosh, *The Doctrine of the Person of Jesus Christ*, 1931 p. 277 : cf. *PRE.*³ vol. 9 p. 427). We find in J. C. K. v. Hofmann of Erlangen the statement that Christ will " have desired His human nature to be the means of manifesting His personal communion with God, but manifesting it within human nature as limited and conditioned by sin " (*Der Schriftbeweis*, I, 1852, p. 45). Or according to the second edition of the same book : " He will thus have so made human nature His own, that in it He belonged to humanity as it was in consequence of sin, but without being a sinner, and that He used it as the means of manifesting His eternal communion with God, but manifesting it within human nature as limited and conditioned by creation and sin " (p. 46). In the same way, according to H. F. Kohlbrügge, Christ was " born flesh of flesh, not by a birth pure in the fleshly sense to cover up a quasi-original sin, but flesh as we are flesh, i.e., not ' spirit,' but utterly emptied of God, removed from the sphere of God's glory ; held in the very same condemnation or eternal death and curse as we are from our birth ; given over to him that hath the power of this death, that is the devil, as we are from the start. So He was born for us of a woman and in this whole nature of ours, with all human affections, appetitions and needs. He was made sin for us here in the likeness of a flesh of sin in our stead " (*Betr. üb. das I. Kap. des Ev. nach Matth.* 1844, p. 92). Emmanuel, God with us, means that the Word was made flesh. But flesh means that " God has adopted a lost humanity, sinful men and women " (p. 132). Again, with a bolder interpretation of the situation or position of sinful man, as Christ assumed it for our benefit : " Why was the death on the cross cursed by God ? In it the Most High God has willed to condescend to men on earth, wherefore it behoves men to remain on the ground and to live by the Word, by grace, by faith ; but this man refuses to do, he will always be soaring above his reach, so he comes to grief and the curse overtakes him. For thus saith God in Exodus, 19¹², ' Take heed to yourselves, that ye go not up into the mount ! ' Hence it is a God-deriding enterprise of the flesh to aim at raising itself up to God by its own power and wisdom and righteousness ; and it remains suspended between earth and heaven. For these sins of ours over which death impends our Lord died, hanging between heaven and earth, with hands and feet tight nailed, i.e., as one who can accomplish nothing " (*Fr. u. Antw. zum Heid. Kat.*, 1851, *Quest.* 39). To the same effect Edward Bohl writes : " The Logos entered our condition thus alienated from God, or the nature which sinned. But our condition is that through Adam we have passed into guiltiness and become liable to death, in consequence of which we

are enemies of God and hated by Him. . . . Either the Son of God brings salvation to pass under conditions of life like ours or else everyone has to start all
over again and to fulfil independently God's claims upon us " (*Dogmatik*, 1887,
p. 299, 302). And similarly we must say with H. Bezzel : " Jesus' becoming
man had never redeemed us, only His becoming flesh. . . . His becoming man
had but intensified the pain of the question, ' Why could'st thou not also be a
man like Him ? ' and He had but consummated the proof that of course we
could have been so, if we had not fallen. His becoming man would have been
a sneer at my misery, as surely as a man in the glow of health and strength,
when he is brought to a sickbed, will always be felt like a pain by the sick." " Not
alone the form of a man, but the form of a manhood dishonoured and devalued
by sin, the form into which sin has long and fiercely thrust its sting and on which
the world has stamped its awesome memories, the form ofttimes so utterly unlike
a man, so deformed and worthless and unconsecrated." " He not merely bore
the body, but the body of weakness, and in virtue of the divine realism chose
Himself not merely the being of man but the actual being of the entire solid
poverty of cosmic impotence, the entire limitations of fleshly being." He experienced " humanity in caricature," He entered upon " the entire seriousness of
man's perverted image, He took the form of a servant, with which sin stamps
its slaves." " The Christian's comfort is not that He was a man, but that He
ceased to be the man with whom God was well pleased and was forced into the
caricature of man produced by sin." " Thy pervertedness is only a weak copy
of His inward impoverishment and desolation ; He not only bore sin, but He
became sin itself " (quoted by J. Rupprecht, *H. Bezzel als Theologe*, 1925, p. 61 f.).

4. In becoming the same as we are, the Son of God is the same in
quite a different way from us ; in other words, in our human being
what we do is omitted, and what we omit is done. This Man would
not be God's revelation to us, God's reconciliation with us, if He were
not, as true Man, the true, unchangeable, perfect God Himself. He
is the true God because and so far as it has pleased the true God to
adopt the true being of man. But this is the expression of a claim
upon this being, a sanctification and blessing of this being, which excludes sin. In it God Himself is the Subject. How can God sin,
deny Himself to Himself, be against Himself as God, want to be a
god and so fall away from Himself in the way in which our sin is
against Him, in which it happens from the very first and continually
in the event of our existence ? True, the Word assumes our human
existence, assumes flesh, i.e., He exists in the state and position, amid
the conditions, under the curse and punishment of sinful man. He
exists in the place where we are, in all the remoteness not merely of
the creature from the Creator, but of the sinful creature from the
Holy Creator. Otherwise His action would not be a revealing, a
reconciling action. He would always be for us an alien word. He
would not find us or touch us. For we live in that remoteness. But
it is He, the Word of God, who assumes our human existence, assumes
our flesh, exists in the place where we exist. Otherwise His action
would again not be a revealing, a reconciling action. Otherwise He
would bring us nothing new. He would not help us. He would leave
us in the remoteness. Therefore in our state and condition He does
not do what underlies and produces that state and condition, or what

we in that state and condition continually do. Our unholy human existence, assumed and adopted by the Word of God, is a hallowed and therefore a sinless human existence ; in our unholy human existence the eternal Word draws near to us. In the hallowing of our unholy human existence He draws supremely and helpfully near to us.

That God sent His own Son ἐν ὁμοιώματι σαρκὸς ἁμαρτίας is at once explained in Rom. 8³ by περὶ ἁμαρτίας, i.e., for sin, in matters of sin and so not in order to do sin Himself ; and then the main clause unambiguously declares that κατέκρινεν (ὁ θεὸς) τὴν ἁμαρτίαν ἐν τῇ σαρκί. That is, in the likeness of flesh (unholy flesh, marked by sin), there happens the unlike, the new and helpful thing, that sin is condemned by not being committed, by being omitted, by full obedience now being found in the very place where otherwise sin necessarily and irresistibly takes place. The meaning of the incarnation is that now in the flesh that is not done which all flesh does. " He hath made him to be sin for us " (2 Cor. 5²¹) does not mean that He made Him a man who also sins again —what could that signify " for us " ?—but that He put Him in the position of a sinner by way of exchange (καταλλάσσων, in the sense of the Old Testament sin-offering). But whom did He put in that position ? τὸν μὴ γνόντα ἁμαρτίαν. Because this man who knew no sin is " made to be sin," this " making " signifies the act of a divine offering περὶ ἁμαρτίας, ὑπὲρ ἡμῶν, judgment upon sin, its removal. *Ipse ergo peccatum, ut nos iustitia, nec nostra sed Dei, nec in nobis sed in ipso, sicut ipse peccatum, non suum, sed nostrum* (Augustine, *Enchir.* 41). This is the obvious definition of *vere homo* on this side—but its definition, not its limitation, not its secret sublimation. The commission of sin as such is not an attribute of true human existence as such, whether from the standpoint of its creation by God or from that of the fact that it is flesh on account of the Fall. And that is why it says that He was tempted in all things like as we are χωρὶς ἁμαρτίας (Heb. 4¹⁵). He is the suitable Highpriest for us because He is· holy, harmless, undefiled, κεχωρισμένος ἀπὸ τῶν ἁμαρτωλῶν (Heb. 7²⁶). The Lamb of God which taketh away the sin of the world is " a lamb without blemish and without spot " (1 Pet. 1¹⁹) ; ἁμαρτίαν οὐκ ἐποίησεν (1 Pet. 2²²). He was manifested (ἐφανερώθη) to take away sins, καὶ ἁμαρτία ἐν αὐτῷ οὐκ ἔστιν (1 Jn. 3⁵). The prince of this world cometh—καὶ ἐν ἐμοὶ οὐκ ἔχει οὐδὲν (Jn. 14³⁰). And " which of you convinceth me of sin ? " (Jn. 8⁴⁶). It was on just these lines that the Early Church developed its thought and teaching : *Confirmamus eam fuisse carnem in Christo, cuius natura est in homine peccatrix, et sic in illa peccatum evacuatum, quod in Christo sine peccato habeatur, quae in homine sine peccato non habebatur* (Tertullian, *De carne Christi*, 16).

But if we ask where the sinlessness, or (positively) the obedience of Christ, is to be seen, it is not enough to look for it in this man's excellences of character, virtues or good works. For we can only repeat that the New Testament certainly did not present Jesus Christ as the moral ideal, and if we apply the canons usually applied to the construction of a moral ideal, we may easily fall into certain difficulties not easy of solution, whether with the Jesus of the Synoptics or with the Jesus of John's Gospel. Jesus Christ's obedience consists in the fact that He willed to be and was only this one thing with all its consequences, God in the flesh, the divine bearer of the burden which man as a sinner must bear.

According to Phil. 2⁸ this was found in His human form : " He humbled himself, by becoming obedient unto death, even the death of the cross." He learned obedience ἀφ ὧν ἔπαθεν (Heb. 5⁸) " For the joy that was set before him he endured the cross, despising the shame " (Heb. 12²). " Therefore doth my Father love me, because I lay down my life " (Jn. 10¹⁷). We learn from the story of Gethsemane what its opposite would be, the sin which Jesus does not do. It would have consisted in His willing against God's will that " this cup " should pass from Him (Mt. 26³⁹). And positively, from the temptation story, it would have consisted in His exercise (and consequent denial) of His Sonship to God in the manner and style of a human hero for His own advantage and glory, i.e., in worshipping the devil (Mt. 4¹ᶠ·). That is why Peter, wishing to restrain Him from going up to Jerusalem, receives the answer : " Thou thinkest not of the ordinance of God but of the ordinance of men " (Mt. 16²³). And that is why the rich young man is rejected with his greeting, " Good master." " Why callest thou me good ? There is none good but God alone " (Mk. 10¹⁷ᶠ·). " The Son of man came not to be ministered unto, but to minister, and to give his life a ransom for many " (Mk. 10⁴⁵). That this should be the rule of His life and that it should be kept is the sanctification, the obedience of the Man Jesus.

Jesus' sinlessness obviously consists in His direct admission of the meaning of the incarnation. Unlike Adam, as the " second Adam " He does not wish to be as God, but in Adam's nature acknowledges before God an Adamic being, the state and position of fallen man, and bears the wrath of God which must fall upon this man, not as a fate but as a righteous necessary wrath. He does not avoid the burden of this state and position but takes the conditions and consequences upon Himself.

It is just this that we continually refuse to do. In this consists the rebellion of sin, in which daily and hourly man repeats the ancient rebellion of Adam. For as Adam refused to preserve the order of Paradise, i.e., the limits of his creatureliness, man as Adam's child refuses to fit into the order of restoration. He will not understand and admit that he is flesh, stands under judgment, and can only live by grace. He will not admit that God is right in His verdict upon him, and then cling entirely to this God's mercy. At the very least he insists upon still standing and walking on his own feet. He wants, at least in co-operation with what God does, to " save his life " (σῶσαι τὴν ψυχὴν αὐτοῦ, Mk. 8³⁵). By that very process he loses his life. On that very rock he suffers shipwreck. For by that very process sin in the flesh is not judged, but rather is committed afresh. By that very process man does afresh what Adam did. It is otherwise with Jesus. He made good what Adam perverted. He judged sin in the flesh by recognising the order of reconciliation, i.e., put in a sinner's position He bowed to the divine verdict and commended Himself solely to the grace of God. That is His hallowing, His obedience, His sinlessness. Thus it does not consist in an ethical heroism, but precisely in a renunciation of any heroism, including the ethical. He is sinless not in spite of, but just because of His being the friend of publicans and sinners and His dying between the malefactors. In this sinlessness He is according to Paul the " second Adam " (1 Cor. 15⁴⁵ᶠ·), the One who by His obedience sets the many before God as righteous, whose righteous act confronts in reconciliation the transgressions of the many who by following Adam are involved in hopeless death. In this righteous act there is achieved a justification for all, a justification that brings life (δικαίωσις ζωῆς, Rom. 5¹²ᶠ· ; 1 Cor. 15²²). By the Word of God becoming Adam the continuity of this Adamic existence is broken and the continuity of a new Adamic existence is opened up. But the continuity of the old Adamic existence is broken, just because unshielded by illusions, circumvented by no artifices, its truth is simply recognised, its needs are borne openly and readily.

This is the revelation of God in Christ. For where man admits his lost state and lives entirely by God's mercy—which no man did, but only the God-Man Jesus Christ has done—God Himself is manifest. And by that God reconciled the world to Himself. For where man claims no right for himself, but concedes all rights to God alone—which no man did, but only the God-Man Jesus Christ has done—the world is drawn out of its enmity towards God and reconciled to God.

Upon the actual basis of the New Testament understanding of the statement as to the sinlessness of Jesus we cannot describe the questions involved as altogether opaque, even though we cannot and will not try to solve the mystery to which they point. On the one hand the New Testament has treated the *vere homo* so seriously that it has portrayed the obedience of Jesus throughout as a genuine struggle to obey, as a seeking and finding. In Lk. 2⁴⁰ it speaks of a " growing and waxing strong," and in Lk. 2⁵² it speaks of a προκόπτειν (strictly speaking, an extension by blows, as a smith stretches metal with hammers, *Griech. H.W.B.* by Pape-Sengebusch, *s.v.*) of Jesus in wisdom, in stature and in favour with God and men. Moreover the temptation narrative (Mt. 4¹ᶠᶠ·) obviously describes the very opposite of a mock battle, and it would be wrong to conceive of it as a merely " external molestation by Satan," to reject it as an " inward temptation and trial " of Jesus. To the *vere homo* there also belongs what we call man's inner nature. (Opposing B. Bartmann, *Lehrb. d. Dogm.*⁷ vol. I, 1928, p. 360.) Equally vital is the saying περίλυπός ἐστιν ἡ ψυχή μου (Mk. 14³⁴), and " My God, my God, why hast thou forsaken me ? " (Mk. 15³⁴). Jesus " in the days of his flesh, when he had offered up prayers and supplications with strong crying and tears unto him that was able to save him from death, καίπερ ὢν υἱός yet learned obedience by the things which he suffered " (Heb. 5⁷ᶠ·). The New Testament has nowhere attempted to describe this " learning," and it is always an impertinence on our part to attempt to imitate it. The New Testament simply points to the facts of the case. But from the facts of the case no deductions can be made without obscuring the point at issue in the assertion of sinlessness. The point is that, faced with God, Jesus did not run away from the state and situation of fallen man, but took it upon Himself, lived it and bore it Himself as the eternal Son of God. How could He have done so, if in His human existence He had not been exposed to real inward temptation and trial, if like other men He had not trodden an inner path, if He had not cried to God and wrestled with God in real inward need ? It was in this wrestling, in which He was in solidarity with us to the uttermost, that there was done that which is not done by us, the will of God. " In that he himself hath suffered, being tempted, he is able to succour them that are tempted " (Heb. 2¹⁸)—not otherwise. From this may be seen how right was the attitude of those who in the so-called monothelite controversy of the 7th century upheld and eventually led to victory the doctrine that along with the true human nature of the God-Man there must likewise not be denied His true, human will, different from the will of God although never independent of it.

Of course, the meaning of the New Testament is that Jesus cannot sin, that the eternal Word of God is immune from temptation even in the flesh, that Jesus is bound to win in this struggle. But that this is the case is the mystery of revelation which it attests. It is the truth of the event of the reality of Jesus Christ. It can be understood only as this truth breaking forth in event. The sinlessness of Jesus thus does not admit of a systematic connexion with the fact that here a true man had a serious struggle, but only of establishment and acknowledgment in its historical connexion with that fact. He who struggled here and won is He who was bound to win, He who when He entered the contest

had already won. He really had no awareness of sin. That is the truth of the
vere Deus. The New Testament makes this assertion because it is aware of His
resurrection. The resurrection was the revelation of the *vere Deus*, the revelation
of the fact that the Word was made *flesh*. But this revelation is in contrast to
its background that the Word was made flesh. To understand, we shall have
to travel together, here as everywhere, the way indicated from the cross to the
resurrection of Christ.

III

" The Word became flesh," ἐγένετο, we read in Jn. 1¹⁴. To this
decisive factor in the whole christological question we must now turn.
" The Word became "—that points to the centre, to the mystery of
revelation, the happening of the inconceivable fact that God is among
us and with us. If there is any synthetic judgment at all it is this
one, that " the Word became." But can or will the Word of God
become ? Does He not surrender thereby His divinity ? Or, if He
does not surrender it, what does becoming mean ? By what figures
of speech or concepts is this becoming of the Word of God to be
properly described ? " The Word became "—if that is true, and true
in such a way that a real becoming is thereby expressed without the
slightest surrender of the divinity of the Word, its truth is that of a
miraculous act, an act of mercy on the part of God.

That this is the case results exegetically from the context of Jn. 1¹⁴. The
statements about the Logos which precede the verse are to the effect that He
was (ἦν), and was in the beginning, and with God, and in such a way that He
was Himself God (Jn. 1¹) ; and next, most impressively, that by Him all things
became (δι' αὐτοῦ τὰ πάντα ἐγένετο), and without Him did not anything become
that actually became (Jn. 1³). Becoming is therefore ascribed to His creatures,
as distinct from Him, the Creator. If they all became by Him, there is nothing
we expect less than to hear that He, too, is Himself the subject of an ἐγένετο
or becoming, that He can exist Himself in the same way as the things created
by Him. Further, in Jn. 1⁶ᶠ·, ἐγένετο describes the historical appearance of the
witness John. As " a man sent from God," who was not the light, i.e., not
revelation, but only the witness to it, he is quite clearly distinguished from the
Logos. And yet it must also be said of the Logos that ἐγένετο, He appeared in
history, just as the Baptist appeared shortly before Him, and as did many
others before and after Him. Finally in Jn. 1¹²ᶠ· it speaks of those that believe
on His name and thus receive Him, to whom He gave ἐξουσία to become (γενέσθαι)
what they obviously are, the children of God, not by nature, but solely by the
grace of God. And then the Giver takes His place with the recipients and to
Him Himself a γενέσθαι is ascribed. The whole problem of Jn. 1¹⁴ is thus expressed in this copula ἐγένετο. The very thing happens which is the last thing
we should expect after what has gone before (although for the Evangelist it is,
of course, the presupposition of all that has gone before). The divine Word
leaves His eternal throne and descends below, where the creatures, where His
witnesses, where His called and chosen are. His action is that He, so to speak,
loses Himself among those who can still be only the objects of His action. He
the eternal Subject now exists—a stumbling-block to all Jewish ears and foolishness to all Greek ears—just as anything else or as anyone else exists. That is
the meaning of ὁ λόγος ἐγένετο, if the words are taken in the sense they bear in
the context, that is, if no reduction is made which softens or weakens either

the ὁ λόγος or the ἐγένετο. If not, a challenge is offered to think together these two concepts, with their strictly opposite contents, as definitions of one and the same subject. That Subject is Jesus Christ whose glory it is the aim of the Fourth Gospel and of the New Testament generally to attest. It is in respect of this Subject and only this Subject that we arrive at the statement ὁ λόγος ἐγένετο. This Subject and only this Subject is indicated by the statement. This at once implies that we are not challenged to combine the two concepts in a third higher concept and so to abolish their object. In this case there can be no higher object in which the opposition between the two concepts would disappear. In place of this higher concept stands the name of Jesus Christ. In this case, therefore, to " think together " can mean only the responsibility which we owe to this name, so long as we keep to what is already given us in Scripture. It can mean only to think both the ὁ λόγος and the ἐγένετο with the strict simultaneity with which they are given us in Scripture.

To understand the miraculous act of this becoming, we must reach back to what we have acknowledged under I, that it is to be understood as an act of the Word who is the Lord. As from its own side the humanity has no capacity, power or worthiness by which it appears suited to become the humanity of the Word, there is likewise no becoming which as such can be the becoming of the Word. His becoming is not an event which in any sense befalls Him, in which in any sense He is determined from without by something else. If it includes in itself His suffering, His veiling and humiliation unto death —and it does include this in itself—even so, as suffering, it is His will and work. It is not composed of action and reaction. It is action even in the suffering of reaction, the act of majesty even as veiling. He did not become humbled, but He humbled Himself. Accordingly we have to give a closer explanation of the act peculiar to this miracle, the incarnation of the Word. As the Word of God becomes flesh He assumes or adopts or incorporates human being into unity with His divine being, so that this human being, as it comes into being, becomes as a human being the being of the Word of God.

In the sense of the concept familiar to us, we can therefore assert " becoming " only of the human being, in order by that very means to give expression to the inconceivable becoming of the divine Word. The expression " assumption," which in accordance with an early conceptual tradition we use to give an appropriate description of ἐγένετο, we find already in Phil 2⁷, μορφὴν δούλου λαβών, and in Heb. 2¹⁶ σπέρματος Ἀβραὰμ ἐπιλαμβάνεται. Its prominence must date from as early as the 2nd century. We find it in *Pseudo-Justin's Cohort. ad gentiles*, 38, ἀναλαβὼν ἄνθρωπον ; in Tertullian, *Adv. Prax.* 27, *indutus carnem* ; in Origen, Περὶ ἀρχῶν, I, 2, 1, *Humana natura, quam* . . . *suscepit* ; in Hippolytus, *De Antichristo*, 4, ἐνεδύσατο τὴν ἁγίαν σάρκα. The standing Latin term in mediæval and early Protestant scholasticism was that of *assumere* or *assumptio*.

If we paraphrase the statement " the Word became flesh " by " the Word assumed flesh," we guard against the misinterpretation already mentioned, that in the incarnation the Word ceases to be entirely Himself and equal to Himself, i.e., in the full sense of Word of God. God cannot cease to be God. The incarnation is inconceivable, but it is not absurd, and it must not be explained as an absurdity. The inconceivable fact in it is that without ceasing to be God the

Word of God is among us in such a way that He takes over human being, which is His creature, into His own being and to that extent makes it His own being. As His own predicate along with His original predicate of divinity, He takes over human being into unity with Himself. And it is by the paraphrase " the Word assumed flesh " that the second misunderstanding is also guarded against, that in the incarnation, by means of a union of divine and human being and nature, a third is supposed to arise. Jesus Christ as the Mediator between God and man is not a third, midway between the two. In that case God has at once ceased to be God and likewise He is not a man like us. But Jesus is the Mediator, the God-Man, in such a way that He is God and Man. This " and " is the inconceivable act of the " becoming " in the incarnation. It is not the act of the human being and nature. How can it be capable of such an act ? Nor is it the act either of the divine being and nature as such. It is not the divine nature that acts where God acts. But it is the triune God in His divine nature, One in the three modes of existence of Father, Son and Holy Spirit. So, too, in this assumption of human being by the eternal Word. He, the eternal Word, in virtue of His own will and power as well as in virtue of the will and power of Father and Holy Spirit, becomes flesh. The unity into which the human nature is assumed is thus unity with the Word, and only to that extent—because this Word is the eternal Word—the union of the human with the divine nature. But the eternal Word is with the Father and the Holy Spirit the unchangeable God Himself and so incapable of any change or admixture. Unity with Him, the " becoming " of the Word, cannot therefore mean the origination of a third between Word and flesh, but only the assumption of the flesh by the Word.

Unitionis formale exprimit τὸ ἐγένετο, *quod non per transmutationem aut conversionem, sed per assumptionem explicandum est* (Quenstedt, *Theol. did. pol.* 1685, III, *c.* 3. *m.* 1, *sect.* 1, *thes.* 23). Thus by the whole of early dogmatics the unity of God and man in Jesus Christ is described primarily as an *unio personalis* sive *hypostatica* and only secondarily as an *unio naturarum*. And, moreover, the *unio naturarum* is decidedly always regarded from the standpoint of the *unio personalis*. The characteristic definition of the incarnation is thus unanimously to this effect : *Est autem incarnatio opus Dei, quo Filius Dei secundum oeconomiam divini consilii Patris et sui et Spiritus Sancti . . . carnem in unitatem personae sibi assumpsit* (*Syn. pur. Theol.*, Leiden, 1624, *Disp.* 25, 4). Or : *Incarnatio est actio divina qua Filius Dei naturam humanam . . . in unitatem suae personae assumsit* (Hollaz, *Ex. theol. acroam.*, 1706, III, *sect.* 1 *c.* 3 *qu.* 20).

In the Early Church the Greek tradition, and, after the Reformation, the Lutheran scholastic tradition, diverge from the Latin and later from the Reformed, in that the former take a well-nigh independent interest in the *unio naturarum*, whereas the latter stress the more urgently the relation of the union of natures to the hypostatic union. The two occurred in Protestantism with such liveliness that in the 16th and 17th centuries there was actually a formal opposition between the Lutheran and the Reformed Christologies. Pushed to an extreme, behind Reformed Christology might be seen the nestorian error with its separation, and behind the Lutheran the eutychian error with its identifi-

6

cation, of the two natures.   And this was in fact the mutual objection.   For
the moment, however, it is enough to maintain that Lutheran and Reformed
were at one in their starting-point, that the unity involved, Jesus Christ, is
originally and really the unity of the divine Word with the human being assumed
by Him.   But this unity also implies the unity—a unity to be thought of neither
as identity nor as· duality—of the divine being of the Word with the human
being assumed by Him, the unity of the two natures.   In essentials, we may say
at once at this point, discussion can take place only upon the common ground
presupposed by these two statements, and in essentials· it can consist only in
a mutual questioning and being questioned as to the validity of these two statements.   What is involved is a serious opposition between two schools of tradition,
not an opposition of faith.   At an earlier point we have seen that it goes back
to the difference between the Synoptic and the Pauline-Johannine witness to
Christ.   But that difference is certainly not a difference in faith.

The unity of God and man in Christ is, then, the act of the Logos
in assuming human being.   His becoming, and therefore the thing
that human being encounters in this becoming of the Logos, is an act
of God in the person of the Word.   Therefore God and man, Creator
and creature cannot be related to each other in this unity as in other
men or in creation generally.   We can and must, indeed, speak of a
presence, even of a personal presence of God in all created being, and
to that extent of a unity also of God with all created being.   But
then this created being has an independent existence in relation to
God.   It is real only in virtue of creation and preservation, through
God, and to that extent only in unity with God.   But it is real in
this unity, not as though it were itself God, but in such a way that,
being in God, it is different from God, in such a way that through God
it possesses an existence of its own different from the existence of
God.   It is the same with God's gracious presence in the word preached
and in the sacrament (so far as by that is meant the outward creaturely
sign of word and elements), and with God's gracious presence in the
hearts of those chosen and called by faith.   Unity with God in the
former case means that man's speech, that water, bread and wine,
are real not only through God, but as inseparably bound to God, and
similarly in the latter case, that believing man may live not only
through God but inseparably bound to God.   But unity with God
cannot mean in the former case that man's speech, that water, bread
and wine, or in the latter case that believing man, is identical with
God.   What is proclaimed by the unity of God and man in Jesus
Christ the God-Man is as follows.   This Man Jesus Christ is identical
with God because the Word became flesh in the sense just explained.
Therefore He does not only live through God and with God.   He is
Himself God.   Nor is He autonomous and self-existent.   His reality,
existence and being is wholly and absolutely that of God Himself,
the God who acts in His Word.   His manhood is only the predicate
of His Godhead, or better and more concretely, it is only the predicate,
assumed in inconceivable condescension, of the Word acting upon us,
the Word who is the Lord.

The earlier dogmaticians tried even more explicitly to distinguish from every other kind of unity, and in that way to characterise, the uniqueness of the unity of the Word and human nature. I quote J. Wolleb : *Non (humana natura) unita est ei (τῷ λόγῳ) συνουσιωδῶς ut personae divinae sunt unitae. Non οὐσιωδῶς tantum καὶ δραστικῶς, essentia et virtute, ut essentia Christi omnibus praesens est. Non παραστατικῶς seu praesentia gratiae tantum. Non φυσικῶς ut forma et materia uniuntur. Non σχετικῶς ut amicus amico. Non μυστικῶς tantum, ut Christus habitat in fidelibus. Non sacramentaliter ut in S. Coena, sed ὑποστατικῶς personaliter (Christ. Theol. Comp.* 1624, I *c.* 16 *can.* 4, 3). But from the utter uniqueness of this unity follows the statement, that God and Man are so related in Jesus Christ, that He exists as Man so far and only so far as He exists as God, i.e. in the mode of existence of the eternal Word of God. What we thereby express is a doctrine unanimously sponsored by early theology in its entirety, that of the *anhypostasis* and *enhypostasis* of the human nature of Christ. *Anhypostasis* asserts the negative. Since in virtue of the ἐγένετο, i.e., in virtue of the *assumptio*, Christ's human nature has its existence—the ancients said, its subsistence—in the existence of God, meaning in the mode of being (*hypostasis*, " person ") of the Word, it does not possess it in and for itself, *in abstracto*. Apart from the divine mode of being whose existence it acquires it has none of its own ; i.e., apart from its concrete existence in God in the event of the *unio*, it has no existence of its own, it is ἀνυπόστατος. *Enhypostasis* asserts the positive. In virtue of the ἐγένετο, i.e., in virtue of the *assumptio*, the human nature acquires existence (subsistence) in the existence of God, meaning in the mode of being (*hypostasis*, " person ") of the Word. This divine mode of being gives it existence in the event of the *unio*, and in this way it has a concrete existence of its own, it is ἐνυπόστατος. The statement occurs clearly as early as Hippolytus (*C. haer. Noeti* 15) : Οὔθ' ἡ σάρξ καθ' ἑαυτὴν δίχα τοῦ λόγου ὑποστάναι ἠδύνατο διὰ τὸ ἐν λόγῳ τὴν σύστασιν ἔχειν. " The Word of God Himself became the mode of being of the flesh " (Joh. Damascenus, *Ekd.* 3, 2). . . . *Ita ut caro illa nullam propriam subsistentiam extra Dei Filium habeat, sed ab illo et in eo vere sustentetur et gestetur* (*Syn. Pur. Theol.* Leiden, 1624, *Disp.* 25, 4). The aim of this doctrine, erected into dogma at the Second Council of Constantinople in 553 (*Anath. de tribus cap., can.* 5, *Denz.* No. 217), was to guard against the idea of a double existence of Christ as Logos and as Man, an idea inevitably bound to lead either to Docetism or to Ebionitism. We have seen earlier that what the eternal Word made His own, giving it thereby His own existence, was not a man, but man's nature, man's being, and so not a second existence but a second possibility of existence, to wit, that of a man. We have to take seriously sayings like Lk. 1[32], cf. [35] : οὗτος . . . υἱὸς ὑψίστου κληθήσεται.

It was just at this point that the disagreement started in the 17th century between Lutheran and Reformed theology. What is the meaning of the eternal Word having given His own existence to a man's possibility of existence, to a man's being and nature, and so having given it reality ? We have learned from a typically Reformed explanation that it was *Ita ut caro . . . ab illo et in eo vere sustentetur et gestetur*. We must consider the *ab illo et in eo* as well as the *sustentetur et gestetur*. Nevertheless the latter, already found in Melanchthon (*Enarr. symb. Nic.* 1550, *C.R.* 22, 341 f.), strikingly emphasises the act of the Word as such ; the flesh has existence, so far as it acquires it through the Word. Upon this formulation the question arises, how far existence, especially in the form of the Word's existence, really belongs to it, whether in such a *sustentatio* God and Man are really being thought of as one and not perhaps secretly as two. There have, of course, been Reformed theologians who have spoken even more strongly in this direction. So Wolleb : *Personalis unio est qua persona Filii Dei ὑπόστασιν suam humanae naturae communicavit* (*op. cit.* I, *c.* 16, 4). But the Lutherans' interest at this point was already in the *unio naturarum*, i.e., in the result of the act as such. They wanted to go even further than the *communicavit*, and say that *Λόγος ita sibi univit humanam naturam, ut ei suam divinam et indivisam subsistentiam vere et realiter largitus sit ad communem participationem, ita ut non minus vere jam sit humanitatis ὑπόστασις quam ipsius divinae naturae λόγου* (Quenstedt, *Theol. did. pol.*, 1685, III, *c.* 3 *m.* 1, *sect.* 2 *qu.* 4 *th*). This *communis participatio* does, in fact, go far beyond the Reformed *sustentare* or even *communicare*, and anticipates the peculiarly Lutheran doctrine of the unity of the natures and of the consequent *communicatio idiomatum*. But instead of the one-sided relationship of the *ἐγένετο*, instead of the *assumptio* in which the Logos is and continues to be the Subject, does not this give us a kind of reciprocal relation between Creator and creature? Do we not have revealedness instead of revelation, a state instead of an event? This is the question directed at Lutheran Christology (in criticism, cf. Wendelin, *Chr. theol. libri duo*, 1633, I *c.* 16 *ed.* 1657, p. 265 f.). Anyhow, if in view of what they actually said and intended the Reformed must be defended against the Lutheran objection that the *assumptio* for them is a " *nuda* " *sustentatio*, a mere presence lent to human nature by the Word of God—which would, of course, be a second denial of the unity of Christ's person—it is to be noted that the Lutherans for their part did at least see the danger in which their own thesis stood. In the passage just adduced Quenstedt continues thus: that along with His existence in His divine nature the existence of the Word becomes the existence of the human nature, . . . *licet in modo habendi sit disparitas ut scilicet divina natura λόγου eam habeat πρώτως et κατ' αὐτό, humana vero δευτέρως et κατ' ἄλλο, secundario et propter unionem personalem, adeoque perpetuo sit et maneat λόγῳ propriissima, licet participetur ab humana natura a λόγῳ assumpta.* Then later Lutherans like Hollaz (*Ex. theol. acroam*, 1705, III, *sect.* 1, *c.* 3, *qu.* 22) expressly explained this limitation by saying that, although *particeps divinae subsistentiae*, the *natura humana* is not as such a *persona* but only *personata*, i.e., receptive of existence. Even such strict Reformed statements as that of Wendelin, *Humana Christi natura nec propriam habet hypostasin nec aliunde communicatam* (*op. cit.* p. 266), or that of Keckermann, that the *natura humana* is *ita unita* to the Logos, *ut extra eum ne ad momentum quidem consistere possit* (*Syst. S. S. Theol.* 1611, p. 315, quoted from Heppe, *Dogmatik d. ref. Kirche*, 1861, new edn. 1935, Eng. tr. p. 417), are understandable in the light of this. This was the concern of the Reformed school, and it brought a return to the original meaning of the dogma, from which in the whole dispute the Lutherans at least with their *communis participatio* had to some extent departed, however justifiable in itself their intention had been. If instead of polemical utterances both sides had developed more intensively the thoughts by which the interests of their opponents could be met—in the case of the Reformed the *in eo vere sustentetur*, and in that of the Lutherans the primacy of the existence of the Logos, it ought not to have been impossible to reach an understanding on what was in the last resort their common intention.

In recent times the doctrine of the *anhypostasis* and *enhypostasis* of Christ's human nature has occasionally been combated by the primitive argument, that if the human nature of Christ is without personality of its own, it is all up with the true humanity of Christ and the Docetism of early Christology holds the field. In other words we moderns should be aware that personality really does belong to true human being. This argument is primitive because it rests simply upon a misunderstanding of the Latin term *impersonalitas* used occasionally for *anhypostasis*. But what Christ's human nature lacks according to the early doctrine is not what we call personality. This the early writers called *individualitas*, and they never taught that Christ's human nature lacked this, but rather that this qualification actually belonged to true human being. *Personalitas* was their name for what we call existence or being. Their negative position asserted that Christ's flesh in itself has no existence, and this was asserted in the interests of their positive position that Christ's flesh has its existence through the Word and in the Word, who is God Himself acting as Revealer and Reconciler. Understood in this its original sense, this particular doctrine, abstruse in appearance only, is particularly well adapted to make it clear that the reality attested by Holy Scripture, Jesus Christ, is the reality of a divine act of Lordship which is unique and singular as compared with all other events, and in this way to characterise it as a reality held up to faith by revelation. It is in virtue of the eternal Word that Jesus Christ exists as a man of flesh and blood in our sphere, as a man like us, as an historical phenomenon. But it is only in virtue of the divine Word that He exists as such. If He existed in a different way, how would He be revelation in the real sense in which revelation is intended in Holy Scripture ? Because of this positive aspect, it was well worth making the negation a dogma and giving it the very careful consideration which it received in early Christology.

'Εγένετο, the event of the incarnation of the Word, of the *unio hypostatica*, has to be understood as a *completed* event, but also as a completed *event*.

What the New Testament tells us of the reality of Jesus Christ is undoubtedly meant to be heard as the news of an accomplished fact, namely, that in the fulness of time it became true—and it was this that made this time fulfilled time—that once and for all God became Man and so His Word reached the ears of us men, and so we men were reconciled to God. The reality of Jesus Christ is an objective fact. It is this that gives Christology, so to speak, its ontological reference. And we undoubtedly have to do justice to this reference.

What the New Testament says about Jesus Christ is all said in the light of Easter and Ascension, that is, in the light of the union, achieved once for all, between the eternal Word and the human existence assumed by Him. God's Son, so the Christian message runs, is now what we are for all time, nay for all eternity ; He is Emmanuel, He is " with us alway, even unto the end of the world " (Mt. 28[20]), i.e., until we on our side " shall be ever with the Lord " (1 Thess. 4[17]). How can that be said, if Christ's exaltation means even remotely the abolition, the laying aside of His lowliness, the reversing of the incarnation, and not on the contrary the revelation of His divine majesty in His lowliness, the resurrection of the Crucified, the triumph of the Word in His actual human existence ? The Christian message declares that in this form, as the *Logos incarnatus*, He exists in the recollection of the Church, exactly as in this form, as the *Logos incarnandus*, He existed for the patriarchs in the expectation of Israel. To that extent it is the message that the incarnation of the Word is an accomplished event. From this point of view it is the answer to the Pauline-Johannine problem. Is the name of Christ, is Christ the Son of God, really Jesus of Nazareth ? Yes, it replies ; and so with all its might it must maintain that this and no other is His name, that such He is and not something else. " Ask ye who is this same, Christ Jesus is His Name, the Lord Sabaoth's Son, He, and no other one."

The miracle of the incarnation, of the *unio hypostatica*, is seen from this angle when we realise that the Word of God descended from the freedom, majesty and glory of His divinity, that without becoming unlike Himself He assumed His likeness to us, and that now He is to be sought and found of us here, namely, in His human being. There is no other form or manifestation in heaven or on earth save the one child in the stable, the one Man on the cross. This is the Word to whom we must hearken, render faith and obedience, cling ever so closely. Every question concerning the Word which is directed away from Jesus of Nazareth, the human being of Christ, is necessarily and wholly directed away from Himself, the Word, and therefore from God Himself, because the Word, and therefore God Himself, does not exist for us apart from the human being of Christ.

What we have just described is the christological position of Luther, at any rate his favourite one, as already familiar to us. Moved, and as a rule moved exclusively, by the question of the grace of God, he clutched with both hands, like Anselm of Canterbury and Bernard of Clairvaux before him, at the answer of the Pauline-Johannine Christology, that God's grace was manifested to us really, concretely and surely in the stable and on the cross in the human existence of Jesus Christ, that everything was done and completed for us by God Himself in this very human existence and only in it, that our justification was accomplished in His sight and had only to be received in faith. In consequence, here and only here is God's Word to be found. Pushing forward in this direction Luther could quite well say: " I will know of no other Son of God, except Him who was born of the Virgin Mary and has suffered " (*Wochenpred. üb. Joh.* 6–8, 1530 f. on Jn. 6⁴⁷ *W.A.* 33, 155, 1). And in the famous passage : " If He is natural and personal where He is, there too He must also be a Man, for there are not two detached persons, but a single person. Where it is, there is a single undetached person. And where thou canst say, here is God ! thou must also say, Then Christ the Man is also there ! And where thou wouldest point to a place where God was and not man, the person would be finely split, since straightway I could say with truth, Here is God who is not man and never was man. But to me that is not of God. For it would follow, that space and positions separated the two natures from each other and split the person, whereas death and all devils could not separate them or rend them from each other. And he would always be a bad Christ who at no more than one place was at once a divine and human person and at all others had to be nothing but a mere separated God and divine person without humanity. Nay, friend, where thou presentest me with God thou must also present me with humanity. They admit not of separation or detachment from each other. It was a person that became, who doth not sever humanity from Himself as Master John putteth off his coat and layeth it aside when he goeth to sleep " (*Vom Abendmahl Christi. Bekenntnis*, 1528, *W.A.* 26, 332, 28). This assertion of Luther's was then built up doctrinally by Lutheran orthodoxy in the form of an idea which expressly maintained a perichoresis between the Word of God and the human being of Christ, i.e., a reversal of the statement about the *enhypostasis* of Christ's human nature, to the effect that as the humanity only has reality through and in the Word, so too the Word only has reality through and in the humanity. Λόγος *ita praesens est carni et caro ita praesens est* τῷ λόγῳ *ut nec* λόγος *sit extra carnem, nec caro extra* λόγον, *sed ubicunque est* λόγος *ibi et praesentissimam sibi habet carnem, quippe quam in personae unitatem assumit, et ubicunque est caro, ibi praesentissimum sibi habet* λόγον, *quippe in cuius hypostasin est assumta* (J. Gerhard, *Loci theol.* 1610 f. L, IV, 121). *Uti post factam unionem hypostaticam* τοῦ λόγου *et carnis, assumpta caro nunquam et nuspiam est extra et citra* τὸν λόγον *ita et* λόγος *nunquam et nuspiam est extra vel citra suam carnem* . . . *Quicunque totus totus est* ἐνσαρκωθεὶς, *ille totus totus est intra carnem ;* for Ἐν αὐτῷ κατοικεῖ πᾶν τὸ πλήρωμα τῆς θεότητος σωματικῶς, Col. 2⁹. All the fulness bodily. That is, none of its fulness not bodily, nothing *extra carnem* (Quenstedt, *Theol. did. pol.* 1685, III, *c.* 3 *m.* 1 sect. 2 qu. 5th).

The problems raised by this idea may be plainly reduced to the following questions. Does it take such account of the freedom, majesty and glory of the Word of God that they are in no way merged and submerged in His becoming flesh ? And if such account is taken of it, then does the same hold true also of the flesh which He has become ? And if the concept " Word " and the concept " flesh " are both taken seriously but are considered as mutually conditioning one another, is the statement of Jn. 1¹⁴ an understandable statement at all ? On the assumption of such a mutual conditioning does it not mean that either the *vere Deus* or the *vere homo* is taken less than seriously, is in fact weakened down and altered in meaning ?

The early Lutherans were quite aware of this doubtfulness in their doctrine. In practice they wished to adhere as much to the *vere Deus* as to the *vere homo*, and not to infringe upon the Word as God in His divinity or upon the flesh as a creature in its creatureliness. Thus J. Gerhard (*op. cit. sup.*) explained that the unity of the flesh with the Word, in virtue of which the Word was never anywhere henceforth without the flesh as the flesh is not without the Word, must be thought of in the *modus illocalis, supernaturalis et sublimissimus*. And Quenstedt (*op. cit. sup.*) continued his exposition with the qualification . . . *ita tamen, ut nec caro immensa sit, nec λόγος includatur, finiatur vel circumscribatur, sed et illa finita et hic infinitus permaneat.* But what does a limiting of the Word to the flesh mean, if it is specifically not to assert a really spatial limiting, i.e., one appropriate to the concept " flesh ", yet just as little an unlimitedness in the flesh appropriate to the concept " Word " ? Have not Luther and the Lutherans ventured too much in their attempt at such a simple reversal of the statement about the *enhypostasis* of the humanity of Christ, or at the completion of it by a statement about the " enfleshment " of the Word in the exclusive sense ? Does such a statement make any clear assertion at all, seeing its aim is to deny neither the *vere Deus* nor the *vere homo* ? The road which led to this crowning statement is understandable and illuminating. But would it not have been better either not to make it, or to explain it at once by a counter-statement, since it obviously cannot be explained in and by itself ?

Let us now try to take the other line possible here. As readers of the same New Testament we may find the emphasis laid on the fact that it explains to us the ἐγένετο, the reality of Jesus Christ, as an accomplished *event*, as a completed *act*. The fact that God became Man, that His Word became hearable and we ourselves became reconciled to God, is true because it became true, and because it becomes true before our eyes and ears in the witness of Scripture, in the movement which it attests from non-revelation to revelation, from promise to fulfilment, from the cross to the resurrection. In the tracks of this event and by following these tracks we recognise the reality attested to us. The relevance of Christology from this standpoint will acquire a noetic character, and we cannot deny that this is meaningful and legitimate.

While the New Testament speaks wholly from the standpoint of Easter and ascension, let us be quite clear that Easter and ascension as such constitute the end and the goal of its witness, to which we are led by a definite way. To begin with, we are set a riddle. From the very start we are also shown that the solution of it is to hand. But it is still a riddle which is followed by the solution. Man in his humiliation, God in His exaltation, or the God-Man in His veiling and also in His unveiling : these constitute two coherent steps, inseparably linked yet also clearly distinct. Some sort of meeting between God and man takes place in the figure of Christ in the New Testament, and in this meeting is the event which is the object of New Testament witness, *vere Deus vere homo*. The resurrection of the Crucified is important as the revelation of this event, as the triumph of the Word in His human existence. The Christian message states that the Word became flesh. But it is not enough merely to state this. It tells a story : the story of how this state of affairs came to pass, how it became true that God the Lord took man to Himself by becoming man. From this point of view the Christian message is the answer to the problem of the Synoptists, whether Jesus of Nazareth is really the Christ, the Son of God. Its answer is Yes, and now it lays all its emphasis on the fact that the sole source of this human being's existence and power is the agency of the Word of God, that in Him the Word of God wills to be taken up and grasped, believed and understood, the Word as the mystery of the flesh, but the flesh as the shell and form of the Word.

Under this aspect the miracle of the incarnation is seen in the fact that it was the Word of God in the freedom, majesty and glory of His divinity who condescended to us and became in all things like unto us, and that in His human existence, in Christ's birth and cross He, the Word of God, is to be sought and found in His complete transcendence. In the understanding of the miracle that God is man, that is, in the vision of faith, the act of " God becoming man " is, as it were, repeated ; the inconceivable path is trodden again from the closed to the open mystery, from the cross to the resurrection. Faith, as it were, discovers that this Man is God. God's personal action as such is its object. Can it be otherwise, seeing the reality of Jesus Christ which is here contemplated is revelation, and revelation is the object of faith, and so knowledge of it is knowledge of faith ? The very reason why a distinction is here made between God and man— and obviously the better to understand the unity—is in order that their unity may be seen always as an act of God, and that in this act God Himself may always be seen as the Lord.

From this concern there resulted a protest on the part of Reformed theology in the 16th and 17th centuries against the crowning assertion of Luther and the Lutherans about the existence of the Word solely in the human existence of Christ. The " solely " was contested, and it was asserted in reply that since the Word is flesh, He also is and continues to be what He is in Himself, He also exists outwith (*extra*) the flesh. *Etsi in unam personam coaluit immensa Verbi essentia cum natura hominis, nullam tamen inclusionem fingimus. Mirabiliter enim a caelo descendit Filius Dei ut caelum tamen non relinqueret ; mirabiliter in utero virginis gestari, in terris versari et in cruce pendere voluit, ut semper mundum impleret sicut ab initio* (Calvin, *Instit.* II, 13, 4). " Because the divinity is inconceivably and everywhere present, it must follow that it is indeed outwith its adopted humanity and yet none the less also in the same and remaineth in personal union with it " (*Heid. Cat. qu.* 48). To understand this protest we must keep constantly in mind that the Reformed theologians maintained this not as a theological innovation, but in continuation of all earlier Christology. The description *Extra Calvinisticum* which was given to their doctrine by the Lutherans was apt only to the extent that it actually was Calvinists who reverted to this tradition to meet the innovation introduced by Luther and the Lutherans. Thus it is not only substantially erroneous, but also historically impossible, to try to prove from this *Extra* the catch-phrase that Reformed theology thought

" generally of the divine and the creaturely-human in separation " (so H. Stephan, *Glaubenslehre²*, 1928, p. 168). Already Athanasius writes quite definitely in the sense of Calvin's assertion : Οὐ γὰρ δὴ περικεκλεισμένος ἦν ἐν τῷ σώματι. οὐδὲ ἐν σώματι ἦν, ἀλλαχόσε δὲ οὐκ ἦν . . . Ἀλλὰ τὸ παραδοξότατον, Λόγος ὤν, οὐ συνείχετο μὲν ὑπό τινος· συνεῖχε δὲ τὰ πάντα μᾶλλον αὐτός . . . ὥστε καὶ ἐν τούτῳ (in the human nature) ἦν καὶ ἐν τοῖς πᾶσιν ἐτύγχανε, καὶ ἔξω τῶν ὄντων ἦν καὶ ἐν μόνῳ τῷ Πατρὶ ἀνεπαύσατο (*De incarn.* 17). Gregory of Nyssa was equally clear in rebutting the idea that on the basis of the incarnation the infinity of God became enclosed in the limits of the flesh as in a vessel and in opposition to it thought of the divinity of the Word as laying hold of the humanity, which might be illustrated by the unity and separateness between fuel and flame (*Or. cat.* 10). Augustine makes the same distinction : *Quando in forma servi et mediator esset, infra angelos esse voluit in forma Dei supra angelos mansit ; idem in inferioribus via vitae qui in superioribus vita* (*De civ. Dei,* IX, 15, 2). It is no Christian doctrine, he held, *quod ita sit Deus infusus carni, qua ex virgine nasceretur, ut curam gubernandae universitatis vel deseruerit vel amiserit, vel ad illud corpusculum quasi contractam materiam collectamque transtulerit* (*Ep.* 137, 2 *ad Volusianum*). And John of Damascus : " Without separating from the Father's bosom, the Word dwelt in the bosom of the holy virgin . . . thus in all and over all He was Himself, when He existed in the bosom of the holy bearer of God " (*Ekdos.* 3, 7). And Thomas Aquinas : Christ descended from heaven *non ita quod natura divina in coelo esse desierit ; sed quia in infimis novo modo esse coepit scil. secundum naturam assumptam* (*S. theol.* III, qu. 5, *art.* 2, *ad.* 1). *Nec etiam in unione quae est secundum esse personale natura humana comprehendit Dei Verbum sive naturam divinam ; quae quamvis tota unita fuerit humanae naturae in una persona Filii, non tamen fuit tota virtus divinitatis ab humana natura quasi circumscripta* (*ib.* qu. 10, *art.* 1, *ad.* 2). And so even Luther himself could still write : *Neque enim tum verbo suo definivit sese, sed liberum sese reservavit super omnia* (*De serv. arb.* 1525 *W.A.* 18, 685, 23). It is further to be noted that the Reformed position was by no means directed against the positive content of Luther's, not to speak of St. Paul's saying (Col. 2⁹), but against a negative conclusion derived therefrom ; and so not against the *totus totus intra carnem* but against the *numquam et nuspiam extra carnem.* And when in the " Children's Christmas Hymn " he sings :

> And were the wide world e'er so great
> With gold and precious stones ornate,
> Yet were it far too small to be
> A narrow cradle, Lord, for Thee,

even Luther has indicated the *extra* in due and proper form. When they negated this negation, when they maintained this *extra*, which was only meant as an *etiam extra* (Wendelin, *Chr. Theol.*, 1633, I *c.* 16, VI, 4 f.), it could as little occur to the Reformed as to the early doctors to question, in the sense of the nestorian error, the Chalcedonian unity of the two natures in the person of the Word or, in consequence, the hypostatic union itself. They wished the *extra* to be regarded, not as *separative*, but as *distinctive.* Along with the *extra* they also asserted the *intra* with thoroughgoing seriousness. With the Lutherans they asserted a *praesentia intima perpetua* of the Logos in the flesh, i.e., in the sense of what Luther really meant to assert, an *ubiquitas humanae naturae* in virtue of the *operatio gloriosa* of the exalted God-Man (Wendelin, *op. cit.*). They merely wished to maintain the *extra* too, beyond the *intra*, i.e., on the one hand the divinity of the God-Man, on the other hand His humanity as such. They did not want the reality of the λόγος ἄσαρκος abolished or suppressed in the reality of the λόγος ἔνσαρκος. On the contrary, they wished the λόγος ἄσαρκος to be regarded equally seriously as the *terminus a quo*, as the λόγος ἔνσαρκος was regarded as the *terminus ad quem* of the incarnation. And so they wanted to reject that reversal of the *enhypostasis*, by which, it seemed to them, either the divinity or the humanity as such was imperilled. Maresius' trenchant formulation expresses everything : *sic λόγος humanam naturam sibi univit, ut totus eam inhabitet et totus quippe immensus et infinitus extra eam sit* (*Syst. breve univ. theol.*, 1662, p. 118, quoted from H. Heppe, *Dogm. d. ev. ref. Kirche* 1861, new ed. 1935, Eng. tr. p. 418). So earlier Augustine had sought already to compress both views : *Per distantiam divinitatis et infirmitatis Filius Dei manebat in coelo, filius hominis ambulabat in terra—per unitatem vero personae, qua utraque substantia unus Christus est, et Filius Dei ambulabat in terra et idem ipse filius hominis manebat in coelo* (*De pecc. merit.* I, 31, 60).

Obviously this view, too, is afflicted by its own doubtfulness. It visualises the dynamic element in the ἐγένετο and it preserves the noetic interest of the Christology. But it may be asked whether the static element in the ἐγένετο and therefore the ontic relevance of the Christology are equally conserved on this view. Over and above the visualising of the way (with its inevitable distinction between the Word who assumed flesh and the flesh assumed by the Word), has not the end of the way, namely the unity of both, become obscured ? Yet is it not upon this end that everything depends ? And in order to speak without obscurity of this end, had we not better drop all reflections upon the way to it as such ?

As we have seen, the Reformed theologians asserted—and asserted in harmony with tradition—that this end is made quite clear without the Lutheran innovation, that the hypostatic union is quite beyond question without this innovation. But as the Lutherans failed to show how far, by their elimination of the *extra*, the *vere Deus* is, as they allege, preserved to the same extent as the *vere homo*, so now the Reformed too failed to show convincingly how far the *extra* does not involve the assumption of a twofold Christ, of a λόγος ἔνσαρκος alongside a λόγος ἄσαρκος, and therefore a dissolution of the unity of the natures and hypostatic union, and therefore a destruction of the unequivocal Emmanuel and the certainty of faith and salvation based thereon. In short it cannot be denied that the Reformed *totus intra et extra* offers at least as many difficulties as the Lutheran *totus intra*.

To summarise : We may look at the ἐγένετο from the standpoint of the *completed* event, or we may look at it from the standpoint of the completed *event*. Christology may have a static-ontic interest, or it may have a dynamic-noetic interest. But either way, when fully developed, it will give rise to very definite questions against it, which are very difficult to answer. The achievement of a synthesis of the two views, with a satisfactory answer to the questions on both sides, proved to be unattainable, at least in the great dispute within Evangelical theology in the 16th and 17th centuries in which it was last debated. Reflection may be extended in different ways from this factual starting-point. So far as it has not always been the view of the entire Christian Church, the former of the two views, thanks to the impressive manner in which Luther presented it and in which it can still be seen in its later representatives, has the importance of expressing an immediate need of faith, an expression which has established for all time a claim to be heard, and to be heard with even greater attention than was the case even in the early and medieval Church. On the other hand, in view of the unanimity of the Early Church as well as of the more comprehensive and to that extent superior way in which the Reformed theologians put the question, we have to ask if the former view is not one which is justifiable on the basis and in the framework of the second : a question which could not be asked quite so definitely the other way round. Does not the question of the completed *event*, the view that revelation is a divine *act*, merit a position of primacy and superiority, in so far as from this standpoint it is at least easier to do justice to the second view ? Is not the first view more directly, more naturally tenable in the second itself than *vice versa* ? In the second view, is it not a matter of a necessity of faith, which ought as such to take precedence of the former need for faith, however justifiable ? If this is so, the practical result is that in future Reformed theology will have to express itself even more clearly than was the case at least in the 16th and 17th centuries, how far, as it maintained at the time, it does not mean to abandon one iota of what Luther rightly intended to express. But Lutheran theology will have to abandon or to modify the isolated assertion of its view, its denial, its inherited distrust of the more comprehensive way of putting the question ; it will have to expound its special thesis on the basis and in the framework of the superior orderliness of a theology of the divine action. But when we recollect that in the centuries after the Reformation both sides strove genuinely and seriously, but unsuccessfully, in this direction for unification, when, above all, we recollect that there is a riddle in the fact itself, and that even in the New Testament two lines can be discerned in this matter, we will at least be on our guard against thinking of oversimple solutions. Perhaps there can be no resting from the attempt to understand this ἐγένετο. Perhaps there can be no amicable compromise in Evangelical theology as regards the order of merit between these two views. Perhaps if it is to be Evangelical theology at all—and truly so, it may be, only when this necessity is perceived—there always has to be a static and a dynamic, an ontic and a noetic principle, not in nice equilibrium, but calling to each other and questioning each other. That is, there must be Lutherans and Reformed : not in the shadow of a unitary theology, but as a twofold theological school—for the sake of the truth about the reality of Jesus Christ, which does not admit of being grasped or conceived by any unitary theology, which will always be the object of all theology, and so perhaps inevitably of a twofold theology—object in the strictest sense of the concept. It may even be that in the unity and variety of the two Evangelical theologies in the one Evangelical Church there is reflected no more and no less than the one mystery itself, with which both were once engrossed and will necessarily be engrossed always, the mystery that ὁ λόγος σάρξ ἐγένετο.

3. THE MIRACLE OF CHRISTMAS

God's revelation in its objective reality is the incarnation of His Word, in that He, the one true eternal God, is at the same time true Man like us. God's revelation in its objective reality is the person of Jesus Christ. In establishing this we have not explained revelation, or made it obvious, or brought it into the series of the other objects of our knowledge. On the contrary, in establishing this and looking back at it we have described and designated it a mystery, and not only a mystery but the prime mystery. In other words, it becomes the object of our knowledge ; it finds a way of becoming the content of our experience and our thought ; it gives itself to be apprehended by our contemplation and our categories. But it does that beyond the range of what we regard as possible for our contemplation and perception, beyond the confines of our experience and our thought. It comes to us as a *Novum* which, when it becomes an object for us, we cannot incorporate in the series of our other objects, cannot compare with them, cannot deduce from their context, cannot regard as analogous with them. It comes to us as a datum with no point of connexion with any other previous datum. It becomes the object of our knowledge by its own power and not by ours. The act of knowing it is distinctive as one which we actually can achieve, but which we cannot understand, in the sense that we simply do not understand how we can achieve it. We can understand the possibility of it solely from the side of its object, i.e., we can regard it not as ours, but as one coming to us, imparted to us, gifted to us. In this bit of knowing we are not the masters but the mastered. It is when we are in the act of knowing God's revelation, amid the objective reality of it, in the act of knowing the person of Jesus Christ, that this must be said. If we do not know this person, if we are unaware of the reality of " very God and very Man," we will certainly not say this, but confidently ascribe to ourselves the possibility of knowing it. If we are aware of it and declare that it is true, we will also be aware and will not hesitate to declare, that it can be manifest to us in its truth only by its own agency and not because of any capacity belonging to us ; just as a man justified by faith in Christ, and he alone, is aware and confesses that he is a lost sinner, whereas one who has not received forgiveness will definitely regard himself as a man with power to justify himself. Thus it is in the act of knowing revelation that it will always be and become a mystery to us. It is indeed the prime mystery, because strictly, logically and properly, it is only of this object, of the person of Jesus Christ, that all this can be said. That is the outcome of our christological foundation and it remains for us now to make its content quite explicit and understandable.

" Incarnation of the Word " asserts the presence of God in our

world and as a member of this world, as a Man among men. It is thus
God's revelation to us, and our reconciliation with Him. That this
revelation and reconciliation have already taken place is the content
of the Christmas message. But even in the very act of knowing this
reality and of listening to the Christmas message, we have to describe the meeting of God and world, of God and man in the person of
Jesus Christ—and not only their meeting but their becoming one—as
inconceivable. This reality is not given nor is it accessible elsewhere.
It does not allow us to acknowledge that it is true on the ground of
general considerations. Our experience no less than our thought will
rather make constant reference to the remoteness of the world from
God and of God from the world, to God's majesty and to man's misery.
If in knowledge of the incarnation of the Word, in knowledge of the
person of Jesus Christ we are speaking of something really other, if
the object of Christology, " very God and very Man," is objectively real
for us, then all that we can arrive at by our experience and our thought
is the realisation that they are delimited, determined and dominated
here by something wholly outside or above us. Knowledge in this
case means acknowledgment. And the utterance or expression of this
knowledge is termed confession. Only in acknowledgment or confession
can we say that Jesus Christ is very God and very Man. In acknowledgment and confession of the inconceivableness of this reality we
describe it as the act of God Himself, of God completely and solely.
If we speak of it in any other way, if we deny its inconceivability,
if we think that by our statements we are speaking of something
within the competence of our experience and thought which we can
encounter and master, we are speaking of something different from
the dogma and from the Scripture expounded in the dogma. We are
not understanding or describing revelation as God's act in the strict
and exclusive sense. We are speaking of something other than God's
revelation. In the very act of acknowledgment and confession we
must always acknowledge and confess together both the distance of
the world from God and the distance of God from the world, both the
majesty of God and the misery of man. It is the antithesis between
these that turns their unity in Christ into a mystery. Thus we must
ever acknowledge and confess the inconceivability of this unity.

Ἐννόησον γὰρ ἡλίκου ἦν ἀκοῦσαι καὶ μαθεῖν ὅτι ὁ Θεός, ὁ ἄρρητος, ὁ ἄφθαρτος, ὁ
ἀπερινόητος, ὁ ἀόρατος, ὁ ἀκατάληπτος . . . οὗτος ὁ πάντα νοῦν ὑπερβαίνων καὶ πάντα
λογισμὸν νικῶν, παραδραμὼν ἀγγέλους, ἀρχαγγέλους, πάσας τὰς ἄνω νοερὰς δυνάμεις,
κατεδέξατο γενέσθαι ἄνθρωπος καὶ σάρκα τὴν ἀπὸ γῆς καὶ πηλοῦ πλασθεῖσαν ἀναλαβεῖν
(Chrysostom, *Hom. in quosdam locos N.T.*, on Mt 26³⁹). We also recall the
prominence given to the *Et incarnatus est* in the recitation of the creed in the
Missale Romanum by the prescribing of a genuflexion.

It is this mystery of Christmas which is indicated in Scripture
and in church dogma by reference to the miracle of Christmas. This
miracle is the conception of Jesus Christ by the Holy Ghost or His
birth of the Virgin Mary.

The passages with which the Church dogma is directly connected and with which we, too, must start are Mt. 1[18-25], with its reference back to the sign of Emmanuel in Is. 7[14], and Lk. 1[26-38] (esp. [34-35]). The formulation of the dogma is as follows :

In the Roman baptismal symbol of the 4th century according to Rufinus : *qui natus est de Spiritu sancto ex Maria virgine.*

Acc. to the *Psalt. Aethelstani* : τὸν γεννηθέντα ἐκ πνεύματος ἁγίου καὶ Μαρίας τῆς παρθένου.

In what has become the official form of the so-called *Apostolicum* : *qui conceptus est de Spiritu sancto, natus ex Maria virgine.*

In the Eastern form of the so-called *Apostolicum* (and in the *Nic. Constant.*) : σαρκωθέντα ἐκ πνεύματος ἁγίου καὶ Μαρίας τῆς παρθένου.

In the Latin version of the *Nic. Constant.* : *et incarnatus est de Spiritu sancto ex Maria virgine.*

By taking up this reference and so making confession of this dogma as a statement grounded in Holy Scripture, we do not by any means show disinterested respect for the fact that it is a dogma after all, and that up to the present day it has been a dogma which Catholics and Protestants have on the whole believed and taught unanimously and as a matter of course. The respect paid in the Church to this dogma cannot be sufficient reason in itself for us to adopt it as our own. In dogma as such we hear merely the voice of the Church and not revelation itself. If we make it our own and affirm it as the correct Church interpretation of revelation, this can be done only because we realise its necessity, and this realisation will have to be substantiated in an attempt to understand it.

For what follows cf. Schleiermacher, *Der chr. Glaube*, § 97, 2 ; Fritz Barth, *Die Hauptprobleme des Lebens Jesu*[5], 1918, p. 257 f. ; C. Clemen, *Religionsgeschichtl. Erklärung des NT*, p. 114 f. ; R. Seeberg, *Chr. Dogmatik*, 1925, vol. 2, p. 178 f. ; E. Brunner, *Der Mittler*, 1927, p. 288 f. ; M. Dibelius, *Jungfrauensohn und Krippenkind*, 1932 ; K. L. Schmidt, " Die jungfraüliche Geburt Jesu Christi," *Theol. Bl.* 1935, p. 289 f.

As regards the necessity of the dogma, we must begin with the admission that both in extent and form the grounds for the dogma in the statements of Holy Scripture are not at first sight so strong or so clear as one might wish for such a dogma in the strict sense of the term.

It is unreasonable and fanatical for B. Bartmann (*Lehrb. d. Dogm.*[7], 1928, vol. 1, p. 423) to assert that " the sole and invariably effective ground for denying " the doctrine of the Virgin birth is " the rationalistic dogma of the impossibility of miracle." Against this is to be set the credible explanation of F. Kattenbusch (" Die Geburtsgeschichte Jesu als Haggada der Urchristologie," *Theol Stud. u. Krit.*, 1930, p. 472) who rejects the Virgin birth and yet can say : " There is nothing in it that offends me—not even the idea of a ' miraculous conception.' In principle the idea of a ' nature miracle ' is to me neither alien nor objectionable." On the contrary, it must be granted that in respect of this doctrine, quite apart from the miracle it involves, objection may be taken to making it a dogma, because biblically it is only thinly and in one of the main passages dubiously attested, and it seems in addition to involve factual contradictions. The objections which can be taken to it from this angle are, of course, not insuperable. The view that objection here is inevitable may go back to a very deep-seated error in the entire theological thinking. But this error cannot be exposed merely by accusing people of a fear of miracles. On the contrary, it is right that we should clarify the exegetical position in the light of which doubts can be and have been cast upon the doctrine of the Virgin birth quite apart from the question of miracle. A few indications as to why we can regard the present difficulties as not insuperable may follow point by point.

1. It is a fact that the Virgin birth is not expressly mentioned in the Gospels of Mark and John, that above all Paul and also the Catholic Epistles nowhere expressly betray acquaintance with it, that after the close of the childhood narrative even Matthew and Luke themselves never expressly return to it, and that in the summaries of the *Kerygma* in Acts it is not expressly mentioned. But not every element, not even every important element, in Jesus' existence lent itself as much as His passion and His resurrection to regular and frequent mention as an express part of oral and written tradition and proclamation. It may well be significant that it is in the two childhood narratives—where the general question raised by the Synoptists : Who is Jesus of Nazareth ? is answered with specific reference to His earthly human origin—that the Virgin birth is expressly indicated. Mark was less occupied with this particular question. Paul and John, together with the Catholic Epistles, were likewise less occupied with the other general question. This does not rule out the possibility that the statements in Mt. 1 and Lk. 1 belonged to those presuppositions of all the New Testament witnesses which were taken for granted and were familiar and undisputed. The persistent, and to a certain extent very peculiar, mention of the mother and the equally persistent omission of the father of Jesus in the course of the Gospel narratives should be considered as providing evidence for early and particular attention to this point.

2. It is a fact that *Syr. Sin.*, confirmed by some other traditions, offers the following text for Mt. 1^{16} : " Jacob begat Joseph ; Joseph, to whom the Virgin Mary was betrothed, begat Jesus, who is called the Christ " ; for Mt. 1^{21} : " She will bear thee a son " ; and for Mt. 1^{25} : " She bore him a son." But alongside the variant readings of *Syr. Sin.* for Mt. 1$^{16. \ 21. \ 25}$ stand the passages 1$^{18. \ 20. \ 23}$, in which it, too, indicates the Virgin birth. At best we may conclude from this MS. that already at an early date there actually existed, alongside the one which became canonical, a tradition with this other content.

3. It is a fact that both the genealogies Mt. 1$^{2-16}$ and Lk. 3$^{23-38}$ end not with Mary but with Joseph, and so, if Joseph is not the father of Jesus, do not prove what they ought to prove, Jesus' descent from David, so important to Paul (Rom. 1^3 ; 2 Tim. 2^8), also to John (Jn. 7^{42}), but also and particularly to the Synoptists (Mt. 1^1 ; Mk. 10$^{47f.}$ and par. ; 12$^{35f.}$ and par ; Mt. 12^{23}, 21^9, etc.). We will certainly do well to renounce the attempts of early Church commentators to convert the genealogies of Joseph into those of Mary. But attention should be drawn to the fact that at the important points, Mt. 1^{16} and Lk. 3^{23}, both genealogies contain expressions which at least leave open, if they do not actually indicate, the idea that Jesus was not the bodily son of Joseph. Can the Evangelists really have failed to notice that in this way they were compromising these genealogies and with them the descent of Jesus from David ? And if they thought that by these indications they were not compromising them, could they not have tried to say at the critical juncture that although Jesus was not the physical or natural, He was still the legitimate and legal son of Joseph and therefore of David, i.e., introduced into the family tree on the ground of adoption ? The other problems of these genealogies show that, in accordance with the Old Testament view, their authors understood the idea of descent quite differently from the way in which we do. And linguistic usage shows (cf. K. L. Schmidt, p. 290 f.) that the crucial word ἐγέννησεν can also be used improperly, i.e., in a non-biological sense. " Neither the thought that connexion with David dispenses with miracle, nor the idea that miracle dissolves Jesus' connexion with David

were possible for Matthew. What he expected of Christ lay beyond nature and history and was God's very own revelation which makes His almighty grace effective. Hence the genealogy by itself never proved the kingly rights of Jesus. But just as little did miracle invalidate Scripture or disrupt nature and history. It rather strengthens and completes them. So Matthew narrates that an express direction of God assigned Jesus to Joseph the Son of David. The link forged by nature could not from Matthew's standpoint have bound Jesus more firmly to the house of David than did the will of God made manifest " (Adolf Schlatter, *Der Evangelist Matthäus*, 1929, p. 5 f.). Accordingly Schlatter entitles his exposition of Mt. 1[18-25] " The Grafting of Jesus into the Tribe of David." In the same way, too, the word γενόμενος ἐκ σπέρματος Δαυὶδ κατὰ σάρκα, Rom. 1[3], need not exclude the thought of another than the purely physical descent from David. Γενόμενος κατὰ σάρκα need not altogether signify biological provenance.

4. In itself it is not surprising that the question was asked whether, especially in the narrative of Luke, another simpler account did not shine through the original one, a conception which would be made explicit with the assistance of one or two easy erasures, the ἐπεὶ ἄνδρα οὐ γινώσκω of Lk. 1[34] and the ὡς ἐνομίζετο of Lk. 3[23]. This would mean that an act of God was implied which would not exclude the generation of Jesus by Joseph. But we must still ask ourselves whether the text of Luke is really simplified by these erasures, whether the events and patterns of this narrative of the childhood are really made clearer without the Virgin birth. Even if such a purge of the text of Luke is possible and helpful, what can be excised from the account of Mt. 1[18-25], where even according to the contradictory version of *Syr. Sin.* the Virgin birth is the actual theme and is also clearly presupposed through the whole of the second chapter ?

It certainly cannot be denied that the outward, explicit evidence for the dogma in the statements of Holy Scripture is hedged about by questions. But still less can it be asserted that the questions raised are so hard to answer that one is forced by exegesis to contest the dogma.

Decision as to the necessity of the dogma cannot ultimately be made on the ground where such questions are to be raised and answered. No one can dispute the existence of a biblical testimony to the Virgin birth. The questions to be raised and answered are literary questions ; they are concerned with the tradition, the age and the source-value of this testimony. The final and proper decision is whether in accordance with the demands of Church dogma this testimony is to be heard, and heard as the emphatic statement of the New Testament message, or whether in defiance of Church dogma it is not to be heard, i.e., only to be heard as a sub-statement of the New Testament message which is not binding. This decision can be supported by answering the literary questions in one sense or the other. But it does not stand or fall with the answer to these questions. It certainly was not their age and source-value that brought the narratives of the Virgin birth into the text of the Gospels and out of this text into the creed. But a certain inward, essential rightness and importance in their connexion with the person of Jesus Christ first admitted them to a share in the Gospel witness. At first this was announced with great reserve but in the last resort quite definitely, and then admitted also to a share in Church confession and dogma in contrast to some other elements in this testimony which outwardly (and apparently inwardly too) were much more distinctive. The question to which we must address ourselves here and give a serious answer is, whether this right-ness and importance, which they must have had at the rise of the canonical New Testament, and then again at the framing of the dogma, are so compellingly illuminated for us that we, too, must acknow-ledge the essential rightness and importance of the narratives of the Virgin birth. By putting the question in this way we shall be quite clear that in answering it we are concerned only with an *a posteriori* understanding of the rightness and importance which belong to this matter in revelation itself, for only in so far as this rightness and importance arise out of revelation can they shine upon us with com-pelling light. Behind literary as behind dogmatic investigation there arises the *quaestio facti*, which cannot be answered either by literary or by dogmatic investigation. It is fitting, however, that in the realm of theology literary and dogmatic investigation should both be under-taken in the first instance (i.e., until the utter impossibility of this procedure is demonstrated) *sub conditione facti*.

In order to reach the dogmatic *a posteriori* understanding we have in view, it is, above all, necessary to realise that the dogma of the Virgin birth, in fact the New Testament basis of the dogma, is of a different kind, and lies, as it were, on a different level of testimony from the dogma or New Testament knowledge of the true divinity and true humanity of Jesus Christ. It denotes not so much the christological reality of revelation as the mystery of that reality, the inconceivability of it, its character as a fact in which God has acted solely through God and in which God can likewise be known solely through God. The dogma of the Virgin birth is not, then, a repetition or description of the *vere Deus vere homo*, although in its own way it also expresses, explains and throws light upon it. As a formal dogma, as it were, which is required to explain the material, it states that when the event indicated by the name Emmanuel takes place, when God comes to us as one of ourselves to be our own, to be ourselves in our place, as very God and very Man, this is a real event accom-plished in space and time as history within history. In it God's revela-tion comes to us, in it our reconciliation takes place ; yet it is *such an event* that to every Why? and Whence? and How? we can only answer that here God does it all Himself. The dogma of the Virgin birth is thus the confession of the boundless hiddenness of the *vere Deus vere homo* and of the boundless amazement of awe and thankful-ness called forth in us by this *vere Deus vere homo*. It eliminates the last surviving possibility of understanding the *vere Deus vere homo* intellectually, as an idea or an arbitrary interpretation in the sense of docetic or ebionite Christology. It leaves only the spiritual under-standing of the *vere Deus vere homo*, i.e., the understanding in which God's own work is seen in God's own light.

In this sense the New Testament passages about the Virgin birth draw a boundary line around the reality of Jesus Christ, a line barely indicated yet quite definite, clearly establishing itself in spite of the small amount of material, impressive and unforgettable to every reader of the New Testament. Those who seek with A. v. Harnack (*Dogmengeschichte*[4], vol. I, p. 113) to explain the content of these passages simply as a postulate derived from Is. 7[14] must come to terms with the fact that even if with the LXX Judaism regarded *almah* as equal to παρθένος, nevertheless it certainly did not explain it messianically. How did the Palestinian community, to which the Matthaean account in particular points, achieve this innovation ? Early Judaism in general " never expected that the promised Messiah would see light in this world by way of supernatural generation ; even with regard to Him the Canon held that He was man born of man. Thus Mt. 1[18] signifies an absolute novelty for Jewish thought " (Strack-Billerbeck, *Kommentar zum N.T. nach Talmud und Midrasch*, vol. I, 1922, p. 49). And against those who regard these passages as borrowed from Buddhist, Egyptian, Greek and other myths, we may hold that alike in their New Testament context and in the decided intention of each, these passages point in quite a different direction from the myths in question. The presence of the account of the Virgin birth in the New Testament cannot be understood at all, or else it is to be understood as the drawing of a line, in terms of what is demanded by the nature of this reality, against any possibility of explaining the *vere Deus vere homo* as an interpretation grounded upon a general truth otherwise known to man, or, as the expression and symbol of a oneness between God and man which in the ultimate analysis is always to be found everywhere. In face of this possibility, the passages in Matthew and Luke that are concerned with the earthly human origin of Jesus say: No, His earthly human origin is a mystery; it can be understood only as a unique and peculiar act of God ; the *vere Deus vere homo* and with it the revelation of God as a whole is not an intellectual but a spiritual reality. Obviously, therefore, these passages in the New Testament have their own quite definite, distinct but necessary function, and it is understandable that the statements they make are taken up into the church creeds and have become a dogma. R. Seeberg's objection (*op. cit.* p. 179) is, therefore, to be rejected that " the entire revelation of God in Jesus and His redemptive work might quite well be conceived in all its stages, without any claim being made for birth of the Virgin." In reply, we may say that whether " God's revelation in Jesus " is really " conceived " in dogmatics and in the Church, depends upon how we conceive it. To describe this How ?, i.e., to describe this mystery of revelation, is the aim of the doctrine of the Virgin birth. And it is not calculated to inspire confidence when Seeberg continues that in his Christology he has made " no·use at all " of the Virgin birth and yet " can do justice in every way to the idea of becoming man so far as it means anything for redemption." Is Seeberg's Christology an intellectual or a spiritual explanation of the *vere Deus vere homo* ? The answer to this question would provide a splendid illustration why in certain circumstances a theologian can actually make no use at all of the Virgin birth while in others he is literally forced to make use of it.

It is the mystery of revelation that our dogma describes. If revelation is a mystery and is understood as such, then it is at least possible in principle for the necessity of it to begin shining through. But now we must emphasise the fact that it is the description of this mystery that is the purpose of the dogma.

" Here God will not hold to His order of creation but make a new one. A virgin shall conceive ; and that shall be a ' sign ' or miracle " (Luther, *Preb. üb. Lc.* 1[26ff.], 1552, *E.A.*, 6, 195). Is. 7[14], at any rate, speaks of a sign.

Objections might, of course, be raised to what we have said up till now. Is acknowledgment and confession of this mystery of the divine origin of the person of Jesus Christ completely tied up with acknowledgment and confession of the Virgin birth in particular ? Is the form in which we speak here of this mystery as if it were the content of it inseparable from this content, or this content from this form ? Must it not be left to Christian liberty or even to the historical judgment of the individual whether he can and will acknowledge and confess this content in precisely this form ? To this the answer is that the doctrine of the Virgin birth is merely the description and therefore the form by and in which the mystery is spoken of in the New Testament and in the creeds. Similarly we might say that so far as the New Testament witness to Easter is the account of the empty grave, it merely describes the mystery, or the revelation of the mystery, " Christ is risen." It describes it by pointing to this external fact. No one will dream of claiming that this external fact in itself and as such had the power to unveil for the disciples the veiled fact that " God was in Christ." But was it revealed to them otherwise than by the sign of this external fact ? Will there be real faith in the resurrection of the Lord as revealing His mystery, as unveiling His divine glory, where the account of the empty grave is thought to be excisable as the mere form of the content in question, or where it can be left to Christian liberty to confess seriously and decisively the content alone ? With this form are we not also bound in fact to lose the specific content of the Easter message for some other truth about the resurrection ? Sign and thing signified, the outward and the inward, are, as a rule, strictly distinguished in the Bible, and certainly in other connexions we cannot lay sufficient stress upon the distinction. But they are never separated in such a (" liberal ") way that according to preference the one may be easily retained without the other. Are the signs of which the biblical witness to revelation speaks arbitrarily selected and given ? Is the outward part, in which according to this witness the inward part of revelation is brought to ear and eye, merely an accidental expression of the inward ? From what standpoint will we really want to establish this point, if we are clear that revelation is something else than the manifestation of an idea ? But if we cannot establish it, how can we really want to achieve this abstraction, holding to the thing signified but not to the sign unless we freely choose to do so ? When we do this, is it not the case that openly or tacitly we have in mind something quite different ? This is the question we have to put to ourselves even in regard to the Virgin birth. Ultimately, the only question that we can ask here, but we very definitely have to ask it, is this : When two theologians with apparently the same conviction confess the mystery of Christmas, do they mean the same thing by that mystery, if one acknowledges and confesses the Virgin birth to be the sign of the mystery while the other denies it as a mere externality or is ready to leave it an open question ? Does the second man really acknowledge and confess that

in His revelation to us and in our reconciliation to Him, to our measureless astonishment and in measureless hiddenness the initiative is
wholly with God ?   Or does he not by his denial or declared indifference
towards the sign of the Virgin birth at the same time betray the fact
that with regard to the thing signified by this sign he means something quite different ?   May it not be the case that the only one who
hears the witness of the thing is the one who keeps to the sign by
which the witness has actually signified it ?

Among those who dispute the sign we must first discover the man concerning
whom we can at the same time unhesitatingly admit that he shows a reliable
acquaintance with the thing signified by this sign. Is it chance that in all of
them recognition of the mystery of Christmas is menaced and weakened by being
related to some form of natural theology ? Is it the case that denial of the
Virgin birth involves the assertion of a point of contact ? Or does the assertion
of this point of contact produce blindness to the miracle of the Virgin birth ?
A fatal connexion does actually exist here. It is particularly instructive to
re-read Schleiermacher's (*The Christian Faith*, Eng. tr., p. 404 ff.), disquisitions
on this point. At first sight Schleiermacher appears to know exactly what is
at issue in the Virgin birth. In his phraseology he calls it the " supernatural "
element in the person of the Redeemer, and says regarding it : " The reproductive power of the species cannot be adequate to produce an individual through
whom something is to be introduced, for the first time, into the species, which
was never in it before. For that it is necessary to postulate, in addition to this
reproductive power, a creative activity combined with human activity. . . .
In this sense everyone who assumes in the Redeemer a natural sinlessness and
a new creation through the union of the divine with the human, postulates a
supernatural conception as well. . . . The general idea of a supernatural conception remains, therefore, essential and necessary, if the specific pre-eminence
of the Redeemer is to remain undiminished. But the more precise definition
of this supernatural conception as one in which there is no male activity has
no connexion of any kind with the essential elements in the peculiar dignity
of the Redeemer ; and hence in and by itself is no constituent part of Christian
doctrine. . . . And everyone has to reach a decision about it by the proper application of those principles of criticism and interpretation which approve themselves
to him." We simply comment : " The general concept of a supernatural generation " is quite enough to denote what Schleiermacher means by the mystery of
Christmas as he sees it, namely, the miraculous manifestation of a creative activity
united to the activity of the human species to produce the peculiar being Jesus
Christ. In other words, this thing signified needs no sign at all. What Schleiermacher calls " a new creation " is really the completion of the creation of the
human species, a completion the necessity of which we may know *a priori*,
and the achievement of which may therefore be postulated in the union of
the divine with the human in Christ as " a supernatural generation." Of this
we are not forced to say that it is new, and so it does not require a sign. In
this connexion the view of P. Althaus (*Grundriss d. Dogm.* II, 1932, p. 98 f.)
is also instructive. He attributes to the *natus ex virgine*, so to speak, a contingent
significance, depending upon the decision as to the age and source-value of the
Matthaean and Lukan passages. If a positive decision can be reached here,
then it is true that " the God who could let His Son become Man and make
the new man by natural generation, here takes a different road, in order also (!)
to prove by it that in reality the new Man has been born and God has become
Man." But for those who decide the historical question in the negative, who
thus see in the passages in question an untenable postulate derived from docetic
ways of thinking, Christ's birth must be a "creative miracle of God," consisting

in the fact " that He suffers the Son to become Man in the context of human life, creating the Man who ' without father, without mother, without descent ' (Heb. 7³) breaks through the context of sinful humanity as the new Man of God, the First-born of the new creation." To this we must reply : If this " creative miracle " is actually attested otherwise than by the sign of the *natus ex virgine*, if this sign is therefore unimportant and may be abandoned to the mercy of historical judgment, then does not this " creative miracle " belong to the presupposition of Althaus' Christology ? I refer to what he himself calls the " prime revelation " which, though it is admittedly insufficient and points beyond itself, he regards as present to all men in every age in and through their own reality in the world. According to Althaus, it is in virtue of this " prime revelation " that Christology is at once the recognition and the conquest of the offence (*op. cit.* p. 10, 13 f., 83 f.) ? Where the sign can be dispensed with, any conquest of the offence seems to be superfluous and recollection as such leads to the goal. Possibly (if it is so in the historian's view) God did take this road to attest the " creative miracle," but we are still aware of this " miracle " even if it is not the case. Does not then this " miracle "—and this makes everything plain—mean something else, something different from what we have described as the mystery of the *vere Deus vere homo* ? In this connexion we may reply briefly to the question of popular theology, whether in order to believe in a really Christian way " one " would have to believe fully in the Virgin birth. We must answer that there is certainly nothing to prevent anyone, without affirming the doctrine of the Virgin birth, from recognising the mystery of the person of Jesus Christ or from believing in a perfectly Christian way. It is within God's counsel and will to make this possible, just as it cannot be at all impossible for Him to bring anyone to the knowledge of Himself even beyond the sphere of the Church visible to us. But this does not imply that the Church is at liberty to convert the doctrine of the Virgin birth into an option for specially strong or for specially weak souls. The Church knew well what it was doing when it posted this doctrine on guard, as it were, at the door of the mystery of Christmas. It can never be in favour of anyone thinking he can hurry past this guard. It will remind him that he is walking along a private road at his own cost and risk. It will warn him against doing so. It will proclaim as a church ordinance that to affirm the doctrine of the Virgin birth is a part of real Christian faith. It will at least require of its servants, even if there are some who personally cannot understand this ordinance, that they treat their private road as a private road and do not make it an object of their proclamation, that if they personally cannot affirm it and so (unfortunately) withhold it from their congregations, they must at least pay the dogma the respect of keeping silence about it.

According to the dogma the mystery of revelation is described as the occurrence of a miracle, " miracle " taken in the special concrete sense, not in the general one just mentioned above. At this stage, we do not inquire into its special content : *conceptus de Spiritu sancto, natus ex Maria virgine*. We merely make the point that by these assertions is meant an event occurring in the realm of the creaturely world in the full sense of the word, and so in the unity of the psychical with the physical, in time and in space, in noetic and ontic reality. It cannot be understood out of continuity with the rest that occurs in this world, nor is it in fact grounded in this continuity. It is so unusual an event that it may be misunderstood subjectively as an error, illusion, poetry or symbol, or objectively as a creaturely mystery unexplained to begin with but explicable in principle. It can be properly understood, however, only as a sign wrought by God Himself, and by God Himself solely and directly, the sign of the freedom and immediacy, the mystery of His action, as a preliminary sign of the coming of His Kingdom. This is because in itself it really is nothing other than such a sign. A sign must, of course, signify. To do so it must have in itself something of the kind of thing it signifies ; it must be in analogy with it noetically and ontically. In this respect the miracle of Christmas is in analogy with what it signifies, the mystery of Christmas. But it also consists in the fact that amid the continuity of the creaturely world, yet independently of it, both as regards our understanding of His action and as regards His action itself, God Himself has the initiative.

Quoniam inopinata salus hominibus inciperet fieri Deo adiuvante, inopinatus et partus virginis fiebat, Deo dante signum hoc, sed non homine operante illud (Irenaeus, *C.o.h.* III 21, 6).

Now it is no accident that for us the Virgin birth is paralleled by the miracle of which the Easter witness speaks, the miracle of the empty tomb. These two miracles belong together. They constitute, as it were, a single sign, the special function of which, compared with other signs and wonders of the New Testament witness, is to describe and mark out the existence of Jesus Christ, amid the many other existences in human history, as that human historical existence in which God is Himself, God is alone, God is directly the Subject, the temporal reality of which is not only called forth, created, conditioned and supported by the eternal reality of God, but is identical with it. The Virgin birth at the opening and the empty tomb at the close of Jesus' life bear witness that this life is a fact marked off from all the rest of human life, and marked off in the first instance, not by our understanding or our interpretation, but by itself. Marked off in regard to its origin : it is free of the arbitrariness which underlies all our existences. And marked off in regard to its goal : it is victorious over the death to which we are all liable. Only within these limits is it what it is and is it correctly understood, as the mystery of the revelation of God. It is to that mystery that these limits point—he who ignores them or wishes them away must see to it that he is not thinking of something quite different from this.

Τὸ πρὸ τῆς γεννήσεως καὶ τὸ μετὰ τοῦ θανάτου τὴν τῆς φύσεως ἡμῶν ἐκφεύγει κοινότητα . . . εἰ γὰρ ἐντὸς ἦν τῶν τῆς φύσεως ὅρων τὰ περὶ τοῦ Χριστοῦ διηγήματα, ποῦ τὸ θεῖον ; (Gregory of Nyssa, *Or. cat.* 13).

The mutual relationship between these two limits may perhaps be defined thus. The Virgin birth denotes particularly the mystery of revelation. It denotes the fact that God stands at the start where real revelation takes place—God and not the arbitrary cleverness, capability, or piety of man. In Jesus Christ God comes forth out of the profound hiddenness of His divinity in order to act as God among us and upon us. That is revealed and made visible to us in the sign of the resurrection of Jesus Christ from the dead, but it is grounded upon the fact signified by the Virgin birth, that here in this Jesus God Himself has really come down and concealed Himself in humanity. It is because He was veiled here that He could and had to unveil Himself as He did at Easter. The empty tomb, on the other hand, denotes particularly the revelation of the mystery. It denotes that it is not for nothing that God stands at the beginning, but that it is as such that He becomes active and knowable. He has no need of human power and is free from all human caprice. Therefore even the ultimate extremities of human existence, as He submits to them and abandons Himself to death, offer no hindrance to His being and work. That God Himself in His complete majesty was one with us, as the Virgin birth indicates, is verified in what the empty tomb indicates, that here in this Jesus the living God has spoken to us men in accents we cannot fail to hear. Because He has unveiled Himself here as the One He is, we may and must say what the Christmas message says, that unto you is born this day the Saviour. The mystery at the beginning is the basis of the mystery at the end ; and by the mystery of the end the mystery of the beginning becomes active and knowable. And since this is so, the same objective content is signified in the one case by the miracle of the Virgin birth, in the other by the miracle of the empty tomb. Once we have looked into this self-enclosed circle, we shall have to meet the attack upon the *natus ex virgine* with the further reflection that by it an indispensable connexion is destroyed which is actually found in the creed, so that the *tertia die resurrexit a mortuis*, too, is actually called in question.

At this point we must recall the extraordinary section in E. Brunner's book, *The Mediator*, in which he deals with our theme. Beyond everything that has been said since Schleiermacher, Brunner develops the queer objection that the doctrine of the Virgin birth means a " biological interpretation of the miracle " (meaning the miracle of the incarnation), and is in fact an expression of " biological inquisitiveness." The divine miracle, he contends, is supposed to be explained here in its How, whereas we should be content in faith with the That. The Virgin birth is an event in space and time, a fact of observation, of the reality of which we may be aware without having faith in it. For that reason we ought to declare our indifference toward it. In reply to this we must first of all make an exegetical statement (cf. recently and particularly M. Dibelius) : neither in the New Testament nor in the creed is the doctrine of the Virgin birth a " biological " explanation. There is not a single word in which it takes anything to do with the biological happening as such—even on the analogy of the Easter story. It is content to indicate the fact prospectively and retrospectively. This fact is, of course, of such a kind as to belong to the area of biological enquiry. But on this point it must first of all be said that what happens here in the field of biology is in itself, as Irenaeus (see above) has already said, only the *signum*, or sign, of that inexpressible reality of revelation which lies on the borderland of every field of human study, the *vere Deus vere homo*. If we cannot separate the sign from the thing signified, as, with so many others, even Brunner unfortunately wishes to do, the sign is still not the thing signified. It is certainly true that up to the date of canonical and credal formulation assuredly no one who acknowledged the Virgin birth as its sign even remotely thought of anything like legitimate or illegitimate inquisitiveness in this connexion. The sign itself was always left as free of explanation as possible. More important still is the fact that the sign did not in the least explain the thing signified. Rather it brought to light essentially and purposefully its very inexplicability, its character of mystery. That Brunner should object to the sign undeniably taking place in the sphere of biological enquiry is very strange. How and where could there be signs if not in this field and in other fields of human enquiry, in the " sphere of space and time occurrence " ? Might not Brunner's annoyance at it also be voiced against the appearances of the risen Jesus, against the empty tomb and against all Jesus' miracles ? Of course one could and can be " aware apart from faith " of a sign of revelation. In relation to the Easter miracle this awareness without faith will take the form of a hypothesis of vision or deception or apparent death, and in relation to the Christmas miracle it will take the form of one of those arbitrary Jewish legends, through which awareness of the fact was thought to be actually possible without faith. It may even be thought that a naive cosmo-logical supernaturalism made it possible in earlier times (although certainly not to the universal extent usually assumed) to talk oneself into an awareness of facts of this kind which does not require faith. The awareness which either explains the miracle away or is a mere awareness of *portenta stupenda* must be described from the standpoint of faith as an erroneous or false awareness. As signs of revelation, in their descriptive function and so in their only real nature, these miracles cannot be known in either of these ways. What does the possi-bility of this " awareness without faith " avail against the reality and gravity of its object ? Brunner's denial of the Virgin birth is a bad business. As is also the case with Althaus, it throws an ambiguous light over the whole of his Christology. The sigh of N. Berdyaev is mine too : " I read Brunner's book with tremendous interest, because I felt in him tenseness and acuity of thought, religious sensibility. But when I reached the passage in which Brunner confesses that he does not believe in Jesus Christ's birth of the Virgin, or at least confronts it with indifference, my mood became sad and the matter grew tedious. For it seemed to me as though everything had now been cancelled, as though every-thing else was now pointless " (*Orient u. Occident, Heft* 1, 1929, p. 19). Brunner's contribution to this matter in his more recent book, *Man in Revolt*, is so bad that my only possible attitude to it is silence.

Have we now proved the need for our dogma ? Undoubtedly not. We have made the point that, however scattered and problematic the relevant statements may be, the content of the dogma answers to biblical attestation. In particular, it is related to the mystery of the person of Jesus Christ. It is connected with it as sign with thing signified. It describes this mystery by a miraculous event in analogy with the mystery. In this way, and by incidentally disputing the various denials of the Virgin birth, we have merely hinted at its necessity. We have called attention to the points of view from which this necessity can be made clear. It becomes clear only as we hear the biblical witness, in spite of and amid its reserve. If we hear it as it was obviously heard in the Early Church, we will discern the uniqueness of its content as a sign and the relation between this sign and the mystery of revelation, and so come to understand the miracle constituting this content in its essential appropriateness. Everything in the end depends on the one thing, on the mystery of revelation speaking and being apprehended through this sign. Theo-logical explanation at this point can as little anticipate this or compel it to happen as in the case of revelation generally. To this extent the necessity for this very dogma cannot be proved. It can only be shown what the elements are which lead us to acknowledge its necessity. If we affirm this necessity, we must regard the acknowledgment involved as a decision, which in the last resort can only authenticate itself by virtue of its conformity to the object which is demanded of it. It can and will receive further confirmation, however, in the detailed exposition of the dogma, to which we have now to turn.

1. The most suitable starting-point is the quite unambiguous second clause : *Natus ex Maria virgine*. It is unambiguous because it describes the sovereignty of the divine act, and therefore the mystery of Christmas, by an express and extremely concrete negative. " Born of the Virgin Mary " means born as no one else was born, in a way which can as little be made clear biologically as the resurrection of a dead man, i.e., born not because of male generation but solely because of female conception. The first and in substance more important clause, *conceptus de Spiritu sancto*, which is interpreted by the second, describes in positive terms the same sovereignty of God in the coming of His Word into human existence. It states that the free will of God is the meaning and solution of the enigma. But we must at once make it clear that the negative in the first clause also includes a positive, a very important, positive assertion. It does not speak only of something utterly enigmatic that becomes an event within human reality, and therefore of the sovereignty of God which has to be borne in mind in view of this event. It also speaks of the human reality of Jesus Christ, although it speaks of it with unheard-of limitation, and by the proclamation of a pure enigma. Otherwise it would not describe this mystery, the mystery of Christmas, the sovereignty of God manifested in the fact that here God's reality becomes one with human reality. By its *natus ex Maria* it states that the person Jesus Christ is the real son of a real mother, the son born of the body, flesh and blood of his mother, both of them as real as all the other sons of other mothers. It is thus that Jesus Christ is born and not otherwise. In this complete sense, He, too, is a man. In this complete sense, then, He is man in a different way from the other sons of other mothers. But the difference under consideration here is so great, so fundamental and comprehensive, that it does not impair the completeness and genuineness of His humanity.

The location of this miracle within human reality is stressed by the *ex Maria*, which is so strictly insisted upon, particularly in the Latin forms of the creed ; cf. Gal. 4⁴ : ἐκ γυναικός. The *Symbolum Quicunque* has described it correctly in the formula, *Homo est ex substantia matris in saeculo natus* (Denz. No. 40). And in the earlier credal constructions, too, the clause *natus ex Maria* had without doubt already acquired the sense and at least the practical significance of a protection against gnostic and docetic ideas like those of Valentinus, according to whom Christ had received nothing from His human mother, but had assumed a heavenly body newly created for this purpose, had thus passed through Mary merely as water through an aqueduct, in other words had only apparently been born and become man. The Church was right to reject the doctrine of this Valentinian miracle. For if this miracle could also be regarded as pointing to a mystery, it was certainly not the mystery of Christmas attested by Holy Scripture, nor the inconceivable reality of the *vere Deus vere homo*, but an arbitrarily invented *mysterium*, the meaning of which could not be God's revelation to us, and our reconciliation to God.

Thus in the words *natus ex Maria* the second clause also defines the positive fact that the birth of Jesus Christ was the genuine birth of a genuine man. And in this way the sign signifies the thing signified, the inexpressible mystery that the Word was made flesh. That and nothing else is the act of the divine sovereignty which we call the mystery of Christmas. Only because that really happened is it the mystery of God's revelation to us and of our reconciliation to God. It is important for the whole concept of revelation, grace, faith and in the last analysis for all departments of theological investigation and teaching, to be quite clear that this *natus ex Maria* is included in the dogma, that the miracle of Christmas has as one of its elements the not at all miraculous reality of man. If Emmanuel is true the miracle is done upon him. It is man who is the object of sovereign divine action in this event. God Himself and God alone is Master and Lord. This cannot be stated strongly enough, exclusively enough, negatively enough against all synergism or even monism. It must not be so stated, however, that what is simple and definite is forgotten or obscured. It is he, man, who is central in this event. It is not an event in the loneliness of God, but an event between God and man. Man is not there only in a supplementary capacity. In his own place, his own sharply defined manner, he participates in the event as one of the principals ; not as a cipher or as a phantom, but as the real man that he is. The Word became flesh. He participates in it as a real man can, where God Himself, God alone is the Subject, Lord and Master. It is not that he is not in it. But even the more refined and precise statements we make regarding the sovereignty of God in this event can only describe how real man participates in it and to what extent he can do so.

To glance aside at the dogma of creation, we have to say here, that although revelation and reconciliation are no less inconceivable than it, they do not, like it, involve a *creatio ex nihilo*. Revelation and reconciliation can also be called a creation, the " new creature " (2 Cor. 5[17]). But with G. Thomasius (*Christi Person und Werk*, 3rd Edn., 1886, vol. I, p. 401) we have to speak in this case of a " creative act in and upon the old natural man." In place of the *ex nihilo* we now have this old natural humanity, or in the symbol the *ex Maria*. The new or second creation presupposes the old or first, not as a reality familiar to us in its nature and at our disposal, but as one given beforehand, presupposed by God, i.e., as the existing reality to be freshly enlightened and shaped by judgment and grace. It is to be treated and understood by us in its relation to God, not immediately (not with the results of a " natural theology "), but only in the knowledge of judgment and grace, yet all the same as the existence upon which action is as miraculously taken in the one case, as it is miraculously based in the other, in creation. Against the creaturely self-glorification which might creep in here and interpret man with his existence as God's partner, against all natural theology, the *ex virgine* with its positive background in the *conceptus de Spiritu sancto* will provide the necessary safeguard. But unless constant attention is given to the *ex Maria virgine*, the mystery will still be denied.

But now let us turn to the main point, *ex virgine*. What is meant by that? Certainly the general and formal fact that the becoming, the actual human existence of the Revealer of God who is God Himself, (the γένεσις Ἰησοῦ Χριστοῦ, Mt. 1¹·¹⁸), is a miracle. That is to say, it is an event in this world of ours, yet such that it is not grounded upon the continuity of events in this world nor is it to be understood in terms of it. It is a sign set up immediately by God, and can only be understood as such. But just because like all biblical miracles the *ex virgine* is essentially a sign, in our interpretation of it we ought not to be content merely to make clear its discontinuity, its "super-naturalness." Miraculous and marvellous are two different things. Merely by establishing the marvellous as such, indispensable though that is, we still remain in the sphere in which there are marvels according to heathen religion and cosmology too, marvels with a strong resemblance to the biblical marvel, even to the *natus ex virgine* itself. The way in which the *natus ex virgine* appears in the New Testament and the way in which it has been expounded in the Early Church give us no right to abide by that finding and to regard the marvellous as the original motive of the dogma. With full recognition of its formal importance we can as little abide by this finding as by the *ex Maria* which has an equal claim on our notice and emphasis. By the *ex virgine* the essential point is plainly expressed that by the Word being made flesh, by God's Son assuming "human nature," this human nature undergoes a very definite limitation. Grace is imparted to it. But this cannot happen without its coming under judgment as well.

That both are involved is made specially clear in the text of Lk. 1²⁶⁻³⁸. In the first place the angel's message there clearly has the quality of a joyous message : χαῖρε, κεχαριτωμένη, ὁ κύριος μετὰ σοῦ (v. 28), εὗρες χάριν παρὰ τῷ θεῷ (v. 30). But its effect on Mary is still devastating : ἐπὶ τῷ λόγῳ διεταράχθη (v. 29). To her as to the shepherds in Lk. 2¹⁰ must come the call : μὴ φοβοῦ, Μαριάμ. The decisive words of the promise are not altogether free from exegetical difficulty : Πνεῦμα ἅγιον ἐπελεύσεται ἐπὶ σέ, καὶ δύναμις ὑψίστου ἐπισκιάσει σοι (v. 35). But they certainly have a rather menacing ring. Finally, the famous concluding answer of Mary : ἰδοὺ ἡ δούλη κυρίου· γένοιτό μοι κατὰ τό ῥῆμά σου (v. 38), reminds us most naturally of the Lucan version of the prayer in Gethsemane : μὴ τὸ θέλημά μου ἀλλὰ τὸ σὸν γενέσθω (Lk. 22⁴²). And still deeper shadows rest upon the parallel text Mt. 1¹⁸⁻²⁵, where in the dream Joseph's conversation with the angel is directed towards helping Joseph over the stumbling-block which he must see to be involved in the pregnancy of Mary. Manifestly the *natus ex virgine* according to these texts not only runs counter to nature in the biological sense, but deals positively with a genuine experience belonging to man as such. In that grace is imparted to him he is given not simply to be the spectator of an unusual event, but to participate in an event which contradicts and withstands him. Something decisive befalls him—and here the concept of "nature-miracle" begins to acquire its full biblical meaning—something with which he cannot come to terms without pain and astonishment, without humiliation, which he can affirm and appreciate only in faith and not otherwise. Of course, in the judgment in which he is placed grace is concealed. Indeed it is of grace and of grace alone that the texts purport to speak. This becomes quite clear in the continuation of the Lucan narrative in v. 39–56. And it is contained in the creed, in the preceding *conceptus de Spiritu sancto*, and is to be stressed in the interpretation of it. But grace does not come except through the strait gate and along the narrow way of judgment. It is from this standpoint that it must be understood in the *ex virgine*.

In the *ex virgine* there is contained a judgment upon man. When Mary as a virgin becomes the mother of the Lord and so, as it were, the entrance gate of divine revelation into the world of man, it is declared that in any other way, i.e., by the natural way in which a human wife becomes a mother, there can be no motherhood of the Lord and so no such entrance gate of revelation into our world. In other words, human nature possesses no capacity for becoming the human nature of Jesus Christ, the place of divine revelation. It cannot be the work-mate of God. If it actually becomes so, it is not because of any attributes which it possessed already and in itself, but because of what is done to it by the divine Word, and so not because of what it has to do or give, but because of what it has to suffer and receive—and at the hand of God. The virginity of Mary in the birth of the Lord is the denial, not of man in the presence of God, but of any power, attribute or capacity in him for God. If he has this power—and Mary clearly has it—it means strictly and exclusively that he acquires it, that it is laid upon him. In this power of his for God he can as little understand himself as Mary in the story of the Annunciation could understand herself as the future mother of the Messiah. Only with her *Ecce ancilla Domini* can he understand himself as what, in a way inconceivable to himself, he has actually become in the sight of God and by His agency.

The meaning of this judgment, this negation, is not the difference between God as Creator and man as a creature. Man as a creature— if we try for a moment to speak of man in this abstract way—might have the capacity for God and even be able to understand himself in this capacity. In Paradise there would have been no need of the sign *ex virgine* to indicate that man was God's fellow-worker. But the man whom revelation reaches, and who is reconciled to God in revelation and by it, is not man in Paradise. He has not ceased to be God's creature. But he has lost his pure creatureliness, and with it the capacity for God, because as a creature and in the totality of his creatureliness he became disobedient to his Creator. To the roots of his being he lives in this disobedience. It is with this disobedient creature that God has to do in His revelation. It is his nature, his flesh, that the Word assumes in being made flesh. And this human nature, the only one we know and the only one there actually is, has of itself no capacity for being adopted by God's Word into unity with

Himself, i.e., into personal unity with God. Upon this human nature
a mystery must be wrought in order that this may be made possible.
And this mystery must consist in its receiving the capacity for God
which it does not possess. This mystery is signified by the *natus ex
virgine*.

The decisive point of view, from which the *natus ex virgine* was always regarded
in early dogmatics, was rightly, therefore, the recollection of inherited sin, or
original sin as it is better expressed in the Latin *peccatum originale*, i.e., sin so
far as man does not live it out primarily and only in individual thoughts, words
and deeds, but lives it in the inevitability and totality of his existence as one
already fallen in Adam, because the *liberum arbitrium* of obedience to God is
missing, while the *servum arbitrium* of disobedience is peculiarly his own. This
human nature is limited and contradicted by the *natus ex virgine*. It indicates
the existence of a Man who as a man like all of us in this sinful nature of ours,
in the flesh, bears with us the way and the curse of sin, but who as God does
not live out the sin, because even now He does not live it, because the *servum
arbitrium* of disobedience is foreign to Him while the *liberum arbitrium* of obedience is His own. If He did not bear sin with us He would not be one like us ;
the *vere homo* would not be true. He could not be God's Revealer and Reconciler
on our behalf. But if He lived it and lived it out like all of us, how could *vere
Deus* be true ? How could He be the divine Revealer and Reconciler ? If it is
God Himself who here steps forth as man, then it is unthinkable that there steps
forth here a sinner like us. But then His existence in our old human nature
posits and signifies a penetration and a new beginning. Standing in the continuity of historical humanity He breaks through it and opens up a new humanity.
Fuit in Adamo, nec tamen cum ipso et in ipso peccavit (F. Turrettini, *Instit. Theol.
el.* II, 1682, *Loc.* XIII *qu.* 11, 15). The sign of that is *natus ex virgine*.

But how far is it the *ex virgine* that points to this penetration
and new beginning ?

It is well to remember again at this point that the *ex virgine* must always
be understood as a *pointer* to this penetration and new beginning, but not as
the conditioning of it. (Failure on my part to make this distinction in the first
draft of this book, p. 276 ff., meant that the questions and answers involved
were obscured.) If there is a necessary connexion between this sign and this
thing signified, the connexion is not a casual one. We shall say, then, that God
willed this content in this form, and therefore we shall keep to its actual form.
But we shall not say that God could not have given it quite a different form.
Therefore we can separate form and content, sign and thing signified. But we
cannot derive them from each other, any more than we can separate them from
each other, by any method of calculation. From this standpoint it becomes
clear why there is nothing in the objection unanimously raised at this point by
Schleiermacher, R. Seeberg, Brunner and Althaus, that the *ex virgine* is inadequate for understanding Jesus as the penetration and new beginning in
question, as One free from original sin, because even apart from Joseph He was
connected with sinful humanity on His mother Mary's side. This objection can
only be to the point if the miracle attested by Scripture and proclaimed by the
dogma bears the meaning that it made possible or effected the penetration and
new beginning. But we can as little say that as we can say on Mk. 2¹⁻¹² that
the truth and reality of the fact that the Son of man has power on earth to forgive
sins was made possible and effected by the healing of the paralytic. The forgiveness of sins is manifestly the thing signified, while the healing is the sign, quite
inseparable from, but very significantly related to, this thing signified, yet neither
identical with it nor a condition of it : " That ye may know . . ." Thus—a

point frequently missed in early dogmatics—we must not under any circumstances expect elucidation of the *ex virgine* to provide us, so to speak, with a technical proof of the conquest of original sin that took place in Jesus Christ—that would mean proving the mystery of His person. According to Scripture and creed, Jesus Christ is not the second or new Adam because He was born of the Virgin. His being the second or new Adam is indicated—" That ye may know . . ."—by His being born of the Virgin. What is to be elucidated here is not a causal connexion, but the extent to which this particular sign, or this element in the sign, points to the mystery of Christmas, and so to the conquest of original sin that took place in Jesus Christ.

Virgin birth means birth without previous sexual union between man and woman. Speaking generally, it is what it lacks that distinguishes the birth of Christ, that marks it as the mystery of God, the penetration and new beginning within humanity. But what is it in this lack that acts as a sign? Here we cannot consider the quite un-biblical view that sexual life as such is to be regarded as an evil to be removed, so that the active sign is to be sought in the fact that this removal is here presumed to have taken place.

The passage Ps. 51[5]: " Behold I was shapen in iniquity and in sin did my mother conceive me," by no means implies condemnation of the natural event as such. For all the high value put upon virginity, for all the tendency to look for the seat of sin, or inherited sin, especially in sexuality, even the Catholic Middle Ages never taught that. Calvin formulated what was a common view even among Scholastics when he said, *Hominis generatio per se immunda aut vitiosa non est, sed accidentalis ex lapsu* (*Instit.* II, 13, 4).

But if, to be precise, we add that it is not the natural but the sinful element in sexual life which caused it to be excluded here as the origin of the human existence of Jesus Christ, we still do not give a valid account of the *ex virgine*. It is not because of the sin actually involved in all sexual life that man is altogether a sinner who continually lives in disobedience by living it out. He is altogether a sinner from birth, who all through his life lives out the disobedience in which his life is already involved. And so all sexual life is involved in sin as well, and is itself sin. Thus the exclusion of this sinful sexual life does not mean the exclusion of sin in the sense of *peccatum originale*, and so this exclusion is still as unsuitable as ever to be the sign of the penetration and new beginning in the existence of Jesus Christ, to be the sign of His sinlessness.

If we fail to see this, if we wish to prove the Virgin birth of Christ by the fact that the sinless Son of God could not owe His human origin to the sin actually involved in all sexual life, or to sexual concupiscence, we can hardly escape the following question. Why could not the penetration and new beginning be achieved just as well—after the manner in which the *immaculata conceptio* of Mary is described in Catholic dogmatics—in the form of an extraordinary sanctification of a sexual event unsanctified in itself because of the Fall? Instead of the *natus ex virgine*, why do not Scripture and creed speak of the natural fruit of an elect and specially blessed human married couple? Undoubtedly, if the actual sinfulness of sexual life as such constituted the problem to which a sign had to be the answer here, then Scripture and creed might have spoken, in fact would really have had to speak, in this way. They would have had to say that the actual sinfulness of the act of Joseph and Mary was forgiven them, was wholly taken away from them, so that under the protection of this grace Jesus was the natural yet sinless Son of these human parents. How much simpler it would all have been, and how valuable it might have been for Christian ethics, especially for the Christian doctrine of marriage and the family, if Scripture and creed had said this at this point ! But this is just what they do not say. Therefore we cannot be content with an explanation of the *natus ex virgine* which properly conforms only to this non-existent text.

In the form of the *natus ex virgine* sinful sexual life is excluded as the origin of the human existence of Jesus Christ. But this is understandable and significant only if we keep in mind the fact that the limitation of man achieved in the *ex virgine*, the meaning of the judgment on man therein expressed, cannot be discerned at all from the side of that which is limited or judged, that is, of the sin of man, but only from that of Him who limits or judges, that is, of what God is, wills and does here in excluding the sinful life of sex. The mystery of revelation and reconciliation consists in the fact that in His freedom, mercy and omnipotence, God became man, and as such acts upon man. By this action of God sin is excluded and nullified. And to this particular action of God the *natus ex virgine* points. It is the sign that the sinful life of sex is excluded as the origin of the human existence of Jesus Christ. In that God in His revelation and reconciliation is the Lord and makes room for Himself among us, man and his sin are limited and judged. God is also Lord over His sinful creature. God is also free over its original sin, the sin that is altogether bound up with its existence and antecedent to every evil thought, word and deed. And God—but God only—is free to restore this freedom to His creature. This freedom will always be the freedom of His own action upon His creature, and so the negation of a freedom of this creature's own. Since it lives by His grace, it is judged in its own will and accomplishment. If the *natus ex virgine* with its exclusion of the sinful life of sex points to this gracious judgment of God, it really signifies the exclusion of sin in the sense of *peccatum originale*. That it does actually point to this gracious judgment of God, we realise when we consider that in the birth without previous sexual union of man and woman (of which Scripture speaks), man is involved in the form of Mary, but involved only in the form of the *virgo Maria*, i.e., only in the form of non-willing, non-achieving, non-creative, non-sovereign man, only in the form of man who can merely receive, merely be ready, merely let something be done to and with himself. This human being, the *virgo*, becomes the possibility, becomes the mother of God's Son in the flesh. It is not, of course, that she is this ; but she becomes it. And she does not become it of her own capacity ; she acquires capacity by the act of the Son of God assuming flesh. It is not as though this non-willing, non-achieving, non-creative, non-sovereign, merely ready, merely receptive, virgin human being as

192

such can have brought anything to the active God as her own, in which her adaptability for God consists. It is not as if virginity as a human possibility constitutes the point of connexion for divine grace.

The objection that by his descent from Mary Jesus will still stand in the context of sinful humanity even without a human father is in substance quite correct. The *virgo*, the human possibility of virginity, does actually stand in this context. We are not concerned to deny that, but we are concerned with the knowledge, and the sign awakening this knowledge, that in this context a penetration and new beginning has taken place, so that the context itself has been changed. "What Jesus Christ sanctifies is not the absence of a human father at His begetting, but the circumstance that in this child the eternal Word was made flesh" (Eduard Böhl, *Dogmatik*, 1884, p. 313).

Human virginity, far from being able to construct for itself a point of connexion for divine grace, lies under its judgment. Yet it becomes, not by its nature, not of itself, but by divine grace, the sign of this judgment passed upon man, and to that extent the sign of divine grace. For if it is only the *virgo* who can be the mother of the Lord, if God's grace considers her alone and is prepared to use her for His work upon man, that means that as such willing, achieving, creative, sovereign man is not considered, and is not to be used for this work. Of course, man is involved, but not as God's fellow-worker, not in his independence, not with control over what is to happen, but only —and even that because God has presented him with Himself—in his readiness for God. So thoroughly does God judge sin in the flesh by being gracious to man. So much does God insist that He alone is Lord by espousing the cause of man. This is the mystery of grace to which the *natus ex virgine* points. The sinful life of sex is excluded as the source of the human existence of Jesus Christ, not because of the nature of sexual life nor because of its sinfulness, but because every natural generation is the work of willing, achieving, creative, sovereign man. No event of natural generation will be a sign of the mystery indicated here. Such an event will point to the mighty and really cosmic power of human creaturely *eros*. If our aim is to discover and set up the sign of this power, the event of sex still forces itself upon us as the sign which is unmatched by any other in importance and persuasiveness. The event of sex cannot be considered at all as the sign of the divine *agape* which seeks not its own and never fails. It is the work of willing, achieving, creative, sovereign man, and as such points elsewhere than to the majesty of the divine pity. Therefore the virginity of Mary, and not the wedlock of Joseph and Mary, is the sign of revelation and of the knowledge of the mystery of Christmas.

In extension and elucidation of what has been said, it is not illegitimate to adduce one other consideration at this point, regarding a secondary but all the same a necessary question. What is the significance of the fact that in the sign of the *agape* there is excluded not only the sign of *eros* as such but particularly the function of the male? I would like the attempt to answer this to be regarded only as a *parergon*, as compared with the exposition on pp. 277–281 of the first edition of this book, where it dominated the field of view to an excessive extent.

The early dogmaticians (e.g., Polanus, *Synt. Theol. chr.* 1609, p. 2360 ; F. Turrettini, *Instit. Theol. el.* 1682, Bk. XIII, *qu.* 11, 19), in proving the *natus ex virgine*, usually adduced in connexion with the ἀπάτωρ, ἀμήτωρ of Heb. 7³ the consideration that just as Christ could not have a mother as the eternal Son of the Father, He could not have a father as the Incarnate. But underlying the second part of this statement, which is of interest to us here, is the recognition (worked out in the second part of this section under III) of the *enhypostasis* of the human nature of Christ, namely, that He also exists as man, not in virtue of a possibility of existence proper to his humanity, but solely in virtue of His divine existence in the eternal mode of being of the Word or Son of God. His existence in time is one and the same as His eternal existence as the begotten of God the Father. Now it is precisely the human father whom a human son has to thank for everything that marks his existence as belonging to him—his name above all, and with it his position, his rights, his character as such and such an individual, his place in history. Thus His begetting by a human father could not be the sign of the existence of the man Jesus alone as the Son begotten of the Father in eternity. This sign would rather describe Him as a man whose existence is different from the existence of God, and is proper to Himself. A sign which really describes the mystery of *enhypostasis* must then consist in the actual elimination of the other sign, and so in the lack of a human father, i.e., *natus ex virgine*. And now to complete our previous deliberations we can go on to say that willing, achieving, creative, sovereign man, man as an independent fellow-worker with God, man in the impulse of his *eros*, who as such, where God's grace is concerned, simply cannot be a participator in God's work, is *a parte potiori* man the male and the father of man in the sexual act which man has to thank for his earthly existence. We certainly have to say that the wife has also a share in this determination of man. For she, too, is man. Only a foolish ideology of manhood or an equally foolish ideology of womanhood can deny her her share in this determination of man. Nevertheless there can be no talk of an equality of the two sexes in this respect. God alone knows whether the history of humanity, nations and states, art, science, economics, has in fact been and is so predominantly the history of males, the story of all the deeds and works of males, as it appears to be, or whether, for all that, the hidden factor of female co-operation and participation has not, in fact, always turned the scale in a way of which chronicles, acts and monuments give us no information, because it involves an element which is deeply concealed both psychologically and sociologically, although it was not and did not need to be less potent for that reason. Be that as it may, if there had been a matriarchate instead of a patriarchate and if perhaps there actually still is a matriarchate, nevertheless it is—well, " significant," that the historical consciousness of all nations, states and civilisations begins with the patriarchate. Male action is significant for the world history and characteristic of the world history with which we are acquainted, as it has been and actually is for us, even if it is not so in itself. The biblical witness to revelation assumes this, and subsequent thought in the Christian Church has also taken it over without ado. But it is worth while in this respect to see exactly what the starting-point of the biblical testimony is. In view of the fateful conversation with the serpent in Gen. 3¹⁻⁶, we might first inquire whether the name of the one human being by whom sin entered the world (Rom. 5¹²) was not (cf. 1 Tim. 2¹⁴) really Eve rather than Adam. But according to Gen. 3¹⁶, it is definitely part of the curse imposed on male and female in consequence of the Fall that the male becomes lord of the woman. This would hardly follow from the fact that according to Gen. 2¹⁸ the woman was made a " helpmeet " for the male and according to Gen. 2²¹ᶠ· was made of the rib of the male, and so Paul in his allusion to

7

this passage in 1 Cor. 11$^{8f.}$ could hardly regard this super- and sub-ordination as an " order of creation," but only—which is rather different—as a divine ordinance valid in the sphere of the Fall. In the sense of this ordinance, and so against the background of the Fall, it happens (surprising though it be at first sight) that straightway in Gen. 3^9 Adam the male is summoned by God and made responsible. Thus, not because of an original mark of distinction, but because of the common Fall of man and woman, in which both step out of a relationship in which there is no word at all of super- or sub-ordination, there arises the unlikeness, and man becomes the lord of woman and therefore significant for world history. It is from this angle that the countersign, the sign of the mystery of Christmas, the sign of the lack of a human father for Jesus, becomes understandable as a sign. Willing, achieving, creative, sovereign man as such cannot be considered as a participator in God's work. For as such he is the man of disobedience. As such, therefore, if God's grace is to meet him, he must be set aside. But this man in the state of disobedience is *a parte potiori* the male. So it is the male who must be set aside here, if a countersign is to be set up as the sign of the incarnation of God. In this sign the contradiction of grace is directed against the male because he is peculiarly significant for the world history of human genius. What takes place in the mystery of Christmas is not world history and not the work of human genius. And as the sign of this fact—" That ye may know . . ."—the γένεσις Ἰησοῦ Χριστοῦ, in contradiction to the becoming of all other men, is in no sense a history of males. " Again the Word insisteth that, since God promiseth blessing upon all heathen in Christ, Christ could not come of a man or man's work, for the work of the flesh which is accursed is not suffered along with that which is pure blessing and is blessed. So this blessed fruit had to be only the fruit of a woman's body, not of a man's (although the same woman's body is descended from man, yea even from Abraham and Adam), that this mother should be a virgin and yet a right natural mother, not through natural power or strength, but through the Holy Ghost and God's power alone " (Luther, *Dass Jesus ein geborener Jude sei*, 1523 *W.A.* 11, 318, 20). If woman demands justification and rehabilitation in face of the significant preeminence of the male for world history—and it is better that she should not—let her keep to this sign. By its limitation of man and his sin it means at the same time the limitation of male pre-eminence. The sign declares that if Christ were the son of a male He would be a sinner like all the rest, and that therefore He cannot be the son of any male. Thus the human existence of the sinless Son of God, and with it God's revelation to us and our reconciliation to God, is made possible and real, because in the special way so much emphasised in Mt. 1 Joseph is completely set aside, while God takes his place, not in the creative function of a creative father, but simply as God, as the Creator who performs a miracle, creating and instituting something new. In terms of the doctrine of *enhypostasis* we can say quite simply—as the God who as the eternal Father of His eternal Son will not have a human father side by side with Himself. His eternal generation of this eternal Son excludes a human generation, because a human father and human generation, the whole action of man the male, can have no meaning here. Therefore it is the very absence of masculine action that is significant here. Hence, *natus ex virgine*.

There is the further question whether in contrast to this significant inappropriateness of the male to be the father of Emmanuel something positive should be said about a corresponding significant appropriateness in the female to be his mother. Our language here cannot be too careful. The appropriateness in question can be assigned only to that determination of the nature of the female which remains when everything is deduced which in and with the genius of the male is put under the divine judgment by the *ex virgine* as sinful. Nor does the female fail to be implicated in this. To her there belongs, as already stated, that which in the form of receptivity, readiness, etc., represents the human possibility of female virginity. In addition there is also what Goethe may have meant by " the eternal feminine," although it cannot be said in any important theological sense that it draws us " upwards." Again, the answer which Mary gives the angel in Lk. 1[38] is not nature but grace. It is not the female-human which from its own standpoint is readier for God's work than the male-human. But it belongs itself to the miracle indicated in the answer (Lk. 1[45]) : " Blessed is she that believeth," as Mary is told later. Certainly the suggestion which Schleiermacher ventured to make in his *Weihnachtsfeier* (ed. Mulert, p. 28), that essentially the female has no need of conversion as opposed to the male, would have been better left unsaid. And if, finally, we are to think further along the lines of certain exponents of Roman Catholic Mariology and regard the *virgo* simply as the representative of human nature, who in the incarnation of the Word is honoured as a partaker of the divine nature (2 Pet. 1[4]), it may perhaps be said in its favour that the female is as significant for human nature as such as the male is for human history, and that if in the sign of the miraculous birth of Christ the male as representing human history must withdraw, still (so far as she represents man as such who acts in this story) the female can and must be there, be there for God, if God on His part wishes to act on man and with man. We are thus brought back to what we said about the positive significance of the *natus ex Maria* when we began elucidating this formula—that both God and man are really involved in the mystery to which the miracle of Christmas points us. By now it should have become somewhat more apparent why it is the female and not the male that is singled out as the human being actually involved here. But we must take care to avoid traces of Roman Catholic Mariology and must not regard the human creatureliness represented by the *virgo* as in principle an openness for the work of God which still belongs to man in spite of the Fall. According to Eph. 2[3] men are " by nature the children of wrath." It is not as if somewhere behind wicked human history there is still hidden a good human being, worthy of communion with the divine being as such. The Fall is the fall of the whole man ; i.e., man is what he does, when he is disobedient to God. There is no plane upon which the meeting between God and man can be possible or real except in virtue of the mystery of the divine mercy. The whole basic position of Neo-Protestant dogmatics is brought to light when R. Seeberg (*op. cit.* p. 183 f.), discussing the content of truth in the *natus ex virgine*, comes to the conclusion that it was the mother and not the father of Jesus " who had a feeling and presentiment of the Holy One, which was given them with this child." Mary, that is, must have been " a pious mother and so accessible to ecstatic stimulations." The Spirit of God which moved her, therefore, laid hold of her Son, too, from early days onwards. His utterances in later life point back to " eager preoccupation with Scripture because of His profound accessibility to religion," to " a moral purity right from His beginnings," to " a spiritual aptitude of peculiar depth and harmony "—and all this with a constancy which can only be explained on the assumption of " a revelation of God disclosed in the soul of Jesus from the beginning." *Natus ex virgine*, then, simply means that Jesus had a religious mother and that He was Himself a religious child from the very first. In opposition to this view the early Protestant dogmaticians were rightly at one in declaring that no kind of immanent aptitude for God's work, whether in Mary in particular or in human nature in general, can be expressed by the *ex virgine*. *Beata virgo Maria Deum hominem factum et concipere et parere non humanis meritis, sed concepti nascentisque ex ea summi Dei dignatione promeruit.* For human nature, even in Mary, was *obnoxia et infecta peccato* (Polanus, *Synt. Theol. chr.* 1609, p. 2356, 2358). *Nulla est ex creaturis, quantavis virtute polleat, quae mundum ex immundo possit educere* (F. Turrettini, *Instit. Theol. el.* 1682, L. XIII *qu.* 11, 10). The virginity of Mary does not exclude her from having been *homo peccatorum non expers* (Quenstedt, *Theol. did. pol.* 1685 P. 3, *c.* 3, *m.* 3, *sect.* 1, *th.* 19). As already stated by Gregory of Nazianzus (*Or. theol.* 30, 21), it is the " wholly condemned " (κατακριθὲν ὅλον) which the Son of God unites to Himself in His incarnation in order to free it from condemnation. As will be shown subsequently, it is only on the ground of an act of divine justification and sanctification that human nature (at this very point, too) becomes a partaker of the divine nature. It is not, then, as if at this point a door is opened which can lead to Mariology and thus to a doctrine of the goodness of the creature and its capacity for God, to a doctrine of the independent holiness of the Church. This only can and must be said here : in the form of this act of divine justification and sanctification, and so in the mystery of the divine mercy, human nature (apart from sinful human history and in spite of the corruption proper to human nature itself) is made worthy to be a partaker of the divine nature by grace and by a miracle of grace. In token of that the woman is adopted apart from the male and her relation to him, and in spite of the sin of which she is guilty along with him, to be conceiver of the eternal God Himself on earth, to be the θεοτόκος. That is the positive thing which has to be said about her significative appropriateness in this matter. And for that reason too : *natus ex virgine.*

2. We now turn to the previous clause in the confession, *conceptus de Spiritu sancto.* The *natus ex virgine* described the negative side of the miracle of Christmas. The birth of the Lord was a birth without a previous sexual event, without a male to beget. It is thus the sign of the inconceivable, of the incarnation of the Word, the Holy One, the Lord of all things. As just shown, an independent meaning cannot attach either (in the sign) to the person or the sex of Mary, or (in the thing signified) to human nature. Actually no one is left to be God's fellow-worker. All that " Mary the *virgo* " actually signifies is that man is really the other upon whom and with whom God acts in His revelation. We have had to say all this already in elucidation of the negative formula. Its necessity, i.e., that it is spoken with exegetical correctness, is established by the first and positive formula, *conceptus de Spiritu sancto.* It states that the conception of Jesus Christ prior to His birth of the Virgin Mary was the work of God the Holy Spirit. To that extent it was a miraculous birth and as such the sign of the incarnation of the eternal Word. The formula *conceptus de* `Spiritu sancto* thus fills the blank, as it were, indicated by the formula *natus ex Maria virgine.* It indicates the ground and content, where the latter indicates the form and shape, of the miracle and sign.

To that extent, although it, too, refers to the sign, it stands in a closer relation to the thing signified. In itself the mystery of the incarnation of the Word might also be expressed by saying of Jesus Christ that in the freedom and majesty appropriate to the merciful act of revelation and reconciliation His human existence is peculiarly the work of God the Holy Spirit. It is, therefore, no accident that by the more discerning of those who dispute the Virgin birth the *conceptus de Spiritu sancto* is not usually disputed, but more or less gladly adopted, and given some sort of positive explanation, as a good description for the mystery of the existence of Christ. But even so, these two formulæ cannot be separated in such a way as to let the *conceptus de Spiritu sancto* refer to the thing signified, and the *natus ex Maria virgine* refer to the sign, because obviously it is the *conceptus de Spiritu sancto* which is, so to speak, direct citation from the biblical account of the miracle in Mt. 1[18] or Lk. 1[35], while the *natus ex Maria virgine* (of course a reminiscence of Is. 7[14]) gives, so to speak, dogmatic precision to it. The older credal forms, and even the *Nicaeno-Constantinopolitanum*, did not offer two formulæ but only one when they put the two factors, the Holy Spirit and the Virgin Mary, side by side and summarised the one event between the two in the verbal forms of γεννηθείς (*natus*) or σαρκωθείς (*incarnatus*). There are proper exegetical grounds, therefore, why the formula *conceptus de Spiritu sancto* (treated in the so-called Apostles' Creed as a special first assertion) should not be treated as an independent assertion about the mystery of the person of Christ which has no connexion with the Virgin birth. Rather, it belongs to the *natus ex virgine* ; it states positively what the latter states negatively, it states from God's side what the latter states from man's side, regarding the sign of the mystery of the person of Jesus Christ. (Quite apart from the fact that among the more discerning as among the less discerning of those who dispute this sign it is very doubtful whether by their *conceptus de Spiritu sancto* they really mean the mystery of the person of Jesus Christ, the mystery of the free grace of God, and not perhaps some quite different mystery, a mystery which in reality is no mystery.) Thus the closer relation just indicated between the *conceptus de Spiritu sancto* and the thing signified can be discerned only if in it, so to speak, the *tertium comparationis* between the two is in full view, namely, that God has acted. That is the mystery of grace itself. That is also the ground and content of the miracle, the form and shape of which consist in the *natus ex virgine*.

To the full elucidation of the *conceptus de Spiritu sancto* belongs the recollection that where in the sphere of Christian revelation and the Christian Church legitimate and significant language is used about the Holy Spirit, what is meant is invariably God, God Himself, God in the fullest and strictest sense of the term—namely, the Lord of all lords, He who is Lord because of Himself and not because of another, the Lord to whom man belongs before ever, and to an infinitely greater extent than, he belongs to himself, to whom he owes himself entirely, and to whom he remains in utter obligation, the Lord upon whose grace he is utterly thrown, and in whose promise alone his future consists. He and no other and nothing else is the Holy Spirit by whom Jesus Christ was conceived according to His human nature, in order to be born of the Virgin Mary. It is important to make this quite clear, first, because in so doing we reject in anticipation the attempt to parallel the saying about the Virgin birth of Christ by assertions from the realm of heathen mythology which sound very similar. In the case of these alleged parallels the similarity can never be more than verbal, because the divine agents in the miraculous births spoken of in this connexion are definitely not God in the full and strict sense of the word, but at best gods, that is, hypostatisations of the feeling of man for nature or his reflection on history, hypostatisations behind which man is everywhere only too visible as the proper lord of the world and as the creator of its deities. Accordingly, these mythical miracles are not real miracles, i.e., signs of God, the Lord of the world, signs which positively limit this world of ours as a created world. They are prodigies, i.e., extraordinary occurrences within this world of ours, and therefore objects of our human world-view. It follows from this, secondly, that when we regard the Holy Spirit by whom Jesus Christ is conceived as in the strictest sense God Himself, God the Lord, we forestall and eliminate any attempt to come to the assistance of the saying about the Virgin birth of Christ with any speculation from physics or with any more or less genuine scientific information of a biological sort. In other words, if we are clear that with the Holy Spirit God Himself is declared to be the author of the sign of the Virgin birth, then we know that in acknowledging the reality of this sign we have *a priori* renounced all understanding of it as a natural possibility, even when we are tempted to do so by a consideration so inviting as that of natural parthenogenesis, for example. We are already committed, then, to an acknowledgment of a pure divine beginning, of a limiting of all natural possibilities, and this forbids us at the very outset to indulge in any reflection as to whether and how this reality can be anything else but a pure divine beginning. It is this strict acceptance of the divinity of the Holy Spirit by whom Jesus Christ is conceived, and along with that the strict acceptance of the miraculous character of the Virgin birth, that makes the latter the sign of the mystery of Christmas. It is of significance for the thing signified, of which it is the sign, because here, too, in the incarnation of the Word in the strict sense, we are concerned with the action of God Himself, with a pure divine beginning.

But why is it precisely God the Holy Spirit who is named here? The answer to this question follows from what we have to learn from Holy Scripture of the significance of this the third person or mode of God's being for the act of divine revelation or reconciliation, understanding it in terms of what the Church has expressed and laid down as right knowledge of Scripture in its dogma of the three-in-oneness of God and particularly in its dogma of the Holy Spirit. The Holy Spirit is God Himself in His freedom exercised in revelation to be present to His creature, even to dwell in him personally, and thereby to achieve his meeting with Himself in His Word and by this achievement to make it possible. Through the Holy Spirit and only through the Holy Spirit can man be there for God, be free for God's work on him, believe, be a recipient of His revelation, the object of the divine reconciliation. In the Holy Spirit and only in the Holy Spirit has man the evidence and guarantee that he really participates in God's revealing and reconciling action. Through the Holy Spirit and only through the Holy Spirit does God make His claim on us effective, to be our one Lord, our one Teacher, our one Leader. In virtue of the Holy Spirit and only in virtue of the Holy Spirit is there a Church in which God's Word can be ministered, because it has the language for it, because what it says of revelation is testimony to it and to that extent the renewal of revelation. The freedom which the Holy Spirit gives us in this understanding and in this sphere—gives, so far as it is His own freedom and so far as He gives us nothing else and no less than Himself—is the freedom of the Church, of the children of God.

It is this freedom of the Holy Spirit and in the Holy Spirit that is already involved in the incarnation of the Word of God, in the assumption of human nature by the Son of God, in which we have to recognise the real ground of the freedom of the children of God, the real ground of all conception of revelation, all lordship of grace over man, the real ground of the Church. The very possibility of human nature's being adopted into unity with the Son of God is the Holy Ghost. Here, then, at this fontal point in revelation, the Word of God is not without the Spirit of God. And here already there is the togetherness of Spirit and Word. Through the Spirit it becomes really possible for the creature, for man, to be there and to be free for God. Through the Spirit flesh, human nature, is assumed into unity with the Son of God. Through the Spirit this Man can be God's Son and at the same time the Second Adam and as such " the firstborn among many brethren " (Rom. 8[29]), the prototype of all who are set free for His sake and through faith in Him. As in Him human nature is made the bearer of revelation, so in us it is made the recipient of it, not by its own power, but by the power conferred on it by the Spirit, who according to 2 Cor. 3[17] is Himself the Lord.

This train of thought is particularly clear in Jn. 1[12f.], 3[3f.]. Here the existence of believers is traced back to an ἐξουσία bestowed on them, to a begetting from God different from their natural begetting, to a birth " from above." And in Jn. 3[5f.] it is expressly traced back to a birth of the Spirit. All this is naturally in view of the event in the existence of Jesus which radically precedes and is the primary realisation of every such event among men. The sign of this primary realisation of grace is the Virgin birth of Christ especially in view of His conception by the Holy Spirit.

It has, moreover, in this respect two important parallels in the New Testament. The one is the baptism in Jordan in Mk. 1[9f.]. This story naturally does not assert that because God the Spirit descended upon Jesus like a dove He became the Son of God, but it states (cf. Jn. 1[32f.]) that He upon whom the Spirit descended, as the sign of the dove bore witness, actually is the beloved Son of God. The sign of the baptism in Jordan, like the sign of the Virgin birth, points back to the mystery of this Man's being which was real in itself apart from this sign, and like the Virgin birth the baptism in Jordan also means that the Holy Spirit is the mystery of this being. The second parallel is Rom. 1[4], where His resurrection is mentioned as the sign of the installation of the Man Jesus as the Son of God, but this installation is itself likewise traced back to the Holy Spirit.

The specific mention of the Holy Spirit as a more precise determination of the sign of the Virgin birth is obviously significant in a twofold sense. In the first place, it refers back the mystery of the human existence of Jesus Christ to the mystery of God Himself, as it is disclosed in revelation—the mystery that God Himself as the Spirit acts among His creatures as His own Mediator, that God Himself creates a possibility, a power, a capacity, and assigns it to man, where otherwise there would be sheer impossibility. And the mention of the Holy Ghost is significant here in the second place, because it points back to the connexion which exists between our reconciliation and the existence of the Reconciler, to the primary realisation of the work of the Holy Spirit. For it is on this ground that the same work, the same preparation of man for God by God Himself, can happen to us also, in the form of pure grace, the grace manifested in Jesus Christ, which meets us and is bestowed upon us in Him.

The assertion *conceptus de Spiritu sancto* must now be protected from an imminent misunderstanding. It does not state that Jesus Christ is the Son of the Holy Spirit according to His human existence. On the contrary, it states as emphatically as possible—and this is the miracle it asserts—that Jesus Christ had no father according to His human existence. Because in this miracle the Holy Spirit takes the place of the male, this by no means implies that He does what the male does. Because Jesus was conceived by the Holy Spirit, it does not, therefore, mean—or can mean only in an improper sense—that He is begotten by the Holy Spirit. The idea is completely excluded that anything like a marriage took place between the Holy Spirit and the Virgin Mary.

Such marriages are, of course, spoken of in the myths about Jupiter and other gods that lust after the daughters of men. It was a complete misapprehension of the facts when Justin (*Dial.* 69 f.) thought that he could actually make apologetic use of these parallels in the history of religions. For M. Dibelius (*op. cit.* p. 27, 35, 41 and *passim*) has put it exegetically beyond doubt that the New Testament passages on the Virgin birth definitely do not speak of a ἱερός γάμος. In all the Latin credal forms (even in the Latin version of the *Nic.-Const.*), the *de Spiritu sancto* is emphatically distinguished from the *ex Maria*, although in Mt. 1[18, 20] it expressly says ἐκ πνεύματος ἁγίου. As early dogmatics had already correctly seen, this ἐκ is to be explained in the sense of ἀπό, i.e., on the analogy of Rom. 11[36] (all things are ἐξ αὐτοῦ) and of Jn. 1[13]; 1 Jn. 3[9] (believers are born ἐκ τοῦ θεοῦ), where the ἐκ obviously does not signify the *causa materialis*, the substantial procession of the world or of Christians from the being of God, but the *causa efficiens* of their existence, the transcendent ground of their being. The heathen idea of the substantial procession of certain men from the essence of Godhead because of preceding theogamy involves a compromising either of the begetting deity as such or of the begotten man as such. It would, therefore, be an exceedingly misleading sign of the mystery of Christmas. If we are to allow any notion at all of the nature of this *conceptio*, it can only be that of the creative Word, a command or a blessing uttered by God Himself. It was the Word of wisdom and omnipotence which effected the miracle of this conception.

The meaning of *de Spiritu sancto* is to be expanded as follows: *tanquam creatore humanae Christi naturae*. For *conceptus est non de substantia Spiritus sancti sed de potentia, nec generatione sed iussione et benedictione* (Augustine (?), *Sermo* 234, 5, *in append.*). Οὐ διὰ συνουσίας, ἀλλὰ δυνάμεως . . . *non* σωματικῶς *sed* δημιουργικῶς (Polanus, *Synt. theol. christ.*, 1609, p. 2356). *Falsum est, Deum ipsum hoc praestitisse, quod in generatione vir praestare solet ; Dei enim operatio non* σπερματική *fuit, sed tantum* δημιουργική, *non interna sed externa, non formalis sed effectiva* (Quenstedt, *Theol. did. pol.*, 1685, III *c.* 3 *m.* 3 *sect.* 2 qu. 2 obs. 6). *Uti enim initio terra nullo proscissa vomere, nullo foecundata semine, solo Dei verbo germinavit herbam virentem, sic integerrima Virgo . . .* ἀμέσως *operante Spiritu sancto in illa concipiendi* δύναμιν . . . *virtutem divinitatis Verbi susceptivam simul et generativam concepit, peperit et germinavit illum qui est germen gratiae . . .* (ib.

sect. 1 *th.* 2 *obs.* 3). " God wrought without any anthropomorphism as the Creator, not as a lover ; but for the child divine origin was attested " (M. Dibelius, *op. cit.* p. 37).

The Holy Spirit by whom the Virgin becomes pregnant is really not a kind of divine spirit, and therefore not in any sense an apotheosised husband, but He is God Himself and therefore His miraculous act is to be understood as a spiritual and not a psycho-physical act, not in any way analogous to the effects of creaturely *eros.*

It is not, therefore, an illegitimate spiritualisation but a necessary interpretation of the miracle when Augustine says of Christ that He was conceived in faith or in grace and not in the sexual *libido* or *concupiscentia* of His mother (*Enchir.* 34 ; *Sermo* 152, 8). And in the same sense it is essentially right when John of Damascus (*Ekd.* 4, 14) describes Mary's ear as the bodily organ of the miraculous conception of Christ. " The operation of the Holy Spirit at the conception of Jesus is one mediated through Mary's faith, Mary believes . . . and by believing in the Word of God spoken by the angel she is thereby enabled to take the eternal Word into herself and independently to bring about the beginning of the Redeemer's life " (Ed. Böhl, *Dogmatik,* 1887, p. 311).

By being called the work of the Holy Spirit the conception of Christ is actually withdrawn from any analogy save the analogy of faith and, like every genuine miracle, from any explanation of its How. The comment of F. Turrettini (*Instit. Theol. el.,* 1682, *L.* XIII, *qu.* 11, 9) on the remarkable passage (Lk. 1³⁵) : δύναμις ὑψίστου ἐπισκιάσει σοι, is that the *modus operationis Spiritus sancti* is at once described as (1) *potentissimus ad protectionem et praesidium, ne B. Virgo divina maiestate consumeretur* ; (2) *efficacissimus ad foecundationem . . . allusive ad creationem, in qua spiritus dicitur incubuisse aquis, ut ea virtute oriturus iste foetus dicatur, qua mundus exordium sumpsit* ; (3) *arcanus et incomprehensibilis, qui nec ratione pervestigari, nec sermone enarrari potest,* comparable with the effect of the cloud which filled the tabernacle (Ex. 40³⁵), or the outspread wings of the cherubim over the ark of the covenant (2 Chron. 5⁸)—so that this very saying about the overshadowing is at the same time the answer to Mary's question (Lk. 1³⁴) : " How shall this be ? ", i.e., *si quidem hoc non sit futurum humana opera sed virtute Dei, cui nihil impossibile, et modo plane admirabili, quem mirari deceat, non scrutari.*

The positive fact which fills the space marked off by the *natus ex virgine* is God Himself, i.e., in the inconceivable act of creative omnipotence in which He imparts to human nature a capacity, a power for Himself, which it does not possess of itself and which it could not devise for itself ; in the inconceivable act of reconciling love by which He justifies and sanctifies human nature in spite of its unrighteousness and unholiness to be a temple for His Word and so for His glory ; in the inconceivable act of redeeming wisdom in which He completely assumes His creature in such a way that He imparts and bestows on it no less than His own existence.

In these words I am paraphrasing an exposition by J. Gerhard (*Loci theol.,* 1610, *L.* IV 107), according to which we have to distinguish in the miracle of this conception, or of the *actio Spiritus sancti* in this miracle, three points of view : *Primum est* ἄμεσος ἐνέργεια *quod dederit virgini facultatem sine virili semine praeter naturae ordinem concipiendi foetum. Alterum est* θαυμάσιος ἁγιασμός *quod massam illam, ex qua corpus Filii Dei formatum, sanctificaverit, id est a peccato mundaverit. Tertium est* ἄρρητος ἕνωσις, *quod divinam et humanam naturam in· unam personam univerit.*

Here, as so often, it is not true that such statements by early dogmaticians are the products of an idle and irrelevant scholastic cleverness. Rather is it the case that in these statements an attempt is made at a spiritual understanding of the spiritual ; and no one who at this particular point takes the trouble seriously to think himself into the task set him will deny that in the decisive issue this was the right line to take. In conclusion, let us remember that it is particularly this positive factor in the miracle, expressed in the *conceptus de Spiritu sancto*, that belongs to the sign of the miracle of Christmas which the dogma aims at stressing. Noetically, i.e., for us to whom this sign is given, who have to recognise it in and by this sign, the fact that Jesus Christ is the Son of God come in the flesh stands or falls with the truth of the *conceptio de Spiritu sancto*. But it could not be said that ontically, in itself, the mystery of Christmas stands or falls with this dogma. The man Jesus of Nazareth is not the true Son of God because He was conceived by the Holy Spirit and born of the Virgin Mary. On the contrary, because He is the true Son of God and because this is an inconceivable mystery intended to be acknowledged as such, therefore He is conceived by the Holy Spirit and born of the Virgin Mary. And because He is thus conceived and born, He has to be recognised and acknowledged as the One He is and in the mystery in which He is the One He is.

διὸ . . . υἱὸς θεοῦ κληθήσεται, Lk. 1³⁵. Jesus Christ would be and would be called the true Son of God even without this sign—on this point the early dogmatics was quite united. He is so as the eternal Son of Father who was made flesh in Him. *Dicendum, quod absque ulla dubitatione potuisset Deus concipi et generari ex muliere opera viri* (F. Suarez, quoted from Bartmann, *Lehrb. d. Dogm.*⁷ vol. I, 1928, p. 427). *Filius Dei debet dici, non quod conceptus sit ex Spiritu sancto ratione humanitatis, sed quod genitus sit ex Deo ratione divinitatis* (F. Turrettini, *Instit. Theol. el.*, 1682, L. XIII, qu. 11, 6). *Sanctus ille homo . . . erit et cognoscetur Filius Dei non propter conceptionem sanctam sed propter unionem personalem* (Quenstedt, *Theol. did. pol.*, 1685, P. III c. 3, m. 3 sect. 1 th. 18). It is difficult to understand how a scholar so well versed in the history of dogma as A. E. Biedermann can constantly make of the doctrine of the Virgin birth a " doctrine of the physical sonship of God " (*Dogmatik*, 1869, §§ 582, 823). In the understanding of Scripture and Church doctrine there is neither a physical nor, as Biedermann would have it, a " religious " Son of God, but only the one eternal, if you like, " metaphysical " Son, who becomes a man like us in the mystery of Christmas and yet is and continues to be the eternal Son of God. As a sign of this mystery there is the miracle : *conceptus de Spiritu sancto*.

The mystery does not rest upon the miracle. The miracle rests upon the mystery. The miracle bears witness to the mystery, and the mystery is attested by the miracle.

Per hoc ergo, quod de Spiritu sancto esse nativitas Christi dicitur, quid aliud quam ipsa gratia Dei demonstratur, qua mirabili et ineffabili modo Verbo Dei est adiunctus atque connexus et divina gratia corporaliter repletur (Petrus Lombardus, *Sent.* III *dist.* 4 B).

PART III

THE OUTPOURING OF THE HOLY SPIRIT

§ 16

THE FREEDOM OF MAN FOR GOD

According to Holy Scripture God's revelation occurs in our enlightenment by the Holy Spirit of God to a knowledge of His Word. The outpouring of the Holy Spirit is God's revelation. In the reality of this event consists our freedom to be the children of God and to know and love and praise Him in His revelation.

1. THE HOLY SPIRIT THE SUBJECTIVE REALITY OF REVELATION

We have now to take the third and last step in our development of the concept of revelation as the necessary basis of a Church doctrine of the Word of God and to that extent as the basis of a Church dogmatics, in accordance with the rule of Holy Scripture and with due regard to Church dogma. When we put the question about the self-revealing God, we could not raise it in a vacuum, or in the light of revelation generally, but only in the light of the revelation attested in the Bible. Necessarily, therefore, two other questions forced themselves upon us : the question of the event in which God is revealed as God ; and the question of that aspect of the event which is, as it were, turned towards us, the revealedness of God for us. Hence the answer to that first question, the question of the Subject in revelation, developed into a threefold knowledge of the God who is Himself the Revealer, Himself the act of His revelation, and Himself His revealedness, in the doctrine of Father, Son and Holy Spirit in their oneness and threeness, threeness and oneness. But in the light of the very doctrine of the Trinity the second question, the question of the reality of revelation from God's side, had also to be put and answered independently. We did this in the christological section which is now behind us, the doctrine of the incarnation of the Word. What we have now to do is to give the third question a central place in our deliberations, and, in the closest connexion, of course, with both our trinitarian and our christological inquiries, to give it an independent answer.

Let us again think of its particular meaning, especially in relation to the second question. From the doctrine of the Trinity we know that to the question, how the state of revealedness is achieved for us men, there can be only one answer. The one true God and Lord Himself, in the " person " of the Holy Spirit, is His own state of revealedness for us. The answer is, therefore, the same as we had also to give to the question, what was the event in revelation, except that then its special content was the indication of the Son or Word. Over and above the identifying in essence of God the Son and God the Father, the question of the How of revelation is quite a legitimate one because it is in fact answered quite definitely by the biblical witness to revelation. In the same way we ought not and cannot be satisfied with finding, important in itself, that the Holy Spirit in His essential identity with the Father and the Son, in His divinity, is therefore once more God Himself, is also His own revealed state for us. We ought not to be satisfied with this finding, because from the standpoint of Scripture there has been prescribed for us a definite declaration of the aim or end of revelation, we might also say, a definite declaration of the How of God's actual state of revealedness for us. In the light of this declaration the further question is not only legitimate and meaningful, but imperative and necessary. For where definite answers are prescribed for us by Scripture, we not only ought, we should and must ask them in order to achieve the imperative knowledge and understanding of the biblical answers and therefore the proper knowledge of them by the Church, which is the task of dogmatics. But the imperative question here is this. What is the meaning of revelation as the presence of God Himself, so far as it is not only an event proceeding from God but also an event that reaches man. To what extent, in the occurrence of revelation, are we men free for God, so that He can be revealed to us ? To what extent is there in this occurrence a revealed state of God for man, and to that extent a human receptivity for God's revelation ? The object of this question we call " the subjective reality of revelation." By this is meant no less than the answer prescribed in Holy Scripture, namely, the outpouring of the Holy Spirit.

At the corresponding point in § 13, 1 we asked how in the freedom of God it was real that His revelation reached man. Our question now is : In what freedom of man's is it real that God's revelation reaches him ?

By our first answer, the doctrine of the Trinity, and ultimately and decisively by Holy Scripture as the source and norm of all our present answers, our whole investigation of the concept of revelation is directed to a very definite area which we cannot quit without abandoning objectivity. If we remain objective and so pursue our thinking in this area, one thing can and must be regarded as fixed *a priori*. This freedom of man's can only be a freedom created by God in the act of His revelation and given to man. In the last resort it can only be God's own freedom. The question of a freedom originally proper to man, the question how it is real from man's side that God's revelation reaches him, does not tally with any answer prescribed by Holy Scripture. In this regard the Bible nowhere speaks of anything that is real from man's side. It does speak of God and His action as an action for man and on man. But it speaks of God's action and man's action only so far as they have their possibility in God. Even the fact that God's revelation reaches man, and therefore man's freedom for God, cannot be explained from man's side if we mean to hold fast to the answer prescribed in the Bible. What we have to explain is how there is such a thing as faith and obedience, i.e., in the Bible sense, God's work and gift in man's freedom to believe in Him and to obey Him. It is in this sense, which we must, of course, consider in detail, that we have to regard the concept of " the subjective," when we speak of the " subjective reality of revelation."

And so our first question is this : How does this freedom in man become real ? It is not : How does it become possible ? The latter question will also have to be raised and answered, but *secundum ordinem*, and therefore not first. Only when raised second is it the genuine question of our attitude to God's revelation. If raised first it again leads to lack of objectivity. It means that we are first trying to lay down the conditions upon which we can regard the way from God to man as traversible. And it is in the framework or through the spectacles of these conditions that we later have to realise how far God in the reality of His revelation has actually trodden a traversible way to man. We are thus putting ourselves in a place where we have no right. For what do we know of the traversibility of this way ? We cannot imagine that we even know ourselves, man, so well, that we can make clear from our side which way from God to man is a traversible one ! And we cannot presume to think of understanding the way which God has actually trodden in the light of conditions which we ourselves have discovered and set up. If we do, then on either side our claim is an immediate denial of revelation, whatever our results. Therefore the claim must be dropped at once, i.e., in this context the question of the reality of revelation must come first, the question of its possibility follows. The former is the question of fact, the latter the question of our attitude to it.

At this point, too, our exposition in the first draft of this book (§ 17, p. 284 ff.) involved a parlous obscuration at least in form. Even at that time I was aware that in this case too a " renewed recourse to the reality of God " is obviously the only possible answer (p. 285). I knew that in all inquiries into the possibility of God's revelation we had first to reckon with the reality of it (p. 291). I was aware that I had to express this if only in the form of numerous " reservations." But I did it only in the form of "reservations" within an investigation, in which, by pointing to grace confirmed by baptism, I aimed to advance from a description of the subjective possibility of revelation to the description and valuation of its reality, or, as it were, from the problems raised by this concept to their solution. No " reservations " could be of any avail against the uncertainty of this method, although I might appropriately have raised a good many more. It was most instructive that in spite of all the reservations Karl Heim (*Glaube und Denken*, 1st edn. 1931, p. 417 ff.) claimed to find in this exposition the question of the certainty of faith, the question of " man in despair about himself," and an attempt to answer it. In other words, Heim saw an answer to a question of his own, and as such he certainly and very rightly found it highly unsatisfactory. I suppose I must have seemed to be on the way from possibility to reality, from the riddle of man in despair about himself to the solution of the riddle in the certainty of faith. And if I was, it must have looked like an illegitimate pallia- tion, when after rejecting all other attempts at solution, " in a manner almost Roman and sacramental," I pointed to baptism as the basis of the knowledge of grace, as Heim reproached me with doing, instead of speaking like an ordinary Reformed theologian about the certainty of election on the basis of being sealed by the Holy Spirit. How painfully I felt that I had been misunderstood on this point ! When I pointed to baptism my intention was to say the strongest thing I could think of about the utterly supreme truth of grace and the Holy Spirit, and therefore about real " sealing," as compared with any immanent certainty in the soul. But I was myself to blame if this was not patent. Within a line of thought which Heim could so easily confuse with his own—in fact in one place (p. 301) I spoke specifically of " sacramental self-knowledge "—it could so easily not be patent. We can end with baptism only if we have begun with baptism. And this I had not done ; I had begun " by inquiring *in abstracto* into the conditions of the subjective possibility of revelation." But this possi- bility necessarily remains in the air, so long as it is not regarded strictly as the possibility already realised in revelation, and therefore so long as the question is not in terms of its realisation, and the answer to this question is not regarded. For, when we talk obscurely about the possibility of revelation, what perhaps we say quite seriously about its possibility is bound to revert to obscurity, and there- fore leave the impression that even the indication of baptism, the ultimate and strongest point which we can produce here, is perhaps no more than a palliation on the part of self-despairing man, and not a very attractive one at that. Heim has really done me a great service by his criticism. He has forced me still further from his own way, the way of reflection upon the possibility of certainty in faith. The right way—which makes the very reservations superfluous—can only be the reverse of that way which I then thought it necessary to take in Heim's company, in spite of all the reservations. Certainty of faith, i.e., a grounded awareness that God's revelation reaches man and how it does so, has first to be regarded simply in its reality, and only then, and on that basis, in its possibility, and in the various conditions of that possibility. Even in theology we can end in certainty of faith only if we have already started in certainty of faith.

First of all, then, we have to speak of the reality of God's revealed- ness for man. This must be our exclusive starting point. But if that is the case, then first we have to make one thing clear. The existence of men who render faith and obedience to the Word of God ; the fact that there is such a thing among men as faith and obedience to the Word of God ; the entire correspondence on man's side to the divine act of revelation : all this is just as seriously the content of the biblical witness to revelation as is the objective reality of revela- tion, i.e., Jesus Christ as the incarnate Word of God. Scripture did not attest for us the existence and work, the deeds and words of God in Jesus Christ, and yet leave open the question of the result of it all

on the men whom it is supposed to reach. As distinct from objective
proclamation we are not here abandoned to quite a different field of
inquiry. We are not left to our own field of inquiry. We do not have
to raise such questions as " Where do I begin ? " or " What has
this to do with me ? " or " How did I get here ? " simply from a standpoint which we have discovered or selected for ourselves, and then
answer them with a corresponding self-possession and arbitrariness.
Quite the contrary. The fact and form of the coming of God's Word
to man so that man becomes a hearer and doer of it, the fact that
Jesus Christ the Son of God acquires many brothers and His eternal
Father many children, the fact of the fulfilment of grace : these very
facts constitute an integral part of the biblical testimony to revelation
and of revelation itself, and that part belongs directly and indispensably
to the substance of the record. We can say, not only that " *God*
with us " is a fact, but also, and included in the former statement,
that " God with *us* " is a fact. We cannot say this of ourselves—
the latter statement any more than the former. God's revealedness
among us and in us really comes to us in revelation. It is part of
revelation. We cannot meditate upon it *in abstracto*. No arbitrary
decisions can be reached in relation to it. But if it does exist for us,
then we have to listen to it and acknowledge it very much in the form
in which Scripture tells us of that occurrence from God's side which
is its objective presupposition. Not God alone, but God and man
together constitute the content of the Word of God attested in Scripture. Yet the relation between the two is not an indifferent one. It
is not reversible. It is not a relation in which man can be, as it were,
the partner and workmate of God. It is not of such a kind as to
permit us to intrude ourselves in place of biblical man with our
own reflections and meditations upon ourselves, and with the viewpoints and principles by which we usually make up our minds. God
and biblical man confront one another as the Lord confronts the
servant, the Creator the creature, the Reconciler the pardoned sinner,
the Redeemer the one who never ceases to expect His redemption,
the Holy Spirit the Virgin Mary. It is this man who together with
God (this God) constitutes the content of the Word of God attested
in Scripture. And it is as the witness to this man that Scripture is
meant to win our ear, having something to tell us about man in the
sight of God and therefore about God's revealedness for us. But
in this sense and with this restriction Scripture does in fact have
something quite definite to say not only about God but also about
man, and with a like seriousness also about man. The Holy Spirit
acting upon man is also God. Hence his work upon us is also revelation, and knowledge of him is knowledge of revelation, and therefore
rests upon knowledge of the witness to revelation. We have no
right, then, to expect to import into the reality of God's process of
revelation to and among men any contribution learned from a source

of knowledge different from Holy Scripture. In this respect also, we must realise the adequacy of Holy Scripture as the source of our knowledge. We must submit to our bondage to Scripture. We must submit to be content with it. We must do so no less because man is in the very presence of God. Indeed, because of the special parlousness of this point, we have to say, *just* because man is in the very presence of God. Actually Scripture does not abandon us even on this its subjective side. We are not left to our own guess-work or to the findings of a religious anthropology—not even to those of a Christian anthropology, which claims to assert something different from what it has previously been told.

That the Bible is not dumb on this side is revealed clearly by the contrast between Law and prophets in the Old Testament, and in the New Testament by the corresponding contrast between Gospels and Epistles. In the Old Testament particularly the subjective element which is represented in the first instance by the prophets is further strengthened by the third section of the Canon, the *ketubim*. In this section the community which adopts the revelation, and the individual within it who is moved by the needs and hopes of Israel, express themselves in the most varied literary forms. With sublime naturalness both Synagogue and Church took account of this subjective element as well when constructing the Canon. It was regarded as an integral part of the witness to revelation and of revelation itself. On principle, therefore, we must not think of speaking about its subordination to the objective element, because any subordination in principle would indirectly call in question the *homoousia* of the Holy Spirit, compared with the Father and the Son ; *qui cum Patre et Filio simul adoratur et conglorificatur*. From this standpoint the emphatic insistence upon Gospel before Epistle in the first part of the Roman Mass carries with it an awkward reminder of subordinationist trains of thought. And the dispute about " Jesus and Paul," or " Jesus or Paul," which has preoccupied Protestant theology since the 18th century, is incontestably painful. There is an element of tragicomedy in the development of Neo-Protestantism. Its desire was to enforce the problem of man in his relation to God. But in its polemic, it unwittingly rejected the only branch on which it might have sat with honour. The desire was and is no doubt a legitimate one. In relative distinction from the aim of the trinitarian and christological dogmas of the early Church, it wished to see and to understand not only God in His relation to man but also man in his relation to God. We may say that even in the early days this was always the special desire of the Western Church and it found its active representative especially in Augustine. At the peak of mediæval Scholasticism, in the *Summa* of Thomas Aquinas, it was enforced on a broad front over against the objective dogma, which for its part was not neglected. At the Reformation it came to the very forefront : so much so that unreflecting historians of a later date could believe that the objective dogma had now become a *caput mortuum*. It was no accident that the favourite and best exploited books were the Psalms and Romans, not the Law and the Gospels. Luther orients his whole theology by the reality of the justification of the sinner, Calvin by the reality of the sanctification of the same sinner. Their interest is as onesided as that of Athanasius, who had formerly oriented his whole theology by the reality of the incarnation. There was both an inner and an outer necessity for this onesidedness of interest on the part of the Reformers, and the danger involved in it never came to anything as long as the divinity of the Holy Spirit was the self-evident presupposition upon which they prosecuted their interest. It is this which in the same sense converts both Luther's doctrine of justification and Calvin's doctrine of sanctification into proclamation of the mystery of revelation, as had formerly been the case with the Christology of Athanasius. If we are to call the special dogmas of the Reformation subjective dogmas, we can do so only in the sense—and this is what turns them into genuine Church dogmas—that they treat particularly, not so much of God's freedom for man become an event in Christ, as man's freedom for God actualised in the Holy Spirit. And it was at this point that Neo-Protestantism failed. It claimed to be fostering the particular interest of the Reformers. Indeed, it appeared to do so. But it was so interested in man's freedom that it forgot the divinity of the Holy Spirit. At the outset the " freedom from man's side " was still problematically confronted with a freedom from God's side. But logically the latter freedom was drawn in and sucked up by its opposite pole. Man came to be understood quite apart from all mystery or revelation. And the final result was that God's freedom became simply a more precise establishing of the all-dominating "freedom from man's side." This being the case, it was only logical that they should be compelled to read the Gospels with critical spectacles, the necessary result being a Christology emptied of all mystery. And not only that, but they were completely baffled when confronted with the epistolary part of the New Testament, with the " apostle." They thought that either in part or as a whole they could invalidate the apostle as a witness to revelation in favour of what was left of the Gospel when all critical deductions had been made, i.e., of the " historical Jesus." It was inevitable that this theology should come into conflict with the specific witness of biblical man represented by the apostle as distinct from the Evangelist. For at its heart this theology was not concerned as the Reformers were with the creature man, the pardoned sinner, the mortal who, together with the God who acts upon him, constitutes the content of the biblical witness to revelation. It was concerned with man in himself, the man who understands himself because he controls himself. The very conflict makes it plain that they accepted the Bible as witness to revelation only conditionally, conditionally, that is to say, upon the parallel presupposition that there is another and primary witness in respect of a revelation in man *per se*, a witness which is self-given, and in the light of which the former witness has now to be understood. But if such a primary witness to revelation is presupposed, the second is already rejected, however seriously we protest our continued acceptance of it. For the claim of the alleged second witness is this : that we men cannot witness to ourselves of a revelation of God within us, so that no such primary witness to revelation is possible. If we refuse to acknowledge this, we obviously cease in any real sense to confront Scripture as a witness to revelation, and we can no longer understand it as a single whole, either according to the objective or to the subjective content of its witness. Not even according to its subjective content, where we might have found the legitimate answer to the question about man as the Reformers did, but quite a different answer, of course, from the one which we think we ourselves can give in that alienation from Scripture to which we have fallen victim.

Now if we ask Scripture about its witness to man as he stands before God and receives His revelation, at the very outset the following point is basic. By God's election and calling, by his hearing of the Word, by the witness of the Holy Spirit, this man is distinguished not only invisibly and inwardly, but also and in spite of all that remains invisible and inward in the reality of the revelation which comes to him, very visibly and outwardly. He stands at a definite place in history, which not by accident, but by a most definite necessity, is this particular place and not another. Revelation does not encounter man in any general way, as though it were the eternal definition or eternal meaning of all time, or the general solution of the riddle of temporal occurrence. As we saw in an earlier context, revelation has its own time, which is just this one and not another, which can reach men of all times only as the revelation which has entered this time. To this objective particularity in revelation there corresponds a subjective. The men who receive it are quite special men. They are special men not only invisibly and inwardly, but in their very existence, in their visible outward position. In the Old Testament they belong to the nation with which God has made His covenant, which He has put under His judgment and His promise, to the nation of Israel. In the New Testament they belong to the Church in which Jesus Christ is present as the real acting subject, as the head of all the members gathered in the Church with their definite tasks and functions. Certainly it cannot be said that this membership of the nation or Church turns these men into recipients of revelation. God turns them into that. And God is not forced to turn them into that because of this membership : at the given place in the Old Testament as well as the New Testament we always find men who appear not to be recipients of revelation at all. And God is not bound to this membership ; in the Old Testament, at all events, figures are constantly turning up, who, quite away from the given place, outside the nation Israel, seem nevertheless to have become genuine recipients of God's revelation. But this last possibility appears more and more to have the significance of a corrective. Those who perhaps boast of their membership instead of boasting in God must be checked and shamed. Those who within this membership do not become recipients of revelation must be given a sign of judgment. The freedom of grace which is so easily forgotten and so lightly treasured must be made manifest. And to do this, every now and then there turns up, at least in the given place in the Old Testament, a heathen who standing in his own quite different place has nevertheless heard God and obeyed God. When such heathen turn up in the New Testament as unexpected confessors of the Messiahship of Jesus, it occurs as a continuation of the Old Testament corrective for Israel, not as a corrective for the Church. The Church is not limited by the addition of the heathen, but confirmed and revealed as the body of Him before whom every knee shall bow. So indeed Israel itself, so far as it points to and prophesies the Church, is not limited but confirmed and manifested by the corrective, against a confusion of the Israelite community and the Israelite nationality. The exception, therefore, proves the rule. God Himself and God alone turns man into a recipient of His revelation—but He does so in a definite area, and this area, if we may now combine the Old Testament and the New Testament, is the area of the Church. The Old Testament corrective retains its validity for those who are in the Church. It indicates the separation between good and bad, the judgment of God to which they are subject. But it does not call in question the reality and clarity, the finality and exclusiveness with which the Church is the place in which God turns men into recipients of His revelation. That the world contains such a place created and indicated by God is declared to be true and not untrue by the development of the universal Church from the national community of Israel. This truth cannot be ignored. Put pointedly and to be taken *cum grano salis*, there exist over against Jesus Christ, not in the first instance believers, and then, composed of them, the Church ; but first of all the Church and then, through it and in it, believers. While God is as little bound to the Church as to the Synagogue, the recipients of His revelation are. They are what they are because the Church is what it is, and because they are in the Church, not apart from the Church and not outside the Church. And when we say " Church ", we do not mean merely the inward and invisible coherence of those whom God in Christ calls His own, but also the outward and visible coherence of those who have heard in time, and have confessed to their hearing, that in Christ they are God's. The reception of revelation occurs within, not without, this twofold coherence.

This significance of the Church for the subjective reality of revelation is not a Roman Catholic but a biblical and therefore of necessity a universally Christian doctrine. As in the Old Testament the individual as such who fears Yahweh and walks before Yahweh only exists so far as the people of the covenant exists and Himself as one of this people, so according to the Gospels Jesus by no means addresses men in any abstract individuality of their existence, but *a priori* as members of the community which, now that the time is fulfilled, is to be summoned forth and called together by His word out of the relative darkness of the nation-community as its completed form. The real function of the Messiah is to save His people from their sins (Mt. 1²¹) ; He is the ἡγούμενος, who shall feed my people Israel (Mt. 2⁶). In order that this saving and feeding may come true, it is to this people Israel that the call of Jesus is directed : " Repent ye ; for the kingdom of heaven is at hand " (Mt. 3²). And how are we to understand either the introduction to the Sermon on the Mount (Mt. 5²ᶠ·), or from that standpoint its whole content, if we do not consider that it is not this or that individual with his definite religious and moral possibilities, but again the people that is called blessed, summoned forth, and called together, namely the spiritually poor, the mourners, the meek, etc., in short the nation of those who with Simeon (Lk. 2²⁵) wait for the " consolation of Israel " and are as such the true Israel. Thus it is that from the very first the result of Jesus' call is not the existence of a medley of more or less convinced and reliable adherents, but, in the company of the Twelve who suddenly shoot up as it were out of the ground (in whom the twelve tribes of Israel reappear), the existence of the foundation, the rock upon which He will build His ἐκκλησία (Mt. 16¹⁸). To them the Lord promises that He will be with them alway even unto the end of the world (Mt. 28²⁰). To them He gives ἐξουσία (Mt. 10¹). Whoso receiveth them receiveth Him (Mt. 10⁴⁰). He that heareth them heareth Him (Lk. 10¹⁶). He is in the midst of them, even if only two or three of them should be gathered together in His name (Mt. 18²⁰). To them the Holy Spirit is promised (Ac. 1⁴ᶠ·) and upon them—note that already beforehand they were " all with one accord in one place "—He is actually poured out at Pentecost, with the result that they receive the gift of speech and that men of every nation can understand them : " we do hear them speak in our tongues τὰ μεγαλεῖα τοῦ θεοῦ." And then there were " added unto them " the same day about three thousand souls (Ac. 2¹ᶠ·). For " neither pray I for these alone, but for them also which shall believe on me through their word·; that they all may be one " (Jn. 17²⁰ᶠ). If this is what we find already in the first part of the New Testament, how much more is it the case in the second part, the Epistles, where we cannot understand a single word in relation to either' writers or recipients, unless we discern the tightly closed circle within which the speaking and hearing takes place. I will refer to only one decisive point, Paul's account of his conversion in Gal. 1¹⁵ᶠ·. Who had this Paul been till then ? Someone *in vacuo* ? No, but one set apart and called by God's grace from his mother's womb, like the prophet Jeremiah. And what does he become now that God reveals His Son in him ? A Christian ? Amongst other things, yes : and yet no mention is made of it, but there is immediate mention of his duty to proclaim Christ among the Gentiles. Therefore he did not and he will not exist except in his function in the life of the Church. And it is on the same assumption that he now addresses his congregation, quite irrespective of whether he is dealing with former Jews or Gentiles. It is upon their being κλητοὶ ἅγιοι (Rom. 1⁷ ; 1 Cor. 1²) that everything that is real between him and them is based. The very fact that it is comparatively rare for such explicit mention to be made of the Church as such, as in Rom. 12³ᶠ·, 1 Cor. 12⁴ᶠ·, Eph. 4¹ᶠ·, 1 Pet. 2⁵ᶠ·, shows how naturally existence in Christ and existence in the Church are seen and understood as an actual unity, although the difference between them is as great as that between existence in heaven and existence on earth.

From this standpoint we ought at least to understand what was the intention in the utterances of the fathers on this matter ; though to a certain extent they are already overshadowed by the developing Roman Catholic conception of the Church. Ὅσοι ἂν μετανοήσαντες ἔλθωσιν ἐπὶ τὴν ἑνότητα τῆς ἐκκλησίας, καὶ οὗτοι Θεοῦ ἔσονται, ἵνα ὦσιν κατὰ Ἰησοῦν Χριστὸν ζῶντες (Ignatius of Antioch, *Ad. Philad.* 3, 2). *Ubi enim ecclesia, ibi et Spiritus Dei et ubi Spiritus Dei illic ecclesia et omnis gratia ; Spiritus autem veritas* (Irenaeus, *C.o.h.* III 24, 1). *Si de illo populo vult aliquis salvari, ad hanc domum veniat, et salutem consequi possit.* . . . *Extra hanc domum, id est extra ecclesiam, nemo salvatur* (Origen, *In Jesu Nave hom.* 3, 5). *Habere non potest Deum patrem, qui ecclesiam non habet matrem. Si potuit evadere quisque extra arcam Noe, et qui extra ecclesiam foris fuerit, evadit.* . . . *Hanc unitatem qui non tenet ; non tenet Dei legem, non tenet Patris et Filii fidem, vitam non tenet et salutem* (Cyprian, *De cath. eccl. un.* 6). *Hic est fons veritatis, hoc domicilium fidei, hoc templum Dei quo quis non intraverit vel a quo si quis exierit, a spe vitae ac salutis alienus est* (Lactantius, *Div. inst.* IV 30, 11). *Nec deputabo te inter Christianos, nisi in ecclesia Christi te videro* (Augustine, *Conf.* VIII 2, 4). It is obvious what points of interrogation and exclamation have to be affixed to such statements. In any case it is good to be alive to the fact that Luther related very closely to the Church the sentence in the *Smaller Catechism* : " The Holy Ghost hath called me by the Gospel, illumined me by His gifts, sanctified and sustained me in the true faith," for he immediately continued : " like as He calleth, gathereth, illumineth, sanctifieth and by Jesus Christ sustaineth the whole of Christendom on earth in the one true faith," and then concluded quite unmistakably : " in which Christendom He daily forgiveth me and all believers all their sins and shall at the last day raise me and all the dead and to me together with all believers in Christ shall give an eternal life." And in the *Larger Catechism*, to the question how and wherewith the Holy Spirit makes us holy, the answer is : " By the Christian Church. . . . For firstly He hath a special community in the world, which is the mother that begetteth and supporteth every Christian by the Word of God which He revealeth and plieth, lightening and kindling hearts that they grasp it, adopt it, cling thereto and abide thereby " (*W.A.* 30¹, 188, 22). And at the corresponding point in one of the sermons which precede and are the basis of the *Larger Catechism*, we read expressly, and with the same exclusivism as that of the patristic citations : *Et in hac ecclesia* thou too art, that the *Spiritus sanctus* leadeth thee thereinto, *per praedicationem Evangelii. Prius nihil nosti de Christo, sed Christiana ecclesia annuntiat tibi Christam. . . . Per . . . officium eius sanctificaris . . . alioqui nunquam Christum agnosceres et audires (ib.* 92, 13). " Therefore whoso would find Christ must first find the Churches. How would we know where Christ and His faith were, if we wot not where His faithful are ? And whoso would know somewhat of Christ must not trust himself nor build a bridge to heaven by his own understanding, but go to the Churches, visit and question the same. For outwith the Christian Church is no truth, no Christ, no blessedness" (*Pred. üb. Luc.* 2¹⁵ᵗ⋅, *Kirchenpost.* 1522, *W.A.* 10¹, 140, 8). Similarly, Calvin heads his chapter *Instit.* IV 1 : *De vera ecclesia cum qua nobis colenda est unitas, quia piorum omnium mater est,* and in clear reminiscence of the quotation from Cyprian, he says : *Haec enim quae Deus coniunxit separari fas non est, ut quibus ipse est pater, ecclesia etiam mater sit (ib.* IV 1, 1). Whoever separates himself from the *communio ecclesiae* must be held *pro transfuga et desertore religionis.* He renders himself guilty of an *abnegatio Dei et Christi (ib.* IV 1, 10). We must, of course, make many reservations in face of the Roman Catholic interpretation of the necessity of the Church to salvation. But the necessity itself it would be unwise either to reject or to avoid. Indeed, it is necessarily prescribed for us, when we ask concerning the subjective reality of revelation.

To understand this we must above all try to see that over against Jesus Christ the Church is not a chance, i.e., an arbitrary construction. It is not created, formed and introduced by individual men on their own initiative, authority and insight. It is not the outcome of a free undertaking to analyse and come to terms with the self-revealing God by gathering together a community which confesses Him, by setting up a doctrine which expounds and proclaims His truth in the way that seems most appropriate to these men. Applied to such a church, the *extra ecclesiam nulla salus* would in fact be an enormity. In face of such a church we should all have not only the right but the duty, a duty to faith, to appeal to the free grace of God to be made blessed outside of it. In face of such a church we should have to insist at least upon civil toleration, not only in the name of humanity but in the name of God. A church of that kind has nothing to do with the subjective reality of revelation. We can say quite simply that a church of that description is not the Church but the work of sin, of apostasy in the Church. Naturally none of the fathers whom we mentioned could possibly be thinking of that kind of church. We can and must say, of course, that where the Church is, there also we have always this church which is not the Church, i.e., that in the Church the work of sin and apostasy is always going on as well. There is no time at which to a greater or less degree the Church does not also have the appearance of such a church. There is no time at which to a greater or lesser degree it is not actually a church in this sense. There is no time at which it is quite inappropriate to remember that Jesus Christ is the Lord of the Church, and not the Church the Lord of Jesus Christ. There is no time at which the Church is not compelled by the arbitrary human action which constantly arises at its very heart to remind itself through Holy Scripture of its origin, and to let itself be ruled and therefore corrected from the standpoint of this origin against upstart arbitrarinesses. But the nature of the Church cannot be gathered from man's upstart arbitrarinesses in it. Just as, similarly, Jesus Christ cannot be understood from the standpoint of man's nature and kind, which He assumed and adopted, and which are only too familiar to us. What we men apprehend is ultimately and at bottom an accidental or arbitrary search after God, in which we can see only sin against God and a falling away from Him—never the unity between God and man, in which our nature and kind are in Jesus Christ genuinely and finally liberated from such strivings. That there took place in Him revelation and reconciliation between God and man we can comprehend only when we see and understand that the eternal divine Word was here made flesh. It is that which at this point brings light into our darkness. It is that which signifies liberation and purification. It is that which effects revelation and reconciliation. It is that which is the unique reality of the person of Jesus Christ. And the same is true of the Church of Christ. Because it is true of Jesus Christ, it is also true of His Church. The place or area in history at which—and at which alone—reception of revelation is achieved, the visible and invisible coherence of those whom God in Christ calls His own and who confess Him in Christ as their God, in other words the Church, has no reality independent of or apart from Jesus Christ. It is not that because of the sovereignty of their reason, will or feeling men have concluded for Christ or have become " Christians," i.e., subjects of the predicate Christ. Where that occurs you have sin or falling away. And where any church is only the Christian Church in this sense, namely the church in which Christ is the predicate and not himself the subject, it has itself become the church of sin and apostasy, an heretical church. But the Church of Christ, which really is what it is called, does not exist in this independent reality. Although there is in it no lack of man's upstart arbitrariness, it exists in dependence on Jesus Christ. And it is because it lives by Jesus Christ, not because it is constantly involved in upstart and arbitrary action, that it is the true Church.

Cf. for what follows K. L. Schmidt, " Die Kirche des Urchristentums " (in *Festgabe für A. Deissmann*, 1927, p. 258 ff.) ; E. Thurneysen, " Christus und die Kirche," *Z.d.Z.* 1930 p. 177 ff. ; E. Fuchs, " Die Auferstehung Jesu Christi und der Anfang der Kirche," *Z. f. Kgsch.*, Vol. 51, pt. 1–2, 1932, p. 1 ff.

That the Church has its origin in Christ means four things.

1. It derives from the Word that became flesh. That the Word was made flesh was not without meaning for the world of flesh. It was not a superfluous occurrence which might have happened anywhere and at any time. The fact of the occurrence has not passed unnoticed by the world and it has not left it unaffected. This was the Word by which all things were created. It was the Word by which God supports all things. It was the Word which only came to its own when it came into the world. Above all it was the omnipotent

Word of God which cannot return void, the Word which when it is spoken always has the result that what is declared in it occurs. And one thing at least is declared in it (by the very fact that the eternal Word of God is spoken in our world), and that is that it should be heard in this world of ours. And so the result of its being spoken is that it is now heard in this world of ours. In Jesus Christ our human nature and kind were adopted and assumed into unity of being with the Son of God. And this was no futile or superfluous occurrence. Necessarily, therefore, there are among the men whose nature and kind were met by this occurrence in Jesus Christ those who live in this adoption and assumption. They are the children of God because, in spite of the sinfulness of their nature and kind, they are justified and sanctified by that which meets their nature and kind in Jesus Christ. This life of the children of God for Jesus Christ's sake is the reality of the Church, the subjective reality of revelation. In virtue of the omnipotence of the Word of grace, there is this meeting, this life of the children of God. And for that reason and to that extent, the saying *extra ecclesiam nulla salus* holds good. There is no reality of revelation outside the circumference described by this meeting.

In New Testament passages like Rom. 12[4f.] ; 1 Cor. 10[16f.], 12[12f.] ; Col. 1[18. 24] ; Eph. 1[22f.], 4[12], 5[23. 29f.], etc., the Church is described as the body of Christ. One meaning of this description is undoubtedly this : that the existence of the Church involves a repetition of the incarnation of the Word of God in the person of Jesus Christ in that area of the rest of humanity which is distinct from the person of Jesus Christ. The repetition is quite heterogeneous. Yet for all its heterogeneity it is homogeneous too (although the uniqueness of the objective revelation forbids us to call it a continuation, prolongation, extension or the like). The fulness of the Godhead dwelt in Him " bodily " (Col. 2[9]). In Him God immediately (but also, of course, externally and visibly) delimited, touched and determined human history. In this particular history one man or person (for that is at least one meaning of $\sigma\tilde{\omega}\mu\alpha$) delimited, touched and determined another and all others, so that now they are no longer what they are without this One who delimits them. And all this is proved to be real in the history of the Church, in the historical, the externally and visibly actual form of the totality of those who are delimited, touched and determined by Him as the Son of God. *Verbum Patri coaeternum in utero virginali domum sibi aedificavit corpus humanum et huic tanquam capiti membra, ecclesiam, adiunxit* (Augustine, *De civ. Dei* XVII 20, 2). " He was by his sufferings buried in the earth and, like a root unset, hidden in the world, and there grew from it that fair tree, the Christian Church, outspread over all the world " (Luther, *Pred. üb. Röm.* 15, 4 f., *Adv. Post.*, 1522, *W.A.* 10[12], 91, 10). " He will not be content that the story occurred and he fulfilled it for his person, but he mingleth it with us and maketh thereof a brotherhood, that he might be a common good and heirship for us all ; he setteth it not in a *praedicamento absoluto*, but *relationis*, to say that he hath done so not for his own person or sake, but as our brother and for our sole good ; and will not be otherwise regarded and known of us, save as he who with all this is ours and we in turn his and so we belong together most intimately, so that we cannot be more closely tied, like those who alike have one father and are set in the like common and undivided inheritance and can assume, glory and take comfort in all his power, glory and goodness as in our own " (*Pred. üb. Mc.* 16[1f.] ; *E.A.* 11, 208).

2. But this life of the children of God is always a life for Christ's sake. The foundation of the Church is also its law and its limit. We might say that it corresponds to the *anhypostasis* of Christ's human nature. By its inmost nature the Church is forbidden to want independence of Jesus Christ, or sovereignty in thought or action. If it did, it would relapse into the unjustified and unsanctified nature from which it is withdrawn in Christ. This will always find plenty of means to assert itself in its life. But it cannot want to relapse into it. It is born of the omnipotent Word of grace ; it would only die if it were to become or to be anything but the fulfilment of that Word. Grace holds good only where grace rules. The rule of grace which is unfailing where men are God's children for Christ's sake, the dependence of these men upon the Word of which they are reborn— this is the reality of the Church, the subjective reality of revelation. And in the light of it, it is and must be true that *extra ecclesiam nulla salus*. There is no reality of revelation apart from this dependence on the Word.

A second meaning of the description of the Church as Christ's body is undoubtedly this : that the repetition of the incarnation of the Word of God in the historical existence of the Church excludes at once any possible autonomy in that existence. The Church lives with Christ as the body with its head. This means that the Church is what it is, because in consequence of what human nature and kind became in Jesus Christ, human nature and kind are made obedient to the eternal Word of the Father and are upheld by that Word. " The cup of blessing which we bless, is it not the communion (κοινωνία) of the blood of Christ ? The bread which we break, is it not the communion of the body of Christ " (1 Cor. 10[16f.]) ? In and by this participation the Church lives. It lives by the fact that within it as the circumference nothing happens except a real repetition of what has happened in its midst, in Jesus Christ, to men and for men. It lives by growing up to him who is the head, Christ (Eph. 4[15]), i.e., by receiving its whole existence, comfort and direction from Him and only from Him. He is always the subject of the Church. " What believest thou concerning the holy, universal, Christian Church ? That the Son of God out of the whole human race gathereth, guardeth and sustaineth for himself an unworldly Church unto eternal life, by his spirit and word in unity with true faith, from the beginning of the world unto the end, and that I am and shall eternally remain a living member of the same " (*Heid. Cat. qu.* 54). *Nostre Seigneur Jésus Christ ne nous donne pas quelques instructions, comme si on enseignoit l' A B C à un enfant, et puis qu'on le baillast à un maistre plus excellent : nostre Seigneur donc ne parle pas ainsi à demi à nous : mais en toute perfection, tellement que et en la vie et en la mort il nous fait tousiours persister à ce que nous tenons de luy et renoncer à ce qui viendra du costé des hommes : car tout meslinge ne sera sinon corruption. . . . Il faut que l'Eglise se bastisse tellement que Jésus Christ nostre chef ait tousiours la preeminence. Car si on vouloit tellement exalter les hommes que Jésus Christ fust obscurci au milieu, voilà un bastiment espouvantable, et qui n'emporte que ruine et confusion. Et de faict, si un homme devenoit gros comme un pilier de ce temple, et que ca teste fust comme un poing et qu'elle fust cachée dedans ces espaules, ce seroit un monstre : il vaudroit beaucoup mieux qu'il retinst sa mesure commune* (Calvin, *Serm. on Gal.* 1[11t.], 1557 ; *C.R. Calv.* 50, 329 f.). " Askest thou what the Christian Church is, or where the Christian Church is to be found ? I will tell thee. The Christian Church thou must seek, not that it lie at Rome or at St. James or at Nuremberg or at Wittenberg or among countryfolk, townsfolk or nobility, but it

1. The Holy Spirit the Subjective Reality of Revelation

saith, ' the government shall be upon His shoulders ' . . . that a right Christian and true member of the Churches is he who believeth that he sitteth upon Christ's shoulders, that is, that all his sins are hung on Christ's neck, so that his heart saith, I know no other comfort save that all my sins and misdeeds are laid upon His shoulders. Therefore those who lie on Christ's shoulders and let themselves be carried by Him, are called and are the Church and proper Christians " (Luther, *Pred. üb. Jes.* 9, 1 f., 1532, *E.A.* 6, 59 f.). *Rectus itaque confessionis ordo poscebat, ut trinitati subiungeretur ecclesia, tanquam habitatori domus sua et Deo templum suum et conditori civitas sua. . . . Unde nec tota, nec ulla pars eius vult se coli pro Deo, nec cuiquam esse Deus pertinenti ad templum Dei, quod aedificatur ex diis, quos facit non factus Deus* (Augustine, *Enchir.* 56).

3. Seeing then that the life of the children of God is a dependence upon the incarnate Word, it is a common life. Not secondarily, but primarily and radically, it is the life of a community. A Church community or congregation, as distinguished from all mere association, is grounded in the essential being of those who are united within it. But they are what they are from and by the Word. Their existence is none other than that of the Word. Therefore they are one, and originally one, as surely as the Word in which they exist is one. They could only be disunited without the Word—but they are not without the Word, for they would not yet be, or would have ceased to be what they are, if they were disunited. Thus the Church as a collection, coherence, or unity of many does nòt rest upon the sense of association in any love or brotherliness with which the many might be filled. In this respect also it rests directly upon Christ, in whom the many are what they are. And it is only on the basis of this existence that brotherliness and love are possible and necessary, even though they do not constitute the Church as such. Those who are in the Church are brothers and sisters. They are simply confirming their own existence and in it the Church's basis, when this becomes visible in their attitudes and modes of action ; and they are denying the Church's basis and nothing less than their own existence, if this remains invisible in their attitudes and modes of action. But the unity of the Church is grounded upon the one Christ. And whatever the case with the attitudes and actions of the men who participate in it, the Church is the congregation ; subjective reality is the congregation. And *extra ecclesiam nulla salus* necessarily means : that by belonging to Christ we belong to all who belong to Him—not secondarily but *a priori*, not by the exercise of Christian virtue, but according to our nature, i.e., for Christ's sake, and therefore not by accident or disposition or choice, but in the strictest possible sense, by necessity.

The third meaning of the description of the Church as the body of Christ now becomes clear. Those who live within the circumference of which Christ is the centre do not constitute, but they are as such a single and indivisible whole. Each in his own place—as a member, is drawn into the identity of the body with its head. If the members are not equal but unequal, they are still not different but one. They are just as much one as they are one with Jesus Christ by participating in the justification and sanctification of His human nature and kind. This connexion between justification and the congregation is well seen in the Epistle of Barnabas (4¹⁰) : Μὴ καθ' ἑαυτοὺς ἐνδύνοντες μονάζετε ὡς ἤδη δεδικαιωμένοι, ἀλλ' ἐπὶ τὸ αὐτὸ συνερχόμενοι συνζητεῖτε περὶ τοῦ κοινῇ συμφέροντος.

" By the Word Christ goeth up into the heart and illumineth it. All hearts behold one kind of light, have one faith and one knowledge. This is the day He hath made here, and hath so made as it departeth not therefrom. As the sun abideth during the day and uplifteth the day, so too the sun Christ maketh day of Himself and from Him goeth radiance into every believing heart, and He is at once in all. And as so many eyes all together see the sun perfectly and entirely, nor doth it give but one ray of itself but everyone hath radiance and all have it in common, so too here is one Christ, all have Him in common and yet each hath Him wholly in his heart. When He cometh, He so illumineth us and ruleth us all by one faith. So the false view departeth and the heart beholdeth God's word and work aright, so there is a new world, a new people and a new light " (Luther, *Pred. üb. Luc.* 24¹³ᵗ·, 1521, *W.A.* 9, 669, 6). " Christ then sayeth not that they have one will or mind, however true it is that all Christians are of one faith, love, mind and thought, as those that have one Christ, spirit and faith, notwithstanding all the differences between individuals in respect of their external function and works. But here He speaketh not of the unity which we call an equality, but the Word layeth it down *ut sint unum*, that they be one thing, just as ' the Father and I ' are one thing ; so that it is said concerning the essence and meaneth much more than to be one in heart and mind. But what the one or one sort of thing is, we shall never see or grasp, we have to believe. . . . Therefore as the body is one thing and is called one, so the whole of Christendom is called one body or one cake, not simply because of a oneness or similarity in outlook but rather because of a oneness in essence. Now there is a much greater unity between the member and the body than between thine and another's thoughts. For His thoughts are in His body and also thine in thine and it cannot be said that my and thy thoughts are one thing, in the way that all members are together one thing, i.e., one body, so that if a member is away from or out of the body, it is not one thing or essence with the body, but a body or essence of its own ; but so long as they are all together, it remaineth one cake, without any difference or separation of essence. So then here also Christ meaneth that His Christians must depend on each other, so that they are altogether a single thing and unseparated body and continue so, like as He and the Father are one. . . . There standeth therein a mighty great comfort for all who believe in Christ and hold to His word, namely, that we are all members of one body as one flesh and blood. And have the advantage that all that befalls a member befalls the whole body, which doth not occur in the likeness or harmony alleged. For although many have one heart and will, one doth not partake of another as in a body. . . . For it belongeth to such unity that there is no bit or part that liveth and feeleth for itself alone and hath not the life and feeling of every other, that is, of the whole body. Where then the meanest member of Christendom suffereth, the whole body soon feeleth it and is aroused so that they all at once begin to run and cry and shriek. For so our head Christ heareth it and feeleth it. And although He holdeth in a little, yet when He beginneth to smell trouble and to wrinkle the nostrils, He maketh not light of it. For so it saith in the prophet Zechariah : ' he that toucheth you toucheth the apple of mine eye.' Lo! there thou hast a precious promise of exquisite comfort and courage to Christians. . . . But in none other wise can we attain it but by this, that God (as He hath said) sustain us in His name, that is, if we abide in the word which we have received from Christ. For the word holdeth us together, that we all remain under one head and depend on Him, see none other holiness or aught that should hold for God save in Him. . . . By the word are we incorporated in Christ, all that He hath is ours and we can take to ourselves what is His as of our own body, furthermore He too must take to Himself all that befalleth us, which neither world, devil nor any ill chance can spoil or overpower. There is no power on earth so great that it has any effect upon this unity. But the devil goeth about to break this bond and by his cunning and craft to snatch us from the word. Where that hath happened, he hath already won. For apart from the word there is no more unity, but futile fission, unhallowed sects and schisms, which he casteth amongst us by his nets and snares, that is, by men's teaching " (*ib., Pred. üb. Jn.* 17[11f.], 1528–9, *W.A.* 28, 147–152).

4. The life of the children of God, and therefore the Church, the subjective reality of revelation, is divine and human, eternal and temporal, and therefore invisible and visible. It is also human, also temporal, also visible. Always in its entire hiddenness in God it is also an historical reality. How can it be otherwise, seeing it has its origin, its ground, its centre in the incarnation of the Word ? According to His human nature Jesus Christ was also an historical reality. Otherwise revelation would not be revelation, reconciliation would not be reconciliation. Otherwise even after the incarnation God would continue to live and be only on high and in Himself, far from man. He is on high. But He is also with them that are of a broken and contrite heart. In eternity He is God in Himself and God with us. But if He is God with us, then He is so in historical reality ; for we live and have our being in historical reality. And if this revelation of His in historical reality did not take place in vain, if to the time which He had for us there corresponds a time which we ought to have for Him, then that which corresponds to His incarnation, the life of the children of God, the Church, is also visible. Invisible, too, of course. Even in the incarnation, it still cannot be seen that it is the eternal Word that there became man. At that point, too, temptation and offence are still possible. It is only through God that God can become manifest even in the flesh. Yet when He does become manifest, He becomes manifest in the flesh, visibly. In the same way the Church is not only invisible in virtue of divine election, calling, illumination, justification and sanctification, which turn the children of God into what they are. It is not only invisible in virtue of the invisible grace of the invisible Lord who rules it. It is not only invisible in virtue of the Word invisibly spoken to it, in which they all are one. But in all these things it is also visible. The children of God are visible men. A visible event brings them together. A visible unity holds them to each other. The fact that they have received God's revelation is invisible, but they themselves are visible as those who have to remember that fact, and are glad to do so. That the event is the call of God is invisible ; but the event of their being brought together is visible. That their unity is the Word heard is invisible ; but that they belong together and keep together is visible. The problem of their existence as the Church can be perceived with a perspicacity which is proportionate to our constant perception of the problem of the God-manhood of Jesus Christ. But at the very least the problem

of their existence as the Church is set in a complete visibility, and as a problem at least it cannot be denied. Therefore we have always to look for the Church on the plane of temporal things, of things which can be seen and thought and experienced. And so *extra ecclesiam nulla salus* is always an assertion that for every man, at every time and place, the subjective reality of revelation is fulfilled in a temporal encounter and decision, an encounter and decision which can be seen and thought and experienced.

If from this standpoint we again reach back to the description of the Church as Christ's body, we shall now have to insist upon a fourth meaning. The Church has a further point in common with the incarnate Word of God. As distinguished from the eternal nature of God, it has a spatio-temporal form and extension. It is therefore visible in the same way as any other σῶμα. It has this form and extension only from the incarnate Word of God, i.e., only by the free gracious will of the Son of God, who gives it this visible reality of existence by assuming it into communion with His own existence in space and time. Apart from Him there would be no visibility of the Church, because apart from Him there would be no Church at all. Apart from Him that which is visible as the Church will never really be the visibility of the Church. But in Him and through Him there is not only the invisible reality of the spiritual life of the Church proceeding from His Word. In Him and through Him there is also its bodily life, without which it could not be a gathering of real men and the permanent setting of witness to Him amid human history. In Him and through Him the Church is the wholly concrete area of the subjective reality of revelation. Within this area the justification and sanctification of men may become an event. At the gates and borders of this area concrete encounters and decisions may be reached. By the existence of this area revelation is concretely recognised and attested by men. By this area the question of faith is concretely put to men. In his *De Fide rerum quae non videntur* (4, 7 f.) Augustine has expounded the thought in this way. The Church, he says, by its visibility stands security to outsiders for the reality of the invisible, which it proclaims as happening at God's instance and as coming from God. *Me attendite, vobis dicit Ecclesia, me attendite quam videtis etiamsi videre nolitis. . . . Haec aspicite, in haec attendite, haec, quae cernitis cogitate, quae vobis non praeterita narrantur, nec futura praenuntiantur, sed praesentia demonstrantur.* In expounding Ga. 4²⁶ Luther declared most emphatically that by the words " Jerusalem which is above, the free " we are not to think of the *ecclesia triumphans* but of the *ecclesia in hoc tempore*. It is upon earth the Church must be, *ut sit omnium nostrum mater ex qua nos sumus generati et quotidie generamur. Ergo necesse est hanc matrem nostram, ut et eius generationem, esse in terris inter homines. Generat tamen in Spiritu* (*Komm. zu Gal.*, 1535, *W.A.* 40¹ 663, 18). And Melanchthon, in rebutting a misunderstanding on the part of Counter-reformation polemics, made it clear that *neque vero somniamus nos Platonicam civitatem, ut quidam impie cavillantur, sed dicimus existere hanc ecclesiam, videlicet vere credentes ac iustos sparsos per totum orbem. Et addimus notas : Puram doctrinam evangelii et sacramenta. Et haec ecclesia propria est columna veritatis* (*Apol.* VII 20).

Thus reception of revelation, into the reality of which we are now inquiring, occurs in the Church, namely, in the twofold coherence of those whom God confesses in Christ and who in Christ confess God. We have insisted (1) that it involves the coherence of those who are raised by the omnipotent grace of the incarnate Word from the world of the flesh to the life of the children of God ; (2) that in this coherence it involves the lordship of the grace of the incarnate Word ; (3) that it involves a coherence which from the standpoint of the creative and ruling Word is a unity of those who cohere in it ; (4) that it at least also involves, once more from the standpoint of the creative and ruling Word, the fact that this coherence may, as well or as ill as any other historical reality, be seen, experienced, thought and recognised by man. It is this coherence which is meant when we describe the Church as the area by which the subjective reality of revelation is invariably enveloped. In our description of this area we have used the most general term, which is yet the most concrete and indeed decisive that could be used in a statement about this reality, if we are to say anything about it from the standpoint of Holy Scripture. On our human side, on the world's side, that which corresponds to the objective reality of revelation in Jesus Christ is the existence of the coherence which arises, consists and is articulated in the way which we described, the existence of the Church. According to what we have just said, this corresponding factor, the Church, even though it is a human gathering and institution, cannot therefore be regarded as a human production. Although it is in the world, it cannot be thought of as owing its existence to this world. Although we are in the Church, are indeed ourselves the Church, the Church cannot be thought of otherwise than as the reality of God's revelation for us, i.e., it is in strict relation to the revelation of God to us, it is in complete subordination to it, yet in that relation and subordination it is equally revelation, it is equally God's own act. If we tried to say anything else, we should have grievously misunderstood the biblical image which so far has served as our main statement, that the Church is the body of Christ.

In our concrete description of the subjective reality of the revelation of God, we have made a fundamental statement, which we must now make clear to be such, if the description is to possess the character of a genuine recognition of reality. Strictly speaking, the indication of the Church, with which we had to begin, was in the first instance a demarcation of the area of the reality, although we could not speak of the area without at the same time speaking of the reality itself. But what fills this area ? What happens in it ? What is the Church ? We shall have to extend our inquiries much further afield, with an inquisitiveness for definitions of content. The decisive answer and therefore the expression of what is fundamental in the description must certainly be to the effect that it involves the outpouring of the Holy Spirit, i.e., it involves the fact that, after He has become man in Christ for us, God also adopts us, in such a way that He Himself makes us ready to listen to the Word, that He Himself intercedes with us for Himself, that He Himself makes the speaking and hearing of His Word possible among us. Therefore the decisive answer to the question of the existence of the Church must certainly be to indicate the mystery of Pentecost, the gift which men who themselves are not Christ now receive in their entire humanity for Christ's sake, the gift of existing from Christ's standpoint for Christ and unto Christ, " the power to become the sons of God " (Jn. 1^{12}).

But in order to understand this decisive answer we must distinguish between what has to be said about the divine giving and what has to be said about man's being endowed. The problem of the subjective, the question how man becomes a recipient of revelation, breaks up, as it were (in a way corresponding to the two-sidedness of the christo-logical question), once again into an objective and a subjective question, (1) How does revelation come from Christ to man ? and (2) How, as such, does it come into man ? And clearly even the first of these questions has not yet been answered by the doctrine of the incarnation of the Word. This first question, too, must obviously be answered in the doctrine of the outpouring of the Holy Spirit.

The distinction which we have to make at this point does not rest upon a logical abstraction. Ac. 2 cannot be understood without Ac. 1. In Ac. 1 we are told that those upon whom the Holy Spirit subsequently came were men. He had already been promised to them, promised by the risen Christ Himself. And they were already προσκαρτεροῦντες ὁμοθυμαδὸν τῇ προσευχῇ (1^{14}). The gift of the Holy Spirit is thus imparted to men who expect it with a quite definite awareness and by a quite definite method. They are already on Christ's side, since their existence is to be given them from Christ's side. Here, of course, we can and must at once think of some similar two-sided statements in the Old Testament. For instance, Ps. 51^{10} : " Create in me a clean heart, O God, and renew a right spirit within me." Or Ezek. $36^{25f.}$: ." I will sprinkle clean water upon you and ye shall be clean. . . . A new heart also will I give you, and a new spirit will I put within you . . . and will make of you people that walk in my statutes and keep my judgments to do them." Or the relation between Jer. $1^{4f.}$, where his election and calling is imparted to the prophet, and Jer. $1^{9f.}$, where we find expressed his equipment and institution as a prophet. The stylistic form of *parallelismus membrorum* in this particular passage does not explain everything. On the contrary, this is the very place at which we may ask whether the style itself does not point to situations like that which we are now considering. And we must also remember that passage in the Nicodemus dialogue which is always so startling when we read it (Jn. 3^5) : ἐὰν μή τις γεννηθῇ ἐξ ὕδατος καὶ πνεύματος, οὐ δύναται εἰσελθεῖν εἰς τὴν βασιλείαν τοῦ θεοῦ. Again Eph. $5^{26f.}$: Χριστὸς ἠγάπησεν τὴν ἐκκλησίαν καὶ ἑαυτὸν παρέδωκεν ὑπὲρ αὐτῆς, ἵνα αὐτὴν ἁγιάσῃ καθαρίσας τῷ λουτρῷ τοῦ ὕδατος ἐν ῥήματι, ἵνα παραστήσῃ αὐτὸς ἑαυτῷ ἔνδοξον τὴν ἐκκλησίαν. Again Tit. 3^5 : κατὰ τὸ αὐτοῦ ἔλεος ἔσωσεν ἡμᾶς διὰ λουτροῦ παλιγγενεσίας καὶ ἀνακαινώσεως πνεύματος ἁγίου. Above all we have to think at this point of the fact which is expressly recalled in Ac. 1^5. Christ baptises us with the Holy Spirit. But according to the account given in all the four Gospels, most emphatically in John, He had a predecessor in His activity. According to Mt. 3^2, cf. 4^{17} this predecessor preaches nothing but Jesus Himself. According to Jn. $1^{6f. 15f.}$, etc., he has no other function except only to point to Jesus. According to Mt. 3^{11} he is distinguished from Jesus because he baptised " with water unto repentance." In him all the Evangelists see the obviously necessary fulfilment of Is. 40^3 : " It is the voice of one preaching in the wilderness, Prepare ye the way of the Lord ! " So necessary is this fulfilment that Jesus Himself, before entering on His own activity, has Himself baptised by him in order " to fulfil all righteous-ness." What does it all mean ? Simply this. Let us suppose that God's revela-tion is real on God's side, that the Word has become flesh, that Christ exists. Then two things are still required for revelation to be revealed to men, for Christ to become the Saviour of men. First something which is again objective, if you like, a special presentation of revelation on man's behalf, so that it may find and reach him, so that his heart may be pure, open, ready for it—and only then something subjective, in the narrower sense that he now really receives and possesses the Holy Spirit and with it receptivity for Christ, the actual power to listen to the Word spoken to him.

1. The first point we have to make is that in its subjective reality God's revelation consists of definite signs of its objective reality which are given by God. Among the signs of the objective reality of revelation we have to understand certain definite events and relations and orders within the world in which revelation is an objective reality, and therefore within the world which is also our world, the world of our nature and history. The special determination of these events and relations and orders is that along with what they are and mean within this world, in themselves, and from the standpoint of immanence, they also have another nature and meaning from the side of the objective reality of revelation, i.e., from the side of the incarnation or the Word. Their nature and meaning from this transcendent standpoint is that by them the Word which entered the world objectively in revelation, which was spoken once for all into the world, now wills to speak further in the world, i.e., to be received and heard in further areas and ages of this world. By them it will have " free course " in this world. They are the instruments by which it aims at becoming a Word which is apprehended by men and therefore a Word which justifies and sanctifies men, by which it aims at executing upon men the grace of God which is its content. And their instrumental function is to veil the objective of revelation under a creaturely reality ; and yet to unveil it, i.e., in the actual form of such creaturely reality to bring it close to men, who are themselves also a creaturely reality. They point to revelation. They attest it. No, the Word of God made flesh attests by them that it was not made flesh in vain, that it was spoken once for all, that it is the valid and effective Word. All the formulations just attempted point at once to what we must now state directly : that it cannot depend upon our caprice whether we see or do not see that these events and relations and orders are signs ; not only from the standpoint of immanence but also from that of transcendence. There is no world view which can prevent us from doing so. Even ontically, the fact that these events and relations and orders are signs in the sense indicated does not rest upon a determination proper to them in their creatureliness, but upon a determination acquired by them in addition to what they are and signify in their creatureliness, because the Word of God actually avails itself of them. They are not instruments in the sense in which a hammer or shears are instruments in the hand of a workman who avails himself of these instruments because, prepared by another workman, they now possess the qualities required for the purpose for which he handles them. The instruments of the Word of God become what in its service they ought

to be, solely because of the Word of God itself, which makes it possible
for men to see them from the transcendent standpoint that lies beyond
the immanent, that is, to meet the signs and to understand them.
Their nature as signs does not rest upon a capacity resident in these
particular creaturely realities as such, either to be or to become testimonies to revelation. Nor does it rest upon any *analogia entis*. It
rests upon the divine foundation and institution. It is in virtue of
this that, as distinct from the host of other creaturely realities, they
become what once they were not and could not become, yet now do
become and are. They do so by the omnipotence of the divine will
to manifest itself to the world, to reconcile the world to itself. That
is, they do so by the omnipotence of the same gracious will which in
Christ adopted the human nature which in itself is incapable of revelation, and by its own agency made it capable thereof. But, again, even
the actual manifestation of the sign, even the fact that it is now seen
and understood as that which it is and signifies, is not its own work.
God has not, as it were, handed over His own work to it and departed.
His foundation and institution does not mean that it now contains
grace, as a vessel contains a liquid with which it has been filled. The
activity of the sign is, directly, the activity of God Himself. The
manifestation of the sign is God's manifestation, even though it is
always a creaturely reality. Again, therefore, it takes place by the
omnipotence and yet also the freedom of God's gracious will. God
has bound us, but not Himself, to the signs of His revelation. They
are testimonies, but they are not limitations to His majesty and glory.

It is because these signs have been given, and by way of them,
that men may receive direction and promise from the side of the
objective reality of revelation, of the incarnation of the Word. The
fact that God's revelation is also a sign-giving is one side, the objective
side, as it were, of its subjective reality. We are saying the same thing
when we say that this giving of signs is the objective side of the Church
as the sphere in which God's revelation is subjectively real.

To make this point, the biblical material with which we must begin is as
follows. According to the Holy Scripture of the Old Testament and New Testament, God's revelation always comes to man both immediately and mediately.
Immediately, for whatever mediators or media God makes use of, in order to
speak to man and to act on him, He always remains Himself the subject of
this speaking and acting. Immediately, for the fact that He does make use of
particular mediators and media never means a withdrawal by God Himself, or
a transfer of His properties and activities to the creatures concerned. But
God's revelation comes mediately to man in that it actually never does come
without creaturely mediators or media, and it always occurs in a creaturely
area and framework which is fixed in outline and unvarying in appearance.
For according to His man-ness—which we always have to recall in this connexion—Jesus Christ was one particular man and not another, with all the
spatio-temporal contingency which that involved. Similarly, that which corresponds to Jesus Christ in the world is one specific thing which cannot be confused
with any other. There is no accidental or uncontrolled occurrence of this, that,

and the other thing which in themselves might quite well be a divine sign-giving—and why not ? According to Holy Scripture even the divine sign-giving in the world has the character of contingence, of factuality, and therefore a quite definite character. Definite signs are as such chosen and set up. They constantly recur. They stand in definite relations to each other. They are, and signify with a certain regularity, what they are supposed to be and signify as such signs.

Let us think of a sign which is the most visible and in a certain sense includes all the rest, the sign of the election of the people of Israel. It is not identical with objective revelation, the incarnation. Yet in an extremely comprehensive way it obviously corresponds to it. It belongs to objective revelation, to the extent that that revelation does not remain objective, but reaches man, and for that very reason, on its subjective side it has a place in history. We might as well eliminate the whole of the biblical witness and its object, the incarnation, or replace it by some other witness and its object by another, if we ever thought of eliminating the election of the people of Israel or substituting another sign. The manifestation of Jesus Christ has this to correspond to it, or it is not the manifestation of Jesus Christ ; for in its utter concreteness it points to this sign and this very sign points back to it, in the sense that He is the seed promised to Abraham. But why this sign in particular ? Why particularly the election of Abraham ? Why the particular confirmation of it in Jacob ? Why the deliverance of these particular tribes from Egypt ? Why God's dwelling on Sinai and later in Jerusalem amidst this particular people ? Why the judgments of God which indicate the close of their particular place and function in history ? Why finally Jesus Christ as the Messiah of the Jews in particular ? Why indeed ? We can only give a negative answer. It was certainly not because the people of Israel was specially adapted for such a sign-giving, or because the achievement of the sign-giving required that it should be led in this particular way. Of course, everything might equally well have been quite different. There might have been no election of a particular people, or the election of quite a different people from this one, or the election of this people, but with quite different circumstances and results. But the weighing of such possibilities is a matter which clearly never entered the minds of the biblical witnesses in the Old Testament and New Testament. For that reason we must put it right out of our minds when we read their testimonies. It is just because they escape all positive proof that the contingency and factuality constitute the election of Israel a genuine sign. This is the way in which the Son of God elects and calls and justifies and sanctifies His own people in and from the midst of the world.

It is exactly the same with other relevant factors in the biblical testimony. In itself, what has it to do with Christ that this people was set apart and separated from other peoples by the sign of circumcision ? It only helps to clarify our understanding that to-day we know that other Near Eastern peoples were also familiar with the same rite. In itself nothing depends upon the rite ; but everything depends upon its founding and institution. Everything depends upon the Lord of the covenant, who among this people promises by this rite the judgment which is to be fulfilled and His grace which is to come in Christ. And therefore because of the Lord of the covenant who has so willed and done, once again everything depends upon this rite. It is a genuine sign, not because it is this rite, but because it is the sign of the divine command and promise.

But the main sign-giving, in the sense of a manifestation of the covenant between God and man concluded in Christ, is the existence and activity of the prophets in Israel. These are men of God who again are specially elected from among the elect people. They speak the Word of God to meet special situations among that people. They always do it by proclaiming to them the salvation and condemnation, the condemnation and salvation which come from God. Their existence and their word as such are something quite different from the objective

8

reality of revelation in the incarnation of the Word. We see nothing but what is human. Men speak to men because they have a specific human understanding of a human situation. They are human, too, in their depiction of the coming of salvation and condemnation. Only as the intangible margin of the whole, i.e., in the shape of the unheard-of claim and emphasis with which they speak, and only in the equally intangible form of the divine source of the salvation and condemnation announced, is there any sign here that God's Word is central. That it really is central here we can only affirm from our awareness of the incarnation of the Word of God in Christ. For what we see here is obviously only a sign, only something that corresponds to the Word of God. But what is meant here by " only " ? The fulness of revelation in the Old Testament word of the prophets is just this. Here amid the world of men the Word of God Himself is inconceivably laid upon the lips of these men. It is inconceivably uttered to meet this or that situation in human history. It is just as inconceivably heard by the men of that time. And in the whole process it possesses this sign, this thing that corresponds to it. The Old Testament attests that the existence and activity of the prophets is the Word of God. In so doing it plainly and comprehensively declares that there is a human way of uttering this Word and a human way of hearing it ; and that inconceivably but in fact this utterance and hearing are so related to God's own Word, that God's own Word can be heard in it. There is a " Thus saith the Lord " on human lips, which the Lord not only acknowledges subsequently but which He has already acknowledged before it was spoken, because what is here said by men is actually His commission, because He Himself has willed and constituted this creaturely correspondence to His own Word. The same is true of the other form-concepts of the Old Testament which we have already touched upon in an earlier context. The king, the priest, the Law, sacrifice, the tabernacle, the temple, the holy land : all of them have to be assessed as a coherent group of signs pointing to a common centre.

But, of course, we have also to see a sign—the sign, as it were, of the superiority and freedom of the thing signified as compared with any of the signs—in the fact that this whole world of Old Testament signs disappears, so to speak, in a flash at the manifestation of Christ. Or rather, it is recognised as the " shadow of good things to come " (Heb. 10[1]). And it is prolonged in the New Testament Church by only a small number of new signs, which merely indicate, as it were, the indispensability of the signs and also their continuity with the ancient sign-world. Into the place of the whole ancient sign-world steps the Church with its apostles and its *kerygma*, with baptism and the Lord's Supper ; for that is really all there is to be said about the Church and its visibility. Obviously, the change and reduction in the signs and the things corresponding is conditioned by the transition from the age of Messiah expected to that of Messiah come. The substance remains the same, but the *oeconomia*, the *dispensatio*, the *exhibitio*, the *manifestatio* of revelation has been changed (Calvin, *Instit.* II 9-11). *Christum aliis signis et absentem figurari et venturum praenuntiari oportuit ; aliis nunc exhibitum repraesentari decet* (II 11, 14). It should be noted, however, that this does not amount to the removal or abolition of sign-giving as such. Even the manifestation of Christ Himself can be seen and understood to be what it is only in the form of sign-giving. The sayings of Jesus in this world rang in human ears, and His acts in this world took place before human eyes : they are the language of the incarnate Word. Even the Church after the manifestation of Christ is in the world and consists of men who as such continue to require sign-giving. The Church is not Christ. The Church does not possess His incomparable authority, that of the eternal Word itself. Neither has it authority to do His deeds. According to Acts, prophecy and miracles were at first still active among His disciples. But obviously they were only a reflection of the manifestation of Christ Himself, a reflection which was bound to cease. What does not cease is the calling, commissioning and sending forth of the twelve apostles by the crucified and risen One. What does not cease is the extension of the Church's work on the basis of its witness to Christ : the proclamation of Christ by the preaching of Christ, the institution of baptism, and the festival of the Lord's Supper ; and the gathering of the people out of all nations by this proclamation. That is the new and simplified and concentrated sign-world of the New Testament. In a further derivative sense requiring careful demarcation, it can also be said that the whole existence and history of the Christian Church, so far as it actually has an existence and history of its own, belong to this sign-world of the New Testament. But as such they must submit to continual measurement by the original sign-giving at the calling, commissioning and sending forth of the twelve apostles, and they must be justified at that tribunal. Even the sign-world of the New Testament, whether in the former and narrower or in the latter and broader sense, is dependent upon the reservation " till he come " (1 Cor. 11²⁶). Measured by the reality of the coming of God's Kingdom at the end of our time, it is certainly also the " shadow of good things to come." But with this reservation, that is, within our time, it stands and holds good. It cannot be separated from the objective revelation in Christ. It belongs to it just as strictly as the earlier sign-world of the Old Testament. The Church, the body of Christ, and therefore Christ Himself exists and exists only where there are the signs of the New Testament, that is, preaching, baptism and the Lord's Supper, in accordance with their institution fulfilled at the inauguration of the apostolate. We can conclude our biblical deliberations quite simply at this point with the declaration from the *Conf. Aug. art.* 7 : *Item docent, quod una sancta ecclesia perpetuo mansura sit. Est autem ecclesia congregatio sanctorum, in qua evangelium pure docetur et recte administrantur sacramenta.* Even less than in the case of the Old Testament signs do we either expect or desire to have to prove or demonstrate the necessity and the utility of these particular signs except by pointing to their contingent, factual given-ness. We are not asked whether a quite different sign-giving from this particular one might not have been possible for the objective revelation of God in Jesus Christ. Nor are we asked whether we could think of or would prefer a quite different sign-giving from this particular one. With God all things are possible, and with us at least very many. But in the revelation of God in Jesus Christ one possibility is selected and thereby set up and finally confirmed as God's reality. And so, too, it is with the sign-giving which attests this revelation. Our reflection upon it can start only with what it actually is.

Since this sign-giving stands in the closest possible connexion with objective revelation, like that revelation it must be regarded as a divine act. It is the moving of an instrument in the hand of God. God is still the Lord over it and therefore free. In the mystery of His mercy He does not suffer any diminution because He avails Himself of this instrument. The given-ness of these signs does not mean that God manifest has Himself as it were become a bit of the world. It does not mean that He has passed into the hands or been put at the disposal of men gathered together to form the Church. On the contrary, what it does mean is that in Christ the world and man have fallen into the hands of God. It means the setting-up of God's lordship, not of a sacral human lordship. We stand here at the point at which the Evangelical conception of the Church diverges abruptly from the Roman Catholic and also the Modernist Protestant (whose innermost tendencies have recently been unmasked). But the act of the objective revelation of God is an act in the existence of Jesus Christ

as very God who is also very man. So, too, the act of sign-giving
by which the objective revelation comes to us is an act in the existence
of these signs as they were given us once and for all at the inauguration
of the apostolate. And since it is a sign-giving which awaits the seeing
eyes and hearing ears of ever new men, this sign-giving must receive
an ever new recognition and understanding in the Church with each
succeeding generation. And it must do so in such a way that never
even in part can the Church believe that it has mastered it, that
it has learned what Christ really wants of us in the message of the
apostles, what preaching and sacrament ought really to be in our
midst. It must do so in such a way that at any time in the Church,
naturally with respectful consideration for what the fathers apprehended and taught, there exists a challenge to render an account *ab
ovo* and to discharge one's own responsibility thoroughly, whether it
stands with this sign-giving as it was primarily intended to stand. In
this respect, too, the Evangelical concept of the Church and that of
the Roman Catholic Church, as well as that of a Protestantism which
knows only of an " intact " confession, are widely divergent. Yet at
every fresh recognition of revelation, an act which devolves upon the
Church in every age, it must always be strictly a matter of interpreting
the sign-giving which belongs inseparably to revelation. There cannot
be in the Church any valid recognition which is really new, i.e., a real
recognition of revelation at some new date and under some new conditions, which bypasses the institution of the apostolate, and that means
concretely, Holy Scripture, which is concerned with something other
than the exercise *pure* and *recte*, i.e., in accordance with Scripture, of
preaching and the administration of the sacraments. No matter what
arguments may be adduced in their favour, innovations which have
their norm in a different *pure* and *recte* are achieved only outside the
Church and *eo ipso* apart from Jesus Christ, as He has really made
Himself known to us. To summarise : we shall see to it that with
revelation itself the signs of it are always made new, as much because
they are God's act as because they extend to the Church that lives in
time. But we shall also see to it that as there is no new revelation,
there are likewise no new signs. We need none of them. There is
no way in which we could have any knowledge of them. So we have
no need to inquire about them. We shall have all our work cut out
to apprehend and understand both revelation itself and its one and
only sign-giving. The Church as the sphere in which God's revelation
is subjectively real does have this strictly objective side.

It is of more than historical value for us to remember at this point that
originally the concept *sacramentum* (the translation of μυστήριον) had a far more
comprehensive sense than was later given to it (as is particularly clear from the
usage of Tertullian and Cyprian). It formerly denoted the mysteries of the faith
as such, as they were offered to humanity in the Church—the very thing we have
just been describing as sign-giving. And in fact, even in the later special sense,

no general definition of a sacrament can be given which does not unintentionally coincide with the definition of a sign in the comprehensive sense just described. *Sacramentum est signum rei sacrae in quantum est sanctificans homines* (Thomas Aquinas, *S. th.* III *qu.* 60 *a.* 2c). *Sacramenta instituta sunt . . . ut sint signa et testimonia voluntatis Dei erga nos ad excitandam et confirmandam fidem in his, qui utuntur, proposita* (*Conf. Aug. art.* XIII). *Sacramentum . . . externum esse symbolum, quo benevolentiae erga nos suae promissiones conscientiis nostris Dominus obsignat* (Calvin, *Instit.* IV 14, 1). *Sacramentum est sacra et solemnis actio divinitus instituta qua Deus mediante hominis ministerio sub visibili et externo elemento per verbum certum bona coelestia dispensat ad offerendum singulis utentibus et credentibus applicandam atque obsignandam promissionem de gratuita remissione peccatorum Evangelii propriam* (J. Gerhard, *Loci theol.* 1610 *L.* XVIII 109). *Sacramentum est actio sacra divinitus instituta, in qua gratia per Christum foederatis promissa a Deo, visibilibus signis obsignatur atque hi vicissim in ipsius obsequium adiguntur* (J. Wolleb, *Chr. Theol. Comp.*, 1626, I *c.* 22 § 1). " Sacraments are the regular means of grace given by Christ to the Church which He founded, by which the gracious fruits of the redemption once effected by Him on the cross are applied to man " (J. Braun, *Handlex. d. kath. Dogm.*, 1926, p. 249). Obviously the whole objective side of the Church could be intended in all these definitions just as well as the sacraments in the special and narrower sense of the word. Note the metaphors with which Calvin, for example (*Instit.* IV 14, 5 f.), seeks to represent the general meaning of sacraments. They are, so to speak, seal-impressions, or paintings, or reflections of the divine promise of grace ; they are supporting pillars of faith, or exercises (*exercitia*) to develop certainty about the Word of God. These figures are just as suited to the more comprehensive concept of sign-giving, which belongs to revelation and mediates objectively to the human subject. And this is not an accidental but a necessary coincidence. This may be shown in two ways.

1. The concept of sacrament in the later and narrower sense has obviously a special meaning within the concept of sacrament in the older and wider sense and so, too, within the general concept of divine sign-giving which is occupying us here. In the definitions quoted, the concepts emphasised were *externum symbolum, elementum, signum visibile, actio sacra*. Now, of course, these do indicate baptism and the Lord's Supper in particular. But they also emphasise marks which are proper to divine sign-giving as such. Think in particular of the concept of *signum*, which has been so decisive for Western sacramental doctrine since the time of Augustine. Of course in the narrower sense the sacrament is called *signum visibile*, since it is a matter of symbols and actions which are visually apprehensible. And at first glance it might be thought that in this way we exclude the element of man's word which is generally so important for divine sign-giving. But Augustine himself counted man's spoken or written word among the signs. *Nihil aliud sunt verba quam signa* (*In Joann. tract.* 45, 9). What is decisive is not the concept of the *visibile* as such, but the superior one of the *sensibile*, under which the *audibile* also falls. And without a *visibile*, i.e., without man speaking or without Scripture, there is no *signum audibile* either. " The Word is also an external thing, which can be grasped with the ears or read with the eyes " (Luther, *Pred. üb. Luc.* 11[14f.], *Hauspost.* 1544, *W.A.* 52, 185, 17). *Visibile* declares (pretty much as in the concept *ecclesia visibilis*) that the sign belongs by nature to our world as well, to the sphere of our observation and experience. It may be met, as other realities are met. As such a *signum visibile* the sacrament is a *symbolum*, and an *externum symbolum*, i.e., an inalienable sign of the coherence, indeed the unity of the Church, on the basis of the objective revelation in Christ to which it owes its origin. This unity of the Church is, of course, hidden and invisible. Yet it is also public and visible. It is so from Christ Himself ; and to that extent the Church contains the *symbola* instituted by Him as *symbola externa*. No doubt the things involved in the sacrament

in its narrower sense are *elementa*, i.e., elements of a spatially extended, corporeal nature, water, bread and wine. And this fact seems to assert an out-and-out distinction of the sacrament from all other elements in the divine sign-giving in general. But only in appearance. For the spiritual, historical and moral being of man is also steeped in the elemental sphere, in the cosmos of corporeality, in an ultimately inextricable unity with his natural being, of which it is the counterpart. Finally, the sacrament is emphatically described as an *actio sacra*. And we naturally think of the nature of baptism and the Lord's Supper as being the Church's action as opposed to the Church's word in preaching. But we have to note that while not all the Church's speaking is a completed act, at least it is an action. The same is true of all the other elements in our definitions. For example, the sacrament has been instituted by Christ as a sign of the *res sacra*, namely, the divine grace in Christ. Its purpose is the *sanctificatio* or *iustificatio* of man. Its function is that of applying, *obsignare* (confirming a superscription by a seal fixed beneath it), the reconciliation that occurred and was expressed objectively, by the ministry of certain men. But these features obviously do not belong to anything distinctive in a sacrament as compared with preaching. They merely underline the general context to which a sacrament also belongs. It is simply that a sacrament gives prominence to something special within the general context. As a *signum visibile*, a *symbolum externum*, a sign in the *elementum* and in an *actio*, a sacrament asserts clearly, and with relatively greater eloquence than the word in the narrower sense can ever do, that the *iustificatio* or *sanctificatio hominis*, which is the meaning of all divine sign-giving, does not rest upon an idea but upon reality, upon an event. And the event upon which it rests is of such a kind that it does not merely possess the relevance which a powerfully disseminated philosophical doctrine or a popular conviction may have. It is the event which has shown itself to be both spiritual and corporeal, the act of a Creator who is above the antithesis between the corporeal and the spiritual, the event of the entry of this Creator into our history, the event of the rolling up of our history by His presence. That is why *iustificatio* or *sanctificatio hominis*, which is the meaning of all divine sign-giving, cannot be treated as a problem and isolated, as we can always do with an idea or a doctrine or a conviction. It can no more be dealt with like this than can the Rhine or Mont Blanc; indeed far less so. For while we can at least interpret nature in any way we like without, of course, having any hold upon it, there is absolutely nothing to interpret when it comes to the presence of God in Christ, the action of God Almighty, Maker of heaven and earth. God is and God exists, exactly as nature uninterpreted is and exists. He is and exists with a necessity beside which all the imperturbability with which nature is and exists can only be regarded as fortuitous. Ὁ λόγος σάρξ ἐγένετο (Jn. 1[14])—preaching, too, can and must say this. But in a way which preaching can never do, the sacrament underlines the words σάρξ and ἐγένετο (cf. Heinrich Vogel, *Das Wort und die Sakramente*, 1936, p. 6 f.). And we have to think of these words as underlined if we are to understand and treat the divine sign-giving as the objective side of the Church, that is to say, in its given-ness, indeed in its pre-given-ness, comprehensive, undiscernible from any angle, unassailable from any angle. The sacrament's insistence upon this quality in divine sign-giving is its special feature as compared with preaching and its special feature in the whole life of God's people assembled to form the Church. We will not be always noting about a theology whether it has any knowledge of baptism and the Lord's Supper, or whether these things are at bottom an embarrassment to it, which it must pester itself to say anything sensible about. If this is indeed the case, it will surely be revealed at some quite different (though only apparently different) point. We shall perceive that it has no proper knowledge of the distinct validity of the prophetic and apostolic word in the Church, or of the value of dogma, or of the theological relevance of the decision of Nicaea or the decision of the

Reformation. And certainly it will not be able to value preaching as the central part of the Church's liturgy. And we shall have to ask whether a theology of this kind can have any awareness of the comprehensive and unassailable given-ness of revelation itself. On the other hand, it may well be that a theology allows itself to learn from the very simple fact that in the Church baptism must always be administered and the Lord's Supper celebrated. By this fact it is reminded that, since it is the reality of revelation, the subjective reality of revelation necessarily has an objective side. It is from this objective side that our thinking must invariably derive. It is in this way (this way and not another) that it becomes thinking with a definite content, thinking which is really connected with the object here set before us. It is from the standpoint of baptism and the Lord's Supper that the prophets and apostles, and in their turn the fathers and Reformers, are really fixed : and fixed in such a way that we cannot evade them. And it is when regarded in the light of baptism and the Lord's Supper that, parallel to every temporal movement in time in which it must occur, preaching too must and will always acquire that peculiar element of fixity, of unchanging similarity to itself, without which it ceases in any really effective way to bear witness by the mouth of man. *Et incarnatus est.*

2. The inter-relationship to which we have just pointed can also be approached from the opposite angle. At every point, the divine sign-giving in which revelation comes to us has itself something of the nature of a sacrament. For in its totality it is always a *signum visibile*, a *symbolum externum*, a sign both in the realm of nature and also in an action executed by men. John the Baptist is the prototype of all sign-giving, of all attestation, in the biblical sense. And John says everything that can be said about himself in distinction from and in relation to Christ when he describes himself as him that baptises with water. And so it is quite right that in Jn. 3[5], Eph. 5[26f.], Tit. 3[5], the " laver of baptism " should be set plainly and directly against the inner work of the Holy Spirit. It is quite right that we should learn from Jn. 6[52-58] that to our eating and drinking unto eternal life there necessarily corresponds a perfectly definite corporeal eating and drinking. We can never understand these and similar passages too realistically. And in so doing, we will not be guilty of any serious blunder, so long as we remember, as we certainly ought to remember, that in the isolation in which it is manifested as the sign, as the objective witness which man must receive, a sacrament has naturally to be conceived as *pars pro toto*. It is in this living and concrete way, as a creative event in history, that revelation comes to us and seeks to be received and adopted. It comes in exactly the same way as in a sacrament, stressing the objective quality of grace which it possesses. It is no mere matter of the water in baptism or of the bread and wine in the Lord's Supper. For we have also to remember Jn. 6[63]: " It is the spirit that quickeneth ; the flesh profiteth nothing." To ask whether there are not times when the divine revelation and salvation can be received without the necessity of baptism is a childish question. Neither in salvation nor in revelation can we speak of an absolute and, as it were, automatic necessity for the administration of the sacraments. The possibility has never seriously been discussed in the Church, for to tie us to the divine sign-giving would also be to tie God. But again this does not in any way alter the fact that baptism is once for all enjoined upon us. And, of course, what is involved in the water of baptism and in the bread and wine of the Lord's Supper is the establishment and recognition of the sign of the concrete, living, creatively active lordship of God. And, of course, what is involved in our understanding of the whole divine sign-giving—and to that extent *pars pro toto* is true of the passages quoted—is exactly the same as what is involved in the water of baptism and in the bread and wine of the Lord's Supper. The authority of the prophets and apostles and through it the grace of the incarnate Word of God is set at the beginning of the Christian Church and therefore at the beginning of our existence as the children of God, just as

baptism is put at the beginning of our Christian life as an objective testimony pronounced upon us. And we live by the word of the prophets and apostles, i.e., by the proclamation based upon their testimony and again by the grace of God's Word through this proclamation, just as we are fed with bread and given wine to drink in the Lord's Supper. We are bound to baptism and the Lord's Supper in token of this ordering and maintenance of life by the Word mediated through the prophetic and apostolic word. For this ordering, this maintenance of life is inseparable from this life, the life of the children of God. It is this life only because and in so far as it is life by the grace of our Lord Jesus Christ, that is to say, only when it is ordered and maintained in the way indicated by the sacraments. For that reason and in that sense we have to say in all seriousness that sacraments are an indispensable " means of grace." (In this concept, we have only to stress the word " grace " to understand it correctly !) And no complaints about " Roman sacramentalism " will prevent us from declaring that on its objective side the Church is sacramental ; that is to say, it has to be understood on the analogy of baptism and the Lord's Supper. In other words : The sphere of subjective reality in revelation is the sphere of sacrament. This has nothing to do with the Roman *opus operatum* or with heathen " magic." The sphere of sacrament means the sphere in which man has to think of himself as on the way from the baptism already poured out upon him to the Lord's Supper yet to be dispensed to him, the sphere in which he begins with faith in order to reach faith, ἐκ πίστεως εἰς πίστιν (Rom. 1¹⁷). On this way our perception will certainly be a true one if we think of ourselves as the recipients of revelation. And it is in this sphere that theology has to seek both its beginning and its goal, and by the law of this sphere that it must direct its methods.

To balance this first finding we have now to frame a second. The revelation of God in its subjective reality consists in the existence of men who have been led by God Himself to a certain conviction. They believe that objective reality in revelation exists for them. They believe that it exists for them in such a way that they can no longer understand their own existence by itself, but only in the light of that reality : not apart from it, therefore, but only in relation to it. They cannot, therefore, understand themselves except as the brethren of the Son, as hearers and doers of the Word of God.

It will be noted at once that we have taken a leap in thought. We had been speaking of the divine sign-giving by whose mediation revelation, or Jesus Christ, reaches man. We had previously intended to go on to speak of the way in which revelation comes to man. And now we are suddenly speaking of men who are already convinced, who by divine conviction have already discovered that they are brethren of the Son, hearers and doers of the Word of God. Obviously we have not said a single word about the decisive thing, namely, about the way in which it comes about that, when the signs have been given, a man encounters and receives them as the signs of revelation, and therefore in and with them encounters and receives revelation itself. It is quite true that we have not said a single word about this : we have simply taken a leap at this point. But this was not due either to forgetfulness or embarrassment. For that is exactly what has to take place at this point : it is the positive side of that which has to take place. God's revelation in its subjective reality is the person and work of the Holy

Spirit, i.e., the person and work of God Himself. This does not mean that we cannot say anything about it, that we have to be silent. How can it possibly mean that ?   In this matter we have to follow Holy Scripture, which testifies that the person and work of God are manifest. Silence about the person and work of God means only that we reject the witness of Holy Scripture, and ultimately that we deny God's revelation. But we do not deny it. We acknowledge it. Therefore we must be clear that just because the person and work of God are concerned in it, our acknowledgment necessarily means that we start from the fact of it. That is our presupposition. And we really start from it. We get out into that world in the midst of which and for which revelation takes place, and the person of God comes, and the work of God becomes an event—into that world which is not itself the person and the work of God. It is only by starting at this point, by getting away from revelation and out into this sphere, that we can make definite assertions about revelation, though revelation itself, to the extent that it is identical with the person and the work of God, can never be the object of specific assertions. We see this in the case of Christology. Christology can proceed only from the fact of Jesus Christ. On the basis of that fact, and with a proper awe for the mystery of Christmas, its function is to denote in this world the one specific point in the world : that the Word became flesh. And even as it does this, it can never add the decisive thing, that is, how it all happened, how revelation became objectively real within this world. It is exactly the same with the outpouring of the Holy Spirit by which the objective reality of revelation becomes a subjective reality. We have to respect the mystery of the given-ness of this fact as such, i.e., as the inconceivable and therefore the unspeakable mystery of the person and the work of God. We show this respect by following the example of Holy Scripture and taking it as our starting-point. Again, this means two things : first, that we do accept and use it as our presupposition even on the subjective side ; and second, that we are content to accept and use it as our presupposition, without making any rash or subversive attempt to understand its How. And that means in practice that when we are asked how objective revelation reaches man, we can and must reply that it takes place by means of the divine sign-giving. In this sign-giving objective revelation is repeated in such a way that it can come to man in genuinely human form. But the presupposition still remains a mystery. All that we know is that God Himself does really avail Himself of this medium, and that therefore objective revelation is actually shown to man by the signs. To the question how revelation reaches man, our first finding enables us to give only a penultimate and not an ultimate answer. It is always by the free grace of God that objective revelation is really shown to man so that he really sees it. We have no insight into the exercise of this grace, and therefore we can never say the last word on this matter. When we have described the objective side of the Church we are still faced with the need for a leap in thought. We cannot penetrate the possibility of this need, and therefore there is nothing special to say about it. Similarly, to the question how objective revelation reaches men, we cannot give a first but only, as it were, a second and consequent answer. We can answer it only by pointing to man on the far side of that necessary leap, where the subjective reality of revelation in the strict sense of the concept, where the person and work of God, where the event of the free grace of God in the same sense, are already behind him ; just as they were still before him according to our first finding, i.e., from the standpoint of the divine sign-giving. In this before and behind God wills to be loved and praised. What lies between them we can never express or state, because it is not revealed to us. And it is not revealed to us because it is revelation itself. Any attempt to state or express anything concerning what lies between would be foolhardy, because it could consist only in arbitrary speculation, based on the presupposition that we can actually bypass God. But it would also be fatal, because it would reveal that we regard the leap not as the divine necessity but as a necessity which we can penetrate, that with the mystery of revelation we do not acknowledge but deny revelation at the critical point. Acknowledgment of revelation necessarily means that we presuppose revelation and therefore look away from that holy centre to what precedes and follows it. It means that we look away to the Old Testament and the New Testament. To be more explicit, it means that we look away to the human form in which revelation does encounter man *Deo bene volente*, i.e., to the existence of sign-giving. But again that means that we look away to the human form in which revelation has penetrated to man *Deo bene volente*, i.e., to the existence of men who are already convicted by God by means of the sign-giving, who have therefore already discovered that they are the children of God. We have to allow full weight to the leap which does in fact intervene, with all its inferences. We have to maintain complete silence in relation to it. We have not to try to incorporate it into our system of knowledge as a kind of paradoxical bridgework. We have to lay down our weapons with an indication of Scripture, preaching and sacrament on the one side, and on the other the indication of man, who by the goodness of God can discover that he is the child of God. When we do these things we declare that the leap is not a *salto mortale* which, if need be, can always be learned and explained and taught and recommended to others. There can be absolutely no question here of anyone either making a leap or challenging others to make it. All that we have to consider is that here the leap has already been made, the unheard-of and to us impossible leap from God to man. In that fact revelation is already a reality. And it can and must call for our consideration that at this point in our exposition we make a leap in thought, in order to draw attention to the proper object of our discussion both on the one side and on the other, both before the leap and after.

This leap in thought will necessarily look like theological forgetfulness or embarrassment. It will fall under suspicion as such. But we must not allow that fact to tempt us. A genuinely forgetful or embarrassed theology will not make a leap at this point. It will offer a synthesis instead. For the same reason we must strenuously resist even the slightest suggestion that this leap involves theological "irrationalism." On the contrary, it takes place precisely in view of the obvious reasonableness of God in His revelation. A genuinely irrationalistic theology, not being aware of its true character—and of the fact that it is very rationalistic as such—is usually very talkative at this point.

If it is now clear that at this point a *silentium altissimum* is far more eloquent than any attempted demonstration, it is also clear that at this point only a *silentium altissimum* can say positively what has to be said without demonstration. Therefore we can look back and calmly make our second point concerning the subjective reality of revelation.

We began by stating that the subjective reality of revelation consists in the existence of particular men. We recall what was said at the beginning of this section. There is no question of something in the divine act in revelation which emanates " from man's side," but only of something which is " directed towards man." The fact that man's existence is involved does not mean that we can ascribe to man, or to these particular men, the role of autonomous partners or workmates with God co-operating in the work of revelation. Man's existence is involved only as the humanity of Christ is necessarily involved in the doctrine of the incarnation, or the *virgo Maria* in the doctrine of the mystery of the incarnation. We are concerned with the existence of man or of definite men only as an existence posited from God's side, and posited afresh in the act of His revelation. For neither of the existence of man as posited by himself, nor of his existence posited by God as his Creator, can we posit the assertion which we have to make at this point, the decisive assertion that he can discover himself to be the child of God. In our creaturely existence we are always the kind of people who think that they can posit themselves, and as such we can never discover, at least never legitimately, that we are the children of God. Therefore from God's side, and from God's side in a new way, which transcends their obscure creaturely being, on the basis of the revelation which comes from God, there exist men who in their existence are the subjective reality of revelation. The basis of it all is the divine movement towards man in revelation. It is the divine condescension in virtue of which the Word assumed humanity. That is what makes these men what they are. That is what incorporates them in revelation from their own side. That is why they themselves not only have but are the revelation in their existence. Of course, it is only as recipients that they are the revelation. It is only in subjective reality. We cannot, therefore, confuse them with Jesus Christ. They are never anything except from Him. And yet they are themselves the revelation. But this is revelation as it is " directed towards man." Revelation now is not only Jesus Christ. " In Jesus Christ " it is also the existence of these men. If it were not, how could it ever attain its goal ? How could it really be revelation ? If it really is revelation, if it does attain its goal, if there is in fact a revealedness of revelation, then necessarily it must be revealed—and previously it was not revealed—both in the being and, in fact, as the being, of men. But the incorporation of these men in revelation means that they are convinced by God Himself. It means that the objective reality of revelation, i.e., Jesus Christ, exists just for them. What it all amounts to is this. In this work of conviction, materially they do not think of anything but the work of divine sign-giving, the work of the prophetic and apostolic word in Holy Scripture, the work of preaching and sacrament. The conviction about which we are thinking means simply that this work attains its goal. We may be tempted to think that it means something else as well. By the testimony of the Holy Spirit we may be tempted—as happens often enough—to understand some hidden communication of revelational content in addition to and beyond the divine sign-giving. We may be tempted to find in this material addition of an immediate spiritual inspiration the very essence of the divine conviction. But if we are, then it can only mean that we are again casting eager side-glances away from objective revelation as it objectively reaches us in the divine sign-giving. We are trying to find a something better which God might have told us, instead of looking at the supposedly less good which He has actually told us. We may later harmonise this something extra with the divine sign-giving. We may re-express it in biblical and confessional terms. But if our starting-point is the material addition which comes from immediate spiritual inspiration, we are not convinced by God Himself. Whatever starts in that way is a concealed or open sectarianism. It forgets that the Holy Spirit is not only the Spirit of the Father but also the Spirit of the Word. It forgets that the Holy Spirit certainly comes to us, not by an independent road which bypasses the Word and its testimonies, but by the Word and its testimonies. We remember that the Word is not bound to the sign-giving. But we also remember that we are bound to the sign-giving. We cannot know anything or say anything about any other Word or Spirit except that which comes to us through the divine sign-giving. If God wishes by immediate spiritual inspiration to create new prophets and apostles of the Word—as of course He can—that is His affair. If He does, they will prove themselves to be such, just as the old prophets and apostles did, through whom the Word of God comes to us not as a possibility but as an actuality. The divine conviction, the witness of the Holy Spirit, can, as it were, be checked by our relationship to the divine sign-giving. For that reason we do really know them and can say something about them. We can say that they attest the Word of God to us. They do not attest a kind of spiritism. They do not consist in the transmission of a material addition, of a new revelational content. They consist in the attestation to us of the one revelation which has taken place for us. " For us," of course, does not mean the selfish desire for salvation of those who will accept Jesus Christ as a good man because they think that they find in Him the satisfaction of the private religious needs of man, and are therefore bound to honour Him. Real revelation puts man in God's presence. It is quite different from a mere answering of questions raised by the sublime egoism of man, who, in addition to all his other requirements, also wants to go to heaven. Pietism is quite right. We speak of real revelation only when we speak of the revelation which is real for us. It is the revelation which is attested to ourselves. It is the revelation which we ourselves adopt when it is attested. It is the revelation which reaches us. An objective revelation as such, a revelation which consists statically only in its sign-giving, in the objectivity of Scripture, preaching and sacrament, a revelation which does not penetrate to man : a revelation of this kind is an idol like all the rest, and perhaps the worst of all idols. But it is not by our arrangement or contrivance that it is not an idol, that it is the real objective revelation which therefore penetrates to man, that it is objective revelation which becomes subjective in man himself. On the contrary, the fact that this takes place is something which we must accept as quite beyond our understanding. It was not we who have introduced revelation even in its objectivity. Of ourselves we cannot find any arguments to convince us of its credibility and validity. We do not stand at the summit of some moral or religious undertaking, which has enabled us to manipulate revelation in such a way that it has now become subjectively real as well. In this event, by His objective revelation (i.e., by Himself), God Himself has spoken to us on behalf of His objective revelation (i.e., on behalf of Himself). Therefore He Himself has interceded with us on His own behalf. Objective revelation exists for us because God exists. And it exists in the way that God exists. But, of course, it also exists for us, and because we exist and in the way that we exist. For if God really exists for us, we also exist for Him. And this inconceivable event means no more and no less than that we are caught up together into the event of His revelation, not as co-workers but as recipients, not alongside God but by God and in God—and yet really caught up. Our own existence is revealed to us not as a divine but as a very human existence. Yet it is also revealed as an existence which God in His graciousness had adopted and assumed as such, as the existence of the children of God. This taking up of man into the event of revelation, on the basis of which he is revealed to himself as the child of God, is the work of the Holy Spirit or the subjective reality of revelation.

Let us try to clear this up in detail. We described the inconceivable event in which objective revelation exists for man as his being convinced by God. And indeed what takes place at this point does involve a conviction, an opening up, an uncovering of the truth of objective revelation before the eyes and ears and in the heart of man. It means that he himself recognises it to be true and therefore regards it as true and valid for himself. It means that his reason apprehends it, that he himself is entirely in the truth, i.e., he regards himself entirely from the standpoint of the truth. The truth itself does not undergo any addition. It is the truth, even if man is not in the truth. It is true that God is with us in Christ and that we are His children, even if we ourselves do not perceive it. It is true from all eternity, for Jesus Christ who assumed our nature is the eternal Son of God. And it is always true in time, even before we perceive it to be true. It is still true even if we never perceive it to be true, except that in this case it is true to our eternal destruction. " God was in Christ reconciling the world unto Himself " (2 Cor. 5[19]). " It is finished " (Jn. 19[30]). To this " perfect " of the truth of revelation nothing either need be added or can be added. It is not that there are, as it were, two different points : at the one the Son of God assumes humanity ; and then, at quite a different point, the question of our destiny is necessarily raised and answered. In the one reality of revelation He is, in His assumed humanity, the Son of God from eternity, and we, for His sake, are by grace the children of God from eternity. Therefore the " perfect " of the truth of revelation already includes the conception of its existence for us. In objective revelation as such (if we may for a moment speak of such an abstraction) the only thing which is not included is that we also exist for it, that our eyes, ears and hearts are as open to it as it is to us, i.e., that we actually adopt the truth as truth and so are in the truth. To that extent the distinction between objective and subjective revelation is unavoidable. But on neither side need this distinction mean that we are speaking of a revelation which exists apart. Subjective revelation is not the addition of a second revelation to objective revelation.

If we think of the subjective as something which has later to be added, then necessarily we have thought of the objective as an idol, and it is hardly likely that the added subjective will not also be portrayed as an idol. There have always been fateful moments in ecclesiastical and theological history when men have had to be arrested in the very act of treating abstractly of objective Christian truth as sign-giving, e.g., in the form of what is supposed (but only supposed) to be a correct dogmatics. That is to say, they have treated of it without asking about their own existence in the truth. And they have then imagined that they can make good the undeniable damage by putting objective truth aside for a while as something which has already been adequately confessed and expounded. And in order to escape the obvious " danger of intellectualism " they give themselves temporarily to the theme of its appropriation by man. The illusion induced by that abstraction drove them away from a dead orthodoxy straight into the arms of pietism and rationalism. And the same mystification seems to be exercising a not inconsiderable influence on some modern theological contemporaries. We have only to consider the high value which they place on the "Oxford Group Movement." The illusion in this abstraction consists in the fact that they cannot answer the very justifiable question of their own existence in the truth by taking the question of the truth itself less seriously (because it is suspected of being too intellectual), but only by taking it more seriously, which obviously they do not do when they believe that they have found a great lacuna (as we always must) in respect of man's existence in the truth. There has simply never been a really correct dogmatics which expounded objective revelation as such and *in abstracto*. Revelation is objective only in its irruption into the subjective, in its redemptive objective assault upon man. We have to follow objective revelation through its whole unified movement from God to man. It is no use confronting an incorrect dogmatics with an equally incorrect ethics, biology, or pastoral theology. This is simply to fight one error with another.

Subjective revelation can consist only in the fact that objective revelation, the one truth which cannot be added to or bypassed, comes to man and is recognised and acknowledged by man. And that is the work of the Holy Spirit. About that work there is nothing specific that we can say. We can speak about it only by sheer repetition, that is, by repeating what is told us objectively, that " God was in Christ reconciling the world unto himself." The work of the Holy Spirit is that our blind eyes are opened and that thankfully and in thankful self-surrender we recognise and acknowledge that it is so : Amen. Therefore we cannot say anything else about this work, we cannot speak about it in any other way than by repeating over and over the Amen which has been put into our mouths by this work. Here, too, we must remember that the Holy Spirit is the Spirit of the Father and also of the Son. He is not a Spirit side by side with the Word. He is the Spirit of the Word itself who brings to our ears the Word and nothing but the Word. Subjective revelation can be only the repetition, the impress, the sealing of objective revelation upon us ; or, from our point of view, our own discovery, acknowledgment and affirmation of it. Any subjective revelation or discussion of subjective revelation which claims that it is more than repetition, which claims our interest in any way except as a repetition, which claims that it ought to be considered independently, like ethics or biology or pastoral theology, which claims even for a moment that it is distinct from proclamation, the proclamation of objective revelation : any such revelation involves and necessarily involves an immediate and radical break with revelation of any kind. If we are investigating existence in truth—as we always must—we have to investigate truth. For it is upon truth itself that our existence in truth rests, and it is in truth that we have to look for it. It is in Jesus Christ as the objective reality of revelation, and nowhere else in all the world except in Him, that we are the children of God, and nowhere else in all the world except in Him that we come to recognise ourselves to be such. On principle, we literally cannot assign any other definition of content to the new existence of men convinced by God Himself than that they know, and that they cannot and do not want to know, anything else except that they are in Christ by Christ. That is how we must now expound the phrase " in God by God." " In Christ " means that in Him we are reconciled to God, in Him we are elect from eternity, in Him we are called, in Him we are justified and sanctified, in Him our sin is carried to the grave, in His resurrection our death is overcome, with Him our life is hid in God, in Him everything that has to be done for us, to us, and by us, has already been done, has previously been removed and put in its place, in Him we are children in the Father's house, just as He is by nature. All that has to be said about us can be said only by describing and explaining our existence in Him ; not by describing and explaining it as an existence which we might have in and for itself. That is why the subjective reality of revelation as such can never be made an independent theme. It is enclosed in its objective reality. If we try to assert anything but that we are really and finally helped in Christ, that we have to cast all our care upon Him—" for he careth for you " (1 Pet. 5⁷)—then what we say is no longer said about God's revelation. For by Christ we will never be anything else than just what we are in Christ. And when the Holy Spirit draws and takes us right into the reality of revelation by doing what we cannot do, by opening our eyes and ears and hearts, He does not tell us anything except that we are in Christ by Christ. Therefore we have to say, and in principle it is all that we can say, that we are brethren of the Son of God, hearers and doers of the Word of God. We are invited and challenged to understand ourselves from this and not from any other standpoint. When we do say this, we are men convinced by God. His revelation exists for us in such a way that we also exist for it. And are free for it. In fact, we ourselves are revelation, that is, to the extent that there takes place in us the revealedness of God, the life of the children of God which is hid with Christ in God, existence in grace. It is men convinced by God in this sense who constitute the subjective aspect of the reality of the Church.

For the biblical background and the historical context of this exposition, the wealth of adducible material is so great that we must confine ourselves to only one classical document, the foundation which Calvin prefixed to his great exposition of the *modus percipiendae Christi gratiae* (*Instit.* III 1). As the chapter heading reveals, the point at issue is the recognition that *quae de Christo dicta sunt, nobis prodesse*, i.e., that what is proclaimed to us by Christ as very God and very man belongs to us, helps us and is made our own. This takes place *arcana operatione Spiritus*, i.e., by that work of the Spirit which is done in secret.

1. *Non in privatum usum*, not for a divine in-Himselfness, did the eternal Father give to His Son the life of which He was the bearer when He appeared

among us, but *ut inopes egenosque locupletaret*, i.e., with one final determination
and direction from all eternity, to be wealth to our poverty and need. And the
first thing which we have to say about our receiving the grace of Jesus Christ is
necessarily that it concerns this *locupletatio*, the occupation by Him of the empty
space which is ourselves. As long as He is *extra nos* and we *ab eo separati*, He
there and we here, this *prodesse* is not actual, the divine will in Christ's presence
in the world is unfulfilled, and His presence is without significance for us, *inutile
nulliusque momenti*. *Communicatio*, impartation of the grace manifested in Him,
demands that He be not only there but here. He has to become our own. He
has to dwell in us, *nostrum fieri et in nobis habitare* : in us, in the sense in which
Eph. 4¹⁵ tells us that He is our Head, Rom. 8²⁰ that He is the firstborn among
many brethren, Rom. 11¹⁷ that we on our side are grafted into Him like a shoot
into a tree, and Gal. 3²⁷ that we put Him on as a man puts on a garment. *Communicatio* of grace is *communicatio* of Christ Himself. It consists, therefore, in
this, that He and we are no longer two but one, i.e., that we *cum ipso in unum
coalescimus*. This is what occurs when we believe the Gospel. But the Gospel
is proclaimed to many people and they do not believe it, and so that does not
occur. When it does, it is just the secret of the activity of the Spirit, the *arcana
Spiritus efficacia*. This is what leads to *frui*, participation in Christ and His
grace. The Christ " that came by water and blood " became identified with us
and died for us (1 Jn. 5⁶, cf. Jn. 19³⁴ ; the Early Church was quite right to connect
these passages with baptism and the Lord's Supper). And the Spirit is His
witness. The same Spirit is the eternal Spirit of the Father and of the Son,
and His testimony in our hearts is therefore the analogue, the seal-impress of
the grace of Father and Son applied to us in Christ in water and blood. Receiving
this testimony, man has a right to participate in that grace which is simply the
ablutio (purification) of human nature accomplished in Christ and the sacrifice
offered by Christ for all men, and therefore Christ Himself. It becomes His very
own. As we are told in 1 Pet. 1², God's elect are those in whom this *sanctificatio
Spiritus* takes place, i.e., those for whom the decision of God in Christ avails,
so that they are put into *oboedientiam et aspersionem sanguinis Christi*, i.e., into
the position of the obedience of faith and of the forgiveness of sins accomplished
in the death of Christ. It is in this position that these men exist. But the position has reality for them only in the *arcana irrigatio Spiritus*, in the testimony
of the Spirit and therefore in Christ of whom the Spirit testifies. Of this position
we must also say, with 1 Cor. 6¹¹, that its basis and power are in " the name of
the Lord Jesus Christ " and " the Spirit of our God." In short, the Holy Spirit
is the bond of peace (Eph. 4³), by which Christ has bound us to Himself and
united us to Himself, just as already and on high He is *vinculum pacis* in which
the Father and the Son are united.

2. Therefore the work of the Spirit is nothing other than the work of Jesus
Christ. The Spirit is present in His own as the seed of *coelestis vita*, pointing
them away from every here and now. By the Spirit He separates them out
from the world and gathers them to the hope of their eternal inheritance. In
this way He creates His Church. By the Spirit He calls to Himself prophets,
i.e., pupils and teachers of revelation. By the Spirit all men go in the body of
death to meet resurrection. As the Spirit of Jesus Christ who, proceeding from
Him, unites men closely to Him *ut secum unum sint*, He distinguishes Himself
from the Spirit of God who lives as *vita animalis* in creation, nature and history,
and to that extent in the godless as well. And just because He is Christ's Spirit,
the work of Christ is never done without Him. Nor is it done except by Him.
The grace of our Lord Jesus Christ does not exist except in the fellowship of the
Holy Spirit (2 Cor. 13¹⁴), and the love of God is not poured out into our hearts
except by the Holy Spirit (Rom. 5⁵).

3. Scripture speaks about Him in many ways. It calls Him (Rom. 8¹⁵ ;
Gal. 4⁶) the *Spiritus adoptionis* : the One who attests the kindness revealed in

the only-begotten Son of God, of Him who wills that we too should call Him Father. It calls Him the secret and earnest of the hope which constantly gives life and confidence to us who are *peregrinantes in mundo et mortuis similes* (2 Cor. 1[22]). It calls Him the water that makes the unfruitful field fruitful (Is. 44[3], 55[1]), or that gives drink to the thirsty (Jn. 7[37]), or that cleanses their filthiness (Ezek. 36[25]). It calls Him the unction that strengthens and quickens (1 Jn. 2[20]), or the fire which destroys yet is also beneficial (Lk. 3[16f.]). And all this in the sense that He imparts to us a life consisting in the fact *ut non iam agamus ipsi a nobis sed eius actione ac motu regamur, ut si qua sunt in nobis bona, fructus sint gratiae ipsius, nostrae vero sine ipso dotes, mentis sint tenebrae cordisque perversitas.* If, therefore, we do not think of this life by the Spirit when we speak about Christ, but of a sort of ineffective Christ confronting us somewhere at a distance, we are only speculating. It is only in the *coniunctio*, only in the *coniugium* which Eph. 5[30] describes as a mystery, only in the fact that we are flesh of His flesh, spirit of His Spirit, *adeoque unum cum ipso*, members in Him as the Head, only therefore by the Holy Spirit—for *solo Spiritu unit se nobiscum*—that Christ is the One who has come to us as Saviour.

4. The work of the Holy Spirit within us, by which He effects decisively and comprehensively our oneness with Christ, is faith. And faith as the work of the Holy Spirit is not a magical transformation. It is not a higher endowment with divine powers. It is simply that we acquire what we so much need—an *internus doctor*, a teacher of the truth within ourselves, *cuius opera in mentes nostras penetrat salutis promissio, quae alioqui aerem duntaxat vel aures nostras feriret.* From 1 Jn. 3[24], cf. 4[13], we know that we are not only approached and reached by the promise or external Word, and in the Word Christ Himself. By the Holy Spirit whom He has given us, we know that the Word, that is Christ, abides with us, and so becomes ours and we His. All other teachers would exert themselves to no purpose, all other light would be offered to the blind in vain, if Christ had not constituted Himself our *interior magister* by the Spirit, if He Himself had not opened our eyes to Him, and drawn us to Himself, as those who were given Him by the Father (Jn. 6[44]). He and He alone is *perfecta salus.* Yet to make us participant in the salvation accomplished by Him He Himself must baptise us with the Holy Spirit. In other words, He Himself must give us light to believe the Gospel, which is to make us new creatures, the temples of God.

2. THE HOLY SPIRIT THE SUBJECTIVE POSSIBILITY OF REVELATION

The subjective reality of revelation consists in the fact that we have our being through Christ and in the Church, that we are the recipients of the divine testimonies, and, as the real recipients of them, the children of God. But the fact that we have this being is the work of the Holy Spirit. Therefore the Holy Spirit is the subjective reality of revelation.

And now we must investigate its subjective possibility. This means simply that we must try to understand what we are told about this reality as an answer to the question to which the reality itself challenges, which is so to speak forced upon us by the reality. Our concern cannot be merely with a general question, with any undisciplined " How is this possible ? " which might be hurled at us. Nor

2. *The Holy Spirit the Subjective Possibility of Revelation* 243

can we treat of it merely from the standpoint of a general concept of
possibility and impossibility which may perhaps illuminate us. In
this respect, too, the reality of revelation is in no sense an answer
to all kinds of questions originating elsewhere than in itself. They
may be thought to be the most essential, or at all events the most
relevant questions, and with the best claim to be raised. But that
does not make the slightest difference. The reality insists upon being
understood in its own light, on its own merits, and therefore with the
help only of the questions to which it challenges us itself. And indeed
it does challenge us to questions, and it does will to be understood.
Again, we must make it clear that whatever we say, we say personally
to ourselves, as something said to ourselves. Otherwise we cannot
seriously commit ourselves to the statement. Obedience to revelation
consists in following it, which means that at the very least we wish to
understand it. But the question of understanding cannot precede the
question of fact. It must invariably follow it.

We will formulate the question of understanding as we did our
first question. It will then run as follows : How in the freedom of
man is it possible for God's revelation to reach man ? Man is free for
God by the Holy Spirit of the Father and the Son. In that consists
the reality of revelation. But how can he be free ? To what extent
is he so ? To what extent is the work of the Holy Spirit the reality
of revelation, i.e., the adequate ground of man's freedom for God, and
therefore of his receiving what God offers him ? To what extent has
the Holy Spirit the possibility or power to do this work ? We are
not asking whether He has it. We cannot do that without calling in
question His reality. And to call it in question would already be to
deny it. Our question is : In what consists the possibility and power
already recognised and acknowledged in reality ? In that reality, how
far do we find a problem solved, a question answered, a condition
fulfilled, a need met ? We are not putting the question independently
of the question of fact. As we face and answer it, we are not withdrawing to an independent point of consideration, where we know
from the first what problem has to be solved, what question answered,
what condition fulfilled, what need met. On the contrary, we confine
ourselves to the problem which this reality has solved, to the question
which it has answered, to the condition which it has fulfilled, to the
need which it has met.

We must start very much as we did in the christological investigation of the concept of revelation. We have to show that the reality
of the Holy Spirit in His work on man has also a strictly negative
meaning. It is real in the Holy Spirit that we are free for God. And
this settles the fact that we are not free for God except in the Holy
Spirit. The work of the Holy Spirit itself cuts away from us the
thought of any other possibility of our freedom for God. It encloses
this possibility within itself. How could it be otherwise ? As God,

the Holy Spirit is a unique person. But He is not an independent divinity side by side with the unique Word of God. He is simply the Teacher of the Word : of that Word which is never without its Teacher. When it is a matter of instructing and instruction by the Word, that instructing and instruction are the work of the Holy Spirit. Without that work there is no instruction, for the Word is never apart from the Holy Spirit. And it is by this very work of the Holy Spirit, and because in the Holy Spirit we recognise that God's Word is the truth, that we are convinced of the futility of the only remaining possibility, i.e., that in some sense we already have the Holy Spirit, in other words, that we have a prior knowledge of the Word of God, that we have been instructed in it from the very first, that we are even in a position to instruct ourselves in it. It is God Himself who opens our eyes and ears for Himself. And in so doing He tells us that we could not do it of ourselves, that of ourselves we are blind and deaf. To receive the Holy Spirit means an exposure of our spiritual helplessness, a recognition that we do not possess the Holy Spirit. For that reason the subjective reality of revelation has the distinctive character of a miracle, i.e., it is a reality to be grounded only in itself. In the actual subjective reality of revelation it is finally decided that apart from it there is no other possibility of being free for God.

It should, of course, be noted that when we say that man is not free for God apart from the reality of the Holy Spirit, we are not making a generally self-evident statement after the manner of philosophical agnosticism. Indeed, no agnostic statement can even remotely attain to what is intended by this theological statement. The agnostic informs us that the upward view is blocked. He calls the man a fool who blinkingly turns his eyes in that direction. The incapacity of which he speaks is dreadful enough, but it is certainly not the radical incapacity which is involved when we state theologically that man is not free for God. Again, when the agnostic speaks about the above to which our view is barred, he does not mean God (who, fundamentally, is the only possibility of our life here, and therefore of our upward view to that which is Himself). It is an above of which there is unfortunately no actual view, although, of course, there could be. If there were, it would be at our disposal. And renunciation of it is also at our disposal. It is upon the certainty of our disposing that the agnostic ultimately depends. That is why he dare make his renunciation so absolutely, and therefore proclaim the very system of agnosticism. Because he makes his renunciation so absolutely he cannot possibly mean God when he speaks of the above which is barred to us. If he did mean God, he would have to allow the renunciation he makes so absolutely to be bracketed and relativised by the reality of the Holy Spirit. But what relation could there be between the upward view which this reality opens up and the upward view of which agnosticism speaks,. or between the fact that man is not free for God and his ceasing to peer in the direction in which agnosticism looks for the beyond ? There can be no doubt that acknowledgment of the reality of the Holy Spirit would necessarily compel the agnostic to speak quite differently. Instead of an absolute claim to renunciation, he would have to forego all claims and speak about the humility enjoined upon us. Instead of eyes which blink (and blink continually), he would have to speak about our blindness and the healing of the blind. In fact, he would have to surrender his agnosticism all along the line.

This incidental note has nothing to do with apologetics. The only reason for it is to make it clear that when we say that apart from the reality of the Holy Spirit we are not free for God, this has nothing whatever to do with the above philosophical theory. The agnostic does not know what he is saying when perhaps he agrees with us that man is not free for God. As an agnostic he knows nothing about it. For this is something which can be known only by revelation, only by the Holy Spirit.

It is exactly the same here as it is with the objective reality of revelation. For only by the knowledge of that revelation, the knowledge of Jesus Christ, do we learn that God is a hidden God. Similarly, it is by the same Holy Spirit by whom God takes up His abode in us and makes us His temple, that God and man are separated with such power and finality, that their unity can no longer be understood except as the unity of the free grace of God with His unconditional adoration by man. We have only to look at it strictly to see that there is not the slightest contradiction between the offices of the Holy Spirit as Comforter and as Judge, between the unity and the distance which He creates. For necessarily as the Teacher of the Word who reconciles us to God, He informs us both about God and also about ourselves. God He sets before us as the almighty Lord, and His kindness as infinite, just because it is so unmerited, so absolutely unconditioned by our encounter with it. But ourselves in the first instance He does not reveal as petty finite creatures of little account in His presence (for this contrast would still not signify that we are not free for Him ; the infinite needs the finite just as the finite needs the infinite). In the first instance we are revealed as rebels against this Lord, as unthankful for His kindness, as resisters of His call. Only then and from that standpoint are we shown to be creatures who, not only in their finitude, but as men created by Him out of nothing, are really dust before Him, whose existence is forfeit and would be lost, were it not that we might wait for Him. The Holy Spirit puts God on the one side and man on the other. And then He calls this God our Father and man the child of this Father. He brings God straight to those eyes and ears and hearts of ours which are so utterly unfitted for Him. And He takes us straight to the reality of God's action, the God who so utterly does not need us. Therefore the line is really drawn about which the agnostic wisdom of this world can never even dream, let alone perceive. And this line is not expunged or removed in the Holy Spirit. It remains drawn. The miracle does not cease to be a miracle. It will remain a miracle to all eternity of completed redemption. The children of God are those in whom the miracle of their sonship persists, and with it free grace, and unconditional adoration, and the line, and the knowledge that man is not free to step beyond that line of his own accord. There is no other knowledge apart from this. We cannot pull down God from His throne and set man over against Him in a kind of fore-heaven. There is no other synthesis than that which is achieved solely in the Word of God and in His

Holy Spirit. If we suppose that there is, it is simply a product of that theological dilettantism which is no sooner recalled from speculation by a glance of the real subject than it reverts at once to fresh speculation, i.e., to unfettered thought and language about that subject, and all because it does not know the meaning of consistency even at this point. In the Holy Spirit we know the real togetherness of God and man. We do not need to deny what agnosticism denies without even knowing what it is denying. In the Holy Spirit we are confronted by what we cannot deny even if we willed to do so. We know, therefore, that we cannot ascribe to man any freedom of his own for God, any possibility of his own to become the recipient of revelation. And we know it in a way which does not admit of any question. For the Holy Spirit is not a dialectician. And the negation is not our own discovery. Unlike our own positive or negative discoveries, it is not open to revision.

But once we have established that there is no other freedom of man for God, the question arises all the more imperiously, how far the possibility really does exist in that miracle which is the work of the Holy Spirit. Almost everything that we can say about man from the standpoint of revelation tells against the possibility that God can be revealed to us. But the work of the Holy Spirit is in favour of that possibility. Now we cannot make either statement except from the standpoint of revelation. Therefore we cannot mean the same thing when on the one side we say God cannot, and on the other we say God can. " God cannot " means that He cannot do it on the basis of a human possibility. " God can " means, of course, that He can on the basis of His own possibility. It is the possibility which is proper to God in the work of the Holy Spirit which we now have to consider. Let us see to it that we do not look for it anywhere but in the work of the Holy Spirit Himself. There is no independent standpoint from which we can survey and either approve or disapprove the ways of God (as though we could suggest other ways to God). We can only keep God's actual ways before us. We can only try to understand both the fact and the extent that they are actual ways. In so doing we shall not even dream that we can know what actual ways are except from our consideration of the actual ways of God. We can give only one basic answer to the question how in the freedom of man it is possible for God's revelation to reach him. This is that it is possible, as it is real, only in the outpouring of the Holy Spirit. We have now to develop this statement.

1. By the outpouring of the Holy Spirit it is possible for God's revelation to reach man in his freedom, because in it the Word of God is brought to his hearing.

In expounding the subjective reality of revelation we everywhere insisted that it is not only strictly bound to its objective reality, but that it is simply the process by which that objective reality becomes subjective. The Holy Spirit is the Spirit of the Father and of the Son, of the Father who reveals Himself in His Son and only in His Son. But that means that He is the Spirit of Jesus Christ. That is why we insisted at the very outset that to speak about the Holy Spirit and His work we must expound the biblical testimony to the revelation in Jesus Christ. Even on the subjective side this testimony does not let us down, but is perfectly adequate. Again, that is why we had to point so explicitly to the Church. The Church is the one particular spot which corresponds to the particularity of the incarnation. It is there that revelation is really subjective, for there Jesus Christ the Head has in His own people His body, there the only-begotten Son of God has in them His brethren. Again, that is why in the concept of the Church we had to insist so strongly upon the objective sacramental element, and only in the last instance and in relation to it could we speak of man as the recipient of revelation, i.e., of man won by Christ for Christ. That is the reality of revelation as it reaches man from God's side. And at the outset we can only repeat and underline the fact that that and that alone is its possibility. The reason, and the only reason, why man can receive revelation in the Holy Spirit is that God's Word is brought to his hearing in the Holy Spirit. For the capacity of man to do this depends upon the fact, and only upon the fact, that it is God's Word which is brought to his hearing in revelation. God's Word, i.e., God's revealed, incarnate Word spoken to all other men in the man Jesus of Nazareth. According to Scripture, everything which can be, everything which is either objectively or subjectively possible in relation to revelation, is enclosed in the being and will and action of the triune God. All capacity in this respect is His capacity, and we can read it from His working. Again according to Scripture, His working is the working of His Word, the work of His Son. Everything distinct from that is directly or indirectly our working, and it must first receive revelation, it must first be reconciled to God by the divine working and work. Therefore in relation to revelation all capacity is concretely the capacity of the Word, the capacity of Jesus Christ. There is no alternative : when we ask how a man comes to hear the Word of God, to believe in Christ, to be a member of His body and as His brother to be God's child, at once we must turn and point away to the inconceivable, whose conceivability is obviously in question ; and we must say that it depends upon the inconceivable itself and as such, that it can become conceivable to men. The Word creates the fact that we hear the Word. Jesus Christ creates the fact that we believe in Jesus Christ. Up there with Him it is possible for it to be possible down here with me. All the other possibilities which I have and of which I may think are perhaps very fine and significant possibilities in another direction. The fact that we have them means, perhaps, that we are free and open and ready in every conceivable direction : but not in this direction. For the thing for which we have to be free and open and ready at this point does not itself derive from our reality. It does not belong to it. It has only assumed our reality. Therefore it confronts us as a new reality. In the whole range of our possibilities there is nothing to correspond to it or to explain it. And if this is true of the thing itself, it is also true of the reality and the possibility of our communion with it. There is such a thing " because the love of God is shed abroad in our hearts by the Holy Ghost which is given unto us " (Rom. 5⁵). But if it is possible for it to exist, the possibility is not in our hearts but in the love of God. Similarly, the " through the Holy Ghost which is given unto us " cannot have its possibility except in the love of God. In other words, the work of the Holy Spirit means that there is an adequate basis for our hearing of the Word, since it brings us nothing but the Word for our hearing. It means that there is an adequate basis for our faith in Christ and our communion with Him, because He is no other Spirit than the Spirit of Jesus Christ. It is, therefore, the subjective possibility of revelation because it is the process by which its objective reality is made subjective, namely, the life of the body of Christ, the operation of the prophetic and apostolic testimony, the hearing of preaching, the seeing of that to which the sacraments point. Of course for us, in our knowledge of revelation, it is something quite new, and strange, and not at all self-evident, that there should be this process of making subjective, this life, this work, this hearing and seeing : that an event in our life should really correspond to the event of Jesus Christ, that a here below should correspond to a there above. Easter and Whitsunday are— and not merely within our knowledge—two different things. So, too, are the objective state and subjective process, Word and Spirit, divine command and human reception. But when we inquire into the possibility of the second, we can only reach back to the first and say that it is there that its whole possibility is to be found. The Holy Spirit is the Spirit of God, because He is the Spirit of the Word. And that is the very reason and the only reason why we acquire eyes and ears for God in the Holy Spirit. If, then, we want truly and properly to understand the Holy Spirit and His work upon us, we can never try to understand them abstractly and in themselves.

Supposing we do look at the work in itself, at the occurrence as it becomes an actual event in our lives. And from it we try to discover how far in this occurrence Christ can be an event in our lives. The result will certainly be either that we merely find something extremely human, in which Christ is unrecognisable, and we completely misunderstand the work of the Holy Spirit, or that we most inappropriately confuse and equate the occurrence which we know, and therefore our human something, with Christ Himself, which means that we will seek Christ anywhere and everywhere and expose ourselves to every possible heresy. And either way we can never more mistake the work of the Holy Spirit, and discredit it either in our own eyes or others', than by making it the object of an independent investigation. For when we do that, the result may be disillusionment or gratification, but the possibilities which we will certainly consider have nothing whatever to do with the great possibility that we might receive revelation. There can be no doubt that our feet are already on the road either to scepticism or to a mild or even a violent fanaticism.

If we want truly and properly to investigate the subjective possibility of revelation, and therefore to understand the Holy Spirit and His work, we must never look at subjective realities in which he might presumably or actually be seen and experienced. We must look rather at the place from which He comes and at what He brings. We must look at the contents of God's hand stretched out to us in Him. We must look at the love of God shed abroad in our hearts by Him. We must look to the objective possibility of our communion with Christ. In other words, we must look at Christ Himself.

It is only when we look in this direction that we can answer the very relevant question: Have I the Holy Spirit? Certainly, " if any man have not the Spirit of Christ, he is none of his " (Rom. 8⁹). But just because He is the Spirit of Christ, this question of " having " is not decided by what we can never do more than think we " have," but only by Christ. For it is only from Christ that we can have it, and therefore we can have it for ourselves only by continually turning to Him. And He says always: " Him that cometh to me I will in no wise cast out " (Jn. 6³⁷). The Church and Holy Scripture and preaching and the sacrament are therefore again the only possible criteria in any practical investigation.

And true and proper proclamation of the subjective possibility of revelation, true preaching from the Holy Spirit of Pentecost, will not consist in pointing to our own or other men's seizure, but in pointing to the divine seizing, and therefore once again to Christ Himself.

Consciously or unconsciously, every hearer is necessarily faced with the question whether and how he can be a real hearer and doer of the Word. And true preaching will direct him rather " rigidly " to something written, or to his baptism or to the Lord's Supper, instead of pointing him in the very slightest to his own or the preacher's or other people's experience. It will confront him with no other faith than faith in Christ, who died for him and rose again. But if we claim even for a moment that experiences are valid and can be passed on, we find that they are marshy ground upon which neither the preacher nor the hearer can stand or walk. Therefore they are not the object of Christian proclamation. If it is really applied to man in a thoroughly practical way, Christian proclamation does not lead the listener to experiences. All the experiences to which it might lead are at best ambiguous. It leads them right back through all experiences to the source of all true and proper experience, i.e., to Jesus Christ.

To sum up : It is Christ, the Word of God, brought to the hearing of man by the outpouring of the Holy Spirit, who is man's possibility of being the recipient of divine revelation. Therefore this receiving, this revealedness of God for us, is really itself revelation. In no less a sense than the incarnation of the Word in Christ, it is the divine act of lordship, the mystery and the miracle of the existence of God among us, the triumph of free grace. The more important the idea and proclamation of this receiving is for a man, and the more seriously he takes his problem, and the more definitely he can speak to it, the more emphatically he must again and again insist upon this fact.

We hardly need any specific evidence to show that this statement and finding has not been spun out of the void, but derives from the New Testament and therefore, implicitly and explicitly, from the Old. Not only in the message of the New Testament Gospels, but also of the Epistles and Apocalypse, it is one of the most self-evident themes that the Holy Spirit, and with the Holy Spirit all that makes the Church the Church, and Christians Christians, does not come from any place but only from Christ. And that means that grace—it may be pardoning grace or sanctifying and enabling grace—is always His grace. It means that faith is always faith in Him. Only as it is awakened and imparted by Him is it faith in God. It means that the gifts of the Spirit in the community are literally subordinated to Him and measured by Him as the Lord of the community. It means that the apostles are His servants. It means that the Word is His commission. It is constantly applied in new ways, but in content it is always an indication of Him and of Him alone. There may be many detours, but they are genuine detours. They may appear to lead us to a subjective whose interest is only abstract. But they always return to what the New Testament has to say, namely to the objective. They return to it as it has to be the objective for the sake of the subjective. It is the one unique thing, the centre. We may draw a circle around that centre, but it can never be anything more than a circle : *Διὸ ἀναζωσάμενοι τὰς ὀσφύας τῆς διανοίας ὑμῶν, νήφοντες, τελείως ἐλπίσατε ἐπὶ τὴν φερομένην ὑμῖν χάριν ἐν ἀποκαλύψει Ἰησοῦ Χριστοῦ* (1 Pet. 1¹³).

We have here the root of that recognition on whose basis the Western Church assumed into the creed, in relation to the eternal procession of the Holy Spirit, the *Filioque* as well as the *ex Patre* (cf. Vol. I 1 p. 500–511). Its intention was to recognise the fact that in God's revelation the Holy Spirit is the Spirit of Jesus Christ, that He cannot be separated from Him, that He is only the Spirit of Jesus Christ. And it did it with such definiteness that it found it necessary to confess that He is the Spirit of the Father and of the Son not only here and now and for us, but also from all eternity, in the hidden triune being of God which is revealed to us in revelation. It is because the Holy Spirit is from all eternity the communion between the Father and the Son, and therefore not only the Spirit of the Father but also the Spirit of the Son, that in God's revelation He can be the communion between the Father and those whom His Son has called to be His brethren. It is grounded from all eternity in God that no man cometh to the Father except by the Son, because the Spirit by whom the Father draws His children to Himself is also from all eternity the Spirit of the Son, because by His Spirit the Father does not call anyone except to His Son. In respect of revelation the Western Church did not recognise any Spirit to be the Holy Spirit except the Spirit of Christ. But it also spoke of the God who meets us in His revelation as the eternal God. If it was right in this, then we must stand firmly with it on this particular question of the *Filioque*.

The same recognition will also help us to understand the later development in the medieval West of that objectivism in the concepts of both sacrament and the Church, which was upheld successfully and with stern consistency by the Popes, e.g., against the spiritual kingdom of the Franciscans. The doctrine of the third kingdom of the Spirit first arose with Francis of Assisi and it was added to by his spiritual successors. To understand the struggle we have to remember that with its emphasising and practice of life and love in the discipleship of Christ the Franciscan Christianity of the Spirit obviously claimed to represent a sub-jectivisation of objective revelation. It imagined that the historical Christ could now be left behind as something antiquated. The disciple would now replace Him as the vehicle of His Spirit. In effect, this meant a dissolution of the recognition stated in the *Filioque*, and therefore of the recognition of the New

Testament unity of Christ and Spirit. Where the Holy Spirit is sundered from Christ, sooner or later He is always transmuted into quite a different spirit, the spirit of the religious man, and finally the human spirit in general. The threads are visible which lead from Franciscan Pneumatology to the anthropology of the humanistic Renaissance. To that extent the Papacy had the better case theologically in this controversy.

In the 16th century the same position was maintained by the Reformers, headed by Luther. " In these words St. Peter assigneth to this person called Jesus of Nazareth the divine work of pouring forth the Holy Ghost. For to pour forth the Holy Ghost belongeth not to any creature, though he were an angel from heaven, but to God alone " (*Pred. üb. Act.* $2^{14f.}$, 1534, *E.A.* 4, 100). " And mark well this text, how here Christ bindeth the Holy Ghost to His mouth and setteth Him His goal and measure that He go not beyond His own word : ' All things whatsoever have proceeded from my mouth He shall call to your remembrance and transmit by you.' Therewith he sheweth that henceforth in Christianity naught else must be taught by the Holy Ghost than what they, the apostles, heard from Christ (but did not yet understand) and were taught and reminded of by the Holy Ghost, that therefore it always pass out of Christ's mouth from one mouth to the other yet remain Christ's mouth, and the Holy Ghost is the schoolmaster, to teach and recall such " (*Pred. üb. Joh.* $14^{23f.}$ *Cruz. Somm. Post. W.A.* 21, 468, 35). To the question, why the Holy Spirit is called a " witness," Luther replied : " Because He witnesseth of Christ and otherwise of none other ; apart from this testimony of the Holy Ghost to Christ there is no certain, lasting comfort. So all dependeth upon this text being surely grasped and retained ; so say thou : ' I believe in Jesus Christ who died for me and know that the Holy Ghost who is called and is a witness and comforter, preacheth or testifieth of none other in Christendom to comfort and strengthen the afflicted, than of Christ. I will also abide thereby and otherwise hold to no other comfort.' For should there be a better or surer comfort than this, the Holy Ghost would bring it also : but He is not to do more than witness to Christ. The comfort shall not fail, if we but hold fast thereto and gladly believe that it is true and the Holy Ghost's witness " (*W.A. Ti.* 6, 6654). Of course, in contrast to the earliest controversy Luther directs all these statements not only against the fanaticism of his time but also and supremely against the Papacy. He lays against the Papacy exactly the same charge as the Papacy itself had formerly made, that it presupposed and asserted a presence and operation of the Holy Spirit apart from and side by side with Christ. There are many contexts in Luther in which on the one front or the other he concretely and uncompromisingly expounds this unity of Christ and the Spirit. He lays it down that the work of the Holy Spirit on our behalf is tied down to Scripture, preaching and the sacraments. He Himself is the measure of its operation, and we can never regard it in any way as the work of an absolutely " subjective " illumination, inspiration or enthusiasm. In the case of Luther the problem of the subjective, of man receiving divine revelation and reconciliation, was, we might almost say, *the* theological problem. There is no doubt, therefore, as to the meaning of the relentlessness with which, when he speaks of the Spirit, he points away from the Spirit and to Christ and therefore to all the objective side of the Church. His aim was to reveal and constantly to recall the descent in virtue of which the subjective reality of revelation is not any reality, but the one reality of the breaking in of God to man, the breaking in of objective revelation into our subjective realm. *Observa autem quaenam sint illa omnia, quorum doctorem fore spiritum promittit : Suggeret, inquit, vel reducet in memoriam " quaecunque dixi." Unde sequitur non fore novarum revelationum architectum. Hoc uno verbo refutare licet quaecunque sub praetextu spiritus in ecclesiam figmenta ab initio hucusque Satan invexit. Mahometes et papa commune habent religionis principium, non contineri in scriptura perfectionem doctrinae, sed quiddam altius revelatum esse a spiritu. Ex eadem lacuna nostro tempore Anabaptistae et Libertini sua deliria hauserunt. Atqui impostor est Spiritus, non Christi, qui extraneum aliquod ab evangelio commentum ingerit. Spiritum enim Christus promittit, qui evangelii doctrinam quasi subscriptor confirmet* (Calvin, *Comm. Jn.* 14²⁶, *C.R.* 47, 335). It is not a *novum regnum* which the Holy Spirit sets up amongst us, but the glory which was given the Son by the Father. *Simul ac spiritus a Christi sermone divellitur, quibuslibet deliriis et imposturis aperta est ianua.* . . . *Quorsum igitur spiritus doctrina? Non ut nos abducat a schola Christi, sed potius ut rata sit vox illa qua iubemur ipsum audire (Jn.* 16¹⁴ *ib.* 363). To understand what it was that Protestant orthodoxy of the 17th century was trying to safeguard at all costs, it is necessary to bring out the content and bearing of this particular aspect of Reformation thinking—and that quite irrespective for the moment of whether orthodoxy played its part well or badly.

The case is far otherwise with Neo-Protestantism. This has its forerunners in the *Anabaptistae et Libertini* of the Reformation period. Even in its best and purest form it rests upon a declension from the height of this insight. It did not at first instal the human factor in its many forms as a second divine revelation side by side with the revelation in Christ. It did not at first allow this second revelation to evolve into the real revelation. But long before, and even where it still did not appear to do this, or concealed the fact that it did, it separated itself from the New Testament Church by setting over against the knowledge and life of faith in Christ an autonomous knowledge and faith deriving from the Holy Ghost. In the first instance, of course, it claimed, and still claims, only to represent the interests of the subjectivisation of objective revelation as against an objectivism which is actually or apparently dead. Neo-Protestantism in its noblest and earliest form was in every sense a godly and serious piety. It was godly and serious in all the important forms of its second or Enlightenment stage. Even to-day we shall miss the mark if we accuse it of a lack of seriousness or godliness. On the contrary, it must be soberly admitted that as far as seriousness and godliness go it has often enough had the advantage over the representatives of the official teaching. The one reproach we can and must bring against it is that it abandoned an insight which was unambiguously indicated in the New Testament, not so unambiguously asserted in the Middle Ages, and unforgettably renewed in the Reformation theology of justification and sanctification. This was the insight that the Holy Spirit is none other than the Spirit of Jesus Christ. By abandoning it, it opened the doors with only too much seriousness and godliness *quibuslibet deliriis et imposturis*, i.e., to a recognition of all possible idols, including those with which we have to do to-day.

The clearest monument, accessible to everyone, of this development and of these open doors is the collection of church hymn-books current in Evangelical quarters (cf. for what follows Lukas Christ, "Das evangelische Kirchenlied," *Z.d.Z.* 1925, p. 358 ff.).

It is no accident that in the Evangelical service it is the praise of the congregation which particularly represents the element of subjective reality in revelation, i.e., man as he becomes the recipient of it in the Holy Spirit. In Eph. 5¹⁹ there is an early reference to ᾠδαῖς πνευματικαῖς. But what is the meaning of πνευματικαῖς in this context? What sort of possibility is it that man possesses here? If we are contemplating the Reformation period the answer is simple. At the end of 1523 Luther writes to Spalatin of his intention to publish a collection of psalms in German, and asks him for his co-operation in the task. The purpose of such *cantilenae spirituales* is simply *quo verbum Dei vel cantu inter populos maneat* (*W. A. Br.* 3, 220, 3). And more explicitly in 1524 in the preface to the so-called *Walther'schen Chorgesangbüchlein*: " . . . in order that thereby God's Word and Christian doctrine may be applied and exercised in every sort of way. Accordingly I have also . . . brought together some spiritual songs, to apply and make current the holy Gospel which hath now by God's grace once more arisen, so that we too may boast, as Moses doth in his song in Exo. 15, that Christ is our praise and song, and that we would know nothing else to sing or to say save Jesus Christ, as Paul saith in 1 Cor. 2 " (*W.A.* 35, 474, 8). The intention of this programme is outwardly reflected in the fact that with four exceptions Luther himself did not compose freely, but imitated the Bible or the early and mediæval Church. In Luther's case this was no makeshift : he was a poet of ability. It is simply that his concern was " not for his own interests, but for the Church and her faith " (L. Christ, *op. cit.* p. 367). This is decided by the actual content. Luther's hymns are completely lacking in all lyrical quality, i.e., in all emphasis upon the emotion of the subject. The one who speaks in them is neither giving to himself all kinds of accusatory, heartening, instructive and hortatory advice, nor is he constraining others with the challenge or invitation or demand to lay this or that upon their hearts. What these hymns contain is adoration and solid communication, confession of faith, confession of sins, proclamation. It would have to be a very strange reading that did not find in them the language of the Christian heart and its experience, or rather—no matter whether " I " or " we " is in the forefront as the subject of the hymn—of the community of God's children. It was in its name and on its behalf that Luther composed his hymns. But in these hymns we never find either God's child or God's Church preoccupied with themselves, but always turning to the recognition and praise of God and His acts, with the greatest concentration upon the second article as understood in all its biblical simplicity. It is in this way that there speaks the life, love, experience and actuality of subjective reality in revelation. And as regards purpose and basis the same is true of most of the hymn-writers of the 16th century, for instance, J. Decius, M. Weisse, J. Zwick, N. Hermann, Paul Speratus, J. Gramann, M. Schalling or N. Selnecker. The Reformed Church was marked by a strict adherence to the biblical psalms (in the renderings of Jorissen and Lobwasser). The result was that, although it had no very sure merit as poetry, in content its Church praise did maintain the same high level. It maintained it longer than the Lutheran, and in the stricter Reformed circles still does so to-day. But by the end of the 16th century, when academic orthodoxy had reached its peak, there had already been a remarkable change in the sphere of hymnology. It was not always equally radical, but its effects were felt at every point. In the first instance, of course, the object of faith is retained in spite of the change. But there is now a new preoccupation, and whole stanzas are devoted, not to this first theme, but to what is obviously a second centre of reflection, the heart, the soul, the I, the We, in all the problem of its relation to the former object. P. Nicolai, for example, is still deeply rooted in the 16th century in his " How sweetly shines the morning star." And the interesting feature of it is not that the bridal mysticism of the Song of Songs finds expression in the Evangelical Church. What really is interesting is that this is only a symptom of the formation of this new epicentre, which is almost palpable in this particular hymn. In the 17th century it made irresistible progress in men like J. Heermann, J. Rist, J. Franck, J. J. Schütz, Joachim Neander —and theologically there can be no doubt that Paul Gerhardt belongs to this series. Certainly the old Reformed note is not lacking in any of them. Paul Gerhardt is naturally the best from this standpoint. In fact, for broad stretches —in so far as they compose as orthodox theologians—it is impressively sounded. But the other note becomes clearer and clearer. On the one hand there is an intensifying of interest in the depths of the believing subject, his sin, his pardon, his sanctification, and in the perceptions, moods and feelings accompanying these processes. On the other hand, there is a widening of the element of religious meditation and reflection on the many aspects of the external existence of the subject in the various divisions of day and year, in calling, in good times and more particularly in bad, in life and especially in the expectation of death. In place of the drama of creation, reconciliation and redemption, which is the work of the triune God, another drama is staged. We hear a monologue of the soul, or a dualogue between the soul and God, or even at this early date of one soul with another. It is a serious and depressed and almost melancholy voice which we hear, and one which corresponds to the gloomy character of the history of the century. We must believe of these men that they struggled and strove and despaired and were comforted and established in faith. Sometimes they found unforgettable words to express it. But overlooking the change in the Reformation content of their hyms, it is in them and their self-confessions that we are forced to believe. And it is as self-confessions that their hymns harmonise remarkably well and not unnaturally with those of their contemporary, the convert and mystic J. Scheffler, *alias* Angelus Silesius. For good or evil, we must believe that he, too, was serious and ardent and profound in intention. But in what or in whom are we really believing ? And in the glory of a newer, more gladsome and more self-conscious age this self-confession becomes richer, more luxuriant and more emotional as we pass into the 18th century. In the so-called rational theology, pietism triumphs theologically with its great slogan " not only doctrine but life too " ; and at once the rivulets of poesy begin to gush in the direction of " not doctrine but life." It is a downright exuberant Christian feeling for life—quite in accordance with the general spirit of the age—which now meets us (even the tunes of the period begin to acquire a suspicious swing) in the songs of a Christian F. Richter, L. A. Gotter, B. Schmolck, J. J. Rambach, P. F. Hiller, Ernst Gottlieb Woltersdorf, and in his own particular way N. v. Zinzendorf. What first strikes one about them is the sometimes rather pompous but always very impressive way in which—the orthodox facade is still unbroken—they relate themselves to dogma and particularly to Christology. Nothing could be more moving, more triumphant or more solemn than, say, their language about Christ's active God-manhood in the three offices of prophet, priest and king. But the fanciful and fancy-breeding elaboration used shows at once the extent to which things have gone awry : confession and proclamation have now really given way to religious poetry. The objective element is now filled out and carried along by the ardour and the thankfulness and veneration and the laudatory rejoicing of the subject. It is true that even this poetry is not devoid of confession and proclamation. The hymns do contain statements and verses which we are glad to read and sing, so gripped are we not merely by their emotional content but by their content of knowledge, biblical and reformed. But on the whole participation in the singing of these hymns implies a congregation which is highly self-impelled, highly self-activating and highly self-exalted, and no longer—we cannot fail to remark it—the congregation of Luther which is moved simply by hearing the Word in faith. It is a congregation which has grown far more godly, which makes far greater demands on itself. But above all it takes things much more seriously and importantly even in regard to its religious possessions. Children of God ? Yes, but children of precocious wisdom and maturity, almost ready to leave school, already, it would seem, on a footing of comradeship with the Father. And then at the very peak of the century, there arise the two last great Evangelical hymn-writers, Gerhard Tersteegen and Christian Fürchtegott Gellert. The objective substance of the hymn has still not been abandoned : indeed it has hardly been touched. A fairly complete compendium of biblical and Church Christology could still be compiled from these hymns. But in both Tersteegen and Gellert is it not quite evident that that second epicentre has finally settled and hardened ? The real substance of what they make the congregation sing definitely relates to this and not the former centre. The traditional Christology has turned unnoticed into an exoteric garment. In Tersteegen it is a garment for the exposition of a mystical experience of the Presence. In Gellert it is a garment for the exposition of a solid moral attitude. In both cases, however, it is a foreign body which adheres to the real substance not necessarily but a little accidentally. Listen to Tersteegen himself in the Foreword to his *Geistlichen Blumengärtlein inniger Seelen*, 1768 : " Alas, that so many hungry souls have so long allowed themselves to be supported and fed on dry, strengthless husk-and-shadow figures of truths, in which the spirit can find no solid or abiding satisfaction and peace, since in them the essential core-truths of the inward life of a Christian, still by God's grace to be experienced here in this pilgrim way, are, where not contemned, yet so little realised and known in their beauty and preciousness, that sympathy can never sufficiently lament it. Alas, men search far and wide and with many an effort for a treasure which they cannot properly find ; yet they could have it so easily and so intimately, if only by God's help they would give themselves a chance of entering into the appropriate preparedness or disposition of the heart. Come, O souls called of God to His pure service of the spirit ! Let us in the Lord's strength rid ourselves and let ourselves be rid of all visible things, of the senses, of reason, and of all idiosyncrasies, in order that, properly separated, simplified, pure creatures, we may enter into our spirit and soul-ground, and there find, behold and love God who is also a Spirit, and enjoy His peace which passeth all understanding." And listen to Gellert in the Preface to his *Geistlichen Oden und Liedern*, 1757 : " Songs for the heart, for which music is particularly suited, must be so composed, that they let us feel everything that is lofty and touching in religion : the holiness of faith, the divineness of love, the heroism of self-denial, the greatness of humility, the loveliness of thankfulness, the nobility of obedience to God and our Redeemer, the good fortune of having an immortal soul created and redeemed for virtue and for eternal life ; that they let us feel the shamefulness of vice, the bestiality of the desires and of sensuality, the vileness of greed, the pettiness of conceit, the frightfulness of lewdness, in a word, the attractions of virtue and the hatefulness of vice ; of virtue as it is loved and commanded by God, and commanded for our good ; of vice as it is rebellion before God, and for us shame, timeless misery, eternal pain." Compare with this what Luther wrote about the contents of a similar collection of hymns. It is hardly necessary to draw attention to the distorted products of pietism and rationalism which were so plentiful both then and later. It is not in the light of distortion but in the light of the pure form of the Neo-Protestant hymn as it reached maturity in Tersteegen and Gellert that we shall see what really happened. And it makes no essential difference whether we have a preference either for Tersteegen or for Gellert. Mysticism and morality are complementary opposites, which cannot seriously be played off one against the other except as a result of misunderstanding. If we really have to seek the subjective possibility of revelation, the Church, at the point where it has been unequivocally sought since the middle of the 18th century, it is better that this Church should sing both Tersteegen and Gellert, so as not to be guilty of partiality. What really happened at the peak of the development of the Evangelical hymn as it was reached in Tersteegen and Gellert was this. Not in a distorted form, but in its twofold classical form, the confession of Christ remains, but in the last resort, in relation to what those poets really intend and the congregation really sing and chant, it has become superfluous. Because it is no longer the one and all, because it has now become (unmistakably and irrevocably) a first side by side with a second, it is clear that it could be taken away altogether and nothing essential would be deducted from what was really intended to be sung and chanted. In the generation which followed Tersteegen and Gellert the Evangelical Church acquired a purely subjective hymnody. This was the age when 16th- and 17th-century hymns, including those of Luther and Paul Gerhardt, were allowed to disappear entirely or almost entirely from the hymn-books, or were subjected to such a lengthy transformation that they too came to say the only thing which people now wanted to say and to hear. Perhaps it would have been healthy and certainly instructive if this tendency had carried the day. It would have brought it home clearly to the Church's consciousness that the Holy Spirit as men now thought they knew Him, being separated from Jesus Christ, was, in fact, a different spirit from the Spirit of Jesus Christ. He was the spirit of mysticism and morals but not the Spirit in whom the Early Church and the Church of the Reformers had heard and believed the Word and nothing but the Word. But further development obscured rather than clarified the situation. When we turn to specifically modern hymnody, to men like Novalis, E. M. Arndt, A. Knapp, P. Spitta, we come across two facts. First, pietism and rationalism have now united in a single and all the mightier stream. But more than that, the radical tendency of the 18th century has obviously worked itself out and even been suppressed. The bias of tradition which clings to the life of public worship in a particular way, and the newly awakened sense of the value and dignity of history, have seen to it that the objective content of hymnody has apparently been restored. But, of course, there has not really been any change in content. The preponderance of the subjective element is still constantly increasing. In the 19th century the religious inwardness and moral seriousness of the Christian temper expressed in the hymn have really become its heartbeat and the measure by which it is measured. For obvious reasons, different from those in the 18th century, the congregation's confession has now really become its confession of itself. The further lesson has been learned, in a manner which was not even remotely possible in the 18th century, of poetically projecting the subjective, which is the real object of singing and speaking, upon the objective. The objective itself is thus transmuted into the subjective. Christ is glorified as the original type of all that is deepest and most powerful in the Christian heart and in the Christian congregation, as the aim, object and essence of all Christian convictions, wishes and longings. Here and there in this poetry one can still catch reminiscences of what the " spiritual song " of Luther and his contemporaries had still been in the century of the Thirty Years' War. And this awkward turning to the object involves automatically and involuntarily the possibility of the objective becoming articulate as such. But in principle we still have to say that the situation is now well-nigh hopelessly involved—doubly involved : for we are again in a position to compare the value of the old Protestant hymn with that of the modern. We again find it intelligible and usable. We can promote it to new honour. The idea arose out of the delightfully rich *Liederschatz der Evangelischen Kirche*, in which Luther and the Reformed Psalms, Paul Gerhardt and the poets of the late Baroque, Tersteegen and Gerhardt and the Romantics and Idealists, the poets of the Awakening and those of the mediating theology of the 19th century were all set peaceably side by side. Congregations were accustomed to the assumption, indeed, they were specifically educated in it, that the whole development had been normal and legitimate. In other words, even the very different first stage can confidently be regarded from the standpoint of the present. If Luther's " A safe stronghold our God is still " is sung with the same breath and intention as, say, E. M. Arndt's " I know whom I believe," then it just ceases to be Luther's hymn. Even Reformation praise of God disappears in the gurgling gullet of modern religious self-confession. All the same, the situation is not quite so involved that we cannot see the meaning of the way which the Evangelical Church has gone in this respect. Originally it did mean by a " spiritual song " a song in which, as in preaching and sacrament, but this time in the form of the congregation's answer, the Word of God is preached and heard. Then it found an interesting subsidiary theme in the experience which man produces by means of the Word. Then the sub-theme was allowed to become an independent theme. Then it was found to be obviously more interesting than the principal theme. Then it was raised to the status of principal theme. And finally, and most important of all, it was found that the most appropriate and effective way to treat this new principal theme was intensively to attract to it the old one, which in itself was now obsolete, but, regarded as an allegorical text, acquired a fresh although secondary glory. It is just this last and conservative turn in the 19th century which should make clear to us the full extent of the reversal. In the 18th century it was thought for a time that the objective content of the hymn could simply be rejected. In the 19th century, however, it was found that it could be subjectively interpreted and utilised. And it is the latter fact which more clearly supports the view that so far as this way is to be considered the true way of its own inner development, Protestantism has followed the way of apostasy from the Reformation. The history of the hymn reveals to us the inner secularisation which has taken place. And it is the very sphere in which we find practically nothing in the way of its outward secularisation ; in our modern hymn-books at least it is relatively seldom that we can fix an open heresy. It is far easier to find the hidden heresy involved in the whole development. This can be more or less clearly demonstrated in every section of our hymn-books. It is the heresy of the third article. The Holy Spirit has ceased to be the Spirit of Jesus Christ. To all appearances He is still a spirit of God, even a Christian spirit. In fact, however, He is the spirit of human inwardness and seriousness, the spirit of mysticism and morals. In that spirit we do not yet enjoy, or enjoy no longer, the communion with God which is realised in the revelation of God. On the contrary, for all our seriousness and with all our piety, we are simply alone with ourselves and by ourselves, ἐλπίδα μὴ ἔχοντες καὶ ἄθεοι ἐν τῷ κόσμῳ (Eph. 2¹²). Necessarily this hidden heresy had to manifest itself in other spheres. In the last resort the whole external secularisation of Protestantism in the specific form of modernistic Neo-Protestantism is only a symptom of the inner secularisation visible in the evolution of the hymn.

2. By the outpouring of the Holy Spirit it is possible in the freedom of man for God's revelation to meet him, because in it he is explicitly told by God's Word that he possesses one possibility of his own for such a meeting.

The Word of God which is revealed in revelation declares that man is not actually free for God. This is already expressed by the fact that it is actually the Word or the Son of God who is revealed. What happens is not just anything. It is the last and most peculiar thing which could happen from God's side. God comes forward Himself to be man's Saviour. This presupposes, and it is already proclaimed as a truth of divine judgment, that man cannot be helped in any other way. It is not merely that man lacks something which he ought to be or to have or to be capable of in relation to God. He lacks everything. It is not merely that he is in a dangerous and damaged state, but in his being toward God he is completely finished and impotent. He is not only a sick man but a dead one. It was because the world was lost that Christ was born. Therefore from the very standpoint of Christ's birth we have to say, in the very strictest sense, that the world was lost. A statement like that is only possible from the standpoint of Christ's birth. But from that standpoint we have to make it. Man is free in many respects. He possesses many of the possibilities common to all creatures. And he possesses all the specifically human possibilities which do not appear to be realised except by him. But he does not possess the possibility of communion with God. He cannot be together with God in the way in which he can be together with his equals, and above all with himself, and

9

in a wider sense of the term with all other creaturely realities. He
does not possess a special possibility for this, nor do the rest of his
possibilities give him any capacity for it. In this respect he is not
free. We cannot say that to be a man means to be without God.
But we can and must say, negatively, that to be a man does not mean
to be with God. To be a man can certainly include to be with God,
but only when it is overlapped by the definition : in Christ, that is,
as a hearer and doer of the Word of God, in the Church. But this
is the new thing added to our being as men by revelation. It is not
included in our being as such. In fact, it is excluded. And as long as,
and to the extent that, it is not added to that being as something new,
the being is itself excluded from it. All this is as true as the Word of
God itself. When the Word of God is acknowledged, it is also acknowledged that man is not free for God. But to acknowledge the Word
of God means that he is actually free for God. Therefore it is part
of the acknowledgment that his actual freedom to acknowledge is a
miracle. It is not grounded upon any freedom or possibility for this
acknowledgment which he possessed in his own right. It is grounded
solely upon the freedom of the Word of God which has come to him.
We cannot think away or ignore the negative content of this acknowledgment. On the basis of our own freedoms and possibilities we
should never acknowledge the Word of God to all eternity. And an
acknowledgment, grounded or even partly grounded in our own freedoms and possibilities, would *per se* not be recognition of the Word
of God. The very intention of making our acknowledgment of the
Word of God on the basis of our own freedoms and possibilities would
make that acknowledgment quite impossible. And any subsequent
attempt to explain that acknowledgment by our own freedoms and
possibilities is to deny and therefore to destroy it. It is only as a
miracle that it occurs at all. Similarly, it is only as a miracle that
it is received and understood. Our own freedom and possibility to
meet revelation must be completely talked out in order that the
meeting may be possible. To become free for God we must be convinced that we are not already free. We must make room for the
miracle of acknowledging the Word of God. The Word of God comprises in itself the necessary negation. If we do hear the Word of
God, the question whether we could hear it on the basis of some
freedom of our own has already been discounted. If we do hear it,
then *eo ipso* we know no other freedom but that of the Word of God
itself. It is not a freedom which we have taken, but a freedom which
God has given to us in His mercy, and in virtue of His omnipotence.
And that is the very reason why it is in the act of hearing that we
obviously know the force and validity of the negation. It has to be
fulfilled in us, so that it is no longer expressed only in the Word as
it is spoken by God, but in the Word of God as it is heard by us,
and therefore in our own selves. It has to be made our own, so that

we are quite unable to offer either the practical or theoretical resistance which denies and destroys the miracle of the acknowledgment, and therefore the acknowledgment itself.

But it is not our business either to talk out our freedom for God or to talk in the negation of that freedom. If we could, it would mean that we had in fact a freedom for God and His Word, and a very sovereign freedom at that. For before we heard the Word of God we should obviously know at least this much about its nature and essence : that what will meet us contrary to all our own capacity will be a miracle. But we should also know that our own abilities cannot attain to hearing this Word. And this twofold knowledge would enable us to teach ourselves about the negation, and therefore to dispose ourselves negatively, thus creating the condition by which we may be hearers of the Word of God. But the Word of God excludes every other freedom except its own. Therefore even the freedom to convince ourselves of our own unfreedom, to talk in the negation, is quite untenable. On the contrary, the fact that we are compelled to try to secure at least this freedom for God, the freedom to deny our freedom, is the proof that in practice we cannot attain that renunciation which the hearing of God's Word demands of us.

There is a way of asserting the *servum arbitrium* and discoursing against the doctrines of the *liberum arbitrium* (" God is everything, man is nothing and thou art a madman ") which is too triumphant not to betray that the renunciation is still not made. It is the idea of a *liberum arbitrium*, of man's pride in his own decision, which triumphs in the very assertion of its opposite. That pride may only too well and gladly assume the form of a publican's Pharisaism. And even if we perceive this, our own last word will still be one form of that pride in decision.

What we concede to the Word of God will always be an attempt to make good a claim to our own freedom, to go on believing in our own possibilities. If we imagine that we can talk out this freedom ourselves, we have already talked it in again. Our talking out, however radical (and the more radical it is the more obviously this is true), is quite unable to talk out what really has to be talked out. It is better for us to recognise our total inability in this respect, to admit to ourselves that on the basis of our own possibilities we shall always be men who require to believe in their own possibilities. The only power for this talking out is simply the power of the Word itself. In so far as we ourselves do the talking out, it is the power of the Holy Spirit. We must remember that what we have to do here is just to receive revelation as revelation. We have to see that this reception is the reception of revelation. We have to see that man is finally and actually confronted with God, with the Lord, as Creator, Reconciler and Redeemer. We have to realise that God's revealedness for us is God's own person and God's own work. All the comfort, all the power, all the truth of this revealedness depends upon the fact that it is with God that we are dealing. All our understanding of this revealedness depends upon the fact that we identify it with God Himself, ruling out all other possibilities but God's possibility. We have therefore to realise that as the recipient of revelation man is brought under God's judgment. It is only because of this that he is brought under God's promise. It is only because of this that God meets him as the One who intercedes for him, who undertakes and directs his cause, who does not therefore quench his own ability and will and accomplishment but subordinates it to His own, since man must always be subordinated to God, if God's glory is to triumph and man is to be helped. We are to understand, therefore, that for God to be revealed involves the dislodging of man from the estimation of his own freedom, and his enrichment with the freedom of the children of God. This negation, the negation of man through God's eternal grace and mercy, is only the obverse of his position as a child of God, as a member of the covenant between God and man. But this obviously means that the negation of man cannot be put into effect any more than his position as a child of God except through God's own action. Thus God's possibility triumphs over the very imprisonment in which we are involved, where we only fulfil our own possibilities and only believe in our own possibilities. The self-enclosed uniqueness of man, who only has and knows his own freedom, is overarched and enclosed and finally relativised through the uniqueness of God and His freedom, the freedom in which He is resolved to have fellowship with this man and once and for all to be his Lord. How could man ever foresee this triumph and the wonder of it ? How could he ever anticipate this triumph or prepare himself for it ? It is God's triumph. It is a state or position in which man may very well find himself, but only with amazement, only with gratitude, only in humble recognition of an accomplished fact, without any opportunity to think how it might come to pass, without possessing any need or capacity to derive it from his earlier state or to indicate the way which led from the one to the other. That earlier state was one of self-glorification and self-will. Apart from the triumph of God it would still be his state to-day. How else can he understand it, then, except as a state which is marked off as the old one, the state of his impossibility for God ? He would again be forgetting or denying the triumph of God if in his new state or in the isolation, the relativising and the outdistancing of the old, he saw the activity of any other power than that which is the power of God on and in us, and which with Holy Scripture we call the power of the Holy Spirit. That power and that power alone is his possibility. It is the possibility of that saving poverty, that saving humility, or that saving death, which carries with it existence in Christ, and the wealth and exaltation and life of that existence.

We read in Mt. 19²³ᶠ· that it is hard—it is easier for a camel to go through the eye of a needle—for a rich man to enter into the kingdom of heaven. The disciples are amazed at this saying (obviously and rightly they give it universal significance) and ask : " Who then can be saved ? " But Jesus looked at them and said to them : " With man this is impossible, but with God all things are possible." It is from the same angle, of course, that the saying about the strait and narrow way (Mt. 7$^{14f.}$) has to be understood. The " few " that find this way are not the clever or pious who might be supposed capable of finding it. They are those who are chosen by God (Mt. 22^{14}) and who are therefore enabled to find what the many do not find. According to Mt. 7$^{24f.}$ the proclaiming and hearing of the Word of Jesus means a judgment upon men, comparable with the storm and flooding which threaten a house. The encounter with Jesus will show whether the builder was a wise man, whether he has ears to hear (Mt. 11^{15}) ; for if so, he will be not only a hearer but also a doer of His word : ὁ δυνάμενος χωρεῖν χωρείτω (Mt. 19^{12}). But who can " receive it " ? He to whom the Son wills to reveal it (Mt. 11^{27}), those to whom it has been given to know the secrets of the kingdom of heaven (Mt. 13^{11}). Why is this the only possibility ? Obviously because what has to take place is a " becoming like children " (Mt. 18^3), a being " born again " (Jn. 3^3) ; which clearly means to begin one's life all over again and quite differently. But that is just what no man " can " do— he has no possibility for it. " Repent and believe the gospel " (Mk. 1^{15}). Yes, but what does μετανοεῖτε mean ? Do we, then, have the possibility or the ability to change our νοῦς, and, if so, where and how did we get it ? No, it is with an unheard-of possibility that we have to do here. We hear of a lost son : " this thy brother was dead and is alive again " (Lk. 15^{32}). Who can that be ? We hear also (Jn. 5^{24} ; 1 Jn. 3^{14}) that faith is a μετάβασις from death to life. Who has the freedom for such a μετάβασις ? In Rom. 8^{10} we hear : " If Christ be in you the body is dead because of sin ; but the Spirit is life because of righteousness." In Eph. 2^5 we hear : " Even when we were dead in sins he hath quickened us together with Christ." How can this happen ? In 2 Cor. 4^{16} we hear : " Though our outward man perish, yet the inward man is renewed day by day," and in 2 Tim. 2^{11} : " If we be dead with him, we shall also live with him." And in Col. 3$^{9f.}$ we hear a command : " Put off the old man σὺν ταῖς πράξεσιν αὐτοῦ and put on the new man, which is renewed εἰς ἐπίγνωσιν κατ' εἰκόνα τοῦ κτίσαντος αὐτόν." Who can be obedient to such a command ? Let us be quite clear : the problem of this and of similar statements does not derive from their second part, as if it were dark and mysterious that we should come out of death into life, for then the first part, our being in death, is, as it were, a natural and self-evident starting-point. No, the starting-point, dying, destruction, putting off the old man, being dead, this too is obviously outside the range of our own possi-bilities, whether in the narrower sense of the terms, or in the more comprehensive sense intended in these passages. Death is the boundary, the surrender and abandonment of our own possibilities. Dying is a sheer *contretemps*. Therefore when Scripture speaks of this dying of the old life as the first step to the new, it never means a work which it is in our hands to fulfil. It most definitely does not mean what all the great mystics have described as the achievable process of self-surrender and ultimately of absorption. It means an event unachievable by man. It means a death which genuinely and properly confronts man. In Rom. 6$^{3f.}$ (" Are ye ignorant that all we who were baptised into Christ Jesus were baptised into his death ? We were buried therefore with him through baptism into death ; that like as Christ was raised from the dead through the glory of the Father, so we also might walk in newness of life "), and Phil. 3$^{10f.}$ (" that I may know him, and the power of his resurrection and the fellowship of his sufferings, becoming conformed unto his death ; if by any means I may attain unto the resurrection from the dead "), this dying is brought into the closest connexion with Christ's death and with baptism which is given to us as the sign of it. " Because one died for all, therefore all died " (2 Cor. 5^{14}). For " if any man be in Christ he is a new creature " ; therefore it is true of him that " the old has passed away " (2 Cor. 5^{17}). " In the Spirit " we have to break away from the ἐπιθυμία σαρκός (Gal. 5^{16}), indeed, we must mortify the πράξεις τοῦ σώματος (Rom. 8^{13}). It was the same in the Old Testament. It needed the presence of Jehovah to achieve the cry of " Woe is me ! I am undone " (Is. 6^5), without which the prophet could not be a prophet. " The breath of the Lord bloweth upon it," therefore " the grass withereth and the flower thereof fadeth " (Is. 40^7). " Thine anger causeth us to pass away, and thy wrath that we must suddenly go hence " (Ps. 90^7). " Thou hidest thy face, they are troubled; thou takest their breath, they die, and return to their dust " (Ps. 104^{29}). Of itself the world cannot punish itself : but according to Jn. $16^{8f.}$ it is the Comforter, the Holy Spirit, who shall punish them, who shall " judge them and kindle a fire " (Is. 4^4). The judgment upon man is not his own but God's business. For that reason, in the Bible it is always associated with the righteousness of God. In the very act of judging God makes room for His own glory and co-opts man as His covenant partner (Is. 9^6, Ps. 33^5, Ps. 103^6). The humiliation of man by God becomes something for which he is glad and thankful : " When thou humblest me, thou makest me great " (Ps. 18^{35}). " I thank thee that thou humblest me and helpest me " (Ps. 118^{21}). " It is good for me that I have been afflicted " (Ps. 119^{71}). " I know, O Lord, that thy judgments are righteous and that in faithfulness thou hast afflicted me " (Ps. 119^{75}). Genuine repentance will never speak in any other way. It will regard itself and therefore the subjective possibility of revelation even on its negative side as a divine and not as a human possibility.

In his 1516–17 lectures on the Romans, Luther does great honour to Christian repentance and humility in God's gracious judgment. But we should seriously misunderstand him if we missed the constant emphasis and reminder that it is the work of God and not of man if we are led to Christian repentance and humility. As Luther saw, the avowed purpose of the Epistle to the Romans was *destruere et evellere et disperdere omnem sapientiam et iustitiam carnis . . . et plantare et constituere et magnificare peccatum* (on Rom. 1^1 ; Fi. II, 1, 2). *Deus enim nos non per domesticam, sed per extraneam iustitiam et sapientiam vult salvare non quae veniat et nascatur ex nobis, sed quae aliunde veniat in nos, non quae in terra nostra oritur, sed quae de coelo venit (ib.* 2, 7). But man can grasp and confess this only when he himself has become a real sinner. Has become— *est enim non naturalis* (Rom. 3^5, *ib.* 71, 9). And : *rarum et arduum est peccatorem fieri (ib.* 71, 1). To become a sinner means to become a liar and fool, to be stripped of all our own righteousness, truth, wisdom and virtue, to be inwardly (in our own eyes), that which we are outwardly (before God) *(ib.* 67, 10). But this is the very thing which of ourselves we cannot do : *nos non possumus introire ad nos et mendaces ac iniusti fieri (ib.* 67, 24). We have to believe that we are sinners : *sicut per fidem iustitia Dei vivit in nobis, ita per eandem et peccatum vivit in nobis, i.e. sola fide credendum est nos esse peccatores (ib.* 69, 10). But this means that we have to believe in God, and, of course, believe on His word, that *Deus per suum exire nos facit ad nos ipsos introire et per sui cognitionem infert nobis et nostri cognitionem. Quia nisi Deus ita prius exiret et verax fieri quaereret in nobis, nos non possemus introire ad nos et mendaces ac iniusti fieri (ib.* 66, 24 ; 67, 21). *Revelationi suae sive sermonibus suis debemus cedere ac sic iustificare et verificare eos ac per hoc nos ipsos (quod non cognoveramus) secundum eos peccatores confiteri (ib.* 67, 31). Therefore that *peccator fieri* can be a reality only *spiritualiter (ib.* 71, 8) ; *humilitas* can be real only as *spiritualitas* (on Rom. 7^{24}, *ib.* 175, 23). *Spiritualis et sapientis hominis est scire se esse carnalem et sibi displicere* (on Rom. 7^{14}, *ib.* 170, 5). Only the spiritual man can speak of himself as Paul does in Rom. $7^{14f.}$. *Si non esset in luce spiritus, malum carnis sibi adiacere non videret nec gemeret* (on Rom. 7^{21}, *ib.* 174, 32). *Qui odit peccatum, iam extra peccatum est et de electis* (on Rom. 8^{28}, *ib.* 213, 6). *Verbum Dei facit opus suum* i.e. *pavorem Dei in illis (ib.* 214, 17). God's way *(natura)* is : *prius destruere et annihilare, quicquid in nobis est, antequam sua donet* (on Rom. 8²⁶, *ib.* 203, 4). In His *opus proprium*, as it stands before us in the humiliation and exaltation of Christ Himself, He is for us a hidden God, i.e., hidden behind the contradiction which it presents to our own thinking and being (*ib.* 204, 11). . . . *cum suam potentiam non nisi sub infirmitate, sapientiam sub stultitia, bonitatem sub austeritate, iustitiam sub peccatis, misericordiam sub ira absconderit* (on Rom. 8²⁸, *ib.* 208, 4). He attests His power (*virtus*) to the elect, by showing them their impotence, and hiding and destroying their own power, so that they cannot boast of it any more (on Rom. 9¹⁷ ; *ib.* 229, 21). When this happens, it is evidence (*signum*) that we really have the Word of God and bear it within ourselves (on Rom. 10¹⁵ ; *ib.* 249, 12 ; cf. 214, 18 ; 227, 16).

Directly alongside this reminder of Luther's teaching we must set the well-known introductory chapter of Calvin's *Institutio* (I, 1). Calvin begins by insisting that the essence of all wisdom (*sapientia*) lies in the twofold *cognitio Dei et nostri*—this raises the question which of the two precedes the other, which is the basis of the other. *Non facile est discernere* ! Calvin concedes at once that knowledge of God seems to be wholly based on self-knowledge, indeed on the knowledge of our *tenuitas*. It is the *miserabilis ruina*, to which the Fall has reduced us, which compels us to lift our eyes upwards. It is the sight of that whole world of wretchedness (*mundus omnium miseriarum*) which we now discover in man, the feeling of our own ignorance, fatuity, indigence, weakness, even perversity and corruption, which makes us realise that power, goodness, righteousness and truth have their *locus* solely *in Domino*. Before we begin to be dissatisfied with ourselves, we cannot long for Him. The self-satisfied man rests upon himself and has no need of God. Therefore it is *cognitio sui* which impels us to seek God and sets us on the way to find Him. But how do we achieve a real self-knowledge ? Only in the presence of God, condescending *ex illius intuitu ad se ipsum inspiciendum*. Of ourselves we always regard ourselves as righteous and wise, unless we are convicted by unambiguous arguments to the contrary. But we can never be convicted by abstract self-examination. The eye is only able to grasp light in a very small measure, but we do not realise this as long as we direct it to the earth, only when we try to point it to the sun. Similarly, it is only when we think of God and His righteousness and wisdom and power that we see our own righteousness as *iniquitas*, our own wisdom as *stultitia*, our own power as *impotentia*, and we arrive at a real self-knowledge. That is why, according to Holy Scripture, man has no knowledge of his lowliness except when he stands terror-struck in presence of the revealed majesty of his God. Our knowledge of God may be limited by our corresponding knowledge of self, but in this conditioning relationship the first place decidedly belongs to the knowledge of God. That is why Calvin's exposition of the doctrine of man's unfreedom for God (*Instit.* II 2, 1) begins with a reminder that sinful man has to renounce all wisdom and power of his own, because he must give God the glory. That is why repentance is derived strictly from faith, from *participatio* in Christ (III, 7, 1). That is why *abnegatio nostri*, in which Calvin discerns the *summa vitae Christianae*, is derived from the statement: *Nostri non sumus, sed Domini* (III 7, 1). That is why it is clear that the *humilitas* of faith in justification must not be confused with the virtue of modesty (*modestia*), but consists in the fact that when God is known in His Word nothing else remains except to hope in Him (III 12, 6).

At this point we must mark off our teaching from a view which has recently been advanced in many quarters. This involves at least the possibility that we may have a bad conscience, that we may be disappointed in our arbitrary imaginings, even to the point of complete disillusionment. It involves the possibility of a collapse, and of our knowledge of the collapse, of all our ideologies and enterprises, the possibility of despair, the possibility that we may find in despair the controlling factor in our existence. In other words, it involves the possibility of a negative determination of our existence, a possibility which is integral to man, an immanent anthropological point of contact with the revelation of God. Indeed, this possibility of a negative determination of our existence might objectively be identical with the wrath and judgment of God, and therefore subjectively, as our own experience, at least a necessary indication of it, and something which we should have to see and know as such. Therefore, to the extent that revelation is the manifestation of wrath and judgment (and yet indirectly, too, as the revelation of grace and salvation), it comes in answer to an existing possibility of our own, in answer to what man himself can already know about himself : it comes right into his own life. In that case what the Word of God talks us out of is only the positive possibility of receiving revelation. And at the same time we talk ourselves into the possession of a great negative possibility : in fact we must. In the very discontinuity which arises at this decisive point there is to be found a continuity between man and God, nature and grace, reason and revelation. In fact, we have here a neutral " feeler," the object of a natural theology under the third article. The truth behind this construction is, of course, self-evident. According to 1 Cor. 1[26f.] God has chosen that which in the world's eyes is foolish and weak and ignoble and despised. According to Mt. 11[25] He has revealed the truth to babes. According to Lk. 1[52] and James 1[9] He exalts the meek. According to Lk. 6[20] and James 2[5] the poor are blessed. According to Mk. 2[17] the sick need the physician. According to 2 Cor. 12[9] the power of God is mighty in the weak. In fact the connexion between God's revelation and the uncovering of the radical need for man's redemption is indissoluble. God's unveiling in revelation is invariably His veiling. Jesus Christ's resurrection and exaltation has for its presupposition His passion and His death, His profoundest humiliation. But not for one moment, even, can we abstract from this truth the fact that the connexion has its basis and meaning in Jesus Christ. Folly, humility, weakness, suffering and death—in short, the negative determination of man's existence as such does not in any way enjoy this connexion either generally or in itself. As an immanently anthropological possibility it has no merit or advantage compared with the various possibilities of a positive determination of our existence. According to 2 Cor. 7[10] Paul knows of a " sorrow of the world " which " worketh death," just as sin does according to Rom. 7[13]. And in 1 Cor. 1[26] he says of those things which are foolish and weak and ignoble and despised, that God has chosen them—obviously from amongst similar things—and chosen them, " that no flesh should glory before God " (v. 29). If Luke, like James, emphasises particularly the connexion between Christ and the poor, the publicans, etc., on no less than three occasions (Lk. 7[36], 11[37], 14[1]), the same Evangelist makes Him accept invitations actually to the table of a Pharisee—almost as if to warn them against the possible misunderstanding. A negative determination of existence is not as such identical with the saving exposure of our radical need of redemption. Moreover, the saving exposure of our radical need of redemption need not consist in a negative determination of our existence. On the contrary, if it is the exposure and therefore the foolishness and poverty and humility of which the New Testament speaks, it does not have its basis in a more or less negative determining, in an immanently anthropological limitation or even overthrow of our existence. To these latter, when we have exhausted every other aid, we can always react with irony, with scepticism, with apathy, with the greatest of all illusions, a so-called lack of illusion, and finally and in the last resort with suicide. It is not for the sake of these that we deserve to be blessed. Paul does not rejoice that the Corinthians were sad, but that they were sorry unto repentance, κατὰ θεόν (2 Cor. 7[9-11]). This λύπη κατὰ θεόν is distinguished from " worldly sorrow " by the fact that we cannot react to it as we choose, that we can, therefore, very definitely be blessed for its sake. For that reason we must also say that it is not one of our own possibilities. It is not a determination of human existence which can be fixed and understood according to an immanent anthropology. Luke's (6²⁰) '' Blessed are the poor '' is correctly interpreted by Matthew (Mt. 5³) in his " Blessed are the poor in spirit." This poverty, true and saving despair, is the gift of the Holy Spirit, the work of Jesus Christ. In this it resembles faith, of which it is a part. As the gift of the Holy Spirit and the work of Jesus Christ it is known decisively in the knowledge of our own sin and therefore and primarily in the knowledge of the divine compassion, forgiving us our sins. Before Damascus Paul first sees and hears his Lord, then he falls to the ground, a trembling comes over him, and he is blinded. As the gift of the Holy Spirit and the work of Jesus Christ, this poverty is a reality of faith. That is, it does not consist abstractly in our own experiences of poverty, no matter how powerful. It consists concretely in the poverty of Christ as it became an event upon Golgotha. This alone is the radical and the final exposure of our poverty and in that way the ground of our riches (2 Cor. 8⁹). As the gift of the Holy Spirit and the work of Jesus Christ, this poverty is a fundamental and comprehensive poverty. It is genuine despair, because it is saving despair. What is destroyed by it is not only our certainty, but also our uncertainty, and the disillusionments which lead up to it : not only our defiance but also our desperation, not only our illusions but also our complete absence of illusions, not only our good but also our bad conscience. It is despair about ourselves. Therefore it is despair even about the negative possibilities of the defining of human existence. Of course, it can and often enough—perhaps usually—does coincide with such negative possibilities. Concrete human folly, abjectness and weakness, which can be fixed and understood as such, are naturally intended in all those New Testament passages. And on the basis of divine election they may be sanctified as signs of that laudable poverty in spirit, of that divine sorrow unto repentance, of that true and saving despair. As such, they attest and declare it. To that extent they declare and attest God's revelation. But they are not necessarily correlated to it. We cannot maintain any general or necessary or logical connexion between them. If they are '' feelers '' on man's side, it is not in any neutrality as general human possibilities. It is only as signs sanctified by divine election. It is only on the basis of a revelation which has already been enacted and received. They do not belong, then, to anything that man can know about himself from his own standpoint. Consequently they are " points of contact " newly posited by God, not present already in the nature of man. Therefore they are not the object of a natural theology under the third article.

3. By the outpouring of the Holy Spirit it becomes possible for man in his freedom to be met by God's revelation, because in it the Word of God becomes unavoidably his master. From what has been said under 1 and 2, we are aware that we have to seek the subjective possibility of revelation, our freedom for the Word of God, only in the Word itself, in Jesus Christ. We have not to abstract from this objective factor and seek it in its effects on and in us. Therefore, in so far as it now becomes our freedom, we have to understand it as a miracle, and not in any sense as a natural freedom and capacity. But what is the significance of this miracle of Jesus Christ actualised in us in the outpouring of the Holy Spirit ; what is the import of this encounter, so that we can and must assert positively that it can confront us, that we do acquire a part in the divine possibility which is realised in it ? That is the question which we now have to answer. In trying to answer it we need to keep before us what we established in 1 and 2. For the sake of saying something positive, we must not

let ourselves be tempted into speaking about a quality of grace poured into man, or a natural capacity and power for revelation. If we do, we turn our eyes away from Christ and towards man. And we do not say the positive thing that we really have to say. It is still the case that the subjective possibility of revelation is God's possibility, just as its objective and subjective reality is God's reality. But if that is so, what after all is the meaning of a man's participation in this possibility? One thing is certain. We can never make it comprehensible as our own participation, i.e., as our taking, conceiving, grasping and appropriating the share given us in this possibility. We can and should understand that it is to us that the possibility is given. Participation in it does not signify an abolition of our identity with ourselves. It is a frightful misunderstanding to try to interpret it along the lines of a possession or a trance. There are such states, but only when the consciousness of identity is removed. For that reason we must not interpret the miracle of the divine possibility along the lines of such unusual but not miraculous phenomena. In this miracle we are dealing with that miracle of God which is performed upon ourselves in our own identity with ourselves. Even if we did have to reckon with a removal of the consciousness of identity in the recipient of the revelation, if we were dealing with the miracle of this receiving, we should still have to say quite emphatically that it is performed upon a man who is really identical with himself. It does not take place in one who is outside himself—even the doctrine of the Holy Ghost must not lay itself open to a charge of Docetism. It takes place in the man who is himself and with himself. It is not to a transcendent *alter ego* (if there are such things) that the divine possibility in revelation is given to apprehend. It is given to me myself. I am the old and I am also the new man on the basis of this possibility. I in my apparently unrepeatable selfhood apprehend, or do not apprehend, am called or not called, am elected or rejected: I am judged, I am blessed. Therefore it is a question of our taking, receiving, laying hold of, appropriating the share in the divine possibility which is allotted to us. Moreover, we can and must realise that this participation is achieved in our own experience and activity, in that act of self-determination which we call our human existence. This participation has nothing whatever to do with a magical invasion of the inter-related totality of our physico-psychical human life by supernatural factors and forces. It does signify a limitation and interruption of our existence. Our existence is confronted by something outside and over against it, by which it is determined, and indeed totally determined. But it is determined as the act of our self-determination in the totality of its possibilities. Yet not in such a way that we know in advance and can usually tell what form the fulfilment of this self-determination will take. Not as though we ourselves can decide upon a specific attitude to which the process of determination necessarily has to conform. Not as though, e.g., a passive, receptive attitude necessarily corresponds to the divine possibility : in certain circumstances an active, spontaneous attitude may correspond much better. Not as though the process of determination is necessarily fulfilled subjectively in the form of a state of uncertainty and despair. In certain circumstances it may be fulfilled subjectively in the form of an intensified or simply a healthy, normal sense of life. Antitheses of this kind are immanent antitheses. They belong together to the extent that they represent all the different possibilities within the act of our self-determination. But *per se* they have nothing whatever to do with our being determined from without, with the divine possibility which is given to us in revelation. This is a relationship which they only acquire. It is important to make this point. We have to realize clearly that participation in the divine possibility does not mean that somewhere within our being, there is, so to speak, a vacuum for which we are not responsible and over which we have no control, but which we can abandon on the assumption that the divine possibility which is given to us will intervene. Where this happens the result is either enthusiastic magic or magical enthusiasm. This is related to the possibility given us by the outpouring of the Holy Spirit in the same way as idol worship is related to the worship of God. It approximates no less closely to the doctrine of an inpouring of grace than to that of the capacity of the natural man for revelation. But the possibility given us by the outpouring of the Holy Spirit is the possibility of a direct confrontation of the whole man by God. Man is confronted in the totality of his own possibilities, and therefore in all possible conditions and attitudes. In revelation, the whole man is addressed and challenged, judged and pardoned by God. In view of this totality of revelation to us we must not refer the revealedness in us to some obscure or even luminous place apart from our own experience and activity. We must not refer it to a place where we can exempt ourselves from all responsibility. We must not refer it to a place which enables us to count on the fact that God or " it " believes in us, from which we are therefore onlookers both of ourselves and God. In the presence of God there is no such back room. There is only the one well-known place for our physico-psychical existence, although it does include within it many alternative possibilities. It is in this totality that our existence participates in the divine possibility, or else we have no part in it. The point is that the whole area of our possibilities is again enclosed by the divine possibility. That is what we have to reckon with if we would understand our participation in this possibility. Therefore if we do not understand it, or if we can understand it only as a miracle, this does not mean that it is not we ourselves who are participators, we ourselves in our own experience and activity. What it does mean is that as participators in this possibility we are a riddle to ourselves. We know that we are set before God, but we do not know how it happened. We do not know how we as such can stand and be before God. We do not know how we are worthy or capable of it. Again, we can and must know that all our experience and activity is involved in this standing before God. But we can never say how far this or that impression is our calling, this or that discovery our awakening, this or that decision our conversion, this or that conviction our faith, this or that emotion our love, this or that expectation our hope, and this or that attitude our responsibility and justification before God. For as participators in God's possibility, all that we see and find is simply ourselves, and all the very selfish, very human states and conditions and attitudes in which we actually find ourselves. We never can and never will comprehend how far the concretion of our situation and our attitude is the concretion of our participation in God's possibility. And this contradiction does not emanate from outside. It has nothing whatever to do with the philosophical difficulty of holding together our presence and God's presence, the visible and the invisible, reality and the idea. Philosophical hedges can be surmounted philosophically. And the necessary ways to do it have been discovered long ago, and are constantly rediscovered and applied according to the needs of the age. In an earlier context we have already said that the need for God, of which we are now speaking, is known only by the children of God. They alone really know the miracle of revelation. And in the light of this miracle they alone know the contradiction between the clear and certain fact and the not merely obscure and uncertain but utterly unknown means which alone corresponds to the fact. They know that they are accepted with God. But they know that they are great sinners. They know that they do stand before God. But they know that they cannot stand and live before Him. They know that the possibility of God which is given us is a content which the vessel of our activity and experience cannot contain. In face of the subjective possibility of revelation, as it is incontestably present in the reality of God's revealedness, they are bound to be a riddle. And they know that the riddle is insoluble. For it is not only that we cannot perceive the mystery of the Holy Spirit. We must not. That is the reason why we cannot. The one who crosses our way is God, and He is and will be the Lord. It is only in the most profound and wilful forgetfulness, or in the strict sense, only as we fall away from our status as the children of God—and because there can be no question of a child of God falling away, we have to say that we cannot possibly try to escape the contradiction between the clarity of the fact and the obscurity of the means. Yet this is our life in God's possibility, the receiving of God's grace in His judgment, clarity in obscurity, rest and peace and joy in those who, although they are awakened and called and converted and believing and loving and hoping, know themselves only too well before God, and are quite aware of the frailty of their impressions and discoveries and decisions and emotions and expectations and attitudes. It is because the contradiction remains in force —not by them, nor by their insight and knowledge, but by God's gracious work and in God's knowledge—that their life in the divine possibility is grounded and maintained. God Himself maintains the contradiction in force. It is in Him that we do actually have Himself, the mystery of grace which we do not understand, or understand only as miracle. And what God does and knows in this context is the mystery of His Word as it has newly come to us. It is exactly the same if we say : the mystery of Jesus Christ. For the mystery of the Word of God coming to us and apprehended by us is this : that the mystery of Jesus Christ now stands in our life as a miracle, that as God there became man, for that reason we here have God. In Jesus Christ, the incarnate Son of God, the contradiction is maintained from above, from God : in all the almightiness of the merciful, condescending love of God. But in the same omnipotence the contradiction is also maintained downwards, towards man, when Jesus Christ comes to us as the Word of God. It is, therefore, maintained by the divine omnipotence. And the fact that it is maintained is manifested and manifest to us. For that reason, the contradiction is not one of those paradoxes which owe both their origin and their solution to our own acuity. It is not one of those contradictions which can be overcome if we have the sagacity and strength to bring them together in our own lives, to co-ordinate them in our thinking, to harmonise them in our feeling. The solution of the contradiction is not only in appearance. It is a genuine solution, proceeding from the reality of Christ's resurrection from the dead. Therefore life in this contradiction is not merely a life of acceptance, as we do actually accept some necessary and unnecessary contradictions, because we cannot remove them. On the contrary, life in this contradiction is already a life in reconciliation. Of course, there is still the contradiction and the conflict between the spirit and the flesh, between the new and the old man, between what we see and what God alone sees. But this very life in conflict is still a life in reconciliation. Our hearts and minds are preserved in the midst of conflict by the peace of God, which passes all understanding. They are preserved because and to the extent that Jesus Christ or the Word of God is unavoidably the Master of this life of ours.

We have now arrived at the two most relevant and helpful concepts in our attempt to describe positively the freedom of man for God's revelation. That freedom exists where the Word of God or Jesus Christ is to man the Master, and unavoidably the Master. Instead of master we might also say teacher, leader or lord. In this context the word " master " is particularly rich in content. Its counterpart may equally well be pupil, scholar, follower or adherent, or servant. And all this is involved in the freedom of man for the Word and by the

Word, of which we are speaking. But for the sake of clarity, we must at once add to the concept of "master" that of "unavoidable." *Analogia fidei* it will be understood what is now meant by "master." There are indeed many masters and teachers, and leaders and lords. They are all of them distinguished from this Master by the fact that they can be totally or partially avoided either altogether or from some particular point in time. To stand unavoidably under any other master is a sign of sickness. But to stand under this Master is not only the normal thing, it is the only possible thing. The outpouring of the Holy Spirit exalts the Word of God to be the master over men, puts man unavoidably under His mastery. The miracle of the divine revealedness, the power of Christ's resurrection in a man, consists in this event. In it the "God became man" is actualised in us as "man has God." It is a removal of the contradiction between a possibility which obviously is only God's possibility, and the human experience and activity, which only an unredeemed arrogance could claim as a fitting and worthy vessel for such a content. In this event man is a participator in this divine possibility. Through God he is free for God. We will now try to analyse the event.

(*a*) To have our master unavoidably in Jesus Christ means always to have found someone over against us, from whom we can no longer withdraw. We can withdraw from everything else that is over against us, whether it is the world or men. It is at once our misery and comfort, the source of our most serious aberrations and the help of which we simply must avail ourselves from time to time, that again and again we can withdraw to an inward solitude. The outpouring of the Holy Spirit makes this withdrawal impossible, at any rate in relation to the Word of God. We can say at once, of course, that it makes it impossible in principle. No matter who or where we are, whether we like it or not, whether we are worthy of it or not, parallel to our line of life, as a second constant, there runs the accompanying presence of the Word which is spoken to us, a presence which we can never frighten away. A man does not become a different person when he receives the Holy Spirit : why should he ? But as the man he is, he cannot flee from this specific partner to any solitude. As the man he is, he stands in this specific relationship which he can no longer leave. In this specific relationship he must be secretly responsible. He must reckon with the fact that he is always engaged in a dialogue, whatever the content of that dialogue may be. Concretely, it may perhaps be with an element of biblical truth which has once illuminated him. It may be with a man in whom the Church once met him. It may quite simply be with the fact of his baptism. Generally speaking, it is with a *signum* which was once factually a *signum* of the Word of God as it confronted and met him. And the puzzling fact that he is bound in this way is the new life which he has as the child of God, a life which is independent of his own will and accomplishment but which carries with it the possibility of receiving the divine revelation.

We are not speaking of the omnipresence of God as philosophy understands it, but of the concrete theological omnipresence of which we read in Ps. 139^{1-10} : " O Lord, thou hast searched me, and known me. Thou knowest my down-sitting and mine uprising, thou understandest my thought afar off. Thou searchest out my path and my lying down, and art acquainted with all my ways. For there is not a word in my tongue, but lo, O Lord, thou knowest it altogether. Thou hast beset me behind and before, and laid thine hand upon me. Such knowledge is too wonderful for me ; it is high, I cannot attain unto it. Whither shall I go from thy spirit ? or whither shall I flee from thy presence ? If I ascend up into heaven, thou art there : if I make my bed in Sheol, behold thou art there. If I take the wings of the morning and dwell in the uttermost parts of the sea ; Even there shall thy hand lead me, and thy right hand shall hold me." The man who can join in that prayer is through God free for God. What it involves is that " abiding " as the word is so pregnantly used, especially in the first epistle of John ; the abiding in us of Jesus Christ (3^{24}) ; of the Word ($2^{14, 24}$) ; of the love of God (3^{17}) ; of the anointing (2^{27}) ; of the divine seed (3^{9}) ; even of eternal life (3^{15}) ; even of God Himself ($4^{12, 15f.}$). It has, of course, its counterpart in our own " abiding " in the Word, in love, and in God.

(b) To have our master unavoidably in Jesus Christ means that we have discovered His supreme authority, to which in all our obedience or disobedience we are always responsible and subject. To other authorities we may make the most profound surrender. We may accept the strictest discipline in relation to them. But over against all of them we can still remain independent, at the deepest and truest level of reality. For every other authority is the kind which we still have to choose and recognise as such. Consequently our attitude to it stands or falls with our own choice and recognition of it. It has no power to dominate us unavoidably. Our thoughts at least—even if only our subconscious thoughts—are always free in relation to it. But the outpouring of the Holy Spirit means that man is placed under the Word, because it is God's Word. Obviously this does not involve any pronouncement upon the capacity or performance of man. Again, it is not a question of what he is in himself, but of the reality of the relationship in which he stands. Again, he has not become another person by receiving the Holy Spirit, and yet he is another person, so far as he stands in this relationship. The man who is really subject to the Word will not refuse to recognise that by the Word he is accused of disobedience at the very heart of his being. But this very impeachment of him confirms the reality of the relationship in which he is placed : supremacy on the one side, subordination on the other ; claim on the one side, responsibility on the other ; all the irreversible inequality of the relationship, in which he is now a partner. And this authority is not one which is freely chosen and later recognised : it is an original authority which has its basis in itself. In so far as man has to do with this authority, without any assistance or co-operation of his own, but concretely, in his own life, he is put in a position where freedom for God and the possibility of hearing His revelation is self-evident.

At this point we have to remember that in the Old Testament and New Testament the basic relationship between God and man is created by the establishment of an unequivocal superiority of God over man. Of Yahweh as of Jesus Christ the first thing which must be said concerning His action on man is that He rules over him. This is the case before anything else. Everything else is simply the working out of the reality that irresistibly and definitively man has acquired his King. The occurrence of revelation takes place within and on the basis of this basic relationship. It is not merely the background. It is the very atmosphere and setting in which reconciliation, grace, assistance, even judgment and punishment can arise on God's side—and faith and unbelief, obedience and disobedience on man's. The element which constantly surprises us, and the impression we receive from the whole Bible, is that in it not only the existence of God but His transcendence over man is proclaimed without any problems ; it is the permanent presupposition of everything that we are told and taught. It all lives by this presupposition. It is true only because God's transcendence is already true. The Bible knows nothing of man in himself, man who can first hold himself aloof from God and then perhaps—or perhaps not—choose and recognise what is the will of God. In the Bible man appears at once as either the pious man or the sinner, either the servant of God or an arbitrary rebel against Him, either the believer or the unbeliever, either the one who gives thanks or the one who is in despair. He is never neutral. He never has the word or the breath for autonomous discussion. At the very points where he seems to speak most strongly, say in Job, or Ecclesiastes, or many Psalms, or, in the New Testament, in 2 Corinthians, where Paul seems to have such a surprising amount to say about himself, he is in fact most securely bound to that relationship, to that absolutely real relationship of super- and sub-ordination, which precedes all the expressions and experiences of his life with God, and which withdraws only in appearance, but is never completely obscured. It is in this relationship that the prophets and apostles see and hear the revealed God, and become His witnesses. The outpouring of the Holy Spirit which enables us to hear their witness, to apprehend revelation, obviously and necessarily consists in the fact that fundamentally we are placed in the same position, brought into the same relationship. It is here that the new life of the children of God begins. In this relationship we have ears to hear what is told us by God.

(c) To have our master unavoidably in Jesus Christ means that we are subject to a command, in face of which there can be neither subterfuge nor excuse. We can find excuses and subterfuges for the commands of all other masters, even when we obey them in whole or in part. We can have doubts about their meaning. We can insist that we did not hear or understand. We can reply that we have already fulfilled them ; or, *vice versa*, that we cannot fulfil them, at any rate in the strict sense. But in face of this command those devices are impossible. The outpouring of the Holy Spirit means that men have received an order, by which they can now mark off their very existence. The outpouring of the Holy Spirit means that they themselves are utterly and absolutely commanded. No place is left to them at which they can devise subterfuges and excuses. The Word of God spoken to them strikes absolutely their very being. The content of the command is that their existence is an existence before and with

Him, and in conformity with Him, that they must fear Him and love Him. And as such it is always meaningful, perspicuous and clear. As such it is never fulfilled, but always unfulfilled. If we cannot actually fulfil it, that is the revelation of our guilt. It does not absolve us from the duty of obedience, from allegiance to Him. It simply lays that duty upon us. In this respect, too, it is not a matter of what man is in himself and becomes in himself. It is a matter of his real standing and walking in relation to the word spoken to him. This relationship consists in the fact that he is taken and bound and ruled. In this context what he is or becomes in himself, even his better efforts, is always shown to be disobedience. But it does not follow in the least that he has failed or that he ought to let himself fail; the result is that for the first time, however limited he can and must be in himself, he is really upheld from above. In his very disobedience he is called, challenged, claimed for obedience. He cannot take refuge either in activity or in passivity. It is not his activity or passivity, it is he himself in his activity or passivity who is the target. Therefore, as the target is aimed at and reached by this irresistible command, that which confronts us, that supreme power of which we were speaking, acquires actual concrete form. We cannot add anything to the fact that we are bound. We cannot alter it. Our human self-determination is still active, but it is imposed upon us. And in this fact we are free for God. We are capable of hearing His revelation.

At this point we may legitimately speak of the Pauline " bringing every thought into captivity to the obedience of Christ" (2 Cor. 10⁵). We may recall the ἀνάγκη, under pressure of which Paul exercises his apostolic office, for " woe is unto me, if I preach not the Gospel " (1 Cor. 9¹⁶). We may remember the καταλαμβάνεσθαι ὑπὸ Χριστοῦ, which compels him to say: οὐχ ὅτι ἤδη ἔλαβον as well as διώκω δὲ εἰ καὶ καταλάβω (Phil. 3¹²). We may recall the equivocal way in which he describes himself in Philem. 1, Eph. 3¹, 4¹, and 2 Tim. 1⁸ as the δέσμιος Ἰησοῦ Χριστοῦ, or again, the subordination of his apostolic dignity to the prior δοῦλος Ἰησοῦ Χριστοῦ, Rom. 1¹, or again, the qualification of it by the added διὰ θελήματος θεοῦ of 1 Cor. 1¹, etc., in accordance with which we then find the goal and content of his apostolate stated in the words : ἀποστολὴ εἰς ὑπακοὴν πίστεως ἐν πᾶσιν τοῖς ἔθνεσιν (Rom. 1⁵). We recall further that the relationship of reconciled man to the righteousness of God and to God Himself is described in Rom 6¹⁸· ²² as a δουλοῦσθαι, and his relationship to the Holy Spirit in Rom. 8¹⁴ as an ἄγεσθαι. To look back from this point to theGospels, it will surprise us how self-evidently the tone which Jesus adopts in His addresses is quite simply and directly the tone of command. It will surprise us how frequently the relationship of lord and servant or of king and subject seems to be the model for His relationship to His disciples. It will surprise us how frequently the Messianic challenge to faith is asserted as a challenge to obedience. In short, it will surprise us how clearly and powerfully the title *Kyrios* is applied to Jesus. A single example will illustrate the point : " But who is there of you having a slave plowing or keeping sheep, will say unto him, when he is come in from the field, Come straightway and sit down to meat ; and will not rather say unto him, Make ready wherewith I may sup, and gird thyself, and serve me, till I have eaten and drunken ; and afterward thou shalt eat and drink ? Doth he thank the slave because he did the things that were commanded ? Even so ye also, when ye shall have done all the things that are commanded you, say, We are unprofitable slaves; we have done that which it was our duty to do " (Lk. 17⁷·¹⁰). That is how the children of God hear the Word of God. Their hearing is really the hearing of an order and therefore obedience, a hearing which as such is necessarily a doing of the Word (Jas. 1²² : " Be ye doers of the word, and not hearers only, deluding your own selves "). When we remember this we shall be on our guard against thinking that the commanding, ordering, or lawgiving of the Old Testament belongs specifically to the Old Testament, and confusing it with the *nomos* of the Jews against which Paul contends in Romans and Galatians. In these epistles Paul demonstrates the impotence of the Law for righteousness in God's sight. But the Law to which he refers is the commandment as it is heard unspiritually and without Christ. It is the commandment as it is heard without hearing the command within the commandment, without a fear and love for God the commander. It is the commandment which is not really a compulsory command. According to the *nomos* of Israel the first of all the commandments is that we should fear and love God the commander : " I am the Lord thy God, which brought thee out of the land of Egypt, out of the house of bondage " (Ex. 20²). Paul himself stood under this Law, when he regarded and described himself as the servant and captive and bondman of Jesus Christ. He saw that believers, too, stand under the νόμος τοῦ πνεύματος τῆς ζωῆς (Rom. 8²). In spite of the Reformers' dialectic of Law and Gospel, we can and must regard the whole possibility of our participation in God's revelation under the familiar concept of the divine Law. The Law speaks to us the command within the commandment. It demands that we should fear and love God. Therefore its purpose is not only to instruct and direct, to judge and to terrify. It is also to comfort, to give us hope and joy and help, to give us the very presence of God Himself in the act in which He Himself is ours, in which He binds Himself to us to save us. In the 119th Psalm we have an almost inexhaustible song of praise to the testimonies and commandments and statutes and laws and precepts and words and ways of God. But of the scriptural testimonies to revelation the 119th Psalm is one which we must not despise, but carefully consider. It is, as it were, a concretion of the saying about the omnipresence of God in Psalm 139 : " Thy Word encompasseth me on every side."

(*d*) To have our master unavoidably in Jesus Christ is to exist in an ultimate and most profound irresponsibility. All other masters and teachers and leaders and lords load and burden us with responsibilities, i.e., with questions which we answer out of our own knowledge, with obligations which we satisfy by our own wish and action, with programmes which we have to fulfil and realise by our own achievements. For that very reason their power to command has exactly the same limitations. They give the orders, but then they leave us to execute those orders alone. They cannot command from us either fear or love. They cannot represent us. It is for that very reason that we can so easily make excuses and apologies in relation to their commands. But the Word of God has a limitless power of command. For it does not impose on us a new and final and frightful, because unending, responsibility. It claims our response. It claims our own will and action. It claims the achievement which is, of course, required of us. It claims all this, not as an autonomous work, the success of which we ourselves must guarantee, but as an act of service, in the fulfilment of which we are borne and covered by the work it does

itself. From this aspect, too, the outpouring of the Holy Spirit signifies the relativising of the question who and what we are in ourselves.
By it we are put into this relation under the Word and under the
command of the Word. And that means, of course, that as the people
we are we have to participate in that work of the Word. Not as
those who have to finish the work, to reach the goal, to bring in the
results. In our very participation it is foreseen that we are men, and
disobedient men, and therefore quite unsuitable for the work. Our
participation does not depend upon our fitness for this work. It is a
participation in spite of our unsuitability. It rests upon the forgiveness of sins. It is grace. It is a participation in fear and in love to
the God who has mercy on us in that He calls us to it and permits it.
That is just why it is not a participation which involves anxiety and
worry whether we can really do what we are required to do. Of
course we cannot do it. That is the presupposition of our participation. Only one thing is required of us. As those who cannot do it
of ourselves, and never could, we have to participate when the Word
does it. It is a matter of the receiving and adopting of man into
participation in the Word of God. This participation corresponds to
what took place in the incarnation of the eternal Son of God. It is
the basis of the life of the children of God, that non-autonomous life
which is a life only of grace and of faith. And when man is placed
under the Word and under the command of the Word, he is really
free. Free from worry about himself. But also free from worry
about others. And free from worry about the whole development of
human affairs in the Church and the world. In the ultimate and
decisive question, the doing of the will of God in all these things, he
has no worries at all, even when he ought to be weighed down in all
the penultimate questions regarding himself and others and the Church
and the world. That the will of God should be done in all things is what
he can and should pray when the other burden seems likely to crush
him, and then it will not crush him. But the very prayer, Thy will
be done, is in fact an admission that I need not worry about it, because
that is not my business. I am not responsible. This burden, the
burden of my own and others' sins, does not lie upon me. It lies
solely and entirely upon Jesus Christ, upon the Word of God. In the
fact that I am bound to this Word of God consists the one and only
thing which I can do for myself and others, for the Church and the
world. What happens in this relationship will be good ; what does
not happen in this relationship will be bad. And when I am bound
in this way I can never again take the burden on myself, I can never
invest myself with the dignity of the Word, the dignity of Jesus Christ.
Jesus Christ alone bears it and can bear it. Our relationship to Him
must always consist in our knowing and saying and confirming and
attesting and living out the truth : that He careth for you. And
in this very freedom, in this ultimate absence of responsibility, it is

self-evident that we have to hear the freedom of God and the revelation of God.

The attitude of the men of the Bible and the recipients of revelation will again help us to see our way clearly at this point. It is marked by the fact that the strictness with which they are claimed for the things of God is directly paralleled by a particular attraction to the things of God. In the Old Testament prophets and especially in Paul in the New Testament, particularly in the latter case, we do not see anything of the rigidity or Zelotism or anxious zeal, in short, the spiritual cramp which always results when men think and act as if the *causa Dei* were really their own anxiety and concern. They do not really aim to do what God does. They aim only to participate. They do not do the work: they assist. It is in this way that they are the recipients and witnesses of revelation. The commandments which they keep in love to God are God's commandments (ἐντολαὶ αὐτοῦ), and therefore not grievous (1 Jn. 5³). His yoke is easy and His burden is light (Mt. 11³⁰). They need not be ashamed of the Gospel, because it does not need their own dynamic. And it does not need it, because it is itself the δύναμις θεοῦ, and indeed εἰς σωτηρίαν (Rom. 1¹⁶).

(e) To have our master unavoidably in Jesus Christ is to be subjected to a definite formation and direction. We can adapt ourselves to other masters. We can imitate them. We can model ourselves on them, or even on the caricature of them. No other master has the power to subordinate another man to his direction and leadership in such a way that the latter is completely himself and not a cast, and yet completely represents the form and the way of the master and not a caricature. The arbitrariness of all imitation is also its weakness. Just what imitation really intends, imitation cannot achieve. Therefore we can call it the tragedy of all other mastery, that at the very best it produces only imitation. The formation and direction of a man by the Word of God, which becomes a reality with the outpouring of the Holy Spirit, has nothing to do with imitation. We must again insist that under this formation and direction man remains the man he is. His own nature and thinking and willing and feeling, both in general and in detail, is not lost. But in the light of this his own being, he remains a sinner before God. Yet this very being of his as a sinner before God is subjected to the Word of God, and is therefore formed and directed by that Word. And because the subordination and therefore the formation and direction are perfect, there takes place at this point what imitation intends but can never achieve: the master acquires a pupil, a servant, a scholar, a follower, in whom he finds himself again and in whom accordingly he, the master, can also be found again by others. But the master is the eternal Word, which has assumed flesh. We are not the eternal Word, but flesh of that flesh, which in Him was made partaker of the divine nature. In that we are subjected to Him, the eternal Word, we are not only flesh, but in the flesh we are the children of God, the brethren of the First-born. That is the subjection of our being to the Word. Subjected to the Word, this being is no longer left to its own devices. It no longer grows wild. It still exists in the flesh. But in spite of and even because of this, its direction is from the Spirit, from the new birth, to the Word. It is the object of an attraction, a formation, a leading by the Word. From the standpoint of the being itself, this is, of course, inconceivable. It does not deserve it, nor can it contribute to it or co-operate in it. But that is just what makes it so necessary and irresistible. Only by a denial and rejection of Jesus Christ Himself, i.e., only in the absence of the Holy Spirit, can this attraction, formation and direction by Him be denied and rejected and rendered ineffective. Where and to the extent that He now acts in the Holy Spirit, He forms and directs the man who still exists in the flesh, who is still wandering as a sinner. Certainly this is a strictly hidden formation and direction, just as He Himself, the Master, is a hidden master. But His action upon us is just as real as He Himself is. And the aim of His action is that out of man's life there should come a repetition, an analogy, a parallel to His own being—that he should be conformable to Christ. Conformable to Christ does not mean that a man is a second Christ—which involves all the arbitrariness and weakness of a mere *imitatio*. Conformable to Christ means that in all his humanity, for Christ's sake and in Christ, he is a child of God. It means, therefore, that he is directed away to the one for whose sake and in whom he is a child of God. This directing and integrating into Christ is the work of the Holy Spirit, and in it he can hear and receive the divine revelation. The possibility into which we have been inquiring is to be found in this actuality.

For a right understanding of this point, the decisive New Testament concept is one which is very important for the Synoptists, but also quite prominent in John. It is that of following Jesus. Ἀκολουθεῖν points in quite a different direction from *imitatio*. In the first place it is descriptive of someone who accompanies another, who takes the same road as he does. But more pregnantly, it indicates the follower who respectfully walks behind a master or prince, the scholar who strides along at a distance behind his teacher. And in cases like this imitation is not only unnecessary, but impossible. Further, we have to note that this following is distinguished from an arbitrary action, like imitation, by the fact that it is conditioned by the call of Jesus. It is therefore a Messianic gift. The individual who decides (" Lord, I would follow thee ") to tread this way on his own initiative, at once proves that he is not suited for the kingdom of God (Lk. 9⁶¹ᶠ·). Finally, the frequent inter-relating of the idea of following with that of self-denial ought also to prevent us from thinking that this is the kind of formation and direction which a man can undertake of himself. It is allowed and granted to him to participate in the existence of Jesus, in the salvation manifested in Him, and in His passion—that is what following is. In this following he becomes a μαθητής. He can be taught by Jesus and can learn from Him. But he who does not follow Him is not worthy (ἄξιος) Mt. 10³⁸, and cannot be His disciple (Lk. 14²⁷). In the same way we are told in 1 Pet. 2²¹ that in His passion Christ has left us a ὑπογραμμός, that we should follow in His steps, i.e., fashion our life according to the form of His passion. In the same connexion we must also think of Heb. 12², where Jesus is called the ἀρχηγός καὶ τελειωτής of our faith, to whom we have to look if we are to run properly in the race which is set before us. But Paul also addresses the Galatians as children who seeing that Christ was still " openly set forth " before them in vain (Gal. 3¹) were not yet born again—in, as it were, the personal unity of the apostolic Word with the working of the Holy Spirit—but whom He had still to labour to bring forth : μέχρις οὗ μορφωθῇ Χριστὸς ἐν ὑμῖν (Gal. 4¹⁹). It is a matter of the μορφὴ δούλου of Him who emptied Himself of His own God-form and humbled Himself to the death on the cross. It is of this that Christians must think if they are to revert from disunity to unity ἐν Χριστῷ Ἰησοῦ (Phil. 2¹·¹¹). By the Spirit who is the Lord they are " changed into his (Christ's) likeness." The result is, therefore, that they become a mirror of the glory of the Lord. And in that very fact it is shown that, unlike the Jews whose hearts are covered when they read their Moses, they have freedom (ἐλευθερία) and therefore open eyes (ἀνακεκαλυμμένον πρόσωπον) for God's revelation (2 Cor. 3¹²·¹⁸). In that they become σύμφυτοι τῷ ὁμοιώματι τοῦ θανάτου αὐτοῦ, implanted into the Church, which by baptism we understand to be the image of His body given up to death for us, they will also participate in His resurrection (Rom. 6⁵). We have to put all these things in their general context if we are to gain even an inkling of what is meant by the very simple but pregnant Johannine τηρεῖν of the Word and the sayings (Jn. 8⁵¹, 14²³) or commandments of Jesus (Jn. 14¹⁵· ²¹, 15¹⁰ ; 1 Jn. 5³).

(*f*) To have our master unavoidably in Jesus Christ means finally and comprehensively that we have no concern of our own, but that His, Christ's concern, is our concern. No other master can master us so thoroughly, either for good or evil, that although we are in his service, or school, or following, we cannot still have our own concerns, and in the last resort have him as our master only for the sake of those interests of ours. But where the Word of God is master by the outpouring of the Holy Spirit, there enters in an interest or concern which does not allow any rivals, for the simple reason that in the Word of God it is always a matter of our own interest and concern. But it is our own interest and concern not as seen from our standpoint, but as seen from the opposite but beneficent standpoint of the wisdom of God, as judged by the righteousness of God, as adopted by the goodness of God. That is the Word of God : the work of God upon us : for us and therefore against us : the work of the kindness which we cannot grasp, which we have outraged, which does good to us, as to those who always do evil. Where it is heard as such, there is still an active will to assert and help ourselves, to maintain and justify and advertise ourselves, but it has been fundamentally broken and its vital power destroyed. At any rate it cannot exist in face of the Word of God— so that fundamentally it cannot exist at all. It can exist only as and to the extent that we exist under the Word. If that means humiliation, it also means comfort. If it means limitation, it also means liberation. If it means Law, it also means Gospel. It is a great affliction when our right to have our own desires and to pursue them is so radically questioned and finally taken away. But, of course, it is an even greater help, when the common necessity of worrying about our own situation is so radically relativised and in fact basically set aside. But however that may be, a central convulsion, indeed a revolution, has brought about the supplanting of our *causae* by the *causa Dei* (which does not demand our anxiety and activity but only our faith and obedience). In the light of this decrease on our side and increase on the other, we are again reminded of all that we have tried to say positively about the possibility of the revelation of God to man.

We will close with some words of John the Baptist in the Fourth Gospel, which again confront us with the riddle of the subjective possibility of revelation and the solution of this riddle : " A man can receive nothing, except it be given him from heaven. Ye yourselves bear me witness, that I said, I am not the Christ, but that I am sent before him. He that hath the bride is the bridegroom : but the friend of the bridegroom, which standeth and heareth him, rejoiceth greatly because of the bridegroom's voice : this my joy therefore is fulfilled. . . . He that hath received his testimony hath set to his seal that God is true. . . . The Father loveth the Son, and hath given all things into his hand. He that believeth on the Son hath eternal life " (Jn. 3[27-29. 33. 35f.]). Calvin (*Comm. on Jn.* 3[33] *C.R.* 47, 74) writes concerning the saying about confirmation of the veracity of God by our receiving of the witness of Christ : *Quantus est hic honos, quo miseros homunciones dignatur Deus, ut qui natura nihil sunt aliud quam mendacium et vanitas, idonei tamen censeantur, qui sacram Dei veritatem subscriptione sua comprobent.* And concerning the saying about faith in the Son, into whose hand the Father's love hath given all things (on *Jn.* 3[35], *ib.* 47, 75) : *Facit enim hoc amor, quo Filium amplexus nos quoque in eo amplectitur, ut per illius manum nobis bona sua omnia communicet.*

THE REVELATION OF GOD AS THE ABOLITION OF RELIGION

The revelation of God in the outpouring of the Holy Spirit is the judging but also reconciling presence of God in the world of human religion, that is, in the realm of man's attempts to justify and to sanctify himself before a capricious and arbitrary picture of God. The Church is the locus of true religion, so far as through grace it lives by grace.

1. THE PROBLEM OF RELIGION IN THEOLOGY

The event of God's revelation has to be understood and expounded as it is attested to the Church of Jesus Christ by Holy Scripture. It is within this concrete relationship that theology has to work. That is why when we asked how God does and can come to man in His revelation, we were compelled to give the clear answer that both the reality and the possibility of this event are the being and action only of God, and especially of God the Holy Spirit. Both the reality and the possibility! It was only for the sake of a better understanding that we could distinguish between the two. And what we had to understand was ultimately just this, that we must seek both of them in God, and only in God. Therefore we could not take the distinction seriously. We could not fix the reality of revelation in God, and yet find in man a possibility for it. We could not ascribe the event to God, and yet attribute to man the instrument and point of contact for it. We could not regard divine grace as the particular feature and man's suitability and capacity as the universal. We could not interpret God as the substance and man as the form. We could not, therefore, regard the event of revelation as an interplay between God and man, between grace and nature. On the contrary, as we tried to be faithful to Holy Scripture as the only valid testimony to revelation, we saw that we were committed to the statement that as an event which encounters man, this event represents a self-enclosed circle. Not only the objective but also the subjective element in revelation, not only its actuality but also its potentiality, is the being and action of the self-revealing God alone.

But this revelation is in fact an event which encounters man. It is an event which has at least the form of human competence, experience and activity. And it is at this point that we come up against the problem of man's religion. The revelation of God by the Holy Spirit is real and possible as a determination of man's existence. If we deny this, how can we think of it as revelation ? But if we do not deny it, we have to recognise that it has at least the aspect and character of a human phenomenon. It is something which may be grasped historically and psychologically. We can inquire into its nature and structure and value as we can in the case of all others. We can compare it with other phenomena of a more or less similar type. We can understand it and judge it according to that comparison. But the sphere to which this problem introduces us is the sphere of religion. On their subjective side, too, we have tried as strictly and logically as possible to expound the reality and possibility of revelation as the divine reality and possibility. But how could we do that without having to speak no less definitely and concretely about an encounter and fellowship between God and man, about the Church and the sacrament, about a definite existence and attitude of man in the presence of God ? And in speaking about these things we have spoken about things which are human. They are singular, perhaps, but not unique. They are astounding, but not inconceivable. And they are not unparalleled elsewhere. From this aspect what we call revelation seems necessarily to be only a particular instance of the universal which is called religion. " Christianity " or the " Christian religion " is one predicate for a subject which may have other predicates. It is a species within a genus in which there may be other species. Apart from and alongside Christianity there is Judaism, Islam, Buddhism, Shintoism and every kind of animistic, totemistic, ascetic, mystical and prophetic religion. And again, we would have to deny revelation as such if we tried to deny that it is also Christianity, that it has this human aspect, that from this standpoint it can be compared with other human things, that from this standpoint it is singular but certainly not unique. We have to recognise the fact calmly, and calmly think it through. If we are going to know and acknowledge the revelation of God as revelation, then there is this general human element which we cannot avoid or call by any other name. It is always there even apart from Christianity as one specific area of human competence, experience and activity, as one of the worlds within the world of men.

Cf. for what follows, Edvard Lehmann, " Die Erscheinungs-und Ideenwelt der Religion " (in Chantepie de la Saussaye, *Lehrbuch der Religionsgeschichte* 1925 vol. 1, pp. 23–130).

Always and even necessarily men seem to feel that they are confronted by definite forces which stand over their own life and that of the world and influence it. Even at the most primitive cultural levels they seem to be aware not only of nature but also of the spirit and of spirits and their operation. Human culture in general and human existence in detail seem always and everywhere to be related by men to something ultimate and decisive, which is at least a powerful rival to their own will and power.   Both culture and existence seem to have been determined or partly determined by a reverence for something ostensibly more than man, for some Other or wholly Other, for a supreme Relative or even the Absolute.   There seems always and everywhere to be an awareness of the reality and possibility of a dedication, or even a sanctification of the life of man, on the basis of an individual or social striving, which is almost always and everywhere referred to an event which comes from beyond.   As a result, the representation of the object and aim of the striving, or of the origin of the event, has always and everywhere been compressed into pictures of deities, with almost always and everywhere the picture of a supreme and only deity more or less clearly visible in the background.   It is difficult to find any time or place when man was not aware of his duty to offer worship to God or gods in the form of concrete cults : by occupying himself with pictures and symbols of deity, by sacrifice, acts of atonement, and prayers, by customs, games and mysteries, by the formation of communions and churches.   It is difficult to find any time or place when it was not thought that the voice of the deity had been heard and that it ought to be asserted and its meaning investigated.   The Veda to the Indians, the Avesta to the Persians, the Tripitaka to the Buddhists, the Koran to its believers : are they not all " bibles " in exactly the same way as the Old and New Testaments ? Are not at any rate the elements and problems in the basic outlook of all religions the same as those of Christian doctrine : the world's beginning and end, the origin and nature of man, moral and religious law, sin and redemption ?   And even in its supreme and finest forms, although it may be at the highest level, is not Christian " piety " on the same scale as all other forms of piety ?   And what are the criteria by which the highest place is necessarily accorded to it ?

To allow that there is this whole world apart from and alongside " Christianity " is to recognise that in His revelation God has actually entered a sphere in which His own reality and possibility are encompassed by a sea of more or less adequate, but at any rate fundamentally unmistakable, parallels and analogies in human realities and possibilities.   The revelation of God is actually the presence of God and therefore the hiddenness of God in the world of human religion.   By God's revealing of Himself the divine particular is hidden in a human universal, the divine content in a human form, and therefore that which is divinely unique in something which is humanly only singular. Because and in so far as it is God's revelation to man, God Himself, and the outpouring of the Holy Spirit, and therefore the incarnation of the Word, can be seen from this side too, in the hiddenness which is obviously given to it along with its true humanity as a religious phenomenon, as a member of that series, as a particular concept within general observation and experience, as one content of a human form, which can have other contents and in which the divine uniqueness of that content cannot be perceived directly.

We have to make the point even sharper by adding that the impression that we are dealing with human religion is no less strong and certain when the Church feels bound to speak about the divine revelation. Indeed, it is even stronger and more pronounced here than in other departments of religious history. It is no accident that expositions of the general phenomenology of religion usually take their most striking examples of the most various types of religious formation and action from the Bible (and the history of the Christian Church), as though we had here—in the phrase of A. v. Harnack—a " compendium of the history of religion." If it is true, as A. v. Harnack thinks, that the man who knows this religion knows all religion, then we certainly cannot isolate the " Christian religion " more easily from the general world of religion than we can all other religions. D. F. Strauss deserves a hearing at least when he makes the following criticism of those who defend the supernatural revealedness of Christianity : " Because the fruit is now before us, separated as ripe fruits usually are, from the twig and stalk which bore them, it is supposed not to have grown on a tree, but to have fallen direct from heaven. What a childish idea ! And even when we can point out the very stalk by which it was attached to the maternal branch ; even when in its growth we can see clearly its unmistakable relationship to other similar fruits ; even when we can still find on its surface traces of the sun which has irradiated it and the hailstones which have bruised it, and the prick of evil insects which have attacked it : it is still argued that it cannot have sprung from any earthly stem or ripened in our atmosphere " (*Die chr. Glaubenslehre*, vol. 1, 1840, p. 352).

If we do not wish to deny God's revelation as revelation, we cannot avoid the fact that it can also be regarded from a standpoint from which it may in certain circumstances be denied as God's revelation. In fact, it can and must also be regarded as " Christianity," and therefore as religion, and therefore as man's reality and possibility. In this section we will have to show what exactly we mean by this " also." But first we have to see clearly the question which it poses, and the basic elements in the twofold possibility of answering it.

The question raised by the fact that God's revelation has also to be regarded as a religion among other religions is basically the plain question whether theology and the Church and faith are able and willing to take themselves, or their basis, seriously. For there is an extremely good chance that they will not take themselves and their basis seriously. The problem of religion is simply a pointed expression of the problem of man in his encounter and communion with God. It is, therefore, a chance to fall into temptation. Theology and the Church and faith are invited to abandon their theme and object and to become hollow and empty, mere shadows of themselves. On the other hand, they have the chance to keep to their proper task, to become really sure in their perception of it, and therefore to protect and strengthen themselves as what they profess to be. In this decision the point at issue cannot be whether God's revelation has also to be regarded as man's religion, and therefore as a religion among other religions. We saw that to deny this statement would be to deny the human aspect of revelation, and this would be to deny revelation as such. But the question arises how the statement has to be interpreted and applied. Does it mean that what we think we know of the nature and incidence of religion must serve as a norm and principle by which to explain the revelation of God ; or, *vice versa*, does it mean that we have to interpret the Christian religion and all other religions by what we are told by God's revelation ? There is an obvious difference between regarding religion as *the* problem of theology and regarding it as only one problem in theology. There is an obvious difference between regarding the Church as a religious brotherhood and regarding it as a state in which even religion is " sublimated " in the most comprehensive sense of the word. There is an obvious difference between regarding faith as a form of human piety and regarding it as a form of the judgment and grace of God, which is naturally and most concretely connected with man's piety in all its forms. That is the decision which has to be made.

We are touching upon one of the most difficult historical puzzles when we assert that in the manifestations of modern Protestantism in the 19th and 20th centuries, as it developed from its 16th and 17th century root, the great characteristic decisions have all gone on the side of the first alternatives. It was and is a characteristic of its theological thinking, so far as it here concerns us (in relation to its conception and formulating of the Church and its life), that in its great representatives and outstanding tendencies what it has discerned and declared is not the religion of revelation but the revelation of religion.

As a text for what follows : " The word religion is introduced in the most decided opposition to the word faith so prevalent in the Lutheran, Reformed and Catholic Churches, and it presupposes the Deistic criticism of the universally Christian concept of revelation. Do we still want to assert that we are in the sphere of the Reformation ? " (Paul de Lagarde, *Deutsche Schriften*, 4th impression, p. 46).

Thomas Aquinas (*S. Theol.* II 2 *qu.* 81 f.) spoke of the general (moral) virtue of *religio* and (*ib. qu.* 186 f.) of the specifically monkish *religio*. Occasionally he described the object of theology as *christiana religio* (e.g., in the Prologue to the *S. Theol.*) or as *religio fidei*. But when he did this he had obviously no thought of a non-Christian " religion." What we call that seems then not to have been known by that name. And the concept of religion as a general concept, to which the Christian religion must be subordinated as one with others, was obviously quite foreign to him. In substance, the problem had been raised early in the Middle Ages by Claudius of Turin, John Scot Erigena and Abelard. But it did not and could not have any great importance until after the Renaissance.

After the humanistic fashion, Calvin spoke of the *religio christiana* even in the title of his *chef d'oeuvre*. But when he did so he was not conscious of making *christiana* the predicate of something human in a neutral and universal sense. What Calvin (*Instit.* I 2, 2) describes as *pura germanaque religio : fides cum serio dei timore coniuncta, ut timor et voluntariam reverentiam in se contineat et secum trahat legitimum cultum qualis in lege praescribitur*—is obviously a normative concept which he has derived from Holy Scripture, and in which the universal is sublimated in the particular, religion in revelation, and not *vice versa*. Certainly Calvin ascribes to fallen man an inalienable *semen* of this religion (I 3, 1 f.).

But over against it he sets the knowledge that this *semen* cannot ripen, let alone bear fruit in anyone (I 4, 1 ; 12, 1). Therefore the concept of *religio* as a general and neutral form has no fundamental significance in Calvin's conception and exposition of Christianity. For him *religio* is an entity x, which receives content and form only as it is equated with Christianity, i.e., because as it is taken up into revelation and fashioned by it.

In general the older orthodox (J. Gerhard and L. Huttêrus among the Lutherans, Bucan and H. Alting, Gomarus and Voetius, and even J. Cocceius among the Reformed) avoided any systematic treatment or discussion of the concept " religion." This was true even of some of the later ones, J. W. Baier on the one side, and F. Turrettini and P. v. Mastricht on the other. For Baier (*Comp. Theol. pos.*, 1686, Prol. I 7 f.) religion is still only the essence of the possibilities of a *theologia naturalis* which is inadequate for the knowledge of salvation. Neither materially nor formally is revelation related to religion. The two Basel men, Polanus and (his obvious disciple) Wolleb, are a striking exception even at the beginning of the 17th century. But even in these two the doctrine of religion is not placed at the head of the system under the theological principles of knowledge. Perhaps on the model of Thomas Aquinas, it is introduced under ethics, as an introduction to the exposition of the commandments of the first table, and especially to commandments 2–4. And as in Calvin, it is filled out as the doctrine of the true, i.e., the one, necessary religion founded by God Himself, which is identical with the Christian religion, i.e., the Christian religion as inwardly apprehended by man (A. Polanus, *Synt. Theol.*, 1609, p. 3694 f.). Apart from Christianity there is only false and hypocritical religion and irreligiosity (p. 3718). For the natural man, who is a liar, is incapable of true religion, not only from the standpoint of the will but also from that of knowledge (p. 3710). *Vere religio sola proprie est, aliae non sunt, sed dicuntur esse* (p. 3697). Therefore there can be no question of a freedom of choice between this and other religions (p. 3718). At the same time, we can find in J. Wolleb (*Christ. Theol. comp.*, 1626, II 4, 1) the very thing which Polanus obviously tried to avoid. It is concealed and rendered innocuous by the context, but it is there all the same : a general and neutral definition of the concept " religion " (*Religio . . . generali significatione omnem Dei cultum, specialiter cultum Dei immediatum, specialissime vero aut internum solum aut externum et internum simul denotat*), to which the concept *vera religio* (*ib.* 4, 3) can be subordinated as a species. In a Dutch pupil of Polanus, Anton Walaeus (*Loci comm.*, 1640, p. 31 f.), and in the *Synopsis purioris Theol.*, Leiden 1624 *Disp.* 2 17–20 (this disputation took place under the presidency of Walaeus himself), the concept " religion " occurs in a quite different and more captious context, namely in the proofs for establishing the authority and necessity of Holy Scripture. According to Walaeus this is supported by the fact that in Holy Scripture the *vera et salutaris religio* is transmitted, i.e., the *christiana religio*, which has all the notes (*notae*) of the *vera et divina religio*. The *notae* are given as follows : (1) the *vera veri Dei notitia*, (2) the *vera ratio reconciliationis hominis cum Deo*, (3) the *verus Dei cultus*. These *notae* are found in the Christian religion taught in the Bible and not elsewhere. In them we recognise—and this is an unfortunate phrase—*conscientia hominum id ipsis dictante* (*Syn.* 2, 18) : *haec natura ipsa docet in religione vera requiri* (Walaeus, p. 32)—the signs of true religion. And because of them we believe that the Bible is of divine origin and therefore necessary. This is an unambiguous hint at a general concept of religion which is known by virtue of the voice of conscience or of nature. It may be regarded as innocuous because it has importance " only " apologetically, in the content of arguments for the authenticity of Holy Scripture as against atheists on the one hand and the Papacy on the other. But once it is introduced, how long will it have " only " an apologetic importance ? Does it not actually have more weight with Walaeus than he himself concedes ? We have to raise the question, for in him and in the Leiden Synopsis only a very incidental part is played by the reason for the recognition of the divine nature of Holy Scripture which was for Calvin (*Instit.* I 6–8) the one and only reason beside which all other arguments (I 8, 13) could be considered only as *secundaria nostrae imbecillitatis adminicula* (with no mention at all of any argument *e vera religione*). That reason is the *testimonium Spiritus sancti internum*. But now does not the recognition rest upon these secondary arguments and therefore, as far as the *argumentum e vera religione* is concerned, upon the general idea of religion which is supposedly known to us by conscience and nature ? And what will that mean for the exposition and application of Holy Scripture ? For Walaeus and the Leiden men it does not actually amount to much. But we can already foresee what it will amount to some day. A. Heidan (*Corp. Theol. chᵛ.*, 1676, L I p. 7 f.) took up a highly individual position. Like many of his theological contemporaries, particularly in Holland, his obvious aim was to unite Calvin and Descartes. To the salvation of the Calvinist components, he equally obviously succeeded only in drawing some very remarkable parallelisms. No one can emphasise more strongly than he did the fact that faith and theology must be based on revelation. *Cum religio sit rectus Dei cultus, atque ille in vero de Deo sensu et recto erga eum affectu consistat, atque ille a nobis effingi non possit aut debeat neque sit partus ingenii nostri, a Deo ipso cui cultus ille praestandus est, praescribi nobis debuit. Ille enim solus ideoneus est de se testis* (Calvin, *Instit.* I 7, 4 !) *qui quod sibi gratum est, docere nos possit et cui nihil gratum esse potest, nisi a se profectum et naturae suae conveniens. Quod quale sit nemo novit nisi ipse. At id quomodo innotescat, nisi nobis ab ipso patefiat et reveletur ?* (p. 12). It must seem that a general conception of religion was impossible on these premises. But then Heidan remembers the atheists of his time, and his Cartesian heart begins to flutter. There is a *naturalis Dei cognitio, quae singulis hominibus innata est* (p. 8). If this were not the case, how could it become a reality in us by tradition and instruction ? (p. 9). The existence of God can be proved *a priori*, by way of the ontological argument (p. 11). *Cum Deum cogito, concipio ens perfectissimum, numen potentissimum, sapientissimum* . . . (p. 12). And *ex hac notitia Dei ortum habet religio* (p. 13). It seems that a general concept of religion has been reached. But Calvin stirs again and for his sake the deduction that *rectam rationem fuisse normam primaevae religionis* is indignantly rejected : in fact, Adam had knowledge of God only by revelation (p. 13). *Deus non potest concipi sine verbo.* Without revelation we can have no knowledge of God (p. 14). *Illa recta ratio est mera chimaera, cerebri humani commentum* (p. 15). Obviously the introduction of the general concept is only an apologetic interlude. As soon as he forgets the atheists, Heidan again speaks only as a theologian of revelation. In his doctrine of Holy Scripture it is noticeable that he does not make any use of the *argumentum e vera religione*. In his case, too, the coming of a new outlook is only intimated. He obviously took it for granted that the contradictions amid which he moved would not be felt as contradictions by him personally. But it is evident that the problem could not be left at that stage. An important and serious step forward was made when M. F. Wendelin (*Chr. Theol. lib. duo*, 1634, I, 1) tried to make the *vera religio* the *objectum theologiae*, distinguishing it from God as its *causa efficiens principalis* and from Holy Scripture as its *causa efficiens instrumentalis*, and putting it at the head of his theological system as a form-concept. How does it come about that this subject, which was hardly referred to even incidentally by most of the older men, and was treated by Polan and Wolleb only in the context of ethics and by Walaeus as one " argument " with others in the doctrine of Holy Scripture, is now promoted to this high position ? Now Wendelin is not guilty of filling out the concept *vera religio* from *conscientia* and *natura*, nor does he introduce it as an apologetic element into his doctrine of Scripture. On the contrary, the concept is filled out by him in a wholly objective and Christian way ; *vera religio* is the *ratio agnoscendi colendique Deum a Deo praescripta ad hominis salutem Deique gloriam* or the *norma agnoscendi colendique Deum perfecta et mere divina in sacris literis consignata* ; to that extent it is *divinum quiddam et infallibile, a quo provocare nemini fas est.* Wendelin obviously means that it is God's revelation in its subjective reality. But why is it emphasised in this way ? we may ask—just as it is in the contemporary hymn. Yet it is still characterised and emphasised as God's revelation, and the secret catastrophe has not yet come to light! The same can still be said of F. Burmann. Of course, more striking accents are now noticeable : the compromises of Walaeus and Wendelin, an apologetic rationalising of the concept of religion on the one hand, and its systematic over-emphasis on the other, are now seen in heightened form. As opposed to his teacher Cocceius, Burmann opens his *Synopsis Theologiae* (1678) with a big chapter, " *De religione et theologia,*" in which the main concept is that of the *creatura rationalis* striving after God, but attaining to God by God (I 2, 1). Again we find the definition that *religio* is the *ratio cognoscendi et colendi Deum.* But now an ambiguous *recta* replaces the addition which pointed expressly to revelation (2, 4) : *a Deo praescripta* or *in sacris literis consignata.* And of this *religio* as the *ratio recta cognoscendi et colendi Deum* it can be said that *fluit ex ipsa Dei hominisque natura cum creaturam rationalem nihil aeque deceat, quam Dei . . . excellentiam summasque virtutes venerare ac colere. Inde religio necessaria et naturalis rationis sequela est ; atque adeo datur religio naturalis* (2, 6–7). Yet the possible and apparently necessary deductions are not drawn by Burmann. As he sees it, the natural religion of the sinner does not attain its goal because he is a sinner (2, 11) : *vera religio a solo Deo eiusque revelatione dependet,* and the only *vera religio* is the *christiana religio* (2, 19). It is known to be *vera* by the fact that it has the characteristics of true religion ; i.e., it gives us the *verum medium* and the *vera ratio* for communion with God (2, 18). We were told similar things in Walaeus. But as distinct from Walaeus, Burmann did not expressly point to conscience or to nature as the source of these *notae.* And yet, like Wendelin, he did not expressly point to Holy Scripture. Perhaps in his case, too, we can accept the explanation : *huic ergo verae religioni unice adhaerescendum est* (2, 29) ; and the fact that from this point his Synopsis is a straightforward theology of revelation and Scripture. There were similar developments on the Lutheran side. This is true even of the representatives of Lutheran High Orthodoxy in the second half of the 17th century, e.g., in A. Calov, *Syst. loc. theol.* I, 1655, c. 2, in J. F. König, *Theologiae pos. accroam.* 1664, § 57 f., in A. Quenstedt, *Theol. did. pol.*, 1685, I 2. In all of them (except Baier) we find that the chapter on Holy Scripture, the *principium Theol. cognoscendi,* is preceded by one entitled " *De religione christiana,*" which is described as the *obiectum theologiae generale.* But both theoretically and practically the *religio christiana* arises only in relation to the *religio paradisiaca* of Adam prior to the Fall. It is expressly declared that the concept *religio* can be applied only *improprie, abusive, per nefas* to the worship of God by the heathen, Turks and Jews, or even Roman Catholics. And theoretically and practically the concept is filled out only from scriptural sources, or, to be more exact, only from what is regarded as Christian. *Religio vera* and *religio falsa,* or, better, *religio* and *superstitio,* are still opposed the one to the other like heaven and earth. In the entity described as *religio christiana* we can still recognise what we call the subjective reality of revelation. It is just that there is a change of emphasis. The question of the *religio christiana* has acquired an autonomous interest. Even worse, as in Calov (*c. 2 sect. 2 qu.* 6), the discussion of the dangerous problem : *Utrum religio christiana vera sit ?* reveals a strange vacillation between spiritual and carnal argumentation. Yet even here no one can point to a single passage in which there is any notable deviation from the line adopted by Calvin. As a Lutheran parallel to Burmann we might mention D. Hollaz (*Ex. theol. acroam,* 1707). The corresponding chapter in his work is entitled " *De religione et articulis fidei* " (Prol. 2). The problem of a general concept of religion occupied him for the length of two questions. And he is distinguished from Calov, König and Quenstedt, as Burmann is from Wendelin, by the fact that in the definition of *religio christiana* as *ratio colendi Deum* the addition of *A Deo praescripta* is missing. Instead, the declaration of his predecessors, that this *ratio* definitely consists in faith in Christ, is in his case enriched by the addition *sincera in Deum proximumque caritas*. Hollaz is one of the last and strictest representatives of the theory of verbal inspiration. Therefore theoretically he was a scriptural theologian. Yet the Bible was not so important to him that he had to mention it consistently at the point where mention of it has such a basic importance. Such was the power of that concern which was then about to make itself autonomous and all-powerful under the caption *religio*. And yet later when he defines *vera religio* (more clearly than in a Walaeus or a Burmann) he has at the very heart of it the qualification *quae verbo divino est conformis*. And there can be no question that he finds the one true religion in that which is built upon the foundation of Jesus Christ (and which he identifies with the *religio evangelica, quae a ministerio Lutheri cognomen accepit*).

In this as in other matters the catastrophe occurred, and Neo-Protestantism was truly and openly born, in the movement of so-called rational orthodoxy at the beginning of the 18th century. We can watch it happen in two theologians, on the Reformed side Salomon van Til (1643–1713, *Theologiae utriusque compendium cum naturalis tum revelatae* 1704), and on the Lutheran J. Franz Buddeus (1667–1729, *Institutiones Theologiae dogmaticae*, 1724). In form Buddeus was a disciple of Baier. But the difference in content is apparent at once, particularly in the present question. Dogmatics now begin quite openly and unilaterally—and in van Til it is the complete dogmatics of a *theologia naturalis* constituting a first and autonomous section—with the presupposition of the concept and the description of a general and natural and neutral "religion," which **as** *religio in se spectata* is the presupposition of all religions. *Ut enim a natura homo habet, quod ratione sit praeditus, ita, quod et Deum esse et eundem rite colendum agnoscit, non minus naturae ipsi acceptum ferre debet* (Buddeus I 1, 3). As is the intellectual equipment, so is the knowledge of God ? As a convinced Cartesian van Til appears ready to take even a further step when he declares : *Principium ex quo religio naturalis, quoad certam de Deo eiusque cultu demonstrationem hauriri debet est ipsum lumen rationis in mente hominis per notiones insitas et communes conspicuum, ita ut nemo attentior et praeiudiciis liberatus illud ignorare possit* (*Prael.* 4, 1). The definition of this *religio naturalis* is as follows : It is the *certum hominum studium, quo quisque pro sua sententia facultates suas in certi luminis contemplatione et observantia ita tenet occupatas, prout sibi existimat convenire, ut numen illud reddat sibi quocunque in casu propitium* (*Prael.* 2, 1). On the basis of this *religio naturalis* Buddeus (I 1, 5–13) holds that there is knowledge of a supreme being (*ens perfectissimum, quod Deum vocamus*) who unites in Himself the perfection of knowledge, wisdom and freedom, who is eternal and almighty, and perfectly kind and upright, and true and holy, who is the final cause and ruling principle in all things, who is absolutely unique, to whom we owe obedience and responsibility, who opens up for us the prospect of an immortal life of the soul and an ultimate reward,, without whose love we cannot be happy because He alone is the supreme good, who wills to be worshipped by us in word and work and thought, who imposes on us definite duties towards ourselves, our fellow-men and finally Himself. Van Til, in part I of his compendium, develops this natural theology in a broad doctrine of the nature and attributes of God, creation and providence, the moral law of nature, the immortality of the soul, and even sin. And all this can be known by man *facili negotio* (Buddeus I 1, 5). *Cum ratio omnes homines luculenter edoceat eaque ita comparata sint, ut, siquis usu rationis polleat, sanaque mente sit praeditus, quam primum ista intelligit, statim praebere assensum teneatur* (I 1, 14). Buddeus will not concede a substantial *verbum* or *lumen internum*, as taught by many mystics, i.e., he will not assert formally the existence of a second source of revelation (I 1, 15).

Nor will van Til allow anything of this kind; at all events in the *Dedicatio* of his work he warns young theologians, *ne principium rationis eodem cum principio fidei habeant loco*, because the two are not equally evidenced. But what about that *prima scientia*, man's original knowledge of himself and God, which he then defines and describes as the presupposition of natural religion (*Prael.* 3) ? Once we accept this knowledge, how far can we or ought we to say that after all it is not so well evidenced as that which comes from revelation ? Be that as it may, at least Buddeus does not forget to make the immediate and well-known reservation of all exponents of natural theology : that the *religio naturalis* and its knowledge of God do not extend to eternal salvation, because with all these insights the means of fellowship with God, the supreme Good, and the right use of that means, have not yet been given to man. He therefore points us away to the indispensable supplementing of the *religio naturalis* by revelation (I 1, 16–18). At a later stage, at the end of the first and the beginning of the second part of his compendium, we finally come to the same reservation in van Til. And yet, according to Buddeus, we still have to say of this *religio naturalis* that it contains the *notiones* which are the *bases et fundamenta omnis religionis*. It is by these *notiones* that man has to be measured in respect of religion. It is on the ground of these *notiones* that we can recognise as such the *religiones, quae revelatione nituntur*. Whatever contradicts these *notiones* of *religio naturalis* is either not revelation at all or revelation misunderstood. According to Buddeus natural religion does us a twofold educational service. By its insufficiency it enables us to see the necessity for revelation. And by its directions it enables us to find true revelation. Buddeus thinks that he can guarantee that natural religion and revelation will never contradict each other, but always correspond (I 1, 19–20). And in van Til natural theology culminates in a doctrine *De praeparatione evangelica*, in which : (1) from the presuppositions and data of natural religion there is logically postulated the necessity of a reconciliation between God and man ; (2) again on the principles of natural religion the conditions of such a reconciliation are adduced ; and (3) and lastly, the heathen, Jewish, Mohammedan and Christian religions are mutually compared, and the latter is shown to answer to the adduced conditions and is therefore recognisable as the revealed religion. *Theologia naturalis . . . ad ista rationes dictamina religiones qualescunque explorat, ut inde elicias, religionem christianam (licet mysteria agnoscat naturalis scientiae limites excellentia) tamen plus quam reliquas cum lumine naturae consentire (Praef. ad lectorem)*. That is the programme which van Til and Buddeus set themselves and carried out to the best of their ability (the first time that such a programme was ever put forward in Protestantism without being condemned as unconfessional).

What they achieved, and all the leading theologians of the time co-operated, in the movement, can never be overestimated either in its basic significance or in the seriousness of its historical consequences. With these theologians there emerged clearly and logically what was perhaps the secret *telos* and *pathos* of the whole preceding development. Human religion, the relationship with God which we can and actually do have apart from revelation, is not an unknown but a very well-known quantity both in form and content, and as such it is something which has to be reckoned with, as having a central importance for all theological thinking. It constitutes, in fact, the presupposition, the criterion, the necessary framework for an understanding of revelation. It shows us the question which is answered by revealed religion as well as all other positive religions, and it is as the most satisfactory answer that the Christian religion has the advantage over others and is rightly described as revealed religion. The Christian element—and with this the theological re-orientation which had threatened since the Renaissance is completed—has now actually become a predicate of the neutral and universal human element. Revelation has now become a historical confirmation of what man can know about himself and therefore about God even apart from revelation. " The light of nature goes even further. It shows me the true characteristics of this revelation. No revelation is true, except it conform to the light of nature and increase it. . . . A true revelation must prove itself such in my heart by a divine power and conviction which I clearly feel . . . which the light of nature teaches, which therefore leads me on and gives me a desire to seek out and challenge such a revelation and in that way to demonstrate the true religion " (C. M. Pfaff, *Einl. in d. Dogmat. Theol.* 1747, p. 27 f., quoted from A. F. Stolzenburg, *Die Theol. des Jo. Franc. Buddeus und des Chr. Matth. Pfaff*, 1926, p. 219 f.).

There is no need to tell in detail the sad story of more recent Protestant theology. Our two examples, Buddeus and van Til, and the other theologians of that generation (C. M. Pfaff, S. Werenfalls, J. A. Turrettini, J. F. Osterwald, J. L. von Mosheim) were all men of an admitted seriousness and piety. And in points of detail they were outspokenly conservative. They knew how to safeguard in their theology the full rights of revelation, at any rate in appearance. Their aim was to find a more or less perfect agreement between the Bible and traditional teaching on the one hand and on the other the postulates of *religio naturalis* and the claims to a genuine religion of revelation to which they give rise. Materially, therefore, they did not make any very striking deviations from the line of 17th-century orthodoxy. And they were still a long way from the parlous stabilising of the relation between reason and revelation which was so soon to emerge in the philosophy of C. Wolff. The main point of this new development was the fact that much the same evidence can be produced for both, and that they should therefore give mutual guarantees of their right of ownership and also of peaceable intercourse in a sphere common to both of them. This untenable compromise preceded the work of the so-called Neologians of the second half of the 18th century. The Neologians could not convince themselves that all or even most of what had so far been regarded as revelation could be substantiated before the critical authority of reason. They thought it right, therefore, to submit Christian dogma, as well as the Bible, to a very severe criticism on the basis of the *notiones* of *religio naturalis*. They were followed by Kantian rationalism which abolished the Neology, reducing *religio naturalis* to an *ethica naturalis*, and ultimately rejecting revelation, except as the actualising of the powers of moral reason. Then Schleiermacher tried to find in religion as feeling the essence of theology, revelation being a definite impression which produces a definite feeling and then a definite religion. Then, according to Hegel and D. F. Strauss both Christian and natural religion are only a dispensable prototype of the absolute awareness of philosophy purified by the idea. Then, according to L. Feuerbach in particular, there is room only for natural religion as the illusory expression of the natural longings and wishes of the human heart. Then A. Ritschl taught that the Christian religion must be regarded as revealed and true, because in it the supreme value of human life, i.e., (the opposite of Feuerbach) its liberation from the world regarded as sensible nature, is most perfectly realised. Then E. Troeltsch taught us that the main task of the theologian is to exercise himself in " entering hypothetically " into the phenomena of general religious history, so that by a comparative assessment of the various worlds of religion he may then see that Christianity is relatively the best religion at any rate for the time being and probably for all conceivable time (this side of the incursion of a new ice age). And then at last and finally there came that tumultuous invasion of the Church and theology by natural religion whose astonished witnesses we have been in our day. Of all this, of course, the doughty van Til and the equally doughty Buddeus never even dreamed. Yet they and their generation must still be regarded as the real fathers of Neo-Protestant theology, for which the way was not unprepared by the very different Reformation tradition. All these more or less radical and destructive movements in the history of theology in the last two centuries are simply variations on one simple theme, and that theme was clearly introduced by van Til and Buddeus : that religion has not to be understood in the light of revelation, but revelation in the light of religion. To this common denominator the aims and the programmes of all the more important tendencies of modern theology can be reduced. Neo-Protestantism means " religionism." Even the conservative theology of these centuries, the supra-naturalistic of the 18th and the confessional, biblicistic and " positive " of the 19th and 20th, has, on the whole, co-operated, making such concessions to the prevailing outlook that in spite of the immanent resistance which it has put up it cannot be regarded as a renewal of the Reformation tradition. C. E. Luthardt (*Kompend. d. Dogm.*, 1865, 2) quietly admitted the fact that since the 18th century theology has been " the science of religion " ; " the science of Christianity only in the sense that the Church is the *locus* of Christianity "—no more. And at the end of the Foreword to vol. I of his dogmatics (1925) R. Seeberg calmly remarks that it might have been better to write a " philosophy of religion " instead of a dogmatics ; but interested philosophers and historians would, of course, take it in that way without sharing his particular theological presuppositions. Weighing all the circumstances, we must regard an utterance of this kind as a more significant and serious symptom than the very worst pages in the books of a Strauss or a Feuerbach. It shows that at the end of the period which started with Buddeus theology had lost any serious intention of taking itself seriously as theology.

Why have we to judge this development negatively as a disruption of the life of the Church, and ultimately as a heresy which destroys it ? Those who carried through the development, the great and with them the countless lesser theologians of Neo-Protestantism, have always felt that in opposition to mere tradition and its concerns they were the representatives of a free investigation of the truth even in relation to God and the things of God. They felt that they were this legitimately and by commission. And those who more or less resolutely opposed them demonstrated the purely immanent character of their opposition by the fact that on the whole they would not go so far in accepting the consequences of that reversal of revelation and religion. They made it clear that if not quite so logically they themselves stood right in the centre of that development. From the standpoint of a merely conservative outlook and attitude no serious objection or amendment could or can be alleged against the development. Against the basic proposition that truth must be freely investigated even in the field of theology, there is nothing to be said. As two hundred years of the history of theology have consistently shown, the man who rejects that proposition will inevitably and rightly cut a poor figure. Even if he does really represent the Church's interest as against that development, he is a poor and dangerous representative of that interest. And the question whether he really does intend the Church's interest, and is not at bottom howling with the wolves, can never be put to him too sharply as occasion offers. The motive for resisting that reversal ought not to be fear of its consequences.

It ought not to be fear of that reconstruction of dogma and biblical doctrine, as it was carried through in the 18th century by an application of the criterion of *religio naturalis*. It ought not to be fear of Kantian moralism or Schleiermacher's theology of feeling, of Feuerbach's illusionism, of the Bible criticism of a D. F. Strauss or an F. C. Baur, a Harnack or a Bousset, of the relativism of the history-of-religion school, etc. Of course, all these and much else are possible and actual consequences of that reversal, and they are still active to-day in spite of its relatively respectable antiquity. But we cannot be afraid of the consequences and repudiate them unless it is perfectly clear that we are not co-operating in that reversal of revelation and religion. To put it concretely, we are defenceless against the " German Christians " of our own time, unless we know how to guard against the development which took place in van Til and Buddeus, and even earlier : as early as König and Quenstedt, Wendelin and Burmann.

If we do not know this, if we argue against them in detail and not as a whole, and only from conservatism, i.e., fear, and not from know-ledge, then we are lost, no matter how good may be our intentions or what victories we achieve in points of detail. What serves and helps the Church is not to soften or weaken the heresy which has infiltrated into it, but to know it, to fight it and to isolate it. If the dreaded results of the reversal of revelation and religion could really be claimed as the results of free, theological inquiry into the truth, then however novel or dangerous they might appear to be, the Church would have to recognise them as good and necessary, or at any rate as open to discussion and not disruptive of the fellowship of the Church. It is not because they are novel and dangerous, but because in fact they certainly are not the results of free, theological investigation of truth, that they can and should and must be opposed, radically and seriously opposed. The opposition must be directed—not contrary to the free investigation of truth but for the sake of it—against the point at which the results arise and emerge. But the point at which they arise and emerge is an uncertainty in the conception of revelation and the resultant relationship between God and man, which simply means an uncertainty, or decline of faith. If we are to try to explain that historical development, then—with all the caution and reserve which a judgment of this kind demands—we have to say that Protestant theology would never have conceived of reversing the relationship between revelation and religion if it had not shared with the whole Church of the time in a widespread vacillation concerning something which the Reformers had so clearly perceived and confessed. This was that the decision about man has been taken once and for all and in every respect in Jesus Christ. Jesus Christ is now his Lord, and man belongs to Him, and lives under Him in His kingdom, and serves Him, and therefore has all his consolation in life or death in the fact that he is not his own but is the property of Jesus Christ. Of course the Neo-Protestant theologians have said this. In fact they have usually left the confession of the Reformation " untouched." But the older Protestant theologians did not leave it untouched. They made use of it, i.e., when they pursued theology they thought or at any rate tried to think in accordance with this confession. They reck-oned inflexibly with the fact that things actually are as they said in the confession, and they did not reckon with the fact that in part they might be otherwise. That is why the theology of the Reformers, and at bottom of all the older Protestantism, was a free investigation of truth. For it meant that their theological thinking as such could always be free, free for its own inexhaustible object. It meant that having that object, it would remain true to itself. It did not need any other attractions or distractions or enslavements from alien points of view. Their theological thinking had the freedom of unconditioned relevance ; the freedom of faith, we must say, because this unconditioned relevance was none other than that of faith. Of course, we cannot and must not reproach the later theology because the problem of human religion—we can put it more comprehensively and say the problem of man in general—both came to its notice and laid claim to its attention. The period of the 16th–18th centuries was in its own way a great period, when European man resumed the powerful offensive which had been made by Græco-Roman antiquity, beginning to discover himself as a man, his nature, his possibilities and capacities, humanity. The discovery of " religion " belonged, of course, to the same movement. It was in the very nature of things that theology should have its part in that discovery.

To that extent we can only give partial approval to the belief of the older orthodoxy that the problem of religion ought not to be considered at all. It is a sign of the superiority of Calvin's theology that he was able quietly to incorporate this problem into his discussion and exposition. And if the development in the 17th and 18th centuries had been only a sign that Protestant theologians were openly participating in the spiritual movement of their day, we could hardly withhold our approval.

Ignorantly or stubbornly to ignore the anxieties and hopes of the immediate present is something which we do not expect or demand of theology for the sake of the Church. But it is quite a different thing openly to champion the predominant interest or even the demonism of an age, openly to identify oneself with that interest and to become the prisoner of that demonism. This is the very thing which theology must not do. Yet it is what it began to do in the 17th century, and was doing openly in the 18th. It fell prey to the absolutism with which the man of that period made himself the centre and measure and goal of all things. It was its duty to participate in this trend and lovingly to investigate it. But it was certainly not its duty to cooperate in it, which is what it did when in the time of Buddeus it openly turned " religionistic." But it was not what theology did that was really serious. It was what it did not do : its weakness and vacillation in the very substance of faith. In fact and in practice it ceased to regard the cardinal statements of the Lutheran and Heidelberg confessions as definite axioms. Originally and properly the sin was one of unbelief. It was that belittling of Christ which begins the moment He is no longer accepted as our One and All and we are secretly dissatisfied with His lordship and consolation. Without denying the catechetical statements, this later theology thought that it should reckon seriously with man from another standpoint than that of the kingdom and ownership of Christ. It separated his own piety from the Word of God spoken to him, making of it a distinct and prior chapter. The danger was obvious that the chapter might become autonomous and, in fact, predominant, ultimately absorbing the chapter on the Word of God. And this was the inevitable result of that negation, that surrender in the very substance of faith. The real catastrophe of modern Protestant theology was not as it has often been represented. It was not that it retreated in face of the growing self-consciousness of modern education. It was not that it imperceptibly allowed itself to be told by philosophy and history and natural science what the " free investigation of the truth " really is. It was not that it unwittingly turned into a rather illogical practical wisdom. Of themselves, the modern view of things, the modern self-conception of man, etc., could not have done any harm. The real catastrophe was that theology lost its object, revelation in all its uniqueness. And losing that, it lost the seed of faith with which it could remove mountains, even the mountain of modern humanistic culture. That it really lost revelation is shown by the very fact that it could exchange it, and with it its own birthright, for the concept " religion."

It is always the sign of definite misunderstanding when an attempt is made systematically to co-ordinate revelation and religion, i.e., to treat them as comparable spheres, to mark them off from each other, to fix their mutual relationship. The intention and purpose may be to start at religion, and therefore man, and in that way to subordinate revelation to religion, ultimately perhaps even to let it merge into it. Again, the intention and purpose may be to maintain the autonomy and even the pre-eminence of the sphere of revelation by definite reservations and safeguards. But that is a purely secondary question. For all the many possible solutions, it is not decisive. The decisive thing is that we are in a position to put human religion on the same level and to treat it in the same way as divine revelation. We can regard it as in some sense an equal. We can assign it an autonomous being and status over against revelation. We can ask concerning the comparison and relationship of the two entities. And the fact that we can do this shows that our intention and purpose is to start with religion, that is, with man, and not with revelation. Anything that we say later, within this systematic framework, about the necessity and actuality of revelation, can never be more than the melancholy reminder of a war which was lost at the very outset. It can never be more than an actual veiling of the real message and content. In fact it would be better, because more instructive, if we accepted the logical consequences of our point of departure, and omitted our later efforts on behalf of revelation. For where we think that revelation can be compared or equated with religion, we have not understood it as revelation. Within the problem which now engrosses us it can be understood only where *a priori* and with no possible alternative we accept its superiority over human religion, a superiority which does not allow us even to consider religion except in the light of revelation, far less to make pronouncement as to its nature and value and in that way to treat it as an independent problem. Revelation is understood only where we expect from it, and from it alone, the first and the last word about religion. The inquiry into the problem of religion in theology involves an either-or, in which the slightest deviation, the slightest concession to religionism, at once makes the right answer absolutely impossible.

We may well ask whether this is not much more clearly seen by the opposite side, by the strict exponents of a pure—a really pure—" science of religion," than it is by the theologian whose thinking and activity is informed by the " science of religion." A " pure " science of religion is one which does not make any claim to be theology. For such a science revelation is either (1) the phenomenon common to almost all religions, whereby their cultic, mythical and moral structure is traced back to the activity, imparting and ordering of the Deity, or (2) the strictly defined limiting concept of truth beyond and within the plenitude of religious realities, a concept which cannot as such be treated by the science of religion, let alone filled out in any concrete way. It would be too much to say that the concept of revelation is even respected by this procedure, for genuine respect would necessarily involve a quite different procedure. The purer the science of religion becomes, the more it drinks in that sea of religious realities (in which the phenomenon of revelations is only too plentiful), and the more it is reduced *ad absurdum*. Yet from the standpoint of theology we must still describe its procedure as more sober and instructive and promising than the adulterated science of religion of theologians who, on the one hand, usually spoil the peaceful course of this investigation of religious realities by suddenly taking account of a religious truth of revelation, and, on the other, give evidence, by the philosophical standards of assessment and value which they apply, that they are dealing with something which they are in no position either to understand or to take seriously.

If we are theologically in earnest when we speak of revelation, we shall speak after the manner of those passages in the Catechism. It is a matter of Jesus Christ the Lord. It is a matter of man, therefore, only as he is reached by revelation in order that he may live under Him and serve Him, in order that he may belong not to himself but to Jesus Christ, in order that belonging to Him he may have comfort both in life and in death. But if we deviate only a nail's breadth from this confession, we are not theologically in earnest and we do not speak about revelation at all. Revelation is God's sovereign action upon man or it is not revelation. But the concept " sovereign "— and in the context of the doctrine of the Holy Spirit we can presuppose this as " self-evident " (although not at all self-evidently)—indicates that God is not at all alone, that therefore, if revelation is to be understood, man must not be overlooked or eliminated.   And the same is true of religion, whether by that we mean the Christian religion in particular or human religion in general, to which the Christian religion belongs.   But one thing we are forbidden.   We must not try to know and define and assess man and his religion as it were in advance and independently.   We must not ascribe to him any existence except as the possession of Christ.   We must not treat of him in any other sphere than that of His Kingdom, in any other relationship than that of " subordination to Him."   We must not try to relate him to God's revelation only when we have first taken him seriously in this in-dependent form.   If we do, we say *a priori* that—at least in the un-conditional sense of those passages of the Catechism—Jesus Christ is not his Lord, and he is not the property of Jesus Christ.   We have regarded both these truths as open to discussion.   We have therefore denied revelation, for revelation is denied when it is regarded as open to discussion.   In relating them in that way, we have not spoken about revelation, even though we may later have tried to do so in very earnest and clear and emphatic terms.   We always have to speak about revelation from the very outset if we really want to speak about it later and not about something quite different.   If we only speak about it later, then we are speaking, e.g., about a postulate or an idea. What we are really and properly speaking about is not revelation, but what precedes it, man and his religion, about which we think that we know so much already which we are not ready to give up.   There lies our love, there our interest, there our zeal, there our confidence, there our consolation : and where we have our consolation, there we have our God.   If we only come to revelation later there is nothing that can be altered.   On the other hand, if revelation is not denied but believed, if man and his religion are regarded from the standpoint of those state-ments in the Catechism, then to take man and his religion seriously we cannot seek them in that form which has already been fixed in advance. There can, therefore, be no question of a systematic co-ordination of God and man, of revelation and religion.   For neither in its existence, nor in its relation to the first, can the second be considered, let alone defined, except in the light of the first.   The only thing we can do is to recount the history of the relationships between the two : and even that takes place in such a way that whatever we have to say about the existence and nature and value of the second can only and ex-clusively be made plain in the light of the first, i.e., in the course of God's sovereign action on man.   It is man as he is revealed in the light of revelation, and only that man, who can be seriously treated theologically.   Similarly, the problem of religion in theology is not the question how the reality, religion, which has already been defined (and usually untheologically), can now be brought into an orderly and plausible relationship with the theological concepts, revelation, faith, etc.   On the contrary, the question is uninterruptedly theological :

What is this thing which from the standpoint of revelation and faith is revealed in the actuality of human life as religion ?

If we are to maintain the *analogia fidei* and not to fall into untheological thinking, we must be guided by the christological consideration of the incarnation of the Word as the *assumptio carnis*. The unity of God and man in Jesus Christ is the unity of a completed event. Similarly the unity of divine revelation and human religion is that of an event—although in this case it has still to be completed. As God is the subject of the one event, so, too, He is of the other. The man Jesus has no prior or abstract existence in the one event but exists only in the unity of that event, whose Subject is the Word of God and therefore God Himself : very God and very man. Similarly in the other, man and his religion is to be considered only as the one who follows God because God has preceded the man who hears Him, because he is addressed by God. Man enters, therefore, only as the counterpart of God. If we hesitate to trace back the different attitude of the older Protestant theology from that of more recent times to a deep-seated difference in faith, we can think of it simply and, as it were, technically in this way. It did not praise and magnify Christ in word only, as the newer theology definitely does in its own way. It could also praise and magnify Him in deed, i.e., by the practical ordering of its thinking about God. In other words, the discipline of the christological dogma of the Early Church was still a self-evident presupposition with a real practical importance. On the other hand, it is obvious that the christological dogma was bound to become strange and incomprehensible to more modern theology, once it had ceased to be the practical presupposition of its actual thinking.

To sum up : we do not need to delete or retract anything from the admission that in His revelation God is present in the world of human religion. But what we have to discern is that this means that *God* is present. Our basic task is so to order the concepts revelation and religion that the connexion between the two can again be seen as identical with that event between God and man in which God is God, i.e., the Lord and Master of man, who Himself judges and alone justifies and sanctifies, and man is the man of God, i.e., man as he is adopted and received by God in His severity and goodness. It is because we remember and apply the christological doctrine of the *assumptio carnis* that we speak of revelation as the abolition of religion.

2. RELIGION AS UNBELIEF

A theological evaluation of religion and religions must be characterised primarily by the great cautiousness and charity of its assessment and judgments. It will observe and understand and take man in all seriousness as the subject of religion. But it will not be man apart from God, in a human *per se*. It will be man for whom (whether he knows it or not) Jesus Christ was born, died and rose again. It will be man who (whether he has already heard it or not) is intended in the Word of God. It will be man who (whether he is aware of it or not) has in Christ his Lord. It will always understand religion as a vital utterance and activity of this man. It will not ascribe to this life-utterance and activity of his a unique " nature," the so-called " nature of religion," which it can then use as a gauge to weigh and balance one human thing against another, distinguishing the " higher " religion from the " lower," the " living " from the " decomposed," the " ponderable " from the " imponderable." It will not omit to do this from carelessness or indifference towards the manifoldness with which we have to do in this human sphere, nor because a prior definition of the " nature " of the phenomena in this sphere is either impossible or in itself irrelevant, but because what we have to know of the nature of religion from the standpoint of God's revelation does not allow us to make any but the most incidental use of an immanent definition of the nature of religion.   It is not, then, that this " revealed " nature of religion is not fitted in either form or content to differentiate between the good and the bad, the true and the false in the religious world.   Revelation singles out the Church as the *locus* of true religion. But this does not mean that the Christian religion as such is the fulfilled nature of human religion.   It does not mean that the Christian religion is the true religion, fundamentally superior to all other religions. We can never stress too much the connexion between the truth of the Christian religion and the grace of revelation.   We have to give particular emphasis to the fact that through grace the Church lives by grace, and to that extent it is the *locus* of true religion.   And if this is so, the Church will as little boast of its " nature," i.e., the perfection in which it fulfils the " nature " of religion, as it can attribute that nature to other religions.   We cannot differentiate and separate the Church from other religions on the basis of a general concept of the nature of religion.

For a truly theological treatment of religion and religions the problem of *Nathan der Weise* is therefore pointless.   Christian, Jew and Mussulman as such —and that is how Lessing sees them all, including the Christian—have no advantage over one another and have no real fault to find with one another. The way which Nathan/Lessing proposes as the solution to the conflict : " Let each be zealous for his uncorrupted, unprejudiced love . . ." will only lead them deeper into the conflict from the theological standpoint, the standpoint of revelation.   For religion and the conflict of religions arise from the very fact that each is striving after his love, which he will, of course, always regard as uncorrupted and unprejudiced.   Where and when have religious men ever had anything but, at bottom and in general, good intentions ?   In the " eternal evangel " at the end of his *Education of the Human Race* Lessing was probably thinking only of the starting-point and goal of all religious history.   Even theologically, he was justified to the extent that the mutual rivalry between religions is half-hearted and insincere.   But Lessing did not see that after overcoming the false conflict between the various " religionisms," including the Christian, a genuine religious conflict might begin at a point which seems to lie quite outside the possibilities of his templars or his patriarchs.   It might begin at the point where in opposition to all " religionisms " the proclamation of the grace of God is introduced as the truth of the Christian religion.   Where Christianity does that— even as one religion with others—its self-consciousness is more than religious fanaticism, its mission is more than religious propaganda, and even in the form

of one " religionism " with others it is more than a "religionism." But it will
have to be radically different, or better : the grace of God will have to be very
effective to be essential to Christians as grace, if we are to be able to say that
about Christianity.

A truly theological treatment of religion and religions, as it is
demanded and possible in the Church as the *locus* of the Christian
religion, will need to be distinguished from all other forms of treatment
by the exercise of a very marked tolerance towards its object. Now
this tolerance must not be confused with the moderation of those who
actually have their own religion or religiosity, and are secretly zealous
for it, but who can exercise self-control, because they have told themselves or have been told that theirs is not the only faith, that fanaticism
is a bad thing, that love must always have the first and the last word.
It must not be confused with the clever aloofness of the rationalistic
Know-All—the typical Hegelian belongs to the same category—who
thinks that he can deal comfortably and in the end successfully with
all religions in the light of a concept of a perfect religion which is
gradually evolving in history. But it also must not be confused with
the relativism and impartiality of an historical scepticism, which does
not ask about truth and untruth in the field of religious phenomena,
because it thinks that truth can be known only in the form of its
own doubt about all truth. That the so-called " tolerance " of this
kind is unattainable is revealed by the fact that the object, religion
and religions, and therefore man, are not taken seriously, but are
at bottom patronised. Tolerance in the sense of moderation, or
superior knowledge, or scepticism is actually the worst form of intolerance. But the religion and religions must be treated with a tolerance
which is informed by the forbearance of Christ, which derives therefore from the knowledge that by grace God has reconciled to Himself
godless man and his religion. It will see man carried, like an obstinate
child in the arms of its mother, by what God has determined and
done for his salvation in spite of his own opposition. In detail, it will
neither praise nor reproach him. It will understand his situation—
understand it even in the dark and terrifying perplexity of it—not
because it can see any meaning in the situation as such, but because
it acquires a meaning from outside, from Jesus Christ. But confronted
by this object it will not display the weak or superior or weary smile
of a quite inappropriate indulgence. It will see that man is caught
in a way of acting that cannot be recognised as right and holy, unless
it is first and at the same time recognised as thoroughly wrong and
unholy. Self-evidently, this kind of tolerance, and therefore a theological consideration of religion, is possible only for those who are ready
to abase themselves and their religion together with man, with every
individual man, knowing that they first, and their religion, have need
of tolerance, a strong forbearing tolerance.

We begin by stating that religion is unbelief. It is a concern, indeed, we must say that it is the one great concern, of godless man.

Outwardly crude things are only trifling compared with what is taught about growing pious with works, and setting up a worship of God according to our reason. For in this way the innocent blood is most highly dishonoured and blasphemed. The heathen have committed far greater sin by their worshipping sun and moon, which they regarded as the true worship of God, than they have with any other sins. Therefore the piety of man is vain blasphemy and the greatest of all the sins that he commits. Similarly the creature which regards it as an act of worship and piety to flee from the world is far worse in God's sight than any other sin, and this is the state of popes and monks, and of everything that seems good to the world, and yet is without faith. Therefore whoso will not obtain grace by the blood of God, for him it is better he should never come before God. For he but enrages the Majesty more and more thereby (Luther, *Pred. üb.* 1 *Pet.* 1¹⁸ᶠ·, 1523, *W.A.* 12, 291, 33).

In the light of what we have already said, this proposition is not in any sense a negative value-judgment. It is not a judgment of religious science or philosophy based upon some prior negative judgment concerned with the nature of religion. It does not affect only other men with their religion. Above all it affects ourselves also as adherents of the Christian religion. It formulates the judgment of divine revelation upon all religion. It can be explained and expounded, but it cannot be derived from any higher principle than revelation, nor can it be proved by any phenomenology or history of religion. Since it aims only to repeat the judgment of God, it does not involve any human renunciation of human values, any contesting of the true and the good and the beautiful which a closer inspection will reveal in almost all religions, and which we naturally expect to find in abundant measure in our own religion, if we hold to it with any conviction. What happens is simply that man is taken by God and judged and condemned by God. That means, of course, that we are struck to the very roots, to the heart. Our whole existence is called in question. But where that is the case there can be no place for sad and pitiful laments at the non-recognition of relative human greatness.

That is why we must not omit to add by way of warning that we have not to become Philistines or Christian iconoclasts in face of human greatness as it meets us so strikingly in this very sphere of religion. Of course it is inevitable and not without meaning that in times of strong Christian feeling heathen temples should be levelled to the earth, idols and pictures of saints destroyed, stained glass smashed, organs removed : to the great distress of aesthetes everywhere. But irony usually had it that Christian churches were built on the very sites of these temples and with materials taken from their pillars and furnishings. And after a time the storm of iconoclasm was succeeded by a fresh form of artistic decoration. This goes to show that while the devaluation and negation of what is human may occasionally have a practical and symbolical significance in detail, it can never have any basic or general significance. And it must not, either. We cannot, as it were, translate the divine judgment that religion is unbelief into human terms, into the form of definite devaluations and negations. From time to time it has to be manifested in the form of definite devaluations and negations. But we must still accept it as God's judgment upon all that is human. It can be heard and understood, strictly and exactly as intended, only by those who do not despair of the human element as such, who regard it as something worth while, who have some inkling of what it means really to abandon the world of Greek or Indian gods, China's world of wisdom or even the world of Roman Catholicism, or our own Protestant world of faith as such, in the thoroughgoing sense of that divine judgment. In this sense the divine judgment, which we have to hear and receive, can actually be described as a safeguard against all forms of ignorance and Philistinism. It does not challenge us to a venal and childish resignation in face of what is humanly great, but to an adult awareness of its real and ultimate limits, which do not have to be fixed by us but are already fixed. In the sphere of reverence before God, there must always be a place for reverence for human greatness. It does not lie under our judgment, but under the judgment of God.

To realise that religion is really unbelief, we have to consider it from the standpoint of the revelation attested in Holy Scripture. There are two elements in that revelation which make it unmistakably clear.

1. Revelation is God's self-offering and self-manifestation. Revelation encounters man on the presupposition and in confirmation of the fact that man's attempts to know God from his own standpoint are wholly and entirely futile ; not because of any necessity in principle, but because of a practical necessity of fact. In revelation God tells man that He is God, and that as such He is his Lord. In telling him this, revelation tells him something utterly new, something which apart from revelation he does not know and cannot tell either himself or others. It is true that he could do this, for revelation simply states the truth. If it is true that God is God and that as such He is the Lord of man, then it is also true that man is so placed towards Him, that he could know Him. But this is the very truth which is not available to man, before it is told him in revelation. If he really can know God, this capacity rests upon the fact that he really does know Him, because God has offered and manifested Himself to him. The capacity, then, does not rest upon the fact, which is true enough, that man could know Him. Between " he could " and " he can " there lies the absolutely decisive " he cannot," which can be removed and turned into its opposite only by revelation. The truth that God is God and our Lord, and the further truth that we could know Him as God and Lord, can only come to us through the truth itself. This " coming to us " of the truth is revelation. It does not reach us in a neutral condition, but in an action which stands to it, as the coming of truth, in a very definite, indeed a determinate relationship. That is to say, it reaches us as religious men ; i.e., it reaches us in the attempt to know God from our standpoint. It does not reach us, therefore, in the activity which corresponds to it. The activity which corresponds to revelation would have to be faith ; the recognition of the self-offering and self-manifestation of God. We need to see that in view of God all our activity is in vain even in the best life ; i.e., that of

ourselves we are not in a position to apprehend the truth, to let God
be God and our Lord. We need to renounce all attempts even to try
to apprehend this truth. We need to be ready and resolved simply
to let the truth be told us and therefore to be apprehended by it. But
that is the very thing for which we are not resolved and ready. The
man to whom the truth has really come will concede that he was not
at all ready and resolved to let it speak to him. The genuine believer
will not say that he came to faith from faith, but—from unbelief,
even though the attitude and activity with which he met revelation,
and still meets it, is religion. For in faith, man's religion as such is
shown by revelation to be resistance to it. From the standpoint of
revelation religion is clearly seen to be a human attempt to anticipate
what God in His revelation wills to do and does do. It is the attempted
replacement of the divine work by a human manufacture. The divine
reality offered and manifested to us in revelation is replaced by a
concept of God arbitrarily and wilfully evolved by man.

*Hominis ingenium perpetuam, ut ita loquar, esse idolorum fabricam. . . . Homo
qualem intus concepit Deum, exprimere opere tentat. Mens igitur idolum gignit,
manus parit* (Calvin, *Instit.* I 11, 8).

" Arbitrarily and wilfully " means here by his own means, by his
own human insight and constructiveness and energy. Many different
images of God can be formed once we have engaged in this undertaking,
but their significance is always the same.

*Imagines Deus inter se non comparat, quasi alterum magis, alterum minus
conveniat : sed absque exceptione repudiat simulachra omnia, picturas aliaque signa,
quibus eum sibi propinquum fore putarunt superstitiosi* (Calvin, *Instit.* I 11, 1).
In nihilum redigit quicquid divinitatis, propria opinione sibi fabricant homines (*ib.*).
In the sense of this undertaking the final principles of the various philosophical
systems are just as much idols as the idea of the uncanny in the outlook of the
animistic religions ; and the view of God expressed, say, in Islam, is no less
defective than absence of any unitary idea or image of God in Buddhism or
ancient and modern atheistic movements.

The image of God is always that reality of perception or thought
in which man assumes and asserts something unique and ultimate and
decisive either beyond or within his own existence, by which he believes
himself to be posited or at least determined and conditioned. From
the standpoint of revelation, man's religion is simply an assumption
and assertion of this kind, and as such it is an activity which contradicts revelation—contradicts it, because it is only through truth that
truth can come to man. If man tries to grasp at truth of himself,
he tries to grasp at it *a priori*. But in that case he does not do what
he has to do when the truth comes to him. He does not believe. If
he did, he would listen ; but in religion he talks. If he did, he would
accept a gift ; but in religion he takes something for himself. If he
did, he would let God Himself intercede for God : but in religion he
ventures to grasp at God. Because it is a grasping, religion is the

contradiction of revelation, the concentrated expression of human unbelief, i.e., an attitude and activity which is directly opposed to faith.
It is a feeble but defiant, an arrogant but hopeless, attempt to create
something which man could do, but now cannot do, or can do only
because and if God Himself creates it for him : the knowledge of the
truth, the knowledge of God. We cannot, therefore, interpret the
attempt as a harmonious co-operating of man with the revelation of
God, as though religion were a kind of outstretched hand which is
filled by God in His revelation. Again, we cannot say of the evident
religious capacity of man that it is, so to speak, the general form of
human knowledge, which acquires its true and proper content in the
shape of revelation. On the contrary, we have here an exclusive
contradiction. In religion man bolts and bars himself against revelation by providing a substitute, by taking away in advance the very
thing which has to be given by God.

> *Non apprehendunt (Deum) qualem se offert, sed qualem pro temeritate fabricati
> sunt, imaginantur* (Calvin, *Instit.* I 4, 1).

He has, of course, the power to do this. But what he achieves and
acquires in virtue of this power is never the knowledge of God as
Lord and God. It is never the truth. It is a complete fiction, which
has not only little but no relation to God. It is an anti-God who has
first to be known as such and discarded when the truth comes to him.
But it can be known as such, as a fiction, only as the truth does come
to him.

> *Notitia Dei, qualis nunc hominibus restat, nihil aliud est, quam horrenda idolo-
> latriae et superstitionum omnium scaturigo* (Calvin, *Comm. on Jn.* 3[6], C.R. 47, 57).

Revelation does not link up with a human religion which is already
present and practised. It contradicts it, just as religion previously
contradicted revelation. It displaces it, just as religion previously
displaced revelation ; just as faith cannot link up with a mistaken
faith, but must contradict and displace it as unbelief, as an act of
contradiction.

In the Old Testament the rejection of heathen religion is directed with a
surprising onesidedness against its idolatry. Whatever god it may apply to,
idolatry is to be rejected. As a reason for this judgment, it is consistently maintained, e.g., in Jer. 10[1-16] and Is. 44[9-20], that in all heathen religions man himself
is originally the creator of his own god. I do not think it a likely explanation
of these passages that the biblical authors did not know, or for the sake of
vilification did not want to know, what the Catholic Church has always said in
explanation and defence of its customary veneration of images, and what is
to-day almost a commonplace of the science of religion, that the image of God
is never originally and properly regarded as identical with the Deity represented,
that the Deity is adored and worshipped in the image only as in its representative
and substitute, and that to the image as such only a loosely intended δουλεία is
offered. I think it more likely that the reproach of " making idols " (Is. 44[9],
45[16]) is made with a full knowledge of this fact, and that it is directed against
the spiritual idolatry which finds expression in the making of images. The

people of Israel are forbidden to " cleave " or " fall away " to " other " or " strange gods," which is the one great sin. But these other gods are not called " other " just because they are the gods of other nations. And Yahweh is not zealous against them only for the sake of His own honour, because He is the one God of the people of Israel. On the contrary, they are " other " and " strange " first of all to Himself. They are of a different nature and kind. And for this reason, that they can have such representatives and substitutes in the images which are made by human hands, whereas He, Yahweh, cannot be represented by any human work. For His name is holy. In His work, in His revelation, in His activity as the Lord of the covenant, in His commandments, in His Word enjoined upon the prophets, He wills to give exclusive testimony to Himself, to be His own Mediator. Behind the worship of other gods, as its idolatry reveals, there stands the caprice and arbitrariness of man. That is why Israel must not fall away to them. And this ban is emphatic ; just as the ban on images is emphatic even though they may be meant to represent Yahweh. And they are emphatic because Yahweh is the God of the divine self-revelation, which contradicts the caprice and the arbitrariness of man. It is as such that He wills to be recognised and honoured. It is to be noted that what in the heathen seems primarily to be just folly, for Israel, and in the sphere of revelation and the covenant, is concretely revealed as the sin of unbelief. Because Israel has become participant in the divine self-revelation, it must neither participate in the idolatry of heathen religions nor make and venerate images of Yahweh. The latter no less than the former involves a radical repudiation of Yahweh.

The most remarkable New Testament development of this thought is to be found in the passages Rom. $1^{18f.}$ and Ac. $14^{15f.}$, $17^{22f.}$ (The passage Rom. $2^{14f.}$ does not come up for discussion here—for the general context of the chapter makes it clear that the heathen in whom the prophecy of Jer. 31^{33} has been fulfilled are Gentile-Christians.) The revelation of righteousness, i.e., of the will of God in Jesus Christ, graciously creating and bestowing righteousness on the earth—this fulfilment of all revelation has now made the distinction of the heathen from Israel a secondary one. The Messiah of Israel appeared and was rejected and crucified by Israel itself. In that way He has revealed Himself as the Lord of the whole world. This does not mean only that there is now a grace of God for all men of all nations. It also means that they are all drawn into the responsibility and accountability which formerly only Israel had experienced. It does not mean only that the covenant made between God and man has now to be proclaimed to all nations as good news which affects them too. It also means that the complaint of apostasy is now expressly and seriously levelled against them all. To use the words of Ac. 14^{16} : " The times have passed since God in the generations gone by suffered all the nations to walk in their own way." And with Ac. 17^{30} : " The times of ignorance therefore God overlooked ; but now (in and with the Now inaugurated by Jesus Christ) he commands all men everywhere that they should repent." Where the forgiveness of sins is manifest, there sins are revealed and condemned and punished as such. The very revelation of the righteousness of God is also the revelation of the wrath of God against all ungodliness and unrighteousness ($\dot{\alpha}\sigma\acute{\epsilon}\beta\epsilon\iota\alpha$ $\kappa\alpha\grave{\iota}$ $\dot{\alpha}\delta\iota\kappa\acute{\iota}\alpha$) of men (Rom. 1^{18}). What is meant by that ? According to Rom. 1 and Ac. 14 and 17 it does not mean what we usually understand by " ungodliness " and " unrighteousness." It does not mean a profane and secular attitude orientated away from the divine. It is rather the worship offered by man in a fine loyalty to what he regards as the divine. This loyalty and the truth of the divineness of this " divine " is roundly denied by God's revelation in Christ and man's confrontation by that revelation. It is this supposedly very best that men do, this worship of theirs, which is " ungodliness " and " unrighteousness." Their piety is " fear of demons " (superstition) Ac. 17^{22}. They worship the things which by nature are not gods at all (Gal. 4^8). So in and with their piety they are ἄθεοι ἐν τῷ κόσμῳ (Eph. 2¹²). And in the light of the revelation made and fulfilled in Christ we now have to say of all men what formerly, in the light of the revelation in Old Testament prophecy, we could only say of the renegade Israelites, that in the very best that they have done they are guilty of apostasy from God. It is in this way that they have " held the truth in unrighteousness " (Rom. 1¹⁸). But when Christ appeared and died and rose again, the grace of God became an event for all men, and all men are made liable for their being and activity, for their being and activity as it is revealed in the light of this event. For as the ultimate and profoundest human reality, this event is the self-revelation of the truth, and therefore of the truth about man. In the light of the self-revelation of the truth, our human being and activity is seen to be in its ultimate and profoundest reality a fight against the truth. It stands over against the truth self-revealed there at an angle of 180°. It is the assumption of Rom. 1 as well as of the speeches in Acts that in and with the proclamation of Christ the men to whom this proclamation is made and who in it learn about the relationship of God and man, i.e., about God's grace, have to admit that in this opposition they have a relationship to truth, which they deny and betray by this opposition. When the grace of God is proclaimed to them in Christ, they have to concede that " God has not left Himself without a witness " (Ac. 14¹⁷). For in and with the proclamation of the grace of God in Christ there is disclosed to them the witness of God, from which they have fallen away and with which they have been brought into radical contradiction. As they come under the light of this proclamation, the witness awakens and arises and speaks and testifies against them, so that they stand before the God who meets them in this revelation unexcused and inexcusable (Rom. 1²⁰).

In the speeches of Acts the witness which is disclosed and awakens and accuses in this way, the witness which is promised to all men in and with the proclamation of Christ, is its knowledge of God as the Creator. " He did you good and gave you rain from heaven and fruitful seasons and filled your hearts with food and gladness " (Ac. 14¹⁷). Yes, He ! They come to know this afresh. And they come to know afresh that this was what they already knew. Is not this what they confirmed when " in ignorant worship " (ἀγνοοῦντες εὐσεβεῖτε, Ac. 17²³) they built an altar to the " unknown God " ? In proclaiming to them God in Christ, Paul tells them : You knew about this, but this God has become an unknown instead of a known God, for now you worship Him ignorantly. Before this God, whom I now make known to you again, you stand therefore as men accused who cannot excuse themselves. I now tell you, from my own knowledge of Christ, I now guarantee to you as your own knowledge even in and in spite of your utter ignorance : that this God created the world and everything in it ; that He is the Lord of heaven and earth ; that He created man and directs the history of men. It is because this is the case, because men belong to this God, that they seek after God, if haply they might feel after Him and find Him, although—o folly of man !—He is not far from any one of us. For we actually live and move and have our being in Him. We do not need to seek after Him. The unknowing knowledge of one of your poets itself attests that " we are His offspring " and therefore that He is as near to us as a father is to his children. If that is true (and it is true), and if we know it (and we do), what is the meaning of this seeking and feeling after God, this trying to find God by which I see you gripped ? It is only because God is the Creator and therefore the Lord—and in Christ this has been revealed for time and eternity—that we can commit the sin of idolatry. But why do we commit it ? It is because we have to recognise that God is the Creator and therefore the Lord, as we are told—and in Christ we are told it as something well-known, something we have been told already—it is because of this that we have to recognise our idolatry as sin, as " ungodliness " and " unrighteousness "—why do we not do it ? How can the Lord of heaven and earth, in whom we have our life and breath and everything, dwell in a temple made by hands and be served by human hands ? How can we who are His offspring and children and who therefore already belong to Him, worship the Godhead in an image of our seeking and feeling and finding, an image made of gold, or silver or stone, graven by art and man's device, the image of our own attempts to draw near to Him ? If God is the Creator, how can there be such a thing as a mediation which we ourselves establish ? How impossible all these things are ! And yet how real is the struggle against the grace of revelation in favour of a capricious and arbitrary attempt to storm heaven ! In this struggle against grace the known God has become an unknown one. There is no future for opposition to the truth, now that it has as such been marked upon our body in God's revelation (Ac. 17[24-29]). All that really remains for us—personally—to do is to " turn from these vanities unto the living God " (Ac. 14[15]).

We meet with the same line of thought in Romans, but with a characteristically different emphasis. The witness which the apostle declares to the heathen in and with the preaching of Christ, which he therefore awakens in them and makes valid against them, is here emphasised to be their knowledge of God the Creator. The invisible and unapproachable being of God, His everlasting power and divinity, are apprehended and seen in His works from the creation of the world (Rom. 1[20]). It is from a knowledge of God, a knowledge of Him on the basis of revelation, that men always start when revelation comes to them in Christ (Rom. 1[19]). That is why they can be accused of a " holding of the truth," a *corruptio optimi* (Rom. 1[18]). We must bear in mind that the very words which are so often regarded as an opening or a summons to every possible kind of natural theology are in reality a constituent part of the apostolic *kerygma*, whatever contemporary philosophemes may be woven into them. To bring out the real meaning of the revelation of the righteousness of God in Christ (Rom. 1[17], 3[21]), Paul reminds us in Rom. 1[18]–3[20] that the same revelation is a revelation of the wrath of God, i.e., that as we are told of the grace which has come to us, we have to perceive and believe our own abandonment to judgment. Grace and judgment are for both Gentile and Jew, both Jew and Gentile, Rom. 1[16], 2[9], and for both Jew and Gentile in the very best that they can do, their worship of God. It is a Christian statement presupposing revelation when in relation to the Jews Paul says that a knowledge of sin comes by the Law (Rom. 3[20]). Similarly, it is presupposing the event which took place between God and man in Christ that he says that the knowledge which the Gentiles have of God from the works of creation is the instrument to make them inexcusable and therefore to bring them like the Jews under the judgment and therefore under the grace of God. Here, too, there is no difference. Because Christ was born and died and rose again, there is no such thing as an abstract, self-enclosed and static heathendom. And because Paul has to preach this Christ, he can claim the heathen on the ground that they, too, belong to God and know about God, that God is actually revealed to them, that He has made Himself known to them in the works of creation as God—His eternal power and divinity, which are none other than that of Jesus Christ. Therefore he can tell them that because of their knowledge they are inexcusable before God, if they have " imprisoned " the truth with their ungodliness and unrighteousness. We cannot isolate what Paul says about the heathen in Rom. 1[19-20] from the context of the apostle's preaching, from the incarnation of the Word. We cannot understand it as an abstract statement about the heathen as such, or about a revelation which the heathen possess as such. Paul does not know either Jews or Gentiles in themselves and as such, but only as they are placed by the cross of Christ under the promise, but also under the commandment of God. The witness of the hope of Israel, the prophetic revelation, is fulfilled in Christ. By smiting its Messiah on the cross Israel founders on that revelation. It has now become a revelation to both Jews and Gentiles. It now concerns the Gentiles. Therefore the Gentiles have to bow just as emphatically as the Jews to the claim and demand of revelation. Like the Jews, they are addressed on this basis : that from the creation of the world (ἀπὸ κτίσεως κόσμου, Rom. 1²⁰, i.e., in and with their own existence and that of the whole world)—not of themselves, but by virtue of the divine revelation—men know God, and therefore know that they are indebted to Him. The status of the Gentiles, like that of the Jews, is objectively quite different after the death and the resurrection of Christ. By Christ the Gentiles as well as the Jews are placed under the heavens which declare the glory of God, and the firmament which telleth His handiwork (Ps. 19²). They are therefore to be claimed as γνόντες τὸν θεόν (Rom. 1²¹) ; but only to the extent that, like the Jews, they have not remained such (οὐκ ἐδοκίμασαν τὸν θεὸν ἔχειν ἐν ἐπιγνώσει Rom. 1²⁸). It is, therefore, not the case that Paul was in a position to appeal to the Gentiles' possession of a knowledge of the invisible nature of God as manifested from creation. He could not link up pedagogically with this knowledge. In his proclamation of Jesus Christ he could not let it appear even momentarily that he was speaking of things which were already familiar by virtue of that " primal revelation." At bottom the Gentiles did not achieve even in the slightest the knowledge of Ps. 19. That is, they did not give God praise and thanks as God (Rom. 1²¹). As the sequel shows, this does not mean only a quantitative falling away of their service towards Him nor an imperfection of their relationship to Him. It means rather that the δοξάζειν καὶ εὐχαριστεῖν which they owe God are not there at all. They have been ousted by another mind and thought and activity which at its root (in negation of the fact that God is revealed to man from the creation) does not have God as its object. " Their thoughts became vain and their foolish heart was darkened " (Rom. 1²¹). " They professed (themselves and others) to be wise, and in this they became fools " (Rom. 1²²). And the result was sheer catastrophe : " They changed the glory of the incorruptible God into the likeness of the image of corruptible man, yea of flying and four-footed beasts and creeping things " (Rom. 1²³). In this idolatry " they exchanged the truth of God for a lie, they worshipped and served the creature instead of the Creator, who is blessed to eternity. Amen " (Rom. 1²⁵). And in due course the exchange had terrible consequences in the indescribable moral confusion of the human race. Paul says nothing at all about the heathen maintaining a remnant of the " natural " knowledge of God in spite of this defection. On the contrary, he says unreservedly that the wrath of God has been revealed against this defection : " they which do such things are worthy of death " (Rom. 1³²). Just as revelation had always contradicted heathen religion in the sphere of Israel and on the soil of Palestine, so now, when Jesus Christ has died for all, it contradicts it " publicly," in its own heathen area, in an apostolic letter which remarkably enough is addressed to the Christians in Rome. There is no such thing now as an undisputed heathendom, a heathendom which is relatively possible, which can be excused. Now that revelation has come and its light has fallen on heathendom, heathen religion is shown to be the very opposite of revelation : a false religion of unbelief.

2. As the self-offering and self-manifestation of God, revelation is the act by which in grace He reconciles man to Himself by grace. As a radical teaching about God, it is also the radical assistance of God which comes to us as those who are unrighteous and unholy, and as such damned and lost. In this respect, too, the affirmation which revelation makes and presupposes of man is that he is unable to help himself either in whole or even in part. But again, he ought not to have been so helpless. It is not inherent in the nature and concept of man that he should be unrighteous and unholy and there-fore damned and lost. He was created to be the image of God, i.e.,

to obedience towards God and not to sin, to salvation and not to destruction. But he is not summoned to this as to a state in which he might still somehow find himself, but as one in which he no longer finds himself, from which he has fallen by his own fault. But this, too, is a truth which he cannot maintain : it is not present to him unless it comes to him in revelation, i.e., in Jesus Christ, to be declared to him in a new way—the oldest truth of all in a way which is quite new. He cannot in any sense declare to himself that he is righteous and holy, and therefore saved, for in his own mouth as his own judgment of himself it would be a lie. It is truth as the revealed knowledge of God. It is truth in Jesus Christ. Jesus Christ does not fill out and improve all the different attempts of man to think of God and to represent Him according to his own standard. But as the self-offering and self-manifestation of God He replaces and completely outbids those attempts, putting them in the shadows to which they belong. Similarly, in so far as God reconciles the world to Himself in Him, He replaces all the different attempts of man to reconcile God to the world, all our human efforts at justification and sanctification, at conversion and salvation. The revelation of God in Jesus Christ maintains that our justification and sanctification, our conversion and salvation, have been brought about and achieved once and for all in Jesus Christ. And our faith in Jesus Christ consists in our recognising and admitting and affirming and accepting the fact that everything has actually been done for us once and for all in Jesus Christ. He is the assistance that comes to us. He alone is the Word of God that is spoken to us. There is an exchange of status between Him and us : His righteousness and holiness are ours, our sin is His ; He is lost for us, and we for His sake are saved. By this exchange ($\kappa\alpha\tau\alpha\lambda\lambda\alpha\gamma\dot{\eta}$, 2 Cor. 5[19]) revelation stands or falls. It would not be the active, redemptive self-offering and self-manifestation of God, if it were not centrally and decisively the *satisfactio* and *intercessio Jesu Christi*.

And now we can see a second way in which revelation contradicts religion, and conversely religion necessarily opposes revelation. For what is the purpose of the universal attempt of religions to anticipate God, to foist a human product into the place of His Word, to make our own images of the One who is known only where He gives Himself to be known, images which are first spiritual, and then religious, and then actually visible ? What does the religious man want when he thinks and believes and maintains that there is a unique and ultimate and decisive being, that there is a divine being ($\theta\epsilon\hat{\iota}ov$), a godhead, that there are gods and a single supreme God, and when he thinks that he himself is posited, determined, conditioned and overruled by this being ? Is the postulate of God or gods, and the need to objectify the Ultimate spiritually or physically, conditioned by man's experience of the actual superiority and lordship of certain natural and supernatural, historical and eternal necessities, potencies and ordinances ?

Is this experience (or the postulate and need which correspond to it) followed by the feeling of man's impotence and failure in face of this higher world, by the urge to put himself on peaceful and friendly terms with it, to interest it on his behalf, to assure himself of its support, or, better still, to enable himself to exercise an influence on it, to participate in its power and dignity and to co-operate in its work ? Does man's attempt to justify and sanctify himself follow the attempt to think of God and represent Him ? Or is the relationship the direct opposite ? Is the primary thing man's obscure urge to justify and sanctify himself, i.e., to confirm and strengthen himself in the awareness and exercise of his skill and strength to master life, to come to terms with the world, to make the world serviceable to him ? Is religion with its dogmatics and worship and precepts the most primitive, or better perhaps, the most intimate and intensive part of the technique, by which we try to come to terms with life ? Is it that the experience of that higher world, or the need to objectify it in the thought of God and the representation of God, must be regarded only as an exponent of this attempt, that is, as the ideal construction inevitable within the framework of this technique ? Are the gods only reflected images and guarantees of the needs and capacities of man, who in reality is lonely and driven back upon himself and his own willing and ordering and creating ? Are sacrifice and prayer and asceticism and morality more basic than God and the gods ? Who is to say ? In face of the two possibilities we are in a circle which we can consider from any point of view with exactly the same result. What is certain is that in respect of the practical content of religion it is still a matter of an attitude and activity which does not correspond to God's revelation, but contradicts it. At this point, too, weakness and defiance, helplessness and arrogance, folly and imagination are so close to one another that we can scarcely distinguish the one from the other. Where we want what is wanted in religion, i.e., justification and sanctification as our own work, we do not find ourselves—and it does not matter whether the thought and representation of God has a primary or only a secondary importance—on the direct way to God, who can then bring us to our goal at some higher stage on the way. On the contrary, we lock the door against God, we alienate ourselves from Him, we come into direct opposition to Him. God in His revelation will not allow man to try to come to terms with life, to justify and sanctify himself. God in His revelation, God in Jesus Christ, is the One who takes on Himself the sin of the world, who wills that all our care should be cast upon Him, because He careth for us.

... by this article our faith is sundered from all other faiths on earth. For the Jews have it not, neither the Turks and Saracens, nor any Papist or false Christian or any other unbeliever, but only proper Christians. So where thou come into Turkey, where thou canst have no preacher nor books, there say to thyself, be it in bed or at work, be it in words or thoughts, Our Father, the Creed and the Ten Commands ; and when thou comest to this article, press thy finger with the thumb or give thyself some sign with hand or foot, so that thou layest good hold of this article and makest note of it, And specially, where thou shalt see some Turkish stumbling-block or have temptation. And with thine Our Father, pray that God may keep thee from stumbling and hold thee pure and stedfast in this article, For in the article lieth thy life and blessedness. (Luther, *Heer-pred. wid. d. Türcken*, 1529, *W.A.* 30 II 186, 15.)

It is the characteristically pious element in the pious effort to reconcile Him to us which must be an abomination to God, whether idolatry is regarded as its presupposition or its result, or perhaps as both. Not by any continuing along this way, but only by radically breaking away from it, can we come, not to our own goal but to God's goal, which is the direct opposite of our goal.

Therefore I have often said that to speak and judge rightly in this matter we must carefully distinguish between a godly man (what philosophers call a *bonus vir*) and a Christian. We too approve of being a godly man and there is nothing more praiseworthy on earth and it is God's gift, just as much as sun and moon, corn and wine and all things made. But that we may not mix and brew them indiscriminately, let a pious man have his praise from the world and say : A godly man is indeed a precious man on earth, yet he is not there- fore a Christian. For he may be a Turk or a heathen (as in early times some have been highly praised). As indeed it cannot otherwise be, that among so many bad a good man must at times be found. But be he as pious as he will, he is and remains still for all such piety Adam's child, that is, an earthy man, under sin and death. But if thou ask about a Christian, you must go much higher. For this is a different man, who is not called Adam's child and hath no father and mother on earth. But he is God's child, an heir and nobleman in the kingdom of heaven. For he is called a Christian, because with all his heart he depends on the Saviour, who hath ascended to the Father, and believes that for His sake and by Him he hath God's grace and eternal redemption and life. That is neither mastered nor grasped, achieved nor taught by our own life and virtue and work by which we are called godly folk on earth, neither by righteousness according to the Law and ten commandments, which is yet neces- sary, as was said, and is found in every Christian. But this chief thing and righteousness is still far from achieved, of which Christ speaks and calls it right- eousness. (Luther, *Pred. üb. Joh.* 16^5-15, *Cruc. Somm. Post.*, 1545, *W.A.* 21, 365, 12).

A mistake which is not justified by its respectable antiquity, and which Luther himself had a share in confirming, is that of regarding the Old Testament as a document, and, where possible, as the classical document, of a religion of works, and therefore, because all religion as such is a religion of works, of religion in general. The Israel which understands the " Do this and thou shalt live " (Lk. 10^28) to mean that man has to justify and sanctify himself in his own works by fulfilling the Law, is not the true Israel. He wants to be under the Law, without wanting to listen to the Law (Gal. 4^21). Sin has become " exceedingly sinful " καθ᾽ ὑπερβολὴν ἁμαρτωλός (Rom. 7^13), making use of the Law (Rom. 7^8, 11), com- mitting the grossest act of treachery by means of the Law (Rom. 7^11). In face of the Law with its "Thou shalt not covet" it causes "desire" (ἐπιθυμία) to spring up in us (Rom. 7^7). What is this desire and the sin that dwelleth in us (Rom. 7^17) ? According to the narrative of the fall of the first man (Gen. 3^1 f.), it obviously did not consist primarily in the desire for fruit as such, but in the spiritual or pseudo-spiritual desire, by the enjoyment of this fruit to become as God, and to know good and evil. This is the " desire " which acquires a new and indeed its real power in Israel by the treacherous act which sin commits through the Law (Gal. 3^19, Rom. 5^20, 1 Cor. 15^56). " They have a zeal for God, but not according to knowledge. For being ignorant of God's righteousness and seeking to establish their own, they did not subject themselves to the righteousness of God" (Rom. 10²³). To the question of the scribe : " What must I do to inherit eternal life?", Jesus replies by simply directing to the Law. And how does the man take the direction ? " But he wished to justify himself" (Lk. 10²⁵⁻²⁹ ; cf. 16¹⁵). That is the " desire " of a man betrayed by sin by means of the Law. It is not the true Israel which has succumbed to this desire, and it is not the intention of the Old Testament which is realised in this desire. This is the zeal of an Israel upon whose heart a veil has been put, even to this day when Moses is read (2 Cor. 3¹⁵). It is the zeal of an Israel which, in pursuit of a " law of righteousness," fails to attain the real Law (Rom. 9³¹). Israel is wrecked on the rock upon which it is built, because it will not believe (Rom. 9³²⁻³³). The Law given it by God is in truth a spiritual Law (Rom. 7¹⁴). It is not contrary to the promises (Gal. 3²¹). Christ is the end of the Law : to justification for everyone that believes (Rom. 10⁴). By the Israel that crucifies his Messiah, the Law is not kept but " weakened " (Rom. 8³) and broken (Rom. 2¹⁷ᶠ·). And that is why here as always the Law is directed against Israel (Rom. 2¹², 3¹⁹). The Law worketh wrath (Rom. 4¹⁵). It killeth (2 Cor. 3⁶ ; Rom. 7⁵· ¹³). The same curse which once came upon the fathers because of their disobedience to Moses, their persecution of the prophets, their whoredom with the Baalim— the same curse now comes upon Pharisaic Israel, whose legalism is another form of its old lawlessness. " Thou gloriest in the law and dishonourest God by transgression of the law " (Rom. 2²³). " All the day long did I spread out my hands unto a disobedient and gainsaying people " (Rom. 10²¹). At root the new righteousness of works is simply the old idolatry. And at root the old idolatry was simply a righteousness of works. To understand this equation we have to read the speech of Stephen in Ac. 7²⁻⁵³, which closes with the annihilating verdict : " Ye received the law by the ordinance of angels and kept it not " (Ac. 7⁵³). The way of the true Israel, of the nation which the Lord by His Word has made to be the people of His covenant, cannot have been the way from idolatry to the righteousness of works. The true Israel, i.e., the Isaianic remnant (Rom. 9²⁹), the seven thousand in Israel that did not bow the knee to Baal (Rom. 11⁴), was obedient to the Law of God in that it held all the other commandments in and with the first one, which means that it received and accepted grace as grace, that it lived by the Word of God, that it waited on God, that it looked to the hands of God, as the eyes of a servant look to the hands of his master (Ps. 123²). The true Israel could not depart from the Law, but also it could not attempt to justify and sanctify itself by a misuse of the Law, because the Law was put in its heart and written on its mind (Jer. 31³³; Rom. 2²⁸ᶠ·), as " the law of the spirit of life " (Rom. 8²) : and in addition its transgression was forgiven and its iniquity remembered no more (Jer. 31³⁴; Rom. 4⁶). Given in this way, the Law was for it the direct power of God, which necessarily preserved the justified and sanctified Israel from going aside either to the left hand or to the right. The witness of this Israel, and therefore the witness of the coming Jesus Christ, is the real meaning and purpose of the Old Testament. It is not, therefore, the document of a religion of works. But with the New Testament it is the document of the revelation which contradicts every religion of works and therefore all religion as such. Luther's attitude to this question is not reducible to a single denominator. As an expositor of the Old and New Testaments, he often distinguished between Law and Gospel, commandment and promise, Old Testament and New, in a way which was utterly abstract and schematic, with a Paulinism which was not that of St. Paul himself. But then (cf. Theodosius Harnack, *Luthers Theologie*, 1862, new Edn. 1927, vol. 1, p. 450 f.) he would again perceive and understand the original and ultimate unity of the two with an astonishing clarity. We prefer this second Luther. At the end of his life, at the close of his Preface to the Romans (1546), he reduced the content of this apostolic writing to the following remarkable formula : So it seems as though St. Paul would in this epistle bring into small compass the whole of Christian and Evangelical doctrine, and prepare an entrance into the whole of the Old Testament. For undoubtedly he who has this epistle well at heart has the light and power of the Old Testament beside him. Therefore let every Christian be constantly exercised in it. For which may God give His grace, Amen (*W.A. Bib.* 7, 27, 21). But if with Romans we have the light and power of the Old Testament, then it is clear that even the Old Testament, and the light and power of its holy and righteous and most excellent Law, are necessarily grace, and the contradiction of grace against justification and sanctification by works as the chief sin of man.

As regards the New Testament, do we not have to point out that, like the Old Testament, it is a Law, that is, an order and command and direction for the new life of the people and children of God ? But it is not for that reason—not even partially—an authorisation and challenge to self-justification and self-sanctification. It is not a book of religion. From first to last it is the proclamation of the justifying and sanctifying grace of God. It is, therefore, a revelation of the unbelief which is in all religion. Again and again we have to point expressly to this fact. For the simple insight, that the New Testament is testimony to Jesus Christ and nothing else, can never be an insight which we have already won and can leave behind. It is one which we must win again and again as we wrestle with the errors of our ears and hearts. We constantly overlook the fact that the form of the New Testament witness, not only in the Sermon on the Mount, and the Epistle of James, and the parænetic chapters of Paul, but everywhere, is the Law. We forget the clear and self-evident fact that the essence of the gracious work of Jesus Christ and the Gospel as it is experienced in the New Testament Church is His lordship over man. We forget that there can be no more direct or absolute an imperative than the simple claim made on man in the New Testament : that he should believe in this Jesus Christ. We forget that there can be no more stringent obedience than that which the New Testament describes as faith. None of the forcefulness with which the Old Testament claims man only and wholly for Yahweh has here been lost. We overlook this point. We break up the New Testament into evangelical and promissory and comforting sayings on the one hand, legal and ethical and imperative sayings on the other. We do not perceive its unity even as Law. We do not hear in the preaching of John the Baptist about the Lamb of God that taketh away the sin of the world the same preaching of repentance as is ascribed to him in the Synoptic Gospels. And then there easily creeps in a second error. It seems as though there is a kind of *nova lex* in the New Testament side by side with the Gospel, i.e., side by side with the message of the reconciliation of the world with God achieved in Christ. It seems as though the Gospel only acquires a moral character because its appeal is not only to faith, but to something more and different, the free decision of the human will, because man is challenged to confirm the justification and sanctification achieved in Christ by specific attitudes and actions. It seems as though that word of reconciliation only becomes a serious matter in the light of this second word about the new life. The result is that when we listen to the New Testament message we constantly have to shift our gaze from one direction to another. At one time we have to think of Christ and His work, at another of the improvement of our own position. At one time we have to put everything into God's hands, at another to take everything into our own. At one time we have to believe, at another to love and to do all kinds of good works. Then the second error is almost inevitably followed by a third, the reversal of the relationship of the two constituent parts of the New Testament message as abstracted and characterised in this way. The second group of New Testament pronouncements, misunderstood as a *nova lex*, is undoubtedly much easier to understand and its meaning and bearing are more readily perceived than the first. From this we can tell that it speaks of supernatural grace, and Jesus Christ and His work, and the forgiveness of sin, and the gift of the Holy Ghost, only in an abstract way. Who is going to give time and attention to this obscure and lofty matter, which can so easily be misunderstood as intellectualistic ? What we want to see is deeds. Life is urgent, with all its questions and tasks, and with all the possibilities which man always thinks that he has in relation to them. It is especially to these possibilities that the *nova lex* seems to point as we think we see it in the New Testament. At bottom we are still alone when we weigh up the New Testament in this way. We are still in the sphere of our own ability and daring and enterprise and achievement. The whole mystery of the New Testament is our own mystery, with all the burdensome but beneficent responsibility which that involves. And why should we not weigh it up primarily in this way ? Why should we not suppress the other side of it for special occasions, for the new efforts at ethical self-assertion which are necessary from time to time ? Is it as indispensable as we affirm both before and after ? Have we still any real place for it ? Do we not find it a little disturbing that the New Testament seems consistently to have this other aspect ? Be that as it may, the attentiveness and love and emphasis and zeal are no longer on this aspect, but on the much more practical matter of self-justification and self-sanctification, against the background of the assurance that either way the work of Christ and the gift of the Holy Spirit are, of course, the decisive starting-point. This threefold development is the process with which every reader of the New Testament is continually tempted to retranslate its message into a document of religion. It is, therefore, our task to make the process impossible at the very root : that is, at the point where the New Testament usually divides up into the two categories of (*a*) placatives and (*b*) motives. This division is quite unfounded. It would perhaps be better for us in the first instance to regard the New Testament as altogether Law than to think of it as divided into Law and Gospel. For, of course, it is true that faith in its message is both our justification and also our sanctification, both our new status in the sight of God and also our new life. And it is both, because it is simply faith in Jesus Christ. And we rightly understand it as such if in the first instance we understand it as outright obedience to the Lord Jesus Christ : which means that in the first instance the message of the New Testament is regarded as altogether Law. There is a good deal to be said for the view that sanctification, the fact that man is claimed by God, the fact that he belongs to God by grace (as Calvin develops the thought in Bk. III of the *Institutio*), is the main or at any rate the formally prior reality in faith. But whatever conceptual order we may adopt, in the New Testament faith is always faith in Jesus Christ. It may be taken more as trust or more as obedience. It may be taken first as trust and then as obedience, or *vice versa*. But one thing is always certain, that it can be understood only in the light of its object, Jesus Christ, i.e., in opposition to any claim which the believer might make for his own work. The believer in the New Testament sense is claimed by Jesus Christ with all his activity and work. He belongs to Jesus Christ. Therefore any claim on behalf of his own activity and work is decisively destroyed. He cannot expect to be able to help himself ; he is not allowed even to wish to do so. Faith in the New Testament sense does not mean merely the superseding but the abolishing of man's self-determination. It means that man's self-determination is co-ordinated into the order of the divine predetermination. In faith, it loses its autonomy outside this predetermination, and therefore its significance over against God or in competition with God. It loses its significance as a sphere of ultimate and genuine decision, and therefore its character of ultimate and genuine seriousness. The only ultimate and really serious determination for the believer is that which proceeds from Jesus Christ. Ultimately and in the true sense he is no longer the subject. In and with his subjectivity he has become a predicate to the subject Jesus Christ, by whom he is both justified and sanctified, from whom he receives both comfort and direction. Proclaiming this faith, the New Testament has no room for a *nova lex*, which would have to be sought elsewhere than in the Gospel itself and as such. If John the Baptist preaches the Lamb of God, which takes away the sin of the world, it is in the same word, and not in a second which has to be heard along with the first, that he preaches repentance and amendment of life. An autonomous interest in the latter means the introduction of a foreign element into the New Testament message. For an autonomy of this kind can mean only that we have the " desire," first in secret, and then publicly, to resume that being as subject which we lost in Jesus Christ, our self-determination outside the divine predetermination, and therefore to abandon our faith. All other desires are rooted in this desire, just as transgression of the first commandment inevitably involves that of all others. Sin is always unbelief. And unbelief is always man's faith in himself. And this faith invariably consists in the fact that man makes the mystery of his responsibility his own mystery, instead of accepting it as the mystery of God. It is this faith which is religion. It is contradicted by the revelation attested in the New Testament, which is identical with Jesus Christ as the one who acts for us and on us. This stamps religion as unbelief.

We cannot make this point without insisting expressly that it is only by the revelation of God in Jesus Christ that we can characterise religion as idolatry and self-righteousness, and in this way show it to be unbelief. Religion can, of course, be called in question from within, and we have to be aware of this and to distinguish it from the abolishing of religion by revelation. It is an observation which we can more or less clearly verify from the history and phenomenology of every religion that the religious man does not at all face up to his theoretico-practical aims, like a man who is sure of his business, straightforwardly. In his striving, then, he involves himself in a peculiar inward dialectic. He strangely contradicts himself. He scores through his thinking and willing, and uplifts and outbids it by a thinking and willing which he believes to be higher and better. In this way he necessarily calls himself in question, unsettling himself and plunging himself into uncertainty. But he also jeopardises more or less radically the whole of his religious activity—although without abandoning the religious attitude and appetite—but also without directing it to its real goal in this new and critical turn in the matter. The observation will not surprise us if we know the judgment which revelation has pronounced upon all religion. It is a confirmation of the fact that the verdict is true : Religion is always self-contradictory and impossible *per se*. But we have to note that the critical turn at which the self-contradiction and impossibility are brought out is itself a moment in the life of religion. It has only an immanent significance. It does not give any ultimate or definitive answer to the question which it tries to answer. Therefore—and this is the point—it must not be confused with revelation. It does not show religion to be unbelief. For it falls under the same judgment. Even at the supposedly higher level where it tries to overcome idolatry and self-righteousness in its own strength and its own way, religion is still idolatry and self-righteousness. To be more specific, religion is called in question by a twofold movement which at root is only one : by mysticism on the one hand and atheism on the other. Our task is to show that even in these two supposedly higher and apparently inimical forms, whether in good or evil, in failure or success, religion is still thoroughly self-centred.

The two primitive and as it were normal forms of religion are, as we have seen, the conception of the deity and the fulfilment of the law. It is always in these two forms that religious need first seeks its satisfaction. But it seeks satisfaction because it already has it—and that is why religious need differs from the need of man in faith in God's revelation. It is, of course, the need of man for a truth above and a certainty within, both of which he thinks he can know and even create for himself. Since the need is there, have not the starry heaven above and the moral law within long since brought this truth and certainty into the range and realm of his perception ? He is not in any way lacking in advice or help. He knows that truth and certainty exist and are attainable, and he is confident of his own ability to achieve them. His need is not an absolute need, a strictly needy need, in face of which he does not know where to turn. His need is not in the least like the neediness of the believer, who with empty heart and hands finds himself thrown back entirely upon the revelation of God. To satisfy this need, he steps out in a bold bid for truth, creating the Deity according to his own image—and in a confident act of self-assurance, undertaking to justify and sanctify himself in conformity with what he holds to be the law. And in so doing he betrays the fact that even as he seeks satisfaction, potentially at least, in respect of his religious capacity he is already satisfied. He is like a rich man, who in the need to grow richer (which cannot, of course, be an absolute need) puts part of his fortune into an undertaking that promises a profit.

From this it follows that there is always an ultimate non-necessity about the origin and exercise of all religion. The life of religion, in which religious need seeks satisfaction and provisionally finds it, is fundamentally only an externalisation, an expression, a representation and therefore a repetition of something which previously existed without form or activity, but still quite powerfully, as the real essence of religion and to that extent as the peculiar religious possession of man.

Has the religious life as expressed and manifested any other necessity than the limited, loose, incidental and purely ornamental necessity of a children's game, or of serious or light-hearted art ? If need be, could not religion's thoughts of God not be thought, its doctrines not be stated, its rites and prayers not be fulfilled, its ascetic and moral prescripts·be freely disregarded ? Does the religious outlook and desire really have to express itself in this way ? Is it really bound to this expression once it has been made ? Does it in any way cease to be what it is apart from it ? The history and phenomenology of all religion show us that this is not actually the case : the outward and actual satisfaction of the religious need is a relative, but only a relative, necessity. If need be, the conception of Deity and justifying and sanctifying work of man are not indispensable.

And now we can add a second point. In all originated and applied religion, in all external satisfaction of the religious need, there is a very definite weakness deriving from the inward satisfaction which precedes it. At bottom, the external satisfaction will never be anything more or other than a reflection of what the man is and has who thinks he should proceed to this external satisfaction of his need. But what becomes of this reflection, if the original, religious man, changes ? Is it compatible with religion that it should change with him ? Is it compatible with religion that it should not ?

The religion of man is always conditioned absolutely by the way in which the starry heaven above and the moral law within have spoken to the individual. It is, therefore, conditioned by nature and climate, by blood and soil, by the economic, cultural, political, in short, the historical circumstances in which he lives. It will be an element in the habit or custom with which, quite apart from the question of truth and certainty, or rather at the very lowest and most rudimentary stages of his inquiry into it, he compounds with the terms of existence imposed upon him. But the terms of existence, and therefore custom, are variable. Nature and climate, or the understanding and technique with which he masters them, may change. Nations and individuals may move. Races may mix. Historical relationships as a whole are found to be in perhaps a slow or a swift but at any rate a continual state of flux. And that means that religions are continually faced with the choice : either to go with the times, to change as the times change, and in that way relentlessly to deny themselves any claim to truth and certainty ; or else to be behind the times, to stick to their once-won forms of doctrine, rite and community and therefore relentlessly to grow old and obsolete and fossilised ; or finally, to try to do both together, to be a little liberal and a little conservative, and therefore with the advantages of both options, to have to take over their twofold disadvantages as well. That is why religions are always fighting for their lives. That is why they are always acutely or chronically sick. There has probably never been a religion which in its fateful relation to the times, i.e., to change in man (or rather in its own liberalism or conservatism or in both at once) has not been secretly or openly sick. And it is a familiar fact that religions do actually die of this sickness, i.e., of an utter lack of fresh believers and adherents. They cease to exist except as historical quantities. The link between religion and religious man in his variableness is the weakness of all religions.

These two factors, the non-necessity and the weakness of all religions, constitute the pre-supposition for that critical turn which plays its specific part in the history and form of more or less every religion.

Usually the weakness of religion supplies the cause, its non-necessity the opportunity for this development. With the change of the times, that is, with his own alteration in time, man cannot be satisfied with the previous satisfaction of his religious need, i.e., as taught him by his fathers. The characteristics of the conception of God and the norms of the law of his religion are far too stiff or even far too fluid for him still to be able to feel at home in it. Its truth no longer speaks to him, its certainty is no longer valid. Doubt is aroused, and the desire for freedom—and, of course, because his religion has only that relative necessity both are possible—and they both seem to be trying to break out from the religion which has been passed down to him and taken over by him. It now seems—but only seems—that he is quite near to realising what revelation has to say of his religion, that he has been pursuing idolatry and self-righteousness, and that all his previous thinking and activity have been the activity and thinking of unbelief. Apart from revelation he will never reach this, the absolute crisis of his religion. He would have had to believe first to be able seriously to accuse himself of unbelief. And to believe, the revelation of God would have had to encounter him. Without this the outcome of the relative crisis in which he finds himself in relation to his religion will perhaps be this. A new religion with a new conception of God and a new law will quickly emerge and be established and proclaimed, being applauded and gaining historical breadth and form at the expense of the old. If this happens, then however great the historical catastrophe in which the change from religion to religion is consummated, the critical turn, at which religion as such is called in question and the self-contradiction and the impossibility of religion as such are revealed, has not been reached. Where there is a more radical issue, as compared with the first possibility, it is a far more quiet and unassuming but also much more significant event. Of course, it is not as radical and significant as it pretends to be. But it is undoubtedly more radical and significant than the dying of an old religion and the emerging of a new.

Always presupposing the actual weakness and non-necessity of religion, it can happen not merely that the conception of God will be uncertain and the law oppressive, but that our own activity, the desire to form a conception of God, religious dogmatics, the fulfilling of the law, religious ethics and ascetics, will also be open to suspicion and doubt, and indeed impossible. It can happen that we become aware in principle of those presuppositions of the crisis of our religion, its weakness and non-necessity, as data which prevent us from escaping from our former religion to another or it may be to a new one, because we see only too clearly that the same problems will still meet us. But, of course, this is a proof that the need which has impelled our former religious life and activity was not in the strictest sense a needful need. It was the playful need to externalise a religious possession which exists prior to that externalisation and apart from it. In the crisis of our religion we are confronted by the real or supposed failure of that externalisation. In that externalisation as such we cannot accept even ourselves. We cannot participate in it any longer, at any rate inwardly and responsibly. Secretly or openly we abandon it. But we do not abandon our religious possession, which we have been trying to externalise. We do not abandon the formless conception of God, already present in the soul. We do not abandon the unrealised self-justification and self-sanctification, which we have already followed in the heart. We give up only in the sense that we consciously withdraw to the inner line from which we originally started. We do not lose anything by the withdrawal. We simply withdraw our capital from an undertaking which no longer appears to be profitable. The vitality and intensity which we applied to the conception of the divine image and the fulfilling of the law of our religion are now turned inwards and exploited in favour and in the direction of the formless and unrealised reality, unthought and unwilled, out of whose richness religion once sprang, only to be reabsorbed into it. The same acuteness of thought and the same power of will with which we once exerted ourselves positively and constructively, when we could still accept ourselves as religious believers, are now active negatively and destructively. The religious interest and desire which was once in play, expressing and manifesting itself, now prefers to live itself out without expression or manifestation. The same non-needy, religious need now seeks its satisfaction in a solemn non-satisfaction, in a pathetic renunciation of self-expression, in a pathetic silence, in a pathetic cessation of the soul, in the solemn emptiness which it thinks it would now prefer to its former equally solemn fulness. In our thinking and willing we have enough to do to define this vacuum in which there will be neither conception nor realisation, as in fact there never has been. Our religious task is one of clearing out and tidying up in preparation for the expected fulness of the self-enclosed and self-sounding religious reality which will follow our emancipation from all representations. In view of this goal, there can be no thought of transition to another religion or the founding of a new one. That would only mean a loss of time and strength. Far better—and this is where our thinking acquires a new task—to convince ourselves that the previous attempt to externalise the conception of God was a misunderstanding which deceived us right at the outset when we were really wanting and seeking what is now known to be true : the religious reality of that formless and unrealised vacuum. Far better—and this is where our will is also claimed—that all the energy which we once directed to fulfil an outward law should now be concentrated on the task of inward loyalty, and therefore of loyalty to that nameless and impersonal and undirected will, which struggles within us for truth and certainty.

This is the new road on which religious man now moves towards the old theoretico-practical goal. He thinks the same thing, but he thinks it quite differently. At least he thinks that he thinks it quite differently. From a lofty watch-tower he looks down fiercely or sadly or indulgently on those who still think quite differently from what he does, but who possibly, probably, do not understand for a moment how very, very differently he now thinks. At any rate, in attitude, in seriousness, in the inwardness of faith, in the exaltation with which he gives himself to his task, the task of withdrawal, to his negations and destructions, to his work of liberation, probably even in what we might call his religious fanaticism, he still resembles his former self and all other religious men. Is it perhaps that he is mistaken in thinking that his road is so completely new ? Still, even if it is in principle only a continuation of the old way, it cannot be denied that there has been at least a very sharp bend in the road.

So far we have described this relatively new road as a single one. But at a certain point in this road there is a fork, and it becomes the twofold way of mysticism and atheism. The difference derives from the relationship to the existing and hitherto accepted or predominant religion. Mysticism means that practically and basically we renounce that religion as regards its expression, externalisation and manifestation

We do not think that we shall find truth in its conception of God, or salvation and assurance in obedience to its law.

The word " mysticism " has, of course, two meanings : the one from μύειν, the other from μυεῖν. Μύειν means to close eyes and mouth ; μυεῖν means to consecrate. Mysticism is the higher consecration of man, which he secures by exercising towards the external world, both passively and actively, the greatest possible reserve. Or it is the passive and active reserve towards the external world, which is at the same time dedicated to a higher consecration of man.

Mysticism means the basic liberation of man from that satisfaction of the religious need which hitherto he has sought " outside." Yet in its relationship to this " outside " it is the conservative form of that critical turn. For mysticism does not attack religion openly and directly. It does not negate it. It is not interested in iconoclasm or the refutation of dogmas or other open acts of liberation. It subjects itself to the prevailing doctrine and observance, and even respects it. It leaves religion in peace. Sometimes, indeed, it can apparently enrich religious dogmatics by certain particularly profound and serious epigrams, and contribute certain particularly meaningful forms (mysteries) to the cultus, and give new life to the universal fellowship by a particularly impressive expression of its principles and the assembling and exercising of the most faithful of its believers. Gladly and honestly it purports to be true " friendship with God." There is a radical withdrawal from the outwardly religious position. But in its mystical form it consists only in this : that the mystic insists upon interpreting everything that is taught and practised in any particular religion according to its inward and spiritual and vital meaning, i.e., in relation to the reality of that formless and unrealised vacuum, and not in any abstract externality. The mystic will give prominence to the fact, and emphasise it, that everything external is only a form and picture, that the transitory is only a parable, that its truth is only in its relation to the inexpressible, because undirected, essence from which it proceeded and to which it must also revert. The specifically mystical experience of renunciation, of silence, of the way of quietude, is that of understanding and indicating and interpreting an external form which has to be accepted and respected. The mystic will say the most dangerous things, e.g., about the secret identity of the within and the without, of the ego and God. But he will say them quite piously and always in connexion with a religious tradition which apparently asserts the opposite. He will, as it were, try to make the latter a witness against itself. He will claim freedom only for this interpretation of tradition, not freedom to supersede tradition. He may even go far beyond ordinary believers in outward conservatism. And all this not because of fear or dishonesty, the common complaints against the mystic, but because in his own way he has a sincere affection for the whole system of external religion. That is, he has an affection for it because he needs it. It is the text for his interpretations. It is the material for his spiritualising. It is the external of which he has to show the inward meaning. It is the point of departure for the great withdrawal, on which, as he thinks, a knowledge of the truth will be achieved. Where would mysticism be without its opposite numbers, religious dogmatics and ethics ? If the latter perished, mysticism would " give up the ghost for want," just as it says that God would if man were to perish. It lives in fact by its opposite number, and for that reason it deals with it gently and even carefully.

There is therefore no contradiction, and it must not be taken as a mistake, when, e.g., Johann Scheffler, having caused the Ego and God to rise and set together, could then go on to sing :

> " Claim thou never thy wisdom, however so clever thou art,
> None there is wise in God, except in a Catholic part,"

and he could express himself similarly over a wide range of his poetical work. " This sensitive bard, who came from the very depths to dogmatics, who knocked at the door, who thought that he could remove stones with his seer's eyes, who tried to make dried rice green again by throwing himself into the thorns, by thrusting into the dead undergrowth with bared breast—he experienced something. A spider crept out of the thornbush, which sucked him dry of his heart's blood. And, suddenly, he hung in the thorns, himself like dry rice unsouled. The wind touched it, it still sang, in a last indestructible echo of its loving power. But intermingled with it there was the horrible sound of a crackling ghostlike twig. Scheffler became an orthodox fanatic . . ." (Wilhelm Boelsche, in his edition of *Der Cherubinische Wandersmann*, 1905, p. LXIV f.; similarly Fritz Mauthner, *Der Atheismus u. seine Gesch. in Abendland*, Vol. 3, 1922, p. 190 f.). Even the champions of a radical mysticism could not show a greater lack of comprehension. As though mysticism did not claim to be the complement of existing and accepted religion ! What is it to abandon, gouge out, reduce, or negate, if there is no such thing as religion ? And how is it to exist as mysticism, if there is nothing left to negate ? It is the genius and circumspection and economy of Angelus Silesius, in his investigation and presentation of this question of mysticism, that he recognised the fact that in this activity—together with friends in China and India and Arabia, who are much cleverer than their admirers in the modern West—he was always acting as an " orthodox fanatic."

From the same standpoint of its relationship to existing religion, atheism might be called an artless and childish form of that critical turn. Atheism means a blabbing out of the secret that so far as this turn involves anything at all it involves only a negation. Of course, even in its most radical forms, it is ultimately aiming at something positive. And in this respect its aim is the same as that of mysticism. Its positive goal is religious reality in that formless and unrealised vacuum, where knowledge and object are or again become one and the same thing—the Chinese *Tao*, the Indian *Tat tvam asi*, Hegel's in-and-for-itself of the absolute Spirit. For the sake of this positive goal, mysticism too must negate, and is prepared to do so. In the last resort it can only say No. Existing religion with its dogmatics and ethics is a structure which is taken over only to be broken up. But as far as possible, it will conceal this fact and say nothing about it. Atheism, however, shouts it out to the world. It hurls itself against religion in open conflict. It loves iconoclasm, the refutation of dogmas, and, of course, moral emancipation. It denies the existence of God and the validity of a divine law. And its whole interest is in the denial as such. That is its artlessness. It fails to see what mysticism does not fail to see : that absolute denial can have no meaning except against the background of a relative affirmation. A herd cannot be periodically slaughtered, unless it is continually fed and tended, or at any rate kept in being. Atheism lives in and by its negation. It can only break down and take away, and therefore it is exposed to the constant danger of finishing at a dead end. But again, as compared with mysticism, atheism set out to be a purer and more logical denial of religion as such, of its God and its law. Much more clearly than in mysticism, the meaning of that common, critical turn is here seen to be a withdrawal from the dogma of religion and the way of certainty, which we once thought out and maintained, but now find incredible. Intensively atheism is more energetic than mysticism, but extensively it is more modest. It is satisfied to deny God and His law. It fails to see that, apart from religion, there are other dogmas of truth and ways of certainty, which may at any moment take on a religious character. In this respect, too, mysticism is the more astute and far-sighted. Sooner or later it extends to everything. It not only queries God ; it carefully does the same of the cosmos and the individual as well. It proposes and practises a programme of comprehensive negation. But it keeps clear a way of retreat, or thinks it can. Atheism, on the other hand, does not deny the reality of nature, history and civilisation, of man's animal and rational existence, of this or that ethic or the lack of it. On the contrary, these are authorities and powers to which the atheist usually subscribes with the happiest and most naive credulity. Atheism nearly always means secularism. And more than that, atheism usually allies itself with these secular authorities and powers in the conflict with religion, with God and His law. It argues from their existence and validity. It accepts them as irrefutable data, from which it raises against religious authorities and powers the objection that they do not exist. But in so doing it exposes itself to the danger that all kinds of new and disguised, and sometimes not so disguised, religions may arise behind its back and wherever possible with its support.

It is because it is unguarded at these two points that atheism is the more primal, and unitary, and ultimately the stronger form of the critical turn that we are now considering. The meaning of this turn is here negation pure and simple. Specifically and concretely, it is the negation of the over-world of religion, the weakness and non-necessity of which are perceived, and which has become superfluous and irritating as a result of a change in the conditions of human existence. In essence, mysticism too is negation in ever new forms and degrees. Except in negations it cannot speak of the positive thing at which it ostensibly aims, the glory of the vacuum which takes into itself everything outward. And it is only to provide the necessary material that it deals gently and even carefully with religious positions. It goes to work more comprehensively, but in the last resort mysticism does specifically and concretely mean the negation of the over-world of religion. This world, not the cosmos or the ego, is the true and ultimate external which has to be made " inward," i.e., to be negated. Mysticism is esoteric atheism. But atheism still carries the banners and laurels of the work of liberation which is their common purpose. If the joint programme is practicable, it has the disadvantage of a lesser wisdom, but the advantage of a more direct and logical method—if only it did not betray right at the outset the fact that the common programme is not practicable. Its impracticability is shown by its inability to answer the following questions : (1) where does a denial of that over-world of religion finally lead ? ; and (2) how is the emergence of new and concealed " over-worlds " effectively to be prevented ? Can the critical turn in religion—mysticism aiming at atheism, and atheism interpreting mysticism (that great artist in interpretation), lead anywhere, but nowhere : which in practice certainly means the stimulation of old religions and the formation of new ?

When the atheist sees the danger of the sterile negation in which he finds himself, at the very last moment he usually borrows from his more cautious and far-seeing partner. That is why the great work which F. Mauthner wrote in praise of Western atheism concludes in the 4th vol. (1923), p. 372 f. with a section entitled " Der Friede in gottloser Mystik." In this section he again speaks of a " concept of God purified from the nonsense of theologians." He commends this to his readers, presupposing that they will regard it only as an " ordinary deception, a healthy lie, an unavoidable lifelong illusion," and that they will not accept it. Of course, the concepts consists only in a " halting ' it ' " (p. 446). Perhaps some may think that he does not let us go far enough. But others may be of the opinion that it is from this " halting ' it ' " that all idolatry and self-righteousness derives. They may believe that at bottom and in spite of all reservations even this limited permission throws the door wide open again to every conceivable religious glorification. For if the atheist does not remain a pure atheist, if he tries to become a mystic again, let him see to it that, after the manner of Angelus Silesius, he does not finally and necessarily become a dogmatician and a moralist as well. And what if the atheist sees his other danger : that when his negation of the God of religion and of His law is complete, new religions may lift up their heads out of the nature and culture and history which are not negated, and out of man's own animal and national existence ? Well, he may perhaps do as Otto Petras (*Post Christum* 1936) did. He may address to himself and others (on the basis of some philosophy of history) a master-word to the following effect. To-day not only some but all ideologies and mythologies are dead, definitely dead, dead to all futurity. All that remains to modern man is a venture stripped of every dream of an over-world, the venture of a naked and dangerous existence, absolutely sterile and always confronted by death. This existence is typified already in certain soldiers in the world war, in the ocean flyer roaring forward in space between heaven and earth, or in this or that perverted modern industrialist : the man who, stripped of all illusions, hopes and fears, marches for the sake of marching, he knows not whence, he knows not whither. Very well! But then the dilemma arises. Either this new form of existence is simply lived out and not preached by some who gladly surrender to this master-word. If that is the case, atheism is a private affair, and its critical function towards religion is at an end. Or this new form of existence is not only lived out but publicly proclaimed. But if that is the case it cannot dispense with some sort of basic, declarative ideology and mythology, i.e., some sort of over-world has to be dreamed into it too. And the result of this critical turning against religion is simply the founding of a new religion—and perhaps even the confirmation of an old.

To summarise : the critical turn against religion signifies in any case the discovery of its weakness and only relative necessity. But in its mystical form it cannot avoid combining its denial with a naturally not at all naive affirmation, but an affirmation all the same. And if it tries to escape this in its atheistic form, unwillingly but in fact it cannot avoid, if not preparing, at least opening up, a wide field for new religious constructs. But this means that even in these two extremely basic forms the critical turn against religion is not so radical and powerful that it knows how to make it clear, even in theory, how it really thinks to achieve the negation of religion, its God and its law. Of course, the will and purpose are clear enough : but the way is not clear. Historically we must say that those religions which have the innate capacity to be both conservative and liberal have so far given evidence of the longer wind and the more vital substance in face of mysticism and atheism. If a religion died, it died because of the victory of another religion, not because of the more fundamental attack of mysticism or atheism. In fact, therefore, the weakness and the limited necessity of religion are not so fatal in their results as they might be. In its weakness and limited necessity religion is always there in different forms. And in the last resort mysticism and atheism can never prove that it might be otherwise, 'or how far it might be otherwise. For their own existence is far too closely bound up with the existence of religion. And if we tried finally to conceive the inconceivable and, according to all historical experience, the quite improbable ; the historical existence of pure mysticism, which would necessarily be identical with that of pure atheism, its purity would obviously consist only in this : the negation which is ostensibly only a means to the end, a work of liberation, the dangerous negation— dangerous even to mysticism and atheism—which is so well adapted to bring in religion in one way or another, has now reached its goal. Man is finally and ultimately free of God and His law. He is free of all religious works and all religious working. He is free from all that striving for representation and expression. He is happy in that formless and unrealised vacuum, happy alone by himself, and therefore, alone, happy in the real world beyond the antithesis of the within and the without. But why should there not sometimes have been mystically or atheistically inclined individuals, able at any rate to imagine that they are happy in this way ? If so, they will have tasted and felt the great positive, which lies behind the critical turn against religion, and from which its negations alone derive their relative power, without mysticism and atheism always being exposed to betrayal to religion. But then, what about this positive? It is not so diametrically opposed to religion as its few fortunate and countless unfortunate devotees usually asseverate. It is really opposed to religion only as the spring is to the river, as the root to the tree, as the unborn child in the womb to the adult. It is the quiet religious possession. It is the contemplation of the universe and the creative power of the individual feeling which gropes after it in its nameless and formless and unrealised oneness. It is the power to be in the world and a man, which always precedes the " halting ' it,' " but which will project out of itself that " halting ' it ' " and later and quickly enough some sort of religion. The power to be in the world and a man, as man's own power, is identical with the power to devise and form gods and to justify and sanctify oneself. This power, and therefore the great positive beyond all negations, and therefore the happiness which the presence and the enjoyment of this positive can create, and therefore —if there ever has been or will be such a thing—pure mysticism or pure atheism can never be the real crisis of religion. This power belongs to the magic circle of religion: it is indeed its creative and formative centre and real point of departure.

If this statement is not accepted, its immortal proof is in Schleiermacher's *Talks on Religion* (" to the educated among its despisers "), 1799. Not only as an apologist, but as an expert expositor of religion, Schleiermacher was right not to accept at its face value the scorn of the all too uneducated, but to address them boldly in the name of the God " who will be in you."

A real crisis of religion is needed to affect this power, and this power first and decisively. It will not have to be content with easy successes against the theologies and ideologies and mythologies of external religion, extending only to temple buildings and ceremonies and observances. It will have to rush into that inner chamber shouting: Here is the *fabrica idolorum*! Here we lie and murder and steal and commit adultery! Here the cry must be: *Ecrasez l'infame!* Here or nowhere: for if not here, religion and religions will grow from here like the heads of the Lernæan hydra, however zealously we may deny God outside and destroy His law. But a turning against the religions which can make this judgment on religion is manifestly impossible, whether in the form of mysticism or in that of atheism. For in making this judgment it will have to judge itself. We can be quite definite upon this point: it is as little likely to emerge in the future as in the past. The real crisis of religion can only break in from outside the magic circle of religion and its place of origin, i.e., from outside man. It is only in a quite different antithesis than that of religion and religious ability, only in the light of faith, that the judgment " unbelief, idolatry, self-righteousness " can be made on this sphere and therefore

Great ←

on man as a whole, so that he can no longer flee from one refuge to another. This is what happens in the revelation of God. But to the extent that it does not happen in any other way, religion and religions are left at peace. There is development, but there is also a certain continuance, so that religion and religions are always there. Mystics and atheists cause a certain incidental and limited disquietude—when a greater or lesser historical transformation is due—but this belongs just as much to their innermost life as do the positive expressions and representations, the deities and laws, against which mystical and atheistical criticism is directed. The ebb as well as the flow belongs to the innermost life of the ocean. And it is in the purer forms—so far as they can be achieved—that the critical turn of religion is least hostile.

For to the extent that the purity of mysticism and atheism increases, and the work of liberation is achieved in specific individuals, and they attain either a real or an ostensible peace in that which is positively intended—to that extent the hostility to religion and religions will be definitely reduced. All the great " friends of God " and " deniers of God " have ultimately attained at any rate to a kind of toleration of religion ; proving once again that the mother can never quite deny her child.

But the abrogation which is a genuine and dangerous attack on religion is to be found in another book, beside which the books of mysticism and atheism can only be described as completely harmless.

3. TRUE RELIGION

The preceding expositions have established the fact that we can speak of " true " religion only in the sense in which we speak of a " justified sinner."

Religion is never true in itself and as such. The revelation of God denies that any religion is true, i.e., that it is in truth the knowledge and worship of God and the reconciliation of man with God. For as the self-offering and self-manifestation of God, as the work of peace which God Himself has concluded between Himself and man, revelation is the truth beside which there is no other truth, over against which there is only lying and wrong. If by the concept of a " true religion " we mean truth which belongs to religion in itself and as such, it is just as unattainable as a " good man," if by goodness we mean something which man can achieve on his own initiative. No religion is true. It can only become true, i.e., according to that which it purports to be and for which it is upheld. And it can become true only in the way in which man is justified, from without ; i.e., not of its own nature and being, but only in virtue of a reckoning and adopting and separating which are foreign to its own nature and being, which are quite inconceivable from its own standpoint, which come to it quite apart from any qualifications or merits. Like justified man, religion is a creature of grace. But grace is the revelation of God. No religion can stand before it as true religion. No man is righteous in its presence. It subjects us all to the judgment of death. But it can also call dead men to life and sinners to repentance. And similarly in the wider sphere where it shows all religion to be false it can also create true religion. The abolishing of religion by revelation need not mean only its negation : the judgment that religion is unbelief. Religion can just as well be exalted in revelation, even though the judgment still stands. It can be upheld by it and concealed in it. It can be justified by it, and—we must at once add—sanctified. Revelation can adopt religion and mark it off as true religion. And it not only can. How do we come to assert that it can, if it has not already done so ? There is a true religion : just as there are justified sinners. If we abide strictly by that analogy—and we are dealing not merely with an analogy, but in a comprehensive sense with the thing itself—we need have no hesitation in saying that the Christian religion is the true religion.

In our discussion of " religion as unbelief " we did not consider the distinction between Christian and non-Christian religion. Our intention was that whatever we said about the other religions affected the Christian similarly. In the framework of that discussion we could not speak in any special way about Christianity. We could not give it any special or assured place in face of that judgment. Therefore the discussion cannot be understood as a preliminary polemic against the non-Christian religions, with a view to the ultimate assertion that the Christian religion is the true religion. If this were the case, our task now would be to prove that, as distinct from the non-Christian religions, the Christian is not guilty of idolatry and self-righteousness, that it is not therefore unbelief but faith, and therefore true religion ; or, which comes to the same thing, that it is no religion at all, but as against all religions, including their mystical and atheistical self-criticism, it is in itself the true and holy and as such the unspotted and incontestable form of fellowship between God and man. To enter on this path would be to deny the very thing we have to affirm. If the statement is to have any content, we can dare to state that the Christian religion is the true one only as we listen to the divine revelation. But a statement which we dare to make as we listen to the divine revelation can only be a statement of faith. And a statement of faith is necessarily a statement which is thought and expressed in faith and from faith, i.e., in recognition and respect of what we are told by revelation. Its explicit and implicit content is unreservedly conditioned by what we are told. But that is certainly not the case if we try to reach the statement that the Christian religion is the true religion by a road which begins by leaving behind the judgment of revelation, that religion is unbelief, as a matter which does not apply to us Christians, but only to others, the non-Christians, thus enabling us to separate and differentiate ourselves from them with the help of this judgment. On the contrary, it is our business as Christians to apply this judgment first and most acutely to ourselves : and to others, the non-Christians, only in so far as we recognise ourselves in them, i.e., only as we see in them the truth of this judgment of revelation which concerns us, in the solidarity, therefore, in which, anticipating them in both repentance and hope, we accept this judgment to participate in the promise of revelation. At the end of the road we have to tread there is, of course, the promise to those who accept God's judgment, who let themselves be led beyond their unbelief. There is faith in this promise, and, in this faith, the presence and reality of the grace of God, which, of course, differentiates our religion, the Christian, from all others as the true religion. This exalted goal cannot be reached except by this humble road. And it would not be a truly humble road if we tried to tread it except in the consciousness that any " attaining " here can consist only in the utterly humble and thankful adoption of something which we would not attain if it were not already attained in God's revelation before we set out on the road.

We must insist, therefore, that at the beginning of a knowledge of the truth of the Christian religion, there stands the recognition that this religion, too, stands under the judgment that religion is unbelief, and that it is not acquitted by any inward worthiness, but only by the grace of God, proclaimed and effectual in His revelation. But concretely, this judgment affects the whole practice of our faith : our Christian conceptions of God and the things of God, our Christian theology, our Christian worship, our forms of Christian fellowship and order, our Christian morals, poetry and art, our attempts to give individual and social form to the Christian life, our Christian strategy and tactics in the interest of our Christian cause, in short our Christianity, to the extent that it is *our* Christianity, the human work which we undertake and adjust to all kinds of near and remote aims and which as such is seen to be on the same level as the human work in other religions. This judgment means that all this Christianity of ours, and all the details of it, are not as such what they ought to be and pretend to be, a work of faith, and therefore of obedience to the divine revelation. What we have here is in its own way—a different way from that of other religions, but no less seriously—unbelief, i.e., opposition to the divine revelation, and therefore active idolatry and self-righteousness. It is the same helplessness and arbitrariness. It is the same self-exaltation of man which means his most profound abasement. But this time it is in place of and in opposition to the self-manifestation and self-offering of God, the reconciliation which God Himself has accomplished, it is in disregard of the divine consolations and admonitions that great and small Babylonian towers are erected, which cannot as such be pleasing to God, since they are definitely not set up to His glory.

To see how self-evident this standpoint is in Holy Scripture we have only to note the contexts in which from time to time the people Israel or the New Testament Church appears abstractly in its human existence—certainly as this nation or Church—but for a moment, as it were, behind the back of Yahweh or of Jesus Christ. We can think of Ex. 32 : the scene which follows at the foot of Sinai immediately after the conclusion of the covenant and the giving of the Law : Israel, the congregation of Yahweh, the people of the revelation, under the leadership of Aaron, the head of his priestly class, in the full panoply of its religion. But Moses is temporarily missing, and with him obviously the concrete presence of the grace of Yahweh, which would make this religion true. The result : it is true, as we are expressly told in verse 5, that a feast of Yahweh is celebrated ; but lo ! it consists in adoration and sacrifice before the molten image of a calf. With a sacrificial zeal which cannot be denied they all gave of their best toward it. Aaron himself designed and made it. " And they cried : This is thy God, O Israel, which brought thee out of Egypt " (v. 4). " And the Lord said unto Moses, I have seen this people, and, behold it is a stiffnecked people " (v. 9). That is revealed religion as such. That is the actuality of revealed religion. That is revealed religion as seen for a moment in abstraction from the grace of revelation. And that was how above all the prophet Amos saw it. He described the sacrifices offered to Yahweh at Bethel and Gilgal by the bitter term " scandals " (transgressions R.V. 4^4). He warned them : " Seek not Bethel nor enter into Gilgal " (5^5). In the name of Yahweh he proclaimed : " I hate, I despise your feasts and will not smell your solemn assemblies. Yea though ye offer me your burnt offerings and meal offerings I will not accept them, neither will I regard the peace offerings of your fat beasts. Take thou away from me the noise of thy songs : for I will not heed the melody of thy viols " (5^{21-23}). In the most bitter earnest he flings the question : " Did ye bring unto me sacrifices and offerings in the wilderness forty years, O house of Israel ? " (5^{25}). He also raises a question which relativises the whole of Israel's existence in a devastating way : " Are ye not as the children of the Ethiopians unto me, O children of Israel ? saith the Lord. Have I not brought up Israel out of Egypt, and the Philistines from Caphtor, and the Syrians from Kir ? " (9^7). In the light of all this we can quite understand why the priest Amaziah thought that he ought to denounce this man to the king as a " rebel," and to expel him from the royal temple of Bethel ($7^{10f.}$). It is equally significant that Amos expressly refuses to be a prophet or of the prophetic guild ($7^{14f.}$). With Amos there seems to open up an irreconcilable gulf between revelation and the religion of revelation. We have a similar uncovering of nakedness, of inward disobedience, and even of the religion of revelation in its actuality, its human exercise, in Is. $1^{11f.}$, Jer. $6^{20f.}$, Ps. $50^{7f.}$ It can (Jer. 7^{21}) be intensified to the cutting opposition : " Add your burnt-offerings unto your sacrifices, and eat ye flesh. For I spake not unto your fathers nor commanded them in the day that I brought them out of the land of Egypt concerning burnt-offerings or sacrifices : but this thing I commanded them, saying, Hearken unto my behests, and I will be your God, and walk ye in all the ways that I command you, that it may be well with you." And in Jer. $8^{8f.}$: "How do ye say, we are wise and we have disposal over the law of the Lord ? How do ye say, We are wise and the law of the Lord is with us ? But, behold, the false pen of the scribes hath wrought falsely. The wise men are ashamed, they are dismayed and taken : Lo, they have rejected the word of the Lord : and what manner of wisdom is in them ? "

But, of course, we do not understand these pointed statements correctly, unless we understand them in the context of the general prophetic message of criticism, repentance and judgment. Of course, this, too, belongs to the life of

Old Testament religion as such. It is directed from within against apostasy, against its falsification and degeneration, against cultic disloyalty and moral licence. But it has an unheard-of breadth of form. The radical nature of its criticisms and judgments and warnings beggars all comparisons. It cannot be explained until we see that we always have here something more than the opposition to the specific concrete aberrations and sins of Israel, which, of course, have to be taken seriously as such. What we have here is at every point the inevitable struggle of revelation against the religion of revelation, a struggle in which the prophets did not even spare prophecy itself. Is it not as if the whole religion of Israel is ground as between two millstones, between the Word of God, which so definitely institutes and orders and forms it, and the Word of God by which, one must almost say, every concrete obedience to this command is no less definitely unmasked as unbelief ? May we not ask whether in this gruesome process an injustice is not done to this people, which is obviously so deeply and seriously religious, which in the end, in spite of all its mistakes and aberrations, tenaciously holds on to its religion through a thousand years of the most trying and difficult circumstances ? We shall not ask this question, but we shall understand the process, if we realise that in it—and in this respect, too, the Old Testament has exemplary significance—the judgment of revelation upon religion as such does actually fall upon the religion of revelation. For that very reason the process can, and indeed must, close almost as a matter of course with the promise of salvation, which psychologically and historically is so difficult to explain. It has nothing whatever to do with a sentimental touch of sunset glow after the storm. It belongs so necessarily to the Word of judgment, because the Word of judgment is so comprehensive and profound. It points to the inconceivable divine acquittal. It shows us that the chastened are those whom God loves, that the killed are those who are to live. The Word always remains. The covenant of Yahweh remains, though broken and disgraced. Therefore Israel remains the people, and its religion the religion, of revelation : that is, up to Jesus Christ. With His rejection Israel did not as formerly commit one specific sin. With it, it did not merely break and disgrace the Word and covenant. It denied and abandoned it in substance. Again, and this time comprehensively, the fate of Israel is exemplary. The religion of revelation is indeed bound up with the revelation of God : but the revelation of God is not bound up with the religion of revelation. The prophetic criticism of religion is now seen to be prediction. The abstraction which for a thousand years was only a burning question threatening on the horizon is now achieved. What appeared only from time to time, invariably to be overcome by its opposite, is now revealed in all its nakedness, as human religion. Once it was the human answer to the divine revelation as demanded and ordered by God Himself. In its exercise it was accused and condemned of unbelief, but always readopted into grace. But now—the example had to be recorded—it is a rejected and an emptied religion. It is a religion deprived of its basis and object. It is the Jewish religion from which God has turned away His face. It is one amongst other religions and no more than they. Its only advantage is the terrible one that once it was more than they, but only once. It is so absolutely by the grace of God that the true religion is the true one, that it has to let itself be unmasked and condemned by grace as false religion. If it rejects grace, and therewith its unmerited acquittal, it can never be anything more than false religion, unbelief, idolatry and self-righteousness. If the Church knows what it is doing when it regards its religion, the Christian religion, as the true one, it must never close its eyes to this example or its ears to the warnings of Amos and Jeremiah.

It is just the same in the New Testament. When the disciples are seen as men, independently, as it were, of their commission, and of the directing and sustaining word of Jesus, when they stand for a moment on their own feet the far side of Easter and Pentecost, then in a transition no less sharp than that of

Old Testament Israel, and obviously under the same order, they at once enter that peculiar shadow-world where their religion is seen to be a religion and therefore unbelief. The chief exemplary figure in this respect is the apostle Peter. The Roman Church would have been right to claim succession from this particular apostle if it had considered his part a little more closely. When Peter stands on his own feet, he is the man who does not mean the things of God but the things of men (Mt. 16²³). He is the doubter who ventures, and then immediately withdraws (Mt. 14²⁸ᶠ·). He can cut off the right ear of Malchus (Jn. 18¹⁰), but then deny Jesus thrice. He is the one to whom Jesus unequivocally says : When thou hast turned again, stablish thy brethren. (Lk. 22³²). But what strange figures the rest of the disciples also cut. We remember the recurrent question : Who is the greatest in the Kingdom of heaven ? (Mt. 18¹). We remember the sons of Zebedee with their wish to sit the one on the right hand of Jesus and the other on the left (Mk. 10³⁵ᶠ·). We think of the despair of the disciples in the storm on the lake : " Why are ye so fearful ? " " How is it that ye have no faith ? " (Mk. 4³⁵ᶠ·). We recall their sleeping in the garden of Gethsemane (Mk. 14³⁷), and their rashness and helplessness in so many other cases. " Behold, Satan hath desired to have you, that he might sift you as wheat ! " (Lk. 22³¹). There can be no doubt that what we are dealing with here is not just isolated or even frequent cases of omission and denial on the part of the disciples, but the extremely fundamental fact, that while Jesus has called them, and they are His followers, they belong to a γενεὰ ἄπιστος (Mk. 9¹⁹). They are wholly and utterly outside even while they are wholly and utterly inside. So far as they stand on their own feet, the four Gospels make it quite clear that they are wholly and utterly outside. It is clear that they have their religion, but it is equally clear that their religion is unbelief. If not, as in the confession of Peter (Mt. 16¹³ᶠ·) or the confession of Thomas (Jn. 20²⁴ᶠ·), then it is at once characterised as grace. Μὴ γίνου ἄπιστος, ἀλλὰ πιστός, says the risen Christ to Thomas, when He lets him touch His wounds (Jn. 20²⁷). We have an explicit statement of the matter in Jn. 15¹ᶠ· The disciples are the branches in Jesus Christ the Vine. If a branch brings forth no fruit it is cut off. If it brings forth fruit, it is cleansed, that it may bear more fruit. " Ye are already clean for the word's sake, which I have spoken unto you. Abide in me as I in you. As the vine cannot bring forth fruit of itself, if it abide not in the vine, so neither do ye, except ye abide in me. I am the vine, ye are the branches. If a man abide in me, as I in him, he bringeth forth much fruit : without me ye can do nothing (χωρὶς ἐμοῦ οὐ δύνασθε ποιεῖν οὐδέν). If a man abide not in me, he is cast out as a branch, which dries up and men gather them and cast them into the fire and burn them." The Acts, of course, shows us the acts of the same disciples, now as apostles, as fruitbearing branches " in the vine." But that " in the vine " must not be overlooked, the reminder " without me ye can do nothing " must not be suppressed, when in their person Christianity confronts the false religions of the Jews and the heathen as the religion which is unequivocally true. And it is not their person, but their office which is characterised in this way. It is the outpouring of the Holy Spirit which gives us the indispensable key to the story. That now as formerly the Christian religion can still be unbelief, when it is not by the grace of God faith, we see in the figures of Ananias and Sapphira (Ac. 5¹ᶠ·), or in the form of Simon Magus (Ac. 8¹³ᶠ·), or in a different way in the disciples of John at Ephesus (Ac. 19¹ᶠ·). In the apostolic letters the main passage which points in this direction is 1 Cor. 13 (which we shall best understand if for the concept " love " we simply insert the name Jesus Christ). The chapter summarises the whole religious life of a Christian community at the time of Paul : speaking with tongues, prophecy, knowledge of mysteries, a faith that removes mountains, giving all one's goods to the poor, martyrdom in the flames to close—and of all this it is said that it helps the Christian not at all, absolutely not at all, if he has not love. For love alone never fails. Prophecy, speaking with tongues, knowledge, all these will be " done away." Their work is only partial. It is not the whole, and therefore it is nothing. It is childish thinking which must be left behind. It is the indirect reflection in a glass. At the very heart of the apostolic witness (which accepts the Christian as the true religion) Christianity could not be more comprehensively relativised in favour of revelation, which means a crisis even for the religion of revelation.

Now it is not the case that this relativising of the Christian religion means that Christian faith is made weak or uncertain or hesitant, or that the decision for the truth of the Christian religion is robbed of its firmness and confidence. Christian faith does not live by the self-consciousness with which the Christian man can differentiate himself from the non-Christian. There is such a self-consciousness, and in its own place it, of course, is both right and necessary. But this self-consciousness has its natural limitations. It cannot possibly mean that the Christian would try to assert himself before God in a righteousness and holiness of his own. Unbroken in relation to man, it is broken in relation to God. It is because it is broken in the one case that it is unbroken in the other.

At this point we can adduce analogically what Paul says in 1 Cor. 4²¹· about his attitude to criticism levelled against him in Corinth. He is not only not afraid to be judged by the Corinthians or by any other human court. He does not even think of judging himself; οὐδὲν γὰρ ἐμαυτῷ σύνοιδα—an unbroken self-consciousness indeed ! But—" I am not hereby justified : but he that judgeth me is the Lord . . . He will reveal the hidden things of darkness, and make manifest the counsels of the hearts ; and then shall every man have praise of God." The apostolic self-consciousness which is unbroken in relation to man is therefore breached in this way. Similarly in Rom. 4¹· Paul did not simply deny to Abraham as the father of Israel and all believers any " justification by works " or corresponding καύχημα. He pointed to the fact that according to the word of Scripture there can never be any question of boasting before God. The justification of Abraham before God is the justification of a godless man. His faith is faith in that justification and not trust in his own works, in circumcision and the Law. In brief, it is not his religious self-consciousness.

It is with this delimiting of the religious self-consciousness that the knowledge of the relativising of even the Christian religion by divine revelation is concerned. We reach this delimiting in faith and by faith. How can it possibly signify a weakening of faith ? On the contrary, faith will prove its power, and in the power of faith the Christian will live, in the very fact that faith continuously compels him to think beyond his religious self-consciousness, and therefore constantly to reckon with the relativising of his Christian religion by divine revelation. And, of course, in this light and only in this light the decision for the truth of the Christian religion can be taken with real power. Strong human positions are only those which are fully abandoned to God : that is, positions which are seen to be quite untenable when measured by His will and judgment. Even from the standpoint of our own being and activity, we do not act prudently, but the very reverse, when we entrench ourselves against God in some tiny chink of our own being and activity, and try to secure ourselves. Not only our security before God, but the very security of our being and activity, and therefore our security in relation to men, rests absolutely upon our willingness in faith and by faith to renounce any such securities.

In this connexion we ought to consider the remarkable passage 2 Cor. 12$^{1f.}$. There can be no doubt that Paul is not here speaking of the religion of the Christian Church, as in 1 Cor. 13, but very personally of his own most intimate religious experience. There are great things of which he might glory in this sphere, of which, indeed, he could glory in truth, and without talking nonsense. He has been the recipient of ὀπτασίαι καὶ ἀποκαλύψεις, and in particular, " fourteen years ago " he has known a rapture into the third heaven, into Paradise, associated with the hearing of " unspeakable words," which cannot be repeated. But who is it who can really glory in all these things ? Three times (vv. 2, 3, 5) Paul speaks of him impersonally : " I know a man. . . ." He calls him a " man in Christ." Undoubtedly he means himself. But—and this is the distinctive thing in the description of this ecstasy—he puts a space between himself and this man. And it is only at this remove that he will take part in the glory which this man—himself—has by virtue of these high things. " To the honour of this man I will boast ; but to my own honour I will not boast, though it be because of weakness " (v. 5 acc. to Schlatter). He is restrained from being lifted up by these experiences (v. 7 f.), and is forced into this paradoxical glorying because of weakness. For, like a thorn in the flesh, an angel of Satan stands at his side to buffet him. Not even the most earnest prayer to Jesus Christ can frighten away this enemy. Indeed, Paul obviously does not now want to frighten him away. In his presence and activity he now sees the order in the power of which he is held outside the circle of these experiences : at the place where Christ dwells beside him, i.e., in his weakness. The Lord's answer to his prayer is this : ἀρκεῖ σοι ἡ χάρις μου · ἡ γὰρ δύναμις ἐν ἀσθενείᾳ τελεῖται (v. 9). He will therefore glory only in his weakness : " For when I am weak, then am I strong." But what is his weakness ? Well, it is what is left of his Christian existence after deducting the religious experience of which he might reasonably and truly boast, i.e., humiliations, emergencies, persecutions, distresses for Christ's sake (v. 10). In these he sees the power of Christ dwelling in him. In these he knows that he is strong. In these he glories. And in Paul we can see how the real security of his being and activity, the power of his decision, the strength of even his outward position, the whole energy of his religious self-consciousness in relation to that of others, is rooted in the fact that he let everything, the Christian religion, and *in concreto* his own specific " revelations," be most definitely limited by revelation, by the Lord Jesus Christ : for " when I am weak, then am I strong."

We are here concerned with an order which can be forgotten or infringed only to the detriment of a real knowledge of the truth of the Christian religion. Again, to ascribe the demonstrative power for this truth to the religious self-consciousness as such is to the dishonouring of God and the eternal destruction of souls. Even outwardly, in its debate with non-Christian religions, the Church can never do more harm than when it thinks that it must abandon the apostolic injunction, that grace is sufficient for us. The place to which we prefer to look is only mist, and the reed upon which we have to lean will slip through our fingers. By trying to resist and conquer other religions, we put ourselves on the same level. They, too, appeal to this or that immanent truth in them. They, too, can triumph in the power of the religious self-consciousness, and sometimes they have been astonishingly successful over wide areas. Christianity can take part in this fight. There is no doubt that it does not lack the necessary equipment, and can give a good account of itself alongside the other religions. But do not forget that if it does this it has renounced its birthright. It has renounced the unique power which it has as the religion of revelation. This power dwells only in weakness. And it does not really operate, nor does the power with which Christianity hopes to work, the power of religious self-consciousness which is the gift of grace in the midst of weakness, unless Christianity has first humbled instead of exalting itself.

By its neglect of this order Christianity has created great difficulties for itself in its debate with other religions. We can see these difficulties developing in three historical stages.
1. It was at the very least noticeable in the days of the early Church before Constantine. At that time Christianity had one great advantage. As a *religio illicita*, an *ecclesia pressa*, it was, as it were, automatically forced into something like the apostolic position, i.e., the apostolic weakness. The adherents of the Christian religion could not acquire any great credit by their cause, at any rate externally, in the field of politics, society or culture. They and their faith were alone against a hopeless, external super-power. They were fighting in a lost position. The angel seemed indeed to be buffetting them to prevent their reaching up to high revelations. They seemed to be automatically directed to boasting of nothing but this weakness of theirs, i.e., to resting in the sufficiency of grace. But the external super-power by which they were opposed, the later heathendom of antiquity, was a Colossus with feet of clay, as the apologists, the more primitive Church fathers and, of course, all the keener-sighted leaders of the contemporary Church were very well aware, in spite of all the pressure of persecution. Christian doctrine and practice possessed all the necessary qualities to commend itself against this heathendom, as the more profound and universal and serious religion. It was a real temptation, not merely to validate Jesus Christ against or for the sinful men of heathen religion, as the sacred books of the Church, the Old Testament and New Testament, demanded, but at the same time (and very quickly on a fairly broad front) to play off the Christian religion as better than the heathen, to contrast Christian possession—which can easily be demonstrated in many if not all spheres of the spiritual life—with heathen poverty. When we read the apologetics of the second and third centuries, can we altogether avoid the painful impression that what we have here—as though the persecuted can only regard themselves as spiritually undeserving of the external pressure brought to bear on them—is, on the whole, a not very happy, a rather self-righteous, and at any rate a not very perspicacious boasting about all those advantages of Christianity over heathen religion which were in themselves incontestable but not ultimately decisive ? In these early self-commendations of Christianity a remarkably small part is played by the fact that grace is the truth of Christianity, that the Christian is justified when he is without God, like Abraham, that he is like the publican in the temple, the prodigal son, wretched Lazarus, the guilty thief crucified with Jesus Christ. Instead, we have the—admittedly successful—rivalry of one way of salvation, one wisdom and morality with others, of a higher humanity consummated and transfigured by the cross of Christ with a decadent and defeated humanity which has rightly grown weary of its ancient ideals. How strangely did a man like Tertullian see the danger which threatened at this point, and at the same time never really

see it at all, but actually help to increase it. And to the extent that the fact that grace, that Jesus Christ, is the truth of Christianity was never completely concealed in the doctrine and proclamation of the Church, did not the fact that Christianity is the special religion of grace and redemption easily appear to be its final and supreme advantage, although it was robbed of its real meaning and power to convince by the fact that the Church was not content with grace ? Both materially and formally that which is centrally and uniquely Christian was abandoned or replaced. To the extent that that took place, material and formal comparisons were everywhere made with the world, with the intention of prevailing over it at any rate spiritually. Against the power of syncretism, which was so integral to that passing spiritual world, only the might of spiritual poverty and the power of revelation within it could have emerged successfully. To the extent that this power constantly reappeared, the truth of Christianity spoke and shone forth. So far as the Early Church was great, it was so by this power. If only the Early Church had not already trusted far too much to other powers, and thereby weakened itself, and paved the way for further weakenings.

2. At first the Church was exposed to external pressure. Because of this there was an external resemblance to the original apostolic situation. The Church was compelled constantly to reflect and to return to that which is ultimate and real. But all this came to an end with the developments which took place after Constantine and it quite disappeared in the whole period which was dominated by the idea of the *Corpus Christianum*. Certainly this idea of the unity of Church and state has to be regarded as an extremely promising offer made to the Christianity of that period. But we must hasten to add that it then proved itself to be quite unprepared for the offer, not having outgrown the temptations associated with it. As already the Early Church had reflected more upon its intellectual than its spiritual superiority over against the heathen world around it, and had presumed more upon its monotheism, its ethics, its mystery, than upon its spirituality, upon the grace of Jesus Christ, so now as the acknowledged Imperial Church, in open alliance with the higher and lower political factors, it could find its greatness in the fact that it became increasingly a second world-power. It could make it its ambition—under the plea that it was, of course, a matter of the glory of God—to try to become the first and real world-power instead of the second. Where was the awareness of grace as the truth of Christianity in the days of the investiture-conflict and the crusades, or in the world of Gothic ? To what extent was this a real concern in the great reform movement of Cluny and monasticism generally ? To what extent could heathen and Jews find in the mediæval Church a power which was genuinely different, a novel and unfamiliar power, not the power which men can always demonstrate, but the power of God which humbles and therefore blesses all men, the power of the Gospel ? To what extent could the Church confront the Islam which oppressed it in South and East as something which was really original ? To what extent could the Christian opponents of the Church, the imperial and national parties or the heretical sects, deduce from the action and attitude of the Church that there was any concern for the glory of God and not its own glory ? Obviously much less as the spiritual alienation of the Church from its own centre and the inward secularisation that accompanied it, both of which had been prepared in the early period, now increased more and more. Christianity was moulded according to a definite universal, intellectual-moral-æsthetic form, which made possible, and inevitable, the complementary formation of all kinds of particular national Christianities, each with its own particular national-religious self-consciousness. To what extent was this form, either in itself or in its individual variations, an evidence of the truth of Christianity ? Certainly it was evidence of a unique and rich religious self-consciousness, i.e., a testimony to the glory of Western man, educated and formed or stimulated and influenced by the Church as the (only too legitimate) heiress of ancient civilisation. But it could be an evidence of

the supreme, victorious truth of Christianity only in so far as in it it is secretly and ultimately a matter of the grace of Jesus Christ. And in spite of its zealous and absorbed activity in other respects, in this decisive respect the Church showed far too little vigilance and loyalty. The evidence of grace was not destroyed. It maintained its quiet force. Even in this world revelation shone out in the spiritual poverty of those who believed it as it is meant to be believed. But it did so in the Church only against the Church (i.e., against the tendency which dominated the Church, against the proud but treacherous idea of the *corpus christianum*). On the very road on which it sought its strength, the Church of this time did the thing that was bound to weaken it at the critical point.

3. The way was prepared for the so-called " modern period " by the trends of the later Middle Ages, and the Renaissance. As concerns Christianity, it is characterised by a fresh collapse of the unity of the Church and state. Western humanity has come of age, or thinks it has. It can now dispense with its teacher —and as such official Christianity had in fact felt and behaved. Man finds himself as a " universum," and although he cannot at once throw off his respect for the teacher, he feels that he can at last go his way with head erect. Grateful for what they have received, but determined upon a secular factuality, politics, science, society and art all dare to stand on their own feet. The floods have receded, and behold, there is nothing much left after the thousand years of the apparent domination of Christianity except a little monotheism, morality and mysticism. As a whole, the humanity of the West does not seem to find in the Church or to ascribe to it anything more. Because of that, it does not feel compelled to remain tied to the Church. That is the joyous discovery which it now makes. Nor does the heathendom which surrounds the tiny peninsula of Europe and its transmarine colonies, or the fierce Judaism which continues to exist in the midst of Christianity, seem to have heard any more than this, or heard it with any emphasis from the mouth of the Church. In spite of the most favourable conditions of the Middle Ages, the Christian Church obviously could not impress world consciousness as anything more than a religious society. Under these favourable conditions it tried to bind and to dominate. But the increased secularisation of culture makes it plain that it has not been able to do this. So now again, as at the first, it is forced on to the defensive. At first, of course, there is no hint of outward repression or persecution. There is no reason for this. Certainly, it is opposed until well on in the 19th century, so far as it is a matter of liberation from mediæval claims. But the moment it decides on a certain reserve and toleration, its freedom is conceded. There is no question of its being dangerous and of having to be radically persecuted, as had happened with full consciousness under the dying rule of antiquity. What is primarily in question in these centuries is the possibility that, assigned to its proper limits, the Church or Christianity may be an important and, under suitable oversight, a useful and usable force for education and order in the service of the new secular glory of Western man. And the non-Christian religions are on exactly the same level as inward Christian secularism, being content with a certain reserve and toleration on their own part and maintaining a mild indifference to the newer Christianity, so far as they come into contact with it. Of course, it might be dangerous for modern secularism and the non-Christian religions if the truth of Christianity, the grace of God in its radical and critical power, again found expression. It is significant that the only case in which there has been hostility to the Church in modern times, the persecution which early Protestantism had to suffer so long in many lands, was connected with the very fact that this truth had again found utterance. But that is long ago. When the mediæval dream was over, even Protestantism had, and knew how, to adapt itself to the existence of a religious society which modern man regards as ultimately unnecessary and innocuous. And as a whole the more modern Christian Church never even gave a thought to retracing the false path prepared in early days or following what

was openly neglected in the Middle Ages. In the reconsideration of itself and
its possibilities imposed by the new situation, it did not attain again to the
weakness in which alone it can always be strong. Instead, it inwardly affirmed
the new situation, as it had previously affirmed the old. That is to say, it
accepted modern man with his energetic attitude to himself, asking how best
Christianity could be commended to that man. It took up the role allotted to
it, and was at pains to make itself indispensable in it, i.e., by pointing out
and demonstrating that if there is a truth in the Christian religion which can
profitably be heard and believed, especially in the modern age, it consists in this,
that properly understood, the doctrine of Jesus Christ, and the way of life which
corresponds to it, has the secret power of giving to man the inward capacity to
seek and attain the aims and purposes which he has independently chosen. In
seeking after this new self-commendation, on the converging lines of Jesuistry,
Pietism and the Enlightenment, it became secular anthropologically, in the same
way as in the Middle Ages it had been secular theologically. And it was in seeking after this new self-commendation that it arrived, among other things, at the
discovery of the general concept of " religion," the theological history of which
we have briefly considered. Therefore it all amounted to this : that within the
general anthropological concept, recognised by the non-Christian world as well,
the particular " nature of Christianity " should be reliably disclosed and declared
at the same human level, from the same viewpoints and on the plane of the same
arguments used by those who thought that they could dispense with it, i.e., in
the area of human and humanly perceived advantages and disadvantages, strong
points and weak points, probabilities and improbabilities, hopes and fears. There
was a certain resemblance to the situation under the Roman Empire—although
without the corrective of outward persecution. But Christianity was now represented as a better foundation for philosophy and morality, as a better satisfaction of ultimate needs, as a better actualisation of the supreme ideals of modern
man, than any of its various competitors. Just at this time and on these presuppositions, and supported by the Jesuits and the Protestant Pietists, there
was a comprehensive re-adoption of the missionary task of the Christian Church.
The result was a fresh confrontation of Christianity with the non-Christian
religions. It was inevitable that both the mission and the confrontation should
suffer most heavily from the fact that the sending Church was itself seeking its
strength at a different point from where it could be found. And the debate
whether the aim of the mission was the representing of an Americo-European
or the founding of an autochthonous African and Asiatic Christianity, could
not help towards a solution of the hidden difficulty that either way the main
concern was the " glory " of this or that Christianity in its relation to the needs
and postulates of man. Now, in this third period, both in the Christian West
and on the mission fields, it has always been the case that the truth of Christianity,
the grace of Jesus Christ, has spoken, shone through and interpenetrated in
the spiritual poverty of those who in this age believed in Him. But in this age,
too, this was in contradiction to the tendencies and directions that dominated
Church history. So far as these tendencies and directions dominated and determined the situation, it was inevitable that Christianity should surrender its truth
to the continual fluctuations of modern man, that tossed about from one unclean hand to another its truth should seem to be the now absolutely authoritarian,
now individually romantic, now liberal, now national or even racial truth of man,
but not the truth of God which judges and blesses, and which it continually
claimed to be according to the original and strangely enough unsilenced documents of Christianity. During this third period of its history Christianity and
the Church have had experience of many victories—more than would have been
dreamed at the peak of the period in the 18th century. But no one should be
deceived about the fact that they were Pyrrhic victories. And the no less
numerous reverses, which it suffered on the same road, were more significant

of the real state of things than the victories. And it may be that modern secularism for its part is still far from the end of its ways and possibilities. It may be that the powers of the heathen religions are far from being exhausted. If this is the case, it might become an ever more burning question, whether from the very standpoint of its existence as such, of its validity and task in the world, Christianity does not have cause to give a body blow to its own secularism and heathenism, which means—for everything else is secular and heathen—to set its hope wholly and utterly on grace.

We must not allow ourselves to be confused by the fact that a history of Christianity can be written only as a story of the distress which it makes for itself. It is a story which lies completely behind the story of that which took place between Yahweh and His people, between Jesus and His apostles. It is a story whose source and meaning and goal, the fact that the Christian is strong only in his weakness, that he is really satisfied by grace, can in the strict sense nowhere be perceived directly. Not even in the history of the Reformation ! What can be perceived in history is the attempt which the Christian makes, in continually changing forms, to consider and vindicate his religion as a work which is in itself upright and holy. But he continually feels himself thwarted and hampered and restrained by Holy Scripture, which does not allow this, which even seems to want to criticise this Christian religion of his. He obviously cannot shut out the recollection that it is in respect of this very work of his religion that he cannot dispense with the grace of God and therefore stands under the judgment of God. At this point we are particularly reminded of the history of the Reformation. But in the very light of that history we see that the recollection has always been there, even in the pre- and post-Reformation periods. Yet the history of Christianity as a whole reveals a tendency which is quite contrary to this recollection. It would be arbitrary not to recognise this, and to claim that the history of Christianity, as distinct from that of other religions, is the story of that part of humanity, which, as distinct from others, has existed only as the part which of grace lives by grace. In the strict sense there is no evidence of this throughout the whole range of Christianity. What is evident is in the first instance a part of humanity which no less contradicts the grace and revelation of God because it claims them as its own peculiar and most sacred treasures, and its religion is to that extent a religion of revelation. Contradiction is contradiction. That it exists at this point, in respect of the religion of revelation, can be denied even less than at other points. Elsewhere we might claim in extenuation that it simply exists in fact, but not in direct contrast with revelation. But in the history of Christianity, just because it is the religion of revelation, the sin is, as it were, committed with a high hand. Yes, sin ! For contradiction against grace is unbelief, and unbelief is sin, indeed it is *the* sin. It is, therefore, a fact that we can speak of the truth of the Christian religion only within the doctrine of the *iustificatio impii*. The statement that even Christianity is unbelief gives rise to a whole mass of naive and rationalising contradiction. Church history itself is a history of this contradiction. But it is this very fact which best shows us how true and right the statement is. We can as little avoid the contradiction as jump over our own shadow.

We cannot expect that at a fourth or fifth or sixth stage, the history of Christianity will be anything but a history of the distress which Christianity creates for itself. May it not lack in future reformation, i.e., expressions of warning and promise deriving from Holy Scripture ! But before the end of all things we cannot expect that the Christian will not always show himself an enemy of grace, in spite of all intervening restraints.

Notwithstanding the contradiction and therefore our own existence, we can and must perceive that for our part we and our contradiction against grace stand under the even more powerful contradiction of grace itself. We can and must—in faith. To believe means, in the knowledge of our own sin to rely upon the righteousness of God which makes an infinite satisfaction for our sin. Concretely, it means, in the knowledge of our own contradiction against grace to cleave to the grace of God which infinitely contradicts this contradiction. In this knowledge of grace, in the knowledge that it is the justification of the ungodly, that it is grace for the enemies of grace, the Christian faith attains to its knowledge of the truth of the Christian religion. There can be no more question of any immanent rightness or holiness of this particular religion as the ground and content of the truth of it, than there can be of any other religion claiming to be the true religion in virtue of its inherent advantages. The Christian cannot avoid abandoning any such claim. He cannot avoid confessing that he is a sinner even in his best actions as a Christian. And that is not, of course, the ground, but the symptom of the truth of the Christian religion. The abandoning and confessing means that the Christian Church is the place where, confronted with the revelation and grace of God, by grace men live by grace. If this were not so, how would they believe ? And if they did not believe, how would they be capable of this abandoning and confessing ?

The passage in Gen. 32²²ᶠ·, on Jacob's wrestling at Jabbok, can throw light on this. It says of Jacob, who undoubtedly is already elected and called by God, that he wrestles with God until morning, and that God—obviously—does not overcome him. From the immanent standpoint he is and continues to be an enemy of grace. This is indicated by the new name Israel, which he acquires : " Thou hast striven with God and with men and hast prevailed "—a great distinction, but at bottom a shattering one, which reminds us of the religious history of the people whose ancestor Jacob was. The giving of this name to Jacob is a fulfilment of the judgment. But that is not the meaning and object of the history. After the conflict the sinew of Jacob's thigh is touched and dislocated by God. So, then, although he is not overcome by God, he is and continues to be a man weakened by God. Again, in his wrestling against God, Jacob will not let God go, because he desires to be blessed by Him. Again, God actually does bless this stedfast opponent of His. And finally, Jacob calls the place of this conflict with God " Peniel " : " For I have seen God face to face and my life is preserved." The place where there is knowledge of the truth of the Christian religion will have to be such a Peniel, and it can be such a Peniel only where a man stands wholly and utterly against God, and in this resistance against God he is marked by God, and therefore cannot make any other request than : " I will not let thee go, except thou bless me," and in this very prayer of his he is heard and blessed, and in this very blessing he sees the face of God and in it he knows the truth.

We describe the victorious grace of God as the mystery of the truth of the Christian religion. But it must again be emphasised expressly that this means something more than that in its Reformation form at any rate Christianity claims particularly to be the religion of free grace, i.e., a religion whose doctrine and life is now directly concentrated upon the reality described in the concept " grace." When we ground the truth of the Christian religion upon grace, it is not a question of the immanent truth of a religion of grace as such, but of the reality of the grace itself by which one religion is adopted and distinguished as the true one before all others. It is not because it is a religion of grace that this happens, nor is it because it is so perhaps in a particularly insistent and logical way. But conversely, it is because this happens that it is a religion of grace in an insistent and logical way. Of course, in its decisive features, the historical aspect of a religion of grace, even of a logical religion of grace, does not differ from that of other religions. In its immanent constitution it is involved absolutely in the contradiction against grace. Indeed, and at this point we cannot really try to save Protestantism—it may even assume the character of a particularly emphatic revolt against grace. Even the religion of grace can be justified and constituted the true religion only by grace and not of itself. Of course, its election and truth are manifested in the fact that it is the religion of grace, and in consequence always understands and forms itself as such. The symptom of the surrender of every human claim, the confessing that we continually contradict God, will certainly not be wanting. It is inevitable that in contradicting we know that we are thrown upon the One whom we contradict and who in a different way contradicts us, and we cannot fail to thank Him for the blessing of which we are so entirely unworthy. It is in this way, in the very encounter with God, the site of which we call Peniel or, it may be, Evangelical Reformed Christianity, that the face of God is seen, and therefore Peniel or Evangelical Reformed Christianity is the true religion. But we must not forget that it is not the symptoms, and therefore not the site we call by this name, which demonstrate the true religion, but that it is the truth itself which is the basis of the symptoms and distinguishes the site, so that we can call it this without being tied down to the site and symptoms. The truth itself is indispensable if in our consideration of the site and symptoms, however plain, we are not to be deceived concerning the truth of the Christian religion.

We can regard it as a wholly providential disposition that as far as I can see the most adequate and comprehensive and illuminating heathen parallel to Christianity, a religious development in the Far East, is parallel not to Roman or Greek Catholicism, but to Reformed Christianity, thus confronting Christianity with the question of its truth even as the logical religion of grace. We are referring to the two related Buddhist developments in 12th and 13th century Japan (i.e., during the life-times of Francis of Assisi, Thomas Aquinas and Dante) : the Yodo-Shin (" Sect of the Pure Land," founded by Genku-Honen) and the Yodo-Shin-Shu (" True Sect of the Pure Land," founded by Genku's pupil Shinran). (Cf. for what follows : K. Florenz, " Die Japaner," in Chantepie de la Saussaye, *Lehrb. d. Rel. Gesch.*[2] Vol. 1, 1925, p. 382 ff., and Tiele-Söderblom, *Komp. d. Rel. Gesch.*[6] p. 197 ff.). The movements are a turning-point in the religious history of Japan. Their point of departure is the belief of Genku that the earlier forms of Japanese Buddhism, particularly that of the Zen-sects which flourished in the 12th century, were honourable and right, but that they were too severe for the mass of the people and therefore unattainable. What they had demanded had been that man should redeem himself by his own efforts, i.e., by his striving after a higher morality, mystical absorption, and contemplative knowledge as the " path of holiness." In its place Genku wished to see substituted a fundamentally much easier way of salvation. For this purpose he gave a central position to the god " Amida-Buddha." This god had been preached in China since the 7th century—there was a possible connexion with the Nestorian mission —and in Japan since the 8th. It was named " infinite light " or " infinite life," and in the popular mind at least was regarded as the supreme and personal God. This Amida, it was taught, is the Creator and Lord of Paradise, a " pure land (*yodo*) in the West." The life-problem of man is to be born again there after death, and from there to attain to Nirvana. " There in blessedness we shall sit cross-legged on lotus flowers, and in contemplation of Amida gradually develop to a full ripeness of knowledge, in order at last to enter Nirvana " (Florenz, p. 387). But how do we arrive at this new birth ? Not by our own power, answers Genku, in sharp opposition to the other Buddhist sects. And he fastens decisively on a text which he took over from the Chinese tradition about Amida, heavily underlining it as the " primal promise." This text contained a vow of the God Amida himself, in virtue of which he himself, Amida, does not wish to accept complete enlightenment (Buddha-hood), unless all living creatures, who sincerely believe in him, and ten times desire of him regeneration into his country, participate in the fulfilment of this wish. So, taught Genku, we have to put all our trust not in our own strength, but in that of this other, Amida. We have to fulfil the one condition which he has attached to the attainment of salvation. We have to believe in Him, who has compassion on all, even sinners. We have to call on his name, and as we do so all his good works and meritorious acts stream into our mouths and become our own possession, so that our merit is Amida's merit, and there is no difference between him and us. We have to do this calling as often as possible. Particularly in the decisive hour of death we have to be sure when we call on this name that Amida will not reject even the greatest sinners, but will give them a corner in the paradise, which is the forecourt of Nirvana. Those who called on him, but with secret doubts, will be locked up for 500 years in the cup of a lotus flower in some corner of Paradise. And in a particularly significant way, those who did not succeed in relying wholly on faith and therefore on the efficacy of this calling, but who tried to secure themselves by the execution of so-called good works and religious practices, will find a preliminary lodging in the extreme West. The place provided is replete with heavenly delights, singing and dancing and playing. The obvious purpose of the purgatory is instruction, and from it they will depart to the fields of supreme blessedness. It was this doctrine of Genku and the Yodo-shin which was systematically developed by Shinran, the founder of the Yodo-Shin-Shu. Both doctrinally and practically he made it basic. Everything rested on the primal promise of the compassionate redeemer Amida and on faith in him. But whereas Genku knew the worship of another Buddha as well as Amida, this was now strictly forbidden. In short, Buddha-Gautama took second place as a mere herald of the Amida doctrine. Genku had not contested the possibility of meritorious works. Shinran denied them absolutely. As he saw it, everything depends on the faith of the heart. We are too firmly embedded in fleshly lusts to be able to extricate ourselves from the vicious circle of life and death by any form of self-activation. All that we can do is simply to give thanks for the redemption assured by Amida without any activity at all on our part. In the Yodo-Shu doctrine the hour of death loses its emphatic and critical character, and calling on Amida loses the last remnant of the character of an achievement or a magical act. It becomes simply a sign of our thankfulness. Genku had said : "Even sinners will enter into life ; how much more the righteous." But this was significantly reversed by Shinran : "If the righteous enter into life, how much more in the case of sinners." The redemptive significance of faith in Amida has nothing to do with feelings or joy of heart, or even the strength of the longing for salvation. There are, of course, ways of awakening and strengthening faith. For example, we ought to avail ourselves of the opportunity to be instructed in sacred doctrine. We ought to ponder its meaning. We ought habitually to hold discussions with religiously minded friends. We ought to recite the Amida-prayer in a gentle voice. In face of our utter sinfulness we ought to strengthen ourselves with the marvellous thought that because of the primal promise we are not rejected. But we must also know that even faith in this primal promise is ultimately a gift of God. Yet faith is for everyone, even for women—an unheard of innovation in the world of Buddhism. We shall not be surprised, then, to learn that Yodo-Shin-Shu knows nothing of bidding prayers, magic formulas and actions, amulets, pilgrimages, penances, fasts and other kinds of asceticism, monasticism. The cult-object in its rich temples is simply a picture or statue of Amida. Its priests have no mediatorial significance. Their function is to instruct believers and to carry out the practices of the church. They wear vestments only in the temple. They are subject neither to special laws of food nor to celibacy. Great emphasis is laid upon their activity in the way of instruction, preaching and edifying popular literature. The effect of faith in Amida, inculcated into the laity, is morality of life in the framework of family, state and calling. They are " to exercise self-discipline, to live in harmony with others, to keep order, to be obedient to the national laws, and as good citizens to care for the welfare of the state " (Florenz, p. 397). As distinct from the other Japanese sects Yodo-Shin-Shu has never let itself be supported legally or financially by the government. From the outset it has been completely free from the state, its main activity being in the large cities. We are not really surprised that St. Francis Xavier, who was the first Christian missionary to live in Japan (1549–1551), thought that he recognised in Yodo-Shin-Shu the " Lutheran heresy." But the question raised has an importance which is more than historical, for (according to Florenz, p. 398) half of the total population of Japan, at any rate a good third, still adhere to this church.

(In the same context we are also reminded of the Indian Bhakti religion. But even if we accept the parallel, it is not nearly so forceful as the Japanese one. Bhakti is an act of utter surrender and resignation. In it our own will is placed absolutely at the service of another's. It can easily be intensified into a personal act of inward inclination and love. The high or supreme God to whom Bhakti is offered can have any name or character. It is the emotion of love itself and as such which redeems man, which enables him to participate in the answering love of God, which even in earthly things allows him to be sympathetic and kindly, unselfish, patient and serene. There is mention of a certain neutralising of all other means of salvation. As a kind of modest counterpart to the Protestant doctrine of justification, there is mention of a "cat rule," by which the soul of everything can be surrendered to God and does not need to make any effort, because God leads it to salvation in the same way as a cat carries its kitten. This is in contrast to a "monkey-rule," in which God's relation to the soul is characterised by the she monkey, to which the young must still cling even while they are carried. The most uncertain part played by the idea of God, the substitution of surrender and love for faith, and the utter and complete formlessness even of the concept of love, show that we are in a quite different world from that of the Japanese religion of grace, and an absolutely different world from that of Evangelical Christianity. It would be a very degenerate form of modern Evangelical Christianity which felt that the Bhakti religions could claim kinship with it.)

It is only the "Japanese Protestantism" of Genku and Shinran which calls for serious consideration. When I said that its existence is a providential disposition, I meant that we ought not to be startled even momentarily by the striking parallelism of it to the truth of Christianity, but that we should be grateful for the lesson which it so abundantly and evidently teaches. And the lesson is this : that in its historical form, as a mode of doctrine, life and order, the Christian religion cannot be the one to which the truth belongs *per se*—not even if that form be the Reformed. For obviously the form, even if Reformed, can never be proved to be incontestably original. Of course, no one in his senses would ever dream of speaking of an identity between Christian and Japanese "Protestantism." In practice no two natural or historical forms are ever the same. It is, therefore, well to note (1) that the starting-point of the Yodo-movement is obviously the popular demand for an easier and simpler road to salvation ; but no one can say of either Luther or Calvin that they begin at that point. The consequence is (2) that among the Yodoistic ideas parallel to the Reformed, we miss any doctrine of the law and also of the holiness, or wrath of Amida. There is nothing to relieve the goodness and mercy of this God. There is nothing dramatic in his redemption of man. It does not have the character of a real solution. From this it seems (3) that in the Yodoistic antithesis to cultic-ethical righteousness by works there is lacking that accent of a struggle for the glory of God against the arbitrariness and boasting of man which is given its proper stress in Paul and later in the Reformers, especially Calvin. In this case it seems to be based entirely on a pastoral concern which, as such, is held to be obviously incontestable. (4) Yodoism and all Buddhism stand or fall with the inner power and validity of the stormy desire of man for redemption by dissolution ; for entry into Nirvana, to which the "pure land" attainable by faith alone is merely the forecourt ; for the Buddha-hood, whose perfection even the God Amida has not yet reached. In the Yodo religion it is not Amida or faith in him, but this human goal of desire which is the really controlling and determinative power. Amida, and faith in him, and the "pure land," to which faith is the entry, are related to this goal only as the means to the end. On a closer examination, therefore, there are not wanting noteworthy immanent distinctions between the Japanese and Christian "Protestantism." An ever closer examination would show that they are even wider and deeper than stated. But to point out these distinctions is not to state the decisive factor. Yodoism can certainly be compared without violence to the simple Christian "Protestantism" which countless souls have thought of as the true Protestantism ever since the 16th century, which has found a definite self-conception and self-expression in Lutheranism especially, and which was to some extent that of Luther himself. Without being arbitrary, we can think of the magicians of Pharaoh, Ex. 7, who could at least do the same miracles as Aaron, even though he was the brother of Moses :

the similarity was enough to make Pharaoh harden his heart. With so many similarities even the distinctions might give rise ultimately—perhaps as a result of contact with Christianity—to a further immanent development of Yodoism to an even purer form and in that way to an almost complete equality with Christian Protestantism. And this would mean that Yodoism would take its place with the purest form of Christianity as a religion of grace. But even if there were no question of this, we should still have good reason to see in the distinctions symptoms, but only symptoms, of the real difference between true and false religion. As symptoms they have no decisive or really determinative force. They are not as such the truth as against a lie. They are only the seal of a truth which we must first receive elsewhere. We have to reckon with them in theory. But in the last resort even if they were lacking we should still have no doubts concerning the difference between truth and error. In other words, the Christian-Protestant religion of grace is not the true religion because it is a religion of grace. If that were the case, then, whatever our view of the distinctions, we could quite reasonably say the same of Yodoism, and, with a rather more blunted sensibility, of the Bhakti religion. Indeed, why should we not say it of a whole range of other religions, for which grace in different names and contexts is not a wholly foreign entity ? Only one thing is really decisive for the distinction of truth and error. And we call the existence of Yodoism a providential disposition because with what is relatively the greatest possible force it makes it so clear that only one thing is decisive. That one thing is the name of Jesus Christ. Methodologically, it is to be recommended that in face of Yodoism, and, at bottom, of all other religions, our first task is to concentrate wholly upon this distinction, provisionally setting aside whatever other deference we think we recognise. It is not merely a matter of prudentially weighing the various possibilities of heathen development, which might eventually catch up with the differences we teach, but of a clear insight that the truth of the Christian religion is in fact enclosed in the one name of Jesus Christ, and nothing else. It is actually enclosed in all the formal simplicity of this name as the very heart of the divine reality of revelation, which alone constitutes the truth of our religion. It is not enclosed, therefore, in its more or less explicit structure as the religion of grace, nor in the Reformation doctrines of original sin, representative satisfaction, justification by faith alone, the gift of the Holy Ghost and thankfulness. All this, as Figura shows, the heathen, too, can in their own way teach and even live and represent as a church. Yet that does not mean that they are any the less heathen, poor, and utterly lost. Our knowledge, and the life and churchmanship which correspond to it so badly, genuinely distinguish us from the heathen only to the extent they are at any rate symptoms of the grace and truth which is only Jesus Christ Himself and therefore the name of Jesus Christ for us—only to the extent that they are absolutely conditioned by this One and no other, and therefore tied to this name, their goal and content determined and fixed by it, strengthened and preserved by it. Christian Protestantism is the true religion to the extent that the Reformation was a reminder of the grace and truth determined in this name, and that this reminder is effective in it. The reminder was more a being reminded. And in the reminder it formed itself, or was formed (and with it in some measure the rest of Christendom) into what we now call accordingly an explicit religion of grace. Out of the reminder there sprang the doctrines of justification and predestination, the Evangelical doctrines of the Church, the sacraments, and the Christian life and all the other distinctive features, which more or less clearly mark it off in this way. As symptoms, as predicates of the subject Jesus Christ—and we can take them seriously in retrospect—they have acquired, and had, and do have the force of truth : the force of the confession and attestation of the truth. How should it not be demanded and proper to proclaim the name of Jesus Christ, and in it the truth of the Christian religion ? And now : in this symptomatic, confessional and attesting power, the not inconsiderable distinctions between the Christian and all non-Christian religions of grace become serious and important. We have good grounds for believing that even in respect of the twin-sided structure there is no real possibility of confusion. There can be no question, even in the future, of a real parallelism or coincidence between the doctrine and the life of the Christian and non-Christian religions of grace (however consistent). Instead, certain symptomatic distinctions will be visible here and there, in which the true and the essential distinction can always be perceived. But a conviction of this kind can be well-grounded only if it is based exclusively upon faith in the one and only Jesus Christ, for it is only from Him that the relative distinctions can have and constantly derive their relative light. Therefore the true and essential distinction of the Christian religion from the non-Christian, and with it its character as the religion of truth over against the religions of error, can be demonstrated only in the fact, or event, that taught by Holy Scripture the Church listens to Jesus Christ and no one else as grace and truth, not being slack but always cheerful to proclaim and believe Him, finding its pleasure in giving itself as promised to the service offered to Him, and therefore in being His own confessor and witness in the confession and witness of the Church. In fact, it all amounts to this : that the Church has to be weak in order to be strong.

That there is a true religion is an event in the act of the grace of God in Jesus Christ. To be more precise, it is an event in the outpouring of the Holy Spirit. To be even more precise, it is an event in the existence of the Church and the children of God. The existence of the Church of God and the children of God means that true religion exists even in the world of human religion. In other words, there is a knowledge and worship of God and a corresponding human activity. We can only say of them that they are corrupt. They are an attempt born of lying and wrong and committed to futile means. And yet we have also to say of them that (in their corruption) they do reach their goal. In spite of the lying and wrong committed, in spite of the futility of the means applied, God is really known and worshipped, there is a genuine activity of man as reconciled to God. The Church and the children of God and therefore the bearers of true religion live by the grace of God. Their knowledge and worship of God, their service of God in teaching, cultus and life, are determined by the realisation of the free kindness of God which anticipates all human thought and will and action and corrects all human corruption. For it does not leave anything for man to do except to believe and give thanks. And it teaches him to do this—not as his own work but as its own gift —which will never be denied to the man who believes and gives thanks. The Church and the children of God live under this ordinance. To that extent they live by the grace of God. But the fact that they do so is not the basis of their existence as the Church and the children of God. Nor is it the thing which makes their religion the true religion. From the standpoint of their own activity as such, they do not stand out decisively above the general level of religious history. They do not escape the divine accusation of idolatry and self-righteousness. For one thing, their life by grace hardly ever appears in history except as an occasional obstacle to the effective fulfilment even amongst them of the law of all religion. If the thought and will and action of Christians as those who live by grace were really the criterion of their existence as the Church and the children of God, with what confidence we could maintain their existence as such and the truth of their religion! But we cannot maintain it on the ground of that criterion because it is not unknown for an apparent and sometimes a very convincing life of grace, and the phenomenon of the religion of grace, to appear in other fields of religious history. And yet by biblical standards we have no authority to speak of the Church and the divine sonship or of the existence of true religion in these other spheres. The decisive thing for the existence of the Church and the children of God and for the truth of their religion is something quite different. And therefore the decisive thing for their life by grace, in itself so equivocal, is also different. It is the fact that by the grace of God they live by His grace. That is what makes them what they are. That is what makes their religion true. That is what lifts it above the general level of religious history. But " by the grace of God " means by the reality of that by which they apparently but very equivocally live ; by the reality of that by which men can apparently and equivocally live in other spheres of religious history. " By the reality" means by the fact that beyond all human appearance, beyond all that men can think and will and do in the sphere of their religion, even if it is a religion of grace, without any merits or deservings of their own, God acts towards them as the gracious God He is, anticipating their own thought and will and action by His own free kindness, arousing in them faith and thankfulness, and never refusing them. They are what they are, and their religion is the true religion, not because they recognise Him as such and act accordingly, not in virtue of their religion of grace, but in virtue of the fact that God has graciously intervened for them, in virtue of His mercy in spite of their apparent but equivocal religion of grace, in virtue of the good pleasure which He has in them, in virtue of His free election, of which this good pleasure is the only motive, in virtue of the Holy Spirit whom He willed to pour out upon them. It is of grace that the Church and the children of God live by His grace. It is of grace that they attain the status of the bearers of true religion. But we can see the concrete significance of this, we can see how different it is from any kind of higher principle of religion, which might be used in the assessment of all human religion, only when we are clear that " by the grace of God " means exactly the same as " through the name of Jesus Christ." He, Jesus Christ, is the eternal Son of God and as such the eternal Object of the divine good pleasure. As the eternal Son of God He became man. The result is that in Him man has also become the object of the divine good pleasure, not by his own merit or deserving, but by the grace which assumed man to itself in the Son of God. In this One, the revelation of God among men and the reconciliation of man with God has been fulfilled once and for all. And He gives the Holy Ghost. It is because of all these things and by means of them that there is in this One a Church of God and children of God. They are what they are, and they have the true religion, because He stands in their place, and therefore for His sake. They cannot for a single moment think of leaving Him with the intention and purpose of trying to be what they are in themselves, or to have the true religion in themselves. When they do in fact leave Him—as they are always doing—the result is that they become uncertain of their existence as the Church and the children of God, and therefore of the truth of their religion. But there can be no alteration in the objective content, that they are what they are, and therefore bearers of the true religion, only in Him, in the name of Jesus Christ, i.e., in the revelation and reconciliation achieved in Jesus Christ. Nowhere else, but genuinely so in Him. Therefore by the grace of God there are men who live by His grace. Or, to put it concretely, through the name of Jesus Christ there are men who believe in this name. To the extent that this is self-evident in the case of Christians and the Christian religion, we can and must say of it that it and it alone is the true religion. On this particular basis we must now expound and explain this statement under four specific aspects.

1. In the relationship between the name of Jesus Christ and the Christian religion we have to do first with an act of divine creation. That means that its existence in historical form and individual determinations is not an autonomous or self-grounded existence. The name of Jesus Christ alone has created the Christian religion. Without Him it would never have been. And we must understand this not only in the historical but in the actual and contemporary sense. The name of Jesus Christ creates the Christian religion. Apart from Him it would not be. For if we would speak of the Christian religion as a reality, we cannot be content merely to look back at its creation and historical existence. We have to think of it in the same way as we think of our own existence and that of the world, as a reality which is to be and is created by Jesus Christ yesterday and to-day and to-morrow. Apart from the act of its creation by the name of Jesus Christ, which like creation generally is a *creatio continua*, and therefore apart from the Creator, it has no reality. If we would speak of the Christian religion apart from the name Jesus Christ, only two possibilities remain. The first is the general religious possibility. Now, of course, this is open to the so-called Christian as well as to other men. But as such it can be realised in other non-Christian religions as well as in the Christian. In fact, as a possibility which is general by nature, it can be clearly realised only in a known or unknown non-Christian religion. In any case it is only an empty possibility, and therefore not a reality. The second possibility is the swiftly crumbling ruin of a construct very like religion which was once called and perhaps even was

Christianity. But now that the root of life has been cut off from it, it no longer has the capacity for life of a non-Christian religion. It can only decay, being replaced by another religion which has at least the power to be. That the Christian religion could never have entered history and therefore never existed without the creative power of the name of Jesus Christ in the strictest sense, is something which we hardly need to demonstrate. Without that name the men of the time could have existed as the bearers of a general religious possibility under the specific conditions under which it was the possibility of those men. There would then have existed a fairly quiet religious Hellenism of Jewish and Oriental and Occidental provenance and colouring. But Christianity as a missionary and cultic and theological and political and moral force has existed from the outset only in an indissoluble relationship with the name of Jesus Christ. And from the history of the Church during the last centuries we can learn that the existence of the Christian religion is actually bound up with this name and with the act of divine creation and preservation to which it points. Eliminate this name and the religion is blunted and weakened. As a " Christianity without Christ " it can only vegetate. It has lost its only *raison d'etre*. Like other religions, for other reasons, it can look only for a speedy dissolution. If we try to look away from the name of Jesus Christ even momentarily, the Christian Church loses the substance in virtue of which it can assert itself in and against the state and society as an entity of a special order. Christian piety (no matter whether it vaunts itself as a piety of head or heart or action) loses the substance in virtue of which it can be something distinctive alongside morals, art and science. Christian theology loses the substance in virtue of which it is not philosophy, or philology, or historical science, but sacred learning. Christian worship loses the sacrificial and sacramental substance in virtue of which it is more than a solemn, half insolent and half superfluous pastime—its substance, and therefore its right to live, and at the same time its capacity to live. The Christian religion is the predicate to the subject of the name of Jesus Christ. Without Him it is not merely something different. It is nothing at all, a fact which cannot be hidden for long. It was and is and shall be only in virtue of the act of creation indicated by this name. And it is because of this act of creation that along with its existence it also receives its truth. Because it was and is and shall be through the name of Jesus Christ, it was and is and shall be the true religion : the knowledge of God, and the worship of God, and the service of God, in which man is not alone in defiance of God, but walks before God in peace with God.

But note this. Because this name describes no less than the creation and the Creator of the Christian religion, we cannot act as though it were at our disposal, adding it to our supposedly Christian doctrines as an expository or confirmatory addendum, or even as a critical proviso, conjuring with it in relation to our supposedly Christian enterprises as with a magic force, interposing it as the pretext and purpose of our supposedly Christian institutions, like a stained-glass window in an otherwise completed Church. The name of Jesus Christ is certainly no mere *nomen* in the sense of the famous mediæval controversy. It is the very essence and source of all reality. It stands in free creative power at the beginning of the Christian religion and its vital utterances. If not, then what we bring in at the end or climax is not in any sense the name of Jesus Christ. It is simply a hollow sound which cannot transform our human nothingness into divine fulness. There is fulness instead of nothingness only where the name of Jesus Christ as the Creator of our doctrine and enterprises and institutions is really the beginning of all things. To understand the theory of this, it is best to look at it this way. The Christian religion is simply the earthly-historical life of the Church and the children of God. As such we must think of it as an annexe to the human nature of Jesus Christ. And we must remember what we are told concerning His human nature in Jn. 1¹⁴. There never was a man Jesus as such apart from the eternal reality of the Son of God. Certainly in the fulness of human possibilities, along the line from Abraham to the Virgin Mary, there was the possibility which found its realisation in the man Jesus. But it did not find this realisation independently, but in virtue of the creative act in which the eternal Son of God assumed the human possibility into His reality, giving to it in that reality the reality which previously and *per se* it did not possess, and which, when it acquires it, it does not possess apart from His reality. The human nature of Jesus Christ has no hypostasis of its own, we are told. It has it only in the Logos. The same is true, therefore, of the earthly-historical life of the Church and the children of God, and therefore of the Christian religion. It is the life of the earthly body of Christ and His members, who are called out of the schematic, bare possibility into the reality by the fact that He, the Head, has taken and gathered them to Himself as the earthly form of His heavenly body. Loosed from Him they could only fall back into the schematic possibility, i.e., into the non-being from which they proceeded. They live in Him, or they do not live at all. By living in Him they have a part in the eternal truth of His own life. But they have the choice only of a part in His life or of no life at all. But a part in the life of the Son of God, as the heavenly Head of this earthly body, is simply the name of Jesus Christ.

2. In the relationship between the name of Jesus Christ and the Christian religion we have to do with an act of the divine election. The Christian religion did not possess any reality of its own. Considered in and for itself it never can. It is a mere possibility among a host of others. It did not and does not bring anything of its own to the name of Jesus Christ which makes it in any way worthy to be His creation and as such the true religion. If it is real, it is so on the basis of free election, grounded in the compassion and inconceivable good pleasure of God and nothing else. In a secondary sense we can, of course, explain the necessity of the rise of Christianity in the light of Judaistic development and the political, spiritual and moral circumstances of the Mediterranean world in the Imperial period. But in its reality we can never explain or deduce it from that source. Historically, we cannot seriously explain and deduce it except from the history of the covenant made with Israel. And we cannot do that with any strictness or discernment except when we explain and deduce it from the fulfilment of that covenant in the name of Jesus Christ, from the revelation as it is actually made and acknowledged and believed, and

therefore on the presupposition of that name. That it pleased God at that time and place and in that way to reveal Himself in the name of Jesus Christ, is something which had its necessity in itself, and not in circumstances and conditions prior to that name. From that day to this it is election by the free grace and compassion of God if in virtue of the name of Jesus Christ the Christian religion is a reality and not nothingness. As there is a *creatio continua* so also there is an *electio continua*, better described, of course, as God's faithfulness and patience. The name of Jesus Christ is not something mechanical. It is not under any external constraint. It is not bound to what seems to have, and claims reality as Christianity, as Christian doctrine and conduct and institutions, as pursued by ostensibly Christian men or the ostensibly Christian portions of humanity. Where it is bound, it has bound itself. And the fact that it has done so is always grace and not human or Christian merit. Grace, and to that extent election, i.e., free grace, is simply the faithfulness and patience of God. It is election if the Church is not only a favourite religious society, and there are others, but the body of Christ, if it not only has aspirations but inspirations, if its relation to state and society is a relation of genuine antithesis and therefore of genuine fellowship. The fact that it controls the Word and sacraments, and has Holy Scripture and the Creeds, does not in any way alter the fact that it is all election, unmerited grace. It is election if its worship is not only a remarkably mixed development of Jewish Synagogue worship and the later mystery cults, but worship in the Spirit and in truth. No tradition, however faithful, and no consciousness of immediacy, however vital, can ever prevent it from being only the former. If it is otherwise, if the alleged spiritual element is genuinely of the Spirit, then it is only by the Holy Spirit who breathes as He will, it is only because of a free and merciful turning on the part of God, it is only by election, and not by any immanent aptitude for genuine spirituality. It is election if theology is not a science without an object, if it does not hear and expound the Word of God only in appearance, if it labours to serve the purity of ecclesiastical doctrine. There is no method, or enlistment, or alignment which compels us to say that theology is in any way different from Rabbinic scholarship or Greek speculation. If it is different, if it is the real learning of the Church, it is so at every point on the basis of election, and not otherwise. We could say the same of Christian piety, Christian custom, Christian philanthropy, Christian education and Christian politics. We have to remember that the important adjective " Christian "—with which we expressly name the name of Jesus Christ—can never be a grasping at some possession of our own. It can only be a reaching out for the divine possession included in this name. It can only be an inquiry about election. It can only be a prayer that God will not turn away His face from us, that He will not weary of His unmerited faithfulness and patience. Where the adjective really means anything, election has already taken place. And it is election, and only election, which makes the Christian religion the true religion. For there need be no fear that the thought of the decisive grace of God, which is not bound to any human or even Christian possession, will mean a weakening of the Christian certainty of truth. On the contrary, the thought may have a shattering effect upon all our self-confidence in regard to truth, and indeed it must. But it opens our eyes to the basis of real certainty. For the Christian religion is true, because it has pleased God, who alone can be the judge in this matter, to affirm it to be the true religion. What is truth,·if it is not this divine affirmation? And what is the certainty of truth, if not the certainty which is based solely upon this judgment, a judgment which is free, but wise and righteous in its freedom, because it is the freedom of God?

From the standpoint of election, too, all the stress must be laid on the fact that the relation between the name of Jesus Christ and the Christian religion cannot be reversed. We remember Luther's translation of Ps. 100[3] : " Know that the Lord is God. He hath made us—and not we ourselves—to be his people and the sheep of his pasture." And Jn. 15[16] : " Ye did not choose me, but I chose you, and appointed you to go and bring fruit, and that your fruit should abide." Both these " sayings " are particularly directed to the religious community of the religion of revelation as such. For the Church and for the children of God there is a recurrent temptation to regard themselves as those who elect in this matter. It is their faith and their love, their confession, tradition and hope which is its proper substance. Its grounding in the name of Christ Jesus can then appear as a free concession. We may perhaps decide upon it very seriously, but by thinking that it is something which we ourselves can and should decide, we show that we no longer realise with what name we have to do. It is in this role of an elected and continually re-elected, but ultimately only an elected King, that the name of Jesus Christ occurs in almost all the theology and piety and Church life of the 18th to 20th centuries. In these centuries the Christian religion quite openly thought that it could live on its own substance, i.e., on Christian experience and morality and universal order as such. As a rule, this did not, of course, mean that the name of Jesus Christ was dispensed with, or that it was refused the necessary love and worship. The *beneficia Christi* were thought to be seen in the substance of the Christian religion. Even within liberal, let alone conservative Protestantism, the individual radicals of the period, like Reimarus in the 18th, D. F. Strauss in the 19th and A. Drews in the 20th centuries, were like unwelcome brawlers in a passionately pious community. And it was as such that they were everywhere treated. But the mixture of pity and anger and obvious anxiety with which it was done was suspicious. So, too, was the pious and learned apologetic zeal, which all parties and not least the liberals displayed, on one pretext or another to safeguard, or to restore and re-establish to the name of Jesus Christ, in opposition to the radicals, the traditional place of honour at the centre of everything. If it had actually enjoyed or regained that place, we might have been spared the trouble. Luther and Calvin did not need to aim at a " christocentric " theology, like Schleiermacher and later A. Ritschl and his pupils, because their theology was christocentric from the very outset, and without the singular attempt to make or call it so. It did not need to become christocentric. And how can theology or piety or Church life become christocentric, if it is not so at the very outset? The strainings and the unhealthy zeal and historical and systematic devices by which the moderns have tried to become christocentric bear clear and eloquent testimony that they were not christocentric at the outset and therefore cannot be. In a word, they bear testimony that, like the radicals, they believe that this is something which we can choose for ourselves, though the actual choice is different. The belief that the name Jesus Christ is something we can choose is the radically unauthentic element in the Jesus-cult of Pietism and the revival movements of the period. It may well be said that the positive concern of the period for the name of Jesus Christ is the clearest indication of the basic rebellion of the Church of the time. For it was rebellion, if only pious rebellion, when it was thought that we can affirm the name of Jesus Christ and therefore can and ought to choose it from the secure haven of a religion which satisfies us in any case : when there was the possibility of entering into a discussion of the matter. It was, of course, no accident when in its concern with Jesus Christ—obviously for apologetic reasons—the theology of the period made an abstract, human and historical life of Jesus Christ the particular object of its endeavours. Here again that other aspect, which was so obvious to the Christology of the early Church, was forgotten : that the human nature of Christ to which such an ingenuous appeal was now made was not an independent reality, but even as a possibility, realised in the eternal Son of God, it was the object of an externally unmerited and unpredictable election. In a strange forgetfulness of what the New Testament itself clearly states, the piety or moralism or even demonism of Jesus of Nazareth was regarded as the element which can always be acknowledged and presupposed, whereas His so-called " Messianic consciousness " gave rise to a problem, and could be affirmed only after considerable thought, and with great reserve and tentativeness. It escaped notice that in dealing with Christology in this way the theologians of the period merely revealed themselves in their own embarrassment : the great certainty with which they claimed to be Christians, and in possession of Christian experiences and thoughts, and representatives of the Christian attitude, and the great uncertainty with which they finally decided the question whether or not the name of Jesus Christ is necessary. The very emphasis, the fact that no question is seen in relation to the one but a real question in relation to the other, the naivete with which their own Christlikeness is affirmed as compared with the hesitance of the final affirmation of Jesus Christ : all this meant that directly as well as indirectly everything was lost and the confession of the name of Jesus Christ was already abandoned. And it was tragic how the scientific seriousness, and sincerity and profundity, and the deep and genuine piety, which were undoubtedly applied to this hesitant affirmation, could only make the harm more apparent. Again, therefore, it is not an accident if the psychology particularly of the theologians and churchmen of the period (and especially about the turn of the 19th century) has for the most part been one of a pronounced lack of humour, of weariness and depression, even of melancholia. Could it be otherwise when for all the subjective solidity of the effort they were fighting for a kind of lost cause ? It might, of course, be objected : Is not the confession of the name of Jesus Christ a free human decision and therefore a choice of this name ? Of course it is : that is the unequivocal teaching of Mt. 16¹³ᶠ·, Jn. 6⁶⁷ᵗ· We might also recall Josh. 24¹⁵ᶠ· : " And if it seem evil unto you to serve the Lord, choose ye this day whom ye will serve ; whether the gods which your fathers served that were beyond the River, or the gods of the Amorites, in whose land ye dwell : but as for me and my house, we will serve the Lord." But there is, of course, a considerable difference between " choosing " amongst the Mesopotamian and Canaanite gods, which is always possible for the people, and the being chosen by Yahweh, which Joshua already has behind him. In fact there is no doubt that an election does take place : but it is an election upon which, just because it is our own election, we can only look back as upon something which has taken place already. In the act of electing we are not confronted by two or three possibilities, between which we can choose. We choose the only possibility which is given to us : " Lord, whither should we go ? " Those who confess and therefore choose the name of Jesus Christ choose the only possibility which is given to them, the possibility which is given to them by Jesus Christ : " Thou hast the words of eternal life." They elect, but they elect their own election. There can be no question of a substance of the Christian religion which is their own, which antedates their electing and can play a part as a motive or criterion for electing the name of Jesus Christ. On the contrary, its decision has no independent validity. It is simply the recognition of a decision already made regarding them : and it is in the decision already made that they will alone find the substance of their more or less estimable religion. Their own decision, the decision of obedience to the decision made in the freedom of God, is what Scripture describes as the decision of faith and especially of faith in the name of Jesus Christ. The Reformers and the older Protestantism knew well enough what they were doing when with one breath they challenged man to this decision and to that extent undoubtedly appealed to his freedom, and then immediately (with greater or lesser emphasis) described predestination, i.e., the choice in the eternal decree of God, the election effected and perceived in Christ, as the proper object and content of the decision of faith. It is only in the decision of faith as ordered and understood in this way that we really have to do with the name of Jesus Christ. Ordered and understood in any other way, it may seem to be the name of Jesus Christ. It may be supposed to be that name. But in fact it is only a *nomen,* and as such it has no power and therefore it can never be affirmed with any power. The power of affirming the name of Jesus Christ is either its own power or it is impotence. And it is only in the decision of faith as ordered and understood in this way that the truth can emerge and become certainty. The truth illumines and convinces and asserts itself in the fulfilment of the choice whose freedom and power is only that of the name of Jesus Christ Himself. As such it becomes, it makes itself, the truth of the Christian religion, whereas in the alleged possession of an abstract Christianity we always look in vain for the truth of the name of Jesus Christ and therefore strive in vain for certainty of the truth of the Christian religion.

3. In the relationship between the name Jesus Christ and the Christian religion we have to do with an act of divine justification or forgiveness of sins. We already stated that the Christian religion as such has no worthiness of its own, to equip it specially to be the true religion. We must now aver even more clearly that in itself and as such it is absolutely unworthy to be the true religion. If it is so, it is so by election, we said. And now we must be more precise : it is so in virtue of the divine justification of sinners, of the divine forgiveness of sins. The structure of this religion (most acutely in its Protestant form) is certainly quite different from that of others. And this, too, we can understand and assess only as the work of the name of Jesus Christ. But it is not so decidedly different from others that in respect of it we can evade the judgment of the divine revelation that all religion is idolatry and self-righteousness. On the contrary, history in the Christian sense, whether the history of the Church as a whole or the life-story of the individual child of God in particular, stands always under this sign. The more closely we study it, or rather, the more clearly the light of revelation from Holy Scripture falls upon it, the more evident this is. Both as a whole and in particular it is a sinful story. It is not justified in itself. It is sinful both in form and also in its human origin. It is no less so than can be said of the story

of Buddhism or of Islam. The hands into which God has delivered Himself in His revelation are thoroughly unclean. In fact, they are seriously unclean. If our knowledge of the truth of the Christian religion were determined by the life of an immanent purity of the Church of God as its *locus*, or of the children of God as its vehicles, it would have been permanently concealed. Both are clean (even in their uncleanness) for the sake of the Word which is spoken to them. Otherwise it would be all up with our knowledge of the truth of the Christian religion. For we should be looking at the redeemedness of the redeemed. Or what is worse, we should be looking at our own redeemedness. We should not hear the Word by which the Church and the children of God are clean in their uncleanness and in all their unredeemedness redeemed. We should feel that the creation and election of this particular religion to be the true religion, even if it could be supported by many arguments, would ultimately be only a matter of arbitrary assertion, not borne out by the facts.

There is, of course, one fact which powerfully and decisively confirms the assertion, depriving it of its arbitrary character and giving to it a necessity which is absolute. But to discern this fact, our first task—and again and again we shall have to return to this " first "—must be to ignore the whole realm of " facts " which we and other human observers as such can discern and assess. For the fact about which we are speaking stands in the same relationship to this realm as does the sun to the earth. That the sun lights up this part of the earth and not that means for the earth no less than this, that day rules in the one part and night in the other. Yet the earth is the same in both places. In neither place is there anything in the earth itself to dispose it for the day. Apart from the sun it would everywhere be enwrapped in eternal night. The fact that it is partly in the day does not derive in any sense from the nature of the particular part as such. Now it is in exactly the same way that the light of the righteousness and judgment of God falls upon the world of man's religion, upon one part of that world, upon the Christian religion, so that that religion is not in the night but in the day, it is not perverted but straight, it is not false religion but true. Taken by itself, it is still human religion and therefore unbelief, like all other religions. Neither in the root nor in the crown of this particular tree, neither at the source nor at the outflow of this particular stream, neither on the surface nor in the depth of this particular part of humanity can we point to anything that makes it suitable for the day of divine righteousness and judgment. If the Christian religion is the right and true religion, the reason for it does not reside in facts which might point to itself or its own adherents, but in the fact which as the righteousness and the judgment of God confronts it as it does all other religions, characterising and differentiating it and not one of the others as the right and true religion. We must observe that it is not a whim or caprice which is this confronting and decisive fact but the righteousness and the judgment of God. What takes place at this point is already perfectly in order, because however surprising it may be from our standpoint it is God's order which is manifested and operative. We are, of course, confronted by an acquittal which is utterly inconceivable from our standpoint. But the acquittal is a judgment. And although we have no insight into its motives, it is a righteous judgment. Therefore we cannot say that on the basis of that fact of God some other religion might have become the right and true religion. We perceive and acknowledge the judgment pronounced in this fact of God. And in doing so we have to accept it as it stands. We cannot juggle with the possibility that it might have been different. And we should again forfeit the absoluteness of the perception if we did not let it stand as wholly and utterly a perception of the divine judgment and therefore of the fact of God, if instead we tried to squint past the fact of God and to find certain conditioning factors of the judgment in the nature of the Christian religion as such. If we look at the Christian religion in itself and as such, we can only say that apart from the clear testimony of the fact of God some other religion might equally well be the right and true one. But once the fact of God is there and its judgment passed, we cannot look at the Christian religion in itself and as such. And it is only secondarily that we come to those thoughts of equality. They express the fact that in face of the righteous acquittal pronounced on the Christian religion in this judgment we have no merits or deservings of our own, to which we might point in confirmation. As we receive and accept it, we can cling only to the sentence itself, or the divine fact which proclaims it, and not to any glorious facts from the sphere of the Christian religion as such. The justification of the Christian religion is a righteous acquittal. It rests entirely on the righteousness of God. It is not in any way conditioned by the qualities of the Christian religion. It cannot, therefore, be understood in any way except as an act of forgiveness of sin. In that it is justified by that fact of God, its various qualities, far from being adduced as the basis of its justification, are not even considered or taken into account, but covered up. Of course they have to be covered up, and they cannot be considered or taken into account, if there is to be an acquittal. For the sum total of the qualities of even the Christian religion is simply this, that it is idolatry and self-righteousness, unbelief, and therefore sin. It must be forgiven if it is to be justified. And we can understand and receive its justification only if we understand and receive it as sheer forgiveness. If we understood or received it in any other way, we should again be by-passing the actual fact of God, by which the Christian religion is justified. We should again be missing the absoluteness of the knowledge of its truth. It is only as forgiveness that the truth adopts the Christian religion. It is only as forgiveness that it can be known as a definition which in the last resort is inalienably peculiar to the Christian religion.

We ask : How is this justification in the form of forgiveness an act of the righteousness and judgment of God ? On the basis of what right does God forgive, and forgive at this and not at some other point ? And in answer to this question we have not only to point to the freedom and inscrutability of the divine judgment. We have also to bear in mind that this freedom and inscrutability is identical with the revealed fact of the name of Jesus Christ. It is quite in order to find forgiveness at this point and not at any other. It takes place according to the ordering of this act of God, that is, the name of Jesus Christ. It is this name which stands in relation to the world of religions, as does the sun to the earth. But it denotes a definite event, in which the world of religions acquires a definite part. For it denotes the unification of the eternal divine Word with the nature of man, and therefore with the rectification of that human nature, notwithstanding and in spite of its natural perversion, to humility and obedience to God. This rectification of human nature is the work of Jesus Christ from birth to death, and it is revealed to be such in His resurrection from the dead. But to the human nature readjusted in Jesus Christ there belongs the capacity from which, because of that nature, only religion as unbelief can and does proceed. In the human nature of Jesus Christ, instead of resisting God in idolatry and self-righteousness, man offers the obedience of faith. In that way he satisfies the righteousness and judgment of God. Therefore he really merits his acquittal, and therefore the acquittal, the justification of his religion. In the Christian religion it is a matter of the earthly life of the Church and the children of God. It is a matter of the life of the earthly body of which Jesus Christ is the Head ; i.e., of the life of those whom He has brought into fellowship with His human nature and therefore to a participation in the acquittal which He has rightly and righteously merited. Christian religion is faith in the discipleship of the justifying faith of Jesus Christ which no man can imitate. If this is the case, then as a human faith it needs the divine forgiveness just as much as the faith of other religions. But it does actually receive and enjoy this forgiveness. And the forgiveness which it receives and enjoys is not a matter of whim or caprice. It is a strict and righteous award. In the first instance, of course, it is made only to Jesus Christ, the only man who has maintained and demonstrated the obedience of faith. But for the sake of Jesus Christ, i.e., for the sake of the fellowship and participation guaranteed to men by Jesus Christ, for the sake of the solidarity of our humanity with His bestowed by Him, for the sake of the faith in Him of discipleship, those whom He calls His brethren, and who in that faith in Him recognise and honour their first-born brother, are also (with their religion) the objects of that righteous award of God.

For them—as distinct from Him—this acquittal is a free and inconceivable forgiveness, a forgiveness which they did not merit, a forgiveness on the ground of His merit, yet a forgiveness with all the seriousness and emphasis of a valid award, a forgiveness which cannot be disputed or overturned. And in the same unconditional way it is a forgiveness even of their religion, of which, regarded in itself and as such, they would have to admit that it is unbelief, like the faith of other religions. The one decisive question which confronts the Christian religion, or its adherents and representatives, in respect of its truth, is this : who and what are they in their naked reality, as they stand before the all-piercing eye of God ? Are they really His Church, His children, and therefore the adopted brethren of His eternal Son ? If they are not, if their Christian religion is just a mask, then even if it is the most perfect and logical form of Christianity it is unbelief like all other heathen religions. It is falsehood and wrong and an abomination before God. But if they are, if they live by the grace of God, if they participate in the human nature of His eternal Son, if they are nourished by His body and His blood as earthly members of His earthly body in communion with Him as their heavenly Head : then for the sake of this fellowship their sins are forgiven, even the sin of their religion is rightly pardoned. Their Christian religion is the justified religion and therefore the right and true religion. Beyond all dialectic and to the exclusion of all discussion the divine fact of the name of Jesus Christ confirms what no other fact does or can confirm : the creation and election of this religion to be the one and only true religion. Of course, the one decisive question can never be spared the Christian religion and its adherents and representatives. It can never become irrelevant. It can never be regarded as settled. Whenever Christianity confronts other religions, or a Christian the adherent of another religion, this question stands over them like a sword. From that standpoint we can and must say that, in the world of religions, the Christian religion is in a position of greater danger and defencelessness and impotence than any other religion. It has its justification either in the name of Jesus Christ, or not at all. And this justification must be achieved in the actuality of life, of the Church and the children of God. But the achieving of this life is grace, the grace of the Word, which begets faith, and the Church and children of the Word, according to its free and inconceivable compassion. The possibility of a negative answer to that question is the abyss on the fringe of which the truth of the Christian religion is decided. A positive decision means a positive answer to the question. It means that the Christian religion is snatched from the world of religions and the judgment and sentence pronounced upon it, like a brand from the burning. It is not that some men are vindicated as opposed to others, or one part of humanity as opposed to other parts of the same humanity. It is that God Himself is vindicated as opposed to and on behalf of all men and all humanity. That it can receive and accept this is the advantage and pre-eminence of Christianity, and the light and glory in which its religion stands. And as it does not have this light and glory of itself, no one can take it away from it. And it alone has the commission and the authority to be a missionary religion, i.e., to confront the world of religions as the one true religion, with absolute self-confidence to invite and challenge it to abandon its ways and to start on the Christian way.

The Christian religion will always be vital and healthy and strong as long as it has this self-confidence. But it will have this self-confidence only as its adherents and proclaimers can look away from themselves to the fact of God which alone can justify them. In so far as they still rely on other facts, this self-confidence will inevitably receive one inward blow after another and in the long run completely disappear. It makes no odds whether these other facts consist in ecclesiastical institutions, theological systems, inner experiences, the moral transformations of individual believers or the wider effects of Christianity upon the world at large. To glance aside at such facts will always and very quickly mean uncertainty regarding the truth of the Christian religion. For all these things may quite well be facts ; but together and in detail they are facts which themselves need justification and therefore cannot be claimed as the basis of it. If the Christian or Christians who ask concerning the truth of their religion are wrapped up in themselves and their Christianity, forgetting that in this matter they have to do first with forgiven sin, then let them see to it how long they can protect themselves from the scepticism in this question which so irresistibly wells up in them. And if they can, if they are able to assign to these facts a credibility which in this field they cannot possibly have, that will be all the worse for them and the Christian religion than any open outbreak and admission of doubt. And again, those who believe in their Church and theology, or in changed men and improved circumstances, are on exactly the same road, the road to uncertainty. This is betrayed by the fact that all of them, incidentally but quite openly, and with the unteachable ferocity of a secret despair of faith, have to take refuge in reason or culture or humanity or race, in order to find some support or other for the Christian religion. But the Christian religion cannot be supported from without, if it can no longer stand alone. If it does stand alone it does not allow itself to be supported from without. Standing alone, it stands upon the fact of God which justifies it, and upon that alone. There is therefore no place for attempts to support it in any other way. Such attempts are a waste of time and energy. In fact, they are a renewal of the unbelief which is not unnoticed or unassessed by God, but covered up and forgiven. But such attempts are bound to be made if once we glance aside at other facts side by side with the one justifying divine fact. In that case unbelief has already returned. It already has the decisive word. And it will see in such attempts, not a waste of time and energy, but an urgent necessity. The secularisation of Christianity is then in full train, and no subjective piety will avail to halt it. And the result will be a loss of all outward health and strength and vitality.

4. In the relationship between the name of Jesus Christ and the Christian religion, we have to do with an act of divine sanctification. We said that to find the basis of the assertion of the truth of Christianity we must first look away from it to the fact of God which is its basis, and that we have constantly to return to this " first." When we ask concerning this truth, we can never look even incidentally to

anything but this fact of God. We cannot try to find the justification of the Christian religion apart from the name of Jesus Christ in other facts, not even in the inward or outward state of justification of the Christian religion. Yet this justification of the Christian religion only by the name of Jesus Christ obviously involves a certain positive relation between the two. Christianity is differentiated from other religions by that name. It is formed and shaped by it. It is claimed for His service. It becomes the historical manifestation and means of its revelation. We have compared the name of Jesus Christ with the sun in its relation to the earth. That must be an end of the matter. But the sun shines. And its light is not remote from the earth and alien to it. Without ceasing to be the light of the sun, it becomes the light of the earth, the light which illuminates the earth. In that light the earth which has no light of its own is bright. It is not, of course, a second sun. But it carries the reflection of the sun's light. It is, therefore, an illuminated earth. It is the same with the name of Jesus Christ in relation to the Christian religion. That name alone is its justification. But it cannot be transcendent without being immanent in it. For it is only the Christian religion which is justified by it. And that means that it is differentiated and marked off and stamped and characterised by it in a way peculiar to itself. In the light of its justification and creation and election by the name of Jesus Christ, the fact that it is the Christian religion and not another cannot possibly be neutral or indifferent or without significance. On the contrary, even though Christianity is a religion like others, it is significant and eloquent, a sign, a proclamation. There is an event on God's side—which is the side of the incarnate Word of God—God adopting man and giving Himself to him. And corresponding to it there is a very definite event on man's side. This event is determined by the Word of God. It has its being and form in the world of human religion. But it is different from everything else in this sphere and having this form. The correspondence of the two events is the relationship between the name Jesus Christ and the Christian religion from the standpoint of its sanctification. It is not by the laws and forces of human religion and therefore of man, but in virtue of the divine foundation and institution, that this particular being and form are an event in the world of human religion. What becomes an event is unjustified in itself. It has no autonomous role or significance. It has simply to serve the name of Jesus Christ which alone justifies it. It can never—even incidentally—replace and suppress this name by its own substance. It can only attest it. It can only kindle and maintain the recollection and expectation of it. It can never claim to be itself the fact of God denoted by this name. It can only try to be its exhortatory and consoling sign. It can have a part in the truth only as it points to it and proclaims it. And in this pointing and proclaiming it can never have or claim any power or authority of its own. It will

3. *True Religion* 359

speak or be silent, work or rest, be known or not known, in virtue of
the power and authority of the name of Jesus, effectual in the outpouring of the Holy Spirit. That name alone is the power and mystery
of the declaration which is the meaning of this particular being and
form. That name alone expresses this being and form as the being
and form of true religion. It is not justified because it is holy in
itself—which it is not. It is made holy because it is justified. And
it is not true because it is holy in itself—which it never was and never
will be. But it is made holy in order to show that it is the true religion.
At this point we link up with what we earlier described as the twofold
subjective reality of revelation, which is the counterpart in our realm
of the objective revelation in Jesus Christ. The Christian religion is
the sacramental area created by the Holy Spirit, in which the God
whose Word became flesh continues to speak through the sign of His
revelation. And it is also the existence of men created by the same
Holy Spirit, who hear this God continually speaking in His revelation.
The Church and the children of God do actually exist. The actuality
of their existence is quite unassuming, but it is always visible and in
its visibility it is significant. It is an actuality which is called and
dedicated to the declaration of the name of Jesus Christ. And that
is the sanctification of the Christian religion.

The covenant of God founded on grace and election acquired at once even
with the people of Israel the evidence of a visible form, a seal which could be
perceived by both the obedient and the disobedient, by both Israel itself and
the heathen nations round about. It did so with the establishment of the Law.
The whole aim and purpose of the Law was that it should be the sign of Yahweh's
grace and election. But as the sign of Yahweh's grace and election, as the evidence
of the covenant, the Law had to be observed and kept and sought out day and
night. The founding of the covenant did not take place with the establishment
of the Law, let alone with Israel's observing and keeping and searching of it.
It took place prior to the Law with the reiterated calling of Abraham, Isaac and
Jacob, and the sending of Moses, and the liberation of Israel out of Egypt. But
because it took place as the basis of the covenant of God with this people, which
had a human and historical existence like all other nations, it did not take place
without the establishing of the Law, without claiming this people for obedience
to the Law, without the promise of cursing and blessing attached to the observance or non-observance of it. The acceptance and observance of the Law was
a recurrent guarantee that this people was the people of the covenant. The gift
of the Law was the sanctification of this people, in answer to the grace of Yahweh,
the necessary consequence of the revelation of grace, the inevitable historical
form which could not be separated from it. And sanctification meant its separation and differentiation and characterisation as this people. How could it exist
both as a human and historical nation and also as the people of Yahweh without
undergoing a visible separation, differentiation and characterisation as this
people ? And how could it experience and adopt the grace which encounters
it with its existence as this people, without being continually reminded of this
visible separation, differentiation and characterisation, and constantly acknowledging it ? Clearly the observance of the Law can only be a sign and testimony.
It is only relative to the thankfulness for the promise, I am the Lord thy God,
which can never be exhausted even by the strictest observance of any one of
the commandments. But it is obviously a necessary sign and testimony. Its

absence casts doubt both upon their thankfulness and even their existence as this people, automatically transforming the promise into a threat.

It is of a piece that in the New Testament we not only have the reconciliation of the world to God in Jesus Christ, but also, as a consequence and necessary adjunct, a " ministry of reconciliation," the establishing of a " word of reconciliation," a human request instituted in and with the reconciliation accomplished by God in Jesus Christ : " Be ye reconciled to God " (2 Cor. 5$^{18f.}$). It is a ministry " even as we have received mercy " (2 Cor. 4^1), a " ministration of the Spirit " (2 Cor. 3^8), a " ministration of righteousness " (2 Cor. 3^9). It consists in this, and only in this, that men may " reflect " the glory of the Lord " with unveiled faces " (2 Cor. 3^{18} ; cf. 1 Cor. 13^{12}). Furthermore : " We preach not ourselves but Christ Jesus as the Lord " (2 Cor. 4^5). It is, therefore, a strictly subordinate and relative event, tied absolutely by the divine act of justification and the divine creation and election upon which it rests, absolutely dependent upon it. Where is the reflection which can last even for a moment without the object reflected ? Where is the reflected light of the earth without the sun which illuminates it ? Yet although tied and dependent in this way, the event which occurs in this " ministry of reconciliation " is a very real and necessary one. And the ministry must be executed without " fainting " (2 Cor. 4^1, 4^{16}) and in " joyfulness " (2 Cor. 3^{12}). Replacing the Old Testament Law, it is the sanctification of the congregation formed by the divine revelation and reconciliation. As the whole problem is presented to us in Paul's description of the sanctification of the apostolic office in the New Testament, it is the sanctification of the Christian religion which is accomplished once and for all in the name of Jesus Christ, but has to be continually reacknowledged and reaffirmed in obedience. It is because of this that we have to take seriously the fact that the Christian religion has a concrete historical nature and a concrete historical form : the distinction of that nature and form from those of other religions, the problems which arise concerning them, the possibility and danger of erring in respect of them and the need to make constant decision in relation to them. The name of Jesus Christ is not only the justification but also the sanctification of the Christian religion. But for that very reason these things have to be taken just as seriously as Israel had to take the Law, if it was to remain the people of the covenant. They have to be taken seriously in faith and obedience to the justifying name of Jesus Christ and therefore in the inescapable light of the question of truth which continually raises itself and demands an answer. The name of Jesus Christ justifies the Christian religion, without it being able to make even the slightest contribution to its justification as a human religion. This name is the authority and power which moves and transforms it in all its human sinfulness, continually erecting and maintaining a sign in this sphere, and seeing to it that it is observed. It is the authority and power which by this sign, by the sign of the Church and of the existence of the children of God assembled in the Church, continually exhorts and consoles this religion throughout its history, being revealed not only in the past, but by means of this sign in the present and future. It is perfectly true that Christians are sinners and that the Church is a Church of sinners. But if they are justified sinners—as Christians are—then in virtue of the same Word and Spirit which justifies them, they are also sanctified sinners. That is, they are placed under discipline. They are put under the order of revelation. They are no longer free in all their sinfulness. They remember the Lord who justifies them and they are bound to wait upon Him. To that extent, although they are still sinners, they are ready for Him and at His disposal. Both in general and in particular, Christianity as an historical form is readiness for the Lord, by whose name those who profess this religion, and with them the religion itself, are created and elected and justified. That is why the problems of the nature and form of this religion are serious problems : the question of canon and dogma, the question of creed, cultus and Church order, the question of correct theology and piety and ethics. They are not serious problems in the sense that to win through to certain answers would enable Christianity to justify itself as the true religion. But they are serious problems in the sense that by the answers made to them it is decided whether Christianity is here and now ready for the Lord who justified it long ago, whether it really is justified and therefore the true religion, whether it does still participate in the promise which was made long ago and does not depend upon its merit or co-operation for validity. It is not a question of acquiring and maintaining an advantage when Christians and Christianity seek the truth concerning the visible nature and form of their religion, suffer and fight for the truth when it is known. The fact remains that the highest results of their seeking, suffering and fighting do not give them any advantage. It all amounts to this, that as they have to keep on breathing for animal life, so they have continually to struggle for their existence as Christians and Christianity, to be those who already have the advantage of knowing the name of Jesus Christ, and of being named after Him. It is a matter of the exercising and repeating of their existence as the Church and the children of God. They would not be what they are from eternity to eternity, if they were not so in time. They would not be what they are invisibly, if they were not so visibly and therefore in this exercise and repetition. But the sanctification, to which they are subject in this exercise and repetition, is quite beyond their own striving and its successes and failures. No less than their justification, it is the work of Him for whose sake they are called Christians and Christianity.

§ 18

THE LIFE OF THE CHILDREN OF GOD

Where it is believed and acknowledged in the Holy Spirit, the revelation of God creates men who do not exist without seeking God in Jesus Christ, and who cannot cease to testify that He has found them.

1. MAN AS A DOER OF THE WORD

We have come a long way. We asked concerning the Word of God in its original form, and therefore concerning the revelation which is the object of the testimony of Holy Scripture, the source and norm of the proclamation of the Christian Church. Three answers were given, each of them complete in its own way. The first had special reference to the subject presupposed in the concept of revelation; the doctrine of God in His unity and trinity as Father, Son and Holy Spirit. The second had special reference to the event indicated in the concept; the doctrine of the incarnation of the Word of God in Jesus Christ. The third had special reference to the effect and goal of this event; the doctrine of the outpouring of the Holy Spirit. But there is still a gap in the last circle. We began both the christological and the pneumatological sections of our doctrine of revelation with a presentation first of the reality, then of the possibility of revelation, both on its objective side, as it derives from God, and also on its subjective side, as it comes to man. To put it in another way, we began with an exposition of faith, then of the related understanding, in regard to the freedom which God has for us and the freedom which we have for God, in regard to Jesus Christ and the Holy Spirit. There then followed an investigation of the concept of time in the christological section, and a corresponding investigation of the concept of religion in the pneumatological, which we have just concluded. But the christological section closed with a positive description of the real mystery of the person of Jesus Christ as the divine-human Reconciler, and of the miracle to which this mystery points. A corresponding discussion has still to be added to the pneumatological section. And since the section as a whole is concerned with revelation in its man-ward aspect, it is obvious that the object of this final discussion can only be man himself as the recipient of revelation, i.e., believing and perceiving man. In the true manhood of the Son of God, all those who believe in Him are taken up into unity with Him and into the unity of His body on earth. They become partakers by grace of the

divine sonship which is proper to Him by nature. That is the full
meaning and content of the revelation made in Jesus Christ as the
Word of God by the Holy Spirit.

What has preceded will be a sharp warning that there is still no
room for lyricism. We must not let ourselves be involved in a discussion of the Christian man abstracted from divine revelation instead of
revelation itself, with a direct vision as the way and condition of knowledge instead of faith instructed by Holy Scripture. If we follow Scripture, there is no psychology of the Reconciler, but the strict doctrine
of His true Godhead and humanity. Similarly there is no psychology
of the reconciled. In both cases the only possible object of direct
vision or psychology is the " flesh," of which we are told in Jn. 6[63]
that it profiteth nothing. Again, in Christology we had to hold to
the Word that is made flesh. Similarly, if we are not to be betrayed
into irrelevant prattling, we must now hold to the Spirit, who is
involved in the redemptive conflict with our flesh. At this point we
are specifically warned by the last section, in which it became evident
that revelation is the removal of all religion, including the Christian.
Christianity is the true religion only in virtue of the name of Jesus
Christ, in the act and hiddenness of the divine grace, by dint of the
divine creation, election, justification and sanctification. It is not the
true religion in itself, or in such a way that the Christian is as such the
master of truth. If we ignore this warning, if we insist upon the postulate of the Christian as such, apart from the Word and the Spirit and
faith, we have to ask ourselves whether by allowing the Christian as
such to assume such an unnecessary importance we are not risking
something of vital importance : for the Christian abstractly considered
is no longer a sinner, at any rate in any actual or serious sense. He is
considered and explained only in his antithesis as a sanctified sinner.
But the actual revelation which we receive in Jesus Christ by the Holy
Spirit never ceases to tell us that we are sinners, in the strictest and
most serious sense. It is only in and with this judgment upon us, not
in ourselves but in Jesus Christ, that we are reconciled with God and
therefore sanctified. Actual revelation does not know man in a partly
achieved state of sanctification beyond the act of divine grace, but
only as the object of this particular act, and therefore not in a peace
or truce between the spirit and flesh, in which he can, as it were, be
photographed psychologically, but only in the midst of the conflict
which at no point reflects the predetermined issue to which it moves.
If, then, we try to deal with the Christian *in abstracto*, or even think
that we can, we must ask ourselves whether we have not lost sight
completely of actual revelation, and whether in these circumstances
we can catch any real glimpse of the Christian. For where else can he
be seen except in the light of revelation ?

But bearing in mind this limitation of our theme, which is the
limitation of all theological discussion, we are forced to concede that

man as he receives and believes and confesses revelation does constitute
a problem which has to be dealt with if our doctrine of the outpouring
of the Holy Spirit, and therefore of revelation and the Word of God
generally, is not to be incomplete at a critical point. According to
Holy Scripture, revelation is the incarnation of the eternal Word and
the outpouring of the Holy Spirit upon flesh. But if this is the case,
then we must heavily underline the fact that it would not be revelation
if man were to remain outside the closed circle of it, if the circle of
his own existence were not intersected by this circle of revelation. The
Christian *in abstracto* we must avoid—the Christian *in concreto* we
cannot avoid. It is to him that the Word of God is directed and the
gift of the Holy Spirit is made, and upon him that the light of revelation
falls. We cannot see this light, which is, of course, always and exclusively the light of God, without seeing this man as well. But when
we see man, we do not see any kind of being. Whatever it may or
may not signify in detail or in a more general context, we see the
being which is constantly realising its existence in acts of free determination and decision. And we the observers are ourselves the primary
evidence.

To use the older terminology, we see a *creatura rationalis*, a thinking, willing,
feeling creature, a spiritual being which, with the angels, so far as we can gather,
is unique of its kind. The well-known passage in the Formula of Concord (*Sol.
decl.* II, 19) does not say that man is a *lapis et truncus*, but that Holy Scripture
compares his heart with a *duro lapidi, qui ad tactum non cedat, sed resistat, item
rudi trunco, interdum etiam ferae indomitae.* The passage then continues : *non
quod homo post lapsum non amplius sit rationalis creatura, aut absque auditu et
meditatione verbi divini ad Deum convertatur ; aut quod in rebus externis et civilibus
nihil boni aut mali intelligere possit, aut libere aliquod agere vel omittere queat.*
In every respect but one, man is " witty, intelligent and accomplished." But
in *spiritualibus et divinis rebus* he is *similis* (!) *trunco et lapidi ac statuae vita carenti,
quae neque oculorum oris aut ullorum sensuum cordisve usum habet.* For he cannot
see the wrath of God against his sin ; he cannot see that he is threatened by
death and hell ; he will not receive either exhortation or instruction : *antequam
per Spiritum sanctum illuminatur, convertitur et regeneratur* (20–21). As is said
later, without the Holy Spirit he is actually worse than a stock, *quia voluntati
divinae rebellis est et inimicus* (24). But : *Ad hanc Spiritus sancti renovationem
nullus lapis, nullus truncus, sed solus homo creatus est* (22). As man and therefore as a *creatura rationalis* man becomes the object of the divine action. But
this means that *haec agitatio Spiritus sancti non est coactio, sed homo conversus
sponte bonum operatur* (64). *Sic eum trahit, ut ex intellectu caecato illuminatus
fiat intellectus, et ex rebelli voluntate fiat prompta et obœdiens voluntas* (60). If
it does not belong to our freedom to put ourselves in this position, it is none
the less our freedom which we exercise in this position. If there is no *cooperatio
voluntatis nostrae in hominis conversione* (44), there can and must be once we
assume the work of the Holy Spirit on man : *quantum et quamdiu a Deo per
Spiritum sanctum ducitur, regitur et gubernatur*—if God were to withdraw His
gracious hand from us, in that case *ne ad minimum momentum* (66).

We said earlier that in the very self-determination, without which
he would not be a man, man becomes an object of the divine predetermination. It is in this way that the circle of his existence is

intersected by the circle of revelation. The grace of revelation is not
conditioned by his humanity, but his humanity is conditioned by the
grace of revelation. God's freedom does not compete with man's
freedom. How could it be the freedom of the divine mercy bestowed
on man, if it suppressed and dissolved human freedom ? It is the
grace of revelation that God exercises and maintains His freedom to
free man.

It will be instructive to turn to the passage in Jas. 1²¹⁻²⁵, which is very important in this context. The emphasis is all upon man as the recipient of the
Word of God. According to verse 21 this Word has " the power to save your
souls." It is only of itself, only of the One who has spoken it, only " from
above," that it has this power. James does not leave us in any doubt about
that. But in this power this Word is " engrafted " in the man who believes
and confesses it. It is something alien, the element of a new order. Yet it is
as near to him as he is himself : " on thy lips and in thine heart " (Rom. 10⁸).
But if it is really near to him, that means that it will be " received " by him.
But this receiving means a very definite humbling of man. The self-righteousness
which corresponds to his old and impure nature is reversed. He is reduced to
that " meekness " which alone can do what is right in the presence of God. If
the Word is really engrafted in us, this receiving and reversal are merely the
self-evident and inevitable consummation of our existence as it is newly posited
by God. We merely deceive ourselves if we try to be only hearers of this Word,
and not doers because we are hearers (v. 22). As real hearers we are indeed taken
prisoner by this Word. We surrender to it. Inevitably, therefore, the totality
of our existence is evidence of what we have heard. According to Calvin's
exposition of the passage (*C.R.* 55, 395), a doer of the Word is : *qui sermonem
Dei ex anima complectitur vitaque testatur, serio se credidisse, iuxta hanc Christi
sententiam : Beati qui audiunt sermonem Dei et custodiunt eum* (Lk. 11²⁸). To
want to be hearers only would mean to want to isolate the Word from our existence, to make ourselves onlookers at heart, and independent judges in our own
consciences, to debate with the Word. In short, it would mean that we maintain
our autonomy over against it as those who know the Word and are interested
in it and reverence and adore it. But although we can do this with the word of
man, we cannot do it with the Word of God. Because it is the Word of the Lord,
to hear the Word of God is to obey the Word of God. Not to obey the Word of
God is therefore to deceive oneself. The deception is twofold : first by dealing
with the engrafted Word, as though it were not the Word of the Lord ; and
then by imagining that to ignore the engrafting is to rob it of its power, as though
resisted grace does not become judgment by the very same power by which it
may be blessing. As it says, vv. 23–24, we can see our natural face in a mirror,
and then turn away and forget it again. But in the mirror of the Word of God
we see ourselves as we are before God and therefore in truth. Once we have
heard what this Word has to say to us, we can never forget it. We can only
be what it says that we are. If we do not want to fall into the pit of iniquity,
we must be doers of the Word. The man who, like Peter looking down into the
empty grave of Jesus (Lk. 24¹², Jn. 20⁵), stoops down and looks into the mirror
of the Word of God, attains, as Calvin said, a *penetrabilis intuitus, qui nos ad Dei
similitudinem transformat.* This Word, this Law lays claim to us, and in doing
so it lays claim to our freedom, i.e., our own free and spontaneous obedience. It
does not claim individual works. It claims ourselves as the doers of the work
which corresponds to its content. That is to say, it demands our confession,
the confession of our existence. It demands our heart. It demands that we
leave the sanctuary of an abstract " inwardness," and give ourselves to the
decision not merely of obeying, but of obedience, of accepting it as the truth

without reserve, of submission to the truth. In this doing of the Word, which is true hearing, we are saved and blessed, the object of the divine good-pleasure— not otherwise : *in ipsa actione sita est beatitudo* (Calvin). A right understanding of this passage in James will show us at once why the concept " work," so long as it is not an evasion of Jesus Christ and of faith, has a very positive significance for Paul as well. For him, too, God will requite each " according to his works " (Rom. 2⁶), and it is not the hearers but only the doers of the law who are justified (Rom. 2¹³). Upon the one foundation, Jesus Christ, each individual builds his work, and it is this which will be made manifest one way or the other at the last judgment (1 Cor. 3¹³). We all have to stand before the judgment seat of Christ and receive according to what we have done in this life (2 Cor. 5¹⁰). In Gal. 6³ᶠ· it is deliberately emphasised that to avoid self-deception we must all look to our own work, by which we have both our own praise and our own burden. At times (Phil. 2¹²ᶠ·) Paul can even regard the attainment of eternal redemption from the standpoint of κατεργάζεσθαι (in the context the accent is not on this but on the ἐν φόβῳ καὶ τρόμῳ), but, of course, he at once points to the obvious basis of it all : For it is God that worketh in you to will and to do of His good pleasure. Conversely, in Eph. 2⁸ᶠ·, when he has just stated most strongly that we are saved by grace through faith, as a gift and not by virtue of our works, he can then continue : " We are His creatures, created in Christ Jesus to good works, for which God hath prepared us, that we should walk therein." From 1 Thess. 1³ and 2 Thess. 1¹ we see that the concept ἔργον πίστεως is a familiar one to Paul. And he can describe his own activity as an apostle as an ἐργάζεσθαι ἔργον κυρίου (1 Cor. 16¹⁰) and himself as the συνεργὸς of God (1 Cor. 3⁹). And we must add all those passages in which on very different grounds but always with the most unequivocal imperatives he summons Christians to good works. In none of these does he envisage any possible rivalry of the work of man with the work of Jesus Christ or the Holy Spirit. In Phil. 2¹²ᶠ· and Eph. 2⁴ᶠ· we can see clearly that although the presupposition of work or works cannot be thought away, it consists for Paul in an act whose Subject is God Himself and God alone, and whose power cannot be increased or diminished by the work or works, but only confirmed. In the Pauline doctrine of Christian works the question of anything more than this necessary confirmation does not arise. And after the uncompromising pronouncements of Romans and Galatians, there can be no question of any rivalry between human work and human faith. There can be no doubt that, according to Paul, it is in faith, and only in faith, that man is the object of that divine act, and therefore justified before God, because justified by God. And that is so because in faith he has Jesus Christ as his object, the One to whom he is drawn and committed and in whom he is established. In faith he confirms and acknowledges and affirms the divine act as something which has been done for him and to him. Because faith is faith in Jesus Christ, in faith it is true that he is a man reconciled to God. We can therefore describe faith as that work which confirms the divine action, upon which Paul lays such great stress. And in all the passages in which he describes that work as the criterion of our perseverance or non-perseverance before God, from his other statement it is obvious that he does not mean anything but the " work of faith," i.e., our life-work as ultimately and decisively defined as something which happens in faith. This work is our justification in the sight of God, not, of course, as a work of man, but for the sake of its object, because it is the work of faith in Jesus Christ. But this does not alter in the very least the fact that it is necesarily a human work, our life-work. It is man who believes. This does not justify him. What justifies him is the fact that he believes in Jesus Christ. But man believes. And when he believes, his faith is not an accidental or partial, but a necessary and total, determination of his existence. It may be a weak and tiny faith, but if it is not necessary and total even in its weakness and tininess, it is not faith, and Jesus Christ is not its object. It does not justify man because of its necessity and totality, but because of its object, for the sake of Jesus Christ. And yet it is not faith, it does not have Jesus Christ for its object, and therefore it does not justify, if it does not have this necessity and totality—or to put it more simply, if it is not man, man himself, the whole man, who believes. When we say man himself, the whole man, we come to what is in fact both in James and also in Paul, not the strict, mathematical centre (which can only be the name of Jesus Christ and faith in Him), but the central area which necessarily circumscribes and indicates that centre : the man who comes necessarily and totally under a new determination is the ἐν Χριστῷ, the man who is the object of that divine act, the man who believes in Jesus Christ. His existence under this determination, his existence therefore under the determination of Jesus Christ and faith in Him, is what Paul so strikingly describes as his work or works. It is obvious that for Paul this work could as little be a rival of faith as it could of Jesus Christ and the Holy Spirit—or as little as in James the doing of the Word could be of the hearing. It is not additional to faith. It is the expression, the true and necessary expression of faith. In actual fact, faith is alone. But real faith—as opposed to what James calls a dead faith—is not an upward faith, as directed to Jesus Christ and therefore to justification. If it is to be faith at all, it is actually and necessarily a downward faith, as the faith of man, of man himself, of the whole man. We might also say that work is faith and faith is work, to the extent that it is the creation of the free God, and within those limits necessarily and totally the free decision and act of man.

If we are to speak fully and rightly of the grace of the Holy Spirit we cannot avoid the Christian *in concreto*. And the Christian *in concreto* is the free man, whose freedom is safeguarded and maintained by God. If we remember that man's self-determination in Jesus Christ by the Holy Spirit stands under the sign and within the limits of the divine predetermination, we are faced with the problem which is usually described as the problem of theological ethics, or more practically as the Christian life. In this content we cannot do more than give a first and general outline. The fact of God's revelation as such raises the question what are we to do ?—the question of the shaping of our life in conformity with this fact. Better, it commands our obedience. It is within these limits that we are forced to deal with the matter at this point. We will do so under the title " The life of the children of God."

I have to thank A. v. Harnack for this title. In 1925 I had a last direct conversation with him, upon the possibility and problem of an Evangelical dogmatics. He told me that if he had to write such a work himself, this would be his title. There is no doubt that if an Evangelical dogmatics did have to have a special title—and better not—this one could be used. Of course, even under this title its basic and decisive theme and centre would be the one Son of God and the Holy Spirit, its source would be Holy Scripture and its *locus* the Church. And obviously that is not what Harnack meant. His proposal was that dogmatics in the older sense ought now to be replaced by the personal confession of someone who has attained the maturity and serenity of final convictions and spiritual certainties, a confession determined at its very heart by the history of Christianity. For myself, I cannot see that this kind of confession is in any way a real substitute for the function of dogmatics in theology and the Church. Harnack was obviously speaking for Neo-Protestantism, whose proper object of faith is not God in His revelation, but man himself believing in the divine. As it thinks and speaks under Holy Scripture and in the Church, theology cannot ascribe any such value or significance to man. But the impulse which led Neo-Protestantism on this particular track need not be repressed. It has a legitimate place within the doctrine of the Holy Spirit. I can perhaps do justice to it outwardly by adopting Harnack's proposal, even if not in his own sense. For the revelation of God does in fact create the life of the children of God. After what has been already said, I need hardly say that without any change in material significance we might just as well use the title " The Life of the Church."

Human self-determination, and therefore the life of the children of God, is posited under the predominant determination of revelation. In a double sense our first definition of it is negative : God creates men who do not exist unless they seek Him, and who cannot cease to testify that He has found them. These negative formulations will later have to be replaced by positive ones. I use them first in order again to bring out the predominant determination, by which human self-determination is posited. The free decision of man, the act and work of man, the life of real men, is revealed in the fulfilment of revelation as the outpouring of the Holy Spirit. But it does not have its character as the life of the children of God from itself, but from the light in which it is placed. No positive—and we must add at once, no negative—description of what man does or does not do can clearly reproduce, in the strict sense, the " Christian " character of his life and activity and suffering. It acquires this character only " from outside," that is, from God. What is essentially " Christian " in this life and doing and not doing can only be the declaration : He and not I ! He and not we ! He, the Lord ! He for us ! He in our stead ! The predominant determination of man by revelation, the basis of the life of the children of God, is the fact that this " He " avails for them, comforting, exhorting, ordering and limiting—and all with an unrivalled emphasis, because it is the reality of their own existence which is vindicated in it all, a reality which they can as little avoid as they can escape ourselves. But it is the hidden reality of their own existence. It is He, He who is the reality. He is not I. He is not we. Only indirectly is He identical with us and we with Him. For He is God and we are men. He is in heaven and we are on earth. He lives eternally and we live temporally. There is always this eschatological frontier between Him and us. But this means that it is only indirectly and not unequivocally that we can grasp that He and not I, that He and not we, as it is declared in the life and doing and not doing of man, and the effects of its comforting and exhorting and ordering and limiting in our human life. The reality of which we are trying to speak in respect of the life and doing and not doing of man is greater than, indeed utterly different from, anything that we can say about it, because He is this reality. It is clear that even with negative formulations like those mentioned we must not think that we can pass on to direct communication. In relation to Him they always say too little, in respect of human life and doing and not doing they say too much to be able to do more than give a general indication or point in the right direction. But the pointing can be known as such and with its limitations by the fact that it takes place first in the negative formulation.

A first thing that we have to say is that if we think of the life of the children of God as a creation of the Holy Spirit we have to do with a determinateness of human life understood as *being* and *doing*. And with the necessary caution we can also say that we have to do with a determinateness of the inward and outward aspects of human life : its isolation and its fellowship.

These preliminary distinctions will all have to give way later to biblical concepts, and are only relative. In justification of them we can point at once to the biblical distinctions between regeneration and conversion, justification and sanctification, faith and obedience, the children of God and the servants of God. There can be no question of an antithesis between two quite different determinations of man ; for He who determines, Jesus Christ and the Holy Spirit, is only One. We shall also find that the two lines which we are now separating constantly intersect. But it belongs to the indirectness of all our present consideration that we cannot possibly reduce what we have to perceive and state to a single denominator, or describe it in a single term. Apart from the loan-words " Christ " and " Christian," there is nothing in human life answering to that one name of Jesus Christ, in which, as we have seen, the two lines of our thinking converge in that quite different context.

In the revelation of God, man is claimed on the one hand as a specific subject and being. He is not merely newly qualified but really new, because newly made in the relationship created between himself and God. This is the Christian life regarded as being—and it is rightly and properly a benefit of revelation. But we have to remember that this being, as the being of a man, does not subsist of itself, but only in a specific doing on the part of the subject. The claim of revelation comes into force in this doing. In this doing, and to that extent in this being—because it is, of course, the doing of this subject and therefore of this being—we can, repeating the distinction, differentiate between the inward aspect, i.e., its meaning, intention and bearing, and the outward, i.e., the action and its effect, neither of which can exist without the other any more than being without doing, or doing without being. We again repeat the distinction when we say that, so long as we look at the being and inward aspect of man, as claimed in revelation, we see him in his isolation. For in his being as a new subject or in the intention of his activity he is isolated even in his social life, an individual even in the Church. He is confronted only by God, and no one can represent him in that confrontation. But if we look at the doing or outward aspect of this same man, we find that in spite of his isolation this same man is united in society as an individual with the whole Church, related, of course, to God, but in God to others. The impossibility of regarding him strictly from the one standpoint or the other means that we cannot treat either of these insights as exclusive. The fact is that they belong together. It is only relatively that we can separate them.

Negatively defined, the first of the two, the being, the inward nature, the isolation of the Christian means that he cannot exist without seeking God in Jesus Christ. He is denied any other being than that which consists in the specific act of seeking. He is forced out of every other being and forced into that of being a seeker after God, and after God in Christ. Behind him there is only the impossible, the sin which he has committed and the abyss of death. It is true that that is always behind him and to that extent he is still a sinner, and under sentence of death. He is saved only in Christ. But it is behind him. He is saved in Christ. He is a sinner pardoned, a *peccator justus*. He lives in his activity as a seeker after God. That is his new creation by the Holy Ghost. In the Holy Ghost he actually hears and believes the Word of God, and the Word of God is the eternal Word, which assumed flesh and in that flesh raised up our flesh and the flesh of all those who hear and believe that Word to the glory of the Father. For that reason it is taken away from us, from the children of God. They can have it only as they have the Word, and therefore only as they seek the Word, only as they seek God in Christ, only as they " seek that which is above " (Col. 3[1f.]). By the fact that, having heard and believed, they are forced into this search, they are new subjects, born again by the Holy Spirit. And this very search is the core of their life, the intention of their activity, the thing which in all their fellowship they can only be and do in isolation. And now we can name the biblical concept which speaks of this seeking after God by those whom He has found in His word. It is the love of God in the transitive sense, the love of man to God. That is the only being which remains when his other being is taken away from him, because he has risen with Christ.

Again, negatively defined, the second of the two, the doing, the outward aspect, the social nature of the Christian means that he cannot cease to testify that God in Christ has found him. Therefore his being makes necessary a very definite doing. He simply cannot suppress or conceal or keep to himself what he is. What is he ? He is a man found by God. He did not seek, he was sought. He did not find, he was found. God in His eternal Word was free for him. And by the Holy Spirit he, man, was free for God. In the freedom of God he himself became free and the child of God. This is the irresistible summons to action. This is what he has to reveal and declare. This is what his whole existence has now to proclaim and attest and affirm. It is in this decision that he now lives. The freedom to decide otherwise is now behind him. It is true that it is always behind him. Again and from this angle, too, it is true that he is always a sinner, under sentence of death. For whatever is behind him is again the impossible, the sin which he has committed and the abyss of death. He is saved in Christ, but only in Christ, and therefore in the decision to witness to Him. In face of the sin and death, from which he has come, as a real *justus peccator*, he can only live out and reveal and attest his salvation. The Spirit who has regenerated him compels him to do this work of revealing and attesting and confessing. And this inescapable confessing becomes the outward side of his life, his activity as a doing and working. And just at this point, for all the isolation of his inner path, he suddenly finds himself in the fellowship of the Church. And now again we can give the biblical concept which marks this fact. It is the attesting and confessing that we are found and saved : the praise of God. The praise of God is the action inescapably laid upon us when our freedom is transferred to another action under the sentence and judgment of God when we are dead with Christ.

All things considered, the Christian life, the life of the children of God, consists in these two concepts of love and praise. The children of God are those who seek after God and find their answer in God. It is in this apparently contradictory unity that they are what they are and do what they do. In fact, both sides are true : they ask because they already have the answer ; they answer because they themselves are first asked. They are both true in Jesus Christ. And the two concepts together are the principle of what we call theological ethics : the love of God is our only remaining being and the praise of God is our necessary doing. Even in its consideration and doctrine of revelation dogmatics has already to ask what becomes of the man to whom the revelation of God comes ? What have we to do who know that we have heard and believed the Word of God ? And because it finds the problem of the Christian man in its basic considerations and treats it as its own problem, it takes ethics into itself, thus making a special theological ethics superfluous . For without ceasing to be dogmatics, reflection upon the Word of God, it is itself ethics.

2. THE LOVE OF GOD

The Christian life begins with love. It also ends with love, so far as it has an end as human life in time. There is nothing that we can or must be or do as a Christian, or to become a Christian, prior to love. Even faith does not anticipate love. As we come to faith we begin to love. If we did not begin to love, we would not have come to faith. Faith is faith in Jesus Christ. If we believe, the fact that we do so means that every ground which is not that of our being in love to God in Christ is cut away from under us : we cannot exist without seeking God. If this were not the case, we should have failed to come to faith. And the fact that it is so is a confirmation that our faith is not an illusion, but that we ourselves as men do really believe.

We remember what James says about doing and Paul about work. The faith of which Paul speaks is not an imaginary faith. According to Gal. 5⁶ it is a faith which is active in love, i.e., effectual, i.e., actual : ἐνεργουμένη. He that loveth not knoweth not God, 1 Jn. 4⁸. If it is a matter of the way of faith, the way of the Christian, then love is the way, ἡ καθ' ὑπερβολὴν ὁδός (1 Cor. 12³¹).

But there is also nothing beyond love. There is no higher or better being or doing in which we can leave it behind us. As Christians, we are continually asked about love, and in all that we can ever do or not do, it is the decisive question.

Paul expressly says of love in 1 Cor. 13⁸ that it οὐδέποτε πίπτει. He means that it will still apply to the being and activity of the redeemed in the world to come. In eternity when we see God face to face, either we will be those who love, or we will not be.

Love is the essence of Christian living. It is also its *conditio sine qua non*, in every conceivable connexion. Wherever the Christian life in commission or omission is good before God, the good thing about it is love.

According to Rom. 13¹⁰ love is the πλήρωμα νόμου. According to 1 Tim. 1⁵ it is the τέλος τῆς παραγγελίας. If ye keep my commandments, ye shall abide in my love, Jn. 15¹⁰. That is why in Mk. 12²⁹f· the Law and the prophets are summed up in the twofold commandment : Thou shalt love—God and thy neighbour. Love beareth all things, believeth all things, hopeth all things, endureth all things (1 Cor. 13⁷). In love the truth is honoured (2 Thess. 2¹⁰ ; 1 Cor. 13⁶ ; Eph. 4¹⁵). Love builds up the Church (1 Cor. 8¹ ; Eph. 4¹⁶). R. Rothe is right when he says " that every moral function (all the doing and non-doing) of the individual (apart from all else) is normal only in so far as, whatever else it may be, it is an act of love, and is done in love " (*Theol. Ethik²*, Vol. I, 1867, p. 536).

But from this we may gather that as the living expression of the human children of God, as the self-determination of human existence, neither in essence nor in actuality can love be understood in itself, but only in that sphere or light of the divine predestination, in which we stand when we hear and believe in the Word of God and are born again as the children of God. If love is the essence and totality of the good demanded of us, how can it be known that we love ? Obviously it can be said that we do so only because something else can first be said of us, that we are loved, that we are men beloved. If there is nothing in the Christian life which can precede love, the love of God for man must first precede the Christian life as such, if it is to begin with love. It is not the case that we ourselves can put ourselves in the position in which all that we can do is to seek what is above. We do, of course, put ourselves in many awkward positions. We can even plunge ourselves into despair. But we cannot put ourselves in the position, that saving and blessed despair, in which we can only seek refuge in God. But God plunges us into this despair when He reveals Himself to us, when His Word is made flesh and the judgment of our flesh by the Holy Spirit, who opens our eyes and ears and therefore kindles our faith. When that occurs, the Christian life begins. We are born and live as the children of God. And then we are real men who really love. But only then.

So it is a rare plant which groweth not in our garden, to love God with all our heart, etc. For " to love God " and to seek God's glory means to be hostile to ourselves and to the whole world. As Christ also says in Lk. 14 : " If any man comes to me and hates not his father, mother, wife, child, brother, sister, even his own life, he cannot be my disciple." But we do not find that in us. Perhaps we love the letters GOD, but we do not love what the letters signify. We only curse and complain, especially when we are assailed and suffer (Luther, *Pred. üb. Lk.* 10^{23-37}, acc. to Rörer, *E.A.* 5, 70 f.). We have to think particularly of the passage in which we are told of Christian love that " the love of God is poured into our hearts by the Holy Spirit which is given unto us " (Rom. 5^5)— and for this reason, because in the death of Christ, God first showed His own love for us while we were yet sinners (Rom. $5^{7f.}$). Herein is love, not that we loved God, but that He loved us (note the aorist ἠγάπησεν), and sent His Son to be the propitiation for our sins (1 Jn. 4^{10}). " Abide in My love " says the commandment ; " for as the Father hath loved me, so have I loved you " (Jn. 15^9). " For the great love wherewith He loved us " God has given us this new status, quickened us together with Christ, saved us by grace and therefore set us on the way of good works (Eph. $2^{4f.}$). Paul now lives his life in the flesh in the faith of the Son of God, " who loved me, and gave himself for me " (Gal. 2^{20}). The meaning of Deut. 30^6 is exactly the same (and we must note it if we are to understand Deut. 6^5) when Israel is told : " Yahweh thy God will circumcise thine heart, and the heart of thy seed, to love the Lord thy God with all thy heart, and with all thy soul, for thy life's sake." Of course love is our being and doing, if we love. But the fact that we love, and are those who love, which is the essence and totality of the life of the children of God, is no less a gift and work of God, a virgin-birth (in the extended sense of Jn. $1^{12f.}$), than is the human existence of the eternal Son of God. It is for those who love God that there is prepared " what eye hath not seen, nor ear heard, neither have entered into the heart of man " (1 Cor. 2^9). Love is of God, and whoso loveth is born of God and knoweth God (1 Jn. 4^7). The fact that Christian love is grounded in the love of God for us was made a dogma at the *Conc. Araus.* II (529) : *Prorsus donum Dei est diligere Deum. Ipse ut diligeretur dedit qui non dilectus diligit. Displicentes amati sumus, ut fieret in nobis, unde placeremus. Diffundit enim charitatem in cordibus nostris Spiritus Patris et Filii, quem cum Patre amamus et Filio* (*Can.* 25, *Denz.* No. 198). It is difficult to see what relationship there is between this and what Thomas Aquinas obviously thought that we should say, that *Deus potest a nobis amari naturaliter, etiam non praesupposita fide vel spe futurae beatitudinis* (*S. Theol.* II, 1 qu. 65 art. 5, 1). The biblical passages do not know anything of a natural love to God which is proper to us apart from divine revelation, or of a natural capacity for love which is prior to revelation. It is only the children of God by grace who love and can love God.

On the other hand, we must insist that the love of the children of God does become an event in an act or acts of human self-determination : it is a creaturely reality. A creaturely reality, let us say, which as such, as human self-determination, is re-created by God Himself in the sphere or light of the divine predetermination, thus being transformed, becoming love instead of non-love, but not ceasing on that account to be human self-determination and therefore a creaturely reality. We cannot therefore say that it is the product of a transformation of the creaturely into divine reality, nor can we say that

in it the divine reality has taken the place of the creaturely. In strict
analogy with the incarnation of the Word in Jesus Christ, what takes
place in man by the revelation of God is this : his humanity is not
impaired, but in the Word of God heard and believed by him he finds
the Lord, indeed in the strict and proper sense he finds the subject
of his humanity, for on his behalf Jesus Christ stands and rightly stands
in His humanity at the right hand of the Father. For that very
reason all that he can do is in his humanity to seek God in this Jesus
Christ, and therefore to love Him. When the children of God love,
they are the earthly members of His body, longing for their heavenly
Head. The earthly members—that is why their loving, grounded as
it is in the love of God, is not transmuted into a heavenly or divine
loving.

As distinct from the sayings in Jn. 4^{24} : πνεῦμα ὁ θεός, or 2 Cor. 3^{17} : ὁ δὲ κύριος
τὸ πνεῦμά ἐστιν, the saying in 1 Jn. $4^{8.\ 16}$: ὁ θεὸς ἀγάπη ἐστίν is an irreversible
one. It does not say that even in any consummation God is what we know
as love in ourselves. It does not know that what we know as love in ourselves
is God. It does not teach the deity of love, but the love of the Deity. We have
to take it quite strictly. The fact that God is love means not only that we ought
to love but can and must love. According to 1 Jn. 4^9 the love of God is manifested in the fact that He sent His only-begotten Son, that we might live through
Him. That is the incomparable and unattainable love of God. Only of that
love can it be said that God is love. And as such, in essential contradistinction
from all our loving, it is the basis of the loving of the children of God in all its
creaturely reality.
It was Peter Lombard (*Sent.* 1 *dist.* 17) who maintained the doctrine that
the love with which we love God and our neighbour is nothing but God. Indeed,
as he saw it, it is the Holy Spirit Himself. For in the Trinity, according to
Augustine, the Holy Spirit is the love of the Father for the Son and of the Son
for the Father, and it is this Holy Spirit who is given to us. In the Christian
life of man the Holy Spirit Himself replaces the human *motus animi*, although
its effect is the same. Thomas Aquinas cautiously but very definitely rejected
this view. Our love, he says, is only *quaedam participatio charitatis divinae.*
In itself, however, it is a human act of reason and will, with a human *principium.*
*Oportet quod si voluntas moveatur a Spiritu sancto ad diligendum, etiam ipsa sit
efficiens hunc actum.* How else can our love be meritorious ? (*S. Theol.* II, 2
qu. 23 *art.* 2c). Apart from the last argument, we have to admit that Thomas
is right. Furthermore, we must point out that at this point Lombard's conception
of the operation of the Holy Spirit approximates closely to the magical and is
in any case inadequate—as if the fact that the Spirit is given to man does not
mean that man himself can hear and believe the Word of God ; as if the miracle
of the Holy Spirit does not therefore take place in the natural man as such,
who is in himself free.

We must not do violence to the miracle of the Holy Spirit, the
founding of the love of the children of God, even in its more precise
form, by letting God be God and man man, but trying to explain the
origin of love in man as a supernatural extension of natural human
capacity. If we ask how it is possible for man to love, according to
Holy Scripture, we have first to go back to faith, and then from faith
to its object, Jesus Christ. It is in spite of and within the limitation

of his natural capacities that man is met by Jesus Christ in faith in
the promise. He is still a creature, afterwards as well as before. He
is still a sinful creature. But he is met by Jesus Christ and sees and
knows Him as very God and very Man, and therefore as the Reconciler.
And that is the miracle of the Holy Spirit and therefore the founding
of love in man.

It is at this point—as we saw a moment ago—that we part company with
Thomas. In the passage cited he felt that he could make a concession to Lombard,
and in line with his doctrine of grace generally he certainly could and indeed
had to make it. It was this. He claimed that the *actus caritatis* was possible
only if there was added to the *potentia naturalis* a *forma habitualis superaddita,
inclinans ipsam ad charitatis actum et faciens eam prompte et delectabiliter operari.*
What can we say about the introduction of this third *principium* which operates
midway between the divine and the human ? If we stress its divine character,
we are involved in the same difficulties as those which Thomas himself raised
against Lombard : where is the real man in this *forma habitualis*, who is, of course,
supposed to be the subject of love ? But if we stress its human character, where
is the mystery of the origin of love, the miracle of the Holy Spirit ? And with
what right or consistency dare we introduce into the debate a third factor in
the strict sense ? No, if we want to find an answer to the question of the human
possibility of love, i.e., a possibility which is in the sphere of man, we cannot take
refuge either in the " docetic " anthropology of a Lombard or the " Ebionitism "
of a Thomas. We can only point to the fact that we live in the sphere of the
Church, that we are therefore baptised and look to the fulfilment of the promise,
that Jesus Christ died and rose again for us. This is the true *forma habitualis
superaddita*, which does not ascribe to us either a miraculous extension of our
own capacity, nor under the guise of this supernatural quality a liberty which
abolishes grace *qua* grace. If we do not entrust to the Church and baptism and
the promise, the power of the Holy Spirit and therefore the power to found this
love, what confidence can we have in this supernatural capacity ? But if we
do trust in the promise, how can we doubt that man as he is, real man without
deduction or addition, can participate in the promise, and that the miracle of the
outpouring of the Holy Spirit consists in the fact that this man with his natural
capacity, which in itself is utter incapacity, does in faith participate in the
promise and in faith begin to love ? It was not the love of Lombard, which is
identical with the Holy Spirit, or the love of Thomas which is thought of as a
supernatural quality, but this love which in the human sphere is grounded only
in the power of the promise and of faith, that Luther had in mind when in his
exposition of 1 Jn. 4[8. 16] he dared to say of love : " He hath praised love, then,
above everything else that can be named upon earth. For he maketh of it that
which is called God ; and he who hath it he honoureth not as a man or prince,
a King or Emperor, but as a God, and setteth up that God not merely above
lords and princes, nor yet in Paradise, but above all creatures, in God Himself ;
so that the two are one and the same. What then can we desire or think more
precious or glorious than to be one with God and to abide where is High Majesty ?
What are all the Carthusians and monks compared with that man ? " (*Pred. üb.*
1 *Jn.* 4[16ff.], 1532, *W.A.* 36, 441, 30).

But it cannot be otherwise than that the love of God for us is the
basis not only of the reality but also of the knowledge of Christian
love. This means that we must not deduce the real meaning of love
in this context from some arbitrarily if profoundly chosen master-
concept of love in general, comprising the love of God for us on the
one hand and our love for God on the other. Even in love there is

only an indirect identification of the believer with God in Christ. How then can we ever set up or apply a master-concept of this kind ? To know what love is, we have first to ask concerning the unique love of God for us. What our love is will necessarily appear when we ask about our response to this love of God for us and the confirmation and acknowledgment which we owe it. Only then, and by means of the standard which is given us in that way, can we assess the rightness or wrongness of a concept of love which is otherwise completely arbitrary.

To say the least, the definition of Christian love given by Thomas Aquinas (*S. Theol.* II, 1 *qu.* 65 *art.* 5 c) is not very relevant. He speaks of *charitas* as *amicitia quaedam ad Deum, quae quidem super amorem addit mutuam redamationem cum quadam communicatione.* Is it not topsy-turvy to regard Christian love as merely a particular instance of the general possibility of " friendship " ? As though in Christian love the *mutua redamatio* had first to be reduced to a presupposed *amor*, and the *communicatio* between God and man to the *mutua redamatio*. As though in Christian love the direct opposite was not the case : first and basically, a very onesided *communicatio* in God's revelation, which is as such the divine love ; then and for that reason, although quite different from it (and not placed on the same level by the addition of the word *mutua*) man's *redamatio* ; and only finally what we mean by the concept *amicitia*. As a second example of what it is not, I will quote the description which Hegel (*Vorles. ub. d. Phil. d. Rel.* III 1 *ed.* Lasson p. 75) gives of love : " Love is a differentiating of two, who are not at all divided for one another. The consciousness, the feeling of this identity, this being outside myself and in the other, is love : I have my self-consciousness, not in myself, but in the other. But this other in whom alone I am satisfied and am at peace with myself—and I only am as I am at peace with myself ; without it, I am the contradiction which falls apart—this other, by being outside himself, has his self-consciousness only in me, and both are just the consciousness of apartness from self and identity, the perception and feeling, and awareness of unity. That is love, and all talk about love is empty talk if we do not see that it is the differentiating and the removal of the differentiation. God is love, i.e., the differentiating and the unreality of the differentiation is a game of differentiating, which cannot be taken seriously, the differentiation is posited as at once removed, i.e., the simple, eternal idea." The general possibility which Hegel equates with love is obviously that of an identity between identity and non-identity. But what resemblance is there between Christian love and this " game of differentiating which cannot be taken seriously " ? God in His love for us acts in serious distinction from us, without either having his self-consciousness in us or losing it to us. " Not that we loved God, but that he loved us " (1 Jn. 4[10])—that is how it is. And if we return God's love, that does not mean that we have our self-consciousness in God or lose it to us. Our differentiation before God is a serious thing, and it is only in this differentiation that we can and will love Him. The connexion between God's love for us and our love for God is not of such a kind that in the last resort it makes no difference whether it is God who speaks or man because the result is always the same, that both have their self-consciousness in one another ; possessing and losing it, losing and possessing it in a movement which can cease and yet not cease only in the idea of this movement, which therefore deserves to be called God in a special sense. On the contrary, we have here an irreversible order of that which is above and that which is below, of predetermination and self-determination, of God and man. Finally, the relationship does not have the character of a continuous swinging or circular movement, or of the " simple, eternal idea " of it. It is essential to it that it should not be an idea but a drama or a history. On every side, therefore, the Hegelian presupposition proves unsuitable as an interpretation of the concept of Christian love. And when we criticise current ideas of love, it would be as well not to forget the Hegelian, i.e., the Romantic, concept of the mutual losing of oneself in another. As a third example of what it is not, I take the definition of A. Ritschl (*Unterricht i. d. chr. Rel.*, 1875, § 12 note d) : " Love is the constant will which promotes another spiritual, i.e., like-minded, person to achieve his true and highest destiny, and indeed in such a way that the one who loves pursues his own final purpose (3rd edn. : individual purpose). This appropriating of the lifework of another does not mean a denial but a strengthening affirmation of ourselves." Here again—but this time in a more open anthropological, not to say *bourgeois* form—love is equated with a general possibility, i.e., that of correspondence and equilibrium between the individual determination of the will and the social. That God in His loving pursues His own purpose is something which Ritschl would never have conceived or written if he had kept before him the revelation of the triune God, and particularly the person and work of Jesus Christ, instead of that master-concept. It is self-evident, of course, that in all that He does God does pursue His own individual purpose. But to insist upon this and to connect it with what He does to us in His love is to do such violence to the idea of divine love as almost to destroy it. On the other hand, Ritschl's definition does not fit our love to God, because in this case there can be no question of the one who loves (man) promoting " another spiritual and like-minded person (God), to achieve his true and highest destiny." On the same ground, we might even ask whether this can really be said of God in His love to us ; and conversely whether the pursuit of our own individual purpose is a constitutive part of our love to God. In short, even in its Ritschlian form, the process by which we think we know what love is, and then apply this knowledge to divine and human love, does not hold out any invitation to follow it.

We will now try to give the briefest possible outline of what the love of God is which is the real basis of our love to God, determining its character. One thing is certain, that according to Holy Scripture it has nothing to do with mere sentiment, opinion or feeling. On the contrary, it consists in a definite being, relationship and action. God is love in Himself. Being loved by Him we can, as it were, look into His " heart." The fact that He loves us means that we can know Him as He is. This is all true. But if this picture-language of " the heart of God " is to have any validity, it can refer only to the being of God as Father, Son, and Holy Spirit. It reminds us that God's love for us is an overwhelming, overflowing, free love. It speaks to us of the miracle of this love. We cannot say anything higher or better of the " inwardness of God " than that God is Father, Son, and Holy Spirit, and therefore that He is love in Himself without and before loving us, and without being forced to love us. And we can say this only in the light of the " outwardness " of God to us, the occurrence of His revelation. It is from this that we have to learn what is the real nature of the love of God for us.

In this historical context we can point already to the sayings of Hosea and Jeremiah and Deuteronomy in the Old Testament : " When Israel was a child, then I loved him, and called him, my son, out of Egypt " (Hos. 11¹). " With cords as a man useth them, drew I them to me, with bands of love " (Hos. 11⁴). " I have loved thee with an everlasting love, therefore with lovingkindness have I drawn thee to me, for me to have compassion on thee " (Jer. 31³). " Because the Lord hath loved you and because he would keep the oath which he sware unto your fathers, hath the Lord brought you out with a mighty hand and with outstretched arm, and hath redeemed thee out of the house of bondage " (Deut. 7[8]). " Behold the heaven and the heaven of heavens, and the earth and all that is upon it, unto the Lord thy God it belongeth. Only the Lord had a delight in your fathers to love them, and he chose their seed after them, even you, above all peoples, as at this day " (Deut. 10[14f.]). Perhaps we might also add the distinctive abbreviations of the same message in passages like Pss. 11[7], 33[5], which say of Yahweh that He loves " righteousness " and the " law," at any rate to the extent that these concepts denote His redemptive action in Israel. We find the same teaching in the New Testament : " Behold, what manner of love the Father hath bestowed upon us, that we should be called the sons of God " (1 Jn. 3[1]). " Greater love hath no man than this, that a man lay down his life for his friends. Ye are my friends . . ." (Jn. 15[13f.]). " Walk in love, as Christ also hath loved us, and hath given himself for us " (Eph. 5[2]). " In all these things we are more than conquerors through him that loved us " (Rom. 8[37]).

In Holy Scripture the love of God to us speaks the language of this fact—the fact of His election, guidance, help and salvation—and it is in this language that it has to be heard and understood. But all the expressions of this factual language meet in the name of Jesus Christ. In this name the approach of God to man consists in one fact alone. This is, of course, the event of revelation and reconciliation in the one Word, which is the Son of God. It is the fact that God intercedes for man, that He takes upon Himself the sin and guilt and death of man, that laden with it all He stands surety for him.

At this point, above all other texts, and remembering the many others which say the same thing, we recall the central saying of Jn. 3[16] : " God so loved the world, that he gave his only begotten Son, that whosoever believeth on him should not perish, but have everlasting life." In the light of this we understand Luther's anger against Erasmus : *Christi ne uno quidem iota mentionem facis, ac si sentias, christianam pietatem sine Christo esse posse, tantum si Deus natura clementissimus totis viribus colatur. Quid hic dicam Erasme ? (De servo arb.,* 1525, *W.A.* 18, 609, 18).

This self-sacrifice of God in His Son is in fact the love of God to us. " He gave Him," which means that He gave Him into our existence. Having been given into our existence He is present with us. Present with us, He falls heir to the shame and the curse which lie upon us. As the bearer of our shame and curse, He bears them away from us. Taking them away, He presents us as pure and spotless children in the presence of His Father. That is how God reconciles the world to Himself (2 Cor. 5[19]). We can, indeed, speak of the love of God to us only by pointing to this fact. It is the work and gift of the Holy Spirit that the fact itself speaks to us, that in the language of this fact God says : " I have loved thee . . . fear not, then ; for I am with thee " (Is. 43[4f.]). No other saying is needed, for this one says all there is to say.

" If God be for us, who can be against us ? He that spared not his own Son, but delivered him up for us all, how shall he not with him also freely give us all things ? . . . Christ Jesus that died, yea rather, that is risen again, is even at the right hand of God, who also maketh intercession for us " (Rom. 8[31f.]).

In this passage it is as well to note that the love of God for us—how else could it be ?—is the love of our Creator. When in that fact He says, " I love thee," He speaks as to One to whom we owe our existence, without whom we did not exist and without whom nothing existed, the One who has made heaven and earth. If we hear this fact we hear that the Creator of all things loves us : in other words, in face and in the midst of His creation, and our existence as such in the content of the natural and historical cosmos which is " our world ", we can no longer feel that we are unloved or only partially loved. The act of creation was and is itself an act of the love of God to us. Jesus Christ is the " first-born of all creation "—" by him were all things created, that are in heaven, and that are in earth, visible and invisible " (Col. 1¹⁵ᶠ·). But if this is the case, then how can we who are beloved of God in Jesus Christ be unloved or only partly loved within this creation, in the sphere of nature and history ? Nay, " I am persuaded, that neither death, nor life, nor angels, nor principalities, nor things present, nor things to come, nor powers, nor height, nor depth, nor any other creature, shall be able to separate us from the love of God, which is in Christ Jesus our Lord " (Rom. 8³⁸ᶠ·). There is, of course, no question of any actual or known basis of the love of God apart from Christ. We are the beloved in nature and history, not through any powers of reconciliation and revelation proper to nature and history, but because nature and history are in the hand of their Lord, who causes everything to work for good to them that He loveth (Rom. 8²⁸). " It was the good pleasure of the fulness (of God) to dwell in him (Jesus Christ) and by him (in the life of his ἐκκλησία) to reconcile all things to himself, making peace by him through the blood of his cross : by him, whether things in earth or things in heaven " (Col. 1¹⁹ᶠ·). By Him and therefore not by any powers and orders of the created world in itself and as such. He is the Son of God who according to Heb. 1³ upholds all things τῷ ῥήματι τῆς δυνάμεως αὐτοῦ, i.e., in His revelation — and as the Reconciler καθαρισμὸν τῶν ἁμαρτιῶν ποιησάμενος, the One who sat down on the right hand of the Majesty on high, and is greater than all the angels (Heb. 1⁴). We cannot speak of a love of God the Creator *in abstracto*, supposedly active and manifest in nature and history as such. The *Heidelberg Catechism* was right when in its exposition of the first article of faith (*Q.* 26) it laid down as its main assertion, that " the eternal Father of our Lord Jesus Christ . . . for the sake of His Son Christ is my God and my Father," adding all its other statements about the operation of God as Creator and the benefit which we owe to God as Creator merely as the predicates of this subject.

Therefore when we try to describe to ourselves the love of God, we can only express and proclaim the name of Jesus Christ. That is what it means to speak concretely of the love of God, i.e., in face of the complementary question : What then shall we do ? In this connexion it is perhaps as well to remember only one thing. We have touched upon it already : that God has no need to love us, and we have no claim upon His love. God is love, before He loves us and apart from it. Like everything else that He is, He is love as the triune God in Himself. Even without us and without the world and without the reconciliation of the world, He would not experience any lack of love in Himself. How then can we for our part declare it to be necessary that we should be loved by Him ? It is, in fact, the free mercy and kindness of God which meets us in His love.

This is a thought which is emphasised by Augustine : *Ibi enim gratia amor est, ubi non aestuat indigentiae siccitate sed ubertate beneficentiae profluit.* That is why the love of God necessarily kindles our answering love : it comes to those who could not be prepared for any such thing to come to them. It is the love of *Deus iudicans* for *homo peccans* (*De cat. rud.* 4, 7). And in another passage it is asked whether the love of God means that He needs us (*frui*) or that He uses us (*uti*). There is as little question of His needing us as there is of the light needing the radiance which it spreads itself : the good which we have is either God Himself or that which comes from God—how then can He need us ? But if that is the case there can be no question of God using us as though this were necessary to meet a divine need. If God uses man, it is only in the service of His kindness to man : *Ille igitur usus, qui dicitur Dei, quo nobis utitur, non ad eius, sed ad nostram utilitatem refertus, ad eius autem tantum bonitatem De doctr. chr.* I 31–32). " That there should be a God and that He should love the world and grudge it no good thing, passeth all our reason, mind, comprehension and skill. If I were God, who knoweth the world inside out, of what sort it is, I should have wished it hell fire, and done it. That is what I should have done. But what doth God ? Instead of His wrath which the world hath well deserved, He hath loved the world, and in such surpassing and incomprehensible wise, that He giveth His only Son to the world, His bitterest enemies. I have no rhetoric or eloquence to encompass this *Artificium*, or adequately to draw out these *magnificas figuras*. Were it not more than enough that God had bidden the world good morrow ? But He goeth further and loveth the world, the shameful fruit. For it is *omnium odibillissimum et maxime inamabile objectum*, the image of all that is most hostile and unholy. That is what the world is in very truth. A stall full of wicked and shameless people, who misuse most shamefully all the creatures of God, blaspheming God and ascribing all their ills to Him. And it is these shameful folk that God loveth. That is a love transcending all love. Verily He must be a good God, and His love must be a great, inconceivable fire, much greater than the fire which Moses saw in the bush, yea much greater than the fire of hell. Who would despair, for that God is thus minded towards the world ? It is too high and above my skill, I cannot amplify nor adequately represent it, as it is in fact and in verity " (Luther, *Pred. üb. Jn.* 3[16-21], 1532, *E.A*.4, 124 f.).

We now turn to the second question, that of our loving, which we can understand as an answer to the love of God for us. This must be the standard for all that we have to say. It must be set over against our presentation of the fact. It must be a description of the human self-determination which occurs in the sphere and light of the divine pre-destination. It must correspond on man's side to that which is said by God on His side. We cannot deny or hide the fact that in one way or another we all think we know already about human loving, and we continue to do so even when confronted by the fact of the love of God to us. If, then, we are asking about Christian love, let us say what we know. But only in the limits and under the discipline of this canon. If we forget it or pass it by in favour of some preconceived idea of love in general, to that extent we will derive our definition of Christian love from a false source. At this as at other points, there is no absolute guarantee against such a possibility. But at this point, too, we can find a relative guarantee. In other words, we can use the concrete method of exegesis, as we did in § 15, 2, when we took Jn. 1[14] as the *locus classicus* on the incarnation. The biblical witness of revelation and therefore of the love of God to us does not leave us in the lurch even in respect of a proper human love to God, because the outpouring of the Holy Spirit is an element in this revelation. Without arbitrary selection, we can take as our *locus classicus* the words of the synoptic Jesus in Mt. 22³⁷ᶠ·, Mk. 12²⁹ᶠ· and Lk. 10²⁷ᶠ· In these passages He is asked which is the " first " or " great " commandment, or (acc. to Luke) : " What must I do to inherit eternal life ? " And He replies with a conflation of the Old Testament sayings in Dt. 6⁵ and Lev. 19¹⁸.

In Mt. and Mk. these two sayings are divided into a " first " or " great " commandment and a " second " (which according to Matthew is " like " unto the first). But in Luke, who does not even repeat the verb ἀγαπήσεις, they can obviously only be understood as a single command. In point of fact, of course, the unity as well as the distinctness is brought out in all the versions.

We must now examine point by point its most explicit form as we find it in Mk. 12²⁹⁻³¹ : The first (commandment) is this : Hear, O Israel ; the Lord our God is one Lord : and thou shalt love the Lord thy God with all thy heart, and with all thy soul, and with all thy mind, and with all thy strength. And the second is this : Thou shalt love thy neighbour as thyself.

1. Only Mark records the address and presupposition of the commandment in Dt. 6⁴ : Hear, O Israel, the Lord our God is one Lord. But this is most helpful in placing us in the right context. First of all, the address : Hear, O Israel. The commandment to love is not directed to humanity, or to men in general in their natural or historical groupings. Humanity or men in general are not even considered as the recipients of this commandment and as those who will fulfil it. The commandment is given to Israel. Indeed, it is given to Israel only in the sense of the synoptic Jesus. It is given to the community declared in the twelve apostles as representing the new twelve tribes. It is given to the community of believers in the Messiah, both Jews and Gentiles. It is given to the true Israel, the Church of Jesus Christ. The decision which it demands is, of course, possible for everyone. But it is not possible for everyone to hear the commandment which claims this decision. Even at its roots, in the invitation and summons to love as a Christian, Christian love is something actual. Not every man is in fact what it is decisive to be : Israel elect and loved of God, an earthly member of the earthly body, whose heavenly Head is Jesus Christ. Israel, the people of believers, is indissolubly bound to the redemptive Word of God, to the only-begotten Son of God who was sacrificed for us. But who is Israel, who is it that belongs to this people, to this community ? The " Hear, O Israel " shows that this is something which is constantly being decided afresh. According to the witness of the Old Testament, Israel in the national sense, Israel " according to the flesh " has as such no claim to be this Israel. Even if it be hearing Israel, which observes the commandment to love, it has to remain Israel by ever hearing anew. If no one can hear without being a child of God, no one can be a child of God without

ever hearing anew. Let us imagine for a moment that both conditions
are fulfilled : men who hear because they are children of God, children
of God who as such hear—human self-determination in the sphere and
light of the real, divine predestination, yet in that sphere and light
a corresponding self-determination which is no less real. The result
is a very definite understanding of the commandment itself. Then :
Thou shalt love, as the text itself suggests, also and basically means :
Thou wilt love. Loving becomes a self-evident and necessary act on
the part of the beloved, hearing Israel. To hear this command means
to hasten to fulfil it. But the power and seriousness and value of the
fulfilling do not lie in what the beloved, the men of hearing Israel, can
do in themselves, but wholly and utterly in what the beloved have
heard as the men of hearing Israel, in the promise under which their
being stands, that God is for them. Because it is true that they are
therefore the beloved of God, it is also true that their activity will be
love. When they hear the commandment and in that way maintain
themselves as Israel, the beloved of God, they lay hold of their own
future as men who love, but in such a way that their love consists only
in the fact that they are loved and therefore has its power and seriousness and value only in the One who loves them, in Jesus Christ. In
Jesus Christ God is for them. Therefore in Him, when they hear the
commandment, they lay hold of their own future as lovers, their fulfilment of the Law.

2. This is even more plain when we consider the presupposition of
the commandment, that the Lord our God is one Lord. Even in the
Old Testament passage it is remarkable enough that the emphasis on
the commandment to love is linked up with a reference to the uniqueness of Yahweh. The Lord is referred to by Moses as " our God,"
i.e., the God who has entered into covenant with us from the days of
the Fathers. And according to the saying of the synoptic Jesus, the
same Lord is " one Lord " for those who believe in Him, i.e., as their
Master He does not belong to a *genus*, in which there are others who
can also rule over them. Apart from His, there may be all sorts of
other so-called, supposed and apparent spheres and therefore all sorts
of other so-called, supposed and apparent lords. But no one else rules
and is the Lord as He is, i.e., in deed and in truth. That is, He is the
only one who does what He does. He acts towards them in a matter
in which none but He can act : in the matter of their deliverance from
the shame and curse of their human existence, from sin and death.
And in this matter He again does what He alone can do : He intercedes for them ; He gives Himself to be the bearer of their shame and
curse ; He suffers in their place, that they may be acquitted and free.
For that very reason His control is a unique control. It is a control
which at first sight is quite definitely not what we mean by ruling and
commanding. It is not a matter of demands and claims and orders.
On the contrary, it is all gift and offer and promise. But just because

it is this promise made to man, it is an unparalleled rule with its demands and claims and orders. In virtue of His promise, God takes the place of man. He takes the matter which is for man a matter of life and death right out of his hands and makes it His own business. Therefore man belongs to this Lord. What other lords can be compared with Him ? They are only so-called, supposed and apparent lords. Therefore "the Lord our God is one Lord." But when we say this, the content of the commandment is in fact decided : what it is that God who is the one Lord will order and demand of man. Certainly He does not require that man should again take into his own hands this matter which is a matter of life or death, either wholly or in part. Certainly He does not require that he should try to purify himself from the shame and curse, to free himself from sin and death, to make himself out to be holy and righteous and living. Certainly He does not require that he should try to do something to repay God for what He is and does for him : " All this I did for thee : what wilt thou do for Me ? " If he were to do things of this kind man would be disobedient to the one Lord. He would in fact insult and deny God as the one Lord. For he would deny the necessity and sufficiency of His unique work. And in so doing he would deny the uniqueness of His lordship and therefore of His being as God. Ceasing to acknowledge the uniqueness of his Lord, and therefore His being as God, he would open up the way for the thought that there may perhaps be other real lords side by side with this Lord. And then it is not long before the hour comes when he calls upon other gods and worships them side by side with the real God.

What was the recurrent sin of Israel against its God ? Obviously it was the constant tendency to forget that God and God alone had delivered it out of the house of bondage, Egypt. It was the constant arrogance of wanting to dispose of its own weal and woe, of triumphing or murmuring as though it were not the people of God's own possession, by virtue of the deliverance which God accomplished for it. There was an incipient idolatry in this emancipation from God as sole helper, even before the emergence of actual idolatry. And what was and is apostasy in the Church of Jesus Christ ? Is it not again and again the refusal to let Jesus Christ be Jesus Christ ? Is it not the attempt to set up alongside Him a specifically Christian righteousness, holiness and vitality ? And for all its appearance of obedience, this attempt is in fact profoundly disobedient. It always involves secularisation : an inevitable surrender of faith and love and hope, the betrayal of the Church and its message and order to the powers and values and principles of the world.

The commandment of God as the one Lord is obviously heard and respected only where it is interpreted as a commandment to love Him. Love and love alone can correspond to the uniqueness in which He is the Lord. And whatever love may consist in, by virtue of the uniqueness of God, it will always be the one *diligere*, the one choice, in which man chooses God as his Lord in the sense in which God has already chosen Himself and decided on His own lordship—that is, as the One who interceded for us and represents us, as the One who already loved man before man could and would love Him, as the One who has done literally everything for man, so that there is nothing left for man himself to do. To choose this Lord, to let Him be the Lord, means to love Him, and that is what man is enjoined to do by this Lord. Again, when we say " the Lord our God is one Lord," the fulfilment of the commandment to love God is also decided. For although it is enjoined upon man and man himself has to achieve it, neither inwardly nor outwardly nor in any other way will the fulfilment be in something which man can accomplish of himself. The uniqueness of the lord-ship of God is again denied and trampled underfoot if man presents Him with a love which is his own. Love to God consists decisively in recognising that we have nothing of our own to offer Him. We cannot offer a love which is the work of our own hands or heart. We have to recognise that He intercedes for us and represents us, that what is our own, even our own love for Him, can never be anything but our shame and our curse. The love with which we reply to the love of God for us can begin and grow only when we go beyond what we can claim as our own love, when we recognise that we the unloving are beloved by Him. In other words, it can begin and grow only in the recognition of Jesus Christ and therefore in Jesus Christ Himself. That is how—in all the seriousness of our reality before God and in God as the one Lord—it really becomes our own love to God.

3. The commandment tells us " Thou shalt." As we have already seen, within the " Thou shalt " there is a " Thou wilt " which is indeed the presupposition of the " Thou shalt." But this does not indicate any weakening of the " Thou shalt." On the contrary, how can the commandment as such have real and ultimate seriousness and em-phasis if it does not demand the fulfilment of man's nature, if it comes to him, as it were, as an alien body, which he can deal with as he him-self decides, which he can assimilate or not as he pleases, the choice being left entirely to himself ? The law which does not have its basis and meaning in the Gospel, in the declaration of a revelation, benefit and election which are made already, of the grace of God as it is already operative in Jesus Christ—that law is no real Law. For an abstract law like that, however fiercely it may be represented and asserted as the Law of God, can never really claim man, and therefore judge him and therefore force him to obey. From the " Thou shalt " which is not rooted in the " Thou wilt " of the Gospel we can always withdraw in a light-minded despair or a despairing light-mindedness. And if it is the commandment of God which is compressed into " Thou shalt love," how can it be a commandment if as such it stands, as it were, in the air, if it comes to man from without, if it does not demand the fulfilment of his inmost being ?

It is singular to read in G. Kittel's *Wörterbuch zum Neuen Testament*, concern-ing the concept of love in the Old Testament (vol. 1, p. 25 f.), that clothed in the garments of law the commandment to love reduces the Law *ad absurdum*, since it is the border at which all human *and* divine lawgiving ceases, and it demands an ethical way of life that transcends the Law. What the commandment to love reduces *ad absurdum* is not the Law, but the idea of a law which confronts man from outside, instead of being posited with his being in covenant with God and therefore claiming him from within. What the commandment to love reduces *ad absurdum* is the kind of formulation which we find in the same passage (p. 29) : " Thou shalt exercise the totality of the power which indwells thee, so as by the affect (!) of love to give rise to a disposition which will determine life's conduct (!) ; thou shalt give thy whole personality to the development of thy relationship with Yahweh." How we can ever come to be challenged by so fantastic a demand is quite inconceivable.

Love to God can be demanded and is demanded from those who already belong to God—to the God who is Lord in this unique sense. From them, as we have seen, *love* is indeed demanded. And it is *demanded*. God intercedes for them. God takes their affairs, their life's concern in the strictest sense of the concept, out of their hand. Therefore with all their existence they are cast back upon God and directed to Him. Their choice, *diligere*, has already been fixed. Love to God is the only possibility which is open to them. The " Thou shalt love " summons them to this sole remaining activity, which they themselves now find to be necessary, self-evident and indispensable. For them it is a real " Thou shalt," like an imperious physical demand. It is a genuine " Thou shalt," beside whose obedient fulfilment disobedience is a manifest impossibility, an absurdity.

At first sight, it might appear that there is a contradiction in the fact that love to God is demanded from the children of God and is therefore an act of obedience. But this is not the case. On the contrary, only love can make a real demand, i.e., the demand which really comes from God and really comes to man. And it is only in love that there can be real obedience. And conversely real love, which is the love of God, can only be the fulfilment of a command and therefore obedience. It would not be the commandment of God if, whatever else its content, it did not demand from us the most voluntary thing of all, love. And it would not be the love of God if it were not a voluntary decision for Him, if it had any taint of an act of human caprice.

Is vere demum se Deo in obsequium addicet, qui eum amabit. . . . Deus coacta hominum obsequia repudiat, vultque sponte et liberaliter coli : discamus interea, sub Dei amore reverentiam, quae illi debetur, notari (Calvin, *Comm. on Mt.* 22³⁷, *C.R.* 45, 611). It was therefore significant that when Polanus (*Synt. Theol. chr.* 1609, p. 3856 f.) gave eight reasons which ought to move us to love God, numbers 2–8 were as follows : because God is our supreme good, because He overwhelms us with His benefits, because love to Him is the necessary proof of the knowledge of God, because it is the sign of our fellowship with Him, because it is the sign of the love of God for us, because it conforms to the example of Christ, the angels and the saints, because God Himself is its reward—but the first and obviously decisive reason is : *Quia ipse nobis hoc mandat*, in proof of which he adduces this text and also Deut. 11¹, 30¹⁶ ; Josh. 22⁵, etc. S. Kierkegaard (*Leben und Walten der Liebe* 1847, ed. Schrempf p. 29 f.) has rightly taken the

13

phrase " Thou shalt love . . ." to mean that what is Christian " does not have its origin in the heart of man," from which he deduces that " only the obligation to love forever protects love against all change, making it eternally free in its blessed independence, and safeguarding its happiness eternally against all despair." But in order that it may become for us this happy obligation, in the words of H. F. Kohlbrügge (*Pred. üb. Luke* 10²⁵ᶠ·, 1854, *Schriftausl. Heft* 15, 2, p. 507), " we must completely renounce the love of God as a commandment." " Having come to Christ, having come under the lordship of free grace, we continue as we are under this grace, clinging to Christ—and as we continue clinging to Him, our experience is that His yoke, i.e., the obedience of faith, is easy and His burden, that is, the keeping of His commandments, abiding in His word, is light." Obviously a hard yoke, or a heavy burden, in the sense of the words of Mt. 11²⁹ᶠ·, upon which Kohlbrügge plays, would not be the happy obligation intended by Kierkegaard, and for this reason, that it would not be the obligation imposed upon us. If it is to be imposed upon us we have to " cling to Christ," i.e., to be in faith the beloved of God in Him. But as His yoke and His burden, it is " easy " and " light," because although it does not have its origin in our hearts, it is not an alien demand which comes to us from without, but it is the demand to be what we are. It is only in this way that it is the commandment of God, not one which proceeds from our own heart, but one which is inserted into our heart by Him, which is appropriated by our heart and which in its divinity is a means of blessing to us in the sense of Kierkegaard. Neither the obligation nor its fulfilment is " hard " and " heavy." What is " hard " and " heavy," impossible and absurd, for those who " cling to Christ," is its non-fulfilment, the disobedience, which would be a denial of their very being. It is by an abstract " law," i.e., by an abstract consciousness of duty, that we become " weary and heavy-laden." But when we respond to the " Come unto me " of Jesus Christ, we are neither burdened by the fact that love is now demanded of us, nor are we absolved from obedience to the commandment by this demand to love, nor pointed to some " ethical way of life " which transcends the law. But by responding in faith to the Saviour's call and coming to Christ, we become what we are, i.e., we love in all our actions. What is inserted into us and appropriated by our hearts as we " cling to Christ " is Christ Himself, the One who loved us and took our place as Saviour. Being loved by Him, and having Him as our Lord, we have no future apart from Him, and therefore no future without love. For us " Thou shalt love " can only mean : Thou shalt not try to evade or escape thy future as opposed to thy present. Thou shalt go further. Thou shalt live. Is there any other categorical imperative apart from this ? It is categorical, even though and indeed because it is an easy yoke and a light burden.

4. " Thou shalt love the Lord thy God." As the children of God are what they are and in that way fulfil the law, their love has its counterpart or object in God. That is so even though, and indeed because, He gives Himself to be theirs in faith. How else could He be objective for them, if He did not become theirs in faith ? But how could He become theirs in faith, if He were not objective for them, if He did not confront them as another ? God alone—because He is God and man's Creator—can confront man as another. But His confrontation means that He gives Himself to be man's own. And therefore in this confrontation, which is not the removing but the form of His presence in the heart, He can and will be loved by man. The decisive element which is revealed in this fact is that love is love for another. Of course, this element is real only in love to God,

and in the love to the neighbour which it includes and posits. All other loving is compromised as such by the uncertainty of the objectivity or otherness of the one who is loved, by the possibility that the one who supposedly loves is perhaps really alone. Where there is no otherness of the one who is loved, where the one who loves is alone, he does not really love.

It is at this point that we must guard against an idea which played a singular part in the theological concept-world of the Early Church and has continued to do so right up to the present time. That is the idea of a " self-love " which is not merely justified but commanded. The main biblical support for the idea is to be found, of course, in the " Thou shalt love thy neighbour as thyself." But appeal can also be made to Mt. 7¹² : " All things whatsoever ye would that men should do unto you, even so do ye unto them " ; Phil. 2¹² : " Work out your own salvation . . ." ; and 1 Tim. 4¹⁶ : " In doing this thou shalt save both thyself and them that hear thee ; " and with a touch of humour (Polanus *op. cit.* p. 4183) Prov. 12¹⁰ : " A righteous man regardeth the life of his beast." Concerning the " as thyself " we shall have to speak later. But in any case the " as thyself " does not stand side by side with God and our neighbour in such a way that we can agree with Augustine, who was guilty of reading into the passage when he commented : *in quibus tria invenit homo, quae diligat : Deum, se ipsum et proximum* (*De Civ. Dei* XIX, 14). Similarly, the presupposition that according to Mt. 7¹² we will all manner of things that people should do unto us cannot be equated with a commandment. And if Phil. 2¹² does not teach self-redemption, neither does it teach self-love : even faith, in which we affirm and grasp our redemption by Christ, ought to be very different from an act of self-love. Now Augustine (and before him Tertullian and Chrysostom) was of a different opinion. *Nihil est tibi te ipso propinquius. Quid id longe ? Te habes ante te,* he could declare (*Sermo* 387, 2), concluding with the exhortation, to love ourselves first, then our neighbour, although both, of course, in God and in the corresponding limits (*De Doctr. chr.* I, 22 f.). Thomas Aquinas gave to this view its speculative basis, that love is a *virtus unitiva. Uni cuique autem ad se ipsum est unitas, quae est potior unione ad alium. Unde sicut unitas est principium unionis, ita amor quo quis diligit seipsum, est forma et radix amicitiae* (*S. Theol.* II, 2 qu. 25 art. 4 c). Even Polanus (*op. cit.* p. 4182 f.) has a chapter entitled " *De caritate hominis erga seipsum,*" beginning with the luminous statement : *Unusquisque sibi ipsi primum proximus est, deinde aliis.* And the 18th-century Church used to sing—

> That I should love myself, O God, it is Thy will,
> And as Thou hast prescribed, let me this task fulfil,
> Hold back in holy bounds the urge in me,
> Which Thou implantedst, happy and blessed to be.

(*Lieder für den öff. Gottesdienst,* edited by J. J. Spalding, 1780, p. 213.

Even Kierkegaard (*op. cit.* 24 f.) still thought that the commandment to love our neighbour states, in the right sense, the reverse as well : Thou shalt love thyself in the right way. But there were two who did not agree, Luther and Calvin. *Igitur credo, quod isto precepto " sicut te ipsum " non precipiatur homo diligere se, sed ostendatur vitiosus amor, quo diligit se de facto, q.d. curvus es totus in te et versus in tui amorem, a quo non rectificaberis, nisi penitus cesses te diligere et oblitus tui solum proximum diligas. . . . Sicut et Adam est forma futuri i.e. Christi, alterius Adam. Sicut in Adam mali sumus, utique sic in Christo boni esse debemus ; comparatio hic, non autem imitatio exprimitur* (Luther, *Röm. Brief,* 1515–16 on Rom. 15² ; *Fi.* II 337, 8). And irrespective of the authority of Augustine, Calvin inveighed against the representatives of this view : *Evertunt non interpretantur verba Domini, qui inde colligunt (ut faciunt omnes Sorbonici) amorem nostri semper ordine priorem esse : quia regulatum inferius sit sua regula. Inprobitas, inscitia* and *fatuitas* were revealed in this exposition. *Asini sunt, qui ne micam quidem habent caritatis.* Our self-love can never be anything right or holy and acceptable to God. It is an affection which is the very opposite of love. God will never think of blowing on this fire, which is bright enough already. His demand is that the impulse should be " reversed," *evertatur in caritatem* (*Comm. on Gal.* 5¹⁴, *C.R.* 50, 251 f. ; cf. *Comm. on Deut.* 6⁵, *C.R.* 24, 724 ; *Comm. on Mt.* 22³⁹, *C.R.* 45, 612). We have to admit that the Reformers were right. Of course, there is the man who loves himself : this is assumed in our text and in Mt. 7¹². But there is no commandment to do this. Self-love is not on the same level as the commanded love to God and our neighbour. Where the latter begins, the former ceases, and *vice versa.* Loving himself, man does not love or no longer loves in the sense of the children of God : and to the extent that this love is the only true love, we must add that loving himself he does not love or no longer loves at all. Loving himself, he is alone. That is the predicament of most of what passes for " love." Man is supposed to love, but the truth is that man is concerned only with himself and therefore does not love at all. Love must always have an opposite, an object. It is only an illusion that we can be an object of love to ourselves. But it might be objected at this point that there is a self-knowledge. But in the only real self-knowledge (which is radically different from the " know thyself " of antiquity), the self-knowledge of repentance, we are not in any sense objective to ourselves. It is by the mirror of the Word of God, by Jesus Christ, that we learn the truth about ourselves. What we love—if we love at all—is always something else or someone else. Of much apparent loving of another we have to ask whether the other really is another, whether it has in fact a basic object, and therefore whether it is real love at all. And in spite of Augustine the invention of a commandment to love oneself was a cardinal error. As the wrath of Calvin rightly felt, it meant the elevation of something negative in itself into a principle. It was obviously the dictum of a " natural " theology and anthropology, that there is in man—manifestly unaffected by the Fall—the life principle of an original *unitas ad se ipsum* of all life, on the basis of which self-love is something good and possible, taking precedence over love of one's neighbour. If that was the real view, it ought to have been subjected to a critical examination in the light of our text and Holy Scripture generally, which would no doubt have led to its dissolution. But it was preferred uncritically to take the " natural " view as a standard for the exposition of our text. The right thing is to avoid this result from the outset.

In love to God man is not alone. On the contrary, in love to God he has to do with a genuine partner—with the One who loving him first has given Himself to be his own, and therefore made Himself a genuine partner. Only of love to God can it be said that it has a genuine partner, for it is only in love to God that there is love to one's neighbour. For that reason only the love of God can be called real love. And it is the Lord who wills to be loved as the other. We again think what that means. The one Lord, the Lord of all lords, the Lord who is not only called Lord but actually is the Lord by coming to man as the Revealer of Himself and by taking his place as the Reconciler, that One is Lord in such a way that His lordship is known by man in every circumstance : if not in goodness, in severity, if not as assistance, as opposition, if not in the presence of His revealedness, in the times of His forbearance which can also be times of warning : times to remember and await His revealedness. In all these things He never ceases to be the Lord, and in that eminent sense in which it can be said only of the Son or Word of God who became flesh for us. It is a matter of the love of this Lord, and of this Lord as " thy God." Being this Lord, i.e., acting upon me as this Lord, He is in fact my God. All that I know of God and can know and should know and indeed ought to know, I know by an exercise of lordship, of which I am the object. It is not possible for me even to think of a God who is not this Lord. And how can He be the Lord He is, if He is not God ? His lordship is the action of deity. This Lord is identical with God Himself. And the uniqueness of the Lord in whose hands I am means the uniqueness of God. The knowledge of the uniqueness of God is not the result of a philosophical consideration of the nature of God. It is the answer to His revelation as the Lord. The philosophical consideration of the nature of God can never lead us beyond the dialectic of the concepts of monotheism and polytheism, pantheism and atheism. It is only in the revelation of God as the Lord that the decision is made : I am the Lord thy God—I : not the idea of the unity of God, not the beings which want to be gods, not anything or everything which can be divine, not thou thyself in thine own divinity, but I—thou shalt have none other gods but me.

In this text the New Testament κύριος is an exact equivalent for the Old Testament name for God, Yahweh. The meaning of the Old Testament formula, " Yahweh thy God " or " Yahweh our God," does not differ in the slightest from the developed form. When Yahweh reveals His name to Moses, He makes (or re-makes) the covenant between Himself and Israel. The decisive factor in this covenant is that the Yahweh revealed to Israel should act towards Israel in the way peculiar to Himself, to salvation, and that in this action He should be acknowledged by Israel as God, and in view of the uniqueness of His action as the only possible Lord of Israel, to be respected and worshipped as the only God. It is customary to distinguish the so-called " henotheism " of certain strata of Old Testament tradition as an earlier, and from the standpoint of the history of religion a lower, stage as compared with the later and supposedly higher " monotheism " of the prophets. But as such, even where it is not explicit on the point, even where, like St. Paul (1 Cor. 8⁵), it actually recognises the existence of other gods, faith in Yahweh has as its main point a recognition of the uniqueness of the deity of Yahweh. And the strength of the later " monotheism " of the prophets —that which distinguished it more sharply from heathen monotheism than from the so-called earlier henotheistic stage in its own area—was the simple power of faith in Yahweh, the power of the knowledge of the unique history, in which Israel was confronted by its Lord.

5. But what does it mean to love ?—to love this other, the Lord thy God ? As we have considered the text we have already formed certain preliminary definitions. To love means to become what we already are, those who are loved by Him. To love means to choose God as the Lord, the One who is our Lord because He is our Advocate and Representative. To love means to be obedient to the commandment of this God. In every case, therefore, love is an accepting, confirming and grasping of our future. In it this future is identical

with the reality of God, who in the most pregnant sense of the word is
" for us." It is therefore an accepting, confirming and grasping of
the God who is our future. And as such it takes place in an order
and connexion which proceed from God, and is therefore an act of
obedience. But from what we have just said we learn the following
further lessons. If love, as distinct from the illusion of self-love, is
love for another, and if this other is God the Lord, then our loving
must be defined as the nature and attitude of man, conscious that he
is of a different kind from that object. Love to God takes place in
the self-knowledge of repentance in which we learn about ourselves
by the mirror of the Word of God which acquits and blesses us, which is
itself the love of God to us. The man who loves God will let himself
be told and will himself confess that he is not in any sense righteous
as one who loves and in his loving before and over against God. On
the contrary, he is a sinner who even in his love has nothing to bring
and offer to God. The love of God for him is that God intercedes for
him and represents him even though he is so unworthy, even though
he can never be anything but unworthy and therefore undeserving of
love. He is accepted and confirmed and grasped by this love of God
to him. In it is both his own future and the commandment of God :
how can that have any other meaning than that he is driven to repentance and held there ? He can and will love only as even in respect
of his loving he allows and willingly allows this to happen.

At this point I should again like to quote H. F. Kohlbrügge : " The feeling
of sin and misery begins and remains in us, the more we are irradiated by the
sun of righteousness. Whoso is born of God has his supreme good in God alone ;
nothing else can satisfy him. Idols must all give place one after the other. But
the more the love of God increases in the heart, the more knowledge there is of
inability, and, even with the best of wills, unwillingness, to love God the Lord,
and to love Him with all the heart and soul and mind and strength. The spirit
will not come from the flesh. The love of God and neighbour cannot be found
in man, in the flesh, but only hatred of God and neighbour. The love of God
is poured into our hearts by the Holy Spirit given to us. That is the knowledge
and experience of all the saints. In themselves, that is, in their flesh, they find
no good thing and therefore no love to God. . . . Only by the fact that they
are. perfect in Christ Jesus do they have the assurance that they are perfect
in love. But the more Christ has become their peace, the more they humble
themselves in the dust before God, and are rejected utterly because of their
lovelessness, and find the basis of their hope only in the love with which God
has first loved us, and in the grace of Jesus Christ, in which He is so rich towards us in all patience and mercy." According to Kohlbrügge there are
definite marks of a sorrowful kind by which the children of God can know that
the love of God is in them. These are weeping, groaning, crying, sorrow and
concern because in their hearts they find only perversity and hostility, only the
love of sin and the world and the things which are seen, because they have no
desire at all for God and His love, but a cold, sluggish, hard and stony heart,
filled with all kinds of evil considerations and other sinful thoughts. Therefore
the children of God must at all points humble themselves before the holiness of
God. They must bow beneath His holy law. They must be crushed and broken
in respect of the love of God and neighbour. They must be humbled to the very

core. They must apply to themselves what the apostle Paul says in the seventh chapter of Romans, especially of the sin which the regenerate find in themselves in the light of God's law. For the fact that they are overwhelmed in this way proves that the love of God is in them (*ibid.* pp. 502–504).

The very necessity of this knowledge of the otherness of the one who loves as compared with the one who is loved will perhaps make it clear that to love God is to seek God. Those who are found by God in His great love for us are the very ones who must and will seek Him. In seeking Him they assure and affirm and apprehend their own future and therefore Himself. They are obedient to His commandment. In seeking Him, therefore, they love Him. We cannot be satisfied with repentance as such (especially if it is sincere). We cannot be satisfied with self-knowledge (especially if it does not mean assurance but a burning need). Beyond our own quite conscious lovelessness, and therefore without even dreaming that with our love we can offer anything to God, we begin genuinely, and in need, and with a consuming desire to know, to ask about the One who has first loved us. As those who are in need but also have a consuming desire to know, we know God as the one God, the one God because He is the one Lord, one in His revelation, one in His activity on our behalf, the One who is Himself alone our hope. As those who are in need but also have a consuming desire to know, we know that this one God is our only refuge and salvation—indeed He is the only possibility of our existing at all. In all the otherness in which He confronts us, we actually belong to Him—in all our otherness over against Him. If we are quite clear about His lordship and therefore His love on the one hand, and our own lovelessness and unworthiness of love on the other, it will strike us quite clearly that the autonomy of our existence has been taken from us. He has taken it to Himself; He has not taken away our existence from us. We have not ceased to be ourselves. We are still free. But in that existence He has left us without root or soil or country, " having transferred us to the Kingdom of the Son of his love " (Col. 1[13]), having Himself become our root and soil and country. From the standpoint of His incarnation and exaltation, the fact that we are " translated into the kingdom of the Son of God " means that as the Second Adam He has assumed human nature, that He has united it to His divine person, so that our humanity, our existence in this nature, no longer has any particularity of its own, but belongs only to Him. And from the standpoint of the reconciliation and justification effected in Him, it means that, bearing our punishment, achieving the obedience we did not achieve and keeping the faith we did not keep, He acted once and for all in our place. We cannot, therefore, seek our own being and activity, so far as they still remain to us, in ourselves but only in Him. Strictly speaking, our being and activity as such can only be this seeking. We misunderstand this seeking if we think of it as a special art or striving on the part of those who have already proposed and undertaken the task, or as a wonderful flower of piety which has grown in the garden of those who are already particularly situated and gifted for it.   Even the works and wonders of mystical love to God are still part of our own being and activity, which has as such to be abandoned in its entirety in the sight of God, as something which is loveless and unworthy of love.   Our own being and activity stands wholly and utterly under this judgment (including, therefore, all the works and wonders which are possible within it, but also in its dark lethargy and wildness).   Yet this being and activity acquires a direction at the point where everything is done for us, the direction Godward in Jesus Christ.   And this is no special work.   It is far more.   It is the work of all works.   It is no special miracle.   It is far more.   It is the miracle of all miracles.   And as such it is the simplest necessity of nature : even more necessary than breath to our body.   But it takes place quite irrespective of any works or wonders of which we may be capable, or of the lethargy and wildness which is inherent in all our being and activity, including our highest efforts as well as worst periods of unconcern.   What matters is emphatically not the fact that we are seeking.   What matters is that if we accept and adopt this direction, we are always seekers.   Of course, that means that we are seeking.   But in all that seeking we are again in the sphere of our lovelessness and unworthiness of being loved.   In spite of our seeking, we can still be rejecting.   Our seeking may be upright, inward and profound, but as such it will stand in constant need of the forgiveness of sins.   What justifies the seeking is only the fact that we seek as real seekers.   And that means that it is only He whom we seek and who has again and again made us seekers, who in our existence has thrown us back utterly upon the forgiveness of sins through Him. That we should be those who always seek Him is what the command-ment to love enjoins.   It is the love which is the fulfilling of the law.

And now there is really only one other thing to add.   If we are seekers of God, and to that extent lovers of God, this can be definitely and unequivocally proved and maintained of the children of God only by the one thing : that in all circumstances and in every connexion they rejoice if their seeking is not in vain, if therefore the One whom they seek allows Himself to be found by them, if in that way He con-firms the fact that He has sought and found them, before they ever sought Him.   How can they not rejoice when God really confronts them, when the One whom they loved loves them again and anew, as He had already loved them before, when He is therefore present to them in His Word, in Jesus Christ, when He speaks with them, and acts on them ?   Is He not a faithful God, because He does so ?   And how can they not rejoice that He is so faithful ?   But we have every reason to think that it is not self-evident that we should rejoice.   We seek many things in which we do not rejoice when we find them— which shows, of course, that even our seeking is impotence and error.

Supposing that this is the case here, with the children of God in their seeking after God ?

Often enough we can see in others, and especially in ourselves, that it is possible to be a regular and genuine and serious seeker after God, out of a passionately sincere heart, or a real sense and experience of the many compulsions of life and conscience—only to give it all upwhen our apparent seriousness is suddenly taken seriously, in a situation in which our seeking could really be a finding, because a being found; and simply because the God we find, who has let Himself be found, is not the One of whom we can joyfully confess that it is Him we have sought. We love Him or think that we love Him at a distance, but we do not love Him near at hand. We prefer to withdraw to that pretended love at a distance. But is not that love unmasked and adjudged as non-love ?

Let us be more precise. This is something which can never happen with the children of God. They will prove and maintain that they are what they are, those who really love, not merely subjectively honest, but quite genuine seekers after God, by the fact that they do not withdraw but stand fast, and joyfully, with a Yes which comes from all their heart and soul and mind and strength, even when they find God. When they do find God, when the love of God reaches its goal, this means that they hear and feel and taste afresh that they have an incomparable Lord and that they can be free only in obedience to Him. When they do find God, they are met by grace, which means that they accept, that they receive the gifts proffered, that they approve what is done for them, that it may be done to them. But grace shows that in themselves they are poor and impotent and empty : indeed, that they are adversaries and rebels. Grace points them away from self, frightens them out of themselves, deprives them of any root or soil or country in themselves, summons them to hold to the promise, to trust in Him, to boast in Him, to take guidance and counsel of Him and Him alone. Grace is the discipline which does not permit them any idolatry or self-righteousness, but bids them say, even when they have done all that it is their duty to do, that they are unprofitable servants. Grace does not allow of any arrogance, even at a later stage. Grace keeps down. Grace reveals the lethargy and wildness which lie like a heavy load upon even their best thoughts and undertakings. Grace demands of them that they trust only in grace, and live only by grace—and by grace really live. If that be God, the Son of God and the Word of God, who can rejoice at it ? Who in seeking after God ever sought after that ? We can only reply that the children of God rejoice in it. This and this alone is what the children of God have sought. Therefore the children of God are not disillusioned or embittered. They do not turn away, they do not return to that pretended love at a distance, when the Beloved One is seen to be like this, and meets them in this way. For the children of God there is nothing bitter about the severity of the Law from which there is no escape, the mercy which reveals our misery, the freedom and glory of God, which take from us all claim, the order which obtains here and which right to the very core of our being is always and unreservedly an order of humiliation, the light which falls right into our darkness. There is nothing shameful about it. They do not need to flee from it. It is all sweet. It is the greatest possible honour. They seek after it with the greatest possible diligence. They do not ask anything more, or different, or higher, or more dignified. They love it just as it is. They can never let it be repeated too often, or hear it or see it too often, or allow it to sink into their feelings and conscience and will too often. It is in this way that they desire to be treated and ruled. They love the One who deals with them in this way. And that proves that they have really sought after God and loved God. It is proved by the fact that they continue to love God, that they love the One whom they sought all the more now that they have found Him, now that He has found them afresh. God sees and knows that they do. He knows His own. At heart, man is a hypocrite. In respect of love he can easily make out to himself and others that he is something which he is not. We have to answer to God, if we think we should confess that we love Him, not only in the way in which we seek Him, but in the way in which He gives Himself to be found, because that is what He is. God sees and knows whether we love Him in this way. But if it is true before Him, that we love Him in this way, if we can say before God that it is true—as the children of God can—then we are not only permitted to be sure about our loving and therefore our fulfilment of the Law, but we are forbidden to doubt. If we rejoice to hear the actual Word of God to man, we love God. The very fact that we rejoice to hear the Word of God means that the assurance which we are not only permitted but commanded has nothing to do with the forbidden arrogance of the *homo religiosus*.

6. It might be asked whether the addition, that thou shalt love God, " with all thy heart, with all thy soul, with all thy mind and with all thy strength," really adds anything new and specific to what we have already said. I think that this is actually the case. For obviously these concepts, which we must not isolate, of course, but take as a whole and in their total effect, are an emphatic reminder that man himself, the whole man, is challenged by the commandment to love, not only that he love, but that he should be one who loves, and therefore (in the twofold sense of the word) one who is condemned, and therefore a seeker after God, as we have seen already. It is to be noted that the words " all " and " thine " are repeated four times. And the four main words, heart, soul, mind and strength, which obviously describe the sphere of human capacity as such, at once indicate that when the commandment claims this being for love, it is concretely the actual and whole being of man which is claimed. We ourselves, with all that we have and are as men (and have not and are not), are either those who love or those who do not. There can be

no division between the man I am visibly in myself and the man I am invisibly in Jesus Christ, and then on the basis of this division a dismissal of the former because of the duty to love. It is as the man I am visibly in myself that I am invisibly in Jesus Christ. And it is the fact that I am invisible in Jesus Christ that imposes upon me as the man I am visibly in myself the duty to love. Rightly, then, there can be no question of any division of my visible being, or of any restricting of the duty of love, to particular aspects and capacities of this being, whether to my so-called inward parts or to my so-called deeds. Of course the commandment to love claims my inward parts. But in doing so, it claims that I should not only think and feel but, as I do so, live and act out of the love for which it claims me. It claims my life and activity, but in doing so it claims that they should be love from the inmost parts. Again, there is no question of a division between the different times and situations and tasks of human love ; as though love were commanded at one time and not commanded at another, as though it were left to our judgment to love, or not to love or to love less. The addition is a guarantee, therefore, against every division, and therefore against every reservation or exception in love. Or positively, it means that Christian love is characterised as a total constitution and attitude of man. It is one man who is pardoned by Jesus Christ, one man who is the sinful creature which he is in himself : one in his existence within and without ; one at every stage and in all the circumstances and encounters of his way. As this one man he is either a man who loves or a man who does not. Clearly, the addition reaches back to the presupposition, that " the Lord our God is one Lord." It is, as it were, a proof that the One who is loved in Christian love is really God. God is the one Lord. That He is the One who is loved is shown in the fact that He is loved without division, reservation and exception ; either in that way or not at all : there is no question of any other alternative. It will be rewarding to take a backward look from this standpoint.

In its relationship to that presupposition, the addition shows us that there is a similarity between the love with which God loves us and the love for Him which He has enjoined upon us. For all the majestic superordination of the one over the other, we can still describe them both by the same concept. To the exclusiveness with which God and God alone is our Lord, there corresponds the exclusiveness with which our being and activity must be a seeking after God and that alone. From a new angle this similarity may draw our attention to the grace in the law of love imposed upon us. It is grace that God wills not only to love us but to be loved by us in return. Just as He does not need to love us, in the same way and even less He does not need to be loved by us. But that is what He wills. And as He is our exclusive Lord, He wills our exclusive love : all thy heart, all thy mind, all thy might for this one thing, to love Him. He therefore wills

— and by His Word and His Holy Spirit He creates—that similarity between Him and us. What He is for us in His sphere as God, Creator and Reconciler, we can be for Him in our sphere as sinful creatures. We can therefore love. And in loving we can participate in His perfection.

" Ye shall be perfect, even as your Father in heaven is perfect " (Mt. 5[48]). This is not a law which crushes and kills. It would be so only if we were to hear it, not from the mouth of Jesus Christ, from which it comes to us as a law fulfilled by Him, but as a human regulation, which we would have to fulfil. Heard from Him it is indeed the Law, but the Law as the promise and form of the Gospel, the Gospel in the Law. Is there any news more glad and comforting than that God wills this similarity between Him and us and has already created it in Jesus Christ ?

In the second place, the addition again and especially lights up the voluntariness of the obedience given in Christian love. We shall seek after God undividedly and unreservedly, as the commandment demands, only when the commandment to do it has reached and touched not only our heart, our soul, our reason, but all these as our own capacity and all of them completely ; so that all of them, in their good points and bad points, in the strength and splendour which may be proper to them as such, and in the perversity and shame which are quite certainly proper to them before God, become our own total act of love. Love as the totality of our being and activity excludes the slavery of law, which obeys only out of fear or has an eye for the gifts of God instead of Himself. Love as a totality excludes an obedience which is melancholy and burdensome because it is secretly resisted. Love as a totality cannot leave in us any fear of God because of sin unforgiven. Where forgiveness reigns, there is, of course, an inevitable fear of God, but it is only a form of love, the seeking of that without which we can do nothing. Again, as a totality love cannot play with God, as though He were a means to achieve all kinds of good ends. Of course, we do have all kinds of good and not so good ends. And a kind of heathen automatism often lets us ascribe to God the role of Fulfiller of the wishes corresponding to them. But in love to God do not our wishes necessarily become of themselves the desire that His will should be done ? Again, love as a totality cannot co-exist with a fear of the world or of ourselves : as though there were still powers and forces, which made us obey only sluggishly and under duress. Such powers and forces do, of course, exist. But what is the concern which they cause us compared with the one concern, to love God aright ? Love is the freedom into which the love of God has transferred us. Does it not absorb and suck up all the reservation which we can and do make against it. Does it not transform them into reasons for and not against a willing and joyful obedience ?

Calvin was a preacher especially of the majesty of God and the Law and obedience, but it was the voluntariness of love which he particularly emphasised

in his comments on this passage in both its Old and its New Testament contexts :
Deum non oblectant extorta et coacta obsequia. . . . Nihil Deo placet quod affertur
ex tristitia vel necessitate, quia hilarem datorem quaerit . . . Deus se nobis amabilem
reddit, ut libenter et qua decet alacritate amplectamur quicquid iubet (Comm. on Deut.
10^{12} *C.R.* 24, 723), . . . *vultque sponte et liberaliter coli (Comm. on Mt.* 22^{37} *C.R.*
45, 611). From these words of Calvin we turn to the texts in Rom. 8^{15} and
2 Tim. 1^7, which speak of the " spirit of adoption " or the " spirit of power and
of love and of a sound mind " which we have received, and of the " spirit of
bondage to a new fear," and " the spirit of despondency " which we have not
received—and above all to 1 Jn. $3^{19f.}$, $4^{17f.}$, which speak of our heart condemning
us and not condemning us, that if we are of the truth we can assure our heart,
that God is greater than our heart and knoweth all things, while we, on the other
hand, can be confident that whatsoever we ask we receive of Him, as those who
keep His commandments and do those things that are pleasing in His sight.
They also speak of the judgment of God in which we stand, that in it love may
reach its end with us, giving us the same confidence : φόβος οὐκ ἔστιν ἐν τῇ
ἀγάπῃ ἀλλ' ἡτελεία ἀγάπη ἔξω βάλλει τὸν φόβον. Fear can only be the punishment of those who are not perfect in love. We are perfect in love and therefore
without fear ; for we love, because God has first loved us.

Third, we learn from the addition that love cannot be lost. The
expressions " all thy heart," " all thy soul " undoubtedly point not
only to a cross-section of man's existence but to a long section. From
this standpoint, in respect of the individual acts of human life in their
temporal succession, they say of that existence : The commandment
to love claims you totally and therefore undividedly and without
reserve. There can be no question of any limitation of that love.
The addition underlines the fact that, because the divine " thou shalt,"
is a true and proper one, as distinct from all law which is not real or
which we do not count as real law, it affects the body, and in such a
way that we cannot distinguish our own existence from it. " Thou
wilt love," it says with an emphasis from which there can be no escape,
because it does not point us to any acts which we can do or not do,
but to our future life. If we accept this, we cannot think of love
as a possibility beside which our future might hold other possibilities.
We can think of ourselves only as its captives, and as its captives
for our whole future. The same is true when we remember that in
love there is actualised a similarity between God and His children,
the similarity between the exclusiveness with which He is the Lord,
and the exclusiveness with which we must therefore seek after Him.
Once this circle is closed, once the similarity is actualised, how can
there be any going back, or giving up, or limitation ? The same is
true again when we remember the voluntariness of love. Obviously
we can think of love ceasing only if in or with it there is a place for
those elements of fear whose presence would mean that it is not
voluntary and therefore not love. If love does not have these elements
of fear and is therefore real love, how can it possibly cease ? The
addition " all thy heart, all thy soul " (and this must be decisive for
our whole consideration of the matter) reflects the once and for all
revelation and reconciliation which has come to us as the Word of

God, for which the Holy Spirit has opened us, which is the basis of the
love to God in us, which has irresistibly challenged us to love, which
has made it possible for us to love even in our total incapacity for
love. Are we to think the absurd thought that God, the triune God,
can cease to be God, and that that kingdom of His into which we have
been placed by faith can actually have an end? The operation of human-
creaturely impressions and experiences can certainly cease. Human
purposes and enterprises can cease. What we have called the works and
wonders of love, what takes place in the sphere of the human being and
activity even of the children of God, and therefore stands under the
judgment of God, and therefore has its visible limits : all that can cease.
But how can love itself cease, that direction of man's being and activity
which involves a judgment upon even the greatest works and wonders
possible in this sphere, but in which above all the forgiveness of sins
and the covering of shame is already achieved and thankfully accepted?
How can it ever be really possible for man to lose this direction again?
Whatever can be lost has never been love.

Against the fact that love cannot be lost, the text in Mt. 24¹² has been alleged,
in which we are told that in times of persecution the increase of ἀνομία will
mean that the love of many will grow cold (ψυγήσεται). But does this really refer
to those who are genuinely obedient to Jesus' commandment to love? There
are, of course, all kinds of other love : the love of relatives and friends, which,
according to the sayings of Jesus, can in time of temptation turn not only into
indifference but even into hate. It is impossible that Jesus should have meant
and said the same thing about the love to God and neighbour of the commandment. The verse in Rev. 2⁴ has also been recalled : " I have this against thee,
that thou didst leave thy first love." But does not this epistle speak of the
constancy (ὑπομονή) of the then Church? Can ἡ ἀγάπη σου ἡ πρώτη—whatever
it may be—signify Christian love as such? As we see from what follows, does
it not refer to specific works in which it no longer reveals itself and ought to do
so? Against these two texts we can set 1 Cor. 13³: ἡ ἀγάπη οὐδέποτε πίπτει.
And Rom. 11²⁹: ἀμεταμέλητα γὰρ χαρίσματα καὶ ἡ κλῆσις τοῦ θεοῦ. And Rom.
6¹⁴: " Sin shall not have dominion over you : for ye are no longer under the
law, but under grace." Also the passages from 1 Jn. : " Whosoever abideth in
him sinneth not : whosoever sinneth hath not seen him, neither known him "
(3⁶). " Whosoever is born of God doth not commit sin, for his seed remaineth
in him ; and he cannot sin, because he is born of God " (3⁹). And (of particular
significance as the basis) 5¹⁸ : " We know that whosoever is born of God sinneth
not ; but He that is born of God (Christ) keepeth him, and that wicked one
toucheth him not." This is in the same letter, in the opening of which it is
so strongly declared, that " if we say that we have no sin, we deceive ourselves,
and the truth is not in us. If we confess our sins, he is faithful and just to
forgive us our sins, and to cleanse us from all unrighteousness. If we say that
we have not sinned, we make him a liar, and his word is not in us " (1⁸ᶠ·).
There cannot, therefore, be any reference to or recommendation of a perfectionist
self-righteousness, complacency or assurance in these passages. Obviously, we
have to speak of sin as a reality when it is a question of knowing ourselves on
the basis of truth and the Word of God with reference to what we have been
right up to the present moment. But we cannot speak of sin as a possibility
when it is a question of knowing ourselves on the basis of the same truth and
Word of God, in relation to what we will be in the knowledge of the commandment and its promise given to us. It is only as the impossible, the excluded and

the absurd, only on the supposition that we are not we, and that Jesus Christ is not Jesus Christ, that sin can be thought of as our future. The same consideration has to be taken into account in the difficult chapter Heb. 6. To understand it, we have to start at the end of the chapter (vv. 13–20). We are told that God had given to the heirs of the promise a " strong encouragement " by " two immutable things " (διὰ δύο πραγμάτων ἀμεταθέτων, v. 18), first by the promise itself and as such, and then by the oath which (acc. to Gen. 22[16f.]) He sware by Himself, seeing there was none greater than Himself (v. 13). " The oath serves for confirmation to the ending of all strife " (v. 16). On the basis of this twofold certainty—that we have the Word of God and have it as God's Word—we can and should " flee to lay hold of the hope set before us. We have it as an anchor of the soul which is sure and stedfast, and enters into that which is within the veil, whither as a forerunner Jesus entered for us, that he might be the high priest for ever according to the order of Melchisedek " (6[18-20]). On the basis of this very presupposition we cannot think of resting on what the beginning of the chapter (vv. 1–8) calls the λόγος Χριστοῦ τῆς ἀρχῆς, i.e., we cannot be content with a promise which is still empty and unfulfilled, as though it were not fulfilled in advance in view of the oath which God sware by Himself, and the divinity of the One who has made it. We cannot stop at a foundation upon which there is to be no further building. But on the basis of this presupposition we can and should " go on to perfection " (ἐπὶ τὴν τελειότητα φερώμεθα). " And this will we do if God permit " (vv. 1–3). But this perfection is a future from which there is no return. Those who hear and receive the Word of God are like the earth watered by the rain, which, thus blessed by God, brings forth fruits meet for use (v. 7). Could it not bring forth thorns and thistles as well ? Of course, but it is then accursed, and its fruits are to be burned (v. 8). As the blessing of God the Word would not then be heard or received. There would be no returning from the future posited by the Word, only a proof that for us that future had not been posited at all. The Son of God would then be crucified and put to shame by us. We would participate afresh in the transgression with which Israel confirmed its rejection (v. 6). Now, of course, this transgression is the past which we have to confess openly. And again and again we shall have to realise and confess that we are guilty in respect of our past as this transgression. But it cannot at the same time be our future. " For it is impossible for those who were once enlightened, and have tasted of the heavenly gift, and were made partakers of the Holy Ghost, and have tasted the good word of God, and the powers of the age to come "—the text continues : " if they shall fall away, to renew them again unto repentance " (vv. 4–6). Therefore in the context of the letter, we have here an obvious warning against the idea that the future quietly includes both the possibility of sin and also the possibility of a fresh renunciation of sin. This idea of a divided future alternating between sin and repentance is the very thing which is excluded by the presupposition—or as we might say in our own context—by the totality of the commandment to love based on the presupposition. Those who have heard the good Word of God and tasted the powers of the world to come cannot reckon with this bilinear but only with the unilinear future : that they will love as they are loved. How can they have that sure and certain anchor of their hope " within the veil," how can they see Jesus, who stands as High Priest at the right hand of the Father, how can they be His contemporaries, if at the same time they can and want to compromise the turning-point of all ages, and therefore of their own age, which is His age, by the idea of a twofold future of sin and repentance ? As such, they neither know a present repentance, nor will they owe that future repentance which is always commanded of those that love God, when they look back to the sin which they have done and do and time and again will do, as those that belong to the past. The possibility of future repentance presupposes that we love God with all our heart and soul, and therefore affirm and accept Him, and in

Him our only future. There is a saying which in the Middle Ages and even later was ascribed to Augustine, and in content it is quite right : *Charitas, quae deseri potest, nunquam fuit vera* (*De salutaribus documentis* 7). By comparison, the biblical testimony was weakened when Thomas Aquinas conceded the impossibility of losing love *ex virtute Spiritus sancti*, the impossibility of sin in the act of love itself, and the impossibility of losing *charitas patriae*, i.e., the love with which we shall meet God face to face, but then continued : *charitas autem viae . . . non semper actu fertur in Deum, unde quando actu in Deum non fertur, potest aliquid occurrere per quod charitas amittatur* (*S. theol.* II, 2 qu. 24 art. 11 c). It was, of course, a mistake to set against this the doctrine of love as a *habitus a Spiritu sancto infusus*, as occasionally propounded by the later Calvinists (e.g., by Polanus, *Synt. Theol. chr.*, 1609, **p.** 3867), for the concept *habitus* approximated too closely to the quite unbiblical idea of a supernatural qualifying of the believer and therefore a jeopardising of the knowledge of the freeness of grace in respect of the believer. In and with the love of God, our loving of God, too, is a promise addressed to us, and grasped as such in faith. It is not, therefore, a supernatural quality, a " *habitus*." Yet the meaning behind this equivocal expression is a right one : that we cannot perceive and understand love in those " acts " in which it is offered or not offered to God, but only in the being of man as determined in faith by the Word and the Holy Spirit. And it would involve a negation of this, and indirectly of the Spirit of God, to carry through the thought that it can be removed and lost by the vacillations which we can definitely anticipate in relation to the " acts " of love (by the judgment under which these acts as such invariably stand and will stand). Christian love does not find comfort in itself and its acts, but only in its foundation and object. Its cessation, therefore, does not belong to any possible future, but only to the impossible.

The fourth thing we learn from the addition " with all thy heart . . ." is that Christian love cannot be understood except as the thankfulness which the believer owes to God in His revealing and reconciling work. The totality in which God wills to be loved by us according to His commandment excludes all self-glorying, all claims which he who loves might make to the loved One on account of his love. If he does make such claims, to that extent he ceases to love. His heart, or reason, or some part of his nature or capacity, moves to dispense him from loving, at any rate in part, allowing him both to search and to have edifying but vain thoughts about the beauty and value of the search. Where this happens, his gaze is not exclusively upon God in Jesus Christ. His heart is divided, and his attention vacillates between God and himself. The similarity between his loving and God's loving tends in the same direction, because he obviously does not let God be the one Lord. Nor can there be any further question of a genuine voluntariness in his love. And what is to prevent it degenerating into a love which can be lost, if it is not only confidence in God, but also to some extent confidence in self, in the power and beauty of the being and activity of the children of God, or even in the works and wonders corresponding to this being. No, it can only be understood as thankfulness. Negatively that means that love is grace, but not *gratia gratum faciens*. Its relationship to the love with which God loves us is irreversible. The love of God is its basis, and it rests upon it. It cannot therefore justify itself. How indeed could it, if it is the seeking of that Other who justifies us, and therefore the recognition that we cannot justify ourselves by our own being and activity, even by our being and activity as the children of God ? And the positive meaning of it is that love is nothing more and does not wish to be anything more than the obedient erecting of the sign of divine grace. Indeed, what God in His love wills from us to His glory is that our existence in the determination which we ourselves give to it should be a sign of the fact that we stand under His predetermination. The fulness of His love is not only that He rescues us from the sin and death to which we would fall victim if left in the determination which we would have given ourselves, but that He claims us for the proclamation of His glory. That is what takes place in the fact that we may love Him. Therefore the love of God—and it is at this point that it merges into the praise of God—means that in our own existence we become a sign of what God as the one Lord has done and is for us. How can love to God be inactive ? It is all activity, but only as man's answer to what God has said to him. As this answer it is a work, and it produces works. But it is a work, and produces works, in the fact that it is the witness of God's work, and therefore a renunciation of all self-glorying and all claims.

3. THE PRAISE OF GOD

Rather strangely, the emphasis in Mk. 12 falls on the last part, the " second commandment," " Thou shalt love thy neighbour as thyself." From what we said at the outset, and fundamentally, about the relationship between the love and the praise of God, and from what we have just said in our exposition of the commandment to love, this really comes under our new heading. As anticipated, the whole meaning and content of the commandment to love our neighbour is that as God's children, and therefore as those who love Him with all our heart, soul, mind and strength, we are summoned and claimed for the praise of God as the activity and work of thankfulness which, by reason of our being as those who love, we cannot avoid. The " second " commandment has no other meaning and content apart from and in addition to : " Bless the Lord, O my soul, and all that is within me bless his Holy name." And *vice versa*, it is by the " second " commandment that we experience point by point and exhaustively what is the praise of God, what is the meaning and content of the revealing, manifesting, attesting, confessing, living out and showing forth of the lordship and redemption which has come to the children of God. Therefore we have to say just as strictly that no praise of God is serious, or can be taken seriously, if it is apart from or in addition to the commandment : " Thou shalt love thy neighbour as thyself." Whatever else we may understand by the praise of God, we shall always have to understand it as obedience to this commandment.

Cf. for what follows, R. Bultmann, *Jesus*, 1926, p. 102 f. ; E. Fuchs, " Was heisst : ' Du sollst deinen Nächsten lieben wie dich selbst ? ' " *Theol. Bl.*, 1932, PAGES 417–448

First, we will simply continue the exposition which we have begun and ask what we are to think of the remarkable duplication or repetition of the commandment to love as such ? In what sense is there obviously a second loving of the children of God alongside the first ? In what sense does the " neighbour " obviously stand alongside God as the object of this loving of theirs ? We cannot be too cautious in our reply—at any rate in relation to all preconceived and imported concepts of God and man and love.

In the sense of the text as we have so far expounded it, as a commandment to love God, the commandment to love is one of unequivocal absoluteness and exclusiveness according to all our present findings. To think back for a moment over what we have said, it is obviously *the* commandment, the one commandment, the commandment of all commandments, and the commandment in all commandments. Therefore, if the commandment to love our neighbour is placed alongside it and expressly described as a separate " second commandment," there seem to be only three possible explanations. Either we have another absolute demand in the strict and proper sense. If that is the case, we will have to repeat all that has been said about love to God and apply it to love to our neighbour. Or there are not really two demands at all, but one absolute demand. Love to God and love to the neighbour are identical ; the one has to be understood as the other. If that is the case, we will have to show that God is to be loved in the neighbour and the neighbour in God, and in what way. Or there is only the one absolute demand of love to God, and the demand of love to the neighbour approximates to it as the first and most important of the particular, relative and subordinate commands, within which, as in Luther's catechism, the commandment to love God forms the real nerve and content, the commandment in the commandments and the commandment of all commandments.

First, we must abandon at once as quite impossible the idea that there are two absolute commandments side by side. Exegetically, it is not legitimate to compare the brief saying on love to the neighbour with that about love to God simply by transferring all the definitions of the one to the other. On this explanation, it is impossible to see any way of avoiding the conclusion that the text speaks of the love of two Gods. But God is the one Lord and God. We are enjoined to love Him, and to love Him with that totality and exclusiveness. The same love cannot, therefore, be demanded as love to the neighbour.

The second solution, to regard the two loves as identical, is in itself a useful and illuminating solution. But it does not stand up to closer investigation. It is only by the severest pressure that it can be introduced into the text : it does not say, as on this presupposition it would have to say, that we must love our neighbour with all our heart, with all our soul . . . and the Lord God as ourselves. Certainly, the two commandments belong together. That is clear. But it is just as clear that the commandment to love our neighbour is a " second " commandment. The final and almost unavoidable logic of this solution would be the damnable confusion and blasphemy : that God is the neighbour, the neighbour is God. But we need not press it as far as that. If we try to interpret love to God as love to the neighbour and love to the neighbour as love to God, we have to make certain anthropologico-theological presuppositions which are quite illegitimate because they cannot be based on the biblical witness to revelation, and are in fact contrary to it.

In other words, as the basis of this identification we have to ascribe an inherent value (1) to the neighbour as representing the human race, and (2) to our relationship to him as the fulfilment of individual humanity, to the human thou, and therefore to the human ego in its relationship to the thou. And this value is not derived but autonomous, and therefore has to be brought into a more or less direct connexion with God or with something divine. It is because of this twofold value, because of the self-based sanctity and dignity and glory both of man in himself and also of the fellowship between man and man as such, that according to this conception religion is also humanity and love to God is love to the neighbour (meaning love to man). Of course, it is usually more or less strongly emphasised that humanity must also be religion and love to man must also be love to God. But it is inevitable that the distinctive features of a love to God which cannot be seen should be known and therefore necessarily determined by a love to man which is very much seen and supposedly well known. Love to God is, then, the quintessence and hypostasised expression of what we know in a concretely perceptible and practical form as love to man. Love to God is the idea, the supreme norm of this known love to man. But it is clear that in these circumstances love to God cannot be what it is in Holy Scripture, the response of man to the being and activity of One who has first loved us. The converse, that true love to man must also be love to God, comes too late to be a real converse. The statement has no importance, if the real cardinal and interpretative principle of love is in the preceding statement, that true love to God will have to be love to man. It is too late for love to God to be decisive and meaningful in the biblical sense. There is no praise of the God who has first loved us, breaking forth in love to the neighbour. Instead, there is praise of the sanctity and dignity and glory of man, with a somewhat equivocal love for the God created according to the likeness of this man. The meaning and place given by Holy Scripture to love to God are quite different. Holy Scripture speaks of man always and exclusively from the standpoint of his sin and reconciliation. It addresses man only in the name of Jesus Christ. It does not, therefore, participate in this praise of man. As Scripture sees it, man as such has no dignity of his own, nor has the fellowship of man with man. What he is as an individual and in fellowship, he is under judgment and as a new creation of the love of God. The only humanity there is is this lost humanity, founded anew by the Word and Spirit of God, revealed in Jesus Christ and to be grasped in faith in Him. There is no humanity based on itself. If such a humanity has to be presupposed in order to identify love to God and love to the neighbour, then the identification cannot be made. Love to God in the sense of Holy Scripture, and this love to the neighbour, are opposites which mutually exclude each other.

Of course, we might find some other basis for the identification. We do not need to base the commandment to love the neighbour in the idea of humanity, and therefore in a doctrine of the inherent dignity of man and of the fellowship of man with man, and certainly not in a general doctrine of man existing either as an individual or in society, as it were, in a vacuum. There are other ways of showing the identity of this commandment with the commandment to love God. Inveighing roughly against all forms of idealism, we can replace the idea of humanity by an appeal to history, that is, to all those real and historically visible orders, marriage, the family, calling, nationality, the state, in which we all undoubtedly exist and in which we no less definitely have to recognise and respect the ordinances of creation and therefore the ordinances of God. The reason why I live as a human I in relation to the human thou is because in virtue of my creation it is arranged that I should stand in these orders and therefore be a father, son, brother, husband, compatriot, citizen, etc., and as such that I should definitely confront and be confronted by the thou, that I should be directed and pledged and indebted to it, in short, that I should be wholly and utterly bound up with it. The thou appointed for me by the ordinances of creation, is my neighbour. It is not that he has a value in himself or for me. It is rather that he is ineluctably posited for me in the framework of these ordinances. That is the basis of the commandment to love one's neighbour. Love to God is, therefore, necessarily love to the neighbour, because obviously I can only honour God by submitting to what He as Creator disposes regarding me and therefore by accepting my responsibility to the thou in the framework of His ordinances. But is this historical basis of the identity of love to God and love to man really so very different from the first humanitarian basis as it pretends to be? Is the idea of order which lies at the root of it so very opposed to the earlier decisive idea of humanity, because when the Bible speaks of God it will not at any price speak of man, but speaks all the more confidently and

definitely of these ordinances ? Have not the idea of humanity and
that of order this in common, that they both rest upon an inherent
value which is presupposed without question—although there is perhaps the distinction that in the one case the emphasis is upon the
presupposedness, in the other upon the value ? Can we not interpret
humanity as an order of creation and all the orders of creation as
orders of humanity ? Do we speak any the less about man when
for a change we prefer to speak more about the supra-personal bonds
in which he stands than about the inner freedom of his humanity ?
Here, too, under another aspect, are we not really speaking about
love to man rather than love to the neighbour ? It may be objected
that the idea of order is obviously superior to that of humanity because
it derives from the divine creation. But in the last resort cannot the
champions of humanity claim that in dealing with it as a pure presupposition they, too, are thinking of the divine creation ? We have
to put the same question to both the humanitarian and the historical
schools : whether the so-called humanity or the so-called ordinances
are given and known by us in the sphere of the created world in such
a way that in them we can recognise the divine creation ? whether
in this sphere of sin and reconciliation there can be any direct knowledge of God and His commandments, i.e., a knowledge which is based
directly upon creation apart from revelation ? Only if this is the case
dare we openly equate what humanity or the ordinances seem to
command with the biblical commandment to love the neighbour, and
therefore this commandment with the commandment to love God. If
it is not the case, then the idealism of the humanitarians and the realism
of the historicists both lead us to the same empty cistern : to the
knowledge of a God who is made in our own image, the content and
idea of our own freedom and our own relationships. The freedom of
the children of God begins only where the freedom, which we think we
experience in our humanity, ends. Their real relationship begins only
where the relationship with what they think they experience and know
as ordinances in history ends. If we compare the connexion with our
fellow-man, which seems to be laid upon us in virtue of the freedom
and relationship supposedly learned from creation, with the biblical
commandment to love our neighbour, and if we again compare the
latter with the commandment to love God—how far we have gone
from the commandment to love God as it was laid down by Jesus and
fulfilled in Him ! Instead—and either way—how near we have come
to the blasphemous inference (which was not, of course, intended either
way), that God is the neighbour, i.e., man, and that man is God !

But it might still be argued that we do not need to define and fill
out the concept neighbour according to the teaching of philosophical
idealism or realism. Can we not define and fill it out quite legitimately,
i.e., from the standpoint of the biblical testimony to revelation, and
still identify the commandment to love God and the commandment to

love the neighbour ? Now we must certainly affirm that what the neighbour is can and ought to be determined, not by the idea of humanity or order, but by Holy Scripture. And we can already anticipate and say that in the light of Holy Scripture the neighbour certainly cannot be identified with God, but must always be thought of as a man and therefore as a creature. But that means that love to him cannot be equated with love to God, but must be distinguished from it, and that only in that distinction can it be brought into a most definite connexion with it. If we have a legitimate concept of neighbour the chances of establishing an identity of the two commandments are at their very slenderest.

The collapse of the second possibility regarding the relationship of love to God and love to the neighbour seems logically to leave only the third alternative : to separate the commandment to love the neighbour from the absolute commandment to love God, and to regard it as one of the relative, derived and subordinate commandments, although perhaps the first and most important ; to regard it perhaps as a summary of the commandments of the second table, and yet as such only a repetition and commentary on the first commandment, the commandment to love God. This solution, too, is in its way simple and illuminating. It means that, ultimately and in fact, the life of the children of God can still be described in a single phrase. Fundamentally only the one thing has to be said of them, that they live in love to God and therefore in rendering obedience to the absolute commandment of the Father. Beside the fulness of this life, their life in love to the neighbour can have only the significance of a free sign. Now there can be no doubt that in view of all that we have said about love to God this third solution brings us nearer to the underlying truth than either of the other two. Yet it cannot be worked out in this form. For at the very outset we meet the difficulty that Holy Scripture does not treat the commandment to love the neighbour in such a way that when it is a question of the neighbour we are, as it were, at a lower stage of the divine commanding, on a field of secondary decisions, which merely follow or accompany love to God. It is the praise of God which breaks out in love to the neighbour. And in Holy Scripture the commandment to praise God rings out on at any rate the same note of central and absolutely decisive urgency as that of love to God. If we look at the texts with this in mind, we might even ask whether the first solution with its two absolute commandments is not preferable to this third with its contrasted absolute and relative commandments ; or whether after all we will not have to come back to the doctrine of the identity of the two commandments.

In the text in Mark the two commandments are referred to as πρώτη and δευτέρα. But there is no indication that this enumeration is meant to express a subordination of the second to the first. Indeed, we can only understand the statement in Mk. 12³¹ : μείζων τούτων ἄλλη ἐντολὴ οὐκ ἔστιν, if in it their parity over against all other commandments is presupposed. And in Mt. 22³⁸ᶠ· we are told expressly that αὕτη ἐστὶν ἡ μεγάλη καὶ πρώτη ἐντολή. δευτέρα ὁμοία αὐτῇ· ἀγαπήσεις τὸν πλησίον σου ὡς σεαυτόν. And it then adds that " on these two commandments hang all the law and the prophets." Note further that " Love thy neighbour as thyself" appears in Mt. 19¹⁹ as Jesus' answer to the question : What must I do to inherit eternal life ? this time as the conclusion and summary of a recapitulation of the commandments of the second table (and quite apart from the commandment to love God). In Jas. 2⁸ again " Love thy neighbour as thyself " is called " the royal law " quite apart from the commandment to love God, and in what follows it is equated with the " law of freedom " which in James undoubtedly embraces the totality of the divine Law. And we find the same in Paul : in 1 Thess. 4⁹ he calls Christians θεοδίδακτοι εἰς τὸ ἀγαπᾶν ἀλλήλους. " The whole law is fulfilled in one word, even in this ; Thou shalt love thy neighbour as thyself " (Gal. 5¹⁴), and in the same epistle : " Bear ye one another's burdens, and so fulfil the law of Christ " (Gal. 6²). And unequivocally in Rom. 13⁸ᶠ· : " He that loveth another hath fulfilled the law." All the commandments of the second table are " summed up " (ἀνακεφαλαιοῦνται) in the saying : " Love worketh no ill to his neighbour. Therefore love is the fulfilling of the law," or according to Col. 3¹⁴ the σύνδεσμος τῆς τελειότητος. We are also definitely told in Jn. 13³⁴ (cf. 15¹², ¹⁷) : " A new commandment give I unto you, that ye also love one another." In addition and finally, there is a whole series of extremely emphatic pronouncements in 1 Jn. According to 1 Jn. 2⁸ᶠ·, to live in light or in darkness is the same as to hate or to love one's brother. It is a lie for a man to think that he can love God and hate his brother, for a failure to love the brother that he has seen, proves that he cannot love the God whom he has not seen (4²⁰). In 3¹¹ " the message that ye have heard from the beginning is that we love one another." It is because we love the brethren, that we know that we have passed from death to life (3¹⁴). If we recognise love in the fact that He laid down His life for us, then " we ought to lay down our lives for the brethren " (3¹⁶, cf. 4¹¹). The commandment which God has given us is that we should believe in the name of His Son Jesus Christ and that we should love one another (3²³, cf. 4²¹). We may well ask whether the effect of all these passages as regards the life of the children of God is not to put love to God to some extent on the periphery as no more than a presupposition, making love to the neighbour the true and essential act of Christian decision ? If the life of the children of God had been described in a phrase, would it not be love to the neighbour rather than love to God ? Well, such a conclusion would be foolish. And it would be no less foolish to allow these considerations to force us back to the assumption of two absolute commandments or to the awkward doctrine of the identity of the two commandments. Yet on these grounds it is obviously impossible to assign to the commandment of love to one's neighbour a position which is in any way subordinate. If there can be no question of restricting the first commandment, obviously we have always to reckon with the fact that in its own way the second comes no less seriously or urgently or incisively than the first.

We must also ask the radical question whether it is even possible to conceive of a commandment of God which is subordinate, derived and relative ? Is not the commandment of God always and whatever it says an absolute commandment ? If we postulate two commandments of God, a primary one which demands love to Him, and a secondary which, comprising all sorts of individual injunctions, demands " only " love to the neighbour, does not this inevitably give rise to the idea that in the latter we do not have to do with the commandment and judgment and grace of God in the same sense, that we are not bound to obey with all our heart, and all our soul . . . , that we have entered the sphere of free human interpretation and explanation of the Law, that basically it is not a matter of obedience, but of our own selection of what is most fitting according to the dictates of conscience and our view of the existing situation ? Such an idea cannot be held in relation to any of the individual commandments of the so-called second table, or in fact to any commandment of God, which might be its occasion and actual content ; how much less, therefore, to the summary of all individual commandments (as opposed to the " great one " of love to God), as we have it before us in Holy Scripture in the commandment to love one's neighbour ! If Jesus calls this a " second " commandment, He is obviously pointing us to a way which is different from the first and cannot be substituted for or confused with it ; to a distinctive sphere or meaning of the love which is commanded. But in the one case as in the other, it is obviously a question of the love which is commanded, not in a weaker sense, but in the emphatic sense of the first commandment. There is certainly no question of conduct in which we can even partially excuse ourselves from obedience and go our own way. According to Holy Scripture there is no freedom except as we are bound to the commandment of God. Obedience itself is what Holy Scripture means by freedom. If, therefore, it speaks so clearly of a " second " commandment, we must ask carefully how far we are commanded to love in a second and different way, in a second sense or sphere. And we shall have to insert quite definitely that without any reservation, distinction or diminution we are still dealing with the question of the commandment and of obedience to it.

The connexion and the difference between the two commandments are plain when we remember that the children of God, the Church, now live, as it were, in the space between the resurrection and ascension of Jesus, and in the time of the forbearance of God and their own watching and waiting. In effect they live in two times and worlds. And in both of these their one undivided existence is claimed absolutely by God, subjected to His command and engaged to obedience. There can be no question of any other Lord but God claiming our love, or of any other object but God wanting to be loved. But the love of the children of God corresponds to their twofold existence in two times and worlds. The resurrection and ascension of Jesus Christ have taken place. On this basis they are already members and participants of the new world created by Him, by faith in the manifestation of the Son of God in and with the human nature which He has adopted, in and with the flesh which He has united to His deity and glorified by His power. Represented by Him, *peccatores iusti*, in His person they are already assembled before the throne of God, citizens of His everlasting kingdom, participators in eternal life. They are in Christ ; and it is in the totality of this their hidden being, which is none other than their actual human and creaturely existence here and now, that in the way described they are put under the commandment to love God, to seek after the One who has first sought and found them. But by virtue of the coming but not yet visible lordship of Jesus Christ, in faith in His coming, comforting themselves with the promise of the forgiveness of sins, given in the Word made flesh for all flesh, they always stand in need of the comfort and warning of this promise, because although the former time and world are past they still lie, indeed are, behind them. They have to wait and watch for their Lord as *iusti peccatores*. They have to serve Him in the relationships, connexions and orderings of a reality which has, of course, been overthrown and superseded by His resurrection, but not yet visibly abolished and replaced by His second coming, in the space between the times, where it doth not yet appear what they shall be. They " walk " in the light in face of darkness, and in this visible pilgrimage in all its hope and peril, which is simply the totality of their actual human and creaturely activity here and now, God has placed them under the commandment to love their neighbour. With this in mind we can try to bring out the elements of truth in the three rejected answers to the question of the relationship between the two commandments.

1. We are in fact (and this is the basic truth in the first solution) dealing with two different demands, both of which have to be regarded as in the same sense the commandments of God. They are both commandments of the one God. They are both concretely directed to His children living between and in the two times and worlds. They both claim them absolutely, and absolutely for God. And yet because of the twofoldness in which they exist before God and for God, they are not one but two commandments. The first one, the commandment to love God, is intended for the child of God in his completed existence in Jesus Christ as the heavenly Head of His earthly members. The second commandment, to love the neighbour, is intended for the child of God in his not yet completed walk and activity as an earthly member of this heavenly Head. It is the same God speaking to the same man. He speaks to him in two ways, because he exists in two ways. But because it is the same God who speaks and the same man who listens, in both cases an absolute obedience is demanded. Two absolute commandments ? No, but two commandments of the one absolute Lord, so that they both have absolute significance for the same man as God has determined and without competing the one with the other.

2. In both commandments (and this is the basic truth in the second solution) we have to do with the one claim of the one God on the whole man. In both cases we are concerned with His revelation in Jesus Christ by the Holy Spirit, with the order of grace, in which His Church, His children, are placed. It is His revelation which underlies the twofold reality and aspect of human existence. It is by means of this revelation and in the light of it that there is the transition, the movement of the one time and world to the other, and therefore the twofoldness of the demand made upon man. In the revelation of

God it is indeed a unique and absolute demand, just as the God who gives it and the man who receives it are one. But again, by positing and illuminating the twofoldness of our existence, the divine revelation underlies the fact that the demand is also a twofold demand, the unity of which can be believed but not perceived. To dissolve love to God into love to the neighbour, or love to the neighbour into love to God, would be to deviate from the divine revelation, and to lose again the unity in which love to God and love to the neighbour are commanded. If we try to love God as the neighbour, it will not be the God whom we are commanded to love. And if we try to love the neighbour as God, it will not be the neighbour whom we are commanded to love. If we are not to deviate from the divine revelation, if we really want to obey the one commandment of God, we can only love God and our neighbour. The desire to experience the unity of these commandments, and corresponding speculation about that unity, must be suppressed for the sake of the true unity of the commandment and of obedience to it. The Word and the Spirit of God are the true unity which we seek. But to find this true unity we have to listen to the Word and the Spirit and therefore to listen to the twofold commandment of love in the divine revelation.

3. To the extent (and this is the basic truth in the third solution) that the commandment to love God refers us to our existence in the time and world which comes and remains, the commandment to love the neighbour in the time and world which now is and passes, we are in fact dealing with a first and a second commandment, a primary and a secondary, a superior and a subordinate, an eternal and a temporary. The two times and worlds are not symmetrical. They do not balance each other. The one prevails over the other. That which comes and remains has the priority and superiority over that which now is and passes. This is something which belongs to the nature and essence of both of them as they are posited and illuminated by the divine revelation. It is therefore quite right that in the text of Matthew the commandment to love God should be described not only as the first, but also as the " great " commandment. It is in fact the basic and comprehensive commandment, the greater circle which includes in itself the lesser commandment of love to the neighbour. Because of the time and world which comes and remains, by virtue of the shadow which it has thrown, by virtue of the light of divine forbearance which it has cast, our present time and world is that which now is and passes. And therefore love to the neighbour is undoubtedly commanded for the sake of love to God and in and with the commandment to love God. Love to God is the real cause and expository principle of love to the neighbour. Love to the neighbour is in fact the token of love to God. To that extent, as something commanded in respect of our existence which now is and passes, by its very nature it can be the erecting of a sign, and not of a completed and eternal work. But we must be

careful not to treat it arbitrarily. It is also right that the second commandment should be put alongside the " first " and " great " with the
express declaration that it is " like " it. If we do not want to deviate
from revelation, we can never think of achieving the unity of the
two commandments by identifying love to God and love to the neighbour. But on the same presupposition, we cannot express the priority
and superiority of the first commandment, as though they were of our
disposing, by ascribing to the second a lesser degree of divine seriousness and emphasis, by regarding and treating the sphere designated
by the second commandment as a sphere of free human reflection and
decision side by side with the sphere of the divine predestination. No :
the commandment of love to the neighbour is enclosed by that of
love to God. It is contained in it. To that extent it is inferior to it.
But for that very reason it shares its absoluteness. In and with it, it
has all the seriousness and emphasis of the commandment of God, in
face of which there is no room for arbitrariness, but only for unceasing
responsibility. The sign of love to the neighbour is a sign which is
demanded from us. It is not one which is left to our own arbitrary
choice. For the time and world, as members of which this second
demand addresses us, is the time of the judgment and patience of
God. It is, therefore, no less the time of God than the time and world
which comes and remains, as members of which we are summoned
to love to God.

Now that we have purified the presuppositions in respect of the
relationship between love to God and love to the neighbour, we can
turn to the specific question : What is love to the neighbour ? What
does it mean when it says : " Thou shalt love thy neighbour as
thyself ? "

1. Here again our best plan is to go forward step by step. We
will begin by considering what can be the force of the " thou shalt."
According to the findings we have just made, there can be no doubt
that in the full range of the concept it has the significance of the commandment and the claim of God regarding His children. In this case
it applies to His children, so far as they are still members of the world
which now is and passes, when it doth not yet appear what they shall
be ; but even so it is still the commandment and claim of God. It
does not cease to be true that they should love Him with all their
heart and all their soul . . ., that in their totality they are challenged
by Him and for Him. But now the totality and absoluteness of the
commandment acquires the concrete shape which corresponds to the
world which now is and passes.

That is why Polan (*Synt. Theol. chr.*, 1609, p. 4187) gives as the main reason
why we should love our neighbour *sedulo et libenter* : *quia a Deo nobis mandata est.*

It is actually the case that in the midst of the world which now is
and passes, they cannot cease to attest that God has found them. For

they cannot exist without seeking Him as members of the eternal time and world, for which He has made them. The twofold determination of their existence, that they are members of both the coming and the passing world, cannot involve any limitation of the commandment and of obedience to it. On the contrary, it is because they are found, and therefore members of the coming world, that they are also members of the passing world. The second commandment, that they should love their neighbour, reminds them of the unity and therefore of the totality of their existence as the children of God. But if we think of love to the neighbour as in this sense based on love to God and therefore enclosed by it, here, too, we cannot understand the " thou shalt " apart from the promise : " thou wilt." When it is a matter of the neighbour, it is a question of our walk and activity as those who love God, of the inevitable outward side of that which inwardly is love to God. If love to God is its content, the " thou shalt " simply shows to the children of God the future which is definitely before them : thou wilt be what thou must be as one who is loved by God ; thou wilt seek the One who hath found thee. But this being the case, obviously the second commandment, if love to the neighbour is its content, can only show them the future which is before the one who hears the first command and is therefore to be addressed as one who loves God. The one who loves God, the second commandment tells us, will love his neighbour as himself. This is no less the Gospel than the first commandment. If not, if it does not presuppose the renewal of our being in Jesus Christ, if it does not come to us as those to whom it can come, how can it really be to us a law, how can it really claim us ? Neither from the content nor the form of this commandment can we abstract Jesus Christ as the One who utters it any more than we can in the case of the first commandment. If those to whom the commandment comes only love God because they are first loved by Him, it is only on this presupposition that they will actually love their neighbour as themselves, and that the fact that they do so can be stated and understood.

Il est certain, que jamais nous n'aimerons nos prochains, sinon que nous ayons aimés Dieu auparavant : car la vraye charité procède de ceste source là (Calvin, Serm. on 1 Cor. 10[151.], C.R. 49, 668).

But on this presupposition it is a real fact, and it can be stated and understood, that the children of God will love their neighbour as themselves. We will take this first in its general significance : in their existence as members of the world which now is and passes, they cannot lose or surrender or suppress the characteristic that they are citizens of the world which comes and remains. It is provided that this citizenship should continue to be hidden so long as this world lasts, so long as they live this side the second coming and the bodily resurrection of the dead. For they are not Jesus Christ Himself, but the earthly members of the earthly body of this their heavenly Head and Lord. The praise which Jesus Christ has offered to God in His resurrection and ascension, the Gospel of the forty days, is something which they His Church will not repeat. But they could not be what they are if their life did not stand under the constraint to declare and attest that unique and irrepeatable praise of God, under the presuppositions and conditions of this present passing world, and in the flesh which still clings to them. They are still in this world. They are still in the flesh. But in that they believe in the risen and exalted Jesus Christ, they are held and moved here in a very definite way by the commandment of God. The commandment constrains and compels them even in this world, but as citizens of the world which comes, to live by their faith and therefore to seek God in Jesus Christ. And the same commandment obviously constrains and compels them, as citizens of the world which comes, but in this present world, to live by their faith. From this standpoint it is simply the commandment to love their neighbour. It is not now a question of seeking the One without whom they cannot live. In that sense it is only the One in whom they believe who can be the object of their love. We cannot believe in our neighbour, nor are we required to do so in this second commandment. To confuse or confound the two demands, to be related to our fellow-man in such a way that we believe in him, that we give to him what we owe to God, is to make us incapable of fulfilling what we do owe to him. Yet we cannot seek the One in whom we believe and without whom we cannot live, we cannot love God, without this loving, as it were, manifesting itself, not as a second, repeated light of revelation, but as the light of our human and earthly witness to revelation, in the praise of God commensurate with us in our humanity within this world and time. This love is our answer to His loving. It is a loving with all our heart, all our soul. . . . It therefore puts us in a position of sheer thankfulness. And being put in that position in the totality of our existence, we cannot allow ourselves to understand and treat it, and with it our relation to God, as an affair of the heart, as the matter of a self-sealed inwardness. Nor as men living in the limitations of their humanity and under the presuppositions and conditions of this world, can we take refuge in the excuse that we are not Jesus Christ, and that we cannot praise God in some miraculous intervention like His resurrection and ascension. By the very fact that Jesus Christ is risen and ascended, we are compelled and constrained in our simple sphere, which has not to be confused with His, which is the very sphere in which we can and must be the children of God, to let our walk and activity be the walk and activity of those who are thankful. Not to do this, not to desire it, to hold back, is to deny the position in which we are put, to deny our love to God and therefore the fact that we are loved by Him, to deny in fact our very status as children. If we cannot do this, we cannot help but testify. By what we might again call a necessity of nature, in our very existence we become a sign and testimony.

It is obviously in this sense that in the Sermon on the Mount Jesus says to His disciples : " Ye are the light of the world," explaining that a city which is set on a hill cannot be hidden, and that there is no sense in a man trying to put a light under a bushel instead of on a lampstand (Mt. 5[14f.]).

Yet although this is something which we become ourselves, we have no arbitrary choice in the matter. It is God in His revelation who defines and ordains the testimony, when it is really the testimony of His own children, born again by the Word and Spirit. How can the praise which freely breaks forth from heart and soul and mind and strength be the praise which is well pleasing and acceptable to God, unless it takes place in strict obedience to His commandment ? If we were left to ourselves in this matter, the most marvellous constraint and unconditional enthusiasm and ecstasy by which we might feel impelled could, of course, lead to unusual and even sensational eruptions and explosions, to all kinds of remarkable movements and evanescent developments—but with all our enterprises and achievements we would still be exposed to the corruption and transitoriness of this world and of our own old nature as determined by this world. There would certainly not be any real testimony to the resurrection and ascension of Jesus Christ, any serious and as such effective manifestation of our love to God. We must be quite clear that every expression of our love to God, however well intended, is inexorably exposed to the law of the corruption and transitoriness of this world and of our old nature, to the extent that it is only an expression of our own arbitrariness or is accompanied or followed by it. What comes from our own experiences and discoveries is most certainly not the praise which is well pleasing and acceptable to God. For it to be such, the order of divine revelation and the commandment of God must be established and revered. And this commandment is the commandment to love one's neighbour. It is this commandment with its " thou shalt " which once again, in this second dimension, shows us the future which is before us. This time it is our future in this world, our future in the time still left to us under the judgment and forbearance of God. But for us even this future is an assured one. More than that, it orders us and it is therefore ordered. That is the first general lesson of the second commandment side by side with the first.

2. But who and what is the " neighbour " of whom this commandment tells us that we should love him as ourselves ? How does he come to be, as it were, the material of this sign and testimony of our thankfulness ? The explanation that he has this role and significance because of some inherent value in himself as such, or in the relation to him as such, is one which we have already rejected. We have also rejected the cognate explanation that we are directed to our fellow-men because of the existence of certain original orders of human life in society. If

we are to regard the commandment as a genuine commandment, our best plan at first is not to give place to any explanation. To obey a command does not mean to be convinced by its import that it is good, and then to applaud it and, of course, actively to endorse it. If we first tried to reason out why we should love our neighbour, we would never love him at all. Do we even know why we should love God ? All that we can say on this point is merely a later explanation of the fact that we should do so. To continue asking what is the import of the first commandment is necessarily to continue breaking it. In respect of the second commandment we shall have to try later to explain what it is all about that we are commanded specifically to love our neighbour. But the fact that it is commanded is a fact of revelation which is quite independent of this explanation and which claims primarily to be understood and evaluated as such. The true content of the two explanations remains, of course, and we can assume it at once : that in the neighbour set before us by the commandment we have to do (in a sense which has still to be defined more accurately) with our fellow-man, whom we did not choose as such ourselves, but who is posited as such.

That is the meaning of the biblical terms πλησίον, ἕτερος, ἀδελφός, and the reciprocal genitive ἀλλήλων, all of which obviously try to describe both the proximity and the distinctiveness, and also the givenness, of the entity referred to, and invariably mean our fellow-man. But in quite a number of important passages express use is made of the vocable ἄνθρωπος: Mt. 6[14], 7[12], 10[32f.] ; Lk. 5[10] ; Rom. 12[17f.] ; 2 Cor. 3[2] ; Col. 1[28], etc. There can, therefore, be no objection when Calvin on one occasion sums up the content of the commandment in this way : *Ubi ergo cognoscitur Deus, etiam colitur humanitas* (*Comm. on Jer.* 22[16], *C.R.* 38, 388).

The fellow-man posited as such constitutes, as it were, the material, the opportunity for the necessary maintaining of our faith in the sphere of this world. It is in relation to him that our love to God is manifested.

In this connexion Calvin was quite ready to speak of a *probatio* or *examen* or *experimentum* of our faith (e.g., *Comm. on Ps.* 15[2], *C.R.* 31, 144 ; *Sermon on Gal.* 5[4f.], *C.R.* 50, 680 ; *Comm. on Gal.* 5[14], *C.R.* 50, 251).

As those who love God we have to accept the fact that this is the only way in which we can maintain our faith. Therefore we do not need to try to find other and supposedly better and more impressive ways. To do so is only to deviate from the revelation and command-ment of God. No matter who or what he is, the neighbour is our future, and indicates the order in which God wills to be praised by us. It will always be to Him and before Him and in relation and responsibility to Him that this praise of God can take place, if it is to be a praise which is well pleasing and acceptable to God. The same God who willed to love us, and wills to be loved by us, also wills that we should love this neighbour. He wills both in the same unsearchable compassion. To try to withdraw from His compassionate will in relation to our neighbour is necessarily to renounce His mercy for ourselves. In this respect, too, He is unsearchable. But not more so than in respect of love to Himself. If it is a real miracle that we can love God, it is necessarily a real miracle that we can love our neighbour.

When we try to come to closer grips with the question, who or what is this neighbour, we must not be confused by the fact that loving our neighbour is described in Holy Scripture as serving, helping, doing good, sacrificing ourselves, in short as a payment of something which we owe, so that with corresponding frequency reference is made to his poverty and want and need of assistance and the like. It is not the fact that he is in need, and there is something we can give him, which makes him the neighbour whom we should love.

In this respect we shall have to treat with some reserve the advice frequently given by Luther, that we must seek our neighbour within the orders of life and society in which we actually find ourselves : the husband in his wife, the children in their parents and brothers and sisters, the master in the servant, the inferior in the superior and *vice versa*, the national in the fellow-national and so on. This advice might easily lead to the idea that the neighbour is one to whom we have a definite duty, who has a claim upon us. Of course, he has : but we cannot possibly think of our neighbour as Holy Scripture does if we think of him from that standpoint as an embodiment of the Law, or rather of a Law separated and emptied of the Gospel. It is right that when the Old Testament speaks of the neighbour who is to be loved, the primary reference is to fellow-Israelites. But note that in the Old Testament the " people " is not primarily a national community of blood. The " neighbour " also includes the frequently mentioned and by no means unimportant " stranger that is within thy gates." And the nation itself and as such is primarily the people of God, the people of the covenant and the *cultus*. Even in the Old Testament it is only secondarily that it is this within the framework of a closed, but never absolutely closed, national community of blood. The neighbour in the Old Testament sense is primarily the member of the covenant of Yahweh. In the light of the New Testament the secondary definition of neighbour cannot become primary (not even by extending it to all sorts of other orders of life and society). The neighbour cannot, therefore, be thought of as a kind of content of the mandate, claimed by human society in all its various forms. The mandate does, of course, exist, but it owes its dignity and validity to a form of the neighbour in which he does not face us as the representative of the mandate, or as an authority to which we owe obedience and service.

The primary and true form of the neighbour is that he faces us as the bearer and representative of the divine compassion. Where he is only Law, where he means confusion, accusation, the discovery of our wickedness and helplessness, wrath and judgment, we see him in a veiled form. And even if we cannot have him or see him in any other way, he could not meet us even in this veiled form, he could not seriously claim and judge us unless he were primarily and properly set before us in quite a different way, as the instrument of that order which is so necessary and indispensable for us in this time and world, in which God wills to be praised by us for His goodness. That there is this instrument of the order is itself divine goodness which we ought to recognise and praise as such before we ever ask about the claim to which it gives rise.

It is the context of the Lucan version of our text, the pericope of the Good Samaritan (Lk. 10²⁵⁻²⁷), which is calculated to help us most in this respect. What first strikes us in this account is that the twofold commandment of love is not introduced as a saying of Jesus, but as a saying of the lawyer (νομικός), who is trying to " tempt " Jesus. To his question : What shall I do to inherit eternal life ? Jesus answered with a counter-question : " What is written in the law ? How readest thou ? " (v. 26). And it is by way of answer to this counter-question that the lawyer recites the twofold commandment (v. 27). Purposely in his mouth, the unit, of the two commandments seems to be more strongly emphasised, by omitting the distinction into a first and second, than is the case in Matthew and Mark, where the twofold commandment is introduced as a formulation of Jesus Himself. There is, therefore, in the third evangelist an awareness of the fact that a twofold love is demanded of the one man who as the rest of the account makes clear is neither ready for nor capable of it. Of course, it is not by nature or of himself that the lawyer knows what he recites. He is in fact a doctor of the Law in Israel. Therefore outwardly and in appearance, by his very calling, he belongs to the community of Yahweh. In an important function he lives in the sphere and by the tradition of this community, claiming to be a member and in fact a prominent member of it, with a special claim to participate in the associated promises. The word of faith is nigh him, as it says in Rom. 10⁸, in his mouth and in his heart. It is false exegesis to assume that he is necessarily guilty of subjective insincerity. But whatever his subjective sincerity, he betrays the fact that he does not really know the near word, the two commandments, which he can recite so faithfully. Jesus praised him for his good knowledge and faithful recitation : ὀρθῶς ἀπεκρίθης. But he then challenges him to do the very thing which he knows and can express so well, and in that way (for this was his original question) to inherit eternal life. Why does he not go and do it ? Why does he ask what he should do when he obviously knows so well ? Indeed, why ? The reason is evident, for he goes on to ask : " And who is my neighbour ? " (v. 29). He had answered rightly, very rightly, in respect of love to God. But he does not ask : And who is God ? That is something which he seems to know and thinks he knows. He asks only in regard to the unperspicuous latter part of the doctrine which he has so weightily advanced. He asks only in regard to a single concept in the second of the commandments advanced by him, the concept neighbour. It is only this concept which he wants clarified. But from the very fact that he can ask this question the physician Luke regards him as mortally ill. He thinks that the question reveals that this doctor of the Law does not actually know the second commandment at all, and therefore not the first. Luke does not, of course, express it in this way. He goes further back. He finds the real reason for the question in the fact that the man " wished to justify himself " (v. 29). The lawyer does not know that only by mercy can he live and inherit eternal life. He does not want to live by mercy. He does not even know what it is. He actually lives by something quite different from mercy, by his own intention and ability to present himself as a righteous man before God. Or he thinks that he can live in that way. He wished to justify himself. That this is the case is revealed by the question : And who is my neighbout ? If a man does not know who his neighbour is, if he does not or will not know what mercy is, if he does not live by mercy, then obviously his intention and effort is to justify himself. But how can he understand the second commandment if this is his relation with his neighbour ? And how can he understand the first apart from the second ? Why does he not go on to ask : Who is God ? what is loving ? above all—the most obvious question in the light of what Jesus had just said : what is the " doing " which these commandments

14

require ? But, of course, if he had asked all the things which have to be asked he would have known the two commandments and stopped asking. But by asking " only " about his neighbour, he shows that he does not really know either of them, even though he can recite them : and that is why he wants to justify himself. The converse must also be stated : that because he wishes to justify himself, he does not really know the two commandments at all, although he can recite them. If he had no wish to justify himself, he would know the commandments in that case, and he would then know who is his neighbour, and everything else that has to be known at this point. Again, if he had known who is his neighbour, he would know the commandments, and would not wish to justify himself. Which is the first and basic element in his perversion ? His self-righteousness, or his lack of knowledge of revelation ? Who is to decide ? The one certain thing is that in this man the two go hand in hand and confirm each other. So then, to the question : And who is my neighbour ? and the background that " he wished to justify himself," Jesus answers in the Lucan version (vv. 30–35) with the story or parable of the good Samaritan : the man who fell among thieves, who lay wounded and half-dead by the roadside, whom the priest and Levite saw and passed by on the other side, until at last the Samaritan appeared, who took charge of him without hesitation and with unsparing energy. What is the meaning of this story as an answer to the question ? We might expect—and current exegesis of the text is in accordance with this obvious expectation—that Jesus would have said to the teacher of the Law: This Samaritan did not ask questions like you. He found his neighbour in the man that had fallen among thieves. He treated him accordingly. Go and do thou likewise. But the assumption on which (v. 37b) this final challenge is reached, according to the statements of the text, which in themselves are quite clear, although obstinately surrounded by traditional exposition, is really quite a different one. The question with which Jesus concludes the story is which then of the three (i.e., priest, Levite and Samaritan) proved to be a neighbour to the man who fell among thieves ? And the teacher of the Law himself had to reply: " he that showed mercy on him," i.e., the Samaritan. This man as such, as the one who showed mercy, is the neighbour about whom the lawyer was asking. And that is the only point of the story, unequivocally stated by the text. For the lawyer, who wants to justify himself and therefore does not know who is his neighbour, is confronted not by the poor wounded man with his claim for help, but by the anything but poor Samaritan who makes no claim at all but is simply helpful. It is the Samaritan who embodies what he wanted to know. This is the neighbour he did not know. All very unexpected : for the lawyer had first to see that he himself is the man fallen among thieves and lying helpless by the wayside ; then he has to note that the others who pass by, the priest and the Levite, the familiar representatives of the dealings of Israel with God, all one after the other do according to the saying of the text: " He saw him and passed by on the other side ; " and third, and above all, he has to see that he must be found and treated with compassion by the Samaritan, the foreigner, whom he believes he should hate, as one who hates and is hated by God. He will then know who is his neighbour, and will not ask concerning him as though it were only a matter of the casual clarification of a concept. He will then know the second commandment, and consequently the first as well. He will then not wish to justify himself, but will simply love the neighbour, who shows him mercy. He will then love God, and loving God will inherit eternal life. But now the text takes a last surprising turn. In fact, the lawyer does not see his own helplessness. He does not see that the priest and the Levite bring him no help and the Samaritan does. He does not really know his neighbour. Therefore he does not know either the second commandment or the first, although he can recite them so well. Therefore he does not love, he does not do what he must do to inherit eternal life. What advice or help can be given to him ? The section closes with the again quite unexpected challenge flung out at him by Jesus, v. 37b : " Go and do thou likewise " (ὁμοίως). From what precedes, we might have thought that He would summon him to that threefold knowledge. But that is not the case. He is merely summoned to do what the Samaritan did. He is summoned to be the neighbour who must bring comfort, help, the Gospel to someone else. Once he is, he will no longer want or need to ask : And who is my neighbour ? He who is merciful—at this point we can and should remember Mt. 5[7]—will receive mercy. We see and have a neighbour when we show mercy on him and he therefore owes us love. We see and have a neighbour when we are wholly the givers and he can only receive. We see and have him when he cannot repay us and especially when he is an enemy, someone who hates us and injures us and persecutes us (Mt. 5[43f.]). The Samaritan also receives : he receives from the man who fell among thieves, by giving to him. The fact that he becomes a good neighbour to him is merely a witness that he himself has found a compassionate neighbour in the man who is half-dead. And those who do likewise, as neighbours who exercise mercy—and who therefore themselves see and have a neighbour—really know both the second and the first commandments. They know them because they keep them. Their intention and attempt to try to justify themselves is smashed. They can only respond to the mercy which has met them. They can only love. They praise God. And in so doing they know what they must do to inherit eternal life. At this point we might ask whether and how it was possible to summon the lawyer—who obviously does not see or have a compassionate neighbour, who lacks all the necessary presuppositions—to go and do likewise and in that way to praise God. Well, it is Jesus Christ who gives the summons, and we cannot abstract Jesus Himself from the summons which He gives. On His lips the " Go and do thou likewise " is only Law because it is first Gospel. The good Samaritan, the neighbour who is a helper and will make him a helper, is not far from the lawyer. The primitive exegesis of the text was fundamentally right. He stands before him incarnate, although hidden under the form of one whom the lawyer believed he should hate, as the Jews hated the Samaritans. Jesus does not accuse the man, although judgment obviously hangs over him. Judgment is preceded by grace. Before this neighbour makes His claim He makes His offer. Go and do likewise means : Follow thou Me. There the story ends. We do not hear what becomes of the lawyer, whether he finally learns to know the Law in doing it or whether he only continues to recite it. But his question : Who is the neighbour, his neighbour ? has been unmistakably answered.

In the biblical sense of the concept my neighbour is not each of my fellow-men as such. It is not, therefore, a matter of telling myself and realising that humanity as such consists of mere individuals, who are all my neighbours.

This is a point at which Calvin's exegesis is obviously wide of the mark. He thought that instead of telling him the parable, Jesus might just as well have said to the lawyer : *proximi nomen ad quemvis hominem promiscue extendi, quia totum humanum genus sancto quodam societatis vinculo coniunctum sit.* As he sees it, " Love thy neighbour as thyself " can be *clarius* (!) put in this way : *Dilige unumquemque hominem sicut te ipsum.* For : *ut quis nobis sit propinquus, sufficit esse hominem, quia nostrum non est communem naturam delere.* The contrasting of the priest and the Levite with the Samaritan signifies a *propinquitatem, quae nos ad mutua officia obligat, non restringi ad amicos vel consanguineos, sed patere ad totum humanum genus.* And the attitude of the Samaritan *demonstrat natura duce et magistra, hominem hominis causa esse creatum : unde colligitur mutua inter omnes obligatio (Comm. on Lk.* 10[30], *C.R.* 45, 613 f.). This is more a Stoic than a New Testament doctrine. It is not supported either by the text or by any other part of Holy Scripture. To prove it, Calvin had to do what so many other expositors have done and studiously overlook the fact that according to vv. 36–37a of this chapter it was not the three, let alone the whole *genus humanum*, but only the Samaritan who was neighbour to him that fell among thieves.

In the biblical sense of the concept my neighbour is not this or that man as such. Nor is he the member of this or that larger or smaller group, or of the group which comprises the whole of humanity. It is not therefore the case that the question : Who is my neighbour ? really means : Is this or that individual one of my neighbours ? On the contrary, my neighbour is an event which takes place in the existence of a definite man definitely marked off from all other men. My neighbour is my fellow-man acting towards me as a benefactor. Every fellow-man can act towards me in this way, not, of course, in virtue of the fact that he is a man or that he is this particular man, but in virtue of the fact that he can have the commission and authority to do so. But not every fellow-man does in fact act towards me in this way. Therefore not every man is my neighbour. My neighbour is the man who emerges from amongst all my fellow-men as this one thing in particular, my benefactor. I myself, of course, must be summoned by Jesus Christ, and I must be ready to obey the summons to go and do likewise, that is, to be myself a benefactor, if I am to experience as such the emergence of a fellow-man as my benefactor, and therefore to see and have him as my neighbour. Therefore I myself have a decisive part in the event by which a fellow-man is my neighbour. But when we say this, do we not simply say that the whole matter is that of an event ?

What is the meaning and content of this event, and therefore of the benefit which comes to me through my neighbour ? To begin with, we can only reply that it consists in this : that through my neighbour I am referred to the order in which I can and should offer to God, whom I love because He first loved me, the absolutely necessary praise which is meet and acceptable to Him. It is not at all self-evident that in the midst of the world which now is and passes the children of God are referred to this order and borne along by and concealed within it. It cannot be taken for granted that they really can here and now really praise God. In this present transitory world they might have had to manage without any such reference. Here and now they might have been left to themselves. And in that case, what they offered as praise of God would, as we have seen, be subject to all the corruption and transitoriness of this world and of their own former nature. And in that case and in those circumstances what would become of their faith, of their love to God, of their citizenship in heaven ? Being lost here, would they not also be lost there ? Could they and would they still believe and love and hope in this world and therefore belong to that world ? No : they would " fall among thieves " and be left half-dead and helpless by the roadside. And in that need there would be no man to help them; not even the representative of the Church, to the extent that he is only a man, as the parable so drastically shows with its assessment of the priest and the Levite. They would simply die. They would simply cease to be what they are. They can only be what they are as the children of God if in respect of their twofold existence they are surrounded and borne along by the mercy of God. In their existence in the world which comes and remains they are surrounded and borne along by virtue of the high priestly advocacy and intercession of Jesus Christ. But this advocacy and intercession of Jesus Christ has its counterpart in the world which now is and passes. There is a painstaking mercy of God which follows them even here, seeking for them the very best, even in respect of the praise of God which is so necessary to them and so inseparable from their love of God and their existence as the children of God. The bearer and representative of this temporal as well as eternal mercy of God is simply my neighbour, i.e., the fellow-man who emerges from amongst all others as my benefactor. To what extent my benefactor? To the extent that, in virtue of a special commission and authority here and now, he proclaims and shows forth Jesus Christ within this world, thus giving to my praise of God direction and character: the character and direction in virtue of which it is meet and acceptable to God, not arbitrary and subject to the corruption of everything which takes place in this world, but confirming and maintaining my love to God, enabling me even as I offer it really to live in this world really by faith. That is the Samaritan aid which my neighbour gives to me. That is the meaning and content of the event in which he is to me a neighbour and not merely a fellow-man. Of course, I have my own part. I have to go and do likewise. I myself have to be a neighbour and therefore a bearer and representative of that divine mercy in the world. I have to be a child of God. It is only then that this will come to me through the neighbour. But again that does not alter the fact that this thing has to come to me through my neighbour. In respect of the necessary offering of my praise of God, I am referred to the fact that I am not alone. It is in virtue of the presence of my neighbour that I stand under and in the order in which God receives the praise which is proper and acceptable to Him.

We ask further: To what extent has a fellow-man commission and authority to emerge in this way, and therefore to be in a position to act towards me as the bearer and representative of the mercy of God? Our first general and decisive answer is: To the extent that there is within the world a Church, created by the Word and Spirit of God to be the earthly body of the heavenly Head, Jesus Christ, the great sign of revelation in the time between the ascension and the second coming of Jesus. It is the Church which introduces the Good Samaritan. To understand this, we must first remember that the Church as such and in itself is simply the work of the service which men render one another by mutually proclaiming and showing forth Jesus Christ. For the proper praise of God within this world the Church and this ministry are necessary. In the Church it is true that the Lord does not leave His own as orphans in this world, in this sphere of the judgment and the patience of God (Jn. 14¹⁸). In the Church He is with us alway even to the end of the world (Mt. 28²⁰). He is this by means of the service which is offered in the Church. Who and what a neighbour is, we can best realise from those who founded the Church, the biblical prophets and apostles. What they do is the purest form of that work of divine mercy which is assumed by the children of God. They bear witness to Jesus Christ. In that way they order the praise of the children of God ; they make it possible as a real praise of the real God. But the same thing happens wherever the Church is the Church. Where it has the form of the priest and Levite, that is, where this service is not offered, it is not the Church. In the Church we cannot wish to justify ourselves, we cannot try to live by self-will, but only by mercy. In the Church we flee to Jesus Christ proclaimed, that is, to our neighbour, who offers us the service of proclaiming Jesus Christ.

But although this general reply is decisive, it is not of itself enough. It is not enough for this reason. As the Bible sees it, service of the compassionate neighbour is certainly not restricted to the life of the Church in itself and as such. It is not restricted to those members of the Church who are already called and recognisable as such. It is not restricted to their specific action in this capacity. Humanity as a whole can take part in this service. The Samaritan in the parable shows us incontestably that even those who do not know that they are doing so, or what they are doing, can assume and exercise the function of a compassionate neighbour. The Church in fact does not exist only for itself, inwards. It does not exist only for those who are already consciously and visibly its adherents and members. The fact that there is a Church has also a significance outwards. Within world-history, humanity, it points to the fact of a calling, a limitation and determination, which applies both to the whole and to each individual within the whole. By virtue of the reconciliation effected in Jesus Christ the existence of the Church in the world has a representative significance. Even though the humanity around it does not belong to the Church we can no longer think of it as untouched by or not participating in the mission which in the Church man acquired and accepted for his fellow. The existence of the Church means that a summons is given to the humanity which is around it but does not belong to it. It means that a *character indelibilis* is imparted to man as such. In this, although he may not be aware of the Church, although he may be indifferent or hostile to it, yet even as one who is outside and over against it, he still has a part in its existence in his own way. Not as though every man as such is my neighbour. Even within the

Church it is only a promise that he is this, and that this service is
done to man. The actuality of it is always an event. But because
there is a Church every man does actually stand under the promise
of this event. It is impossible to be absolutely outside the Church,
to have absolutely no part in it. We will see why in a moment. Whatever a man makes or does not make of it, whether it means for him
grace or judgment, whether he himself will sooner or later belong to
the Church or not, every man is actually related to the Church by
the fact that he exists with it in the space between the ascension and
the parousia of Jesus Christ. To that extent he is actually involved
in the calling to that service which is offered in its true and explicit
form in the Church : the service of proclaiming Jesus Christ. It is
in the light of this summons, of the fact that simply as he is, as a man,
he can be a neighbour to me here and now at any moment, as the
Samaritan was to the man half-dead by the roadside, it is in this
light, and not in the light of the fact that he is an outsider, that I must
regard him from within the Church. I could not believe in the Church
if in it and by it I did not find hope even for man as such.

We could call this awareness of the destiny of man the Christian conception
of humanity. It is distinguished from the Stoic in three ways. First, it is not
based on the perception and assessment of a so-called " nature " of man. Second,
in ascribing to man as such a *character indelibilis* it does not mean statically a
quality of his own. Third, it does not ascribe to him only—which is not enough—
a so-called disposition or capacity which may perhaps be developed by instruction and education. It means actually and concretely his destiny, a historical
differentiation of man and humanity, which consists in a mission and authorisation, and is fulfilled in an actual confrontation with the Church of Jesus Christ.
It was in the light of this historical differentiation that in a particularly impressive way Paul (and, of course, all the mission of the primitive Church) considered the Gentiles, and the possibilities of order and culture amongst them, and
the fact that in more than one connexion it can be claimed expressly that they
render considerable services to the Church for which all thanks are due : not
in the light of a significant and promising nature of man, not in the light of an
education which is always due for future completion, but in the light of the
actual and therefore significant and promising encounter of the Gentiles with
the Church of Jesus Christ. The Church would not take itself seriously if confronting the world it did not regard it as a world already changed by this fact,
if it did not find hope for man, not as such and before it has claimed him, but
simply because it exists and will claim him. How can it ever cease to see him
in advance in the light of " thou wilt," by which it lives itself ? How can it
rest towards him in a barren " thou shalt " and therefore " thou art not " ?
The Christian conception of humanity is, therefore, a very different one from the
Stoic. But it is to be distinguished from it not by a lesser, but by a dispro-
portionately much greater intensity and definition. What kind of power can
and will that conception have which deals only with the " nature " of man and
the still to be realised possibilities of education which must be weighed against it ?
Again and again it will be corroded by a very justifiable scepticism, not only in
respect of human nature, but also in respect of all human education. It is only
in the Church or from the Church that there has ever been a free, strong, truly
open and confident expectation in regard to the natural man, a quiet and joyful
hope that he will be my neighbour, a conception of humanity which is based
on ultimate certainty.

How do we ever come to the point, either within or of necessity also without the Church, where we can count at all on the possibility of this fellow-man emerging to help, and therefore on the event of the neighbour, as described in the parable of the Samaritan ? How can we ever trust that a man will be my neighbour like that ? What is the real mission and authorisation in which he can ? In answering this question we must keep strictly to what the biblical testimony to revelation has to say concerning it. Our fellow-man becomes to us the compassionate neighbour because he is seen in the reflection of the sign which gives to the great sign of the Church, in all its meaning for humanity generally, its origin, basis and stability, in the reflection of the human nature of Jesus Christ. In the resurrection and ascension of Jesus Christ there took place a glorification of suffering, crucified, dead and buried man in his unity with the person of the Son of God. And it was in that glorification, in the Gospel of the forty days, that the praise which is meet and acceptable to God became event in its original and most proper form. Proclaiming Himself, Jesus Christ has rendered us the benefit of setting up the order of praise without which we would be lost in this world. It is really an order which is set up at this point, a destiny which is fulfilled. Because in this One human existence became once for all and uniquely a testimony to the fact that God has assumed it, there can and must be a praise of God by other men, even by those who are not Jesus Christ, even by those who, like all of us, have to move within the limitations of this present, passing world and their own former nature. This original order, this new destiny of man is operative in the existence of the prophets and apostles, by whom Jesus Christ is proclaimed, and of the Church, in which this proclamation is perpetuated. In this proclaiming we again have an event, in a secondary form : a glorification of man the sinner abandoned to death. Man himself now becomes a sign. He can and must show mercy. He can and must summon to a genuine praise of God, and in that way render to the children of God that necessary service. He can and must be my compassionate neighbour. He can and must and will, not by his own capacity and will, but because the Son of God has made Himself my neighbour in His incarnation and revealed Himself my neighbour in His resurrection. The service of the Church—where the Church really is the Church—rests on the fact that Jesus Christ won human brethren of this kind, that He has become a neighbour to individual men who can as such be good neighbours to us, because in them Jesus Christ is present to us, and in hearing them, we hear Him (Lk. 10[16]). The Church means the service of testimony. But the Church and all that takes place in it exists only representatively for the world, just as it has its own life only representatively in its heavenly Head. It is not the churchman in particular, but man generally, every man, who in the Church comes into the light of the promise : " Ye shall be my witnesses " (Ac. 1[8]). For that reason we must expect to find the witness of Jesus Christ, and therefore our neighbour, not only in the Church, but, because in the Church, in every man. Not simply to find : if we are to find him, the event of divine beneficence has to be real. But to expect to find : for if in the prophets and apostles we see men to whom Jesus Christ has become a neighbour, and they themselves have become helpful and compassionate neighbours by bearing witness to Him, if it has become a general possibility in the Church that men can have this function, then we must obviously be prepared and ready for the fact that man, our fellow-man generally, can become our neighbour, even where we do not think we see anything of the Church, i.e., in his humanity he can remind us of the humanity of the Son of God and show mercy upon us by summoning us in that way to the praise of God.

We can expect this hidden neighbour, who stands outside the visible Church, just because there is a visible Church. We are obviously referred to him by at least some of the statements made in Scripture about the Gentiles. The Gentiles, with their worship of false gods, are the dark background before which the re-demptive dealings of God with His people and Church take place. They are also the object of the Church's mission and proclamation. As those who are one day to be assembled on Mount Zion, they are the content of one of the prophecies of the last days. But in individual figures whom we must not overlook, they also have a present place in the redemptive history attested by the Bible. They are strangers, and yet as such adherents ; strangers who as such have some very important and incisive things to say to the children of the household ; strangers who from the most unexpected distances come right into the apparently closed circle of the divine election and calling and carry out a kind of commission, fulfil an office for which there is no name, but the content of which is quite obviously a service which they have to render. We can think of the Balaam, Num. 22–24, who is to curse Israel, but instead he must irresistibly bless. We can think of the harlot Rahab who, according to Josh. 2¹², " had mercy" on the Israelite spies, and who was therefore justified by her works according to Jas. 2²⁵, and saved by her faith according to Heb. 11³¹. We can think of the Moabitess Ruth and her loyalty to the humiliated Israelitess Naomi, a loyalty which has no less reward than that she is made the ancestress of David and given prominence as such in Mt. 1⁵. We can think of the co-operation of Hiram, King of Tyre, in the building of Solomon's temple (1 K. 5¹⁵ᶠ·). We can think of the sayings and gifts of the Queen of Sheba (1 K. 10¹ᶠ·). We can think of the Syrian captain Naaman (2 K. 5¹ᶠ·). We can think of the wonderful role which is ascribed to the Persian king Cyrus, not only in Deutero-Isaiah but also in the book of Ezra. And in the New Testament we can think of the wise men who come with their offering from the East (Mt. 2¹ᶠ·) ; of the centurion of Capernaum, who, according to Mt. 8¹⁰ᶠ·, had such a faith as Jesus had not found in Israel, and led Him to speak of the many who shall come from the East, from the West and shall sit down with Abraham and Isaac and Jacob ; of the Syro-Phœnician woman (Mk. 7²⁴ᶠ·) ; of the centurion at the cross with his messianic confession (Mk. 15³⁹) ; of the centurion Cornelius at Cæsarea, in whose house Peter learns that " in every nation he that feareth him and worketh righteousness, is acceptable to him " (Ac. 10³⁵). That these biblical figures must be regarded as in any way the representatives of a general revelation is excluded by the context of all these passages. The most remarkable of them all is the Melchisedek, King of Salem, and a " priest of the most high God," who brings bread and wine to Abraham, and blesses him and receives from him a tithe (Gen. 14¹⁸ᶠ·). He reappears in the royal Ps. 110[4], again mysteriously as the representative of an otherwise unmentioned priestly order, by which even the Elect of Yahweh seems to be measured. According to Heb. 5[6f.], 6[20], 7[1f.], he is the type of Jesus Christ Himself and of His supreme and definitive high priesthood. It is therefore not merely legitimate but obligatory to regard the figure of Melchisedek as the hermeneutic key to this whole succession. It is not on the basis of a natural knowledge of God and a relationship with God that all these strangers play their striking role. What happens is rather that in them Jesus Christ proclaims Himself to be the great Samaritan : as it were, in a second and outer circle of His revelation, which by its very nature can only be hinted at. It must be noted that no independent significance can be ascribed to any of the revelations as we can call them in a wider sense. There is no Melchisedek apart from Abraham, just as there is no Abraham apart from Jesus Christ. They have no Word of God to preach. They are not witnesses of the resurrection. They have no full power to summon to the love of God. In this they differ permanently and fundamentally from the prophets and apostles, as does their function from that of the Church. Their witness is a confirmatory and not a basic witness. But granted that there are prophets and apostles, granted there is a people of God and a Church, granted that God is already loved, they have the authority and the power to summon those who love God to the praise of God which is meet and acceptable to Him. If we know the incarnation of the eternal Word and the glorification of humanity in Him, we cannot pass by any man, without being asked whether in his humanity he does not have this mission to us, he does not become to us this compassionate neighbour.

By virtue of this characterisation our fellow-man becomes to the children of God a confirmatory witness to Jesus Christ. In Holy Scripture the characterisation is brought out by the use of the strong term brother. In the Old Testament it is used with neighbour to describe a member of the nation or covenant. In the New Testament, with one or two exceptions, it completely replaces the term neighbour. What the Church expresses and affirms when it makes this term the term for our fellow-man is the nearness of our neighbour, his indispensability, the, as it were, natural impossibility of leaving him, of trying to be the children of God alone and without him. But as the term which institutes the neighbour, in its biblical sense it can only be understood christologically, i.e., from the standpoint of the incarnation, the resurrection and ascension of Jesus Christ. The fatherhood of God and the sonship of man is originally and properly true in Jesus Christ. It is only true for us by transference, through Him. Similarly, brotherhood and brotherliness amongst men are not a requisite of their humanity, but a new creation of the revelation and reconciliation of God. Brotherhood arose amongst men because Jesus created it between Himself and individual men, by calling them into relationship with Himself, that nearness of brothers which cannot be destroyed or doubted but is absolutely necessary and indisputable ; by allowing their humanity to enter into blood relationship with His ; by giving them His Father to be their Father. It is that way, in Himself and not otherwise, that He made them brethren one to another. Any confirmation of their brotherliness one to another can consist only in the fact that each recognises in the other the original and proper

brother Jesus Christ and is therefore summoned to the praise of God
by him—or in the strict sense—by Jesus Christ through him.

How little natural brotherhood is to be expected between us men, i.e., how
little proclamation of it as a universal, ethical truth, is shown by the story of
Cain and Abel, Gen. 4[8f.], of which there are warning reminders in Mt. 23[35] and
1 Jn. 3[12f.] The story also has the significance of a promise. According to Heb.
11[4], by faith Abel offered a better sacrifice, by which, even though he is dead, he
still speaks on behalf of the murderer. But this is because Abel and Cain were
brothers, as the sons of Adam and Eve. It is because of the new brotherhood
based on the fact that his sacrifice is prophetic of Jesus Christ and His sacrifice.
The first-born among many actual brethren, the true and proper brother is,
therefore, Jesus Christ (Rom. 8[29]). It is only in Him and through Him that
there can and shall be others. They are ἀδελφοὶ ἐν Χριστῷ (Col. 1[2]), because
He is not ashamed to call them brethren (Heb. 2[11]) and as such to be equal to
them in all things (Heb. 2[17]). He speaks of them as His brethren (Mk. 3[34], Mt.
28[10], Jn. 20[17]). He it is who gives this name to their mutual relationship (Mt.
23[8], Lk. 22[32]). They are brethren as " brethren beloved of God " (1 Thess. 1[4]) ;
and the word ἀγαπητοί must always be understood in this sense.

It must be observed that this qualified description of the neighbour
as a brother is not noticeably applied in Holy Scripture to any but
those who have already recognised each other as companions in the
faith, and members of the Church. This does not exclude, but includes
the fact that in every man we have to expect a brother (for that only
means a neighbour in the full sense of the word). What man is there
who might not one day meet us as a messenger of the Word of God,
a witness to the resurrection ? At this meeting we would, of course,
be reverting to the qualified usage of the New Testament in calling
him brother. If in his humanity he reminds me of the humanity of
Christ, irrespective of whether or not he shares my faith in Christ,
and summons me to the proper praise of God in that way, that in
itself is not the encounter which justifies this name. But how can it
help but point beyond itself to that encounter ? We will have to
return to this point when we come to speak of love to the neighbour.

And now, in the christological context, we can at last understand
why not consistently but very often in Holy Scripture the neighbour
is represented as a fellow-man in great suffering and therefore in need
of help, a fellow-man whom we have to love by bringing the help
which he needs. If we are to keep strictly to the biblical witness to
revelation we cannot answer this question with a doctrine which is
roughly as follows : That suffering fellow-man in need of help directs
the children of God to the task which God has appointed for them.
God does not will the many griefs and sufferings and burdens under
which we men have to sigh. He wills their removal. He wills a better
world. Therefore we, too, should will this better world, and a true
worship of God consists in our co-operation in the removal of these
sufferings. Therefore our neighbour in his distress is a reminder to
us and the occasion and object of our proper worship of God.

This kind of ("religio-social") teaching overlooks too many things and arbitrarily introduces too many things for us to be able to accept it. That God does not will the evil under which we men have to suffer is true to the extent, but only to the extent, that as His revelation shows, He does not will its cause, the alienation of man from Himself, and the world as fashioned by this alienation, which as such is necessarily a world full of evil. On the contrary, in drawing man to Himself in Jesus Christ, He inaugurates a new world and causes it to break through. This work of reconciliation, in the consummation to which Jesus Christ pointed and which He is to fulfil, is the divine removing of the things under which we now see both ourselves and others suffer. We are not told that we have to co-operate in this removing as such. We are not told that we have to undertake the amelioration of the world in fulfilment of a divine programme of amelioration. We are not told that we shall find a neighbour in our fellow-man because his pitiable condition stirs us to do something along these lines. What we are told is that we should love our neighbour by proclaiming to him—not only in word, of course, but in deed—the true amelioration and therefore Jesus Christ.

Our neighbour in the sense of that doctrine of world-amelioration would again mean Law (instead of Gospel first and then as such Law). This is the very perversion which our previous discussion has shown to be untenable. Even our suffering fellow-man in need of help does not primarily confront us with a task. On the contrary, he has something to impart, to give, to present; the most important thing in life and the most indispensable. For revealed in that way he is to us primarily and decisively the compassionate neighbour. Only then and as such does he confront us with a task, and the task must be understood only from the standpoint that he has already been of benefit to us. And his benefaction to us as a suffering fellow-creature in need of help consists in the fact that even in his misery he shows us the true humanity of Jesus Christ, that humanity which was not triumphant but submissive, not healthy and strong, but characterised by the bearing of our sins, which was therefore flesh of our flesh—the flesh abandoned to punishment, suffering and death. Our fellow-man in his oppression, shame and torment confronts us with the poverty, the homelessness, the scars, the corpse, at the grave of Jesus Christ. The indigence and helplessness of our fellow-man need not be particularly crying. It need not always be what we, in our human way of thinking and speaking, call trouble and need. The plight of man does not begin or consist only in what we can see. It may just as well be hidden behind an aspect of soundness, strength and victory, as revealed in sickness, weakness and defeat. It is enough that it should be there, crying or merely complaining, openly revealed or hiding under the appearance of its opposite. If we tried rashly and self-confidently to find the straits and helplessness of our fellow-men in what we see, we might easily overlook his actual misery and not recognise in him our neighbour. We say his actual misery, for our fellow-man is actually in misery and he can be recognised as a neighbour only in his actual misery. It is not necessary that when we recognise him as such we should feel pity. We may feel surprise and awe at his human greatness, or terror at his fate, or horror at his nature or lack of it, or resignation at his character and conduct, whatever they are. His actual misery consists in the fact that he wills, wills to live, and yet—with or without mask, openly or secretly, perhaps indeed without knowing it himself— he cannot, cannot live, and is therefore caught in an always hopeless and hopelessly repeated and varied attempt to do so. If I recognise him in this, if with whatever feelings I see this as his oppression, shame and torment, I recognise in him my neighbour. And it is in this actual misery of his that there consists his actual similarity to the crucified Christ. We repeat, his actual similarity, for it is there, quite independently of his belief or unbelief. It is there without his having to give any account of his attitude to Christ. He resembles Him, even though he is His enemy. For it is this actual misery of man, the curse of an attempt to live which is foredoomed to failure, that Christ has taken upon Himself and carried, in that He became man, in that the eternal Word became flesh. For the sake of this misery, in His faithful actualisation, He became poor and homeless, tormented, dead and buried. What Is. 53 says of the suffering Servant of God is true at any level of any man so far as it simply speaks of his suffering. In the reflection of the prophecy about Christ there is a reflection of my neighbour, if I have the grace to recognise him in my fellow-man. And in recognising my neighbour in my fellow-man, I am actually placed before Christ. We repeat—actually. It does not make any difference to the actuality whether or not we recognise in our fellow-man the poverty and homelessness, the scars, the sufferings and the grave of Christ. Indeed, we shall certainly not recognise Christ in him in the first instance.

In what Jesus says about the last judgment in Mt. 25[1f.], both those on the right hand and those on the left declare quite definitely that they did not know that they had or had not given Jesus to eat and drink and sheltered and clothed and visited Him. This must be a warning to us that it is not a question of seeing Jesus in our fellowman. The text does not say that He is to be seen in these " least " as His brethren, but that He actually declares Himself to us in solidarity, indeed in identity with them. And of the recognition of this solidarity and identity it says that it is only transmitted later by the saying of Jesus the Judge both to those on the right hand and those on the left, and to the great surprise of both. Therefore the encounter with the neighbour and the decision in relation to him precede this recognition. For the significance of the encounter and decision consists in the content of this recognition, i.e., in the fact that Jesus actually encounters us in our neighbour, and that we decide for or against Him in making this decision in relation to our neighbour.

The afflicted fellow-man offers himself to us as such. And as such he is actually the representative of Jesus Christ. As such he is actually the bearer and representative of the divine compassion. As such he actually directs us to the right praise of God. For him to be and do this, we do not need to know anything about his mission, about the sacramental character of his existence. At first we will not be able to know anything about it. We need to take him simply as what he actually is : as the neighbour who is near us *propinquissimus* in his misery. That is how the purpose is fulfilled which God has with him and for us. That is how we have to do with Jesus Christ Himself in this world, in the time of waiting and watching. For that reason we need to have to do only with our fellow-man. In a purely secular, profane and human way, this fellow-man confirms to the children of God the Word of God, by which they are begotten : the Word of their reconciliation by Him who although He knew no sin, was made to be sin. How can it be confirmed to them more powerfully and clearly than by their recognising in their fellow-man the afflicted one, the sinner, the one who is punished for his sin ?

3. We go on to ask what is meant by " Thou shalt *love* thy neighbour." In view of all that we have said about " shalt " and " neighbour " we can only reply that in the sense of the second commandment to love means to enter into the future which God has posited for us in and with the existence of our neighbour. Therefore to love means to subject ourselves to the order instituted in the form of our neighbour. To love means to accept the benefit which God has shown by not leaving us alone but having given us the neighbour. To love means, therefore, to reconcile ourselves to the existence of the neighbour, to find ourselves in the fact that God wills us to exist as His children in this way and this alone : in co-existence with this neighbour, under the direction which we have to receive from him, in the limitation and determination which his existence actually means for ours, in the respecting and acceptance of the mission which he actually has in relation to us. Would we rather have it otherwise ? Is there a kind of secret unwillingness in us, that this is how it is intended and ordained, that we are not really alone, that even in the world we are not left to ourselves, that necessarily, inescapably and indispensably we have to have the neighbour ? In relation to what we have just said, there might well be a reason for this unwillingness. Our fellow-man reveals himself to us as a neighbour in the sense of the second commandment when he stands before us, and we know him, as a man who is actually wretched, when the futility and the powerlessness of his attempt to live is manifest to us. It is our fellow-man who is sinful and punished for his sin who is our neighbour. So long as that is not clear, the possibility of that unwillingness will not be any problem to us. Why should we not be on relatively quiet and comfortable terms with our fellow-man so long as we do not see his actual misery and are therefore in a position, either to rejoice and find strength in what we regard as his strength and health and victoriousness, or in his tragic greatness, in relation to what we regard as his plight and need of help, to use our own surplus energies to improve his position and in that way, in the enjoyment of the superior position which we thereby adopt, to do ourselves a real kindness and perhaps more ? The fellow-man who is unaware of his actual plight, the fellow-man to whom we can look

and about whom we can concern ourselves, above all the fellow-
man who helps to confirm and enhance us in the role of benefactor,
mentor and ameliorator : this fellow-man does not constitute any
serious problem, and any headaches which he may incidentally cause
will not be mortal. But this in the last resort not at all disconcerting
fellow-man is not our neighbour in the sense of the second commandment. He is not the one who, sent and authorised by God, shows
mercy upon us. He is lacking in the most important quality, in which
alone he could do so, an actual similarity to the crucified Jesus Christ.
At least, he is so in our eyes and in his relation to us. That is why
he is not at all disconcerting. That is why we do not experience any
serious unwillingness in relation to him. But that is also why he
cannot help us seriously. This fellow-man will not summon us to the
praise of God. Only afflicted, sinful fellow-man can do that. Only
this man is my neighbour in the sense of the second commandment.
But this neighbour will cause me a really mortal headache. I mean,
he will seriously give me cause involuntarily to repudiate his existence
and in that way to put myself in serious danger. In face of this neighbour I certainly have to admit to myself that I would really prefer to
exist in some other way than in this co-existence. I would prefer this
because from this neighbour a shadow falls inexorably and devastat-
ingly upon myself. The wretched fellow-man beside me simply reveals
to me in his existence my own misery. For can I see him in the futility
and impotence of his attempt to live, without at once *mutatis mutandis*
recognising myself ? If I really see him, if as *propinquissimus* he is
brought into such close contact with me that, unconfused by any
intersecting feelings which may influence me, I can only see his misery,
how can it be otherwise ? This is the criterion : if it is otherwise, if
I can still see him without seeing myself, then for all the direct sympathy I may have for him, for all the zeal and sacrifice I may perhaps
offer him, I have not really seen him. He remains at root that in no
way disconcerting fellow-man. He is still not my neighbour. The
neighbour shows me that I myself am a sinner. How can it be otherwise, seeing he stands in Christ's stead, seeing he must always remind
me of Him as the Crucified ? How can he help but show me, as the
reflection of myself, what Christ has taken upon Himself for my sake ?
The divine mission and authority which the neighbour has in relation
to me, the mercy which he shows me, is not to be separated from this
revelation. But for that very reason it is a question whether I will
accept this neighbour. The whole nature of the time and world for
which the redemptive order of the second commandment is instituted
and obtains is revealed in the fact that this question is put to us. The
children of God themselves in this time and world are still afflicted
men, sinners. They not only participate in the divine justification ;
they also stand in need of it. They stand in need of it just because
they participate in it. No virtue, sanctity or beauty can permit them

to live by anything else but grace and in any other way than in faith in the righteousness of Jesus Christ. What we have is a human life and activity which, apart from the light of grace which falls on it from above, is completely covered by the same darkness as that which lies over all the world which now is and passes. Here and now the children of God are caught in the futile and impotent attempt to live which constitutes the plight of man. As sinners, therefore, they must be helped, or there will be no help. And for that very reason in this present passing world they are helped by the afflicted neighbour, answering to the fact that in relation to the world which comes and abides they are helped only by the crucified Jesus Christ. But for that reason their neighbour always and necessarily means a question. If they are to be helped by him, he must touch them at the very point where they really are : in their status as members of this world, as children of Adam. The accommodating fellow-man with whom they come to terms without any unwillingness is in his very harmlessness no real bearer and representative of the divine compassion. He is not the surgeon's knife which, by bringing them pain, is here and now their true blessing. It is, therefore, quite natural for us to confess that we would rather not accept the service of our neighbour. When it is a question of the indispensable praise of God in the life of the children of God, it seems as though there is an attempt to repeat the crisis of our abandonment and our redemption by the revelation of God in Jesus Christ. As those who are already redeemed in faith, we may easily prefer to be left to ourselves, to praise God according to our own fancy and free choice, bringing forth, and offering of ourselves, in a splendid isolation with the invisible God, what we think to be the work of thankfulness appropriate to His glory. Have not the Word of God and the Holy Spirit, which as the children of God we think we have received, put us into a position to do this ? In faith, are we not free and good and quite capable of doing it ? And now it again proves to be the case that everything is quite different. Even for the children of God, even for the pardoned, there is no freedom outside the divine order. God wills from them, from them particularly, not an arbitrary but an obedient praise. Their neighbour is put before them for that very reason, that their praise may be obedience. And their neighbour is the afflicted neighbour. But the afflicted neighbour reveals that they are themselves afflicted, are sinners, as he is. And the fact that they are, even as the children of God, is nowhere more clearly seen than in their unwillingness as the children of God to be revealed and recognised as such. It seems as though the age-old revolt of Adam, all the wickedness of idolatry and self-righteousness, is again trying to become an event. There is a new and we might almost say a more frightful danger : that even as those who are saved, we might still be lost. That is the surgeon's knife. That is how God's mercy comes to His children. That is how He holds and bears and guides them

The neighbour is indeed and necessarily a problem—not to their perdition but to their salvation. For we have to continue that their meeting with the neighbour cannot be an insoluble problem, a problem in face of which they are helpless, a danger to life. It comes to them from the God whose children they are, from whom they come, who has loved them, and whom they love in return. It is a matter of the terrible seriousness of confirmation. If they are not God's children at all, if their love to God is a lie, then the seriousness of this encounter is the mortal seriousness of non-confirmation. How, then, can it be otherwise than that the confirmation of the children of God is also accomplished in the shadow of this dark possibility? But however near to the brink of this abyss their way may actually lead them, we can no more expect a fulfilment of this possibility in the life of the children of God than that their love to God should cease. If they cannot cease to testify that God has found them, they cannot finally and ultimately want to withdraw from the order in which God wills to be praised, from the neighbour that He has appointed, however difficult it may be to find themselves in co-existence with him, and even though they might prefer a thousand times to have it otherwise. They will, therefore, accept the fact—and this is where love to the neighbour really begins—that as the man he is, and therefore as a sinful, afflicted fellow-man, he is what they themselves are, and holds up to them a mirror in which they would rather not look. In face of this mirror they naturally have the greatest desire to revolt as Adam did. And that fact is a confirmation how much the mirror is needed. It will compel them to trust again and this time absolutely in grace, and not to entertain any illusions about the fact that, without their new birth by the Word and Spirit of God, they would be lost like everyone else. For that reason they can only repeat what they know already, but never know too well. For that reason they can only thankfully confirm their existence as the children of God. There cannot actually be a new outbreak of the revolt of Adam. Forgiven sin can, of course, still continue in all its guilt and corruption, but it cannot again become sin unforgiven and triumphant. The crucified Jesus Christ does not contract out of the mediatorial position which He adopted in His resurrection and ascension. He does not, therefore, contract out of that solidarity and identity with sinful and afflicted fellow-man, in which as neighbour He crosses the path of His own. If it is He who meets them as the neighbour, this meeting can again reveal to them all their peril, again remind them of the lostness from which they are redeemed—but it cannot lead them to a new catastrophe, a new lostness. The neighbour can be to them avenging Law only in the framework of the Gospel, only as the bearer and representative of the mercy of God, which always involves chastisement. Therefore the meeting with Him will be to their salvation. They will praise God, according to the will of God. They will therefore love their neighbour. And this will begin with the fact that, however unwillingly, they accept his existence : and indeed in the last resort, beyond all unwillingness, they accept it willingly.

In concrete terms, this will mean, negatively, that faced with the problem of the neighbour whom they must love they will not take refuge in any form of religiosity under the title of love to God. In his well-known and familiar way, A. Ritschl sponsored the statement that " love to God has no free play for action apart from love to the brethren " (*Unterricht i.d. chr. Religion*, 1875, § 6, note *a*). And unfortunately R. Bultmann repeated that " there is . . . no obedience apart from the concrete situation in which I stand as a man among men, no obedience directed straight to God . . . so I can love God only by willing what He wills, by really loving my neighbour " (*Jesus*, 1927, p. 106). But that cannot be true, since for the community no less than for the individual it would exclude not only the practice of meditation, contemplation and oblation, but in the last resort prayer as well and Sunday worship and Sunday itself as the Lord's Day. The relationship between love to God and love to the neighbour is not that love to the neighbour is the only possible form of love to God and as such, as it were, absorbs the latter, or makes it invisible. In fact, the two relationships in which the children of God exist, the one to the invisible God and the other to the visible brother, come together in certain concrete activities, which do not coincide completely and of which we must not deny the one in favour of the other. It is, of course, true that all the activity of the children of God in the world which now is and passes is subject to the law of obedience and therefore to the law of neighbourly love. This is no less true of prayer than of work, of Sunday than week-day, of the solitariness than the fellowship of our existence. There is, therefore, no action of which we cannot also be asked concerning its relation to the neighbour posited for us (just as there is nothing of which it is irrelevant to ask whether it takes place in love to God). There cannot, therefore, be any question of using love to God as a refuge from the problem of the neighbour whom we must love. Meditation, contemplation, even theological activity and the like, cannot be advanced as an excuse for failure towards our neighbour, or as a mitigation or evasion of the embarrassment which he causes us. This is impossible because we cannot do anything meaningful or serious in these other spheres without at once being reminded of what we are trying to escape. If we really can find refuge in a safe sphere of religiosity, devotional edification and theology, quite apart from the plight and task created by our neighbour, then this is only a sign that we cannot do anything serious or meaningful in this sphere, that it has already become for us a heathen temple which can only be destroyed. We come under the saying in Hos. 6[6] : " I will have mercy and not sacrifice," as expounded in Mt. 9[13], 12[7]. Not that we are called away from true sacrifice, from a genuine religiosity, devotional edification and theology—as is often rashly concluded—but we are called back from that heathen temple to a real obedience to the twofold commandment in its unity and therefore to true sacrifice. There may, of course, be an equally arbitrary and impossible flight from love to God to a wrongly understood love to the neighbour. The children of God renounce all movements of flight. The life of the children of God is fulfilled in a rhythm of this twofold love, and there is nothing more senseless and impossible than to play off the one against the other. The children of God " abide " in love : and this applies to both, because they know that, once they have fled to God, there is no other place to which they can flee.

But that they accept the existence of the neighbour, and willingly so, can never be the last word on the subject. To accept my neighbour necessarily means to accept his service. As we have seen, if I really recognise him as my neighbour, he serves me by showing me in his own person my sin and misery, and in that way the condescension of God and the humanity of Jesus Christ the Crucified. We had to lay all the emphasis upon the fact that this is the actual content of my meeting with the neighbour as such. Of course, Jesus Christ is always concealed in the neighbour. The neighbour is not a second revelation of Jesus Christ side by side with the first. When he meets me, the neighbour is not in any sense a second Christ. He is only my neighbour. And it is only as such and in his difference from Christ, only as a sign instituted by Christ, that we can speak of his solidarity and identity with Christ. Therefore once again to love the neighbour necessarily means that we actually allow him, just as he is, and as we see him, to do the service which he has to do us. But again that means that we allow him to call us to order, to remind us of our place. Our place is not that of those who boast of a possession and have therefore to substantiate a claim. It is only by forgiveness that the children are saved from the judgment of God. That they have received forgiveness is their new birth, the work of the divine Word and Spirit within them. That they ought to live by forgiveness is the new life which is given them with all the gifts of faith, knowledge, holiness, joy, humility and also love, which are included in this life. The neighbour cannot bring us to this place. How could he ? If we are not forgiven, our neighbour has nothing at all to say to us when he exemplifies our sin and misery. Our meeting with him can only lead to another act in the great revolt of Adam. We certainly will not let him say what he has to say to us. We certainly will not love him for fear he might try to say it. But if we are forgiven, if we find it necessary to remain in this place, if we know how pressing is the temptation secretly to leave it for an apparently nobler one, if we see the precariousness of our existence as the children of God and know that it is not in our power to maintain ourselves in an existence which we have not even founded for ourselves, then we shall obviously be grateful for every factual reminder that this and this alone is our place, and for every barrier which prevents us from leaving it. And this factual reminder and barrier is the neighbour. The neighbour cannot forgive me my sin. But if my sin is forgiven, my neighbour can say to me that I need this forgiveness, that I cannot choose between a life of forgiveness and some other life which will perhaps illumine me better. The neighbour can keep me to the fact that a choice and decision has already been made concerning me in this respect. The neighbour can speak to me about my own confession of sin. He can ask me whether I am still resolved and ready to stand by it. He can ask me whether I am still resolved and ready actually to live as the one I have confessed before God to be. He can ask me whether my confession is a real confession, i.e., a decision which cannot be withdrawn. He asks me this as he holds before me that mirror. I will not let this question be put without resistance, but I will be grateful that it is put. I will say to myself that I cannot be questioned too much or too seriously and stringently on this matter. I so easily forget the thing I am questioned about. And if I really did forget it, it would mean the collapse of my existence as a child of God. I will therefore willingly and joyfully accept what the neighbour has to show me, because I am actually in need of it. Whether willingly and wittingly or not, in showing it, my neighbour acquires for me a sacramental significance. In this capacity he becomes and is a visible sign of invisible grace, a proof that I, too, am not left alone in this world, but am borne and directed by God. But this fact alone means that I am actually bound to this neighbour. He does me the service of reminding me of my place. He reveals my lostness, and in that way he tells me indirectly but quite definitely that I can only live by grace. And in so doing he comes right into my existence. His co-existence with me loses its external, incidental and unnecessary character. Because I exist, therefore, and in the same way, he exists. How can I help loving him when he does me this service ? And we get exactly the same result from the particular content of his service. He tells me what I am and where I belong by what he himself is. He calls me to order by calling me into line, and in the first instance into line with himself. He tells me that I am such an one as himself. Therefore at any rate in personal relation to himself, he takes me right out of the private existence which I perhaps thought I could achieve for myself. He shows me that there is a fellowship of sin and misery : a place where it is concretely true between us men that we cannot accuse each other ; that we cannot claim any advantages, any superiority or superior position ; that we all have to proclaim our common bankruptcy.

This is not in itself the fellowship of grace and forgiveness. But when I see myself placed with a fellow-man in this fellowship, the fellowship of sin and misery, I can hardly help understanding it as at least a pointer to the fellowship of grace and forgiveness and so taking it quite seriously for that reason. The reality of the common need in which I see us both would be no less even if it were an open question whether it is matched by the reality of a common aid. The fact that I myself know the reality of a help in need cannot divide me from the man who does not seem to know it, who seems only to know his need, and even that not properly. If I know my own need and see another in the same need, that is enough to drive and bind and engage me to him. Because I know the help of God, I shall also know that the need in which God helps is the judgment of God. And under the judgment of God I shall not be separated from the other, but see myself bound to him, even if I do not know whether he knows with me the help of God. How can I help loving him when I see him placed with me under the judgment of God ? This reality on which I have stumbled with him is it not of itself strong enough to create a strong fellowship between him and me ? Certainly we cannot say that this fellowship has any ultimate and real strength, any autonomous strength, if we consider it purely as such. Its true and abiding strength is only in the strength of the fellowship to which it points. Fellowship in sin and misery is not usually true and abiding as such, and therefore in the last analysis it is not usually strong, but where it is, it quickly and distinctly dissolves into its opposite. The judgment of God certainly places men in a common need. But considered purely as such it would necessarily tear them apart and set them against one another, thus increasing their need. And the fact that they are torn apart and set against one another, the totality of isolation and dissension, is far more characteristic of the world which stands under the judgment of God than is the solidarity of folly and wickedness, sorrow and anguish, which is not wanting in the picture, and in the promotion of which it is thought that not a little help can be found. The neighbour puts the child of God in all seriousness and without any reserve into this fellowship, the fellowship of sin and misery. When he sees himself put there, when he loves his neighbour even in this fellowship, the fellowship has already secretly ceased to be *only* this. If it is a child of God who loves, even in this fellowship of sin and misery love to the neighbour cannot possibly mean that he can be satisfied and content to be characterised by the other as " such an one himself," or to recognise in him " such an one as himself." But this result of his meeting with the neighbour will inevitably have the consequence that he knows himself to be summoned afresh to the love of God, the God who first loved him in his sin and his misery. The encounter has certainly done him the service of pointing him afresh to the grace of God by reminding him of his lostness. It will therefore cause him to seek anew the one without whom he can be nothing. But it was the neighbour who mediated this reminder. It was the neighbour who came into his life with this benefit. He cannot therefore make this movement of new love to the gracious God by himself. He cannot dispense with the neighbour. For him, the child of God, the dissolution of his private existence by the known solidarity of need cannot be reversed. He cannot forget the one with whom he has seen himself in the same condemnation. He cannot leave him to his own devices.

For the one who not only knows the need, but also the help in need, a very definite obligation to his neighbour arises out of the fellowship which he has with him in need. Note that only now, even from the standpoint of Law, can we speak meaningfully and seriously about the claim of our neighbour and our responsibility to him. His claim and our responsibility are a direct result of the fact that he has done us a service and benefit as a living sign of the grace of God. In relation to our neighbour, then, the road does not lead, as we are often told, from Law to Gospel—there is no road that way—but from

Gospel to Law. We shall, of course, have to speak very definitely of our neighbour as a sign of the Law, of his claim and our responsibility to him. There can be no question of our being content simply with the fact that we ourselves are summoned afresh to the love of God. If we are, then the meeting with the neighbour has not really taken place at all. We have not really participated in his service and benefit. A solidarity of need has not really been established between him and me. But if this has really taken place, if I have entered into an indestructible relationship with him, then the moment I draw the conclusion that I must love God afresh and this time truly, the bond between us will inevitably turn into a question : What is to become of him, the other ? And now the fact that the fellowship of sin and of misery is not as such the fellowship of grace and forgiveness becomes a difficulty. I do not know whether the neighbour who has shown me my need with his need, and in that way has done me service, also knows about the help in need. If I did, if I could assume without more ado that I also stand with him in the fellowship of grace and forgiveness, I could leave him to himself without concern. He would have no claim on me, and I would have no responsibility to him. I would know in advance that without any effort on my part, he has the same comfort as I have and will therefore do as I do. I would know that he, too, is summoned afresh and this time truly to the love of God, and this knowledge would exclude any concern about him.

We might almost hazard the conjecture that the angels know each other in this fellowship which is ultimately and finally freed from the Law. They do not, therefore, have any concern for one another. For that reason they live and move before God in the truest possible unity. And before us too, in the coming world of eternal life, there is a similar relationship one to another, a relationship which is absolutely free and therefore indissoluble.

But it belongs to the conditions of the present, passing world, of which we are members even as the children of God, that here and now we do not know each other in this way. We cannot, therefore, achieve this unconcern. We know our own redemption in need only as we look to God in Jesus Christ, only as we listen to His Word, and not as we look to our own being and activity as such. And we know of ourselves that this looking and listening is always necessary. As the children of God we know that this looking and listening can never be left behind as unnecessary. It is always before us as something which we have to do afresh. The fact that in our need we look to God in Jesus Christ and listen to His Word and then love God afresh and this time truly, is something which, if it happens, we can only accept as grace. And that is how we stand here and now towards our neighbour, with the difference that while we can, of course, accept grace for ourselves, we cannot accept it for him. We can know that God loves him, and that His Word is for him. But we cannot know that in his need he looks to God and listens to His Word and is comforted. We cannot know that we also stand with him in the fellowship of grace and forgiveness. Even the closest personal acquaintance will not allow us any unconcern in this respect. Even the strongest conjectures we have of him in respect of this fellowship will not reduce the definite assumption that he is always just as much in new need of this looking and listening as we are. And for that reason, I cannot discharge my duty to him simply by summoning him to love God with me.

It was Augustine who (e.g., *De doctr. chr.* I, 22 ; *De civ. Dei* X, 3, 2) deduced from the *diliges proximum sicut te ipsum* that the *diligere* must consist in moving the neighbour (*hoc cum eo debet agere . . ., ut ei quantum potest commendet . . .*) to love God. If we cannot make any use of the doctrine of self-love presupposed by Augustine, we can hardly give this content to love for our neighbour.

I myself do not love God either of my own volition or because someone has told me that I should do so. I myself cannot suppose that I shall find help in my need by loving God. If I love God in my need, I do so because I must. But I must do so, because God has already helped me in that need by His love. If it is not true of my neighbour that he loves God because he must love Him—and I cannot know whether this is true of him : I must therefore reckon with the fact that it might not be true of him—then the summons to love God might only mislead him. It would lead him to assume that I can do something that he cannot do, as though a child of God were a kind of technician, whose hands he has only to watch closely to become the same. It would be to him a law whose fulfilment could not take him any further than to a love of the most terrible gods and idols. It would awaken the false hope of having found a means to help himself in his need. I cannot, therefore, satisfy the claim which my neighbour has upon me by this summons. Any attempt to do so would be an attempt to evade the claim, a clear token that at bottom I have no real concern for him. By summoning him to do something which, as I well know, can only happen when something has already been done for him, I repudiate any responsibility for the latter being done. I break off fellowship with him at the decisive point of answering the question : how can he ever come to love God ? how does it help him to say that he must love God, as I myself must love Him ? And if I can break off fellowship with him at this point, how does it stand with myself ? How little thankful I evidently am for the service and benefit which the neighbour has done me. How superficially I am related to him in the depth of need. And how dark is my own way before me. How doubtful is my own love to God if I dare to enforce it upon my neighbour as a demand to make it a law.

We must be very clear that much well-meant and even Christian concern for the neighbour is actually in this forbidden direction of Law. What we have and intend to offer to our neighbour in alleged fulfilment of our duty towards him is an open or concealed " thou shalt," a counter-claim which is made upon him. It need not be only a moral claim. Even as a religious and Christian claim it may still be Law : the belief that the other man ought to believe, to examine himself, to be converted, to subject himself to God, and therefore to love God in his need. And when this belief does not find any or any adequate justification, how quickly it is followed by the conclusion that the other will not let himself be helped, or helped in the right way. We have not really begun to help him at all. We have probably not noticed at all that he wanted to help us and has helped us, and that all that we have to do is therefore to respond : to realise the fellowship which his service has created between himself and us. We are probably completely deceived about ourselves, thinking that we can help ourselves, in the way which we so confidently think we should commend to him. This commendation—of which we ourselves know very well that it does not work out in practice—can, in fact, only mean that we want to be rid of our neighbour, while apparently doing the best we can for him. Is it surprising, then, if so much apparent love to the neighbour does not attain its object in spite of all the enthusiasm put into it, but only meets with misconception, ingratitude and hostility ? If it were genuine love, that could and would not happen. Genuine love would desist even in the smallest and minutest things from putting the neighbour under the Law.

If this way cannot be considered, that does not mean that I will seek refuge in the excuse that I am not God, and therefore that I am not in a position to let the grace of the Word and Spirit be imparted to my neighbour, and in that way to stir up in him the love to God which is irresistible where this help is a reality. Indeed, I am not God, but only a man. Indeed, I cannot help another with what alone deserves to be called help. But does that mean that I am discharged from my responsibility to that other ? Discharged from responsibility that this real help should be imparted to him ? Because I am only a man, have I to choose between " Am I my brother's keeper " and the way of the Law ? On the contrary, there is another alternative—and it is this which I owe to my neighbour—not as a God I am not, but as the man I am—and which gives him the most definite claim upon me. But this alternative consists in the fact that I praise God, i.e., bear witness to my neighbour of the love with which God in Jesus Christ has loved me and him. To love the neighbour, therefore, is plainly and simply to be to him a witness of Jesus Christ. That the duty of love is the duty of witness results from the fact that I am summoned by my encounter with the neighbour to expect to find in him a brother of Jesus Christ and therefore my own brother. I do not know this. I cannot perceive it in my neighbour. All the more reason, therefore, why I should definitely believe it of him when he actually proclaims to me the grace of God, when he acts towards me as a servant of God, when he has acquired for me this sacramental significance. If he has reminded me that I live by forgiveness, how can I not be summoned to assume the same of him ? How can I believe that he will have a different future from myself ? How can I not think of him that as one who is loved by God he will love God in return ? It is this faith in respect of him that I now have to live out. And the living out of this faith is the witness to which he has a claim and which I owe him. It will be as well—just because it is a question of helping the neighbour—not to connect the concept of witness with the idea of an end or purpose. Witness in the Christian sense of the concept is the greeting with which, if and when I believe, I have to greet my neighbour, the declaration of my fellowship with one in whom I expect to find a brother of Jesus Christ and therefore my own brother. I do not will anything and I may not will anything in rendering this witness. I simply live the life of my faith in the concrete encounter with the neighbour. The strength of the Christian witness stands or falls with the fact that with all its urgency this restraint is peculiar to it. Neither to myself nor to anyone else can I contrive that help will actually be given in need. Therefore in my testimony I cannot follow out the plan of trying to invade and alter the life of my neighbour. A witness is neither a guardian nor a teacher. A witness will not intrude on his neighbour. He will not " handle " him. He will not make him the object of his activity, even with the best intention. Witness can be given only when there is respect for the freedom of the grace of God, and therefore respect for the other man who can expect nothing from me but everything from God. It is in serious acknowledgment of his claim and our responsibility that we do not infringe this twofold respect. I only declare to the other that in relation to him I believe in Jesus Christ, that I do not therefore meet him as a stranger but as my brother, even though I do not know that he is. I do not withhold from him the praise which I owe to God. In that way I fulfil my responsibility to my neighbour.

Now there are three decisive forms of this witness. We cannot draw up any general order of precedence or define the relationship between them. We can only say that if I really love the other—without withdrawing from, but also without intruding on him—all three are equally complete and adequate in themselves and yet all three are equally indispensable. Therefore my love and witness are basically fulfilled in each of the three forms, but basically they must always assume all the three forms.

(*a*) The first form of witness is that I do not grudge my neighbour the word as a word of help in his and my need. If I have really been helped myself and I now find myself in the company of another in that fellowship of sin and misery, then I shall have something to say to him and must say something to him about the other side which this need has for me. I would not be the man I am, if I wanted to withhold this knowledge. The only word of real witness is indeed that which is a declaration of this knowledge. How uncertain we really are of this knowledge (even if we think we are ever so certain of it), we only experience perhaps at the moment when we know that we are summoned to such a word of real witness. If the heart were full of the knowledge of the grace of Jesus Christ, the mouth would speak out of itself. But if neither is the case, then there is a pressing temptation to avoid what ought to be said, and merely for the sake of saying something to talk of things which are irrelevant.

There are two ways especially in which we may fail to bear true witness. The first is by talking about our own sin and need as such. It cannot, of course, be contested that when we bear witness we have to speak about our sin and need, for if we have to speak about the hope of a fellowship in help we cannot omit to speak about a fellowship in need. But while we have to speak about this, the witness itself does not begin there. We have to speak about it, but it must not become too prominent, it must not become the main theme. When I speak about it, I am not really praising God. It is not in any way helpful to my neighbour, indeed it is nothing new, to tell him how bad I have been and to what extent I am just such an one as himself. The story of my misery which I can tell him will at best be an interesting story. And it is more than probable that as the narrator of the story I will indulge my vanity, and evoke a corresponding vanity in the other in relation to the story of his misery. I cannot, of course, suppress the knowledge of my misery. I ought not to suppress it. But so long as I dwell on it, I do not express the knowledge of my salvation. There is, therefore, no witness. The second way in which there is no true witness is when I talk about those experiences, states and events in my life, in which I apparently think that I can see an alleviation or even a removal of my need. Here, too, we must say : how can it be otherwise than that we should also speak of our experience of help in need, when we want to speak about the help itself ? How can we suppress this note, or why should we ? But even this note as such is not itself the note of that witness which we owe to the neighbour. What I give him with the story of my positive experiences will only be relatively new, because he himself may not be entirely devoid of such experiences in his own way. And if I still make an impression on him, it is more than likely that this impression will be a legal one, which will lead him into error instead of helping him. Thus, while I can and must say that I know from my own experience the help which I have to attest, this experience of mine must not be put in the centre, it must not be the autonomous theme of what I say, if my word is not to lose the character of true witness. Either way, the temptation is strong, because it has to do with elements of our knowledge about which we cannot and must not omit to speak. But it is also strong because we are never at a loss for words when we come to speak of our sin and our positive experiences. Either way, that is, we seem to have a rich and certain knowledge. How easy to confuse this knowledge of ourselves with the much less intimate and tangible knowledge of the help itself. How easy, therefore, to speak of these things in and with the witness which is required of us. All the more urgent the need to distinguish and separate. To that end, we must remember that if I am a genuine sinner and have a real

experience of God's help, then that is true, and in its simple truth
it will speak for itself, and it will have the power of a sign pointing to
the help itself : just as another man may by the very fact of his
existence be to me a sign of the grace of God. In the witness required
of me, a right to speak cannot be denied to my knowledge of these
two things. But this self-knowledge is not important in proportion
to what I say about it, but in proportion to the fact that it *is* as I
say, and is *seen* to be so, irrespective of what I say. But it *is* as I
say, and is *seen* to be so, when knowing myself—and we may grant
occasionally speaking about myself—I am not really concerned to
speak at all about myself and my sin and my experiences as an
independent theme, but only about the help itself and as such.

When it is a matter of bearing testimony, there can be only one
theme and centre of what I say. And that is the indication of the
name of Jesus Christ as the essence and existence of the loving kindness in which God has taken to Himself sinful man, in order that he
should not be lost but saved by Him. This name, and in the strict
sense only this name, the name of the Helper, is what we know about
help in need, and therefore can and must speak. This name is the
word which we do not grudge our neighbour, but with which we have
to greet him as a future brother. Where there is genuine love for the
neighbour this name cannot and must not be withheld. The only
word which is praise of God and a witness to the neighbour is a word
which is praise of Jesus Christ and witness about Him. Every word
which is that is true praise of God and a true witness to the neighbour.
Such a declaration of the name of Jesus Christ will be a full recognition
of what Jesus Christ is and of what has been done by Him. It will
be a critical word, unsettling, pointing away, excluding the claims of
all other names in which we might seek refuge. It will always be a
word of thankful adoration before the majesty of free grace revealed
in this name. But necessarily it will also be a word of confession, i.e.,
a word in which our recognition of this name as the name of the Lord
is irrevocably revealed. But it will depend upon and maintain that
assertion of the name which the name has created for itself among
men. That means that it will be a churchly word, i.e., a word proceeding from the Church and calling to the Church. And its churchly
character will consist concretely in the fact that it is basically an
expository word, the explaining and applying of Holy Scripture as
the primal witness to Jesus Christ which underlies and sustains all
the rest. It is when I speak a word like this to my neighbour that I
fulfil my responsibility to him. I tell him what I know of the other
side of my and, as I hope, his need. This other side of the need, if
indeed there is this other side, i.e., if God is manifest to man, is simply
Jesus Christ. That God should be manifest to the neighbour in his
need, that his need should have this other side, is something which I
cannot control or foresee. But God can make use of my service to

make it true. I have to show myself prepared and ready for this service by not refusing to the neighbour my word of witness. I refuse it if I am silent or if I speak of things which are irrelevant. In the latter case my words are just words : I do not love my neighbour in deed and in truth. If my witness is a witness to the name of Jesus Christ, it is not just a word, but as a word it is the most concrete act, in the strictly literal sense it is the " expression " of praise of God and love to the neighbour. That it is not in my power to give this work the efficacy by which it is to the neighbour the fulfilment of revelation, the imparting of the Word and Spirit of God, by which therefore his need takes on that other side—this limitation belongs to its very nature as witness. We cannot try to transcend the limitation without destroying its nature as witness. We have to respect the limitation, especially if we do not want to cease loving our neighbour. But within this limitation there can be no doubt that we not only say the right thing but in doing so do the right thing to our neighbour when, because we are really concerned about him, we speak to him freely about the name of Jesus Christ.

(b) The second form of the witness consists in the fact that I give assistance to my neighbour as a sign of the promised help of God. At this point we touch the sphere in which love to the neighbour or the active expression of that love is particularly or even exclusively to be sought, according to a widespread view. But there is no place here for an emphasising or exclusive emphasising of this sphere. Certainly there can be no question of my duty to speak to my neighbour being limited or replaced by my duty to assist him, as though this were a different duty. The question could only arise—and also the notion that the witness of deed only begins here—if I did not properly comply with my duty to speak to my neighbour. But in that case it would already be decided that I do not properly comply with my duty to assist my neighbour, and that even my supposed actions in this new sphere are not at all in order. In point of fact it is simply a question of another, if necessary, form of the same duty. The need of my fellow-man, the need of his impotent attempt to live, the revelation of which makes him my neighbour, expresses itself like my own need in specific sicknesses, derangements and confusions of his psycho-physical existence. It expresses itself in the fact that his attempt to live is foredoomed to failure and confronted with death. I cannot really arrest this process either in its inner necessity or in its manifestations. I cannot help my neighbour to the extent that I can as little save him from death as I can myself. It is in the helplessness, in which we confront ourselves, that there consists the fellowship of sin and misery into which I see myself placed by him and with him. And for that very reason I shall not speak to him of myself but of Jesus Christ : of Jesus Christ as the Helper who is the end of this process, of Jesus Christ as life in death and beyond death. But how can I speak my word of witness without substantiating it, making it my own word, by showing that I participate in the sicknesses, derangements and confusions of his psycho-physical existence : participate not only as a fellow-sufferer— the concept sympathy is inadequate, as many in the world have more truly found than many in the Church—but as one who knows where help is to be found : knows, because I have already been actually helped in Jesus Christ in respect of my own sufferings. I can as little help my neighbour as myself. But I cannot be helped, as I am helped, without being laid under an obligation to tell my neighbour what help there might be. The help will be alien (as compared with the sin and misery of his attempt to live in his own strength). It will be help from without, the help of a brother. But it is a help which he needs and can use, and that help does exist. I myself am not the alien, the one who comes from without, the brother who can really help him. Christ alone is this brother ; I can be so only by His commission. But how can I have this commission ? How can I speak to my neighbour about Jesus Christ, without also witnessing to this real and helpful brother by my attitude to the psycho-physical manifestation of his need ? My word of witness is a lie if I do not substantiate it in such a way that my attitude is a declaring of the brother, Jesus Christ. If my attitude is not a confirmation of what I say, if in my existence I fall short, as it were, of my word, I speak but I do not believe, I do not actually affirm what I say. And what kind of praise of God is that ? If I believe, if I affirm what I say, if I affirm Jesus Christ to be the real, helpful brother of my needy neighbour, then I must act towards this neighbour as a brother. Certainly as a brother only by commission. Certainly as a brother who is incapable of any help on his own account. But all the same a brother who is summoned to a definite action. This brotherliness, this action, can only be an indication. But because and in so far as I have to say this word to him, it is always an action, and a brotherly action at that. To substantiate this word to the neighbour necessarily means that I assist him as one brother assists another, that my action is an action for him. The limit within which I can act for him is clear : I can do nothing for him, which as my doing is identical with the only truly helpful assistance which God gives in Jesus Christ. By my assistance, I can only set up a sign of that assistance. But even in this limited sense I can and should and must act for him. And for the neighbour the sign of this real assistance can be all that may show and remind him that the vital need, in which he cannot help himself and no other man can help him, has nevertheless a limit. We cannot set the limit to this need. But we—who ourselves know its limitation by Jesus Christ—can and must act in such a way that it becomes clear to the neighbour in his life that there is this Nevertheless, this limit. How can that become clear to him ? Obviously because he is granted certain, even if only temporary and partial, reliefs and mitigations of his evident need, when a halt is called to that need at some definite point and in some definite measure. And I can purposefully see that this happens, i.e., with a view to this result. If I do so, this is the assistance, the brotherly action, the action on his behalf which within the clear limit of my commission and capacity is required of me. If I fail to give him this assistance I make the word which I may perhaps try to speak to him a lie. And I cannot excuse myself by saying that I was required to do the impossible. If I give him this assistance, I still owe him the real help which he needs. I cannot therefore pride myself on my action. But within this obligation I have fulfilled my responsibility to this extent : I have set up a sign of real help. I have done what I am required to do, and what I actually can do, in terms of my obligation. The fact that I have done so, that my efforts in this direction have been accepted as the required setting up of a sign, I cannot, of course, ascribe to myself. It is grace, and as such I can only receive and believe it. And that I have done what I have done successfully, i.e., that the sign has really shown him what it is supposed to show him in his need, is not in my power, nor in the last resort is it in the sphere of my knowledge. In this respect, too, I can only be ready for service with my brotherliness, to be used by the true brother Jesus Christ as and when He wills. These are two further considerations which will keep us humble even in the most zealous and sincere activity for others. But they cannot destroy the clear necessity and possibility of that activity.

Supposing we take the most obvious and illuminating case of possible assistance which one man can give another in this sphere. By sacrificing himself he can save the physical life of another. (This is the case which is, of course, emphasised in 1 Jn. 3[16], cf. Jn. 15[13], as a confirmation of love for the brother.) Can he really help him by doing this ? No, he has not saved him from death ; for sooner or later death will overtake the one who is saved. Can he give his act the character of a sign of real help in face of death ? No, for even the purest intention which he may have in this expressive act cannot create for it this character if it does not have it already, whatever may be his intention. Can he give to this expressive act the effect that the one who is saved does, in fact, recognise the sign of real help in face of death, the witness to Jesus Christ which is given him by it ? Again : No, he cannot do that. Many a person has been saved from death by another without receiving and accepting in that event the witness of the one who saves him. He cannot really make the one who is saved see what there is to see in the act. Even, then, in this simplest and clearest instance of one man assisting or acting for another there has to be at least a threefold divine miracle if witness is to be borne by the service of the one to the other and if that witness is to be real assistance. Even the one who saves life cannot escape humility : for what has he done, if this threefold miracle does not occur ? But how can it be disputed that the saving of physical life, which the one can do for the other, can actually mean for this other a knowledge of the limit of his need, a redemption in the light of which he learns to believe in the redemption, a comfort which will not fail, when the death which has for the moment been averted comes ? Why should we not be summoned, in specific instances, at least to offer our neighbour this promising service ? Why should we not trust in its efficacy, when it is plainly demanded of us in certain cases ?

We shall have to be clear that our action does not give us control of the decisive miracle. But we act rightly, and therefore with the promise that it will be a brotherly action, only when we count on the decisive miracle as a miracle of God. All this can be meaningfully applied to other less obvious and illuminating possibilities, when it is " only " a matter of helping the sick life of another to rather better health, of lightening a little the burden he has to carry, of comforting him a bit in his trouble, of bringing a bit of joy into his sadness, of helping him in one way or another in the fight with inward difficulty or the outward hindrances to which he is subject. " Only ? " There are no quantitative distinctions here. Love can be small or non-existent in the greatest act for another, and it can be real and strong in the smallest. As we are told in 1 Cor. 13³, I may give all my goods to the poor and let my body be burned, without it being any use to me, because in spite of it all I have not love. But " whosoever shall give to drink unto one of these little ones a cup of cold water only, in the name of a disciple, verily I say unto you, he shall in no wise lose his reward " (Mt. 10⁴²). And " pure religion and undefiled before our God and Father is this, to visit the fatherless and widows in their affliction . . ." (Jas. 1²⁷). Love to the neighbour is weighed, not measured. We are nowhere dispensed either from the great thing, if it is a matter of the great, or from the small, if a matter of being faithful in that which is the least. Everything must be done by us at the right time and in the right place : everything with the clear knowledge that we are unable even to give the sign, let alone to make it effective, to bring the help which it attests ; but everything with the even clearer knowledge that we are required to give the sign, and to give it in deed as well as in word, that from the one motive of real obedience we will be content with the promise ; and that therefore as far as we understand and are able there must be this helping, lightening, comforting, and bringing of joy, and it is our task. If it does take place, and, quite apart from any claim, if we are in a position to cause it to happen, why should we not be confident to bear witness of Jesus Christ to our neighbour in this second form, the form of our little assistance, and therefore be obedient to the commandment to love him ? It is unnecessary to say that both the obedience in which alone this can happen and the spontaneity in which alone we can obey are possible and actual only in faith.

(c) The third form of witness consists in this : that I substantiate to my neighbour by my attitude what I have to say to him by word and deed. Here again it is not a question of a third thing, which has to be added to a first and second. If it had still to be added, then the first two, even my word and deed, would not be the witness which I owe to my neighbour. Again there can be no witness by an attitude apart from the word and deed. The witness in question is that of an attitude in the word and deed, of the word and deed as they become event in a definite attitude. By attitude as opposed to word and deed we have to understand the disposition and mood in which I meet my neighbour, the impression of myself which I make on him in speaking to him and acting on his behalf. The only attitude which we can regard as consistent with witness is the evangelical attitude. If my words and acts are real witness to Jesus Christ, then in, with and under them there is an additional and decisive something of my own subjection to the lordship of Jesus Christ, of the comfort of forgiveness, by which I myself live, of the liberty of the children of God in which I myself move. It is additional, i.e., it too speaks to

my neighbour in my words and deeds as such.   It is an atmosphere
which touches and surrounds him.   The neighbour hears my few words
and enjoys my little assistance.   But he also notices that I myself
look and listen where my words and deeds seem to invite him to look
and listen.   What I have to say to him is perhaps in itself very clear
and true, a very clear and firm indication of the one thing necessary.
And at the same time my practical attitude is perhaps one which has
in itself the whole nature and possibilities of sincere illuminating assistance.   But supposing the picture which the other gains of me does
not harmonise with these expressions in the sense of witness ?   Supposing with my person I say something quite other than with my word
and deed ?   In speaking and acting, have I also considered that these
two can only be witness to the extent that they are the witness of
my person ?   Naturally my person cannot claim to replace to the other
man the only convincing and helpful person of Jesus Christ.   And
it is not in my power even to be a witness of Jesus Christ with my
person.   And especially I have no power to make an impression by
the witness of my person.   But that does not alter the fact that I
am summoned to give my neighbour the witness which is the witness
of my person and attitude.   And if this is not done, again there is
no witness at all.   It is no witness if the picture which I present in
my words and deeds is in the last resort that of someone who is indifferent, who is busied with his own sufferings and joys, who is
enmeshed in his own activity.   Where, then, is the indication of the
lordship of Jesus Christ ?   If this is the picture I present—and my most
earnest words and sympathetic deeds will not of themselves prevent
me offering it—how can I praise God and love my neighbour, when
my attitude is ultimately heathen ?   It will be surprising if in these
circumstances my sacrifice, however great, is either accepted by God
or respected by men.   Again, my witness is not witness if I come to
the other in a movement which is strong and apparently quite selfless,
yet not in the patience which sees him in the hand of God, but in an
impatience which would take him into my own hand ; not in faith in
the forgiveness which is prepared for him by God, but in a false belief
that I am the man who has to forgive him (which will certainly lead
finally to a knowledge that I cannot forgive him) ; not in the hope on
Christ, in which I can freely give to him, but in a false confidence in
what I have to say to him and he has to be told by me, in what I have
to do for him and he has to receive from me.   If this is my attitude,
then with the best will in the world the picture I present is not a sign
of the reconciliation which took place in Jesus Christ, but only a sign
of the law which is not the Law of Christ.   It is not, therefore,
witness to Christ. It is not the praise of God. It is not the love of my
neighbour, however clear and true my word may be and however
helpful in itself my action.

    For sure, a consideration of this third form of the witness required of us again throws doubt on the whole possibility of loving our neighbour, by witnessing to him of Jesus Christ. To speak to our neighbour about Jesus Christ and to show him brotherly assistance both appear at first sight to be realisable possibilities. But what can I do to ensure that the picture which I offer in my person is evangelical and not heathen or legal? What can I do about the disposition and mood and atmosphere which I spread? " The redeemed must look redeemed." But can we do anything to make this so? Now it cannot be denied that at bottom this is not a question of things right outside the realm of human possibility and decision. If it is required of us that we should be ready for the service to which we are appointed not only in word and deed but also in attitude, too much is not required of us. The limits of our responsibility do not, of course, coincide with the limits of our consciousness of responsibility, to which we might perhaps appeal. Once our attention is drawn to it, there is much we can do in relation to our inward and outward attitude ; not everything, but one thing at least and perhaps the most important thing of all. The redeemed can very well look a little like redeemed. But it is true that here in this question of attitude, more clearly than in that of word or deed, we are reminded that the task appointed us in this time and world, to praise God and love our neighbour, demands more than an isolated doing and not doing—it demands the whole life. Here more clearly—and that is why it is so important that especially this third question should be put—we are reminded that we, who should love our neighbour, are the same who should love God with all our heart, and soul, and mind, and strength. The question of our attitude, of the picture we present, of the impression we make, is not, of course, identical with the question of the totality of our obedience. What is required of us cannot really be reduced to the concepts of sentiment, mood, atmosphere, personality, etc. And we cannot understand the tasks of word and deed without it becoming plain that what is involved is the task of staking our existence, without which neither our word nor our deed can be a witness to Jesus Christ. Yet obviously with the question of our attitude we touch particularly upon the comprehensive question of our existence as such. If in this third sphere there are possibilities, freedom, decision, if we cannot deny that we may be just as conscious of our attitude as of our words and deeds, that we can speak about it and knowingly and willingly alter and amend it, then from this point more nearly than from that of our doing we look out and back to the presupposition of it in our existence before God. Of course, we can and must differentiate between our petty attitude, as well as our petty word and deed, and our existence before God : for the one is only our activity as the children of God in this present, passing world, whereas our being before God is our being in Jesus Christ and in membership of the age which comes and remains. But this differentiation can be made only within the unity of our existence as

15

the children of God. It is we who are involved either way. And the question of our attitude reminds us of this identity in word and deed and to that extent of our existence before God. Who are we—we, who for the praise of God, for the love of neighbour, are summoned to stake our existence in its totality ? What is it that we have to stake and offer ? What is it that we can give our neighbour in word and deed and ultimately and decisively in attitude ? What if this giving is obviously not exhausted when we bear a witness which is apart from ourselves ? What if it is the case rather that we ourselves, the witnesses, must be the witness in word and deed and attitude ? Now we have already indicated that the reality, the work and the effectiveness of our witness can never be in our own power and disposal, but that if there is to be a real praise of God and love of our neighbour in our activity, there has to take place an activity of God which we with our activity can only serve, and which from the standpoint of our activity can only have the character of a miracle. In a few concluding sentences we must now try to clear up this relation between God and us, between His activity and ours, in the service to which we are summoned by the commandment to love our neighbour.

4. We will do this in our survey of the final part of the text of Mk. 12, which so far we have not discussed. What does it mean when it says : " Thou shalt love thy neighbour *as thyself*." One explanation is that by these words, alongside the commandments to love God and the neighbour, a third commandment is set up, that of love to self, and that this love to self is the measure and principle of love to the neighbour. But this explanation we have already rejected. It is true, of course, that we do love ourselves. And in the second commandment—but only here, notice—this is presupposed to be true. But we are not commanded to love ourselves. And this self-love is not mentioned as though it were, so to speak, the normal type and pattern of love to the neighbour. Self-love means, and must mean, to be alone with ourselves, to seek ourselves, to serve ourselves, to think of ourselves. Now it is true that we do this. It is true that we do it even when we love our neighbour. It is true that this self-love is the visible and tangible reality of the one who loves his neighbour. The commandment itself recognises and establishes it to be true. But the commandment : Thou shalt love thy neighbour, is not a legitimation but a limitation of this reality. If I love my neighbour, that is the judgment on my self-love and not its indirect justification. When I love my neighbour I do not apply to him the same good thing as I do to myself when I love myself. Far from it. When I love my neighbour I confess that my self-love is not a good thing, that it is not love at all. I begin to love at all only when I love my neighbour. The only positive meaning of " as thyself " is, then, that we are commanded to love our neighbour as those who love themselves, i.e., as those who in reality do not love, as the sinners that we are. It is as those who in

fact and absolutely and constantly seek themselves and serve themselves and think of themselves, in this reality that we are addressed and claimed by the revelation and commandment of God and therefore concretely by the commandment to love our neighbour. This reality of self-love and therefore of sin is the reality of the life of the children of God in this present, passing world and therefore in relation to this activity. We have already asked who are we who are summoned to love our neighbour ? and what have we to stake and offer who have not only to bear witness but to be witnesses in word and deed and attitude ? We are now given the answer—by the commandment itself —that we can stake and offer ourselves only as sinners. Even as we love our neighbour, it will always be true that we love ourselves, that there is, therefore, no love in us. Our existence is that of those who absolutely and constantly withdraw from love. That, and the fact that we stand under the judgment of the commandment, is the answer which we must give to the question which is made particularly urgent by the problem of our attitude.

Now we must not overlook the fact that even in this final turn the commandment is full of the Gospel. It stamps us as the people we are, and it claims us as such. And in so doing it tells us that we are not to give way to boasting, when we dare to meet our neighbour not only as partners of his need but as those who know of help in his and our need. We are not to take anything to ourselves which does not belong to us, when we dare to do this. The commandment itself states that we are sinners, that there is no love in us. The one who commands us accepts this, as it were, on his own responsibility. In this present passing world he wants us for obedience to his commandment. He wants us as the people we are, i.e., in and with our self-love and therefore our lack of love. The commandment passes judgment on us, but in so doing it does not exclude, but includes us. It seriously accepts us as the children of God, as those who know of help in need, as those who can acquire and execute a divine commission. It summons us to love as those who are without love. It gives us the status of witnesses. And in so doing it cuts us off from all those enervating reflections on the worthiness of our own words and deeds and attitude which might hold us back or call us away from the venture of obedience. It sets us completely free. We are already judged. Even as we are told to love it is decided that we love ourselves and are therefore without love. God knows our existence, and indeed better and more radically than we can ever do even with the most profound of our reflections. When we think about this venture of meeting our neighbour as witnesses —as witnesses of that which is greater than his and our need—all that we can do is to recall that which is told us by the divine commandment itself. No reflections of ours could put it better or more strongly or radically than this critical " as thyself." It is rather to be feared that our reflections would end optimistically, which would poison our supposed obedience to the commandment at the very root, because we would then rely on ourselves rather than wholly and absolutely on the promise. Or else they would end pessimistically, and we would regard ourselves as dispensed from all further attempts to be obedient because too much is required of us in word and deed and attitude. The " as thyself " tells us that *a priori* our obedience is thought of only as the obedience of sinners, and in that way it cuts off both these false paths. For this annihilating " as thyself " invites us to put our trust simply in the fact that the commandment is given us. That we have the commandment is our true being, with which we can and should be satisfied, leaving it to God to decide what will come of our doing and fulfilling of the commandment in view of that other fact which is simultaneously revealed to us, that it is a being of sinners. We have no foreknowledge of it except in Jesus Christ. The justification of our activity, the acceptability of the little praise we offer to God, the truth of the love we give our neighbour, we really have to leave to God. That we can do so, that as we are commanded to love we are invited to cast upon God all our care in respect of the fulfilling of the commandment is again, in this context, the Gospel within the commandment. But if this is the case, it is unequivocally clear that the reality, the work and the effectiveness of our witness—if we do bear witness, if we are witnesses—are not at our own power and disposing. There is, in fact, a risk in which we have no assurance apart from our faith in Jesus Christ. Apart from our faith in Jesus Christ we simply have to accept that risk when we dare to meet the neighbour of whom we know only that he is in need, in the same need as ourselves, meet him in word and deed and attitude as those who have something to say, to show, to give to him, who can be something to him. For what can we be to him ? We can only love him as ourselves, i.e., as those who love themselves and are therefore without love. We have in fact no guarantee—but the one—that all that we say and do and are to him will not betray our self-love and lack of love. Can we believe or hope that in a kindly illusion the other will not be aware of this ? Ought we perhaps to try to support the illusion ? Unfortunately there can be no doubt that very much so-called concern about the neighbour is at bottom only the concern to hide from each other the judgment under which we all stand. However wholesome and good may be our intentions, we do not really love our neighbour. Our words and deeds and attitude cannot in these circumstances be real witness. This hardly needs to be proved. We have only to subject ourselves to the judgment of God. We have to see that we can obey the commandment only as those who are judged by the commandment, that it is the Gospel within the commandment that we should obey as those who are judged by the commandment. When we do, we shall cease trying to hide from each other. There is nothing to hide : we can and should love our neighbour only as the people we are, and therefore " as ourselves." We cannot meet him in a self-invented mask of love. We can only venture, as the men we are, to do what we are commanded in word and deed and attitude, relying entirely on the fact that the one who commands that we—who are without love— should love, will see to it that what we do will be real loving. There can be no question about it—this fidelity to the Gospel in the commandment belongs to our obedience to the commandment as such— we have to rely on the miracle, the free grace of God, to make good what we with our own foresight can only bungle. We have to trust in the fact that Jesus Christ will be present in this meeting with my neighbour. It will be His business, not mine, and however badly I play my part, He will conduct His business successfully and well. We have to rely on the fact that it is Jesus Christ who has given me a part in His business ; that He has not done so in vain ; that He will make use of my service, and in that way make it real service, even though I do not see how my service can be real service. We have to rely on the fact that Jesus Christ is the Lord, in whose hand the other is the neighbour ; that He became man and died for him ; that my lack of love cannot and will not prevent Him calling the other to Him by me. These are not guarantees. They can only be an assurance. But this assurance is required of us when we are commanded : Thou shalt love thy neighbour as thyself. It is only in this assurance that obedience is possible. We can define it in two ways.

(a) The courage with which in obedience to the commandment, without foresight, indeed against all foresight, a man turns to his neighbour to fulfil the commandment by what he does, to be to him a witness in word and deed and attitude—this courage can only be the courage of humility, in which he puts himself at the disposal of the ministry and mission and commission of the Church. The commission to testify is in fact the commission of the Church. And the promise of this commission—the presence of Jesus Christ, His control in the midst of man's perversity, the power of the forgiveness of sin which He pronounces, the power of an action in His name—this promise is the promise which is given to the Church. In holy baptism I am placed by the Church under the promise of the Holy Ghost. I am instructed and comforted and led by the Church. In the Lord's Supper I am nourished by the Church on the true body and blood of Christ to eternal life. And it is in this sacramental positing and ordering of my existence that I lay hold of that assurance and put it into action. It is as I accept this sacramental determination of my existence in all its concreteness that I have the concrete courage for that assurance, and therefore for the obedience whose result I cannot foresee, and therefore for the love of my neighbour. We know, in fact, that the life of the children of God is simply the life of the Church of God.

(b) To lay hold of that assurance and to put it into action means calling upon God in prayer. The promise given to the Church has

still to be received again and again by each of its members. The
Church with its commission and promise lives in its sinful members.
And as the Church for its own sake cannot wish to crowd out and
replace the Lord and the free grace in which He speaks individually
to each individual, again for its own sake it cannot take away from
the individual the calling on this Lord, the direct appeal to His free
grace. Prayer is the subjective determination of the assurance in
which we can love our neighbour, just as the Church and baptism and
the Supper are its objective determination. Praying is the decisive
thing, which makes this assurance possible for us : the casting of our
care upon God : our care about ourselves—how it is with our loving ;
and our care about the other—whether our love will reach him. In
the last resort we can only love the neighbour by praying for ourselves
and for him : for ourselves, that we may love him rightly, and for
him, that he may let himself be loved ; which means that either way
prayer can have only one content and purpose : that according to His
promise Jesus Christ may let His work be done for and to ourselves
and to our neighbour. Praying, asking of God, can consist only in
receiving what God has already prepared for us, before and apart from
our stretching out our hands for it. It is in this praise of God that
the children of God live, who love God, because He first loved them.

CHAPTER III

HOLY SCRIPTURE

CHAPTER III

HOLY SCRIPTURE

§ 19

THE WORD OF GOD FOR THE CHURCH

The Word of God is God Himself in Holy Scripture. For God once spoke as Lord to Moses and the prophets, to the Evangelists and apostles. And now through their written word He speaks as the same Lord to His Church. Scripture is holy and the Word of God, because by the Holy Spirit it became and will become to the Church a witness to divine revelation.

1. SCRIPTURE AS A WITNESS TO DIVINE REVELATION

The theme of dogmatics (cf. *Dogm.* I 1 §7, 1) is the question of the Word of God in the proclamation of the Christian Church, or, concretely, the question of the agreement of this proclamation with Holy Scripture as the Word of God. To answer this question as such we had first to investigate that form of the Word of God which precedes both proclamation and Holy Scripture, i.e., the revelation of God. It is because God has revealed Himself, and as He has done so, that there is a Word of God, and therefore Holy Scripture and proclamation as the Word of God, and therefore a relation and correspondence between the two, and therefore the possibility and necessity of this question of their agreement. We have already answered the question of the concept of revelation presupposed in both these other forms of the Word of God. We have not sought or found this answer at random. We have taken it from the Bible. For the Bible is a sign which, it cannot be contested, does at least point to a superior authority confronting the proclamation of the Church. In contrast to Roman Catholicism and Protestant modernism, we felt that we ought to take this sign seriously. For that reason, at every decisive point we took our answer to the question of revelation from the Bible. And the Bible has given us the answer. It has attested to us the lordship of the triune God in the incarnate Word by the Holy Spirit.

But in so doing it has answered that question concerning itself which we have not yet asked. We now know to what extent it points to a superior authority confronting the proclamation of the Church : obviously to the extent that it is a witness of divine revelation. It is not in vain that we have taken notice of this sign. It has proved itself a true sign. It has shown us something. It has in fact indicated a higher, judicial, decisive authority superior to all the proclamation which takes place in the Church and can claim the authority of the Church. Does the Church recognise this authority ? Does it, therefore, recognise the concrete significance of the Bible as the sign which points to this authority ? Does it recognise that the question of dogmatics must also be its question ? the question of the agreement of its proclamation with this sign, because in, with and under this sign that proclamation is confronted by the Word of God with which it must be in agreement if it would itself be the Word of God ? Dogmatics cannot answer this question for the Church. It can do so only at its own specific place in the Church. But if it is a church dogmatics, how can it give any but a positive answer ?

Now that the content of the biblical witness is before us, we see better than we did that the actual recognition of this witness and the willingness to follow it will always be something which takes place miraculously and very simply, without any special claim. If the biblical witness is obeyed in the Church, it happens quite unassumingly, without the adornment of special grounds and reasons, or any appeal to a prophetic mission or experience or illumination. Looking back on the content of this witness, we can now say that the lordship of the triune God has shown itself to be a fact. If this is so, if therefore obedience to this witness is also a fact, if therefore the proclamation of the Church is actually subjected to and measured by and executed according to this witness, then we will not ask : why the Bible ? and look for external or internal grounds and reasons. We will leave it to the Bible itself, if we are to be obedient to it, to vindicate itself by what takes place, i.e., to vindicate the witness to divine revelation which we have heard in it, to repeat itself in such a way that it can again be apprehended by the obedient man and everyone else. If the obedient man tries to base his obedience on some other calling, as though that were necessary, then at once his obedience is called in question as obedience. Where the lordship of the triune God is a fact, it is itself the basis, and a sufficient basis, for obedience.

Presupposing this obedience, what it means for the proclamation of the Church to be subjected to and measured by and executed according to the biblical witness, is, of course, a very necessary topic of discussion, and we shall take up the question in the last chapter of these prolegomena, when we give the theme and task of dogmatics its final, concrete formulation. Before we come to this question, there is an obvious need—again presupposing that tacit obedience—to think about the Bible as such : its nature as sign, its relation to the thing which it signifies, its normative and critical character in relation to the Church's proclamation, its limiting and determinative significance for the life of the Church both as a whole and in each of its members.

1. *Scripture as a Witness to Divine Revelation* 459

We have to be quite clear about this : that in that tacit obedience in
face of the biblical witness, expressed or unexpressed, there is a quite
definite perception with regard to that witness. Even the statement
we have made already, that it is the witness of revelation, is of itself
important and full of content. But it needs to be elaborated and
explained. And it must not be the only statement. If it is a witness
of revelation, and if, however tacit, there is a genuine and necessary
obedience to it, then the witness itself and as such—as well as the
revelation which it attests—is necessarily in the power of the revelation of the Word of God attested by it, and it necessarily acquires in
the Church, as distinct from all other words and signs, the dignity and
validity of the Word of God. It is not superfluous to think this through
and to state it, for the very reason that our attitude to this witness has
constantly to be re-tested, whether it really is that tacit but genuine
and necessary obedience. The presupposition of this obedience—
which we cannot create, but can only presuppose as a fact—will have
to be clarified by answering the later question of the concrete task
of dogmatics in relation to proclamation. But this clarification is only
possible as we try to bring out the perception with regard to the
character and basic significance of the witness which is contained in
a genuine and necessary obedience to the biblical witness. It is therefore to the doctrine of Holy Scripture that we must turn.

We have now reached the point which, confessionally and doctrinally, the
Reformation Churches of the 16th century found it so important according to
their own conscience and experience expressly to fix and emphasise, as against
the Roman Church on the one hand, and fanatics on the other, that it soon
became the rule, and an increasingly strict rule, to introduce the official explanations of the Confession, and then theological expositions of Evangelical teaching,
with an exposition of this very perception : the perception with regard to the character and significance of Holy Scripture. *Fallitur quisquis aliunde christianismi
formam petit, quam e sacra scriptura*, Melanchthon had already written in the
Preface to his *Loci* of 1521. And the invitation, which at the beginning of 1523
the Council of the city of Zürich issued to the decisive disputation, was significant
for the development of this doctrine. It not only says that " divine Scripture "
ought almost as a matter of form to be the decisive and wholly decisive general
presupposition of the proposed discussion of the division which has arisen in
the Church. But rather threateningly in view of the expected results of this
discussion, it also lays down that " when we have found according to divine
Scripture and truth, we will send everyone home, with the injunction to proceed
or abstain, that none may henceforth preach what is right in his own eyes, without foundation in divine Scripture. . . . And if any is contumacious in this, and
does not come with true divine teaching, we will deal further with him according
to our perception, enjoining that which we will should be maintained." In the
same way the theses which Zwingli drew up for the disputation of Berne in 1528
begin with the clear-cut statement that " the holy Christian Church, whose one
Head is Christ, is born of the Word of God, is incorporated in the same, and
heareth not the voice of a stranger." It has often been remarked that the 1530
Lutheran *Augustana*, as opposed to the contemporary *Confessio tetrapolitana*
with its Zwinglian orientation, does not expressly mention, but only tacitly
assumes this Scripture principle. It must be noted, however, that the memorial
which Zwingli himself then directed to the Emperor (*Fidei ratio*) did not contain

it either, and that there was no emphatic assertion of the principle in the Zürich
" Introduction " of 1523, the Synod of Berne of 1532 and the Confession of Basel
of 1534. If Luther omitted it in his catechisms of 1529, the same must also be
said of Calvin's catechism of 1545. We are not dealing, therefore, with something
which is specifically Reformed : this becomes clear later, when insistence on the
Scripture principle came to be more generally adopted. Since the *Conf. Helv.
prior* and the Genevan *Confession de la foy* (both of 1536) it has been the typical
introductory article of Reformed confessional writings. And the famous opening of Calvin's *Institutio* can only be understood if we see that its bearing is to
assert the Scripture principle in opposition to all those other sources of the knowledge of God which have been destroyed by the Fall. But it also comes right at
the beginning of Melanchthon's *Examen ordinandorum* (1559), of the *Examen
concilii Tridentini* of Martin Chemnitz (1565) and of the two parts of the Formula
of Concord (1579). And if we compare the older orthodox dogmatics, e.g., on
the one side the *Loci* of J. Gerhard (1610 f.) and the *Compendium* of Leonard
Hutter (1610), and on the other the *Loci* of Peter Martyr (1576), the *Institutiones
theologicae* of W. Bucan (1602), the *Syntagma* of Polan (1609) and the *Compendium*
of J. Wolleb (1626), we shall find that if possible the Lutherans put the Scripture
principle at the very peak of their theological system even more ardently and
obviously than did the Reformed. It maintained this role as formally the
basic doctrine of the Evangelical Church until it was first challenged, then replaced
in fact and finally in theory, by the new dogma *De religione*. For the theology
of the 18th and 19th centuries it was generally a respected historical survival
and something of an embarrassment. But we must not overlook the latent
continuity of its existence even at that time. The Bible has always remained
in the Church as the regular textual basis of proclamation. Biblical criticism
and later biblical scholarship, which were now the main interest of theology,
bore indirect, but for that reason all the more impressive, witness to its authority.
And when more recently German Protestantism especially was forced to examine
and give account and defend itself by an internal danger which threatened to
bring to a head the creeping sickness of the previous centuries, it was neither
accident nor caprice that in May 1933 at the head of the so-called Dusseldorf
theses we again find word for word the statement made by Zwingli in 1528.
Again, it was neither accident nor caprice that the Free Reformed Synod of
Barmen-Gemarke in January 1934, the first of the free Synods in which the
Confessional Church was constituted, and then once more and with a definite
polemical delimitation at the Reich Synod of Barmen in May 1934, the Scripture
principle of the Reformation was affirmed and confessionally stated with almost
automatic necessity. It seems to be the case that whether the principle is
expressly formulated or not the *dixit* and *contradixit* contained in it, the attitude
of obedience which answers to it, is essential to Protestantism as such. If there
was no longer the same reaction as at the time of the Counter-Reformation and
again in our own days, if the Church dared simply to abandon the sign of the
Bible dominating its worship and instruction, it would be the end of Protestantism. For in so doing it would cease to protest—the only protest which concerns
it. In the measure that it must and will protest, according to the law of the
concrete twofold antithesis which it has followed, the formulation of this principle
is always unavoidable.

The doctrine of Holy Scripture as such involves therefore the confession in which the Church clarifies that perception which corresponds
to a right and necessary attitude of obedience to the witness of revelation, and in that way adopts and maintains such a position. It is
important to be on our guard at once against the view that we have
to prove and justify this position. When the Bible has spoken as a

witness to divine revelation, and when it has been recognised and acknowledged as such, we are forced into this position ; we have our work cut out to do what we have to do in this position ; we have neither room nor time to ask whether and why we can and will maintain it in the future ; we are neither able to find reasons nor justifications for our attitude. Therefore the doctrine of Holy Scripture can only confirm that we are placed in this position by the witness of revelation. We admit the fact and therefore the necessity of all that that position involves.

We might ask : Is such a confession necessary ? Is it not enough that we are put in this position ? Is not the obedience which we have to give in it itself enough ? Is not every doctrine of Holy Scripture as such a superfluous saying of " Lord, Lord " ? Might we not ask whether such a confession is not even dangerous as a confirmation of our attitude, whether it will not lead again to an attempted defence and justification which will jeopardise our obedience ?

To the first of these questions our answer is that confession of Holy Scripture as a witness to divine revelation is necessary, whenever and to the extent that we are questioned concerning our attitude to it. But in fact we are always being questioned concerning it : by Scripture itself, which always wants us to know what we are doing when we obey it ; by other men, who propose that we should take up some other attitude, and sincerely or insincerely want to know whether we are aware or not of the meaning and the consequences of what we are doing ? and finally by ourselves, inasmuch as obedience and disobedience are constantly at war with each other especially in ourselves. Therefore since the boundary has to be marked out between obedience and disobedience, the confession of Scripture is itself a necessary part of obedience to Scripture.

When in Mt. 7$^{21f.}$ Jesus said that not all who say to Him Lord, Lord shall enter into the kingdom of Heaven, but those who do the will of His Father in Heaven, He did not say that where the will of the Father is done we can or should omit to say Lord, Lord. The fact that confession can be only the confession of obedience does not alter the fact that obedience must still confess itself to be obedience as against the disobedience of ourselves and others, recognising and overcoming the temptation which constantly threatens.

Our answer to the second question is that a confession of Holy Scripture only involves a defence of our position to the extent that in our attitude to it we order ourselves by this confession, i.e., by the clarifying and expressing of the character and value peculiar to the witness of revelation as such. When we do this rightly, when we ground and maintain ourselves in it, there can be no question of a defence and justification of our attitude, but only of a constant indication of its necessity. The content of a true doctrine of Holy Scripture will simply be a development of our knowledge of that law which has its basis and justification in itself, the law under which we stand when we really have to do with the witness of revelation. If our obedience is called in question by a knowledge of this law, this is something which it needs, for we are summoned by it to an obedience which is pure and not confused by defences and justifications.

But as the genuine content of these two questions, we gladly accept the reminder that confession of Holy Scripture, i.e., the explication of the knowledge of its reality and nature contained in obedience to it, is in fact a superfluous and dangerous and in spite of its exactness and completeness an incredible protestation, if the obedience which it presupposes is itself alien to us. On the other hand, if the doctrine of Holy Scripture is simply the necessary exponent of its correct exegesis, we do not forget that the right doctrine of Holy Scripture cannot claim abstract validity, but its confirmation must always be sought and found in exegesis and therefore in Holy Scripture itself.

The basic statement of this doctrine, the statement that the Bible is the witness of divine revelation, is itself based simply on the fact that the Bible has in fact answered our question about the revelation of God, bringing before us the lordship of the triune God. Of course, we could not have received this answer, if as members of the Church we had not listened continually to the voice of the Church, i.e., if we had not respected, and as far as possible applied the exposition of the Bible by those who before and with us were and are members of the Church. About this important definition of true obedience to Scripture, in which there emerges a definition of Scripture itself, we will have to speak explicitly in § 20. And, of course, even then we could not have received this answer if we had not also read and searched and pondered the Bible with our own eyes, if we had not ourselves accepted the responsibility for its correct exposition. That is the second definition of obedience to Scripture, which again points back to a definition of Scripture itself, with which we shall have to deal in § 21. But just as we should ask Holy Scripture in vain about the revelation of God, if we were to sidetrack the exposition of the Church, or to try to spare ourselves the trouble of individual exposition, what is equally necessary, and even more so, is that it should be Scripture which actually does and alone can answer us. The Church can expound, and we can expound, and there is authority and freedom in the Church, only because Scripture has already told us what we are asking about when we ask about God's revelation. The statement that the Bible is the witness of divine revelation is not, therefore, limited by the fact that there is also a witness of the Church which we have to hear, and in addition witness is also demanded of us. The possibility both of the witness of the Church and of our own witness is founded upon the reality of which that statement speaks. Yet all statements which we have still to formulate about those secondary definitions of our obedience to Scripture, all the statements about the necessary authority and equally necessary freedom in the Church itself, can only be expositions of the basic statement that there is a Word of God for the Church : in that it receives in the Bible the witness of divine revelation. Therefore it is the truth of this basic statement which has been tested and proved in the fact that seeking in the Bible we have found in the Bible the answer to our question about God's revelation.

When we examine this statement more closely, we shall do well to pay attention to the particular determination in the fact that we have to call the Bible a witness of divine revelation. We have here an undoubted limitation : we distinguish the Bible as such from revelation. A witness is not absolutely identical with that to which it witnesses. This corresponds with the facts upon which the truth of the whole proposition is based. In the Bible we meet with human words written in human speech, and in these words, and therefore by means of them, we hear of the lordship of the triune God. Therefore when we have to do with the Bible, we have to do primarily with this means, with these words, with the witness which as such is not itself revelation, but only—and this is the limitation—the witness to it. But the concept of witness, especially when we bear clearly in mind its limiting sense, has still something very positive to say. In this limitation the Bible is not distinguished from revelation. It is simply revelation as it comes to us, mediating and therefore accommodating itself to us— to us who are not ourselves prophets and apostles, and therefore not the immediate and direct recipients of the one revelation, witnesses of the resurrection of Jesus Christ. Yet it is for us revelation by means of the words of the prophets and apostles written in the Bible, in which they are still alive for us as the immediate and direct recipients of revelation, and by which they speak to us. A real witness is not identical with that to which it witnesses, but it sets it before us. Again this corresponds with the facts on which the truth of the whole proposition is founded. If we have really listened to the biblical words in all their humanity, if we have accepted them as witness, we have obviously not only heard of the lordship of the triune God, but by this means it has become for us an actual presence and event. If we want to think of the Bible as a real witness of divine revelation, then clearly we have to keep two things constantly before us and give them their due weight : the limitation and the positive element, its distinctiveness from revelation, in so far as it is only a human word about it, and its unity with it, in so far as revelation is the basis, object and content of this word.

To avoid this, there is no point in ignoring the writtenness of Holy Writ for the sake of its holiness, its humanity for the sake of its divinity. We must not ignore it any more than we do the humanity of Jesus Christ Himself. We must study it, for it is here or nowhere that we shall find its divinity. The Bible is a witness of revelation which is really given and really applies and is really received by us just because it is a written word, and in fact a word written by men like ourselves, which we can read and hear and understand as such. And it is as such that we must read and hear and understand it if this is to happen at all and there is to be any apprehension of revelation.

The demand that the Bible should be read and understood and expounded historically is, therefore, obviously justified and can never be taken too seriously. The Bible itself posits this demand: even where it appeals expressly to divine commissionings and promptings, in its actual composition it is everywhere a human word, and this human word is obviously intended to be taken seriously and read and understood and expounded as such. To do anything else would be to miss the reality of the Bible and therefore the Bible itself as the witness of revelation. The demand for a " historical " understanding of the Bible necessarily means, in content, that we have to take it for what it undoubtedly is and is meant to be : the human speech uttered by specific men at specific times in a specific situation, in a specific language and with a specific intention. It means that the understanding of it has honestly and unreservedly been one which is guided by all these consideration. If the word " historical " is a modern word, the thing itself was not really invented in modern times. And if the more exact definition of what is " historical " in this sense is liable to change and has actually changed at times, it is still quite clear that when and wherever the Bible has been really read and expounded, in this sense it has been read " historically " and not unhistorically, i.e., its concrete humanity has not been ignored. To the extent that it has been ignored, it has not been read at all. We have, therefore, not only no cause to retract from this demand, but every cause to accept it strictly on theological grounds.

But when we do take the humanity of the Bible quite seriously, we must also take quite definitely the fact that as a human word it does say something specific, that as a human word it points away from itself, that as a word it points towards a fact, an object. In this respect, too, it is a genuine human word. What human word is there which does not do the same ? We do not speak for the sake of speaking, but for the sake of the indication which is to be made by our speaking. We speak for the sake of what we denote or intend by our speaking. To listen to a human word spoken to us does not mean only that we have cognition of the word as such. The understanding of it cannot consist merely in discovering on what presuppositions, in what situation, in what linguistic sense and with what intention, in what actual context, and in this sense with what meaning the other has said this or that. And the exposition of his word cannot possibly consist only in the exposition which, as I listen to him, involuntarily or even consciously I try to give of the speaker himself. These things do not mean that I penetrate to his word as such. At best, they mean only that I am prepared to listen and understand and expound. If I were to confuse this preparation with the listening, understanding and expounding, and concern myself only with the word as such and the one who speaks it, how I should deceive myself ! As far as I am concerned, he would have spoken in vain. We can speak meaningfully of hearing a human utterance only when it is clear to us in its function of indicating something that is described or intended by the word, and also when this function has become an event

confronting us, when therefore by means of the human word we ourselves in some degree perceive the thing described or intended. It is
only then that anyone has told me anything and I have heard it from
him. We may call other things speaking and hearing, but in the strict
sense they are only unsuccessful attempts at speaking and hearing.
If a human word spoken to me does not show me anything, or if I
myself cannot perceive what the word shows me, we have an unsuccessful attempt of this kind. Understanding of a human word presupposes that the attempt to speak and hear has succeeded. Then I
know what is being said. On the basis and in the light of the word
I understand what is said to me. Now understanding is, of course, a
return to the word, an inquiry into the word itself : the word with
all its linguistic and factual presuppositions ; an inquiry in which even
as I turn afresh to the word and speaker, I take up a standpoint outside
the word and speaker, that is, in that perception of the thing described
or intended in the word which is mediated to me by my hearing of
the word. Again, if the word does mediate any such perception, if
the thing described or intended by the word is still not known by me
even when it has been spoken, then I have not heard that word at
all, and in that case how can I understand it ? But if I have heard it,
how can I understand it except in the light of what it says to me, i.e.,
of the matter, the perception, which it mediates to me ? Of course,
concretely this understanding can consist only in my returning from the
matter to the word and its presuppositions, to the speaking subject in its
concrete form. But it is only in the light of what is said to me and
heard by me, and not of myself, that I try to inquire of the word and the
speaking subject. The result of my inquiry in this form will be my interpretation of this human word. My exposition cannot possibly consist in
an interpretation of the speaker. Did he say something to me only to
display himself ? I should be guilty of a shameless violence against
him, if the only result of my encounter with him were that I now knew
him or knew him better than before. What lack of love ! Did he
not say anything to me at all ? Did he not therefore desire that I
should see him not *in abstracto* but in his specific and concrete relationship to the thing described or intended in his word, that I should see
him from the standpoint and in the light of this thing ? How much
wrong is being continually perpetrated, how much intolerable obstruc-
tion of human relationships, how much isolation and impoverishment
forced upon individuals has its only basis in the fact that we do not
take seriously a claim which in itself is as clear as the day, the claim
which arises whenever one person addresses a word to another.

At this point the question arises : What is the source of the hermeneutic
teaching which we have just sketched ? Well, the fact that in spite of its inherent
clarity it still does not enjoy general recognition is in itself an indication that it
does not arise out of any general considerations on the nature of human language,
etc., and therefore out of a general anthropology. Why is it that, as a rule,

general considerations on the nature of human language do not lead to the propositions indicated ? My reply would be : because the hermeneutic principles are not dictated by Holy Scripture, as they are in our case. If we ask ourselves, and as readers of Holy Scripture we have to ask ourselves, what is meant by hearing and understanding and expounding when we presuppose that that which is described or intended by the word of man is the revelation of God, the answer we have given forces itself upon us. Hearing undoubtedly means perceiving revelation by the word of man—understanding, investigating the humanly concrete word in the light of revelation—expounding, clarifying the word in its relation to revelation. It is in view of the only possible explanation of Holy Scripture that we have laid the principles of exposition indicated—not, of course, believing that they apply only to biblical exposition, but believing always that because they are valid for biblical exposition they are valid for the exposition of every human word, and can therefore lay claim to universal recognition. It is not at all that the word of man in the Bible has an abnormal significance and function. We see from the Bible what its normal significance and function is. It is from the word of man in the Bible that we must learn what has to be learned concerning the word of man in general. This is not generally recognised. It is more usual blindly to apply to the Bible false ideas taken from some other source concerning the significance and function of the human word. But this must not confuse us into thinking that the very opposite way is the right one. There is no such thing as a special biblical hermeneutics. But we have to learn that hermeneutics which is alone and generally valid by means of the Bible as the witness of revelation. We therefore arrive at the suggested rule, not from a general anthropology, but from the Bible, and obviously, as the rule which is alone and generally valid, we must apply it first to the Bible.

The fact that we have to understand and expound the Bible as a human word can now be explained rather more exactly in this way : that we have to listen to what it says to us as a human word. We have to understand it as a human word in the light of what it says.

Under the caption of a truly " historical " understanding of the Bible we cannot allow ourselves to commend an understanding which does not correspond to the rule suggested : a hearing in which attention is paid to the biblical expressions but not to what the words signify, in which what is said is not heard or overheard ; an understanding of the biblical words from their immanent linguistic and factual context, instead of from what they say and what we hear them say in this context ; an exposition of the biblical words which in the last resort consists only in an exposition of the biblical men in their historical reality. To this we must say that it is not an honest and unreserved understanding of the biblical word as a human word, and it is not therefore an historical understanding of the Bible. In an understanding of this kind the Bible cannot be witness. In this type of understanding, in which it is taken so little seriously, indeed not at all, as a human word, the possibility of its being witness is taken away from the very outset. The philosophy which lies behind this kind of understanding and would force us to accept it as the only true historical understanding is not of course a very profound or respectable one. But even if we value it more highly, or highest of all, and are therefore disposed to place great confidence in its dictates, knowing what is involved in the understanding of the Bible, we can only describe this kind of understanding of the reality of a human word as one which cannot possibly do justice to its object. Necessarily, therefore, we have to reject most decisively the intention of even the most profound and respectable philosophy to subject any human word and especially the biblical word to this understanding. The Bible cannot be read unbiblically. And in this case that means that it cannot be read with such a disregard for its character even as a human word. It cannot be read so unhistorically.

Even the best and finest results, which were to be and have actually been achieved by the methods based on this understanding, will not prevent us from making this rejection, but only strengthen us in it. In accordance with the only remaining possibility of exposition, the best and finest results of this method usually consist in a certain clear knowledge of the biblical men in their concrete state, of their personality and piety in relation to their position and role in the historical circumstances in which they lived, their specific speech and being, greatness and limitation, significance and weakness as microcosmically or macrocosmically determined. We certainly cannot despise such knowledge as worthless. When their word is heard, and in the hearing attention is paid to what is signified and intended in this word, and there is an understanding of the full meaning and scope of their humanity in the light of this object of their word, then a proper exposition of their word can take account of their humanity in all its scope and meaning—not, however, *in abstracto* but in its connexion with the object revealed in their word as it is heard and understood. An exposition of their humanity *in abstracto* may be very full historically. It may be informed and penetrated by a very great understanding for their religion. It may be carried out with the greatest possible zeal. But we still have to reject it as an interpretation of the Bible — and on the very ground that it does not take the human word of the Bible as seriously as according to the Bible itself it ought to be taken. Therefore Calvin is really right from this, the historical point of view (let alone any other), when he believes that the Bible itself excludes any interpretation of the Bible which puts biblical man in the centre of consideration. And he is probably also right when he brings such an interpretation of the Bible into connexion with the false intentions of the doctrine of the Papal Church. *Retenons bien que saint Paul en ce passage, pour monstrer que nous devons tenir l'Escriture saincte indubitable, ne dit pas, Moyse a esté un homme excellent : il ne dit pas, Isaie avoit une eloquence admirable : il n'allegue rien des hommes pour les faire valoir en leur personnes : mais il dit qu'ils ont esté organes de l'Esprit de Dieu, que leurs langues ont esté conduites en sorte qu'ils n'ont rien advancé de leur propre, mais que c'est Dieu qui a parlé par leur bouche, qu'il ne faut point que nous les estimions comme creatures mortelles, mais que nous sachions que le Dieu vivant s'en est servi, et que nous ayons cela pour tout conclu, qu'ils ont esté fideles dispensateurs du thrésor qui leur estoit commis. Or si cela eust esté bien observé, on ne fust pas venu en telle et si horrible confusion comme encores sont tous les povres Papistes. Car sur quoy est fondee leur foy, sinon sur les hommes ? ... Il est vray qu'ils alleguerons bien le nom de Dieu : mais cependant ils mettront en avant leurs songes et resveries, et puis c'est tout. Or au contraire, voici sainct Paul qui nous dit qu'il nous faut tenir à l'Escriture saincte. Voilà pour un item. Et à quelles enseignes ? Pource que Dieu parle là, et non point les hommes. Nous voyons donc comme il exclud toute authorité humaine, qu'il faut que Dieu ait sa preeminence par dessus toutes ses creatures, et que grans et petis s'assuiettissent à luy, et que nul ne presume de s'ingerer pour dire, Je parleray ...* (Serm. on 2 Tim. 3[16f.], C.R. 54, 286). And Luther was no less right when he drew attention to the fact that in his well-known saying : " If any man preach any other Gospel unto you than that ye have received," Paul undoubtedly subordinates himself completely to the Word which he preached : Paul *simpliciter seipsum, Angelum e coelo, doctores in terra et quicquid est Magistrorum, hoc totum rapit et subiicit sacrae scripturae. Haec Regina debet dominari, huic omnes obedire et subiacere debent. Non eius Magistri, Judices seu Arbitri, sed simplices testes, discipuli et confessores esse debent, sive sit Papa, sive Lutherus, sive Augustinus, sive Paulus, sive Angelus e coelo. Neque alia doctrina in Ecclesia tradi et audiri debet quam purum verbum Dei, vel doctores et auditores cum sua doctrina Anathema sunto* (Comm. on Gal. 1[9], 1535, W.A. 40[1] 120, 18). For *hoc vitium insitum est nobis, quod personas admiramur et plus respicimus quam verbum, cum Deus velit nos inhaerentes et affixos esse tantum in ipsum verbum. Vult, ut nucleum, non testam eligamus, ut plus curemus patremfamilias quam domum. In Petro et Paulo non vult nos admirari vel adorare Apostolatum, sed Christum in eis loquentem et ipsum verbum Dei, quod de ore ipsorum egreditur* (on *Gal.* 2⁶ *ib.* 173, 18). All the care and love which we may apply to the biblical text within the framework of that other understanding cannot alter the fact that the understanding as such is inadequate. Luther and Calvin, on the other hand, have at this very point shown a real historical understanding for the Bible.

It is not only not an abuse or violation either of the human word of the Bible in particular or of human words in general, but it has importance as an example when the Christian Church bases its understanding of this word, or of the two humanly composed and selected collections which we call the Bible, not only in relation to the hearing but also in relation to the exposition of it, upon what is said in this word. That it derives this hermeneutic principle from the Bible itself, i.e., that the Bible itself, because of the unusual preponderance of what is said in it over the word as such, enforces this principle upon it, does not alter the fact that this principle is necessarily the principle of all hermeneutics, and that therefore the principle of the Church's doctrine of Holy Scripture, that the Bible is the witness of divine revelation, is simply the special form of that universally valid hermeneutic principle. The Church not only has to hold this in respect of the understanding of the Bible itself. In demanding a historical appreciation of the Bible, it must also require—and self-evidently of every reader of the Bible—that his understanding of it should be based on what is said in the Bible and therefore on God's revelation. It cannot, therefore, be conceded that side by side with this there is another legitimate understanding of the Bible, that, e.g., in its own way it is right and possible when we hear and understand and expound the Bible not to go beyond the humanity as such which is expressed in it. There is indeed a very definite humanity expressed in it, as, for example, that of the apostle Paul. But as the Reformers felt and saw with true historicism, as it is expressed and as the reader of the Bible honestly and unreservedly accepts it, it does not speak of itself, but of God's revelation, and no honest and unprejudiced reader of the Bible can ignore this historical definiteness of the word. No one, of course, has ever dared to say that from their own standpoint—and that is what we have to take into account in understanding this word as a human word—the biblical writers said nothing, and that therefore the problem of what is intended or signified in their word, the problem of the matter or object of it, simply does not exist. And similarly there can hardly be any controversy concerning the fact that what is said by them, that what at least from their standpoint has the character of matter or object, on a closer consideration, is simply God's revelation. It has to be conceded, of course, as in relation to every human word, that there might be a slip somewhere between the word and the reader, whether in the attempt to speak or the attempt to hear : that what is said does not appear to the hearer or reader in its factuality, that it cannot do anything with him, and that he for his part does not know how to make anything of it. If that is the case, he will, as it were, be left in the air in relation to the word. He will certainly not be able to understand it, because he has no *locus* from which he can understand it. Self-evidently, therefore, he will not be able to expound it either. But this possibility of failure cannot alter or destroy the validity of the general hermeneutic principle. If it is really the case that a reader of the biblical Scriptures is quite help-less in face of the problem of what these Scriptures say and intend and denote in respect of divine revelation, that he sees only an empty spot at the place to which the biblical writers point, then in a singular way this does set in relief the extraordinary nature of the content of what these writers say on the one hand, and on the other the state and status of the reader. But all that it actually proves is that there can be no question of a legitimate understanding of the Bible by this reader, that for the time being, i.e., until his relation to what is said in the Bible changes, this reader cannot be regarded as a serious reader and exegete. There can be no question of his exegesis being equally justified with one which is based upon the real substance of the Bible, divine revelation.

There is a notion that complete impartiality is the most fitting and indeed the normal disposition for true exegesis, because it guarantees a complete absence of prejudice. For a short time, around 1910, this idea threatened to achieve almost canonical status in Protestant theology. But now we can quite calmly describe it as merely comical.

Now this does not mean that the hermeneutic principle is destroyed or altered. For it is characteristic of what is said and intended and denoted in the Bible, again in the sense of those who said it, that if it is to reveal and establish itself at all as substance and object, it must do so of itself. How can it be otherwise, when what is said is God's revelation, the lordship of the triune God in His Word by the Holy Ghost ? To what is said—and even as they say it, and the biblical witnesses themselves attest it—there belongs a sovereign free-dom in face of both speaker and hearer alike. The fact that it can be said and heard does not mean that it is put at the power and disposal of those who say and hear it. What it does mean is that as it is said and heard by them it can make itself said and heard. It is only by revelation that revelation can be spoken in the Bible and that it can be heard as the real substance of the Bible. If it is to be witness at all, and to be apprehended as such, the biblical witness must itself be attested by what it attests. We shall have to return expressly to this peculiarity of the biblical witness in the second section of this chapter under the title " Scripture as the Word of God." But at this point already we can and must lay down that even this property of biblical witness does not give us permission to depart from the historical understanding of the text as we have described it, or to accept the possibility and legitimacy of any understanding which deviates from it. In exegesis, too—and especially in exegesis—there is only one truth. In face of it, the unfortunate possibility that the matter of which the word speaks may be alien to us does not excuse us. Nor does it permit us, instead of proceeding from the substance to the word, to go first to the word, i.e., to the humanity of the speakers as such. But if that is the case, we are obviously not excused or permitted by the mystery which is the obvious source of this fatal possibility : the mystery of the sovereign freedom of the substance. On the contrary, the knowledge of this mystery, even when it is only a matter of hearing as such, will summon us as readers of the Bible to hear, really to give ear, in a way in which we would probably never do otherwise. Not knowing this mystery, we will, of course, hear as we always do, as though we know already, and can partly tell ourselves what we are to hear. Our supposed listening is in fact a strange mixture of hearing and our own speaking, and, in accordance with the usual rule, it is most likely that our own speaking will be the really decisive event. We have to know the mystery of the substance if we are really to meet it, if we are really to be open and ready, really to give ourselves to it, when we are told it, that it may really meet us as the substance. And when it is a matter of understanding, the knowledge of this mystery will create in us a peculiar fear and reserve which is not at all usual to us. We will then know that in the face of this subject-matter there can be no question of our achieving, as we do in others, the confident approach which masters and subdues the matter. It is rather a question of our being gripped by the subject-matter—not gripped physically, not making an experience of it and the like, although (ironically) that can happen—but really gripped, so that it is only as those who are mastered by the subject-matter, who are subdued by it, that we can investigate the humanity of the word by which it is told us. The sovereign freedom of this subject-matter to speak of itself imposes on us in face of the word as such and its historicity an ἐποχή, of which there can be no inkling if we presuppose the comical doctrine that the true exegete has no presuppositions, and against which we consistently and most flagrantly offend if we presuppose that doctrine. And the knowledge of this mystery will see to it that the work of exposition, which is the goal of all hearing and understanding, at least enters the stage of convalescence from the sickness with which all exposition is almost incurably afflicted, the sickness of an insolent and arbitrary reading in. If the exposition of a human word consists in the relating of this word to what it intends or denotes, and if we know the sovereign freedom, the independent glory of this subject-matter in relation both to the word which is before us and to ourselves, we will be wholesomely restrained at the very least in our usual self-assured mastery of the relationship, as though we already knew its content and our exposition could give something more than hints in its direction. We shall be at least restrained in our evil domination of the text (even though in this age we can as little rid ourselves of it as we can of our old Adam generally). And then the way will no longer be radically closed to a real relating of the word and subject-matter. It is not, then, that by a knowledge of the mystery of what is said in the Bible we acquire the right to turn to some other understanding of the Bible than that which is based upon this subject-matter and therefore upon God's revelation. It is rather that knowledge itself brings this understanding before us and makes it possible to us as the only possible one. It is as the sovereign freedom of the subject-matter of the Bible is presented to us that its character as a subject-matter becomes unshakably and unequivocally certain, so that we can no longer confuse it with the word or the humanity of those who speak, and even less with ourselves. Characterised as the matter which speaks of itself, it will be respected by us as that which claims our interest for its own sake.

We have described the mystery which we have to recognise at this point as the peculiarity of the biblical word, i.e., of the subject-matter of the biblical word. But we must now add that there is no question of a peculiarity of the biblical word or its subject-matter, beside which we have normally to ascribe to other human words and their subject-matter a different peculiarity. It is rather that the peculiarity of the Bible has the force of an example, i.e., that we learn from it what is to be learned concerning the peculiarity of the human word in general. Everything that is said in a human word is as such always wrapped in a mystery, in this mystery, even when it is not divine revelation. But it is because what is said in the biblical word of man is divine revelation, and as such the *analogia fidei*, that everything which is said by human word is drawn into the darkness and light of its mystery. Is it not the case that whatever is said to us by men obviously wants— and it is with this claim that it confronts us with something said to us—to make itself said and heard ? It wants in this way to become to us a subject-matter. It wants us for our part to bring it a true objectivity, i.e., interest for its own sake. Therefore the human word, by means of which it is told us, wants to be heard openly and not with that mixture of hearing and our own speaking and interrupting. In order to be understood by us, it wants not to be mastered by us, but to lay hold of us. It wants to be evaluated in its relation to what is said in it, when this has been spoken to us and made itself intelligible to us. In short, whatever is said to us by men always demands of us what God's revelation in the human word of Holy Scripture—but that alone—can actually achieve in relation to us. God's revelation in the human word of Holy Scripture not only wants but can make itself said and heard. It can become for us real subject-matter, and it can force us to treat it objectively. And as it does so, the human word in which it is told to us is heard openly and understood without being mastered, and expounded rightly, i.e., in relation to its subject-matter. God's revelation in the human word of Holy Scripture is distinguished from everything else that is said to us by men by the fact that a majesty belongs to the one which obviously is radically lacking in the other, a majesty without which the latter would be meaningless if the former were only an exception and not the law and the promise and the sign of redemption which has been set up in the sphere of all other human words, and of all that is said by them. How can we deny or ignore the distinction between what merely wants to be the thing said by other men, and what can be God's revelation in the human word of Holy Scripture? We have to accept this distinction. But knowing this distinction, how can we regard the false hearing and understanding and expounding of the human word, and therefore the meaninglessness with which it is delivered, as the norm and law of our words, just because it is the rule under which they labour, and the power of the revelation of God in the human word of Holy Scripture only as an outside exception? Even though as an exception it may confirm the rule, it necessarily breaks through it and reveals itself to be the norm and law in the light of which all human words now actually stand. Their aim and intention cannot possibly be concealed if we start with the hearing and understanding and expounding of the human word of the Bible. They cannot themselves become witnesses of revelation. Good care is seen to that. But when we start with the witnesses of revelation, we have to approach all other human words with at least the question what it is that however feebly and ineffectively they want to say, and what would make itself said and heard in them. There will then be no question of the assurance of an hermeneutics which is based on the necessity of irrelevance, nor of the meaninglessness to which human words generally would in fact be condemned, were it not that they had with them with all its promise the human word of Holy Scripture, and their own future was revealed by this human word. In view of the future of every human word which is already present in Holy Scripture, we will, of course, read Homer and Goethe and even the newspaper rather differently than if we did not know the future. It is not our present task to pursue this line. Our present concern is to establish that when we have to do with revelation as the content of the biblical word and with the hermeneutics prescribed by this content, we are not dealing with a mysterious thing apart which applies only to the Bible. Biblical hermeneutics must be guarded against the totalitarian claim of a general hermeneutics. It is a special hermeneutics only because hermeneutics generally has been mortally sick for so long that it has not let the special problem of biblical hermeneutics force its attention upon its own problem. For the sake of better general hermeneutics it must therefore dare to be this special hermeneutics.

2. SCRIPTURE AS THE WORD OF GOD

If what we hear in Holy Scripture is witness, a human expression of God's revelation, then from what we have already said, what we hear in the witness itself is more than witness, what we hear in the human expression is more than a human expression. What we hear is revelation, and therefore the very Word of God. But is this really the case ? How can it be ? How does it come about that it is ? We will postpone the answer to this question—the two succeeding sections of the chapter will be devoted to it—in order first of all to clarify by rather more exact definitions the meaning and scope of the question itself, the meaning and scope of the positive side of our basic principle, that Scripture is the witness of divine revelation.

1. If we say that Scripture is this witness, or if we say that this witness is Scripture, we say this in the Church and with the Church, i.e., we say it of that Scripture which the Church has discovered and acknowledged as Holy Scripture, of canonical Scripture. When we say it with this qualification and restriction, we say that it is not for us or for any man to constitute this or that writing as Holy Writ, as the witness of God's revelation, to choose it as such out of many others, but that if there is such a witness and the acceptance of such a witness, it can only mean that it has already been constituted and chosen, and that its acceptance is only the discovery and acknowledgment of this fact. If in respect of what we regard as Holy Scripture we accept the qualification and restriction made in the Church's Canon, this does not mean that although it is not for the individual Christian to-day to constitute or choose Holy Scripture, it was once the task of the Church to do it, round about the year 400. " Canon " means " rule," i.e., the " rule of truth," and most significantly this conception was originally connected with the dogma as well as the constitution of the texts which are recognised to be holy. In no sense of the concept could or can the Church give the Canon to itself. The Church cannot " form " it, as historians have occasionally said without being aware of the theological implications. The Church can only confirm or establish it as something which has already been formed and given. And it can do so only to the best of its knowledge and judgment, in the venture and obedience of faith, but also in all the relativity of a human knowledge of the truth which God has opened up to men. This establishment of the Canon is the work of the Church, both in those matters which relate to the constitution of Holy Scripture and in those which relate to dogma.

As is well known, the establishment of the Canon has had a long and complicated history. Basically, we cannot yet say that that history is closed. In evaluating the history we have, of course, to discriminate the means and motives and criteria from the establishment itself. It is quite true that in this question of the rule of truth the Church was always affected *in concreto* by historical, theological and even ecclesiastico-political considerations. This fact marks its judgment as a human judgment in the same way as it does its judgments with regard to dogma. But the question actually discussed from these various angles and finally decided at various stages was simply a question of faith in relation to those Scriptures in which we can recognise the rule of truth. This object as such the Church could neither form nor reveal by means of the discussions conducted according to those considerations. In discussions of that kind it could not see either the fact or the extent to which the rule of truth has already been created and already revealed to it. For the obvious core of the history of the Canon is this, that within the various churches, and with all kinds of vacillations, particular parts of the oldest tradition have gradually been distinguished and set apart from others in the appreciation and acceptance of Christendom, a process which proper and formal canonisation by synodic resolutions and the like could only subsequently confirm. At some time and in some measure (with all the chance features which this appreciation and acceptance may have strengthened) these very writings, by the very fact that they were canonical, saw to it that they in particular were later recognised and proclaimed to be canonical.

Therefore we hear the judgment of the Church, but we do not obey its judgment, when we accept the settlement which the Church has, of course, made. In and with the Church we obey the judgment which was already pronounced, before the Church could pronounce its judgment and which the Church's judgment could only confirm. Just as the question of the witness of revelation can only be a question of faith, so too the answering of that question can only be a knowledge of faith. When we adopt the Canon of the Church we do not say that the Church itself, but that the revelation which underlies and controls the Church, attests these witnesses and not others as the witnesses of revelation and therefore as canonical for the Church.

Nous cognoissons ces livres estre canoniques et reigle trescertaine de nostre foy : non tant par le commun accord et consentement de l'eglise, que par le tesmoignage et interieure persuasion du sainct esprit, qui les nous faict discerner d'avec les autres livres Ecclesiastiques. Sur lesquels (encores qu'ilz soyent utiles) on ne peut fonder aucun article de foy (Conf. Gallic. 1559, Art. 4). *Non potest ecclesia ex libris non canonicis canonicos facere, sed efficit tantum ut ii libri pro canonicis recipiantur, qui revera et in sese sunt canonici. Ecclesia inquam, non facit scripturam authenticam, sed tantum declarat. Illud enim authenticum dicitur, quod se commendat, sustinet, probat et ex se fidem et autoritatem habet* (W. Bucan, *Instit. theol.*, 1602, loc. 43, qu. 15). *Divino instinctu . . . (hi libri) acceptati sunt, idque non libero aliquo actu ecclesiae sed necessaria susceptione* (Syn. pur. Theol., Leiden, 1624, disp. 3, 13). Is this also the Roman Catholic doctrine of the Canon ? In the Vatican Council it was indeed decreed that *Eos* (libros) *vere ecclesia pro rectis et canonicis habet . . . propterea quod Spiritu sancto inspirante conscripti Deum habent autorem atque ut tales ipsi ecclesiae traditi sunt* (Const. dogm. de fide cath. cap. 2). And B. Bartmann (Lehrb. d. Dogm.[7] 1928, I, p. 14) writes as follows : " The books are canonical *in actu primo* and *quoad se* because they are inspired, *in actu secundo* and *quoad nos* because they were adopted into the canon as inspired. By the divine act they were adapted to canonicity, by the Church's act this was formally accorded to them." Now the meaning may well be that this " according " of the Church can consist only in a recognition of that property, that when the Church adopts this or that Scripture into the Canon all that it does is, in the light of its inspiration and in deference to it (otherwise might it not just as well omit it ?), to confirm that it already belongs to the Canon. We cannot think that the Church can give authority to a sacred writing, but only that it can establish its authority. Yet at the time of the Reformation Sylvester Prierias (in the *Dialogus de potestate Papae*, 1517, p. 15, which he wrote against Luther) could say that the doctrine of the Roman Church and of the Roman Pope is the *regula fidei infallibilis, a qua etiam sacra scriptura robur trahit et auctoritatem*. And John Eck (*Enchir.*, 1529, *De ecclesia, c. objecta* 3) could boldly declare, and he was not for long the only one, that *Scriptura non est authentica sine autoritate ecclesiae*. And there were controversialists who actually expressed the opinion that Æsop's Fables would have just as much or even more weight than a Bible which did not have the authority lent it by the Church. The saying of Augustine was constantly appealed to in this sense : *Ego vero evangelio non crederem, nisi me catholicae ecclesiae commoveret auctoritas* (*C. ep. Manich.* 5, 6). Now even at that time there were some Roman Catholic writers who did not share this view, so that it would not be right to see in these utterances the doctrine of the Roman Catholic Church. However that may be, the true doctrine of the canon can be re-stated in the words of John Gerhard : *Non est duplex, sed una scripturae auctoritas, eademque divina, non dependens ab ecclesiae auctoritate, sed a solo Deo. Auctoritas scripturae quoad nos nihil aliud est quam manifestatio et cognitio unicae illius divinae et summae auctoritatis, quae scripturae est interna atque insita. Ecclesia igitur non confert scripturae novam aliquam auctoritatem quoad nos, sed testificatione sua ad agnitionem illius veritatis nos deducit. Concediumus ecclesiam esse scripturae sacrae* (1) *testem,* (2) *custodem,* (3) *vindicem,* (4) *praeconem,* (5) *interpretem, sed negamus ex eo effici, quod auctoritas scripturae sive simpliciter sive quoadnos ab ecclesia pendeat* (*Loci. theol.*, 1610 f., LI c. 3, 39). Or in the words of Joh. Wolleb : *Ecclesiae testimonium prius est tempore ; Spiritus sancti vero prius est natura et efficacia. Ecclesiae credimus, sed non propter ecclesiam ; Spiritui autem sancto creditur propter seipsum. Ecclesiae testimonium* τὸ ὅτι *demonstrat, Spiritus sancti vero testimonium* τὸ διότι *demonstrat. Ecclesia suadet, Spiritus sanctus persuadet. Ecclesiae testimonium opinionem, Spiritus sancti vero testimonium scientiam ac fidem firmam parit* (*Comp. Christ. Theol.*, 1620, *Praecogn.* 9). As the Protestant theologians of the time liked to expound it, the Church may be compared with the Samaritan woman, of whom it first says in Jn. 4[39] that many of that city believed in Christ because of her saying, but then in v. 42 that they say unto her : " Now we believe, not because of thy saying : we have heard him ourselves, that this is indeed the Christ, the Saviour of the world." We cannot suppose, of course, that this is the doctrine of the Canon held by the Catholic Church.

Holy Scripture is the Word of God to the Church and for the Church. We are, therefore, ready to know what Holy Scripture is in the Church and with the Church. We do not regard ourselves as unrestrained in this matter or restrained only by our own direct knowledge of the rule of truth. Therefore we know that we have to listen to the Church in matters of the Canon, as we have also to listen to it at all points in matters of the exposition of Holy Scripture and faith and order. But even though it is in and with the Church that we ask what is that Holy Scripture which is the Canon given in the Church and forcing itself upon it by its own inspiration, we cannot take our answer from the Church but from Holy Scripture itself. We will not be obedient to the Church but to the Word of God, and therefore in the true sense to the Church.

This answer is in itself a divine and therefore an infallible and definitive answer. But the human hearing of this answer, whether that of the Church or our own to-day, is a human hearing, and therefore not outside the possibility of error, or incapable of being improved. This is true of our answers to the question of faith and order ; it is also true of our answer to the question of the Canon. As we give this answer, believing in and with the Church, as we recognise certain Scriptures (e.g., the sixty-six of our Authorised Version) to be canonical in and with the Church, we have the right and duty to accept this answer as good and sufficient, and with the help of these Holy Scriptures seriously to ask concerning the witness of God's revelation and the Word of God itself. Every bit of real witness of God's revelation—we cannot without error deny the presence of such witness among the sixty-six books—is also a portion of God's Word and is all-sufficient for the life of the Church and for our own life in time and in eternity. An absolute guarantee that the history of the Canon is closed, and therefore that what we know as the Canon is also closed, cannot be given either by the Church or by individuals in the Church according to the best and most satisfactory answers to this question. In the past there has already been more than one proposal to narrow or broaden the human perception of what ought to count as canonical Scripture, and if the proposals never came to anything they were at least seriously considered. The insight that the concrete form of the Canon is not closed absolutely, but only very relatively, cannot be denied even with a view to the future.

Even if we ignore the considerable variations in the first four centuries, it is worth noting that the Council of Florence in 1441—a thousand years after our present-day New Testament had gained general acceptance—for the purpose of the understanding which was then sought with the Eastern Churches, could still think it necessary to put out an express list of the Old and New Testament writings recognised to be canonical (*Denz*. No. 706). This act had to be repeated in 1546 by the Council of Trent (*Sess*. IV *Denz*. No. 784), the problem of the Canon having meanwhile been reopened by the Reformation. The Protestant Churches—the Reformed very definitely, and at bottom too the Lutheran quite decidedly—thought it right to exclude from the Canon as " Apocrypha " a whole series of Old Testament writings which had been recognised as wholly canonical for a thousand years (the books of Judith, the Wisdom of Solomon, Tobias, Sirach and the two Maccabees). But even the question of the New Testament Canon seemed to be reopened at that time. It is well known what Luther thought about Hebrews, James, Jude and Revelation. He did not wish to deprive anyone of them, but for his own part he could not number them with the " right, sure, principal books." What is not so well known is that in the table of contents of his September Bible of 1522 he openly separated them from the other twenty-three and according to him true New Testament writings, thus characterising them at once as deutero-canonical. And Luther did not stand alone. Before the Council of Trent with its new tradition, not only Erasmus but even Cardinal Cajetan expressed open doubts concerning the authenticity and authority of Hebrews, James and Jude as well as 2 and 3 John. Zwingli thought especially that the Apocalypse should be rejected. And it is at least noteworthy that Calvin omitted the Apocalypse in what was otherwise a complete exposition of the

New Testament. From his introductions to the commentaries it emerges clearly that he had doubts not only concerning the books mentioned by Luther but also concerning 2 Peter and 2 and 3 John. In the *Apol. Conf. Württ.* 1555 J. Brenz dismissed these seven writings in the same gentle but decisive way as Luther had done the Old Testament Apocrypha in his well-known formula. They were edifying and wholesome, but not normative. Among the Reformed the same view was held and taught by the Bernese W. Musculus (cf. H. Heppe, *Dogm. d. ev. ref. Kirche,* new edn. 1935, p. 15). It seemed for a moment as though the separation of the Old Testament Apocrypha might be paralleled in the New Testament sphere by a return to the Eusebian Canon with its distinction between the homologoumena and the antilegomena, the seven books in question being reckoned with the latter. J. Gerhard (*Loci theol.,* 1610 f.) can still speak (in chap. 9 and 10 of his *Locus de Scriptura*) quite openly *De libris Novi Testamenti canonicis primi et secundi ordinis,* meaning by the *libri secundi ordinis* precisely the seven Eusebian antilegomena. But in spite of the authority of Luther himself, this was still only a private opinion. And in the debate with the Roman Church and theology this private opinion soon proved embarrassing and was therefore rejected on internal grounds. Even J. Gerhard had reasons to show that all the books which he described as *libri canonici secundi ordinis* must still be counted *canonici.* This meant that the older objections had to be contested, and it was obvious that the distinction made by Eusebius could not be sustained. That is how it turned out. Already in 1545 the Confession of Zurich had attacked Luther's view : In the aforesaid books of the New Testament we are not misled by any stubborn fool, nor do we believe that any among them are strawy, or have been inserted wrongly. And although the mind of man may not agree to Revelation or other books, we set no store by such agreement. For we know that we men ought to be judged by Scripture and not Scripture by us (in K. Müller, *Bek. Schr. der ref. Kirche,* p. 155). The *Conf. Gallic.* (1559 Art. 3) and the *Conf. Belgica* (1561 Art. 4) follow the example of the Tridentinum and give a solemn list of all the sixty-six canonical Scriptures, not trying to make any distinction between the New Testament books. And J. Gerhard's Reformed contemporary, Polanus, declares concisely and authoritatively that *Novi Testamenti (libri) omnes sunt vere, univoce et proprie divini et canonici, nullo excepto.* Of course there were some (*quidam*) Evangelicals who disputed the canonicity of the seven books. But their opinion was now felt to be a *pudendum : Horum opinio erronea, quia paucorum est, communitati ecclesiae evangelicae seu reformatae impingi non debet* (*Synt. Theol. chr.* 1609, p. 283 and 307). All the same even Polanus still took the trouble to give an explicit counterproof in relation to each of the contested books. By the end of the 17th century the matter had passed to the stage of historical reminiscence in Reformed circles. It was not mentioned at all, for example, by F. Turrettini (*Instit. Theol. el.,* 1679, *Loc.* 2 *qu.* 9, 13). On the other hand, Quenstedt among the Lutherans was still conscious of the distinction between *libri primi et secundi ordinis* in the New Testament (he also calls them *protocanonici* and *deuterocanonici*). And he still accepts the distinction, although not so obviously as J. Gerhard had done. The point which he tries to make with regard to the latter is that there has for a time been doubt concerning their human author—not their divine. And he goes to great lengths to try to conceal as much as possible certain hints in Luther's works which point quite definitely in a different direction (*Theol. did. pol.,* 1685 P I *cap.* 4 *sect.* 2, *qu.* 23, *th.* 2 *dist.* 5 and *font. sol. obs.* 23 f.). For practical purposes the whole process was only an interlude. But that it was possible at all is of fundamental significance : for the later writers, who did not share the doubts of the earlier ones, never formally disputed that questions may be raised concerning the constitution of the Canon as they had in fact been raised in the 16th century. On the contrary, by the express numbering of those books which must be recognised as authentic, both the Church of Rome (in the Confession of

Trent) and the Reformed Churches (in the *Gallicana* and *Belgica*) accepted the legitimacy of the question. And we can see something of the same in the tenacious maintaining of a formal distinction between the protocanonical and the deutero-canonical writings by the later Lutherans.

At this point we must not forget, of course, a general phenomenon which points in the same direction. And that is that even where there is no question of a direct attack on the traditional constitution of the Canon, not only the in-dividual readers of the Bible, but the Church as a whole, as it has made its mind known in its symbols, confessional writings, its theology, preaching and devotional literature, does not in fact and practice treat all parts of the Bible alike, or without tacit questions in relation to one or other of them. Holy Scripture has always been defined in the Church with varying degrees of emphasis on the constituent parts. The well-known criterion of Luther was to test every Scripture by whether " it sets forth Christ or not." " What teacheth not Christ is not apostolic, even though Peter or Paul teacheth it. Again what preacheth Christ is apostolic, even though Judas, Annas, Pilate and Herod doth it " (*Preface to the Epistles of St. James and St. Jude*, 1522). And with a varying insight into what can be called Christ, this is the criterion which in all ages the Church has in its own way applied to the Canon. Yet in so doing it has not reached any conclusions or made any demands concerning an alteration in its public constitution. In spite of its 1000 years and in spite of the Florentinum and the Tridentinum, the Roman Church was the very last (we have only to think of its flagrant exalting of the Gospels above the prophets and apostles in the *Missale*) actually to treat all parts of the traditional Canon alike. The Church, even the Roman Church, even Luther, has always had to ask concerning the traditional Canon as a whole whether we are not right to value some parts more and others less highly, whether in so doing we do not neglect essential parts of the witness of revelation to the detriment of our knowledge of the Word of God. But if that is true, it is also true that on the basis of the knowledge of the Word of God, which it has perhaps gained from some parts of the witness of revelation as distinct from others, the Church can and must continually ask concerning the legitimacy of the traditional Canon. But if it can and must do this, as in fact it always does, then we cannot rule out a consideration of the possibility of an open alteration in its constitution, either a narrowing as in the 16th century or an extension. We know that there once existed an unknown letter of Paul to the Laodicaeans, and two letters of Paul to the Corinthians no longer extant. There are also some known but " un-recorded " sayings of Jesus, unrecorded, that is, only in the canonical Gospels. And for all we know—and certain recent discoveries ought to prepare us for any eventuality—there may be things awaiting us in the sands of Egypt, in the light of which not even the Roman Church will, perhaps, one day—i.e., the day of their discovery—be able to accept responsibility for dogmatically insisting upon the concept of a closed Canon. Yet it is not the consideration of possibili-ties such as these, but the basic consideration of the positive nature and meaning of the Canon, which forces us to re-accustom ourselves to the thought that the Canon is not closed absolutely.

Clearly a change in the constitution of the Canon, if it arises as a practical question, can take place meaningfully and legitimately only as an action of the Church, i.e., in the form of an orderly and responsible decision by an ecclesiastical body capable of tackling it. Individuals can think and say what they like on theological and historical grounds. But what they think and say can have only the character of a private and non-binding anticipation of the Church's action. Whether it is genuinely of the Church will again depend entirely on the question whether it is a matter now as before of a *necessaria susceptio*, i.e., an actual instruction of the Church by writings which either prove or do not prove themselves to be canonical. As long as no decision is publicly reached in the Church, we have stead-fastly to accept the force and validity of decisions already taken both in respect of the faith and also of the Canon. In the decisions already taken, the Church still tells us that this or that, this particular *corpus*, is Holy Scripture. The individual in the Church certainly cannot and ought not to accept it as Holy Scripture just because the Church does. He can and should himself be obedient only to Holy Scripture as it reveals itself to him and in that way forces itself upon him, as it compels him to accept it. But he still has to remember that Scripture is the Word of God for and to the Church, and that therefore it is only in the Church that he can meaningfully and legitimately take up an attitude to Scripture. Whatever his private judgment may be, even his private judgment of faith, however much it may diverge, he must always listen to the Church. The so far unaltered judgment of the Church radically precedes as such the judgment of the individual, even if it is the judgment of quite a number of individuals who have to be reckoned with seriously in the Church. It is not, of course, the absolute judgment of God, but the judgment of the *majores*, the πρεσβύτεροι (Irenaeus), the judgment of those who were called and be-lieved before us. As such, so long as the Church does not revise it, i.e., restrict or widen it, we have to respect it. As such, it has the character of a direction which no one can simply ignore. Until the Church itself is better instructed, we must expect to find Holy Scrip-ture, Scripture as the witness of divine revelation, Scripture as the Word of God, where the Church itself has found it in virtue of its own decision. We must expect it there and only there, i.e., we have no authority on the basis of our own decision to proclaim in the Church any other Scripture but this. We personally may accept it. But we cannot act as though we speak in any way but in and with the Church, as though we have a right to speak without first listening to the Church. It is where the Church declares that it has found Holy Scripture that we have actually to expect Holy Scripture. That is, whatever may or may not be our own experiences of this or that part of it, we have always to approach the Scripture which the Church calls holy, the witness of revelation, with instructions to see whether what has been heard by the *majores*, although not perhaps by us, may not have something to say to us.

We have to accept the concept of the Canon in a more guarded way than was actually the case in 17th-century Protestantism. That is, we cannot definitely reject the fact that the Church does establish the divine authority of the Scripture contained within this or that limit. In this question of the Canon we cannot ascribe to the Church the role of a mere witness and spectator, however honour-able. We cannot attribute the true and binding divine authority, which decides upon the Canon, so entirely to Scripture itself as the Word of God, as the older Protestant orthodoxy rightly did, and then say to individuals in the Church—

as though Luther and Calvin had never had any doubts on the question—that in certain Scriptures, for the limit of which they are still primarily referred to the testimony of the Church, they will hear in equal measure as the Word of God. If that is so, then it will be so, i.e., the Word of God will really speak to them in just these Scriptures. But if the negative and positive presuppositions are true, if the Church really takes seriously its assurance that only the Word of God itself can dispose and decide in relation to the revelation of the Word of God, the Church cannot speak of its Canon as though in its decision it had made the decision of the Holy Ghost Himself, and therefore decided in its own power for all ages and as against all individuals in the Church. The Church can only regard and proclaim its decision as a direction—an indication seriously meant and therefore to be taken seriously. If it is not to call in question the lordship of Jesus Christ and of the Holy Spirit, and therefore revelation and its own being—it cannot regard and proclaim it as a divine law. In respect of the Canon, it will always be open to further instruction. Towards individuals within it it will show patience in respect of their practical relationship to the Canon. It can and must require of them respect for its indication. To the fluctuations of time and temporal movements, to particular gifts and illuminations, but also to the dangerous caprices of individuals and individual groups, it can and must attest the totality of the Canon, and of the Canon which it itself recognises to be such. It can and must see to it that in the name and applying of Luther's criterion, there does not arise a neglect of specific aspects of the biblical witness, a heretical onesidedness and over-emphasis. It can and must in its own sphere prevent the attempting of arbitrary alterations of the Canon in the limit entrusted to it, or the treatment of some of its parts as alone truly canonical in opposition to others. But even in respect of the limit of the Canon entrusted to it, it cannot and must not be closed *a priori* to further instruction. By its witness in respect of this limit it cannot and must not anticipate the witness of the Holy Spirit to the individual within it. All that it can and must say to him is that in the limit attested by it he has to expect the witness of the Holy Spirit, and with Him to expect that the promise which it has the right and duty to give him will be confirmed. This is the distinction in respect of the truth of the biblical Canon which the doctrine of the Canon held by Protestant orthodoxy has obscured. It had every right actually to contend for the seven antilegomena in opposition to Luther and others when on inward grounds, and decidedly in obedience to Holy Scripture itself, it had the consciousness that it ought to do so. But it had no right to overlook and suppress the basic significance of the fact that in the 16th century the Canon had proved to be an uncertain quantity as far as its constitution was concerned. It claimed too much, and plunged too far, when it equated the Canon which it recognised with the Canon revealed by God. It had no right to make the Church take up any other position in relation to the Canon (in flagrant contradiction with its own accusation of the Roman Church) than that of a witness and spectator, i.e., that of a guarantor of its divine authority. To the extent that it did this, the orthodox doctrine of Scripture, as we shall see again when we discuss the concept of inspiration, simply prepared the way for Neo-Protestantism. It gave to the Church, that is, to men in the Church, power and assurance, which, according to its own presuppositions, could only be the power and assurance of God as opposed to all men, and therefore men in the Church. Had they not said that the divine authority of Scripture must speak for itself, and therefore alone be listened to as itself speaking for itself ? Why were they not content to attest its spiritual authority ? Instead, they arbitrarily made a divine law out of the Church's decision of faith. They did not proclaim it in faith, as the law of the Church and therefore the law of the Spirit. They made it a divine law, which ended the possibility of any further instruction, and which it was believed could be laid on the neck like a yoke. But in so doing they brought out its contradiction to the real law of Christ and of the Holy Ghost—indeed they were themselves unwittingly enmeshed in the contradiction. They cast their pearls before swine. They had, therefore, no reason to be surprised if for long periods the Church's direction in regard to the Canon was not even accepted as the spiritual law of the Church, if the doctrine of Scripture was forced and dissolved by the far more prominent doctrine of religion. Therefore for the sake of the real authority of the biblical Canon we must again learn to regard its establishment as a witness of faith, its recognition as the obedience of faith, and therefore its actual constitution, even if we have no reason to oppose it, as not finally closed.

2. When we have to do with Scripture, i.e., canonical Scripture, the Scripture which the Church has defined and we in and with the Church have recognised as canonical, when we have to do with Holy Scripture as a witness, in fact the witness of divine revelation, we have to do with the witness of Moses and the prophets, the Evangelists and the apostles. What is meant (and in this formulation we are merely repeating certain biblical passages) is the witness of the Old and New Testament, the witness of the expectation and the recollection, the witness of the preparation and the accomplishment of the revelation achieved in Jesus Christ. Concerning revelation as time and between these two times we have already spoken explicitly in the doctrine of revelation itself (§ 14). We are speaking now of its attestation, of the records of it as such. And in the light of what we have already said about their content, of these we have to say that in the content created by their context, and in the variety conditioned by their varied relationship to that content, they all belong together in the sense that they are all equally Holy Scripture and have this content. The Old and the New Testament both have as their distinctive feature to attest in the one case the Messiah who is to come, and in the other the Messiah who has already come. In the Old Testament the Law is distinguished from the prophets by the fact that in the Law it is the calling of Israel, in the prophets the direction and instruction of Israel already called by the Word of Yahweh, which constitutes the material of the prophecy inherent in both. Similarly in the New Testament the Gospels are distinguished from the apostolic writings by the fact that the Gospels look back to the words and acts of Jesus as they point us to the resurrection, whereas the apostolic writings look back from the resurrection to the human situation as illumined and altered by it. But the two lines, of the Old Testament witness on the one hand and of the New Testament witness on the other, always intersect at a single point. The same is true of the Old Testament and New Testament lines as a whole. In detail we shall often find that the distinctions disappear. There is a legal element in the prophets and a prophetic element in the Law, an evangelical element in the apostolic writings and an apostolic element in the Gospels. Only two distinctions really remain : the first consists in the fact that in the Old Testament Christ is not attested as the One who has already appeared,

16

whereas in the New Testament He is not attested as the One who has not yet appeared. Yet we have to allow an exception to this rule in the early chapters of the Gospels of Matthew and Luke and the Baptist and Mary episodes, where the New Testament still uses the terminology of the Old. And the on the whole irreversible distinction between the two witnesses is again completely relativised by the unity of its object. Within all the groups there is a second irreversible distinction, the distinction between the various individualities of the known and unknown writers with whom we have to do in the Biblical witness. Isaiah is not Qoheleth, and Paul is not James. Yet although this is obviously a permanent distinction, it too is relativised by the unity of what is said by all these individuals. When we speak of the biblical witness, we mean this witness as a whole. The distinctions in the content of the witness do not mean a distinction in the witness itself. The Church arose when the witness as a whole was to hand. For the Church arose through the record of Jesus Christ and the message of the power of His resurrection. These two, the record and the message, even before they were fixed in writing, and more especially when they were, were from first to last an exposition of the Law and the prophets. The one necessarily belongs to the other. We cannot separate either the Law and the prophets, or the Gospels and apostolic writings, or the Old and New Testaments as a whole, without at each point emptying and destroying both. If the Church had not from the very first heard this whole, it could not have heard what it did hear. It would not have arisen as the Church. It is only in this unity that the biblical witness is the witness of divine revelation. And remembering this unity, the Church holds fast to this witness. In it it recognises the ruling, divine authority. It busies itself with its exposition. It exists by itself attesting what it finds attested in it. The Church has no control over the unity of this witness. It has it, but it is not of its power that it is the witness of divine revelation. How can it control this unity? How can it be of its power that this witness, although it has it, is in its totality the witness of divine revelation? Apart from the witness itself, all that it can have is the recollection and therefore again the expectation bound up with it. It is in its recollection and expectation that it is the witness of divine revelation, and Scripture is Holy Scripture. The Church has no control or power over what may lie between, over the event that this witness is the witness of divine revelation not only in recollection and expectation, but here and now. This is also true of the totality, the unity of this witness. But as the recollection is generally enough to awaken, confirm and justify the expectation, it allows the Church no expectation but that of the totality, the unity of this witness. This is what the Church means when it teaches the holiness and therefore the unity of Scripture. It means the holiness and unity of God in His revelation, as revealed and confirmed first of all in the founding of the Church and then again and again in the human variety of this witness. Again, it means the holiness and unity of God in His revelation, which in possession of this witness, it is summoned and authorised to expect of Him. Therefore bound by past and future, its present can be only a very humble and claimless, but unbroken, assent to this witness, and therefore to the fulness of this witness in its unity. It does not in this way anticipate what only God Himself in His revelation can create and give, the event of the perception of this unity. But it affirms that God in His revelation can create and give this perception, as He has created and given it already. In this sense it will lay hold of the whole biblical evidence, the Law and the prophets, the Gospels and the apostolic writings, the Old and New Testaments. In this sense it will have a concern for the exposition and proclamation of the whole. In this sense it will confront each of her members with the promise and task of listening to the Word of God in this totality. In this sense, as we have already seen when investigating the concept of the Canon, it will be on its guard not only against any exclusions, but also against preferences of this or that part which may compromise the unity of the witness, against devaluations which may isolate the part from the whole. Even if only in recollection and expectation, it knows of the peace in which this witness has its origin and its goal. It is in its willingness to participate in this peace that it subjects itself to this witness and therefore to the whole of this witness.

Rightly understood, the unity of Holy Scripture gives rise to a conclusion and demand to which the Church must pay good heed. But this conclusion and demand is not that we should abstract from the Bible some concealed historical or conceptual system, an economy of salvation or a Christian view of things. There can be no biblical theology in this sense, either of the Old or New Testament, or of the Bible as a whole. The presupposition and the organising centre of such a system would have to be the object of the biblical witness, that is, revelation. Now revelation is no more and no less than the life of God Himself turned to us, the Word of God coming to us by the Holy Spirit, Jesus Christ. But in our thinking, even in our meditation on the biblical texts, it is only improperly, i.e., only in the form of our recollection and expectation, that we can " presuppose " Jesus Christ and then add to this presupposition other thoughts, even those which are derived from our exposition of those texts. Properly, and that means, in living fact, revelation can only be presupposed to our thoughts, even to those based on exposition, that is, it can only be their organising centre, by revelation itself. Therefore a biblical theology can never consist in more than a series of attempted approximations, a collection of individual exegeses. There can never be any question of a system in the sense of Platonic, Aristotelian or Hegelian philosophy. For the basic thought essential to such a system is not only, as even the philosophers say, the thought of an ultimate, inconceivable reality, but as such—and it is here that the inconceivability of the theologian differs from that of the philosopher—it is not at our disposal. We cannot attain to it as the thought of a true, i.e., a present reality, or we can do so only improperly, i.e., in the form of recollection and expectation. Even the biblical witnesses themselves cannot and do not try to introduce revelation of themselves. They show themselves to be genuine witnesses of it by the fact that they only speak of it by looking forward to it and by looking back at it. How can we wish to complete the totality of their witness by treating revelation as a presupposition which we can control ? How can we expound it except by surrendering ourselves with them to the recollection, their recollection, and to the expectation, their expectation ? It is only in this surrender—and not in an arbitrary doing of what they omitted to do—that our exposition of that witness will be kept pure and will become our own witness. Biblical theology (and self-evidently dogmatics too) can consist only in an exercise in this surrender, not in an attempt to introduce the totality of the biblical witness.

At this point we must ask whether the older Protestant theology of the 17th century did not do too much, and therefore too little. Intrinsically, there can be no objection to the fact that in its exposition it made such active use of the instruments of Aristotelian and later Cartesian philosophy. How can we find fault, and not take as a model, the comprehensive thoroughness and accuracy which it obviously sought and in such surprising measure revealed ? If only it had kept itself freer from the temptation to be inspired to go further and to seek that which is theologically impossible, a systematics of revelation, a system in which revelation can be used as a presupposition ! It attempted to bring in the witness of revelation as such in its unity and entirety. But in so doing it did violence to it. And it was on this that it foundered when the Philistines came upon it in the 18th century as once they had come upon Samson. We must leave it to revelation itself to introduce itself either in its unity and entirety or indeed at all. Revelation is never behind us : always we can only follow it. We cannot think it : we can only contemplate it. We cannot assert and prove it : we can only believe it, believe it in recollection and expectation, so that if our faith is right and well-pleasing to God in what we then think and say, it can assert and prove itself. This, then, is the conclusion and demand to which we are led by a right understanding of the unity of Holy Scripture. And the Church must see to it that we never forget that by virtue of the content and object of canonical Scripture, which are not at our disposal, we have to do with a single witness, i.e., a witness which points in a single direction and attests a single truth. If we accept it in and with the Church to which it was given, then that is the recollection and it is also the expectation in which we have to read it. In this direction the surrender, the following, the contemplation, the believing, can never cease. They cannot and must not be replaced by an arbitrary questing and searching and striving for all other possible directions. Luther once spoke about the unity of Holy Scripture in this way : " For Holy Scripture is the garment which our Lord Christ has put on and in which He lets Himself be seen and found. This garment is woven throughout and so wrought together into one that it cannot be cut or parted. But the soldiers take it from Christ crucified, i.e., heretics and schismatics. It is their particular mischief to want to have the coat entire, persuading everyone that all Scripture agrees with them and is of their opinion . . . they fashion another meaning, apart from and without the Word, this meaning is continually before their eyes, and like a blue glass through which they see everything blue and of their meaning. But they are rogues, as Paul calls them, in Eph. 4, when he warns them not to be driven about by every wind of doctrine through the sleight of men. In Greek this little word " sleight " is *kybia*, in German dicing or cheating. For just as rogues are masters of dicing, and it yields them whatever they desire, so the schismatics and sectarians deal with Scripture, each of them wanting it all and dicing for it " (*Pred. üb. Mt.* 26³³ᶠ· *Hauspostille*, 1545, *W.A.* 52, 802, 1). Now the question raised is one which with all due respect we must put to Luther himself. For instance, in his doctrine of the Law and the Gospel, ought he not to have mastered dicing in the best sense and not parted the robe of Christ ? We can also put it to the later doctrine of a redemptive history working itself out in many different and ascending stages. We can put it to the idea of a development of revelation, which can and necessarily does so easily become that of a development of biblical religion. We can put it to the exalting of the Synoptists over John, or the Gospels over the apostolic writings, or in the Old Testament to the customary exalting of the prophets in the narrower sense : all of which correspond to the onesidedness of Luther. In all these cases the failure to recognise the unity of Scripture involved sooner or later, and inevitably, a failure to recognise that it is Holy Scripture. For when we have such arbitrary preferences, we do not read even the parts which we prefer as Holy Scripture. The same is true of any preference, even the most detailed. This criterion ought to be applied to the most commonly accepted doctrine of the Church, even that which we find in the confessional documents. And particularly should it be applied to individual teachers, even the greatest of them. For fundamentally, whenever anything which is " written " is overlooked in the exposition of Scripture, whenever for the sake of the exposition we are forced to weaken or even omit what is written, there is always the possibility that the exposition has really missed the one thing which Scripture as a whole attests, even when it thinks that it has found it. An exposition is trustworthy to the extent that it not only expounds the text in front of it, but implicitly at least expounds all other texts, to the extent that it at any rate clears the way for the exposition of all other texts. Among the older Protestant theologians there were some (e.g., B. Bucan, *Inst. theol.*, 1602, *Loc.* 4, 11 ; *Syn. pur. Theol.*, Leiden 1624, *Disp.* 3, 20), who argued that when the prophets were added to the Law, which alone constituted Holy Scripture in the first instance, they did not make it more complete as such, i.e., as the Word of God, but as the expounding and confirming of the first witness by a second they made it clearer. But the same can also be said of the adding of the New Testament to the Old. Salvation is in fact already proclaimed and can be accepted in the Pentateuch as such. We can say that this is too bold a view. In any case it is gratuitous, for we do not have to do now only with the Pentateuch. But I cannot see where it is actually wrong. If all Scripture does in fact attest one thing, it cannot be denied that if we only know one part of it, it attests it perfectly even in that part. It does not consist only of such a part, but of the whole. Therefore this consideration does not absolve us from taking it seriously as a whole. But it is a constant reminder that, instructed and restrained by the whole, we have in fact to seek the one thing in the individual part as well.

3. It has often been asked whether and to what extent the doctrine of Holy Scripture, and especially the proposition that of all the literature of the world, ancient and modern, we must recognise in these writings Holy Writings, is based on the Bible itself ?

That this statement does correspond with what Holy Scripture teaches about itself rests first of all, and generally and indirectly, upon the uniqueness and contingency of the revelation attested in it. We can put it even more simply and say that it rests on the true humanity of the person of Jesus Christ as the object of its testimony. What else is the Bible but the proof of the existence of the historical environment of this reality and, to that extent, of the historicity of the reality itself ? But of all world literature it is only the Bible which offers this proof : or other literature offers it only because it has first been offered by the Bible. In general, therefore, the witness of Holy Scripture to itself consists simply in the fact that it is witness to Jesus Christ. And the knowledge of the truth of this self-witness, the knowledge of its unique authority, stands or falls with the knowledge that Jesus Christ is the incarnate Son of God. But because this knowledge coincides with the knowledge of faith in His resurrection from the dead, we must say that Scripture attests itself in the fact that at its decisive centre it attests the resurrection of Jesus Christ from the dead. But the attestation of the resurrection of Jesus, which awakens faith and its knowledge, is itself again only the self-attestation of God by the Holy Spirit. In the final analysis, therefore, we have to say that Holy Scripture testifies to and for itself by the fact that the Holy Spirit testifies to the resurrection of Christ and therefore that He is the incarnate Son of God.

To this general and implicit self-witness, however, there corresponds a specific and explicit. Everywhere the Bible speaks not only of the revelation of God in Jesus Christ as opposed to all men, man and humanity generally. It does, of course, do that. In fact, we must say that this is the real content of the Bible. We have seen earlier that the man addressed and claimed in revelation belongs as such to its content, is taken into revelation itself. But now we must go further and say more concretely that the content of the Bible, as understood in this setting, has a definite form, which cannot be separated from it as this content. The Bible as witness of divine revelation comes to every man, all men, and in a measure includes them in itself. Rightly understood, all humanity, whether it is aware of it or not, does actually stand in the Bible, and is therefore itself posited as a witness of divine revelation. But that this is the case is made possible and conditioned by the fact that in the first instance not all men but certain specific men stand in the Bible : that is, the men who in face of the unique and contingent revelation had the no less unique and contingent function of being the first witnesses. Because there were and still are those first witnesses, there could and can be second and third witnesses. We cannot speak about Yahweh's covenant with Israel without at once speaking of Moses and the prophets. Similarly in the New Testament, indissolubly bound up with Jesus Christ, there are the figures of His disciples, His followers, His apostles, those who are called by Him, the witnesses of His resurrection, those to whom He Himself has directly promised and given His Holy Spirit. The Church can say anything at all about the event of God and man only because something unique has taken place between God and these specific men, and because in what they wrote, or what was written by them, they confront us as living documents of that unique event. To try to ignore them is to ignore that unique event. The existence of these specific men is the existence of Jesus Christ for us and for all men. It is in this function that they are distinguished from us and from all other men, whom they resemble in everything else. Therefore the specific and explicit self-witness of Scripture consists in the fact that, from the standpoint of the form in which its content is offered and alone offered to us, it is the witness of the existence of these specific men.

It is the unique and contingent fact of the New Testament apostolate from which we may best begin if we are to hear and understand what the Bible means by this witness. (Cf. for what follows : E. Fuchs, " Die Auferstehung Jesu Christi und der Anfang der Kirche," *Zeitschr. für. Kirchengesch.* 1932, vol. I–II p. 1 f.) Jesus Christ as the revelation of God does not remain alone and therefore unhistorical. He can therefore come to us and to all men. He has primary witnesses, who can be succeeded by secondary and tertiary witnesses. This fact, which is just as unique as revelation itself, is expressly described as a special creation of Jesus Christ : καὶ ἐποίησεν δώδεκα ἵνα ὦσιν μετ' αὐτοῦ καὶ ἵνα ἀποστέλλῃ αὐτοὺς κηρύσσειν (Mk. 3¹⁴). Like so many evangelical passages embedded in the passion narrative, we have to regard this saying as proleptic, i.e., it acquires its proper sense only through the message of the resurrection. Another creative word, but the real content of which can again only be understood in the light of Easter, is that when Jesus (e.g., Mk. 2¹⁴) challenges a man with His ἀκολούθει μοι. Eph. 4¹¹ also speaks of a creation of the resurrected Christ when it says : αὐτὸς ἔδωκεν τοὺς μὲν ἀποστόλους, τοὺς δὲ προφήτας, τοὺς δὲ εὐαγγελλιστάς. . . . It is " by Jesus Christ, indeed by God the Father, who raised him from the dead " that Paul is an apostle and was " set apart from his mother's womb " (Gal. 1¹· ¹⁵, cf. Jer. 1⁵). Apostles are those who were chosen as such by Jesus " through the Holy Spirit " (Ac. 1²). In this light we can understand the unusual characteristics in which not only Paul spoke of his apostolate, but which are everywhere peculiar to the evangelical part of the New Testament. "Whoso heareth you heareth me " (Lk. 10¹⁶). " He that receiveth you receiveth me " (Mt. 10⁴⁰). We must not weaken this. It does not say : " also heareth me " or " also receiveth me." The meaning already is that to hear and receive the disciples is to hear and receive Christ. There is no hearing or receiving of Christ which does not have the form of a hearing and receiving of His disciples. For " as the Father hath sent me (ἀπέσταλκεν), even so send (πέμπω) I you " (Jn. 20²¹). " The words which thou gavest me I have given unto them ; and they received them and knew of a truth that I came forth from thee, and they believed that thou didst send me " (Jn. 17⁸). In the relationship between Jesus Christ and the apostles there is therefore repeated or reflected in some degree the economy of the incarnation of the Word. That is why in the one breath Jesus prays for them, and yet not only for them, but for them that believe on Him through their word (Jn. 17²⁰). That is why He spoke to Peter as He did. Peter by the confession revealed to him by the Father in heaven showed himself to be the rock on which Jesus would build His Church, the man to whom He would give the keys of the kingdom of heaven for a human binding and loosing on earth, with which the divine binding and loosing in heaven would be utterly identical (Mt. 16¹⁸ᶠ·)—a power which we know from Mt. 18¹⁸ and Jn. 20²³ is not only (as the well-known Roman Catholic exposition has it) ascribed and attributed to Peter, but in the person of Peter to the whole apostolic band, to the primary witnesses as such. That is why these primary witnesses are told that, when challenged by the world to give an account of themselves, they should not be anxious how and what they should speak : " . . . For it shall be given you in that same hour what ye shall speak. For it is not ye that speak but the Spirit of your Father which speaketh in you " (Mt. 10¹⁹ᶠ·). " Ye shall receive the power of the Holy Ghost which shall come upon you ; and ye shall be my witnesses " (Ac. 1⁸). For " the Comforter, which is the Holy Ghost, whom the Father will send in my name, he shall teach you all things and bring all things to your remembrance whatsoever I have said unto you " (Jn. 14²⁶). As the Spirit of truth He " will guide you into all truth " (Jn. 16¹³). The fulfilment of this promise is the specific theme of the story of Whitsunday in Ac. 2¹ᶠ·, and it is the presupposition of all the apostolic activity and proclamation which begins there. " Look on us," is what Peter can and must now say to the lame man before the beautiful gate of the Temple, although he has nothing to give him

other than the Word in the name of Jesus Christ of Nazareth (Ac. 3[41.]). It is
the fact that they have to speak this Word, that is, therefore, that they have to
speak in fulfilment of the revelation accomplished in Jesus Christ of Nazareth,
in such a way that He Himself is with them always (Mt. 28[20]) ; it is this which
marks them out, so that now we have to look at them. In the light of these
passages we cannot speak of Paul's sense of his office and mission as extraordinary.
It was in keeping with the New Testament as a whole when in 2 Cor. 5[18] he described the reconciliation accomplished in Jesus Christ, and the " gift " of the
" ministry of reconciliation," as two sides of one and the same thing. In the
analogia fidei there is again a similarity between God and man, between the
heavenly and the earthly reality. " We are ambassadors for Christ, as though
God did beseech by us : we pray you in Christ's stead, be ye reconciled to God "
(2 Cor. 5[20]). In this saying we could easily find the whole biblical basis of the
Scripture principle.

And it was not the case that the Early Church arbitrarily expanded the
evangelical-apostolic witness to Jesus Christ, when out of a pious regard for the
sacred records of God's former people, or a need to vindicate itself by an attachment to this tradition, it added as a preface the Canon of the Synagogue. Both
in the early days and more recently there have been many proposals and attempts
to shake off the so-called Old Testament altogether or to reduce it to the level of
a deutero-canonical introduction to the real Bible (i.e., the New Testament),
which is good and profitable for reading. In face of such attempts we cannot be
too clear that for the most primitive Church, not only for Jews but also for the
Gentiles, the New and not the Old Testament was the addition, the enlargement
and the extension of the Canon, and that not the Gospels and the apostolic writings,
but the Canon of the Synagogue, Moses, the prophets and the psalms (Lk. 24[44]),
constituted the self-evident basis of Holy Scripture. Neither in the New Testament nor in the documents of the 2nd-century post-apostolic period do we find
the slightest trace of anyone seriously and responsibly trying to replace the Holy
Scriptures of Israel by other traditions of other nations, all those nations within
which the first Churches sprang up, or to proclaim those traditions as prophecies
of Christ and therefore as a more suitable introduction to the New Testament
Bible. Yet this would have meant a great easing of the missionary task, and
apologetics often tended in this direction, although hardly ever with reference
to the problem of the Canon. Even Marcion never plunged in this direction,
although he was near enough to it. We cannot plunge in this direction, we cannot even try to do what Marcion and after him the Socinians and Schleiermacher
and Ritschl and Harnack tried to do, without substituting another foundation
for the foundation on which the Christian Church is built. The Old Testament
is not an introduction to the real New Testament Bible, which we can dispense
with or replace. We cannot eliminate the Old Testament or substitute for it
the records of the early religious history of other peoples, as R. Wilhelm has
suggested in the case of China, B. Gutmann in some sense in that of Africa, and
many recent fools in the case of Germany. If we do, we are not merely opposing
a questionable accessory, but the very institution and existence of the Christian
Church. We are founding a new Church, which is not a Christian Church. For
not only is the canonicity of the Old Testament no arbitrary expansion of the
evangelical-apostolical witness to Christ. It existed before and when the first
Church arose, even in the evangelical-apostolical witness to Christ, which as
the witness of recollection has rightly been placed alongside the original Canon,
the witness of expectation. It was so embedded in the New Testament Bible
itself that only if we wanted to make the latter unreadable could we try to assess
and understand it as the witness of divine revelation apart from the original
Canon. Whether we like it or not, the Christ of the New Testament is the Christ
of the Old Testament, the Christ of Israel. The man who will not accept this
merely shows that in fact he has already substituted another Christ for the

Christ of the New Testament. It was not to dissolve the Law and the prophets
but to fulfil them that the real Christ of the New Testament came (Mt. 5[17];
cf. Jn. 10[35]). Let us remember what is said on this score by that Gospel of
Luke, which Marcion preferred but also assiduously. corrected. " This day,"
says Jesus when He first appears, " is the scripture fulfilled in your ears " (Lk.
4[21]). In the suffering of Jesus " all things that are written by the prophets
concerning the Son of man shall be accomplished" (Lk. 18[31]). The revelation
of the risen Christ in the episode of the walk to Emmaus (Lk. 24[13f.]) consists
in nothing but the opening, expounding and confirming of what Moses, the
prophets and all the Scriptures have prophesied. That is why it says in Jn. 1[45]:
" We have found him, of whom Moses in the law, and the prophets, did write."
That is why the Jews are reproached in Jn. 5[39], " Ye search the scriptures ;
for in them ye (rightly) think ye have eternal life : and they are they which
testify of me." " For had ye believed Moses, ye would have believed me ; for
he wrote of me " (Jn. 5[46]). The tenor of the New Testament witness to Christ
can really be seen from the verse of the Psalm quoted in Heb. 10[7] : " Lo, I come
(in the volume of the book it is written of me) to do thy will, O God." The " Gospel
of God," which Paul too, and especially Paul, proclaims, is none other than that
which God " promised afore by his prophets in the holy scriptures " (Rom. 1[2],
3[21], 16[26]). Again and again Paul stresses (Rom. 4[23f.], 15[4] ; 1 Cor. 9[10], 10[11]) that
what happened and was recorded in the Old Testament was " for our sakes,"
and therefore that it takes place and is recorded in an actuality which does not
diminish but is only now fully demonstrated. It is decisive for Paul that the
death and resurrection of Christ took place κατὰ τὰς γραφάς (1 Cor. 15[3f.]). At
the very points where we might expect the word " God," he uses " Scripture " :
" the scripture saith unto Pharaoh . . ." (Rom. 9[17]), " the scripture hath concluded all under sin " (Gal. 3[22], cf. Rom. 11[32]). It is evident, therefore, that
the desire of the Evangelists and apostles themselves was simply to be expositors
of the former Scriptures. According to Ac. 26[22], Paul will say nothing (οὐδὲν
ἐκτός) but what the prophets and Moses had said in relation to the future.
And they obviously instructed their followers to do the same, as we see from
the story of the Christians of Beroea (Ac. 17[11]) or of the conversion of the Jew
Apollos (Ac. 18[24f.]), or from passages like 1 Tim. 4[13], 2 Tim. 3[15f.]. We have " the
sure word of prophecy." And " ye do well that ye take heed thereunto as unto
a light that shineth in a dark place, until the day dawn, and the day star arise
in your hearts " (2 Pet. 1[19]).

And now we have only to answer the question whether the Old Testament
witnesses understood themselves in the same way, i.e., as called and separated
witnesses of the one revelation of the one God in Jesus Christ, as they undoubtedly
came to be understood by the men of the New Testament. This is the decisive
issue between the Church and the Synagogue. In denying Christ, the Synagogue
denies the one revelation of the one God. Its answer is therefore in the negative.
But the Church gives an affirmative answer, as does also the New Testament :
Christ has risen from the dead, and has revealed the fulfilment of Scripture and
therefore its real meaning. In the light of this, how can the Church understand
the Old Testament witnesses except as witnesses to Christ ? A religio-historical
understanding of the Old Testament in abstraction from the revelation of the
risen Christ is simply an abandonment of the New Testament and of the sphere
of the Church in favour of that of the Synagogue, and therefore in favour of an
Old Testament which is understood apart from its true object, and content.
Already, in an earlier context, we have stated the basic considerations which
have to be stated in this regard, and all that we can now do is to say once more
that this question of the self-understanding of the Old Testament witnesses is
ultimately identical with the question of faith. If Christ has risen from the
dead, then the understanding of the Old Testament as a witness to Christ is not
a later interpretation, but an understanding of its original and only legitimate

sense. Moses and the prophets do not belong only because the New Testament undoubtedly says so, but—when the New Testament has undoubtedly said so on the basis of the resurrection of Jesus—they belong, not as the representatives of an earlier religion prior to the Evangelists and apostles, but as the prophetic heralds of Jesus Christ side by side with them. Therefore the Church cannot be released from its task of expounding and applying the Old Testament witness too, and of respecting its authority as the Word of God.

Scripture not only attests to us the objective fact of the revelation which has taken place, its expectation and recollection. It also attests itself in the existence of these specific men, Moses and the prophets, the Evangelists and apostles. And in so doing—and this is what we now have to emphasise—it has in view the function in which passively and actively these men were what they were, and in their writings are what they are. Passively, as distinct from us and all other men, they were those who have seen and heard the unique revelation as such, and seen and heard therefore in a unique way, fashioning their historical environment.

" That which was from the beginning, which we have heard, which we have seen with our eyes, which we have looked upon and our hands have handled, περὶ τοῦ λόγου τῆς ζωῆς (perhaps : surrounding the word of life). . . . For the life was manifested, and we have seen it " (1 Jn. 1¹ᶠ·). But we must also remember the remarkable passage in Num. 12¹⁻¹⁶, which tells us of a rebellion of Miriam and Aaron against Moses : " Hath the Lord indeed spoken only by Moses ? hath he not spoken also by us ? " The following is the answer given to them : " If there be a prophet among you, I the Lord will make myself known unto him in a vision, and will speak unto him in a dream. My servant Moses is not so, who is faithful in all mine house. With him will I speak mouth to mouth, even manifestly, and not in dark speeches ; and the form of the Lord shall he behold : wherefore then were ye not afraid to speak against my servant Moses ? " But there is another rather stronger view of the idea of prophecy, and in some contexts the same directness of meeting with God is ascribed to the prophets as well. With all other Israelites the prophets are witnesses to the internal and external history of Israel. But at the same time—and it is this that raises them out of the mass of the nation—they are witnesses to the will of God concealed in this history, challenging and ruling, promising and threatening. " The Lord God doeth nothing, but he revealeth his secret unto his servants the prophets " (Amos 3⁷). To that extent they, too, are obviously amongst those who see and hear according to 1 Jn. 1¹ᶠ.

But the function of these men has also and necessarily another and active side. As distinct from us and all other men, they were those who have to proclaim to others, and therefore to us and all other men, revelation as they encounter it.

Reading on in 1 Jn. 1³ᶠ· : " That which we have seen and heard declare we unto you, that ye also may have fellowship with us : and truly our fellowship is with the Father, and with his Son Jesus Christ. And these things write we unto you, that our joy may be fulfilled." We are now reminded that right throughout the Old Testament, to those to whom He speaks, and by the very fact that He does speak, Yahweh gives a mission and authority, a commission and command, that they too should speak. We are reminded that everywhere the Old Testament claims to speak with authority, because it repeats in human words what has first been said by Yahweh Himself. Not every man can do this.

Not every man can speak God's Word. For not every man has heard it. But those who have heard it can and must repeat it. This speaking the Word of God is the second thing which makes prophets prophets. And at this point we have striking evidence of the unity between the Old Testament and the New. For as Yahweh does with His prophets, so Jesus calls and sends and commissions His disciples, to speak of the Kingdom of God, i.e., of His own presence as the presence of the Messiah. No Old Testament witness had spoken of it. Therefore no one in the Old Testament, not even Moses, exercised such a mission. All of them, even Moses himself and the greatest prophets, are themselves sent. Yahweh alone is the subject of this sending. In the New Testament only Jesus is the subject of the sending, and compared with Him the others are all sent by Him. Apart from this unheard-of innovation everything is exactly as it was in the Old Testament. It is part of the concept of εὐαγγελιστής, and ἀπόστολος, as it is also of that of prophet, that they do not have to speak in their own name but only in the name, i.e., in fulfilment of the revelation of Jesus : to speak of Him, to speak by His commission, to speak according to His ordering, to speak of the ability which is to be expected from Him. If we interpret these men as free religious thinkers, from the very outset we are guilty of an interpretation which the texts not only do not substantiate but openly contradict : at a decisive point we are understanding them in a way in which they did not understand themselves and did not wish to be understood at any price. " And such trust have we through Christ to Godward : not that we are sufficient of ourselves, to think anything as of ourselves : but our sufficiency is of God, who also hath made us able ministers of the new covenant " (2 Cor. 3[4f.]). " I will not dare to speak of any things save those which Christ hath wrought by me, to make the Gentiles obedient by word and deed " (Rom. 15[18]). In fact : " Christ . . . speaketh in me . . ." (2 Cor. 13[3]). That is why Paul has to say : " Woe is unto me, if I preach not the Gospel " (1 Cor. 9[16]). That is why in the Acts and Epistles the preaching of the apostles is often regarded as equivalent to the Word of God itself. The active side of the function of these men has to be understood wholly and utterly in the light of the passive.

And now a necessary and self-evident delimitation : these men are holy men and the authors of Holy Scripture in this function, but only in this function, only in the exercise of this office. Not therefore as thinkers, not as religious personalities or geniuses, not as moral heroes, although they were these things too in the right sense and in varying degrees. What they were as witnesses to revelation, and therefore as those who saw and heard and were sent on a commission and empowered, was neither the greater nor smaller, the better nor the worse, for what they were from the intellectual or religious or moral standpoint.

In relation to many of these spokesmen, the Bible itself has unintentionally and often enough intentionally made it clear that it holds out little reward for those who try to find its meaning at this kind of level. At this level they are only like us and all men. Perhaps there have been much more pious men and cleverer and better men than these prophets and apostles. Indeed, J. Wichelhaus ventured to say rather morosely that " as men Paul and Peter do not deserve our confidence at all " (*Die Lehre der Heiligen Schrift*[3], 1892, p. 221). Now, there is no reason why as men they should not deserve as much faith as we usually give to other men—but no more, and of no other kind.

The decisive confidence, i.e., a confidence in what they say, is something which they certainly cannot create by the incidental glimpses of their humanity. On the contrary, it is only what they say that by its own credibility can create confidence in their humanity. But necessarily this means—and it applies to all of them—a judgment on their humanity. To look on them, as we are requested to do in Ac. 3⁴, always means, to look on Him who has sent them.

4. As the witness of divine revelation the Bible also attests the institution and function of prophets and apostles. And in so doing it attests itself as Holy Scripture, as the indispensable form of that content. But because this is the case, in this question of divine revelation the Church, and in and with it theology, has to hold fast to this unity of content and form. The distinction of form and content must not involve any separation. Even on the basis of the biblical witness we cannot have revelation except through this witness. We cannot have revelation " in itself." The purpose of the biblical witness is not to help us achieve this, so that its usefulness is outlived when it is achieved. Revelation is, of course, the theme of the biblical witness. And we have already seen that the perception of it is absolutely decisive for the reading and understanding and expounding of this biblical witness. But it always.is the theme of this, the biblical witness. We have no witness to it but this. There are, therefore, no points of comparison to make it possible for us even in part to free ourselves from this witness, to put ourselves into direct relationship to the theme of it. And it is in keeping with the nature of this theme that (in the form of the calling and enlightening and empowering of these specific men) it has been indissolubly linked with its witness, i.e., their witness. In this question of revelation we cannot, therefore, free ourselves from the texts in which its expectation and recollection is attested to us. We are tied to these texts. And we can only ask about revelation when we surrender to the expectation and recollection attested in these texts.

" It holdeth God's word," is what Luther once said about the Bible (*Pred. üb. Rom.* 15⁴ᶠ·, 1522, *W.A.* 10¹· ² 75, 6). It only " holds," encloses, limits and surrounds it : that is the indirectness of the identity of revelation and the Bible. But it and it alone does really " hold " it : it comprehends and encloses it in itself, so that we cannot have the one without the other ; that is why we have to speak about an indirect *identity*. The idea against which we have to safeguard ourselves at this point is one which has tacitly developed in connexion with modern theological historicism. It is to the effect that in the reading and understanding and expounding of the Bible the main concern can and must be to penetrate past the biblical texts to the facts which lie behind the texts. Revelation is then found in these facts as such (which in their factuality are independent of the texts). Thus a history of Israel and of Old Testament religion is found behind the canonical Old Testament, a history of the life of Jesus, and later of course a Christ-myth, behind the canonical Gospels, a history of the apostolic age, i.e., of primitive Christianity behind the canonical Acts and epistles. The intention is to subject the biblical Canon to the question of truth as formulated in the sense of modern historicism. The Bible is to be read as a collection of sources. In the first instance this was all done in all good faith even from the ecclesiastical and theological standpoint. There was such confidence

in the rightness and utility of the question of truth formulated in the sense
of modern historicism that it could be thought the highest honour for the Bible
and the greatest benefit for oneself, i.e., for Christendom, to proceed from a study
of the texts to the formation, with the help of observations gained from them,
of a conception or conceptions of what is true and proper in them, of a form of
the spirit apart from the letter. Now we must not overlook the human significance not only of the genuine scientific concern but also of the religious earnestness which went to the making of these pictures, or of the enthusiasm with
which it was thought they should be presented to the Church : " These be thy
gods, O Israel." But at the same time we cannot ignore the fact that in substance it was a mistake from the very first. From the very first : not therefore
from the moment when the Canon was approached critically as a collection of
sources ; not from the moment when it was read with caution, with actual
doubt whether things did take place exactly as we read, with an assessment of
the varying so-called " values " of the different sources, with the disqualification of this or that constituent part, with conjectures on the true connexions of
what actually took place instead of those given or omitted in the texts, with a
more or less comprehensive correction of the biblical in favour of an " historical "
truth, and finally with a partial or total reconstruction of reality as it is thought
to be better seen over the heads and shoulders of the biblical authors. It was a
long way from Zacharias to Gunkel and Reimarus to Wrede. But once the way
was entered we need not be surprised if the eventual results were so radical that
they caused pain in the Church. And they could not be prescribed or suppressed.
But it is not because of the results, which were, of course, opposed by other
more harmless, i.e., conservative ones, that this road must be called the wrong
one. It is so, because at bottom it means succumbing to the temptation to read
the Canon differently from what it is intended to be and can be read—which
is the same thing. The universal rule of interpretation is that a text can be
read and understood and expounded only with reference to and in the light of its
theme. But if this is the case, then in the light of the theme—not *a priori*, but
from the text itself—the relationship between theme and text must be accepted
as essential and indissoluble. The form cannot therefore be separated from the
content, and there can be no question of a consideration of the content apart
from the form. We cannot therefore put the question of truth in the direct way
that it was arbitrarily thought it should be put. It is not that, when we have
consulted Genesis and the Synoptics as unfortunately our only sources, the real
question concerning the early history of Israel or the life of Jesus is a question
of history, i.e., the history of the world of culture, of religion, somewhere behind
Genesis and the Synoptics. Except in historical terms—in terms of the history
of literature—these writings cannot be read merely as sources. If we have a
particular interest in antiquities, we can read them in this way at our own risk,
at the risk of failing to serve even our own interest and missing the real nature
and character of the writings. Why should there not be occasional items of this
kind in the Bible ? But by obstinately putting this question of truth, by acting
as though the interest in antiquities is the only legitimate interest, the true
nature and character of the writings has been missed for over a hundred years.
And that this should be so—even if there were more agreement than there actually
is on the validity of this hermeneutic principle—we can only describe as a scandal
even from the celebrated standpoint of " pure scholarship." At any rate it was
a scandal in the Church ; not, of course, that D. F. Strauss and Wellhausen
came to all sorts of extreme results, but that theology allowed itself to be decoyed
into this trap (without even being able to advance in excuse the pretext of being
nominally a non-theological discipline). Theology at least, even and especially
historical theology, which applies itself particularly to the biblical texts, ought to
have (let us say it at once) the tact and taste, in face of the linking of form and
content in those texts of which it must still be aware, to resist this temptation,

to leave the curious question of what is perhaps behind the texts, and to turn
with all the more attentiveness, accuracy and love to the texts as such. In its
arbitrary attempt to sketch and create those pictures, it largely failed to do the
work really laid upon it. It is only to-day that we can see how little we have
really gained from that intensive and extensive ploughing of the field of New
Testament literature to help us to explain even the simplest individual concepts,
not to speak of commenting on the texts both as they stand and in relation one
to another. It is no accident that, when about 1920 Protestant theology made a
kind of rediscovery of the objectivity of the New Testament and of the biblical
witness generally, at almost the same time—with the emergence of the so-called
" *formgeschichtlich* " method introduced by M. Dibelius, R. Bultmann and K. L.
Schmidt (F. Overbeck was, of course, a forerunner)—in the case of the New
Testament at least it came to a consciousness of the form of the witness corresponding to that objectivity. And it is also no accident that in our days it is
to the preparation of a biblico-theological dictionary that the most powerful
forces of biblical research are applied, although unfortunately we cannot say
that the advance which we must now make is equally clear to all those who are
co-operating in this enterprise. The real decision whether in this field we are
going to make a move for the better will depend on two things. The first is
whether there will be the rekindling of a similar interest in Old Testament
scholarship. But the second is whether in both fields the time has not passed
when we can select arbitrary themes, whether the exegesis of canonical Scripture
as such, the coherent exposition of Genesis, Isaiah, the Gospel of Matthew, etc.,
according to their present status and compass is again recognised and undertaken
as in the last resort the only possible goal of biblical scholarship. As material
for the carrying out of this true and long neglected task, we must not and cannot
ignore the insights won under the perverted sign of the earlier source-investigation
of the Bible. There cannot, therefore, be any question of sealing off or abandoning
so-called " criticism," as it has been so significant for this investigation. All
relevant, historical questions must be put to the biblical texts, considered as
witnesses in accordance with their literary form. And the differences in exposition which result when we answer them can only be to the good, so long as
criticism is clearly made to serve this task, so long as it no longer has to serve
the foolish end of mediating an historical truth lying behind the texts. The
historical truth which in its own way biblical scholarship does have to mediate
is the true meaning and context of the biblical texts as such. Therefore it is not
different from the biblical truth which has to be mediated. When that is seen
and understood, when the foolish pursuit of an historical truth *supra scripturam*
is on all sides abandoned in favour of a circumscribed investigation of the *veritas
scripturae ipsius*, then we can and must give the freest possible course to critical
questions and answers as demanded by the character of the biblical witness as
a human document, and therefore an historical quantity. For in these circumstances the questions and answers can and will indicate only that Scripture is
taken seriously as it actually is before us. And the questions and answers can
and will help to safeguard our reading and understanding and expounding of
Scripture from the arbitrary desire, by which it was continually threatened in
the earlier days of the Church, which knew nothing of these questions and
answers, to express its concrete form plastically, and in that way to direct and
hold in definite lines the question of its objective content, the question of God's
revelation. As I see it, this does not mean an annulling of the results of biblical
scholarship in the last centuries, nor does it mean a breaking off and neglect of
efforts in this direction. What it does mean is a radical re-orientation concerning
the goal to be pursued, on the basis of the recognition that the biblical texts
must be investigated for their own sake to the extent that the revelation which
they attest does not stand or occur, and is not to be sought, behind or above
them but in them. If in reply it is asked whether Christianity is really a

book-religion, the answer is that strangely enough Christianity has always been and only been a living religion when it is not ashamed to be actually and seriously a book-religion. Expounding the saying in 2 Cor. 5[7] (" We walk by faith, not by sight ") and linking it up with 1 Cor. 13[12], Calvin coined the statement, *videmus enim, sed in speculo et aenigmate ; hoc est loco rei in verbo acquiescimus* (*C.R.* 50, 63). Biblical theology can be as critical as it will and must—but if it carries out the programme outlined in this statement, it will always do good work as ecclesiastical scholarship : better than that done in recent centuries in spite of all the seriousness and industry applied to it. And it will have an honourable place as scholarship in the general sense.

5. When we regard the prophets and apostles as witnesses of divine revelation, in this their function as witnesses we ascribe to them, as under 3, a very definite separation from us and all other men, a singular and unique position and significance. The thought of this separation is obviously sharpened when it is clear to us that we cannot separate between the form and content of this witness, that in order to arrive at revelation we should not and cannot go beyond the prophets and apostles, and their expectation and recollection, to the pseudo-presence of revelation in itself. Among the many other quantities and factors, which together constitute our human-historical cosmos, the Church sees that these men, this collection of Scriptures (not in the first instance and directly in opposition to the so-called world, but very definitely and in the first instance in opposition to the Church itself) are underlined and singled out and appointed to a role and dignity peculiar to themselves alone.

" They have received the gift of miracles and instruction as distinct from us, to whom it can only belong to speak what has been delivered to us by this declaration of grace " (John Damascene, *Ekd.* 1, 3). *Hoc esse*, writes Calvin, *rectae intelligentiae initium, cum fidem, quae Deo debetur, tribuimus sanctis eius prophetis.* They can be described as " holy men of God " because they *iniunctum sibi munus fideliter exsequentes, divinam in suo ministerio personam sustinuerunt* (*Comm. on* 2 *Pet.* 1[20] *C.R.* 55, 458).

But this setting apart and singling out are ascribed to them by the Church because it belongs to them, and because they have shown and proved themselves to be singled out and set apart, as we have seen already in our discussion of the concept of the Canon. It lies in the nature of this separation and differentiation that it has a limit. Scripture is Holy Scripture as the witness of divine revelation, in the passive and active function of the men who speak in it, in the event of this function, i.e., in such a way that the revelation of God is manifest in its witness demanding and receiving obedience as the Word of God. But only in this way. We have already indicated that the intellectual and moral and religious qualities of these men can neither confirm nor compromise their differentiation. We must now go on to say that between the Bible and the other quantities and factors of our human cosmos there is no difference in so far as the Bible is incidentally a historical document for the history of ancient Israel and its religion, in so far as it is also a document for one aspect of the religious history of Hellenism and can therefore be used as a collection of historical sources—although with little prospect of success in view of its peculiar literary form. Again, as a timeless document of the human longing and seeking for the unconditioned, the Bible can, if we like, be read alongside documents of a similar kind. And we shall find that fundamentally at any rate it is not different from other documents of this kind. Therefore we need not be surprised if we have to say that in other documents of this kind we may perhaps find more edification, i.e., a stronger impulse to this longing and seeking, that in Goethe's *Faust* or even in the sacred books of other religions we can better attain this end. On our own account and at our own risk we can go further and widen the concept of man of God, or prophet, or perhaps even apostle. And on all sorts of pretexts (not without approximation to the Catholic principle of tradition, and even perhaps assimilation to it) we can extend the concept of the witness of revelation to all the realities in which we think we can see an actual mediation of Christ, or more generally a divine impulse from man to man.

For the sake of clarity I will quote what Horst Stephan (*Glaubenslehre*[2] 1928) wrote about " gradation " within that sum of the sources of Christian doctrine which is for him the " Word of God " : " If we give Jesus the special place due to Him, the first rank is taken by the God-sent figures whom we call prophets. They are the leaders from the great days of Israel to Paul and the founding of Protestantism. We can provisionally describe Luther as the last of the prophets. Even this series of prophets demands in detail a more exact differentiation in type and importance. But the second rank stands in even greater need of grouping and individuation. It comprises all the pious who have had influence at particular periods, especially those who have given classical formulation to the Christian faith in definite cultural epochs : figures like Origen and Augustine in late antiquity ; Saint (!) Thomas or Meister Eckart in the Middle Ages ; Melanchthon, Zwingli and Calvin in the older Protestantism (together with Luther, who in the main motifs of his activity rose to the height of prophecy . . .), Herder and Schleiermacher in German Neo-Protestantism. In the third place we might mention those who are children of their age in their Christianity, but who transcend it in certain aspects, e.g., Saint (!) Francis in the Middle Ages, and more recently a Zinzendorf or John Wesley or even (at a considerable remove) a Wichern and Kierkegaard. It is only after the figures of the second and third groups that we encounter all those other spirits whose achievements are only small or preparatory, but who do at times formulate items of knowledge with particular clarity and impressiveness ; as for example the many religious poets or great theologians " (p. 28). In a later passage of the book (p. 217) we find that " the skill of a Paul Gerhardt, Bach or Dürer " comes " under consideration " in this sense, and we are told that " living faith is conscious that not only in the Bible is it touched by God's address " (p. 216). " The living God addresses His men where and how He will ; therefore many a word can become ' God's Word,' which at a first glance seems to be purely of the world. If the present congregation leads to Jesus Christ, if a man of the present can become Christ to another man, and win a part in the divine nature, every kind of human speech, of proclamation but also of concept or visible sign or action, can bear within itself the divine speech. In short, the story of faith must be full of the Word of God " (p. 217). Indeed, there can be no question of a separation of the Bible if we take it on ourselves to introduce all kinds of gradations and to call that revelation and the Word of God in which according to individual taste and judgment we think we see revelation and the Word of the so-called " living " God for a so-called " living " faith. We can only ask whether the representatives of this view seriously deny that in the sphere of the Christian Church there can only be revelation and the Word of God, the living God and a living faith, where it is a matter not of an arbitrary human valuation and selection, but of a divine command and on our part obedience ? Or do they regard all these voices of the peoples and centuries as commands enjoining obedience ? And if so, will they seriously claim that there is only a distinction of degree between the divine command heard in the " prophet " Luther or " Saint " Thomas and " Saint " Francis and that heard in the apostle Paul and, " in the special place which belongs to Him," in Jesus. If they do seriously deny the former or assert the latter, and think that they can rightly read and understand and explain the Bible on this presupposition, then we shall have to grant that there is no differentiation of the Bible. It is only rhetorically that we call it " holy " Scripture.

If we ascribe to it the character of Holy Scripture, we can do so only because we remember at least its witness to revelation and the event of its prophetic-apostolic function. We can do so only because we reconcile ourselves to its effective power of command, as we ourselves recognise and acknowledge it to be effective. We can do so only as we reconcile ourselves to it, not as one of the living powers and forces of Christian history, but as the one power and force which has created and bears and rules the Church and with it all Christian history, which therefore confronts as the critical norm the Church and all the forces active in the sphere of the Church—all that we might regard as the witness of revelation and the Word of God according to our individual taste and judgment. It is only in virtue of this separation of itself that the Bible can be set apart. But in virtue of it, it is actually and truly and radically set apart. The objection is to hand : To what extent after all can and should an historical quantity like the Bible be given this basic priority over against all other historical quantities ? When the Christian Church makes the act of remembrance and the corresponding self-reconciliation, in which it gives to the Bible the authority of Holy Scripture, and expects to hear in the Bible and only in the Bible the Word of God, does there not take place something which cannot be squared with the majesty of God : the absolutising of a relative, that is, of a word which is always human, and which cannot stand side by side with the One who Himself is and wills to be God alone ? And if it cannot do that, as a relative does it not belong to the other relativities of our human cosmos ? Does it not belong, in fact, as something which can be compared although it has not yet perhaps been excelled, to that series in which Neo-Protestantism and in another way Roman Catholicism can see it ? Does not the Protestant principle attribute too much to the Bible, and too little to God Himself on the one hand, and to all other witnesses of His revelation on the other ? The answer is that there is indeed only one single absolute fundamental and indestructible priority, and that is the priority of God as Creator over the totality of His creatures and each of them without exception. Yet how strange it is that we learn of this very priority (in the serious sense, in all the compass and power of the concept) only through the Bible, and only through the Bible as it is read and understood and expounded as witness of revelation and therefore as itself the Word of God. We learn of it only through the Bible as it is itself apparently absolutised. The distinction between absolute and relative seems so easy, and it seems childishly easy to say that God alone is absolute and everything else relative, and that there can be no mixture of the two and no third thing between God and everything else. But we have to ask ourselves how we ever come to make this distinction, how human thinking can achieve the thought of the priority of the absolute over against the relative, without either positing the alleged absolute relatively or the relative as quite unreal over against the absolute ? We have also to ask how we succeed not only in thinking this distinction, i.e. achieving it as an idea and concept, but—and this is what makes it a serious thought—in so making it our own that it is not merely a *theoria*, a drama played out in front of us, but that we ourselves achieve it with our lives, in our existence, and the drama of it is our drama ? For what sort of a knowledge of the priority of the absolute would that be which did not mean our acknowledgment of it, which did not include the authority of the absolute and our obedience to it, which was not in fact based on this obviously not self-evident acknowledgment, authority and obedience ? And we have also to ask how after all we can achieve this distinction without coming up against the reality of the judgment in which our existence and with it our thinking are destroyed ? Who then can see the priority of God the Creator and live ? Who or what can be drawn into this drama and not inevitably perish ? It is not, therefore, quite so easy to achieve the distinction on the basis of which we can and must query the differentiation and separateness of the Bible. Even if it is actually achieved in the Bible, with a clear answer to these three questions, this must make us think concerning the nature and status of the Bible itself. According to the Bible, the in itself unthinkable coexistence of absolute and relative is made possible by the fact that it does not speak of the absolute but of the goodness and patience of the Creator of all things revealed to us in Jesus Christ, nor does it speak of the relative, but of the creatures of this Creator. This God is always the Lord of a creation which genuinely exists after its kind. Further, the Bible certainly does not offer us any mere *theoria*, but what takes place in it as a proclamation of the divine Law is the attack on our existence, the act in which we have to recognise the priority of God, in which His authority is set up and our obedience to it becomes an event, and in all these things this distinction becomes reality. Yet according to the Bible this attack is not simply and of itself the judgment on our existence ; but as the proclamation of the Gospel in the Law it is mercy even in judgment, the promise that we can live and shall live, our preservation in the death which encompasses us for the resurrection of the body and eternal life. The knowledge of the priority of God as achieved in the Bible is the knowledge of the divine benefit, again—and here the circle closes—permitting and commanding us in the thought of Creator and creature to achieve calmly and clearly the unthinkable thought of the co-existence of absolute and relative, no, of the gracious God and of the men saved by His grace. But how can we use this knowledge which we owe to the Bible to query the peculiar status and significance of the Bible ? It is certainly impossible for us to ascribe to it this status and significance arbitrarily, i.e., in any act of free valuation. For that reason, for the serious representatives of the Evangelical Scripture principle there was not the remotest question of the " absolutising " of a strictly relative quantity, of the divinisation or quasi-divinisation of men. On this principle nothing was absolutised and no one divinised. Rather the absolute, no, God was present in His Word as the Lord, as the One who commands and the One who shows mercy, as in the human word of the Bible. And the achievement—for the first time seriously—of the distinction between absolute and relative did not mean that the Bible only came later and arbitrarily, with a knowledge of its nature, to stand on the former side. It was there already. It spoke from that side. The distinction could only seriously be made from that side as it was already made. And the so-called Scripture principle, by which it does stand singly and uniquely on this former side, by which it is the Word of God, can only try to be the later statement of an existing content. Again it is quite impossible that there should be a direct identity between the human word of Holy Scripture and the Word of God, and therefore between the creaturely reality in itself and as such and the reality of God the Creator. It is impossible that there should have been a transmutation of the one into the other or an admixture of the one with the other. This is not the case even in the person of Christ where the identity between God and man, in all the originality and indissolubility in which it confronts us, is an assumed identity, one specially willed, created and effected by God, and to that extent indirect, i.e., resting neither in the essence of God nor in that of man, but in a decision and act of God to man. When we necessarily allow for inherent differences, it is exactly the same with the unity of the divine and human word in Holy Scripture.

What Calvin said of the presence of God in the flesh of Christ can, *mutatis mutandis*, be applied to the presence of God in the word of the prophets and apostles : *Sacramenta . . . iustitiae et salutis materiam in eius carne residere docent, non quod a se ipso iustificet aut vivificet merus homo, sed quia Deo placuit, quod in se absconditum et incomprehensibile erat, in mediatore palam facere* (*Instit.* III, 11, 9).

Even here the human element does not cease to be human, and as such and in itself it is certainly not divine. And it is quite certain that God does not cease to be God. In contrast to the humanity of Jesus Christ, there is no unity of person between God and the humanity of the prophets and apostles. Again, in contrast to the humanity of Jesus Christ, the humanity of the prophets and apostles is not taken up into the glory of God. It cannot independently reveal, but only attest, the revelation which did and does take place in the humanity of Jesus Christ. But at this remove and with this difference, as this word of testimony, as the sign of the revelation which has taken place and does take place, and indeed, as we saw, as the sign posited in and with revelation itself, as the witness of witnesses directly called in and with revelation itself, Scripture, too, stands in that indirect identity of human existence with God Himself, which is conditioned neither by the nature of God nor that of man, but brought about by the decision and act of God. It too can and must—not as though it were Jesus Christ, but in the same serious sense as Jesus Christ—be called the Word of God : the Word of God in the sign of the word of man, if we are going to put it accurately.

There is still a third quantity of which we have to say the same thing in its relation to Holy Scripture as we now say of Holy Scripture in its relation to Jesus Christ : the proclamation of the Christian Church by word and sacrament. And there are other signs of revelation of which we cannot say that they are the Word of God, at any rate in the strict and proper sense. The Church as such, e.g., is one great sign of revelation. But it is not the Word of God. On the contrary—and this is something different—it is created by the Word of God and it lives by it. Again, the dogmas of the Church, the constitution of the Canon as recurrently recognised and accepted, the existence of teachers of the Church and their doctrine, the actions and experiences of the Church or of Christians in the world : all these are indeed signs of revelation, but they cannot on that account be called the Word of God in the true and autonomous sense. They are, to the extent that they are proclamation, and to the extent that as proclamation they attest the witness of Holy Scripture and therefore revelation. On the other hand, Holy Scripture is marked off as a sign of revelation from the sign of the true humanity of Christ by the fact that because of the uniqueness and therefore the temporal limitation of revelation, because it has terminated in the ascension of Christ, the latter is hidden from us, i.e., it can be seen only as it is attested by Scripture and the proclamation of the Church and in faith. But since Holy Scripture is the original form of its attestation, since, unlike the proclamation of the Church, it attests revelation in its uniqueness and temporal limitation, it belongs to the first and original sign, the true humanity of Christ. That the Word has become Scripture is not one and the same thing as its becoming flesh. But the uniqueness and at the same time general relevance of its becoming flesh necessarily involved its becoming Scripture. The divine Word became the word of the prophets and apostles by becoming flesh. Because the man Jesus became for these men the Word of God and therefore said to these men, " Receive ye the Holy Ghost," and "He that heareth you heareth me," and " Behold I am with you alway, even unto the end of the world," they have entered into the gap created through the uniqueness and temporal limitation of revelation. To the Church founded by Him, but *in concreto* by their Word—as mediators, as those who bear His commission, as heralds of His lordship—they now stand in the originality which is proper to Him. They share *ministerialiter* the honour which *principaliter* is proper to Him. It is decided by them whether the proclamation of the Church, which corresponds to the original Word of God entrusted by them to the Church, will be the actual Word of God. If the Church really wishes to live by the Word of God and therefore really to be the Church, it can as little overlook and ignore them as it can Jesus Christ Himself. We again recall Calvin's *loco rei in verbo acquiescimus*. Calvin also formulated the same perception in this way: *Mysteria Dei enim, cuiusmodi sunt, quae ad salutem nostram pertinent, in se, suaque (ut dicitur) natura cerni non possunt : verum ipsa in eius verbo duntaxat intuemur : cuius veritas sic persuasa esse nobis debet, ut pro facto impletoque habendum sit quicquid loquitur (Instit.* III, 2, 41). It should now be clear that the word (i.e., the word of Scripture) takes the place of the thing itself (i.e., the Word of God). This does not mean that it is " only " the word of Scripture and not the Word of God which now confronts us. What it does mean is that the Word of God is now the word of Scripture which is its sign ; or more generally, that the thing itself is present and active in the Word.

As the Word of God in the sign of this prophetic-apostolic word of man Holy Scripture is like the unity of God and man in Jesus Christ. It is neither divine only nor human only. Nor is it a mixture of the two nor a *tertium quid* between them. But in its own way and degree it is very God and very man, i.e., a witness of revelation which itself belongs to revelation, and historically a very human literary document. As such it does not violate the majesty of the one God in His distinctness from all that is not Himself. On the contrary, in its existence, i.e., even in its form (which is, of course, entirely grounded in its content) as the only word of man distinguished and separated in this way, it attests the uniqueness of the divine Majesty. The fear that the holiness of Scripture might prejudice the holiness of God will always prove superfluous where the holiness of Scripture is believed in and respected. But in its uniqueness Scripture does not violate the dignity and significance of the other signs and witnesses of revelation. This is primarily because apart from Jesus Christ Himself there is still this other form of the Word of God, which Scripture needs to be the Word of God, just as it needs Scripture. Preaching and the sacrament of the Church do indeed need the basis and authority and authenticity of the original Word of God in Scripture to be the Word of God. But Scripture also needs proclamation by preaching and sacrament, for it wills to be read and understood and expounded and the Word of God attested in it wills to have actuality. Therefore Holy Scripture cannot stand alone as the Word of God in the Church. And far from the voice and the voices of the Church and its teachers and its experiences and decisions and its history and tradition in the manifoldness of its various epochs and gifts being suppressed by the existence of Scripture as the basic and normative and regulative form of the Word of God, it is the very existence of this original form of the Word of God which sees to it that the voice of the Church and all these voices in the Church are heard as voices and have something to say, and have sufficient reason and cause to rise up again and again, receiving a stable direction and order calculated to keep them from chaos and cacophony in spite of all the aberrations and follies of man, so that as the Church is reminded of its existence in Jesus Christ, there is held out to it in concrete reality the promise under which it lives. When the Church has suffered seriously, i.e., not from without but inwardly and essentially, it is never because it has lived too much but too little under the Word of Scripture. But the Church has become increasingly strong and self-conscious and bold, and produced heroes and geniuses and benefactors, and been able to establish comfort and hope for all people, not only within but without its walls, and gained genuine respect for itself, even in the world, when it has had a humble mind, and been prepared to live not above or alongside but under the Word. The existence in all ages of a Church which is really alive is therefore a concrete answer to the objection that an acknowledgment of the priority of the Bible in the Church will be detrimental to the living God and a living faith. The very opposite is the truth. Death usually reigns in the Church when it is thought that this acknowledgment should not be made.

6. We believe in and with the Church that Holy Scripture has this priority over all other writings and authorities, even those of the Church. We believe in and with the Church that Holy Scripture as the original and legitimate witness of divine revelation is itself the Word of God. The words " has " and " is " in these two sentences proclaim the same truth. But they need to be explained and delimited rather more exactly. For the sake of perspicuity we must anticipate the result : the " has " and " is " speak about a divine disposing, action and decision, to which when we make these statements we have on the one hand to look back as something which has already taken place, and on the other to look forward as something which has yet to do so. They do not speak, therefore, about a content which we can see clearly or control. They do not say that we have the capacity and competence to ascribe to the Bible this priority, this character as the Word of God, and that this priority and character of the Bible are immediately clear to us. If we venture to make them, we do so in obedience and therefore not on the basis and according to the measure of an *a priori* understanding and judgment made by us and applied to this object (as though its holiness were a quality open to our observation and judgment), but in obedience to a judgment of God already made in the light of the object, and in preparation for one which has again and again to be made in the light of it. We venture to do so in thankfulness for what we remember we have already heard in Scripture and in hope of what we may expect to hear again. If we say : the Bible has this priority, it is the Word of God, we must first replace the " has " by a " had " and " will have," and the " is " by a " was " and " will be." It is only as expounded in this way that the two words correspond to what we can actually know and say : we who are not in a position to carry through that divine disposing, action and decision or to handle them as though they were ours. But again when we expound the saying in this way—and it does say " has " and " is "—we must not lose sight of, or forget, or (in a superiority

and power which demand this exposition but scoff at all exposition) weaken the fact that the truth of this " has " and " is " cannot be denied by dissolving it into a past and future. The life of the " had " and " was " and " will have " and " will be " derives entirely from the centre, the present " has " and " is." And our explanatory statements about the recollection and expectation, in which alone we can know and say anything about this present, can be genuine exposition only when they are related entirely to this centre, to the present which we do not know, for which we have no word, over which we have no power, of which as such we cannot say anything except this extravagant " has " and " is," because it is the event of what God Himself decides and wills and does in divine freedom and superiority and power. In the reality and truth of this event nothing is past or only future, nothing is only recollection and nothing only expectation, nothing is doubtful and nothing uncertain, nothing is after or before, nothing has to be repeated and nothing confirmed. It is round this event that the whole doctrine of Holy Scripture circles, and with it all Church dogmatics, and with it, too, preaching and the sacrament of Church proclamation. If our thinking and speaking cease to circle round this event, if we begin to think and speak about the Word of God in Holy Scripture only historically or only eschatologically even, and therefore in one way or another with doubt and uncertainty, we do not think and speak in and with the Church, in faith, we do not think and speak at all about the Word of God in Holy Scripture, but about something else which has consciously or unconsciously taken its place. But when we try to avoid this, we have to be clear that we can only circle round this event; we cannot attain to it of ourselves any more than we can—as we saw earlier—to the unity of Scripture. If it desires and wills to come, taking place within our own encircling exposition—well, it will simply do so, and it will do so the more strongly and gloriously the less we interfere with our clumsy and insolent attempts to attain to it. It is when we are clear that in all our exposition we can only think and explain this event, that we are equally clear that for our part we can never do more than think and explain it. All the possible denials and dissolutions of this present into all kinds of pasts and futures have their source in the fact that this present is not respected as the divine present. It is thought that we can and should turn everything upside down and treat this present as a created human present which we can seize and control. There is no patience to continue circling round that centre, to stick to that faithful exposition and therefore that recollection and expectation which in face of this present—because it is this present—is our place and portion, our task and yet also our comfort. This is the insight which we must now consider and defend in detail.

It will be in place for us to remember first at this point the two important and always much noted statements in which in the New Testament itself there is explicit mention of the priority and character of Holy Scripture as such. Both passages refer primarily to the Old Testament, but according to the fundamental meaning of the two authors in whom they are found, the expressions can and ought and must be applied to all the witness of revelation and therefore to the New Testament witness as well.

The first passage is in 2 Tim. 3¹⁴⁻¹⁷, where Paul orders Timothy—it is noted that we are almost on the edge of the Canon—to " continue " in the things which he has learned, and received in faith (ἔμαθες καὶ ἐπιστώθης). He is to remember those of whom he has learned them, and that from a child he has known the Holy Scriptures (the ἱερὰ γράμματα) which have the power (τὰ δυνάμενα . . .) to make him " wise unto salvation through faith in Christ Jesus." All that he has said so far has been said in clear and express remembrance of the fact that the Scriptures have already played a definite, decisive role in the life of his reader, that they have already given the proof of what they claim to be, that they have already shown their power, the specific power of instruction in the faith which saves him, and, concretely, in the faith which is founded on Jesus Christ, directed to Him, and actual through Him. But then Paul goes on to give the assurance that these same Scriptures will also be profitable to thee " for doctrine, for reproof, for correction, for instruction in righteousness " (all obviously as much for himself as through him for others), " that the man of God may be perfect, thoroughly furnished unto all good works." The same Scriptures have now become the object of expectation. The content of the expectation does not differ from that of the recollection of which he spoke earlier, but all that was previously represented as a gift now acquires the character of a task which has still to be taken up and executed. But the ὠφέλιμος corresponds exactly with the δυνάμενα : Scripture was able and it will be able for what is said about its meaning for the life and activity of the reader both before and after. In the middle of these two statements, throwing light both backwards and forwards, there stands the sentence : πᾶσα γραφὴ θεόπνευστος, all, that is the whole Scripture is—literally : " of the Spirit of God," i.e., given and filled and ruled by the Spirit of God, and actively outbreathing and spreading abroad and making known the Spirit of God. It is clear that this statement is decisive for the whole. It is because of this, i.e., in the power of the truth of the fact that the Spirit of God is before and above and in Scripture, that it was able and will be able for what is said of it both before and after. But it is equally clear that at the centre of the passage a statement is made about the relationship between God and Scripture, which can be understood only as a disposing act and decision of God Himself, which cannot therefore be expanded but to which only a—necessarily brief—reference can be made. At the decisive point all that we have to say about it can consist only in an underlining and delimiting of the inaccessible mystery of the free grace in which the Spirit of God is present and active before and above and in the Bible.

The other passage which calls for consideration is 2 Pet. 1¹⁹⁻²¹. The author had been speaking (vv. 16–18) about the visual witness to the " greatness " (μεγαλειότης) of Jesus Christ. Side by side with this—and he uses a most remarkable comparative (βεβαιότερον)—he places the " prophetic word," calling it " a light that shineth in a dark place, until the day dawn, and the daystar arise in your hearts." It is said of this word that we have (ἔχομεν) it and that in the future we must take heed thereto (προσέχοντες). Here too, therefore, although not quite so clearly in relation to the " prophetic word " as such, we stand between the two times. The pointing to the coming dawn, which corresponds to the recollection of the visual witness, undoubtedly puts what is said into this framework. And here again, and in fact more clearly than in 2 Tim. 3, the centre is revealed from which we have to look backwards and forwards. The " prophecy of Scripture " is rightly read in the sense of what precedes, it is our light in a dark place, when it is not made the object of an ἰδία ἐπίλυσις : i.e., when we allow it to expound itself, or when we allow it to control and determine our exposition. This is because, as the text goes on, it is not given " by the will of man," but in it men spoke as they were " moved by the Holy Ghost," ὑπὸ πνεύματος ἁγίου φερόμενοι, they spoke " from God " (ἀπὸ θεοῦ).

The decisive centre to which the two passages point is in both instances indicated by a reference to the Holy Spirit, and indeed in such a way that He is described as the real author of what is stated or written in Scripture. It should be noted that the expressions used in these passages merely confirm what we have already seen concerning the sending and authorising of the prophets and apostles. In their function as witnesses to revelation they speak in the place and under the commission of Him who sent them, that is, Yahweh or Jesus Christ. They speak as *auctores secundarii*. But there can be no question of any ignoring or violating of their *auctoritas* and therefore of their humanity. Moreover what we experience elsewhere of the work of the Holy Spirit on man in general and on such witnesses in particular, and our recollection of the *conceptus de Spiritu sancto* in Christology, does not allow us to suppose that we have to understand what we are told here about the authors of the Holy Scriptures, as though they were not real *auctores*, as though in what they spoke or wrote they did not make full use of their human capacities throughout the whole range of what is contained in this idea and concept. Exegetically Calvin was right when in his note on 2 Pet. 1[21] he wrote : *Impulsos fuisse dicit, non quod mente alienati fuerint (qualem in suis prophetis ἐνθουσιασμὸν fingunt gentiles), sed quia nihil a se ipsis ausi fuerint : tantum obedienter sequuti sint Spiritum ducem, qui in ipsorum ore tanquam in suo sacrario regnabat (C.R. 55, 458). Theopneustia* in the bounds of biblical thinking cannot mean anything but the special attitude of obedience in those who are elected and called to this obviously special service. The special element in this attitude of obedience lay in the particularity, i.e., the immediacy of its relationship to the revelation which is unique by restriction in time, and therefore in the particular nature of what they had to say and write as eye-witnesses and ear-witnesses, the first-fruits of the Church. But in nature and bearing their attitude of obedience was of itself—both outwardly and inwardly—only that of true and upright men. In particular, it did not mean any abolition of their freedom, their self-determination. How could their obedience be obedience unless it was rendered freely ? But if it was rendered freely, we can only say that they themselves and of themselves thought and spoke and wrote what they did think and speak and write as genuine *auctores*. They did so individually, each within his own psychological, biographical and historical possibilities, and therefore within the limits set by those possibilities. Their action was their own, and like every human action, an act conditioned by and itself conditioning its temporal and spatial environment. That as such it acquired this special function, was placed under the *auctoritas primaria*, the lordship of God, was surrounded and controlled and impelled by the Holy Spirit, and became an attitude of obedience in virtue of its direct relationship to divine revelation—that was their *theopneustia*. In order to understand this biblical concept we cannot make any essential distinction between the thinking and speaking of the prophets and apostles and their writing, either in the sense in which many attempts have been made recently to limit inspiration to their thinking and speaking, or even to the prophetic experience which precedes and underlies their thinking and speaking, or in the sense that it rests distinctly in their writing. What we are told of it in the Old and New Testaments generally, and especially in 2 Tim. 3 and 2 Pet. 1, gives us no cause to adopt either of these explanations. As men, who lived then and there and not here and now, the prophets and apostles do, of course, exist for us only in what they have written. But in what they have written it is they themselves who do exist for us. In what they have written they exist visibly and audibly before us in all their humanity, chosen and called as witnesses of revelation, claimed by God and obedient to God, true men, speaking in the name of the true God, because they have heard His voice as we cannot hear it, as we can hear it only through their voices. And that is their *theopneustia*. That is the mystery of the centre before which we always stand when we hear and read them : remembering that it was once the case (the recollection of the Church and our own recollection attest it) that their voice reproduced the voice of God, and therefore expecting that it will be so again. The biblical concept of *theopneustia* points us therefore to the present, to the event which occurs for us : Scripture has this priority, it is the Word of God. But it only points us to it. It is not a substitute for it. It does not create it. How can it, seeing it is only a description of what God does in the humanity of His witnesses? But as it occurs in these two passages, it points us to what Holy Scripture was and will be. Yet even by this circuitous route it points to what it is. Therefore if we are to read and understand and expound Holy Scripture as the Word of God, it will always have to be a matter of taking the road which Scripture itself lays down for us.

In the statement : we believe that the the Bible is the Word of God, we must first emphasise and consider the word " believe." Believing does, of course, involve recognising and knowing. Believing is not an obscure and indeterminate feeling. It is a clear hearing, apperceiving, thinking and then speaking and doing. Believing is also a free human act, i.e., one which is not destroyed or disturbed by any magic ; but, of course, a free act which as such is conditioned and determined by an encounter, a challenge, an act of lordship which confronts man, which man cannot bring about himself, which exists either as an event or not at all. Therefore believing is not something arbitrary. It does not control its object. It is a recognising, knowing, hearing, apperceiving, thinking, speaking and doing which is over-mastered by its object. Belief that the Bible is the Word of God pre-supposes, therefore, that this over-mastering has already taken place, that the Bible has already proved itself to be the Word of God, so that we can and must recognise it to be such. But when and where there is this proof, it must be a matter of the Word of God itself. We must say at once, that of itself the mere presence of the Bible and our own presence with our capacities for knowing an object does not mean and never will mean the reality or even the possibility of the proof that the Bible is the Word of God. On the contrary, we have to recognise that this situation as such, i.e., apart from faith, only means the impossibility of this proof. We have to recognise that faith as an irruption into this reality and possibility means the removing of a barrier in which we can only see and again and again see a miracle. And it is a miracle which we cannot explain apart from faith, or rather apart from the Word of God in which faith believes. Therefore the reality and possibility of it cannot be maintained or defended at all apart from faith and the Word. Nor can there be any assurances of it apart from faith and the Word. It is not only that we cannot attribute to ourselves any capacity or instrument for recognising the Word of God either in the Bible or elsewhere. It is also that if we are serious about the true humanity of the Bible, we obviously cannot attribute to the Bible as such the capacity—and in this it is distinguished, as we have seen, from the exalted and glorified humanity of Jesus Christ—in such a way to reveal God to us that by its very presence, by the fact that we can read it, it gives us a hearty faith in the Word of God spoken in it.   It is there and always there as a sign, as a human and temporal word—and therefore also as a word which is conditioned and limited.   It witnesses to God's revelation, but that does not mean that God's revelation is now before us in any kind of divine revealedness.   The Bible is not a book of oracles ; it is not an instrument of direct impartation.   It is genuine witness.   And how can it be witness of divine revelation, if the actual purpose, act and decision of God in His only-begotten Son, as seen and heard by the prophets and apostles in that Son, is dissolved in the Bible into a sum total of truths abstracted from that decision—and those truths are then propounded to us as truths of faith, salvation and revelation ? If it tries to be more than witness, to be direct impartation, will it not keep from us the best, the one real thing, which God intends to tell and give us and which we ourselves need ?   But if it does not try to do this, if it is really witness, we must understand clearly what it means and involves that in itself it is only witness.   It means the existence of those barriers which can be broken down only by miracle. The men whom we hear as witnesses speak as fallible, erring men like ourselves.   What they say, and what we read as their word, can of itself lay claim to be the Word of God, but never sustain that claim.   We can read and try to assess their word as a purely human word.   It can be subjected to all kinds of immanent criticism, not only in respect of its philosophical, historical and ethical content, but even of its religious and theological.   We can establish lacunæ, inconsistencies and over-emphases.   We may be alienated by a figure like that of Moses.   We may quarrel with James or with Paul.   We may have to admit that we can make little or nothing of large tracts of the Bible, as is often the case with the records of other men.   We can take offence at the Bible.   And in the light of the claim or the assertion that the Bible is the Word of God—granting that the miracle of faith and the Word does not intervene—we are bound to take offence at it. But this is a miracle which we cannot presuppose.   We can remember it.   We can wait for it.   But we cannot set it up like one chessman with others, which we can " move " at the right moment.   Therefore we are bound to take offence at the Bible in the light of that claim. If we do not, we have not yet realised the importance of that claim. Only the miracle of faith and the Word can genuinely and seriously prevent us from taking offence at the Bible.   But the *theopneustia* of the Bible, the attitude of obedience in which it is written, the compelling fact that in it true men speak to us in the name of the true God : this—and here is the miracle of it—is not simply before us because the Bible is before us and we read the Bible.   The *theopneustia* is the act of revelation in which the prophets and apostles in their humanity became what they were, and in which alone in their humanity they can become to us what they are.

In the *De servo arbitrio* Luther made the important assertion : *Duae res sunt Deus et scriptura Dei, non minus quam duae res sunt creator et creatura Dei* (*W.A.* 18, 606, 11). And again : " Thus Scripture is a book, to which there belongeth not only reading but also the right Expositor and Revealer, to wit, the Holy Spirit. Where He openeth not Scripture, it is not understood " (*Pred. üb. Lk.* 24[13f.] 1534, according to Rörer, *E.A.* 3, 334). But whoso knoweth not Christ, may hear the Gospel or hold the book in his hands, but its import he doth not have, for to have the Gospel without understanding is to have no Gospel. And to have the Scripture without knowledge of Christ is to have no Scripture, and is none other than to let these stars shine and yet not to perceive them (*Pred. üb. Mt.* 2[1-12], *Kirchenpostille* 1522 *W.A.* 10[1], 1, 628, 3). According to Augustine there is only one reason why Scripture is not understood : *Nam dicere ut est, quis potest ? Audeo dicere fratres mei, forsitan nec ipse Joannes dixit ut est, sed et ipse ut potuit ! quia de Deo homo dixit : et quidem inspiratus a Deo sed tamen homo. Quia inspiratus, dixit aliquid ; si non inspiratus esset, dixisset nihil ; quia vero homo inspiratus, non totum quod est, dixit, sed quod potuit homo dixit* (*In Joann. tract.* 1, 1). Augustine was here pointing to something which the older Protestant orthodoxy almost completely overlooked, especially with its doctrine of the *perspicuitas* and *perfectio* of Holy Scripture. We know what we say when we call the Bible the Word of God only when we recognise its human imperfection in face of its divine perfection, and its divine perfection in spite of its human imperfection. In relation to the obvious uncertainty of the traditional Canon, whether in respect of its compass or of its textual form, this could be conceded by many writers. F. Burmann, for instance, could say in this respect : *Doctrina ipsa et hoc verbum Dei vivum sese ipsum ostendit et cordibus electorum per operationem Spiritus sancti potenter insinuat, non obstante defectu vel vitio quocunque in organis istis externis. Non enim ab illis fides vel salus nostra pendet sed a doctrina ipsa iis contenta. . . . Doctrina sacra vi sua propria pollet et defectum organorum superat et licet per homines fallibiles praedicata, tamen plenam sui fidem in cordibus fidelium facit* (*Syn. Theol.*, 1678, I, 5, 21). This very distinction between inspiration and therefore the divine infallibility of the Bible and its human fallibility has now to be carried through more radically.

First, there is the truism that we cannot expect or demand a compendium of solomonic or even divine knowledge of all things in heaven and earth, natural, historical and human, to be mediated to the prophets and apostles in and with their encounter with divine revelation, possessing which they have to be differentiated not only from their own but from every age as the bearers and representatives of an ideal culture and therefore as the inerrant proclaimers of all and every truth. They did not in fact possess any such compendium. Each in his own way and degree, they shared the culture of their age and environment, whose form and content could be contested by other ages and environments, and at certain points can still appear debatable to us. *Quod potuit homo dixit.* This means that we cannot overlook or deny it or even alter it. In the biblical view of the world and man we are constantly coming up against presuppositions which are not ours, and statements and judgments which we cannot accept. Therefore at bottom we cannot avoid the tensions which arise at this point. We must reckon with the fact that this may be possible in points of detail, and we must always be ready for it. Instead of talking about the " errors " of the biblical authors in this sphere, if we want to go to the heart of things it is better to speak only about their " capacity for errors." For in the last resort even in relation to the general view of the world and man the insight and knowledge of our age can be neither divine nor even solomonic. But fundamentally we certainly have to face the objection and believe in spite of it !

Not for all ages and countries, but certainly for our own, it is part of the stumbling-block that like all ancient literature the Old and New Testaments know nothing of the distinction of fact and value which is so important to us, between history, on the one hand, and saga and legend on the other. We must be clear that we cannot attach any final seriousness to this distinction and therefore any final difficulty to the objections to which it gives rise. But if we cannot deny that this distinction is now part of our apparatus of apperception, we cannot try to suppress or artificially to remove the doubts arising from it. We have to face up to them and to be clear that in the Bible it may be a matter of simply believing the Word of God, even though it meets us, not in the form of what we call history, but in the form of what we think must be called saga or legend.

But the vulnerability of the Bible, i.e., its capacity for error, also extends to its religious or theological content. The significance of a fact which was known to the early antiquity weighs on us more heavily to-day than formerly : that in their attestation of divine revelation (from the standpoint of the history of religion) the biblical authors shared the outlook and spoke the language of their own day—and, therefore, whether we like it or not, they did not speak a special language of revelation radically different from that of their time. On the contrary, at point after point we find them echoing contemporaries in time and space who did not share their experience and witness, often resembling them so closely that it is impossible to distinguish between them. Not only part but all that they say is historically related and conditioned. It seems to be weakened, and therefore robbed of its character as witness to revelation, by the fact that it has so many " parallels." That they speak of Yahweh and of Jesus Christ, and not of other entities, is something we have laboriously to work out and prove from their usage as compared with that of their environment—and we can never do it with unimpeachable evidence, but in the last resort only on the presupposition of our faith. It amounts to this, that, as we see it, many parts, especially of the Old Testament, cannot be accepted as religious and theological literature, but only as documents of secular legislation and history and practical wisdom and poetry, although the Synagogue and later the Church claimed to find in them witness of revelation. It amounts to this, that not one of the biblical authors has done the Church and us the pleasure of giving his witness to divine revelation the form of a more or less complete and thorough-going theological system, that even in relation to the theology of a St. Paul and St. John we can only arrive later and by dint of much laborious construction at a certain hypothetical scheme. It amounts to this, that the biblical authors wrote with all the limitations imposed by their most varied possible historical and individual standpoints and outlooks, so that the content of their writing as a whole, for all the " harmony " upon which we touched earlier, does not in any sense constitute a system. But depending on how we can and want to look on them, there are distinctions of higher and lower, of utterances which are more central and peripheral, of witnesses which have to be understood literally and symbolically. There are obvious overlappings and contradictions—e.g., between the Law and the prophets, between John and the Synoptists, between Paul and James. But nowhere are we given a single rule by which to make a common order, perhaps an order of precedence, but at any rate a synthesis, of what is in itself such a varied whole. Nowhere do we find a rule which enables us to grasp it in such a way that we can make organic parts of the distinctions and evade the contradictions as such. We are led now one way, now another—each of the biblical authors obviously speaking only *quod potuit homo*—and in both ways, and whoever is the author, we are always confronted with the question of faith. Again, we must be careful not to be betrayed into taking sides into playing off the one biblical man against the other, into pronouncing that this one or that has "erred." From what standpoint can we make any such pronouncement ? For within certain limits and therefore relatively they are all vulnerable and therefore capable of error even in respect of religion and theology. In view of the actual constitution of the Old and New Testaments this is something which we cannot possibly deny if we are not to take away their humanity, if we are not to be guilty of Docetism. How can they be witnesses, if this is not the case ? But if it is, even from this angle we come up against the stumbling-block which cannot be avoided or can be avoided only in faith.

To all this, however, we must still add as an independent matter something the importance of which the Church has only begun to recognise in our own day, although it has actually exercised a definite effect in every age. The Bible as the witness of divine revelation is in its humanity a product of the Israelitish, or to put it more clearly, the Jewish spirit. The man who in these Scriptures has said *quod potuit* is *homo Judaeus*. This is true—and no devices can avail us, for it is so closely bound up with the content—of the whole of the Bible, even of the whole of the New Testament Bible. It is once and for all the case that the content of these writings is the story of the divine election and calling and ruling of Israel, the story of the founding of the Church as the true Israel. And it is Israelites—and since, as we were told, the witnesses of revelation belong to the revelation themselves, it is necessarily Israelites—who attest all this to us in these Scriptures. If we want it otherwise, we will have to strike out not only the Old but all the New Testament as well, replacing them by something else, which is no longer a witness of divine revelation. The cry of dismay which is heard so strongly to-day is quite justified : we and the men of all nations are expected by Jews not only to interest ourselves in things Jewish, but in a certain and ultimately decisive sense actually to become Jews. And we may well ask whether all the other offences which we may take at the Bible, and will necessarily take if we are without faith, are not trifles compared with this offence. We may well ask whether there is any harder test of faith than the one which we see here. For the Bible itself does not hide the fact, but shows relentlessly that this is a hard demand, that the Jewish people is a hard and stiff-necked people, because it is a people which resists its God, the living God. It is characterised as the people which in its own Messiah finally rejected and crucified the Saviour of the world and therefore denied the revelation of God. It is in this way that the Bible is a Jewish book, the Jewish book. What has later Anti-Semitism to say compared with the accusation here levelled against the Jews ? And what can it do compared with the judgment under which they have been put at the hand of God Himself long ago ? But in all its folly and wickedness Anti-Semitism, which is as old as the Jewish nation itself, is not based, as its liberal critics think, upon an invincible and therefore recurrent arbitrariness and caprice, which can be kept in bounds by occasional pleas for humanity. Anti-Semitism is so strong to-day that it can hammer out a whole racial theory which claims to be a science, but in the last resort is naively directed against the Jews. And on this basis, which is ultimately an anti-Jewish basis, it can fashion a state. But this Anti-Semitism sees and intends something real which liberalism has never actually seen. This real thing is not, of course, identical with what it accuses and attacks. If it knew what it is, it would not accuse and attack it, for it would know—this is not the only reason, but one reason—that no power in the world can match what confronts it here. Modern German Anti-Semitism is concerned about Jewish blood and Jewish race. At best, these are signs of the real thing which encounters humanity unperceived and uncomprehended. But the real thing itself is the one natural proof of God adduced by God in the existence of the Jewish nation amongst other nations. It is hardly seen by Anti-Semites and liberals, but here a part of world-history gives the most direct witness to the biblical witness of revelation, and therefore to the God who is attested in the

Bible. To this very day Israel confronts us as the people of God rejected by God. To this very day Israel shows us that it is only in judgment that God exercises grace and that it is His free decision that He exercises grace in judgment. Israel reminds the world that it is the world, and it reminds the Church from what it has been taken. And because it is this people, the other nations are constantly enraged by its existence, revolting against it and wishing its destruction. Because it is this people, something hostile arises in all non-Jews against every Jew without exception, even the best and finest and noblest of Jews — and this quite apart from ethical or biological feelings and considerations. We cannot attribute the hostility simply to foreign blood and the like. If all the foreign blood which meets us every day in the welter of nations in the modern Western world were to give rise to this hostility, we could never escape it. By being hostile to Jewish blood, the world simply proves that it is the world : blind and deaf and stupid to the ways of God, as they are visibly before it in the existence of this people. And if the Church tries to co-operate in this hostility to Jewish blood, it simply proves that it too has become blind and deaf and stupid. In fact in the Jew, the non-Jew has to recognise himself, his own apostasy, his own sin, which he himself cannot forgive. And in the Jew he has to recognise Christ, the Messiah of Israel, who alone has made good his apostasy and pardoned his sin. Confronted in this way by the divine severity and goodness, he is necessarily alienated by the existence of the Jew, and it is devilish madness if instead he abandons himself to a biological and moral alienation, working out his perverted hostility—as all perversions necessarily work themselves out—in accusations and attacks upon the Jews because of their national alienation. In this way he persists in his own apostasy. He acts as though he could forgive his own sins. In rejecting the Jew he rejects God. But that means that in this perversion we have to do not only with a real thing, but with the most real thing of all. And it is no accident if at the point where we have to do with this most real thing, in the Bible, we are asked point blank whether we are guilty of this perversion or not. For the Bible as the witness of divine revelation in Jesus Christ is a Jewish book. It cannot be read and understood and expounded unless we openly accept the language and thought and history of the Jews, unless we are prepared to become Jews with the Jews. But that means that we have to ask ourselves what is our attitude to the natural proof of God adduced in world-history by the continuing existence of the Jews, whether we are ready to accept it or to join the wolves in howling against it. And once we are clear that the liberal solution, i.e., the liberal evasion of the Jewish problem cannot help us, this question will necessarily be a very hard one. We may not always be alienated by the goodness and severity of God. But the Jew brings this alienation right into national and social life to-day, even in the Bible. Salvation means alienation, and " salvation is of the Jews " (Jn. 4²²). And because man will not be alienated, even for his own salvation, he rolls away the alienation on to the Jew. In that way it all becomes so simple. We can find so many grievances against the Jew. Once we have raised even our little finger in Anti-Semitism, we can produce such vital and profound reasons in favour of it, and they will all apply equally well to the Bible, not only to the Old but also to the New Testament, not only to the Rabbi Paul but also to the Rabbi Jesus of Nazareth of the first three Gospels. And we have to ask : What offence that we can take at the Bible is more pressing and goes deeper and is more general than the offence which it offers here ? For if the liberal solution, which is no solution, collapses, how can we not be Anti-Semitic ? At this point we need the miracle of the Word and faith if the offence is to cease, the perversion to be overcome, the Anti-Semitism in us all eliminated, the word of man, the Jewish word of the Bible, heard and accepted as the Word of God.

We started with Luther's saying : *Duae res sunt, Deus et scriptura Dei.* We have learned from Augustine the one reason why this is the case. Luther is right, because the Bible is vulnerable. At every point it is the vulnerable word of man. Luther did not stop at this saying. For faith, God and Holy Scripture are not two things but one. We believe that Scripture is the Word of God. But when we say that, we say more than we can say in view of our own present : in recollection and expectation we look to the present of an event which God alone can bring about. It is not only in regard to the ultimately harmless question of tradition, but at every point, that the saying is true which points us to the miracle of God which we cannot bring about : *Doctrina sacra vi sua propria pollet et defectum organorum superat et licet per homines fallibiles praedicata, tamen plenam sui fidem in cordibus fidelium facit*. Nothing else, or less, can lead to the decision which has to be made here.

But now in order to see the full acuteness of the problem, we must also emphasise and consider the concept " Word of God " in the statement : We believe that the Bible is the Word of God. What we have said so far cannot mean that the miracle just mentioned consists in our having to believe in a sort of enthusiastic rapture which penetrates the barriers of offence by which the Bible is surrounded. Of course, the whole mystery of this statement rests on the fact that faith is not for everybody, and that even if we have it, it is a small and weak and inadequate because not a true faith. Therefore the miracle which has to take place if the Bible is to rise up and speak to us as the Word of God has always to consist in an awakening and strengthening of our faith. But the real difficulty of the statement does not rest in the side which concerns us men, but in that which concerns God Himself. It does not rest, therefore, in the severity of the offences caused by the humanity of the Bible. Although the question of faith of which we have just been speaking is central, it is only the secondary form of the question which has to be decided at this centre. Faith can in fact only be obedience and cling to the Word as a free human decision. And it can do so only because the Word has come to it and made and introduced it as faith. Therefore faith cannot simply grasp at the Bible, as though by the energy of its grasping, perhaps that highest energy which may even rise to enthusiasm, the Word of God would come to it in spite of all the offences (which are therefore overcome by the enthusiasm). Rather, the energy of this grasping itself rests on the prior coming of the Word of God. Faith does not live by its own energy and therefore not even by its arousing and strengthening by the Word of God. It lives by the energy of the movement in which the Word of God in Holy Scripture has come to us in spite of all the offences which we might take at it, and has first created our faith. Whether this has happened or not is the objective mystery which confronts and precedes the question of faith, the mystery of the statement that " the Bible is the Word of God." In the statement that " the Bible is the Word of God," we cannot suddenly mean a lesser, less potent, less ineffable and majestic Word of God, than that which has occupied us in the doctrine of the Trinity and in the doctrine of Christ and of the Holy Spirit. There is only one Word of God and that is the eternal Word of the Father which for our reconciliation became flesh like us and has now returned to the Father, to be present to His Church by the Holy Spirit. In Holy Scripture, too, in the human word of His witnesses, it is a matter of this Word and its presence. That means that in this equation it is a matter of the miracle of the divine Majesty in its condescension and mercy. If we take this equation on our lips, it can only be as an appeal to the promise in virtue of which this miracle was real in Jesus Christ and will again be real in the word of His witnesses. In this equation we have to do with the free grace and the gracious freedom of God. That the Bible is the Word of God cannot mean that with other attributes the Bible has the attribute of being the Word of God. To say that would be to violate the Word of God which is God Himself—to violate the freedom and the sovereignty of God. God is not an attribute of something else, even if this something else is the Bible. God is the Subject, God is Lord. He is Lord even over the Bible and in the Bible. The statement that the Bible is the Word of God cannot therefore say that the Word of God is tied to the Bible. On the contrary, what it must say is that the Bible is tied to the Word of God. But that means that in this statement we contemplate a free decision of God— not in uncertainty but in certainty, not without basis but on the basis of the promise which the Bible itself proclaims and which we receive in and with the Church. But its content is always a free decision of God, which we cannot anticipate by grasping at the Bible—even if we do it with the greatest faith of which we are capable, but the freedom of which we will have to recognise when we grasp at the Bible in the right way. The Bible is not the Word of God on earth in the same way as Jesus Christ, very God and very man, is that Word in heaven. The being of Jesus Christ as the Word of God even in His humanity requires neither promise nor faith. The act in which He became the Word of God in His humanity requires neither repetition nor confirmation. But in His eternal presence as the Word of God He is concealed from us who now live on earth and in time. He is revealed only in the sign of His humanity, and especially in the witness of His prophets and apostles. But by nature these signs are not heavenly-human, but earthly- and temporal-human. Therefore the act of their institution as signs requires repetition and confirmation. Their being as the Word of God requires promise and faith—just because they are signs of the eternal presence of Christ. For if they are to act as signs, if the eternal presence of Christ is to be revealed to us in time, there is a constant need of that continuing work of the Holy Spirit in the Church and to its members which is always taking place in new acts. If the Church lives by the Bible because it is the Word of God, that means that it lives by the fact that Christ is revealed in the Bible by the work of the Holy Spirit. That means that it has no power or control over this work. It can grasp at the Bible. It can honour it.

17

It can accept its promise. It can be ready and open to read and understand and expound it. All these things it can and should do. The human side of the life of the Church with the Bible rightly consists in all these things. But apart from these things, the human side of its life with the Bible can consist only in the fact that it prays that the Bible may be the Word of God here and now, that there may take place that work of the Holy Spirit, and therefore a free applying of the free grace of God. Over and above that : the fulfilment of this prayer, that the Bible is the Word of God here and now in virtue of the eternal, hidden, heavenly presence of Christ—that is the divine side of the life of the Church. Its reality cannot be doubted : the fulness of the reality of the life of the Church with the Bible lies in this its divine aspect. Also the certainty of the perception of it cannot be doubted : it is mediated to us in the promise, it can be grasped in faith. But the very fact that this happens, that the promise speaks to us and that we are obedient in faith, is always before us as the question which has to be answered again and again by the work of the Holy Spirit. This is the event we look to, if—here on earth in the Church non-triumphant, but militant—we confess that the Bible is God's Word. For in doing so we acknowledge God and His grace, and the freedom of His grace.

By means of this criterion we must now test what the Church has said about the inspiration of Holy Scripture in relation to the sayings in 2 Tim. 3[16] and 2 Pet. 1[20f.] In the so-called doctrine of inspiration the point at issue was and is how far, i.e., on the basis of what relationship between the Holy Spirit as God opening up man's ears and mouth for His Word and the Bible, the latter can be read and understood and expounded as a human witness of His revelation as the Word of God and therefore in the strict sense as Holy Scripture. On the basis of our latest consideration the criterion will necessarily be this : that the doctrine of inspiration will always have to describe the relation between the Holy Spirit and the Bible in such a way that the whole reality of the unity between the two is safeguarded no less than the fact that this unity is a free act of the grace of God, and therefore for us its content is always a promise.

Now first we will show the need for this criterion from two New Testament passages.

In 2 Cor. 3[4-18] Paul made it clear how he primarily wanted the reading of the Old Testament as a witness of the revelation of Jesus Christ to be understood by the Christian congregation. The Old Testament Scripture as such is described by Paul (v. 6) as γράμμα, i.e., as that which is simply written and indeed prescribed as holy and necessary for salvation. There is *per se* no disqualification of Scripture in this designation. Nor is there when Paul goes on to say that the γράμμα kills but the Spirit gives life. This is said in favour of the Spirit but not against Scripture, or only against a Scripture received and read without the Spirit. From this standpoint we ought calmly to reflect on Mt. 5[17f.], where it says that not one jot or tittle can pass from the law until it is completely fulfilled, and that therefore even the least of its commandments must not be " broken." Paul claims for himself the ministry of the new covenant (v. 6), the ministry of the Spirit (v. 8), the ministry which has an incomparably greater " glory " (v. 9). Yet he does not contest, but expressly presupposes, that even the ministry of the γράμμα as such has its " glory " (v. 9 f.). And Paul does not exclude the ministry of Scripture when he contrasts it with his own ministry, the spiritual ministry of the new covenant. On the contrary, he regards his own ministry as the true ministry of Scripture, i.e., its fulfilment. This is proved by the fact that in this very section he is commenting on Ex. 34. It makes no difference that as such and apart from the work of the Holy Spirit the written not only does not minister life, but ministers death; indeed, in its own way it proves that it is and remains that which is prescribed by divine authority. Paul must have known the theories of Talmudic and Alexandrian Jewry concerning the divine-human origin of the Torah, i.e., all the Old Testament Canon. If, as we can certainly assume, he for his part affirmed a special inspiration of Scripture by God, it was obviously only in connexion with his view of the present attestation of the same God by the work of the Holy Spirit. For in 2 Cor. 3 everything depends on the fact that without this work of the Spirit Scripture is veiled, however great its glory may be and whatever its origin. This is the case in that reading of the Scripture by the Synagogue, which is foreshadowed by the veiling of Moses' countenance (Ex. 34). What God has prescribed is there and the men who read it are also there, but over their hearts there hangs a veil. Their thinking is rebellious. For them the open book is in fact a closed book. Only a return to the Lord could set aside the curtain and open up for them access to Scripture. But the Lord, by whose presence the freedom which has already been objectively created " in Christ " (v. 14) can now be achieved, is the Spirit (v. 17). All we who are Christians, and as such, are an unveiled mirror of the glory of the Lord. We know how to read and receive what the Jews read but do not know how to read and receive. But we do so, not by virtue of any capacity of our own as distinct from them, but only of the Lord who is the Spirit—or from the Lord the Spirit (v. 18). We do so, not as though we had made ourselves capable of it, but because God makes us capable of it, as it tells us in vv. 4–6 with a primary reference to the personal ministry of Paul. We could hardly say more clearly that the holy and redemptive nature of Scripture is only a preliminary. The Christian community cannot stop at this preliminary. It is as little helped by the reality of it as the world or the Synagogue. Indeed, like the world or the Synagogue, it is brought under judgment by this reality. But of itself it cannot go on to fulfil and complete this preliminary. If it finds life where the Synagogue can only meet its condemnation, it is the grace of the Holy Spirit, an event for whose occurrence only God can be praised.

We have an interesting parallel in 1 Cor. 2⁶⁻¹⁶ to the extent that Paul here speaks of his own addresses and therefore of what he has written as an apostle from exactly the same standpoint. Paul is conscious of speaking wisdom, " the wisdom of God in a mystery," the hidden wisdom which was predetermined by God before all times to our glory, the wisdom which was not recognised by the powerful of this æon and therefore smitten on the cross : that which in itself is not accessible to the eye or ear or heart of man, but " which God hath prepared for them that love him " (vv. 6–9). Of this " wisdom in a mystery," i.e., of the revelation of God which took place in Jesus Christ, he says no more and no less than that he, Paul, speaks or says or expresses it. Λαλοῦμεν σοφίαν. How can he ever come to do this unless God opens up the way to it, unless it is first of all revealed, and indeed revealed by the Spirit ? As the human spirit knows human things, so it is the divine Spirit—He alone, but He perfectly and without doubt—who knows divine things. This Spirit he, Paul, has received, that he may know as such the divine benefits of the divine wisdom (τὰ ὑπὸ τοῦ θεοῦ χαρισθέντα ἡμῖν vv.10–12). But as he sees it, this does not exhaust the work of the Holy Ghost. In exact correspondence with this knowledge of the benefits indicated to us by God's wisdom he now believes he can and must express them : οὐκ ἐν διδακτοῖς ἀνθρωπίνης σοφίας λόγοις, ἀλλ ᾽ἐν διδακτοῖς πνεύματος : not in the words which man's wisdom teacheth but which the Spirit teacheth : πνευματικοῖς πνευματικὰ συγκρίνοντες : measuring and embracing in spiritual words that spiritual reality (v. 13). In face of this self-utterance we cannot assume

that Paul did not take account of an inspiration, even a real and verbal inspiration, of the Old Testament hagiographa. We have therefore no reason to think
that the θεόπνευστος of 2 Tim. 3¹⁶ is non-Pauline. At all events Paul distinctly
describes himself, not merely as a witness of the divine benefits, so that his statements about them have the value of an historical record, but more than that,
as one who by the Spirit is enabled and led to know these benefits, and even
more, as one who by the same Spirit is authorised and taught to speak about
them. There now follows the expression which is decisive in this connexion.
Paul is aware that man in himself and as such, the living creature man, the
ψυχικὸς ἄνθρωπος, does not receive what on the basis of the work of the Spirit is
said in this way about the benefits of God (τὰ τοῦ πνεύματος τοῦ θεοῦ). It is
foolishness to him, because he cannot know it. It is only spiritually, i.e., on the
basis of the same work of the same Spirit, by which he can know and therefore
speak about these benefits, that they can be known and therefore received :
πνευματικῶς ἀνακρίνεται (v. 14). There is therefore a state of man which is radically
different from that of the ψυχικὸς ἄνθρωπος. This is the state of the πνευματικός,
of the man who is endowed with the Spirit and enlightened and led by the Spirit.
But what is the particular feature of this state ? Simply and yet very strongly
this, that as a man he sees and understands what that other who is himself
taught and led by the Spirit says : ἀνακρίνει τὰ πάντα. The circle which led
from the divine benefits to the apostle instructed by the Spirit and authorised
to speak by the Spirit now closes at the hearer of the apostle, who again by the
Spirit is enabled to receive as is necessary. The hearer, too, in his existence as
such is part of the miracle which takes place at this point. No less than the
apostle, indeed no less than the wisdom which is not known by this æon but
revealed to the apostle, the hearer of the apostolic word is himself a mystery to
everyone (and as Paul sees it especially to himself). As a hearer, he is understood by no one. αὐτὸς δὲ ὑπ' οὐδενὸς ἀνακρίνεται (v. 15). At every point, Paul
concludes, we have to do with the thoughts of the Lord, to whom no one can
give counsel, i.e., who has no equal, no one therefore who is able to think with
Him and to know His thoughts : τίς γὰρ ἔγνω νοῦν κυρίου, ὃς συμβιβάσει αὐτόν.
To know Him three keys are necessary. Paul is conscious that he has two of
them, indeed that he himself represents them in his existence as an apostle—
between the hidden wisdom of God, i.e., the benefit of its revelation, and the
spiritual man, there stands the man who has the " thoughts of Christ," the
apostle, who himself is empowered by the Spirit to know and declare that which
is hidden : ἡμεῖς δὲ νοῦν Χριστοῦ ἔχομεν (v. 16) ; faced by it—and here the
question arises whether the third key is available—the hearer has to decide whether
as a ψυχικὸς ἄνθρωπος he will not receive or recognise it but regard it as foolishness—whether by the help of the same Spirit, who has spoken to and through the
apostle, he will himself be a spiritual man who will listen to what the apostle
has to say to him ?

If we keep the two parts side by side, we get a fairly complete picture of
how the function of a witness to revelation appeared on both sides at any rate
to Paul according to its true character and limits. With all other men the witness
stands before the mystery of God and the benefit of His revelation. That this
mystery is disclosed to him is the first thing, and that he can speak of it the
second, in the miracle of his existence as a witness. But the mystery of God,
now entrusted to the human witness, will still remain a mystery, as it encounters
the Synagogue, which only has and reads the γράμμα, and as it encounters the
living creature, man, for whom the word of the apostle is always foolishness,
if its self-disclosure does not go a step further, even in its form as human witness,
if the same Spirit who has created the witness does not bear witness of its truth
to men, to those who hear and read. This self-disclosure in its totality is *theopneustia*, the inspiration of the word of the prophets and apostles. It is justifiable
to regard the content of these two passages as a commentary on the brief data

which we have on this matter in 2 Tim. $3^{16f.}$ and 2 Pet. $1^{19f.}$ And it is justifiable to measure by the content of these passages what was later said about it in the Church.

But already in the literature of the Early Church we must be struck by three things.

1. There is soon displayed a striking inclination to concentrate interest in the inspiration of Scripture upon one particular point in that circle, and to limit it to it : namely, to the work of the Spirit in the emergence of the spoken or written prophetic and apostolic word as such. We have seen that Paul, too, does take serious cognisance of a holy γράμμα, of something prescribed by divine authority in the Canon of the Old Covenant. We have seen that he also considers even his own words to be " taught of the Spirit." Now this point in the circle of the work of the Spirit cannot be denied or regarded as unimportant. The way of inspiration does actually go through this phase. But what was the significance of the one-sided concentration of the Church's interest on this particular point ? Can we understand what it means that the prophets and apostles spoke and wrote by the Holy Spirit, if we do not keep equally before us that that of which they spoke and wrote, the object of their witness, the beneficent revelation of the mystery of God, was mediated to them only by the Spirit, and that the hearers and readers of what they spoke and wrote have need of the work of the same Spirit if they are really to read and hear it ? Paul is clearly speaking about an act of the free grace of God. But is not the contemplation of this act necessarily obscured to the extent that the one aspect is, as it were, pushed into the fore-front as a conclusion and datum which we can easily grasp ; that it was and still is the case that these men spoke and wrote what they did by the Holy Spirit ? Of course, they did speak and write in that way and in no other. We cannot possibly reject this truth which comes from Paul himself. But is the grace and the mystery of God, which we rightly see in it, really the grace and mystery of the Word of God in the full biblical sense of the concept, if we think of it as reduced to this act of speaking ? To what sphere do we now belong ? Is it an accident that we find the apologists of the 2nd century pushed in this direction ? Is it not the attempt to make the miracle of God in the witness of His revelation perspicuous to everybody, conceivable in its inconceivability, natural for all the emphasising of its supernatural character, a factor with which we can reckon even though we do ascribe it to the Holy Spirit, just as in the last resort the Jews could reckon as given factors with their inspired Torah and the heathen with their Sibylline and similar books ? What are we to think of Theophilus of Antioch (*Ad. Autol.* 2, 9) and Pseudo-Justin (*Coh. ad Graecos* 37) when they did actually ascribe the same inspiredness to the prophets and the Sibyllines ?

2. Already in the Early Church we see a tendency to insist that the operation of the Holy Spirit in the inspiration of the biblical writers extended to the individual phraseology used by them in the grammatical sense of the concept. If I am right, the first express statement along these lines is to be found in the *Protrepticus* of Clement of Alexandria (IX, 82, 1) : that the fact that according to Mt. 5^{18} not even the slightest jot or tittle of Scripture can be destroyed is based on the truth that it has all been spoken by the mouth of the Lord, the Holy Spirit. And a hundred years later Gregory Nazianzus (*Orat.* 2, 105) writes that every slightest line and stroke of Scripture is due to the minute care of the Spirit and that even the slenderest nuance of the writers is not in vain or dis-played to us in vain. Here, too, in the light of Mt. $5^{17f.}$ we must be on our guard against trying to say anything different. If in their concrete existence and there-fore in their concrete speaking and writing the witnesses of revelation belong to revelation, if they spoke by the Spirit what they knew by the Spirit, and if we really have to hear them and therefore their words—then self-evidently we have to hear all their words with the same measure of respect. It would be arbitrary to relate their inspiration only to such parts of their witness as perhaps appear

important to us, or not to their words as such but only to the views and thoughts which evoke them. If inspiration is co-ordinated into that circle of God's manifestation by the Spirit only for our illumination by the same Spirit, the inspiration of the biblical witnesses which is the link between the two, between God and us, can and must be regarded quite definitely not merely as real but as verbal inspiration. But the question is whether it has not been taken out of the circle and regarded as verbal-inspiredness, something for which we give thanks to the grace of God, but which is itself no longer understood as grace but as a bit of higher nature ? What those Church fathers said was in itself correct. But where do we find in them the context in which Paul certainly did speak implicitly of verbal inspiration ? He did not speak of verbal inspiredness—otherwise he would have spoken very differently of the Old Testament in 2 Cor. 3 and of his own word in 1 Cor. 2. And we must not speak of verbal inspiredness in the sphere of the Church if the Church is not to have that false assurance of the Word of God which the Jews and heathen have betrayed by the very fact that the real Word of God is strange to them.

3. Already we find a tendency to explain the event of the inspiration of the biblical authors in a way which suggests that there is a secret desire to evade the asserted mystery of this matter : that here a real human word is the real Word of God, the real humanity of it being more or less compromised by a foolish conception of its divinity. Again we cannot object but only approve when Irenaeus (*C.o.h.* II 28, 2) bases the perfection of the Holy Scriptures on the fact that they are *a verbo Dei et Spiritu eius dictae*. That God Himself says what His witnesses say, that those who hear them hear Him, is something that we often read in the Bible itself and quite patently : in itself it is the right expression for the mystery of its speech. But it is obviously going too far, or, in view of the magnitude of the mystery, not far enough, when Gregory the Great (*Moralia praef.* 1, 2) will not let the human writers of Holy Scripture weigh at all as the authors of it, or allow them to be considered as such : it being all one to the recipient of the letter of a great man, in whose hand he has actually dictated the letter. *Ipse igitur haec scripsit, qui scribenda dictavit*. Where there is this idea of a " dictation " of Holy Scripture through Christ or the Holy Spirit, is not the doctrine of inspiration slipping into Docetism ? If I am right, it was Augustine (*De consensu evang.* I, 35, 54) who first spoke clearly about a divine dictation, or the encountering of it through the biblical writers : *Quidquid enim ille (Christus) de suis factis et dictis nos legere voluit hoc scribendum illis tamquam suis manibus imperavit*. Of course this could and can be regarded non-docetically as a picture of the strictness of the control under which the hagiographers stood and the strictness of their obedience. But if it was not intended docetically, how else can we think of it except—again on the Jewish and heathen model—as a mantically-mechanical operation ? And if it is not to be regarded as mantically-mechanical, how can it not be docetic ? The same choice is even more stringently imposed when we are told by the 2nd century Athenagoras (*Leg. pro Chr.* 7 and 9) that the Holy Spirit moved the mouths of the prophets as His organs, snatching away from them their own thoughts (κατ' ἔκτασιν τῶν ἐν αὐτοῖς λογισμῶν), and using them as a flute-player blows on his flute ; or by Pseudo-Justin (*Coh. ad. Graecos* 8) and later by Hippolytus (*De Antichristo* 2), that the Logos was the plectrum, by means of which the Holy Spirit played on them as on a zither or harp. The obvious aim in all these passages was a stabilising of the word of man as the Word of God and an accompanying assurance in respect of the Word of God. But the price which had to be paid for this apparent gain was far too high. By, as it were, damping down the word of man as such, by transmuting it into a word of man which is real only in appearance, a Word of God which can be grasped in human speech, the whole mystery was lost, the mystery of the freedom of its presence both in the mouths of the biblical witnesses and also in our ears and hearts. And the miracle which took its place,

which was recounted in various forms about the biblical writers and the result of which was admired in the Bible, has only the name in common with the miracle of the presence of the Word of God.

Already the doctrines of inspiration of the Early Church were leading to a rather naive secularisation of the whole conception of revelation. Certainly the existence of the prophets and apostles, the existence of the Bible, is a very surprising and praiseworthy phenomenon. But instead of being placed at once into the circle of the mystery which proceeds without a break from the revelation of the triune God to the present illumination of our hearts, this fact was incorporated into a view of things in which inspirations and inspired men and states have a place with all kinds of other things : have their place, that is, in the Bible, to which in a more or less well-fenced circle there may be added what we accept of saints recognised by the Church and the teaching office of the Church itself. From this standpoint we understand at once how it was possible for the unique authority of Scripture to be so relativised in relation to Church tradition as it actually was in the doctrine of Catholicism and as it was officially recognised to be at the Council of Trent. In the secular compression of inspiration on which it rests, as opposed to the inspiration in which it is known, it obviously cannot be regarded as a unique reality compared with similar phenomena both outside and inside the Church. Probably the struggle and reaction against Montanism had already contributed quite early to this secular compression of inspiration to an objective inspiredness and its continuations as authorised by the Church. But however it took place, in this compression, in the change to an objective inspiredness, even the doctrine of an objective inspiration of the Bible necessarily lost its meaning as one moment in the doctrine of the Word of God, i.e., the doctrine of the Word of God itself necessarily lost its original and comprehensive meaning. The doctrine of Scripture acquired the character of a description of a phenomenon of history and nature which is certainly remarkable, but which can still be established and studied neutrally, which as such could in the last resort be the phenomenon of the origin of the documents of any sort of religious foundation. This is the doubtful element in what is usually accepted as the standard doctrine of inspiration. On this point read the very acute and cautious but in their purely phenomenological character very disturbing expositions of Thomas Aquinas on the nature of prophecy (*S. Theol.* II² *qu.* 171 ff.). How obscure it now is that it is the Holy Spirit of God who in the revelation of Jesus Christ has made prophets prophets, and who alone can guide and enlighten us to recognise them as such. We can and certainly should take comfort in the fact that the Bible was actually read in the early and medieval Churches, even though on other presuppositions than those we find in the teaching of the Bible as such. We can come across the fine thought in Augustine (*De civ. Dei* XI, 4) that the author of Gen. 1¹ at once proved himself to be a true witness of God by the fact that, by the same Spirit in which he himself knew the revelation of God, he also prophesied our future faith. And we can hear him pray (*Conf.* XI, 3, 5) : *Qui illi servo tuo dedisti haec dicere, da et mihi haec intelligere.* Obviously, a recollection of the actual setting of the inspiration of the Bible was never completely lost. But this being the case, we must anxiously ask why it was not strong enough to win recognition in the doctrine of the Bible and in that way to exert an influence upon the actual relationship of the Bible and the Church.

What took place in the 16th century proved itself a Reformation of the Church by the fact that with the restoration of the authority and lordship of the Bible in the Church there now arose a new reading and understanding and expounding of Scripture in accordance with this authority and lordship. On the same lines there grew up a new doctrine of Scripture, and especially of the inspiration of Scripture, corresponding to Scripture itself (cf. for what follows Paul Schempp, *Luthers Stellung z. heiligen Schrift*, 1928. The teaching of Luther really ought to be taken together with that of Calvin, but so far the latter has

not been expounded on the basis of these essential insights.) In the Reformation
doctrine of inspiration the following points must be decisive.

1. The Reformers took over unquestioningly and unreservedly the statement
on the inspiration, and indeed the verbal inspiration, of the Bible, as it is explicitly
and implicitly contained in those Pauline passages which we have taken as our
basis, even including the formula that God is the author of the Bible, and occasionally making use of the idea of a dictation through the Biblical writers. How
could it be otherwise ? Not with less but with greater and more radical seriousness they wanted to proclaim the subjection of the Church to the Bible as the
Word of God and its authority as such. Even in his early period Luther demanded, *ut omne verbum vocale, per quemcunque dicatur, velut Domino ipse dicente
suscipiamus, credamus, cedamus et humiliter subiiciamus nostrum sensum. Sic
enim iustificabimur et non aliter (Comm. on Rom.* 3^{22}, 1515–16, Fi. II 89, 31).
And on the same passage (obviously appealing to Jas. 2^{10}, Fi. II 86, 10) : *Fides
enim consistit in indivisibili, aut ergo tota est et omnia credenda credit aut nulla,
si unum non credit.* At least, therefore, Luther is not inconsistent when we hear
him thundering polemically at the end of his life : " Therefore, we either believe
roundly and wholly and utterly, or we believe nothing : the Holy Ghost doth
not let Himself be severed or parted, that He should let one part be taught or
believed truly and the other part falsely. . . . For it is the fashion of all heretics,
that they begin first with a single article, but they must then all be denied
and altogether, like a ring which is of no further value when it has a break or
cut, or a bell which when it is cracked in one place will not ring any more and is
quite useless " (*Kurzes Bekenntnis vom heiligen Sakrament* 1544 *W.A.* 54, 158, 28).
Therefore Calvin is not guilty of any disloyalty to the Reformation tendency
when he says of Holy Scripture that its authority is recognised only when it
is realised that it *e caelo fluxisse acsi vivae ipsae Dei voces illic exaudirentur*
(*Instit.* I, 7, 1), when it is realised that *autorem eius esse Deum. Itaque summa
Scripturae probatio passim a Dei loquentis persona sumitur (ib.* 7, 4). *Constituimus
(non secus acsi ipsius Dei numen illic intueremur) hominum ministerio ab ipsissimo
Dei ore ad nos fluxisse (ib.* 7, 5). In Calvin's sermon on 2 Tim. 3$^{16f.}$ (*C.R.* 54,
283 f.) God is constantly described as the *autheur* of Holy Scripture and in his
commentary on the same passage we seem to hear a perfect echo of the voice
of the Early Church, when we read : *Hoc principium est, quod religionem nostram
ab aliis omnibus discernit, quod scimus Deum nobis loquutum esse, certoque persuasi
simus, non ex suo sensu loquutos esse prophetas, sed, ut erant Spiritus sancti organa
tantum protulisse, quae coelitus mandata fuerunt ; quisquis ergo vult in scripturis
proficere, hoc secum inprimis constituat, legem et prophetas non esse doctrinam
hominum arbitrio proditam, sed a Spiritu sancto dictatam (C.R.* 52, 383). It is
clear that in themselves the questions we raised in relation to the corresponding
statements of Augustine and Gregory the Great could also be raised here. But
it is no less clear that here they are set in a context which in fact makes them
innocuous. In spite of the use of these concepts neither a mantico-mechanical
nor a docetic conception of biblical inspiration is in the actual sphere of Calvin's
thinking. This does not mean, of course, that these statements, like Luther's,
could not later lose this context and give fresh rise to the questions.

2. The Reformers saw and stated once more the fact that the inspiration
of the Bible as inspiration by the Holy Spirit is not any kind of miracle, nor is
it comparable with any other alleged or real inspiration. For it rests on the
relationship of the biblical witnesses to the very definite content of their witness.
It is indeed this content which inspires them, i.e., which in their speaking and
writing gives them a part in the Holy Spirit and therefore makes their writing
Holy Scripture. It is not of itself, but—as Luther especially always insisted—
of Christ as its Lord and King that Scripture has and again and again acquires
for us its clarity as the divine Word : Others have strange thoughts and remove
themselves from Christ, and want something new. But Holy Scripture refuses

to know or put before us anything but Christ. And whoso therefore goes to Scripture or is led by Scripture to Christ, it is well with him and he is on the right path (*Pred. üb. 2. Buch Mose* 1524 on *Ex.* 7³, *W.A.* 16, 113, 22). All Scripture has its light from the resurrection : *Quid enim potest in scripturis augustius latere reliquum, postquam fractis signaculis et voluto ab hostio sepulchri lapide, illud summum mysterium proditum est, Christum filium Dei factum hominem, Esse Deum trinum et unum, Christum pro nobis passum et regiturum aeternaliter ? . . . Tolle Christum e scripturis, quid amplius in illis invenies* ? (*De servo arb.* 1525, *W.A.* 18, 606, 24). But in this way the doctrine of the inspiration of the Bible is restored as the doctrine of a divine mystery which we cannot grasp and which is therefore true and redemptive. For : *Deus incomprehensibilis.* Christ cannot be understood, *quia est Deus.* He cannot be mastered or conceived, because we live here (*W.A. Ti.* 2, 125, 4). No man, be he apostle or prophet, much less I or those like me, can know Christ fully in this life, can so know and understand truly who and what he should be. For He is true, eternal, almighty God and yet He hath taken on Himself mortal nature, and shown the highest obedience and humility even unto death ; hence He Himself saith, " I am meek and lowly of heart." Now I cannot adequately express how it is with my own mind and heart when I am merry or sad ; how can I then express the lofty affections and emotions of Christ ? (*W.A. Ti.* 6, 65, 36). We must insist that on this retrospective side Calvin spoke rather less clearly and acutely than Luther. But he, too, sees that *hoc animo legendas esse scripturas ut illic inveniamus Christum. Quisquis ab hoc scopo deflectet, utcunque discendo se fatiget tota vita, nunquam ad scientiam veritatis perveniet. Quid enim sapere absque Dei sapientia possumus* (*Comm. on Jn.* 5³⁹ *C.R.* 47, 125). According to Calvin it is also part of the equipment of the biblical writers in their speaking and writing of the Word of God that they had a prior *firma certitudo* in their hearts regarding the divine nature of the experiences to which they then speak and write. *Semper enim Deus indubiam fecit verbo suo fidem.* It is clear that our knowledge of their inspiration must in the first instance rest on the basis on which they themselves stand (*Instit.* I, 6, 2). Therefore for the Reformers the question as to the inspired Word was as such always the question of that which inspires and controls the Word. For them the literally inspired Bible was not at all a revealed book of oracles, but a witness to revelation, to be interpreted from the standpoint of and with a view to its theme, and in conformity with that theme.

3. The Reformers restored the context in which the inspiration of the Bible must be understood on the other side as well. As Luther insisted in innumerable passages the word of Scripture given by the Spirit can be recognised as God's Word only because the work of the Spirit which has taken place in it takes place again and goes a step further, i.e., becomes an event for its hearers or readers. How else will God be recognised except by God Himself ? *Spiritus solus intelligit Scripturas recte et secundum Deum. Alias autem, etsi intelligunt non intelligunt* (*Comm. Rom.* 7¹, Fi. II, 165, 25). The nature of the heretic can be understood from this standpoint : *haereticus est, qui scripturas sanctas alio sensu quam Spiritus flagitat, exponit* (*Ad librum . . . Ambr. Catharini* 1521, *W.A.* 7, 710, 16). And it was on the same point that Calvin expressed himself so vigorously. As he worked it out in *Instit.* I, 7, 4 and the *Commentary on 2 Tim.* 3¹⁶, *C.R.* 52, 383, his view was this. There exists an exact correspondence between the certainty with which the word of the apostles and prophets was the Word of God in itself, or for them, and the certainty with which it as such illumines us. In both cases only God can bear witness to God : *Deus solus de se idoneus est testis—in suo sermone*, first, and then *in hominum cordibus.* And in both cases the God who attests Himself is the Spirit : no one else, but the same Spirit ; *idem ergo Spiritus, qui per os prophetarum loquutus est, in corda nostra penetret necesse est.* In the very same power in which the Word of God dwells in the human word of the biblical writers and goes out from it, it must come to us, i.e., must be known and

received by us as the Word of God, so that we see that God has used the prophets to teach us (*eorum se ministerio usum esse ad nos docendum*) and they faithfully transmitted what was commanded them (*fideliter protulisse quod divinitus erat mandatum*). That is how the concept of inspiration begins and ends on this side. We cannot speak of the inspiration of the Bible without that royal act of the original inspiration in which the risen Christ gave His own a part in His own divine Spirit. But no more can we speak of it without that other royal act—which is only a continuation of the first—in which the inspiration is imparted to us, in which here and now we are forced out of our position as spectators of the word and work of the biblical writers, in which the calling of the prophets and apostles becomes an event to us by the ministry of their word and work. For . . . *Mutuo quodam nexu Dominus Verbi Spiritusque sui certitudinem inter se copulavit, ut solida Verbi religio animis nostris insidat, ubi affulget Spiritus, qui nos illic Dei faciem contemplari faciat, ut vicissim nullo hallucinationis timore Spiritum amplexemur, ubi illum in sua imagine, hoc est in Verbo, recognoscimus. Ita est sane. . . . Eundem Spiritum, cuius virtute Verbum administraverat, submisit, qui suum opus efficaci Verbi confirmatione absolveret* (*Instit.* I, 9, 3).

If we take Luther and Calvin together, we can say that the way to that universal and moving view of inspiration which answers to the majesty of God, and as we find it in Scripture itself, was again opened up by the Reformation. The Reformers' doctrine of inspiration is an honouring of God, and of the free grace of God. The statement that the Bible is the Word of God is on this view no limitation, but an unfolding of the perception of the sovereignty in which the Word of God condescended to become flesh for us in Jesus Christ, and a human word in the witness of the prophets and apostles as witnesses to His incarnation. On their lips and understanding this is the true statement concerning the Bible which is always indispensable to the Church.

But the post-Reformation period first of all failed really to take the newly opened road to the meaning and understanding of the statement. And then it obviously took a different and mistaken way : mistaken, because it destroyed the mystery of this statement, because it necessarily resulted in a denial of the sovereignty of the Word of God and therefore of the Word of God itself. In this connexion we cannot pay too much attention to a remarkable parallelism : the development of the original Reformed Protestantism into the newer Protestantism which began in the so-called orthodoxy and became visible about 1700 was admittedly characterised by a gradual growth of uncertainty in the knowledge of the sin and justification of man and the judgment and grace of God. This uncertainty, as it concerned the question of revelation, was followed first by a quiet, then by an increasingly open and direct inflow of natural theology. To this development there corresponded, curiously enough, a stiffening in the understanding of the inspiration of the Bible which also began quietly but then developed no less definitely. The strictly supranaturalistic character of the statements which were the outcome of this stiffening tends to create an optical illusion. We first think that we are faced by a contradiction when we see orthodoxy becoming laxer and laxer in relation to natural theology and in secret to the doctrine of grace, but stricter and stricter in relation to the doctrine of the inspiration of the Bible. In reality the two belong intimately together. The gradually extending new understanding of biblical inspiration was simply one way, and in view of its highly supranaturalistic character perhaps the most important way, in which the great process of secularisation on which post-Reformation Protestantism entered was carried through. This new understanding of biblical inspiration meant simply that the statement that the Bible is the Word of God was now transformed (following the doubtful tendencies we have already met in the Early Church) from a statement about the free grace of God into a statement about the nature of the Bible as exposed to human inquiry brought under human control. The Bible as the Word of God surreptitiously became a part of natural knowledge of God, i.e., of that knowledge of God which man can have without the free grace of God, by his own power, and with direct insight and assurance. That the highly supranaturalistic form in which this step was made was only a form used because no better was available is proved by the haste with which it was abandoned almost as soon as it was adopted. It was followed by the enlightenment and the ensuing " historical " investigation and treatment of the Bible, i.e., the character of the Bible as the Word of God was now transformed into that of a highly relevant historical record. And this merely revealed what high orthodoxy had really sought and attained under this apparently supranaturalistic form : the understanding and use of the Bible as an instrument separated from the free grace of God and put into the hands of man. If it should be our aim to-day to go back to the better understanding of the Bible which we find in the Reformers and above all in the Bible itself, then it is not a question of renewing the doctrine of inspiration of high orthodoxy in opposition to the Enlightenment and the development which followed it. Rather, we must carefully and consistently avoid the mistake of that orthodoxy—which is all the more dangerous because its supranaturalistic trend can make it appear advantageous. It is only at this root that the evil which broke out later can really be tackled.

Let us briefly review the historical facts. When we study the doctrine *De Scriptura sacra* in the 16th century confessional writings and in the works of the older Protestant teachers, at this point, i.e., in relation to the question why and how far the Bible is the Word of God, we almost always come across the general statements which we also find in the Reformers : that God or the Holy Ghost is its *autor primarius*; that its content is " given " to the prophets and apostles (cf. *Conf. helv. prior* 1536 Art. 1) ; that it is *mandata, inspirata, dictata,* etc., by divine " impulse." But an at best ambiguous mode of speech now begins to be the rule : in the composition of their writings the prophets and apostles acted as *amanuenses* (W. Bucan, *Instit. theol.* 1602 L IV 2 ; *Conf. Bohem.* 1609 I 2) or as *librarii* (A. Hyperius, *De theol.* 1582 II 10) or as *actuarii* (*Syn. pur. Theol.* Leiden 1624 *Disp.* 2, 3). Can we still take this in the same sense as when Calvin (*Serm. on* 1 *Tim.* 4¹ᵗ·, *C.R.* 53, 338) described them as *ministres* ? Or is there already a return to the idea that they are mere flutes in the mouth of the Holy Spirit ? What is certain is that the whole consideration of the doctrine has now obviously narrowed down again to the particular problem of biblical inspiration. The divinity of the Bible can again be referred to without those backward and forward relationships. Even the *testimonium Spiritus sancti internum*, by which we expect a decisive knowledge in this matter on both sides, is either remarkably separated from the living witness of the Spirit in Scripture itself—as though it were something different—or else brought into a no less remarkable relationship to all kinds of other convincing qualities of the Bible. Of course even at this period there were not wanting lights which blazed out like lightning shafts to show where the way could and should have been. For example, the *Leiden Synopsis* (*Disp.* 3, 7) could still maintain that the attitude of the biblical writers had been to some extent active, not passive : *commentantium et autorum rationem habuerunt.* And in the same work we read (*Disp.* 2, 33) : *Scriptura . . . non nisi a Deo, qui eam dedit et a propria sua luce, quam ei indidit, pendere potest.* A. Heidan (*Corp. Theol. christ.* 1636 L I, p. 24 f.) finely distinguishes the *vis persuadendi verbi intrinseca et nativa a Dei verbo indita* and the *testificatio et obsignatio Spiritus in cordibus fidelium,* going on to say of the latter that *hoc testimonium non est citra aut extra verbum quaerendum, in immediatis afflatibus et raptibus, sed in et cum scriptura est coniunctissimum, ita ut una numero sit actio Verbi et Spiritus sancti. Ut non sit aliud quam illuminatio intellectus, qua capax redditur ad intelligendum et persuadetur.* The desire for certainty, which was rightly thought to be needed in the struggle with Rome and the sectaries, as well as in the dispute between Lutherans and Reformed, and above all in the positive proclamation of the Church, might well have been satisfied and better satisfied along these lines, and the lines of the Reformation concept of inspiration. But ever more clearly and definitely a certainty was sought and found quite different from the spiritual certainty which could satisfactorily have been reached on these lines, and which on these lines would have been recognised as the only certainty but also as real certainty. What was wanted was a tangible certainty, not one that is given and has constantly to be given again, a human certainty and not a divine, a certainty of work and not solely of faith. In token of this change there arose the doctrine of inspiration of the high orthodoxy of the 17th century. If previously the biblical writers had always been *amanuenses*, they now became mere *manus Dei*, indeed *calami viventes et scribentes* (A. Calov, *Syst. Loc. theol.* I, 1655, pp. 453, 551, 556). Even the flute-player of Athenagoras now recurs (H. Heidegger, *Corp. Theol.* 1700, II, 34, quoted by A. Schweizer, *Glaubenslehre der ev.-ref. Kirche* 1844 vol. I, p. 202). Where it had been enough to say generally that God is the *auctor primarius* of Holy Scripture and to believe generally in " dictation," what was called the " extensive " authority of Holy Scripture was now formulated with legal preciseness (Gisbert Voetius, *Sel. Disp. theol.* 1648 I p. 29). *Tenendum est, Spiritum sanctum immediate et extraordinario dictasse omnia scribenda et scripta, tum res, tum verba, tum quae antea ignorabant aut recordari non poterant scriptores, quam quae probe noverant, tum historica seu particularia, tum dogmatica universalia theoretica et practica, sive visu, sive auditu, sive lectione, sive meditatione ea didicissent (ib.* p. 32). And the Helvetic Formula of Consent of 1675 *(can.* 2) was preceded by Polan *(Synt. Theol. chr.* 1609, p. 486) and G. Voetius *(ib.* p. 33) in extending this definition expressly to the pointing—indeed, although this was rejected by most of the later men, Polan (p. 479 f.) actually extended it to the *keri* of the Hebrew text. According to G. Voetius (p. 44) the Scriptures of the New Testament were inspired to their authors, not in the Aramaic or Syrian which was their native language, but in Hellenistic Greek. Even things which the biblical authors knew also by their own experience, reflection and judgment they did not write down on the basis of this human knowledge but on the basis of divine inspiration (p. 46). In composing their writings they had no need of prior *studia, inquisitiones et praemeditationes* (p. 47). Even the greeting of Tertius in Rom. 16[22] (p. 46) is inspired, and self-evidently a saying like that in which Paul speaks about the coat which he left behind in Troas, 2 Tim. 4[13] (Calov, p. 560). Since God puts His Word in a prophet's mouth, as Calov expressly declares (p. 565), it is not the prophet's but God's own Word, *in quibus nihil humani sit praeter organum oris.* The sacred writers were not free to write down anything other— or in any other way than that dictated to them by the Holy Spirit (p. 565 and 570). That each obviously wrote in his own language and in that of his age is to be ascribed only to a special condescension of the Holy Spirit, and not to human co-operation (p. 575). If we ask why all this had to be stated with this almost terrifying pedantry and safeguarded against all possible defections, we always come up against the postulate that Holy Scripture must be for us a *divina et infallibilis historia.* Truth is necessarily diffused over all Scripture and all parts of Scripture (*infallibilis et* θεόπνευστος *veritas per omnes et singulas eius partes diffusa est,* Voetius, p. 31). Polan established the inspiration of the Hebrew, *quia si a Massoritis demum vera lectio et pronuntiatio prophetarum esset ostensa, essemus aedificati super fundamentum Massoritarum et non super fundamentum prophetarum* (p. 487). *Nullus error vel in leviculis, nullus memoriae lapsus, nedum mendacium ullum locum habere potest in universa sancta scriptura* (Calov p. 551). Should there be found even the minutest error in the Bible, then it is no longer wholly the Word of God, and the inviolability of its authority is destroyed (p. 552). The same is true if even the tiniest fraction of it derives from human knowledge, reflection and perception (p. 555). " All Scripture is given by God . . ." is what it says in 2 Tim. 3[16]. Therefore we cannot find in it even the smallest word which is not given by God and therefore infallible truth (p. 563).

If it were otherwise, neither for theology nor for faith would there be any certainty, any certainty of grace and of the forgiveness of sins, any certainty of the existence and divine sonship of Jesus Christ. *Quid vero inde, nisi merus Pyrrhonismus, mera σκεπτική et academica dubitatio, immo merus atheismus ?* And by not taking better care for His revelation God Himself would be the cause of human unbelief. *Principium debet esse certum, indubitatum, infallibile* (p. 579). *Si enim unicus scripturae versiculus, cessante immediato Spiritus sancti influxu, conscriptus est, promptum erit satanae, idem de toto capite, de integro libro, de universo denique codice biblico excipere et per consequens omnem scripturae autoritatem elevare* (Quenstedt, *Theol. did. pol.* 1685 I *c.* 4 *sect.* 2 *qu.* 3 *beb.* 7). *Si verba singula non fuissent scriptoribus sacris suggesta per θεοπνευστίαν, scriptura sacra non proprie, non absolute et simpliciter . . . esset dicique posset θεόπνευστος* (Hollaz, *Ex. Theol. accroam.* 1707 *Prol.* 2, 27). H. Cremer (*PRE³* 9, 192) is right : " This doctrine of inspiration was absolutely new." But it was so, not in its content, which was merely a development and systematisation of statements which had been heard in the Church since the first centuries, but in the intention which underlay the development and systematisation. As we have seen, the earlier statements were not free from ambiguity. They did not escape the danger of a docetic dissolving or of a mantico-mechanical materialising of the concept of the biblical witness to revelation. It is obvious that the " modern " 17th century doctrine of inspiration increased the danger with its development and systematisation of the statements. But there is no point in trying to attack it from this side. We have seen from the example of the Reformers that the statements as such, if only they stand in the right context backwards and forwards, can be made without giving rise to that danger ; the mere " dangers " of a doctrine never entitle us to describe it as false doctrine. And again there is no point in joining the wolves of the 18th and 19th centuries and attacking the 17th-century doctrine of inspiration because of its pointed supranaturalism. We must attack it rather because its supranaturalism is not radical enough. The intention behind it was ultimately only a single and in its own way very " naturalistic " postulate : that the Bible must offer us a *divina et infallibilis historia* ; that it must not contain human error in any of its verses ; that in all its parts and the totality of its words and letters as they are before us it must express divine truth in a form in which it can be established and understood ; that under the human words it must speak to us the Word of God in such a way that we can at once hear and read it as such with the same obviousness and directness with which we can hear and read other human words ; that it must be a codex of axioms which can be seen as such with the same formal dignity as those of philosophy and mathematics. The secular nature of this postulate showed itself plainly in the assumption that we may freely reproach the good God if it is not fulfilled, threatening Him with distrust, scepticism and atheism—a threat which was no less freely carried out in the following generations, when men became convinced that the postulate could not be fulfilled. This secularism was not merely a danger which threatened. It was openly present. Therefore we have to resist and reject the 17th-century doctrine of inspiration as false doctrine. The development and systematisation of the traditional statements concerning the divine authority of the Bible meant an actualising of the Word of God by eliminating the perception that its actualisation can only be its own decision and act, that our part in it can consist only in the recollection and expectation of its eternal presence. This actualisation was arbitrary because it was obstinately postulated and maintained. In it the Word of God could no longer be the Word of God and therefore it was no longer recognised as such. The Bible was now grounded upon itself apart from the mystery of Christ and the Holy Ghost. It became a " paper Pope," and unlike the living Pope in Rome it was wholly given up into the hands of its interpreters. It was no longer a free and spiritual force, but an instrument of human power. And in this form the Bible became so like the holy books of other religions, for which something similar had always been claimed, that the superiority of its claim could not be asserted in relation to them or to the many achievements of the human spirit generally. What product of human inventiveness does not ultimately rest on the same claim to infallibility ? What cannot be similarly invested with it ? The intention in establishing the authority of the Bible along these lines was to avoid historical relativism, but it opened up the way to it, and theology and the Church did not hesitate for a moment to tread that way. In content the 17th-century doctrine of inspiration asserted things which cannot be maintained in face of a serious reading and exposition of what the Bible itself says about itself, and in face of an honest appreciation of the facts of its origin and tradition. Therefore the postulate on which 17th-century man staked everything proved incapable of fulfilment. But although this is important, in the long run it is only of secondary importance, because it is always debatable. What is more important is the fact of dogmatic history that once the doctrine arose it was believed for only a short time, but it remained for many ages, and still is to some extent at the present time, a kind of theological bogeyman, the logically necessary interpretation of the statement that the Bible is the Word of God, which has prevented whole generations and innumerable individual theologians and believers from seeing the true, spiritual biblical and Reformation meaning of the statement, causing them to go past Luther and Calvin and even Paul in order to accompany Voetius and Calov. But the decisive fact is this. As a result of this doctrine of inspiration, the view of the Bible which in the Reformers, being genuinely and strictly a view of the Bible, was also a view of Christ here and the Holy Spirit there, and therefore of God's sovereignty and free grace, was now for long periods and for large sections of the Evangelical Churches restricted to the biblical documents as such and in their historico-literary givenness, about which this doctrine of inspiration had asserted such remarkable things. If the assertions themselves could not be accepted—and it was no evil but right and necessary that they should not—the restriction of outlook was accepted all the more intensively and obstinately. In no sense was it a fresh broadening of outlook when the Bible came to be interpreted as the document of a specific history and the so-called spirit of the Bible as the spirit of this history, as was variously attempted by the rationalists of the 18th century, by Herder, by Schleiermacher and by the conservative and liberal schools of the 19th century up to Ritschl and the religious historicists. All sorts of seemingly and actually more concrete views of the human form of the Bible were undoubtedly gained in these ways. But if we imagine that we shall find the Word of God in a history which can be studied on historico-literary lines, the sources of which we believe we have in the Bible, we escape the Docetism of our forefathers, who tried to close their eyes to the humanity of the Bible, only to fall the more heavily into a complementary Ebionitism. And a loftier manticism may even be advanced by the mystery of the newly instituted cultus of " God in history." What is certain is that the view of the connexion of the Word of God in the Bible with the work of Christ for us and that of the Holy Spirit to us, which was barred by the 17th-century doctrine of inspiration, was hermetically closed off now that the latter could not be sustained on secondary grounds without breaking loose from its restriction of outlook. The knowledge of the free grace of God as the unity of Scripture and revelation had been lost. No wonder that the statement that the Bible is the Word of God was now dismissed as " untrue." Thanks to the happy inconsistency which has always been the best thing in Church history, this statement has survived and with it the Evangelical Church. Without its open or concealed truth, the latter could not have survived for a moment. But that is another story. Of the history of the doctrine of inspiration as such it must still be said that in the Evangelical Church it finally made the statement incomprehensible. After a promising start it was for the most part a chapter of accidents.

Instructed by our consideration of the ways to be taken and avoided, we will now try to state in the form of propositions what we can believe about the inspiration, the divine nature of the Bible and therefore about the statement that the Bible is the Word of God, more particularly in the light of the concept of Word.

1. To say " the Word of God " is to say the Word of *God*. It is therefore to speak about a being and event which are not under human control and foresight. Our knowledge of this being and event does not justify us in thinking and speaking of them as though they were under our control and foresight. We know this divine nature which we cannot control or foresee when we know this Word, when we know, then, what we are saying when we say that the Bible is the Word of God. That we have the Bible as the Word of God does not justify us in transforming the statement that the Bible is the Word of God from a statement about the being and rule of God in and through the Bible into a statement about the Bible as such. When we have the Bible as the Word of God, and accept its witness, we are summoned to remember the Lord of the Bible and to give Him the glory. It would not strictly be loyalty to the Bible, and certainly not thankfulness for the Word of God given and continually given again in it, if we did not let our ears be opened by it, not to what it says but to what He, God Himself, has to say to us as His Word in it and through it. With this recognition and adoration of the sovereignty of Him whose Word the Bible is, the knowledge of its inspiration, its character as the Word of God, will always have to begin.

2. To say " the Word of God " is to say the work of God. It is not to contemplate a state or fact but to watch an event, and an event which is relevant to us, an event which is an act of God, an act of God which rests on a free decision. That God's Word is from eternity to eternity does not allow us to evade it, as though for us who live in time it is not the event of its presence, its communion with us, its promise of our own eternal life. To its eternity there necessarily corresponds in its revelation the fact that for us and to us it is not present as that which is not the Word of God is present. But it happens, and happens as nothing else happens, as something new compared with all that we were or are or shall be, in fact with all that the whole world was or is or shall be. Even the fact that the Bible is present as the Word of God does not allow us to look at it in any other way. Indeed, it forces us to look at it in this way. It reminds us of the act of God achieved once and for all. If we have this recollection, if therefore the Bible is really present to us, we cannot possibly understand the Word of God which speaks of it except as the act of God which is now expected by us. Our knowledge of its character as the Word of God and therefore of its inspiration will thus consist in our willing approach to the Word of God promised in it ; willing to let the new thing happen to us which, if we will

hear it, will become event in our life and in the life of the whole world.

3. To say " the Word of God " is to say the miracle of God. It is not secretly to regard the new thing with which we now have to do in the Word of God as something old, i.e., bound by the presuppositions and laws, the customs and traditions of other happenings in our lives and in the life of our world. We reckon that the event of the Word of God is not a continuation, but the end of all other events that we know. We reckon that a new series of events has begun. Again, the in itself non-miraculous given-ness of the Bible as the Word of God, its existence amongst all the other facts of our cosmos, will not induce us to take any other view but rather to take this view. Yet in speaking of the act of God in Jesus Christ, it does itself speak of the grace of God as a reality which cannot be deduced or conceived in the context of the human existence which we know, a reality which posits the end of all other events and opens up a new series of events. That the Word of God is not under our control or foresight is proved by the fact that its content—and not only its content, but its reality as such—is the grace of God, which we have not deserved, the occurrence of which we cannot claim or bring about, which we can only accept because God is pleased to be gracious to us. If we allow the Bible to say this to us, and in so doing to speak the Word of God, how else can we think of the Word of God in the Bible except as a miracle ? How else or better can we describe the character of the Bible as the Word of God, how can we ascribe to it any higher value and authority than that in it we see the place where we must expect the miracle of the Word of God ? No word can be too high for it if it is a description of this miracle and a confession of its truth. But however pious or well-meant the word which eliminates this miracle, which makes the Word of God in the Bible a part of our own higher nature, a remarkable property of a part of our former nature, which brings the Bible as the Word of God into the sphere of human competençe, this word destroys its real dignity and authority, and denies the statement that it is the Word of God.

4. But if we are speaking of a miracle when we say that the Bible is the Word of God, we must not compromise either directly or indirectly the humanity of its form and the possibility of the offence which can be taken at it. An attempt to do so is tantamount to an attempt in our exegesis of the New Testament to understand the miracles recorded there by telling ourselves that the sick people who were healed according to these narratives were not really seriously sick or even that the Jesus who rose again on the third day did not really die on the cross. As truly as Jesus died on the cross, as Lazarus died in Jn. 11, as the lame were lame, as the blind were blind, as the hungry at the feeding of the five thousand were hungry, as the sea on which Jesus walked was a lake many fathoms deep : so, too, the

prophets and apostles as such, even in their office, even in their function as witnesses, even in the act of writing down their witness, were real, historical men as we are, and therefore sinful in their action, and capable and actually guilty of error in their spoken and written word. If the miracle happened to them that they were called to be witnesses of the resurrection and that they received the Holy Spirit, it was to them it happened, leaving them the full use of their human freedom and not removing the barriers which are therefore posited for them as for all of us. Their existence as witnesses, as it is a visible event in Holy Scripture, is therefore the existence of real men (and therefore not at all crowded out by the existence of God or hampered by any kind of magic in the fulfilment of their existence), men who as such, in the full use of their freedom and within the limits posited by it, have to speak to us the Word of God. That the lame walk, that the blind see, that the dead are raised, that sinful and erring men as such speak the Word of God : that is the miracle of which we speak when we say that the Bible is the Word of God. To the comprehension of this statement there belongs, therefore, the recognition that its truth consists in the removing of an offence which is always and everywhere present, and that this takes place by the power of the Word of God. This offence, like the offence of the cross of Christ, is based on the fact that the Word of God became flesh and therefore to this very day has built and called and gathered and illumined and sanctified His Church amongst flesh. This offence is therefore grounded like the overcoming of it in the mercy of God. For that reason it must not be denied and for that reason, too, it must not be evaded. For that reason every time we turn the Word of God into an infallible biblical word of man or the biblical word of man into an infallible Word of God we resist that which we ought never to resist, i.e., the truth of the miracle that here fallible men speak the Word of God in fallible human words— and we therefore resist the sovereignty of grace, in which God Himself became man in Christ, to glorify Himself in His humanity. If we cannot make up our minds for this hard thinking, let us see to it that we are not shutting ourselves off from the real word of comfort spoken to us by the existence of the Bible as such. And if we want to assert a supposedly stricter concept of the value and authority of the Bible, let us see to it that we are not moving away from the strictness of its true value and authority. If the prophets and apostles are not real and therefore fallible men, even in their office, even when they speak and write of God's revelation, then it is not a miracle that they speak the Word of God. But if it is not a miracle, how can it be the Word of God that they speak, how can their speaking, and our hearing of their human words, possess as the Word of God the character of revelation ? To the bold postulate, that if their word is to be the Word of God they must be inerrant in every word, we oppose the even bolder assertion, that according to the scriptural witness about man, which applies to them too, they can be at fault in any word, and have been at fault in every word, and yet according to the same scriptural witness, being justified and sanctified by grace alone, they have still spoken the Word of God in their fallible and erring human word. It is the fact that in the Bible we can take part in this real miracle, the miracle of the grace of God to sinners, and not the idle miracle of human words which were not really human words at all, which is the foundation of the dignity and authority of the Bible.

5. If, therefore, we are serious about the fact that this miracle is an event, we cannot regard the presence of God's Word in the Bible as an attribute inhering once for all in this book as such and what we see before us of books and chapters and verses. Of the book as we have it, we can only say : We recollect that we have heard in this book the Word of God ; we recollect, in and with the Church, that the Word of God has been heard in all this book and in all parts of it ; therefore we expect that we shall hear the Word of God in this book again, and hear it even in those places where we ourselves have not heard it before. Yet the presence of the Word of God itself, the real and present speaking and hearing of it, is not identical with the existence of the book as such. But in this presence something takes place in and with the book, for which the book as such does indeed give the possibility, but the reality of which cannot be anticipated or replaced by the existence of the book. A free divine decision is made. It then comes about that the Bible, the Bible *in concreto*, this or that biblical context, i.e., the Bible as it comes to us in this or that specific measure, is taken and used as an instrument in the hand of God, i.e., it speaks to and is heard by us as the authentic witness to divine revelation and is therefore present as the Word of God. It is present in a way we cannot conceive : not as a third time between past and future, between recollection and expectation, but as that point between the two which we cannot think of as time, which when it is considered immediately becomes once more either before or after. In this way it is the being present of the eternal Word, which is constitutive for its expectation and recollection, on which our time is based, just as the incarnation and resurrection of Jesus Christ as the centre of time is the basis of time in general. A genuine, fallible human word is at this centre the Word of God : not in virtue of its own superiority, of its replacement by a Word of God veiled as the word of man, still less of any kind of miraculous transformation, but, of course, in virtue of the privilege that here and now it is taken and used by God Himself, like the water in the Pool of Bethesda.

6. As to when, where and how the Bible shows itself to us in this event as the Word of God, we do not decide, but the Word of God Himself decides, at different times in the Church and with different men confirming and renewing the event of instituting and inspiring the prophets and apostles to be His witnesses and servants, so that

in their written word they again live before us, not only as men who once spoke in Jerusalem and Samaria, to the Romans and Corinthians, but as men who in all the concreteness of their own situation and action speak to us here and now. We can know that in the life of the Church, and indeed in its life with the Bible, it is a matter of this decision and act of God or rather of the actualisation of the act of God which took place once and for all in Jesus Christ. In the whole Bible it is always a matter of this act. We can remember that the Bible has really already been for ourselves and others the place of this act. We can and should expect this act afresh. We can and should cling to the written word, as Jesus commanded the Jews, and as the people of Beroea did. We can and should search the Scriptures asking about this witness. We can and should therefore pray that this witness may be made to us. But it does not lie—and this is why prayer must have the last word—in our power but only in God's, that this event should take place and therefore this witness of Scripture be made to us. We are therefore absolved from trying to force this event to happen. This does not allow us to be unfaithful or indolent. It is the man who is faithful in seeking, asking and praying, who knows that the faithfulness of God and not his own faithfulness decides. But we are completely absolved from differentiating in the Bible between the divine and the human, the content and the form, the spirit and the letter, and then cautiously choosing the former and scornfully rejecting the latter. Always in the Bible as in all other human words we shall meet with both. And we may differentiate between them as we do in the understanding of a human word. But the event in which the word of man proves itself the Word of God is one which we cannot bring about by this differentiation. The Word of God is so powerful that it is not bound by what we think we can discover and value as the divine element, the content, the spirit of the Bible. Again, it is not so powerful that it will not bind itself to what we think we can value lightly as the human element, the form, the letter of the Bible. We are absolved from differentiating the Word of God in the Bible from other contents, infallible portions and expressions from the erroneous ones, the infallible from the fallible, and from imagining that by means of such discoveries we can create for ourselves encounters with the genuine Word of God in the Bible. If God was not ashamed of the fallibility of all the human words of the Bible, of their historical and scientific inaccuracies, their theological contradictions, the uncertainty of their tradition, and, above all, their Judaism, but adopted and made use of these expressions in all their fallibility, we do not need to be ashamed when He wills to renew it to us in all its fallibility as witness, and it is mere self-will and disobedience to try to find some infallible elements in the Bible. But finally we are absolved from having to know and name as such the event or events, in which Scripture proves and confirms itself to

us as the Word of God. We have seen that as the events of the eternal
presence of the Word, as the hours of God, they cannot be grasped in
time or can be grasped only in their before and after, in recollection
and expectation. It is enough—and this is all that is required of us
—that we should constantly approach these events and proceed from
them. Similarly we cannot know our faith in its eternal form as our
justification before God, but only as a movement ἐκ πίστεως εἰς πίστιν
(Rom. 1¹⁷), which as such is not justified. We can give to ourselves
and to others an account of our faith ; but we can only do so in thankfulness and hope, without showing the basis of our faith. And that is
how we stand in relation to Holy Scripture. We can and must be
summoned by it to thankfulness and hope. In obedience to this
summons it will be seen in the reality and the judgment of God whether
and to what extent we participate in the event of the presence of His
Word. A consciousness of this presence as such, or an indication of
this presence to others, does not lie in the sphere of human possibility
and therefore cannot be demanded of us. " By their fruits ye shall
know them." Therefore the presence of the Word of God is not an
experience, precisely because and as it is the divine decision concerning us.

7. When we speak of the inspiration of the Bible or when we
confess that the Bible is the Word of God, on the one side, in the
sphere of time and sense, in the concrete life of the Church and of our
own life as members of the Church, we have to think of a twofold
reality. There is first the question of the text of the biblical witness :
or rather of a definite portion of this text, which in a specific time and
situation claims the attention of specific men or of a specific individual.
If now it is true in time, as it is true in eternity, that the Bible is the
Word of God, then according to what we have just said, God Himself
now says what the text says. The work of God is done through this
text. The miracle of God takes place in this text formed of human
words. This text in all its humanity, including all the fallibility which
belongs to it, is the object of this work and miracle. By the decision
of God this text is now taken and used. And in the mystery of God
it takes place that here and now this text acquires this determination.
Yet it is still this text as such of which all this has to be said. It is
as such that it will speak and attest, and be read and heard : and the
Word of God in it and through it, not alongside or behind it, not in
some place which we have first to attain to or even create beyond the
text. If God speaks to man, He really speaks the language of this
concrete human word of man. That is the right and necessary truth
in the concept of verbal inspiration. If the word is not to be separated
from the matter, if there is no such thing as verbal inspiredness, the
matter is not to be separated from the word, and there is real inspiration, the hearing of the Word of God, only in the form of verbal
inspiration, the hearing of the Word of God only in the concrete form

of the biblical word. Verbal inspiration does not mean the infallibility of the biblical word in its linguistic, historical and theological character as a human word. It means that the fallible and faulty human word is as such used by God and has to be received and heard in spite of its human fallibility. Whatever may be the value of the one who is commissioned and of his word, for us he now has the value of his commission. In this dignity he has to be respected, and his word respected. That we not only have him and his word, the biblical text, but in him and through him the Word of God, is something which we must leave to God. In this confidence, which will give us a proper freedom in relation to the human word as such, we do have to abide by the human word. For—and this is the second thing that has to be considered—in relation to the concrete text and no less concretely to ourselves, it is a matter of the event or the events of the presence of the Word of God in our own present : not the experience of its presence, but its actual presence—the presence upon which God decides, which we cannot create or anticipate, but the presence, which as the inconceivable, free presence of God Himself decides our past and future, defining our recollection as thankfulness and our expectation as hope. In face of the biblical text we are not bound to imagine that the Word of God is present. We are not called upon to use any devices to make it present. But in face of the biblical text we are clamped or pincered by thankfulness and hope and we must not try to escape from this clamp or pincer. Imprisoned in thankfulness and hope we must dare to face the humanity of the biblical texts and therefore their fallibility without the postulate that they must be infallible, but also without the superstitious belief in any infallible truth alongside or behind the text and revealed by ourselves—we must dare really to face it, i.e., to let the text speak to us as it stands, to let it say all that it has to say in its vocabulary and context, to allow the prophets and apostles to say again here and now to us what they said there and then. That is how it will always be when they do what we cannot force them to do and speak the Word of God in their human words. The door of the Bible texts can be opened only from within. It is another thing whether we wait at this door or leave it for other doors, whether we want to enter and knock or sit idly facing it. The existence of the biblical texts summons us to persistence in waiting and knocking. Their concrete form is a challenge to concrete effort. We can sum up all that must be said on this point in the statement that faith in the inspiration of the Bible stands or falls by whether the concrete life of the Church and of the members of the Church is a life really dominated by the exegesis of the Bible. If the biblical text in its literalness as a text does not force itself upon us, or if we have the freedom word by word to shake ourselves loose from it, what meaning is there in our protestation that the Bible is inspired and the Word of God ? To say " Lord, Lord " is not enough. What matters is to do the will of God if we are to know His grace and truth—for that is the inspiration of the Bible.

8. But we must remember—and with this we can bring these considerations to a close—that the inspiration of the Bible cannot be reduced to our faith in it, even though we understand this faith as the gift and work of God in us. All that happens in the sphere of time and sense, in the concrete life of the Church and of our own life as its members, the eventuation of the presence of the Word of God in the human word of the prophets and apostles, can only be regarded as a repetition, a secondary prolongation and continuation of the once-for-all and primary eventuation of revelation itself. It was not for nothing, nor was it wrong, that the Early Church wanted assurance of the dignity and authority of the Bible as the Word of God against the accident and self-will to which it is obviously exposed by its humanity in the reading and understanding and expounding of the Bible. We have thought of the divine inspiration of the Bible as an actual decision which takes place in the mystery of God as His work and miracle, and which has to be recollected and expected in faith and obedience and in faithful exegesis. But there is an obvious doubt whether this really does sufficient justice to the objectivity of the truth that the Bible is the Word of God, whether this description is not at least exposed to the danger and may be taken to imply that our faith makes the Bible into the Word of God, that its inspiration is ultimately a matter of our own estimation or mood or feeling. We must not blind ourselves to this danger. But we must ask ourselves how we are to meet it, how we can in fact do justice to the objectivity of the inspiration of the Bible. Yet obviously we can do justice to it only by refraining from even imagining that we can do so. We do justice to it by believing and resting on the fact that the action of God in the founding and maintaining of His Church, with which we have to do in the inspiration of the Bible, is objective enough to emerge victorious from all the inbreaks and outbreaks of man's subjectivity. To believe in the inspiration of the Bible means, because of and in accordance with its witness, to believe in the God whose witness it is. If we do not, how are we helped by even the strongest assurance of the divinity of its witness ? And if we do, how can we ask for any special assurance of it ? Is it not to believe without believing, if we want to make such an assurance indispensable ? Certainly it is not our faith which makes the Bible the Word of God. But we cannot safeguard the objectivity of the truth that it is the Word of God better than by insisting that it does demand our faith, and underlie our faith, that it is the substance and life of our faith. For in so doing we maintain that it is the truth of the living God, beyond which there is none other, the power of which we are not allowed to doubt in face of the forces of human subjectivity, which we have therefore to know and recognise as such. But if this is true, then it stands that we have to understand the inspiration of the

Bible as a divine decision continually made in the life of the Church and in the life of its members. That it took place once and for all in the resurrection of Jesus Christ and in the outpouring of the Holy Spirit, as the establishment of the Church, is not disputed. But this is known and acknowledged in its objectivity by the fact that we recollect and expect the same divine decision in the preservation of the Church, and our own fellowship with Jesus Christ and in the Holy Spirit. That the Bible is the Word of God is not left to accident or to the course of history and to our own self-will, but to the God of Abraham, Isaac and Jacob, the triune God as Him whose self-witness alone can and very definitely does see to it that this statement is true, that the biblical witnesses have not spoken in vain and will not be heard in vain.

In view of what we have just said we will close with an admission of, if you like, a purely formal nature, the significance of which is that it points to the act of confession with which the doctrine of Holy Scripture is really concerned when its content is rightly understood. We have to admit to ourselves and to all who ask us about this question that the statement that the Bible is the Word of God is an analytical statement, a statement which is grounded only in its repetition, description and interpretation, and not in its derivation from any major propositions. It must either be understood as grounded in itself and preceding all other statements or it cannot be understood at all. The Bible must be known as the Word of *God* if it is to be *known* as the Word of God. The doctrine of Holy Scripture in the Evangelical Church is that this logical circle is the circle of self-asserting, self-attesting truth into which it is equally impossible to enter as it is to emerge from it : the circle of our freedom which as such is also the circle of our captivity.

When the Evangelical Churches of the Reformation and later were asked by their Roman adversaries how the divine authority of Scripture could be known and believed by men without being guaranteed by the authority of the Church, the Evangelical theologians gave the hard but only possible answer that the authority of Scripture was grounded only in itself and not in the judgment of men. *Credimus et confitemur, scripturas canonicas sanctorum prophetarum et apostolorum utriusque testamenti ipsum verum esse Verbum Dei et autoritatem sufficientem ex semetipsis, non ex hominibus habere. Nam Deus ipse loquutus est patribus, prophetis et apostolis et loquitur adhuc nobis per scripturas sanctas* (*Conf. hebr. post.* 1562 *Art.* 1). We might just as well ask where we can base the distinction of light from darkness, of white from black, of sweet from sour (Calvin, *Instit.* I, 7, 2). *Quaestio, an scripturae seu sacra biblia sint Dei verbum ? homine christiano indigna est. Ut enim in scholis contra negantem principia non disputatur, ita indignum iudicare debemus, qui audiatur, si quis christianae religionis principium neget* (J. Wolleb, *Chr. theol. comp.* 1626, *praecog.* 7). This is not an embarrassed expediency but the wisdom of serpents and the harmlessness of doves. It is not an evasion of the actual point at issue, but its reference back to the only possible actuality. If only they had remained and gone further along these lines.

For the statement that the human word of the Bible is the Word of God we can obviously give only a single and incomparable basis.

This is that it is true. This basis either exists of itself or not at all It is either already known and acknowledged or it is not accepted.

Auctoritas scripturae quoad nos nihil aliud est quam manifestatio et cognitio unicae illius divinae et summae auctoritatis, quae scripturae est interna et insita (J. Gerhard, *Loci theol.* 1610 f. L I *cap.* 3, 38).

As this one basis posited itself and was known and acknowledged, it became the basis of the Church. And as it posits itself again in the same self-glory and in that self-glory is again known and acknowledged, it alone is the power of its continuance. The Church does not have to accredit it, but again and again it has to be accredited by it. And all that we may adduce on other grounds for the authority of Scripture does not underlie this one ground and its divinity, but at best can be sustained only on the presupposition of this one ground and as pointing to it.

The 16th century was well acquainted with and even accepted—just as it accepted the authority of the Church under Holy Scripture—an apologetic which came down from the Early Church and the Middle Ages, subordinate to but illustrating this one ground : *argumenta testimonia*, human considerations by which it was thought that the divinity of Scripture could later be more oi less clearly brought out. Attention was usually drawn to the antiquity of the Bible, its miracles and prophecies, its decisive and victorious role in Church history. Calvin thought it necessary to devote a whole chapter of the *Institutes* to these considerations as they throw light on the existence of the Bible (I, 8 : *Probationes, quatenus fert humana ratio satis firmas suppetere ad stabiliendam scripturae fidem*). But he himself calls them *secundariae nostrae imbecillitatis adminicula* and warns us in every possible way against thinking that we can regard and apply them as the grounds of faith : *inepte faciunt, qui probari volunt infidelibus, scripturam esse verbum Dei, quod nisi fide cognosci nequit* (I, 8, 13). The verdict that Scripture is the Word of God is not a human but a divine judgment, and only as such can it be adopted and believed by us : *illius ergo virtute illuminati iam non aut nostro aut aliorum iudicio credimus a Deo esse scripturam. . . . Non argumenta, non verisimilitudines quaerimus, quibus iudicium nostrum incumbat; sed rei extra aestimandi aleam positae, iudicium ingeniumque nostrum subiicimus . . . quia inexpugnabilem nos veritatem tenere, probe nos conscii sumus . . . quia non dubiam vim numinis illic sentimus videre ac spirare, qua ad parendum, scientes quidem ac volentes, vividius tamen et efficacius quam pro humana aut voluntate aut scientia trahimur et accendimur. . . . Talis ergo est persuasio quae rationes non requirat, talis notitia, cui optima ratio constet, nempe in qua securius constantiusque mens quiescit, quam in ullis rationibus, talis denique sensus, qui nisi ex caelesti revelatione nasci nequeat. Non aliud loquor quam quod apud se experitur fidelium unusquisque, nisi quod longe infra iustam rei explicationem verba subsidunt* (I, 7, 5). Unfortunately, Calvin found many later imitators in the enumeration and development of these secondary grounds, but not in his definitely expressed perception of the abysmal difference of these grounds from the one primary and real ground, not in his awareness of the superiority and self-sufficiency of that one ground. The *testimonium Spiritus sancti internum*, on which alone he and the Reformation as a whole based faith in the Bible as the Word of God, at a later date gradually but irresistibly became one ground with others, and the other grounds gained an interest and acquired an importance as though they were, after all, autonomous. The unarmed power of the one ground, that in the Bible God has attested Himself to be God and still does so, came more and more to be regarded, as it was never meant to be regarded in the 16th century, as the power of a particular spiritual experience, which at some point we have to have of the Bible. But on this understanding, it could not have the force of a real ground. Calvin had seen in it only the power of an objective proof. But it was now suspected to be only subjective and in the strict sense not a proof at all. Therefore the witness of the Holy Spirit necessarily retired and finally disappeared behind the rational proofs which Calvin had treated only as luxuries. This was the state of things at the end of the 17th century. In S. Werensfels (*De triplici teste, Opusc.* I p. 179 f.) we find the witness of the Holy Spirit transformed into the human conviction which as readers of Scripture we ourselves can form of the meaning and credibility of what we read according to our own knowledge and conscience. And a little later in J. D. Michaelis (*Comp. theol. dogm.* 1760, § 8) we find the blatant assertion that never in all his life has he experienced this testimony of the Holy Spirit, and that he does not envy those who think they have and believe that they must maintain *illa quae in codice sacro insunt divinitatis et argumenta.* At this point the battle was lost. More recently there has been no lack of voices advising us that at least an historical appreciation of the original position has not been forfeited. We can summon A. Ritschl as a witness. He could once write of the *testimonium Spiritus sancti* : " Even if this concept does comprise all that is meant by religious experience, it is formally quite differently constructed from the concept of experience ; in fact it is quite opposed to it. By experience we mean a movement, the subject of which is the human Ego ; but in the *testimonium Spiritus sancti* the Ego is thought of as an object, and its experience of salvation and conviction of the truth as the operation of another power " (*Rechtf. und. Versöhnung*[4] 2 *Bd.* p. 6). But even when it is rightly understood, Ritschl declared the concept to be " unusable."

Scripture is recognised as the Word of God by the fact that it *is* the Word of God. This is what we are told by the doctrine of the witness of the Holy Spirit. According to His humanity Jesus was conceived of the Holy Spirit, to be born of the Virgin Mary for us. Again, according to His humanity, Jesus is redemptively present by the Holy Spirit in the Lord's Supper. And by the Holy Spirit the witnesses of His humanity became and are also the witnesses of His eternal Godhead, His revelation was apprehended by them and through them it is apprehended by us. When we say " by the Holy Spirit " we mean, by God in the free and gracious act of His turning to us. When we say " by the Holy Spirit " we say that in the doctrine of Holy Scripture we are content to give the glory to God and not to ourselves.

H. Alstedt (*Theol. schol.* 1618, p. 27, cited H. Heppe, *Dogm. d. ev. ref. Kirche* 1861, new edn. 1935 p. 24) wrote these words : *Auctoritas et certitudo scripturae pendet a testimonio Spiritus sancti et haec est demonstratio demonstrationum maxima. Auctoritas namque dicti vel scripti cuiuscumque pendet ab ipso eius auctore. Multum situm est in hac regula, quippe basi totius theologiae.* D. F. Strauss was right to criticise this rule : " Who can now attest the divinity of this witness ? Either itself again, which is nobody : or a something, perhaps a feeling or thought in the human spirit—this is the Achilles' heel of the Protestant system (*Die chr. Glaubenslehre*, vol. 1, 1840, p. 136). Indeed, who does attest the divinity of this witness ? What Strauss failed to see is that there is no Protestant " system," but that the Protestant Church and Protestant doctrine has necessarily and gladly to leave his question unanswered, because there at its weakest point, where it can only acknowledge and confess, it has all its indestructible strength.

AUTHORITY IN THE CHURCH

The Church does not claim direct and absolute and material authority for itself but for Holy Scripture as the Word of God. But actual obedience to the authoritative Word of God in Holy Scripture is objectively determined by the fact that those who in the Church mutually confess an acceptance of the witness of Holy Scripture will be ready and willing to listen to one another in expounding and applying it. By the authority of Holy Scripture on which it is founded, authority in the Church is restricted to an indirect and relative and formal authority.

1. THE AUTHORITY OF THE WORD

Holy Scripture attests to the Church (and through the Church to the world) the revelation of God, Jesus Christ, the Word of God. The power in which it does so is the power of the object to which it bears witness and which has also made and fashioned it as that witness. The witness of Holy Scripture is therefore the witness of the Holy Spirit. He is indeed the power of the matter of Holy Scripture. By Him it became Holy Scripture; by Him and only by Him it speaks as such. In doing so it mediates revelation; it presents Jesus Christ; in the servant form of a human word it speaks the Word of God. Those who hear it, hear Him. Those who wish to hear Him must hear it. This is the Evangelical principle of Scripture as such: the universal, fundamental and self-sufficient thing which has to be said about the attestation and mediation of revelation. And on this perception and confession there depends the answer to the question, how it comes about for us, for the Church (and through the Church for the world), that the witness of Holy Scripture is apprehended and accepted in virtue of the witness of the Holy Spirit. How does obedience to the Word of God in Holy Scripture arise? The question is analogous to the basic question: how is the revelation of the triune God effected? And if in the latter case a closer explanation of this very revelation compels us to reply: objectively by the incarnation of the divine Word in Jesus Christ and subjectively by the outpouring of the Holy Spirit of God, so too in relation to obedience to the attestation and mediation of this revelation, in relation to the Word of God in Holy Scripture, we have to distinguish between an objective and a subjective element, i.e., an outer and an inner determination of this obedience. In both cases we are dealing with determinations whose subject is God. The reality of the attestation and mediation of His revelation is in the same sense and just as strictly His work as is revelation itself and as such. But our present concern is to understand the reality of this attestation and mediation to us. Now to understand the reality of revelation itself and as such, the doctrine of the triune God had to divide into the doctrine of the incarnation of the Word and that of the outpouring of the Holy Spirit. The same division will be necessary to understand the reality of its certification and transmission by Holy Scripture. The truth and force of Holy Scripture in its self-attesting credibility is itself—and this is something we must never lose sight of—a single and simultaneous act of lordship by the triune God, who in His revelation is the object and as such the source of Holy Scripture. But if we ask how this truth confirms itself to us, how this power is effective in us—if we ask how the self-witness of Holy Scripture as the Word of God can enlighten the Church (and through the Church the world), then without denying the unity of the divine Word we have to distinguish between that which enlightens and those who are enlightened, between something objective and something subjective, between the external aspect and the internal, or, to put it concretely, between the possibility of God for man and the possibility of man for God. Only by making this distinction can we see them together as is needed, and therefore understand the reality of the witness to revelation in Holy Scripture, i.e., grasp it in the possibilities actualised in it. By attempting to grasp these possibilities as such, we repeat, as it were, on a lower level the division into the doctrine of the incarnation of the Word and that of the outpouring of the Holy Spirit. The possibilities are—objectively the authority of Holy Scripture instituted in the Church, by which the definite authority of the Church itself is established and limited ; and subjectively the over-ruling freedom of Holy Scripture in the Church, which is again the basis and limit of the definite freedom of the Church and its members. We have to consider both the authority and the freedom if we want to reply to the question, how we arrive at obedience to God in Holy Scripture. Authority is the external determination under which this becomes possible for man from God—freedom is the internal determination, the determination under which it is possible for God from man. Either way it is primarily and strictly a matter of the authority and freedom which belongs to Holy Scripture itself in the Church. But either way it is secondly a matter of the authority and freedom of the Church as such, subject to Holy Scripture. Holy Scripture is the ground and limit of the Church, but for that very reason it constitutes it. Having authority and freedom in the Church, it lends that authority and freedom to the Church. We have to take this into account. For only as this takes place does it actually come about that Holy Scripture is obeyed as the Word of God in the Church, and through the

Church in the world. We are not asking now why this happens. We have already answered that question. It happens because Scripture is the Word of God and makes itself known as such. We are now asking genetically how it happens—just as in the doctrine of the incarnation of the Word and the outpouring of the Holy Spirit we could not discuss the " Why ? " of revelation, but, against the background of the doctrine of the Trinity, only its " How ? " To the same question of the method, this time of the mediation and attestation of revelation, we will now reply in this and the following section with the doctrine of authority and freedom in the Church.

When we speak of " authority " in the Church we mean first and generally that there is in the Church an authority which in relation to similar authorities stands in a closer relationship to the basis and nature of the Church, which has a greater part in its historical and material origin, which has therefore a claim to be more closely heard and regarded as more normative than other authorities. Fundamentally and in general, authority in the Church is an authority which has precedence because of its more primitive nature. Holy Scripture itself is such an authority in the Church. It is so in this general sense because it is a record, indeed historically it is the oldest extant record, of the origin and therefore of the basis and nature of the Church. That there are other authorities in the Church, which stand in a definite relationship to its basis and nature, which have a part historically and materially in its origin, and which have therefore in their own sphere a claim to be heard and respected and so in their own way to rank as authorities, is not radically denied by the existence of Holy Scripture. But not all these other authorities possess the character of records and none of them has the character of the oldest record. Therefore Holy Scripture has always in the Church a unique and in its way singular authority. But in its character as authority in this general sense, the authoritative significance of Holy Scripture cannot be exhaustive for the Church.

The appeal to the " written nature " and the age of the Bible never played a decisive part in the Reformation either on the Lutheran or the Reformed side. We find incidental mention of it in the *Conf. Helv. prior* 1536 *Art.* 1 and in Calvin, *Instit.* I, 8, 3 f. On the lips of the Reformers the *Ad fontes !* of the Humanists had another meaning, even in the case of those who like Zwingli were not so far from Erasmus.

In this general sense, Holy Scripture may have a singular authority in the Church, but that authority is still mediate, relative and formal. Mediate means temporal, historical and human. Consequently it is authority in the way in which there is earthly authority in other spheres as well, *iure humano*, authority which is subject to better instruction, to correction, to interpretation by other well-known authorities of a similar nature, to contradiction by an authority which perhaps reaches the same level and is then rated higher, and above all to a *ius divinum* from which it derives its validity. Relative : this means that like all other authoritative powers in the Church it can only represent the divine authority. And if this is the case it is not merely possible but necessary to appeal from Scripture (always recognising its unique value) to a true and original Word of God which we have to conceive of quite differently. The Church can and should go beyond the representative and preliminary judgment of Scripture to the supreme and real Judge and Lord. Formal : this means that at bottom and practically Holy Scripture is on a level with other witnesses to divine revelation, simply as witness, as pure form. It is not therefore the ground on which we know the promise that the revelation of God will and can be present in its attestation. The promise, by which in fact all witness lives, is known on quite a different ground, for which we should have to seek according to our own choice and in our own strength if we did not have it in Scripture.

Therefore on this view we have to say with Schleiermacher that faith in Christ " must be presupposed, if a special place is to be made for Holy Scripture " (*Der chr. Glaube*, § 128).

Now it is true that even in this general sense, i.e., as a very old record, Holy Scripture is authority.

Therefore, like Schleiermacher, who emphasised something on which the Reformers laid no stress at all (*Der chr. Glaube*, § 129, *Kurze Darstellung*, § 105), we can find the authority of Holy Scripture, or at any rate the New Testament, in the fact that it contains what are historically the first records of the Church's life.

Holy Scripture is also, in fact, a human historical record. Therefore in its relation to divine revelation it can also be compared to witness. It is also a mediate, relative, formal quantity. It asks and always has to be also evaluated as such. But to the extent that this has to be the case, the question how we come to obey it can never be answered. The real obedience of the Church is to an authority which has to be distinguished from Holy Scripture, to something immediate, absolute and material, which has to be sought or has already been found side by side with or even beyond Holy Scripture.

Therefore according to Schleiermacher the obedience of the Church is not to this thing as such which is historically the oldest and most primitive, but to it only as it has a " normal dignity," whose presence in Holy Scripture is decided by knowledge from quite a different source.

We then have to ask to what extent this different knowledge can claim to be knowledge of divine revelation, to what extent therefore that direct and absolute and material thing side by side with or above Holy Scripture is rightly equated with God or with Christ or with the Holy Spirit and therefore made the object of the real obedience of the Church. What is certain is that, in this determination of its obedience, in the last resort the Church will necessarily have to rely on its own judgment. It will be itself which necessarily ascribes to that direct and absolute and material authority side by side with or above Holy Scripture, from which Scripture receives its mediate, relative and formal authority, its character as divine revelation. It must seek out Scripture for itself and itself give to it this supreme dignity. To be able to do this it must already be mistress of divine revelation, already know and participate in it. Divine revelation must be an original possession of the Church enabling it to declare with certainty where and what revelation is and therefore where and what the witness of revelation is.

Schleiermacher, the authoritative theologian of Neo-Protestantism, could actually ascribe this original possession of revelation to the Church in his doctrine of Holy Scripture. So, too, could and can Roman Catholicism.

If this were the case, the Church would itself actually be a direct, absolute, material authority. It would always, in fact, be the Church which instituted this authority and necessarily recognised itself in it. Its obedience to this authority would, in fact, be the fulfilment of its own striving and volition. It would then be quite impossible to find in it obedience and not self-regulation, to see in the authority accepted in the Church an authority over the Church and for the Church.

In opposition to this possibility we first have to lay down that where the Church really is the Church, then as the Church of Jesus Christ it finds itself in a known and therefore real relationship of obedience to what constitutes its basis and nature and therefore to Jesus Christ the Word of God. A relationship of obedience, however, is a relationship in an antithesis, an antithesis in which there is an obvious and genuine above and below. To a relationship of obedience two partners are necessary. They have a definite unity but they are no less definitely distinct in this unity. They stand in a definite and irreversible order, united, but distinct. One of them, and only one commands. The other has to submit to this command—just to submit. Now it is in such a relationship of obedience to Jesus Christ that we find the Church in the original act of revelation attested by Holy Scripture, in the confrontation of the apostles with the Crucified and Risen One, which has its Old Testament prototype in the confrontation of the prophets of Israel with Yahweh. Neither in Old Testament nor in New Testament do we find even only a trace of the possibility that this relationship of obedience, in which the biblical witnesses became what they were, recipients of revelation, was later dissolved and transformed into one in which these men could confront Yahweh or Jesus Christ as those who had a control of their own over that which was revealed to them, in which the Church could even partially rule itself. In Holy Scripture there is no sequel of an assured possession of revelation which from the standpoint of these men would be prior to revelation, a view of revelation side by side with or even above revelation. They are never recipients of revelation in the sense that they appropriate revelation and can then recognise and evaluate it for themselves. They are recipients of revelation in the sense that revelation meets them as the master and they become obedient to it. It is because they are obedient that they are prophets and apostles. It is because they are obedient that they have the Holy Spirit. It is because they are obedient that they are appointed and commissioned to be Christ's witnesses to others, to the nascent Church and to the world. The Church of Jesus can exist only when it repeats this relationship of obedience. A revelation which the Church can recognise and evaluate on the basis of its own possession of revelation and from an independent view of revelation, even if it is called the revelation of God or Christ or the Holy Spirit, is not as such the revelation on which the Church of Jesus Christ is founded. And the Church which in such a relationship to revelation ascribes to itself that direct and absolute and material authority is not as such the Church of Jesus Christ, even if it does quite seriously wish to call itself the Christian Church. The existence of the Church of Jesus Christ stands or falls with the fact that it obeys as the apostles and prophets obeyed their Lord. It stands or falls with the known and actual antithesis of man and revelation, which cannot be reversed, in which man receives, learns, submits and is controlled, in which he has a Lord and belongs to Him wholly and utterly.

But the relationship of obedience between the prophets and apostles and their Lord is a unique relationship as such. It is as unique as the incarnation of the divine Word, as the outpouring of the Holy Spirit, as the reconciliation of man with God in Christ's death and the revelation of it in His resurrection, as the forty days after Easter between the times. This between the times is a self-enclosed time, which does not return, or rather returns only in and with the return of Jesus Christ Himself. The Church's time, our time, is a different time. And this time is not simply a prolongation and continuation of that time. Therefore the existence of the Church does not mean the existence of new prophets and apostles who will receive God's revelation in the same direct way, and will be commissioned and empowered as its witnesses. If the Church of Jesus Christ exists only when there is a repetition of this relationship of obedience, then we must say : *Either*, outside that between-the-times there is no Church of Jesus Christ at all. The Church of Jesus Christ existed only once, in the prophets and apostles themselves, or strictly : in the forty days after Easter, in which the apostles saw the promise of the prophets visibly fulfilled before them. Since the appearance of that light the world has returned to its original darkness, and the memory of that light has become only an empty expectation. *Or*, the promise of the forty days is truly and visibly fulfilled before us as was Old Testament

prophecy in the forty days themselves : Ye shall be my witnesses.
and : Lo, I am with you always. The unique revelation did not take
place in vain, nor did that unique relationship of obedience take place
in vain. Both of them, the revelation and the obedience of the
prophets and apostles, continue to exist : indirectly, but in full, unbroken reality, a copy of the revelation in which this is always truly
and validly present, and a model of the obedience, which even though
there are no more prophets and apostles, can and should be seriously
repeated in every age. This authentic copy of revelation and this
authentic model of obedience to it is therefore the content of the
witness of the prophets and apostles in Holy Scripture. It is therefore true that Holy Scripture is the Word of God for the Church, that
it is Jesus Christ for us, as He Himself was for the prophets and apostles
during the forty days. The result is that in their witness the Church
itself has to do personally with its Lord. Therefore in the *per se*
mediate, relative and formal quantity of Scripture, in which their
witness is presented to us, it has to do with the self-subsistent and
self-maintaining direct and absolute and material authority, with its
own existence, nature and basis. Consequently the Church cannot
evade Scripture. It cannot try to appeal past it directly to God,
to Christ or to the Holy Spirit. It cannot assess and adjudge Scripture from a view of revelation gained apart from Scripture and not
related to it. It cannot know any " normal dignity," which has to
sanctify Scripture as the earliest record of its own life and make it
its norm. It cannot establish from any possession of revelation the
fact and extent that Scripture too is a source of revelation. Scripture
confronts it commandingly as Holy Scripture, and it receives revelation from it in an encounter which is just as concrete and concretely
ordered as that which according to Scripture originally took place
between the Lord and His witnesses. It obeys Holy Scripture. Not
as though it were obeying some long deceased men and their humanity
and theology. But it obeys the One whom it has pleased to give
certain long-deceased men, in and with and in spite of their humanity
and piety and theology, a commission and authority. Therefore it
serves the Word of God in the sign and guise of the word of these
men. As it hears *them*, it hears it. And as it hears them, it *hears* it.
The incarnation of the Word of God and the outpouring of the Holy
Spirit has happened, is happening and will happen for the Church
(and through the Church for the world) in every age, because in face
of the uniqueness of revelation the Church is ready to receive its
authentic witness and to accept and transmit it as authentic.

It will be as well to scrutinise sharply this either—or. If the promise " Ye
shall be my witnesses " and " Lo, I am with you alway " is not fulfilled,
and therefore if Scripture is not the Word of God for the Church, then the revelation of God is only a memory, and there is no Church of Jesus Christ. There
may well be a human community which is puffed up with the illusion that in

it the life and influence of the prophets and apostles are perpetuated and that therefore it stands with them in an immediate relationship to the direct, absolute and material authority of God, Christ and the Holy Spirit. This illusion, this forgetting of the uniqueness of revelation and with it of the prophetic-apostolic situation, works its own revenge : by raving about what does not pertain to it, the Church shows itself at once to be incapable of the relationship of obedience in which the prophets and apostles stand to revelation. It will pervert this relationship of obedience into one in which it thinks that by virtue of possession and knowledge and power it can evade God, Christ and the Holy Spirit, in which it has not merely to obey but to control. And inevitably it will more and more be the one who really controls. Inevitably it will more and more approximate to that direct, absolute and material authority, and finally proclaim itself more or less directly identical with it. Inevitably it will become a Church which rules itself under the pretext of obedience to revelation. And it can easily happen that when the illusion as such is more or less clearly felt and discerned, another human fellowship will arise, which, tired of this presumption, will make it its purpose to cherish that lovely recollection. There will then be possible a cultus and theology of the revelation which, according to the sacred books, once took place long ago, a revelation which at bottom does not affect us because it cannot be revelation to us, but which always surprises and claims and solemnises us from afar, not without a certain devotion and enjoyment. If Holy Scripture is not the Word of God, if it has only a mediate, relative and formal authority, it is possible to have a Church of ineffective although quite impeccable orthodoxy. It is possible, therefore, to have the Catholic Church, and the various Neo-Protestant applications and variations of the Catholic concept of the Church : all of which presuppose the great illusion regarding the uniqueness of revelation ; all of which are on the way to a pantheistic identification of Church and revelation. And on the other hand it is also possible either in the Catholic or the Protestant form to have a reflection of the true original : a dead Church, a Church which is assembled around revelation as around a lifeless idol, a Church which sees the uniqueness of revelation and, for that very reason, despairs of itself. But the two Churches are not at bottom two Churches. They are only the two poles between which the life of the one Church would have to swing in a highly unnecessary and dangerous tension, were it not that Holy Scripture is the Word of God. They are the two poles between which the life of the one Church, whether it calls itself Catholic or Protestant, will necessarily swing, if it has not the faith that in Holy Scripture God Himself speaks to it. For without that faith it will alternately be swollen with arrogance and sink in self-despair. In its own eyes and those of the world it will now be great and arrogant, now small and hateful, not in the glory and poverty of Christ, but either way as a representative, like all other worldly constructs, of the darkness in which the world will necessarily lie if God has not revealed Himself, or if He has curiously done so only once, and therefore in vain as far as other ages are concerned.

If this Church in the one form or the other is not the Church of Jesus Christ, if there is a real Church of Jesus Christ distinct from this Church—although perhaps only as the mystery of God which is constantly declared in this Church, then it is because the saying is literally true and fulfilled : Ye shall be my witnesses and, Lo, I am with you alway. If this is true, if it is believed because it is true, then the revelation is determined far above the Church in the word of the prophets and apostles to whom it is said : the word of revelation, not the Church's own word, but the outside word which is spoken to it, so that it cannot seize or possess or control that revelation. And if this is so it will always bow before it. It will learn of it. In genuine obedience it will participate in it. At this level it will not be far from it, but in its garb as a human word, with which we can deal to-day and every day in human form, it will be near.

Then, if the attested God is present to it in human testimony, if Scripture is the Word of God, it will live by the revelation of God, avoiding both arrogance and despair, experiencing and declaring His presence in our present, being the companion of His age in our age, not in an arbitrarily selected garment of pomp or poverty, but in the genuine humiliation and also the genuine glory of Christ.

In this either—or the Church will again and again have to choose. Will and can the Church decide to receive revelation by accepting the authentic witness of it ? Is it therefore resolved to ascribe direct absolute and material authority only to Holy Scripture and not to anything else, not even to itself ? At this point we stand before one of the severest conflicts in its history. Although not felt in all its severity, it was present from the very first. It broke out openly in the Reformation and counter-Reformation of the 16th century. Since then, together with other well-known antitheses, it has constituted the frontier which separates the Roman Catholic Church and the true, Evangelical Church, and which will inexorably separate them, so long as both continue to be what they are. Yet the nearest and most pressing opponent and disputant of the Evangelical Church is not open Catholicism as such, but the heresy of Neo-Protestantism which has broken out within it, and which in this matter has shown itself at the crucial point to be simply the extended arm of the errant Papist Church. The Evangelical, and with it the true Church, stands or falls by the fact that (apart, of course, from the revealed and proclaimed Word of God which is identical with Scripture) it understands exclusively the statement that the Bible is the Word of God, claiming direct, absolute and material authority neither for a third authority nor for itself, and therefore taking in full and, if the objection is made, " narrow " seriousness the confession of the newness, uniqueness and divinity of the revelation attested in Scripture and the acknowledgment that the Church owes this concrete obedience. On the other hand, it is no less essential and important for the Roman Catholic system that it should reject this alleged narrowing down of revelation to its biblical attestation, putting a definite element in Church life which is given the name of divine revelation, the so-called tradition, side by side with Holy Scripture, then broadening this element more and more until the whole of Church life seems to be included in it, then subordinating and co-ordinating Holy Scripture under and with this whole, and finally declaring this whole and therefore itself to be identical with the revelation of God. The same relativising of Holy Scripture first of all in relation to certain elements, then to the totality of Christian history, the same inclusion of Holy Scripture in this history, and finally the same equation of this history as such with divine revelation is also the very essence and characteristic of the Neo-Protestant doctrine of Scripture. The distinction between the two consists in the fact that the reality of the Church equated with revelation has in Catholicism, in the form of the Roman hierarchy, a theoretical and practical definiteness and mobility which the Neo-Protestant " history " of Christianity, lacking any visible form, can never have. Yet the two are one in the fact that behind both there stands the possibility to extend the long line of equations by another line, i.e., by identifying not only Christian history but the history of religion, indeed in the long run all history or human reality generally, with revelation. Therefore we have to say that in this conflict a decision of final magnitude is involved. A historical consideration on the relationship between Scripture and tradition is indispensable at this point. (Cf. for what follows : H. J. Holtzmann, *Kanon und Tradition*, 1859 ; Josef Ranft, *Der Ursprung des katholischen Traditionsprinzips*, 1931).

Even to-day the prejudice still exists that the concrete, polemical sharpness of the Reformed Scripture principle, the unconditional rejection of a Church tradition rivalling Holy Scripture as a source of revelation, is a peculiarity of the Reformed Church. And the same holds of the opinion based on this prejudice that from the standpoint of Lutheranism it is not impossible that an understanding might be reached with Catholicism in this matter. This historical prejudice has support in the well-known fact that the Scripture principle is in fact expressed more or less sharply and explicitly at the head of all the more important confessional writings of the Reformed Church with more or less acuteness and explicitness, whereas in the basic Confession of the Lutherans, in the Augsburg Confession and Luther's Catechisms generally, it does not receive specific mention. Let us take as an example the *Conf. Gallic.* 1559 *Art.* 5 and see what the Reformed Church accepts and rejects in this matter: *Nous croyons que la parole de Dieu qui est contenue en ces livres est procedee de Dieu, duquel elle seule prend son authorité et non des hommes. Et d'autant qu'elle est reigle de toute vérité contenant tout ce qui est necessaire pour le service de Dieu et nostre salut, il n'est loysible aux hommes, ne mesmes aux Anges d'y adiouster, diminuer ou changer. Dont il s'ensuit que ne l'antiquité, ne les coustumes, ne la multitude ne la sagesse humaine, ne les iugements, ne les arrestz, ne les edicts, ne les decrets, ne les conciles, ne les visions, ne les miraclez; ne doivent estre opposez à icelle Escriture saincte, ains au contraire toutes choses doivent estre examinees, reiglees, et reformees selon icelle.* But in view of this and similar passages we must not forget that there are some Reformed confessional writings, like the Berne Synod of 1532, the Basel Confession of 1534 and especially the *Heidelberg Catechism*, in which we need a microscope to find the Scripture principle, as we do in the older Lutheran documents. Consequently the fact that on the Reformed side the matter is made more explicit than on the Lutheran rests solidly upon the fact that in this as in other matters the Reformed Confession represents the common substance of the Evangelical teaching at a later stage, at the stage at which it was already achieving, provisionally, a final form, and therefore with a clarity which had everywhere existed in practice right from the outset, but which was hardly ripe for theoretical expression in the third decade of the century —the great period of the Lutheran reformation. That at the end of the Reformation period the Lutheran Church understood itself to hold the same doctrine and to make the same confession as the Reformed is brought out quite unequivocally in the two parts of the preface to the Formula of Concord, where Holy Scripture, " the prophetic and apostolic writings of the Old and New Testaments " are mentioned as " the one judge, rule and guide," as " the clean, pure spring of Israel," by which as " the only touchstone all teachers should and must be known and judged, whether they are good or bad, right or wrong." " Should an angel from heaven come and preach otherwise, let him be accursed," is quoted from Gal. 1[8]. " But other writings of the old and new teachers, as they are called, should not be equated with Holy Scripture, but all subjected to it and accepted only as witnesses. . . ." And these statements were far from being a later correction and amplification on the part of the Lutheran Church. They simply made explicit what Luther himself at any rate had not only practised, but a hundred times implicitly and explicitly asserted. Do we not have it in his own words in the Schmalkaldic Articles, which were given the status of a public confession, that: " We must not make the work or words of the holy Fathers into articles of faith. . . . We are told that the Word of God must constitute articles of faith, and no one else, not even an angel " (*Bek. Schr. d. ev.-luth. Kirche*, 1930, 421, 18) ? It is hard to see how far the decision taken here is in any way less radical and irrevocable than that of the Reformed confessions. With a good conscience a Lutheran can no more make even slight concessions in this matter to the Catholic position than a Reformed Protestant.

We will compare this Evangelical decision directly with the Roman Catholic one, as determined and made in its basic form on 8th April 1546 at the fourth session of the Council of Trent: the *puritas ipsa evangelii*, the truth and order (*veritas et disciplina*) which was promised by the prophets, expressed by Christ Himself, and proclaimed by the apostles at His behest, is contained in *libris scriptis et sine scripto traditionibus, quae ab ipsius Christi ore ab apostolis accepta aut ab ipsis apostolis Spiritu sancto dictante quasi per manus traditae ad nos usque pervenerunt.* And then the Council declares that the books of the Old Testament and New Testament it *nec non traditiones ipsas, tum ad fidem, tum ad mores pertinentes, tanquam vel oretenus a Christo, vel a Spiritu sancto dictatas et continua successione in ecclesia catholica conservatas, pari pietatis affectu ac reverentia suscipit et veneratur* (*Denz.* No. 783). Hence Holy Scripture is one, but not the only source of our knowledge of revelation. Apart from what we know from Holy Scripture, Christ, or even the Holy Ghost, have told the apostles other things which we have to hear and reverence as " truth and order." These other things are the tradition which has come down to us from them transmitted from hand to hand. Its bearer and guardian has been the Catholic Church in its historical continuity. And to this second visible source of knowledge we have to ascribe the same authority as to the first. At the Council of Trent this decision was not made without difficulties and disputes. Three bishops in particular, of Fiesole, Astorga and Chioggia, according to a Catholic interpretation, " repeatedly evoked the displeasure of the leaders of the Council and other fathers, partly by their tactlessness, partly by their opposition to the obvious standpoint of the majority, especially in relation to the *pari pietatis affectu,*" and it was only by threats that they could be reduced to silence (Ranft, p. 7). The logic of the preceding developments was against them and their doubts, and milder suggestions were necessarily opposed by a council which had made it its appointed task to fight the Reformation. If the Reformed decision was no novelty in the Church, neither was the Tridentine, and we have to concede that the scales had long come down on the latter side. Had it been otherwise, the Reformation would not have had to be carried through in the painful but unavoidable form of a disruption.

Already in Irenaeus we find " true gnosis " defined as ἡ τῶν ἀποστόλων διδαχὴ καὶ τὸ ἀρχαῖον τῆς ἐκκλησίας σύστημα κατὰ παντὸς τοῦ κόσμου (*C. o. h.* IV, 33, 8). And in Origen the *credenda veritas* is that, *quae in nullo ab ecclesiastica et apostolica traditione discordat* (Περὶ ἀρχῶν I *praef.* 2). Basil distinguished among the Church doctrines : τὰ μὲν ἐκ τῆς ἐγγράφου διδασκαλίας—τὰ δὲ ἐκ τῆς τῶν ἀποστόλων διαδοθέντα ἡμῖν ἐν μυστηρίῳ. By oral tradition Basil had in mind a secret tradition. And if it were neglected we would be thoughtlessly ignoring the most important part of the Gospel (*De Spiritu sancto* 27, 66). In Basil, and later in Epiphanius, we find that the need for παράδοσις side by side with Scripture is grounded on the complaint that the apostolic tradition contained in Scripture is incomplete : οὐ γὰρ πάντα ἀπὸ τῆς θείας γραφῆς δύναται λαμβάνεσθαι (*Adv. Haer.* 61, 6). Tertullian had already expressed himself even more plainly on the ambiguity of Scripture : *Non ergo ad scripturas provocandum, nec in his constituendum certamen, in quibus aut nulla aut incerta est victoria* (*De praescr.* 19). And Chrysostom could turn to good account the passage 2 Thess. 2[15] which was so gladly used in later Catholic polemics. From it we learn that the apostles transmitted many things that were not put in writing : ὥστε καὶ τὴν παράδοσιν τῆς ἐκκλησίας ἀξιόπιστον ἡγώμεθα. παράδοσίς ἐστιν, μηδὲν πλέον ζήτει (*In. ep.* II *Ad. Thess. hom.* 4, 2). And at the second Council of Nicea in 787 the stage had been reached when those who reject the παράδοσις ἐκκλησιαστικὴ ἔγγραφος ἢ ἄγραφος can be expressly anathematised (*Denz.* No. 308). But what is this apostolic tradition which is accepted and has to be heard side by side with Scripture ? Even in the 16th century the charge could be brought against the decree of the Council of Trent that it speaks of apostolic traditions without stating what concretely it wants to be understood as such. The charge is well-founded only to the extent that the Council was content to repeat the answer already given with increasing definiteness in the Early Church, pointing to the historical continuity of the Catholic Church. In effect this answer simply means that the recognition and indeed the universal recognition of the Church shows a definite tradition to be apostolic, and therefore authentic, and therefore revelation. We have seen this answer already in the words of Irenaeus. Similarly we find in Jerome that there are many things which are accepted in the Church only on the basis of tradition but which have still gained for themselves (*usurpaverunt*) the *auctoritas scriptae legis*. Who decides where this should be the case ? The *consensus totius orbis* (*Dial. c. Luciferianos* 8). *Quod universa tenet ecclesia nec conciliis institutum, sed semper retentum est, non nisi auctoritate apostolica traditum rectissime creditur* (Augustine, *De bapt.* IV, 24, 31, cf. II, 7, 12 and V 23, 33). Universality as the mark of what is apostolical and therefore ecclesiastical could just as well be regarded temporally (i.e., with respect to the age of a particular tradition) as spatially (with respect to its geographical dissemination). It was in the first sense that Tertullian understood and used the proof of prescription : *id esse dominicum et verum, quod sit prius traditum, id autem extraneum et falsum, quod sit posterius immissum* (*De praescr.* 31). But in the utterances especially of Augustine the emphasis seems to fall rather on spatial universality. Comprehensively the answer to the question would have to be formulated as follows : apostolic and therefore authentic tradition is what the Church which is general and universal in these two dimensions recognises to be such. By the turn of the 4th and 5th centuries what the Church as such has to say side by side with Holy Scripture, even if only in amplification and confirmation of it, already has a particular weight of its own, so that the saying which we have already quoted from Augustine—which the Reformers attempted in vain to interpret it *in meliorem partem*—now became possible : in answer to the question what we are to tell those who still do not believe in the Gospel, Augustine has to confess, obviously on the basis of his personal experience : *Ego vero evangelio non crederem, nisi me catholicae ecclesiae commoveret auctoritas* (*C. ep. Man.* 5, 6). That I have the Gospel and can believe in it is obviously, as Augustine sees it and as he was rightly understood in later Catholic polemics, itself a gift of Church tradition. Therefore the saying foreshadows that inclusion of Scripture itself into the tradition which was expressly accomplished at a much later date.

In spite of all the evidence to this effect, the attitude of the Church fathers on this matter was not unequivocal. The Reformers, too, could appeal to the Early Church. The statement : *quia non possit ex his* (*sc. Scripturis*) *inveniri veritas ab his qui nesciant traditionem ; non enim per literas traditam illam, sed per vivam vocem* is cited by Irenaeus (*C. o. h.* III, 2, 1) as gnostic and heretical. Against the idea that age as such legitimates a tradition, Cyprian especially objects in many of his letters (63, 14 ; 71, 3 ; 73, 13, 23), and supremely in the saying : *consuetudo sine veritate vetustas erroris est* (74, 9). Similarly and even more pregnantly Tertullian, the father of the proof of prescription, could write boldly enough : *Dominus noster Christus veritatem se, non consuetudinem cognominavit* (*De virg. vel.* 1). In Athanasius we find a clear distinction between the " holy and inspired writings," which are self-sufficient (αὐτάρκεις) in the declaration of truth, and other writings which may be used as a commentary on them (*Adv. gentes* 1). Similarly, Augustine could declare that *in iis, quae aperte in scripturis posita sunt, inveniuntur illa omnia, quae continent fidem moresque vivendi, spem scilicet et caritatem* (*De doctr. chr.* II, 9). But we must note that these statements, although they contradict the others, never attain to that clear and critical confrontation of Scripture and tradition which we have in the Reformation decision. The introduction of that " heretical " statement by Irenaeus has only a dialectical significance. Elsewhere Irenaeus (cf. *C. o. h.* II, 4, 1–2 ; IV 24, 3) is one of the first of many who co-ordinated and subordinated Scripture to tradition. What corresponds to *consuetudo* in Cyprian is the ambiguous concept of Church *ratio*. And, of course, in Tertullian the *veritas* which is so impressively opposed to *consuetudo* is not the *veritas scripturae* of the Reformers, but a substance of truth imparted to the Church and developing in history with inward consistency from its original seed, so that its true and normative manifestation could just as easily be its developed rather than its earlier form. Even in Tertullian the proof has a form which is related to the future. Hence he can occasionally say, in what must be

understood as a purely dialectical contradiction he can occasionally tell himself :
In omnibus posteriora concludunt et sequentia antecedentibus praevalent (De bapt. 13).
From the statements of the fathers which point in this other direction I would
not venture to deduce more than that in the development of the Catholic system
there was always a recollection of its opposite and therefore a retarding element.

The classical and in pre-Reformation and counter-Reformation times the
standard representation of the Catholic conception is to be found in a writing
which we may think it significant was composed by a professed semi-pelagian
and, in the first instance, obliquely directed against the Augustinian doctrines of
predestination and grace : the *Commonitorium of* Vincent of Lerins, A.D. 434.
In this work we are told that the way to the knowledge of the *veritas catholicae
fidei* is twofold : *Prima scilicet divinae legis auctoritate, tum deinde ecclesiae
catholicae traditione.* Why must there be the second as well as the first ? Because,
says Vincent, although in itself Holy Scripture is a sufficient authority, in view
of its exalted nature (*altitudo*) it cannot be understood in the same sense by
everybody, because the same passages in the Bible are continually being interpreted by different people in different ways. But it is necessary, and care must
be taken, that the exposition of the prophets and apostles should be an ecclesiastical and therefore a universal or catholic one : *ut id teneamus, quod ubique,
quod semper, quod ab omnibus creditum est.* For this purpose we have to ask
concerning it, taking as our criteria universality, antiquity, consent. *Universitas*
belongs to a definite position which can claim to be ecclesiastical when spatially
and geographically it is everywhere that of the Church : *antiquitas*, when it has
been that of those who have gone before and the fathers ; and *consensio*, when
it is held by all or almost all those who at any time bear the teaching office (the
sacerdotes et magistri). In the *ubique* and *semper* Vincent was obviously only
repeating and summarising what preceding centuries had worked out concerning
the nature of tradition as it has to be distinguished from Scripture. But at the
same time, and it is here that we see the independent significance of his statements, there is added a third criterion, the *ab omnibus*, which is not merely a
repetition of the *ubique*, which does at least indicate the problem which obviously
has to be answered even when the *universitas* and *antiquitas* have been established
as the signs of what is catholic and therefore apostolic. For with the addition
he puts the question : Who does *in concreto* decide the presence of what is universal
in time and space ? Theoretically this question was left open by the Council of
Trent in its declaration on the principle of tradition, though in practice there
can be no doubt what was intended. But even in this instrument of the counter-
Reformation it appears that the retarding element was still at work. In Vincent,
however, it had already been overcome in principle. Vincent gives the theoretical
answer to the question, and although from the standpoint of more recent development we cay say that even in him it lacks final precision, it is clear enough in
its own way. Beyond the constitutive *ubique* and *semper* there is a regulative
ab omnibus. That is, the interpretation of tradition and—because tradition on
its part is the authentic interpretation of Holy Scripture—the interpretation of
Holy Scripture is the concern of the existing teaching office in its *consensio*.
The darkness in which Tertullian had once put the earlier above the later, and
also the later above the earlier, is now illuminated. The *veritas catholicae fidei*,
that of the truly catholic exposition of Scripture which corresponds to its object
and is therefore carried out within the framework of tradition, is on the one hand
according to 1 Tim. 6[20] a *depositum : quod tibi creditum est, non quod a te inventum,
quod accepisti, non quod excogitasti, rem non ingenii sed doctrinae, non usurpationis
privatae, sed publicae traditionis, rem ad te perductam, non a te prolatam, in qua
non auctor debes esse, sed custos, non institutor sed sectator, non ducens sed sequens.*
Therefore *Timotheus*, the *sacerdos, magister, tractator, doctor* of that time, is summoned to guard, preserve and maintain : *quae didicisti doce, ut cum dicas nove
non dicas nova.* But in this *nove* we already meet the second thing which faces

not only backwards but forwards : *preciosas divi dogmatis gemmas exculpa, fideliter coapta adorna sapienter, adice splendorem, gratiam, venustatem, intelligatur te exponente illustrius quod ante obscurius credebatur.* *Per te posteritas intellectum gratuletur quod ante vetustas non intellectum venerabatur.* Its activity is not merely to conserve but in conserving to produce. There is, Vincent declares, progress in the Church. Of course there is no *permutatio : ut aliquid ex alio in aliud transvertatur,* but there is a *profectus religionis : ut in semetipsum res amplificetur. Crescat igitur oportet et multum vehementerque proficiat tam singulorum quam omnium, tam unius hominis quam totius ecclesiae, aetatum ac saeculorum gradibus, intelligentia, scientia, sapientia, sed in suo dumtaxat genere, in eodem scilicet dogmatae eodem sensu, eademque sententia. Imitetur animarum religio rationem corporum, quae, licat annorum processu numeros suos evolvant et explicent, eadem tamen quae errant permanent* (22–23). Therefore the tradition does not change, but it grows, just as a natural organism remains the same in nature and kind and yet grows, and to that extent is always the same yet always made new. But the conserving and producing use of tradition is in one hand and under one guidance and responsibility, and this hand and guidance and responsibility is that of the Timothy addressed by Vincent, i.e., those who at any time bear the teaching office of the Church in their mutual *consensio.* This *consensio* must obviously guarantee that both the conserving, i.e., the care for *ubique* and *semper,* and also the production should be kept free from accident and self-will in the service of this genuine tradition as directed to the future. We cannot assess too highly the contribution made by Vincent of Lerins in his theoretical elucidation of this matter, even when we remember that he was only formulating what had already been put into practical effect in the Church of his time, and continued to be so throughout the Middle Ages, but what even the Council of Trent obviously did not dare to formulate and proclaim as dogma with the same precision. Vincent drew the cords tighter than those who preceded him. He derived the one *corpus* of the *depositum* from the unexplained combination of Scripture on the one hand, with its need of exposition and development, and tradition on the other, which does expound and develop Scripture. He understood this *corpus* as a whole as a living thing, which even as it remains the same, can and must also grow. Above all, he put both the maintenance and development into the hands of the teaching office of the Church, thus making the latter the visible subject of tradition. In all this he shows plainly which way things were moving and had to move once the first steps had been taken. When we remember Vincent, we cannot say of the counter-Reformation decision of the Tridentinum that it was hurried and exaggerated. Rather, the fathers of Trent, with perhaps too much sobriety and moderation, raised to the dignity of a confession a perception which had had a long life in the Popish Church and which it might have confessed much earlier, if it had not been restrained by what is (in the light of more recent developments) a puzzling timidity. But even though we cannot say why it should be the case, it was in fact restrained for a long time from openly making a dogma of the doctrine of the two sources, which is itself only a preliminary word. The proclamation of the truth by the Reformation was needed for the lie to come to fruition even in the measure in which it did so at Trent.

What was really intended was the identification of Scripture, Church and revelation. This lay behind the decree about tradition, and might well have been stated in it in accordance with the meaning of the developments which had preceded it. Indeed we can find a compromising hint of this identification in the Tridentinum itself to the extent that in the utterances on the translation and elucidation of the Bible, which were regarded more as practical injunctions, a statement was adopted which was later incorporated into the *Professio fidei Tridentina,* formulated in 1564, and which forbids the exposition of Holy Scripture even *privatim, contra eum sensum, quem tenuit et tenet sancta mater ecclesia, cuius est iudicare de vero sensu et interpretatione Scripturarum sanctarum, aut etiam contra unanimem consensum patrum* (*Denz.* No. 786).

The Catholic thesis, as laid down in the Tridentinum, was maintained and defended in the 16th century, and from then on right up to the present day, on the following individual grounds. It was pointed out that Christ Himself spoke, but neither wrote nor gave any commission to write, that Scripture is also younger than the Church with its oral tradition, and not only younger but actually based on the latter, a work of the primitive Church and dependent on the Church's decision for its canonical validity. It was said again, as it had been so often in the Early Church, that the Bible is dogmatically insufficient. There are also many decisions and directions of the Church recognised even by Protestants : for example, the doctrine of the Trinity, the baptism of infants and the observance of Sunday, all of which are based only on the tradition of the Church, not on Scripture. It was emphasised—and in view of the internal dissensions of the Protestants the argument had a new and telling force—how difficult it is to interpret the Bible, how great is the danger of an arbitrary subjectivism in its readings and how pressing the resultant need for a secondary authority to regulate the understanding of Scripture. Further, a series of passages was adduced from Scripture itself which seemed to justify the presence and validity of such a secondary authority. By way of example, I will cite those which the greatest Catholic champion of the 16th century, Cardinal Bellarmine, regarded as particularly cogent (acc. to Ranft, p. 29) : Jn. 16[12] : " I have yet many things to say unto you, but ye cannot bear them now " ; Jn. 21[25] : " There are also many other things which Jesus did, the which if they should be written every one, I suppose that even the world itself could not contain the books that should be written " ; Ac. 1[3] : " To whom also he shewed himself alive after His passion by many infallible proofs " ; 1 Cor. 11[2] : " I praise you that ye remember me in all things, and keep the traditions, as I delivered them to you " ; 1 Cor. 11[23] : " I have received of the Lord that which also I delivered unto you " ; 1 Cor. 11[34] : " The rest will I set in order when I come " ; 2 Thess. 2[15] : " Therefore, brethren, stand fast, and hold the traditions which ye have been taught, whether by word or our epistle " ; 2 Tim. 1[13] : " Hold fast the form of sound words, which thou hast heard of me " ; 2 Tim. 2[2] : " The things that thou hast heard of me among many witnesses, the same commit thou to faithful men, who shall be able to teach others also." And last but not least for the validity of tradition, the voice of tradition itself was adduced in the form of well-known testimonies from the Early Church.

Reformed Protestantism did not need to be embarrassed by these arguments. The argument that Christ spoke but did not write anything reveals the basic confusion between the revelation of God and its attestation, and therefore the fatal lack of clarity in relation to the divine ruling of the Church and human ministry within it. It is, of course, obvious that there is a tradition which is older than Holy Scripture and on which Holy Scripture as such is founded : it is the way from revelation as such to its scriptural attestation. This way was the way of the prophets and apostles distinguished by that direct encounter with Jesus Christ Himself. But it certainly was not the way of the Church founded and founding itself on their witness. To the later Church this way was closed when their witness took on written form. When that happened, the Church entered on a new way in so far as it is now the bearer of revelation only as the bearer and proclaimer of that witness—of that witness in the concrete and visible state in which it possesses it and not—as we need to note of all the New Testament passages quoted—in a state which can be manifested only by the perpetuation of prophets and apostles, i.e., the continuance of direct revelation. It is not the Church which has produced the witness, but the witness which has produced the Church : certainly before it was laid down in Scripture ; but in this first form of its operation, on the original way before it became Scripture, it is invisible to the Church. It does not know it except as Scripture. Or by virtue of what insight and authority can it go behind its written form ? If it knows and recognises its canonicity as the Word of God, this is grounded in itself, or in the revelation attested in it, in the manifestation of Jesus Christ and the institution of the prophets and apostles, and not in the judgment of the Church which later acknowledges the fact. Is the Church really taking its own judgment seriously, is it really recognising Scripture as canonical, as the Word of God, if it deduces from it the right to be and act as the bearer of a special Word of God apart from its function in the service of Scripture ? If it does take it seriously, or rather, if it takes seriously what it acknowledges by this verdict, then no tradition however old and universal can prove that tradition has to be heard side by side with Scripture as an authority in the same sense. The equation of these authorities, and concealed behind it that of the Church itself with revelation, was an error and falsehood which we find already in Irenaeus and Augustine. Of course the Church has to preach, to teach, to judge, to decide. It has to do it with authority, and not merely in a repetition of biblical texts, but in the freedom commanded it, i.e., in the exposition and application of these texts, and necessarily going beyond them. But for the proclamation of the Church to try to be more than the exposition and application of Scripture, for it to make an autonomous claim to revelation, appealing to and basing itself on a direct and uncontrollable secret apostolic tradition, for it to be free itself from the discipline and criticism of Holy Scripture, from the possibility of appealing from its own mediate to this immediate authority, for it to ascribe to itself another position than that of a secondary ministry of attestation—that is quite impossible if the Church knows what is meant by its own judgment concerning the canonicity of Scripture. And in view of this we must say of the much deplored difficulty of explaining the Bible and of the fact of the many variations and contradictions in the explanations found, that what has always so widely divided the minds of men in the exposition and application of Holy Scripture has not been too great, but too small, a faithfulness in the perception that the Church must hear in Scripture and only in Scripture the Word of God. What Catholicism has for the most part done is classically typical of all heresies. In the exposition and application of Scripture it thinks that outside of Christ and the Holy Spirit as self-attested in Scripture it can also claim a Christ who may be known directly and a Holy Spirit who can be received and works directly— He may sometimes go by other more secular names, He may even be identical with human reason or vitality or nature or historical consciousness. And where this happens, then Scripture, which is clear in itself and in subject matter, becomes obscure, the demanded freedom in exposition and application becomes self-will, and a divergence of the various expositions and applications becomes inevitable. There is no more dangerous subjectivism than that which is based on the arrogance of a false objectivity. Not the fact that Holy Scripture as the Word of God is obscure and ambiguous, but the fact that it is the Word of God for the Church on earth, and therefore a teacher of pupils who are lost sinners, is what makes the much deplored divergence in its understanding possible, and, unless the miracle of revelation and faith intervenes, quite inevitable. But this divergence can be avoided only by this miracle and certainly not by denying it in advance. It will not be avoided if, instead of accepting in faith the grace which meets them in Scripture, the pupils give way to their own sin, renouncing the relationship as pupils in which all their hope should be set, and each trying to be the teacher of Scripture or at least an equal partner in discussion. But even if in so doing they appeal to Christ and the Holy Spirit, even if ever so many of them should enjoy the finest *consensio* among themselves—on this path they can only increase the fragmentation and make it incurable.

Not too little but much too much traditionalism, i.e., enthusiastic belief in a direct access to revelation granted to the Church, was always true of the older Protestants as well. We have only to think of the fanatics and enthusiasts and mystics of the 16th century, who sowed the harvest of Protestant sectarianism which is so often derided in Roman polemics. But not only of them. Even in the two great official Evangelical Confessional Churches the Scripture principle was not taken too seriously but too little seriously. Too many direct certainties and self-evident truths were presupposed, some of them taken over from the Middle Ages, some of them dictated by the Renaissance, some of them newly developed, but all regarded as an inalienable possession of the Church, with the expressed or unexpressed character of a second source of revelation side by side with Holy Scripture. We have only to think of the alleged natural law, of Aristotle who, in spite of Luther's protest, quickly entered his own again as " the " philosopher (and to whose place and function other philosophers could equally well be appointed later), of the idea of the *corpus christianum* which was so critically important for the status of the Reformation Churches in state and society, but above all of the reality of the Confessional Churches as such, which was posited absolutely or almost absolutely. We have only to think of the magic and the practical influence of the magic exercised by the name of Luther and to some extent of Calvin. We have only to think of the almost magical authority which the Confession of Augsburg, laid before emperor and empire, acquired for Lutheranism. Are not all these non-scriptural authorities no less than the supposed apostolic traditions of the Tridentinum ? On what ground and with what right did they all come—even in the 16th century—to be openly treated with the same seriousness as Scripture ? And it was these authorities which brought about the same disastrous result even in Protestantism. The Protestant exposition and application of Scripture did not become so subjective and self-contradictory in the school of Holy Scripture itself, in which Protestantism ought to have been according to its own programme, but in the school of these other authorities, which were unconsciously accepted and described as *pari pietatis affectu et reverentia* and of equal value with Holy Scripture, not in the school of Luther and Calvin, but secretly very much in the school of Vincent of Lerins and in the spirit of the supposedly disputed Tridentinum. For that reason the 16th and 17th centuries were right when they tried to ensure that the cheap gibes of their opponents at this subjectivism and contradiction did not affect in the slightest the *perspicuitas scripturae sanctae*, when they were fundamentally agreed that the way out of this obvious dilemma did not lie backwards, in concessions to the Catholic principle of tradition, but only forwards, in a more energetic acceptance and application of the Evangelical Scripture principle. If they had only sought and taken that way more seriously ! The real weakness of the older Protestant position is that it did not do so much more definitely. Here, as elsewhere, the weakness was that from the very first it included in itself too much of Neo-Protestantism to be able to confront Catholicism not only with words but more effectively with deeds.

The weakness is betrayed in the fact that in the 17th century attempts were already being made to find the way out not only in practical but in radical contradiction to the Reformation decision and with more or less open concessions to the Tridentine dogma—in other words, backwards.

It was not the first and best who led the way in this direction. The great Dutch jurist and historian, Hugo Grotius, is the one of whom we have to think (cf. Holtzmann, p. 41 f.). That he was an Arminian is in this context just as characteristic as was once the semi-Pelagianism of Vincent of Lerins : the battle against the freedom of grace is the root of Neo-Protestantism as well as of Roman Catholicism. Deeply impressed by the well-known arguments of Catholic polemics, Grotius made the radical concession : *stat omne verbum in duobus testibus, in scriptura et traditione, quae mutuo facem sibi allucent.* Of course when he said this Grotius did not intend to say the same as the Tridentinum. What he had in mind was two sources of revelation, of equal seriousness and mutually self-declaratory. And by tradition he meant the *antiquus et universalis consensus veteris ecclesiae* distorted by the scholastics, as he thought he could see it in the essential and unanimous testimonies of the Church fathers and at the heart of the official Romish tradition. We shall have to ask how this " old " Church can be delimited from the mediæval. But let us suppose that this question can be answered. We then have to ask how the decision of this Early Church can have equal dignity with that of Holy Scripture ? And in seeing and acknowledging in its own past a second source side by side with the first, does not the Church *eo ipso* appoint itself the judge over both and therefore over Holy Scripture ? And by what right does it do so ? If Grotius faced the last two questions even less directly than the fathers of Trent did, there can be no doubt that his historical conjoining of the Bible and the earliest tradition, no less than the Tridentine dogma which extends the concept of tradition right up to the present time, necessarily demanded the idea of a possession of revelation under the control of the contemporary Church, an idea which would necessarily involve an open repudiation of the Reformation decision.

Grotius' counterpart in Lutheran Germany was the much discussed Georg Calixt of Helmstedt (cf. Holtzmann p. 43 f. ; W. Gass, *Geschichte der protestantischen Dogmatik*, vol. 2, 1857, pp. 68–216). He is even more interesting than Grotius, because on the one hand the origins of the thesis are clearer in his case, and on the other the thesis is worked out more carefully and yet more definitely. Calixt could regard himself as a good Lutheran in that he did undoubtedly value the doctrine of justification by faith as the one and important insight and confession of his Church, and stated it fairly correctly as understood by the Reformation. But at the same time he belongs to that increasing number of Evangelical theologians who from the 17th century onwards did not give full weight and content to the concept of faith in this doctrine, but with a strange lack of certainty conceded that faith might unfortunately mean even an inactive and ineffective intellectual belief, and that therefore if the way of salvation is to be fully expounded it is necessary that without altering the doctrine of justification there should be added to it some conclusion on the necessary fruits of faith, on the minimum of moral righteousness in the believer indispensable to eternal bliss. In other words the idea arises, or recurs, that grace must be enlarged by man. The moral disposition and sentiment acquire an independence quite alien to the Reformers. It is of a piece with this that in Calixt the significance of the doctrine of justification has faded compared with that of the common dogma of the ancient Church, against the background and as the result of which he rightly enough understands it. The affection of Calixt is definitely not for the doctrine of justification, but for the general doctrine of the Trinity and the incarnation, and to that extent not for the Lutheran but for the ancient Christian-Catholic Church, out of which the Lutheran proceeded with its doctrine of justification. Calixt could also regard himself as a good Protestant to the extent that he could most sharply differentiate himself from the latest Jesuistic-curial Catholicism now being erected on the foundation of Trent. But again he did it in favour of that Christian Catholicism which he thought could be discovered behind the disruption of the 16th century and the corruption of the Middle Ages, and by which he now measured and criticised and compared the Lutheran and Reformed Churches, trying to indicate their true unity. According to Calixt there is a *consensus quinquesaecularis*, an essential agreement of the teachers, confessions of faith and conciliar resolutions of the first five centuries both among themselves and with Holy Scripture, which itself must be understood as part of this original *corpus*. For in this period the Church received from the Word of God the doctrinal substance indispensable to it, and in receiving it, it gave and appropriated it to itself (Gass, p. 110). Holy Scripture attests the legitimacy and therefore the normativity of the consent of the Church of this period. And conversely the Church of this period attested by its consent the perspicuity and sufficiency of Holy Scripture (Gass, p. 126). Therefore and to that extent the Church of this period is the criterion for the Church and Churches of all later periods, when the emergence of specific and alien doctrines partly destroyed that consent. It is the judgment on the more recent Popish Church, but also the higher, judicial and unifying authority in face of the Popish Church on the one hand and Protestantism on the other, and also in face of the inner dissensions within Protestantism. It constitutes, so to speak, the sound, natural stem of all historical Christianity, the core of truth, which has been maintained and can be recognised in all its excrescences and extuberances, and the rediscovery and universal acceptance of which would restore health and unity to the Church. Now there can be no doubt about the richness and consistency and also the good, i.e., humanly speaking most enlightening, intention of this conception. But for all this we cannot fail to see that it marks a definite and open reaction from the Reformation insight concerning Holy Scripture. With Calixt as with Grotius, we have first to ask whether the doctrine of the *consensus quinquesaecularis* in antithesis to the later Church does not rest on a great illusion ? Whether, in fact, that earlier Church did not very definitely contradict itself ? Whether in many of its agreements it was not very definitely opposed to Holy Scripture ? Whether Roman Catholicism and all sorts of other views later seen to be heresies were not present in the post-apostolic age and especially the succeeding centuries ? Whether from the standpoint of Holy Scripture the Church of that period, as of all periods, was not in need of reformation and therefore not at all in agreement with or one with Scripture, but confronted by and subjected to it to its humiliation and redemption. But even if it were as Calixt presupposed : can we really say in the one breath that the Church has received the Word of God from Holy Scripture and also given and appropriated it to itself, even if the latter takes place in the most perfect way ? Must we not give to the primary witnesses the first word, a word which is radically and qualitatively first, even as compared with the most perfect of secondary witnesses ? Can we bind the Church in the same way to the latter as to the former ? Again, even if the Church did genuinely find itself in agreement with Holy Scripture and pursued a real reciprocity in its relation to it, it must not be overlooked that both the agreement and the ensuing dignity of the Church are radically lost again, or to what extent a full and open restoration of the two is radically impossible. Calixt maintained a latent continuance of that sound stem even in the later Church, and he demanded and prophesied a universal reformation of the Church to restore, i.e., to make visible again its continuity with that normative Church which still had a latent existence. But in this Church, which is secretly present and will again become visibly and actively normative, the Church is not placed under Scripture but side by side with it, receiving the Word of God from it as it gives it to itself. The historical premiss on which Calixt maintains and proclaims the normativity of that Early Church, i.e., that Church as the norm, is actually the premiss of an independent possession of revelation by the Church. Calixt definitely rejects an infallible Pope as the official representative and controller of this possession of revelation. This is to the credit of his desire for Protestantism. But what is the real difference if the Pope is replaced by an expert on Early Church history, or a well-meaning architect of unity, who can now pass judgment ? Behind the fallible professors and ecclesiastical politicians and other representatives of the present-day Church there still stands an infallibility of the Church as such. If the *consensus quinquesaecularis* is really the norm of the Church and can be known as such, somewhere in the present-day Church we can know about revelation *a priori* just as well as by being taught out of Holy Scripture. We are somehow in that original agreement with Holy Scripture which makes possible a reciprocity of receiving and giving. We started from the obvious uncertainty in Calixt in relation to the doctrine of justification. It was inevitable : those who think that it must be enlarged by a special doctrine of the fruits of faith necessary to salvation have not understood its presuppositions and therefore its meaning, even though they may state it correctly. When he asserted the unity of the Lutheran Church with that of the Middle Ages and antiquity, Calixt could do so sincerely and boldly not least because he accepted the doctrine of justification only with this need for expansion and this expansion, not least because he thought he should correct the Reformed doctrine of original sin by teaching that the result of original sin involves only a severe weakness, but not a positive corruption of human nature (Gass, p. 133), not least because he obviously wanted to understand the activity of the regenerate as a co-operation of natural and supernatural acts based on the indwelling of the Holy Ghost (Gass, p. 101). And inevitably, too, Calixt adopted a mediating position even in the question of knowledge, even in the relationship of reason and revelation which had not been thoroughly elucidated by the Reformers : " Revelation does not need violently to enter into its rights, for in the sphere of spiritual activity as a whole there is a position which it has to occupy, there are points of contact which it has to grasp, there are tokens by which the consciousness of its truth is strengthened . . . both kinds of intellectual appropriation (reason and revelation) exist side by side by divine arrangement " (Gass, p. 88). In face of these positions we can only say that the Neo-Protestant parallel to the Catholic principle of tradition which achieved definite shape in Calixt was not only possible but inwardly necessary. In all its shoots the theology which says " and " derives from one root. If you say " faith and works," " nature and grace," " reason and revelation," at the appropriate place you logically and necessarily have to say " Scripture and tradition." The " and " by which the authority of Holy Scripture is relativised in both Roman Catholicism and Neo-Protestantism is only the expression, one expression, of the fact that already the majesty of God has been relativised in His fellowship with man. And in this primary relativising both are equally remote from the Reformation decision.

Because of its weakness in carrying out the principle of Scripture, Protestantism entered on a great crisis. In the course of it, at least in its Neo-Protestant form, it developed into a pseudo-Church only too similar to that of Catholicism. That is, it became a Church which in its history and presence is itself revelation. This development was, of course, always hampered by the recollection of the Reformation decision. But Catholicism had only to express itself more definitely and clearly in the direction which had become unequivocally plain at the very latest in Vincent of Lerins, but which had been immanent in it from the very first and to which—as distinct from the uncertainty of Protestantism in relation to its principle—it maintained a cautious but tenacious loyalty throughout the centuries. Here, too, the children of this world were wiser than the children of light. We saw how in addition to the parallelism of Scripture and tradition the Tridentinum decreed the subordination of all biblical exposition to the teaching office of the Church. But as often asserted for polemical purposes, was not the canonising and transmission of the Bible the work of the Church, and did not this, too, mean the superiority of the Church ? The fact is that even before the Tridentinum Johann Eck (*Enchir.* 1529 *de eccles. resp.* 3) could write : *Scriptura non est authentica sine autoritate ecclesiae. Scriptores enim canonici sunt membra ecclesiae*, and he called this argument the *Achilles pro catholicis*. Indeed, as early as 1517 Sylvester Prierias had penned a statement which at that time even Catholics felt to be daring : *Quicumque non innititur doctrinae romanae ecclesiae ac romani pontificis tamquam regulae fidei infallibili, a qua etiam sacra scriptura robur trahit et auctoritatem, haereticus est* (*Dial.* 15). It corresponds only too well that in the *Professio fidei Tridentinae* (1564 *Denz.* No. 995) tradition—now expressly defined as *apostolicae et ecclesiasticae traditiones*—is mentioned before Holy Scripture. And so, after the Tridentinum, the *Cat. Rom.* (1556 I *c.* 10 *qu.* 14) developed the doctrine that the apostolicity of the Church consists in the fact that its proclamation is true as that which did not arise yesterday or to-day, but was already represented by the apostles. To resist the doctrine of the Church is to resist the doctrine of the apostles themselves, to sever oneself from the faith, to resist the Holy Spirit. *Qui Spiritus primum quidem apostolis tributus est, deinde vero summa Dei benignitate semper in ecclesia mansit.* It is not surprising, therefore, that in the next century (cf. Holtzmann, p. 55 f.), on the one hand the concept of tradition was more and more definitely expanded to cover all the Church's historical development (including Holy Scripture at the outset, and the explicit and implicit decisions of the present-day Church at the close), and on the other the present teaching office of the Church comprised in the Papacy was more and more definitely referred to as the mouthpiece of this tradition. That in the service of the apostolic tradition the Church has not only a conserving function (as the Tridentinum has it) but also a producing one (as we find already in Vincent) is something which is expressed with increasing clarity. Occasionally now (especially in Jesuit literature) there is an openly derogatory mention even of the antiquity of the Church so highly valued in opposition to the Protestants. The ecclesiastical practice of any century can now, it is claimed, be ascribed directly to the Holy Spirit without reference to antiquity. Indeed, that side of Tertullian's proof of prescription which looked to the future now took on new life in the saying of the Jesuit Salmeron : *quo iuniores eo perspicatiores esse doctores.* It is now recognised and openly declared that there are many conciliar findings and episcopal constitutions, many solemn announcements of the Early Church, which now have no practical significance or authority, indeed that the Church fathers were guilty of not a few heterodoxies and errors. In Baroque Jesuitism Augustine especially was fearlessly renounced. Mention is made of the obscurity of this father who was not without importance in the Early Church, just as Catholic polemics used to speak of the obscurity of Holy Scripture : his real views are so recondite and confused that we can only assume either that he does not want to be understood, or that he had not sufficient command of language for the purpose ; and in addition he is of a passionate nature and inclined to extremes, ebbing and flowing like the ocean. In the Jansenist disputes it could be definitely stated that the reputation of Augustine had been more harmful to the Church than useful. And Brisacier (in the struggle against Jansenism) could even go so far as to say that the Early Fathers and Councils are dead rules, which have no relevance to the burning questions of the time, but only serve to impress with the show of antiquity : they are strings to which we do not tie men but beasts ! Statements like this were exaggerations for which later Catholic theology was not responsible and which self-evidently were never the officially stated opinion of the Church. But it is still instructive that, in the century in which we find the Protestants Grotius and Calixt relativising the authority of Scripture by an over-serious proclamation of the authority of the Early Church, the Roman representatives of the same undertaking, the best-known exponents of progressive modern Catholicism, were questioning the authority of that Church. Both could, in fact, take place for the sake of the same alleged possession of revelation by the present-day Church. Yet it was no extravagance, but it had become the common habit of the Church, and still is even in contemporary Catholic dogmatics, not to speak as Trent did of two, but quite expressly of three sources of Christian knowledge, Scripture, tradition and the Church. Actually, of course—and this is an exaggeration, but a very characteristic one—nine co-ordinated sources of knowledge could be mentioned : Scripture, tradition, the Church, the Councils, *Sedes Apostolicae*, the fathers, orthodox theologians, reason, philosophy and history. There is no doubt that Catholic dogmatics and proclamation does even to this day listen to all these authorities *pari pietatis affectu*, just as in its own way Neo-Protestant proclamation and dogmatics also does. Tradition as a second source had in fact included all the eight authorities apart from Holy Scripture. The emphasis on the Church, especially the present-day Church, in what became the more customary triad shows the actual mouth to which we have to listen if we are to know *in concreto* what tradition is in this comprehensive sense, to which we have to listen if we are to know *in concreto* what Holy Scripture is and what is the meaning and content of Holy Scripture. To close the circle, all that was needed was an express decision as to where the mouth of the present-day Church must be sought and heard. And that decision did not remain untaken.

In conclusion, we may also mention it as an interesting fact from this same century that it was not a Protestant but the French Oratorian, Richard Simon, who was the pioneer of a historico-critical science of biblical introduction. Only in the 18th century was he followed on the Protestant side by Johann Salomon Semler and others. For Simon himself the matter stood consciously and expressly in direct relationship to the Tridentine principle of tradition. " Catholics who are convinced that their religion does not depend wholly on the text of Holy Scripture, but equally on the tradition of the Church, cannot be shocked if they find that the unfavourableness of the times and the negligence of the copyists has introduced the same alterations into sacred writings as profane. Only prejudiced or ignorant Protestants can be shocked by it " (*Histoire critique du vieux test.* 1678 1, 1). Even without any Scripture, the Christian religion could have maintained itself by tradition alone according to Simon (1, 4). The freedom to investigate the human form of the Bible, which Simon derived from this genuinely Catholic perception, seemed at that time, at any rate to Catholics like Bossuet, novel and dangerous. Quite wrongly ! The historico-critical investigation of the Bible could only have been dangerous to the Catholic system if it had taken the form of a free investigation of truth and therefore a free inquiry into the original form of the biblical witness of revelation. In its artlessly expressed humanity it would then be self-revealed in its exaltation over the Church both past and present, over every alleged possession of revelation. But that was certainly not the opinion of Simon, just as it was not the opinion of Semler and the Neo-Protestant biblical criticism that followed him. It was the freedom of biblical criticism which Simon so radically claimed—Bossuet did not really need to work so zealously for the suppression of his books—and not the freedom of faith based on the freedom of revelation. It was Simon who openly and unreservedly spoke " the final word in the whole Jesuit development of the principle of tradition " (Holtzmann, p. 60) : *l'écriture, soit qu'elle ait été corrompue, ou qu'elle ne l'ait point été, peut être citée comme un acte authentique, lorsqu'elle est renfermée dans les bornes, que nous avons marquées ci-dessus ; c'est à dire, lorsqu'elle se trouve conforme à la doctrine de l'église* (3, 22). It is not therefore critical investigation, but the doctrine of the Church, which finally decides the authenticity of the Bible. Critical investigation is good enough to make way for the doctrine of the Church by proving that the Bible cannot have authenticity of its own. As a critical investigation it can also do otherwise—because it is not bound and therefore not really liberated by the question of revelation. The biblical tradition may or may not be " corrupted." In any case, if it comes into conflict with the doctrine of the Church, criticism can be honourably suppressed. That is how it was with the Roman Catholic origin of modern biblical criticism. Neo-Protestantism has no *doctrine d'église* or papal Biblical-Commission visibly to direct and control its criticism of the Bible. But beyond all the alleged critical liberty of investigation it has all the better knowledge of the mighty tradition of the human consciousness of self and of history, by which it is decided with no less certainty than by a visible Rome within what limits the Bible is and is not an authority, whose command investigation as such loyally accepts and to whose judgment it is subordinated in the same honourable way as the " free " investigation of an externally known " Catholicism." In this connexion, too, we have to see that there is an underlying unity in the struggle against the authority of the Word, which is really the struggle against the freedom of grace.

We will conclude our historical survey with a glance at the two events in the history of Catholicism in the 19th century which give to the problem a final acuteness.

The first of these events is one to which not enough attention has been paid, the existence of the Catholic so-called Tübingen School. We can summarise the significance of this school as follows. Catholic theology now takes notice of the idealist-romanticist philosophy and theology of the turn of the 18th and 19th centuries, which was a continuation and renewal of the humanistic, enthusiastic and mystical side-movements of the 16th century, and in which Neo-Protestantism reached and passed its peak. It sees that there is an inward relationship between Catholicism and this a-Catholic system, and it makes its aspirations its own. Enriched in this way, it finds that it can gather together theoretically the results of previous Catholic development and represent them with a new power to modern man. (Cf. for what follows, Ranft, p. 46 f.). Already in the course of that 17th-century development of the principle of tradition, especially at the hands of the Jesuits, the expression had been incidentally coined : *Traditio successione continua vivit in animis fidelium semper* (Holtzmann, p. 89). And now, after a century in which there had been no visible advances, at the end of the Enlightment and in relation to its real or supposed overthrow by the " Storm and Stress," idealism and romanticism, in the circle of J. M. Sailer (whom Clement Brentano styled " the wisest, truest, most sincere and consecrated Bavarian ") the idea of a " living " tradition again became powerful. What was meant was the tradition of Christendom in continuity with the inwardness of the God-guided heart in which it has its true being, while its objective form in history and the Church, although we must honour it, has to be understood more as a condescension to man as he now is. This position has a clear affinity to the philosophy of religion of Lessing and Kant. It is naturally only a first attempt in this direction. To assimilate itself to Neo-Protestantism in this form, the form of the older Enlightenment, was too difficult a task for Catholic theology. With an even more open attachment to Neo-Protestantism, this time the Neo-Protestantism of Hegel and Schleiermacher, and better able to safeguard the specific interests of the Catholic Church, the Tübinger J. S. Drey has to take up again the thesis of Sailer and try to overcome its weakness by his view of the Church, i.e., of revelation as a living organism, which has developed and still develops out of the life-principle within it under the guidance of the divine Spirit, so that in its life the static principle, i.e., that which is originally given by God, is continually moved and kept in progress by the dynamically living principle—which is tradition. Drey avoids a conception in which Scripture itself is a fixed system and not a part of life which has its own movement revealed in clear advances (e.g., from the Gospels to the Epistles). For on this view tradition is only an enlargement, a supplementing or adding to Scripture by oral tradition, and Christianity and theology are the stereotyped impress of the *corpus* of Scripture and tradition as now immovably written and mechanically passed down. No, Scripture, tradition and theology are the living movement and development of the Christian spirit in the Church. We have to listen to them because this movement and development takes place in them. We have to listen to them first and decisively in what is the last stage of the development of that spirit : in the objectivity of the living faith of the present and in the subjectivity of the conceptual expression this faith creates for itself in its temporal and historical antithesis. In the distinction made by Drey between the static and dynamic principle of revelation on the one hand, and the subjectively-outward and the subjectively-inward element in theology on the other, we can see an after-effect of the Enlightenment which by the logic of Catholic thinking had to be and was actually carried a step further. But does not Catholicism have within itself these distinctions of the Enlightenment ? Can they not equally well be used by it in its attempt to understand and explain itself ? The Tübingen school from the very first could never quite rid itself of these distinctions. But it understood better how to restore and maintain the balance between the two elements disturbed by Sailer and even Drey, the real dialectic between the static and the dynamic, the objective and the subjective. And it always concluded with the thesis so much emphasised by Drey, that we have to listen to the Church, the present-day Church, if we want to hear revelation. To the extent that it did this it was essentially a genuinely Catholic school. Its idealistic interpretations of revelation (like the Catholic biblical criticism inaugurated by Richard Simon, although in another way) were admirably calculated to repeat the Tridentine relativising of the authority of the Bible in a manner illuminating to the modern consciousness, but without at the decisive point leading or wanting to lead—and how could it ?—to any other conclusion than that of the authority of the Church demanding obedience to-day. The classical exponent of this theology, who gathered the finest fruits of Neo-Protestantism into the Catholic barns, was after Drey the man who is rightly honoured as the father of modern German Catholicism, J. Adam Möhler (*Die Einheit der Kirche* 1825 ; *Symbolik* 1832). Möhler, too, who knew Schleiermacher particularly well, started from the distinction between faith and doctrine, spirit and letter, hidden root and visible shoot, pious self-consciousness and outward ecclesiasticism in the life of the Church, i.e., of revelation. But more clearly than in Drey and in a definite Catholic improvement on Schleiermacher, the two elements are now shown to be originally co-ordinated with each other, so that the Catholic conclusion that we must listen to the Church can now be understood *a priori* from within. According to Möhler's first great book, there corresponds to the unity of the spirit of the Church the unity of its body, to the mystico-spiritual and doctrinal inner unity, in which the individuality of the believer has its place, the outer unity, increasingly represented in the bishop as the unity of the congregation, in the unity of the episcopate (seen in the metropolitan Synods and the General Council) and finally in the unity of the Roman *cathedra*. This correspondence which transcends and organically comprehends the antithesis of idea and history, doctrine and action, inward and outward truth, inward and outward witness, this higher unity of both unities rests on the fact that, as the human spirit is everywhere the same, so too Christ is one and His work one (*Symbolik*[3], p. 342). But the unity of Christ is transferred to the Church, because it is the community founded by Him, " in which the activities developed by Him during His earthly life are continued under the leading of His Spirit to the end of the world by means of an apostolate ordered by Him and persisting without a break " (p. 334). Further : " The Church is the Son of God continuing to appear among men in human form, always renewing Himself, always becoming young, His continual becoming-flesh " (p. 335). " It is His visible form, His continuing and eternally self-rejuvenating humanity, His eternal revelation " (p. 360). What took place between Christ and the apostles can be described as follows : " To the action of the Saviour in proclaiming His Word there corresponded that of the apostles : the Word in their mouth at once became faith, the possession of man, and after His ascension it was no longer present except in this faith of the disciples of the Lord." The divine Word became human faith and in that way, without ceasing to be the divine Word, it passed over into the realm of human comprehension, analysis, reflection and judgment (p. 374). The same thing happens when as the apostolic word it becomes the faith of the first post-apostolic generation : the doctrine of Scripture now becomes the doctrine of the Church, again without any break ; on the contrary, always being understood more fully, always attaining to greater clarity in controversy with heresies (p. 375 f.). That, then, is how it lives and grows and works, always the same, and yet always new. Just as the world is maintained in the reality once and for all posited by God and by virtue of the living power imparted to it by God in and with creation, i.e., as it is renewed in such a way that there is a continual impartation from that which lives now to that which will live in the future—so tradition

is the extended self-impartation of the original, divinely spiritual life-force once
and for all posited with the founding of the Church (*Einheit der Kirche*, p. 11 f.).
" The essential content of Holy Scripture is eternally present to the Church,
because it is its heart's blood, its breath, its soul, its all " (*Symbolik*[3], p. 383).
The Church is therefore " the Christian religion become objective." " As the
Word spoken by Christ . . . entered with His Spirit into a circle of men, and was
adopted by them, it took form, it assumed flesh and blood, and this form is the
Church. . . As the Redeemer by His Word and His Spirit founded a community,
in which He allowed His Word to be living, He entrusted His Word to that
community to be preserved and transmitted, He deposited it in it, in order that it
might go out from it and grow and reach out always the same but eternally new
and with ever new power. His Word can never be separated from the Church
and His Church from the Word " (p. 336 f.). The revelation in Jesus Christ
would either have failed altogether or succeeded only in part if it had been only
a momentary incorporation of the truth, " if the personal manifestation of the
Word had not been sufficiently strong to give its sound the highest degree of
most intensive movement and to create the most complete imaginable activity,
i.e., to breathe in the breath of life and creatively to produce a union, which
would again show forth the truth in a living way and be the example of sufficient
authority for every age : or represent Christ Himself " (p. 343 f.). " The
authority of the Church mediates everything that rests on authority and is
authority in the Christian religion, i.e., the Christian religion itself, so that for us
Christ Himself remains our authority only to the extent that the Church is our
authority " (p. 345). From this it follow that " it must be inerrant " (p. 339).
" If the divine element is the living Christ and His Spirit in it is that which is
inerrant, and eternally infallible, then the human element is also infallible and
inerrant, because the divine does not exist for us apart from the human ; it is
not the human in itself, but the instrument and manifestation of the divine "
(p. 336). " The divine Spirit, to whom the leading and quickening of the Church is
entrusted, in its unity with the human becomes a specifically Christian sensibility,
a deep and sure feeling, which, standing in the truth, leads to all truth . . . a
profoundly inward mind, which is particularly adapted to grasp and accept the
written Word, because it is in harmony with that in which the Holy Scriptures
themselves were composed " (p. 359). " What then is tradition ? It is the
specifically Christian mind as it is present in the Church and continues to develop
under the Church's nurture, a mind which is unthinkable without its content,
which is rather formed on and by its content, so that we have to call it a filled
mind. Tradition is the Word, living continuously in the hearts of believers.
The exposition of Holy Scripture is entrusted to this mind as the common mind ;
the explanation which it gives . . . is the judgment of the Church, and the Church
is therefore the judge in matters of faith " (361 f.). And : " all dogmatic and
moral developments which can be regarded as results of formal universal activities (of the Church) must be respected as utterances of Christ Himself " (p. 364).
" The Church expounds Holy Scripture " (p. 360). Therefore its life is always
one : on the vertical plane of temporal succession as well as on the horizontal
of temporal conjunctivity, whereas heresies are betrayed and judged as such
by the fact that they are and set up innovations and peculiarities outside its
unity. " Nothing sweeter hovers before the imagination of the Catholic, and
nothing speaks to his feelings more beneficially, than the idea of the harmonic
involution of countless spirits, which, scattered over all the surface of the earth,
freely empowered of themselves to enter into every deviation on the right side
and the left, nevertheless, even as they preserve their various peculiarities,
constitute a great band of brothers for mutual development of their life, representing one idea, that of the reconciliation of man to God, and being therefore
reconciled and made one amongst themselves " (p. 339 f.). Möhler thought it
important—and this insight has recently been given an express historical basis

in the book by J. Ranft—that what he represented as the law of the organic unity of revelation and Church, Scripture and tradition, is identical with that law which covers all the ordinances of human life. Just as Christ lives in His Church, so there lives in the history of every people—as long as the people itself lives, Pan is not dead—preserving what is proper to it, rejecting what is alien, self-consistent in the most varied expressions, a national spirit, that is, the particular character of this people, impressed on its deepest, most secret existence, and differentiating it from all other peoples : and so too the history even of heathen religions shows how an original religious view is logically carried through and organically built up and expanded in its later development. It is the law to which Christian heresies too are subject : did not the congregation which the reformer of Wittenberg built up and all Lutheranism develop according to his spirit ? Did it not show itself to be the infallible expositor of his Word ? "The infallibility of the Church in its exposition of the divine Word is formed and has to be judged by this pattern" (p. 362 f.). A Catholic review of Möhler's achievement runs as follows : "The nature of the Church in the union of its eternal divine basis and temporal human development undergoes a radical reinterpretation. The appeal to the principle of tradition which seemed outwardly to be a hampering and retrospective outlook suddenly became an appreciation of the continually living attesting mystery of Christ Himself. At a particularly important point Möhler thus succeeded in throwing light on the darkened picture of ecclesiastical teaching. What the Tridentinum had stated only in simple formulae . . . what the post-Tridentine theologians had saved in a bitter theological contest, he was able to grasp fully with the help of the idealistic understanding of spiritual movements" (Ranft, p. 60). We can set against this the morose verdict of D. F. Strauss : "So Möhler could derive the sole-redemptive Popish Church with no greater difficulty from the Christian consciousness than Schleiermacher could his Redeemer. He could give the Christian consciousness a form, in which it seemed interchangeable with the modern principle of progress" (*Ges. Schriften* II p. 222). How was it possible—we must ask—for Catholic theology to achieve such results as Möhler did with the help of Hegel and Schleiermacher, or (as Strauss thought) so badly to misuse their achievements ? Prudently but foolishly Strauss had nothing to say on this question. But the Catholic author joyfully and confidently let out the secret : "Möhler was able to make use of the finest insights of idealistic philosophy just because they were in some sense an interpretation of the most vital phenomenon of the history of Christian dogma, the progress of the development of Christian doctrine" (Ranft, p. 52). It was really a waste of time for Protestant critics of Möhler's system to accuse him of "Schleiermacherising" and to charge him with transmuting Catholic doctrine. Möhler himself had already given the answer : Why should we not speak rather of a catholicising of Schleiermacher ? (Ranft, p. 52) ; which means that we have to weigh the possibility that in availing himself of his ideas and formulations, Möhler did represent Catholic doctrine, and in doing so understood Schleiermacher at the deepest possible level and rightly applied him in this way ? And do we not have to admit that he is right ? The Catholic and the idealistic interpretation of Christian history both do go back to the same conception. They are at one in what ultimately emerges and is expressed in Möhler : in the identity of the Church and its faith and its Word with the revelation which is its basis. The only point is that the Catholic is the original and proper form of this understanding, and the idealistic a derivative form, which (in a preliminary self-misunderstanding) at first contradicted the former. Aware of its identity with Christ, the Catholic Church can in the last resort, if at all, only be interpreted idealistically. And the finest insights of idealistic philosophy are, in fact, only "in some sense an interpretation" of the phenomenon of the movement of Christian history seen through Catholic, i.e., crypto-Catholic eyes. Möhler as a good Catholic was able to see in the secondary

idealistic form of that conception its primary and Catholic one, and therefore
instead of rejecting it to adopt it into Catholic thinking. At the same time, as
a good idealist, he was able to dissolve the idealistic self-misunderstanding, to
help the modern consciousness to fulfil its deepest intention, i.e., to help it on
the way back to Rome. And that he was able to do this is his really remarkable
historical achievement in this matter. By this personal union he represented the
best interests of both partners, while giving to the authority of the Church the
final word which was also the first. And he did well not to let himself be led
astray either by the doubts of anxious Catholics or by the ill-founded scoffing of
his Protestant opponents. It was along the lines and with different variations
on the ideas of Drey and Möhler that their successors, J. Kuhn and Franz Anton
Staudenmaier taught in Tübingen. The decisive positions of this school have
become the common possession of Catholic theology, although more strongly in
the second half of the 19th century than in the first that theology was to enter
into a new relation to the " earlier theology," meaning especially Thomas
Aquinas : a development which outwardly forced the elements taken over from
German idealism more and more into the background because of their alien
form. But what took place or was brought out with the existence of that school
could not be and was not reversed or concealed again. We must not be surprised
if among the later Catholic dogmaticians we again hear Scripture and tradition
spoken of in the more abstract and old-fashioned manner of sub-Tridentine theology as two separate sources of revelation, and elsewhere of Christ and His revelation as opposed to both. At a first glance we miss the boldness and energy with
which Möhler related and ultimately united these things. But we are much
mistaken if we imagine that there has been a real withdrawal, if we overlook the
fact that these insertions (which were not really the invention of Möhler) had
everywhere become the common possession of the Catholic theological consciousness, that the idealistic construction with which the Tübingers had defended
and justified them could be scrapped or relegated to the museum once it had
fulfilled its purpose—occasionally being brought out, of course, and directly
applied right up to our own time (e.g., by Karl Adam, and also by Erich Przywara). Once the synthesis had been achieved which is indispensable for a German
Catholic theology, and with this synthesis behind one, it was possible again to
think and proceed analytically without revealing at every point the identifica-
tions made by Möhler, but with the decisive content of his views, quite independently of idealism, as the starting-point and goal. In this sense the second, modern
German Catholic theologian of any size, Matthias Joseph Scheeben, who is representative of the new repristination of Thomas, of a Catholic theology of the
older and strict style, stands entirely on the shoulders of Möhler.

In the German-speaking area at least, Scheeben.was *the* theologian of the
pontificate of Pius IX, and especially at the time of the Vatican Council at
which—and here we come to the second event which is decisive for our present
problem—the final term was put to the whole development as concerns the
teaching office of the Church. When Catholic theology related Scripture and
tradition as sources of revelation and then represented them more or less clearly
as a single context of tradition, from the days of Irenaeus their considerations
and assertions had almost always led to a more or less clear indication of a
third authority side by side with Scripture and tradition, or rather as the
elected mouth, or the authentic exponent of both : of the Church itself, i.e.,
the Church of the present day, visible and represented in the authoritative
pronouncements of its teaching office. Therefore the real importance of Möhler's
thinking did not consist in his identifying of what ultimately became the complex
of Scripture and tradition with revelation, with the incarnation of the Word,
with Jesus Christ, but in his attempting to understand the whole divine dignity
and authority ascribed to this complex only as a predicate of the Church, the
present-day Church, as the living bearer of the apostolate, the representative of

Jesus Christ. The Church it is into whose faith the Word of God has come and in whose faith it has actually gone forth. The Church has the Word ; expounds it ; is revelation *in concreto*, not a new revelation, but the old revelation, self-enclosed and for that very reason perfect and complete. The Church is Jesus Christ, speaking, ruling, acting, deciding to-day. Once again, the identification was old, very old. Even in the 2nd century the Roman Catholic Church as such has already its basis in this identification, and it is along these lines, which since then cannot again be new, that all Roman Catholic progress has been made. As a Catholic Möhler had only systematised what all informed and progressive Catholics had always meant and said on this matter. And as an idealist Möhler had only made explicit the relationship between Roman Catholic progress and progress in the sense of the Neo-Protestantism which resisted the Reformation on its other flank. It now needed only a final clarification not yet explicitly made in Möhler but prepared and announced in all Roman Catholic development—and always clearly and logically announced and prepared. The consummation now reached cannot possibly be regarded as an innovation, as was partly the case within the Catholic Church. And on the Neo-Protestant side, it is only as a result of that persistent self-misunderstanding, only because the way home has not yet been found, that it can be received with the horror with which it was partly received when it came. Again, in Möhler the question had not yet been finally made clear, where that Church which is identical with revelation, i.e., where that mouth which declares revelation, where that authority of the Church which is identical with the authority of the Word of God, has to be sought and heard *in concreto*. To this question Möhler still gave the traditional answer, which was correct but incomplete, that it has to be heard in the voice of the whole episcopate united to its popish centre, as the legal successor and bearer of the apostolate proved by unbroken succession, as the visible representative of Jesus Christ. Thus Möhler left unresolved the problem involved in this answer. He set side by side Conciliarism and Curialism, the system of Episcopacy and that of Papacy, " of which the latter, without failing to recognise the divine institution of bishops, specially stresses the strength of the centre, while the former, without denying the divine institution of the primate, tries to find the main strength in the periphery. In so far as each recognises the divine nature of the other, they constitute most useful opposites for the life of the Church, so that by their efforts the individual free development of parts is safeguarded and their conjunction to an inseparable and living whole is also maintained " (*Symbolik*[3], p. 399). Many loyal Catholics would have been glad to maintain the concept of the Church's authority in this dialectical form. But had these loyal Catholics rightly understood the meaning of previous Catholic development and therefore its starting point and origin ? Had not Möhler himself written some time before : " The whole view which the Catholic Church has of itself, as a visible institution taking the place of Christ, would be lost, or rather, would not have arisen at all, without a visible head. With a visible Church a visible head is necessarily posited." Could or should the description of this indispensable head, of this concrete culmination of the authority of the Church, be content with this dialectical parallelism of Council and Pope ? That the Council as representative of the " periphery " of the Church cannot speak or decide as the voice of the Church to-day and therefore as the living Jesus Christ without the Pope, the representative of its " centre," was something which had not only been claimed by the Popes from early in the first Christian millennium, but had actually been acknowledged and even theoretically maintained by the overwhelming majority of standard theologians. In this unique position of supreme teacher and judge, the Pope was what not only Möhler, but also the representatives of certain centrifugal tendencies, like the Gallicanism of the 17th and 18th centuries, had always been prepared to concede : the " centre " of the Church's life as opposed to its episcopal " periphery." But would not the very opposite be maintained, that the

Pope cannot speak and decide authoritatively without the actual and express co-operation, but only with the explicit sanction of the bishops ? To the word and decision of the Pope should there not be ascribed the infallibility which belongs to the divine authority of the visible Church and therefore to its visible head, only if and to the extent that he speaks out of the total consciousness of the Church represented in the episcopate, i.e., as supported by the vote of the bishops united in Council ? Could it be concluded that what Möhler called those " most useful opposites " would never in fact work out otherwise than bene-ficially ? As long as the equipoise between Pope and Council was maintained, was not there always the possibility of a disunity within that " visible head " ? And was it indeed a head ? Had the Church a mouth by which it could speak with authority, infallible, ultimate, absolute authority, and possessing which it could preserve its identity with the living Jesus Christ ? Is the first word, that the visible Roman Catholic Church stands and speaks in the place of Jesus Christ, because it itself is the continually-living Jesus Christ Himself—is that first word a final word, is it really spoken in a way in which it can be received and believed, unless it is unreservedly transferred and applied to the official status and utterance which admittedly constitutes its organising centre, the centre of its teaching office, the episcopate ? Was not the whole transformation of the authority of Scripture into that of the Church, which had been the mean-ing of the development from Irenaeus to Möhler, quite futile, because that meaning was still equivocal and finally obscure, so long as there had not emerged as the last and concrete culmination of the incarnation of the Word one man, who as the living bearer of the tradition identical with revelation, and therefore himself revelation as it has to be heard to-day, represents the Church, or the Christian humanity which has attained possession of revelation, and executes its self-government ? Could the insight which had been ripe for expression so long be suppressed any longer, that this is in fact the nature and function of the Romish Pope ? Could it be suppressed that the official decision of the Pope is quite unreserved and needs no confirmation ; that as such and in itself it is the decision of the whole episcopate and therefore the decision of the infallible Church, the infallible decision of Scripture and tradition, the infallible declaration of revelation and therefore itself infallible revelation for the present age ; that by virtue of his supreme authority and apostolic power according to the Lord's promise, and under the guidance of divine providence, the Pope will never speak except out of the common consciousness of the infallible Church, and in his official speaking utterances will never say anything but infallible revelation for the present age ? Could this be suppressed any longer when it had been true from the beginning and had for so long, although only partially at first, been known to be true ? That was the question with which the Catholic Church was consciously faced under the pontificate of Pius IX (the same Pope who in 1854 had defined the dogma of the Immaculate Conception of Mary, and who, at the same Council at which the infallibility was decided, gave dogmatic authority to the Thomist doctrine of reason and revelation). The answer given by the Catholic Church through the mouth of the Vatican Council, and the latter through the mouth of the Pope himself, is to be found in the *Constitutio dogmatica* I *de ecclesia Christi* of the 18th July 1870. The decisive passage is at the end of Ch. 4 (*Denz.* No. 1839) and it reads as follows : *Itaque Nos traditioni a fidei christianae exordio perceptae fideliter inhaerendo, ad Dei Salvatoris nostri gloriam, religionis catholicae exaltationem et christianorum populorum salutem, sacro appro-bante Concilio, docemus et divinitus revelatum dogma esse definimus : Romanum Pontificem, cum ex cathedra loquitur, id est, cum omnium Christianorum pastoris et doctoris munere fungens pro suprema sua Apostolica auctoritate doctrinam de fide vel moribus ab universa Ecclesia tenendam definit, per assistentiam divinam ipsi in beato Petro promissam, ea infallibilitate pollere, qua divinus Redemptor Ecclesiam suam in definienda doctrina de fide vel moribus instructam esse voluit ; ideoque eiusmodi Romani Pontificis definitiones ex esse, non autem ex consensu Ecclesiae, irreformabiles esse.—Si quis autem huic Nostrae definitioni contradicere, quod Deus avertat, praesumpserit: anathema sit.* Note well that it is not with the consciousness of innovation, but with the consciousness of loyalty to its tradition and development from the very first, that the Church makes this declaration. It is the Pope himself who makes it: with the consent of the Council, which according to its content he did not need, but which he is glad to have stated, not as a violation of his own authority, but rather as a confirmation of its fulness. The declaration states an ecclesiastical or papal doctrine and at the same time describes this doctrine as divinely revealed dogma, i.e., as an interpretation of revelation with the authority of revelation itself. Therefore it already assumes in form what it asserts in content. That is, in the doctrine as fashioned in this way it states that the Romish Pope is in possession of the infallibility with which Christ clothed the doctrinal decisions of His Church. It is not the man himself elected to be Pope who as such possesses this infallibility. It is this man to the extent that in his office as shepherd and teacher of the Church, and as such using his apostolic authority, he pronounces and decides in matters of faith and morals. Yet it is the Pope himself who in the last resort has to decide when these three conditions obtain. He does not possess infallibility of himself, but on the basis of the divine aid promised him in the person of Peter. The Pope does not only possess it, but it is proper to him in his particular office, and that directly and quite independently of any other teaching office. Within these limits, which are not reservations but elucidations, he possesses infallibility and therefore his decisions are authoritative and therefore final decisions in themselves and not on the basis of the consent of the Church. Refusal to accept this doctrine means separation from the Church. This declaration of the *Vaticanum* has a special preliminary history in the history of the doctrine of the primacy of Peter and the primacy of the Roman see. But it has also behind it the history of the doctrine of Scripture and tradition, and properly and definitively it can be understood only from this standpoint. It is the closing of **that** circle, the opening of which is marked by the dualistic formula of Irenaeus (repeated in the Tridentinum), the continuation by the triad of Vincent of Lerins, and the culmination by the synthetics of Möhler. Since the *Vaticanum* we can know what was not previously known, viz., where and what the Church is *in concreto* which teaches revelation. It is interesting that it requires the primacy of Peter and the Popes to make it possible for the Church as it is identical with revelation to have this concrete point. But more interesting is the fact which had for a long time been obvious but was only now admitted: that the Church as it is identical with revelation possesses such a point; that to this day there can be seen from every place and by every man a place and man where heaven and earth meet, where God and man, the Word taught by Christ and proclaimed in faith in Him are directly one, " a living authority resting on divine operation in all the contentions of the world " (Leopold v. Ranke, *Die röm. Päpste, Meisterwerke*, vol. 8 p. 299); that this one place and this one man in their particularity only make manifest the glory which is actually imparted to the whole Church as such and as its own. That there is this man and place, that there is this living authority, that is what the *Vaticanum* has stated—not with the impossible intention of giving something to the Pope or the Church which they did not previously possess, but defining and proclaiming as a dogma essential to salvation something which it had always had in all its fulness, *quod ubique, quod semper, quod ab omnibus creditum est.* It had always been the case everywhere, and as revealed truth, that the Church speaking by the mouth of the Pope was the revelation of truth. On the authority which the Church has, it now confirms—and this is the singular significance of this declaration of the Vatican even from the formal standpoint—to itself and to the world the fact that it has this authority; that is, that it has it in the supreme concreteness of the fact of the office which now delivers this declaration about it and therefore about itself, of the office which—in the greatest formal similarity to the Johannine Christ—is at once the subject and the object of this declaration. The circle is now actually closed. We can now know where and what is the authority of the Church as it is identical with the authority of the Word of God. The Vatican declaration was not made without strong opposition even within the Catholic Church, indeed even within the episcopate which had assembled for the Council. A group of mainly German, but also French and Oriental bishops, made themselves at the Council the representatives of this opposition. Their weakness consisted *a priori* in the fact that it was not fundamental, i.e., that its representatives were always having to explain that in the real point at issue, i.e., the recognition of the revealed truth of this declaration, they were at one with the Pope and the majority of the Council, but that on serious grounds they could not agree that the time was opportune, as they called it, for its proclamation as a dogma. It was argued that this proclamation was not necessary, because the corresponding belief had already been expressed generally, and directly as well as indirectly by the Councils of Florence and Trent. The declaration might be open to misunderstanding as regards the infallibility which still had to be maintained, afterwards as well as before, of the whole episcopate as such. It would make more difficult both reunion with the Eastern Church and the return of the Protestants. It might cause dissension among the bishops and in the Catholic world as a whole. It would threaten the local authority of bishops. It was calculated to centralise the life of the Catholic Church in an unhealthy way. Behind these arguments there was an inarticulate but, in the 19th century, very timely concern—and warning notes could be heard throughout Europe and even in America—that the declaration might stimulate opposition to the Church, that it might bring it into fresh conflicts with the sponsors of modern culture and especially with the more or less liberal powers of state. We can understand all this from the human standpoint, but we cannot be surprised that an effective opposition was quite impossible on this basis. The supporters of the new dogma could reply with every appearance of truth and soberness that the declaration must follow, just because its content, although it had been accepted for a long time, yet in spite of the statements of earlier Councils had always been doubted and disputed in various circles simply because it had not been clearly defined and proclaimed as dogma. The infallibility which we certainly have to assert of the episcopate as a whole cannot be compromised by that of the Pope, but is merely confirmed by it, since the Pope is the head of the episcopate. Union with the Eastern Church and the return of the Protestants cannot be furthered by lowering conditions to a minimum as in a business transaction, but only by making it known as clearly as possible that in the Roman Catholic Church they are dealing with the infallible Church. The declaration cuts away the ground from any possible dissension among the bishops or Catholics generally. " Where the Church has spoken, the faithful are not open to temptation. While the Church is silent, the spirits of error rage " (Archbishop Manning, in *The Ecumenical Council* 1869, vol. 2, p. 37). Silence on a revealed truth because of fear of the opposition it might cause is equivalent to the tacit admission that it is not revealed truth at all. The declaration will not lessen but enhance the authority of the bishops in their local spheres. And since its content relates only to the last and supreme stage of the Church's authority, it cannot exercise a disruptive, centralising effect upon the life of the Church, but lends to the decisions of all episcopal courts certitude and stability. We may add that in face of the tacit concern about the opposition to be expected from modern society and the state, Pius IX and the majority of the Council were of the opinion that in this very declaration the Church would by this re-affirmation of the earlier presuppositions of the Papacy strengthen itself as the Church against all the external and internal forces of hostility or indifference, defending itself most effectively by attack. In this attitude L. v. Ranke could not but see " something grand " (*op. cit.* p. 267 f.). " What is true," the friends of the new dogma argue, " must also be defined as true in the Church. What Jesus Christ thought worth revealing, must also be worth declaring." " In the Church of God and in the truth of revelation it is always opportune to declare what God will have revealed to men " (Manning, p. 39), and especially when it is denied, as it had often been since the Council of Trent. Even as Protestants we cannot avoid the impression that the trend which carried the day at the Council was inwardly stronger, to the extent that, in developing—as we have to see it—the error and falsehood to its supreme point, it had in its favour the logic of all Catholic development within which—if with the Reformed perception we are not to reject it at its source and therefore as a whole—any arrest is impossible, especially on purely opportunist grounds. We cannot deny to the supporters of the new dogma the witness that—always within the anti-Christian sphere which they occupied in common—they did think and act more spiritually than their opponents. Above all, we must understand that it was not due to any lack of conviction or character if the bishops of the defeated minority— and especially the Germans—emerged after the Council as adherents and defenders of its declaration. Their opportunist arguments could not bind them and—once the Church had spoken—it was not right that they should do so. Once we see the inner necessity of the Vatican dogma we shall not be so much surprised by certain outward peculiarities of that Council, as many were at the time both inside the Catholic Church and without. This Council, as distinct from most of the early ones, was summoned without any direct co-operation on the part of even Catholic governments, although the France of Napoleon III especially would have been willing to sponsor it. But was not the former co-operation of the political arm based on the reality or apparent reality of the *Corpus christianum*, which had long since disintegrated ? Were not all modern States now established on religious neutrality ? From this standpoint, was it not right for the Church to take charge of its own affairs ? Moreover, the convening of this Council was only by the Pope, and not by the College of Cardinals, which in earlier councils had always acted with him. Again—and this had given rise to complaints as early as Trent—the order of business given the Council by the Pope laid down that the proponing of subjects for discussion is basically a matter for the Pope, that bishops must first submit their motions to the Pope, or to a papal Congregation, who have full power either to pass or not to pass them on to the Council. Again the presiding power seems to have been used with doubtful good faith, or at least not always as many would have desired it in the sense of a freedom of action and speech after the parliamentary manner. But after all a Council is not a Parliament. We shall have to say of these arrangements that ultimately they only anticipated the result of the Council, since they gave to it a form in which it became itself a witness to what it declared. If this declaration was a circle by which the authority of the Pope was proclaimed on the authority of the Pope—how could it be otherwise than that the Council itself should declare that authority by accepting these arrangements ? If apart from the parliamentary form, for which there was rightly no place in the Church, we recall the possibility of fraternal discussion and a general decision, which can be reached according to the " order of business " of an Evangelical Synod, all that we can say is that the Catholic Church, which includes the so-called " suppressed " minority, had long since renounced this possibility. It would have been a μετάβασις εἰς ἄλλο γένος if the Council had not formally taken, or been given, the actual form which it did. In any other form, that which it intended to and did say concerning the infallibility of the Pope would have been disavowed from the very outset. The minority bishop was quite right who later wrote : *Concilium Vaticanum apertissima principis petitione et circuli vitiosi errore illud tandem definivit, quod ab omni initio definitum stabilitumque praesupposuit. Pontifex semet personaliter infallibilem ab initio usque ad finem gessit, ut semet personaliter infallibilem tandem definiat* (acc. to *PRE*[3] 20, 472). He was wrong only in that as a Roman Catholic bishop he thought he had a right to deplore what he described in this way.

As is well known, the internal Catholic resistance to the Vaticanum, so far as it was maintained, stiffened into the so-called Old-Catholic movement and Church. From the outset it had no great prospects, for it did not and could not live by anything essentially different from those opportunist grounds alleged against the declaration, and this only to the extent that it received help from powerful forces outside the Church. Old Catholicism as such means a maintaining of the dualism which we still find in Möhler. In practice, it means either the return to an episcopal-conciliar system, which could only be an exclusive, limiting possibility in earlier Catholic development, which puts the authority of the Church fundamentally above that of Scripture, as in the papal system, but as distinct from it cannot give to the question, where and what is this authority of the Church, any concrete answer. Or, it means a transition to the Parliamentarianism of modern religious societies, which is now so common in the Protestant Churches, and which cannot basically be improved in opposition to the papal system. In recent years Old Catholicism has become inwardly strong where it has fundamentally tried and succeeded in linking itself to the Evangelical Scripture principle. But in this it is greatly hampered by the fact that it can only do this in principle, while in practice it has to recognise and carry with it a rather arbitrarily composed complex of Church traditions alien to Scripture, and at the same time by this very link it ceases to be Catholicism and therefore Old Catholicism. Old Catholicism means a state of indecision between two decisions, which can be made only with a fundamental and practical Yes, or a fundamental and practical No.

But the opposition to the Vatican dogma aroused in the modern non-Catholic world of culture, including the Neo-Protestant Church, was and is absolutely impossible. In the year 1870 and later only one authority could enable a valid protest to be made against the fully closed circle of the Roman Catholic doctrine of revelation, that is, an Evangelical Church with a good conscience in respect of its own faithfulness to the Reformation Scripture principle, a Church whose authority stood under and not over the Word, whose doctrine and preaching was directed at all points not according to the self-consciousness or historical consciousness of modern man, but only according to the witness of the prophets and apostles. We can quietly assume that at that time and since the right answer to the Vaticanum has been secretly given in many Protestant pulpits in the name of this Church, an answer certainly involving a confession of repentance in the name of the whole of modern Protestantism. But there was then no instrument to gather together these voices and to give expression to and make known the Evangelical verdict on the crime of the Vatican in proper proportion to its flagrant nature. There was no Protestant Church with an unanimous confession. The loudest Protestant voices at that time, and in the years of the *Kulturkampf*, were, for all their loudness, broken voices. And those who used them lacked the one thing which they needed to be able to say No to the Vaticanum with authority. Without that, the Roman stroke—and Pius IX had timed it rightly—caught the modern world of culture at that stage of complete inward dissolution on which it had entered in the second half of the century, when it tired of classical idealism. From what standpoint could the Popish Church be attacked when it equated itself with revelation? From the conception which had been taken over from the 18th century of a universal human reason identical with the highest truth? Compared with the new or rather the age-old doctrine of identity of the Popish Church such a conception, which had in any case paled, could never be more than a weaker and less vital partner, however illuminating it might be to sound commonsense. Or from the standpoint of the still prevalent romantic individualism?

This, too, was emulated in depth and perspicuity by the Vatican dogma, or the older Catholic idea of the representative individual incorporating the Church in the fulness of his competence and authority. From the standpoint of the modern positivistic concept of knowledge? Certainly the empiricism of the recent natural and historical science seemed specially formed as an iron wall against the mystery of newly revived ecclesiasticism. And who amongst those who were educated after this manner did not then believe that they were separated from Pius IX and his Council by unbridgeable antitheses in principle? But did not this science leave too much open, not actually if involuntarily to affirm that mystery in spite of and even in its agnosticism and atheism? And again, in relation to its own principles, did it not make too evident a use of a doctrine of infallibility which for all its contradiction of Rome was bound to act indirectly as a confirmation of the papal claim to infallibility? From the thought of the modern national, legal and welfare state? In the 19th century, both before 1870 and after, the Church was in fact severely attacked along these lines and suffered a considerable weakening in authority. How much it had to concede to Napoleon I and later to the new Italy in the varying stages of its growth and finally to Bismarck's Germany and even to the radical cantonal governments of Switzerland! If only the modern states, with all the jealousy with which they sought to maintain their prestige against the Vatican, had not at the same time felt so deep a need to prop up their never very stable authority against the forces of revolution by leaning on the authority of the Church. And if only in their nationalistic and socialistic developments they had not secretly been on the way to a politico-cultural totalitarianism, which when it emerged openly was bound to confront the absolutism of the Roman system of revelation with a similarity of structure far too close for any serious objections to be made to it, in spite of occasional misunderstandings here and there. Or finally from the freedom of the Protestant conscience? "Luther at Worms" was a favourite figure in the second half of that century, and the motif of a religiously flavoured defiance of the hierarchical claim of Rome was gladly accepted as the deepest note in the universal chorus of protest even outside the circle of the Protestant Church. What was not seen was that Luther's freedom and defiance had been related to the concrete Word of Scripture, whereas the freedom and defiance which were now worked up were just freedom and defiance as such, the "it seems to me" of an autonomous conscience, in virtue of which man was still lord of Scripture, as had always been the case in Catholicism, and was now with a conclusive and demonstrative clarity. That the walls of Jericho would fall down at the sound of the trumpets of the "Evangelical Covenant" was something which the inhabitants had no reason to fear. For centuries the Jesuits had had an incomparably better understanding of the use of this sort of freedom of conscience. The opposition of the modern non-Catholic world to the closed circle of the Catholic system could not be anything more than a blind panic. The Council of Freethinkers which met at Naples at the same time as the Vatican Council was for good reason bound to end as a pitiable farce. It would have been different if the Vatican dogma had come up in the time of Kant and Goethe, Schleiermacher and Hegel, but the world of 1870 was one which was highly disunited in itself, and its arguments were bound endlessly to oppose and cancel out each other. In the ultimate thing in which it was at one by virtue of its origin in the Renaissance and its recent high-water period, it was far too closely related to the now consolidated Catholicism to be in a position to offer it any consistent or dangerous opposition. Had not Möhler shown long ago that it was quite possible, and with comparatively little trouble, not merely to translate its most intimate intentions into Catholic terms, but to make them vital and effective in their Catholic centre? Therefore it was certainly more than diplomatic optimism, and more than contempt, when the German *Kulturkampf* ended by Bismarck, for many years the apparent embodiment of modern non-Catholic opposition, being made a Knight of the Papal

Order of Christ. One of the great moments of the Vatican Council was when a representative of the minority ventured to argue from Church tradition against the opportuneness of the new dogma. In reply Pius IX uttered his now famous saying: "I am tradition!", which is only a variant of the equally famous saying of Louis XIV, to the effect that he, as king, was the state. The latter word is, of course, a genuinely "modern" one. It is unthinkable except against the background of the Renaissance. The same is also true of its Popish variant. Again, that saying of Louis XIV contains within itself the whole French Revolution, just as conversely the sayings of political liberalism with their peculiar emphasising of the individual are notoriously open to the sudden change into an absolutism, in which the individual can again be the state in the sense of Louis XIV. Similarly, the dictum of Pius IX contains in itself all theological and ecclesiastical liberalism—as its opposite, but only the dialectical opposite, which can be changed into it. And conversely, it is not basically impossible that theological liberalism should lead to a recognition that all Christian tradition and authority is comprised in a single individual. The following words were written by a Viennese professor of theology, E. Commer (in an address on the 25th Jubilee of Leo XIII, *PRE*.[3] 20, 474): *Affirmamus, ecclesiae esse unum caput in duabus personis distinctis, Christo scilicet et Petro. Sicut humanitas Christi est quasi instrumentum animatum coniunctumque divinitatis, quae propria filii est, simili quoque modo pontifex maximus dici potest primarum instrumentum humanum animatumque ipsius verbi incarnati ac divinitatis, quacum coniunctus est auctoritate vicarii universa. Recte igitur papa . . . alter Christus appellabatur.* And before we rightly steel ourselves against such blasphemy we should read what, e.g., A. E. Biedermann (*Chr. Dogm.* 1869 792 f.) worked out concerning the general principle of divine sonship as the true meaning of the biblical and ecclesiastical doctrine of the divinity and humanity of Christ. If in the Roman Pope acting in his office we recognise the *alter Christus*, the human instrument of the divinity bound up with him, it is impossible to see why in the individual definitions of the God-man in the Bible and the Church we should not recognise generally the definitions of the relationship between God and man, between the absolute and the finite spirit. And if the latter is possible, why should the former be fundamentally impossible? Between the mythologically singular and the speculatively universal identification of man with divine revelation there can be no final and serious contradiction. If the one is possible, then basically the other is also possible. If the one is false, then basically the other is also false. Those who affirm the one cannot basically reject the other. The rejection of the one is possible only if it is bound up with the basic rejection of the other. The place from which both can be discerned as false and therefore rejected, the place from which Jesus Christ can be seen in His incomparable glory as the Lord of man—that place had been abandoned no less by the Roman Catholic Church than by the modern non-Catholic world which rejected its dogma, and no less by that world than by the Roman Catholic Church. To this we can only add that in the family quarrel between the two the Roman Catholic Church will always enjoy the relative advantage, which it did in the period of the *Kulturkampf* after the Vatican decree. It will do so because its heathenism has a much more comprehensive Christian covering. It will do so because it has a much more pronounced anti-Christian character. It will do so because it consists much more definitely in a perversion of the truth. It will do so because it has a much stronger share of living force of the Word of God falsified by it. Its familiar and opposite has some fragments of Christian knowledge, but for the most part it has to nourish itself on naked heathendom. Its anti-Christian character has still to develop before it can meet the Roman Church with the same weapons and even on the same level. But however that may be, the real decision is not taken in this family quarrel, but on that front where Catholicism and the modern world were encountered—and will be—by an Evangelical Church which stands under Holy Scripture.

All that now remains for us is to describe positively and negatively the nature and the meaning of the Evangelical decision on this matter as it was made at the Reformation, and as it must be made again and again wherever the Evangelical Church is true to its name.

The Word of God in the revelation of it attested in Holy Scripture is not limited to its own time, the time of Jesus Christ and its Old and New Testament witnesses. In the sphere of the Church of Jesus Christ it is present at all times, and by its mouth it wills to be and will be present at all times. This is the Evangelical confession of faith. In this confession of the vitality and therefore of the presence of the Word of God as already actualised and to be actualised again and again there is included the Church's confession of itself, i.e., of its institution and preservation by the Word of God for the authority entrusted to it and the mission enjoined upon it.

The confession includes first a confession of the reality of a fellowship of the Church in space as well as time, i.e., of a unity based upon the Word, which the Church has within itself in past, present and future : a unity in faith and proclamation, a unity of that which it receives in the gift which constitutes it and of that which it does in fulfilling what is enjoined upon it. The confession includes therefore a confession that where the Church is there are also brethren in faith and proclamation. The present-day witnesses of the Word of God can and should look back to the witnesses of the same Word who preceded them and away to those contemporary with them. In this matter it is impossible to speak without having first heard. All speaking is a response to these fathers and brethren. Therefore these fathers and brethren have a definite authority, the authority of prior witnesses of the Word of God, who have to be respected as such. Just because the Evangelical confession is a confession of the vitality and the presence of God's Word actualised again and again, it is also a confession of the communion of saints and therefore of what is, in a sense, an authoritative tradition of the Word of God, that is, of a human form in which that Word comes to all those who are summoned by it to faith and witness in the sphere of the Church and by its mouth—of a human form which is proper to it in the witness of these fathers and brethren, before they themselves come to faith and witness, and which is to that extent prior to their faith and witness—of a human form with which they have always to reckon, and, in virtue of that priority, with a definite respect proportionate to the witness of the Church as such.

Second, this confession includes a confession that the witness of the presence of the Church has a definite authority to the extent that it is the witness of the living and present Word of God, and takes place in that response to its transmission and in recognition of its definite authority. Where men speak in the Church according to the manner of the Church, i.e., in fulfilment of that witness, and where to that extent the Church itself speaks, it means that that priority is again set up and established, that that hearing, which is respectful in the true sense, is presupposed and demanded, that for the hearers there is again created that responsibility, without which, of course, the Church itself could not speak, but which is a matter for the hearers now that it does speak responsibly. But again, in so far as the Church speaks, there arises a human form of the Word of God, which as such always precedes the faith and witness of the hearers, and with which the latter have to reckon in the same way as in the fellowship of saints in faith in the vitality and presence of the Word of God we have to reckon with that prior witness of the fathers and brethren. Once again, therefore, we have a tradition of the Word of God which is authoritative in a definite sense.

In this twofold form, then, the Evangelical confession of the Word of God includes a confession of the authority of the Church. We shall return to the meaning and content of this confession in the second part of the section. But before we say a single word about the authority of the Church—and this is the parting of the ways where the Evangelical decision is ineluctably and irrevocably made—we have to insist that there is an authority *in* the Church which is also an authority *over* the Church. This authority is itself the basis of all authority in the Church, from which it has its definite value and validity and without it would not possess it, without which it never has and never will really exercise it. But this authority limits the authority of the Church, that is, it does not destroy but defines it. By it the authority of the Church is not only instituted but directed, so that whenever the authority of the Church is heard this authority has also to be heard with it as the first and final and decisive word. There is an authority in the Church which at the risk of the complete destruction of the authority of the Church itself cannot be transformed and dissolved into the authority of the Church, or at any cost be identified with it. How, then, can we speak of an authority of the Church in this twofold sense? How does it arise that in the communion of saints there is a tradition of the Word of God, resting on responsibility and demanding and evoking responsibility? The Evangelical confession which has to be set against Catholicism and Neo-Protestantism is as follows. It arises in so far as the existence of the Church, which possesses and exercises this authority, is a unitary act of obedience, an act of subjection to a higher authority. It is in this act of obedience that it is what it is, the Church, ἐκκλησία, *evocatio*. It is not the Church apart from this act. It is not so if and when it repudiates this obedience. But it repudiates it when the authority to which it subjects itself is not really a higher authority distinct from and superior to its own. It repudiates it when it subjects itself to an authority not vested in but instituted by itself and therefore immanent in it. It repudiates it when it subjects itself to its own authority. Even when its own authority has and is the plenitude of authority (and the more so the more it is), obedience to it is the very antithesis of obedience. It is self-government. But self-government is a—indeed it is the great prerogative of God. Self-government in the creaturely sphere can only mean the usurping of this divine prerogative of God and therefore the open disobedience of the creature. But the self-government of the Church is the admitted essence of both Catholicism and also Neo-Protestantism. In the one case the final decision rests with the teaching office of the Church which comprises both Scripture and tradition and expounds them with unchallenged authority, identifying itself with revelation. In the other it rests with the less tangible but no less infallible authority of the self-consciousness and historical consciousness of man. But either way it rests with the Church which then has to obey it. And to the extent that this is the case, the Church knows no higher authority than its own. It invests its own authority with all the marks of a higher authority, an authority which transcends itself as the Church. It is all the more careful to expunge any transcendent authority not identical with its own. It lays its anathema and contempt upon the possibility of obedience to any authority not identical with but transcendent to its own, describing it as separation from the Church. And in doing all this it refuses to obey. It makes itself like God. And it therefore ceases to be the Church. And in addition, it loses its own authority no matter how highly it values and extols it, no matter with what fulness it apparently possesses it. A higher authority which is transformed and dissolved into its own authority, which has been adopted and assimilated into it and has therefore disappeared, is not really a higher authority and obedience to it is not real obedience—even when the authority of the Church into which it has been assimilated arrays itself in all the predicates of divine revealedness, and obedience to the authority of the Church arrayed in this way bears all the marks of the most profound and sincere piety. The Church is no longer the Church where it does not know a higher authority than its own, or an obedience other than that of self-government. And from a Church which does not have an authority different from its own authority there is necessarily taken even the authority which it has. In a state of disobedience it cannot be the recipient and the subject of an authoritative tradition of the Word of God resting on and demanding and evoking responsibility. It cannot be the communion of saints. Bound to no prior human form of the Word of God, it will be unable itself to remain a prior human form of the Word and therefore to bind itself. It will not be able to evoke that respectful hearing of its witness.

The decision in favour of a Church of obedience as opposed to a Church that is self-governed is necessarily and unavoidably imposed upon us by the fact that the Christian Church cannot reflect on its own being, or live by it, without seeing itself confronted by the Lord, who is present to it but as its real Lord, with a real authority which transcends its own authority. Its Lord is Jesus Christ. He has called it into life and He maintains it in life. In Him it believes. Him it proclaims. To Him it prays. It is related to Him as the human nature which He assumed is related to His divinity. It looks up to Him, as He is present to it, and it partakes of His Holy Spirit, as the earthly body looks up to its heavenly Head. He and He alone, with the Father and the Holy Spirit, can have divine glory and authority in the Church. But He does have it. The Church would not exist without Him, just as the creature would not exist without the Creator. It is the same relation as that of the Creator and creature which exists between Him and His Church. In His distinctness from it He is one with it ; and in its distinctness from Him it is one with Him. The relation between Jesus Christ and His Church is, therefore, an irreversible relation. Whatever the glory and authority of the Church may be, the glory and authority of Jesus Christ are always His own. And as the glory and authority of the Church are based on the glory and authority of Jesus Christ, as they are established in the Church and are the very nature of the Church, so they are also limited by them. The glory and authority of Jesus Christ cannot, therefore, be assumed or subsumed, but will always be fulfilled and maintained in a contradistinction between the disciples and the Master, the body and its members and their mutual Head. The basis of the Church, its commission and authorisation, even the personal presence of Jesus Christ in His Church, does not remove the possibility and necessity of this differentiation between its authority and His. It is in this very contradistinction and only in it that there exists and consists the unity of Christ with His Church and His Church with Him. If it lives as His Church and has as such its own authority, it lives in obedience to Him, in an obedience which neither openly nor tacitly can ever be self-government.

But we must give a less equivocal form to all these statements if they are to present a clear picture of the Evangelical decision in matters of the authority of the Word. It may be that many of the cleverer, and to that extent better, representatives of Catholic and Neo-Protestant theology believe that they can follow and agree with us so far in spite of their very different position. Certainly, they may say, above the authority of the Church as its basis and limit there stands the direct and absolute and material authority of God Himself, the authority of Jesus Christ as the Lord of the Church whom it must obey. Certainly this relationship is in itself irreversible. Certainly there is in it an irremovable distinction between the higher and the lower, the glory and authority of God and that of the Church. Certainly, the latter must always be preserved by the former and therefore distinguished from it. But supposing, they then go on to ask, there is this preservation even in distinction, supposing the Church is really obedient, supposing the Word of God is really living and present in it ? Can we and must we not reckon with this possibility ? Is it impossible *a priori* for the teaching office of the Church actually to speak pure, divine and infallible truth by its papal mouthpiece, in virtue of the divine grace promised to the Church—and self-evidently in subordination to the authority of God and in the service of Jesus Christ ? May not something of the same be the case when in Neo-Protestantism the modern consciousness of self and history lays hold of the Word ? But if we may and must reckon with this possibility, then have we not obviously to reckon also with the fact that, without being in itself more than the Church, the Church is itself the tradition of the Word of God and therefore present revelation and therefore Jesus.Christ ? But if we have to reckon with this possibility—by whom or what can its claim to actuality be resisted ? We at once reply to this question that the claim is resisted by the very fact that it is made at all. The Church, whose authority is preserved in the differentiation from the divine authority, the Church which is *obedient* to its Lord and in which the Word of God is living and present, will definitely *not* make that claim. Of course, it will be the tradition of the Word of God and therefore present revelation and therefore actually—as the earthly body of the heavenly Head—Jesus Christ Himself. But this will be true as the act and truth of Jesus Christ in the power and mystery of the Holy Ghost. The glory and authority of the Church will then be a predicate of His divine glory and authority, as once in the incarnation of the Word human nature was a predicate of His eternal Deity and therefore Deity could be beheld in the flesh according to Jn. 1[14]. But the glory and authority of God are not then a predicate of the Church—as little as once the eternal Word was a predicate of the flesh. There can, therefore, be no question of the Church claiming to be as such the tradition of the Word, revelation, Jesus Christ Himself. The grace directed to the Church cannot be transformed into a possession and a glory of the Church. When and where the grace of God is directed in all its fulness to the Church in this differentiation, it cannot and will not try to say of itself what the Catholic and Neo-Protestant Church thinks that it should say of itself. It will receive what is actually given it of divine glory and authority. It will be thankful for it. It will accept it and let it be effective. It will shine in this borrowed light. But it will not boast about it as though it were its own possession. It will not attire itself and act as though it had any claim or control in the matter. Out of the fact that Jesus Christ does actually acknowledge it it will not derive any personal glory, or self-commendation, and it will certainly not make a dogma of it. It will remain in the place, it will always return to the place in which the grace of God has come to it, i.e., the place of obedience, the differentiation between its own authority

and that of Jesus Christ Himself. Not in denial of the fact that it
is adopted by the living and present Word into unity with Him, but
in recognition of and gratitude for this exaltation, it will remain in
this place, it will always return to it, it will not leave it with the
claim that it itself has and is direct and absolute and material authority.
In the knowledge of the eternal Jesus Christ and in fellowship with
Him it will be modest, knowing that He is in it and it in Him in the
distinction of the Creator from the creature, of the heavenly Head
from His earthly body. In this place it recollects and expects His
blessing. This humility, which in the fulness of what it receives and
has constantly turns to the origin and object of faith, is the very
essence of the Evangelical as distinct from the Catholic and Neo-
Protestant decision.

But we have still to give to our description of this Evangelical
decision its final point and sharpness. Where is it that a Church
which derives from the presence and grace of Jesus Christ a claim to
direct and absolute and material authority divides from a Church
which remains in and constantly returns to the differentiation in which
Jesus Christ is present and gracious to it ? The dialectic by which
in the former case the change is made from thankful reception to an
arbitrary attempt to possess, from recognition of the divine authority
of God to the claiming of divine authority, from obedience to self-
government—this dialectic seems always to be so strangely irresistible.
If in the antithesis between God and man there is fellowship created
by God, if there is the self-giving of God to man, if the revelation of
God is made actual to man—is not the antithesis necessarily overcome,
does not the giving of God necessarily mean a possessing by man, no
matter how radically impossible this possessing may be to man in
the first instance ? Is it not imparted miraculously by that divine
giving ? Who knows, if we follow out this dialectic, we might even
accuse the Evangelical decision—and the accusation has been made
—of resting on an unchildlike, unthankful defiance of grace, on an
arbitrary persistence in revolt from Jesus Christ, in the human estrange-
ment from God, which has been overcome by Jesus Christ. It might
be argued against it—and it will be argued against it—that the true
humility of faith consists in the very fact that the Church does assume
the divine glory and authority lent it by Jesus Christ and to that
extent claims and exercises it. What is it, therefore, that concretely
prevents this change and makes it impossible ? What is the necessity
concretely imposed upon the Church, according to the Evangelical view,
to remain in that differentiation and therefore in the distinction
between its authority and the authority of Christ and therefore in
the subordination of the former to the latter, to resist as a temptation
the *Eritis sicut Deus* even in this form—even if it comes in the garment
of the promise and grace of Jesus Christ Himself ? The answer can
only be the simple one that this concrete necessity is the fact of Holy

Scripture. It is not self-will that the Evangelical Church persists in that differentiation, that it claims to be the school in which Jesus Christ is the Master, and the flock in which He and He alone is the Shepherd, the kingdom of which He and He alone is the King, that it takes care not to reverse this order in its own interest. The Church is not in a position to have an opinion on this question. It cannot choose between this possibility and the opposite one in which it itself is Master, Shepherd, King. The latter possibility is in fact closed to it. It is closed to it because Jesus Christ is gracious and present in His Word. This is, of course, by the power and life of His Holy Spirit. Yet this Spirit of His is simply the Spirit of His Word. And His Word, in which He Himself is present and gracious to His Church —and which must not be replaced by or confused with the word which the Church itself has and has to speak—is the word of the biblical witnesses, the Word which He Himself has put in the mouth of His prophets and apostles. Therefore His Word always confronts the word of man in the Church in the form of a human word, i.e., the prophetic-apostolic word. His Word (and therefore His presence and grace) is not an idea which, once it has enlightened the Church, once the Church has made it its own, becomes the idea of the Church itself. And the authority of His Word cannot be assimilated by the Church, to reappear as the divine authority of the Church. His Word —the same Word by which He imparts Himself to the Church, in which He lives in the Church, in which He Himself sets up His authority in the Church—is given to the Church in such a way that it is always His Word as against its word : the Word which it has to hear and proclaim and serve and by which it lives, but which in order that this may happen is prevented from being assumed or subsumed into the Church's word, which asserts itself over against it as an independent Word, as one which is always new to the Church in every age and has to be newly encountered by it. Its form as the word of the prophets and apostles is the safeguard of its independence and newness. It vests it with the healthy strangeness which it needs if it is to be said to the Church of every age as the Word of its Lord. It creates and maintains the healthy distance from the Church of every age which is needed if the Church is to hear it before and as it itself speaks, if it is to serve it before and as it takes its authority and promises on its own lips, if it is to live by it, before and as it lives its life as its own. Its form as the word of the prophets and apostles strengthens the differentiation in which alone the Church of every age can receive revelation and be the bearer of revelation. Because He has entrusted and commissioned His Word to His prophets and apostles, because He has made them the rock on which He builds His Church, the authority of Jesus Christ is a concrete authority. It stands over against the authority of the Church. It cannot be assumed and assimilated by it. Neither gradually nor suddenly, neither with an

appearance of arrogance nor with one of humility, can it be transformed
into the authority of the Church. It is always autonomous, just as
the men of the Old and New Testaments and their human word are
always autonomous, over against the mass of churchmen who have
adopted and reproduced, declared and proclaimed their witness. Beyond anything that the Church itself has said and can say, rightly
or wrongly, loyally or disloyally, there stand these witnesses saying
always to the Church what they have already said. They are not in
any sense the first of a long series with whom those who come later
in the same series can be compared with a like dignity and claim.
They do, of course, initiate this long series, but they do so as those
who were instituted by Jesus Christ Himself in all the uniqueness of
His own reality. They are, of course, a human sign, but the sign
which calls to every other sign and by which every other sign is set
up. They are the first, who not only initiated the series as a whole,
but who must initiate afresh each individual link in it if it is properly
to belong to the series. It is really the Word of Jesus Christ Himself
which as called and instituted witnesses they have to speak to the
Church. They have to speak it, therefore, in a way in which the
Church could never speak it to itself. It can speak it to itself and the
world only as a repetition of their word. According to Eph. 2[20], 3[5]
it can be built up only on their foundation, the foundation of the
apostles and prophets, not alongside this foundation. There is, therefore, no direct connexion of the Church with Jesus Christ and no direct
life by His Spirit—or rather the direct connexion of the Church with
Jesus Christ and its direct life by His Spirit is that it should build
on the foundation which He Himself laid by the institution and calling
of His witnesses, i.e., that it should hold to their word as His Word.
They and they alone in the Church can have direct and absolute and
material authority, the authority of the sign which is given with the
revelation itself. And they do not need to claim it. It does not need
to be ascribed to them. They have it. For without them there would
be no Church. Their existence is the concrete form of the existence
of Jesus Christ Himself in which the Church has the foundation of
its being. In the Church the tradition of the Word of God, obedience
towards Jesus Christ and subjection to His authority are not an open
question but are ordered and regulated from the very first and for all
time by the existence of the apostles and prophets. The life of the
Church has always to fulfil itself in the form of a new subordination
to the prophetic-apostolic word, in the form of a new erection of that
first and basic sign : a subordination and erection which cannot be
considered in relation to any other authority in the Church, because
all other authorities in the Church are themselves conditioned by the
fact that they are subordinated to that word as the concrete form of
the Word of Christ and only to that extent are they authorities in
the Church.

It is at this point, then, that the Evangelical Church on the one hand divides from the Catholic and Neo-Protestant Churches on the other. In the 16th century—not as an innovation, but in re-discovery and restoration of an order disturbed in the very earliest days—the Evangelical decision was taken that the Church has not to seek and find the Word and authority of Jesus Christ except where He Himself has established it, that it and its word and authority can derive only from the word and authority of the biblical witnesses, that its word and authority are always confronted by those of the biblical witnesses, and are measured and must be judged by them. This is what the Reformation was trying to say and did say in its affirmation that Holy Scripture alone has divine authority in the Church. It was not ascribing a godlike value to the book as a book and the letter as a letter—in some sinister antithesis to spirit, and power and life. But it wanted Jesus Christ to be known and acknowledged as the Lord of the Church, whose revelation would not have been revelation if it had not created apostles and prophets, and even in the present-day Church can only be revelation in this its primary sign. But this primary sign of revelation, the reality of the apostles and prophets—and we need not blush to say this, it is not contrary to spirit and power and life but is the strait gate which we will not bypass if we do not want to miss the reality of the spirit and power and life of God—has the form of book and letter in which the apostles and prophets continue to live for the Church and in which with the Word of Jesus Christ Himself they too—to the Church's salvation—are prevented from being assumed and subsumed into the spirit and power and life of the Church, in which form they can always confront the Church as a concrete authority, and therefore as the source of its authority.

The fact that the primary sign of revelation, the existence of the prophets and apostles, is for the Church book and letter, does not rob it of its force as witness. If the book rises and the letter speaks, if the book is read and the letter understood, then with them the prophets and apostles and He of whom they testify rise up and meet the Church in a living way. It is not the book and letter, but the voice of the men apprehended through the book and letter, and in the voice of these men the voice of Him who called them to speak, which is authority in the Church. Why should it be a dead authority because it stands in the book and letter—as though for that reason it could not speak, as though it could not maintain and exercise its authority in the most vital and varied and effective way, as though it had not done so throughout the centuries? The written nature of this primary sign cannot prevent it from being in the Church of every age a real sign, a sign just as powerful and definite as was once the personal existence of the living prophets and apostles to the growing Church of their day. But it is its written nature that is also its protection against the chance and self-will to which it would be exposed without it. Its written nature makes it a sign which, however differently it may be seen and understood and, of course, overlooked and misunderstood, is still unalterably there over against all misunderstandings and misinterpretations of it, is still unalterably the same, can always speak for itself, can always be examined and questioned as it is, to control and correct every interpretation. Its written nature guarantees its freedom over against the Church and therefore creates for the Church freedom over against itself. If there is still the possibility of misunderstanding and error as regards this sign in virtue of its written nature, there is also the possibility of being recalled by it to the truth, the possibility of the reformation of a Church which has perhaps been led into misunderstanding and error. How and along what way could the Church rethink its existence as the Church and reorientate itself accordingly if it could hear the voice of the first witnesses, and in them the voice of Jesus Christ Himself, only through the medium of an unwritten tradition, or, even if written, it silenced the autonomous speaking of Christ Himself through His witnesses by an irrevocable interpretation bound to a definite authority? Would it not then be left to its own devices without any possibility of a reformation in the light of its origin and object? But if behind every alleged or genuine oral tradition, over and above every authority in the Church, there is a Holy Scripture, and if this Holy Scripture is as such recognised as the judge by which from the very outset all ecclesiastical tradition has to be judged and to which all ecclesiastical judges have always to listen, then that means that the Church is not left to its own devices, that the source of its renewal is open, and therefore that it itself is open to be renewed and reformed in the light of its origin and object. In the 16th century this source of renewal was found again in the witness of the prophets and apostles. The Church again became open to renewal by this witness. We can therefore understand that the written nature of this witness was regarded as a gift which had to be received with particular thankfulness from the providence which rules over the Church. Therefore not what was really meant, *De prophetarum et apostolorum testimonio*, or ultimately *De verbo Domini*, but *De sacra scriptura* became the theme and title of the fundamental declarations in which the Evangelical decision for the authority of Jesus Christ against an equivalent authority of the Church found expression. It was in the written nature of the prophetic-apostolic witness that the cogency was found to prove again this witness against the whole weight of the Church and its tradition and teaching office. It was as written that this witness could directly enter the arena side by side with its ecclesiastical interpretations and be directly appealed to as witness and judge. It was as written that it could be the criterion above all warring opinions, no matter how interpretations might differ and continue to differ. It was as written that it then rose up in face of the whole Church from its concealment in a mass of tradition and in the chorus of voices past and present. It was as written that it maintained against the Church the newness and strangeness and superiority of a higher authority.

But this is only one example. Not merely for the 16th century but for the Church of every age Holy Scripture as such is the final point and sharpness of the fact which the Evangelical decision makes unavoidably necessary. In every age, therefore, the Evangelical decision will have to be a decision for Holy Scripture as such. As such, of course, it is only a sign. Indeed, it is the sign of a sign, i.e., of the prophetic-apostolic witness of revelation as the primary sign of Jesus Christ. Of course, the Church can only read Scripture to hear the prophets and apostles, just as it can only hear the latter to see Jesus Christ with them, and to find in Him—and properly, ultimately and decisively only in Him, the prior direct and material and absolute authority on which its authority depends, on which it is founded and by which it is everywhere and always measured. But again, it can distinguish between seeing Jesus Christ, hearing His prophets and apostles and reading their Scriptures, and yet it cannot separate these things, it cannot try to have the one without the other. It cannot see without hearing and it cannot hear without reading. Therefore if it would see Jesus Christ, it is directed and bound to His primary sign and therefore to the sign of this sign—if it would see Jesus Christ, it is directed and bound to Holy Scripture. In it His authority acquires and has that concreteness as an authority higher than the Church which arrests the apparently irresistible revulsion of obedience to self-government. We can appropriate God and Jesus and the Holy Ghost and even the prophetic-apostolic witness in general, and then exalt the authority of the Church under the name and in the guise of their divine authority. But in the form of Holy Scripture God and Jesus Christ and the Holy Ghost and the prophets and apostles resist this change. In this form their divine authority resists the attack which the Church and its authority is always making upon it. Whenever this attack is made and seems to have succeeded, it again escapes it. Rightly or wrongly, in loyalty or disloyalty, the Church may say a thousand things expounding and applying Scripture. But Scripture is always autonomous and independent of all that is said. It can always find new and from its own standpoint better readers, and obedience in these readers, even in a Church which has perhaps to a large extent become self-governing, and by these readers a point of entry to reform and renew the whole Church and to bring it back from self-government to obedience. If the Reformation of the 16th century means the decision for Holy Scripture, conversely we must also say that for every age of the Church the decision for Holy Scripture means the decision for the reformation of the Church : for its reformation by its Lord Himself through the prophetic-apostolic witness which He established and the force of which is revealed and

effective because it is written. Let the Church go away from Scripture
as such. Let it replace it by its traditions, its own indefinite consciousness of its origins and nature, its own pretended direct faith
in Jesus Christ and the Holy Ghost, its own exposition and application of the word of the prophets and apostles. In the proportion in
which it does this, it will prevent that entry upon which its whole
life and salvation rests, and therefore at bottom refuse to be reformed.
All kinds of " life," evolutions and revolutions will be possible in the
Church. It can include conservative and progressive thinking in their
constant action and reaction. There can be undeniable tensions and
party conflicts like those between Catholicism and Neo-Protestantism,
or like the internal Catholic battles between Realists and Nominalists,
Episcopalians and Curialists, Benedictines and Jesuits, or the internal
Neo-Protestant between Orthodox and Pietists, " Positives " and
" Liberals." And these may give the deceptive appearance that the
Church is really alive. But it does not live in the inner movement
of these tensions. In them we see rather the process of decay to
which the Church is at once subject when it ceases to live by the
Word of God, which means by Holy Scripture. What is ultimately
at issue in these tensions is the very secular antithesis of various
human principles which can all be reduced easily to the denominator
of this or that philosophical dialectic, and which ultimately reflect
only the deep disunity of man with himself. And in these tensions
the Church is obviously only disputing with itself. And in this
debate properly both partners are right and both wrong. According
to the circumstance of the age the debate may end with a victory
for this side or that, but neither party, not even the victor, can say
Amen with an ultimate certainty and responsibility, because neither
way is it or can it be a matter of confession, i.e., of responsibility to a
higher tribunal confronting both partners with concrete authority.
These debates in the Church are conducted in the absence of the Lord
of the Church. But are they then really conducted in the Church ?
Has the Church not ceased to be the Church the moment it wants
to be alone with itself ? And does it not want to be alone with itself,
if it will not stand with its authority under the Word in the concrete
sense of the concept, and therefore under Holy Scripture ?

It is here that we come to the final positive meaning of the Evangelical decision : it is taken in the thankful recognition that the Church
is not alone, that it is not left to its own discussions and especially
that it is not left to itself. It would be, the moment its authority
ceased to be confronted by that divine authority. For then clothed
with divine dignity the Church would have to stand and live by itself
like God. And however grand it might seem to be in its godlikeness,
for the creature which is distinct from God that means only misery,
the misery of sin and death. From this misery of the solitariness
of the creature fallen in sin and death the Church is snatched away

by the fact that God in Jesus Christ is present and gracious to it
in concrete authority, which means in an authority which is different
from and superior to its own. It is the Word of God as Holy Scripture
which puts an end to this misery. Because Holy Scripture is the
authority of Jesus Christ in His Church, the Church does not need to
smooth out its own anxieties and needs and questions, it does not
need to burden itself with the impossible task of wanting to govern
itself, it can obey without having to bear the responsibility for the
goal and the result. Because Holy Scripture is the higher authority
established within it, the Church has a higher task than that which
is at issue in those party conflicts, namely, the task of confession,
which itself can only be again a thankful confirmation of the fact that
its Lord is among it in His witness. Under the Word, which means
Holy Scripture, the Church must and can live, whereas beyond or
beside the Word it can only die. It is this its salvation from death
which it attests when it makes, not the Catholic or Neo-Protestant,
but the Evangelical decision.

2. AUTHORITY UNDER THE WORD

All that we have still to say about the authority of the Church itself can be
understood in the light of the commandment in Ex. 20^{12}: " Honour thy father
and thy mother." Obviously there can be no conflict between this commandment and the first: " I am the Lord thy God, which have brought thee out of
the land of Egypt, out of the house of bondage. Thou shalt have none other gods
before me." What it demands is self-evidently limited by the first commandment. But the dignity of what it demands is not reduced and lessened by the
demand of the first commandment. On the contrary, because the first commandment is valid, in its own sphere the commandment to honour father and mother
is also valid. It is in the people which has none other God but the One who
brought them out of Egypt that father and mother are honoured by the children
as the visible bearers and representatives of their own adherence to this people.
The connexion of this commandment with the basic commandment which as
such constitutes the people Israel, and the comprehensive sense in which the
latter has to be understood, are clearly brought out in the saying in Lev. 19^{32}:
" Thou shalt rise up before a hoary head and honour the face of the old man,
and fear thy God: for I am the Lord." We can see the same order in what
the Old Testament says about the blessing which fathers can and should pronounce on their children and the priests on the whole people : the fact that
men bless is not the denial but a confirmation of the real truth that Yahweh
blesses and keeps, Yahweh makes His face shine and is gracious, Yahweh lifts
up His countenance upon those who are blessed and gives them peace (Num.
6$^{22f.}$). Again, the fact that Yahweh blesses and keeps and is gracious is not a
denial but an institution and confirmation of the human blessing, the fatherly
and priestly blessing pronounced on His people. At this point, too, we can and
must recall the prophetic saying in Jer. 6^{16}: " Thus saith the Lord : Stand ye
in the ways, and see, and ask for the old paths, where is the good way, and
walk therein, and ye shall find rest for your souls." And the saying of Bildad in
Job 8^8 points in the same direction : " For inquire, I pray thee, of the former
age, and prepare thyself to that which their fathers have searched out." The

new and strange word of the witness of revelation in the name of Yahweh points
here to an earthly-historical way along which the people has always been led
thanks to the revelation within it : " I have considered the days of old, the years
of ancient times" (Ps. 77⁵)—and which as such has something to say to the
people in which it will again recognise the "good way." The former way is not,
of course, to be regarded as an autonomous word, distinct from the present
revelation of Yahweh, another authority side by side with that of the prophetic
word. But the revelation too, the prophetic word, cannot and should not be
spoken and heard without remembering the former way of Yahweh with His
people. From this standpoint we have to admit basically and generally that
Cyprian was right when he said : *disciplinam Dei in ecclesiasticis praeceptis
observandam esse (Ad Quir.* III 66). We understand it in this way : that there
is an authority of the Church which does not involve any contradiction or revolt
against the authority of Jesus Christ, which can only confirm the *disciplina Dei*,
and which for its part is not negated by the authority of Jesus Christ, by the
disciplina Dei, but is established, confirmed and yet also defined and delimited
by it. *Ut sacrilega esset partitio, si fides vel in minimo articulo separatim ab
homine penderet, sic ludibrio Deum palam habent, qui praeteritis ministris, per quos
loquitur, illum se magistrum recipere simulant* (Calvin, *Comm. on Act* 15²⁸, *C.R.*
48, 362). The Church has a genuine authority.

Under the Word and therefore under Holy Scripture the Church
does have and exercise genuine authority. It has and exercises it
by being obedient, concretely obedient, by claiming for itself not a
direct, but only a mediate authority, not a material but a formal, not
an absolute but a relative. It has and exercises it by refraining
from any direct appeal to Jesus Christ and the Holy Spirit in support
of its words and attitudes and decisions, by not trying to speak out
as though it were infallible and final, but by subordinating itself
to Jesus Christ and the Holy Spirit in the form in which Jesus Christ
and the Holy Spirit is actually present and gracious to it, that is,
in His attestation by the prophets and apostles, in the differentiation
from its own witness conditioned by its written nature. Therefore,
it has and exercises it in the concrete humility which consists in
the recognition that in Holy Scripture it has over it everywhere and
always and in every respect its Lord and Judge : in the incompleteness of its own knowing and acting and speaking which that involves,
in the openness to reformation through the Word of God which constantly confronts it in Holy Scripture. It is in this way, in this
concrete subordination to the Word of God, that it has and exercises
genuine authority. What is meant is genuine, human authority, i.e.,
a genuine capacity to attain and demonstrate it by its words and
attitudes and decisions, by its whole existence : not with the superiority of heaven over earth, of eternity over time, of God over man,
but with that of earthly elders over earthly children ; not only with
the meaning and force of a natural ordering, but, as in the Old Testament commandment, in the sense of the sign to which the natural
order is consecrated and exalted in the sphere of God's people ; in
such a way, then, that the human superiority attained and demonstrated reflects the superiority of heaven over earth, of eternity over

time, of God over man ; in such a way, then, that the latter superiority is reflected in that which it attains and demonstrates like the light of the sun in water. How can the water try to pretend that it is the sun ? How can it try even to make out that the reflecting of the sun is a property immanent to it ? And when and where is water a pure and infallible and final reflector of the sun ? Yet it cannot be denied that when the sun shines it does reflect its light. And in this sense the Church has and exercises a genuine, human authority. It is genuine, therefore, not only in the sense that it is there and has its place in the same way as amongst men it is there and has a place in the relationship between elders and children, or rulers and subjects. But—and here it escapes all creaturely analogies—it is genuine in the sense that within this creaturely subordination and to that extent in the analogy it is also a sign (only a sign but a chosen and appointed sign) of that subordination to the Word of God in which the Church itself lives and to attest which it is commissioned and empowered in virtue of this ordering. In respect of this genuine human authority of the Church we have to go further and say that far from being only a remarkable and doubtful instance of human authority in general, far from there being a human authority in general, in the idea of authority or the reality of natural or historical laws, ecclesiastical authority is a reflection of the authority of God in His revelation in relation to all other authorities in the human sphere. It is true, original, primal authority, the type of all other authority. This is just as certain as that fatherhood is found first not on earth but in heaven, not among men but in God Himself. Similarly, the authority of the Church is the reflection of the heavenly divine fatherhood revealed in Jesus Christ and not of any creaturely fatherhood. Because there is revelation and the Church, there is also the family and the state, not *vice versa*. If the order of the family or the state wants to be and have genuine authority, it can do so only as an imitation of the authority of the Church. It can live only by the fact that there is first of all the authority of the Church. The authority of the Church is not open to question, like all other authority. Yet we must not forget that all this depends on the authority of the Church being genuine. And this depends on the Church itself being obedient, concretely obedient, and therefore standing not above or alongside, but under the Word of God. The authority of the Church disintegrates and ceases to have this typical primal significance in relation to all other authorities if the Church tries to renounce that obedience, if it tries to be and exercise the essential authority of God instead of the human authority which is a sign.

" They alone are spiritual fathers, who rule and direct us by the Word of God "(Luther. *Gr. Kat., Bek. Schr. d. ev.-luth. K.* 1930, 601, 29). *Certe nemo erit in ecclesia idoneus doctor, qui non filii Dei ante fuerit discipulus ac rite institutus in eius schola : quando sola eius autoritas valere debet* (Calvin, *Comm. on* 1 *Jn.* 1[1], *C.R.* 55, 300).

Our first question is how this genuine authority, the authority of the Church under the Word, comes into being. Our starting point in replying is that the Church is constituted as the Church by a common hearing and receiving of the Word of God. The common action of hearing and receiving is partly contemporary : it takes place among those who belong to the same age and period of the Church. But to a much greater extent it is non-contemporary : it takes place among those who belonged to an earlier and those who belonged to a later age in the Church, between the present age and those which preceded it. A common hearing and receiving is necessarily involved either way where the Church is the Church. The life of the Church is the life of the members of a body. Where there is any attempt to break loose from the community of hearing and receiving necessarily involved, any attempt to hear and receive the Word of God in isolation—even the Word of God in the form of Holy Scripture—there is no Church, and no real hearing and receiving of the Word of God ; for the Word of God is not spoken to individuals, but to the Church of God and to individuals only in the Church. The Word of God itself, therefore, demands this community of hearing and receiving. Those who really hear and receive it do so in this community. They would not hear and receive it if they tried to withdraw from this community.

But this common action is made concrete in the Church's confession. We will take the concept first in its most general sense. Confession in the most general sense is the accounting and responding which in the Church we owe one another and have to receive from one another in relation to the hearing and receiving of the Word of God. Confessing is the confirmation of that common action. I have not heard and received alone and for myself, but as a member of the one body of the Church. In confessing, I make known in the Church the faith I have received by and from the Word of God. I declare that my faith cannot be kept to myself as though it were a private matter. I acknowledge the general and public character of my faith by laying it before the generality, the public of the Church. I do not do this to force it on the Church in the peculiar form in which I necessarily hold it, as though I were presuming either to want or to be able to rule in the Church with my faith as it is mine. On the contrary, I do it to submit it to the verdict of the Church, to enter into debate with the rest of the Church about the common faith of the Church, a debate in which I may have to be guided, or even opposed and certainly corrected, i.e., an open debate in which I do not set my word on the same footing as the Word of God, but regard it as a question for general consideration according to the Word of God commonly given to the Church. But because my confession is limited in this way, I cannot refrain from confessing, I cannot bury my talent. Irrespective of what may come of it or whether it may be shown that I have received ten talents or only one—I owe it to the Church not to withhold from it my faith, which can be a true faith only in community with its own, just as conversely it cannot be too small a thing for the Church, in order to assure itself afresh of a true faith in the community of faith, in order not to miss anything in its encounter with the Word of God, to take account even of my confession of faith and to enter into a debate which is open on its side as well.

But it is obvious that before I myself make a confession I must myself have heard the confession of the Church, i.e., the confession of the rest of the Church. In my hearing and receiving of the Word of God I cannot separate myself from the Church to which it is addressed. I cannot thrust myself into the debate about a right faith which goes on in the Church without first having listened. Of course, we must presuppose that I do also myself directly hear and receive the Word of God, but not in such a way that I can be content and satisfied with this direct hearing and receiving. If I do not also hear indirectly, if as a member of the Church I have not heard and received its confession of faith which is prior to mine—heard and received it as is proper to the witness of men who are not themselves Jesus Christ but are members of His earthly body before me—how can I hear and receive the Word of God ? What right have I to confess and therefore to take part and be heard in that debate ? If my confession is to have weight in the Church, it must be weighted with the fact that I have heard the Church. If I have not heard the Church, I cannot speak to it. I have from the very outset excluded myself from the fellowship of the Church's confession, which is the aim of the debate which goes on in the Church. If I am to confess my faith generally with the whole Church and in that confession be certain that my faith is the right faith, then I must begin with the community of faith and therefore hear the Church's confession of faith as it comes to me from other members of the Church. And for that very reason I recognise an authority, a superiority in the Church : namely, that the confession of others who were before me in the Church and are beside me in the Church is superior to my confession if this really is an accounting and responding in relation to my hearing and receiving of the Word of God, if it really is my confession as that of a member of the body of Christ. This is not a direct but an indirect superiority ; not a material but a formal ; not an absolute but only a relative. In the sign of this superiority, in the confession which is superior to my confession, of those who before and with me are members of the body of the Lord, I see a reflection of the superiority of the Lord Himself—only a reflection, but the reflection of His superiority. And in honouring and loving the Church in this sign—under the sign but none the less truly—I honour and love the Lord of the Church. His Word and kingdom is the Church in which I have to confess my faith. By His Word it lives and with His Word He rules it to this day. I have to remember, of course, that this rule of His in the Church was and still is a rule among sinners.

Therefore, in what I hear as the confession of the Church, I will certainly have to reckon with the possibility of falsehood and error. I cannot safely hear the voice of the Church without also hearing the infallible Word of God Himself. Yet this thought will not be my first thought about the Church and its confession, but a necessarily inserted corrective. My first thought in this respect can and must be a thought of trust and respect which I cannot perhaps have for the men as such who constitute the Church, but which I cannot refuse to the Word of God by which it lives and Jesus Christ rules it. How can I know Jesus Christ as the Lord who has called me by His Word if in relation to the rest of the Church I do not start from the thought that despite and in all the sin of the men who constitute it it too has been called and ruled by the same Word? Because my sins are forgiven me, I am bold to believe and, in spite of the sin of which I am conscious, to confess my faith as created in me by the Word of Christ. And if this is the case then in relation to the rest of the Church and its confession I cannot possibly begin with mistrust and rejection, just as in relation to our parents, no matter who they are or what they are like, we do not begin with mistrust and rejection or with the assertion that we must obey God rather than man, but with trust and respect and therefore, in the limits appointed to them as men, with obedience. As in and with the confession of the Church I hear the infallible Word of God, I have to reckon first and above all with the lordship of Jesus Christ in His Church and the forgiveness of sins, which is operative in the Church ; not with sin and therefore with the possibility of falsehood and error which it involves. And this means that I have not primarily to criticise the confession of the Church as it confronts me as the confession of those who were before me in the Church and are with me in the Church. There will always be time and occasion for criticism. My first duty is to love and respect it as the witness of my fathers and brethren. And it is in the superiority posited by this fact that I shall hear it. And as I do so, as I recognise the superiority of the Church before and beside me, it is to me an authority. This is how the authority of the Church arises. It always arises in this way, that in the community of hearing and receiving the Word of God which constitutes the Church, there is this superiority of the confession of some before others, this honour and love, this hearing of the confession of some by others, before the latter go on to make their own confession. Before both and therefore above both is the Lord of the Church with His Word. Only under His Word can some confess and others hear their confession before they confess themselves. But under His Word there does arise this priority and superiority of some over others, the necessity that in the Church we should listen to other men before we go on to speak. Under His Word there is, therefore, a genuine authority of the Church.

Our next question is : In what does the authority of the Church

consist which arises in this way ? In accordance with what we have
just said we will obviously have to put the question rather more
precisely : In what consists or what is the confession of the Church in
the narrower sense of the concept which we have now reached, the
confession of the Church which I have to receive with trust and
respect, the confession of the some to whom others have to listen
before they can confess ? First, we might mean the totality of voices
which together make up the chorus or choruses of the fathers and
brethren, who as such witness to others how the Word of God has
previously been and is heard and received in the Church. But there
must obviously be a chorus or choruses, not a confusion of many
independent voices, if we are to hear not a cacophonous chaos, but
wholeness and therefore the confession of the Church. A single voice
may perhaps reach us and make itself understood as such, but in it
we cannot possibly hear the confession of the Church. We can hear
the Church only where it is spoken out of a community of hearing and
receiving the Word of God and therefore in fellowship. There must
be two or three according to the saying of Jesus if, subjected with
them to His Word, we are to hear from their lips the confession of the
Church. An individual as such cannot in isolation be to us a father
and brother in the Church. But if there is a chorus or choruses self-
expressed in the higher confession of the Church, so that their word
can be heard and heard as a word of the Church, then we have obviously
to put our question even more precisely : How do these choruses arise,
i.e., how does there arise this common speaking out of the community
of hearing and receiving the Word of God ? We have already described
the life of the Church under the Word as a debate which comes into
being because the members of the Church owe and pay one another
and must receive from one another a mutual accounting, responding
and witness of their faith. If this debate is not idle talk, if it really
takes place on the basis and at the instance of the Word of God commonly heard and received, it has a common end. And what can this
end be if not the common proclamation of the Word of God heard
and received which is the task laid upon the Church with this gift ?
For the sake of this task questions have to be asked and answered in
the Church about faith, about the hearing and receiving of the Word
of God. There has constantly to be a common enquiry concerning a
true faith and to that extent concerning the Word of God as truly
heard and received. This task is the compelling practical ground why
the faith of the individual cannot be, as it appears to be, a private
matter, why the individual with his faith is responsible, why he is
forced to come before the public of the Church, why he has to make
his faith known to others and submit to their judgment, if he is
legitimately to play an active part in that general search after a true
faith. The meaning and purpose of the debate conducted in the
Church is obviously not the debate as such, the encounter, the contact,

the stimulating and instructive exchange on the task of the Church's proclamation. Otherwise it would degenerate into mere talk, or at any rate to the level of preparatory academic discussion such as we might find in a poor theological seminar. But the Church is not a poor theological seminar. Much less is it a religious debating club. Its debate stands under a binding purpose and this purpose is that of union or unions in relation to a true faith. The immediate goal cannot be that of remaining apart, but of coming together and standing together in view of the actual coming together in proclamation. The immediate goal and necessary result of a debate on true faith conducted in the Church is that those who take part in it should make a common confession of their faith.

So far all the ecumenical Church conferences, even that of the summer of 1937, have shared with the conferences of ministers customary in all Protestant Churches the peculiarity (emphasised in this case by the solemnity and publicity of the occasion) that for all the honest protestation that they were acting as a Church the majority of those taking part, and even the leaders, did not appear to see that this is the immediate goal and necessary result of a debate conducted in the Church. What are we to make of attempts at discussion and reunion in which a confession is not at least proposed, in which indeed it is basically not even intended ? (Cf. on this Eduard Thurneysen, " Oxford 1937 " *Kirchenbl. f. d. ref. Schweitz*, 1937, No. 19.)

As a work of man this confession is, of course, subject to more than one reservation. The agreement on which it rests can never be more than a partial agreement, an agreement at definite points, points in the knowledge of the Word of God which are particularly important or controversial in the Church of the time. Other points have to be left open for later or similar discussions. Basically this kind of agreement can never lay claim to more than a preliminary significance. In joy and thankfulness at such agreements the Church cannot escape the possibility that in such further discussions as become necessary they may be again questioned, transcended and corrected by the Word of God as newly read and understood. Indeed, the possibility of mistaken agreement and the necessity of rejecting their authority at a later stage cannot fundamentally be denied. Therefore this agreement cannot claim to be more than a partial and temporary agreement, which takes place in faith and in calling upon the Holy Spirit, a human agreement as seen from the standpoint of the Word of God. On the basis of such an agreement we can speak a common word, but a common human word, not commonly the Word of God. In such a uniting we cannot, therefore, speak from heaven, we cannot speak revelation.

In such agreements in the Church it is better not to claim the prophetic " Thus saith the Lord " and the apostolic " It pleased the Holy Ghost and us " (Ac. 15[28]). The prophets and apostles could and had to speak in that way, but not the Church, which only applies and expounds their witness to revelation.

All these reservations do not alter the fact that wherever there is this agreement, and therefore a Church, debate about true faith has reached its goal, and a Church confession has come into being : human, partial, preliminary, but of the Church, audible, and therefore audible as the expression of a common hearing and receiving of the Word of God—they do not alter the fact that this confession has authority, i.e., the claim to be heard by others before they confess themselves. Where two or three, gathered in the name of the Lord, " after there has been much disputing " (Ac. 15[7]), confess their faith in concert, there I as a member of the Church have reason always to consider this before I intervene in the Church's discussion. That these two or three were really gathered together in the name of the Lord, i.e., really in a common hearing and accepting of the Word of God, I will not deny to them in advance—for I believe in a forgiveness of sins and therefore I also see and understand the Church under the forgiveness of sins. On a closer hearing I may not be able, or may be only partially able, to ascribe to them the presence of this basic presupposition of Church confession. I may have to declare the result of their agreement to be more or less false and therefore their authority wholly or partly unfounded. But this is something which I cannot know in advance. What I can and should and must concede in advance—and the fact of their agreement confirms this prior judgment—is that this presupposition has been fulfilled, that what they say in common they say with the authority of the Church, and that therefore I have always to listen to it. If I wanted to have it otherwise, if I wanted not to give them this honour and love, where would be the love and honour which I owe to their Lord and mine, where would be the seriousness of my hearing and receiving and myself believing and confessing the Word of God in the Church and therefore in community with others ?

To sum up : The authority of the Church is the confession of the Church in the narrower meaning of the concept, i.e., the voice of others in the Church reaching me in specific agreements and common declarations and as such preceding my own faith and the confession of it. Church authority always consists in the documented presence of such agreements. If there are definite limitations in the nature of such agreements and their results, this does not hinder the fact that in this limitation they are and have authority, that they have to be heard by others, and indeed heard before these others speak—that is, especially before they question these agreements and their results and their authority either in part or in whole. It is enough for the moment that they are radically questioned by the Word of God. But this is true of others, too, and of the whole Church. Within this common questioning there does exist this precedence—human, partial, preliminary, but set up as a sign of the basic questioning of the whole Church within the Church—of the confession of the Church over the faith and the confessions of faith of others.

We come now, and at this point we must turn to the concrete historical life of the Church, to the question of the form in which the authority of the Church has this existence. According to what we have just said, there can be no question of the form of ecclesiastical life in history and at the present day—in its totality as a confused and varied juxtaposition of many different and neutralising factors and constructs, traditions and customs, personal or general developments and influences, outwardly or inwardly conditioned determinations— embracing as such the confession and therefore the authority of the Church. As such, history, even ecclesiastical history, has neither divine nor even ecclesiastical authority. The form of a Church confession and therefore the form of Church authority is always that of a decision. The movement of Church affairs, the reality of Christian faith, so far as it knows no questions and therefore no need of answers and therefore agreements, even the emergence of all sorts of questions and answers and the genesis of controversies, even the unrestricted debating of the Church, for all their importance and significance in other directions, cannot as such be the form of the life of the Church in which it becomes the authority of the Church. In their indecision they cannot be heard and respected as the confession of the Church. Ecclesiastical history can be heard and respected as ecclesiastical authority only when there is discussion on the basis of a common hearing and receiving of the Word of God, and in that discussion one of those agreements, and in the documenting of that agreement a common confession, in matters of faith—hence, only when answers are given to the question of a true faith by way of speech and counter-speech, agreement and a common declaration in the face of Holy Scripture. It is not at all the case that this kind of happening cannot be distinguished from others and therefore is swallowed up again in the series of other happenings. But can we not see in any happening we like this answer, agreement and decision ? We can, of course, if we are either God Himself or an impartial spectator and student of ecclesiastical history, impartial, that is, as regards the faith of the Church. What all-seeing God perceives in Church history is always and at every moment—in the good and the bad, to salvation and perdition—an answer, agreement and decision in the face of His own Word entrusted to the Church in Holy Scripture. Because He is the Lord and Judge of all, there is no ecclesiastical authority for Him. And for the impartial spectator and student too, although in a different way, the differences in ecclesiastical life are all smoothed out. Everywhere he sees the same thing, the same attempts to state the essence of Christianity, the same two or three arriving at certain agreements, the same preliminary decisions. He finds everything equally important because everything appears equally unimportant. For the unbiassed historian of churches and heresies in his godlikeness there is ultimately only Church history as a whole, and no Church authority. Church authority only exists for the Church, and the Church only exists where there is faith in the Church's sense, i.e., in obedience to the Word of God.

Where there is faith we do not stand above Church history, like God and in his own way the impartial historian. We stand in Church history. Church history is lived. We are concretely claimed for the task of the common hearing and receiving of the Word of God, for the task of its common proclamation and therefore for discussion concerning true faith. We are claimed because we ourselves are always summoned to confess. We will always be open to projected agreements and Church confessions. In fact we will be on the lookout for them. And from the infinite variety of ecclesiastical happenings, certain events will stand out of themselves in virtue of their content, i.e., in virtue of what they have to say to us in our position in the Church, in our confessional situation, in the face of our encounter with the Word of God and the task which evolves out of it. Whatever may be the case with others in another position and another situation, in this event, and not in the many others, we ourselves encounter the confession and therefore the authority of the Church. Others may be responsible for overlooking this event, not hearing in it the confession of the Church, not acknowledging the authority which we think we perceive in it. And we ourselves will be responsible for overlooking events in which others think they hear the confession of the Church and see its authority. But where in our position and our situation face to face with Holy Scripture we receive an answer, an answer given in the light of Holy Scripture to the question of our faith, there we must hear the confession of the Church and affirm its authority and there, and only there, we can do so. Decision therefore is not merely the Church's confession as such, as laid down in the Church. It is also its recognition in the rest of the Church and its validity as Church authority accorded in that recognition. Decision is, therefore, the institution and existence of the authority of the Church in the entire range of this event : a common decision of those who speak—perhaps centuries ago—and of those who hear to-day. It is in these common decisions, in which a word is spoken here and there it is taken as a word to be respected, it is in the existence of these agreements that we live out the Church's history, and that both in the one case and the other, then and now, in them and in us, there lives the one Church of Jesus Christ. It may be that in both cases, then and now, as their decisions and as our own human decisions in which there is no freedom from sin, these decisions are mistaken, sick and under judgment—when was it otherwise ? But in both cases, then and now, they are made in the light of Holy Scripture and therefore for all their sin they are not without grace, because not without the ruling of the Lord of the Church, not without His pardon. If we believe this—and how can we believe at all, if we do not believe it ?— then caught up in these common decisions, as the hearing Church here face to face with the teaching Church there, and together with it as the confessing Church in these decisions, we will know and love and honour the life of the Church of Jesus Christ and His government and His justification and sanctification of sinful man ; which means concretely, we will accept the Church there as an authority to the Church here, we will concede it that precedence, that right to be heard first, we will make our own confession only in response to its confession.

And now in and because of this common decision, the confession of the Church there, which is prior to the Church here, has a specific historical form : the form of the event which answers the question of the Church here in its own position and situation. This confession has therefore a historical meaning and content ; it has form and contour. It consists in letters, words and statements. It is distinguished from so many other authorities, which might in themselves be an authority for the Church but in actual fact are not, by the fact that according to the will of the Lord of the Church it is this confession which speaks to it, and that according to the will of the same Lord it has heard this confession. If over against God it is and has in itself no more authority than any other human answer, agreement and decision reached in the sphere of His Church, it is now by God Himself as the power that rules the Church, through His Word in face of which it has taken place and been recognised, that within the limits appointed by it, it is exalted to be an authority, a word which has precedence and must be respected. And this exaltation is something which even the godlike historian, who does not think that there can be any such exaltation, has grudgingly to acknowledge as a fact. If he does not stand apart but has his place in the Church and accepts his situation and task in the Church, then he will not merely have to accept the fact as such. In principle, and perhaps also in practice, he will have to see the necessity that he in the Church here should confess the confession of the Church there in its specific historical form, because as the exposition and application of Holy Scripture it has spoken to the Church here in such a way that it must always hear and respect it.

To sum up : on both sides, on the side of those who wield it and also on that of those who recognise it, the form of the Church's authority is determined by a decision in virtue of which the one side speaks in the light of Holy Scripture and the other hears what is spoken in the light of the same Holy Scripture. What is spoken and heard, as distinct from much else that is spoken and heard but not in this unity, constitutes, determines and conditions the form of Church authority.

From this it follows that it is not theologically possible to denote and enumerate the authorities which are and have Church authority in this sense. Church authority is spiritual authority : in all its forms it rests on the fact that there and here, then and now, two decisions meet in obedience to the Word of God and constitute one of these unities of common confession. The unities can, of course, be historically established and morphologically described. By custom, agreement and decision they may become Church law. But because of the spiritual character of these unities it is not possible theologically to say that such and such are Church authority, even though they are clearly established historically, or as Church law. It is not possible as it were to list them in a catalogue of Church authorities. Theologically, the mystery of the twofold decision, the mystery of obedience to the Word of God in which an authority becomes a Church authority and is recognised as such, must always be respected as a decision. Theologically, the contingent aspect of this decision, that it does happen in relation to this or that authority, cannot be made a principle. If that were to happen this authority would be equated with Holy Scripture or the Word of God. And that is what must not happen. Theologically, we can, properly speaking, only point out: (1) that wherever the Church exists and lives there will and must also be Church authority, and in a specific historical form ; and (2) that granted the existence of this authority in a specific historical form, it has as such to be respected. We must now address ourselves to the second of these tasks. In doing so we will try to think through what we have said already with the help of some examples.

1. We assume that between the Church now and here and the Church then and elsewhere there exists a unity of confession in respect of the compass of Holy Scripture, the so-called biblical Canon. We have already touched this question in an earlier context, but we must take it up again, because the fixing of the Canon is the basic act of Church confession and therefore the basic establishment of Church authority. The fact that there exists a Canon of Holy Scripture, i.e., a prophetic-apostolic witness of the revelation of God in Jesus Christ which in principle is prior to all the proclamation, teaching and decision of the Church, is posited in and with revelation itself. What this Canon is, of course, is also decided with revelation by God Himself and therefore in heaven, but not in such a way that the Church on earth is spared from having to decide it itself, that is, to know and confess what is *in concreto* the compass of that witness posited with revelation by God Himself. As a human document, this witness waits for human faith in its character as witness, and therefore for the counter-witness of this human faith. It is marked off by God and therefore in itself, but it waits to be taken and understood as marked off in this way and therefore to become the divine-human basis and law of the Church. It is only by becoming this, only in this decision, that it can be. It is only by being taken and understood and attested that it is marked off for us and exercises its function as a first and dominant sign of divine revelation. If the Canon has divine authority from God and in itself, its establishment as the Canon, its designation and delimitation as such, is an act of the Church, an act of its faith, its knowledge, its confession. Does that mean that the divine authority of the Canon is surrendered to human self-will ? We could say that only if we were not confident that the prophetic and apostolic witness

has the power to speak for itself with divine authority, and therefor to awaken a corresponding counter-witness to its authenticity in the Church, if in spite of the fact that that witness has been given it, we regarded the Church as a playground of human self-will instead of the sphere of the lordship of Jesus Christ. If we believe that the Lord is mightier than the sin which indisputably reigns in the Church, if we believe that He is the victor in the struggle against grace which is undoubtedly widespread even in the Church, then we can count on it that a genuine knowledge and confession in respect of the Canon, and therefore a knowledge and confession of the genuine Canon, is not at least impossible in the Church, not because we have to believe in men, but because if we are not to give up our faith we have to believe in the miracle of grace. But if we can count on this, then in what has been believed and known and confessed in the Church regarding the compass and text of the Canon, we cannot basically and exclusively see a work of human self-will. If the decisions made in this respect by the early and earlier Church are not made in heaven but on earth, to the extent that we do not have to oppose to them another witness in the strength of our own faith, knowledge and confession, to the extent that we do not have to contradict them, when we ourselves hear and receive the Word of God, they come to us and concern us and guide us as earthly pointers to the decision made in heaven. They bind us with the power of Church authority. Even our contradiction, even our different witness, can only be a later one, a liberation from a bondage accepted in the first instance but then shown to be wrong. We have still to hear first, to hear the Church, i.e., the others, the elders in the Church, before we can speak lawfully. I have first to be told by the Church which Scripture is Holy Scripture. The Church has had more than one discussion on the subject. Expressly or tacitly it has later repeated and reaffirmed its agreement to meet certain doubts. Upon each new generation, baptised and instructed in it, and hearing its preaching and called to the preaching office, it lays the confession that this or that belongs or does not belong to the Canon of Holy Scripture. It is only with human, not with divine authority, that this can be said to the younger Church by the older. Similarly, it is only with human, not with divine authority, that in this matter a protest can be made by the Evangelical Church against the different Roman Catholic contribution, against its inclusion of the so-called Old Testament Apocrypha in the Canon. But this confession and this protest is the confession and protest of the Church, in whose fellowship the Word of God must have reached us if we ourselves are to believe and confess it. If the Church can only serve the Word of God and if this service is only a human and, as such, a fallible service, we cannot escape this service, what it says to us in this service has authority, we have to accept it as at first normative for us, and therefore until we are better informed we have to approach the Holy Scripture laid before us by the Church—not otherwise, and in its full compass as presented to us, and therefore without addition or subtraction—the collection of those documents in which we too have to seek the witness of divine revelation. The Church with its existing and already attested faith promises us that we shall not seek this witness in it in vain. Except in its ministerial function, in a human way, by its preaching and instruction on the basis of this Canon, the Church cannot ensure that we shall find this witness in this Canon. We shall find this witness only in virtue of its self-witness, that is, in virtue of the authority of the Holy Ghost. The Church can point us to the decision made in heaven in respect of the genuine Canon. But it can do so only on earth and in earthly fashion, which means in the power and framework of its faith and perception. Therefore, if we are to be able to affirm and repeat it (in the power and framework of our own faith and perception), if there is to be that unity of confession between it and us, its indication or decision requires that direct confirmation by the self-witness of what is attested by it, which can take place only in our own encounter with the Word of God in Holy Scripture. But we have already received this direct confirmation in part when we began to believe as members of the Church. For in what but the Word of God in the Scripture which the Church calls holy have we put our faith? And to receive more of this direct confirmation, we will first have to hold to the indication given us by the Church in its confession of this or that form of the Canon if we do not want to deny and abandon again our own membership of the earthly body of the heavenly Lord. Nor will we ever with our own perhaps different confession be able to break this connexion, or renounce the honour and love which we owe our elders and others in the Church. But first and before we on our part can confess at all in the Church, either to agree or disagree, we always have to believe in the Church and therefore upon the basis proposed to us by the confession of these elders and others in the Church.

In practice, then, the course of things for us as individuals, as newcomers coming to the Church to-day, will be roughly as follows. Our starting point will be a definite agreement with the proposal made us by the earlier and rest of the Church, in which we already find ourselves when we believe in the Word of God in Holy Scripture. But we shall then find that the content of this proposal can be used by us only in part, and very much in part, i.e., we shall find the further witness of revelation which the Church promises us only in definite parts of the Canon indicated to us, but in others we shall not find it. It may and probably will be the case that we are not able to find it in the greater part of the Canon indicated to us. But assuming that this is so, it is much more important to establish the positive side : that we have actually found it in one, even if only a small, part of what is proposed. If this is really the case, if we think we have received a direct confirmation in respect of at any rate a smaller part of what is proposed (let us say in respect of certain psalms, or gospels, or epistles, or even specific passages in these books), this may incline us to judge favourably in respect of the rest of what is proposed. And this pre-judgment will at once acquire a practical significance if it is not just a matter of our opinion, if in these few parts of the Church's Canon or even these few passages we have found not merely the probable echo of our own feeling and judgment, but objectively the witness of divine revelation and therefore the Word of God as the Word of our Lord and of the Lord of His Church, if in hearing them we have really come to the obedience of faith. Placed in this obedience and *ipso facto* brought into agreement, even if only partial, with the witness of the Church, we shall definitely be ready to hear further this witness in relation to the Canon, and therefore not to cease but to continue searching the witness of the Word of God in those parts of the proposed Canon so far closed to us. On the basis of our limited but real consent to the confession of the Church, we shall be basically ready to reckon with the fact that if a much bigger section of the proposed Canon is silent for us, the fault may not be in what is proposed, but in some small degree in ourselves. Of course, it may be in what is proposed if it is a human and fallible proposal. But why should it not just as easily be in ourselves ? And if we have to agree with it at one point by virtue of our own faith and perception, if the Lord of the Church has made known to us at one point the human and fallible service of His Church, why should it not be more natural to seek the fault in future in ourselves, and therefore to remain open to the confession of the Church and therefore to continue our investigation of the witness of divine revelation in the rest of the proposed Canon in the light of this confession and its authority ? Again, it will be the case in practice that no individual completes this inquiry in such a way that on the basis of his own faith and perception, his confession always coincides with the then confession of the Church. Rather, we all have to reckon with the fact that for us definite and perhaps very large parts of the Church's Canon will be closed to our life's end, that it will be difficult or impossible for us really to hear the witness of revelation promised in respect of these parts too by virtue of our own faith and perception. But equally definitely we can reckon with the fact that the impulse to seek the blame for this certainly abnormal condition in what is proposed to us rather than in ourselves will have been at any rate diminished. And if we believe that in all honesty we are not conscious of any fault of our own in this matter—why should we not ultimately form our own negative private opinion respecting this or that part of the Canon closed to us in this way ? But why should we want to see more than a private opinion in this negative restriction ? Are we so certain that it is right and is it so important that for the sake of it we must challenge the confession of the Church ? Can we not accept the latter, even if we ourselves cannot wholly agree with it on the basis of our own faith and perception ? Are we so convinced of the rightness and importance of our in part negative restriction— which it is presupposed that we ourselves cannot alter again—that even in relation to the rest of the Church and the later Church we are sure that here, in respect of these parts of the Church's Canon which we have rejected, there can be no fulfilment of the promise, as there was for us in respect of the other parts ? With our rejection of these parts can we presume to oppose the Church or its existing confession in the name of the Church itself ? If we are not sure of this, if at bottom we are only putting questions to the Church's confession, on what grounds can we properly contest its churchly authority ? We can make a serious protest against the Church's Canon only when we are so sure of it in content that we are bold to submit it to the judgment of the Church, not merely as our private opinion, but with the responsible intention of replacing, renewing and correcting the Church's confession in relation to the Canon by a new one. This possibility is not excluded. But how serious and difficult it is may be seen from the fact that Luther did not use it in respect of his well-known doubts on the Epistle of James, nor did the 16th century opponents of the Eusebian *Antilegomena*, but they were satisfied to state their doubts merely as private opinions and not to press them. Again, Luther did not try to have raised to an ecclesiastical confession his opinion that the *Loci* of Melanchthon was a *libellum non solum immortalitate, sed canone quoque ecclesiastico dignum* (*De servo arb.* 1525, *W.A.* 18, 601, 5). And it is also worth noting that out of modern biblical criticism which has been so radical in the sphere of private opinions and discussions the desire for a new confession in relation to the Canon has not emerged and confronted the Church in such a way that it has seriously had to take up the question of a new definition of the Canon.

The question of the genuine Canon is not basically closed by the existence of the Church's Canon. Even in the light of the Church's Canon individuals have every right to raise it. Indeed, it is in practice the rule that it is an open question for the individual. But this does not affect in the least the existence and validity of this Canon. So long as it is not abolished or replaced, its proposal remains, and with it its authority and dignity and validity and the need to take it seriously, to have confidence in its promise, i.e., always to return to it. Future instruction is always reserved. The fault may not actually be in us but in the proposal. But this future instruction, like the past, will have to demonstrate itself as an instruction of the Church by the Church and not merely a private indoctrination of individuals. These individuals, however numerous, have not merely to know what they want, but also to want what they know, i.e., they must be bold to test the churchly legitimacy of their intention, which in the first instance can only be a private intention on the basis of a private opinion, by confronting the Church with the clear and responsible demand for a new confession ; a confession which will mean a narrowing or broadening of the Church's Canon or its replacement by a quite different Canon. They must be bold to appeal to the Holy Spirit of Scripture as the Word of God in proof of the necessity of this intention. And they must be bold to expect that this Holy Spirit will witness to the rest of the Church in this way. So long as they are not bold to do this, so long as they will not accept this responsibility, so long as they perhaps do not have the serious desire for it, so long, therefore, as their new confession has not really established itself as the confession of the Church in place of the old one, their objection to the old confession—however remarkable or deserving of consideration it may in fact be—can never have any greater significance than that of a murmuring compared with the authority of the old one. This murmuring can and must remind the Church that its authority is circumscribed and preliminary, a human authority, against which there may be not only murmuring but even serious protest. It can and must bring before the Church the question whether its existing confession in relation to the Canon is still its confession and can and must continue to be so. It can and must summon it to examine itself in respect of its existing confession, and then either to reaffirm in research and doctrine, preaching and instruction, that this is still its confession, or to make a new and better one. But as long as the old proposal is in force, as long as a new proposal is not

responsibly made and adopted and proclaimed as the new decision
of the Church on the basis of new discussion and agreement, the objection to it is only a murmuring to which we cannot give anything like
the same hearing as we give to the voice of the Church. The voice of
the Church and therefore the existing Canon of the Church must
always be heard first, its content investigated and its possibilities
exhausted.

We may ask how the matter stands in relation to the text of the Bible. Is
it possible and necessary to count on a unity of confession in this respect too,
and therefore on a basic text or perhaps even a translation of Holy Scripture
which is ecclesiastically authoritative and has to be respected in the same sense
as the Canon marked off by the Church ? The Roman Catholic Church gives
an affirmative answer, although strangely and characteristically not in respect
of a normative form of the basic Hebrew and Greek text, but only of a normative
Latin translation. It is as such that the Council of Trent defines (*Sess.* IV,
1546, *Denz.* No. 785) the *vetus et vulgata editio, quae longo tot saeculorum usu in
ipsa ecclesia probata est*, and therefore demands : *ut . . . in publicis lectionibus,
disputationibus, praedicationibus et expositionibus pro authentica habeatur et quod
nemo illam reicere quovis praetextu audeat vel praesumat.* We see in this edict
once again the utter self-glorification with which in Catholicism the Church
controls the witness of divine revelation, subjugating the voice of this witness
to its own Latin voice. The procedure is not calculated to invite imitation,
and it has not been imitated on the Evangelical side in relation either to a translation or even to the basic text, so that we do not have to reckon with a unity
of confession in this matter. Of course the legend of the origin of the Septuagint
(Irenaeus, *C. o. h.* III, 21, 2) has a significance that is not altered by the fact
that it is a legend : it raises the legitimate question of a single and authentic
text of Holy Scripture. And we certainly cannot say that this question, whether
in relation to the basic text or translations, is clearly and exclusively a question
of historical philology. The decision on this matter—especially as regards translations, but also incidentally the basic text—is also a question of faith, i.e., of
theological insight. It is, therefore, right and necessary that the Church should
be interested in the biblical text from both standpoints. It should not entrust
and abandon itself to the decisions necessary in new editions of the Bible
without considering the judgment of all kinds of historical and linguistic experts,
a judgment which may be very limited because of its theological or non-theological
background. But at the same time—and at this point I no longer accept my
exposition in the 1927 *Prolegomena*, p. 371 f.—it corresponds to the facts of the
case if the Church is certainly summoned to a constantly recurring task by the
problem of the text, but does not go on to lay down certain confessional results
as in the fixing of the Canon. The fluidity of the basic text, the fact that it
is known to us only in different traditions, but not in a primal form which can
be clearly fixed as such, the obvious openness of the question of the genuine
text—all this belongs to the human and therefore the divinely authoritative being
and character of Holy Scripture, to the freedom of the Word of God in relation
to its readers and expositors, a freedom which we would clearly transgress with
a confessional decision. This is particularly true of translations. Every translation is obviously an explanation. And by its very nature of course—unlike
a confession of faith—it is an explanation for which an individual must usually
take the main responsibility. Even if a translation can actually acquire a certain
tacit authority in the Church, as Luther's did, it is inadvisable to underline this
factual authority by a formal decision and declaration on the part of the Church,
to tie the Church expressly to the private work of an individual, and in this
way to paralyse all further work in the task of translation. Of translations we

can only desire that as many as possible will arise and be disseminated in the Church in order that those who are not linguistic experts may have a share in the task of translation by a mutual comparison and completion. And of the basic text we can only desire that it may always be made known to the Church with the fullest possible addition of variants, i.e., the contribution of tradition in all its variety, and that there may then be and continue to be—from the historical and philological and also from the theological standpoint—the critical consideration of this contribution which this makes possible. A *textus receptus* is not offered by Church confession, or any court to which we can ascribe authority. There are good reasons for this. And if we are not to reckon with new facts, that is, facts which are still unknown, with the future discovery of a primal form which forces itself upon us as the norm, it is impossible to see how the present-day Church can ever reach the point of confession in this matter, i.e., of setting up and proclaiming a *textus receptus* to the Church of the future.

2. We assume that between the Church now and here and the Church then and elsewhere there exists a unity of confession in respect of the authority of the word of specific ecclesiastical teachers, i.e., specific expositors and preachers of the Bible, whose word has in fact emerged from all the words of other expositors and preachers and spoken to the Church of their day and of a later day, and still speaks to the present-day Church, in a way which cannot be said of other teachers of their own or other periods. Because the Church then and since has heard these teachers especially, because it has received their word with particular attention and gratitude, it has made confession of the point. And as the present-day Church we ourselves are summoned to give our assent to this confession of the particular attention which ought to be paid to these teachers. It is a fact which we cannot prove to be theologically necessary, which we cannot postulate, which theologically we cannot prove to be real, but which we can only explain on the assumption of its actuality : that there are " Church fathers " and that these fathers have a definite ecclesiastical authority.

Ecce quo te introduxi : conventus sanctorum istorum non est multitudo popu-laris ; non solum filii sed et patres ecclesiae sunt (Augustine, *C. Jul.* I, 7, 31). *Talibus post apostolos sancta ecclesia plantatoribus, rigatoribus, aedificatoribus, pastoribus, nutritoribus crevit* (*ib.* II, 10, 37). According to this estimate of one who was himself a father, fathers are members of the Church who have actively taken part in the life of the Church in a way which is so distinctive and so obviously different from what the best of others do that they stand out as a particular " convent of saints." Later generations were able to state with greater precision what are the characteristics of a father. Ecclesiastical fathers (*patres ecclesiastici*), according to Roman Catholic doctrine, are " those writers of the Church's past, who distinguished themselves by age, sanctity of life, purity of doctrine and the Church's recognition " (B. Bartmann, *Lehrb. d. Dogm.*[7] 1928, vol. 1, p. 30). They must be distinguished from mere " ecclesiastical writers " (*scriptores eccl.*), to whom these predicates do not belong or belong only in part, among whom we have to reckon an Origen and Lactantius. And distinguished in this way they constitute one of the sources of Church tradition. Among them, and also among the theologians of later times, the papal proclamation then distinguishes " ecclesiastical teachers " (*doctores ecclesiae*), of whom it is thought to be known that with the holy martyrs and virgins they will wear an aureole in Heaven. Amongst those who qualify as such are Ambrose, Augustine, Jerome, Gregory the Great, Athanasius, Basil, Gregory Nazianzus, Chrysostom, Anselm of Canterbury (from 1720), Thomas Aquinas (from 1567), Bonaventure (from 1588), Bernard of Clairvaux (from 1830) and others.

The Reformation obviously did not recognise this theological hierarchy and its importance as a second source of revelation. Of an uncritical subjection to the so-called *consensus patrum*, which according to Catholic doctrine constitutes the criterion of a completely valid proof from the fathers, let alone to the the authority of any one of even the older teachers, there could be no question on the basis of the Evangelical Church and its Scripture principle. Still, the Reformation did regard certain fathers of the Church as *testes veritatis*, accepting that they have to be regarded as in some sense normative, although always under the norm of Holy Scripture. This can easily be shown from Luther as well as Calvin, especially in relation to Augustine. "Where the holy fathers and ancient teachers, who explained and expounded Scripture, do not fall by this plumbline, we will recognise and accept them not alone as expositors of Scripture, but as elect instruments by which God hath spoken and wrought" (*Conf. helv. prior.* of 1536, Art. 3). *Quia enim Ecclesia est Catholica, Deus semper excitavit in diversis locis aliquos, qui consentientem confessionem de sano verae doctrinae intellectu ad confirmationem posteritatis ediderunt. Et bonae mentes valde confirmantur, quando vident, eandem vocem doctrinae omnibus temporibus in Ecclesia sonuisse* (M. Chemnitz, *Loci*, 1591, *Hypomn.* 6). It was not in accordance with the practice of Protestant theology in the age of orthodoxy if occasionally (as in G. Voetius, *Disput.* I, 1648, p. 74 ff.) the distinction between Church fathers and Church writers was in theory completely obliterated, and it was maintained that there can be no question of anything but an impartial hearing of all the voices of the past, that there can be no special authority of particular fathers in the Evangelical Church and its theology.

This theoretical purity was quite out of place, for in the Evangelical Church and its theology the confession had long since found a place for new fathers and "elect instruments," i.e., the Reformers themselves. It is not unnecessary to recall the excesses of this kind of confession as they occurred even in the century of the Reformation. It is a matter for astonishment when only ten years after Luther's death N. Amsdorf declares: *neminem tanta praeditum sapientia, fide, constantia post apostolos fuisse aut deinceps futurum esse, quantum in reverendo viro D. M. Luthero non sine ingenti administratione donorum Dei conspeximus* (Introduction to the Jena edition of Luther's Works, E. A. *Op. lat.* v.a. I, p. 12); or when we are told by Michael Neander (1576), quoted by W. Gass, *Gesch. d. prot. Dogm.* vol. 1, 1854, p. 228: *Non itaque fervet zelo pietatis, qui huius viri* (sc. *Lutheri*) *historiam, labores, pericula, certamina ac plane coelestia dona non saepe cogitat, admiratur ac pro hoc viro Deo agit saepius gratias et qui post Biblia sacra Lutheri libris non primum locum tribuit et magnificat ut coelestem divinum ac preciosum thesaurum . . . Lutherus suam theologiam a priori habuit i.d. ex coelesti quadam revelatione;* or when Andreas Fabricius (1581, *ib.* p. 228) extols him as *theander, megalander,* φωσφόρος θεολόγων, φωστήρ τε καὶ μέγα θαῦμα οἰκουμένης, the prophet and Elijah of Germany, no less unique than Paul and John the Baptist; or when J. Gerhard (*Loci.* 1610 f. *L* XIV 32) seriously found in Luther a fulfilment of Rev. 14[6]: the prophecy of the *angelus volens per medium coeli habens aeternum evangelium*; or when it could be seen written on a Wittenberg stove: "The Word of God and the teaching of Luther will never fail." But the Reformed, too, sometimes spoke in the same way and it was sung of Calvin's *Institutio*:

> Praeter apostolicas, post Christi tempore, chartas
> Huic peperere libro saecula nulla parem.
> (P. Thurius.)

Now behind all these and similar excesses there is the serious fact that in and
with its reformation by the Word of God and in the service of this divine reformation the Church of that period also heard the human word of Luther and Calvin
in such a way that it could no longer consider its earthly historical existence
as a Church without not only the Word of God but also this human word,
without the teaching and instruction of these Reformers. As the Church reformed by the Word of God it became *eo ipso* the Church of Luther, the Church
of Calvin. Both men, and many of their companions with them, actually
possessed and exercised in their lifetimes (as " doctors of Holy Scripture "—
and therefore as spiritual, but because spiritual, not only spiritual leaders of
their Churches) an authority which far exceeded that which they enjoyed in
their local ecclesiastical and academic offices. And in their own spheres they
undoubtedly possessed and exercised this authority right up to the beginning
of the 18th century. If it could have been forgotten in their respective Churches,
the polemics of Catholic opponents would have seen to it that it was always
revived. Against these polemics, and especially the accusation that the Reformation and its Churches were illegitimate, Lutheran orthodoxy introduced
into its dogmatics a proper article *De vocatione beati Lutheri* (cf. J. Gerhard,
Loci 1610 f. *L* XXIII 118 f.; A. Calov, *Systema loc. theol.* 1677 VIII *art.* 3,
c. 2, *qu.* 2; A. Quenstedt, *Theol. did. pol.* 1685 IV *c.* 12, *sect.* 2, *qu.* 3; D. Hollaz,
Ex. theol. acr. 1707 IV *c.* 2, *qu.* 10). Two points are demonstrated : (1) the
regularity of Luther's calling as priest and doctor and (2) the fact of his extraordinary calling. Everywhere in Scripture there are found *vaticinia de opere
reformationis, quae licet disertam et specialem nominis Lutheri mentionem non
faciant, implicite tamen organi, per quod opus illud perficiendum erat, denota-
tionem continent* (J. Gerhard, XXIII, 124). Not rhetorically, but by way of
argument, attention is drawn to Luther's profound and powerful exegesis of
Scripture, his *animus heroicus et in periculis etiam maximis imperterritus*, his
fulfilled prophecies, his position and successes as a preacher of the Word in the
fight against Antichrist. The first subject of the doctrine of the Lutheran
Church is clearly about to become its object. Now it is no accident that the
Reformed dogmatics of the same period, faced with the same external situation,
never gave rise to an article *De ministerio Calvini* or the like, and that there
could not—and if the Reformed want to be true to Calvin, there never can be—a
Calvinism and a Calvinistic Church in the sense in which there is still a Lutheranism and a Lutheran Church. This is not explained merely by a theological
abnegation of human glory, but more decisively by the fact that Calvin's authority
—which in its own sphere was no less powerful than that of Luther—was of a
radically different kind in that it rested far less than Luther's on the impression
of his personality and life and far more on his ecclesiastical teaching as such.
It cannot be ignored that the Lutheran confession of Luther both then and now
comes far too dangerously near to the proclaiming of the basic ecclesiastical
authority and therefore of the divine authority of this man, and thus to a real
endangering of the Scripture principle. The same phenomenon will meet us
again when we consider the problem of the Church confession. Calvin was a
teacher of the Church in a purer sense in that to him more than Luther it was
given to lead the Church by his doctrine, in spite of and in its Calvinian distinctness, to Holy Scripture itself, binding it to its substance and only in the concern for the substance to himself. But within these limits he undoubtedly exercised in the Reformed Church and its theology the same function as that of
Luther on the Lutheran side. A voice from the 17th century which is also
instructive in content will perhaps attest this in place of many others : that of
Abraham Heidan, who in the prolegomena of his *Corpus Theol. chr.* 1676, in
the context of a review of the most important dogmatic literature which he
could recommend to his students makes honourable mention of Melanchthon
and then goes on to say : *Sed sublimitatis characterem et verum ὕψος in Calvino*

*miror, qui ita me quandoque attollit et sublimen rapit, ut non sim amplius apud
me. Si ab ullo a Calvino me θεολογεῖν didicisse gloriari possum. . . . Hic aliquid
dicam, iuvenes, quod velim vos memori mente recondere : non ab alio autore melius
disci, quomodo et in explicationibus et in disputationibus utendum sit verbo Dei :
hic solus concionari docet.*

With the authority of the Reformation confession (and also with it the acceptance of the Evangelical Scripture principle, i.e., with the divine authority of
the biblical witness of revelation), the ecclesiastical authority of the Reformers
began to fade in the Evangelical Church from the beginning of the 18th century
and was finally eclipsed. One of Luther's " prophecies " was definitely fulfilled :
*Tum enim multi volentes esse magistri surgent, qui praetextu pietatis perversa
docebunt et brevi subvertent omnia, quae nos longo tempore et maximo labore aedific-
avimus. Manebit tamen Christus regnans usque ad finem mundi, sed mirabiliter,
ut sub papatu (Comm. Gal. 4⁰ W.A. 40 I 611, 17).* Certainly the firm popularity
which has been retained by the figure of Luther even in modern developments,
and in particular the estimation as an apostle of freedom of conscience or a
religious personality or a German which he has been accorded more recently
on every possible or impossible count, is no substitute for a recognition of his
ecclesiastical signification as a Reformer and Church teacher. The same is
naturally true of the different strains of " historical Calvinism." The Reformers
enjoyed ecclesiastical authority, and will recover it, only where the Reformation
confession has authority. But this, too, stands or falls with the acceptance of
the Evangelical Scripture principle, or materially with the divine authority of
Holy Scripture. Where this is recognised, the recognition of the ecclesiastical
authority of the Reformers as expositors and preachers of Holy Scripture will
be automatically ensured. So, too, will assent to the former confession of the
Church.

What is certain is that the authority of the Reformers in the Evangelical
Church is analogous to that of the " Church fathers," i.e., " Church teachers,"
in Roman Catholicism. This means that although in the latter case the matter
is wrongly related to the doctrine of tradition as a second source of revelation,
we cannot ignore the problem actually raised, and act as though there were
for us no " elect instruments " but only an equally significant or insignificant
collection of " ecclesiastical writers." Already in the sphere of a true and Evangelical knowledge of the Word of God there are outstanding teachers of Holy
Scripture who as such have to be regarded as outstanding teachers of the Church.
The question is, how and in what limits they have to be regarded in this way.
But it has also to be considered whether in these limits they have not to be
regarded in a much stricter sense as what they are than the fathers of Catholicism.

To get to the root of this matter we have to be clear especially
about this point. Holy Scripture in its divine authority speaks to
each generation in the Church in the form of a definitely defined Canon.
To that extent it speaks with human authority, the authority of the
preceding Church. But similarly, it never speaks to any generation
or individual in the Church alone, as the naked, written word which
has come down to us. It speaks to us as to those who belong to the
fellowship of the Church and have a place in its history. Most frequently, perhaps, it speaks externally not as the word written and
read but as the word preached. But even as direct readers we cannot
withdraw from our particular place in the Church which has baptised
and instructed us, or from its witness with regard to the understanding
of what we now undertake to read and understand. If Holy Scripture
alone is the divine teacher in the school in which we find ourselves

when we find ourselves in the Church, we will not want to find ourselves in this school of the Church without fellow-pupils, without cooperation with them, without the readiness to be instructed by older and more experienced fellow-pupils : as fellow-pupils, but to be instructed. And basically the older and more experienced fellow-pupil is simply the Church teacher. He is, in fact, older and more experienced in a qualified sense of the words. He is not only a son but a father in the Church. We have to be instructed by him. But the fact that he is so is something which can only happen. We have to treat it as a presupposition. Therefore if we are asked how we came to accept the existence of these teachers, we can only reply with a counter-question : how can we be members of the Church and obedient to the Word of God and not do so ? What is sure is that the Church hears—and it is only as its members and not as spaceless and timeless monads that we hear the Word of God in Scripture. But if we hear it as members of the Church, then we also hear the Church, and therefore we do not hear the echo of the Word of God only or first of all in our own voice, but in the voice of others, those who were before us in the Church. All others, and all who were before us ? No, not all, but those who according to the confession of the Church have spoken and still speak in such a way that others had and still have to listen to them. Those, then, in whose voice, according to the confession of the rest of the Church, we have to hear the Church's voice, whom we have to hear therefore with the authority of the Church. Can we deny in principle the existence of these older and more experienced fellow-pupils, and therefore the ecclesiastical authority of particular teachers ? Surely not in principle. And even in practice we could not do so without the danger and suspicion that the real concern of the self-glorifying which we enjoy as those who hear only the Word of God is a secret emancipation from a genuine hearing of the Word of God rather than the assertion of that Evangelical Scripture principle of which we perhaps make such ostentatious parade.

An interesting peripheral phenomenon of Neo-Protestantism is the peculiar behaviour of the so-called Biblicism whose existence and character are strikingly presented in Gottfried Menken (1768–1831) of Bremen, a writer who has never received sufficient notice in dogmatic history. Even in his youth the characteristic complaint was made against Menken that it was " his obsession to try to construct his Christianity out of the Bible alone " (Gildemeister, *Leben und Werke des Dr. G. Menken*, 1861, II, 7). That is the more or less explicit programme of this modern Biblicism. " My reading is very limited yet very extended ; it begins with Moses and ends with John. The Bible and the Bible alone I read and study " (*ib.* I, p. 21). He is not concerned with " what is old or new, with defending or attacking, with assent to the doctrine of any ecclesiastical party, with orthodoxy or heterodoxy, but only with the pure and genuine teaching of the Bible " (*Schriften*, 1858 f. VII, p. 256). And the Church ? Menken prefers to avoid the word. For him and for all modern Biblicists it is a question of " Christianity," " reality " the " truth," the " kingdom of God." The Church is " the eternally pure possessor and preserver of the divine." Yet only too often its doctrine has " come under the influence of a passing philosophy or the superstitiously venerated theology of the fathers " (*Schriften* VII, p. 264). " In any case, where is the Church ? Is it in the East or the West ? Does it gather under the staff of the ecumenical Patriarch in Constantinople or under the threefold crown of the Pope at Rome ? Finding no rest or portion in the world, did it long ago retire with the ancient Syrian Christians into the heart of Southern India or with the Waldenses into the valleys of Piedmont ? In the fellowship of the Holy Ghost did it infallibly and irrevocably express itself at the Diet of Augsburg or at the Council of Trent or at the National Synod of Dort ? Or finally is the true and perfect idea of Christian truth and doctrine to be found in the *Idea fidei Fratrum* ? These few questions point to many things and embrace a large part of Christianity ; but many different events, and systems and confessions and millions of Christians are outside their scope : Nestorians, Monophysites, Mennonites, Arminians, Jansenists, Mystics and Quakers ; and many others, who all make claim to the name of the Christian Church and the treasure of Christian orthodoxy. These few questions are enough to show that, if we are not ignorant, or if after the customary manner and usage of sectarianism which becomes almost second nature, when we use the word Church we do not regard the confession of the Fathers and the sum total of those who agree with it as the only Christian fellowship in which true doctrine is to be found and to which alone, therefore, or primarily the name of Church belongs, it is not easy even to know what the Church believes and teaches. At an informative glance at so many different periods, countries, languages, systems, costumes and customs, at the confusion and tumult of so many different and contradictory and warring sects, at the medley of so many different confessions and catechisms, it seems difficult and almost impossible to find a standpoint where with insight and material truth we can say : I believe and teach what the Church believes and teaches " (*Schriften* VII, p. 238). In these circumstances how can the Church have authority ? " What is offered me as old is honoured by you as such only because it is found in a 16th-century catechism from the Palatinate or Saxony, or because an 11th-century Archbishop of Canterbury or a 5th-century Bishop of Hippo thought in this way and formulated and determined the matter accordingly. But if you could add to these human authorities a greater one in the utterances of a 2nd-century Bishop of Lyons, which you cannot, it would not make any material difference. For it does not matter to me to learn how Ursin or Luther or Anselm or Augustine or Irenaeus thought about the matter and formulated and determined it—they and their decisions are too new. I want that which is old, original and solely authentic : Holy Scripture itself " (*Schriften*, VII, p. 263 f.). If these statements and arguments had been handed down without name or context, we might suppose that their author was of the Enlightenment instead of the passionate opponent of the Enlightenment which Menken actually was. And we find a similar agreement with Neo-Protestant anti-confessionalism in the later writer J. T. Beck, and partly too in Hofmann of Erlangen, and occasionally even in A. Schlatter. What does this agreement mean ? We obviously have to ask whether here the Bible individually read and autonomously understood and expounded is not set up with the same sovereignty as others have exalted reason or feeling or experience or history as the one principle of theology ? In this context does not the special treatment of the Bible—to the extent that it does not come under the relativism with which the Church is considered—take on something of self-glorification ? Are we not dealing with a pious, but in its audacity no less explicitly modern leap into direct immediacy, with a laying hold of revelation, which, involving as it does a jettisoning of the fathers, although it purports to be a laying hold of the Bible, is perhaps something very different from the obedience of faith which only occurs when revelation lays hold of us by the word of the Bible ? By nature is this absolutism of the Bible any different from that other absolutism which constituted the decisive characteristic of the spirit and system of the 18th century as it culminated in the Enlighten-ment ? And can it be very different in its consequences ? Will those who will have the Bible alone as their master, as though Church history began again with them, really refrain from mastering the Bible ? In the vacuum of their own seeking which this involves, will they perhaps hear Scripture better than in the sphere of the Church ? In actual fact, there has never been a Biblicist who for all his grandiloquent appeal directly to Scripture against the fathers and tradi-tion has proved himself so independent of the spirit and philosophy of his age and especially of his favourite religious ideas that in his teaching he has really allowed the Bible and the Bible alone to speak reliably by means or in spite of his anti-traditionalism. On the contrary, in the very Neo-Protestant peculiarities which we find at crucial points especially in Menken but also in J. T. Beck, we are instructed that it is not advisable for serious students of Scripture so blithely to ignore the 16th century catechisms of the Palatinate and Saxony, or that 5th century Bishop of Hippo, or to refuse the guidance and correction afforded by the existence of Church fathers, as that biblicist programme involves. Other-wise there may be too easy and close an approximation to all kinds of other modern Titanisms. The Biblicism of the Reformers, as distinct from modern Biblicism, did not make this approximation because not in spite but in applica-tion of the Evangelical Scripture principle it kept itself free from this anti-traditionalism. J. A. Bengel, whose name is often mentioned in this context, showed at this point much greater wisdom than his more recent followers. Of course, we must not ignore but properly respect the fact that this modern Biblicism did find itself in a relative opposition to Neo-Protestantism generally. It did give a necessary reminder of the Evangelical Scripture principle and in its own way it made an effective modern application of it at a crucial period. By way of it some important and true exegetical discoveries were made, and its outstanding representatives had a great personal dignity. But again that cannot prevent us from definitely rejecting its procedure in relation to the fathers as a basically liberal undertaking, just as we reject the thoughtlessness and lack of respect shown by all Neo-Protestantism in this regard.

Neither in principle nor in practice, therefore, can we deny the existence of the ecclesiastical authority of specific teachers in the Church. But if this is the case, then it is of itself understandable theologically—assuming that it is a fact—that in the Evangelical Churches it was the Reformers who acquired this authority. If our Churches confessed that they were reformed by the Word of God and not simply by Luther and Calvin, their reformation did take place by the witness borne to them by Luther and Calvin. Therefore the witness of Luther and Calvin is decisive and essential for their exist-ence as this Church, as the Churches reformed in this way, and there-fore for the whole contingency of their existence as the Church of Jesus Christ. This may not be true as a constitutive, but it is certainly true as a regulative principle. If they free themselves from this witness they are no longer these Churches and therefore no longer contingently the Church of Jesus Christ. But supposing that by a new contingent fact they were brought beyond the Reformation and therefore loosed from the authority of the Reformers, and that they recognised the fact just as consciously and definitely as they formerly recognised the Reformation and therefore the authority of the Reformers ? Why should such a development be impossible ?

20

That it has taken place has been asserted more than once in the last 400 years. The first time was in the 16th century itself and in the lifetime of the Reformers, when various sectarian groups tried to explain the work of Luther and Calvin as merely preparatory, an introductory stage already passed, to that third kingdom of the Spirit initiated by their own insights. The same process, the replacement of the conviction by a new one which made the Reformation and the authority of the Reformers out of date, was repeated in the 17th century when the English Independents attempted their radical reconstruction of the life of the Church, at the beginning of the 18th century when Pietism enjoyed its first period of expansion, again when Schleiermacher, with his characteristic genius, summed up and gave form to the whole theological contribution of the century, and again at the beginning of the 19th century when the great awakening swept Evangelical Europe. It was repeated again in certain religio-ecclesiastical phenomena which accompanied the recent political revolution in Germany. The remarkable thing is that although in these centuries the Evangelical Churches were widely and deeply separated from their Reformation origin, so far there has never been any actual and decisive severance of these Churches from the authority of their origin. That authority was often more misunderstood than understood, but it was always reasserted and exercised. More than once—at any rate in Pietism and the awakening—the best and most effective feature in these supposed innovations, quite contrary to their original impulse, consisted in a partial rediscovery and renewal of the Reformation inheritance. Constructive power was displayed by only one of the 16th-century communities which separated themselves from Rome and were now moving away from the Reformers. This was the Church of England, which from the very first had been not so much an Evangelical Church as a final achievement of the great reforming attempt of the late Middle Ages carried through with the help of Lutheran and Calvinistic influences. Every other product of this movement sooner or later had to choose between condemning itself to a precarious isolation like the Unitarians in Poland and Siebenbürgen or reversing the movement as far as it had gone, and in some sense and to some degree, perhaps with all kinds of evasions and diminutions, continuing to recognise the authority of the Reformers. Of course, pure Neo-Protestantism means a break with the Reformation. But in these four centuries there was very little pure Neo-Protestantism. If in the 19th century the Evangelical Church and its theology had built on the foundation of Schleiermacher's *Reden über die Religion* and *Glaubenslehre*, it would have become purely Neo-Protestant, and fulfilled the intentions of the humanists and enthusiasts of the 16th century by breaking with the Reformation. But although the Neo-Protestant infection went deep, wisely the Church did not build on Schleiermacher and was not therefore reconstructed. It was a purely literary fancy if about 1900 anyone dared coolly describe Schleiermacher as the "Church father of the 19th century." In spite of the greatness of his achievement and the intensity of his influence, the theology of Schleiermacher became only the starting-point and centre of an esoteric tradition in the Evangelical Church, but not the contingent fact which separated the Evangelical Churches from their Reformation origin and forced them into new paths. In his deepest intentions, as he finally revealed them in his letters—destroying any illusions about his connexion with the Reformation—Schleiermacher did not find any successor among the leading theologians of the 19th century. But his relatively most loyal personal disciples, August Twesten and Alexander Schweizer, made it their life's task to interpret him, the one in the Lutheran, the other in the Reformed sense, as the true fulfilment and continuation of the work of the Reformers. That they did not and could not succeed in this is another matter. But by trying to do so they at least admitted that Schleiermacher's theology was not a factor by which the Church could be refashioned, thus reverting—with all kinds of misunderstandings into a recognition of the supreme authority of the Reformers. And had not

Schleiermacher himself finally prepared the way for this return by his participation in the Reformation celebrations of 1817 and 1830—in spite of his deepest intentions ? In this form the recognition of the Reformers in the 19th century was increasingly reaccepted. Even those who in fact went quite different paths did not want to admit that they were not covered and justified on these paths by their shadow. If it was necessary skilfully to adapt them for this purpose, as was done especially by A. Ritschl and his disciples, there was no longer any desire to cease appealing to them at every opportunity, and wherever possible pretending to be their most loyal followers. Paul de Lagarde, whom we can place alongside Schleiermacher as one of the few pure Neo-Protestants, was completely alone in his fierce aversion to Luther. And even his disciples, the so-called religio-historical school, accepted his verdict only in the weakened form that we find in the historical construction of E. Troeltsch. For the rest they hastened—this time under cover of the hero-worship of Carlyle—to join in the general praise of the Reformers. At root the attitude of more recent Evangelical theology to the Reformers gives rise to many questions. And the same is true of the relation of more recent Evangelical Churches, of the part played in modern proclamation by references and appeals to the Reformers, by the awakening and honouring of their memory, by the utilisation of their writings and individual thoughts. There is no doubt that in doing this there are many who are either the victims of serious illusions regarding their own agreement with the Reformers, or else combine their honouring and celebrating of the persons of the Reformers with variations from their teaching which put in a strange light the loyalty professed to them. There is no doubt that the construction usually brought in to help—an affirmation of the Reformers and a simultaneous and vigorous denial of the " orthodoxy of the 17th century," which is decked out with all the characteristics of a bogey—is historically and in content quite impossible. But the remarkable fact remains that there was a sense of obligation to this loyalty to the Reformers, that there was a hesitation to confess a really new Protestantism, that the most outspoken Neo-Protestants were often the most eager to emphasise their Lutheranism, and even their Calvinism (e.g., at the Calvin celebrations of 1909). How much easier it would have been if they could have freed themselves from this historical burden and left Luther and Calvin as well as orthodoxy quite resolutely behind. But actually to make this break was not so simple, and in view of the difficulties in the way there is no point in bringing against these generations the charge that they were dishonest and illogical. The law which initiated the Evangelical Church in the 16th century was in fact stronger than all the aberrations of which members have been guilty in recent centuries. In spite of Neo-Protestantism there had been no obvious emergence of a new law to reinitiate the Church. Whether it wanted or not, it was still the Church of Luther and Calvin. This is the secret of the strange picture which it presented at this period in its relation to the Reformers. Is it not almost touching to see with what tenderness even the latest form of Neo-Protestantism, the conception of the so-called " German Christians," still thinks that it can and should maintain the relationship at any rate to Luther and in part to Calvin, even though it is also felt necessary to appeal with a greater emphasis than ever before to new revelations sandwiched between ? Would a really emergent " German National Church " actually dare to renounce the claim to stand in this continuity, and the claim which that would mean for it ? And if it won that freedom could it be more than a new sect ? So far the ecclesiastical authority of the Reformers has been stronger than all kinds of attempts at liberation. And now in face of all this unusual development we must not overlook one thing especially : and that is that the remarkable concern of the newer Protestantism for its relationship to the Reformers had as its necessary concomitant a new and active interest in them from the historical standpoint. The same 19th century which, carrying Schleiermacher's

secret tradition, brought Neo-Protestantism to full flower was also so constantly occupied with the memory of the Reformers that by comprehensive
new editions of their writings and a ceaseless historical investigation of their
life and work it was bound to contribute signally to the living maintenance and
in part emergence of their original form, and in this way it involuntarily but
necessarily introduced the Reformers themselves to check its own interpretations
and misinterpretations, as was not the case in much of the age of orthodoxy.
The work of these generations saw to it that the ecclesiastical authority of the
Reformers—they could now speak and be heard again in a new way—was not
merely the shadow of a remote past, but could again acquire the most up-to-date
significance. If that was not the intention, e.g., of the Strassburg editor of
Calvin's works, that is how it turned out apart from and in spite of his intention.
In the light of the last fifteen years, we can now speak of a Luther renaissance
in the Evangelical Churches and their theology, and also of a corresponding
Calvin renaissance. Even to-day the two phenomena are equivocal. But we
cannot deny them. And if we see and understand them in a proper connexion
with preceding developments, we can at any rate see in them a final symptom
that so far there is no question of having to reckon with any turning away from
the authority of the Reformers to the authority of a new fact on which the Church
can be grounded.

If such a development is not fundamentally impossible, we are
taught by our consideration of history so far that much greater things
are necessary for it to take place. Neo-Protestantism has certainly
not been capable of it. One thing after another may arise in the
Church. There may be all kinds of ecclesiastical movements. Strong
reactions may be produced. But these things cannot of themselves
give rise to a fact which will found a Church like the witness of Luther
and Calvin. They cannot compel the Church to a new confession.
But unless this happens and a corresponding new confession emerges,
unless someone feels competent even seriously to demand the replacement of the authority of the Reformers by another authority, not to
speak of the Church as such taking note of this replacement and
pronouncing upon it, unless this is the case, then involuntarily perhaps
but in fact the Church returns to this authority, and there is good
reason—exactly as in the problem of the Canon—to accept the previous
confession of the Church at any rate as a hypothesis, that is, as the
basis on which we have to stand : in other words, not to play truant
from the school of Luther and Calvin until we are better instructed,
but to learn in it what there is to be learned. It is a matter of instruction in understanding Holy Scripture, when and to the extent that the
Reformers are genuine teachers of the Church. This instruction must
never be neglected because of the consideration that there might
ultimately be others who can give us this instruction better. So long
as these other teachers are not to hand, we have reason to stick to
those who are. Indeed it is not impossible that these teachers—who
have not so far been replaced—may with the confirmation of Holy
Scripture itself continue to remain as they have remained till now.
But now we must ask whether and in what sense alongside the
authority of the Reformers there can be any serious question of an

authority of later teachers within the Evangelical Church itself, and also perhaps of certain pre-Reformation witnesses. Neither can be dismissed in principle; but in practice, i.e., in answering the question where and in whom the Church has to recognise these further teachers, we cannot be too careful. Not every Church witness who at some point and period is an example and stimulus to certain members of the Church is for that reason a father, to whom the Church can and must trust itself, in the sense that the line held by him is the right one for it. This real guidance of the Church, as it was exercised by Luther and Calvin, is a rare thing. We must examine closely what we are demanding of ourselves and especially the Church when under some strong impression we believe that here or there we have found this paternal authority. As individuals we can learn from many. We can learn from those who have no significance or only a limited significance. We can learn even from those who are weak and mis-guided. But that does not make it right to regard all those to whom we are indebted for something as teachers of the Church and, where possible, to try to force them upon the rest of the Church. We shall destroy the confidence of the Church and create confusion if we rush on to make announcements of this kind, which by their nature can only be a matter for the experience and confession of the whole Church, and not for individual preference. The questions which we have to ask are as follows.

(*a*) Has the one proposed been an expositor of Scripture who, like the Reformers, has helped and can still help the Church to understand the Word of God rightly? There are many of whom that definitely cannot be said, even though we cannot deny to their Christian think-ing, speaking and writing, depth, seriousness and force, even though they perhaps led a most godly and charitable life. We have to re-member that both these appearances, the intellectual and the religious and moral, are of themselves equivocal: they are to be found even in notorious heretics. The question and only question which has to be asked—in the light of Scripture itself—is whether the teacher in ques-tion has expounded Scripture and proclaimed the Word of God, and done it correctly. It is not the acuity and depth, nor even the holiness of the Christian which builds the Church, but only the Word of God. Therefore when we ask whether and to what extent anyone can have authority in the Church, the question which is ultimately decisive is whether he has served the Word of God.

(*b*) If it is true that we have to recognise this authority first in the Reformers—because they rightly expounded the Word of God, then a second question which we have to put to all teachers before and after them is how their teaching stands in relation to the confession of the Reformation? The primitive and mediæval Catholic Church which had not yet been reformed by the Word of God, but as distinct from the post-Tridentine Church had also not denied the Reformation,

is for us the one Church of Jesus Christ, whose witness we must therefore be ready to hear in principle.   And we also cannot refrain from
believing that there may be a real if secret fellowship of saints and
therefore the Church of Jesus Christ in post-Tridentine Catholicism
and the Neo-Protestant aberration.   We have therefore no *a priori*
cause to stop our ears in any direction when we ask concerning the
fathers of the Church.

An Athanasius and an Augustine were for the Reformers themselves so obviously fathers in this special sense, and their struggles and
achievements were so plainly the presuppositions of the Reformation
confession, that it would be good for us to hear them as they were
heard in the 16th century and in the later Evangelical Church.   In
their case, as in all the others, even the oldest, we must also not hear
them in so far, that is, as they could and did become not so much
the fathers of the Reformation as of post-Tridentine Catholicism.   The
Reformation and the authority of the Reformers does undoubtedly
involve retrospective selection and decision, and of such a kind that
we cannot count unreservedly with the authority of any one of the
older fathers.

The Roman Catholic criterion of the *consensus patrum* must be interpreted
by us in this sense, that the doctors of the Early Church are an authority for us
to the extent that their doctrine did not need to be reformed, but as a correct
exposition of Holy Scripture bore prior witness to the Reformation.   Within
these limits the Evangelical Church and its theology, if it really is to be a Church
of Jesus Christ, can never listen too much to the witness of the primitive and
mediæval Church.   There are elements in this witness which can only be rightly
seen and assessed in the light of the Reformation, which were only really brought
out at the Reformation.   Conversely, there are certain decisive elements in the
witness of the Reformers which can only be understood in their positive relationship to the witness of the primitive and mediæval Church.   Even in the 17th
century the real or supposed awareness of this relationship was so strong that
a comprehensive work could appear in Strassburg under the title *Thomas Aquinas
veritatis evangelicae confessor*.   Optimistically, the most important factor was
overlooked, which makes Thomas—of whom neither the Reformers nor their
contemporary opponents had any exact knowledge—the typical father of post-
Tridentine Catholicism with his doctrine of the *Principia*.   Yet it is the case
that on a careful reading we do find even in Thomas lines of thought which, if
they do not point us to the Reformation, certainly do not point us to Jesuist
Rome.   And there is a lot that the Evangelical theologian can learn in Thomas
as a well-chosen compendium of all preceding tradition.   The same is even more
true of an Anselm of Canterbury and in another way of a Bonaventura.   There
can be no question, of course, of an unreserved attachment to these pre-Reformation authorities unless we are to be hopelessly launched on the way of Roman
Catholicism.

The same question has to be put even more sharply to post-
Tridentine Catholic and Neo-Protestant theologians.   Modern Catholic
or Neo-Protestant teaching may voluntarily or involuntarily state and
accentuate Evangelical truth.   If it does us this service, why should
we not gratefully acknowledge it, and there, too, hear the voice of the

fathers ? There is a right exposition of Holy Scripture and therefore
an attestation of the confession of the Reformation even in the Church
which resists the Reformation and in that which later repudiates it.
As correct exposition it must be heard, no matter where it comes from.
But within the Evangelical Church which holds the Reformation
presupposition we can never put this question too sharply.

It is justifiable and meaningful to regard as Church fathers in this special
sense the in their own way and to some extent great men of the age of orthodoxy
in so far as according to its own conscious intention the theology of that period
did try to be ecclesiastical scholarship, a comprehensive exposition of Holy
Scripture and a comprehensive development of the Reformation confession. We
must be careful in our estimate of the authority of these orthodox theologians,
because the beginnings of later arbitrariness do in fact appear in their dogmatic
systems. Among the later ones, although there is no question of Neo-Protestantism in the narrower sense of the concept, we have to note that they frequently
find themselves in a mutual opposition and reaction which were as such historically necessary and beneficial, but which had their limitations in the incidental
and onesided character of the antitheses and often in the concessions which were
made at the very outset to the opposition. We surely do most honour to these
later writers when we accept their authority only to the extent that they repeated
and renewed for their own age the witness of the Reformers.

(c) A real teacher of the Church who can be seriously accepted as
such can be definitely recognised by the responsibility to the Church
which is peculiar to his witness. There has always been a right exposition of Scripture, in the sense of the Reformers, which has lacked this
characteristic because it has, so to speak, been done in its own strength
and at its own risk. Neither as hearers and learners nor speakers and
teachers have its authors had before them the whole Church, the
universality of its needs and hopes, errors and genuine experiences,
knowledge and confession, but only a specific part, the problems
of their own life and their more immediate temporal, geographical or
spiritual environment. This need not be a lack in every respect. In
some respects it may be an advantage. Exposition and teaching of
this kind has often had most important results. But only that expositor
is qualified to be a teacher of the Church who is not essentially or
strictly an improviser and individualist but who sees clearly that he
must state his case and bear his witness to the whole Church before
and after him, who has not merely been alone with God and the Bible
and the writings of the Reformers, but who has stood before the whole
Church with God and the Bible and the writings of the Reformers,
and is therefore confident and competent to speak not only to himself
or to an incidental or selected circle, but intelligibly, responsibly and
authoritatively to the whole Church.

This forward and backward universality was a particular feature of the witness
of the Reformers themselves, but also of that of the orthodox fathers, whereas
it is completely lacking in the newer theology, which had far too much the stamp
of occasional literature. Yet we have to allow that, measured by this criterion,
Schleiermacher's *Glaubenslehre* would stand, and also the works of many of his

nearest successors like A. Schweizer, J. A. Dorner, A. E. Biedermann, F. H. R. Frank and, in its own way, that of H. Lüdemann and from the Ritschlian school the dogmatics of Julius Kaftan. Indeed, to some extent they have won a kind of ecclesiastical authority in their own definite circles. If genius often prefers other ways, it must be noted that no one can be a teacher of the Church by virtue of genius alone. It must also be noted that a preference for other ways as such does not prove any one to be a genius.

(*d*) It has to be asked further whether as an expositor of Scripture, in agreement with the witness of the Reformers and in responsibility to the Church, the proposed father has spoken and still speaks a word which means actual decision for the later Church. Both in the past and more recently many things have been said which are true and important and also responsible and of universal relevance but which do not have this significance later, and perhaps can never have it again, or may perhaps some day recapture it. Some words which have been spoken in the Church and for the Church come home to us, and others do not come home to us for a variety of reasons. A teacher of the Church is the one who in exposition of Holy Scripture has something to say which comes home to us. But that means that we must always reckon with the existence of latent teachers of the Church. Many of those whom we no longer hear to-day will never be heard again. But there are also others who, although they are not heard to-day, will one day be heard again. What remains of their authority is in the first instance only a memory : the neutral memory of a great name, bound up with facts and relationships and his reactions to them which are also neutral. Their authority is then suspended, as it were. It would be a very arbitrary undertaking to try artificially to assert them again. If they come to life again in the power of the Holy Scripture which they are concerned to expound, Scripture itself will see to their authority. We have to reckon with this possibility. We cannot, therefore, ignore such recollections of former authority which have now become neutral. Their hour might suddenly come. Those who are now silent might speak again, as according to the confession of the Church they once spoke to their age. The facts and circumstances in relation to which their names and reactions and word were once significant may suddenly return—for there is nothing new under the sun—and the decision which they demand may again be a relevant one. We have perhaps overlooked something if this has not already happened. In the modern period the Reformers themselves were for a long time only latent teachers of the Church. And it is to the Church's good that it has not ceased to give them its attention. We have to see to it that we are open and ready on every side. Already the past history of the Church has become its up-to-date story in the most unexpected places. Something which we thought to be a thing of the past perhaps becomes suddenly alive. And as in the case of the Canon it is perhaps our fault if many who can and ought to be fathers to us are simply dead and have nothing to say.

What can be the practical reach and significance of the authority of such a teacher of the Church ? It is quite certain that his figure cannot in any way be equated with those of the prophets and apostles, nor can his writings even remotely try to crowd out and replace their writings or his witness their witness. Again, it is not a matter of the Church being not only directed and bound to Holy Scripture but also committed to give particular honour and loyalty to the ἐξουσία of " Lutheranism " or the ἐξουσία of " Calvinism." A Church perhaps thinks it right and important to value its history and historical form as such, and therefore the memory of its teaching as that of the heroes and leading figures in this history. But it may do this in the purely secular sphere and be commended for doing so on purely human grounds. And this has nothing whatever to do with the recognition of the ecclesiastical authority of its teachers. " Lutheranism " and " Calvinism " are hypostases for which there are many secular parallels. An enthusiasm for them is not in itself blameworthy. But like many similar enthusiasms it stands under the question whether it is not like the angel worship which was so strictly forbidden in Gal. 4⁸ᶠ·., Col. 2⁸· ²⁰ᶠ·, i.e., something which may crowd out that worship of God in spirit and in truth which makes the Church the Church. In point of fact the teacher of the Church and his personality and definite influence and his conception of Christianity and of the Church's past and future and his positive and negative historical relationships all add up to a law which can be comprehended by human reason and fulfilled as an ideal, and as such they are an excellent source of natural theology. Once this law has been set up, once the Church has decided that apart from being a Christian and Evangelical Church, it must also be Lutheran or Calvinist, then we have to reckon with the possibility that the inevitable will happen, that when we give natural theology an inch it will want a yard, it will want everything : the Church will become more and more Lutheran or Calvinist and proportionately less and less Christian and Evangelical. This deflection always threatens when the disciples of a Church teacher acquire even very slightly the character of an independent group. The authority of such a teacher can only be indirect, formal and relative, i.e., it can only be what the concept prescribes : the authority of a human doctor of Holy Scripture whose task it is to acquaint his pupils not so much with himself as with the object which is his and their concern, to point and bind them not so much to himself as to this object. But if something different takes place between a Church teacher and his pupils, if the teacher forces himself—the fault may be his or that of the pupils—into a position side by side with the object which he has to make known and binding, that is not merely an encroachment, but it means that the very thing which cannot and should not intentionally take place in this relationship has taken place. For this object will not tolerate anything side by side with it. We cannot be pupils of

Holy Scripture and also pupils of the person and system of a second master. That is to destroy the Church and the school of the Church. The pupils have no longer to learn from this teacher, they have to beware of him. When this happens there are no real masters, or we do not honour the real masters. The real masters who are honoured as they ought to be are those by whose person and system the pupils are educated and fashioned to be only scholars of Holy Scripture. The honour which we ought to pay these real masters is to let them carry out their service, to be willingly educated and fashioned in this way. We only dishonour them if we make the honouring of their person and system an independent interest. But we also have to remember that where it is a matter of the authority of a Church teacher it is a matter of the confession of the Church as in the Canon and the confessions. A real teacher of the Church has not spoken to and for himself but to and for the Church of his time. Therefore it is not his individual voice as such but in that voice the voice of the Church of the time which gives him the authority of a teacher for us. Again, it may not be wrong to value him as a private person, or his doctrine as a private doctrine, to honour, e.g., in Luther the hero, doctor, poet, theological genius and the like. But it is still the case that this estimation, however great and well-grounded, does not contribute in any way to his recognition as a teacher of the Church. Indeed, it might be a hindrance to his recognition as a teacher of the Church. Infatuated with his private figure, we might not love him in his mission and function. If we love him as a teacher of the Church, then we listen to the Church when we listen to him. Again, that means above all that we accept his instruction in Holy Scripture as such—the Early Church witnesses to him as a servant of the Word of God. But it must also mean that we have to measure him not only by the Scripture which he expounds but also by the confession of the Church whose voice he is : which means concretely by the confession of the Church of his day. Therefore in cases of doubt we do not have to understand and assess Scripture and the confession by the standard of this or that teacher, but we have to understand and assess every teacher by the standard of Scripture and the confession ; we have not to put Socrates above the truth, but the truth above Socrates—and that in order to give Socrates the honour due to him. The real teacher of the Church never can and never will be accepted and treated by us in any other way.

It is the case, then, that the recognition of the ecclesiastical authority of a teacher not only does not exclude but strictly demands a critical, and even a very critical, attitude to him. When we hear him, that means that we have to pay attention to the lines of his exposition and make them our own. But when we do that, we cannot simply repeat what he has drawn. We have to copy it in responsibility to the Scripture and confession which have spoken to us through him. And that means that we have to draw it out and and develop it. And that means also that we have also not to listen to him : at those points, that is, where everything considered we do not find that his voice agrees with the voice of Scripture and the voice of the Church speaking independently in the confession. There can be as little question of a repristination of the teaching of Luther and Calvin as of the orthodoxy of the 17th century in the present rediscovery and reacknowledgment of the authority of the Reformers. If there were, we would not be giving them the honour due to them, but refusing it. Not those who repeat the doctrine most faithfully, but those who reflect upon it most faithfully so that they can then expound it as their own doctrine, are their most faithful pupils. But to reflect on their doctrine means to draw out the line indicated by them as it needs to be drawn in accordance with a new investigation of Scripture and the confession in reply to modern questions. As witnesses accredited by the confession of the Church of their day, they have ecclesiastical authority for the Church of to-day. Therefore the Church of to-day, with all the experience which it has since acquired and the responsibility in which it itself stands, has to listen to them. This may mean deviation and contradiction as regards the historical form of their doctrine. The Church of to-day would not be accepting them if it were simply accepting or reproducing them in their historical form. It would be accepting them not as the Church of to-day, not obedient to its own calling along the lines of the Reformation, but as an institute of antiquities—the worst dishonour of which it could be guilty for all its well-meant veneration.

Therefore the positive significance of the ecclesiastical authority of a teacher consists in this : that in its existence the Church has a " form of doctrine," which with its human limitations can, of course, only be a token and copy of what is called this in Rom. 6^{17}, but which as a token and copy still has a right and necessary function. The existence of prominent teachers of the Church creates a concrete inequality in the Church. If there are many teachers in the Church, not every one is called to be a teacher of the Church. Within the same office some are of higher rank, some of lower, some have to sketch out the Church's line, others to copy it. Does that mean that an ecclesiastico-theological hierarchy is set up ? From this standpoint would it perhaps be possible to justify the special office of the bishop or even the Papacy ? Certainly not, if the teacher of the Church is rightly understood in his character as a copy and token of the form of the doctrine given to us, which can only be Jesus Christ, i.e., Holy Scripture itself. The small inequality in the Church posited, of course, with its own existence cannot then actualise the great inequality between its Head and members—which is the usual intention when a special episcopate is instituted—but only denote it. But it will denote it—and this is the special dynamic of the existence of an ecclesiastical teacher—on the basis of an event which really took place in the life of the Church and of the corresponding confession of the Church itself. Compared with this, of what significance is the existence of an episcopate furnished with even the most exalted prerogatives ? In the existence of a real teacher of the Church the human direction of the Church has become a fact, while the demand for a special episcopate is always based on and leads to the postulate that while this direction is a good thing, and a necessary thing, in effect its existence is always bound up with the charismatic endowment of those who exercise it. As that direction which is event and fact, and recognised and acknowledged as such by the Church, it is the task of the existence of a teacher of the Church, in so far as it is understood as a mission and charge of Jesus Christ, quite independently of the question of charismatic endowment which is unavoidable in relation to a bishop, to denote and display and emphasise the power and the true and in the last resort only direction of the Church by Jesus Christ or by Holy Scripture itself. And the Church always needs this denoting, displaying and emphasising. It is not a matter of indifference whether the Church and especially those who hold teaching office in the Church in their mode of thought and teaching are always looking to the human pattern of the attitude and direction of Luther and Calvin, and also of the fathers of the Early Church, or whether alone with God and the Bible they are looking to create and fulfil individual ideals of prophecy, priesthood and pastorate, or may even be looking to constitute and realise the fortuitous pattern laid down by the then representatives of a superior episcopate. Obviously the authority of a Reformer cannot be replaced either by our own authority on the basis of individual Bible study or by that of the changing representatives of such an office. It is as a spiritual authority, and in its restricted character as a copy and token of the real " form of doctrine," that the authority of an ecclesiastical teacher will be a real and effective and not a fictitious authority, able to exercise with the Canon and confession of the Church that concrete discipline, especially within the teaching Church, for the sake of which authority is necessary.

3. We assume that between the Church to-day and here and the Church then and elsewhere there must be a unity of confession in respect of specific declarations of the common faith, i.e., of confession in the strictest sense of the concept : the confession of the Church. A Church confession is a formulation and proclamation of the insight which the Church has been given in certain directions into the revelation attested by Scripture, reached on the basis of common deliberation and decision. It will be our first task to explain the decisive elements in this definition.

(*a*) The confession of the Church involves the formulation and proclamation of a definite ecclesiastical understanding of the revelation attested in Holy Scripture. Therefore from the outset the confession and its authority does not stand above or alongside, but as a Church confession under Holy Scripture. Therefore it does not speak by direct revelation, and what it says cannot be a source of revelation for the Church which listens to it.

Even believing in the presence and help of the Holy Spirit a council has " no power to make new articles of faith " (Luther, *Von den Konziliis und Kirchen*, 1539, *W.A.* 50, 607, 7). " For articles of faith must not grow on earth through concilia as by new and secret inspiration. But they must be openly given and revealed from heaven by the Holy Ghost. Otherwise they are not articles of faith " (*ib.* 551, 28). Councils "ought to confess and maintain the old faith against new articles " (*ib.* 618, 11). Similarly, e.g., the Nicene Council "did not newly discover or set up the article of the divinity of Christ, as though it had never previously existed in the Church " (*ib.* 551, 15). The truth which had been revealed from the start was rather upheld and confirmed and declared by that Council in relation to the demands of the period, that is, against the Arian heresy.

Self-evidently the confession of the Church cannot speak on the basis of a supposed and immediate revelation which is different from that attested in Holy Scripture. It does not confess God in history or God in nature, as individuals, and it may be many individuals, in the Church think they see Him. It does not confess this or that element of Church tradition and custom. It confesses Jesus Christ, and Jesus Christ as attested by the prophets and apostles. It confesses the one Word of God, beside whom there is no other. This does not prevent it confessing in definite historical situations, in answer to definite questions, contradicting and explaining in a definite antithesis. But it does prevent it speaking on any other ground than Holy Scripture or any other truth than that attested in Holy Scripture.

Non alibi quaeramus Deum quam in eius verbo, nihil de ipso cogitemus nisi cum eius verbo, de ipso nihil loquamur nisi per eius verbum. This general rule has to be observed with particular care when it is a matter of a *publica confessio.* We must see to it, *ut nihil in ea deprehendatur, quam ipsissima scripturae veritas . . . ut non ex variis hominum placitis consarcinata, sed ad rectam scripturae normam diligenter exacta sit.* That it is a *conceptae intus fidei testificatio* does not prevent *ut solida sit et sincera,* and for that reason it must be drawn *e puris scripturae fontibus* (Calvin, *Adv. P. Caroli calumnias,* 1545, *C.R.* 7, 311 f.). *Si hodie suos consessus haberent sancti patres, uno ore clamarent, nihil sibi minus licuisse, vel etiam fuisse in animo, quam tradere quidquam, nisi Christo praeeunte, qui illis unicus, sicut et nobis, magister fuit* (*Comm. Ac.* 15² *C.R.* 38, 341).

The confession of the Church explains Scripture, it expounds and applies it. It is, therefore, a commentary. It is not enough for it to repeat biblical texts. It can point to them in order to make clear in what connexion it wishes to explain Scripture. But at bottom it must speak in its own words, in the words and therefore in the speech of its age.

Neque vero confessionem duntaxat eam recipimus, quae ex solis scripturae verbis superstitiose contexta sit et consuta, sed iis verbis conscribendam esse contendimus, quae et sensum habeant intra scripturae veritatem limitatum et quam minimum habeant asperitatis (Calvin, *C.R.* 7, 312).

But because it is the Church itself which speaks, listening to Scripture and bearing its witness to its truth, the confession cannot be anything more than a commentary, or try to stand on the same level as Scripture.

The other symbols and adduced writings are not judges like Holy Scripture, but only the witness and declaration of faith how in disputed articles Holy Scripture has always been understood and expounded in the Church of God by those living at the time, and contrary doctrines rejected and condemned (*Form. Conc. Epit., De summ. Concept,* 8). *Interpretationis autem humanae seu Ecclesiasticae autoritas est Ecclesiasticae tantum, non divina et Canonica : quia non immediate ab ipso Deo dictata est, sed hominum deliberatione et consilio tradita, quorum alii plus, alii minus habent lucis, alii maiora, alii minora dona intelligendi et explicandi res divinas. Proinde interpretatio Scripturae Ecclesiastica atque ita et Ecclesiastica Confessio seu expositio fidei quaecunque, item et Catechesis et quaecunque piorum hominum scriptio seu tractatio . . . non est simpliciter probanda, admittenda atque acceptanda, sed cum hac exceptione et conditione, quatenus cum Scriptura Sacra, tanquam cum unico fonte veritatis caelestis et salvificae, fundamento immoto et regula fidei et bonorum operum nunquam fallente, consentit* (Polanus, *Synt. Theol. chr.* 1600, p. 711).

(*b*) The confession of the Church involves the expression of an insight given to the Church. Holy Scripture has been given to the Church as the source of its knowledge of divine revelation. It is not individuals, or any group of individuals, but the Church itself, represented by those who can and must speak in its name, which has to give an account of its faith to itself and the world in the confession of the Church. The confession speaks for and to the one universal Church. Obviously we cannot and must not understand this in any legal or statistical sense. We can only understand it spiritually. From the legalistic and statistical standpoint, no confession (not even those of the so-named " general " councils) ever arose and was proclaimed as the confession of the whole Church for the whole Church. From the legal and statistical standpoint every confession has only been a confession in the Church, proceeding from one part and directed to the other parts of the Church. Its calling to speak in the name of the one universal Church to the one universal Church is grounded only on the Holy Scripture which is given to the one universal Church as the witness of the one revelation given to all. Therefore no ultimately decisive justification can be adduced for the summoning and meeting and special authorisation of individual members of the Church as " authors " of a confession except once again Holy Scripture itself. Those who find themselves assembled to draw up and impose a confession (even though in virtue of their office as the representatives of many communities they are a more or less legitimate " synod " or " council ") dare only adduce to others as their authorisation and authority that they have come together in obedience to the Word of God and have to confess this or that. It is quite clear that when they do this they put themselves under the judgment of the Word of God, accepting the risk that they may be publicly disavowed and given the lie by the Word of God to which they appeal and think and declare that they are obedient. There is no confession without this risk and danger. And obviously for those who venture to come before the Church with a confession, there is also the danger that they will have the witness of Holy Scripture in their favour, but that in the rest of the Church they will speak to deaf ears and therefore, isolated with the Word of God, they will necessarily be in their Church heretics and oddities, unauthorised innovators or even invincible reactionaries. But this does not alter the fact that if the claim of their confession to be Church confession is to be heard or even discussed they must dare to speak to the whole Church in the name of the whole Church. How can it be otherwise if they are really trying to speak from Holy Scripture and to attest the Word of God ? The courage to accept the risk involved is at least one test of the genuineness of their enterprise and action. A confession is not a Church confession which seeks only to represent the importance of one group in the Church or to declare and prove the equal justification of particular interests which may perhaps represent only the local or national peculiarity of one part of the Church which is supposed to be the will of God. However limited and oppressed the authors of a confession may be in the church, if they really have to confess, i.e., to confess the Word of God, they cannot possibly dare to speak of themselves and from their own small corner, or in order to secure recognition for themselves and this corner. Not fearing to make the unheard-of claim which this involves, they must be confident to speak from and to the one universal Church. They must accept responsibility for expressing the voice of the *una sancta catholica*. Otherwise they must be silent or at any rate not regard their speaking as the confession of the Church. To confess involves a mission within (and also without) the Church. If we are not conscious of any such mission, if we only want to be heard and suffered on specific points, we cannot make any important, i.e., ecclesiastical, confession.

But in a spiritual and not a legal and statistical sense some of the resolutions of early Church Councils were genuine confession, made with that certainty which can be achieved and proved only in the venture of obedience to Scripture, but with that certainty made with a definite claim to speak in the name of the whole Church to the whole Church. And although outwardly at first it might plainly happen in the name of a fragment of the then Church, that is how the Reformed confessions have also spoken. That is why they were so careful to prove their connexion and agreement with the confession of the Early Church. Their intention was not really to expound a faith which only arose in 1517 and which is only the faith of the adherents of certain territories or spiritual communities. What they were trying to confess again was the one old faith of the Church and therefore in their confession they challenged the whole Church, not merely to tolerate this faith, but as they heard it re-confessed to accept it. And from our own days we can add that the confession of the Evangelical Church in Germany, which is so necessary for the present age, although its legal and statistical basis is open to question, cannot remain only the declaration of a party or school, or the theological justification of the standpoint of those who still wish to maintain a biblical-reformed Christianity. Without considering the external and internal risks we must dare to speak in the name of the German Evangelical Church and " to the public of all Evangelical Churches in Germany," aggressively and with the consciousness of a mission. For that reason the Barmen declaration of May 1934 closes with the words : " The Confessional Synod of the German Evangelical Church declares that in the recognition of these truths and the rejection of these errors they find the indispensable theological basis of the German Evangelical Church. . . . It asks all whom it concerns to

return to the unity of faith, love and hope. *Verbum Dei manet in aeternum."*
Declarations which do not take this line, whatever significance they may have,
do not have the significance of Church confessions or the right to be heard as
such. *Confessio fidei traditur in symbolo quasi ex persona totius ecclesiae, quae
per fidem unitur* (Thomas Aquinas, *S. theol.* II² qu. 1 art. 9 ad. 3).

(c) The confession of the Church involves an insight which is given
or gifted to the Church. This is bound up with the fact that it has
not invented its content, but discovered it only in Holy Scripture and
as a gift of the Holy Spirit. But this discovery has to be distinguished
from the kind of discovery which might at any time be the result of
the searching of the Scriptures enjoined upon us. A confession is
distinguished from a summarising of the results of theological work
by the fact that its authors did not set out to comment on the Bible
or to understand the nature of Christianity or practically to preach
again, except that this time this preaching was to everyone. All that
can and should take place at any time. But not every time in which
it can and should take place is also a time of Church confession.

Both in modern times and from the very first it has been done most lavishly
and certainly not without the gift of the Holy Spirit without necessarily involving
a new confession. The need of the latter may have been felt and tentative
attempts made to supply it. But such attempts could not and cannot succeed
if set only against this background. We cannot confess because we would like
to confess in the belief that confession is a good thing. We can confess only
if we must confess. Theological work of a theoretical or practical kind is not the
instrument of this compulsion. Theological work as such is quite unable to
produce a Church confession, although it is indispensable to its formation when
a confession arises, and if it is serious its final goal must always be the Church's
confession.

Church confession is a Church event. It is the result of an encounter of the Church with Holy Scripture, which in its contingency
cannot be brought about by even the most serious theological work.
When in a special situation in the Church Holy Scripture speaks to
the Church, when in view of definite and urgent questions nothing
remains but what Scripture has to say, when in the avoidance of
definite errors we can take refuge in the scriptural truth which opposes
them, when in the Church we cannot lay hold of scriptural truth, but
only receive it, when therefore the Church has not found this truth
but this truth has found the Church—then and then alone can there
be Church confession. The genuine Credo is born out of a need of
the Church, out of a compulsion which in this need is imposed on the
Church by the Word of God, out of the perception of faith which
answers to this compulsion. Credo in the sense of Church confession
the Church can say only when all its other possibilities are exhausted,
when reduced to silence it can say nothing else but Credo. But
then it can and will say it with certainty and power. If the Church's
confession involves an insight given to the Church, then the confession cannot understand itself or rightly let itself be understood as
an exposition of favourite human ideas, or convictions, or the so-called

reflections of faith. It certainly rests on exegesis, but it is more than biblical inquiry. It certainly arises only with a dogmatic consciousness, but it will proclaim more than theologoumena. It is certainly proclamation, but its power will not be only that of edification. The faith of its authors will certainly be heard in it, but it will not be because of this subjective faith that it has a right to be heard. Because and to the extent that it rests on an insight given to the Church, a genuine Church confession can and must speak authoritatively: it cannot simply publish its findings as a subject for discussion and free choice. What the confession formulates and proclaims claims to be Church dogma. In saying Credo it has characterised its pronouncements as those whose content it cannot and will not force on anyone, but with which it challenges everyone to take up a position, to decision whether he can reject them as contrary to the Word of God or must accept them as in agreement with the Word of God. Here again it is Holy Scripture which is the basis of the certainty of the confession and the judge over it. It is Scripture which—in this twofold sense—stands behind dogma.

If this office of Scripture as judge is either forgotten or denied, the confession is unauthentic and unauthoritative inasmuch as it claims to be itself revelation, like Roman Catholic dogma. It is Scripture which—in this twofold sense—makes a confession authentic and therefore authoritative. If the certainty based on it is denied, the confession is unauthentic and unauthoritative inasmuch as it then falls to the level of a non-challenging exposition of human conceptions, as in the far too anthropocentric understanding of confession in both older and more recent congregationalism.

(*d*) The confession of the Church always involves the statement and expression of the insight given to the Church in definite limits. This limitation does not contradict either the intended universality of the confession or the certainty proper to it as Church dogma. On the contrary, it is in this very limitation that it is universal and Church dogma, and therefore has ecclesiastical authority. The dignity and validity of Church confession cannot rival that divine authority. It would rather be destroyed if it wished to do so. It is based on the fact that it is limited by it. Indeed, ultimate and decisive legitimacy is from Holy Scripture to whose witness the Church replies in confession with its own witness. To be limited by its origin and object does not weaken but establishes and confirms its authority as a Church authority. The impulse and courage to make a confession, to accept responsibility for the claim which it raises and to go through with this claim, the capacity for a strictly theological attitude which is not afraid of any consequences, the joy which is the secret of the power of a Church confession—all these are rooted in the fact it is the statement and expression of the insight which is given to the Church in definite limits. No more than this, but—in this negation of any imaginary and therefore impotent infinitude—this all the more really and

concretely in the finite sphere of the Church. In a confession we
always have to do with a definite limit of insight. This emerges first
in the legal and statistical uncertainty which we have already mentioned. Obviously it is never more than a part of the Church which
stands behind a Church confession. One part of the Church has in
a definite need and in a definite faith in that need accepted something definite as the witness of Holy Scripture, and with its own witness
it makes a definite reply to it in the face of other parts of the Church.
Because and to the extent that Holy Scripture is the determining
factor, there is a limitation in all this, and yet by it the authority of
the Church's confession is also established and confirmed.

In the first instance, the limit of Church confession coincides
remarkably with geographical limits.

In the primal forms of a general Christian confession finally brought together
and formulated in the so-called *Apostolicum* we undoubtedly have first the voice
of the European West grouped around the Church of Rome, although with the
constant influence of the East as well. On the other hand, in the Nicene and
Niceno-Constantinopolitan confessions of trinitarian faith in God, and in the
christological definitions of Ephesus and Chalcedon, we have to do for the most
part with the decision of the East—although it was not made without the strong
co-operation of the West. Again, in the important *Arausicanum* II (529), in
which the Church dealt with the suggestions of Augustine, we have a typically
Western confession. The Reformed confessions can and must be understood as
a statement of the faith of the European North—which was again split territori-
ally—and the *Tridentinum* (and the *Vaticanum*, too, with its essentially Italian
majority) as the corresponding answer of the European South. And now that
there are African and Asiatic mission Churches with an ever increasing consciousness of independence, and American Christianity and Church life, in spite of all
its connexions with the European mother-Church, is beginning to develop more
and more into an entity *sui generis*, the confessional inheritance of the early
Church and the Reformation has automatically become *in globo* a European
matter, i.e., it is felt to be so across the seas. It cannot be denied that the definite
limits which can be seen in all confessions stand in a constantly shifting relationship to political, cultural and economic groupings and movements. An exhaustive
understanding of these limits obviously cannot be gained from this standpoint
or from the geographical aspect generally. But there is no doubt that the
problem has to be considered from this standpoint. It may give peculiar strength,
or weakness, to a confession that it is the confession of this group here or that
group there.

But the definite limit of Church confession may also have a
temporal character.

We speak of old and new confessions and both may mean either an underlining or a questioning of their authority. The temporal limitation of Church
confession is very correctly and clearly expressed in the Latin text of the passage
which we have already quoted from the Formula of Concord : *explicant et
ostendunt, quomodo singulis temporibus sacrae literae in articulis controversis in
ecclesia Dei a doctoribus, qui tum vixerunt, intellectae et explicatae fuerint.* But in
this temporal limitation they are, according to the Formula of Concord, genuine
testes veritatis. For example (according to the introduction to the Book of Concord,
Bekenntnisschr. der ev.-luth. Kirche, 1930, 761, 16) it can be said of the Augsburg
Confession that *ne latum quidem unguem vel a rebus ipsis vel a phrasibus quae in*

illa habentur, discedere, sed iuvante nos Domini spiritu summa concordia constanter in pio hoc consensu perseveraturos esse decrevimus. If the present of such a confession has become past, the antiquity which it acquires can guarantee its value. The Church of a later date can then regard it as particularly important to subscribe to this confession, because in so doing it confesses the one unchangeable faith of all ages. It can then indignantly refuse to try to make or receive any individual or new confession of faith " with any confession which it lays alongside the old one " (Formula of Concord, *ib.* 833, 25). But originally, as we see from the contemporary correspondence of Melanchthon, Luther and others, the *Confessio Augustana* was not called a *confessio* at all but only an *apologia*. It is first called a *symbolum* in the preface to the Formula of Concord (*Bekenntnisschr. d. ev.-luth. K.* 1930, 741, 13). With the same delicacy, in its formal and open confession the German Church to-day has refrained from applying the title " confession " to such newly formulated and circulated statements as the Barmen decision, but has been content to call them a " theological declaration " or, in the case of the first free Reformed Synod of January 1934, a " declaration on the right understanding of the Reformation understanding in the modern German Evangelical Church." Yet there can be no doubt that the *Augustana* and the Formula of Concord and also these modern documents do in themselves have many of the characteristics of confessions and therefore of new confessions as compared with the older ones. The *Augustana* and the other Reformed confessions did not want to be confessions in so far as they had no new faith to confess—but they were confessions in so far as they did confess the old faith anew. The necessity and legitimacy of a new statement and expression of the old faith, the need which in certain circumstances cannot be denied to make new decisions in the face of new questions and the equivocal nature of the old confession in respect of this new situation, the lawfulness and duty of saying clearly to-day in what sense we see ourselves compelled to confess with the old confession the Word of God—that is the peculiar value of a new confession, quite irrespective of whether it accepts the name or not. That is how the Nicene Creed came to stand alongside the Apostles', the Niceno-Constantinopolitan alongside the Nicene, the Ephesian and Chalcedonian alongside the Niceno-Constantinopolitan. That is how the Reformation Churches confessed, looking back to and repeating the confession of the Early Church. That is how confession has been made in our days, looking back to and explaining and confirming the Reformation confessions and under declaration and confirmation of the same. In every case a new confession was needed which could not be a new one but only a new and preciser version of the old. In every case the old confession was still valid, but it could not really be valid except in a preciser form and therefore as enlarged by a new confession. More clearly than the geographical, the temporal limitations of Church confessions are mutually conditioned, and the old and the new can and must mutually create and confirm their authority. But it is obvious and cannot be denied that there is a definite limit of insight, that the old confession is enclosed by the new, to the extent that it must be interpreted by it, and the new by the old, to the extent that it can only be an interpretation of it.

But the definiteness of the limit of Church confession has a wider and above all a material character. A confession does not arise as a free and comprehensive exposition of the faith of the Christian Church in such a way that the various confessions confront each other as different expositions of one and the same theme.

If a Church or ecclesiastical fellowship wants to declare its faith as such, perhaps at the head of its constitution, to make clear its nature in relation to the world around it, it can, of course, do so. But it ought not to do more than

name the name of Jesus Christ as the object and Holy Scripture as the source
of its faith, and then relate itself to a real confession. A Church confession
with Church authority will never arise on the basis of so harmless an intention.

A Church confession with Church authority has always arisen in
a definite antithesis and conflict. It always has a pre-history, which
does not consist in the discussion of an academic or even an ecclesiastico-political desire to re-confess the common faith, or in the discussion of the fulfilment of this desire. It consists rather in controversies
in which the existing confession of the common faith and therefore
the existing exposition and application of Holy Scripture is called in
question because the unity of the faith is differently conceived, and
there is such different teaching on the basis of the existing unity that
the unity is obscured and has to be rediscovered. The expression
which is valid and which was once really the expression of unity no
longer suffices. If the Church wants to preserve its unity, it must
give it a more accurate expression : an expression in which a judgment
is pronounced and a decision made in matters of doctrinal difference,
an expression which recognises the one doctrine or the other or perhaps
a third which mediates between them as the doctrine of the Church,
and is therefore confirmed and confessed by the Church. On the basis
of such a pre-history every confession acquires and possesses its own
particular aspect. It is certainly not that of a truncated *summa
theologiae*. Neither is it—not even if it has the form of a catechism—
that of a popular biblical theology or dogmatics. It is rather the aspect
of the Church declaring itself in the act of that definite decision, the
necessity of which makes the confession necessary. When the Church
confesses or when confession is made in the Church, then the Church
or those who confess in the Church stand face to face with what is
claimed to be a definite exegesis of Scripture, perhaps a new one,
perhaps one that has disturbed the Church for some time : or it may
be with a doctrine which claims to be taken from Scripture or related
to it. This confronting doctrine is the occasion of the confession in
that it claims to be the expression of a possible expression no less
justifiable than others of the existing unity of the Church in faith.

We must be clear that, e.g., Arianism and semi-Arianism, which in this way
constituted the occasion of the 4th century confessions, did not arise only with a
claim to be tolerated but with a claim to be the only legitimate expression of the
existing unity in faith. Similarly the Reformation confession has to do with an
opponent which understands and represents its doctrine exclusively. Again, the
dogma of the " German Christians," at any rate at the outset, was not intended to
be that of a trend in the Church, but the new dogma of the German Evangelical
Church. At a first glance the case was rather different with the liberalism of the
18th and 19th centuries, which made an explicit and provisional claim to be no less
justifiable than other movements, and, as a rule, would even go so far as formally
to postulate the existence of a conservative counter-movement as the dialectical
complement of its own existence, something which, e.g., in Switzerland, has
partially attained to the dignity of dogma in the form of a doctrine of the necessity and value of two or even three ecclesiastical trends. In face of opposition

to this—in itself, of course, very liberal—view liberal toleration has, of course, usually reverted very quickly to a fairly extreme intolerance. How can it be otherwise than that behind the proclamation of the equal justification of a doctrine there should stand the declaration of its sole justification ? How can it be otherwise than that heresy, even if only in the attenuated form of a general doctrine of toleration, should want to be not merely one opinion, but the doctrine of truth, the expression of Church unity, and that therefore it is bound to be intolerant whether it will or no ? Even where there is apparently only a claim for sufferance, we have to reckon with the fact that counter-doctrine of this kind is seeking not merely to expand the existing unity of faith, but to destroy it, replacing it by another. The battle of confession must be waged, therefore, as a battle for the very substance, a battle for the life and death of the Church.

In the face of the counter-doctrine the confession turns away again from the existing and now equivocal expression of the unity of faith as it is perhaps presented in an older confession to Holy Scripture as the judge of the controversy which has arisen. Or rather the authors of the confession see that they are bound by Holy Scripture in a different way and direction from their opponents. Therefore they have to understand differently the existing expression of the unity of faith which the emergence of the counter-doctrine has now made equivocal. But they cannot prevent their opponents from appealing to this existing expression. In the form of a decision a new expression of the old unity of faith must now be sought and found : an expression which brings out the other way and direction, in which (unlike the representatives of the counter-doctrine) we find ourselves bound by Holy Scripture, an expression which makes manifest the judgment of Holy Scripture in the current controversy as the confessors claim to have heard it.

In the 4th century the Arians appealed to the *Apostolicum* as well as the Athanasians. Similarly the Antiochenes in the 5th century appealed to the Niceno-Constantinopolitan Creed as well as the Alexandrians. Again in the 16th century the Catholics as well as the Evangelicals appealed to the great Councils of antiquity, and in 1933 the German Christians appealed to the Reformation confessions as well as their opponents. In every case the confession was an attempt to clarify a situation which had become obscure. The opening words of the Formula of Concord : *Credimus, confitemur, docemus* indicate the seriousness and responsibility of these attempts at clarification. *Credimus :* What is at stake and has to be affirmed is the Christian faith demanded by Holy Scripture, the unity of the Church. Therefore no one should think that the conflict and its issue are incidental, a matter which might be settled in some other and less serious way. *Confitemur :* It is not a matter of a free heart-faith of individuals, which may perhaps be possible or actual *in abstracto*, but of the faith of the Church which has to be attested and made known in the Church and through the Church to the world, if the Church is not to abandon its obedience to its Lord. *Docemus :* It is not a matter of an academic or an individual decision but before and behind the confession stands the actual life of the Church. Preaching and instruction will correspond to the confession. It is, therefore, a part of the recurrent worship and congregational life of the Church which is voiced in the confession.

But it is the meaning and intention of a doctrinal decision which in this way has become the content of Church confession that with the

Yes expressed in it, i.e., with the scriptural exegesis and doctrine positively stated in it, a definite No is also said to the counter-doctrine which is its cause, the latter being rejected as an expression of the Church's unity and its churchly status denied. If this was not its intention, what intention could it have? Without the No the Yes would obviously not be a Yes, but a Yes and No; perhaps Yes, perhaps No, but certainly not the Yes of a *credere, confiteri, docere*, not the Yes of a responsibility bound by Holy Scripture and accepted before God and the Church and the world. It is obviously by the No that the clarification of an obscure situation is accomplished in a confession, the completed decision being characterised as decision by a mention and rejection of the counter-decision.

This clarification is made in the language of the Roman Catholic symbols by the usual formula: *Si quis dixerit . . . anathema sit. Anathema sit* does not mean (not at any rate with the accent of modern usage): let him be accursed, but: in accordance with reality let him find himself in the eyes of the whole Church outside the unity of the Church, with his counter-doctrine. Let him no longer claim to represent with this doctrine the doctrine of the Christian Church. Let him be quite clear that he can defend his counter-doctrine only as one which is alien to the Christian faith. The same is said by the formulæ which we find in the Reformation confessions: *Reprobamus, reiicimus, exsecramus, damnamus . . . secus docentes.* The declaration of the first free Reformed Synod of 1934 put it in this way: "Therewith (with the positive statement) is rejected the view . . ." and the Barmen declaration of 1934: "We reject the false doctrine. . . ." It is natural that such formulæ are not pleasant reading for those who defend the doctrines concerned. It has to be remembered that they have not to be applied rashly. It is also understandable historically that Neo-Protestantism regards them as radically hierarchical, uncharitable and abhorrent. But against all possible objections on this score we have to make it clear that the confession has to state something definite, but cannot do so without making it clear that it is not stating something equally definite. In a confession the opponent, and with him the whole Church, have not to hear the No only, but they certainly have to hear it as well. And it is not the case that this No can and will disturb and destroy an existing unity and has therefore to be condemned as a sin against love. It is rather the case that this No makes clear once more that unity of the Church which had been obscured, that it can and will restore that threatened unity, and that it has therefore to be regarded as a particular work of love. It is, of course, self-evident that the confession, with its exposition of the doctrine which is agreeable to Scripture, is to the whole Church a call to the renewal of unity and to the representative of the counter-doctrine in particular an invitation to return to that unity of faith which has now been expressed in a new and more accurate way. For the sake of this invitation he must be told clearly that he needs it, because he is outside this unity, because in defending his counter-doctrine he is *anathema*. In order that a sick man may be treated by a physician, he has to know and accept the fact that he is ill. Confession helps him to do this with its *anathema* or *damnamus*. Now there is no doubt that the whole venture of a confession emerges in this *damnamus*. It is all to the good that when we think we can and should go on to confess, we should accept it as the acid test: If we have not the confidence (or the explicit confidence) to say *damnamus*, then we might as well omit the *credimus, confitemur* and *docemus* and return to the study of theology as before. The time is not ripe for confession. Fear of the *damnamus* is a sure sign: we are not at all certain that the doctrine confessed is really agreeable to Scripture and the expression of the unity of the Church, which we would be confident to maintain and defend as such against its opposite with all the seriousness and responsibility of the *credimus, confitemur, docemus,* simply because we had to. We are wanting to express only an opinion and conviction or even a mere emotion against the opponents of which it would be highly inconsiderate and unreasonable to pronounce a *damnamus.* There is a danger—it necessarily hangs like a sword over every confession—either that we shall sin against an existing unity of faith if we say *damnamus* in what is only a strife of opinions and emotions, or else that basing ourselves on mere opinions and emotions with our *damnamus* we shall separate ourselves from the real unity of the faith now actually represented by the opponents upon whom we have laid our *anathema.* The actuality of this danger of the *damnamus*—with which we can easily pass judgment on ourselves one way or the other—can never emphasise too strongly the seriousness and responsibility with which alone we can legitimately pronounce the *credimus, confitemur, docemus.* But again the danger is no reason why we should not pronounce the No which is inseparably bound up with the confession made in obedience to the Word of God. That doctrinal decision and its expression is already serious, responsible and dangerous in itself and in its positive content. The representatives of the opposite already regard as arrogant, uncharitable and intolerant the *credimus, confitemur, docemus* as such. We have only harmlessly and positively to repeat, e.g., the clauses from the *Apostolicum : conceptus de Spiritu sancto, natus ex Maria virgine . . . tertia die resurrexit a mortuis,* and at once those who deny these clauses all feel that they are attacked and insulted, even though there is no mention of *anathema.* In the measure that an opponent understands the confessing Yes, he will hear the claim which stands behind it, and with the Yes he will hear the perhaps concealed No to his counter-doctrine. If the Yes does not in some way contain the No, it will not be the Yes of a confession. And if—as clever confessors have sometimes attempted, who were not really confessors at all—we try to express the Yes in such a way that the No concealed in it is concealed to as many as possible, that as many as possible can rally under the banner of a very general Yes, this can only take place as intended at the price of the Yes. If we want to boast of the love which lies in this procedure we forget that in wanting to confess our aim was to be precise for the truth's sake and not to generalise, and that the present renunciation of truth certainly cannot take place in the service of love.

It is the No and therefore the differentiation from another supposed insight which gives to a confession its definite characteristics, displaying it in its material distinction from and opposition to other confessions ; in its material distinction from confessions which precede it and are clarified and made more precise by it, or which will follow it and clarify and make it more precise ; in its material opposition to confessions, against whose content it makes a protest or in which a protest is made against its own content. But the aspect which each confession has in distinction from and opposition to others shows us that we have to do with only a limited part of the insight given to the Church. More clearly than the geographical and temporal, the material limitation of Church confessions shows them to be in a mutual parallelism and contradiction which as such compromises all of them in respect of the compass of the insight expressed in them. This parallelism and contradiction is, of course, that of a mutually asserted exclusiveness. By their utterly opposed contradictory definitions of the unity of faith, by their different exposition of Scripture, by their mutual *damnamus,* the confessions reveal the divided nature of the Church itself. Although there is always a feeling for the relation to Jesus Christ and an appeal to Holy Scripture and to certain documents of an earlier existing unity of faith, the relation and appeal have become so widely ineffective that in the decisions which are now necessary there is no unity in faith in Jesus Christ, in the exposition of Holy Scripture and in the understanding of those documents of an earlier unity. There is so little unity that although we can recognise the common confession of the Christian faith in the fact of that appeal, and of the proclaiming the name of Jesus Christ, in the use of His sacraments and perhaps in the confessions of individual Christians, or in individual utterances of the Church, we cannot do so in the confession made concerning these points. And there is no supra-confessional and supposed ecumenical standpoint from which we can look beyond the dialectic of this controversy, wherever possible understanding it as the organic development of a whole in its separate parts and therefore removing the contradictions of the confessions. We should have to take up a place outside the Church and therefore avoid the need to judge concerning the content of the decisions made one way or the other in the Church, we should have to be without a confession, if we were to be able to think and judge supra-confessionally. And in thinking and judging in that way we should have all the confessions against us. For (including Neo-Protestantism) they all want it to be understood that their Yes and No is not a dialectical link which will be absorbed in a higher unity, but the true and indeed the only true expression of the Church's unity.

It does not make any difference to this self-witness of all the confessions— which is inevitable if we presuppose the seriousness and responsibility of real confession—that in the Lutheranism of the 19th century there was a popular theory which expounded the Lutheran confession as the organic centre between the relative aberrations of the Roman Catholic and the Reformed Churches, or that again the Church of England claims to be the organic centre between Catholicism and Protestantism. We can speak of a removal of confessional antitheses, of an approximation to an ecumenical standpoint, only—and necessarily—when the opposition of the earlier confessions of two Churches has been made obsolete by a new and common confession and has become a mere difference in theological thinking, when therefore the earlier *damnamus* has been retracted in the light of mutual understanding of the two confessions. But where new facts like this do not arise, we have to face up to the other fact, that the confessions do to a large extent mutually oppose and limit one another.

If we are conscious of the seriousness and responsibility of our own exposition and doctrine and therefore confession, if we can be confident in faith that with our Yes and No we are obedient to the Word of God, we have to accept this fact and accept it willingly in all its force. But how can this happen from any standpoint without our confession being seriously understood and handled as an invitation to all existing opposites ? But in this case when do we not face the further fact of

the absolute impotence of this invitation? When is there no occasion
to pray that the Lord of the Church Himself should restore the unity
in His Church which we cannot restore without disloyalty to Him?
When do we not face the broader fact of the incapacity, the obvious
limitation of the insight expressed in our own confession? Does not
that which can obviously gain only a very limited hearing and assent
suffer from the limitation of the perception expressed in it, no matter
how honestly its confessors think that in relation to it they are obedient
to God, and how little for loyalty's sake—for they have no other
understanding of Scripture than their own—they are able of themselves
to break through its limitation? This limitation of all the confessions
is not merely seen in their actual parallelism and contradiction. Is
it not a depressing if necessary fact that although all confessions have,
or claim to have, their basis in Holy Scripture, their occasion is always
the arising of an error, i.e., a confusion in the faith and knowledge of
the Church? But that means that the confession is not the exposition
of a genuinely comprehensive insight. If it were, it would triumphantly
precede the error and confusion, not allowing it to arise and develop,
but nipping it in the bud. But unfortunately the confession usually
comes too late. It is only an attempt to cover the well when some
children at least have been drowned and the great wasting of the
Church has already taken place.

How broadly the majority of great heresies have had to develop, how long
it has almost always been left to individuals to oppose them and their solitary
voices were not recognised as the voice of the Church and the onesidedness with
which perhaps they raised their opposition was corrected by the common witness
of the communion of the saints—until finally things reached such a pass that
these forerunners were vindicated, and general understanding and decision
became possible, and a word of the Church, or a word spoken in the name of the
Church, opposed the error and confusion in the Church in the form of a confession!

Better late than never. But the fact that it is " late " marks the
confession clearly as a document of human and therefore limited insight. There is also a further point. Because a confession is occasioned
by error and confusion in the Church, in content it is an answer to
them, and therefore, although it is based on Holy Scripture, in the
choice of its themes it is determined by a question which is put in what
is admittedly a highly incompetent way. And not only in its choice
of themes. To confess is to react. But where there is a reaction, there
is not merely the danger, but it is inevitable, that our thesis should
be directed at the antithesis which we have to reject and that by our
Yes and No we should keep it alive—even if only as a reflection. At
some point in our thesis of confession—if only in the form of the
questioning which it has to allow—there still lurks the rejected antithesis. And does not that limit the insight expressed in it—not to
speak of the human fallibility of its authors, the temporal limitation
of their exegetical and dialectical methods, their restricted power of

self-expression? When we consider all these points together, the spatial, temporal and material limitations of all confessions, we may well ask how in these circumstances there can ever be any authority at all in any confession.

But, on the other hand, we have maintained that the authority of a confession rests decisively on its limitation. We must now explain this. It is true that the limitation of every confession is the unmistakable sign of its humanity. But so far we have spoken only of the appearance, the visible form of this limitation. We had to speak of it, for if we wanted to see it at all, we had to see it in its visible form. But it is another question whether we have to understand it in the light of its visible form as such : in other words, whether the fact that there always has been and still is confession, confession with all the dangers which this undertaking involves, confession with all the burden of responsibility which it demands, confession with the courage to accept this responsibility and to defy those dangers, although the men in the Church who made the confession could never be ignorant of the spatial and temporal and material limitation of what they were doing—whether this fact can be explained by saying that in a kind of intoxication these men strangely overlooked and forgot the limitation of what they were doing, so that when all the illusions and phantasies have been deducted the only reality which remains is a matter of geography and politics, certain determinative factors in time, and finally a series of dialectical situations in the evolutionary process of Christian thought and utterance as determined by its environment. That would mean that the limiting of the confession was to be understood in the light of its visible form as such. Now it is clear that the confession whose limitation is understood only in this way will in certain circumstances always be regarded as interesting and worthy of historical notice, but that it cannot be Church authority in a serious, theological sense. But that raises the question whether the limitation of a Church confession in these ways, which we cannot deny but have to emphasise, can in fact be understood only from this standpoint. It means that we have not yet understood this limitation as a mark of the particular humanity of the confession, and it is important that it should be understood in that way. The particular humanity of the Church's confession consists in the freedom, the joy of responsibility, the certainty and the love, in which it has always taken place in spite of the limits of those who make it. But do we explain this particular feature by saying that it is only a forgetting of these limits, an enthusiastic accompaniment which we cannot consider when we try to establish the reality involved ? This particular feature may have a quite different meaning which cannot be understood from the general fact that they were men from the West and the East, of this period or that, and in this or that controversy, nor from any enthusiastic overlooking and ignoring of this general fact.

It may well be that they confessed what and how they did in a particular obedience, and the human limitation of their confession was
the concrete form of their obedience. Their confession cannot then
be explained in terms of their geographical or temporal or material
limitation. It can be explained in that way too. There can be no
question of ruling out the "historical" interpretation. Even that
enthusiasm has played a definite role in every confession. But the
very opposite may also be true. The geographical and temporal
and material limitation can be explained in terms of the confession,
in so far as the confession itself (with or without enthusiasm) was
obedience to the Word of God, in so far as it corresponded in this or
that definite form to the will of God. What objection can we make to
the possibility of this second interpretation, if we are not to eliminate
from the list of important considerations the Word and will of God
as the power which rules the Church, and with them the possibility
of the Church's obedience to them, if we are to agree that that Word
and will are the real subject of what happens in Church history? If
we do agree on this, then we will certainly not deny the varied limitation of all Church confessions, but we will also reckon with the fact
that they have a meaning not only from below, but also from above, in
the fact that it is the Word and will of God and not creaturely powers
and forces which have imposed upon these confessions their different
limits. It was Holy Scripture speaking to the Church which at this
or that time and place imparted to different people their definite
measure of the Spirit and of faith, blessing but also judging, spreading
light but also darkness according to the free and right and perfect
will of God. That is why there are necessarily so many confessions
in the Church. That is why these confessions are so different and even
contradictory. That is why there is an ecclesiastical East and West.
That is why there is a primitive Church and a modern Church mutually
confirming one another. That is why one confession is so painfully
but undeniably at odds with another. What has to be said from below,
in the light of the visible form as such, can and must be said. But it
is from above, in the light of the overruling of the Word and will of
God, that the last and decisive thing has to be said. In the visible
form we see only the creaturely material, and in this creaturely
material we see the guiding hand of the Lord of the Church who
determines and disposes in this way or that. If we reckon also with
this second interpretation—and we clearly believe in the Word and
will of God, in the Lord of the Church, if we do reckon with this second
interpretation—then at least it is no longer inconceivable that the
Church's confession may have Church authority and that it always
does have it in the very thing which seems to compromise it, i.e., in the
limitation which betrays its humanity. In this limitation and therefore this humanity, the confession of the Church, once made, is a
palpable and authentic historical document, which can oppose and

confront the rest of the Church and the later Church as a concrete disputant, as flesh of its flesh. When discussion does arise, will the geographical and temporal and material limitation of the confession speak for or against its authority? Either may very well happen. Its origin at this point or that, its early or modern nature, its concrete attitude : all these may tell for or against its value and validity. A final decision cannot be reached in the light of its limitation as such. This decision is reached when we see the basis of this limitation, the ways and judgments of God. In other words, it is reached when confessions are seen in the light of the lordship of the Word of God over and in the Church by means of Holy Scripture and when they are heard and tested in this light. Seen and tested in this light the Church confession acquires a character which does not belong to it in virtue of its limitation : perhaps the character of a document of the wrath and judgment and rejection of God, and therefore that of a negative authority, of a document which warns the Church away because it is a codification of heresy and falsehood ; but perhaps the character of a document, in whose human limitation we do not only see, as we do see, the traces of the wrath and judgment and rejection of God, not only the general disobedience of man to His Word, the general blindness of all human thinking about Him, the general helplessness to speak rightly of Him, but over and above these things His sin-forgiving grace, the power of His Word to assemble and give a new basis to His Church, and therefore even in the sphere of human error and falsehood a definite perception of the truth. With this character the Church confession acquires and is Church authority in its very limitation, as a document which, as we know and cannot conceal, is either Eastern or Western, old or new, corresponding only too well to this or that theological situation in the Church, with all the traces of space-time creatureliness and scars of historical controversy which it bears in itself. And although in this light we can still see that which we may call the enthusiasm necessarily associated with the genesis of every confession, the hazardous human venture of the Yes and No pronounced in the confession, even this particular humanity now stands under another sign. It is still an accompaniment as seen in this light. The freedom of the confessors is as little important, as little the basis of authority, as is the general humanity revealed in their limitation. But if by the test of Holy Scripture and therefore of the Word and will of God this confession has that character of obedience or rather of sin-forgiving grace and therefore of the perception of truth which breaks through human error and falsehood, their enthusiasm can be understood as an outward aspect of the fact that the confession arose under the compulsion of a necessity, which as such was also a permission, that the limit of its insight is that marked out by the Word of God and therefore does not merely humble the confessors but strengthens and encourages them in the human venture of their *credimus, confitemur*, *docemus*, and also their *damnamus*. If this venture to confess took place in the joy of obedience which is grounded in this way, how can it in any way diminish its authority ? On the contrary, why should it not serve to confirm it ?

(*e*) We have defined the Church's confession as " a formulation and proclamation reached on the basis of common deliberation and decision." In so doing we have described the mode of its origination and ratification.

First of all, the mode of its origination. The subject of a Church confession is the Church. There must always therefore be a majority. It is not necessary that they should all be the authors of the confession. It is also not necessary that they should have deliberated and resolved like a Parliament. We can seldom interpret the concept " Synod " or " Council," or the normal functioning of such an assembly, with sufficient strictness in relation to a confession which is just arising. Once it has arisen we have to give it a very generous interpretation. At the same time, it is not a Church confession unless a majority of Church members are responsible for it, and have taken part in the discussion and acceptance of its content at least in principle—by virtue of the fact of their obvious confessional position previously, or in the form of a subsequent express agreement. Is it not inevitable that the first promoters and authors of a Church confession should make every effort not merely to prove that their undertaking is that of the Church but as far as human possibility allows actually to assure that it is so by trying to put the discussion and conclusion in relation to it on the widest possible basis, by finding as many as possible instructed and committed co-confessors, and by seeking to make the whole proceeding as orderly and controllable as possible ? Even if in fact only a single individual is the author of the confession, it is necessary that he should not be alone and speak only for himself, but that several, as many as possible, stand behind and with him sharing the responsibility. A confession has to speak in the name of the Church and to the Church. Therefore two or three must be gathered together— with some order and willingly and publicly—if what is said is to be a confession.

It is on this presupposition and to establish this point that the Augsburg Confession begins with the words : *Ecclesiae magno consensu apud nos docent*. . . . We must not press this expression. Obviously, the Saxon congregations and the great majority of the then preachers had no direct part in what Melanchthon and a few other theologians did at Augsburg with the distant help of Luther. Yet it was right and fitting and necessary that what was said should be solemnly said in their name : *Ecclesiae* . . . *docent*. The case was much the same with the Basel Confession of 1534. Composed by Oswald Myconius, it still has the superscription : " Confession of our holy Christian faith, as held by the Church of Basel." Like that of Geneva, drawn up two years later by Farel and Calvin, it was publicly affirmed by the assembled citizens of Basel, and the view that the congregation was its author was kept alive until 1821 by the fact that every year in Passion Week it was solemnly read in divine service. The *Conf. helv.*

post. of 1561 was originally a purely private work of Heinrich Bullinger. It then appeared as the confession of the preachers of Zurich, Berne, Schaffhausen, St. Gallen, Chur, Mülhausen, Biel and Geneva, was later accepted expressly by almost all the Reformed Churches of the time, and finally with the *Heidelberg Catechism* became *the* Reformed confessional work, as it still is to this day, particularly in Eastern Europe. Similarly the Gallican Confession of 1559 did not win confessional status as the work of Calvin but as the *Confession de Foi des églises reformées du royaume de France,* and it was not as the work of Ursin and Olevian, but as " Christian instruction as given in the churches and schools of the Palatinate," and later on the basis of the willing assent of other Reformed Churches, that the *Heidelberg Catechism* of 1563 attained the same rank. As against that, the same status certainly cannot be ascribed to writings like the so-called *Staffort Book* of the Margrave Ernst Friedrich of Baden-Durlach in 1599 or the so-called *Confessio Sigismundi* of 1614. When at the beginning of the latter it says that " His princely grace graciously and christianly remembers what the Holy Ghost . . . would have noted " in spite of the well-meant intention that " His princely grace would have the gates opened wide to the King of Glory in their land," the result was only a private concern of the prince, i.e., a land-owner's declaration of his will, not the confessional writing of the Reformed Church, and it ought never to have been represented as such. If there is no *consensus ecclesiae* there is no *ecclesia,* and therefore no *confessio ecclesiastica.* The Brandenburg-Prussian Church has had to suffer a great deal right up to the present time because it was thought that the gates could be opened to the King of Glory in this way.

Of course, in almost all ecclesiastical confessions the theological preparation as well as the way in which the decision was made is open to question and dispute.

Most of all, perhaps, when as at the Council of Trent or the Synod of Dort, the arrangement of the advisory and legislative bodies, the order of business, the formality and explicitness of the theological pronouncements was most highly regular and controlled. What took place at Nicaea has often enough been described and deplored. And even at other Councils it is seldom or never that the opposing faction either present or absent from these consultative and legislative bodies has no reason to complain at the composition of the body in question or the lack of theological preparation or even arbitrariness and violence in the conduct of business, and to dispute the formal validity of the conclusions reached from some standpoint which can only in part be contested.

But it is not the level and content of the theological debates directly preceding its proclamation which decides the authority of a confession, although often they have failed notoriously to reach the height which is to be desired. Nor is it legal correctness nor the human " decorum " observed or not observed in reaching the decision, although it is to be deplored when the latter is wanting. What really decides its authority is simply its content as scriptural exposition, which is necessarily confirmed or judged by Scripture itself. This content can impart something of its own value and significance even to a confession which is open to question on formal grounds. A confession which stands at this point has authority even if it was adopted in the most disorderly tumult. On the other hand, a confession which arose soberly in every respect may have no authority, or only the negative authority of a divine warning and deterrent, if it does not stand at this point. There is no confession whose authority might not seem endangered by the history of its origination. But there is none whose authority might not have the testimony of the Holy Spirit in spite of that history. This is not to excuse the mistakes made in consultation and decision. Where there has been too little concern about Church order in the making of a confession, that has always been avenged in its history, in spite of the sin-forgiving witness of the Holy Ghost. How much of the ineffectiveness of many a confession which is good in itself has perhaps to be ascribed to known or unknown sins in the history of its formation ! Again, when a confession is being made, we cannot be too careful about the greatest possible universality, regularity and fairness of all the proceedings. Speaking in the name of the whole Church to the whole Church we owe this—not merely to a moral scrupulosity, but to the fact itself. But when we have done all that it is our duty to do for the fact's sake, we have still to confess that we are unprofitable servants. The result of our efforts in this direction will always have obvious and concealed limits. But if this limitation will certainly not go unpunished, those to whom the completed confession comes, who are challenged to decision by it, by its content, have no right to point to this limitation in order to evade that decision. The only thing which they have to ask is whether in this limitation—however regrettable—the completed confession has for or against it the judgment of Holy Scripture, which means the testimony of the Holy Spirit. And now concerning the mode of the ratification of a Church confession the following has to be said. To make a confession, *confiteri*, is to proclaim its content, to publish it, to make it known, to make it known as widely and universally as possible. A confession demands publicity. This derives from its nature as the word of the whole Church to the whole Church. It derives from its purpose to reply to the question raised in the Church by the emergence of the counter-doctrine. But it derives primarily from its basis and object : from the witness of divine revelation directed to the Church and through the Church to the world. What the confession has to say does not allow of either a complete or a partial silence. A confession cannot be spoken *mezzo forte*. It cannot be spoken merely to individuals. A confession is quite different from a programme or line, by means of which the adherents of a group try to make their wishes clear without wanting to come too near to those outside the group, which, where possible, they may want to keep secret from others. A confession can only be spoken out loud and with the intention of being heard by everyone. If the claim involved in it is conditioned by a right knowledge of the Word of God, it is not presumption but the most profound and only true humility that this claim should be made without fear. In the desire to publish the confession, which can only be related to the visible sphere of human society, we have a visible representation of the consciousness that it

is made before God and His holy angels, and also before the eyes and
ears of the devil and all demons, in the one case with praise and
thanksgiving and worship, in the other with defiance and triumph.
For that reason we here stand again before the responsible seriousness
of the undertaking of making confession. Should we go on, or would
it be better to make peace and return? This question arises again
with all its force. But where the confession is obedience, the anxiety
implied in this question is removed, for it is self-evident that the
confession should be made public.

In this sense most of the confessional documents of the Reformation must
be regarded not so much as theological ordinances but rather as the trumpet call
of a herald which is sounded out in order to assemble again in the Church all
who are bound by this knowledge, giving a new account of it to its opponents
and extending to them again that missionary invitation. In this respect the
Augsburg Confession occupies a unique position. It is no mere imagination but
an actual fact that in the ecclesiastical and confessional politics of older and
more recent, and the most recent, Lutheranism the dignity of this confession
has played a part which cannot possibly be explained only by the weight or
scriptural character of its content. Theologically it could not satisfy for very
long the needs of 16th century Lutheranism. But in spite of all the trouble it
gave it had to be *the* Lutheran Confession—and as "*invariata*" it acquired that
flavour of something holy, which cannot be changed or improved, that it has
partly retained even to the present day—because it could be ranked under the
saying in Ps. 119[46]: *Et loquebar de testimoniis tuis in conspectu regum et non
confundebar*, because, as the prefaces to the Book of Concord and the Formula
of Concord ceaselessly emphasised, it was laid before the emperor Charles V
and the Imperial Estates at the Diet of Augsburg in 1530. Why is this so important? There is no unequivocal answer. And modern Lutherans would do
well to reflect that to recognise the Augsburg Confession was to put oneself
under the protection and shadow of the religious peace promised to Protestants
of the Augsburg Confession in 1555. Looked at from this standpoint, the
Augustana is simply and soberly the guarantee of the outward right to exist
given to the Lutherans by the emperor and the empire. But unfortunately, of
course, it also guarantees their renunciation of evangelising the rest of the empire
and therefore of the missionary character of their confession. But it would be
wrong not to see the other side of the matter to which the Lutheranism of the
Formula of Concord expressly held at any rate in theory. According to what
we are told in the preface to the Formula of Concord (*Bekenntnisschriften der ev.-
luth. Kirche* 1930, 741, 8), the fact that the *Augustana* was laid before the emperor
and empire gives to it the special value that occasioned in this way this particular
confession *publice ad omnes homines Christianam doctrinam profitentes adeoque
in totum terrarum orbem sparsa ubique percrebuit et in ore et sermone omnium
esse coepit*. We should add by way of understanding that the authors of the
Formula of Concord regarded not merely the Reformation as such, but the
Augsburg Confession in particular, as a direct work of God Himself (*ib.* 740, 5, 14),
and in such a way that, like Luther, they saw in the Reformation the last demonstration of the grace of God before the imminent end of all things (*postremis
temporibus et in hac mundi senecta, ib.* 740, 6). Therefore—and we must weigh
the significance of this passage in relation to the history of missionary thinking—
they believed that in the *Augustana*, as delivered to the emperor and empire,
and in that way acquiring a modified publicity, the last and necessary call to
all men had already taken place as wrought by God Himself. In the short
interval between this and the end of the world they rejoiced in the advantages
of the religious peace assured by the Augsburg Confession. That is certainly a

strange conception, and its easy balancing of eschatology and ecclesiastical politics lays it open to suspicion. All the same, it has this eschatological side, and from this point, according to the Lutheran view, the accomplished confession is identical with an accomplished world mission. It is in this extravagant sense of a kind of an ultimate or penultimate trumpet—loud enough to make all further missions superfluous and also to give the confessors a last earthly assurance—that Lutheranism has wanted its confession to be understood.

The necessary publicity of the confession undoubtedly gives rise to certain criteria in respect of its form and content. What is to be proclaimed by a herald has to be not only right but important. It must accept responsibility and think it worth while to go before the whole Christian public and the world and to claim the hearing and attention of everybody. There are some right and necessary decisions which have to be made by the Church or individuals in the Church quietly and without having to be confessed *urbi et orbi*. What is important or unimportant in this sense is not, of course, immediately apparent. What seems to be unimportant may *in statu confessionis* suddenly become important and therefore a necessary object of public expression. What seems to be important may in a certain situation be unimportant, and its solemn expression an evasion of the real decision which has to be made. In a confession all have to hear that which calls all to decision. Therefore in a confession there can be no statements which are determined or instructive only on a local or regional basis. There can be no decisions which do not recognisably affect faith. It cannot be the theorems of an individual theology which are stated, for now (and we learn from Athanasius and Augustine and Luther that this can happen) the Church can and must on its own responsibility take over these particular elements as its own witness. Again, a confession has to set out its statements in such a way that their basis and inward context is revealed. There can therefore be no confession without the background of solid, theological work. But because of its publicity the confession cannot develop into a summarised dogmatics. It must speak concisely and in thesis form. And it must speak in such a way that without any knowledge of technical theology the whole Church can understand it.

Of many Reformed confessions—at any rate those that are second-class and of doubtful status — we may ask whether these rules concerning the publicity of confession were sufficiently observed when they were drawn up. In the confessions of Hungarian origin we find astonishing differentiations from superstition and local usage. Again, in the German-Reformed there are curiously minute theological and cultic demarcations from Lutheranism and a remarkable prominence of theological jargon. And in the Swiss Formula of Consent of 1675 we find distinctions of which we can only think that they were those of different theological schools, but not a matter of the faith or error of the Church. But we will do well to pronounce such verdicts with reserve. For a long time now many of the definitions in the early symbols, which not only then but even to-day are a matter of life or death for the Church, have been regarded as unnecessary ballast. We must admit that there have been faults in this respect.

21

Yet we must also admit that detailed decisions expressed perhaps in very technical language were once a call to the whole Church, and even though we cannot see in them this quality now, the day may come when they will have it again.

But this publicity also involves that every confession will exert pressure on the rest of the Church and through the Church on the world. Therefore every confession can expect a reaction on the part of the Church or the world or both. If it is a genuine confession it challenges to decision, i.e., it challenges the others to hear its witness to a definite understanding of Scripture, and in that way to test their own understanding of Scripture by its accuracy, i.e., to test it anew, perhaps to realise for the first time that the doctrine and life of the Church must be tested by Scripture, that there is a Holy Scripture whose witness means judgment on the thought and speech and life of the whole world. The confession presents this challenge in the form of a simple Yes and No with which it questions the Yes and No of others : not only incidentally, but in the most definite way, not *disputandi causa*, but in a judgment whether their Yes and No is really of the Church, and their appeal to divine revelation is in order. This questioning means pressure. And pressure begets counter-pressure. It would be too cheap and meaningless a confession, or the confessors of a really important confession would have far too little knowledge of themselves and men generally, if there was the expectation that the confession would find a facile welcome. It is the fact that the confession " only " demands decision, that it " only " challenges others before the judgment seat of Holy Scripture—but inexorably before it—which necessarily makes it pressing. Men, even in the Church, prefer to leave open the question how they stand before this judgment seat, postponing their account before this seat to an indefinite future. If a new doctrine or movement arises in the Church, or an established one is predominant, then its representatives and adherents will not be disturbed in the presupposition that they are confirmed and protected or at any rate not attacked by the Holy Spirit. And the less active majority in and outside the Church prefer the rest of an open question to the unrest of a choice between truth and untruth. For them the danger of perhaps living in an environment in which we only appear to live but have in fact fallen victim to death seems much smaller than that which threatens when we are forced perhaps into a complete change of environment. And it is by this danger that the Church and the world are threatened by a confession. It threatens them by the fact that the question of the environment in which we can live may be decided quite differently from what their presuppositions demand by the One who has the knowledge and power to do so as the Lord of life and death. Therefore a confession demands that they come back to these presuppositions, asking whether they are right, choosing again where they think that they have already chosen rightly and satisfactorily. For that reason a confession presses

and gives rise to counter-pressure. If a confession were a mere change
of mind, it could be adopted by the representatives of other views
with friendly interest, perhaps being regarded as a welcome addition
to the series of the many other open possibilities. But it says Yes and
No—not as God says Yes and No, but in the human sphere, and yet
in that sphere with an appeal to God Himself, and therefore with a
definite assertion and denial of the unity of the Church, and with a
definite indication in what sense and within what limits there is or
is not fellowship in God. It cannot and does not try to anticipate the
judgment of God. But in a way which cannot be ignored, it says that
there is a judgment of God. It imperatively demands that we submit
to this judgment. It is not because it opposes to human statements
other human statements, but because in doing this it makes this
demand, that a confession is necessarily a challenge, an unsettling
factor, a disturbing of the environment, so that that environment
inevitably wishes to silence it. For those who confess, therefore, a
confession necessarily means, because of its publicity, that they are
led by that environment into a struggle, into suffering and therefore
into temptation. It not only can but must be so. Men in the Church
and in the world, if they want to avoid the decision to which a confession summons them, may pretend that they do not see the danger
of it. But in reality the fact that they do this shows that they have
seen it very well. However it may be in detail, basically and in general
they always see it. In some sense—as long as the Church is not completed and heaven and earth are not made new and the new order of
the relationship of God and man based on Jesus Christ is not carried
out by him in His own person—a confession will always bring those
who confess it under counter-pressure and in that way lead them into
temptation.

At this point we come face to face with the connexion made in the Early
Church between the concepts *confiteri*, *confessio*, *confessor*, and that dangerous,
costly and testing, but also hopeful conflict which the Church waged with a
heathen world-power which persecuted and aimed to destroy it, and which at
the time of the Reformation became identical with the might of a secular Church,
which rejected the true Church because it had fallen away from it. In the measure
that the confession ceased to make use of its publicity, this conflict became
latent and for a long time now it has been seen only in certain peripheral phenomena and on the mission fields. But to-day, when confession is coming back
to life, it looks as if this conflict will also flare up again. *Confiteri* means to enter
into this conflict and to accept its hardship and also its promise. There are
many forms of this conflict. It is not serious only when it is a matter of the
opposition silencing confession with physical force, i.e., in some way robbing
the confessors of life or external freedom. Then, of course, it becomes dramatic.
The publicity of confession demands that it should reckon with this form of
counter-pressure, that it should not shrink from engaging in this dramatic form
in certain cases. But we can always count on it that the conflict against confession is either in an unripe and impotent stage and will soon take a worse course,
or else that it is already coming to an end with the defeat of the enemy, when the
latter thinks it necessary to take to the *prima* or *ultima ratio* of force. From the

standpoint of confession itself there are greater and more intensive dangers than that enemies might kill the body. If they do, they are no longer able to do that worse thing which they might do to confession and confessors. From the standpoint of confession, we are, then, forced to be always on the watch, or we have already found relief. The worst attempts to silence a confession consist in making it impossible on its own ground, the intellectual and spiritual. Another confession may be opposed to it which has perhaps a greater appeal, a superior theological technique, or a greater show of legal validity, and is far more impressive by reason of these qualities. Or it may have to sound out in the sphere of a philosophy and way of life in which all its presupposition and conclusions cannot be understood, in which its opponent finds it only too easy to slander and ridicule it as an arbitrary innovation, or an obstinate reaction, or the expression of an uncharitable spirit, or an attack on certain generally accepted sacred interests. It may even happen that the juridical and statistical uncertainty in which it has to move is noted and exploited, that it is triumphantly " seen through " on every hand, that it can be abandoned in the nullity of its claim to speak to the whole Church in the name of the whole Church, in the arrogance of its appeal to the Word of God, in the hierarchical pride of its attempt to assert and state the sole justification of this or that perception, in the uncharitable severity of its No, its *anathema* and *damnamus*. It may be objected that the environment, being deaf and indifferent to confessions of every kind, has no ear for its Yes and No, that the question of truth is dead or apparently dead, that the apparent practical effects of some cheap-working religious enterprise can easily destroy the interest in the decision which it demands. But it may also happen that it is stripped of its character as a call and challenge, that it is given a friendly recognition and hearing, by being guaranteed in a religious peace or concordat as the manifesto of the decision of a recognised group or trend or party in the Church, or as a declaration of the principles of a Church which is itself regarded only as a group or trend or party, and in that way limited and set aside. And the very worst may happen that somebody or something or other has an instinct that it is better not to resist it openly and directly, or simply to put it on one side with those who confess it. On the contrary, it is adopted and affirmed. The leaders and perhaps the masses of the Church (and even of the world) recognise some advantage in accepting it, at any rate officially. It is therefore brought into a context, it is hemmed in by the rest of the Church and possibly the world, it is surrounded and overlaid by presuppositions, which do not " touch " it, which perhaps give it a new ecclesiastical and temporal glory, but—and this is the supreme cunning of the devil—it is made completely sterile by the fact that state and society, school and university all say what it says, as an allocution which demands a response. What are all the weapons of violence compared with the intellectual and spiritual enclosing and suppressing which a confession may suffer at the hands of the Church and the world ?

If a confession is to stand, everything depends on whether the temptation produced by this counter-pressure (indirectly therefore by its own pressure) is recognised and overcome as such. The temptation naturally consists in the possibility of abandoning the confession. And the basic form of this abandonment is always to deny to ourselves and others the character of the confession as a challenge, question and attack on the world around. Its proclamation is renounced. It is regarded once again only as a theory and collection of propositions. With all the loyalty we might still show it in this immanent character, with all our zeal for the integrity of the theory and statements as such, there is now linked another zeal, to spare our environment the collision on the transcendent character of the confession. And it is this second zeal which—although the confession remains " untouched "—now determines our practical attitude in word and action, in our own initiative and our response to the initiative of our environment. In this practical relationship the confessors no longer stand where they must stand if it really were their confession, that is, in the venture and responsibility of its transcendent character. Now that they have experienced what it means for its pressure to create counter-pressure, they no longer desire publicity. They want it to be their confession without this publicity. But this simply means that the confessors have in fact accepted the standpoint of the enemies of the confession. Confession without the desire for publicity, confession without the practical attitude which corresponds to it, is already a confutation of the confession, however " untouched " this may be as a theory and statement, however great may still be their zeal for the maintaining of its immanent character. For what is the meaning and purpose of the hostility and conflict in relation to the confession ? As a theory and statement it will not have to suffer attack, whatever may be its content and however definitely it may be maintained and affirmed. As a theory it does not exert any pressure. As a theory it is quite harmless, indeed it is comforting even to those who do not agree with it. Behind the intention of its opponents to suppress it, there definitely does not stand any ill-will to those statements in the confession which are contrary to their own. Ultimately there stands only the desire that the confession should be a mere theory, that it should not raise the question of the correctness of their presuppositions, that it should not bring them before the judgment seat of Holy Scripture and of God Himself and in that way force them to decision. This is what takes place by means of publicity. A confession has publicity when it has confessors in the Church and the world who in their own person and practical attitude embody the venture and responsibility of its transcendent character as a challenge, question and attack, who in their existence represent what the confession says in words, and in that way consummate its proclamation. But if this does not happen, or no longer happens, even the best confession exerts no further pressure. The desire of its enemies is accomplished. Its confessors have no counter-pressure to suffer. But the confession itself has become so much paper. That it is not is the basis of all hostility to the confession, and that it should be is the purpose of the whole attack upon it. We help this attack, we participate most actively in it, when we think that we can retreat in this way. That there is no venture for the confession means that there is a venture—on the part of the confessors—against the confession. It involves treachery against the confession—pure treachery—if we are again concerned with that distinction between its immanent and transcendent character.

It is a great gain, therefore, if this distinction is soberly recognised for the treachery it is : not merely as surrender, but as agreement and co-operation with the enemy. It is a great gain if to justify it we no longer appeal to humility before the mysteries of God, to which no confession can do justice, or to the love with which we have to spare and carry the weak, or the necessary maintenance of the Church in its existing state, but openly and honestly—and this makes everything else superfluous—to fear of the expected or already present counter-pressure. This fear is in fact the temptation which is inevitably bound up with the publicity of a confession. And it can only be overcome in the conflict between this fear and the other fear, whether the Word of God—to which the confessors have appealed with their confession—commands or permits them to be enemies of the confession because of that first fear. Where the fear of God is greater than fear of men, the temptation has already been overcome. It is recognised that the confession is a demand primarily upon the confessors. Account is taken of that demand, i.e., they no longer yield to the expected or present counter-pressure, but resist it—for that is the demand made upon confessors. This resistance is the true ratification of a confession. The yielding of a confession by the above way of surrendering the practical attitude which puts it into effect always has the result sooner or later of making it impossible and destroying it and rendering it obsolete even as a theory or collection of propositions. The great defeats of the Church have been and are when it has wanted to honour its confession in theory but not in practice, when the living form becomes a mummy, and the mummy unnecessary lumber, and the gift of God is frustrated, when, deprived of its confession and delivered up to every possible force, the Church does not hear the Word of God and has no more to say of it. The great danger in the inevitable conflicts against a confession of the Church is that it may be taken away from it if it yields to temptation and surrenders. But there is also an even greater promise. Even the most modest and inadequate resistance which meets the counter-pressure of an alien church and world, not with surrender, but with new pressure, or rather with the old pressure of the old confession, means the ratification of the confession, and it has the promise that there will be a victory for the confession and new life for the Church.

A confession of faith is always stronger than even the most correct and profound and religious confession of error. Sooner or later a confession of faith will be accepted as superior in every philosophy and way of life in spite of misunderstandings and suspicions. A confession of faith can survive the nullity of its claim being " seen through " by the wise and its arrogance and uncharitableness being condemned by the righteous. A confession of faith has the power to summon to life again that dead or apparently dead question of the truth, and to unmask as such those cheap solutions which are placed in juxtaposition or opposition to it. A confession of faith can allow itself to be tolerated. It can make its voice heard even within a concordat or religious peace. A confession

of faith can ultimately break through and demonstrate the power which
is proper to it alone, and not to its imitators, even where the Church and world
try to enslave and suppress it by apparently accepting and adopting it. And a
confession of faith has always triumphed in the long run where attempts have
been made to suppress it by force. If only it is really a confession of faith—
not necessarily of a heroic and inspired faith, but of a faith lived out and revealed
in practical decisions! This faith does not need any special work and achievements or any special inward qualities. It needs only that it should not merely
formulate the confession but also proclaim it. It needs only that it should not
be forced back into the sphere of a purely theoretical agreement with the confession. It needs only the fact that the fear of God should be a little greater
than the fear of men. In this " little " the pressure of a confession continues
even under the most overwhelming counter-pressure. And that is what must
happen. It is in this continually exerted pressure that the Church lives in the
Church, even in a destroyed and apostate Church—and the Church in the world,
even in a world which resists it in every possible way.

Of the Church confession which fulfils all these conditions we have
to say that it has Church authority, i.e., it can and it must be distinctively heard in the Church as the distinctively articulated voice of the
fathers and brethren in faith. When we say this, we do not formulate
a postulate, but describe a reality : where the Church really lives,
real Church confession is heard in this distinctive way. Or negatively
expressed : the Church does not really live where real Church confession is not heard in this distinctive way. It is not possible that
where Church confession has been made we can ignore this event, i.e.,
ignore its binding and imperative and authoritative character. That
would be to obscure and destroy the continuity between the Church
then and now, the connexion between the Church there and here.
Now in practice, of course, that does happen often enough. Not every
Church confession which has been adopted in some place at some time
has this character always and everywhere. What we said about the
geographical and temporal and material limitation of every confession
works itself out in the actual limitation of the authority of every
confession. But with all the mutual strangeness and division in the
Church, where there is a real Church there is also an unbroken continuity between the Church then and now and an unbroken connexion
between the Church there and here. There is no Church where fellowship is completely lacking in even one of these two dimensions, where
in what appears to be a Church there are no fathers behind us and
no brethren beside us. But having both, in both directions we hear
the voice of a Church confession, within definite limits and on a
definite road we take part in the story of the exposition and application of Holy Scripture, and we have therefore a definite responsibility
to definite decisions made earlier and elsewhere in the Church. This
responsibility can be confirmed and codified in Church law. But it
does not arise because a corresponding decision is made in Church
law. Nor may it be annulled or even weakened by the failure or
flouting of that law. The authority of a Church confession is a spiritual

authority. That is, it is based on its character as correct exposition of
Scripture. As such it is a self-attesting authority, to which nothing can
be added and from which nothing can be taken away by Church law.

Thus the early dogma of the Trinity did not in any sense depend on the
authority with which it was invested for the Roman State Church in 380 by
the edict of the emperors Gratian, Valentinian and Theodosius, as later incorporated in the *Codex Justiniani*. Again, the Confession of Augsburg did not depend
only on the authority ascribed to it in Lutheran territories by the religious
peace of 1555. Even where the ecclesiastical establishment of a confession took
place by the free decision of the Church independently of political powers, it
does not depend on the authority created for it by this codification. Conversely,
the authority of the confessions with whose formulation and proclamation the
Swiss Churches were re-founded in the 16th century is not abolished or weakened by the fact that the liberal 19th century state revoked their canonical
validity, that the Churches at that period lacked the inward resources to reaffirm
them of themselves, and that they have therefore been obliterated from the
present-day law of the Church. What has at one time and place been known
and confessed, as was the trinitarian belief of the 4th century Church or the Scripture principle and doctrine of justification of the Reformation, may at another
time and place have to suffer at the hands of all kinds of spiritual insensibility
and insubordination. It may be ignored and misunderstood or overlooked and
forgotten over long epochs or in large sections of the Church. But it does not
derive its claim to be authority and the power to assert it from its consistent
establishment in the law of the Church, nor does it lose it when the latter is
weak. But where there is the Church and therefore that continuity and connexion of Church life, there genuine knowledge speaks through genuine confession, and it is always heard as an authority with or without Church law.
The fact that they are not assured by Church law does not prevent the trinitarian
confession of the Early Church or the Reformation confessions from speaking
and being heard again in our own days, and perhaps more effectively than if
they still had their former guarantees in Church law. It could not and cannot
diminish the undeniable factual importance, at any rate in Germany, of the
unique witness of the so-called *renitenten Kirche* of Hesse in matters of the right
relationship of Church and State, that it is the witness of a small free Church
which hardly merits external notice. Again it would not be right for us outside
Germany to try to ignore the factual significance of the confessional decisions
taken there since 1934, because formally they are only the decisions of the
German Evangelical Church, or of a small minority in this Church. The authority
of a confession and therefore our necessary responsibility towards it is decided,
not by any outward legitimation, but within the actual continuity and relation
between Church and Church by its own importance, by the perception confessed
in it.

Where the Church is, it does stand in this responsibility. It is to
that extent a confessional Church, i.e., a Church determined by its
responsibility to Church confession. It would be an unconfessional
Church only if it could repudiate and actually deny this responsibility.
Where this is not the case, we can distinguish only between Churches
which are confessional in different ways and to different degrees. It
is the case, then, that the concept responsibility describes and denotes
what we have called the binding and imperative and authoritative
character of the Church's confession. We have seen that confession
cannot in any sense stand beside Holy Scripture, claiming the same

divine authority, the same character as the source and norm of Church proclamation. In substance, no express or tacit obligation to a confession can ever be anything but an obligation to Holy Scripture. But wherever the Church really is, this obligation to Holy Scripture will have a form determined by the particular guidance and history of the Church (through its continuity with the earlier Church and its connexion with Churches elsewhere). Responsibility to the fathers and brethren involves responsibility before God. It is a question of responsibility before God and this alone. But how can there be this responsibility if we try to evade responsibility before the fathers and brethren ? Can we hear them as we hear God Himself in the witnesses to His revelation : that is, in all their words and statements and with a readiness to subject ourselves entirely to them ? Certainly not. But obviously we cannot hear them with the impartiality and neutrality with which we hear various other human voices. *Tertium datur*. This third thing—which is not a middle term between the Word of God and the word of man, but a human word figuratively ranked before all other human words—is the confession or dogma of the Church.

In the sphere in which it has validity, Church confession is an authority to which we must always give a prior recognition. Its authority consists primarily (and at bottom decisively) in the fact that for responsible representatives of the Church's life it is not one of the many old and new texts which we may have read or not read, read thoroughly or cursorily, read many times or only once and then never again, but it is one which has to be read, and read seriously and constantly.

It will be noted that this basic form of the recognition of its authority does not involve any *sacrificium intellectus*—the same can be said of the authority of the Church's Canon and the Church's fathers. We may accept and follow the discipline demanded as binding without being guilty of any kind of neglect of responsibility for our own thinking and deciding. How can it harm this responsibility that these texts are recommended for our particularly intensive and persevering study ?

But why this particular study ? The Church's confession—and this is the second form in which its authority must be respected—is meant to be read as a first commentary on Holy Scripture. We repeat : as a commentary. It cannot replace Holy Scripture itself. It cannot replace our own exposition and application of Holy Scripture. It cannot be the only commentary which—because we have to read Scripture in the Church—we allow between ourselves and Scripture. But as the voice of the fathers and brethren it can and should be the first of commentaries. It can and should be the leader of the chorus or the key witness in that series.

We can hardly object to this as a wresting of Holy Scripture or our own conscience. No one has ever read the Bible only with his own eyes and no one ever should. The only question is what interpreters we allow and in what order we let them speak. It is a pure superstition that the systematising of a so-called historico-critical theology has as such a greater affinity to Holy Scripture itself and has therefore in some sense to be heard before the Apostles' Creed or the *Heidelberg Catechism* as a more convincing exposition of the biblical witness. What we have there is simply the commentary of a theology, if not a mythology. The only thing is that this commentary has not been affirmed by a Church, that so far the theology or mythology has wisely hesitated to claim the character of a real decision. Obviously we cannot choose between the biblical text and a Church confession. We are definitely pointed and bound to the text, and not to the commentary. Again, we cannot choose between the possibility of using all available commentaries for an understanding of the text, including that of the historico-critical theology—or that of using only a few more convenient ones, including, of course, the Church confession. But we have the possibility of giving first place among all the voices which have to be heard to that of the Church confession, i.e., to listen to it first on the assumption that it has something particular to say to us as the solemnly gathered deposit of the significant existing experience of the Church with Holy Scripture. We then have to be constantly ready for corrections of its view either by other voices or by our own insight. But it is hard to see why its view should not be heard with the attention it deserves without having to disturb or destroy the objectivity of our relation to Holy Scripture.

After this, as it were, privileged hearing of the Church confession, we have to go and tread our own way in the understanding, exposition and application of Holy Scripture. The confession cannot and will not deprive us of our own responsibility to Scripture. We shall enter that way " confessionally determined." But fundamentally that can only mean that we have dealt with the confession as an authority of first rank and taken the direction indicated by it.

If we cannot do this, if we have to reject as contrary to Scripture the direction indicated by the confession, we then have to face the difficult problem of an exchange of confessions, that is, an alteration of our ecclesiastical position. Of course, our dealings with the confession may end in this way. They can do so legitimately only in the light of Holy Scripture. But they may also end by our having quite freely to move further in the direction indicated.

That does not mean that we have to make our own its particular theology and the details of its biblical exposition. We can be loyal to its direction and still think that in detail and even as a whole, as our confession, we would rather have it put otherwise. We can still think that we have definitely to repudiate certain of its detailed and perhaps not unimportant statements. Even a positive attitude to the confession can be a genuinely critical one. And moving in the direction it indicates, and therefore a positive attitude to it, means even less that we have to make the content of the confession the content of our own proclamation. For again : the confession cannot in any way constrain the Word of God attested in Scripture, which as such alone can and will be the content of our proclamation.

A confessional proclamation in this sense would not correspond to the meaning of the confession itself, which, as we saw, is not an exposition of the Christian faith *in abstracto*, but a weapon of faith against error in the form of individual concrete decisions. There is certainly no reason why for the purpose of instructing the Church on the antitheses of faith and error we should not occasionally make the confession as such a direct key to the exposition of Scripture, as was obviously done for centuries and to some extent is still done to-day with the *Heidelberg Catechism*, which offers itself at once for this purpose with its division into fifty-two Sundays. But the confession never has the pretension of wanting to become the theme of Church proclamation, which must be provided only by Holy Scripture.

The way of understanding the Bible must be pursued, then, as our own way. We cannot allow this understanding to be prescribed by the confession. We cannot allow ourselves to be bound by the confession as by a law. Does that mean an end of its authority and respect for it ? Not at all—we might say rather that it only begins at this point. For at this point it takes a third and genuinely spiritual form. It becomes a constant antithesis, the horizon of our own thinking and speaking. Naturally, within this horizon it is a question of our own free thinking and speaking, for which we must bear the responsibility, which is not bound by any law except that of its object, and therefore only by Holy Scripture. Our study of the confession, our hearing of it as leader and key witness, is now behind. We must now take the Word itself—but in the sphere of the Church, and now as previously this sphere is denoted by the obtaining confession. It is still, and will continue to be (if no new events intervene), the sphere determined by the trinitarian witness of the Early Church and by the Reformation witness to the lordship of God in His Word and the free grace of God. It is not only we who speak in this sphere but also the fathers and brethren. Therefore in this sphere we are not sovereign in the sense that we are alone, with no antithesis, no horizon. We cannot think and speak as in the absence, but only as in the presence of the confession.

We can make this plain by the external fact that the Christian worship in which our own exposition and application of Holy Scripture is most solemnly expressed usually takes place not freely or in a neutral place, but in a " church " which even by its architecture and furnishings more or less directly and faithfully reminds those who gather in it, including the one who speaks, of their " confessional position." Even if it is mainly a witness to the helplessness of the 19th century the " Church " confronts us with Church history. And what happens in it happens not only in the presence of God and His angels, not only in the presence of the departed spirits of the past, but also—with whatever freedom and responsibility—in the presence of the confession, by which in strength or weakness, in loyalty or apostasy, our " Church " is this particular " Church." In the same way the hymn-book which, good or bad, is always used in worship, confronts us with Church history. Together with the text of the Bible our own exposition and application of the word of the Church's praise is a third trigonometrical point, and at a varying distance behind it there always stands the Church's confession. Finally, even the order of worship can more or less definitely play the same role.

We cannot avoid this fact of the—noted or unnoted—presence of the Church's confession in every present aspect of the Church's life. If we think that we are so free or so committed that after hearing the confession we must go our own way independently of it, the confession does not cease, directly or indirectly to speak, tacitly opposing its word to our word, not as any kind of voice, but as the voice which has been peculiar to our Church from its inception and still character-ises its being to this day. Neither the greatest liberalism nor the boldest catholicising which may be permitted in the Church can alter the fact that the sphere in which it can be disseminated is still and will continue to be the spiritual sphere of the Evangelical, Lutheran or Reformed Church, which, whether we like it or not, opposes the Evangelical confession to all extravaganzas. It is perhaps in this inflexible if non-authoritative antithesis, in a confrontation in which it has, as it were, to be a silent disputant, that the Church confession perhaps speaks most explicitly, even if only in the form of an immanent but irresistible criticism of those who stop their ears against it. In this confrontation we have to recognise and respect its genuine spiritual authority. As we ourselves confront it in a necessary freedom, it retains its own complete freedom as well. If in relation to it we think, rightly or wrongly, that we have to make certain reservations or omissions, if we interpret it critically under the guidance of the Holy Scripture to which it emphatically directs us—side by side with the form, in which we have altered it and made it our own, it still stands in its own original form, in the integrity of its propositions, in the uniqueness of its theology and language, in the historical limitation but also the peculiar greatness of its origin, in its own direct appeal to Holy Scripture. Just as freely as we confront it the confession confronts us, speaking and demanding that we should listen, still intact and including all that we have rightly or wrongly freed ourselves from, all our reservations and omissions. The spiritual authority which it exercises is that it continues to exist in its own form, so that whatever may be our attitude to it as a whole or in detail, because it is the voice of the fathers and brethren in the Church, we can never have done with it. And a spiritual respect for its authority is that we are conscious of this confrontation, that it has been given to us to realise our freedom only in this confrontation or within this horizon, that the realisation of our freedom is always a reckoning or a responsibility which we owe to it. It may be a critical, even a very critical, responsi-bility : but it is still a responsibility.

Even when we feel we must hold something apparently or actually opposed to a statement of the confession, this statement is still before us with all its weight as the confession of the fathers and brethren and with what is perhaps a very galling definiteness. It cannot be forgotten even though at the time we cannot accept and repeat it. As that which also opposes us, it deserves respect, even though we cannot allow its opposition ; it does not cease to occupy us. We can never have done with it, because as a statement of the Church's confession it has not done with us.

This and this alone is the imperative and binding normative authority of a Church confession. Anything more : the elevation of a dogma to the rank of revelation or a law or the content of the Church's proclamation would bring us back ineluctably to Roman Catholic immanentism in which Church and revelation are equated, violating the divine authority of Holy Scripture and therefore returning the Church to that solitariness in which ultimately there can be no Church life at all and therefore no genuine Church authority. Dogma has genuine Church authority only as a word of the fathers and brethren, whose authority is in the strict sense spiritual and has to be respected spiritually. It would be to distrust the power of the Holy Spirit if we were to regard this authority and respect as inadequate. If a confession or dogma, as this word of the fathers and brethren which has authority and has to be respected spiritually, does not oppose any justifiable claim to freedom, if its claim to be heard as such cannot be refused in any justifiable liberty, there is no justifiable claim to be noticed and heard and accepted and obeyed which it cannot proclaim and make good to the extent that it is genuine witness : the genuine counter-witness of the Church to divine revelation and to that extent a genuinely spiritual word. If that is so—or quite simply, if it is a real confession of faith—it will have the power to continue speaking even at a great distance from its own geographical and temporal and historical place in the Church, to make itself directly intelligible and instructive in its application to the faith of a Church in some quite different place, in spite of and even in the particularity of its theses and positions and negations, or even to awaken to new life the dead faith of a Church in some quite different place. It is obviously not the power of an in every way limited and fallible human word, nor is it its canonical recognition, nor is it the fact that it is divine revelation, that explains this. What can explain it except that it is a document of obedience to the Holy Spirit of the Word of God and therefore an instrument of His power and His ruling ? How can it not have and be authority as such, and how else can it have and be authority ? To have and be authority in this sense and therefore to confirm its imperative and binding and normative character, it needs only—but very earnestly—to be seen and understood as the silent but present antithesis of the Church's daily life, as the horizon within which—under the lordship of the Word of God—it is conducted. In this free confrontation faith speaks to faith, and faith awakens new faith, and in the witness which men bear to other men, the Holy Spirit Himself acts and works.

If we are to evaluate rightly the authority of a Church confession, we must hold apart as well as together what we have called its direction and its detailed statements as such. It may well be that the false statements against which the confession was then and there directed are no longer or not yet familiar to the Church here and now in their original form, or at any rate in their actual significance.

What is the significance to us of those statements of Arius or Nestorius to which the christological dogma of the Early Church was the reply ? What is the significance to us of the statements of the later mediæval doctrine of penance

to which the Reformers opposed their doctrine of justification by faith alone ?
Or again we may ask : What is the significance to us in Switzerland or Holland
or England of the statements, to us the very strange and peculiar statements, of
the German Christians against which the Confessional Church in Germany must
set its own statements ?   Or again the missionary Churches of India and China
may ask: What have they to do with all the heresies to which all the dogma of
the European Churches is an answer ?

Similarly, it may be the case that the answering statements of the
faith of the Church then and there as laid down in the confession do
not strike the Church here and now as a necessary expression of its
own faith.   But it is still true that the confession of that time and
place does constitute the antithesis and horizon of our Church life
which we have to hear and regard.   And we can confidently expect
what will happen when this confrontation takes place.   For there is a
notorious connexion, even a unity, between the heresies of every age
and place.

The assertion that 2nd century Gnosticism or Arius and Nestorius or Occam-
ism have nothing to do with us is perhaps a very short-sighted one.   It may be
that these teachings do not have any obvious relevance and we are concerned
with other errors.   But although heresy has altered its form, its content is still
the same.   And it would be premature for us to dismiss as unimportant the
dogma which opposed a strange form of error because in that form it corresponds
to a teaching which no longer occupies or does not yet occupy us.

It may be that in the assertion of the present irrelevance of the
statements and counter-statements presupposed and expressed in
dogma we have a fatal insinuation, an attempt on the part of modern
error, to conceal and withhold from the Church the experience it has
already gained and the decision it has already taken in relation to it
in an earlier and different form, so as to force itself all the more surely
upon it in its new and present form.

The orthodox rational theology of about 1700 knew what it was doing when it
made the Church of that time suspect the Reformation doctrine of predestination
and justification as the superfluous relic of the scholasticism of a former age,
thus rejecting the confessional writings as a horizon.   Verbally, this was a cam-
paign against scholasticism.   But in fact it meant the introduction of a half-
stoical, half-pietistic semi-Pelagianism.   They knew well enough why they did
not want Luther and Calvin as witnesses against what they themselves were
bringing in, although not in the formulæ and expressions of later mediæval
nominalism.   Similarly, it sounded well enough when in the 19th century the
school of Ritschl purported to be able to perceive and unmask the Greek philosophical thinking which lay behind the dogma of the Early Church, and a period
began when scholars could never be sufficiently astonished at the iota of Nicæa
and the prickliness and rigidity of the Chalcedonian Definition, or emphasise
too much the remoteness of our own " piety " and morality and way of thinking
from those distant epochs and controversies of the Church, or relativise sufficiently the significance of the trinitarian-christological dogma.   Historically,
the result was that many true discoveries were made.   But can we doubt that
objectively all this was only a pretext to create a free course for thinking and
teaching about God and Christ and the Holy Spirit, which, if not in words and
statements, all the more certainly in matter, was exactly the same as that of the
early heretics, and against which the continuing presence of early dogma formed

an unwelcome barrier. According to Ritschl, Jesus Christ is a great man who on the basis of our value-judgment is found to be the Son of God. For that reason Harnack has to call the ancient dogma a self-expression of the Greek spirit in the sphere of the Gospel. And we must look carefully to see what is really at stake when we are assured to-day that the Reformation confession was right when it opposed the sacramentalism and monkish moralism of the Catholicism of the period, but that we in the present-day Church are concerned with quite different questions and problems. We are not interested in the question of the grace of God, but the question whether there is a God at all, as was often said thirty years ago. The Christian answer to social and national questions, war, the status of women, is more important than the Scripture principle and the doctrine of justification, as was said later. And to-day, it is not the righteousness of works which is the enemy of the Gospel, but the indifference and the secularism of the masses who are only nominally Christian. Why should there not be much that is right in these assertions ? But we have to note that directly or indirectly they may be aimed at the confession, that their purpose may be to obscure the confession as the horizon of the Church and make it ineffective. We have to note that they may be simply the wings behind which the old enemy, against whom the Reformation drew up its confession, will make a triumphant return into the Church in a new form. Similarly, it may be of fatal significance if the young missionary Churches of Asia think that they can let go the *Apostolicum* because it is only the document of the Church's conflict with a Gnosticism which even in Europe has for a long time been known only historically, a conflict whose results can have no possible interest for modern Japanese and Chinese Christians. Does not Gnosticism always lurk where the Gospel begins to emerge in all its novelty from the background of thousands of years of traditional heathendom ? Is it not there that it is always better to close the doors against it with the formula : *Credo in Deum patrem, omnipotentem creatorem coeli et terrae, et in Jesum Christum, filium eius unicum, Dominum nostrum ?* Is it not a very questionable proceeding if we try to slide them open on the pretext that they are too Western ?

Primarily and decisively it is not the wording of a Church's confession, not its form as geographically and temporally and historically limited, but its direction (which is, of course, only real and recognisable in its statements and form), whose exposition can constitute the necessary horizon of the present-day Church and as such have and be authority. The confession of the Church then and there confronts the Church now and here with its statements. In doing this, it questions it concerning its faith, concerning the obedience of its exposition and application of Scripture. Just as there is a connexion, indeed a unity in heresy, so there is a connexion and unity of faith. The confession speaks to us of this unity of faith. What it desires of us is that we should find ourselves with it in this unity. Its statements give us the direction in which it itself, the Church then and there, has sought and found it. It is not by agreeing with these statements and appropriating them, but by learning the direction from these statements that we respect the authority of the confession. For that reason it may well be that in learning that direction from it we have to oppose critically certain or even many of its statements.

This criticism will mean, therefore, that going in the direction indicated and respecting the authority of the confession we think we ought to prefer other

statements as better following that direction. A certain positive criticism of
the confession cannot be avoided when we respect its authority, when therefore
we go further in the direction indicated by it, and therefore in our own responsibility in relation to the Church here and now. Even if there is no cause to oppose
them directly, its statements have at all points to be extensively interpreted.
They have to be read with underlinings and emphases and accentuations which
they never had then, which they do not have when considered " historically,"
but which they necessarily acquire when they are the antithesis and the horizon
of the present-day Church. The necessity of this positive criticism of the confession may lead to the emergence of a new confession, i.e., a confession which
repeats the old one according to the new knowledge of the present-day Church.
This is not merely reconcilable with the authority of the confession, but may
even be demanded in some way by the authority of the confession as rightly
understood, in that it does not bind us to itself but to Holy Scripture, in that it
does not challenge us primarily to agreement with its statements, but to persistence in the unity of faith and only for that reason and in that sense to agreement
with its statements.

But we must not forget that it does not do this formlessly, but in
the very definite form of its statements. Its statements constitute the
horizon within which we find ourselves in the Church. They give us
the direction to the unity of faith. With their Yes and No they constitute the concrete form which questions us concerning our faith.
It is not, therefore, that we can reverently listen to the confession as
an attestation of any faith and therefore faith in general, so that we
for our part can then enjoy faith in general and therefore any faith,
thinking that in that way we meet its call to the unity of faith. No,
the call takes place in the form of statements. And it is in this form
or not at all that it is the object of our discussion with it. Let those
who think they have to oppose the confession oppose its statements.
Let them do so in obedience to the Scripture to which it itself points
us. Let them do so by continuing in the direction for which it claims
us. Let them see to it that their criticism or interpretation does not
perhaps lead them in quite a different direction and perhaps out of
their Church, or that it is not perhaps based and pursued quite otherwise than in obedience to Holy Scripture. All criticism and interpretation of dogmas is dangerous in both these ways, inevitable though
it may be. The dogma stands before us again after we have dealt
with it, demanding a reckoning. We must see to it that we give this
reckoning. Yet the worst mistake we might make in this respect is
at least better than a relation to dogma in which its statements as
such are no longer heard, in which they cannot speak concretely or be
taken up in some way into our own thinking and speaking. That
there is a dogma attesting the Church faith of the fathers and brethren
is only of significance because this faith speaks in dogma. But it does
so in the statements of dogma. If its statements as such remain or
become alien, how can we find ourselves in the direction in which it
would point us ? If we find ourselves in this direction, then we necessarily also find ourselves in a definite agreement with its statements

which remains even in spite of and in all our criticism and interpretation. We can then understand these statements as statements of faith and accept them with complete freedom. With complete freedom : that is, as our own statements in the sense and understanding in which they have now imposed themselves upon us as true, with the reservations in respect of earlier interpretations (perhaps even of the original understanding) which are the necessary result of our own relation to Holy Scripture, but all the same as the confession of our own faith. In the questions which it answered then and there we recognise the questions which occupy us, and in its answers we see what we have to say here and now in obedience to Scripture. Perhaps we could say it differently. But we must not say it differently. And perhaps we cannot say it any better. What was said there and then is perhaps in its own unaltered form the most clear and definite thing that we can still say here and now even according to our insight. And in order that we too may point to the unity of faith, unless there are compelling reasons to the contrary, we will gladly say exactly what was said there and then, appropriating not only the content but also the form of the dogma, not only the direction but with the direction statements, maintaining not only faith in general but the particular faith of the dogma as defined in its wording. It is only in this way that we can continue discussion with it; that it retains its critical power over against us; that the possibility remains that the meaning and the understanding in which we have affirmed it can be corrected by it ; that the faith of the fathers and brethren has more than ever before to say to our own faith.

This brings us to the last point in our deliberations. As a Church authority the authority of the confession, too, cannot be an absolute, but only a relative one. The infallible and therefore final and unalterable confession is the praise which the Church as the body eternally united to its Head will offer to its Lord in this its own eternal consummation ; it is thus an eschatological concept, to which no present actualisation corresponds, to which every reality of Church confession, everything we now know as dogma old or new, can only approximate. What we know as dogma is in principle fallible and is therefore neither final nor unalterable.

Here again the ways of Roman Catholic and Evangelical doctrine obviously diverge. Dogma in the Roman Catholic sense is the witness of revelation like Holy Scripture itself. Dogma in the Evangelical sense is the Church counter-witness to this witness of revelation. This means there can never be a final word, but only a word which is imperative and binding and authoritative until it is succeeded by something else. The Church confesses, and it also appropriates earlier and other confessions. But even as it does so, it remains open to the possibility that it may be better instructed by the Word of God, that it may know it better and therefore confess it better. In its confessing it has always before it the *eschaton* of the praise of God in its consummation. For that reason, on earth and therefore recognising its incompleteness, it must always be ready to receive such better instruction from the Word of God. In the 16th century it was the Reformed Churches which stated with particular clarity the provisional nature of their confessions and all confession. We confess the Old Church symbols only with the reservation : *pource qu'ilz sont conformes à la Parole de Dieu* (*Conf. Gallic.* 1559, *Art.* 5). In the official introduction to the Synod of Berne in 1532 it says even of the Reformation Confession : " But if ought is adduced by our pastors.or others, which leads us closer to Christ, and according to God's Word is more profitable to fellowship and Christian love than the opinion now recorded, the same we gladly receive, not hindering the Holy Ghost, who does not lead us back to the flesh but forward to the image of Christ Jesus our Lord." And in the introduction to the *Conf. Scotica* 1560 : *protestantes, quod si quis in hac nostra confessione articulum vel sententiam repugnantem sancto Dei verbo notaverit . . . promittimus Dei gratia ex Dei ore id est ex sacris scripturis nos illi satisfacturos aut correcturos si quis quid erroris inesse probaverit.* That even Councils may err, and that God will maintain His truth against the error of a Council (Calvin, *Instit.* IV 9, 13), was a presupposition in the doctrine of all the Reformation Churches, deriving from the recognition of the divine authority of Scripture alone. It was not always and everywhere, especially on the Lutheran side, that the relativity of their own present decisions and therefore of the Reformation confessional writings was so clearly stated as at Berne and Edinburgh, or by Calvin in his work against Pighius (*C.R.* 6, 250) in relation to Luther, Melanchthon and himself. The only meaning we can give to the German text of the passage already quoted from the introduction to the Formula of Concord concerning the *Augustana* is that in these last days (after He allowed the Reformation to happen), Almighty God Himself " composed out of the divine prophetic and apostolic writings " the confession laid before emperor and empire in 1530. And at any rate in the later Lutheran dogmatics (cf. Hollaz, *Ex. theol. acroam.* 1707 *Prol.* II *qu.* 27) we can find pronouncements on the *specialis concursus Dei* under which the symbolic books of the Lutheran Church arose, and on the divine nature of their content, etc., which appear almost to assert their inspiration and canonicity. But on a closer reading we cannot rightly speak of more than an appearance, more than a special emphasis on the ecclesiastical authority of these books, even in Lutheranism. Hollaz does not go further on this point than to say : *periculosum est, sine adiecta declaratione libros symbolicos humana scripta appellare.* We can interpret this statement in *meliorem partem* : it is indeed dangerous to call the dogma of the Church a human word, without adding that as the word of the fathers and brethren whom God has put before us in the Church it is to be read and received as an imperative and binding and authoritative witness to the Word of God. It would have been a fundamental abandonment of the Reformation if there had been any attempt to obscure or remove the line between the divine Word and the human. The only question we can put to Lutheranism in this connexion is whether in speaking so sacrally of " symbolic books," although it is not guilty of any theoretical error, it does not carry this emphasis too far with its strange fancies concerning the *Augustana* and its noticeable magnifying of its own historical form generally ? whether with all the undiminished theoretical support which it unquestionably gives to the Scripture principle it does not in practice exalt itself in its origin and normative form to the level of a second source of revelation, especially treating its confession (and the person of Luther) in this way ? In so far as this is the case, it is also necessarily the case that in practice it has abandoned the Reformation and punished itself with the certain inflexibility and reserve towards new items of knowledge which inevitably results from such practice. We have to remember, of course, that we have here only a specifically Lutheran form of what in other forms has been the fault and fate of Protestantism as a whole.

If divine infallibility cannot be ascribed to any Church confession, then in practice we have to recognise that every Church confession

can be regarded only as a stage on a road which as such can be relativised and succeeded by a further stage in the form of an altered confession.   Therefore respect for its authority has necessarily to be
conjoined with a basic readiness to envisage a possible alteration of
this kind.

Indirectly even the Roman Catholic Church has recognised this.   It does not
admit any perfectibility of dogma, but it does admit a perfectibility of the
Church proclamation of dogma.   And this is confirmed in its history and practice
in which there are obviously dated and antiquated and corrected dogmas and
also those which are new and obviously clearer and more definite.

But what is true of a change in the judgment of the Church regarding the extent of the Canon and the definition of fathers and brethren
is also true of an alteration of the confession.   We cannot regard the
process as any easier or less responsible than that of drawing up
the confession.   It is not for any abstract reason, but recognising the
Word of God in Holy Scripture, that we have now to speak as we do—
and therefore differently from the fathers and brethren.   There has
to be an occasion important enough to justify as necessary the undertaking to speak differently from them.   What we have to say on this
occasion has to be so fresh and different from what they said that it
will be worth disturbing the unity of faith to speak differently from
them.   In some recognisable and compelling way—decisive by reason
of the inner weight of what is stated, in virtue of its agreement with
Scripture—it has to be the Church which undertakes to speak in
another way.   Before the work goes forward, in addition to Holy
Scripture all the voices of the now effective confession have to be
seriously heard, so that nothing is lost of what it has perhaps to say,
in spite of and in our new situation and task.   Our own undertaking
has then to prove its sincerity by its courage in laying it before the
rest of the Church as a decision which we ourselves believe to be
grounded in a divine decision, and therefore with the claim that a
decision has to be made concerning it, and therefore without fear of a
definite Yes or a definite No.   And then a corresponding practical
attitude has to accompany the altered confession from its inception
as the indispensable means of its proclamation.

It must arise out of an ultimate human certainty and an ultimate human
necessity.   We have to speak of it, therefore, as Luther does in relation to the
Articles of Schmalkald :   "These are the Articles on which I will and must stand
to my death, if God will, and I know not how to alter or yield ought that is
therein.   If any wish to concede ought, let him do so upon his own conscience";
and especially in relation to the doctrine of justification (at the beginning of
part 2) :   "Of this article nought can be conceded or withdrawn, though heaven
and earth fall and all that doth not endure : for there is none other name, whereby
we must be saved, saith St. Peter in Ac. 4.   And by His wounds we are healed.
And on this article hangs all that we teach and live against the Pope, the devil
and the world.   Therefore we must be certain and not doubt.   Otherwise all is
lost, and the Pope and the devil and everything that is against us will conquer
and prevail."

We cannot have a new confession on any easier conditions than these—or with the omission of any one of them. If these conditions are present, we not only can but must venture a new confession. But we can also regard all these conditions as the presuppositions on which a new confession must be attempted and the problem of whether we can and ought ceases to be a problem. Attempted on these conditions, it will definitely create for itself authority and respect.

We can only close by asserting that since the Reformation and the time immediately after there has never been a new confession in the Protestant sphere (bracketing the latest developments, whose importance has still to be seen), although there has been no lack of revolutionary movements in this sphere. Neo-Protestantism in particular, which was sufficiently conscious of itself in relation to all prior development even including the Bible itself, has not produced a new confession. It has not had the confidence seriously and consistently to lay before the Church the challenge even of a confession of the non-confessionalism which it has taught and demanded, of a decision in favour of the lack of decision which alone can save. As is well-known, it has never done more than obscure the old confession theologically and to some extent overthrow its canonical legality. The Unitarian Church in Hungary, Siebenbürgen and Poland is an exception which deserves honourable mention. But the question of Julius Kaftan, " Do we need a new dogma ? " (1890), sounded strange, or at any rate impracticable. With many sighs and outcries the old dogma was maintained through every theological development, just as the old Canon was maintained in spite of all the criticism of it. And Neo-Protestantism never went beyond a compromise with the old dogma. Why ? Presumably just because Neo-Protestantism could not fulfil the conditions of a new dogma, because it could not really claim Church authority for its dogmas and therefore with a right insight did not dare to claim it.

§ 21

FREEDOM IN THE CHURCH

A member of the Church claims direct, absolute and material freedom not for himself, but only for Holy Scripture as the Word of God. But obedience to the free Word of God in Holy Scripture is subjectively conditioned by the fact that each individual who confesses his acceptance of the testimony of Scripture must be willing and prepared to undertake the responsibility for its interpretation and application. Freedom in the Church is limited as an indirect, relative and formal freedom by the freedom of Holy Scripture in which it is grounded.

1. THE FREEDOM OF THE WORD

To understand what it means that God has a Word for the Church, we must think of the freedom as well as of the authority of the Church. The Church, called and grounded in the Word of God, is a *communio sanctorum* not only in the sense that here men are gathered into a *communio* and as such are ruled and determined by the *sancta*, i.e., by the sanctuary of the evangelical faith set up in their midst, but—just because of this—in the further sense : that here men participate in this sanctuary, that it is therefore entrusted to their hands and committed to their keeping, that they themselves now become this *communio* of the *sancti* in virtue of the *communicatio* of *sancta* which takes place in this very *communio*, being called to be not hearers only, but also doers of the Word. Authority and respect for authority is only the objective side of the obedience that is demanded, created and implanted within the Church by the Word of God. Had we spoken only of authority, we should have spoken equivocally of the sovereignty of the God of Abraham, Isaac and Jacob, who is not a God of the dead but of the living. His authority is divinely majestic just because it has nothing in common with tyranny, because its true likeness is not the power of a natural catastrophe which annihilates all human response, but rather the power of an appeal, command and blessing which not only recognises human response but creates it. To obey it does not mean to be overrun by it, to be overwhelmed and eliminated in one's standing as a human being. Obedience to God is genuine precisely in that it is both spontaneous and receptive, that it not only is unconditional obedience but even as such is obedience from the heart. God's authority is truly recognised ·only within the

661

sphere of freedom : only where conscience exists, where there exists
a sympathetic understanding of its lofty righteousness and a wholehearted assent to its demands—only where a man allows himself to
be humbled and raised up, comforted and warmed by its voice. Exactly the same is true of the various forms of ecclesiastical authority
and the reverence due to them. If we refuse to see the equally necessary subjective side of obedience as freedom, or see it only as an
incidental factor, if we evade the task of doing justice to this aspect
of the problem as well as to the other, we have to consider whether we
are not involved in a philosophico-political systematisation of theological insights which, though correct in themselves, are partial, and
because they are so, ought not to be thus systematised as if they were
a totality. Otherwise not only do they lose their character and power
as theological truth, but in being thus presented as though they were
the rounded whole of Christian knowledge, they hinder and disturb
the recognition and victory of the truth by a onesidedness which does
not arise from the mystery of God but from the mystery of the arbitrary
human will. They then produce reactions by which they are rightly
affected in their philosophico-political systematisation, but which at
the same time are usually found to injure the abbreviated and mis-
used truth which they contain. The man who is merely mastered
and compelled will certainly not be the man who is reached and born
again by the Word of God ; he will not be mastered and compelled
as the Word of God masters and compels. He is mastered and compelled by powers of a very different sort, up to and including that of
death. Yet there is not a single one of all these powers which so brings
him under its authority as really to remove the possibility of his
rebelling and therefore to make him truly obedient. He can still be
like the Stoic overwhelmed by fate : *si fractus illabatur orbis, impavidum
ferient ruinae.* In the Church the Word of God works differently.
Neither the divine authority governing the Church, nor valid authority
within the Church, is exerted in the manner of these merely mastering
and compelling powers. This is only possible through human misunderstanding and misuse. For this reason those reactions are superfluous in the Church because pointless. The man mastered and compelled is precisely the man whom God loves, who is therefore set upon
his own feet and made truly responsible. To recognise and respect
authority as a member of the Church means to love God in return
and therefore to be willing and prepared to assume responsibility—
real co-operative responsibility. The Christian is not a stone that is
pushed, or a ball that is made to roll. The Christian is the man who
through the Word and love of God has been made alive, the real man,
able to love God in return, standing erect just because he has been
humbled, humbling himself because he has been raised up. Just
because in the Church there is no mere mastery and compulsion,
there is in it a real mastery and compulsion. Just because there is

authority in the Church, there is also freedom. This aspect of the problem also demands attention, and not merely cursory but serious attention.

There is reason to state all this with special emphasis to-day. The Evangelical Church and its theology, in all those countries where it is again beginning to be conscious of its task and mission, is calling to account and analysing the Neo-Protestantism or intermediate stage upon which it entered soon after the Reformation, to which it then almost completely succumbed. If appearances do not deceive, the last term of this development now lies behind us. It is no longer able to satisfy the essence and obligation of this Church and theology as seen from the standpoint of Scripture and the Reformation itself. In this process of analysis the rediscovery of the reality and concept of both divine and ecclesiastical authority is playing an important part at every point. That God is in heaven and man on the earth, that God rules and man must obey, that the Word of God makes a total claim upon men—we have had to learn anew to accustom ourselves again to these simple truths, in contradiction to a theological liberalism which would have nothing to do with them. But this new reference to the authority of God cannot be made without reference above all to its concrete manifestation in the authority of the ecclesiastical Canon, to the authority of the Reformation as something which gives a new basis to the Church; and to the authority of the confession as the documentary form of this new basis. And now of all times all this cannot be formulated or reformulated without exciting to more passionate opposition than ever the same theological liberalism against which, in fact, it must be said. But from the beginning, and to-day more than ever, this theological process of reconstruction is heavily burdened and compromised by the fact that at the same time we are in the middle of a period of philosophico-political reconstruction where similarly authority and freedom are at stake or seem to be so. Apart from the question of divine and ecclesiastical authority, in the world outside the great attempt has been made to oppose to the absolutism of an ostensibly autonomous reason, and therewith to the absolutism of the individual and humanity, the absolutism of a state authority which claims to control men singly and collectively in body and soul, and the basis and justification of which are supposed to have been discovered newly and very impressively in the idea of race. Authority has thus become a favourite secular term, while at the same time liberalism has degenerated into a term of secular abuse. A worse disturbance of the task of ecclesiastical and theological reconstruction to which we have referred can hardly be imagined. How can the life of the Church be more gravely upset than by such an *alter ego* (in this connexion we may think of the story of Pharaoh's magicians) doing apparently what it does with a parallelism which extends even to details ? At an earlier time the Reformation must have been similarly disturbed by the fact that simultaneously and side by side with it there was a movement of renaissance humanism waging war against mediæval culture ; a powerful striving for independence on the part of nationalist monarchies, princes and cities against the imperial power ; a rising of the peasantry against their feudal overlords ; a general attempt to seize ecclesiastical property. How many alive at that time may have understood the Reformation primarily from the standpoint of one of these contemporary movements ? How easy it was to affirm and support it from the standpoint of one of these secular movements and in that way to bring strange fire to its altar ! How easy, on the other hand, where a man was opposed to any. of these secular movements, to reject and fight against the Reformation because of its association with them ! So to-day we must expect the theological and ecclesiastical revival to be viewed in connexion with the nationalist-authoritarian movement, to be derived from the latter in its motives or, the other way round, to be regarded as the religious source of its inspiration, or to be traced back with it to a common root. And obviously it is equally fatal to it whether it is affirmed and supported or refused and opposed by reason of this association. Every word that can and must be spoken in the Church and theology on behalf of true authority and against the abuse of freedom can obviously be both intended and understood in an utterly false sense when brought even into the remotest connexion with the parallel slogans of the contemporary movement. Of course, these parallelisms between Church history and world history are never the result of chance. The Church and the world stand so close together that it is no wonder if events in the Church are always accompanied, whether secretly or openly, by shadows and copies in the events of world history. But it is in the sovereign power of God's wisdom and might that the Church and the world thus belong to each other, and that by the appearance of this parallelism we are reminded of this interdependence and thereby of Himself. If we believe in the providence of God, this cannot mean that we are to think of ourselves as occupying a point of view from which we can systematically perceive and master this interdependence and also this parallelism. Belief in divine providence means rather that we shall not justify and legitimate the way, which the Church must follow in obedience to its mission and to the Word of God, by reference to the ways which we see the world follow. And again, we shall not try to justify and legitimate the course of world-history, about whose meaning and goal we can at most have only suppositions, by reference to the ways of the Church. It is just the obvious system of thought, the obvious connexion between these two apparently parallel things, which constitutes the danger that must be recognised as such and avoided. If it is not recognised and avoided in this way, the Church becomes involved in exertions, antitheses and consequences, to which precisely because its message is intended for the whole world, it ought to stand opposed and superior. Then it loses its authenticity ; for in the very fact that it does not recognise and avoid this danger, but attends to the affairs of others instead of holding fast to its mission and the Word of God, it has shown failure to stand in that obedience which demanded from it nothing but fidelity to its own course. If I am not mistaken, this fidelity to the Church's own path was at the basis of Luther's attitude in the Peasants' War. Yet in other respects neither he nor the other Reformers always recognised and avoided clearly enough this threatening danger. And to the extent in which this did not happen, it turned speedily enough to the ill of the Reformation Church. Therefore we have every reason to make to-day the uncompromising assertion : Whatever in the divine counsels may be the connexion between the process of reconstruction now going on in the Church and theology concerning authority and freedom, and that other crisis which impressively enough is now proceeding in the realm of politics and philosophy—we cannot and must not interpret either by the other. In the present connexion, this means in practice that, when we are concerned to re-establish the authority of God and of the Church, we will have nothing to do with the current proclamation of a secular authoritarianism. We expect as little from it as we should from a new proclamation of a secular liberalism. We are most certainly grateful for all the approval and assistance which may come to us from this source. But we will make no use at all of the arguments and the emotions which it may lend us. Nor, on the other hand, do we have any cause to take part in those secular exertions from the Church point of view, or to offer ecclesiastical arguments and emotions as weapons in that conflict. When the authoritarian state-philosophy of to-day feels that it must fight against the enemy of the human race which it finds in the spirit of 1789 and 1848 and in Marxism, it may or may not be right. But in any case the opposition in which the Gospel finds itself to a false doctrine of freedom is not this opposition. On the contrary, there can be no question that this modern state philosophy will itself be affected by the opposition of the Gospel. With all its authoritarianism it, too, belongs to the doctrine of freedom against which the Gospel is struggling. In just the same way, the idealism of yesterday made itself responsible for what, from the standpoint of the Gospel, is to be opposed as tyranny. We shall find that the Church in its behaviour and discourse before the world must interest itself in that idea of freedom which is now oppressed and persecuted in the worldly sphere, and protect the relative justification of its demands ; not for the sake of freedom in itself, nor because the Gospel is interchangeable with a metaphysic of freedom, but rather that, in the compromising proximity in which it finds itself, it cannot be made interchangeable with a metaphysic of authority. In the period of liberalism the Church quite rightly did not become simply liberal. In spite of quite regrettable concessions to the spirit of the age, and much against its own will, it remained under constant attack from the liberal world as the refuge of the idea of authority. Similarly to-day it does not merely go along with the spirit of the day, nor does it neglect to become the asylum of the truth which to-day is on the losing side—and that is the truth of the idea of freedom. The power and authenticity of its struggle against a philosophy of pseudo-freedom depend wholly upon its refusal to take part in the secular attack on secular liberalism, upon its not being affected by the relatively justifiable criticisms with which liberalism opposes authoritarianism, and, in so far as it has to address itself to a world locked in party conflicts, upon its throwing a compensating counterpoise into the scales in favour of freedom so that justice is done. Its own struggle is too serious and bitter for it to wage except, legitimately, with unburdened back, and good conscience. This legitimacy, unburdened back and good conscience are conditioned by its holding itself " unspotted from the world " even while it keeps an open and attentive mind for what is going on in the world, that is, by its refusing to become a partisan and maintaining the superiority of the Gospel over against all worldly conflicts. For these reasons its own fight against Neo-Protestantism cannot and must not on any account be fought in a common front " on behalf of authority." To be legitimate, it must not be waged at all as a one-sided struggle " on behalf of authority." The Reformation was everywhere spiritually lost and ineffective, becoming a mild or extreme fanaticism, where it turned to its own profit and advantage the general opposition to the Papacy, scholasticism and mediævalism, or where it understood and presented itself one-sidedly within the terms of this opposition. Similarly, to-day, we at once weaken ourselves spiritually if we go so much as a finger's-breadth with contemporary authoritarianism, or even advance with it only along the line on which we seem to run parallel with it. It is, therefore, of supreme importance to pay attention to the other aspect of our problem, that there is freedom in the Church as well as authority. If we refuse to see this, how can we recognise and avoid the great danger presented to us by our environment to-day ? How can we be free from the suspicion of serving the new spirit of the age more than the Holy Ghost ? How can we be trustworthy ? Let it be clearly understood : we must not pay attention to this side of the problem in order to be trustworthy. This attention is required by the nature of our objective. It is required supremely by the fact that God's revelation is revelation in the Word and also by the Spirit. " In the Word " certainly implies that the Church and theology cannot be made over to a subjectivist system. " In the Word " undoubtedly means authority in the Church. But just as certainly " by the Spirit " implies the impossibility of an objectivist system. The other side must be observed : freedom in the Church. Taking God's Word and therefore God's revelation as the point of departure, we find ourselves in fact on the other side of these antitheses. We can no longer play off freedom against authority or authority against freedom. We are not to be concerned about either the one or the other of these two principles as such, but in both only about the will of God. Therefore we must always be prepared to oppose divine authority to every human idea of freedom, and equally prepared to restrict every human idea of authority by reference to the freedom of God.

We are, then, compelled by a real and not merely a tactical necessity to make this second affirmation. But it may be useful to us to remember that in the present-day situation (for the sake of the trustworthiness of the Church and its message) it is also tactically necessary to be relevant and therefore actually to make this second affirmation.

That there is also freedom in the Church must be taken seriously because here, too, in this aspect of the matter, it is clearly a question of the totality. To the question : How does God's Word come to us men in Holy Scripture and how does it exercise sway in the Church of Jesus Christ ? we give this second answer, that it happens through free obedience. In making such a statement we say fully what is to be said to that question. Just as God in His revelation is the Holy Spirit no less than the Son, so God's Word in Scripture is Spirit no less than Word. And we err no less in refusing to appreciate its freedom than if its authority remains hidden from us. The real relationship is this. As the Son can be revealed only by the Spirit, and in the Spirit only the Son is revealed, so authority must necessarily be interpreted by freedom, and freedom by authority. In the Church neither authority nor freedom can claim to be a principle of ultimate validity and power. In the Church both can be understood and considered only as predicates of God's Word, and therefore in the light of this which is their proper subject, and therefore only in the light which they cast upon each other.

This must be particularly remembered in the polemical use of these ideas. It is a temptation, too great a temptation, to say that in the reference to freedom we have the specifically Protestant answer to that question, in direct opposition to Catholicism. We can only issue a warning against this idea. It will fare ill with the Protestant Church if it is more protestant to speak of freedom than of authority, if the demagogic notion is true that in the last resort the aim of the Reformers was to enthrone the reason and conscience of the individual as opposed to the authority and judgment of the Church, that they were, therefore, the forerunners of Pietism, the Enlightenment and Idealism. It is true that, confronted by an authority that was no longer a real, divine or genuinely ecclesiastical authority, they proclaimed the freedom of the Christian man as a free lord of all things and subject to no one. But how can one fail to see that by this very proclamation they were, in fact, fighting on precisely the opposite front ? As though Luther did not see in the enthusiasm of his time, to which all the later forms of liberalism are traceable, the same enemy as in the Papacy ! How can we fail to observe that, according to Luther, the same Christian man is the slave of all things and subject to everyone ? As though Calvin did not do more for the recognition of the authority of God and the Church than all the mediæval popes and scholastics put together ! The Church of the Reformation, provided it does not allow itself to be confused by that demagogic apologetic, need not wait to be reminded by Roman Catholic polemical writers that through an ill-considered affirmation of the principle of freedom it will inevitably fall into heresy and become a sect. Neither in origin nor in essence is it in any way involved in the impasse in which the free individual is suddenly to be the measure of all things. To go no further, how can this optimism be combined with the Reformers' insight into the wretchedness of man, and his incapacity to know God and to do the good ? This part of Reformation theology has had to be prudently erased for the Reformers to be represented and extolled as the fathers of the modern aspirations after freedom. Still more fundamentally, the Evangelical view of the unique glory and saving power of the divine Word excludes the possibility of attaching to Protestantism even the intention or preparation of those aspirations after freedom. By all means let Catholicism fight for authority against freedom in its opposition to all kinds of other heresies. But in opposition to Catholicism itself we do not have to espouse first the cause of freedom, but of authority, and only then and from that standpoint freedom. For with its doctrine of the unity of the Church and revelation (together with its doctrine of nature and grace), it has attributed to man a freedom and capacity side by side with God and over God. So, then, it has really given birth to all the other heresies—however hostile it may be to them. It has made them necessary as opponents on its own level. It has destroyed the recognition of the authority of God, and in so doing—in spite of clericalism—it has destroyed that of a genuine ecclesiastical authority. That is our decisive charge against it. It is also true that with this destruction of authority it has also destroyed the freedom of the mind and conscience, the necessary freedom offered to the individual member of the Church. But how can this be understood and seriously maintained if it is not perceived and maintained first that Roman Catholicism is rebellion against the authority of the Word of God, rebellion against canonical Scripture, rebellion against the fathers too, and against every genuine confession? When at the Reformation the Word of God re-established its rule in the tottering Church, " Catholicism " refused to obey it, and continued to destroy the Church ; not by knowing too much, but by knowing too little about authority, by making new opportunities and new forms for the arbitrary freedom of man to manipulate the Word of God according to its convenience. Therefore the Evangelical Church must not take its stand where according to Roman Catholic theory it ought to be, especially when it has to represent true evangelical freedom over against that theory. It must not define this *libertas christiana* as the inner independence of the soul which is bound immediately and exclusively to God, as though it did not realise how short a step it is from this independence to its counterpart in the form of papal infallibility. But it must define freedom, as it in truth is, as man's real dependence on the God who has mediately addressed and dealt with us. It must define freedom as the faithfulness with which we can and should trace the divine testimonies. It must define it as a cleaving to canonical Scripture, to the fathers and to the confession, and therefore to ecclesiastical authority. It must define it as the unique proud independence which as real submission to real authority is attributed to every individual member of the Church, or rather is conferred by the Holy Spirit of the Word of God. It is only in this way, that is, by a complete reversal of the front on which Catholicism would like to see us stand and where modern heresies would like to push us, that the strong and clear contrast between it and us can be made manifest, as is needful and also hopeful. Again, this must be done in the interests of the truth itself. But again, we must not fail to recognise that Roman Catholicism can listen to us, that a renewal of conversation between us, and at least a common outlook upon the *una sancta catholica* can be achieved, only when it sees that in regard to the recognition and assertion of authority we are not inferior to it but rather superior, that with the proclamation of evangelical freedom we do not aim at a worse but at a better obedience.

The converse is true on the opposite front against Neo-Protestantism. Here the temptation on our side is to commit ourselves to the idea and reality of authority. And, again, a warning is in place. It is true and has already been said that from this angle it is in fact a question of authority : the authority of God, of the Bible and of the confession. It was so already in the struggle of the Reformers against the fanatics and humanists who were the fathers of Neo-Protestantism. But on this side, too, we cannot overlook the fact that for the Reformers this enemy on the left stood very close to that on the right, that is, to the Papacy. They reproached the former no less than the latter with legalism, monkery and the enslavement of conscience, in spite of all their appeals to the Spirit, conscience or immediate revelation. They were right to do so. They were right to oppose to its message of freedom an authority which it rejected, and to oppose it in the shape of the true message of freedom which it was really rejecting. For what did Erasmus or Carlstadt or later Servetus or Sebastian Franck know of the real freedom of a Christian man ? What has the tragic seriousness with which we see all these figures take themselves, what has the portentousness with which in all later Neo-Protestantism man regards the inmost depths of his being and his experience as final reality and highest law—what has all this to do with the real evangelical freedom of the children of God ? Has not Calvin himself with his inexorable proclamation of authority done more for the cause of freedom than all the forerunners of modern ideas who flourished in his day ? When the Reformation Church rightly understands itself, it need not wait to be reminded by Neo-Protestantism that there is perhaps an ill-considered assertion of the idea of authority, by which the Church itself will necessarily become the victim of heresy and degenerate into a sect. Neither the origin nor the essence of the Church is to be found in the blind alley where man would like to be his own lord and law. An absolute principle of authority and an absolute principle of freedom both derive, do they not, from one and the same root, namely, an optimism which is impossible where the thought and effort of the human heart are recognised to be evil from youth upwards, and the sovereign power of the divine Word is discerned and recognised? With just such an absolute and therefore false principle of authority the Reformers reproached not merely the enemy on the right but also the enemy on the left—that is, the fathers of Neo-Protestantism. This adversary of the left may, then, be allowed to continue to fight for freedom against authority. But he must not be allowed to dictate our own attitude. In his case, too, it is safer and more hopeful if we espouse the cause of which he regards himself as champion. However blatantly and energetically he seems to maintain the cause of freedom, it is not in fact true that with him this cause is in good hands. Is there a worse threat to freedom itself than the establishment of man as his own lord and lawgiver ? Who can exercise a worse tyranny over us than the god in our own breast ? And what further tyrannies does not this first and decisive one drag in its train ? It is inevitable that the man who claims to be directly in communion with God, and free from all concrete forms of authority, will all the more certainly be delivered over to the powers of nature and history, to the spirit of the age and of contemporary movements, to the demons of his situation and environment. If you wish to see man enslaved, you have only to free him in the manner in which Erasmus and Carlstadt once wished to see him free. If you wish to awake in him a wild longing for at least an appearance of order and authority, if you want to make him ripe for conversion, then bring him up in the kind of freedom which Neo-Protestantism preaches. Catholic authoritarianism is the inevitable counterpart of this freedom. And that is just the complaint which is to be made from this point of view. Here we are on ground where, as there is no genuine authority, so there is no genuine freedom. There is only action and reaction between a despotic arrogance and an equally despotic despair. We have here the disobedience which wished to evade the reformation of the Church by the Word of God, and does evade it, only to succumb all the more surely to the slavery which, outside the dominion of the Word of God, is in one form or another unavoidable. And therefore we oppose to Neo-Protestantism the very thing which it claims to have and which in reality it does not have, namely, freedom in the Church. Certainly, authority in the Church. Certainly God and the Bible and the Creed. But note well : all this gains validity, not as one of the inventions of the human mind which Neo-Protestantism knows only too well in its own sphere and which it will receive only with obduracy, but as the power which, unlike the powers which man sets up over himself, does not lead him from one tyranny to another, but at last puts him on his own feet, and lifts him into an air in which he can breathe. Therefore, we must not please modern Protestantism by placing ourselves in the position where its own slogans aim at putting us. In face of it—and again the front is completely reversed—the message of the freedom of the Christian man, which it has so astonishingly misconceived, is the victorious truth. Here, too, we do not have to do it in the interests of any sort of strategy, but in the interests of the truth itself. Here, too, we can hardly expect a hearing and discussion and the hope of agreement, until it is clear that the accusation is not of too much but of too little freedom, and that in the representation of its own cause, it is not being underbidden but overbidden.

We have to discuss the question of freedom in the Church, which primarily and properly means the freedom of the Word of God. We have to show that there is not only authority but also freedom in the Church, that there is not only authority but also freedom under the Word. We have to show that this is a genuine freedom which comes to man in the Church, which is not merely allowed him, but conferred upon him, which is not merely permitted but commanded, which is not fortuitous but necessary. This being the case, we obviously have to understand freedom primarily and essentially in concrete terms, that is, as the freedom of the Word of God. Only as such is it truly freedom, immediate, absolute and meaningful. By it the freedom assigned to us men in the Church is established. As human freedom, it is genuine just because it is limited by the former as an indirect, relative and formal freedom. Human freedom, like human authority, means nothing if the Word of God is not primary and basic, containing and exercising both authority and freedom in itself. Because the Word of God has and exercises freedom in itself, for this reason and on this ground, where it is heeded, that is, in the Church where like evokes like, there is also a human freedom. Since this human freedom is thus evoked, it will neither evade the freedom of the Word, nor degenerate into freedom apart from the Word or without the Word or in contradiction to the Word. It can be freedom only under the Word. Again, it is as such, and only as such, that it will be a genuine human freedom.

When we speak of freedom in the Church, in the first instance we mean generally that in the Church, without prejudice to its authority, that is, order, normativeness, guidance and direction, there is also man's own choice and decision, his own determination and resolve. Since the Church consists of men, there is freedom in the Church. Where there is no choice and decision, no determination and resolve, there are no men. Even when we presuppose at once that this freedom can primarily and properly be only the freedom of the Word of God, in view of this primary and proper meaning of the idea, we must first think generally of men in the Church. It is in them and for them that the Word of God has its freedom, although their human freedom is certainly to be distinguished from the freedom of the Word of God itself. We are not speaking, of course, of the eternal Logos as such, but concretely of the Word made flesh which is believed and attested by men. Where men thus believe and attest the Word of God, they are not merely subjected and obedient to it, but because they are so, they participate in its freedom.

In thinking of these men in the Church, we think chiefly of the apostles and prophets themselves. They certainly belong—and indeed as the oldest and first—to the succession of men who have believed and attested the Word of God, and thus, by becoming subject and obedient to it, they have gained a share in its freedom. As apostles and prophets they do not only stand in a succession with all the other men of whom the same may in general be said. As prophets and apostles they stand over against this succession with their word which is the Word of Holy Scripture. To this extent they are also bearers of the Word of God itself, with the direct, absolute and material freedom which is proper to it. But how can they become intelligible to us, if they do not also and as such stand in the succession in which we also may stand as members of the Church founded upon their word, which is the Word of Holy Scripture? Even in the indirect, relative and formal freedom which is proper to their faith and witness also, it must become clear to us that not only this kind of freedom is characteristic of their word, which is the Word of Holy Scripture; the direct, absolute and material freedom of the Word of God must also become clear to us. Otherwise they will not be intelligible to us. Therefore we affirm first of all that the relationship of the prophets and apostles to Jesus Christ, since it has the character of obedience, has also the character of choice and decision. Not a choice and decision of such a kind that in it these men can have control, or by it they can gain control, over that which they chose and for which they decided. This is excluded by the fact that Jesus Christ, the Lord, confronted them, and that they stood to Him in a relation of obedience which could not be reversed. But while there was no reversal in this relation, it was still a relation in which Jesus Christ had in these men something real to confront, in which they really responded to Him, in which, in so far as they gave Him their faith and witness, He was chosen by them, and in which they made a decision for Him. Even obedience is choice and decision, although it is essentially a choice and decision in which the obedient man surrenders his own power to Him whom he obeys. Thus even obedience is freedom. In this sense, the freedom no less than the obedience of the prophets and apostles stands at the beginning of the Church: the freedom which became actual only in the obligations of obedience, only on the basis of the transcendent freedom of Jesus Christ, but still the freedom. There cannot be a Church of Jesus Christ apart from a repetition of this freedom. The existence of Jesus Christ stands or falls by the fact that Jesus Christ makes of such men something real to confront—men who respond to Him in that they choose Him as He has chosen them, who decide for Him as He has decided for them, disciples who follow Him because they are called by Him.

But we must go on to affirm that, even interpreted as freedom, the relationship between prophets and apostles and their Lord is a unique relationship—as unique as revelation itself at the centre of the ages. Therefore, although the continued life of the Church is not possible without a repetition of this freedom, it does not mean a continual succession of prophets and apostles. In the directness of their encounter with Jesus Christ, it is impossible for the disciples of Jesus to have real successors, or for that freedom to be repeatable. Again, everything depends on whether the unique revelation of God in Jesus Christ and the prophetic-apostolic encounter with Him in its uniqueness is futile, or whether the promise : Ye shall be my witnesses, and : Lo, I am with you always, is true and has been fulfilled. If it is true and has been fulfilled, then in the freedom of their faith and witness the prophets and apostles are copies attesting the freedom of Jesus Christ Himself, but at the same time they are prototypes attesting the freedom of all human faith and witness in the Church founded by their Word. In their freedom, the Church must recognise and honour the freedom of their Lord in which the freedom of its members, as members of His body, is grounded. From this point of view also the Church cannot ignore Scripture. Scripture cannot be truly authoritative for it, unless, because it is its authority, it shares in its freedom, that is, in that choice and decision in which the prophets and apostles, on the ground of the choice and decision which befell them, became and were prophets and apostles. Scripture rules within the Church and its members only if they—the Church and those within the Church —share in the movement in which Scripture was born and in virtue of which even to-day Scripture is not mere writing but in its written character is Spirit and life. This is true especially in the narrower sense of these ideas in which they denote the movement of faith and witness in which under the guidance of the Holy Ghost the biblical Word became possible, and was effected and declared not only to bind, but both to bind and also to free. Scripture is a document which does not spring only from obedience as such, but from the obedience of prophets and apostles discharged in this movement. And if that promise is true and fulfilled, the movement is not now dormant and petrified in this document ; rather, in that movement fulfilled in obedience, this document exists as witness to revelation. The Church comes into existence in genuine submission to this authority, but it cannot allow the revelation attested by Scripture to flow over itself as a waterfall flows over a cliff. Rather, because God's revelation is attested by Scripture and because Scripture furnishes the documentary evidence of this movement of revelation and exists only within it, the Church for its part must allow itself to be set in movement through Scripture.

Luther has called Scripture master and judge. " Holy Scripture and the Word of God ought to be regarded as an empress, whom one should immediately follow, obeying what she commands " (*W.A. Ti.* 1, 186, 20) . . . " it is truly the spiritual body of Christ " (*Grund und Ursach aller Artikel* 1521, *W.A.* 7, 315, 24). It is certainly not a merely metaphorical but a literal meaning that is intended when these expressions attribute to Scripture an independent and even personal life of its own in the exercise of its functions with regard to the Church.

If we have to speak of freedom as well as of authority in the Church, there can be no question of setting up a second principle beside Holy Scripture, or of demanding a hearing for a second voice beside that of Holy Scripture. On the contrary, Holy Scripture alone has to be heard in the Church. Therefore it must be heard as the principle and voice of both authority and freedom. For it has both aspects unseparated and inseparably. It has authority as the Word of God, and freedom as man's witness to God's Word—a freedom which does not originate from below, that is, from the humanity of the biblical witnesses, but like authority from above, that is, from the divine Word by which these men were roused to faith and witness. Because they were to testify to God's Word, they were endowed and equipped with authority. Because they were to do this as men, they were endowed and equipped with freedom. And so their testimony in Holy Scripture—because it is the testimony of God's Word—meets us with the claim to be heard and accepted as authentic. But this authenticity is not that of a rigid prescription inscribed, as it were, on a stone tablet, which the Church and its members have to read off mechanically and translate into their own mode of thought and speech. It is a living authenticity ; for Scripture itself is a really truly living, acting and speaking subject which only as such can be truly heard and received by the Church and in the Church. In Scripture we have to see the motivation in which prophets and apostles believed and witnessed. We have to understand this motivation as the life and operation of the Word of God Himself. We have to yield to and follow this motivation of the Word of God which takes place in Scripture. We have to be stirred up and to stir up ourselves by it in our own faith and witness. This is the problem we have to see side by side with that of the authority of Scripture, not as a distinct problem, but as the problem of the concrete understanding of this authority. It is, therefore, really a question of the freedom of the Word, and only then and on this basis, and in the interests of the Word itself, a question of human freedom in the Church—the freedom under the Word which is demanded and at the same time created and bestowed by the Word. The freedom of the Word cannot imply any limitation of the authority of the Word. On the contrary, we have obviously failed to understand its authority, and therefore its loftiness, dignity, value, validity and power, and we are not honouring it as it ought to be honoured, if we do not understand and honour it as the effectual working of Scripture as the present living Word of God in accordance with His true and fulfilled promise, i.e., as a deciding, willing, guiding, governing, determining action taking place in the Church, whose concrete subject is precisely Scripture itself. Thus the superiority of Scripture over against the Church is not the idolatrous calm of icy mountain peaks towering motionlessly above a blossoming valley. The argument of life cannot be played off against the authority of Scripture. Nor can the latter be questioned and assailed in the name of a struggle for the spirit as opposed to the letter. The reason for this is that Scripture is itself spirit and life in the comprehensive and profound sense of these ideas—the Spirit and life of the living God Himself, who draws near to us in its faith and witness, who need not wait until spirit and life are subsequently breathed into the document of His revelation in virtue of the acceptance it finds in the Church or the insight, sympathy, and congeniality which its readers bring to it, but who with His own Spirit and life always anticipates the reactions of all its readers, who in this book really exercises that government in the Church which human church government can only follow by interpreting and applying His Word, by recognising the mighty acts done by Him, by preaching the truth He proclaims, by serving His revealed will. The true freedom of man in the Church, freedom under the Word, consists in this following of the God who at all times precedes us all in Holy Scripture, and in adherence to the action which He takes by Scripture. It will be our next task to illustrate and explain the freedom of the Word itself and as such.

1. The freedom of the Word of God and therefore of Holy Scripture consists primarily in the simple fact that, in contrast to all other elements in the life of the Church and the world, as a direct witness to the revelation of God in Jesus Christ, it has a theme of ineffaceable distinctiveness and uniqueness. This theme—because it has been given to it by God Himself, and because its witnesses are God's own witnesses—constitutes Scripture as a subject which distinguishes itself from all other subjects, and has its own position and activity in relation to them.

At this point we can and must think at once of Mt. 16^{16-19} : It was in the ineffaceable but representative singularity of his existence as this man that Peter uttered his confession of the Lord's Messiahship which is the alpha and omega of all biblical testimony. How did he arrive at this ? He did not arrive at it—flesh and blood did not reveal it to him—but he is extolled as blessed because the confession which he makes was imparted to him by direct revelation, by Jesus' Father in heaven. As the one so blessed, he now receives the promise : " Upon this rock I will build my church." In his singularity as the man Peter which as such is representative of the attitude and function of all who bear witness to direct revelation, he thus becomes a subject distinct from both Jesus Christ and His Church, but mediating between them. He attains independence and a function of his own. This function is obviously the one which he has

22

already exercised in his confession (anticipating, so to speak, the content of the promise). Note how here, distinctively reversed, all the important elements appear : God's revelation, a concrete man, his institution to the ministry of the revelation, his function in that ministry. Note, too, how closely the latter two elements of institution and function are connected with and dependent on the first, God's revelation. An analogous situation occurs in the case of Paul. He is not called by man (Gal. 1¹). He is not naturally fitted to be an apostle (nor can one say of Peter that he was fitted to be that rock). But by the grace of God he is what he is (1 Cor. 15¹⁰). Jesus Christ Himself has made him so. The God who raised Jesus Christ from the dead (Gal. 1¹) also separated Paul from his mother's womb, when it pleased Him to reveal His Son in him, that he might preach Him among the heathen (Gal. 1¹⁵⁻¹⁶). This grace has sufficed him (2 Cor. 12⁹). This grace was not given him in vain (1 Cor. 15¹⁰). Christ is the One who is alive in him (Gal. 2²⁰) and at work in him (Phil. 4¹³). This grace and this Christ are the content of his apostolate. According to all his epistles, Paul cannot be an apostle, or exercise his apostolate, without continually remembering how he has arrived at it, or rather how the apostolate has come to him from Jesus Christ, as " the grace given to him " (1 Cor. 3¹⁰). Therefore it is by his theme that the apostle, like Holy Scripture, is constituted a distinctive subject, differing from and contrasting with all others. It must be understood that in this connexion it is meaningless to emphasise that in Holy Scripture there are, of course, many human subjects. This is true ; but it is more important to realise that in virtue of the unity of their theme the many human subjects of Scripture are visible and operative both to themselves and others as a single subject—of his fulness have we all received (Jn. 1¹⁶).

Therefore, to recognise the freedom of God's Word means primarily to recognise the subject created by God's revelation, the biblical witness. This subject meets us in the most varied forms as a single and unique being who requires to be heard in a single and unitary way. It is a human being. *In concreto* it is always an individual man, a Peter or Paul. But even as a human being it is determined and characterised by the one thing which is said to it and which it has to say. The freedom of God's Word is to be recognised especially in the fact that this subject as such appears and remains ineffaceably and unforgettably before us.

2. The next and really decisive insight may be comprehensively defined as the insight into the peculiar power of this subject in its opposition and relation to all other subjects. Freedom means ability, possibility, power—power in its illimitability or its equality over against other powers. It is such power that the subject has which we find constituted by the theme of Holy Scripture—by God's revelation in Jesus Christ. Because it is the subject constituted by this theme, it has the power of the Word of God.

Let us immediately explain that this power is not to be understood as the power of the religious, cultic, ethical, æsthetical, theological dæmonism which is no doubt naturally proper to the individual biblical subjects and to the biblical subject as a whole, in its humanity—the distinctive characteristic humanity determined by its theme. Both in the Old Testament and the New Testament there is a magic of biblical thought and language, of biblical perspicuity and argumentation, to which we must not on any account remain insensible, but which we can and must allow to have its due effect. As the essential pre-requisite for a biblical exegesis which does not remain confined to grammatical-historical matters, there is needed an intuition, an ability to detect the dæmonic magic of the Bible. But we must not forget that this is still not the power and freedom of the divine Word, however inseparable it may be from its human manifestation, and however important it may be not to overlook this factor. Mt. 11[9] is relevant here: " What went ye out for to see ? A prophet ? Yea, I say unto you, and more than a prophet." Likewise the warning of John the Baptist, Jn. 5[35] : " He was a burning and a shining light : and ye were willing for a season to rejoice in his light." We may add the warning of Paul in regard to himself, 1 Cor. 2[1]: he has come to them οὐ καθ' ὑπεροχὴν λόγου ἢ σοφίας, but to announce the testimony of God. Dæmonism and magic as such constitute a power which is, of course, characteristic of Scripture, but which at bottom it has in common with other writings, and which, therefore, does not basically distinguish this subject from others. To feel this power is still not to recognise the freedom of God's Word. This freedom is not recognised, and the dæmonic magic of Holy Scripture is not correctly appraised, until in these evidences of its human and therefore not unique power (we need not be ascetic and narrow in this respect) the power of the theme, that is of God's revelation in Jesus Christ, is recognised. If the full potency imparted to the biblical testimony by its theme is not to be missed, if a truly inspiring and uplifting power, majesty and profundity characterise it, if it is truly " spirit," even in the human sense of all these notions, then this mighty power is governed by the law : " Without me ye can do nothing " (Jn. 15[5]), and by the confession of Paul in 2 Cor. 3[5f.] : " Not that we are sufficient of ourselves to think anything as of ourselves ; but our sufficiency is of God ; who also hath made (ἱκάνωσεν) us able ministers of the new testament." Everything depends on the recognition of this ἱκανοῦν, whereas if we interpret, appreciate and defend the Bible from the standpoint of its immanent human qualities regarded *in abstracto*, we necessarily remain on a level on which the characteristic power of this subject cannot be unequivocally displayed, and on which it can be rivalled if not surpassed by similar powers.

We are concerned with the power of the Word of God, but, of course, the power of the Word made flesh, believed and attested by men. Therefore not even *in abstracto* with the power which the Word of God has in itself, in its glory as the eternal logos of the Father, where no powers exist beside it, where it simply is the Lord above and utterly beyond all powers. No, our concern is with the Word of God in the humiliation of its majesty, the Word of God in the world where there are powers beside and against it, where it stands until the end of time confronting and opposing these other powers. Many other heavenly and earthly levers will constantly be effective and operative in the sphere of our human world and existence. There seems to be much power and freedom there. Recognition of the freedom of the divine Word will consist chiefly in the simple but not self-explanatory realisation that, in the midst of all other subjects, this subject which is Holy Scripture has, in fact, a real and therefore a concretely limiting and competing power. The Word of God did not remain content with its eternal and in eternity unassailed and unassailable power over all things. It has entered the terrible dialectic of these things. It has become a subject among others. Amongst other things this means that these other subjects are not now left to themselves. They do not have to reckon only with themselves, but also with this new subject, Holy Scripture, by which they are really confronted.

We are reminded of Jer. 23²⁸ᶠ· where the Word of Yahweh is set over against the prophets who have dreams to tell, and it is compared to a fire and a hammer that breaks in pieces the rocks. Also Heb. 4¹²ᶠ·, where it is said of God's Word that it is living and powerful, sharper than any two-edged sword, critically piercing the entire and most hidden existence of man, " neither is there any creature that is not manifest in his sight : but all things are naked and opened unto the eyes of him." " With whom we have to do," the author expressly adds. The opposite of this Word is obviously an imagined Word of God, but, however well and truly imagined, as a mere dream it remains outside the real world and existence of man, leaving the other subjects in the sphere of our world and existence unmolested, but also unillumined and unconsoled in the depths of their creaturely existence. But now God has become man, and therefore Himself a creaturely being, in His Son, and in this human world of ours His Son lives on in the form of His instruments and their witness. So His power in this testimony is also a concrete power at the heart of this sphere, consoling and healing, but also judging and assailing. Therefore no matter how vivid and lifelike it may be, that imagined word which remains aloof is not as such the true Word of God. In all circumstances we must conceive the real Word of God as one among the many subjects which have freedom and power in the same way as others do in this sphere.

But the new subject which in Holy Scripture confronts other subjects—and this is how we must at once characterise its power—involves a radical compromising of the power of all other subjects. We cannot say more. It does not mean their suspension in the sense of destruction. It is not that other powers do not continue really to confront the power of Holy Scripture. It is not that there does not have to be constant opposition and conflict. In God's revelation as such, in the death and resurrection of Jesus Christ, that suspension and destruction have, of course, been completed, and completed once for all. Our age, however, is not itself the age of this revelation, but the age which is encompassed by its beginning and its ending, that is, by the ascension and by the return of Jesus Christ, by the time of this revelation and by the final victory of the Word of God, and the annulment of all other powers. Our world rests in the light of this victory because we have its attestation, but it is not itself the bearer of this light. Jesus Christ Himself and He alone is the bearer of this light. The power of the attestation of this victory, and therefore of God's revelation, consists in the opposition and conflict with the power of the other subjects in the sphere of our world and existence—a power which here and now is still left to them, although they are already threatened with its ultimate cancellation and destruction. It involves the relapse into a comfortable quietism if we see things otherwise, if in the light of the death and resurrection of Jesus Christ we act as though the dominion of the Word of God is opposed by no other dominions, and therefore by no trials, obstacles, adversaries or perils.

It is impossible to understand the special insistence with which the New Testament proclaims God's victory over all other powers, as it is already revealed and is still to be revealed in Jesus Christ, if we do not bring into the closest connexion with it the fact that this message is most emphatically given in the midst of the relativity of this world, with a constant awareness of the present operation of its forces, and a full consciousness of their dangerous character. Through this victory the eyes of those who are its messengers are opened to the fact that in their own human time and situation the Word of God is provisional, assaulted and menaced, and that the conflict in which it is involved is a genuine conflict. Although the divine revelation is complete in regard to its content, it is no less surely incomplete in regard to its effective power as a word addressed in time by men to other men. Precisely in virtue of the absolute content of this testimony, there can be no question of quietism in the sphere of Holy Scripture. This content is identical with the time, action and person of Jesus Christ, set in relief against all other times, actions and persons, so that at the heart of all other times, actions and persons the testimony which has this content will necessarily be an unsettled and unsettling, a suffering and a struggling testimony. The Word of God (or rather what is in this case called the " Word of God ") can be understood in a quietistic sense only if it derives from an absolute which is not identical with Jesus Christ, which is not therefore realised in and by Him alone, but surreptitiously introduced along mystical lines. It is only in this way that there can be a relapse into the view that the Word of God is a transcendent authority above and beyond the dialectic of actual reality and therefore not a fire and a hammer, as in the saying of the prophet, but the telling of a dream.

It belongs, therefore, to the recognition of the freedom of God's Word that we appreciate its exposed position, understanding Scripture as the sign which can be and is spoken against. But it belongs even more to this recognition to realise that its own offensive power is greater (and qualitatively infinitely greater) than the offensive which is mounted against it and from which it has to suffer. If it is true that in the sphere of our world and existence it is actually challenged, it is even more true that it constitutes itself the fundamental challenge to the subjects and powers which exist in this realm and on this level. When it confronts them, it may be that many penultimate words have still to be spoken, but the ultimate word has been already spoken, so that whatever else can and must be said, however serious and difficult it may be in face of the contradiction raised, can, so to speak, be said only in retrospect and by way of recapitulation. Self-evidently, it is by virtue of the content of Scripture that, while it is the sign which can be spoken against, it is at the same time the sign which can never be really and effectually spoken against, which in all its lowliness and assailability confronts all other signs with a decisive because qualitative superiority. The freedom of the Word of God consists in this secret but decisive superiority which it has in face of the totality of world principles, and the recognition of this freedom consists in the quiet and steadfast realisation of this superiority. The outward aspect of the relation between the power of Holy Scripture and other powers will never disclose this intrinsic superiority.

In great things and small, Holy Scripture will always be like the leaven which is really hidden in three measures of meal (Lk. 13[21]). Note well : hidden. It is not a painful and tragic destiny which overtakes the Word of God, when in face of its enemies, and perhaps still more in the company of its friends, always and everywhere in the world, it has to be worsted, pushed into a corner, repulsed, denied, distorted and spurned as the weaker principle. On the contrary, as in the passion and death of Jesus Christ Himself, this is the divine plan and will. Jesus Himself ordained that His disciples should have no silver and gold (Ac. 3[6], cf. Mt. 10[9]). " Behold, I send you forth as sheep in the midst of wolves " (Mt. 10[16]). " The disciple is not above his master, nor the servant above his lord " (Mt. 10[24]). " And he that taketh not his cross and followeth after me, is not worthy of me " (Mt. 10[38]). It would therefore be stupid to bear ill-will to the world, to reproach it, so to speak, because confronted by Holy Scripture it appears to possess and exercise victorious power.

But this external aspect does not disclose the whole truth. The whole truth is that in spite of all appearances to the contrary, Holy Scripture has more power than all the rest of the world together. The whole truth is that all other world-principles are already unmasked and delimited in Holy Scripture, that they are already overcome for all supposedly final and absolute validity, that their power is already surpassed and their triumph outstripped.

The whole truth—hidden but complete—is that of the story of the young David (1 Sam. 17[23f.]). It was not in the helmet and armour of Saul, but with his shepherd's sling, that he overcame Goliath. Very rashly, from a human point of view, he confronted Goliath in the name of Yahweh Sabaoth. " Because the foolishness of God is wiser than men, and the weakness of God is stronger than men " (1 Cor. 1[25]). And therefore : " If any man among you seemeth to be wise in this world, let him become a fool, that he may be wise " (1 Cor. 3[18]). The whole truth is what the " loud voices " in heaven cry at the sound of the trumpet of the seventh angel : " The kingdoms of the world are become the kingdoms of our Lord, and of his Christ ; and he shall reign for ever and ever " (Rev. 11[15]).

The recognition of this full but hidden truth is the recognition of the freedom of God's Word. It will be immediately apparent that this recognition is not possible apart from faith in the resurrection of Jesus Christ. It will also be apparent that we cannot believe in the resurrection without recognising that, in face and in spite of all appearances to the contrary, the world is not victorious over Scripture but Scripture over the world. The Church lives in this faith and in this recognition. But it can only do this by cleaving to the law of revelation, that the Jesus Christ who rose again is He who previously in this world suffered *sub Pontio Pilato*, was crucified, dead and buried. The Church will really live in this faith and in this recognition when it realises that it is a question of the freedom and transcendence of the Word of God, when, therefore, it does not seek and does not hope to find the truth of that hidden kingdom in the reality of its own being as a Church.

A deep insight and a weighty project were fulfilled in the Augustinian antithesis between the *civitas terrena* and *civitas Dei*, which for many centuries became a norm and pattern for the Christian interpretation of history. It is a pity that they did not remain freer from the clerical and secular taint acquired from the fact that the victorious *civitas Dei* was fused with the suffering, struggling and triumphant Catholic Church, and that as a result the transcendence of God's Word became the justification and argument for a specific outlook and policy, the supposed superiority of the cause of one human party over that of another. The comfort, encouragement and hope, which the Church can and should derive from the truth that the Word of God abides for ever, are all quite impossible if it purports and intends to try to actualise and represent this abidingness in itself, if it looks at itself and affirms it instead of looking at the Word of God and believing it. The cross of Jesus Christ is lacking in the Augustinian conception, and therefore it lacks the true divine trustworthiness. The real *civitas Dei* on earth, which is invincible, and can therefore be proclaimed with confidence, is not the rule of the Church, but the rule of Him who in this world had to be nailed to the cross. And for His followers this means the rule of Scripture and the faith in which such a rule finds obedience. Obedience to this rule cannot mean a triumph at the point where prophets and apostles were defeated and slain and where Jesus died on the cross. Therefore faith will not rest for support on its works, nor appeal to its works and therefore to the human structure of the Church, as though the latter as such is the Kingdom of God over against the kingdoms of this world, and in its invincibility in contradistinction to them the manifestation of the superiority of the Word of God. On the contrary, faith will expect this structure to be always in jeopardy, always liable to be destroyed, and at the end definitely to be destroyed like Israel's temple : for in order to enter into its glory, the body of Christ had to die and be buried. The Church must really be content to recognise the hiddenness of the truth of the freedom and transcendence of God's Word, and, through all its visible forms, to believe in its invisibility. Only so can this truth be the comfort of the Church and the inexhaustible source of its life.

Again, the secrecy in which the Word of God is free and transcendent must not be interpreted quietistically. It is true that we cannot expect to see its victory in events, forms and ordinances which are unequivocally recognisable in this sense. The leaven is really hidden. The grain of wheat must really die. All that is humanly visible must always be a picture of this dying and not the picture of a triumphant, divine, world principle. Our faith alone will thus be the victory that has overcome the world (1 Jn. 5⁴). But all the same, it must not be forgotten that with this faith of ours we stand in the midst of the world. Scripture is in the world. Therefore concrete relationships subsist between the Word of God and the powers of this world. Real contacts and reactions take place in which the freedom of the Word of God, which we recognise by faith, demonstrates and establishes its reality. If it is in accordance with the character of the revelation, and therefore provided for, that the war declared upon the world by the testimony of Jesus Christ will constantly assume the visible form of human defeats, human sinning and failure, human suffering and dying, this testimony is nevertheless a challenge to battle, and not the telling of a dream which at the end necessarily leaves everything in the real world exactly as it was before.

If the disciple is not above his Master, we cannot expect that in virtue of the transcendence of the Word we will be led along a different path from that which is definitively prescribed for us in the path of Jesus Christ from the cross to the resurrection. The prophets and apostles and even more so ourselves as their pupils can expect least of all that, as favoured and resolute citizens of a

visible *civitas Dei*, we are destined suddenly or gradually to trample down, overcome and destroy the powers of this world. Yet we have to remember that
beyond all chiliastic errors we also have the true but obviously not contradictory
sayings : " Think not that I am come to send peace on earth : I came not to
send peace, but a sword " (Mt. 10^{34}). And : " I am come to send fire on the
earth ; and what will I, if it be already kindled ? " (Lk. 12$^{49f.}$). And it continues : " But I have a baptism to be baptised with ; and how am I straitened
till it be accomplished ! " This continuation shows that, in the word about fire
on the earth, the great boundary constituted by the cross is not forgotten, but
considered and reckoned with. But since it is the continuation of just this word,
it shows also that the cross as a boundary must not be made a pretext for quietism.

The real world is attacked by Jesus Christ and the testimony of
Jesus Christ. It is victoriously attacked. We can say positively that
it is under a promise which cannot fail. It is dark in itself and therefore the arena of the crucifixion of Christ ; but it is also placed in
the light of His resurrection. It is the same world, yet not the same.
In itself it is the same. Yet it is not the same in that in the Word of
God it is now confronted by a superior power. It is the same in that
its ruling powers, in accordance with their nature, have to withstand
the power of the Word, and the Word has to suffer in it. It is not
the same in that the Word on its own account offers resistance to
these powers, challenging and disputing their claim to be divine,
announcing and preparing their destruction, affirming a new heaven
and a new earth as the final truth. Since Scripture confronts the world
with faith in God's revelation in Jesus Christ, it cannot simply treat
the world as though it is still entirely the same. It reckons soberly
with this outward aspect. And events will, of course, always give
fresh confirmation that it is right, and that the world is still the world.
Therefore the way of Scripture in the world will undoubtedly and in
all circumstances be the way in which the disciples have to bear the
cross like their Master. But beyond this they will know that God is
God, and therefore that although the world is the same, now, in the
light of the resurrection of Jesus Christ, it is also not the same. They
will know that the lie of the world has been contradicted, that its
pretended divinity has been contested, and that its end is near. Faith
in the resurrection of Jesus Christ will not, therefore, be an aimless,
illusionary faith. As an eschatological faith, that is, the faith which
sees in Jesus Christ the beginning and the end of our age and its history,
it will have quite concrete content, which a reference to Holy Scripture as the witness of this beginning and end enables us concretely
to specify and describe.

First, the Word of God demonstrates its freedom and supremacy in
the world in the fact that it has the power to maintain itself in face
of the open and secret, direct and indirect attacks made upon it.

Men with their various (but by nature unanimously hostile) attitudes towards
it come and go. Their political and spiritual systems (all of which to some extent
have an anti-Christian character) stand and fall. The Church itself (in which
somewhere the crucifixion of Christ is always being repeated) is to-day faithful

and to-morrow unfaithful, to-day strong and to-morrow weak. But although Scripture may be rejected by its enemies and disowned and betrayed by its friends, it does not cease to remain true to itself, to say the same thing on all sides and in all situations. It does not cease to present the message that God so loved the world that He gave His only begotten Son. If its voice is drowned to-day, it becomes audible again to-morrow. If it is misunderstood and distorted here, it again bears witness to its true meaning there. If it seems to lose its position, hearers and form in this locality or period, it acquires them afresh elsewhere. The promise is true, and it is fulfilled in the existence of the biblical prophets and apostles in virtue of what is said to them and what they have to say : " I have set watchmen upon thy walls, O Jerusalem, which shall never hold their peace day nor night : ye that make mention of the Lord, keep not silence, and give him no rest, till he establish, and till he make Jerusalem a praise in the earth " (Is. 62$^{6f.}$). The maintaining of the Word of God against the attacks to which it is exposed cannot be our concern, and therefore we do not need to worry about it. Watchmen are appointed and they wait in their office. The maintaining of the Word of God takes place as a self-affirmation which we can never do more than acknowledge to our own comfort and disquiet. We can be most seriously concerned about Christianity and Christians, about the future of the Church and theology, about the establishment in the world of the Christian outlook and Christian ethic. But there is nothing about whose solidity we need be less troubled than the testimonies of God in Holy Scripture. For a power which can annul these testimonies is quite unthinkable. " If these should hold their peace, the stones would immediately cry out " (Lk. 19^{40}).

Further, the Word of God demonstrates its freedom and supremacy in the fact that it possesses the power continually to isolate and distinguish itself from the elements of the world which crowd upon it and affix themselves to it.

The history of the Word of God in the world is not merely the history of the attacks but supremely of the temptations to which it is exposed. Just as the prophets and apostles themselves were not mechanically secured against error, so the Word of God, in its humanness as the prophetic and apostolic Word, is, of course, not beyond the reach of temptation, that is, not absolutely secured against the danger, which is worse than opposition and rejection, of distortion and therefore of falsification under the influence of human ideas alien to it. It cannot be disputed that in this sense, too, it is involved in a struggle as long as it remains the Word of God in and to this world. Every new language into which it is translated, every new mode or system of thought in whose framework and ways it is affirmed and received, the new spirit of each new epoch which in its own way tries to hear it and preach it, each new individual who in one way or another takes possession of it—all these are phases and problems of this perilous struggle in which the purity and therefore the power of Scripture and therefore the salvation of mankind are at stake, in which it has to guard itself against alienation on the part of the men into whose hands it is delivered as their own and in regard to whom—if it is to be appropriated by them for their salvation—it must remain undeviatingly faithful to itself. Church history is the history of the exegesis of the Word of God and therefore of the ever recurrent menace of doing violence to it. But it is also and still more the history of the criticism which it brings and always will bring to bear on all its interpreters. As the orthodox Protestants were fond of saying, Holy Scripture was the *facultas semetipsam interpretandi* which at any rate means the power sooner or later to throw off every foreign sense attributed to it, to mark and expose its perversity, and in contrast to assert itself in its own characteristic meaning. If this is in fact a matter of history, of a struggle where there must always be a victorious outcome, then there is no cause for the scepticism according to which anything and everything may be proved from the Bible, as expressed in the epigram of S. Werenfels :

Hic liber est, in quo sua quaerit dogmata quisque
Invenit et pariter dogmata quisque sua.

If this is a correct account of what might be called the natural law of all biblical exegesis, even the sincerest and best, it must also and even more be noticed with what remarkable independence this book comes through all its better and worst criticism, how carefully it is provided that its serious misinterpretations inevitably cancel each other out, how the occasional arbitrary and one-sided exegesis usually has a short lease of life, how quickly and thoroughly these texts are usually able to free themselves even from the worst bondage under which they may be confined. There is, therefore, good reason to ask whether, side by side with and superior to this fatal natural law of biblical interpretation, there may not be a spiritual law which the Bible itself dictates, which it sets and maintains in force, to which in the end all good and even bad Bible criticism is subjected, which neither the good nor the bad exegete can avoid any more than he can the natural law that can only be the reflection of human laziness or arrogance, but never the living law of the Bible itself. Scripture is exposed but not delivered over to the understanding and misunderstanding of the world. Scripture is in the hands but not in the power of the Church. It speaks as it is translated, interpreted and applied. But always in and even in spite of all these human efforts, it is Scripture itself which speaks.

Further, Scripture demonstrates its freedom and supremacy in the fact that, above and beyond the power of resistance and criticism, it has the power of assimilating and making serviceable to itself the alien elements it encounters.

To these alien elements, which may be open enemies or secret tempters, there belong in the first place all the historical factors which Holy Scripture opposes as the testimony of God's unique revelation in the midst of a sinful world : peoples and their languages, political and philosophical systems, the passing movements of history, the consequent situations of one sort or another, all kinds of human individuals with their secrets. But as there is nothing in this universe which of itself cannot prove inimical and insidious, so there is nothing which has of itself the power to escape the control exercised over it by Scripture. Nothing human is alien to Scripture. It can speak with original force in every language. It can express itself in the language of the most varied political and intellectual systems and win a hearing. It can make the most diverse situations and movements effective and useful, and appropriate to its service the most diverse races and individual personalities. Note well, this does not mean that these natural factors which the Word of God in the course of its history assimilates and makes serviceable have innately a secret affinity and fitness to this end, so that the Word of God uses them as ready-made instruments. The truth is rather that their original character as alien elements has first to be removed, that they have first to receive a new nature, and be awakened and newly created for this service. It is not, therefore, a question of the character native to them, but of the choice which comes upon them, of the grace which meets them and makes of them what they could not be in themselves. And this is just the history of the Word of God in the world. It is not only a history of struggle, but also one of election and grace. It is a history of remarkable transmutations, in virtue of which, even in the midst of the hostile and corrupting world—and certainly not without fatal traces of it—there is still a genuine translation, interpretation and application of Scripture. In this the affirmation and unfolding of its original sense takes place in such a way that human language, institutions and personalities really come into their own in this use and service. This is not because of any particular character of their own. But their particular character is not effaced and suppressed. They are not, so to speak, put into uniform. They are genuinely affirmed. This does not mean a divinisation of historical and natural forces. This is unthinkable even in the case of the human word of the Bible, or the human nature of Jesus Christ Himself. What it does mean is a share in the typological character of the human word in the Bible and of the human nature of Jesus Christ, an inclusion in their characteristic functions, and so a widening, a differentiation and an enrichment, an expansion of the effectual working of the historical forms of God's Word. On the other hand, no enslavement of the Word is implied in this process. It is ensured that the Word is never identical with any of its symbols, and is not itself transformed into a natural factor. There is no absolute necessity or definable universal law on the basis of which these particular transformations must be effected or these particular connexions set up. Where these transformations and connexions are found, they always have the character of special events, not of universal relationships. They never have more than a locally and temporally limited significance. The symbolical value which may attach to a natural historical factor in one place may be wanting in another. If it is appropriate to-day it may be withdrawn to-morrow. There is dissimilation as well as assimilation, dismissal from as well as appointment to service, judgments as well as blessing and consecration upon the various houses of God. The freedom of God's Word would not be freedom if it did not have also a negative significance. But all the same, it still has the positive value that it is not only freedom to repel, but also freedom to attract and accept. The disquieting contact of the Word with the world does not have only a critical but also an atoning and pregnant character. Either way it points to the beginning and end of the world to which testimony is borne by Holy Scripture in the midst of the world.

Finally, and above all, the Word of God demonstrates its freedom and supremacy in the fact that it can change its own form and therefore its effect upon the world.

We understand Holy Scripture falsely, that is, not as Holy Scripture, if we regard it as a fixed, inflexible, self-contained quantity. God is the living God. He is this from everlasting to everlasting. Therefore He is it also as the Lord of our temporal world, as the One who once revealed Himself to prophets and apostles, who once placed His testimonies in their mouth. But this means that He is not buried in this " once," in the writings of these men. They are not a kind of stone mausoleum, in which, so long as it does not crumble and vanish from the earth as is ultimately the way with these structures, He can be known by historical scholars and honoured by other men under their guidance. The Holy Scriptures of the Old and New Testament are to be understood strictly as the Word of God, which means as the forward and backward looking testimony to Jesus Christ. And Jesus Christ is the living Lord of the Church and of the world. But if this is true, the form assumed by the Word of God in the human word of prophets and apostles is not His grave, but the organ of His rule, moved by the living hand of His Spirit and therefore itself alive. Thus we have not only to expect that, by deeper, more precise, more serious, more believing research into Scripture on our part, many a hidden meaning and connexion in these documents will be brought to light ; just as by dint of excavations many important and interesting conclusions are to be expected about the life of those who have lived in the near or distant past. For this expectation is naturally limited by the fact that, however hard we try, more cannot be dug up than was originally there. But the investigation of the Bible does not have to reckon with this natural limitation. For the Bible is a living, indeed, in the light of its content, an eternally living thing, so that from the study of it we can expect new truths to meet us—truths which were not accessible to the most conscientious inquiry of yesterday or the day before yesterday, because the Bible itself has not yet brought them to light. What is true of the content of Scripture, that it is unique in essence, is true also of its form. The word of prophets and apostles was uttered once for all. But while it remains unaltered, this does not in any way prevent it from changing and renewing its form and therefore its range and effectiveness, continually presenting itself to different ages and men from new angles, in new dimensions and with a new aspect. What we call the investigation of Holy Scripture and its results is not at bottom our efforts and their conclusions, of which we usually think in this connexion, but rather the self-initiating movements of the Word of God Himself. In its repudiation of Gnosticism, the Early Church wrestled for a simultaneous recognition of the unity of God and the divinity of Christ and the Holy Ghost. The Reformation championed the understanding of man, as a sinner saved by grace alone. To-day we have to defend against barbarians, and at the same time and above all to realise ourselves, the contingence of the divine revelation, that is, *in concreto*, the revelational character of the Old Testament on the one hand, and on the other, the independence of the Church and its message. To all these processes the contemporary ecclesiastical and non-ecclesiastical movement of ideas in its immanentist evolution has formed the musical accompaniment, but this is quite inexplicable apart from the initiative which proceeded and still proceeds from the Bible itself. The same will have to be said of ages and situations in which we perhaps have to speak more of the suffering than the effective working of God's Word—of its neglect and rejection, its non-recognition and distortion. The sin and error of mankind in times and circumstances like this are as much in place as are at other periods their belief and openness to the truth. For at these times as well it is proper to seek the true motive power, not in the surrounding world, but in the Word of God itself, that is, in the judgments executed in these times and situations. The Word of God hides and withdraws itself from the Church when the latter permits itself to regard and treat itself and its tradition or nature, or the being and history of mankind, as the source of its knowledge of God. The Word of God itself is silent, and yet it speaks even by its silence, when the Church wishes to hear only the human word of prophets and apostles as such and therefore the voice of a distant historical occurrence which does not really concern it or lay any obligation upon it. The Word of God itself veils itself in darkness when the Bible is interpreted with violent and capricious one-sidedness according to the promptings of various spirits instead of under the leading of its own Holy Spirit. We do not truly appreciate either the light which the Church receives from the Bible, or the darkness which enshrouds it from the same source, until we recognise in both, beyond all the human effort and human refusal which is also present, the over-ruling power of the Word of God itself, either to exalt or to abase. Only then do we realise that we cannot read and understand Holy Scripture without prayer, that is, without invoking the grace of God. And it is only on the presupposition of prayer that all human effort in this matter, and penitence for human failure in this effort, will become serious and effective. The Word of God can change its human expression. In different times and circumstances it is the same and not the same. It produces the same effect in continually new forms. Therefore man's encounter and dealings with it have a history which is not the history of a solitary man standing by himself, nor the history of a self-contained, self-centred Church, but a history which on the side of the Church and individual members in the Church has the character of a response, the initiative being always with the Word of God as the first and truly acting Subject. It is no metaphor when we say that the Word of God speaks, acts and rules ; we denote thereby the characteristic and essential feature of the whole movement called Church history. This is the characteristic and essential thing to which the life and deeds and opinions, all the insights and errors, the ways and aberrations, not only of the men who are gathered in power or weakness within the Church, but of the world which surrounds the Church with its good will, hatred or indifference, necessarily have to refer and respond. The Word of God in the form of Holy Scripture is, therefore, the object of the acting, thinking and speaking of the Church and the world—but, of course, only because and so far as it has the initiative, only because and so far as it is the real Subject of this acting, thinking and speaking. All that has hitherto been said about the self-affirmative, critical and assimilative power of the Word of God can be properly understood only when it is realised that the Word is first the Subject and only then the object of history.

We remind ourselves that all this is the content of faith in the resurrection of Jesus Christ as the revelation of the controlling beginning and end of the Church and the world. As the mere statement of a philosophy of Church history and world history these things can all be said or not said, affirmed or contradicted. We say no more than what phenomenologically can be said of the history of the *Iliad* or the Platonic dialogues. But we are not making phenomenological affirmations. We are asserting and developing the promise : Ye shall be my witnesses, and : Lo, I am with you always. What we say is true because Jesus Christ is risen and therefore this promise is true. It is from this point of view that all this about the freedom and supremacy of the divine Word has to be said and heard. But from this point of view it does have to be said and heard.

3. We have seen how in virtue of its theme Scripture becomes a subject. And we have seen something of its power as such. This power of Scripture has a special sphere of influence—the Church. This does not imply a limitation of its power. It constitutes it as free power in contradistinction to a blind, universal, automatically working force of nature. Its operation takes place on the basis of choice, not of necessity. It has, therefore, the form of a decisive, not of a general, event. So long as God is not all in all—and the fact that God is not all in all is the negative sign of this world of ours—it will certainly not be a sign of the divinity of Holy Scripture if its power is that of a universally operative necessity, or if the sphere of its operation is co-extensive with the sphere of this world. The sign of its divinity is rather the fact that its power within this world has its own peculiar sphere. It is not a sphere which is assigned or resigned to it according to the order of nature. It is not a sphere which is conceded to it by the world. It is the sphere of the Church which it has chosen, defined, claimed and conquered itself. Side by side with this sphere there is the sphere of that which is not the Church. The division is provisional in a double sense. It is provisional because of the provisional nature of the whole present state of the world, in which it is not yet identical with the Kingdom of God, but only limited and relativised by the now imminent Kingdom. It is also provisional because of the provisional character of the present, visible demarcation between the

Church and that which is not the Church. The Word of God chooses, defines, claims and conquers the Church as the special sphere of its effective power, not for the sake of the Church itself, but for the sake of God and, in His service, for the sake of the world. And it is not an absolute and rigid, but a flexible boundary which divides it off from that which is not His Church. In His Word God speaks to the Church and in the Church. But He does so in order that through the Church—in the concrete antithesis which arises from the fact that He addresses Himself primarily to the Church and in the Church—He may speak to the world and cause His Church to grow in the world. Again, God is not bound to the sphere which at any one time is created by His Word. On the contrary, this sphere is bound to Him and to His Word. At this point its boundaries may fall back so that there is again no Church where formerly there was the Church. Or they may expand so that now there is the Church where formerly there was none. All the same, as long as this world lasts, the concrete antithesis between the Church and that which is not the Church can as little be removed as, in spite of its fluidity, the relationship between Israel and the Gentiles. In this antithesis of two peoples, God speaks with the world. He speaks with it in such a way that His Word creates the Church first, and then by the ministry of the Church, it becomes a Word to the world.

There is, therefore, no occasion for the impatience which despises and bypasses the Church for the sake of the Kingdom of God, or demands of the Church what can be demanded only of the Kingdom of God, if we can demand anything at all of the Kingdom of God. The Church can and must have a continual awareness of the relativity of its boundaries and therefore of its whole existence in antithesis to what is not the Church. It can and must have a continual awareness that within its boundaries and in its special existence it is not called to serve itself, but to serve God and in the service of God the world. The Church cannot do all this unless within its boundaries and in its special existence it hopes for the consummation of the Kingdom of God and, for that reason, really and selflessly discharges its ministry in the world. But it cannot wish to change or remove, in virtue of its own insight and power, the boundaries that separate it from that which is not the Church, the boundaries over against state and society, for example, or over against every kind of heathenism old and new. It is not in virtue of its own insight and authority that it has been chosen, defined, claimed and conquered as the Church, but by the free Word of God, which according to its own good pleasure called it out of nothingness into existence, into this determinate existence as the Church. It must now leave it to this Word, to which it owes its existence and which it can only serve, to move the boundaries between the Church and that which is not the Church nearer or further away, and eventually, when God will be all in all, to remove them completely. The Kingdom of God is really the Kingdom of God, and therefore its establishment is not surrendered to the power and control of men. Not even the most passionate missionary spirit, not even the deepest sensitiveness to the need and longing of the world, can alter in the very slightest the dividing line between belief and unbelief, obedience and disobedience, which in this world separates the sphere of God's lordship from a world which is not yet reconciled with Him. Nor can it alter the fact that for our human eyes this boundary is determined by the distinction between the service and contempt of the Gospel, between clear and distorted proclamation, between a willing and an impenitent hearing of its message, so that, humanly speaking, it is defined by the boundaries of the Church. We may try to deny this boundary. We may try to unite the world and the Church in another way than by ourselves serving and not despising the Gospel, anxious and ready to hear its message ourselves and to declare it in its purity. In the interests of the Kingdom of God, or our missionary spirit, or our understanding of the need and longing of the world, we may want something other than that there should be a Church and we ourselves members of it. But if we do, how can it be in anything but arrogance, in secret or open opposition to the freedom of God's Word ? And how can the Kingdom of God really be served by this arrogance and opposition ? The freedom of God's Word to which we will submit (if we are really waiting for the Kingdom in which God will be all in all) is not a general possibility which we are free to choose. Nor is it the sum of what we consider possible, or an extract from it. It is the freedom which God has actually assumed in His revelation, of which He has told us that He has actually assumed it. We simply do not know of any other boundary between belief and unbelief, between obedience and disobedience, and therefore between the Kingdom of God and the kingdom of the world, than that which He Himself has drawn through His revelation in Jesus Christ and its apostolic testimony. If we think we do, it can only be a presumptuous surmise. But if we do not, we have to keep to the boundary which has been plainly marked out for us. We will realise its impermanence and its final cancellation. But we will also realise its provisional validity. We will realise that, on this side of its final cancellation and before any of its possible changes in detail, it is within this frontier that we have to serve God if we are going to serve Him at all.

The freedom of God's Word is its freedom to found for itself a Church. This means that it unites with itself and among themselves men of every time and place, of every type and destiny and training, of every kind of natural and spiritual disposition, and in it all of every form of sinfulness and mortality. It does so in such a way that it procures from them a hearing, the hearing of obedience, i.e., the hearing by which, for better or worse, for grace or disfavour, for life or death, they are bound to Jesus Christ. It does so in such a way that in all their sinfulness and sickness and its varied manifestations they have to recognise in Him their Lord. This hearing in obedience is Christian faith and the sphere of Christian faith is the sphere in which God's Word exercises its power. Even if this alters in its outer aspect towards the world, if it contracts or expands, it will always be the sphere of Christian faith. Even its suspension as a separate sphere can only signify that there will not then be any other sphere than that of the Christian faith now elevated to become sight. We know of no other freedom of the Word of God than that which summons us to Christian faith. It is even part of the content of this Word that it has in fact assumed this freedom and this freedom alone : the freedom to create for itself the hearing of obedience. In its founding of the Church, the activity of the Word of God is free in a double sense. It is free, i.e., powerful, over against the sinfulness and sickness of mankind which make the hearing of obedience and therefore Christian faith in itself impossible. It is free also, i.e., powerful, over against the natural diversity of men which has been made disruptive by sin and death, rendering it impossible for them to be at one with God and among themselves by faith. The Word of God is free, and exercises this freedom in the founding of the Church, in overcoming the double limitation of this impossibility, and in imparting to us the possibility of faith.

" The wind bloweth where it listeth " (Jn. 3⁸). " The Son quickeneth whom he will " (Jn. 5²¹). " Father, I will that they also, whom thou hast given me, be with me where I am " (Jn. 17²⁴). On this will that ignores present obstacles the Church rests. In this will we have to recognise at once the freedom of the Word of God. It would be more exact to describe it as its freedom to arouse attention, belief and trust in itself, which means in the biblical testimonies, and therefore to raise up disciples and followers. The Church comes to be because this testimony is accepted and assimilated. This happens in spite of its strangeness, which is both the strangeness of its content as it strives against every man, the strangeness of the form which the content assumes in claiming every man. It is not a matter of course that men will believe the prophets and apostles. The reality and unity of the faith which this witness requires, the power of illuminating to faith and the power of gathering in faith—this is the first secret of the freedom of God's Word.

But this freedom goes further. It is not the case that, when the Word of God has once been conveyed and handed over to the biblical witness of the Church, the Church is left alone like a widow with her deceased husband's legacy.

From this false conception of the biblical revelation as a *depositum* committed to the Church and left to its disposal, the Roman Catholic error has possibly arisen, which claims for the Church the power of ruling itself out of its own resources. It is clear that such a conception involves both the possibility and the need to constitute tradition alongside Scripture as a second ostensible *depositum*. It is also clear that the teaching office of the Church, and its head, will inevitably have to be given the most powerful possible voice as the administrator of these *deposita*. Such a view obviously overlooks the whole uniqueness of the distinction, equipment and authority in which those who stand at the beginning of the Church's history are clothed. Of these it is said : " There be some standing here, which shall not taste of death, till they see the Son of man coming in his kingdom " (Mt. 16²⁸), and : " This generation shall not pass, till all these things be fulfilled. Heaven and earth shall pass away, but my words shall not pass away " (Mt. 24³⁴ᶠ·). They obviously have a function which does not simply pass over into that of the Church. For while the Church is created by their testimony, and their testimony is received and accepted by the Church, it retains its own independent function as distinct from all the functions of the Church. Their testimony is not a *depositum*, but it continues as an event, and in and with this event the Word of God exercises its freedom.

The Word of God does not effect only the founding of the Church, but also its continual preservation. The freedom of Scripture gives evidence that it is divine freedom, the sovereignty of the Creator, in the fact that by it, and by it alone, the Church is what it is. Without Scripture it would inevitably dissolve at once into nothingness, perishing from the impossibility of the actuality and unity of faith. The Church, like the created world as a whole, lives by the divine *creatio continua.* But in its application to the Church this does not mean the patience with which the Word of God holds the created world as such in the being in which it has been created. It means rather the grace of rebirth and new creation spoken by the Word in the midst of the created world. It means the effectiveness of this Word in its continuous attestation from the faith of the prophets and apostles to the faith of the Church. Without this Word and without its continuous attestation, human religions, philosophies and systems, and the human institutions and societies founded upon them, may well live, as in fact they do : on the basis of the universal divine maintenance of all created things. But they live in the shadow of the death to which the whole created order is as such hastening. For the same reason, an erroneous and deformed Christianity, i.e., one which approximates to the form of these human systems, can also live without the Word. It can do so the more easily in proportion as, in virtue of this approximation, it is erroneous and deformed. It is the true Church which, as the sphere of revelation and faith, denies itself this purely natural vitality. Called into existence by the Word of rebirth and new creation, it cannot remain alive except by this Word. What is it profited by any natural will and power to exist ? What is it profited even if they are so great that with their help it gains the whole world ? As one of the human systems which hasten to death, it can maintain a sort of life by such means. But as the Church of truth and of eternal life, even in the most prosperous development which it can enjoy on this plane, it will be already dead if the Word of truth withdraws itself from it.

It hardly needs to be added, and yet it is one of the things which most need emphasising, that prayer for the maintenance of the Church's life ought never to cease. The Church lives and moves solely on the basis which continually has to be offered to it by the living Word. Apart from this basis, it might live like other systems, but never as the Church of truth. And concern for the maintenance of the Church on this strength alone, and therefore for the continual offering of it, will necessarily be the proper criterion of all ecclesiastical action, of all attempts to strengthen and defend the Church, of all apologetic and ecclesiastico-political measures. No concern for the Church can rank above this in importance, or will not have to be brushed aside if it means that the Church will by it escape the living Word. Again, no concern for the Church will not be gladly subordinated to this or allowed to be dissolved in it. If the Church commits itself to the Word of truth, then, and then alone, but confidently and legitimately, it can hope and trust that the universal grace and patience of God to His creation will in some way accrue to its advantage.

The preservation of the Church by the Word of God is accomplished quite simply in the exercise of the freedom of the Word in the manner already described. In the power of the resurrection of Jesus Christ the Word has power to affirm itself in this world and to maintain itself unspotted from the world. But it also has power to draw the world to itself, and continually to express and give itself in new forms. From this inner life of the Word flows the life of the

Church. The Church is alive because it is the theatre of this life of the Word, because it participates in the movements of this life, because by faith it says Yes to these movements, seeking its own salvation only in the fact that they take place, imitating them in so far as its worship and fellowship, preaching and confession occur in the following of these movements. Because this happens, the Church can as little perish as the Word of God itself. In its discipleship of the Word, it shares in its imperishability in the transitory world.

From a human point of view, the preservation of the Church therefore depends upon the selfless attention with which the Church has to accompany the course of the Word of God. It cannot be its business to desire to assert itself as the Church. Let it assert itself by promoting the self-assertion of the Word. Let it not allow itself any criticism of the world on the basis of its own polemical insight. Let it not allow itself any assimilation of secular elements on the basis of its own synthetic wisdom. But let it believe and announce the declarations of war and the conclusions of peace made by the Word of God itself. Let it not allow itself either to cling to the old or to introduce the new unless it be commanded and obliged to do so by the changing form of the Word of God which guides it. Any step away from this path will be a step into the abyss of death. Not that it will immediately reveal and avenge itself as such. It will often enough appear that only a tiny step aside is required, only a little ecclesiastical self-will, for the Church to prosper wonderfully, perhaps after a heavy trial, and for its preservation in the world to God's glory and the salvation of man actually to be guaranteed. On all hands there exist in obvious health and abounding vitality the other human structures of which this selfless attention is apparently not expected, the life of which does not rest upon the grace of rebirth and new creation, and is therefore from the human point of view to be had at a cheaper price than the life of faith. It is only for the Church of truth that what the rest of the world calls life is the abyss of death. Will it see this, although as yet it cannot be seen ? Will it recognise death in what the rest of the world calls life ? Will it choose the life which must inevitably appear to the rest of the world as death ? Plainly everything depends on whether the Church is in fact what it is supposed to be, that is, the sphere in which man has confidence in the Word alone, and therefore in faith alone, acquiring in this confidence the capacity for that self-forgetful attention which with its will to live, its aggressiveness and wisdom, its conservatism and radicalism, the world as a whole does not have. But the Church's being what it is supposed to be depends upon its living in the strength of the Word itself. It depends upon the Word continuing to live in its midst in all its power. It depends, therefore, on the real freedom of the Word for which the Church can only pray and be thankful.

The preservation of the Church by the active freedom of the Word of God means concretely that it is unceasingly under the authoritative claim of Scripture. It is the history of the continuing witness which is given it by Scripture and which it has to receive from Scripture. In place of the sustaining Word of God, if this is not identifiable with Scripture, or if Scripture is a mere " deposit " and not a continuing witness, there can easily enter what the Church has to say to itself or to the world : the Christian idea, outlook and ethic, Christianity or the Gospel in one of the complicated or simplified forms in which man has constantly adjusted it to his needs ; the content, perhaps, of a good or a bad dogmatics or ethics. It is clear that this so-called

Word of God is not free but dependent upon the ecclesiastical and therefore human conceptions in question. To such a Word would belong the animating, inspiring and edifying power which can be and is in fact proper to such conceptions at least at certain times and in certain situations. But to it would not belong the power to maintain the Church, to maintain it, that is, through the revolutions of epochs and situations, through the disillusionments and disappointments which are the inevitable consequence of these vicissitudes. The promise given to Scripture and only to Scripture would be lost. It would not be that Word of truth which alone has power to preserve the Church of truth from death. The Church lives, and it lives also with what it has itself to say, by what is said to it, by the Word which continually comes to it from without, the Word which it hears in Scripture. Because the Word of God is Scripture, it exercises the concrete guidance, government and education of the Church, in virtue of which it is not left to itself, but is continually touched by saving truth and made alive.

From a human standpoint the preservation of the Church depends, therefore, on the fact that Scripture is read, assimilated, expounded and applied in the Church, that this happens tirelessly and repeatedly, that the whole way of the Church consists in its striving to hear this concrete witness. As a rule the step aside which means a step into the abyss of death, the fatal lack of this self-forgetful attention, will scarcely betray itself as such at once. It will normally take the form of great fidelity (to what the Church has said) and great zeal (for what the Church believes that it must itself say). In this way it will apparently bear the seal of divine justification and necessity. Whenever life is exchanged for death, or death for life, in the Church, this fidelity and zeal are usually operative : much good will, much serious piety, wide vision, deep movements, and in it all the sincere conviction of not being in any way self-willed but rather obedient to the Word of God. What is not noted is that this so-called Word of God is only a conception of the Word of God. It may be created freely. More probably and frequently it will take the shape of an old (no longer newly tested), or new (not yet seriously examined) interpretation of Scripture itself, but not the Word of God as it actually lets itself be heard in Scripture. As such, conceptions of the Word of God may be very good, as also, for example, recognised dogmas and confessions, luminous and helpful theological systems, deep, bold and stimulating insights into biblical truth. But in themselves these things are not the Word of God itself and cannot sustain the life of the Church. Similarly, conservatism and radicalism can only deceive and endanger the Church if they try to outshine this and claim it for their conceptions. The criterion whether it is following the Word of God with this self-forgetful attention consists in whether through everything that it says itself, or thinks it has or can receive from Scripture, it is able and willing to hear the voice of Scripture itself as the final verdict which pronounces true death and true life. The continued life of the Church depends, therefore, on whether Scripture remains open to it, whether all its conceptions, even the best, remain transparent to its content—so that it can itself confirm and legitimate, or qualify, or even completely set them aside. But Scripture cannot be the breath of life to the Church apart from this freedom. If the Church is true to itself, it will allow this sovereign freedom to Scripture, and if it departs from Scripture, it will continually have to return to it. We must again conclude that the Church's being true to itself depends on whether Scripture wins and maintains for itself this freedom within it, and whether Scripture compels the Church continually to return to it. How can we give to Scripture this freedom, however faithful we are to it ? Here again we are confronted by the actuality, and we can only give thanks that it is given and pray that it will be continually given.

Looking at the same thing from another angle, we maintain that the freedom of the Word of God is its freedom to rule the Church. It is not for nothing that the Church has been founded, and it is not for nothing that it is sustained. Both things happen that it may serve a purpose, the purpose of the divine revelation, and therefore the glory of God and the salvation of mankind. In the time between the ascension and the second coming, the Church as the communion of those who have been summoned by the Word and have believed the Word is the sign of God's revelation, the sign of the incarnation of the Son of God and the sign of the new humanity redeemed by the Son of God in His coming kingdom. As such a sign, the Church must serve. It must testify in this world to the already accomplished atonement and the coming redemption of its own members and of all mankind in the power of the testimony of Jesus Christ its Lord, who is also Lord over all. But it must not, and cannot, do this in its own strength. It is not the case that the time between the ascension and the second coming is to some extent the kingdom of the believing man autonomous in and by virtue of his faith.

We can only say that this is the mistake especially of Neo-Protestantism. For it sets man on a plane which dispenses with the horizons of the accomplished atonement and the coming redemption. The former has become a dim historical memory and the latter the equally vague goal of a gradual progress in the direction of this memory ; neither of them has any real significance for those who exist in the interval. All that is left to them is faith. But without this twofold reference to the Lord as its proper object, and deprived of the power of the " Glory alone to God on high," this faith can only be a special mode of human capacity, will and activity, and therefore, in comparison with Christian faith, only a false faith. Faith can then be understood only as religion. It is the type of religion in which man is influenced by that historical memory and by that specially coloured expectation of progress. But he is only influenced. At the heart and basis, lacking that horizon, as is the case in all " religions," he is his own master, the master of his own deepest impulses. In this type of religion the fellowship of religious people, what is called the Church, can be only a society with a particular object, a club, which individual believers join for certain enterprises and common endeavours and with the greatest possible mutual forbearance towards the wishes and claims of each individual. The error in this outlook is twofold. It consists in the optical illusion that the plane on which the believer exists is unbounded, and without horizons, and he does not notice the direct proximity of the hills before and behind him, whence comes his help. And it is also the acoustic error that the word " faith " still means Christian faith even though the trust and hope and daring of the human heart which it signifies has lost its direction to these hills, instead of being a promising trust and hope and daring in this direction. In substance an error of this kind must be the same as that of the heretical teachers of 2 Peter, which seems to have consisted in the decisive fact that they no longer understood that a day in the Lord's sight is as a thousand years and a thousand years as a day (2 Pet. 3[8]), so that impudently and obstinately, without respect for the majesty of God, they raised themselves

above angels " to speak evil of dignities " (κυριότητος καταφρονοῦντες, 2¹⁰ᶠ·). The
authority with which these heretics are confronted is : " the words which were
spoken before by the holy prophets, and the commandment of us the apostles
of the Lord and Saviour " (3²).

In the interval between the ascension and the second coming the
believer is certainly responsible, but not autonomous. As a believer
he is a member of the body of Christ. And the body of Christ, the
Church, has its Head in heaven, and therefore on earth it is not left
to the insight and caprice of its members. Although it consists entirely
of human beings, the Church is not a human polity, monarchical,
aristocratic or democratic, in which the discharge of the witness to
Jesus Christ committed to it is left to the good pleasure of its members.
The Church is governed. And as it is created and maintained by the
Word of God, it is also governed by the Word of God : by the Word
of God in the form of the testimony to the revelation of God in Jesus
Christ set down in Scripture. To say that Jesus Christ rules the Church
is equivalent to saying that Holy Scripture rules the Church. The
one explains the other, the one can be understood only through the
other. The Son of God in His human nature, and therefore as God
revealed, allows this revelation of Himself, this prophetic office of
His, to be continued in the prophetic and apostolic witness to His
lordship. In the same way His sovereignty, and therefore the sovereignty of God Himself, confronts the Church in and through this
witness. The Holy Spirit, too, is the Spirit of this witness, the Spirit
who certifies this witness to be true, the Spirit through whom this
witness wins the hearts of men. How else, then, can the Church be
ruled except by this witness ? Any other rule can only turn the Church
into that which is not the Church. Any other rule can only lead the
Church back to the sovereignty of man as he is autonomous in the
strength of his false faith. It can consist only in a denial of the character of our time as the time between the ascension and the second
coming. We have no other time but this. The only other time is the
time of sin and death, which is overcome by the irruption of this time
of salvation. If we are not to live again in this time, if the salt of the
Church, which is the salt of the earth, is not to lose its savour, it must
not be denied that its time has the character of an intervening time.
But this intervening time is a time which is determined by the Word
of God in the prophetic and apostolic witness, and the government of
the Church in this time is, therefore, the business of this Word.

All other forms of Church government are, therefore, false. In some cases
the rule of Jesus Christ may assume merely the role of a decorative flower of
speech, while in truth real control is exercised by the spurious, horizonless faith
of men joined together in the Church. Or in other cases the rule of Jesus Christ
may be seriously acknowledged in form, but it is represented as a direct leadership of the Spirit, and it is only a secondary question whether the point at which
this leadership of the Spirit touches and seizes the Church is supposed to be an
infallible Pope or Council, or the office of an authoritarian bishop, or that of a

hypostatised pastor, or a free leadership or inspired individuals in the community, or finally the whole community as such. The false thing in all these types of Church government is the ambiguity with which the rule of Jesus Christ is (perhaps very seriously) asserted, but Scripture is ignored as though it were not the normative form of this government for this intervening period. If we speak of a purely heavenly lordship of Jesus Christ, and then of one of these earthly manifestations of His sovereignty, we may speak " enthusiastically," but in the last resort we are still speaking of the autonomy of human faith, and therefore not of the Church of Jesus Christ.

The horizon within which the Church of Jesus Christ exists is only seen and grasped—and we only begin to speak of the Church of Jesus Christ—when it is seen and grasped that Holy Scripture is the concrete bearer of Church government. This mediacy was instituted by Him, and made effective by His resurrection. Therefore, far from imperilling the immediacy of the relation between the Lord and His Church, it constitutes the true immediacy of this relationship. And far from resulting in any legalistic hardening of the relationship, it is the guarantee that freedom and therefore inspiration will prevail in this relationship.

Where Scripture exercises authority over the Church, all the things which under the rule of autonomous faith are either declared essential and indispensable with legalistic zeal, or avoided and rejected with a similar legalistic concern, can at different times have a place or not have a place, not merely by permission but by command, not merely because they are harmless, but for salvation : Popes and Councils, bishops and pastors, the dignity of synods and congregations, leaders and inspired teachers, the ministry of theologians and others in the congregation, the ministry of men and the ministry of women. But why this or that ? And not this or that ? It is only if the freedom of God's Word is suppressed, or on the presupposition of an " enthusiastic " supplanting of Scripture, that we can wish legalistically to command or to forbid.

Scripture as the proper organ of Church government will not destroy the immediacy of the relation between the Church and its Lord, and will not impose on the Church the rule of law, so long as the distinction between Scripture itself and all human conceptions of it is maintained and continually made, so long as by constant attention to Scripture, in the unbroken discipline of its reading and exegesis, we allow it to take continual precedence of all human theories in order to follow it faithfully, so long as its government and its being allowed to govern are really taken seriously in the Church.

Over-systematised and rigid conceptions of the Word of God will, of course, necessarily both imperil the immediacy of this relation, and at the same time threaten the Church positively or negatively with some kind of legalism. If it is guilty of these over-systematised and rigid conceptions the Church is not behaving obediently but very disobediently.

This does not mean that these theories may not exist and may not have their own worth and validity. We have seen in the preceding paragraphs that there are conceptions of this kind which, in the sphere under the Word, cannot be denied the highest necessity and the greatest worth. But their existence will not, however, trespass upon the freedom of the Word. They must not destroy the fundamental openness of the Church to the leading of Scripture. On the contrary, they must serve it. The freedom of the Word of God in regard to the government of the Church means that in all circumstances the Church walks in the way which was yesterday indicated to it by Scripture, which has to be trodden to-day, and which to-morrow will again have to be indicated by Scripture ; in a way, therefore, where to-day it is willing and ready to take fresh directions with the obedient spirit it showed yesterday. Just for this reason, exegesis in the Church cannot and must not be discontinued. Each new day its task consists in tracing out the particular freedom which the Word of God takes to-day in the course of its government of the Church. But here again we conclude with the reminder that at this focal point of the Church's action the decisive activity is prayer, the giving of thanks for the reality of this government and the petition that it may never cease to be a reality. Because it is the decisive activity prayer must take precedence even of exegesis, and in no circumstances must it be suspended.

2. FREEDOM UNDER THE WORD

In Phil. 1⁹ we hear Paul praying that the love of his readers may abound more and more ἐν ἐπιγνώσει καὶ πάσῃ αἰσθήσει εἰς τὸ δοκιμάζειν τὰ διαφέροντα, so that they may be sincere and without offence at the day of Jesus Christ, filled with the fruits of righteousness which are by Jesus Christ, to the praise and glory of God. Similarly in Col. 1⁹ᶠ· (cf. 1²⁸, 2²), he writes that he prays unceasingly ἵνα πληρωθῆτε τὴν ἐπίγνωσιν τοῦ θελήματος αὐτοῦ ἐν πάσῃ σοφίᾳ καὶ συνέσει πνευματικῇ, that they might walk worthy of the Lord. Rom. 15¹⁴ speaks also of the same being filled with γνῶσις, this time in express connexion with the allusion to the capability which is obviously rooted in this γνῶσις, to give each other mutual instruction. And in Eph. 3¹⁸ᶠ· the same gift is again solemnly represented as the epitome of that for which Paul prays when he thinks of his congregation : that they " may be able to comprehend (καταλαβέσθαι) with all the saints what is the breadth, and length, and depth, and height ; and to know the love of Christ which passeth knowledge." We should set alongside these passages the saying in 2 Tim. 3⁷ which deplores the γυναικάρια that are constantly learning and never able to reach a knowledge of the truth. From these and similar passages we infer that there is an authentic appreciation and understanding by their followers and congregations of the revelation which they attest. This is distinct from the treasures of wisdom and knowledge hidden in Christ (Col. 2³), just as His love for us is distinct from our love for Him. It is also distinct from the knowledge and doctrines of the apostles themselves. By it their followers and congregations become " wise," i.e., they both show themselves and become capable of judging. Both the frequency and the urgency with which this is mentioned show the central importance which this matter that concerns the human members of the Church has for the apostles as founders of the Church. The fact that in all these passages it is an object of apostolic petition shows on the one hand that we deal here with a pneumatic-charismatic gift to man and not with a human capacity or ability. On the other hand, it shows that its impartation to men in the Church does not take place apart from, but through, transmission by apostles as the original bearers of testimony to Christ, since their testimony borne to the community is also a petition for it. We shall have to think of this gift of knowledge and wisdom mediated by the ministry of the first witnesses to the members of the Church now that we come to speak of the freedom under the Word which corresponds to the freedom of the Word.

The Church as the kingdom in which the freedom of God's Word operates is an assembly of men. They have not assembled themselves together, but they were and are assembled. Nevertheless, they are men, and the divine Word which calls them is also a human word. Now if the freedom of His Church is the characteristic of this divine and human Word which gathers them, if it is true that this Word has the power to affirm itself and to keep itself pure in the world, making its way and continually re-establishing itself and in that way founding, maintaining and governing the Church, then it must also follow that, where this power as such is recognised and experienced, where it is not merely suffered as judgment but is also believed as grace and finds obedience, where then the testimony of Scripture is accepted, there arises and subsists, relatively, mediately and formally, utterly dependent upon that acceptance and related to it, but within these limits quite really, a human power and freedom corresponding to the power and freedom of the Word of God. The men assembled in this sphere cannot escape that which in virtue of the freedom of the Word of God happens in their midst. Necessarily it determines them. It concerns them. It communicates itself to them. They can and must for their part affirm and accept it. For all the distance which separates man from God and the dependence of man upon God, it becomes and is, not only God's affair, but theirs. We have seen in the previous section that the testimony of Scripture cannot be received unless the members of the Church are willing and ready, in its interpretation and application, to listen to each other. Correspondingly, we must now say that this testimony cannot be received unless those who accept it are ready and willing themselves to assume the responsibility for its interpretation and application. This readiness and willingness to make one's own the responsibility for understanding of the Word of God is freedom under the Word.

It is perhaps legitimate to define this freedom as the freedom of conscience, in opposition to the authority of the Church referred to in the earlier paragraph on this subject. According to Calvin the rule of Jesus Christ means (*Cat. Genev.* 1545, edited E. F. K. Müller 120, 35): *quod eius beneficio . . . vindicati in libertatem conscientiarum, spiritualibusque eius divitiis instructi, potentia quoque armamur . . .* In this context "conscience," συνείδησις, *conscientia*, the knowing with God of what God knows, has to be understood strictly as the conscience freed and raised by God for this purpose, and not a universal and always effective human disposition and capacity. Freedom of conscience is not, therefore, the permission, which in the 18th and 19th century sense we all have, to think what we consider fine and desirable. It is rather the power, which God imparts to those who accept His revelation, to think what in His judgment is right, and

therefore true and wise. To avoid the Catholic misapprehension (in contradistinction to the prolegomena of 1927) we could accept the authority of the
Church only under the title " Authority under the Word." Similarly, to avoid
the misapprehension of the 18th and 19th centuries, we now set the freedom of
conscience under the title " Freedom under the Word."

Let us immediately point out a fundamental presupposition of all
that follows. It will have to be borne in mind in everything that we
say. We have seen already that authority under the Word, that is,
the authority of the Church, is not a final and absolute court of appeal,
confronting the authority of the Word with its own dignity and
validity. It exists and can be considered only in proper subordination
to the authority of the Word, to serve its proclamation and establishment. In exactly the same way, freedom under the Word, that is,
the freedom of conscience of individual members of the Church, is not
a final thing which exists in its own right and therefore without
boundaries. That it is contingent is already clear from the fact that
it is counterbalanced by an authority under the Word, that is, by a
willingness and readiness which the reception of the witness of Scripture imposes on members of the Church to listen to each other notwithstanding their individual responsibility. But this counterpoise of
human freedom and authority points beyond itself to the common
origin of both without which there would be neither authority nor
freedom in the Church, nor indeed any Church at all. The original
basis, limitation and determination of human freedom in the Church
is the freedom of the Word of God. This human freedom is, therefore,
neither something which is already proper to man, nor a freedom
which man assumes in reaction to the Word of God. It is an event,
in which the Word of God, in the freedom of God Himself, assumes
the freedom to found and maintain and govern the Church. Because
this happens, and happens within a human gathering, and therefore
happens to men, it results in an emancipation of these men, in their
being endowed with a possibility which they did not have before and
which they could not have from their own resources. In discussing
the freedom of the Word of God as such, we have already found it
necessary to make constant allusion to prayer, since in actual fact
this freedom means that the Church can be present only with thanksgiving and petition at the occurrence of the event by which it is
created, maintained and ruled. Similarly, we now have to say even
more emphatically that the freeing of man which takes place as a
result of this event, our own share in the freedom of the Word, our
own willingness and preparedness for its responsible understanding,
can be only the object of our thankful prayer. As freedom under the
Word, it is not a secure possession, or a merit, but a gift from the
divine mercy, continually to be received as such, and only as such.
We are not responsible in this matter, but we are made responsible.
In so far as it is really a gift, an honour which is vouchsafed to man

as man, we must accept it as a portion which we have not deserved and on which we have no claim. And in that it implies at the same time a task, an obligation of care and concern laid upon man, we must accept it as a vocation in the fulfilment of which we are not our own masters, but servants. The joy, the earnestness and the dignity which it imparts to us, the duty which it enjoins upon us, the whole independence of human being and doing which it confers upon us, cannot for a single moment fall outside the framework of prayer, just as the self-determination which we carry through in the fulfilment of this being and doing cannot for a single moment fall outside the framework of divine predestination.

It was, therefore, no pious flourish, but sober affirmation of objective fact, when J. Wolleb (*Theol. Chr. comp.*, 1626, *Praecogn.* 19) placed *frequens oratio* at the head of the *media verum Scripturae sensum investigandi*. To pray is clearly a free act of man. Certainly the Holy Spirit intercedes for us in prayer with groanings which cannot be uttered, because we do not know how to pray as we ought (Rom. 8²⁶ᶠ·). But this does not alter the fact that " it " does not pray, but we pray when we pray. The other media of scriptural exegesis which Wolleb gives in the same connexion are similar free acts of men : linguistic study, investigation of sources, etc. But prayer is the one free act of man in which he confesses that the initiative lies with the freedom of God rather than with his own freedom. In his own freedom he follows in prayer the freedom of God, and in that way relates himself to God. He knows that he cannot do this of himself, but is disposed and empowered to do it by God Himself. He therefore leaves it to the freedom of God—and this happens in the prayer of thanksgiving and petition—to bring man in his freedom into discipleship, and so, by preceding him, to lead him in the divine way. When we pray we turn to God with the confession that we are not really capable of doing it, because we are not capable of God, but also with the faith that we are invited and authorised to do it. For these reasons, prayer is literally the archetypal form of all human acts of freedom in the Church, and as such it must be continually repeated in all other acts of freedom. Whatever else can and must happen in the special responsibility laid upon the members of the Church for the understanding of Scripture, at least there must always happen in it that which actually does happen in prayer : confession and faith, awestruck shrinking and comforted appropriation, in which faith and appropriation are only obedience to the grace which always precedes and which only as such will constantly suggest that confession and shrinking. And it hardly needs to be said that it is true everywhere that the judgment whether all this happens rightly does not belong to us, that our freedom is only true freedom when the Holy Ghost intercedes for us to enable us to accomplish what out of our own resources we certainly cannot do.

We do not, therefore, need a subsequent safeguard against the possibility that " freedom in the Church " will become dangerous and develop into a freedom in opposition to the Word, an emancipation from the Word. This possibility is excluded from the outset and by the nature of the case. If freedom is under the Word, the possibility is precluded that it will become emancipation, arbitrariness or self-assertion. Therefore we have no need to fear this. We need not suspect that a place is thus being allotted to man which does not properly belong to him in his confrontation by God. That which by

its nature is a recognition of the freedom of the Word of God, that
which by its nature can develop only within the framework of prayer
and of a consciousness of divine predestination, cannot change into
revolt, in spite of the fact that as submission and obedience it is also
freedom, human spontaneity and activity, human dignity and action.
This kind of freedom cannot come into conflict with the authority of
the Church, although it is the opposite pole of the life of the Church
and the process of scriptural exegesis within which it takes place.
How can those who are challenged by the witness of Scripture itself
to a responsible understanding of it fail to be summoned as well to a
mutual listening to one another ?   How can they obey in the one sphere
if they do not listen in the other ?   How can they stand in freedom if
they do not also stand under authority ?   But their standing in freedom
and under authority will both be limited by the fact that first and last
they stand under the Word of God.   We thought of this limitation
when we spoke about authority ; we have also to think of it now
that we are speaking of freedom, and this in the double sense that
human freedom in the Church has in the limiting function of the Word
of God both its foundation and its crisis.

Our present starting-point is that at all events it has in it its foundation.   God's Word comes to man as a human word.   This is the process
in which it exercises its freedom, in which it founds, maintains and
governs the Church.   The purpose of this process consists in the arousing of men so that they become believers and witnesses, believers in
God's Word and witnesses to it.   But this process cannot fulfil such a
purpose except in the form of God's Word coming to man as a human
word.   Just in this form it is the continuing witness to God's revelation,
i.e., to the event that God's eternal Word became flesh for us men.   It is
because God's eternal Word became flesh that there are prophets and
apostles and Holy Scripture, and it comes to us in the form of a human
word.   It is because it became flesh for us men that it comes to us in
this form as to men.   Its condescension, self-surrender and self-
humiliation begin in the fusion with the human nature in Jesus Christ,
continue in the calling of His first witnesses, and are completed in
the fact that by the Word of the first witnesses it comes also to us,
arousing us to believe and to witness.   This coming of the Word to
us can be understood as a claim, a command which meets us, and
a law which is laid upon us.   Of ourselves we do not and cannot know
the Word of God.   But it is now required of us that we take knowledge
of it, since it gives itself to be recognised by us.   Or to put it more
concretely : although our way of life is so different from that of the
prophets and apostles, it is now required of us that we hear their
Word and take it up into our own particular situation, seeing that
in Holy Scripture it has, in fact, already entered into our situation.
The same process can be understood as a gift made to us, a possibility
actually opened up to us : God's Word has for our sakes stepped forth

out of the unapproachable mystery of its self-contained existence into
the circle of those things which we can know. Or, again, to put it
even more concretely : the biblical prophets and apostles did not
merely live for themselves, or speak for themselves, but they spoke
to us, and because their apparently so different and distant walk of
life does actually intersect ours, we have to listen to them. In the
last analysis, over and above both these insights, if this whole process
achieves its goal and purpose by arousing us to believe and testify,
we can only understand it as a mystery which encounters us. It is
by no means a matter of course that God's Word exists for us as this
claim or gift, or that with all the other things we have for good or ill,
we should also have Holy Scripture. And again, it is not a matter of
course that we should render obedience to that claim and accept that
gift. On the contrary, when all this happens, it happens in virtue of
the fact that Jesus Christ intercedes for us, taking our place before
His Father, and in virtue of the illuminating and purifying work of
the Holy Spirit upon us. In opposition to all that we can conceive
as possible, there is then completed both objectively and subjectively
an incomparable renewal. But it is still the case that this claim and
gift, and even this miracle, whose occurrence is always so utterly
inaccessible and incomprehensible, consist concretely in the fact that
we ourselves are aroused to believe and witness, i.e., that the Word
of God in the form of a human word gives itself to be appropriated
by us in our humanity, so that now it is not merely God's Word nor
even the word of apostles and prophets, but, as appropriated to us
and received and accepted by us, it is our very own word. As the
word spoken to us, we now speak it to ourselves and to others. How
can it have reached us, how can its condescension have been completed, if in the last resort it remains foreign to us and outside of us,
if we have not affirmed and accepted it—as, of course, the word which
is appropriated to us, the foreign word which comes to us from without ? How can it have reached us, if this does not mean that we
decide to give it our hearing, and with our hearing ourselves ? How
can we believe if, remaining passive, we do not say to ourselves what
is spoken to us ? And how can we be witnesses if again, remaining
passive, we do not say to others what is said to us ? Even though we
can and must understand what happens here as an unheard-of claim
or gift, though we can and must remember that we do not understand
how this objective and subjective miracle can occur when this claim
is fulfilled and this gift accepted, yet we cannot fail to reckon with the
fact that it does actually happen that in our humanity we ourselves
are now drawn into the process in which the Word of God exercises
its freedom and as the word of the prophets and apostles takes its
course through the world. That we are believers and witnesses will
always be a matter for doubt, and humanly speaking even for despair.
We have to remember that this is a reality for which we can never do

more than give thanks and pray. But we deny this reality, and therefore the whole process of events in which God's Word comes to man as a human word, and therefore the work of the Son and of the Holy Ghost, and therefore the self-revelation of God and even God Himself, if we try to escape the fact that we ourselves in our humanity stand at the preliminary end and goal of this process, not left outside, but drawn into its orbit, not as strangers but as children of the household, not as onlookers but as those who co-operate in responsibility, not passively but actively, not in ignorance, but as participants in the divine knowledge, *conscientes*.

If we ourselves in our humanity stand at the end and goal of this process, this cannot mean only that something encounters us, that we are placed in a receptive position, that something has been decided and ordained for us. But inasmuch as all this happens, because it happens to us in our humanity, it must also and primarily mean that our self-determination, our spontaneity and our activity are engaged in the service of the Word of God. This self-determination may be limited by its creatureliness and perverted by its sinfulness, but it is the characteristic essence of the humanity by which we are distinguished from the life of nature (at least in so far as we know or presume to know the latter). This does not mean that in virtue of this humanity we have, as it were, a disposition towards the service of the Word of God, and can therefore recognise ourselves as naturally responsive to God. In the very fact that our humanity is placed in the service of the Word of God, we recognise rather its incapacity for this service, and can understand the fact that we are called in this humanity to serve the Word of God only as a claim, a gift and a miracle. How can we serve grace if we are in a position to ascribe to our human nature as such a capacity for this service ? Do we not then deny it even before we enter upon this service ? On the other hand, how can we and will we enter upon and exercise this service if we try to refuse and withdraw our humanity from the Word of God ? We cannot even appeal to its powerlessness, its creaturely insufficiency, its sinful perversity. For we are not asked about our disposition for this service. Its realisation is not conditioned by our fitness. The completion of the divine condescension is not limited by the incapacity of our humanity. The Word of God still comes to us even as those who are not disposed for its service. Again, and this time from the other side, it is obviously rebellion against grace if we try to withhold from it our humanity because the latter is so clearly unredeemed nature, because the fact and extent that we can serve grace by it is incomprehensible to us. Its full and real incomprehensibility only appears when we know that the Word of God comes to us only by the miraculous work of the Son and of the Holy Ghost. If we do not realise this, we shall refuse our human service by appealing to our incapacity, and this plea will be just as much a manifestation of self-will as the other in which we appeal to our natural capacity and on this basis exalt ourselves as counterparts to God. The one standpoint as much as the other is alien to the true recognition of divine grace. If we realise that it is the divine claim and gift, the miraculous work of the Son and of the Holy Ghost, that God's Word reaches us, then a pessimistic self-assertion will be just as impossible as an optimistic ; we can just as little withhold our humanity from the service of grace because of its unfitness, as we can flaunt it before God to our own self-glorification. Therefore, whatever may be said about their intrinsically insurmountable limitations, our self-determination, spontaneity and freedom will be placed in the service of the Word of God. It is ourselves that the Word of God concerns, intends and meets. It gives itself to be ours, and it wills us for itself. We are sinful creatures. We are unfit for its service. We cannot in our own strength become either believers or witnesses. In the light that falls upon us when we are taken into its service we have to discover and confess that we are not only useless, but inexcusably recalcitrant. But in spite of this, it concerns ourselves, and, because we are men, our decision and assent. We are not asked whether we are in a position to give or ascribe to this decision of ours the character of obedience, of a plain, clear-cut, honest, total and indeed absolute decision. Rather, we are told by the Word for which we have to decide that we are not in this position and never will be. We are told that the truth and goodness of our decision consists and can be sought only in the fact that it is made in virtue of Jesus Christ's intervention for us in which we can believe and to which we can testify, and in virtue of the gift of the Holy Spirit by which we become believers and witnesses. But on this presupposition, we are asked about our decision, and to be asked about our decision means we are asked about ourselves. Since the Fall, to exist as a human being means to exist in decision. The question put to us by the Word about ourselves or our decision does not concern our goodness or badness, but concerns the agreement of our own decision with the decision that has been made concerning us in the Word spoken to us. Can we evade this agreement ? Is it possible for us to dissent from the decision made about us in the Word of God and therefore continue the alienation described in the story of the Fall. Can we persist in sin ? Or must we identify our own decision and ourselves in our goodness or badness with the divine decision, in order that—irrespective of our goodness and badness—in that identification and therefore under the authority of the Word, we may be what we truly are ? It is about this and this alone that we are asked. It is only in this sense that we are asked about our self-determination, spontaneity and activity. But in this sense we are asked, and to the question put to us in this sense we must reply one way or another.

We add a further consideration. Here at the end and goal of the process in which God's Word comes to us as a human word, it is the individual man who is what he is as a man and therefore identifies himself with the decision made about him in the Word of God. It is not the individual without the Church. It is not the individual apart from the relation to his neighbour indicated to him by his being in the Church. It is not, therefore, the individual who has not heard other men in the Church, who has imagined that he can hear the Word of God in some abstract relation between God and the soul, and the soul and God. It is the individual as a member of the body of Christ and therefore as a member of the Church. But as such the members of the Church are not a mass of interchangeable specimens, but in the whole context of their relationships with each other they are individual men. Although the Word of God is given to them in common and although they can only receive it in common, yet this giving and receiving does not take place in any mechanical way but in a spiritual communion corresponding to the individuality of the man Jesus and of all His witnesses, i.e., in the oneness of the many who as individuals are awakened to believe and testify, through the all-embracing oneness of Jesus Christ and the Holy Ghost, the oneness of the Church and baptism. Therefore the decision which stands at the end and goal of the process must be understood concretely, *concretissime*, as our very own decision, as thine and mine. I am merely recounting a myth if I speak of the coming of the Word of God to man as of something other than the coming of the Word to me. Only as the Word which comes to me can I hear it as the Word which comes to the Church and therefore to others too.

Perhaps it sounds self-evident, but it is not really so, if we say that in the nature of the case it is only as each individual thinks of himself that we can really think through all the matters which have been put forward in this connexion : the coming of God's Word as claim and gift and miracle, the overcoming of the false dialectic of the two forms of self-assertion, and particularly the idea of that decision in which the coming of the Word of God to man reaches its present goal. Those who do not know anything of themselves in this matter can know nothing at all. The conscience that is freed through the Word of God is the personal conscience of each individual, and it is each individual who partakes of the dignity but also of the burden of this freedom under the Word. We shall seek in vain for this freedom elsewhere than in the freedom of the individual.

But here, too, a critical reservation is demanded. As we have seen, it is not the case that our humanity as such, our characteristic existence as men in decision, is something good in itself, and that we have, as it were, to bring it to the Word of God in order that in co-operation with it, as partners with God qualified by our humanity, we may help to fulfil the course of God's Word in the world. We have also seen that no disqualification of our humanity can give us the occasion or the right to evade and resist the course of the Word of God. The case is exactly the same with the second consideration, that it is always an individual who is intended and reached when the Word of God calls man to identify himself with the decision it has made about him. We have said indeed that in the Church it is always this or that individual who is addressed. But it is not at all the case that, not in virtue of our common humanity, but in virtue of our particular humanity as this or that man, we have a capacity for communion with the Word and therefore a claim to that communion. It is not the case that the mystery of the individual, or personality—" the greatest boon of the children of men "—has to be brought to the Word of God as the most precious of gifts. Nor again is it the case that in consideration of the nothingness and lostness of our individuality, in doubt or despair about our strictly personal being, we have the right or warrant to withdraw from communion with the Word of God.

It should be noticed that neither in the Old nor in the New Testament, where it has sometimes been eagerly sought, does there appear an idea of the individual in virtue of which his immediate relationship to God is to be found in his human individuality. The Bible takes no independent interest in the individuality of man determined, as it were, from below or from within. What constitutes the members of the body of Christ, the members of the Church as such and therefore as individuals, is not the peculiar quality which this or that individual brings under his personal name and as his personal contribution to the discipleship of Jesus and to the Church. The Old and New Testaments know nothing of those " biblical character sketches " which people have tried to find in them, especially in modern times. The material sought in them for the characterisation of the most important and " greatest " personalities is obviously scanty and insufficient for the purpose. The investigation of the life of Jesus has foundered because critics have been so slow to see this truth. But as in the Bible universal humanity, i.e., human decision, is of interest only as implicated in the question whether it is identical with the decision of the Word of God concerning mankind, so also the special humanity of the individual is of interest only as implicated in the question whether this individual will accept and use the divine gift conferred upon him. It is only by his conduct as a steward of the talents committed to him, and not by his prior disposition, that it is decided into which category each of the servants in the parable Matt. 25[14f.] will fall. And it is only in relation to the characterisation of the various and yet inter-related *charismata*, that what we would call the problem of individuality is discussed in the Pauline epistles (e.g., Rom. 12[3f.], 1 Cor. 12[4f.], Eph. 4[7f.]).

It is just the grace of God's Word that it always comes in a quite specific, concrete, definitely challenging and self-giving form—for it is the free Word of God—not merely to the Church as a whole, but also in the Church to this or that individual, in order that in the Church he may be this man, this particular member. Confronted by this grace, neither my justifiable self-confidence nor my equally justifiable self-despair can be of the slightest interest. I am not asked who and what I am from below or from within, who or what I may be in my natural state as an individual. I am asked solely about my relationship to the Word of God as it comes specially to me, from above or from without, annihilating my pride and covering my sin. I am addressed by the name I received in my baptism, and not by the title which might

be given me by others as an indication of my personality. The point
is that I, very definitely I, should be what I am in this relationship
and therefore in the process of that annihilation and covering. The
point is that I should take myself, very definitely myself, seriously in
my particular existence created by my new birth by the Word of
God. The point is that I should exist only as this particular man
born again by the Word of God. The point is that I should yield and
surrender my earthly and inner particularity to the particularity of
the gift of grace offered to me. And I am not asked about the richness
or poverty of my personality, but only about the possibility or impossibility of refusing and withdrawing myself from existence as this
new man.

We must bear in mind a third characteristic. We have seen that
at the end and goal of the process in which God's Word comes to
mankind as a human word, a man is what he is as a man, and therefore
decides in his self-identification with the decision of the Word of God
about him. We have also seen that in virtue of the special divine
decision made about him he is precisely this man. Our third point
is that as such he becomes clear to himself in the individual decision
in which his self-identification with the divine Word takes place. We
cannot say that he only comes to exist in this event, but we must
say that in this event alone he becomes clear to himself. As the
founding, maintaining and governing of the Church as a whole has
a history, so the life of its members has a history. The continuity of
its history, the truth that at all times and in all places it is founded,
maintained and governed by God's Word, is hidden from the Church.
The Church cannot see this. It cannot point to it and reconstruct it.
It can only believe it to be the truth : and how can this happen
except in the constant fact of its founding, maintaining and governing ?
That the Church can only believe in this (but, of course, may and must
believe in it) as a truth of God revealed to it, is shown in the fact
that, as this event takes place, the Church will both give thanks and
pray for its occurrence. It is precisely the same with the calling of
the individual man and his awakening to faith and witness. Certainly,
his whole existence is involved, the whole span of his life from his
mother's womb to his death, and also its whole breadth, that is, his
psychico-physical existence in the totality of its presuppositions,
effects and relationships. Only in this totality are we really ourselves.
Even if only a second of my existence in time is lacking, or a hair of
my head, I am no longer I, man, this man. It is either in this totality
that I am a target for the Word of God, or not at all. It is either
in this totality that the decision of the Word of God is taken concerning
me, and I am born again by the Word, or not at all. It is either in
this totality, " with body and soul, in life and death," that I belong
to " my faithful Saviour Jesus Christ," and am a living member of
His body, or else it is not in any sense true. It is impossible to emphasise

23

this too strongly. Its truth is compromised by every qualification. Yet while I may and must believe this truth in this totality—and I do not believe it at all except in this totality—it is still the case that I can only believe it. In faith and only in faith is it clear to me, because and in so far as my faith is faith in the Word of God and therefore in Jesus Christ. In Jesus Christ, I am revealed to myself as he who in the totality of his existence is received and accepted by Him. I shall then accept this revelation as one accepts revelation in faith : I shall accept it with thankfulness and prayer. But apart from faith, and therefore apart from Jesus Christ, this truth is always hidden from me in its totality (without which it is not this truth). But in faith we always have to do with a single event, an individual decision, in which I decide in conformity with the decision of the Word of God. If in this event we link up with the fact that we have perhaps believed before, and if in this event we receive the promise that we will again believe in the future, if there is thus a state of believing which embraces past, present and future, faith itself is not identical with this state of believing. As distinct from it, it is never something which is there already. It is always a gift which has to be seized again and again. We can have it, and the retrospect and the prospect which it gives (and what can truly be called a Christian state of believing), only as it is given to us as a gift, and as we grasp it as such.

Here again we find the same false dialectic with its twofold perversion. On the one hand, there arises the optimistic self-assertion which considers that we can know, name and describe individual events in our own lives or that of others, the actuality of whose content consists in just this gift and its appropriation by us. These events are to be described as special experiences and illuminations, internal and external turning-points. They are extraordinary events in the context of the rest of life, islands in the stream, so to speak, but in this isolation they are to be understood as identifiable happenings, on whose actuality we can definitely count and reckon. But strangely enough, their isolation cannot usually be maintained, and on this presupposition it is not at all the case that the rest of a man's life, the totality of our existence in its determination by the Word of God, is respected as a truth which is concealed from us.

Once such extraordinary events are recognised and admitted in their supposed authenticity, the presumed insights into their occurrence increases, and the corresponding statements about them group themselves into series, patterns and pictures. There arises the so-called " miracle story which we have ourselves experienced." There arises the " testimony " which is supposed to be so edifying both to ourselves and to others. Alongside the confession of the Church in which Scripture is expounded, there arises the confession of the individual Christian, of which he himself is the object, that is, as he thinks he knows himself. There arises, in its main outlines, Christian biography, which, when it is completed, will do away with that hiddenness altogether, and represent the whole life of a man as a more or less uninterrupted sequence of such events.

And again we find the complementary pessimistic form of self-assertion in which we will have nothing to do with events of which the content is the gift and appropriation of faith. We defiantly dispute the reality of such things. We scornfully interpret whatever we hear from others in this respect as illusion and ecstatic fantasy. We contentedly accept the fact that in our own lives such things never have been and never will be. It is obviously not impossible that what in the eyes of some is fire from heaven appears to others as triviality and vanity. Indeed, it often happens in the life of one and the same person that he takes first the one view of these things and then the other.

The worst pessimists in this respect are always those who have been optimists. But again, the worst scepticism and indifference are often enough only the prelude or occasion for an all the more powerful assertion of these personally experienced events, and finally for an all the more complete abolition of every kind of hiddenness of the life in God. The two forms of self-assertion are as close together as this, and as little are they protected from turning into their opposite.

To all this we can only say again that we are not asked about the thing on which both sides believe so passionately that they can hold their views. We are not asked about the faith-incidents as such, which can certainly be seen in our lives, but obviously only in the greatest ambiguity. We are not asked about any sort of humanly demonstrable actuality as such. We are asked about ourselves by the Word of God. Each individual is individually asked about himself. And this means, of course, that we are asked about certain particular events of our life in which the hidden totality of our life in God becomes visible to faith. We have seen, however, how the humanness of the decision for which we are asked, and its distinctive humanness as our own personal decision, are certainly not to be regarded as springing from us, from within and from below, but from the Word of God which alone confers reality upon them. And it is just the same with the particularity of the events of faith. It will fare ill with us if, according to the common presupposition of these two types of self-assertion, as a proof of their actuality we have to perceive and establish them as such by our own resources, from within and below. It will fare ill with us if just at this point, where our whole spiritual life is at stake, we have to rely upon facts which can, of course, be a subject for boasting, but can also very obviously be a subject for despair. It will fare ill with us if even the suspicion can arise that the facts in question have been created and perhaps only imagined by us ourselves. But this is just not the case. For the faith which forms the content of those special events, whether interpreted as a divine gift or as our own appropriation of this gift, is primarily and essentially faith in Jesus Christ. Both it and therefore also those special events of faith are primarily and essentially to be regarded only from above, from Jesus Christ, because they are only real when seen in this way from above, from Jesus Christ. Again, the fact is that both he who boasts of that which is demonstrable on the human level, and he who despairs of it, are missing the mark. Why should it not be the case that at this point—even if with the fluctuating and yet factual certainty which alone is possible in this connexion—a single thing is in fact to be affirmed ? It is not to be denied but rather affirmed that in certain humanly identifiable moments and situations, not simply in recollection or expectation but in the concrete present of faith, we are in fact humbly and thankfully aware in a very special way, not merely of our state of believing, but of our real faith, and therefore of our whole life as a life lived in God, and that in this sense we gladly recall such moments as certainly significant. Of course, this does not mean that we simply have to believe that this has happened. Nor does it mean that when it is a question of proving faith we have the right and duty to refer to them. For how can it be otherwise than that on the other hand at other moments—indeed perhaps already in the same moment—we are just as certainly made aware of the relativity and ambiguity of such an event when humanly affirmed, that therefore to some extent it falls from its special position into the series of other ordinary events in our life, and mingles with the stream of that totality of our life which, being our life in God, is hidden and not revealed to us, and therefore cannot be the object of our faith and witness. In their human identification these special events are obviously subjected to an interplay of light and darkness which can only damage and forbid both the absolute affirmation of the optimist and the absolute negation of the pessimist. The really outstanding events of our life, upon which our faith lives and in which our whole life is revealed to us in faith as life in God, are not those which we can affirm with this human certitude and then have to doubt again. They are not subject to this fluctuation ; they can and must be discussed apart from this false dialectic. These really outstanding events of our life are simply identical with our share in the great acts of God in His revelation. The fact is that according to the testimony of Scripture God's revelation is a unique thing, and yet is completed in certain distinct and definite events. And it is this fact which forms the basis of the real distinctiveness of those moments in which faith apprehends them, and also of their significance for our whole life. We must say further and without hesitation that just those individual and definite events in which, according to the Bible, God's self-revelation is fulfilled, in that they have already happened and we here and now may share in them, constitute the reality of the faith-events of our own life. Whether certain humanly identifiable incidents of this our life remind us of this reality or not, still the reality itself continually breaks through these fluctuating possibilities, and in it these definite revelatory events have taken place in such a way that here and now we are called to share in them. In any event, it is only in their own singularity that the identifiable and yet so insecurely identifiable events of our life have their truth. Whether we can evade participating in those biblical events or not is the question which God's Word puts to us—it does so both when we are conscious of the exalted and exalting events of our life and also when we are conscious rather of their relativity. The truth of such events is determined solely by the content of our faith which is active in them, not by the meaning which, in their fluctuating certainty as the effects of our faith, we sometimes arbitrarily like to ascribe to them, and at other times just as arbitrarily like to deny them.

It is said that H. F. Kohlbrügge once answered the question : When was he converted ? by the laconic reply : On Golgotha. This answer, with all its fundamental implications, was not the witty retort of an embarrassed and unconverted man, but the only possible and straightforward answer of a truly converted Christian. The events of faith in our own life can, in fact, be none other than the birth, passion, death, ascension and resurrection of Jesus Christ, the faith of Abraham, Isaac and Jacob, the exodus of Israel from Egypt, its journey through the desert, its entrance into the land of Canaan, the outpouring of the Holy Ghost at Pentecost and the mission of the apostles to the heathen. Every verse in the Bible is virtually a concrete faith-event in my own life. Whether this is actually the case, whether with my own life I have been present at this or that event here testified to me, this and this alone is what I am asked by the Word of God which bears witness to me of God's revelation in and through all this, and in every single verse of Scripture. In comparison with this, what can be the value of the various more or less reliable insights which, apart from these testimonies, I may have in myself ? Is there a miracle story that I can relate from my own life, which, especially if it is genuine, will not be totally dissolved in this divine miracle story, and which therefore will hardly be worth relating *in abstracto* ? Have I anything to testify about myself which I cannot testify infinitely better if I make my own the simplest ingredient of the Old Testament or New Testament witness ? Have I experienced anything more important, incisive, serious, contemporary than this, that I have been personally present and have shared in the crossing of Israel through the Red Sea but also in the adoration of the golden calf, in the baptism of Jesus but also in the denial of Peter and the treachery of Judas, that all this has happened to me here and now ? If I believe, then this must be the right point of view. If this is the right point of view, what other faith events in my life should I and could I wish to seek ? What, then, becomes of the bold assertion with which I claim first this and then that crisis and turning-point, and then gradually my whole life, as a sacred history ? And what becomes of the defiant and shrinking doubt and despair about all exalted and exalting moments, and finally about my whole life ? However high may rise or however deep may fall the waves of life's events, as they are perceptible to us from within and below, the real movement of my life, the real events in which it is clear to me that in the whole dimension of my existence I belong to God, both at the flood and ebb, are secured from the other side, by the Word of God Himself. And we shall have to answer this question and this question alone : whether, after the Word of God has sought to provide us with this movement and meaning, we have perhaps evaded it ?

All this, therefore, is human freedom under the Word based upon the freedom of the Word of God. We see that it is a question of genuine human freedom, of us ourselves in our decision, of each of us personally, in the special events of our life in which it becomes clear to us that our whole existence is at stake. But we see also that this genuine human freedom is based in its entirety upon the freedom of God's Word, upon the all-embracing decision which through the Word has been pronounced upon mankind, upon the particular grace with which the Word comes to this or that man, upon the uniqueness of the events which form the content of the Word. Therefore, human freedom cannot encroach upon divine freedom. Always and in every respect the latter precedes the former. Yet, on the other hand, divine freedom cannot destroy and suspend human freedom. Always and in every respect the former draws the latter to and after itself. We ourselves are rooted in this genuine human freedom under the Word, prayerfully and thankfully, recognising this reality as it wills to be recognised— we ourselves in our humanity—as the present end and goal of the process whereby God's Word comes to man as a human word ; not as ignorant but as sharing in the divine knowledge, as *conscientes*.

We have still to make clear to ourselves the fundamental scope of this cognisance and of our freedom under the Word. How far is it a fact that God's Word does not remain God's Word, or even the word of apostles and prophets, but gives itself to be appropriated by the Church and therefore is received and accepted by the members of the Church and becomes their own word ? What is the place of interpretation and application of the Word of God under the freedom of the Word ? Here we have to answer the fundamental question, and we must give a fundamental answer. We presuppose that an interpretation and application of the Word actually comes to pass in human freedom under the Word, just as we previously assumed that there was really under the Word a human authority—that of the Church. But as in the former case, in view of the indissoluble connexion of genuine human authority with the authority of the Word, we could not presume to present a system of ecclesiastical authority operating as though it were not the result of the authoritative Word of God itself seen in actual lordship over the Church, so now we may not venture to advance and systematically to represent freedom under the Word, i.e., genuine effective interpretation and application based upon and connected indissolubly with the Word of God, as though this were not the act of the free Word of God itself which is always beyond our control and inscrutable to us. Assuming this act, and also assuming that true interpretation and application of the divine Word is a real event, the one thing which we can—and must now—do is to mention and discuss some of the human possibilities in which it becomes evident that human freedom is actively engaged in this event, and in what sense it is engaged.

1. We have already characterised freedom under the Word, that is, human freedom in the Church, as the assumption of responsibility for the interpretation and application of Holy Scripture. Let us now seek to grasp generally what this means. If the members of the

Church have a responsibility towards Scripture, this clearly means that the founding, maintaining and governing of the Church by Scripture does not happen in such a way that the members of the Church are only spectators or even objects of this happening. It takes place rather in such a way that in their specific place and function they become subjects of it. To be a member of the Church in relation to Scripture which founds, maintains and rules the Church, means not only to hear, receive and believe the Word of God, and so in one's own life to become a man directed and consecrated by the Word ; more than all this it means to take seriously and understand as one's own responsibility the effective operation of the Word, its being continuously expressed and heard, its being continuously proclaimed and made fruitful. The Word of God wills always to be newly and more widely heard in the Church, and beyond the Church lies the world, where by the Church it also wills to be always heard. Because of his freedom which is grounded in this Word, a member of the Church cannot retain a passive, indifferent and merely waiting role in face of this will of the divine Word, as though anyway, in its own time what has to happen will happen. Certainly, it will happen, but not without us. We have seen that we ourselves stand at the present end and goal of the way which the Word of God takes in approaching men. We ourselves are thus present when the way leads on into the Church and the world. Called by the Church into the Church, we ourselves become the Church into which we are called. Yet we cannot merely note that the Church is calling and wait to see whether and how far the Church will continue to call. Rather we ourselves have become the Church in person, and as such have been made responsible for its future. And this means in concrete terms that we are responsible participants in the great event by which Holy Scripture lives and rules in the Church and in the world.

It was not to all men generally, but to His disciples as witnesses, that Jesus said (Mt. 5¹³ᶠ·) : Ye are the salt of the earth ; ye are the light of the world. It follows that, where the original witness of the revelation performs its proper task, it does not function as fructifying salt simply for the private enjoyment and use of those who happen to be called and illuminated ; but in principle the same task is laid upon them, too, differing from that of the prophets and apostles only in the fact that for them Jesus is now the One to whom prophets and apostles bear witness, so that their task has this witness as concrete content. The prayer of Peter in Ac. 4²⁹ : " Grant unto thy servants that with all boldness (μετὰ παρρησίας πάσης) they may speak thy Word," must now be their prayer too, *mutatis mutandis*. And it is certainly not only in a moral sense that Paul speaks concerning the public and private speech of Christians, but (perhaps not without allusion to Mt. 5¹³) he is referring to their commission in the Church, when in Col. 4⁶ he writes : " Let your speech be always with grace, seasoned with salt, that ye may know how ye ought to answer every man," or when again in Eph. 4²⁹ he requires that the speech of Christians be " good to the use of edifying (ἀγαθὸς πρὸς οἰκοδομὴν τῆς χρείας), that it may minister grace unto the hearers." There is a very clear connexion with 1 Pet. 3¹⁵ where the persecuted Christians are told that if they would sanctify the Lord Christ in their hearts, they must be ready to answer (πρὸς ἀπολογίαν) every man who may ask them to justify the hope they entertain. Again, it is in this and not merely a generally moralistic sense that we must understand what is said in the famous passage in Jas. 3¹ᶠ· concerning the judgment under which they stand who have not dedicated their tongue to the service of teaching.

We must always bear in mind how far from self-explanatory it is that there can be any sort of human participation and responsibility in this matter. At this point we have good cause to consider again the whole secret and mystery of the incarnation, of the existence of the man Jesus, and His decisive prophetic office, and the whole riddle of the existence of His plenipotentiary witnesses. It is indeed true that we ourselves with our word are included in this circle ; but what an incomprehensible condescension of God, what an incomprehensible elevation of man is to be observed in this truth ! We have to realise and accept it in all its mystery and incomprehensibility. We are not asked whether we of ourselves hold it to be possible or can make it possible ; we have to observe and accept it in its reality, and then to prove its possibility by the exercise of the freedom which is thereby promised to us. That the responsibility laid upon us is too exalted and wonderful is an aspect of the matter to be considered and pondered. But, on the other hand, it is to be noted that we are asked whether we can well evade such a responsibility. If we accept the fact that we cannot, then we must consider in what exactly this responsibility consists. In order to be proclaimed and heard again and again both in the Church and the world, Holy Scripture requires to be explained. As the Word of God it needs no explanation, of course, since as such it is clear in itself. The Holy Ghost knows very well what He has said to the prophets and apostles and what through them He wills also to say to us. This clarity which Scripture has in itself as God's Word, this objective *perspicuitas* which it possesses, is subject to no human responsibility or care. On the contrary, it is the presupposition of all human responsibility in this matter. All the explanation of Scripture for which we are responsible can be undertaken only on the presupposition that Scripture is clear in itself as God's Word ; otherwise it will at once disintegrate. And all scriptural exegesis for which we are responsible can lead only to the threshold beyond which Scripture is clear in itself as God's Word. But this Word in Scripture assumes the form of a human word. Human words need interpretation because as such they are ambiguous, not usually, of course, in the intention of those who speak, but always for those who hear. Among the various possibilities, the sense intended by the speaker has to be conveyed, and as the sense which they have for the speaker, it has to be communicated to the thinking of the hearer, so that the words have now a meaning for him, and indeed the meaning intended by the speaker. Perhaps this twofold interpretation, which can be distinguished as exegesis and application, can be made at once by the hearer ; perhaps the speaker himself is in a position to offer this twofold interpretation of his words, or, if not their application, at least their exegesis ; perhaps a third party must intervene and perform this service of interpretation for speaker and hearer. All human words without exception need one of these interpretations. Now, since God's Word in Scripture has taken the form of a human word, it has itself incurred the need of such interpretation. Our human responsibility is related to this need of interpretation, and thus to Scripture expressed in human words. When we take into consideration all that is comprised by the term " interpretation," it can be only a partial responsibility. Why should not the prophets and apostles always be heard directly in the interpretation which the hearers themselves are enabled to give ? And why should they not always be in a position to offer an explanation themselves ? It is not, then, the case that by the very fact that it has assumed the form of Scripture, and therefore of human words, God's Word is, so to speak, defencelessly exposed to the need of human interpretation for which we as members of the Church have been made responsible. It is good that in the life of the Church these first possibilities of interpretation in their mutual relatedness both continue to play their part. It is good that, alongside of the clarity which the Word of God has in itself, there is also a self-interpretation of its form as a human word.

This, too, forms a presupposition of the scriptural exegesis in the narrower sense which is incumbent upon us, and without which it cannot itself be realised. All the same, the first two possibilities have their limits. Not every one, and no one at all times and in all circumstances, can be his own interpreter of Scripture, affirming the meaning of the biblical word from his own resources, and affirming it in such a way that it has meaning for him, and indeed its original meaning. We must also add that not always and not to everyone are the biblical authors, who speak from the point of view of their own circle and reveal to us only a small excerpt from that circle, in a position to make the meaning of their words clear and also to communicate it to the thinking of the modern reader. We are thinking of the man (Ac. 8²⁶ᶠ·) who was reading Is. 53 in his chariot— it was not quite unprepared that he had gone to Jerusalem to worship—and who to the question : " Understandest thou what thou readest ? " had to answer : " How can I, except some man should guide me ? " (ἐὰν μή τις ὁδηγήσει με).

At this point there commences what we may call the need of interpretation in the narrower sense, and at this point, too, there also commences the responsibility laid on the members of the Church. A member of the Church is as such called upon to be the third party who, in order to help on both sides, intervenes between the speaker and the hearer, and therefore between the human word of Scripture and the other members of the Church, but also between the biblical word and the men of the world. On the side of Scripture, he helps by attempting to illuminate its sense, on the side of the hearing or reading man, by attempting to suggest to him the fact and extent that Scripture has a meaning for him. The former task has also to be under-stood, of course, as a service to men, the latter as a service to Scripture.

We might glance at this point at the excellent definition which Polanus has given of biblical interpretation : *Interpretatio sacrae Scripturae est explicatio veri sensus et usus illius, verbis perspicuis instituta ad gloriam Dei et aedificationem ecclesiae* (*Synt. Theol. chr.* 1609, p. 635 f.). From this we see that it is a question of (1) the *verus sensus* and (2) the *verus usus* of Scripture. Both remain obviously clear in and by themselves. Both can also speak for themselves, and both do so. Yet both need *explicatio* ; hence there is a need of interpretation and applica-tion. The region of the *verba*, lying between the two, is problematical. Here there is a need, and there arises a responsibility. It is a question of the *verba perspicua* in regard both to the *sensus* and also the *usus* of Scripture. That the necessary work of communication should be done : *ad gloriam Dei et aedificationem ecclesiae*, is the task of *interpretatio*, and therefore a matter of the responsibility laid upon members of the Church.

It will be good to emphasise more strongly than was done in the 16th and 17th centuries that fundamentally this responsibility is laid upon all members of the Church and not upon a specialised class of biblical scholars. The need for the interpreting third party is not an isolated or occasional thing. There are the two first possibilities of interpretation, as a result of which the Word of God, quite apart from the clarity which it has in itself, may even as a human word, so to speak, go its own way on its own feet, so that there is always a direct relationship and possibility of understanding between the biblical authors and their modern readers. Yet despite this, the life of Scrip-ture in the Church and in the world never rests solely upon these two possibilities, and the Word of God has surrendered itself so fully to the need of interpretation that some mediation is always necessary. There is no one who as hearer of the Word does not also and neces-sarily live by the service of such mediators. They may perhaps be remote from him. They may not be known to him as such. But they are in fact effectual, and they have intervened between the scriptural word and himself, and performed for him the service of interpretation and application. We can declare positively that the Church as a whole is an organisation which exists for this mediatorial work. For this reason no member of the Church can remain unconcerned, idle and inactive in face of this duty. If the interpretation of Scripture is not the concern of a special office but of the whole Church, no member of the Church can remain a mere spectator of what is or is not under-taken by this office to this end. Only when every member of the Church realises that the responsibility in this matter devolves upon him too can there be an intelligent critical appreciation of what is or is not done in this regard. If a part—and probably much the greater part—of the Church declines its responsibility for this task, it signifies nothing more nor less than that this section of the Church is renouncing the freedom which it is offered under the Word, and wishes to live only by authority in the Church. In this case, how soon it will be manifest that for this party there is no ecclesiastical authority either. Those who are silent in deference to scriptural learning, the congregation which is passive in matters of biblical exegesis, is committed already to secret rebellion. It is emancipated from the Canon and confession, and therefore from the Word of God and from faith. Therefore it is no longer a true congregation of Jesus Christ. Whoever will have nothing to do with this secret and one day open rebellion, whoever wants ecclesiastical authority for the sake of the authority of God's Word, must affirm freedom under the Word as the freedom of all Christian men, and must wish the congregation to participate in scriptural exegesis with real responsibility.

2. The necessary and fundamental form of all scriptural exegesis that is responsibly undertaken and practised in this sense must consist in all circumstances in the freely performed act of subordinating all human concepts, ideas and convictions to the witness of revelation supplied to us in Scripture. Subordination is not opposed to freedom. Freedom means spontaneous activity in relation to an object, such as is characteristic of human conduct and decision, as opposed to merely passive conduct determined from without and subject to necessary development. But freedom does not necessarily mean the divine sovereignty over the object, nor as human freedom does it necessarily mean a relation of reciprocal influence between the object and the freely acting self over against the object. If there is an object in regard to which any other appropriate reaction is excluded, why should not human spontaneity in face of it consist in man's putting himself under it without at the same time putting himself over it ? We may ask whether there is such an object. Even if there is, we can and must also ask the question whether in fact such a subordination of man over against it will be so realised that all impulses to superiority are effectively excluded. It is easy enough to show that, in point of fact, even in face of such an object man lapses into a relation of reciprocity and further into the presumption of his being divinely and sovereignly controlled, so that, even in the most willing subordination, superiority makes itself felt. But all this does not alter the fact that if there is an object which requires activity in relation to it, and permits no other kind of activity but that of subordination, then the only freedom possible to man consists in the fulfilment of this subordination—and this without its ceasing to be freedom, or being less really freedom than in activity over against objects which evoke the relation of reciprocal activity. He comes to take himself seriously in the exercise of this freedom ; he comes to exercise his freedom in this way, without even asking about the result, about which in the moment of decision he must not ask ; or he comes in this way to discharge the task. In that God's Word is given to us in Holy Scripture, an object is given to us which requires our spontaneous activity, but this activity of subordination.

In Holy Scripture we are dealing with a Word of God coming to us in the form of human words, and, in the activity the Word demands of us, we are dealing with the explanation of this Word, in so far as in its human form it needs an explanation. That the essential form of its explanation must be subordination is based, of course, on the circumstance that it is God's Word in human form. What make the Word of God, in the form in which we encounter it, obscure and in need of interpretation are the ideas, thoughts and convictions which man always and everywhere brings to this Word from his own resources. When the Word of God meets us, we are laden with the images, ideas and certainties which we ourselves have formed about God, the world and ourselves. In the fog of this intellectual life of ours the Word of God, which is clear in itself, always becomes obscure. It can become clear to us only when this fog breaks and dissolves. This is what is meant by the subordination of our ideas, thoughts and convictions. If the Word of God is to become clear to us, we cannot ascribe to them the same worth as we do to it. We cannot try to appraise the Word of God by reference to them ; or to cling to them in face of the Word of God. The movement which we have to make in relation to it—and quite freely, of course—can be only that of yielding, surrender and withdrawal.

Is. 40[12ff.] certainly contains the suggestion of a theory of knowledge : " Who hath measured the waters in the hollow of his hand, and meted out heaven with the span, and comprehended the dust of the earth in a measure, and weighed the mountains in scales, and the hills in a balance ? Who hath directed the Spirit of the Lord, or being his counsellor hath taught him ? With whom took he counsel, and who instructed him, and taught him in the path of judgment, and taught him knowledge, and shewed to him the way of understanding ? " Similarly Is. 55[7ff.] : " Let the wicked forsake his way, and the unrighteous man his thoughts : and let him return unto the Lord, and he will have mercy upon him ; and to our God, for he will abundantly pardon. For my thoughts are not your thoughts, neither are your ways my ways, saith the Lord. For as the heavens are higher than the earth, so are my ways higher than your ways, and my thoughts than your thoughts."

The matter seems further complicated by the fact that God's thoughts in His Word do not come to us *in abstracto* but *in concreto* in the form of the human word of prophets and apostles, which as such is not only the expression of God's thoughts but also the expression of their own. It is the case, then, that the divine Word itself meets us right in the thick of that fog of our own intellectual life, as having taken the same form as our own ideas, thoughts and convictions. It is " a light that shineth in a dark place " (2 Pet. 1[19]). But in fact this apparent complication makes it all simple and easy to understand. The pure Word of God as such needs, of course, no explanation because, like the light of the sun above our atmosphere, it is clear in itself. But as such it would not have come to us, and we could have nothing to do with it. In fact, however, without ceasing to be clear in itself—

clear always by reason of the clarity which it possesses in itself— it has come down to us through the testimony of apostles and prophets. For that reason it has come to need interpretation in so far as it has assumed the mode of our intellectual world and is thus exposed to the risk of being understood, or rather not understood, by us according to the habits of our mentality, in the relationship of reciprocal activity by which we are normally accustomed to understand human words. But just because it has compromised itself in this way, it has become capable of explanation ; not only of fundamental self-explanation in virtue of its intrinsic clarity, but also of the interpretation which its human witnesses are at least partially capable of giving, of the interpretation which the human hearers and readers of these witnesses, again at least partially, are also in a position to give, and finally of interpretation in the narrowest sense of the term, by which the members of the Church serve the Word of God and each man his brother. All this is possible because the Word of God is not given to us *in abstracto*, because it is real light, not merely in the for us inaccessible stratosphere of its inner existence, but also, thanks to the resurrection of Jesus Christ in the witness of the prophets and apostles, in the atmosphere of our own intellectual world. This means that this subordination to the Word, which is the basis for its interpretation in so far as this is our responsibility, is no mere idea or empty postulate, in face of which the only possible actuality is that we set ourselves above the Word of God, and in the end probably in an absolute sense, as we are accustomed to do in regard to other objects.

Such a relation would obtain if we had to do with the eternal Logos of God as such, and with the world as its form of manifestation. As we can see from every form of heathenism, and every philosophy which looses itself even relatively from the revelation of God in Jesus Christ, subordination to it would then simply take the form of a reciprocity of subordinate and superior, behind which it would appear that the real meaning is the attempt to express divine sovereignty over the object. But this is not the true relationship, seeing the eternal Logos has become incarnate, has risen in the flesh, and in the flesh has established a witness for Himself.

Just because we have to do with God's Word in the form of definite human words, the realisation of this subordinate relationship becomes a concrete task. Certainly we are not concerned with its final accomplishment ; but it can be seen and understood concretely as a task imposed upon us. To interpret God's Word must and can now mean to interpret Holy Scripture. And because the interpretation of the Word of God can take place only through man's subordination, this subordination now comes concretely to mean that we have to subordinate ourselves to the word of the prophets and apostles ; not as one subordinates oneself to God, but rather as one subordinates oneself for the sake of God and in His love and fear to the witnesses and messengers which He Himself has constituted and empowered. In

the real contrast between the ideas, thoughts and convictions which
we meet in the words of the biblical witnesses and our own ideas,
thoughts and conceptions, there can and must be practised that proper
subordination in which alone the illumination of the Word of God
can take place at least for us. It is true that in the last resort this
clarity is intrinsic to the Word. It is true that every interpretation
of Scripture consists substantially in the interpretation which the
Word gives of itself. It is true that all the clarity which the words
of the apostles and prophets can have in themselves and for us without
special explanation, and therefore all the clarity which we can lend
to the Word and to the brethren through interpretation in the narrowest
sense of the term, rests ultimately upon the clarity which the Word
of God has in itself. But it is still the case that this self-illumination
does not take place without us, and therefore terminates in that
freedom to which as members of the Church we are called, and therefore in a human activity in the service of the Word of God. This
activity becomes necessary and possible, is commanded and permitted,
by the fact that we have the Word in the form of its human witnesses.
It is over against them that this subordination as the essential form
of human interpretation must take place ; not in regard to the divine
Word in general, but in regard to its human witnesses. Otherwise
it does not take place at all. But in what must it then consist ? It
is not as though we had simply to abandon and forget our ideas,
thoughts and convictions. We certainly cannot do that, just as little
as we can free ourselves from our own shadow. Nor should we try
to do it ; for that would be arrogance rather than humility. Subordination does not mean the elimination and annihilation of our own
resources. Subordination implies that the subordinate is there as
such and remains there. It means placing oneself behind, following,
complying as subordinate to superior. This is what is required in
subordinating our ideas, thoughts and convictions to the witness which
confronts us in Scripture. It cannot mean that we have to allow our
ideas, thoughts and convictions to be supplanted, so to speak, by
those of the prophets and apostles, or that we have to begin to speak
the language of Canaan instead of our own tongue. In that case we
should not have subordinated ourselves to them, but at most adorned
ourselves with their feathers. In that case nothing would have been
done in the interpretation of their words, for we should merely have
repeated them parrot-like. Subordination, if it is to be sincere, must
concern the purpose and meaning indicated in the ideas, thoughts and
convictions of the prophets and apostles, that is, the testimony which,
by what they say as human beings like ourselves, they wish to bear.
To this testimony of their words we must subordinate ourselves—and
this is the essential form of scriptural exegesis—with what we for our
own part hold to be true, beautiful and good. With the whole weight
of our reason and experience we have to follow in the path of this

testimony and become compliant to it. It is another matter that in the process elements in the stock of our experience will be set aside as superfluous and discordant, others receive quite a new form and yet others be newly added to this stock. The decisive point is that in scriptural exegesis Scripture itself as a witness to revelation must have unconditional precedence of all the evidence of our own being and becoming, our own thoughts and endeavours, hope and suffering, of all the evidence of intellect and senses, of all axioms and theorems, which we inherit and as such bear with us.

Scriptural exegesis rests on the assumption that the message which Scripture has to give us, even in its apparently most debatable and least assimilable parts, is in all circumstances truer and more important than the best and most necessary things that we ourselves have said or can say. In that it is the divinely ordained and authorised witness to revelation, it has the claim to be interpreted in this sense, and if this claim be not duly heeded, it remains at bottom inexplicable. The Bible is outwardly, so to speak, accessible only from a certain point below. Therefore we must take our stand at that point below, in order to look up to the corresponding point above. In this connexion we are reminded of Jas. 1²⁵: ὁ δὲ παρακύψας εἰς νόμον τέλειον τὸν τῆς ἐλευθερίας καὶ παραμείνας. . . . Of course, humanly speaking, no one can be obliged or compelled to this παρακύπτειν : it must be an act of human freedom. But if we cannot decide for it, then from the standpoint of our own unshaken intellectual world we can perceive the outlines of the apparently equally unshaken world of the Bible ; and there may then arise the relative understanding which is possible between representatives of different worlds. This may lead on to the corresponding interpretation of the Bible. It cannot in this case be explained as a witness to revelation, not even by one who understands it supremely well in this way. It can be explained as a witness to revelation only to a human intellectual world the inner security of which has been shaken, and which has become yielding and responsive to the biblical world ; and then it will be manifest at once that the biblical intellectual world is not an unshaken quantity, but a moving, living organ existing and functioning in a very definite service. In order that it should perform this service for us, and only for this reason, we must bring to it that subordination. Because it performs this service, it speaks in all its parts with greater correctness and weight than we ourselves can speak to ourselves. We cannot perform this service for ourselves, but only allow it to be performed by the Bible. This service consists precisely in the communication of the witness to revelation which is proper, not to our world, but to the Bible and its world. This is the deeper meaning of the only apparently tautological exegetical rule of the older Protestant orthodoxy, whereby an interpretation of Scripture is to be recognised as true or false by the fact that, if it is true, it is in accord with Scripture so far as this is the Word of God : *Norma interpretandi scripturam et iudicandi de interpretatione scripturae sacrae verane sit an falsa, est ipsamet scriptura sacra, quae vox Dei est. Quaecunque enim interpretatio consentit cum scriptura, illa est vera et ex Deo ; quaecunque ab ea dissentit, est falsa et non est ex Deo.* To this is added the citation, Is. 8²⁰ : " (Hold) to the law and to the testimony : if they speak not according to this word, it is because there is no light in them ; " and Lk. 16²⁹ : " They have Moses and the prophets ; let them hear them ; " and 1 Jn. 4⁶ : " We are of God ; he that knoweth God heareth us ; he that is not of God heareth not us. Hereby know we the spirit of truth, and the spirit of error " (Polanus, *ib.* p. 683).

The decisive basis of this fundamental rule of all scriptural exegesis can be inferred, of course, only from the content of Scripture, and only from there can it become really intelligible. Why must we subordinate the testimony of our own spirit to the testimony of the spirit of Scripture ? Why do we have this peculiar assumption which is so obviously out of accord with the technique of interpretation generally ? Why is it that in this case interpretation is not a conversation *inter pares*, but *inter impares*, although here, too, we have one man confronting another man, and one human intellectual world another ? We will leave aside for the moment what we have already established earlier in another connexion—that perhaps the technique of interpretation generally, in so far as it does not seem to go beyond that conversation *inter pares*, has every cause to learn from the special biblical science of interpretation which in the last resort is perhaps the only possible one. There will be reasons for the fact that it does not desire, and is not able, to do this. But it is certain that biblical hermeneutics must be controlled by this special fundamental principle because the content of the Bible imperatively requires it. The content of the Bible, and the object of its witness, is Jesus Christ as the name of the God who deals graciously with man the sinner. To heed and understand its witness is to realise the fact that the relation between God and man is such that God is gracious to man : to man who needs Him, who as a sinner is thrown wholly upon God's grace, who cannot earn God's grace, and for whom it is indissolubly connected with God's gracious action towards him, for whom therefore it is decisively one with the name of Jesus Christ as the name of the God who acts graciously towards him. To hear this is to hear the Bible—both as a whole and in each one of its separate parts. Not to hear this means *eo ipso* not to hear the Bible, neither as a whole, nor therefore in its parts. The Bible says all sorts of things, certainly ; but in all this multiplicity and variety, it says in truth only one thing—just this : the name of Jesus Christ, concealed under the name Israel in the Old Testament, revealed under His own name in the New Testament, which therefore can be understood only as it has understood itself, as a commentary on the Old Testament. The Bible becomes clear when it is clear that it says this one thing : that it proclaims the name Jesus Christ and therefore proclaims God in His richness and mercy, and man in his need and helplessness, yet living on what God's mercy has given and will give him. The Bible remains dark to us if we do not hear in it this sovereign name, and if, therefore, we think we perceive God and man in some other relation than the one determined once for all by this name. Interpretation stands in the service of the clarity which the Bible as God's Word makes for itself ; and we can properly interpret the Bible, in whole or part, only when we perceive and show that what it says is said from the point of view of that concealed and revealed name of Jesus Christ, and therefore in testimony to the grace of which we as men stand in need, of which as men we are incapable and of which we are made participants by God. From this is to be inferred the basic principle of the subordination of our ideas, thoughts and convictions to the testimony of Scripture itself. Our own ideas, thoughts and convictions as such, as ours, certainly do not run in the direction of the testimony which has this particular content. From the standpoint of what the biblical witness says, the fog and darkness of the human world of thought consist in the fact that, while it arises and subsists as our world, it constantly exposes our nature, the nature of sinful man, without the name of Jesus Christ, and therefore without the God who deals graciously with us. The nature of this man is a striving to justify himself from his own resources in face of a God whose image he has fashioned in his own heart, to make himself as great as possible and therefore at the same time to make God as small as possible. But if the Word of God has actually come into its own, and if it is to be clearly seen, the only thing which can happen to the world of thought which exposes the nature of man is that it should at least give ground (for we cannot simply free ourselves from it, nor ought we to try to do so, since emancipation from it is identical with the resurrection of the flesh), that it should become fluid, losing its absoluteness, subordinating itself and following the Word as a tamed beast of prey must follow its master. To try to hold together and accept *pari passu* both the testimony of the Bible which has this content and the autonomy of our own world of thought is an impossible hermeneutic programme. Its execution founders on the task of scriptural exegesis. To maintain the dualism of this programme implies the renunciation of this task. If we cannot evade this task, we must renounce the dualism of this programme. The fulfilment of the task will then consist necessarily and fundamentally in the surrender of that autonomy. With our whole fund of reason and experience we will let ourselves be led and taught and corrected by the Word of God and therefore by Scripture, that is, by its testimony to Jesus Christ, of which the biblical authors in all their humanity are the instruments. In short, we will concede to Scripture the prescribed primacy and precedence.

We can again refer to some words of Polanus. Immediately after the passage already adduced, he goes on at once to speak very illuminatingly about the continuity between the principle that Scripture is to be interpreted by Scripture, on the one hand, and the special content of Scripture on the other : *Doctrina prophetarum et apostolorum est certus sermo Dei, quem universis totius mundi suffragiis secure opponere necesse est et inde veritatem a mendacio distinguere. Sermo autem ille absque ulla dubitatione est in sacra scriptura.* (Thus : God's speech in Scripture in the form of prophetic and apostolic doctrine is, as such, confidently to be distinguished from all other voices. This distinction must be made and the speech of God must be appreciated as the criterion for the recognition of the true and false.) There now follows the allusion to the question of scriptural exegesis : *Quaecunque igitur interpretatio loci alicuius scripturae consentit cum sacra scriptura, illa est vera ; quae dissentit a sacra scriptura est falsa et repudinanda.* (It ought to be clear from the previous discussion that when Polanus insists that a true interpretation of Scripture must agree with Scripture itself he is not thinking only of the basic principle of all hermeneutics, that each passage must be understood and explained in the light of its parallels, obscure passages by clear ones, etc. What he obviously has in mind is a rule which is valid only for biblical hermeneutics, that if it is to be true an interpretation must agree with the Scripture in Scripture, i.e., obviously with the *sermo Dei* contained in the *doctrina prophetarum et apostolorum*, and that it is false if it deviates from this Scripture in Scripture, that is from this *sermo Dei*.) Is there a material definition of this *consentire* or *dissentire* and therefore of the *sermo Dei* by which all scriptural exegesis is to be measured ? Polanus thinks he knows such a definition, and here, too, he comes to speak of the special content of the Bible as the very palpable criterion of its interpretation : *Illa autem (interpretatio) consentit cum sacra scriptura, quae omnem laudem salutis nostrae aeternae in solidum Deo tribuit et homini prorsus adimit : illa vero non consentit cum sacra scriptura, quaecunque vel minimam partem gloriae salutis aeternae homini adscribit.* He quotes on this point Jn. 7[18] : " He that speaketh of himself seeketh his own glory ; but he that seeketh his glory that sent him, the same is true, and no unrighteousness is in him." It is to be noted that Polanus draws here the extreme conclusion that because the content of the Word of God spoken to us in Scripture is that in matters concerning our eternal salvation the glory belongs only to God and not in any sense to man, this is also the criterion for all scriptural exegesis. Exegesis is true or false according as it makes this clear or not. I see no possibility of disagreeing. Of course, we have to understand clearly that this does not put into our hands a convenient master-key which will open every door. But in relation to every individual text there is given us the serious and specific task of recognising that in every verse the whole glory is given to God. Understood as a fundamental rule, this statement of Polanus is unsurpassable.

3. From the establishment of this basic rule, we come to the individual phases of the process of scriptural interpretation. The first plainly distinguishable aspect of the process is the act of observation. In this phase, exegesis is entirely concerned with the *sensus* of the word of Scripture as such ; it is still entirely a question of *explicatio*, explanation, i.e., as the very word suggests, the unravelling or unfolding of the scriptural word which comes to us in a, so to speak, rolled-up form, thus concealing its meaning, that is, what it has to say to us. We remind ourselves that what is concealed is objectively a self-concealment of the divine Word only in so far as in the form of the scriptural word the latter has adjusted itself to our human world of thought, thus exposing itself to the darkening prism of our human understanding, although, of course, clear in itself (even in the form of the scriptural word). Yet even in this darkening, it still retains its power to explain itself, which means above all to present itself. And as it does this, there arises the corresponding human task : to follow this self-presentation, to repeat it and, as it were, to copy it. Interpretation as presentation is an introductory attempt to follow the sense of the words of Scripture. If interpretation cannot be exhausted by presentation—as the self-explanation of God's Word is not exhausted in its self-presentation—nevertheless it must in all circumstances begin with this attempt. If we ourselves or others are to be in a position to follow the sense of the words of Scripture, they must first be put before us clearly, that is, as in themselves intelligible,

in contrast to mere noises. This presentation of the scriptural word as something intrinsically intelligible is the problem of scriptural interpretation as presentation. Its presupposition and its most important instrument is, of course, literary-historical investigation. I must try to hear the words of the prophets and apostles in exactly the same freedom in which I attempt to hear the words of others who speak to me or have written for me as in the main intelligible words. That means that I must try to hear them as documents of their concrete historical situation. They speak through it ; I must see them in that situation, if I am to hear them speaking intelligibly. It must become for me a speaking situation. At the start of this attempt we still find ourselves wholly upon the plane of general hermeneutics. Obviously, then, the task of investigation will have to be twofold. In the first place we have the documents in their concrete historical situation—the text, as opposed to what is said through it. In this connexion we have to consider the prophets and apostles themselves as speakers.

This is the distinctively literary side of the process, and it may be described in detail as follows. I attempt to bring into the most likely inner connexion the words and phrases of which a certain biblical text is composed. For this purpose I use the methods of source-criticism, lexicography, grammar, syntax and appreciation of style. My aim is to convey the subject-matter or reference of what the author says in this particular text. In this way I obtain a picture of his expression, and I then compare this with other things which the same author has said about the same thing and with what he has said on other matters. To obtain further standards for insight into what he wishes to say in this text I go on to compare what is said on the matter by other authors, who are contemporary or who in other ways stand in a close positive or negative relationship. On the basis of the insight thus gained into the relation of what is said in this text with what has been said elsewhere by the same author or by others, if there seem to be any lacunæ in the text—as though the text itself forbade me—I can then try to complete and round off its presentation. Finally, I shall then try to establish how far in what he says the author has perhaps been dependent upon others, or with others upon a third, and how far again this is perhaps the case of others in regard to him. This will enable me to see clearly how far in what he says I am dealing with his own original, perhaps very original, ideas, and how far I have to do with what is held in common. To grasp the meaning of what is said in any given text, it is basically necessary that I should use all these ways of trying to unfold its meaning as a text.

But investigation is obviously incomplete even in the sense of general hermeneutics, indeed it has not yet reached its decisive stage, if the matter is allowed to rest there. I have to see the prophets and apostles in a concrete historical situation if I am to appreciate the meaning of their words. But to this situation there does not belong only the speaking of the prophets and apostles. As its decisive determination there belongs also that which is spoken by them. The image which their words conjure up reflects a certain object. Again, therefore, exactly as I do in regard to the words of other men, I shall try to reproduce and copy the theme whose image is reflected in the picture of the prophetic-apostolic words and controls those words—for they relate to it.

So we come to the distinctively historical aspect of the process. I now seek to form an idea of what is said in the text—the outward or inner history which it reports or to which it is related. This means that with the help of what I can conjure up, I try to form a picture of what has taken place on the spot to which the words of the author refer, and of what has occasioned the author to use these particular words of his text. To form a picture of this happening means, however, that as it comes to me in the mirror of these words by means of the literary examination, I shall fit it into the series of other pictures which are at my disposal through reconstructing the objective historical situation of the author and of what he has seen. These will include pictures of his own time, its events and typical manifestations, its circumstances and aspirations, its natural and intellectual conception, its objective and subjective assumptions and problems. They will also include pictures of the periods which immediately precede and follow, in the sequence of which the happening which he reports takes its place, and within the process of which it forms an essential member, linking what goes before with what follows. It is not to be forgotten—and here the matter becomes critical—that I have, of course, a more or less definite picture of historical realities generally, and of the whole epoch which forms the framework of the observable process in which the event referred to in the text has its special place. This general picture will certainly determine my picture of the time in which the event referred to in the text falls, my picture of the preceding and succeeding periods, and of the whole historical process. And this applies necessarily also to the particular picture which I form of this event in the narrowest of those various circles. Alternatively, it is possible that this particular picture—not because it is my picture, but because it is the representation of the object spoken of to me—will be so strong that it will determine and modify, shatter and remould my previous picture of that time, then of the whole historical process, and in the end perhaps even of historical reality generally. Even within the framework of general hermeneutics I shall obviously have to reckon with both possibilities. In my attempt to picture to myself the image of what is said to me, I may actually begin with what I could imagine already. But I must not refuse to widen my circle of conceptions, perhaps even to allow it to be widened in a very unexpected fashion. In forming this picture, I cannot and must not fail to exhaust all the possibilities at my disposal. At the same time I must not exclude in principle the idea that what is said, i.e., the object which the words to be interpreted offer for my consideration, might suggest other possibilities than those hitherto known to me, and I might not be able to resist these if I am not to give up the task of interpretation.

In this phase of presentation in the process of scriptural exegesis everything will immediately depend on whether, in the literary and historical examination which underlies the presentation, we really form an accurate picture of the object mirrored in the prophetic-apostolic word. That is to say, it all depends whether as interpreters we are able to allow the text to speak to us, and to take account of the message and its contents, fully prepared, on the one hand, to mobilise and employ in the formation of that picture as the picture of a real occurrence all the possibilities we know from history, world-history and the philosophy of history, but fully prepared, on the other hand, to allow the circle of these possibilities, if need be, to be newly defined and broadened and eventually shattered and re-moulded, and in certain

circumstances even to bring and apply to the task of faithful understanding possibilities which hitherto and in other circumstances we
regarded as impossibilities.

Do the methods of general and those of biblical hermeneutics separate
inevitably at this point ? We cannot admit this. That they diverge in fact is,
of course, obvious. It is only within definite limits that general hermeneutics
is accustomed to take seriously the idea that what is said in a text, that is, the
object which we have to reproduce, might bring into play other possibilities
than those known to the interpreter. To be sure, it realises that the hitherto
accepted picture of a certain epoch, and even the picture ot the historical process as a whole, can be changed in detail and even very radically by what is
said in a text. But it holds fast all the more definitely to a certain preconceived
picture of actual occurrence itself. It thinks it has a basic knowledge of what
is generally possible, of what can have happened, and from this point of view it
assesses the statement of the text, and the picture of the object reflected in it
as the picture of a real, or unreal, or doubtful happening. It is surely plain that
at this point an alien factor is exercising a disturbing influence upon observation.
Strict observation obviously requires that the force of a picture meeting us in a
text shall exercise its due effect in accordance with its intrinsic character, that
it shall itself decide what real facts are appropriate to it, that absolutely no
prejudgment shall be made, and that it shall not be a foregone conclusion what
is possible. If general hermeneutics does, in fact, hold this different point of
view and work with a conception of what is generally possible as the limit which
will be self-evidently presupposed for what can really have happened, it has
to be said that this point of view is by no means inevitable and is not required
by the essential character of hermeneutics. Biblical hermeneutics is not guilty
of an arbitrary exception when it takes a different line. On the contrary, it
follows the path of strict observation to the very end. Certainly, it does this
because of its own definite presupposition. But it is to be noted that this presupposition does enable it to be consistent as hermeneutics. The same cannot
be said of the presupposition of general hermeneutics.

The idea with which scriptural exegesis must begin is that of
fidelity in all circumstances to the object reflected in the words of the
prophets and apostles. This is the fidelity which this object in itself
requires. It also requires all the fidelity which we owe to the object
of every human word if it is to be interpreted. This fidelity does not
imply a necessary suspension of historical orientation and criticism.
In so far as this is essential to its observation and representation, it
must be applied ; and it is not possible to lay down for it in advance
any general limits. How can we appreciate the concrete historical
situation of the prophets and apostles, with regard either to their
speaking or to what is spoken by them, unless we freely survey their
historical existence as speakers, or the existence of that of which they
speak ? How can it be appreciated without critical questions and
answers on both sides ? To observe undoubtedly means to establish
the facts, and so distinguish the real from the unreal or the certain
from the uncertain. And it is in order if we address ourselves to this
task with the presupposition of all that we otherwise know to be real
or think we know to be possible. But, on the other hand, we must
leave to this object, as to any other with which we might have to do,

the freedom to assert and affirm itself over against these presuppositions of ours, and in certain cases to compel us to adopt new presuppositions, as in fact it can do. Our representation of it must be determined by its form, not by the laws of form which we bring with us. Biblical hermeneutics does actually reckon with an object in its texts that claims this freedom. In regard to this object our own presuppositions are not adequate and if we wish to represent it we must be prepared to alter our own ideas of the laws of form. The necessary historical orientation and criticism is not suspended. On the contrary, it is made essential in a qualified form. But unavoidably this object prescribes its own law for our activity, so that we must be prepared to submit to its law if we are not to renounce the task of observation and presentation. How can the freedom of orientation and criticism be in any way limited by this fact ? Indeed, how can it be otherwise exercised than as the freedom of loyalty to this object ? How can it degenerate into freedom from this object, that is, from the text and its contents ? In the freedom of loyalty, therefore, the examination of the biblical texts must do justice both to the texts themselves and also to their object, whatever conclusions and distinctions it may then be necessary to make. From this standpoint it will have to allow itself in certain circumstances to be corrected even on the literary side, because on the assumption of fidelity to the object all the problems may present themselves in a new way. And only in so far as it takes into account the texts in their whole scope and meaning will it be capable of representing what they are trying to say and therefore of drawing out their sense. A representation based on such an examination will allow even the detailed words of the texts to speak exactly as they stand. It will not take away anything from the concrete historical contingency of their origin and their relation to their object. It will not suppress, silence or distort anything which is fitted to illuminate this contingency. It will include the methods of observation used in general hermeneutics. It will have considered all the questions, without exception, which arise from that point of view in forming its general picture of the text. Therefore it will not have to fear any inquiry in respect of historical orientation and criticism. On the other hand, it will not tolerate any restrictions. It will allow the text to speak for itself in the sense that it will give full scope to its controlling object. It will not seek to conceal its ultimate determination for the sake of any preconceived notion of what is possible. It will not distort the text by trying to obscure and level down and render innocuous its real object. It will allow the text to say what, controlled by its object, it does actually say in its historical contingence. In doing this and to this extent, in so far as it can happen in fulfilment of the human task posed, it will explain, unfold and affirm its real historical sense, and thus make it possible to follow the sense of the text itself, what it does actually say.

In conclusion, we must again emphasise that in taking this line biblical, theological hermeneutics is not claiming for itself a mysterious special privilege. The object of the biblical texts is quite simply the name Jesus Christ, and these texts can be understood only when understood as determined by this object. But this insight is not a privilege of theologians. It could also be an insight of the interpreter as such, and biblical hermeneutics might then be only a special case of general hermeneutics, within which it might acquire an instructive significance in the exposition of very different texts. In fact, this insight is not that of the interpreter as such. But this again must not hinder the task of biblical hermeneutics from being undertaken where the insight does exist, and, if possible, carried through quite irrespective of the protest of a general hermeneutics which has not yet been better informed in this regard.

4. The second plainly distinguishable moment in the process of scriptural exegesis is the act of reflection on what Scripture declares to us. What is meant is not, of course, an act which follows the first in time, nor a second act which takes place independently of the first, but the one act of scriptural exegesis considered now in the moment of the transition of what is said into the thinking of the reader or hearer. We are now just at the middle point between *sensus* and *usus*, *explicatio* and *applicatio*. Even in the moment of transition, scriptural interpretation, in which Scripture is primarily explaining itself, is an act of our human freedom and to be valued as such. It is inevitable, as we have already seen, that the way and manner of this transmission will influence and limit our observation and representation of Scripture. Even in the act of observing and representing, no interpreter is merely an observer and exponent. No one is in a position, objectively and abstractly, merely to observe and present what is there. For how can he do so without at the same time reflecting upon and interpreting what is there? No one copies without making this transition. In affirming and representing what is written, and what is because of what is written, we accompany what is written, and what is because of what is written, with our own thinking.

This is self-evident, and it has been formulated by A. Ritschl (*Rechtf. u. Vers.*, edn. 4, III, p. 25), but it is still necessary to state it : " As we only hear with our own ears and see with our own eyes, we can apprehend by means only of our own understanding, not of that of another." Naturally, for if we do not do so, we do not understand at all.

Above the picture observed, like the second rainbow which is distinct from the first, although related to and dependent upon it, there inevitably arises the picture contemplated, in which the reader or hearer tries, as it were, to assimilate the former. It is at this point that we see that it is really quite impossible for us to free ourselves of our own shadow, that is, to make the so-called *sacrificium intellectus*. How can we objectively understand the text without realising it subjectively, in our own thinking ? How can we let it speak to us without at least moving our lips (as the readers of antiquity did visibly and audibly) and ourselves speaking with it. The interpreter cannot help this. Even in what he says as an observer and exponent, he will everywhere betray the fact that, consciously or unconsciously, in cultured or primitive fashion, consistently or inconsistently, he has approached the text from the standpoint of a particular epistemology, logic or ethics, of definite ideas and ideals concerning the relations of God, the world and man, and that in reading and expounding the text he cannot simply deny these. Everyone has some sort of philosophy, i.e., a personal view of the fundamental nature and relationship of things—however popular, aphoristic, irregular and eclectically vacillating. This is true even of the simplest Bible reader (and of him perhaps with particular force and tenacity). But it is definitely true of the educated Bible student, who in appearance and intention is wholly given up to observation.

We have to describe as a philosophy the systematised commonsense with which at first the rationalists of the 18th century thought that they could read and understand the Bible, and later, corrected by Kant, the school of A. Ritschl, which was supposed to be so averse to every type of speculation and metaphysics. It is all very well to renounce the Platonism of the Greek fathers, but if that means that we throw ourselves all the more unconditionally into the arms of the positivists and agnostics of the 19th century, we have no right to look for the mote in the eye of those ancient fathers, as though on their side there is a sheer hellenisation of the Gospel, and on ours a sheer honest exegetical sense for facts. There has never yet been an expositor who has allowed only Scripture alone to speak. Even a biblicist like J. T. Beck patently failed to do this. For, while he let Scripture speak, he also gave very powerful and sometimes very fateful expression to what he had assimilated from the philosophers F. C. Oetinger, Schelling and Baader. In the same way, it is obvious that the famous biblical realism of the older and more recent Swabian schools was not merely a biblical, but also a philosophical and theosophical realism, strangely consistent with the idiosyncrasy of that region. The scholastics of the Middle Ages and the orthodox Protestants since 1600 openly appropriated in the most open manner the luminous conceptuality of Aristotle. But from a philosophical point of view, Luther and Calvin were equally unmistakeable Platonists : Luther probably more of a Neo-Platonist, Calvin a classical Platonist. And Zwingli, in this respect more modern than either, would not have been Zwingli without the Renaissance pantheism of Pico della Mirandola, for which reason he could become not unjustifiably the special favourite of W. Dilthey. The most important historical and exegetical school of the 19th century, the Tübingen school of F. C. Baur, made no less powerful use of the illumination of Hegelian philosophy than the scholastics did once of that of the Aristotelian. But behind the exegesis of the Form-criticism school of to-day there stand unmistakably the presupposition of the phenomenology of Husserl and Scheler. Again, if we elevate the anti-Hegelianism of Kierkegaard into a principle, believing that the key to the mystery of the old and new covenant is to be found in anxiety about the limitation of human existence by its subjection to death, or in its relationship to the Thou stabilised in ordinances, we must remember that we are definitely ranging ourselves with those who " explain " the Bible, i.e., read it through the spectacles of a definite system of ideas, which has the character of a " world-view " and will in some way make itself felt as such when we read and explain the Bible. If we hold up hands of horror at the very idea, we must not forget that without such systems of explanation, without such spectacles, we cannot read the Bible at all. It is, therefore, a grotesque comedy, in which it is better not to take part, that again and again there are those who think that they can point with outstretched finger to all others past and present, accusing them of falling victim to this or that philosophy, while they themselves abide wholly by the facts, relying on their two sound eyes. No one does that, for no one can. It is no more true of anyone that he does not mingle the Gospel with some philosophy, than that here and now he is free from all sin except through faith.

In reading the Bible, as in all other reading and hearing, we use some sort of key or scheme of thought as a " vehicle " in which to " accompany " it. In an exploratory way we attribute to that which confronts us, to the image arising through our observation (we attribute this to it already as it emerges in the act of observation), one or other of the possibilities of meaning already known to us through our philosophy. In the process we think of something—something which we can think in terms of the standard of our philosophy—without regard to the fact that this something as such is not already there in the text and as such is not the object of our observation, but is very properly added in our own mind if in the act of observation we are not to fail completely to find possible clues for interpretation—for after all it is we who observe. This process must certainly be undertaken with great care and circumspection. But it cannot as such be rejected with horror. There would be no sense in wishing to interdict it. It is not only unavoidable as such, but legitimate, just as it was not only unavoidable but legitimate when, just as he was, in his poverty and rags, the prodigal son arose and went to his father.

There is, therefore, not much point in a theological criticism if it rests only on the affirmation that the theological statement under consideration betrays more or less obvious traces of the philosophical culture of its author, and that it makes use of a certain philosophical system of ideas. If a criticism of this kind invites the reader or hearer of the statement to beware and be on his guard, he will have to confess at once that he himself is very definitely involved in a similar system, and as an inhabitant of this glass house he certainly has no cause to throw stones. If he wants to criticise others, he will have to examine himself to see whether he is not perhaps engaged only in the conflict of one philosophy with another—a conflict which has, of course, nothing to do with the interpretation of Scripture. The proper course is first to listen to what the other, using his system of ideas, has to say about the subject itself, i.e., as an exponent of Scripture, and to pass on to criticism only if objections have to be raised on the basis of the subject. If, then, the criticism is to be a positive contribution to scriptural exegesis, in the philosopher-theologian it is not the philosopher but the theologian who will have to be criticised.

In attempting to reflect on what is said to us in the biblical text, we must first make use of the system of thought we bring with us, that is, of some philosophy or other. Fundamentally to question the legitimacy of this necessity would be to question whether sinful man as such, and therefore with such possibilities of thought as are given to him, is called to understand and interpret the Word of God which encounters us in Scripture. If we cannot and must not dispute this, if we are not to dispute the grace and finally the incarnation of the Word of God, we cannot basically contest the use of philosophy in scriptural exegesis Where the question of legitimacy arises is in regard to the How of this use. In this connexion the following points are to be noted.

First, when the interpreter uses the scheme of thought he brings with him for the apprehension and explanation of what is said to us in Scripture, he must have a fundamental awareness of what he is doing. We must be clear that every scheme of thought which we bring with us is different from that of the scriptural word which we have to interpret, for the object of the latter is God's revelation in Jesus Christ, it is the testimony of this revelation inspired by the Holy Ghost, and it can become luminous for us only through the same Holy Ghost. Our philosophy as such—as the philosophy of those who are not themselves prophets and apostles—stands always in contrast to the philosophy of Scripture. Of whatever kind our system of thought may be, as our own thought, in and by itself, it is certainly not identical with biblical thought. It cannot do more than participate in the biblical mode of thought as with its help we seek to pursue what the biblical word has to say to us. Therefore we must not think any of our own schemes of thought is of itself fitted, or even peculiarly fitted, to apprehend and explain the word of Scripture. On the contrary, we should assume from the outset that it is not in itself fitted for this purpose, that at best it can only acquire this fitness through its encounter with and pursuit of the scriptural word. Therefore it can never be a matter of course that we will apply this or that scheme of thought for the apprehension and contemplation of Scripture. It is true that in obedience to our calling we may not refuse to do this. But we must be clear that we can do so only in the venture of obedience, not on the ground of the value, or indeed the special value, of our scheme of thought. Therefore, we have to maintain a constant awareness of the essential distance between the determinative thought of Scripture and our own imitative thought determined as it is by our own philosophy. This imitation must never cease to bear the character of obedience, and indeed of the venturesome obedience which relies solely upon the grace of the Word.

Secondly, the use of the manner of thought we bring with us in reflecting upon what Scripture has to say can have only the fundamental character of an essay, and the use of our philosophy for this end can have only the fundamental character of a hypothesis. On the assumption that I, with my particular mode of thought—not on account of and in virtue of this mode of thought, but in spite of it and with it—am a member of the Church, and that as a member I am invited to undertake the task of scriptural exegesis, I can and must apply this way of thought to the problems of Scripture, in an exploratory and experimental and provisional manner. It is a false asceticism if I am unwilling to do this, if I try to suppress and deny my mode of thought. For this can only mean either that I have to

choose another human system of thought, or that I withdraw from
the task imposed upon me. But as I apply myself to this task, it
will be decided under the Word what becomes of my mode of thought,
whether and to what extent it will be serviceable to me in this activity
—the activity of interpreting Scripture. If it becomes serviceable,
then it will be in the service and under the control of the Word whose
explanation lies in itself, and it will be in virtue of the light which
falls upon my thinking from the object of my thinking, from above.
My mode of thought may not be of any use in and by itself, but by
the grace of the Word of God why should it not be able to become
useful in His service ? In itself, as such, it is a hypothesis : the
hypothesis upon which I must venture in obedience, because I have
only the alternative either of risking some other hypothesis or of not
obeying at all. But it is a hypothesis. In and by itself it is not a
form which is adequate to apprehend and interpret the scriptural
word. And therefore in itself my undertaking to apprehend and
interpret the scriptural word with the help of my mode of thought
is never more than the attempt to perform the necessary task of
reflection. It is not the already successful and completed performance
of this reflection. I shall have to bear in mind the difference between
my mode of thought and that of Scripture, the essential unfitness of
the means employed by me. I shall have to remember that grace is
implied if my attempt and therefore my mode of thought can become
useful to this end. After each attempt I shall also have to be willing
and ready to proceed to new attempts. And I cannot exclude the
possibility that the same attempt can and must be ventured with the
application of quite other philosophies than mine. Therefore I shall
not radically deny to other philosophies than my own the character
of useful hypotheses in the service of the same end. I ought not to
allow the existence of my special hypothesis necessarily to restrain
me from paying heed, for the sake of the task, of the matter itself, to
what is said in the interpretation of Scripture when hypotheses quite
other than my own are applied. I cannot radically exclude even the
possibility that in certain circumstances, and for the better interpretation of Scripture, I myself will decide to use some quite different
hypothesis, and even have to become a more or less consistent " convert " to a different philosophy.

Thirdly, the use of a specific mode of thought and philosophy
brought to the task of scriptural exegesis can claim no independent
interest in itself. It cannot in any way become an end in itself. At
this point we have to remember the danger which philosophy has
always involved, and always can involve, in the matter of scriptural
exegesis.

We must remember Col. 2⁸ in this connexion : Βλέπετε μή τις ὑμᾶς ἔσται ὁ
συλαγωγῶν διὰ τῆς φιλοσοφίας καὶ κενῆς ἀπάτης κατὰ τὴν παράδοσιν τῶν ἀνθρώπων,
κατὰ τὰ στοιχεῖα τοῦ κόσμου καὶ οὐ κατὰ Χριστόν. Similarly, we must recall

Tertullian's savage elucidation of these words of Paul : *Fuerat Athenis, et istam sapientiam humanam, affectatricem et interpolatricem veritatis de congressibus noverat, ipsam quoque in suas haereses multipartitam varietate sectarum in vicem repugnantium. Quid ergo Athenis et Hierosolymis ? Quid academiae et ecclesiae ? Quid haereticis et Christianis ? Nostra institutio de porticu Solomonis est, qui et ipse tradiderat Dominum in simplicitate cordis esse quaerendum. Viderint qui Stoicum et Platonicum et dialecticum christianismum protulerunt. Nobis curiositate opus non est post Christum Jesum, nec inquisitione post evangelium. Cum credimus, nihil desideramus ultra credere. Hoc enim prius credimus, non esse quod ultra credere debeamus* (De praescr. 7).

When and under what circumstances can the use of an imported mode of thought become dangerous in scriptural exegesis ? It obviously becomes dangerous when in using it we cease to be aware of its difference from the biblical way of thought and its original unfitness for the apprehension and interpretation of the latter. It becomes dangerous when we consider it to be a fit and adequate instrument for this purpose. It becomes dangerous, therefore, when—even with the best intention, that of doing justice to Scripture—we posit it absolutely over against Scripture, expecting that by placing it, as it were, on the same high level as Scripture, we can use it to control Scripture. Again, it becomes dangerous when we view its consistent presentation as an end in itself, or when we consider ourselves strictly obliged to be exponents not only of Scripture but also of our own mode of thought, and to remain absolutely loyal to it. In such a use, philosophy becomes κενὴ ἀπάτη, an *affectatrix* and *interpolatrix veritatis*. Scripture is necessarily distorted. The Word of God is not confronted by man as a man, but as a second God, overruling and controlling the Word of the first God, who as such can no longer be the true God. What is said in Scripture is now considered *inter pares*. In the whole history of the Church there is no error or heresy which has not arisen from this *curiositas* which is excluded *post Christum*, from this reversal of the right attitude of the interpreter of Scripture, from this over-valuation of the human mode of thought, from this concession of autonomy to the philosophical interest and therefore from philosophy generally. Every philosophy which is posited absolutely leads necessarily to a falsification of Scripture because to posit absolutely what is man's own and is brought by him to the Word is an act of unbelief which makes impossible the insights of faith and therefore a true interpretation of the Word. In this connexion it is hardly relevant to distinguish between good and bad, between the philosophies of this or that school. Nor is it relevant to seek a philosophy which cannot become dangerous in this way. There is none which must become dangerous, because there is none which we cannot have without positing it absolutely. There is none which cannot possibly become dangerous, because there is none which we cannot posit absolutely, that is, in disloyalty to Scripture erect its presentation into a principle and an end in itself. This, then, is the thing which must not in any circumstances happen when we use our mode of thought in meditating on the word of Scripture. Independent interest can be claimed only by the scriptural mode of thought which takes precedence of ours. Following it, every human mode of thought can be good ; not following it, but affirming and asserting itself over against it, every human mode of thought will necessarily be bad. This is the test, and always will be the test, whether we have assimilated this fundamental rule concerning the subordination of our own thought to the alien thought of Scripture.

Fourthly, in the necessary use of some scheme of thought for reflection upon what Scripture has to say, there is no essential reason for preferring one of these schemes to another. Of course, it can never be a matter of chance for the individual whether his thought takes this or that particular direction ; and it would be stupid to dispute the immanental significance of the difference of philosophical schools and tendencies. Yet it is hard to see how far there follows from this the universal necessity of a definite choice among these various possibilities. The necessity which there is is particular : in a specific situation this or that particular mode of thought can be particularly useful in scriptural exegesis, and it can then become a command to avail oneself of it in this particular instance. But it has always proved fatal when this particular necessity is elevated at once into a general one, when this or that mode of thought is enjoined upon all, when by means of this particular mode of thought it is hoped to apprehend and interpret all the words of Scripture, or even one such word fully, and when it is treated as normative for all situations and times. The freedom of the Word of God then reveals itself in the fact that in defiance of the presumed necessity of what is thought to be a selected philosophy, it will usually acquire at once a new and greater clarity in the language of what is perhaps a diametrically antithetic philosophy. As exponents of Scripture, we should not allow any understanding of reality to impose itself as the normal presupposition for the understanding of the reality of the Word of God. How can we bind ourselves to one philosophy as the only philosophy, and ascribe to it a universal necessity, without actually positing it as something absolute as the necessary partner of the Word of God and in that way imprisoning and falsifying the Word of God ? Thus from the point of view of scriptural exegesis the relevance of the inner conflicts and debates and the whole history of philosophy as the history of human modes of thought can only be contingent and provisional, not basic and ultimate. It is true that in this history there has hardly been a single possible mode of thought which has not been dangerous in itself and as such to the task of scriptural exposition, but has still become fruitful through the grace of the Word. It is also true that it will not be otherwise in the future and that therefore there is every reason, from the point of view of scriptural exposition, to interest ourselves in this history. Yet there is not the slightest ground for the opinion or expectation that in this history the decision either has been, or will be, made, which alone, for purposes of the task, will lead to the establishment of one mode of thought as adapted to the Word of God, thus releasing the expositor from the venture of obedience because it is itself equipped with the *potentia oboedientialis* and can therefore be recommended as universally necessary. This decision is not to be expected from philosophy because according to Scripture itself it is not to be expected from man at all. For true reflection on Scripture as the Word of God cannot be bought under a rule of thought definable by men, and the choice of a particular mode of thought for its service-ableness in this reflection is the business of grace and therefore cannot be our business. In this connexion we have to guard ourselves most carefully against just those representations which are made most eagerly and those possibilities which seem the most attractive.

Fifthly, the use of a scheme of thought in the service of scriptural exegesis is legitimate and fruitful when it is determined and controlled by the text and the object mirrored in the text. We might simply say : when it really becomes contributory to reflection. At this point, therefore, we come to grips with the decisive thing which has to be said in regard to the problem of observation and representation. The truth of our reflection is determined by the object mirrored in the text as the master of our thinking ; as is also on our side the measure of our fitness and adaptability in thinking of this object. The meaning of reflection on what is said to us is that we " go along with " it. But since it is the Word of God that here speaks to us, what can this mean except that with our human thought we are carried along by the Word of God, and therefore that we allow ourselves to be carried along by it, not resisting or evading the movement to which it gives rise, but allowing it to be communicated to our own thinking. We can say, therefore, that the use of a human scheme of thought in the service of scriptural exegesis is legitimate and fruitful when it is a critical use, implying that the object of the criticism is not Scripture, but our own scheme of thought, and that Scripture is necessarily the subject of this criticism. It should now be plain why we had to lay so great a stress on the hypothetical, relative and incidental character of every philosophy used for this purpose. It is not really a question of replacing philosophy by a dictatorial, absolute and exclusive theol-ogy, and again discrediting philosophy as an *ancilla theologiae*. On the contrary, our concern is that theology itself, which in itself and apart from its object can only be the fulfilment of a human way of thought, and therefore a kind of philosophy, should not forget its hypothetical, relative and incidental character in the exposition of Scripture, or become guilty of opposing and resisting its object. It will certainly do this if it fails to heed these warnings in regard to the use of philosophy, if the use which it makes of it is dictatorial, absolute and exclusive. In face of its object, theology itself can only wish to be *ancilla*. That is why it cannot assign any other role to philosophy. Scripture alone can be the *domina*. Hence there is no real cause for disputes about prestige. What must never happen in any circumstances is that some scheme of thought should affirm and assert itself over against Scripture. The mode of thought we bring will automatically become a source of error if we use it to argue against Scripture, if we impose it upon Scripture, if we take Scripture captive by it, if we try to make it a measure of Scripture, if it becomes the ground and nerve of our affirmation and also of our reservations over against Scripture. When this happens, Scripture eludes our interpretation ; it evades and passes it ; its freedom becomes a judgment upon the false freedom which we have wrongly assumed in relation to it. We do not perform the service to Scripture and the Church which as interpreters we ought to perform, and it passes to others who are not guilty of this infidelity. That is why so solemn a warning has to be issued at this point. If the warning is heeded, there is no question of the danger of philosophy for scriptural exegesis, but only of its necessity. Philosophy—and fundamentally any philosophy— can be criticised in the service of the Word of God, and it can then gain a legitimate critical power. It can be elucidated and then elucidate. It can be set in motion and then have power to move. If as exponents of Scripture we do not give it more confidence than we can give to ourselves in our humanity (and this can be confidence in the power of the vocation which comes to us as men), we will not and may not refuse it this confidence (which is always the confidence for which we can answer in Scripture). If we do not commit ourselves unreservedly and finally to any specific philosophy, we will not need totally or finally to fear any philosophy. As interpreters of Scripture, perhaps not in practice but in principle, we will be able to adopt a more friendly and understanding attitude to the various possibilities which have manifested themselves or are still manifesting themselves in the history of philosophy, and to make a more appropriate use of them, if the object on which we reflect has put us on our guard against their particular genius. Even from a human point of view, it is possible to regard scriptural exposition as the best and perhaps the only school of truly free human thinking—freed, that is, from all the conflicts and tyranny of systems in favour of this object. But, however that may be, the task of scriptural exposition demands both caution and also openness with regard to all the possibilities of human thought, because no limits may be set to the freedom and sovereign power of its object. If made with this caution and openness, this transition of the Word of God from the thought of the apostles and prophets into our own—wherever and whenever the Word of God wills to pass over into our own thinking—will become the inevitable and right step to exposition from which no one, if he is to be true to his vocation, may withdraw.

5. The third individual moment in the process of scriptural exposition is the act of appropriation. From *explicatio* we must pass over the bridge of *meditatio* to *applicatio*. The *sensus* must also show itself to be the *usus scripturae*. Again, it is not a question of an act which is to be viewed in abstraction as complete in itself, but of the one totality of scriptural interpretation. No appropriation of the Word of God is possible without critical examination and reflection. But similarly, of course, there is no possibility of a valid and fruitful examination of what is said to us in Scripture or reflection upon it, unless, proceeding further, it develops into appropriation of them. Without this, observation can be only a historically æsthetic survey, and reflection only idle speculation, in spite of all the supposed openness to the object in both cases. The proof of our openness to the object is that our observation and reflection on what is said leads to its assimilation. Or, put the other way round, our openness to the object, through which alone assimilation can properly be carried out, is to be tested by whether it really springs from observation and reflection. By "assimilation" is to be understood that what is declared to us must become our very own, and indeed in such a way that now we really do become *conscientes*, those who in virtue of what is said to them know themselves, and can, therefore, say to themselves and to others what is said to them, those who not only reflect on it but think it themselves. Think it from inner impulse and necessity, just as we think something because we must, because we cannot not think it, because it has become a fundamental orientation of our whole existence. Because the Word of God meets us in the form of the scriptural word, assimilation means the contemporaneity, homogeneity and indirect identification of the reader and hearer of Scripture with the witness of the revelation. Assimilation means assuming this witness into our own responsibility. How can we have heard it, and how can we be its hearers if and so long as we still distinguish our own concern from its concern? How can we have heard its Word if we do not feel compelled to speak it as our own word to ourselves and pass it on to others? Thus assimilation is not a third act which will have to be added to the already complete exposition of Scripture and might possibly not be added. Exposition has not properly taken place so long as it stops short of assimilation, so long as assimilation has the appearance of a work of supererogation by means of which we have to make exposition fruitful by making something for ourselves of the Word of God as already expounded. This act of ours which we call assimilation can only be our activity in view of the free, and indeed the most proper and the most intimate activity of the Word of God itself in the form of impartation.

What is it, then, that the object reflected in the image visible in the biblical text wills in order to become the master of our thinking concerning what is said in the biblical text ? It wills not to be without us, but to be in communion with us, and in this communion to be what it is for us. It wills to be appropriated by us. It wills not merely to master our thinking about it, but our thinking and life generally, and our whole existence. If it is envisaged only as a so-called theory into which our practice has to breathe the necessary life, it has not been properly seen at all. And our observation and reflection on Scripture have been not merely useless but false. False scriptural exegesis at the two first stages usually betrays itself and is avenged at the third stage in the fact that our attitude to Scripture now assumes the dualistic form of this unholy doctrine of " theory and practice," disintegrating into an ostensible righteousness of faith and a suddenly triumphant righteousness of works. From the point of view of the biblical text and its object, concern about a so-called practice limping behind a so-called theory is not only superfluous but impossible.

Ὅσα γὰρ προεγράφη, εἰς τὴν ἡμετέραν διδασκαλίαν ἐγράφη, ἵνα διὰ τῆς ὑπομονῆς καὶ διὰ τῆς παρακλήσεως τῶν γραφῶν τὴν ἐλπίδα ἔχωμεν (Rom. 15⁴). Πᾶσα γραφὴ θεόπνευστος καὶ ὠφέλιμος πρὸς διδασκαλίαν, πρὸς ἐλεγμόν, πρός ἐπανόρθωσιν, πρός παιδείαν τὴν ἐν δικαιοσύνῃ (2 Tim. 3¹⁶). This is the *usus scripturae*. It is to be noted how in these two passages it is not described as something which we have to make out of Scripture, but as a necessary function inseparable from the existence and therefore from the explanation of Scripture.

We have to concern ourselves about this function of Scripture itself if we want to understand the office which at this point again, in freedom under the Word and in the service of scriptural exegesis, devolves upon ourselves. The Word of God remains the Word of God even as that which gives itself to be, and is, appropriated by us. It wills to control us, as it takes up its abode within us. It crosses our threshold as the Lord. This is the state of affairs for which we have to make allowance in every way. It will certainly be the case that we on our side encounter the Word of God with all kinds of specific wishes and needs, hopes and fears. Not man alone in respect of his thinking, but each of us in virtue of our whole fate and character, is a specific system of presuppositions, expectations and restraints. When we assimilate something, this implies that we make it a part of this system. We consume it. We assimilate it to ourselves. We begin to do something with it. We utilise it in accordance with what we are and what we are not, with what we like and what we do not like. The Word of God, however, cannot be used along these lines. When the Word of God is appropriated, it means that each individual who hears or reads it relates what is said to himself as something which is not spoken generally or to others, but to himself in particular, and therefore as something which is to be used by him. If the Church is the assembly of those who hear the Word of God, in the last resort this necessarily means (for what would the hearing amount to otherwise ?) the

24

assembly of those who make use of it. But this, too, can mean only the assembly of those who are ready and willing that the Word of God on its part should make use of them. The customary inverted act of assimilation clearly cannot come into consideration in this context. Or rather, we have to reverse that kind of assimilation at every stage ; instead of our making use of Scripture at every stage, it is Scripture itself which uses us—the *usus scripturae* in which *scriptura* is not object but subject, and the hearer and reader is not subject but object. Man is certainly right to expect something from the Word of God—indeed, something decisive, central and fundamentally necessary for himself and his life : instruction and guidance, consolation and reproof, strengthening and joy. But he is far from right if he stubbornly insists on trying to know for himself in what everything will consist if it is imparted to him. He is far from right if he wants to insist on the feelings and ideas with which he views it. On the contrary, he will have to be prepared for the fact that it may be imparted to him, but in a very different way, one which is perhaps quite contrary to his feelings and ideas, a way which is grounded in the Word of God itself. He will have to have the confidence that the decision, what is good for him and how this good is to be imparted to him, is not his business, but is contained and determined in what is said to him, that in this form it is well determined, and that in this form it is to be accepted by him. Therefore the use which is to be made of Scripture must consist in the fact that man allows the scriptural declaration as such to penetrate his life, executing its own counsel and not that of man, and conveying its own " patience " and its own " consolation," so that man finds satisfaction and endowed in this way can venture to hope.

Therefore it is not the case that in this third and last stage of exposition, the Word is to be conveyed to man (actual, contemporary man) according to the statement of his special claims and hopes, so that *applicatio* means the adaptation of the Word of God to the service of this man. It is not the case that the exposition of Holy Scripture must finally issue in the answering of the so-called burning questions of the present day, that if possible it will acquire meaning and force as it is able to give an illuminating answer to the questions of the present generation. It should and must be carried out in serene confidence that it will in fact do this ; but it must be left to Holy Scripture to decide how far it does so. We cannot try to lay down impatient conditions or ultimata in this respect. We cannot boast about a present-day point of view which it must under all circumstances take into account or to which it must correspond. We must not wish to determine what is interesting, salutary and understandable to the modern man, what he " expects " and so forth. If we do, it can mean only that although we may appear to be eagerly laying ourselves open to it, in fact we are shutting ourselves off from it. And the inevitable result will be that in turn it will conceal itself from us, evading and escaping us as it did when we insisted on apprehending it according to the pattern of some philosophical preconception. In this respect, too, we cannot trifle with the freedom of the Word of God. In face of it, we cannot know beforehand what the real present is, what are its burning questions, who and what we are, " our generation," " the modern man," etc. In a very real sense this will not appear until the Bible opens up before us, to give us correct and infallible information concerning ourselves and our real questions, concerns and needs.

Precisely in order that he may really appropriate what Scripture has to say, the reader and hearer must be willing to transpose the centre of his attention from himself, from the system of his own concerns and questions (even if he thinks he can give them the character of concerns and questions typical of his whole epoch) to the scriptural word itself. He must allow himself to be lifted out of himself into this word and its concerns and questions. It is only from this that light can ever fall upon his own life, and therewith the help which he needs for his life. How can that happen if, on the contrary, he insists on remaining rigidly at the focal point of his own life (or that of the life of his time, as he thinks to know it), as though this could give any illumination ? How can he live out his faith if he repudiates faith itself, that is, a looking away from self and to the word ? Everything depends on the fact that this looking away from self and to Scripture should not be a preliminary stage which we have to leave behind us, but that for the sake of redeeming our life we abide by faith and therefore by this looking away from self and looking to Scripture. This assimilation of Scripture cannot be split again into two parts, of which the first consists in faith and therefore in this looking away from self and to Scripture, and the second, in which we turn our backs on Scripture, because we have now been taught and comforted by it, involves the transition to an independent answering of our own concerns and questions. The impatient question : And now ?, with which we now so easily think that we can finally come to grips with the matter, can only be a sign that in reality we have not got down to the matter at all. The issue in question can only be the unconditional sovereignty of the Word, or, from our standpoint, an unconditional confidence in the goodness of its sovereignty. But this question, and its impatience, is the surest token that in reality we have already evaded the *usus scripturae* in which *scriptura* is the subject, and that we propose to make of Scripture that profane, because arbitrary, use which we are accustomed to make of all other things, but which we cannot make of Scripture. The confidence which we apparently accorded it at the first stage will be shown to be spurious, if later we tire of faith at a second stage. We have failed in advance to expect from its sovereignty everything that we ourselves need. We have failed in advance to give scope to its true sovereignty. We have reserved to ourselves the right to be wise and just again at this later point, and to be able to comfort and exhort ourselves. If there is to be a real appropriation of the Word of Scripture, we must believe wholeheartedly. For always we either believe wholeheartedly or not at all. When we look away from ourselves and to the scriptural word, when we transfer to Scripture the focal point, the centre of gravity of our attention, this cannot be merely an episode. It cannot be followed by a second act under a different rule. Necessarily everything has already happened and will continually happen in this first and single act. Necessarily this first and single act will have been performed and will continually be performed with perfect confidence; not in an abstract confidence in its salutariness as our act, but in a concrete confidence in its object—the object we encounter in the image reflected in Scripture. This object requires and justifies our confidence as perfect confidence. Jesus Christ is this object. Only when this is forgotten can this act remain undone, or become an act in which we wish to consume instead of allowing ourselves to be consumed, to rule instead of to be ruled, or become merely a first act alongside which we have to place a second in which we have something better to do than believe. Only if Jesus Christ is forgotten can we understand the assimilation of Scripture which we have to make as something other than the continual adoption by us of an attitude to the act of appropriation by which in its own wisdom and power it claims us. And only if we forget Jesus Christ can we understand by this attitude something other than faith. By faith we ourselves think what Scripture says to us, and in such a way that we must think it because it has become the determining force of our whole existence. By faith we come to the contemporaneity, homogeneity and indirect identification of the reader or hearer of Scripture with the witnesses of revelation. By faith their testimony becomes a matter of our own responsibility. Faith itself, obedient faith, but faith, and in the last resort obedient faith alone, is the activity which is demanded of us as members of the Church, the exercise of the freedom which is granted to us under the Word.

CHAPTER IV

THE PROCLAMATION OF THE CHURCH

CHAPTER IV

THE PROCLAMATION OF THE CHURCH

§ 22

THE MISSION OF THE CHURCH

The Word of God is God Himself in the proclamation of the Church of Jesus Christ. In so far as God gives the Church the commission to speak about Him, and the Church discharges this commission, it is God Himself who declares His revelation in His witnesses. The proclamation of the Church is pure doctrine when the human word spoken in it in confirmation of the biblical witness to revelation offers and creates obedience to the Word of God. Because this is its essential character, function and duty, the word of the Church preacher is the special and immediate object of dogmatic activity.

1. THE WORD OF GOD AND THE WORD OF MAN IN CHRISTIAN PREACHING

We have reached the final and really critical point in the doctrine of the Word of God, that which is both its starting point and its end : the Word of God as the preaching of the Church. Must the same serious meaning be attributed to this as to the first two aspects, " The Word as God's revelation " and " The Word as Holy Scripture " ? Must this third aspect, the preaching of the Church in the whole sphere of humanity in which it is actualised here and now, be included in the indirect identity between revelation and Scripture ? Is the Church's preaching also God's Word, and to what extent ? Is God's Word also the preaching of the Church, and if so to what extent ? The task of theology and of dogmatics in particular consists in the attempt to answer this question. For the sake of this question, so vital for the life of the Church, it was necessary first to ask about the Word of God as revelation and the Word of God as Holy Scripture. In face of these questions, we now have to establish conclusively the task and limitation of dogmatics. Again, we must begin by stating the problem involved.

What we have to say should first be related to the results attained in the previous chapter on Holy Scripture. The existence of Holy Scripture means that as the Word of God has been spoken once for all in His revelation in Jesus Christ through the Holy Ghost, it is not

743

only distant from, but also near the Church, in the witness of the prophets and apostles. It does not only confront it, but is given to it ; and it is given to it, not only as something perpetually alien, but as its own commission and authority. In the form of Holy Scripture it has and retains its own incomparable authority and freedom, which is as superior to all human authority and freedom as the heavens are higher than the earth. But in the same form, it becomes the foundation in the Church of the human authority and freedom that is legitimate and necessary. In the human authority and freedom thus founded by it and in it, it becomes the object of the Church's preaching, and men, who as such are identical neither with Jesus Christ nor with the prophets and apostles, become indirectly and by faith (upon the sole ground that they are baptised members of the Church and therefore participants in its commission and its authority) the bearers and speakers of the Word of God as it becomes a word spoken by them in the form of their human word. We know that in Holy Scripture the Word of God is the Word of God in a different but no less real sense than it is in revelation. The same is true of the witness of the prophets and apostles as compared with the original witness of the Son of God Himself. However sharply the difference between the Lord and the servants must be stressed, the very solemnity of this relationship, founded and formed as it is by the resurrection of Jesus, forbids us to entertain the notion that, with the transference of the Word of God to its biblical witnesses and the self-communication of Jesus Christ to His followers, anything in the nature of a weakening or dilution, or even a disturbance or distortion of the Word of God has taken place. The same thing is fundamentally true of the relationship of Holy Scripture with revelation on the one hand, and with the preaching of the Church on the other. Once again in a different form, but here too neither diminished nor weakened, we have to do really and truly with the one integral Word of God, with God Himself, with Jesus Christ through the Holy Ghost, just as certainly as Holy Scripture, and in and through it God's self-revelation, is given to the Church. In this case the Word of God is preached only indirectly, formally and relatively in the authority and freedom of Jesus Christ Himself and the authority and freedom of the prophets and apostles, that is, in the authority and freedom accorded to the Church as instituted under the Word and assembled by the Word. But this does not alter in the very least the fact that in this case, too, it is really and truly the one integral Word of God to be believed as such by those who speak and those who hear it. The Church exists as the earthly body of the heavenly Lord and as the community built upon the foundation of the apostles and prophets ; and the connexion between these two things is not torn by the subordination of the first witnesses to Him of whom they bear witness, nor again by the subordination of those who receive this witness to those from whom they receive it. On the contrary, in the very fact of this hierarchy consists the strength of the connecting link by which the Church is held together as a single whole, from Jesus Christ at the right hand of the Father down to the humblest of those who by the word of His witnesses have been called to faith. But this connecting link consists in the one Word of God, which in these three different forms, in none of them less than in the others, in none of them diminished and weakened, but in all three remaining the selfsame Word, constitutes the life and the foundation of the Church. Otherwise how can it be true that in Jesus Christ this Word became incarnate once and for all ? How can it be true that the prophets and apostles appointed and equipped by Him have spoken by His Spirit and still speak ? If it is true that the Son of God has come in the flesh and has risen in the flesh and that Holy Scripture as the witness of God's revelation is God's Word for the Church, the Church certainly has to be reminded of the fact that the Word is conveyed and given to it only by revelation and its biblical witness. But in this reminder there must be no reduction in the validity or completeness of this mediation and gift ; nor must we throw any doubt on the obligation and comfort of realising that in the preaching of the Church as well we have to do with the Word of God in an undiminished meaning of the term and therefore with God Himself. The real problem of God's Word as the preaching of the Church or the preaching of the Church as God's Word can be raised only within the limits of the question put to us by the answer which God has already provided. When we are confronted by the Word of God addressed to the Church as revelation and as Holy Scripture, and therefore giving it its commission and authority, we may well be astonished and terrified, and ask ourselves : Is this so, and how far is it so, and what is going to happen in consequence of the fact that the Church has received this task, and that in and with its fulfilment of this task, God Himself in His Word is involved, and God Himself proclaims His revelation through His witnesses ? But if this question is to be meaningful and practical, we can address it only to ourselves. We cannot address it to God, as though He had not spoken to us in His revelation and His witnesses. Again, as a question addressed to ourselves, we can answer it meaningfully and practically only by listening to God's Word, and not out of the resources of our own insights. The real problem raised by this question cannot burst the framework within which the Church exists ; nor can it go back behind the decision already made in the glory of the Word of God concerning the Church, and concerning the presence and action of the Word of God in the Church. This decision cannot be disputed. It cannot be treated as the goal of our inquiry. It necessarily has to be treated as its presupposition.

Therefore, to state the problem, we must begin with the affirmation that, by the grace of revelation and its witness, God commits Himself with His eternal Word to the preaching of the Christian Church in

such a way that this preaching is not merely a proclamation of human
ideas and convictions, but, like the existence of Jesus Christ Himself,
like the testimony of the prophets and apostles on which it is founded
and by which it lives, it is God's own proclamation. That it is men
who speak here, men who are not themselves Jesus Christ or even
prophets and apostles, does not in any way permit them, in an affirmation and assertion of their humanity, arrogantly to try to say something other than the Word of God. On the other hand, it does not
permit them to be faint-hearted, as though in their humanity they
were not able to speak the Word of God, but only their own human
words. Again, it does not permit those who hear them, because of
the humanity of those who speak, to adhere to their human word as
such, to rejoice or not to rejoice in it, to accept it or to reject it, as
though the word spoken was only this human word and not the Word
of God. That it is men who speak must, of course, be taken into
account with all its consequences. Nothing that this fact implies may
be suppressed. But we can think meaningfully and practically about
it only when we bear in mind first the prime consideration that these
men speak and must be heard as members of the body of Christ and
in the name of the Church, and that the Church is the assembly of
those to whom, in all their humanity, the Word of God is entrusted.
Above all criticism, even above self-criticism, the proclamation of this
insight belongs to the Church's proclamation. It is only in the light
of it that we can exercise the necessary criticism and self-criticism.
This is what decides whether we do it in faith or lack of faith, and
therefore profitably or otherwise. If a man has to say No to himself
at this point for the sake of the Yes, the No must not try to stand
arrogantly or regretfully upon itself—as though the Law precedes the
Gospel. It cannot, therefore, be the starting-point of our deliberations.
On the contrary, it must derive from the fundamental and original
Yes of the grace of God, if it is to be spoken in its right place for the
sake of this Yes. In this connexion the authoritative Yes of divine
grace is the reality of the divine commission laid upon the Church,
and in it and with it the reality of the presence and action of the Word
of God in the proclamation of the Church.

Calvin described the proclamation of the Church in this way: *Nous ne
pouvons point estre prescheurs pour forger et bastir ce que bon nous semblera et pour
abruver le peuple de nos fantasies, mais la parole de vérité nous tient obligez, et
celuy qui parle et celuy qui escoute. Car Dieu veut dominer sur nous, Jésus Christ,
luy seul veut avoir toute maistrise (Serm. on 2 Tim. 2¹⁴ᶠ·, C.R. 54, 151).* And:
*Puis qu'ainsi est donc que nostre Seigneur Jésus Christ s'est acquis une telle authorité,
quand il a esté eslevé là haut au ciel et qu'il a toute superiorité sur toutes créatures:
que nous apprenions de nous ranger sous luy et que cela soit pour nous tenir en bride,
que sa Parole soit receue de nous et que nous sachions qu'il nous gouverne, et faut
que nous souffrions d'estre enseignez en son nom, et que sa Parole qui nous est preschee,
combien qu'elle procede de la bouche des hommes, si est-ce que c'est en l'authorité
de Dieu, et que nostre salut doit estre fondé là dessus aussi bien que si le ciel s'ouvroit
cent mille fois pour nous manifester la gloire de Dieu (Serm. on. Gal. 1¹ᵗ·, C.R. 50,*

286). And at this point we may recall a noteworthy remark of Luther's. At one time I used to think (*Prol.* 1927 p. 415 f.) that its content should be rejected as an exaggeration which leads inevitably to the Catholic doctrine of the infallibility of the Church's teaching office. But a closer examination of the context has convinced me that if Luther was expressing himself forcibly—we might almost say on the razor's edge between truth and error—he was only stating the truth when he said : " It is certainly true, to speak realistically, that holy Church is not without sin, as it confesses in the Lord's Prayer : Forgive us our trespasses. So too John : If we say that we have no sin, we deceive ourselves, and make God a liar who always describes us as sinners. Or, again, Rom. 3 and Ps. 14 and 51. But doctrine is not sinful or culpable ; nor does it belong to the Lord's Prayer when we say : Forgive us our trespasses ; for doctrine is not our doing, but God's own Word which can neither sin, nor do wrong. For a preacher must not say the Lord's Prayer, nor ask forgiveness of sins, when he has preached (if he is a true preacher), but must confess and exult with Jeremiah : Lord, thou knowest that what has gone forth from my mouth is right and pleasing to thee. He must boldly say with St. Paul and all the apostles and prophets : *Haec dixit dominus*, Thus saith God Himself ; or, again : In this sermon, I am a confessed apostle and prophet of Jesus Christ. It is neither necessary nor good to ask here for forgiveness of sins, as though the teaching were false. For it is not my word but God's, which He neither will nor can forgive me, and for which He must always praise and reward me, saying : You have taught rightly for I have spoken through you and the Word is mine. Whoever cannot boast thus of his preaching repudiates preaching ; for he expressly denies and slanders God." (*Wider Hans Worst*, 1541, *W.A.* 51, 516, 15.) We will adduce later a passage which follows shortly after and which clarifies the ambiguity of these words. But even in themselves they are not open to misunderstanding so long as we remember that Luther is speaking here of the grace of God in the Church's commission, which necessarily precedes all criticism, and even more necessarily, all self-criticism. In so far as he speaks in fulfilment of this commission, as a " true preacher," i.e., in so far as he stands in indirect identity with Jesus Christ and the biblical witnesses, the preacher certainly does not need any forgiveness of sins, just as certainly as he does need it in so far as he is the one who discharges this commission in his own words, concerning the doubtfulness of which Luther also realised the essential facts. The threatened " dangers " ought not to be our first concern, but the recognition of the greatness of the divine gift and institution as such. Only as measured against this can we really see the " dangers " as such, and legitimately take the appropriate precautions.

The divine simplicity precedes every man-made complication. Above all the misery of the Church is the glory of the commission with which it is entrusted. All kinds of theoretical and practical difficulties are connected with the fact that the Church's preaching is the Word of God. In relation to them we cannot pause too firmly to survey them from this vantage-point, in undisputed recognition that the Church does have this commission, and that therefore its proclamation is the Word of God. By this is meant that this fact is of the same nature as the resurrection of Jesus Christ, in which we have to recognise in conjunction God's revelation and the divine appointment and authorisation of His witnesses. There is more to it than that, for as a fact which rests only on the power of the revelation and the testimony, it must be understood as included in the resurrection of Jesus Christ. The reason why it is so necessary to understand it in this sense is that we will then value it as an appointment and gift which precedes, transcends and surpasses every human accomplishment or failure. It is only from this point of view that we will acquire the right relation to the subordinate fact of human accomplishment or failure. That the proclamation of the Church is the Word of God implies for the members of the Church both a law and a duty, and it is particularly from this point of view that we shall have to weigh the identification in relation to the work of dogmatics. But it is not the case that this identification gains truth and validity only when in the Church man achieves the fulfilment of this law, or only when he masters the task of preaching the Word of God. It is not, therefore, the case that we have first to look around us and see what is being actually attained and performed in the Church in the matter of proclamation, and then, if the result turns out to be to some extent satisfactory, we can recognise the truth of this identification and admit its validity. It is clear that by this method, as is always the case when we insist on beginning with law and our own fulfilment of the law, we could only end in levity or despair. If we consider what men are doing in the Church, ourselves or others, it is only by a crude self-deception that we can come to the conclusion that the Word of God is really being preached there. And when we have grown tired of this self-deception, if we still consider men in the Church, we shall arrive at the diametrically opposite but no less arbitrary conclusion, that the Word of God is not being preached in the Church. The first thing is that this identification of the Church's proclamation with God's Word is valid ; and then as such it becomes a law and duty for those who are in the Church. The first thing is that it must be believed as it stands ; and it is only then that we can and must give ourselves to the humility, care and exertions which are appropriate to those who are in the Church. In this respect, too, if it is to be taken seriously and held in honour, the Law must be believed and understood as first and foremost the Law fulfilled in Jesus Christ. What has to happen in order that the proclamation of the Church may be the Word of God, and that men in the Church may really proclaim the Word of God, has already happened, as, generally speaking, everything that has to happen in order that the Church may live as the Church of God has already happened. Provision has been made that in the Church men may again and again believe and hope and love, that in it the name of God may be constantly invoked in thankful prayer, that in it the disciples of Jesus may ever and again suffer, and that in it brother may find brother and receive his help. All that has been provided. No presupposition is required from us. We are not even asked whether we see it all performed and fulfilled by ourselves or others. Our business can only be that of accepting as something which has happened for us and to us that which has already been performed and fulfilled in Jesus Christ in respect of the whole life of the Church. It is always in this acceptance that the Church lives its life as created by Jesus Christ and rooted in Him. The same is true in relation to the proclamation of the Word of God, which is only one of the functions of the life of the Church. It can be only a question of accepting what has already been created and founded in Jesus Christ. It is not we who have to care for the truth and validity of the identification of proclamation in the Church with the Word of God. We have to accept that it is so and allow it to be true. Because Jesus Christ has risen, because God's revelation and testimonies are, therefore, given to the Church, it receives and holds His commission, which means that it has Himself in its midst as the Lord of its speaking, the Lord who in and through its speaking bears witness to Himself. Humanly speaking, it is a stark impossibility which here stares us in the face—that men should speak what God speaks ; but it is one which in Jesus Christ is already overcome. At the hands of those for whom it was in fact an impossibility, it brought as a blasphemer to the cross the One for whom it was not an impossibility, in order that it might be revealed in His resurrection as the new possibility for man, to be imparted by Him to His prophets and apostles and to be conveyed by their witness to the Church. Only by wanting to look at ourselves instead of at Jesus Christ can we maintain this impossibility and set it against the truth of that identification. In itself it has been cancelled and transformed into its opposite. We ought not to be concerned on account of this impossibility, for on its own account we are relieved of all responsibility. What ought to concern us is that again and again we so obstinately tend to look to ourselves instead of to Jesus Christ. In Him everything has happened for and to the Church, that it might be true that its proclamation is the Word of God. And it can only be a question of our not resisting the Holy Spirit who says just this to us, and who will uphold us in all circumstances through all the actual human accomplishment or failure which is visible in the Church. It is only when we hold fast to this truth that we can survey this sphere and exist in it with neither frivolity nor despair, and therefore critically, in readiness both to decide and to act. That there is a Word of God for the Church ; that above all human authority and freedom in the Church there is the authority and freedom of this Word of God ; and again that beneath the Word there is a genuine human authority and freedom in the Church : that is something which must first and foremost be apprehended, accepted and reckoned with. This apprehension, acceptance and reckoning is not to be understood abstractly, as though we had to provide that which only Jesus Christ can and has provided, but concretely : as the Church for which Jesus Christ has provided we are now able to struggle manfully against the great human impossibility.

Let it be understood that here again it is not a question of a theory but of the most intimate and decisive practice. In the ministry of the Church's preaching, how can even a single word be said and heard responsibly, without the pre-supposition of Luther : *Haec dixit Dominus* ; i.e., without the presupposition that provision has been made by the Word of God itself for the utterance of the Word of God amid the frailty of what takes place here on the human level ? What presumption it would be to dare to be a Church and to speak and hear as a Church without this presupposition ! But doubt of the presupposition is itself presumption of this kind. And if humanly speaking there is to be any help for that frailty, in what can it consist but in the fact that we do not doubt the presupposition, that we hold fast to the truth that in Jesus Christ every-thing has happened which is necessary to the presence of the Word of God in the Church, and that therefore the human happening in which actively or passively we participate is placed in the light of that which is in fact taking place in its midst : God's own proclamation of His revelation and His witnesses ?

The human impossibility of the Church's proclamation consists simply in the impossibility of the attempt to speak of God. It is this which, humanly considered, is attempted in the Church's proclamation. In this connexion we may think of the term in its narrowest and proper sense, that is, preaching and sacraments. Or we may think of the proclamation attempted indirectly through the medium of the Church's prayer and worship, its confession and instruction, pastoral activity and, not least, of theology itself, although here the real and immediate task is not that of proclamation. Over this whole field the attempt is made to speak of God with the intention that others shall hear of Him. This attempt and intention are as such impossible. God does not belong to the world. Therefore He does not belong to the series of objects for which we have categories and words by means of which we draw the attention of others to them, and bring them into relation with them. Of God it is impossible to speak, because He is neither a natural nor a spiritual object. If we speak of Him, we are no longer speaking of Him. In this matter we cannot do what we want to do and we cannot attain what we should like to attain. This is the iron law under which all Church proclamation without exception stands. That what happens here happens in frailty is far too weak an expression for the real situation. This is not frailty. It is death. This is not difficulty. It is sheer impossibility. What happens here is not some-thing imperfect. Measured by the standard of what is intended, it is simply nothing.

This iron law itself cannot be understood without the prior assumption that the proclamation of the Church is the Word of God. It is not understandable as something in itself, nor as a general truth. The mystic and agnostic philoso-phers apparently use the same phrases. They speak of God and they say the same things about Him in what seem to be very much the same language : that it is not possible for us to speak of Him. But by God they do not mean the Creator of heaven and earth, the Lord and Judge and Saviour of man. They do not mean the One whose hiddenness and incomprehensibility are His own mighty work. They do not mean the One before whom man must bow. They do not mean the One whose interdict and expulsion of man from Paradise makes it impossible for him to speak of God. They do not speak of the One in whose mighty hand it rests to make possible this impossibility and who, in giving to man this new possibility, reveals to him the impossibility of trying to do it out of his own resources. What do the mystics or agnostics know of this God and His hiddenness and mysteriousness ? What they mean is the unutterableness of the ultimate depth of the mystery of the world and the human soul, the unutterableness of a depth in which man can probe far enough to see for himself that it is unutterable, that he cannot speak of it, thinking he knows it so well, and bringing it under his own control, even as a depth which is unutterable. But what is there common between this depth which man himself discovers and controls, and the depth of God ? Nothing but the name. And that this is so is shown by the fact that although we are not supposed to be able to speak of the so-called " God " of this teaching, in virtue of the same competence with which His objectivity was denied He usually becomes the object of the greatest and most comforting eloquence. That man really cannot really speak of God is only realised when it is known that he really can really speak of God, because God Himself with His Word and Spirit steps forth, and has already stepped forth, into the midst, in order to make possible for man that which is not possible for him of himself. It requires the God Who Himself speaks for Himself, it requires the resurrection of Jesus Christ as the power which enables us to speak rightly of God, if man is to be so convinced at the cross of Jesus Christ of God's real hiddenness and incomprehensibility, as determined and effected by Himself, that he sees and confesses that of himself he cannot speak of God. On the basis of this assumption alone does it become transparent to him that proclamation as the human undertaking to speak of God, and let others hear of God, is condemned to failure. It then becomes plain to him that he had not meant God at all when previously as a self-assured mystic or sceptic he had affirmed and denied in the very same breath the unutterableness of God.

If there is proclamation, if the attempt does not fail, it is just at the point where success is achieved that it can and will be understood, not as a human success, but as a divine victory concealed in human failure, sovereignly availing itself of human failure. God then makes good what we do badly. And the fact that God makes good what we do badly cannot be understood as a dialectical change which, so to speak, takes place naturally. It cannot be postulated or assumed as a consequence which in some ways follows necessarily. It can only be hoped by faith in the foundation which God Himself has laid for the Church, that is, by faith in Jesus Christ. What then happens is by no means a matter of course—the very achievement of this divine victory forbids us to think it self-explanatory. For what happens is that men are really able to speak of God, and to let others hear of Him. But, again, it is not self-explanatory that this is not self-explanatory. All the poverty and helplessness and confusion and impotence of Church proclamation to ourselves and others, as we think we see it in our own age and in every age ; the whole sea of impure doctrine in which the Word of God seems formally to be drowned in the Church's proclamation ; everything which might cause us to doubt the truth of the identification as we see the actual state and course of things in the Church : all these things are a reminder that this victory is not achieved self-evidently ; that it can be only a divine victory, a miracle. Yet even the most painful aspect of the Church has not the power to dissuade us from regarding it as self-evident. If we are in fact dissuaded, it is because the identification of the Church's proclamation with the Word of God is true. The achievement of the divine victory stands out miraculously to comfort and to warn, not merely against the bad aspect, but against every aspect that the Church can present. In that achievement grace itself assures us that it is achieved by grace, and not as the result of some self-explanatory dialectical necessity. Jesus Christ in the power of His resurrection is present wherever men really speak really of God. It is not this or that aspect of the empirical Church but the very glory of this event which casts the deep shadow on all human action in the Church, which makes our need plain to us by delivering us from need, and compels us to recognise that of ourselves we are not able to speak of God.

A few pages after the apparently dubious passage about the unhesitating boldness with which the Christian preacher should believe that his word is the Word of God that needs no forgiveness, Luther has the following (*op. cit.* 519, 6 f.) : " Now look, my dear friend, what a strange thing it is, that we, who assuredly teach the Word of God, are so weak and in our great humility so timid, that we do not like to boast that we are the witnesses, servants, preachers, prophets, etc. of God's Church, and that God speaks through us. Yet this is assuredly what we are, since we assuredly have and teach His Word. Such [Luther originally wrote : despairing hearts constitute the sin of being terrified before God and of not being able to think ourselves worthy (as indeed we are not) and of not trusting that God speaks with and through us (as does in fact certainly happen)] timidity arises from the fact that we earnestly believe that God's Word is such a splendid, majestic thing, that we know ourselves all too unworthy that such a great thing should be spoken and done through us, who still live in flesh and blood. But our adversaries, the devils, hordes of papists and all the world, are joyful and undaunted ; in their great holiness they presume impudently to say : Here is God ; we are the ministers, prophets and apostles of God's Church, just as all false prophets have always done. So that even Heintz worst [1] dares to boast himself a Christian prince. But humility and fear in God's Word has at all times been the true mark of the true Church, boldness and audacity in human arrogance has been the true mark of devils, as indeed cannot but be noticed manifestly even in the Pope's " decretals." Thus [note how Luther corrects himself] the recognition of our incapacity does not come primarily from sin, but from the faith (which alone makes possible the awareness of sin) that " God's Word is such a splendid, majestic thing." And it is when this faith is absent, when we can only find the confidence of the Christian preacher dubious and reject it, that there is no place for this recognition.

It is only from the belief that the Church's proclamation is really divine that the recognition of the hopelessness of its humanity follows, and therefore the recognition that in its humanity it can live only by its divinity, that is, by the grace of the Word of God given to the Church. It is not from the more or less blurred aspect of the state and course of Church affairs, but from this faith that the recognition must come that the human preacher in the Church does not cease to be a wholly human preacher. His speech is still a human, all too

[1] Nickname given by Luther to Heinrich II of Brunswick, see *Wider Hans Worst* (1541)—now further complicated by pun on Heinz (for Heinrich).—Trans.

human speech about God. In itself it certainly does not attain its
goal and purpose. It does not matter so much that it is open to the
charges of mysticism and scepticism, which also want to tell us in their
own way that man cannot speak about God. For those who level
accusations from this point of view do not know what they are saying.
Accusations which come from this source do not touch the depth, the
real need of the humanity of Church proclamation. What is quite
intolerable is the judgment of the living God under which the human
aspect stands as participant in His grace. God Himself disputes with
man. God Himself objects that he cannot speak of God, that placed
under God's Word he can speak only in human authority and freedom.
This is what presses upon us an iron law and makes the situation
quite unbearable. This is what occasions anxiety concerning what
man has to say. The demand is that it be said purely, correctly,
seriously, strictly and weightily. This will certainly confront man, in
relation to what he has to say, with a task from whose discharge he
will not be released as long as he lives.

Luther himself in this second passage has shown that it is necessary not to
omit the descent from the height indicated in the first passage to the corresponding depth. It is in this light that we recall the sober sentence of Calvin : *Tamen
retinenda est distinctio, ut quid homo per se valeat, quid Deo proprium sit, meminer-
imus (Instit.* IV 14, 11). When we remember : *quid homo per se valeat*, then the
fifth petition of the Lord's Prayer will certainly be indispensable for the human
preacher in the Church. For : *Nisi ipse nos assiduo sustentet, nihil prodest summa
cognitio et ipsissima Theologia* (Luther, *Comm. ad Gal.* 2[13], 1535 *W.A.* 40[I], 205, 24).

Help in this attack can be expected only from the God from whom
it comes. If the attack of that iron law had an immanent basis in
the human situation as such, immanental victories or alleviations could
and would have to be considered. But in the immanence of the human
situation as such there are no mortal dangers. There are no iron laws
beyond which man cannot see his way, which with more or less good
luck he cannot transform into their opposite and so render innocuous,
which indeed are not really contradicted somehow and somewhere in
the realm of immanence. In so far as it indicates a general human
impossibility, the fact that man cannot speak of God may mean in
practice that in the power of despair which is man's own work he
can actually do so very well. And the despair may be followed at
once by the corresponding and more or less deeply grounded levity.
An attack of this kind is not dangerous. But the real attack which
comes from God is dangerous. The man whose mouth is closed by
God cannot in any circumstances try to open it himself without the
judgment under which he stands becoming a judgment of death. His
mouth can be opened again only in so far as God Himself places His
own Word in it. It is only in the power of the authority and freedom
of the Word which marks and limits his human authority and freedom
that he will not collapse under the judgment which this mark and

limitation implies concerning all his willing and doing, but on the contrary be upheld and blessed in all that he wills and does. And the same applies *mutatis mutandis* to the whole hearing of the Church's proclamation. Because it is God's Word, the human word of Christian preaching always involves opposition. Not the slight opposition which arises from the probably ill-concealed weakness of all words spoken by men. Not, therefore, what man in his human judgment as a hearer of these human words may criticise and miss in them. But the wholly concealed yet utterly real judgment of God under which they stand, because the Church's proclamation is the Word of God, because God exposes man as a sinner even as He is gracious to him, because God opposes man as He receives him, because " God's Word is so splendid and majestic a thing," disclosing the humanity of man in a way which the faults which man may commit in our eyes can never do. If this opposition is to be resolved, it cannot happen immanently, within the sphere in which man speaks to man and tries to understand his fellow-man. Here again we must be helped by the very same Lord who lays the burden upon us.

Adhibetur enim sermo veritatis extrinsecus vocis ministerio corporalis, verumtamen neque qui plantat est aliquid neque qui rigat, sed qui incrementum dat Deus (1 Cor. 3⁷). *Audit quippe homo dicentem vel hominem, vel angelum ; sed ut sentiat et cognoscat verum esse, quod dicitur, illo lumine intus mens eius aspergitur, quod aeternum manet, quod etiam in tenebris lucet* (Augustine, *De pecc. merit.* I 25, 37). *Il ne faut point entendre quand les Sacrificateurs ont office de bénir, que ce soit de leur propre authorité et que Dieu leur ait résigné son office et que sa louange soit amoindrie d'autant. Quand Dieu besogne par ses ministres, ce n'est pas qu'il soit diminué de son costé, ne qu'il faille que sa vertu soit obscurcie : il ne s'oste rien de ce qu'il donne. Mais il luy plait d'user de tels moyens à ceste condition, que touiours on revienne à luy et qu'on ne puise une seule goutte de bien d'autres fontaines que ceste source là* (Calvin, *Serm.* 2 *on. Gen.* 14, *C.R.* 23, 664). *Dominus ubi tantam laudem tribuit externae doctrinae, eam ab arcana Spiritus sui virtute non disiungit. Nam quia Deus homines sibi deligit ministros, quorum opera utatur in ecclesiae suae aedificationem, simul per ipsos operatur arcana Spiritus sui virtute, ut efficax sit ac fructuosus eorum labor. Quoties hanc efficaciam commendat scriptura in hominum ministerio, discamus acceptam ferre gratiae Spiritus sine qua vox hominis irrita in aëre difflueret. . . . Nihil per se, fateor, et separatim potest externa praedicatio, sed quia organum est divinae virtutis in salutem nostram, et organum per gratiam Spiritus efficax, quae Deus coniungit, ne separemus . . . In summa, quos Deus ad se ministri opera convertit, eos convertere dicitur minister, quia nihil est quam Dei manus* (Comm. ad Lc. 1¹⁶, *C.R.* 45, 15). *Certum quidem est, eos qui plantant et rigant, nihil esse, sed quoties Dominus benedicere vult eorum labori, Spiritus sui virtute facit, ut efficax sit eorum doctrina : et vox quae per se mortua est, vitae aeternae sit organum* (Comm. ad 1 Pet. 1²⁵, *C.R.* 55, 231).

Even in relation to what the true Christian preacher says, if we consider abstractly what he has to say as a man in this function, the saying in Rom. 3⁴ is applicable : God is true, but all men are liars. As a true Christian preacher he speaks only as a man, and therefore under the judgment of all human speech. But this fact cannot be considered abstractly without denying the Church as the body of Jesus Christ and Jesus Christ as its Head. We do not say absolutely that it cannot be considered abstractly. We do not say that, armed with the conception of an outpouring of the Holy Ghost upon the Church and its office, one can overlook even for a moment the human fallibility of everything that the Church says about God. We can identify the Church with its Lord only indirectly, in the unity of the body with its head. It is plain that otherwise we return to the channels of Roman Catholic thought about the Church and the Church's authority. The human frailty of the Church's proclamation must be constantly borne in mind to the precise extent that we have to be clear that both those who speak and those who hear in this matter necessarily rely on the free grace of God and therefore on prayer.

But if they are dependent on prayer, undoubtedly they are also dependent on serious and honest work. For how can they pray if, even in praying, they do not also work? How can they pray if they indolently rely upon a spiritual outpouring which is going to come or has already come on them? How can they pray if they do not eagerly and persistently aspire to the Word of God for which they pray? But in saying this, we have already implied that there can be no abstract consideration of the humanity of the Church's proclamation which stands in such need of grace and of prayer. If we depend on the free grace of God, knowing we are lost without it, if we are sincerely humbled by it and led into prayer, in this state of humiliation, of pure dependence, of nothingness in the face of God, we cannot try to be somehow defiant and despondent in ourselves. For how then can it be our nothingness before God? It is a self-contradiction, which is only possible as we deny Jesus Christ, to interpret the relativity of our situation, its human fallibility and sinfulness, as something absolute and final, or, as it were, to let ourselves go down in the assault. If we do, do we not reveal that we have not at all understood the fact that it is God Himself who contends with us and that we have not really submitted and subjected ourselves to this real judgment of God? To make an absolute of human powerlessness is always the sign that true human powerlessness before God is concealed from us. The latter cannot be turned into something unqualified. It is such complete impotence before God that it does not permit us to flee from God, not even in the form of trying to remain staring into the abyss to which it leads us, as though in that way it would become deeper, as though we had to make the judgment under which we stand even more serious, just and terrible by ourselves constituting it our judge in our own case. Really judged by God, man has simply nothing left except to cling to the One who judges him, and therefore to divine grace. We are really judged only by the grace of God. But if we are really judged, how can we assert ourselves in any way before the One who judges us? How can anything happen but that we believe in the grace which He so forcefully offers? There is nothing arbitrary or hypothetical about this change. It is not we ourselves who bring it about. But on the cross at Golgotha this conclusive judgment has been passed upon us, exposing all men as liars and stopping every mouth. And because Jesus Christ is risen from the dead, we are transposed into the Kingdom of God's grace. This transformation is to be accepted as a fact. It is in the light of it (which means, concretely) that our humanity and the humanity of the Church's proclamation is to be seen. It is true that the self-disclosure and self-testimony of the Word of God take place in the Church in a hiddenness which it is God's business and not ours to terminate or even provisionally to disclose. It is true that human words, as the signs by which Christian preaching points to the self-disclosure and self-testimony of the Word of God, only become operative when they are inspired and used by God Himself by the Holy Spirit. It is true that it does not cease to be grace when God acknowledges the human word spoken and heard in His Church. For this Church is a Church of sinners, and it is continually revealed to be such by the fact that God acknowledges its word. It is, therefore, true that the embarrassment remains in which we are involved by the question whether and how far we can speak of God and hear of Him. It is true that to think we can do this is always a venture for which without God's own action we necessarily lack the authority, insight and courage. It is true that God alone can speak about God. Only it is not to be forgotten that all these considerations can only be qualifications and elucidations of the positive affirmation that God gives the Church the task of speaking about Him, and that in so far as the Church fulfils this task God Himself is in its midst to proclaim His revelations and testimonies. These necessary qualifications and elucidations will have to mean that the Church cannot afford to fall into any kind of arrogance or to surrender itself to any kind of self-assurance when in the fulfilment of its ministry it speaks of God. Inevitably the presumption of a clericalism for which miracle ceases to be miracle, grace to be grace, and venture to be venture, is the enemy against which the Church has to contend more fiercely than any other, because this enemy attacks it, as it were, at its most central nerve, and its triumph would necessarily involve the destruction of its very essence. But, secondly, they will have to mean the need to take the task incumbent upon men in the Church, the problem of Christian preaching, as seriously as any human task can be taken. In the Church which is charged with this ministry the commitment of the member is beyond computation. There is no possible place for idleness, indifference or lukewarmness. No appeal can be made to human imperfection where the claim is directed to the very man whose incapacity and unworthiness for this ministry is known and admitted even when he is charged with it, without altering the fact that he really is charged with it. If there is no escape in arrogance, there is no escape in pusillanimity or indolence. He can entertain no illusions, but he has no excuse for diffidence or nonchalance. He can only address himself to the task without pretensions and without reservations. This is what the qualifications and elucidations imply. But they can never become arguments against the positive truth that the members of the Church in all their humanity are invited to share in God's own work of proclaiming His Word. They can never be obstacles to our believing in this positive truth and therefore to our accepting the vocation it implies and holding ourselves in readiness for the service it involves. If they do become obstacles for us, this only shows our failure to understand them, that they are not the great attack of God upon us, from which they derive when they have power. They are the accusations of a kind of scepticism in the guise of piety. We are making them ourselves, not as members of the Church, but in assertion of the arrogance and diffidence of those who wish to evade the power of the resurrection of Jesus Christ and the power of the Holy Spirit. The only power they can have is that of accusations which we ourselves can make. They cannot have real power unless they arise from the realisation that the Son of God has come in the flesh, that His Holy Ghost has been poured out upon the Church, and that the duty of speaking about God has been laid on the Church. They cannot have real power unless they arise, not from unbelief, but from faith. And the power which they then have will be not the power of destruction, paralysis and discouragement, but in a twofold sense, directed against both our pride and our diffidence, the power of salutary criticism. And behind and above this criticism will stand the transformation which was wrought at the cross and on Easter Day. As members of the Church we share in this transformation (which we ourselves certainly cannot effect either in reality or in thought) in so far as we accept its reality in faith. But that means that we do not escape but accept the salutary criticism and the great assault. And to accept this transformation means to recognise and confess : " He is present with us, in the power of His Spirit and gifts." To accept it means, in all our reflection about the humanity of the Church and ourselves, to look beyond it, and beyond all its incapacity and unworthiness, to the foundation and beginning of the Church and to its existence in Jesus Christ. There, in Him, it is not unworthy and not incapable of speaking about God. There it is all that it has to be for this purpose. There it has everything that it needs for it. There it is justified and sanctified, blessed and authorised in its action. There the miracle has already happened which has to happen to a man if he is to speak about God—really speak about God. The Church looks to Jesus Christ. It allows Him to be its own life, and therefore its consolation. It does not cling to its own humanity —either in arrogance or diffidence—but to the task imposed upon it in its humanity. And as it does so, it can confess, but with a final certainty, that as it speaks about God in human words, it proclaims God's own Word. But doing this, how can it fall into arrogance or indolence ? It can do so only if it is uncertain in this confession. And it will be uncertain in this confession only if it allows itself to look elsewhere than to Jesus Christ. If it does not look elsewhere, all the opposition to which this confession can give rise has already been overcome. It can then tolerate the inevitable reproach that this confession is far too audacious and presumptuous. The world outside certainly cannot make this reproach any more sharply than it has already been made from the standpoint of the Church's foundation, origin and life in Jesus Christ. As made by the world, it can touch the Church only if it is not content continually to hear it—again in the sense of salutary criticism—from within, that is, from the source from which it also derives its comfort. If it is content to hear it from this source, it can also be content not to be affected by the reproach which comes from without.

2. PURE DOCTRINE AS THE PROBLEM OF DOGMATICS

Christian preaching is speaking about God in the name of Jesus Christ. It is a human activity like any other. It is not only that. It has its own special necessity and its own special promise, in virtue of which it is a work of God, indeed the Word of God Himself ; and this no less than His revelation in Jesus Christ and its attestation in Holy Scripture. Its life as a human activity derives (objectively) from the fact that this work of God takes place within it, and (subjectively) from the fact that members of the Church believe in this promise. But it is a *human* activity. Its essential character, principles and problems can be described like those of any other human activity. Like any other it can be performed thoroughly or superficially, conscientiously or carelessly, well or badly. We have seen that the Church's commission and therefore the promise of God's own presence and action themselves imply a total claim made upon the member of the Church. This means, therefore, that what he says about God is subjected to a norm and receives an appointed goal. It means that he is faced with the question of the correctness of his action. The promise of the miracle of God's grace cannot exempt him from facing up to this question. Even if grace is grace, miracle miracle and venture venture, even in recollection and expectation, even in the very presence of divine action, man is still man, and although by the divine promise he is relieved of anxiety about the success, justification and sanctification of his action, he is not relieved of responsibility for it. He himself, man, is called to the ministry of preaching. He has the promise of divine grace and miracle—but he is really called. He cannot retreat into the audience from which he can watch comfortably the operation of the grace and miracle of the work which God Himself performs. He and his action, and his human speech about God, are required to be the stage for this work. If this implies, as we have seen, a judgment, and indeed a radical judgment upon his action, it also implies that his action receives a certain definite aim by which it must be measured, and within the scope of which it must run its course. Therefore just because Christian preaching is not merely a human action but also the self-proclamation of the Word of God, a problem arises which we have to tackle seriously and intelligently—the problem of the place of the human action within this self-proclamation, the problem of Christian preaching in so far as it is a human activity comparable with other human activities.

It is to be noted that there can be no real problem of Christian preaching, or serious and intelligent consideration of it, except from this angle. Let us suppose for a moment that we do not have to reckon with this indirect identity between the Word of God and the word of man in Christian preaching, because no such promise has been given to the Church or is believed by it. Its action acquires at once at this distinctive focal point the character of a fantastic undertaking for which there is no real place even on earth, and about whose essential character, principles and problems we can think and speak only in the deepest anxiety and bewilderment. What is preaching if it speaks about God but is not the Word of God Himself? What is the source of its problem and the serious consideration of its problem? Is it part of the life of the community, or of the functions of the civil power, to see that God is spoken about somewhere? Or is preaching a specific form of the moral education of the human race? Or with what it communicates concerning God and the things of God, does it belong to intellectual culture? There have been times, indeed, when a friendly scepticism and tolerance has obtained in these matters on the part of the state, society, philosophy and science. There have been times which have seen a readiness even to demand or to look favourably upon the service of the Church in this sense. There have been times when even the Church itself has thought it necessary to pose the problem of preaching largely in this sense. Such times may come again. But it is quite impossible to understand such times except as an error pleasant for both parties. And in any case, since the 18th century, it has mostly become clear again that Christian preaching declares itself to be superfluous when it allows itself to be used in this way. Uninterruptedly absorbed in progress towards its own deification, the state feels less and less the need that God should be spoken about. The tasks of popular instruction and education seem to depend less and less on the theologians, and more and more to be better fulfilled by others than they could be by theologians even if, as amateurs in these fields, the latter had a better conscience than amateurs can have. Therefore the extraneous and alien tasks are being cancelled and forgotten. Without its own commission, without the justification and authority of God's own speaking, an unauthorised message about God more and more ceases to be a serious problem and more and more becomes an almost illusory possibility. If a message of this kind is not delivered in its own genuine context, growing from its own root and subject to its own criterion, the probability is that sooner or later it will cease to be delivered at all. And perhaps it is the case that our time only makes it apparent that even on the plane of human action it is impossible to speak about God apart from this context, root and criterion. It is as well that we should reckon with the fact that this is the case even if it may again become less apparent in future epochs than it is to-day.

If the assumption is valid that when the Church speaks of God God Himself will and does speak of Himself, then this human action as such is confronted by a definite task. It will have to be an action in the service of what God Himself will and does do. And we shall have to take the term service quite strictly. Neither as a whole nor in detail can there be any autonomous goal. Nor can the form and method of the action be a matter for the independent decision of those taking part. A *minister* in the *ministerium verbi divini* is not in the least comparable, for example, with a subordinate officer in the army, or a civil servant or the head of a business department, who, in the measures he takes and the method by which he proceeds, has to bear a part of the responsibility, and to that extent take independent action and decisions. If the sovereignty of God is to be served, we obviously cannot establish in face of it any such subordinate centres of human control. Or at least, it is only *per nefas* and not of right that this can happen. But that means that the responsibility of this service is incomparably greater than that of any other service. For although the initiative and activity of men are no less intensively demanded, there can be no question at all of any independent decisions. On the contrary, the independent human decisions in their rightness or wrongness depend on the fact that, not only as a whole but also in detail, not only in content but also in form, they are decisions of an obedience in which the only will of man is to co-operate in the realisation of God's work as He Himself has determined it down to its details and form. In this matter every deviation from the way which God Himself treads (even though it takes place after the best and most conscientious reflection), every decision taken freely in disregard of God's own work, necessarily implies disservice. It calls in question the basic assumption that " God Himself declares His revelation in His witnesses." Its immediate and inevitable result is to shake the confidence in which alone this service can be performed. The completeness of obedience to God results from the completeness of faith in His own presence and action ; but, again, it is only when the obedience is complete that the faith can also be complete. The highest degree of exertion in this service implies the greatest selflessness. Then, and only then, can it be fulfilled in the greatest certitude. It is as it renders this service to the Word of God, conceived in the strict sense of the term, that the Church undertakes the task laid upon it, and recognises the divine gift offered to it in the fact that Jesus Christ is the Head by which, in the Word and Spirit imparted to His biblical witnesses, it is founded, maintained and ruled. It is as it renders this service that it thankfully receives this benefit, is built up in its members, and allows itself to be used as the light of God's imminent kingdom kindled in this world. But everything depends on whether it does render this particular service, whether its recognition of God is so deep that without cessation or interruption it advances on its divinely appointed way, and any other action but this service harms and incapacitates it, and it is increasingly pressed into this service as the only kind of activity by which it can really be justified before God and man. How can the Church be legitimated except by manifestation of the supremacy of God's free grace operating towards it and through it ? The service of proclamation demanded of it is bound up with this manifestation. The comprehensive term to denote the content of the service of God as understood in this way is that of pure doctrine.

The well-known definition of the Church in *Conf. Aug.* 7 runs : *Item docent, quod una sancta ecclesia perpetuo mansura sit. Est autem ecclesia congregatio sanctorum, in qua evangelium pure docetur et recte administrantur sacramenta. Et ad veram unitatem ecclesiae satis est consentire de doctrina evangelii et de administratione sacramentorum.* This definition certainly does not say all that can be said about the task of the Church in the execution of its appointed mission. But it does at least say something which has to be said and which has to be given priority over everything else that can be said on the subject. The one Church of Jesus Christ is defined as the congregation of the saints because it is the holy congregation in which the Gospel is purely taught—otherwise it is not the Church. The *recte administrare sacramenta* is related to the *pure docere evangelium* as the sacraments in general are related to the Gospel. They are included in the Gospel. In their own way they are themselves the Gospel. They attest it in the form of a completed action, just as the preaching of the Gospel attests it in the form of the spoken word. Their distinctive feature is that of a corrective to the word of the preacher. In contradistinction to the latter, they expressly testify that the Word of God is not only a word but also an action of God. Therefore in contrast to the *pura doctrina* of the Gospel, their *recta administratio* will expressly remind us that the recommended and intended " purity " of doctrine is not an abstract intellectual business. It is really related to the *rectitudo* necessarily incumbent upon the Church member, to his edification in accordance with the supremacy of God's free grace.

What does it mean when we say : " Pure doctrine as the problem of Christian preaching"? Let us state at the outset that doctrine, *doctrina*, does not mean " theory." Doctrine is distinguished from theory in two ways. First, theory always presupposes a human individual, observing and thinking in his own power and responsibility, forming his own interpretation of a specific object in the whole freedom of reciprocity between man and object in which man will always be the stronger partner, and then giving expression to this interpretation in the form of distinct sequences of ideas. As against this, the idea of doctrine stands in direct connexion with the idea of an object transcending the scope of human observation and thought. In no case does doctrine take place in the freedom of reciprocity. *Doctrina* falls within the framework of a *disciplina*. Doctrinal instruction means always the impartation of something just as we have received it, and in such a way that in relation both to right reception and right communication the one who instructs is responsible not only to himself and the object, but also to all those who have to receive this same thing and impart it. The other difference is that a theory has its value in itself. It can be offered to others for discussion and for the eventual clarification and enrichment of their own theories. But it is possible for this not to take place. It can also form the exclusive enjoyment

and delight of its author. But doctrine by its very nature is directed
towards others. Doctrine may be debatable in fact—of what doctrine
will this not be the case ?—but it cannot wish to be the object of
discussion. Doctrine is not the expression of opinions but of insights.
Doctrine is not intended to complete other doctrines. Doctrine intends
to state the truth and the whole truth. For this reason it is not a
matter of indifference whether it is expressed or not. By its very
nature it has to be applied to one's neighbours. Therefore whoever
makes of doctrine a theory, whether with the intention of recommend-
ing or discrediting it as such, is implicated in a misunderstanding. It
is clear that in the service of the Word of God there can be no question
of theory but only of doctrine.

But what is the meaning of doctrine in this connexion ? What is
the doctrine of the Gospel, of the Word of God ? One thing is clear.
By our use of this concept to characterise the service of the Church's
preaching, we express a qualification. Even pure doctrine is not in
itself the same thing as what God does when He speaks His Word.
Doctrine as such cannot be the endowment of the hearer with the
Holy Ghost. It cannot be his awakening to faith or even his maintenance and advance therein. It cannot be his conversion. Doctrine as
such cannot bring in Jesus Christ. It cannot exhibit or build His
Kingdom. It cannot bring about the event of fellowship between
God and man as a living reality. If we expect these things from it,
we expect too much from it, and perhaps in consequence we expect
too little.

The fact that evangelical doctrine, the human word of the preacher, is indeed
qualified in this way, is perhaps brought out clearly when it is realised that the
recte administrare sacramenta does not stand idly and superfluously alongside
the *pure docere evangelium*. The sacraments are the special witness to the actuality of this event. They, too, of course, can only bear witness to it. They cannot themselves, as on the Roman Catholic view, effect it as a " means of grace,"
in contradistinction to the word of the preacher. What they do do is to bear
witness to a truth which they can attest more effectively than the preacher's
word, because by nature they are not words again, but actions. This is the
truth that what the preacher says is not merely said from one man to his fellows,
but that it exists in Jesus Christ, and, just because it exists in Jesus Christ, it
is spoken with all the strength of participation in this being in Jesus Christ. If
this witness of the sacraments is taken seriously, then the qualification in regard
to doctrine will not imply resignation or weakness. The strength of doctrine
will arise precisely from the fact that, without itself being a sacrament in the
narrower sense of the term, it can refer to the sacraments as the testimony of
the action instituted by Jesus Christ, the testimony to the existence of that which,
as doctrine, it can merely state. It is, of course, to be observed that, in the
customary mode of Evangelical worship and therefore in the Evangelical Churches
generally, this, so to speak, natural strength of doctrine in its relation to the
sacraments is hindered in effectiveness, and perhaps altogether neutralised, by
the fact that the administration of the sacrament does not constitute the rule,
but has become a solemn exception to the rule. Perhaps one of the decisive
questions which will be put to Protestantism in the near future is whether it
can succeed in restoring to Evangelical worship the wholeness intended by both

Luther and Calvin, i.e., whether it can overcome the meaningless divorce of preaching and sacrament and re-establish the natural relationship between them. But it will mean only that we are trying to overcome one evil by a greater if we maintain the divorce, but ignore the qualification to which doctrine as such is subject, thus giving to preaching the character of a direct communication. This is something which can be attributed neither to preaching nor to the sacrament, but both—effectively, of course, only in combination—are intended to serve it, because it is the work of God Himself.

Doctrine means teaching, instruction, edification, *institutio*. It is this function which Christian preaching has to perform. But its instruction is intended for the man called to hear the Word of God. And its task is to instruct him in hearing the Word of God. We remember, of course, that to speak God's Word, and cause it to be heard, is and remains God's concern. It is entrusted to the Church. The Church is engaged in this ministry. It has the duty of preaching in human words the Word of God. It is therefore true that in the performance of this duty human words become the Word of God Himself. But we still cannot say intelligently, if it is a question of understanding the task of these human words as a human task, that in this ministry man has to declare to others the Word of God, to instruct others in the Word of God. For this is the content of the divine promise. Therefore it cannot as such be the content of the human task. It cannot be a description of what man has actually to do. In the performance of this task man can and must attempt to interpret revelation, or concretely the biblical witness of revelation, in the form of a testimony to its truth given to him as his own. Therefore, because what he himself does can as such only be an attempt, it will point beyond itself. When he turns to his hearers and desires to be heard by them, his concern will not be that they should hear himself, the human speaker, but that they should hear Him whose witness the human speaker is. The aim of his discourse will be that others together with him should hear God speak, that they should, as it were, be his fellow pupils in the school of God, or more exactly, the school of Holy Scripture. All that he says about God will be informed and determined by his own hearing of the Word of God. In the last analysis, therefore, it will not consist in the impartation of the material given in this way, even though it is the best scriptural exposition. Rather, under the guise of imparting this objective material, it will be an attempt to incite and inspire the hearers to hear for themselves what the Word of God, in the interpretation which it gives of itself, has to say to them. It will be, therefore, an attempt to put before them, in a kind of exemplary fashion, the movement of faith responding to God's revelation. The aim of all the indirectness with which the Church in its own proper authority and freedom grasps and expounds the Word is the directness of revelation which becomes real, and the directness of faith which becomes alive, at the point where God in His authority and freedom has Himself spoken and is Himself heard. It can only aim at this end ; but it can do so and must do so, in so far as it is the indirectness of the Church which is itself rooted in faith—the Church which knows itself to be called in faith to service, but to service in the strict sense of the term.

Hence it becomes apparent how appropriate it is that the problem of Christian preaching should be discussed under the concept of pure doctrine. If the human word of Christian preaching is to perform the service of leading to the hearing of God's Word, it must obviously have the quality of creating obedience to the Word of God, as it is itself obedient. It must be a selfless human word, a human word which will not say this or that in a spirit of self-assertion, but devote itself only to letting God's own Word say what must be said. Like a window, it must be a transparent word ; or like a mirror, a reflecting word. The more it repudiates and rejects anything which might intervene as a third element between God's Word and the human hearer, the less it obtrudes itself in its own solidity between God and the hearer, the more it is positively an indication, pointer and compulsion to hearing the Word of God itself, and negatively a hushing of all the possible notes of false idolatry and human exaltation—the better it will be. And this is just what is to be understood by purity of doctrine.

We may be permitted to remind ourselves at this point that in mediæval art a frame of clear cut glass was used for symbolic pictures of the Virgin. This was an implied allusion to Lk. 1[38] : " Behold the handmaid of the Lord, be it unto me according to thy word." We may also recall Mt. 26[39] : " Not as I will, but as thou wilt." It is pure vessels like this which the divine Logos seeks, creates and finds in the proclamation of the Church as well. The idea of " orthodoxy " even when one interprets it in *optimam partem*, fails to give the exact meaning of what is intended by " pure doctrine." Orthodoxy means correct opinion. In the problem of Christian preaching it is not merely a question of correct opinion, but of the right kind of teaching. And far more unequivocally than " correct " or " right," the term " pure " denotes the required medial or ministerial character of Christian preaching.

All that we have said concerning the authority and freedom of the Word of God and the authority and freedom of the Church, and our fundamental characterisation of the relation between the divine and human words in Christian preaching, clearly compels us to define the essential character, principles and problem of Christian preaching in this way : that it is what it ought to be and can be if in this sense it is pure doctrine. But if preaching ought to be pure doctrine, pure doctrine can also be understood as a significant characterisation of the objective of what we can do. We can either know or not know this characterisation. We can either care about it or not. We can know and care about it in a better way or a worse. We can adopt specific measures and employ specific means to approach nearer this goal. We can suggest specific standards by which it may be estimated whether and to what extent Christian preaching is or is not orientated towards this goal. In brief, the normative concept of pure doctrine required by the promise of the presence and activity of the Word of God characterises Christian preaching, at any rate in so far as this is also the content of a concrete human action distinguished from other human activities with at any rate, the relative independence which cannot allow the Church to regard itself as being relieved and replaced by other human activities in state and society. This characterisation of the goal applies only to the Church's action.

In all this we do not affirm that pure doctrine is only or decisively a matter of human direction, work and effort. We do not say it in any sense in respect of its realisation. How can we? It is only in view of the fact that God Himself speaks His Word in the proclamation of the Church that we can in any sense set up this criterion of pure doctrine, that is, of the human word completely yielding itself to the divine Word. And if it comes to pass that Christian preaching is pure doctrine in this sense, it will not be the result of human attainment and merit but of the grace of the Word of God, which in fulfilment of His promise is pleased to acknowledge, and has acknowledged, the human word, and has thus itself provided for the necessary purity of this human word. Therefore, it is not the case that the Church only needs the good work of pure doctrine, i.e., what we accomplish on these lines, what we think we can, to the best of our belief and conscience, consider a satisfactory performance, and where this is present God will be compelled, as it were, to acknowledge with His Word the human word so well and purely spoken by us. Even where there is the most serious effort and performance in the matter of pure doctrine, it will always be the result of God's free grace if He does acknowledge our words in this way, and we do well to remember that even the best and sincerest accomplishment of the Church in this respect is, in fact, in need of God's grace. Again, therefore, it is not the case that God's Word may not and cannot recognise even preaching which according to all that we can know in such things we must condemn as supremely impure doctrine, as a medium distorted and spoilt by so many alien elements. Is not the Church completely lost if the grace of the Word of God is not at all points mightier than the weakness of man prevalent at all points, if it is not free to be reflected also in what are, humanly speaking, very tarnished mirrors? We can all take comfort in the fact—and may this consideration have due weight with us when we are inclined to judge the performances of others—that in spite of the impurity of the word with which it seeks to serve the Word of God, the Church cannot place obstacles in the way of the power and grace of this Word or set limits to its operation. Yet all that cannot and ought not to alter the fact that pure doctrine is a task which faces us, and that we are required to have an acquaintance with it and a concern for it. The grace of the Word of God is not magic. It is promised to the Church that is required and ready to serve it. If it makes strong what men make weak, good what men make evil, pure what men make impure, that does not mean that it does everything where men do simply nothing, where men perhaps do not stand under this requirement and in this readiness. When we have done all that was required of us, we must add that we are unprofitable servants. But if we infer from this that we might equally well allow ourselves to be idle servants, we are not trusting in the grace of the Word of God. When we do trust in it, we stand under the law of the Word of God which is laid upon the Church ; we are active in its service (without the presumption of trying to compel its operation, or the folly of trying to see in its presence our own success). We are, therefore, anxious and eager for the purity of the Christian preaching which is to be performed in its service. We know that the effective realisation of this purity of doctrine will always be the result of divine grace. But just because we subject ourselves to the law of divine grace, this purity will always determine the goal of our human activity, the object of our effort and concern. If it is so only in virtue of the grace by which we are called to the Church and its ministry, we withdraw from this grace if we try to be anywhere but in the Church and its ministry, and therefore without eagerness and anxiety for the purity of doctrine.

We have now reached the point where the task of dogmatics again comes under consideration. It is *in concreto* the effort and concern of the Church for the purity of its doctrine. Its problem is essentially the problem of Christian preaching.

At this point we might quite justifiably speak of theology as such and as a whole, that is, of the unity of biblical, dogmatic and practical theology. And in this unity there is certainly no question of precedence. Yet there is in it, as in the Holy Trinity, and not as a sum of the whole, a concrete centre which is constituted by dogmatics. In biblical theology it is a question of the foundation, in practical theology a question of the form, but in dogmatic theology—in the transition from the one to the other—a question of the content of Church preaching, its agreement with the revelation attested in Scripture. These three theological tasks are completely, or almost completely, implicated in each other, so that none can be even correctly seen and defined without the other. Yet the distinction between them arises inevitably from the practical application of the distinction which has compelled our attention in the doctrine of freedom under the Word (§ 21[2, 3-5]) : observation (*explicatio*), assimilation (*applicatio*) and between the two the transition formed by reflection on the Word spoken to us in the biblical witness to revelation. We have seen how the true decision with regard to the right hearing of the Word of God in the Church is made in this reflection. To this reflection corresponds dogmatics, as the theological task which along with exegetical and practical theology is laid upon the Church in its mission and proclamation. But reflection does not take place in the void. It takes place at the central, transitional point between *explicatio* and *applicatio*, between the *sensus* and the *usus scripturae*. In the same way, dogmatics arises only at the central and transitional point between exegetical and practical theology. But it is at this central and transitional point between the question of the origin and that of the method of Christian proclamation that there obviously emerges the really critical theological question, that of its actual content. When the Church asks this question, when it submits to the critical inquiry concerning what it preaches and will preach—honestly and without prejudice, as though it does not yet know what it has to preach—its concern is for the purity of its doctrine (in so far as men can concern themselves in this matter), and therefore for the right fulfilment of the service incumbent upon it. How can it put this question of content without realising that the only source from which it can learn the answer is Holy Scripture ? How, then, can there be dogmatics unless exegesis not only precedes but is included in it ? And, again, how can this question be asked except in view of the proclamation laid upon the Church ? How, then, can there be dogmatics unless practical theology, too, not only follows but is already included in it ? All the same, it is here that we obviously find ourselves at the central point of the path leading from the one to the other, and therefore at the real centre of theology as a whole. The question : who and what sort of a hearer of the Word of God is the man who has so observed the testimony to revelation as to make it his own, is one which is decided in his reflection. Similarly, it is in dogmatics that there lies the decisive answer to the question about the service which theology as an ancillary has to perform in and for the Church. And because, humanly speaking, it is essential for the ministry of the Church that it concerns itself about the purity of its doctrine, that it accepts gratefully the help of theology, therefore— again humanly speaking—the question of the Church's ministry is decided in dogmatics. Bad dogmatics—bad theology—bad preaching. And, conversely : good dogmatics—good theology—good preaching. The suspicion and reproach of *hybris* seem unavoidable when we put it in this way. Therefore let us remember—not in defence but in explanation of the statement—that the grace of the Word of God alone decides concerning the good or bad quality of the Church and its ministry. But if it is true that the grace of the Word of God is the grace which claims the Church for this ministry, setting it in action and therefore making it concerned and zealous about the purity of its doctrine, then it is not apparent how we are to avoid the inference that the decision which is exclusively a matter of God's free grace is made in preaching and therefore (because preaching is impossible without answering these three questions) in theology, and therefore (because the central one of these three questions is the really critical one) in dogmatics. In this connexion, when we speak of dogmatics we do not, of course, think of the work of this or that professor, but of the working out of this central question concerning the content of Church proclamation, in so far as the subject of this labour is the whole Church without excepting even a single one of its members. We think of the labour, the scientific form of which can constitute only its most obvious feature. If such an endeavour to attain pure doctrine is really laid upon the Church as its duty, it cannot spare itself any effort in this matter. It cannot, then, escape the conclusion that it must regard and treat the work of dogmatics as its most essential task.

Next, we must emphasise the fact that in dogmatics it is really a question of the fulfilment of a task. If by the grace of the Word of God it happens that the human word of Christian preaching is pure doctrine, it does not happen in a static situation, but as an action of faith and obedience, an action of the Holy Ghost in the Church. Pure doctrine is a deed, not a thing—not even a matter of thoughts and words. Therefore pure doctrine is not identical with any existing text —whether it is that of specific theological formulæ, or that of a specific theological system ; or that of the Church's creed, or even the text of the Bible. Pure doctrine is an event.

It is the same with the proclamation of the Church as with revelation and Holy Scripture. We have seen that revelation as God's Word is the unity of the act of incarnation and of the outpouring of the Holy Ghost. And we have seen that Holy Scripture as God's Word is the unity of the act of God's speaking to the prophets and apostles and through them to the Church. So the proclamation of the Church is God's Word as the unity of the life-giving act in which the Church hears and speaks. At all these points, especially the second and the third, the older Protestantism of the 17th century fell into the error of splitting up the unity of this act and regarding it synergistically, with an objective divine giving on the one hand, and on the other a subjective human taking and assimilating. In this way, Scripture especially became for it an inspired text, as did also doctrine as the norm of the Church's proclamation. And the result (for we cannot trifle with synergism) was to prepare the way for what was least of all desired, viz. the transformation of the authority and freedom of the Word of God into the very human authority and freedom of those who thought they held the Word of God in the form of these texts, and in that opinion quite consistently went on more and more to control it.

Pure doctrine as the fulfilment of the promise given to Church proclamation is an event. It is the event of the grace of the Word of God and of the obedience of faith created by this grace. It is a divine gift which is only given to the Church as it is both given to it and received by it. Here, too, it is impossible to abstract the divine reality of the Holy Spirit from the prayer for the Holy Spirit in which it is acknowledged and accepted as a divine reality. Just for this reason pure doctrine, in so far as it is the appointed goal of human action in the Church, must be clearly understood as a task, a piece of work which faces us. It cannot in any sense be thought of as a solution already existing somewhere or other, which can quite simply be taken over as such. A simple appropriation of this kind cannot possibly be the business of dogmatics when it is understood as the attempt of the Church to achieve purity of doctrine. Where else can it begin, of course, except with the investigation of the texts of the Bible, or the Church's confession, and of all the perception which has gone to make it ? But it only begins with this investigation. There is far more to it—already it is a matter of reflection—than merely the repetition of those texts. But, again, it cannot aim at the production of a new sacred text, however unavoidable it may be that its work should find its outcome in the production of specific texts, in sentences, formulæ, sequences of thought, systems of ideas. All these things will have an intelligible purpose, and be intelligently received, only if they are intended and understood as milestones on the way, as a provisional outline, and as a proposal for further thought. All the conclusions of dogmatics must be intended, accepted and understood as fluid material for further work. None of the results of dogmatics—really none at all—can be important. The only important thing is the activity of the Church, denoted by the results so far attained, in its striving for purity of doctrine. Whatever stimulates, maintains and guides this activity is good dogmatics ; whatever checks it, lulling the Church into a comfortable sleep, is certainly bad dogmatics, even when the texts it reproduces or itself originates are in themselves excellent.

To teach dogmatics does not therefore mean—however unavoidable it may be that this should also take place incidentally—merely to repeat certain traditional principles, to lay down some new ones, to sketch and explain a specific view of Christian matters, to outline and present a system. While all this does happen more or less inevitably, it really means to take up the Church's work in the direction of pure doctrine, to advance it and deepen it, to carry it out in a new period in the face of new problems. And therefore to study dogmatics certainly and unavoidably means to acquaint oneself with the principles, formulæ and systems taught, handed down or re-shaped in previous dogmatic teaching (because without this acquaintance it is impossible to enter oneself into the work which has to be done). But beyond this preliminary acquaintance, the really important *studere* consists in participating in the work itself, to which all the results attained are intended only to stimulate. It consists in an active concern for the question of pure dogma in which gratitude for previous dogmatic teaching is no constraint on independence.

Before turning to a general description of this work, we have to make some further delimitations. The task of dogmatics is not identical with the task of proclamation. In both cases it is a question of pure doctrine. *In concreto* dogmatics can be preaching and preaching dogmatics. The two are basically inseparable. But, as so often in theological reflection, they have to be distinguished. They have to be distinguished in just the same way as the right thought which necessarily precedes every right deed has to be differentiated from the deed itself.

They differ in exactly the same way as learning and teaching differ : *Oportet enim episcopos non tantum docere, sed et discere, quia et ille melius docet, qui cotidie*

25

crescit et proficit discendo meliora (Cyprian, *Ep.* 74, 10). With due reserve we may say that they differ just as in war the home front and base differ from the front itself. Whether the war at the front is won or lost, what happens at home and behind the lines will be not merely incidentally but decisively connected with what happens at the front itself. It is only *per nefas* that the two aspects can be separated.

We may well expect, therefore, that dogmatics will furnish the necessary preparation for preaching. We may expect from it instruction in the search for pure doctrine, and practice in this search. But we must not expect it to replace this search and to make it superfluous. Proclamation as the pure doctrine of the Word of God will not take place without reflection. But it will not become real in reflection, but through the effective operation of the grace of the Word of God. It will become real in the narrow defile between the testimony to biblical revelation on the one side and the Church and the present-day world on the other. The Church's task at this point is not so much to examine itself and prove its capacity to speak about God. This self-examination is a basis. Not for a single moment is it exempt from it. For that reason it is at the heart of the narrow defile of this self-examination that it fulfils its real task, which is really to speak about God. It is in the thick of the Church's life, i.e., as the hearing Church has to be a teaching Church, that the decision about the purity or impurity of its doctrine is made : in its preaching and instruction, in its pastoral work, in its administration of the sacraments, in its worship, in the discipline which it exercises towards its members, in its message to the world, and last and not least in its concrete attitude over against state and society. Dogmatics, too, does, of course, belong to this life of the Church. But it cannot replace what must become a reality in other aspects of the Church's life. In its own place it can only help to prepare it. In relation to this other characteristic service of the Church, and to what happens or does not happen in that narrow defile, it is the auxiliary of the Church. As such it must be taken seriously— as seriously as the indissoluble unity of reflection and action requires. As this auxiliary it must have its effect on the whole life of the Church. It cannot concede that there are any *adiaphora*. It cannot allow even the slightest responsible expression of the Church's life to escape its control. And in this capacity, it cannot remain only the business of theology, or even academic theology. On the contrary, it must be the concern of the whole Church. If pure doctrine is sought in dogmatics, the same will certainly happen in the other departments of the Church's life. If it does not happen here, then it will certainly not happen elsewhere.

It is not superfluous at least to recall the opposite truth that the task of proclamation cannot be identical with that of dogmatics. The Church pursues dogmatics in order that its preachers may know what they have to say—yet not in order that they may say what they know as dogmaticians, but what they know as preachers. The knowledge of the preacher must be derived exclusively from the biblical witness to revelation. Dogmatics must teach him how to extract from this source pure doctrine. Because he is only a man, this does not go without saying. It must be for him a matter of prayer and also of work. Dogmatics ought to have placed in his hands the knowledge of a standard for all doctrine, and to have taught him and continually to teach him to apply it. He does not have to preach this knowledge. He has to preach on the presupposition of this knowledge, in application and under the control of it. It is not necessary to state in detail how frequently error has occurred, both in the past and present, by deplorably confusing this necessary discipline and its special ends with the aim which this discipline and its special ends are there to serve.

The special task of dogmatics implies that it is the place where, as nowhere else, theology comes into its own. But this situation has a two-edged character of which we ought to be aware. We have said that the work of dogmatics arises at the middle point between that of exegetical and that of practical theology. This means, on the one hand, that theology can exercise itself at this point in a certain security and independence, which is not self-evident elsewhere, but peculiar to it by reason of this middle position. Behind it theology has Holy Scripture as witness to revelation, and its attestation in the earlier confessions and knowledge of the Church. Before it, it has the Church and its activity of proclamation. Thus placed, theology can reveal, unfold and shape itself in dogmatics as a characteristic branch of knowledge. It can do so all the more, the more strictly it stands in this twofold relation and avails itself of the fact that here it is held, nourished and protected in this twofold way. When it asks concerning the content of the Church's proclamation in this sphere and framework, it is confronted by a whole world of problems, each of which is so rich and fruitful because we cannot seriously treat a single one of them without immediately having to treat the one central problem in a new and special way; for there is no real periphery, but each peripheral point immediately becomes another centre. And the details, too, form themselves automatically into a whole, the unity of which we do not merely surmise but also perceive, and then again merely surmise and fail to perceive. And, again, the more definitely we are placed within this sphere and framework, the more conversant we become with the details as such and with their cosmic totality as such: the more reason there is to be astounded, on the one hand, at the complete freedom with which we can work in every question of method, order or sequence of thought, apparently according to the peculiar disposition and talents of each individual worker, and, on the other hand, at the utter impossibility of arbitrariness either in approach or in the basic design, which the very nature of the thing determines. To engage in theology seriously means—and this in proportion to the seriousness with which the task is undertaken—to awaken as a theologian to scientific self-consciousness.

It is still not so very long since dogmatics was felt to be the great embarrassment of a scientific theology. But that was the time when theology in the precise sense had no scientific self-consciousness, but regarded it as necessary and possible laboriously to nourish itself by borrowing, first from philosophy, and then above all from history. It was a time when the middle position occupied by dogmatics and theology between Scripture and the proclamation of the Church was hidden from theologians themselves. Exegesis threatened to be dissolved in Church history, and practical theology in a collection of more or less arbitrarily chosen and imparted bits of technical advice. The two branches were linked, or rather not linked, by a dash of psychological speculation to which in the end there was a justifiable hesitation even to give the name of dogmatics. There was good ground for the bad conscience and dissatisfaction with which dogmatics was then pursued among other theological disciplines and especially other sciences. But if other theological disciplines thought they could bring a better conscience and greater satisfaction to bear upon their problems, this was only in appearance. Without the middle point of an orderly dogmatics to hold them together, they were, if possible, even more in the air than was dogmatics itself in its then disorderly condition. The good order of dogmatics, and therefore of theology generally, stands or falls by whether it consciously and consistently places itself within this framework. When it does so it receives both poise and movement, freedom and strictness in its work, a clear survey of its possibilities and also a clear insight into the secret of its limitations. When it does so, we can again understand what the mediæval theologians meant when they did not only sigh at the toil but also rejoiced in the beauty (*pulchritudo*) of their work. When it does so, there arises a genuine and not simply surreptitious self-consciousness of exegetical and practical theology too. Again, when it does so, and only when it does so, we can understand the independence of a study of Church history as distinct from secular history. When it does so, theology can confront calmly the questions put to it by other branches of knowledge in regard to its scientific character, turning to them with the counter-question, whether in the whole of university learning it is possible to think, teach and speak with equal freedom and necessity as in theology ; whether theology is not still perhaps the true and basic science from which the whole *universitas literarum* has not only derived historically, but to which it can only return, in so far as scientific self-awareness has there its true and original foundation. Let there be no deception : it is only as theology does in fact take up its midway position between the Bible and the Church, only in virtue of this position, that all this is possible. The time of theology's internal disintegration and external impotence and shame will inevitably recur the moment this position is again forgotten or abandoned, instead of being maintained still more strictly than has been possible in the short interval which separates us from the time of which we speak.

But there is another aspect to the fact that in dogmatics, as nowhere else, theology comes into its own. For it undoubtedly involves a real burden and temptation, which we must also consider. It is not, of course, an accident that all the complaints and objections which arise both in the world and in the Church itself against theology are always aimed directly or indirectly at dogmatics. What does this mean ? Is it not the case that the security and independence with which theology can be pursued in this middle position carry with them a relative impregnability for those who pursue it, that they are not immediately exposed, like the biblical theologian, to the direct assault of Holy Scripture, or, like the practical theologian, to the direct assault of the congregation and the world, that they are, indeed, contained and limited on both sides (and, it is to be hoped, most emphatically contained and limited), but that as the transition is there made from

explicatio to *applicatio*, they are implicated in the necessary process
of the reflection which both assimilates and then in the movement to
applicatio utilises ?   It is, of course, on this razor's edge that dogmatics
appears in all its splendour as the central theological discipline, and we
can never rate that splendour too highly.   Here or nowhere, there
awakes the self-awareness of the critical theologian.   But how can this
situation fail to be critical, two-edged and even actually dangerous ?
We are confronted immediately by the question whether that suspicion
is not justified with which even in the Church itself the question is
asked :   What kind of abstraction and aloofness from life is this, in
which dogmatics and therefore theology seems to move ?   Where are
we really led by the innumerable formal reflections, distinctions and
limitations, and all the indissolubly connected objections and negations, in which theology issues at this point ?   Is not the Bible much
simpler than dogmatics ?   Is it not therefore possible and necessary
that preaching and teaching should be much simpler ?   Must this
middle course really be traversed ?   Are not unnecessary refinements
and difficulties artificially introduced only at a later stage to be just
as artificially resolved ?   Is there not at work in the practised analysis
and synthesis a strong vein of humanistic æsthetics, which has no
connexion with the seriousness of the Church's theological task ?   The
temptation offered by such questions is twofold.   It is certainly not a
good thing arrogantly to exclude the probability that the open or tacit
reproaches which such questions imply do always contain a *particula
veri*.   To the extent that in this middle position a man is really concerned with himself instead of with his subject matter, to the extent
that he works himself out in this position, it is undoubtedly a misfortune, for speculations alien to the life of Scripture and the Church
hold the attention, and these can only be aggravated by the natural
brilliance of dogmatic activity, which in this case will immediately
become unnatural.   As dogmaticians, we continually have to put the
question whether, in the whole of our work, we are not more concerned
with ourselves than with the subject matter.   This question will have
to be asked the more urgently in proportion as we may feel our work
to be successful.   But, again, it is wrong if the questions suggested by
this mistrust are allowed to alienate us from the task in hand, that
task which is laid upon us in the middle position between the Bible
and the Church, of critical and systematic reflection with a view to
the discovery of pure doctrine.   Dogmatics has not to be ashamed of
its task as a discipline, its scholastic task.   The reproaches may spring
from inadequate insight into the seriousness and scope of this task.
They may be philistine in character.   Therefore we should not allow
ourselves to be misled by them.   We should treat them with friendly
unconcern.   Often enough there lies concealed behind them the error
which has penetrated into the Church and which scents out in dogmatics its natural adversary.   Often enough apparent simplicity is not

merely complexity and sophistication, but also downright falsehood, which fears to be unmasked by dogmatics. And where this is the case dogmatics has even less occasion to allow itself to be confused by heckling from this source, and so diverted from its post.

But at this point a further question arises, for as dogmatics effects the transition from the Bible to preaching, and constitutes it by its own human reflection, it provides the occasion, as we have already seen in § 21[2], on which the question of the relation between theology and philosophy becomes a burning issue. Is it not inevitable that at this point, where it seems that theology is no longer thinking and speaking exegetically and not yet practically, philosophy will present itself with instruction how critical and systematic thought is to be carried on in this process of transition? Is it not inevitable that in its suggestions—the suggestions which the theologian makes to himself in his capacity as a philosopher—the significant fact will again emerge that it is in dogmatics that the theologian can most easily lay an unauthorised emphasis on self? This is the classical point for the invasion of alien powers, the injection of metaphysical systems which are secretly in conflict with the Bible and the Church. And where this has taken place, it has only separated the Bible and the Church, and after lending to dogmatics a certain false independence, it has caused its disintegration and that of theology generally, at first inwardly and very soon outwardly as well. If the complaints about the aloofness and abstraction of dogmatics from life are justified, if in this matter man is more concerned about himself than his subject, then the reason or the effect will almost always be found in some such interpenetration. We must note again that there is a real source of danger at this point. When theology, as it were, snatches away the biblical word in order to press it into the framework of a scheme of thought which it has already prepared and regards as absolute, and to pass it on in this form to the preaching of the Church, then no matter what the scheme may be, the evil has already been committed, that is, the corruption of doctrine, which it is the task of theology, and of dogmatics at this middle point of theology, to prevent. The keeper himself has opened the gate to the enemy. The contingency needs only to be described to tell us that this is just what must not be allowed to happen. But, again, the opposite temptation must also be resisted. In dogmatics, personal schemes of thought must be shaped in accordance with the word of the Bible, which is now to become the word of the Church, and not conversely. There can never be any question of opposing them to the word of the Bible, as, so to speak, stable elements; nor can there ever be any question in dogmatics of maintaining such a scheme, however necessary and useful it may be, as a norm over against the preaching of the Church. But, again, it is not right to allow a fear of this interpretation, and therefore of the possible corruption of doctrine, to arrest human thinking, as it is no doubt controlled by the criterion of a philosophy, and with it the work of criticism and systematisation which it has to perform. It cannot be good counsel to let an ascetic abstinence prevail at this point, because in practice this can only mean putting aside the work that has to be done here. It is quite wrong, of course, that at this point man should give rein to the arbitrariness of his thought and the philosopher prevail over the theologian. But it is even more wrong that at this point where he is challenged in his whole existence and therefore as a theological philosopher too, man should withdraw and refuse from fear of sin or of being suspected of sin, and should then pass from thinking to not thinking or to an idle and frivolous type of thinking. So long as dogmatics has heeded the warning, it can and must go forward in this respect too with a good conscience.

We now attempt briefly to outline its general task. Even the work of dogmatics can begin only with the hearing of the Word of God, and indeed the hearing of it in the proclamation of the Church. It, too, proceeds from the expectation and the claim which this proclamation arouses, that the human word which is heard may be not only man's word, but God's own Word. Apart from this presupposition, it has no contribution to make, and the questions which it has to put, the criticism which it has to exercise and the counsels which it has to offer will be without root, object and meaning. The sphere in which it thinks and speaks does not lie outside but inside the Church. It does not think and speak, therefore, by ignoring but by acknowledging the promise given to the Church. For that reason it must not approach the preaching of the Church in a mood of distrust, as though the pure doctrine, about which it asks and concerns itself, cannot become a reality. The attitude of dogmatics towards Church proclamation must be critical, but it may not be sceptically negative. In spite of all the objections and scruples which it has to bring forward, in spite of all the changes, however significant, which it has to propose, it must proceed in the confidence that God's Word has never left itself without a witness in the Church, and will never do so. It will listen, expecting to hear pure doctrine and therefore not merely man's word but God's Word. It will listen to the Church's preaching, as listening in faith demands. In this way it will try to hear what the Church has to say about God to the world to-day in the whole scope of its activities. But just because of this presupposition it will listen critically. It will bear in mind the other presupposition that those who speak of God are men, that what happens is a matter of the ministry and liturgy of the Church which cannot as such be perfect and unassailable like the Word of God itself, but which by the Word of God, or, from the human point of view, by prayer and the work of the Church, always has to become what it is. For the Church to which this promise is given, and the preaching of which it therefore approaches with this first presupposition in mind, is undoubtedly a Church of sinners.

If dogmatics is particularly concerned with the work which from the Church point of view must be done in order that its divine worship may be divine worship not merely in form and appearance but in reality, then it cannot be sufficiently emphasised that this work cannot be properly done except in so far as the dogmatic theologian both assigns to prayer a much more important place in the solution of the problems confronting him, and also himself participates in the prayer of the Church for the correctness of its liturgy and the purity of its doctrine. About this, little need be said. The truth is that the quality of dogmatic work depends decisively on its not consisting, for example, merely in a series of conceptual manipulations, but on its being penetrated down to its last and apparently least important details by an unceasing supplication for the Holy Spirit, who is both for the purposes of the Church and for His own sake the *unum necessarium* which no technique nor toil can compel, but for which we can only pray.

We have already seen, however, that the insight that the Church must pray for pure doctrine will not be deep and sincere, if it does not stimulate it to the utmost exertion and set all its activity in motion. If from a human standpoint the preaching of the Church is sick, for it is the preaching of sinful men, and if it can be healed only by the divine physician, it cannot avoid facing the question which is put to it in Jn. 5⁶ by the divine physician Himself : Wilt thou be made whole ? As a human action, Christian preaching has to face concrete human questions even as it stands under the divine promise and is seen under this promise. It does not have to face any kind of human questions. It does not have to face such questions as arise from the desire of the Church to be the Church, or such questions as may entice it to cease to be the Church. It can take note of such questions only as questions which are already answered and superseded by what it has to say. Only as such can it take them up and pay attention to them in what it goes on to say. The task of dogmatics cannot, therefore, be to assume the part of the *advocatus diaboli*, putting such questions to the Church from a general view of truth or reality. On the contrary, it will have the duty of warning the Church about the character of such questions. It will have to instruct and show it how to treat such questions as questions already answered and therefore superseded. But there are some human questions facing Christian preaching which necessarily arise from the being of the Church as the Church and which do, therefore, have to be put : questions regarding the greater or less purity of its doctrine, its greater or less suitability for the service of the Word of God. Wherever the Church's proclamation takes place there is at a first glance in its performance an apparently inextricable dialectic of obedience and self-assertion, consistency and weakening, decisiveness and obscurity, concentration and distraction. This does not mean that purity of doctrine is necessarily absent, but it does mean that it is compromised and threatened. And even the slightest menace to pure doctrine is a serious and fatal menace to Christian preaching and the Christian Church as such. Even behind the most insignificant deviation or obscurity or irrelevance, behind the apparently most harmless whimsicality, which someone or some circumstance may wish to employ in matters of Church proclamation, there may lurk the error and falsehood by which the promise is annulled and the Church destroyed. In every menace to pure doctrine the question arises whether the Church, at the point where it now speaks, has not perhaps rejected grace and is, therefore, itself rejected. In our prayer for the Holy Ghost we commit it to the grace of God, and in so doing we confess that it needs divine grace, and must be continually rescued from death if it is to live. And if we believe in its deliverance from error and falsehood and therefore from rejection and reprobation, if we believe *quod una ecclesia perpetuo mansura sit*, necessarily the questions which we have to put to its preaching in view of that dialectical process will be impelled by the thought of its need, which it is certainly the business of prayer for the Holy Ghost to overcome. Therefore the questions which have to be put to the Church's preaching because they spring from the essential nature of the Church as the Church, the questions which find expression in dogmatics, will never be merely preliminary, formal or supplementary. Certainly dogmatics cannot ask concerning the absolute purity of doctrine—for it is not the work of man, but of God to produce this. It can ask only concerning the greater or less degree of purity. Even on the relative level of the Church's human work it cannot make decisions with regard to the Church's creed. It can do so only in matters arising out of the creed and its repetition. Yet at the same time it cannot be concealed and denied that its questions will not be questions of style, or taste, or feeling, or debatable opinion, but questions in which in some way and in greater or less degree what is at stake is always the life or death, the being or not-being of the Church. This is why in dogmatics there are, strictly speaking, no subordinate questions. Listening always in the confidence that it has to do with the one Word of God, it always has to put the question whether it really has to do with the one Word of God. From this combination of confidence and criticism arises the seriousness of dogmatic questions. Neither must be lacking. Confidence without criticism becomes a profane and forbidden confidence— the false self-confidence of ecclesiasticism. Criticism without confidence becomes a profane and forbidden criticism, the anticipation of divine judgment and the criticism of unbelief. On neither supposition can the questions of dogmatics be serious.

All the questions of dogmatics have fundamentally the same direction. The purity of doctrine is the issue, and therefore it is a question whether the words, the phrases, the sequences of thought, the logical construction of Christian preaching have or have not the quality of serving the Word of God and becoming transparent for it. We have to emphasise that it is the words, phrases, sequences of thought and logical construction which are our concern here. It is not, therefore, a question whether something has been omitted in Christian preaching. It is much rather a question whether something has been done in it, but rightly done.

It is quite understandable that both in earlier times and to-day it could be proposed and the attempt made to achieve pure doctrine quickly, by either silencing the human word entirely, or accompanying it with silence, or by destroying its verbal and so its rational character in an attempt to express it in the speech of primitive poetry. This kind of silence was interpreted as the completest way of letting God speak, and it was thought to be better than speech, and to be what was really meant and intended in speech. Where there is a desire to replace or crowd out preaching by the sacrament and liturgy, no small part is usually played by the theme that pure doctrine is the result of doing nothing, of abstention from human words, which fall under the suspicion of being so solid that they cannot have the transparency required to reveal the Word of God. But the matter is not so simple. That any sort of human words have the required transparency is certainly not the case. But silence is also a human action, as is everything that man does instead of preaching. Even the one thing which does have a place alongside the human word of the preacher, not to displace it, but together with it to constitute the Word of God, is still a human action—namely, the sacrament. And if the sacrament itself is not intended or suited to effect magically what the human word cannot effect magically, this is even less true of an effectual or symbolic silence or any other arbitrarily chosen substitute for the human word. We can, therefore, take note of all proposals of this kind only as attempts to master the real difficulty which cannot possibly succeed, since they are made with inadequate means.

When purity of doctrine is demanded, what is required is not abstention from, but full use of human words, phrases, sequences of thought and logical construction. It is not by their negation, but in their reality, that they are to be pure and transparent. It is demanded that they should serve the Word of God, and therefore cause God's Word to be heard and not man's. Thus the criticism of dogmatics is turned upon them. It both takes them seriously and invites the preaching of the Church to take them seriously, just because it believes in the Church's promise and mission, and in the necessity which demands teaching, but pure teaching, in the Church. Dogmatics asks on what grounds the Church speaks in this way or that, and whether and how far the manner in which it speaks corresponds to these grounds and is or is not, therefore, meaningful. Thus it goes back beyond what is said to what is meant. It seeks to elucidate this and ultimately to correct it. It then returns to what is actually said in order to enquire about its suitability and finally to bring forward proposals for its amendment.

If we ask concerning the subject matter of dogmatics, the reply must be that it consists essentially in the totality of what it hears from the Church—the contemporary Church—as its human speech about God. In practice, however, it will consist in certain key-words and fundamental outlines which in this heterogeneous mass constitute that which is common to the whole and recurs in all its multiple forms. However searchingly the critical inquiry into pure doctrine must be conducted, the fact of such common and recurrent features justifies us from the start in the corresponding faith (without which we cannot approach this task) that what the Church says about God is not just crude material without a pattern, but that by the unmistakable existence of such key-words and fundamental outlines it discloses itself as a system of doctrine, about the unity and therefore the purity of which it is not from the outset a hopeless undertaking to inquire.

Up to and including our own time, when the Church has spoken about God with almost unbroken constancy and completeness, it has spoken in one way or another about a Lord of the world and of man, and about His action in connexion with the coming of Jesus Christ. In one way or another it has described the world as the creation of this God, and man as His creature called to special obedience towards Him. In one way or another it has spoken of the sin of man and of his reconciliation with God, of the life of the Church as a whole and in its members, and finally of a hope of immortality founded in the knowledge of God and of His action. In detail, the question has always been open whether and how far in all this it has spoken out of its being as a Church, or rather out of the being of the Church, or whether it has already ceased to be the Church which it claims to be. As it has spoken about these things, it has never been certain that its doctrine is pure doctrine and therefore the Word of God. But we can say that, by the constancy and completeness with which it has always returned to these themes in its preaching, even when it has fallen into error and falsehood, it has itself become a witness to the fact that in what it says about God it is not by any means left to its own devices, that it is always aware at least of the problem of the unity and purity of its teaching, and that even though it may resist it cannot wholly escape a principle which controls what it says about God.

The material which the Church offers contemporary dogmatics will always be new, as will continually appear on a closer inspection, to the extent that both in content and expression the key-words and basic outlines are caught up in an unceasing movement which dogmatics, if its work is not to be too late, if it does not wish to present historical reports rather than the critical co-operation which it owes to the Church of the present, must meet in its most recent, contemporaneous stage. But, again, there is obviously no lack of continuity in this movement, and so it is implied that the key-words and thoughts with which dogmatics has to deal to-day cannot in practice be any different from those with which it had to deal yesterday or four hundred or a thousand years ago. This continuity of basic words and outlines may sometimes be very formal and neutral, but in practice it does at least mean that dogmatics will find itself in conversation not only with the Church of its own generation, but also with that of all the previous " presents " which have now become " past." Indeed, it cannot take up its critical task in regard to its own present, if it refuses to bear in mind that it can be properly understood only when viewed as part of a single movement, of which it forms the most recent stage.

The task of dogmatics begins with the question with which it approaches this material. Dogmatics springs from the salutary unrest which must not and cannot leave the Church. It is the unrest of knowing that its work is not done simply by speaking somehow about God, or by speaking with some kind of consistency under the remarkable but undeniable compulsion of the basic words and outlines which supply its framework. As the Church occupies itself with dogmatics, it acknowledges that it is aware of the transformation in which its preaching constantly finds itself, in spite of the formal and neutral identity. It acknowledges that this transformation constitutes a problem. It acknowledges its fear that this transformation might be for the worse, but it acknowledges also its hope that it might be for the better. And finally it acknowledges that it cannot leave this matter to fate, or to the course of an immanent and inevitable development which it can comfortably watch as a spectator, but that it has itself a responsibility in this matter. This sense of responsibility arises, as we have seen, from its realisation of the promise given to it that it can and must speak the Word of God. And from the same realisation there also arises the impossibility of confining itself to establishing the material contents of dogmatics, the broad facts of a speech about God which " somehow " takes place and " somehow " finds unity. From it again, therefore, there arises the seriousness of the question with which dogmatics approaches this material.

There exists an exact proportion between the realisation of this promise given to the Church on the one hand, and on the other the strictness of dogmatic inquiry. Where it is not realised, or perhaps where men do not want to realise, that God Himself wishes to speak and will speak to His Church and to the world, men will be more or less content with this " somehow," with the fact that in spite of everything God is still proclaimed (and even with zeal and devotion) in the Church, and they will point with peculiar satisfaction to the undeniable consistency of the key-words and basic outlines. The unceasing changes in their meaning and form will not, then, be felt as a problem, but noted as a gratifying sign of the life and richness of the Church, and there will be no feeling of stimulation either to particular fear or hope. If in these circumstances a dogmatics does set to work in earnest, approaching its material critically and not merely describing it, it will be accompanied from the very first by unconcealed mistrust. It will be felt to be superfluous and disturbing—superfluous, because it cannot improve upon the advantage of the formal and neutral fact that the Church speaks of God with a certain consistency ; and disturbing, because, in so far as its criticism is directed first against the key-words and basic outlines, it casts doubt upon, and even *in concreto* keenly and seriously disputes, the advantage of the fact that in the Church God is truly and consistently proclaimed. It is inevitable that a true and searching dogmatic inquiry will be flatly opposed where men feel they must reject the assumption of the presence and action of the Word of God Himself or fail to realise its scope. On the other hand, when this assumption effectually prevails, we cannot insist too urgently on a true and searching dogmatic inquiry, even to the point of compromising the whole material of dogmatics, compromising the view that God is really proclaimed in the Church, compromising the idea that the formal and neutral unity supplied by key-words and basic outlines is a genuine unity, and compromising the idea that the Church really is what, on the basis of this unity, the Church means and is intended to be. The question will then be raised about the Church of the Word of God and its unity, not merely about the speaking of God as such, but about the proclamation of the Word of God. To ask these questions will then be the special task of dogmatics, which is so vital for the Church. Is it not right, then, that everything that has the name of speech about God, or unity, or the Church, should be summoned and interrogated for the sake of the real thing, which in the constant flux of human appearance is obviously a problem with which we have to wrestle in fear and hope ?

The task of dogmatics consists generally in a critical examination of its material, which means in fact of these key-words and basic outlines of the Church's speech about God. To examine does not mean to reject. It means to take up, in order to test, or weigh, or measure. Its purpose is to see whether the matter to be tested is what it promises to be and really should be. Dogmatics tests the Church's speech about God, in order to find out whether as man's word it is fitted to serve the Word of God. It considers it in the light of the promise that its essential character, order and task are to serve the Word of God and so to be pure doctrine. It does not allow the changing situation in which it stands, and the confusing multiplicity of its meaning and expression, to mislead it into supposing that the Church's speech about God is not worth examining. But, again, it will not wrongly suppose that, because in its reality and its apparent unity this speech would prefer not to be exposed to criticism, it therefore does not need it. About the fulfilment of this criticism we shall have to speak in the last two sections of this chapter. Obviously, an examination of this kind cannot be carried out arbitrarily. As we have seen, the danger is not ruled out that a bad examination of the Church's preaching and therefore bad dogmatics may do more harm than good to preaching. Therefore there is every reason that dogmatics should prove itself to be competent for this task, examining itself first in regard to the method to which it must subject itself if it is to be a good examination and good dogmatics. And if in this preliminary self-examination it is a question of measuring and weighing, it is clear what the questions which dogmatics must first of all put to itself should be : (1) the question concerning the criterion or standard with which it is to conduct its examination ; and (2) the question concerning the right use of this criterion and standard. We can call the first the question of the dogmatic norm, the second that of dogmatic thinking. The dogmatic norm is the objective possibility, dogmatic thinking the subjective possibility of the Church's proclamation, of which the reality is the Word of God itself.

We therefore retrace the path which we traversed in the third chapter. The reality then was the Word of God (as Holy Scripture) for the Church, the objective possibility was authority in the Church, and the subjective possibility was freedom in the Church. We also retread the way which we went in our second chapter. The reality then was the triune God, the objective possibility was the incarnation of the Word, and the subjective possibility the outpouring of the Holy Spirit. The correspondence between the individual components of all these discussions speaks for itself, although there could be little value except perhaps an æsthetic in a detailed presentation. The goal of the prolegomena of a Church dogmatics will have been reached when with the same methodical care as hitherto we have completed this final stage of our journey.

3. DOGMATICS AS ETHICS

To complete this prolegomena to dogmatics the task which is still before us is the presentation of the principle and method of dogmatics, that is, of the dogmatic norm and the dogmatic process of thought. But before addressing ourselves to this task, we must give an explicit answer to a question which is posed by the history of theology and academic custom, and which forces itself upon our notice at this juncture. This is the question whether alongside Church dogmatics there is a special and independent Church ethics. According to our previous assumptions, this would necessarily involve a special and independent examination of Church proclamation with regard to its suitability as instruction for human good conduct in the Christian sense ; or, according to current ideas, a special and independent description of the Christian life. Is there such a thing, and do we not therefore have to do with ethics as well when we treat of dogmatics ? Or conversely, have we to understand and treat dogmatics itself as ethics ?

The history of theological ethics as an independent discipline reveals the following cardinal features. Its presupposition has always been the opinion that the goodness, that is, the holiness of the Christian character, unlike the other objective content of Christian proclamation, is not hidden with Christ in God (in spite of Col. 3³), but can be directly perceived and therefore demonstrated, described and set up as a norm. Moreover, the execution of this enterprise seems always to have involved that the Christian character definable in this way should be construed as a distinctive form of human conduct generally, so that to demonstrate and describe it and set it up as a norm it is necessary to reach back to a general anthropology quite abstracted from the assumptions of revelation. But this process of making ethics independent has always become difficult or impossible in proportion as the opposite opinion has prevailed, that the holiness of the Christian character is not less visible in Jesus Christ, but also not less hidden in the life of Christians, than the remaining content of Christian proclamation ; and therefore in proportion as the exclusive authority of revelation over everything that is to be taught in the Church has been recognised or again come to be recognised. Where there have not been these safeguards, where ethics has therefore been able to secure independence, the fact has always had to be reckoned with that an independent ethics has always shown at once a tendency to reverse the roles, replacing dogmatics as the basic theological discipline, absorbing dogmatics into itself, transforming it into an ethical system with a Christian foundation, and then penetrating and controlling biblical exegesis and pastoral theology in the same way. Since independent ethical systems are always in the last resort determined by general anthropology, this inevitably means that dogmatics itself and theology as a whole simply becomes applied anthropology. Its standard ceases to be the Word of God. It is the idea of the good which controls its investigation of the goodness of the Christian character. But this idea is both sought and found apart from revelation. The Word of God is retained only in so far as it can be made intelligible as the historical medium and vehicle of this idea. The Church which sanctions this theology has subjected itself to an utterly alien sovereignty.

We can see both the suggested motifs in the increasingly independent ethical systems of Christian antiquity and the Middle Ages : the material motif, i.e., insight into the evident perfection of Christian character as developed in monastic life in the 'Ηθικά of Basil of Cæsarea, or the well-known rule of Benedict of Nursia, or the *Imitatio Christi* attributed to Thomas a Kempis ; and the formal motif, i.e., the reaching back to a general or Aristotelian and Stoic anthropology in the *Moralia* of Gregory the Great. The two motifs are combined in Ambrosius' *De officiis*, and again in the *Secunda secundae* of the *S. Theol.* of Thomas Aquinas, in an essay, *De actibus humanis in universali et in particulari*, which has its foundation as unambiguously in Aristotle as it has its illustration in the *vita religiosa* of the religious and the monk. It is certainly remarkable that although Thomas's ethics refers unmistakably to an independent basis it is not presented independently of his dogmatics, but in a subordinate position within it. The same is true of Augustine in his *Enchiridion*, John of Damascus in his *Ekdosis*, and Peter Lombard in his *Sentences*.

Clearly Thomas might have gone to work differently. But the theology of the Reformers, at any rate that of Luther and Calvin, represents an outlook which makes independent ethics inherently impossible. This may be studied in the writing of Luther entitled *Sermon von den guten Werken* of 1520, as also in his other occasional writings on ethics, but above all in the *Institutio* of Calvin, who had so basic an interest in the problem of sanctification. In the classical dogmatics of Reformation theology it would be difficult to point to any passage in which faith or the object of faith is treated without regard to the conduct of the believer. But it would be even more difficult to point to the opposite, that is, to essays towards an independent ethical discipline. Dogmatics itself and as such is ethics as well. This is all the more striking because both Calvin and Luther did not basically repudiate the idea of the law of nature inborn in man, and the recognition of it as something prior to faith, but agreed with the scholastics in giving this point of view their hearty approbation. In practice, however, they did not make any systematic use of the idea. The reason for this was that they held the insight of Col. 3[3] so firmly that they could not lose sight of Jesus Christ as the one object of faith. They were thus prevented from trying to construct an independent system of ethics. They were also safeguarded against the temptation to exploit this scholastic survival of natural theology. It was, therefore, a misunderstanding of Calvin and a disservice to him, when even in the 16th century it was felt to be a duty to publish Ch. III 6–8 of the *Institutio* (*De vita hominis christiani*, etc.) separately as a handbook of Calvinist morals. The ethics of Luther and Calvin is to be sought and found in their dogmatics and not elsewhere.

This cannot, of course, be affirmed quite so unequivocally of Melanchthon.

It can be affirmed of him if we think of his *Loci* and the Apology for the Confession of Augsburg. In these writings, as in the thought of Luther and Calvin, ethics remains embedded in the doctrine of faith and is subordinated to it. But elsewhere, especially in two sketches, *Epitome philosophiae moralis* 1538 and *Elementa doctrinae ethicae* 1550, Melanchthon makes a fresh approach to Aristotle, whom once, like Luther, he so sharply repudiated. This leads him to construct an independent ethical system whose programme he defines as *explicatio legis naturae . . . colligens, quantum ratio iudicare potest . . . praecepta de regenda disciplina in omnibus hominibus, congruentia cum decalogo, quatenus de externa disciplina concionatur* (*C.R.* 16, 167). From this special *philosophia moralis* Melanchthon does not only expect a proof of God's existence, but also an answer to the question : *Qualis sit Deus ?*, a knowledge of divine judgment, and finally a knowledge of the *norma vitae hominum in actionibus externis* as *paedagogia in Christum* (*ib.* 166 f., 169). It is plain that in making these attempts he is not in line with the Reformation, but rather in agreement with scholasticism or the later theology of the Enlightenment. Earlier than Melanchthon, and probably less under his influence than under that of Andreas Osiander, Thomas Venatorius of Nuremberg had written the first Lutheran ethic : *De virtute christiana libri tres* 1529. And if, in Melanchthon, the old formal motif was predominant, that is, the return to a general anthropology and knowledge of God, with Venatorius the material motif appears equally clearly. Faith is now understood as *virtus*, as the power of love and life in its " possessor " (W. Gass, *Geschichte d. chr. Ethik*, vol. 2, I, 1886, p. 108), as *impellentis Spiritus sancti impetus ad recte sentiendum primum de Deo ipso, deinde ad recte agendum cum proximo*, an *impetus*, the idea of which consists again in a Christian interpretation of the four cardinal virtues of antiquity (cf. *PRE* 3rd edn., 20, 490). The faith which was capable of being represented in this way was obviously something quite different from the true Reformation conception of faith as justifying solely by the power of its object. The same is true of the first attempt at a Reformed ethics : Lambert Danaeus, *Ethices christianae libri tres* 1577. The Reformation biblicism and predestinationism of this work offers only a relative safeguard against the dubious view which it opens up, that the will of the elect, which here too is renewed by the grace of God, constitutes (as the subjective principle of the good) a second and independent object for consideration as opposed to grace itself.

By contrast, it was the sign of a healthy instinct when classical Lutheran and Reformed theology persisted in following the example of Calvin and the younger Melanchthon, and presenting Christian teaching in a single system in which ethics was linked with dogmatics. B. Keckermann (*Systema ethicae*, 1577) did try to follow the later Melanchthon and separate ethics not only from dogmatics but from theology generally, presenting it as a philosophical discipline, but this was almost unanimously rejected. Venatorius and Danaeus, too, did not at first find any followers. And even the attempt of Polanus and Wolleb to divide dogmatics itself into two parts : *De fide* and *de operibus*, or *De Deo cognoscendo* and *De Deo colendo*, was not successful. But if on the whole we have to pronounce orthodoxy to have been right in principle, at the same time it must not be overlooked that its attitude was affected by a weakness in substance. Orthodoxy did not understand how to make it clear that it is not only in this or that aspect of Christian doctrine, but in dogmatics as a whole and throughout, that we have to do with ethics, that is, with the being and conduct of man. Further, when in certain connexions it came to speak emphatically about the law, sanctification, the new life, good works, etc., it did not sufficiently insist on the hiddenness of the Christian status. Like the Jesuits and the newly developing Pietism, it spoke of it as if it were a question of perceptible things and not here too of an object of faith. And finally, it not only failed to close the door to a naturalistic basis of ethics which the Reformers themselves had left open, but, especially in detailed ethical teaching such as was offered by individual dogmaticians in astonishing abundance, opened it more widely. These were the breaches through which a rising new wave of suppressed humanism could at last penetrate successfully and introduce an independent theological ethics.

The great forerunner of the movement in this sphere was George Calixtus of Helmstedt, to whom the orthodoxy of his century seemed to impose too much confessional and too little ethical strictness. Against it he renewed the doctrine already advanced by George Major in the 16th century, maintaining that good works are indispensable on man's side for the preservation of the faith. In his *Epitome theologiae moralis* 1634 he also put forward an independent ethics (a doctrine of the life of the new creature, of which the norm is the law of reason or nature, the decalogue which confirms it, and political and ecclesiastical ordinances). The new movement broke through fully at the turn of the 17th century. Both Pietism and the Enlightenment now made it appear that on the whole orthodoxy had not been at all concerned about the problem of ethics. This reproach was justified only to the extent that in orthodoxy neither the pietistic emphasis on the observable effects of grace in the new life, nor the humanistic founding of the moral law on the law of nature, did actually have the significance which it was now desired to assign to them in view of the general victory, both theoretical and practical, of the anthropological view. As if to make up for much lost time, from all quarters and in the most varied combinations of those two motifs, all those who were abreast of the times seized avidly on the so-called " moral teaching " of Christianity, with the result that at the very latest from the middle of the 18th century dogmatics came to be regarded as a dusty compendium of wisdom. Its role was that of a compulsory subject which had now become more or less superfluous and even an obstacle. Where it was still presented systematically and not merely historically by rationalists and supernaturalists, as far as possible it was transformed into a doctrine of ethical principles on a general anthropological basis. The reckoning which necessarily resulted from this transformation was presented with philosophical precision by Kant, when he simplified, or dissolved, dogmatics in his *Religion within the Limits of Pure Reason*. R. Rothe was right when he observed : " The rise of a *theologia moralis* in the Evangelical Church was really a significant sign of a new direction taken by Protestant piety in independence of the Church " (*Theol. Ethik*. vol. I, 1867, p. 68).

We must concede to Schleiermacher, first that from his own particular standpoint he knew how to impart to dogmatics (the " doctrine of the faith ") a new relevance and value, and second, again from his own particular standpoint, he had a nice understanding of the inner nexus and the ultimate unity of dogmatics and ethics. " The doctrine of Christian ethics is also the doctrine of faith. For membership of the Christian Church to which Christian morals always go back, is entirely a matter of faith, and the exposition of the Christian way of life is nothing but the further development of what lies originally in the faith of Christians. And is not also Christian doctrine ethical doctrine ? Of course ; for how could the Christian faith be presented apart from the idea of the Kingdom of God on earth ? The Kingdom of God on earth is nothing but the Christian way of life which must always reveal itself in action " (*Die christ. Sitte*, 1843, p. 12). But, of course, on Schleiermacher's view the common element in doctrinal and moral teaching consists in the fact that both are " only a developed presentation of the principles which make men Christians " (p. 17), i.e., the presentation of Christian piety (p. 21). For this very reason both are subordinated not only to apologetics, which deals with the distinctive characteristics of Christianity as distinct from other religions (*Kurze Darstellung*, 1830, §§ 43 ff.), but in the last analysis to a " science of historical principles," in which it is previously decided what constitutes piety in general, a science which Schleiermacher again entitled " ethics " (§§ 32 f.), and which he advanced as a " philosophical doctrine of ethics." From this last standpoint, that is, from the idea of piety as a universal mode of human feeling, he was unable to overcome the dualism of "ways of knowing" and "ways of conduct" (*Die christ. Sitte* p. 17). He therefore maintained the separation of the two theological disciplines which had become traditional since the 18th century revulsion, although he admitted that this separation could not be regarded as essential and that "it had no original sanction either generally or in the Evangelical Church" (*Kurze Darst.* § 223), and he considered it desirable "that from time to time there should be a unified treatment of the subject" (§ 231). Schleiermacher made only sparing use of his background, but it made it impossible for him to counteract the moralising and secularising movement of theology indicated in the religious philosophy of Kant. R. Rothe was merely taking Schleiermacher's presuppositions seriously when he consigned dogmatics to the sphere of historical statistics, and in its place, as the real central discipline of theology, developed a "speculative theology" under the title of "theological ethics," in which Christian doctrine was dissolved in a freely moulded cultural and philosophical science, just as it was the destiny of the Church, as he saw it, to be dissolved in the state. Rothe and his radicalism remained exceptional. Yet it can be said that both the separation of the two disciplines and also (explicitly or implicitly) the basic subordination of theology to ethics became and remained the rule, to which at any rate the leading theologians of modern times have adhered. This constituted the very nerve of the theology of A. Ritschl, and even at the beginning of our own century it was the firmest point of agreement between the two heirs of Ritschl who are otherwise furthest apart, W. Hermann and E. Troeltsch.

We may note in conclusion that the task of a "unified treatment," which Schleiermacher wanted "from time to time" has actually been attempted in modern times—in 1828 in C. J. Nitzsch's *System der christlichen Lehre*, in 1906 in H. H. Wendt's work of the same name, and above all in 1883 in Martin Kähler's *Wissenschaft der christlichen Lehre*. But the motif which had led the Reformers to this "unified treatment," the concentration of theology on the object of faith offered in revelation (and negatively, respect for the hiddenness of the Christian life and the renunciation of the systematic use of a "natural" understanding of the good), did not lie behind any of these attempts. With Nitzsch and Wendt it is clear that they are at one with Schleiermacher in the anthropological basis and method. They diverge from him only because they are bold enough to credit themselves with the power of systematisation, where he obviously thought that we should hesitate. The success they attained in this was not great enough to call forth a following which might have broken the academic and literary tradition of division. In reminiscence of Reformation theology, Kähler impressively dedicated his "science" to the representation of the man justified by faith: the motives which lead him to faith (apologetics); the foundation of his faith by its content (dogmatics); the bearing of his faith upon the correspondence between his religious certitude and his moral qualities (ethics). In an attempt of this kind, he could hardly fail in detail to make significant advances towards the Reformation inter-connexion of doctrine and life, faith and conduct. But the question arises: Is the starting point really God's revelation in Jesus Christ and not rather abruptly the new born man, and therefore in the last resort man in general? Is anything really said other than what Thomas Venatorius was trying to say? In this respect, is Kähler really to be sought and found on the side of Reformation theology? When it comes to Col. 3[3], has he really gone further than the Pietists, or when it is a matter of general anthropology has he really gone further than Melanchthon and the humanists? We cannot say flatly that he has not. Serious consideration has to be given to this work. But the half-light which pervades it has prevented it from having the success in theological history merited perhaps by its ultimate intention, which may not have been quite clear to the author himself.

In view of the history of the problem it is certainly impossible to say that the unified treatment of dogmatics and ethics necessarily implies in itself an agreement with the Reformers' outlook. What we can say is that the divorce between them involves a necessary alienation from this outlook. This conclusion, and therefore the decision for a unified treatment of the two disciplines is confirmed by a factual investigation of the question.

When this separation takes place, dogmatics itself takes on a negative accent. Its scope then becomes narrowed and emptied in a way which, from our previous understanding of this study of the Church's mission, we cannot approve, and which also can find no confirmation in all that this introduction itself has had to say concerning dogmatics.

We may recall at this point the doctrine of the outpouring of the Holy Spirit developed in §§ 16–18, in which a study of revelation in its subjective reality and possibility quite naturally led us (and especially and in great detail in § 18) to treat " dogmatics as ethics." Again, the problem of ethics concerned us just as explicitly in § 21 (concerning freedom in the Church). Indeed, we may readily ask where the ethical problem has not concerned us in our previous dogmatic discussions ? Is it really true, then, that we can limit dogmatics to a discussion of the purely theoretical content of Christian proclamation, turning neatly to ethics as its practical aspect ? Is there, indeed, any such thing as a purely theoretical content of Christian proclamation ? Can the whole idea of a distinction between "theoretical" and "practical" rightly be sustained, or does it not imply from the very first a πρῶτον ψεῦδος, which has to be resisted in principle ? The question we may put even to Polan and Wolleb is this : Can we really speak separately of *fides*, and only afterwards and in other connexions of *opera* ? *De Deo cognoscendo* and only afterwards and in other connexions *De Deo colendo* ? And we ask some modern representatives of the procedure of separate treatment : Is it really the case, as W. M. L. de Wette supposed (*Lehrbuch d. chr. Sittenlehre*, 1833, p. 1), that doctrine is concerned with the emotional contemplation of eternal being, and moral teaching only with the realisation of ends in life, in finite relations ? Or is it really as Schlatter says (*Die christliche Ethik*, 1914, p. 30) : that dogmatics illuminates our state of mind, but ethics brings light to our will ? or as G. Wünsch puts it (*Theol. Ethik*, 1925, p. 66) : that dogmatics describes what is to be believed, ethics what is to be done on the basis of the fact of the holy, the former expressing the implied world-view, the latter the "characteristic ethical action" based on the former ? If the eternal being, with which doctrine has to do, is not implicated in its realisation in actual life, what kind of a being is it ? What has it to do with the God of biblical revelation ? If the enlightened consciousness is not in itself enlightened will, if faith and its world view is not in itself a deed, how far does this subjective side belong at all to the substance of Christian proclamation and therefore of theology ?

If this separation is insisted on, dogmatics incurs the grave suspicion of being no more than an idle intellectual frivolity. If it really has to accept this disjunction, we ought not to be surprised if at times it acquires the reputation of being aloof from life and of doubtful value, in view of its pure "intellectualism." In these circumstances it has every reason to retire in favour of ethics (even an untheological ethics, if this is regarded as worth while). But perhaps it is the case that dogmatics is not in a position to withdraw, because it has to face a task which cannot be resolved into the abstract question about the goodness of human conduct, but a task which at every point includes the concern of this question.   It is perhaps the case that unless it draws this question into its own discussion, and therefore unless it resolves its independence, as specialised ethics, dogmatics cannot be true to its own nature as a critical inquiry into the content of Christian proclamation.   How can it be otherwise when Christian proclamation undeniably has to do with the relationship founded and completed in the Word of God between the true God and true man, i.e., man in his totality and therefore as an active agent ?   What limits can we legitimately assign to dogmatics, beyond which a specialised ethics can and must begin ?   From the point of view of dogmatics, therefore, the possibility of separating off a distinct ethics must be resolutely rejected.

But, again, the positive accent which ethics acquires by such a separation may well prove to be a source of error in regard to the sense in which human conduct and its goodness can alone be the object of theology.   If we wish to make a fundamental distinction between dogmatics and ethics, we necessarily take it upon ourselves to show the fact and the extent that a distinctive approach and method lies at the basis of each.   But as far as can be seen, it is impossible to show this except where, in a common statement of both questions, the theme of theology has in some way been openly or tacitly surrendered.

We have seen how Venatorius once founded theological ethics on the character of *fides* as *virtus* ; and we ask : From what theological standpoint can we first describe faith as faith in Jesus Christ, and then as a human *virtus* ?   We have seen how Calixtus arrived at a special kind of theological ethics by trying to distinguish from the problem of faith itself the problem of its maintenance ; and we ask : How can this distinction be made ?   According to Schleiermacher (*Chr. Sitte* p. 23), the dogmatic question is : " If the religious form of self-consciousness, the religious disposition exists, what must be ? " ; whereas the question of moral philosophy is : " Since the religious self-consciousness exists, what must be done ? "   This shows us clearly the source of the distinction : it is identical with the dialectic of the religious self-consciousness, romantically understood.   Therefore in dogmatics and ethics alike, as is Schleiermacher's express opinion, we find ourselves in the sphere of anthropology.   The distinction has been made possible and necessary by the law of this sphere, and not by that of an object of specifically theological knowledge confronting this sphere.   According to Christian Palmer (*Die Moral des Christentums*, 1864, p. 21 f.), the difference between dogmatics and ethics is simply the difference between the divine and the human.   Doctrine puts before us " what God through His saving revelation has done and accomplished for us so that we do not have first to act, bring sacrifices, or perform works to save our souls, but need only accept what already has taken place completely, placing ourselves and standing on the ground which has been laid down for all eternity."   But even so, " the Kingdom of God is always the result of human, morally free action as well ; " " every truly moral action is just as much the deed of man as the operation of God."   Ethics has to do with the human side of the Kingdom of God mediated through human will and free human action.   We must ask whether the Kingdom of God is in fact disclosed to us in this sense also, as the deed of man, or whether the change of standpoint from the deeds of God to the deed of man does not necessarily imply a μετάβασις εἰς ἄλλο γένος, which makes it doubtful whether in the co-ordinated doctrine it is really a question of the action of God, and not of a datum of human self-consciousness, as in Schleiermacher? According to A. Ritschl (*Rechtf. u. Vers.* 4 ed. vol. III, 1895, p. 14), dogmatics includes " all the conditions of Christianity in the scheme of God's effectual working ; ethics, presupposing this knowledge, includes the field of personal and communal Christian life within the scheme of independent, personal activity." Again we ask : By what right is the " scheme of independent personal activity " separated here from that of " God's effectual working " ? What is the theological justification for this double question ? Can the Christian life be " handled " in the same sense as its effective causation in God, and if so what does this imply with regard to the " handling " of the latter ? Are not both perhaps to be understood as anthropological " handling " ? According to Theodore Häring (*Das chr. Leben*, 1907, p. 9), doctrine indicates " how the Kingdom of God as the gift of God becomes our personal possession through faith in Christ, moral doctrine how this faith gives us the impetus and the power to work at the task implied in this gift, so that the Kingdom of God may be realised, increasingly coming to us and through us, here in time and hereafter in eternity." We must ask : How can faith in Christ be indicated in theology as the power and impetus to co-operate in the realisation of God's Kingdom ? Human powers and impulses which can be " indicated " are something other than faith in Christ. Similarly that which becomes our " personal possession " is necessarily something other than the Kingdom of God in the biblical sense of the idea. According to O. Kirn (*Grundr. d. theol. Ethik*, 1906, p. 1), dogmatics conceives " the Christian life as based on God's saving revelation and therefore from the standpoint of the receptivity of faith " ; " but ethics surveys it in its active unfolding from the standpoint of the spontaneity of faith." But we ask : How then can dogmatics or ethics view the Christian life in such a way that they can differentiate between the " spontaneity of faith " and its " receptivity " as actuating theological motives in this life ? According to Schlatter (*op. cit.* p. 30) the case stands as follows : We have dogmatics " when we note what we have become and perceive in ourselves, ethics when we make clear to ourselves what we wish to become and make of ourselves. After the dogmatician has shown us God's work which has been done for us and in us, . . . the moralist shows us our own work, which is allotted to us because we are God's work." But we ask : What does it mean in theology to " note " something, to " perceive," to " make clear," to " show " something ? Must not the peculiarity of theological perceiving and showing, that it is determined by its object, imply that the contrast between God's work and our own work is impossible ? And must not theological perceiving and showing be surrendered by the act of noting separately what we wish to become and make of ourselves, by the fact of pointing to our work (in spite of the counter-claim that we are God's work) ? According to C. Stange (*Dogmatik* vol. I, 1927, p. 50 f.), in the light of the various pronouncements of the Christian faith, dogmatics proves that the essence of Christianity, established in symbolic theology, corresponds to the ideal which the philosophy of religion has previously shown to be the essence of religion generally ; it proves, that is, that Christianity is a religion of revelation. Ethics conducts the same proof with regard to the effect which Christianity produces on the development of history. A historical manifestation of a certain type of historical life must be shown to be the result of the essence which is peculiar to this type of historical life. Inasmuch as ethics describes effects which can be understood only as the effects of the essence of Christianity, and Christianity as the essence which produces these effects, it, too, demonstrates that Christianity is a religion of revelation. Here, again, we are obviously in the company of Schleiermacher—even in the case of the other theologians quoted, we have never really been anywhere else—on the elevated platform from which Christianity can be regarded as a " specific form of historical life," which, with the help of an ideal conception of religion, can be compared with similar forms of historical life and " demonstrated " as the fulfilment of the essence of all these forms. How does the theologian reach this platform, and will he succeed in making this demonstration ? Even if for a moment we adopt Stange's presuppositions and speech, we still have to ask concerning his programme of ethics, how the continuity between the " manifestation " and the " essence " of this " particular form of historical life " can be proved ? Can the revelational character of Christianity, as established by symbolic theology, be transferred so naturally to the " manifestation," to its historical " effects," that the former can immediately be inferred from the latter and the latter from the former ? Can the relation between revelation and its " effects " really be brought quite so simply under the Platonic idea of $\mu \epsilon \theta \epsilon \xi \iota \varsigma$ (i.e., the relation between the idea and particular things) ? When revelation is understood in this way, are we really thinking of biblical revelation, and will the description of its " effects " really have the character of a theological ethics ?

The attempts methodically to separate dogmatics and ethics are dubious even from the point of view of ethics itself, because in the process there regularly occurs a change of focus, a fatal interchange of the subjects God and man, which, though impossible in theology, becomes the true constitutive principle of ethics. Appealing to the supposed consequences of dogmatics as the revelation or work of God to man, in ethics we suddenly allow ourselves to open a new book : the book of the holy man which is the sequel to that of the holy God. But in theology we can never have to do with the consequences of God's revelation, or work to man, but only with the revelation and work itself. What theology has to learn and teach with regard to the holy man can be derived only from the one book. In this book it is, of course, very emphatically a question of the holy man as well. But in this book the holy man has no independent existence. Therefore he never becomes an independent object of thought. He exists only in the course of the existence of the holy God and of the study of His speech and action.

Theology in all its aspects is the representation of the reality of the Word of God which turns towards man and therefore redeems him. This definition cannot be filled out by reversing it, as though at the same time it was the representation of the reality of man to whom the Word of God is turned and who is thereby redeemed. How can it have any legitimate authority and competence for this ? It can acquire it only if it ranks itself above the Word of God, in order to gain instruction not only by the Word of God but also by a general human knowledge of man. If it does this in even one of its aspects, it must see whether it is not secretly doing the same in every aspect, or whether it is not a lack of consistency not to do so in every aspect. The problem of ethics is undeniably a theological problem. We can say without qualms that it is the great theological problem. We will have to substantiate and explain this truth. How can it be otherwise if theology is really the representation of the Word of God turned towards man and redeeming him ? Included in the reality of the Word of God, it obviously has to present the reality of man to whom the Word is turned and who is redeemed by it. What is theologically impossible is a study of these two realities as though they are on the same plane, as though there can be between them co-ordination, continuity or interchange, or as though in the last resort they are somehow identical. In this way we can, of course, co-ordinate above and below, receptivity and spontaneity, gift and demand, indicative and imperative, inner and outer, being and becoming (in the general neutral sense of all these conceptions). But we cannot co-ordinate in this way God's Word on the one side and the man who hears God's Word on the other. It is not true that this second reality stands over against the first in a relationship of polarity and tension. It is not true that the believing man must work for the coming of God's Kingdom. It is not true that he is related to the Word of God as the subject to the object. All these are ideas which are possible only on the basis of the view which ruined the old Catholic Church, that there is co-ordination, continuity, interchange and finally identity between nature and supernature. It may all be very true with regard to " nature " and " supernature." But theology is concerned, not with the encounter between nature and supernature, but with the encounter between nature and grace, or concretely, with the encounter between man and the Word of God. The reality of the man addressed by the Word of God cannot be related to the reality of the latter as a subject to an object, but only as a predicate to a subject. That is, in and for itself, it can never at any point or in any respect be this reality. It is only implied in it. It is only to be discovered in it. It can be spoken of only in the context of it. Christians are found only in Christ, not independently. They are seen only from above, not from below, only by faith, not by sight. They do not exist, therefore, as do Mohammedans, Buddhists, atheists, Catholics or Protestants. If we speak of Christians, Christendom and Christianity in this way, we must realise that we are speaking of the Christian world which is a cosmos (like the rest of the world in the sense of St. John's Gospel). We are speaking untheologically. And why should we not speak untheologically of Christianity ? There is no doubt that in himself the religious man and even the Christian can be a rewarding, interesting and instructive object of learned investigation. There is even a whole ancillary theological discipline—Church history—in which dialectically, for the sake of instruction, the object of theological investigation and scholarship is the Christian man as such, and the history of scriptural exegesis rather than Holy Scripture itself. But it is just Church history which makes it so clear that this Christian man is not in himself the man addressed by God's Word, and it can never at any point be a question of a sanctity intrinsic to himself, even though he may be an Augustine or a Luther. It is Church history which shows us that the Christian and Christianity are in themselves phenomena in the cosmos alongside many others. It is Church history which makes it clear, with its (dialectically framed) untheological questioning, that we must ask and answer theologically when it is a question of understanding the Christian as something other than a part and parcel of the cosmos. And that is clearly the question when in theology we ask about the goodness of human conduct and the Christian life, that is to say, when the problem of ethics is raised.

In theology, therefore, the focus and the theme cannot be fundamentally altered, or the subjects of the statements suddenly interchanged. If an ethics rests upon this interchange (and every independent theological ethics does rest upon this interchange), if, as distinct from dogmatics, it suddenly takes as its theme the " believer's spontaneity," what we ourselves wish to become, the effects of the nature of Christianity and so on, such an ethics will have to turn its back on revelation, Holy Scripture and the Christian proclamation, thus ceasing to be a theological ethics. Inevitably it will have to return to a foundation in Platonic, Aristotelian, Stoic or romantic

anthropology and ontology in order to maintain its autonomy in face
of dogmatics. This return will merely be a symptom that theology
as such has been surrendered. And the results of this surrender will
certainly be felt in dogmatics, and in the other parts of a science pursued on this presupposition and calling itself theology, and in the life
of the Church which is governed by this theology.

We now turn to the positive statement of our problem. The
problem of dogmatics is that of the purity of doctrine, or the problem
of the Word of God in Christian proclamation. In dogmatic dialectic
the Word of God is the intended point of departure, the point of reference and the aim. But this Word is the Word addressed to man,
heard by him and continually to be heard by him, the Word which
reaches man, claims him and absorbs his attention. It was impossible
to interpret it in any other way either in revelation and in the witness
to revelation, Holy Scripture. Man, however, is existing man. He is
not mere thinking man. As he thinks, he lives and acts and suffers.
He is absorbed in the actuality of his existence. We are only repeating
what we have often said before when we state again that only the doer
of the Word is its real hearer, for it is the Word of the living God
addressed to the living man absorbed in the work and action of his
life. If a man does not hear it in the actuality of his existence, if he
does not exist as its hearer, then he does not hear it at all. Even if
he tries to think of it, he is necessarily thinking of something else.
And if he tries to speak of it, he is inevitably speaking of something
else. Therefore dogmatics loses nothing more nor less than its object,
and therefore all meaning, if it is not continually concerned as well
with the existence of man and the realities of his situation, if its
problem concerning the purity of doctrine and the Word of God in
Christian preaching is not also the problem of the Christian life of
man, i.e., the life of man as determined by the Word of God : the
problem what we ourselves must do. In dogmatics there is, of course,
a special province in which this latter problem is directly and expressly
raised. This province can be characterised by the key-words law, sin,
sanctification. But the existence of this province cannot really mean
that there are other provinces in dogmatics where these questions are
unimportant or less important. The various departments of dogmatics
do not lie alongside each other, but are implicated in each other, so
that we cannot really work through any of them without expressly
bearing in mind all the others to a greater or less extent, and certainly
not without keeping them all in view. At what point, for example,
does the doctrine of the Trinity cease to have any decisive importance,
or the doctrine of the Church, or of justification, or of the return of
Jesus Christ ? At what point especially can we cease to keep in view
the doctrine of the incarnation of the Word of God ? It is just the
same with the special doctrine of sanctification in which dogmatics
directly and expressly becomes ethics. In every other connexion,

therefore, it will still have to be no less a doctrine of sanctification
and therefore ethics, if it is not to lose its purpose and meaning.

The ethical question, i.e., the question concerning right conduct,
is the existential problem of man. As we will, we are ; and what we
do, we are. It is not as if man first exists and then acts. He exists
in that he acts. The question whether and how far he acts rightly
is the question whether and how far he exists rightly. And so it is
no more and no less than the problem of man's existence which theology
or dogmatics makes its own when it raises the ethical question or
rather recognises and treats it as its most characteristic problem. But
at this point we have to be on our guard against an imminent possibility of aberration. It is not the case that the human problem of
existence as such is the theme of dogmatics and of theology generally.
It is not the case that theology has to give a theological answer to
the question of existence—as though somewhere in the void there is
a problem of existence which, among other things, theology with its
special presuppositions and methods has also to tackle. The Word
of God is not the Word of God unless it precedes this question of man's
existence, unless it is its origin even before it becomes its answer.
And theology has ill understood its task unless it regards this question
as one which is not first answered in the Word of God but already
grounded in it, the question which in the first instance is put by the
Word of God itself. It is only in this way that it can approach it as a
genuine and urgent question. Therefore the theme of dogmatics is
always the Word of God and nothing else. But the theme of the Word
is human existence, human life and volition and action. This is challenged by the Word of God, questioned as to its rightness, and brought
into the right way. It is for this reason and in this sense, not in virtue
of its own previous competence, but by the Word of God, that human
existence acquires theological relevance. But it does in fact acquire it
by the Word of God, and its problem so forces itself upon theology and
also on dogmatics, that neither theology nor dogmatics can be true
to itself if it is not genuinely ready at the same time to be ethics. A
reality which is conceived and presented in such a way that it does
not affect or claim men or awaken them to responsibility or redeem
them, i.e., a theoretical reality, cannot possibly be the reality of the
Word of God, no matter how great may be the richness of its content
or the profundity of its conception. Dogmatics has no option : it
has to be ethics as well. Its dialectics and its whole attitude necessarily
has to be " existential," i.e., because it refers to the Word of God, it
must also refer to human existence.

When P. Althaus (*Grundr. d. Ethik*, 1931, p. 9) says : " Ethics is bound up
in the closest possible way with dogmatics," it is an understatement. Dogmatics
itself is ethics ; and ethics is also dogmatics. If this is understood as a fact,
there is no danger that dogmatics may be dissolved in ethics, or a Christian
existentialist philosophy. God in His relationship to human existence is necessarily

the theme of dogmatics. And in this statement the idea of " relationship " cannot be interpreted merely as any kind of relationship between any two terms —a relationship which in this case might equally well be reversed. God and human life are not any two quantities, but here stands the Creator and there the creature, here the holy One, there the sinner, here the eternal and the everlasting, there the mortal. And their relationship is not any sort of relationship but the one constituted in the Word of God. But the Word of God is Jesus Christ, and so this relationship may be characterised as the free grace of God. How can it be presented without making manifest that it is not self-explanatory but a miraculous act of God, that God is not the prisoner of this relationship, but its founder and its Lord ? Therefore the fact that dogmatics deals with God in His relationship to human existence does not exclude but rather demands the truth that the divine ground of this relationship (which has no corresponding human ground) should be made visible as such—and not only transiently visible but really explicit, as happens in the doctrine of the Trinity and the general doctrine of God. Again, quite apart from the fact that ethics is the real problem of dogmatics and must never be lost sight of, in certain connexions it has to appear specifically and explicitly as a problem in itself. That dogmatics has always to be ethics cannot alter the fact that it is first and foremost and in itself dogmatics. As such it is concerned with the Word of God. Only in subordination to this is it also concerned also with the Christian life. Only in this subordination and dependence can this second theme be properly treated. Therefore in dogmatics there must always be room for the explicit recognition of the precedence and independence of the first theme. If this is remembered, there will be no danger of a dissolution of dogmatics in ethics or in an existentialist philosophy. Of course there is no positive safeguard against an arbitrary perversion along these lines, as, for example, in Gerhard Kuhlmann. But there is at least a safeguard against it in the judgment of those who are not themselves arbitrary.

It is certainly not within human power to give to dogmatics the necessary connexion with the question of human existence, in so far as by this is meant the question put in real life by real men. Similarly, it is not within human power (even less so) to give to it its connexion with the living God. Both these things are done only by God Himself, according to His sovereign pleasure. What does lie within human power in both cases is the scientific neatness and precision which are incumbent upon us in our struggle with the human preoccupation that forgets God on the one hand and human existence on the other, so that we continually have to draw attention to the two relationships at least within the sphere of thought and speech of ideas and words. But if this is humanly possible, it has actually to be undertaken. There is certainly no point in trying to give effective ethical power to dogmatics—for it has it or it does not have it, without our being able to " make " it. But at least we are required, as far as it is possible systematically in ideas and words, to indicate its practical ethical aim, counteracting at any rate in this sphere and with the means at our disposal that second type of preoccupation, in relation to human life and its meaning.

Our task, then, is to include ethics within dogmatics, and it can be undertaken in various ways. Nothing that we have said entitles us to affirm the radical impossibility of a literary or academic treatment of ethics which is outwardly separated from dogmatics. It is feasible if the following conditions are observed : (1) the separation must be merely technical in character, not based on principle and method ; (2) dogmatics thus separated 'from ethics must be pursued in thoroughgoing relation to ethical problems ; (3) ethics thus separated from dogmatics must be pursued in thoroughgoing subordination to dogmatics.

An independent ethics in this sense cannot, therefore, be an independent discipline alongside dogmatics, but explicitly and in fact it has to have the character of an auxiliary branch of theology. Symbolic theology is similarly related to dogmatics ; introduction and the history of religions to exegesis ; ecclesiology to homiletics, catechetics and liturgics ; and Church history — not coordinated but subordinated—to all the three cardinal theological disciplines. For the inner justification of ethics as an auxiliary discipline, it may be said that in a way which is not inappropriate it can make known to theology one of its limits. For if, as it were, by way of an appendix to dogmatics, theology again speaks about the hearing of the Word in a special ethical treatise, it can bear impressive witness to the recognition that its own word is not the decisive word ; that it does not have at its disposal a system by which it can control reality—here in particular the reality of man ; that however good its dogmatics may be, it has not spoken to man from heaven ; that it has to say again on earth what only God Himself can have said once and for all. In the case of the other theological auxiliaries, it can be shown that we have to do with similar and not at all superfluous reservations which theology has to make against itself.

On the other hand, we cannot affirm the radical necessity of an outwardly separate treatment of ethics.

What can be said in this direction in favour of an auxiliary ethics separated from dogmatics does not have such weight that this must be required as absolutely necessary. The necessary reservations in regard to dogmatics can be made effective in other ways than this. The real reason for choosing this way may properly consist only in what P. Althaus (*op. cit.*) calls " difficulties of construction " ; that is, in technical questions concerning the incorporation of special ethical inquiries and expositions into the structure of dogmatics. But this difficulty need not be insurmountable, so that even from this point of view, this method may seem to be a possible mitigation of the problem, but it is not the indispensable solution.

A direct inclusion of ethics in dogmatics has the advantage of greater consistency, unambiguity and clarity. If once it is fundamentally realised that dogmatics itself must be ethics and that ethics can be only dogmatics, then it does not seem quite clear why even externally we should not proceed in accordance with this insight. Further, why should we allow it even to appear, from an externally separate treatment of dogmatics and ethics, that the harmful opinion is maintained that there is such a thing perhaps as an unethical dogmatics or an undogmatic ethics ? And is it not the case that that which necessarily appears as two things, dogmatics and ethics, if treated separately, will gain in intelligibility if presented with the integrality which we cannot deny it in substance ? We decide for this second method. Even outwardly, we understand and treat dogmatics itself and as such as ethics. Therefore, as in the final section of the prolegomena we attempt a general survey of the plan of dogmatics, we shall have to take into consideration the material and problems which according to the modern academic and literary tradition constitute the particular material and problems of ethics.

DOGMATICS AS A FUNCTION OF THE HEARING CHURCH

Dogmatics invites the teaching Church to listen again to the Word of God in the revelation to which Scripture testifies. It can do this only if for its own part it adopts the attitude of the hearing Church and therefore itself listens to the Word of God as the norm to which the hearing Church knows itself to be subject.

1. THE FORMAL TASK OF DOGMATICS

The distinction between the teaching and the hearing Church, *ecclesia docens* and *ecclesia audiens*, which we use in this last section as a guiding thread, originates from the vocabulary of Roman Catholic theology. In itself, apart from the special interpretation it receives there, it is not only instructive and useful, but a term appropriate to the facts, grounded in the Bible, and well suited as a presupposition to the twofold definition of the task of dogmatics to which we must now turn. We effect the necessary reservation in face of the Roman Catholic interpretation first of all by reversing the order of the two ideas : the Church is first and foremost a hearing Church, and only then and as such a teaching Church. Therefore in relation to dogmatics as a function of the Church the following points especially have to be made. Dogmatics is a function of the hearing Church, and stands under the Word of God as the norm to which the Church in its fundamental character as a hearing Church is subject. In consequence it must itself seek above all to listen ; and its primary function consists in inviting and guiding the Church in its second character as a teaching Church to listen afresh to the Word of God. Only from this point of view is dogmatics understood as itself also (§ 24) a function of the teaching Church, of which the Word of God is not only the standard but also the subject matter. Only from this point of view is it in a position to approach the Church as a teacher, or rather in the service of teaching. Only in this order and succession can we carry out and validate the distinction between *ecclesia docens* and *ecclesia audiens* in accordance with all that we have learnt about the relationship of the Church to the Word of God. The second necessary reservation in face of the Roman Catholic interpretation of this distinction consists in this, that by the teaching and hearing Church we are not, of course, to understand two mutually exclusive classes of people to whom are assigned functions that are not interchangeable : on the one side the ecclesiastical teaching office in the form of an episcopate comprised in the papacy and represented by a clergy marked off by its priestly consecration, and on the other side the remaining members of the Church as a whole. We rather understand the Church in the totality of its members to be both a hearing and a teaching Church. There is, therefore, no one to whom special responsibility and functions are on the one hand to be attributed, or on the other hand to be spared or denied. The occasional coincidence of this distinction with the distinction between two classes of people can have only a passing technical significance. The distinction between esoteric and exoteric, theologians and laity, office-bearers and congregation can have no fundamental bearing. Basically, there is on both sides only a common responsibility and participation. All this applies equally to the function of dogmatics in its twofold sense. Dogmatics as a function of the hearing Church, in its submission to the norm to which the hearing Church is subject, is the challenge to the whole teaching Church to be again a hearing Church before attempting to teach, and the esoterics, theologians or office-bearers will ill understand their technical functions if they, of all people, try to elude this challenge. Putting the matter the other way round, dogmatics as defined by the subject-matter given to the teaching Church and as a function of the teaching Church, turns to the hearing Church, indeed to the whole hearing Church, with the invitation to undertake new teaching and preaching, and to make the confession which is inseparable from recognition. But again there are no exoterics, " laity " or " congregation " who can interpret their allotted technical classification as hearers to mean that they have no share or only a passive share in the service of teaching. What a misuse it is of the idea of the congregation to understand by it a group of mere spectators privileged, or disqualified, as such! The truth is that theologians cannot teach except as the mouthpiece of the congregation of Jesus Christ, which does not in any sense consist of listeners only, but of those who, as listeners, are themselves teachers. In this connexion dogmatics is to be understood as a call to the coherence of both sides, and therefore to the unity of the body of Christ.

The fact from which dogmatics starts and to which it returns is the human word of Church proclamation. This fact is equivocal and therefore dogmatics is necessary. The goal of the dogmatic task is that the human word of Church proclamation should no longer be equivocally, but unequivocally, pure doctrine, that there should no longer be various opinions about what men say to each other in this matter but that it should be said and heard as the Word of God. The circumstances are that in the proclamation of the Church men undertake to impart to other men communications about God and man's relation to Him, instruction and advice about this relationship and therefore about their own inner and outer life. This is done with a reference to the Bible and a dependence on its received interpretation, but also under the conditions of the external and intellectual historical situation in which they and their hearers are placed, under the conditions of their own personal being and willing, experience and insight, and subject to the limits thus imposed upon them. The ambiguity arising from these circumstances does not consist in the fact that the position in which preachers and hearers are together placed is in one way or another unfavourable, misleading, oppressive and adverse to these communications, directions and advice. It will always be adverse in some way. Again, the ambiguity does not consist in the fact that the sincerity, genuineness, depth and power of the human word of the preacher may leave something to be desired. This will always be the case in some sense. Even at worst, these possibilities cannot prevent the proclamation of the Church from being pure doctrine. The ambiguity arises rather from the fact that even under the most favourable personal and historical conditions the reference to, and dependence on, the Bible may rest upon and consist in an illusion, that instead of the proclamation of the Word of God a very human error may be the secret of the whole process. The ambiguity is not overcome even when we have reason to note the fellowship of preachers and hearers as evidence of a very vital Church life, and in particular to regard the preacher as a very earnest, tested and experienced Christian.

On the contrary, Church history abounds in examples of the fact that when the relationship of Church proclamation to the Bible rests upon and consists in an illusion, the resultant errors may be compatible with Church fellowship which is impressively vital, and the piety of a preacher which is impressively sincere, so that the only effect is to increase the ambiguity of the whole phenomenon.

We might acquiesce in the ambiguity of this phenomenon, as we must acquiesce in the ambiguity of many another earthly phenomenon, if the proclamation of the Church were not involved, and if the Church had not received the promise that this phenomenon should be identical with the Word of God or, rather, that the Word of God should be identical with it. It is this promise which makes the ambiguity intolerable. It is this promise which makes so dreadful the possibility that Church proclamation might err and lead to error. It is this promise which calls for the unambiguity of pure doctrine.

It is this promise which will not allow us to remain content with a system of doctrine like that of Schleiermacher. For there the phenomenon of Church proclamation is finally understood from and in itself, that is, from and in its connexion with very different types of human proclamation, and its relation to man as historical being in general. And it is always criticised and rectified from the standpoint of its own immanent laws. This dogmatic programme becomes manifestly inadequate when it is realised that, by reason of this promise, Church proclamation is to be classed with Jesus Christ as the external divine Word and with the prophetic and apostolic witness to Him, and that therefore our phenomenon stands in unprecedentedly close relation to the fact that God has spoken, speaks, and will speak. Seen in this connexion, the Church as the subject of proclamation obviously cannot acquiesce in a type of reflection which consists only in conversation with itself. In fact, both itself and its proclamation —even proclamation which objectively and subjectively takes place under the most favourable conditions—are now confronted (and this is what makes the anthropological attempt of Schleiermacher's theology impossible) by a Word of God, different from it and yet pressing towards identity with it. It is therefore faced with the unavoidably acute question, whether it will serve or not serve the Word of God, whether it will accept or deny this irruptive identity, whether it will submit or not to the law which this irruption involves.

Dogmatics now becomes necessary as a critique of this ambiguous phenomenon. At one and the same time it disciplines and honours preachers and their hearers by telling them that in their work they are not left alone. They are not left alone with the favourable or less favourable conditions of their work. Nor are they left alone with its immanent laws and the knowledge obtainable from the understanding of these laws.

Certainly the object of this critique is that Church proclamation should speak of God better. The implications of such an improvement are far reaching and go beyond all the improvement that can be achieved within Church proclamation as a human activity by human standards and in man's own strength. Or, rather, the aim is an improvement deriving from and effected by the fact that the human reflection and action that are seriously demanded are confronted in all their problematic character by quite another reflection and action— that is, God's. From Church proclamation, and therefore from both preacher and hearers, it is required that they should accept as the exclusive possibility and the exclusive norm of their reflection and action the fact that, in what Church preaching says of God, God Himself speaks for Himself. It is on this fundamental truth that dogmatics has to insist in the matter of Church proclamation and its content. It is not a call to piety, to vitality, to sincerity or to depth, but to the realisation of the happening which transcends Church proclamation as such : God has spoken, speaks now and will again speak ; and its aim is that in this realisation this transcendent happening should become immanent within the Church's proclamation, and that proclamation itself should be what in virtue of the promise (the promise which has to be continually apprehended by the Church, in faith and in the obedience of faith) it already is—the Word of God. It is inevitable that in calling the Church to this realisation, dogmatics also calls it to piety, vitality, sincerity and depth. But what this really involves can be seen and understood only as a consequence of this realisation, not as the predicate of the human, but as the predicate of the new divine Subject of Church proclamation. Therefore we may not seek and aspire to it as such and in itself ; it can become actual only as this new subject enters and finds obedience from the old subject which now accepts its service. This does not mean that dogmatics confronts Church proclamation and declares : this or that must be preached. Dogmatics consists in the reminder that over and above the content of all human speech and its possibility what is to be said has plainly been said already and will be said. Therefore in regard to the question : What is to be preached ? there can be no question of the Church trying to give the answer itself, as though it had of itself the power to approve, select and speak. The truth is that in regard to the content of its preaching the Church has to recognise and assimilate and adjust itself to the answer which is already given. Once again, it is a question of realisation. And again it is inevitable that when dogmatics insists upon the necessity of this realisation, it specifies certain subjects of preaching, that is, makes it clear and experimentally evident with reference to certain themes in what consists the recognition and assimilation of the answer which already exists beyond all human speech and its possibility. But this is only another way of saying that the content of Church proclamation is not really the predicate of the human, but of the divine Subject, which the human subject with the content of its speech has to serve. Dogmatic work, the construction of formulæ, dogmatic teaching and systematisation, consists in the reminder of the necessity for this realisation in Church proclamation. The Church teaches. But this fact is not self-grounded or self-effected, nor is it inherently good or inherently capable of improvement. It is not the function of dogmatics to establish this fact, to confirm it, or to repeat it at a higher level of gnosis or philosophical reflection. Again, dogmatics has neither the authority nor the capacity fundamentally to transcend this fact, confronting the Church and its purely human speech as the possessor or representative of the true Word of God, and thus creating a new and better fact. It belongs itself to the teaching Church, indeed to the Church which teaches in human speech. But within the framework of the Church which thus teaches, and in complete solidarity with it, it reminds the Church (and itself first of all), that there exists prior to and above and after every *ego dico* and *ecclesia dicit* a *haec dixit Dominus* ; and the aim of Church proclamation is that this *haec dixit Dominus* should prevail and triumph not only before, above and after, but *in* every *ego dico* and *ecclesia dicit*. That such a confrontation and reminder is possible ; that this can be said in the Church and to the Church ; or, again, that in its work it is not left alone or left to itself and to the legalism belonging to its activity ; and that such an illumination and penetration of its word is possible from outside, that is, from the fundamentally transcendent Word of God—all this is what we term the objective possibility of pure doctrine—the objective possibility which reflects the reality of the promise that the proclamation of the Church is the true Word of the true God.

The teaching and hearing Church of any epoch cannot possibly comfort itself with this promise if its reality is not mirrored in this objective possibility in such a way that the confrontation and reminder of which it is conscious can be genuinely and concretely realised. The new divine Subject really has to encounter and judge the old human subject. The relationship between the two, the intrusion and breaking forth of the transcendent from there to here, really has to be visible and palpable. The instruction of the teaching Church really has to take place. Obviously the objective possibility of pure doctrine is untenable in practice, the reflected promise is itself meaningless, doubtful, and in any case unrecognisable, if the transcendent Word of God does not stand over against the Church concretely and palpably, as something to which appeal can be made. Left alone with the eternal Logos as such, the Church is, in fact, just as much alone and left to itself as, in spite of the presence of the eternal Logos, the world is alone and left to itself apart from the incarnation of the Logos in Jesus Christ, revealing the fact of its creation by Him and bringing it into relationship with Himself by His self-revelation. It is because

26

the Word of God is Jesus Christ, and Jesus Christ is for all time attested in Holy Scripture, that the promise that God Himself will speak in the proclamation of the Church is recognisable and meaningful. It is for this reason that the objective possibility of pure doctrine, the possibility of the confrontation and reminder to which we refer, has practical importance and can be genuinely and concretely realised. It is for this reason that the instruction of the teaching Church can really happen, because it is for this reason that the invasion and irruption of the transcendent, the connexion between the divine and human subjects of Church proclamation, is visible and palpable. It is because the Word of God has a first form in revelation, and a second in Scripture, that it can and must be affirmed that it assumes a third form in proclamation. For this reason the critical question is addressed to proclamation in every age, whether and to what extent it is really the divine Word and not merely a human word, and therefore as a human word really serves the divine Word. For this reason the question is not put idly or arbitrarily, or from motives of human scepticism or uncertainty. For the same reason it cannot be answered arbitrarily, i.e., according to the private opinion and appraisal of the Church or of individuals in the Church. For this reason there has to be in the Church such a thing as dogmatics ; the challenge to effective realisation has to be sounded ; and the challenge can have only one definite meaning, the demanded realisation can take only the one definite course which is already indicated by the first two forms of the Word of God. That Church proclamation is the Word of God means that God speaks as much for Himself in Church proclamation as He has spoken, speaks and will speak for Himself in Jesus Christ and in the prophets and apostles as witnesses to Jesus Christ. Therefore the formal task of dogmatics in regard to Church proclamation consists in confronting it with its own law in all its transcendence, in reminding it that it is the Word of God because Jesus Christ and He alone speaks in the prophetic and apostolic witness.

Dogmatics is, therefore, a call to order and unity in the Church. It is not an indeterminate call. It is one which is quite definitely determined by the existence of the first two forms of the Word of God. And if we are to define the character of this call in its formal sense, we must say that it is first a call to the teaching Church to hear, that is, to listen to Jesus Christ as attested in Holy Scripture. The teaching of the Church is a human action, and as such it is as little guaranteed as any other human action against slipping from obedience into disobedience, from the doing of the Word of God into the doing of human will or fancy.

Church teaching always exists in specific forms, i.e., in sequences of thoughts and ideas which specifically choose, emphasise and underline, or again deny and suppress. If all is well the one aim of these sequences is to explain and apply Holy Scripture, and therefore to proclaim the divine revelation. But *in concreto* they always owe their origin and persistence to the specific currents of Church life (conditioned by the general historical situation), which emanate from the concrete personality of individual preachers and the character of their congregations. Let us suppose the ideal case. We have a form of teaching which in its origin and first appearance, in spite of and in all its human conditioning, can only be traced back to the faithful and true hearing of the Word of God, so that what it says may be defined as the realisation of pure doctrine and as the unadulterated proclamation of the Word of God. Why should we not say so at once, even if we can do so legitimately only in faith ? But then the teaching goes beyond the stage of origin and first appearance. It passes from the first mouth to the second. Or it is even stated a second or third time by its first exponent. And even in the ideal case, it inevitably becomes dubious. For there is uncertainty whether this still happens in the originally faithful and true hearing of the Word of God. Perhaps the teacher concerned and the teaching Church which follows him and uses his formula are already listening to themselves : to the fine and strong and timely things which they themselves have thought about the matter ; to the joyful and pleasant sound which the words in question had in their mouths ; to the echo of the approval and applause which they encountered ; to the consequences of being publicly committed through speaking in this way to the persuasive power of a rapt congregation which wants to hear again and again what has been so wonderfully stated. Even affirmations, denials, syntheses and reservations which, as made in the original hearing of the Word, were well founded and legitimately impressive and—we will suppose —the purest doctrine, now take on a certain independence, or appear only as facile arguments, useful stones in structures with which, as originating in the hearing of the Word of God, they had nothing to do, and which perhaps themselves derive from quite another source than the hearing of the Word of God. In short, the equivocal phenomenon of Church proclamation has again developed from what we will suppose was the unequivocally pure doctrine of the beginning. This development cannot be arrested. This is how it has always gone at the crises of Church history. As such, the teaching of the Church is not guaranteed even for a single moment against the possibility of immediately losing what we will suppose is its recently attained purity, and of again becoming something very different from the speech which obediently listens. A formula may be ever so simple, clear and powerful, an exposition and sequence of thoughts may be ever so transparent and compelling, but it is not guaranteed against this risk. It cannot be protected by any personality, however trustworthy, or any fellowship of believers, however faithful. Here at the very centre of its life the Church experiences the fact that it is in the world. Its proclamation begins, as we will suppose, in the Spirit, but immediately and at every point it shows a tendency to end in the flesh. And, of course, the realities of ecclesiastical history never correspond to this assumed ideal case. In reality, it is inevitable that even in the genesis of this form of doctrine the Word of God is partly heard, and it is partly not heard, but drowned by very different voices ; that unequivocally pure doctrine is not, then, attained, and that instead there is a fluctuating struggle between various, greater and smaller, more or less visible, more or less dangerous ambiguous quantities. At all periods the historical reality of the teaching Church has been necessarily characterised by a continuous embarrassment between various types of doctrine distinguished from each other not as black and white, but by the fact that in the action and reaction of their formation the Word was heard more or less, and that there was more or less admixture of these alien factors. If the Church is only a teaching Church, how can it be understood, and how can it understand itself, except as a Church involved in an unceasing and general lapse from the Word of God, in a more or less pious and well-intentioned resistance to the Word of God ? A more optimistic view may be held, based on the fact that the common source in the hearing of the Word of God is never altogether repudiated, but that something of obedience and pure doctrine is everywhere present and expressed. But even if this is true, even if we must not forget the *providentia Dei* over the *confusio hominum*, it must not be overlooked that we are still brought back to our point of departure. We are confronted by the ambiguity of the phenomenon of Church proclamation. And the Church cannot accept this ambiguity if it is not to deny the promise given to it in Holy Scripture and therefore to betray its very life, and in that way lose its faith in divine providence—unless, of course, when it speaks of God in this connexion, instead of thinking of the Father, the Son and the Holy Ghost who have been revealed to us in a way which binds and commits us, it wants to think at once of an obscure God of history who wills chaos because in the last resort He Himself is nothing but chaos.

If the teaching of the Church is an uncertain action from the human standpoint, the teaching Church will not only have to have heard, if it is to continue to be the Church, but it will constantly have to hear again—not to hear any kind of voice, but to hear specifically the voice which has called the Church into being and to which all Church proclamation must give some sort of answer. If it is not to disown the promise and in that way cease to be the Church, the Church is committed to a struggle against the acute chronic diseases from which its proclamation must constantly suffer. But this being the case, its only resource is to seize the weapon of continually listening. But it must listen in such a way that its whole life is put in question. It must listen in a readiness that its whole life should be assailed, convulsed, revolutionised and reshaped. It must listen for the sake of its teaching. For even allowing that it will not be a perfect work, a new doctrine can be rightly propounded only in so far as it proceeds from a new act of listening. But the word to which it listens must always be the Word of God. It actually has to go back to its starting-point. It has to show the self-denial and determination to start all over again from that point. Of course, it has to do this as the Church which is marked by all that has existed and occurred in the interval, not in unfaithfulness but in faithfulness, not in ingratitude but in gratitude, not with violence but with regard for the various forms of teaching which have so far been granted to it with more or less human clarity or obscurity, in which and with which it has lived up to the present—yet radically prepared for the fact that to-day, to-morrow and the day after the whole of its treasure will again have to be enlightened and illuminated, assessed and weighed by the Word of God. The redemption of Church proclamation consists in its purification, and its purification consists in the fact that it is proclamation of what has been heard afresh. It takes place as the Church which teaches Jesus Christ turns from teaching to hearing Him. This is the necessity which dogmatics has to represent. Its task is to summon to an active consideration of this necessity.

From this point of view it may be seen why of all the various theological disciplines dogmatics has so specially difficult and ungrateful a task and part to perform. It is natural for men, and also for the Church, to prefer to be undisturbed in their proclamation. The action of the teaching Church, like all human action, has a natural momentum in virtue of which it prefers to be as far as possible unimpeded in its course and development. How can the Church like being told that at the first, or at latest the second stage, it becomes guilty of a deviation, and therefore needs to pause and change direction from teaching to listening ? How can it like hearing that it may be attacked and shattered by its original point of departure and that it must begin all over again at that point ? The doctrinal forms to which we have referred have necessarily a certain stability which is not at all to be explained merely as the result of human laziness and self-love, but is certainly connected with the fact that it once listened, and indeed listened to the Word of God. Religious loyalty and human stability of character would seem to bid men hold fast to the formulæ, structures and developments of thought which have originated in obedience and later proved their value. Whole generations of older preachers and hearers may have been bound to such specific forms of doctrine, and with the very best meaning and intention. Putting it the other way round, such a form of doctrine may be the latest novelty (or at least was so yesterday), the triumphant word of the moment, to which all or most of the younger preachers and hearers are about to adhere. It is not natural for men freely to allow themselves to be (repeatedly perhaps) resummoned out of these old or new loyalties. And yet this is the very thing that dogmatics necessarily expects of the teaching Church in every age. It is inevitable, especially in more peaceful situations, in times and places when it enjoys a certain prosperity, and in face of successful personalities and prevailing tendencies, that it should incur opprobrium by introducing an alien and even hostile factor to disturb the peace and activity of the Church's life. But the fulfilment of its formal function undoubtedly means that it has to confront the Church, as a whole and in detail, with questions pulling it up short—not only in respect of traditional development, but also of new movements which have perhaps been adopted with enthusiasm. So far as it is to hear, the Church will undoubtedly have to pause, to stand relatively aside from its own movement and activity, and as far as possible to be ready to face up to incisive questions. It may be that the benefit which accrues from this challenge, the comfort and consolidation which the Church gains from submitting to it, are more noticeable in situations of internal confusion and stagnation or external oppression, when the Church is more open to the suggestion, and to the hope implied in it, that it can renew its teaching on the basis of a new hearing, and to enjoy the hope implied. But however that may be, we always have to reckon with a certain tension between dogmatics and the teaching Church which it addresses, and in every time and place it is essential that dogmatics should not itself grow weary and allow itself to be discouraged. In the long run, if only it is a real summons to hear, it will always penetrate in some way, because its concern is too closely implicated with the concern of the Church itself to be finally overlooked.

Dogmatics can give this summons with so much the more authority and emphasis the more it realises its own solidarity with the teaching Church. It must not speak and think in the manner of a timeless Church discipline, but with full participation in the energies and hopes, the cares and struggles of the Church of its own age. Again, its summons will gain in force the more it can make clear that it does not plead for a hearing on its own account or in the interests of ecclesiastical intellectualism as opposed to voluntarism. Above and beyond all such interests (which by all relative considerations are still carnal), it does so for the sake of Jesus Christ as Lord of the Church. Therefore it does not demand anything but what from the depths of its own inner being and basis the Church necessarily demands of itself.

Its concern must be that Jesus Christ should again be heard in His Church as the Lord of the Church. This is its only possible concern. The fact that it is so always justifies the claim of dogmatics even when it is not made effectively as it should be. But just because of this fact there is danger on both sides in the element of tension between dogmatics and the teaching Church, in the occasional gnostic arrogance of dogmatics over against the teaching Church, and in the occasional stubbornness of the teaching Church over against dogmatics. When it resists dogmatics, is the Church really refusing to listen to the voice of its Lord ? And how is it going to excuse that ? But perhaps dogmatics is not demanding a hearing for the voice of the Lord of the Church, but only for itself, and in that case is not the Church justified in refusing to be disturbed by this type of dogmatics ? But again, is it not disastrous if it then tries to escape the rightful claim of dogmatics ?

The hearing which dogmatics must demand from the teaching Church is a fresh hearing of the promise which is the basis of the Church and its message. The Word of God became flesh. The prophetic and apostolic witness has been proclaimed in the world. The Church itself has its origin and continuance on the basis and in the power of this happening. Therefore the Church has the promise that Jesus Christ wills to be present in its midst and to speak through it, that this presence and voice of His is to be its life, and that living in Him and through Him it is to be the light of the world. To give effect to this promise and to be this Church is its only duty, as well as the only necessity of its life. It is, then, the only law by which it must judge itself.

We can summarise this law once again in the words of Paul's charge to Archippus in Col. 4¹⁷ : Βλέπε τὴν διακονίαν, ἣν παρέλαβες ἐν κυρίῳ, ἵνα αὐτὴν πληροῖς.

But this law has to be heard continually in the Church and by the Church, if it is to find fulfilment. This law is already transgressed, and at every moment and in every situation the Church ceases to be the Church, if it denies the necessity of this hearing, or if, in face of the promise on which it is founded and by which it is maintained, it tries to fall back upon something that it has to teach without first having had to hear again. For how, then, as the earthly body, can it give to its heavenly Head the honour due to Him ? How then can its action be anything but a revolt against Him ? The Church, as the Church, can never do otherwise in any time or situation but to allow its existence and especially its proclamation to be judged, and itself to judge them, by whether it is the ministry which it has received from its Lord. And this judgment will be a true and beneficial and salutary judgment only when it does not consist in a self-selected opinion, as though it is within the Church's competence to decide about the character of the service required of it, but when the Lord of the Church Himself is allowed to judge what its members do by whether their service reflects His own presence and Word, and so whether it is pure doctrine or not.

Habentes regulam ipsam veritatem et in aperto positum de Deo testimonium (Irenaeus *C.o.h.* II 28, 1), we must examine ourselves and also warn the " sheep " against those who are " wolves," *similia quidem nobis loquentes, dissimilia vero sentientes* (*ib.* I Preface).

What the Church does and teaches ceases to be service of this kind the moment, as we have already put it, it slips out of obedience. But slips in what sense ? The fundamental answer is : In the sense of the self-will, the self-righteousness and therefore inevitably the idolatry of the men who compose it. All the Church's members have this self-will implanted in them, and therefore *in nuce* they have self-righteousness and idolatry as well. At every moment and in every situation the danger threatens that members of the Church may want the Word of God without God, bringing it under their power and understanding, and applying it according to their own good pleasure. When Church proclamation is placed by heresy in the service of specific alien interests, when for this end it is intentionally given an alien sense, when its development is palpably distorted by an intentional self-alienation from the Church, it is only a visible outbreak of the danger which constantly threatens the Church, even where there is no such intention and it would be repudiated with horror. No heresy has ever had the original intention of being heresy ; it has become so only when and where a first unintended lapse from obedience has not been noted and resisted in time. For this reason the Church must not wait until the outbreak of open heresy before judging its activity and teaching by its rightness as service of Jesus Christ, before being ready to listen afresh.

It cannot be overlooked how many bitter and painful struggles against heresy would have been avoided if the Church had been on its guard at the right time, at the moment when heresy was still in its early stage, if not of innocence at least of unself-consciousness, or if self-examination, the call to listen again, and a readiness to do so, had been a living reality in the Church in the more peaceful preceding period. We may boldly affirm that if dogmatics had always been on the watch and its claim had always been heeded, there would have been no need for councils, dogmas, anathema, reformation and schism. The fact that these evils were necessary was the inevitable consequence of ignoring the summons to listen or unwillingness to act upon it or a combination of both. There is no sense in deploring the fact that they did become necessary and continually do so. The fact of conscious, outspoken heresy makes them necessary. They are a sign of the penitence and conflict and renewal which the Church may not spare itself once error has crept into its midst. What we can do is to make it clear that although it is useless to deplore these things if we do not know how to avoid them, they could have been avoided if in face of the danger which continually threatens the Church had always allowed itself to be called to heed the promise. In other words, the existence of an orderly Church dogmatics is the unfailingly effective and only possible instrument of peace in the Church.

Before there is such a thing as heresy in the Church, there exists a possibility of forgetting that even the Church which teaches correctly cannot teach in its own name and competence, from the resources of its own wisdom and self-determination. Once this is forgotten, then the position which Jesus Christ occupies in its midst becomes only honorary. He ceases to be the actual ruler of the Church. It bears His name, but in practice it is the Church that governs itself by its own will and action. But where this is the case, every word of the Church's proclamation is a deviation, even if anything seriously deserving the name of heresy is still in the remote distance. The Church has to listen, therefore, in order that this forgetfulness may be combatted at the central point where Jesus Christ Himself reminds the Church of Himself. Again, before heresy arises, there exists even in a Church that teaches correctly the possibility of trifling, as it were, with the work of proclamation. The truth which the Church has to preach will not be the truth of God if it does not have also its own characteristic beauty. But this very beauty can seduce the Church into treating it as we do other beautiful things, i.e., a dilettante contemplation and enjoyment. But it is beautiful only in order that its work may be done all the more joyfully. If instead of calling to decision it becomes an object of contemplation, it ceases to be the truth. The God of whom we make for ourselves pictures is no longer the living God. Deviation has then taken place even though there is no heresy, or only an immediate preparation for heresy. The Church has to listen in order that a swift end may be put to all mere contemplation in its proclamation wherever it swaggers into view. Again, there exists in the Church, before heresy arises, just the opposite possibility that a false moralistic earnestness will dominate proclamation, as though it is man's affair whether it is victorious or defeated, as though man has to make the Word of God powerful by the weight of his own will, as though it lies in man's hands to compel decisions about it. When this is the case the Church strengthens itself to serve the Word of God, as though it is a matter of the organisation and running of a business, or the instituting and carrying through of a great law-suit, or the deployment and operations of an army. But, again, it is impossible to handle the truth in this way. As a rule, this kind of ecclesiastical earnestness involves a trimmed and therefore a truncated version of the truth. It may not be guilty of actual heresy, but it presupposes a deviation which sooner or later will lead to heresy. Therefore the Church has to listen in order to lose the taste for this ecclesiastical earnestness and to become genuinely earnest, so earnest that it is free to consider the necessary objectivity of its action quite unreservedly in the humorous light of the truth that absolutely nothing can be done in our own strength.

The real formal task of dogmatics has particular relevance to such pre-heretical deviations. Over against their possibility, it reminds us of the possibility of listening to the voice of Jesus Christ. To react clear-sightedly and sharply against such possibilities and at the right

point and in the right sense to oppose to them the other possibility of
listening is the proper art of dogmatics, at least on its formal side.
The more quickly, intimately and penetratingly it reacts in this way
against the Church that still teaches correctly, the better it will be
for the whole Church. In dogmatics we do not render any real service
in regard to the teaching of the Church which it has to address, if we
represent this teaching as a confused mixture of true, false and partially
false proclamation. We get this kind of picture if only for a moment
we confront the doctrines of the Church as an individual critical
spectator. But this is just what we must not and cannot legitimately
do as dogmaticians. And it is, of course, even worse if we try to
approach the task of dogmatics with the presupposition that the rest
of the teaching Church is more or less involved in a lapse into heresy.
For the dogmatician as for the Christian generally, the standpoint of
the despairing spectator is quite impossible, however many reasons
he may have for it. The presuppositions of the dogmatician with
regard to the teaching Church cannot in any sense be those of a personal judgment upon it. He must realise his solidarity with it and
take as primary the unambiguous presupposition that in it there is
correct teaching. When he does this, he is not referring to himself,
or to this or that teacher who in his own judgment teaches correctly.
Nor is he optimistically ignoring the many signs which point in quite
the opposite direction. He is expressing the confidence that this is
the Church which stands under the divine promise and in which this
promise has up to the present proved its truth. He can, it may be
hoped, testify to this, in relation both to himself and others. He
finds it confirmed in the great decisions of the Church against the
heresies of the past. But in any case he believes it, because the promise
has been made to himself and others and all who are in the Church
by the Word of God itself. This is the first thing which the teaching
Church ought in all circumstances to hear from the dogmatician—not
a reminder of all the dangers to which it is exposed, but of the fact
that without any merit or value of its own it is in good hands and
therefore on the right road. From this first assumption, and, so to
speak, in its shadow, dogmatics will proceed to admit the second
assumption already discussed : that in the Church men—himself and
all other men—can err, i.e., that they are exposed to the risk of lapsing
from obedience. The dogmatician will understand this possibility
primarily at first hand, that is, as a possibility for his own thinking
and speaking. And on this basis he will be sensitive, clear-sighted
and relentless for its symptoms in the life of the rest of the Church.
The more firmly he is rooted in that first assumption of faith, that in
virtue of the promise and thus upheld by the grace of God the Church
teaches the truth, so much the more sensitive, clear-sighted and relentless he will be in regard to every slightest deviation—not with the
joy of a kind of police detection, but in the realisation that, just where

by God's grace everything is made good, everything is really endangered by human self-will resisting grace, so that everything has to be safeguarded. In this alertness and vigilance, dogmatics will not finally be guided by the memory of ancient decisions of the Church against heresies. As heresies they are judged and overcome and must not return, unless the Church receives from the voice of its Master a fresh illumination compelling it to go back on those old decisions. So long as this is not the case, dogmatics has every reason to take those decisions seriously, to profit by them in regard to the possible deviations of the present, and thus to remind the teaching Church of the voice of its Lord in such a way as to remind it of its own continuity. And now we come to the third and last assumption of dogmatics which harks back to the first : that the teaching Church can and will hear the Word of God afresh. Without this basic confidence, it would be useless to call upon it to do so. In all its human frailty the teaching Church has to be seen and understood as the Church of Jesus Christ which is not forsaken by His Spirit. Thus, it has to be seen and understood, not as any kind of society which to-day we may treat optimistically and to-morrow pessimistically, but as the society which already belongs to Jesus Christ and which will listen to Him when it is addressed in His name. The call of dogmatics to the teaching Church, like Christian preaching to the congregation, must not reckon with the possibility of absolute opposition and resistance. The Church may be very unruly at times, but dogmatics must presume that in the last resort it can do nothing else but listen. Just because of this presumption, the call will have cogency and power, as does preaching in the congregation. It will therefore be radically different from the many other challenges which are made in the world.

At bottom, the deviation of the teaching Church in face of which dogmatics must call to a fresh hearing of the voice of Jesus Christ is only the pre-heretical deviation. We have shown that in this matter dogmatics must use the experiences and decisions of the past in regard to ancient heresies. It will, therefore, remind the teaching Church where it stands with reference to this past, and with the same reference, along what lines it may not develop in the future without betraying itself. Therefore, as Evangelical dogmatics it will necessarily involve opposition both to Roman Catholicism and also to the Neo-Protestantism which is repudiated by the decisions of the Reformers. And it will continually have to unfold this opposition at every point. But the unfolding of this opposition can never really be more than a means to the end of awakening the Church to a new obedience to its Lord and a new loyalty to itself. If dogmatics treats Roman Catholicism and Neo-Protestantism and, reaching further back, Arianism and Pelagianism as heresies, it does not do so, of course, without independent examination and judgment. But it also does not do so on its own authority. It does so on the basis of decisions made in faith by the teaching Church itself, and never subsequently revoked. Its concern can be only to remind the teaching Church to maintain these decisions, to take seriously what it has itself declared and never revoked. Its concern can be only to make clear what its position involves in face of the possible deviations of to-day. And it cannot do this in virtue of an abstract conservatism, but only in the meaning and context of its call that the Church has to listen every day afresh to its Lord alone. This, then, is the bar of judgment where the decisions which the Church has taken already in faith have to be re-tested, where alone they can receive confirmation, and where alone they can be accepted in obedience. Mere loyalty to them cannot itself and as such protect the Church against the possible deviations of to-day.

It cannot be the business of dogmatics to establish and proscribe a new heresy as such, to stigmatise individual personalities and movements in the Church as heretical, i.e., as standing outside the Church. If it has to oppose polemically certain types of teaching, personalities and movements, basically this can mean only that it discloses in them the danger of deviation and of the emergence of a new heresy. Often this will have to be done by showing that they are a renewal and repetition of old errors long since rejected by the Church. Sometimes, then, it will have to note that a particular doctrine is nothing but a recurrence of this or that error, that the error has long since been rejected as a heresy, not by dogmatics, but by the Church, that for many years past the Church has found it quite impossible to proclaim it, and that therefore it can only be repudiated afresh. Of course, we cannot exercise too much care and discretion when in the course of dogmatic investigation and exposition we fasten historical antecedents of this kind on contemporary teachers. Nor can we be too cautious in attaching the labels of ancient heresies. For the real errors which it is desired to check in this way may not really be touched by these analogies with previous historical heresies. In point of fact, we may be dealing with new errors which have never previously existed. Errors of this kind may be characterised and combatted by dogmatics as an increasing danger ; but they cannot be condemned and defined as heresies destructive of the Church, so long as the Church itself has not made any new decision with regard to them. Dogmatics can indeed prepare for this decision, but it cannot try to make it of itself and on its own authority. It can be just as little its business to do this as to raise new credal statements to the rank of dogma.

As a warning against concretely applying decisions against older heresies, or making arbitrary observations and judgments upon new ones, it is salutary to recall the very harsh connotation which the concept of heresy had in the Early Church. According to Polan heretics are : *dissimulati hostes Christi et ecclesiae purae, qui Christum sub ipsius nomine oppugnant.* More precisely defined : *Haereticus est antichristus, qui dogma aliquod erroneum, pugnans cum sacris literis et fidei aliquem articulum oppugnans atque convellens, quod sibi sive sponte sua sive aliena seductione delegit, quamvis convictus autoritate verbi divini etiam in* *conscientia sua, voluntaria animi obfirmatione pertinaciter tuetur.* And the *mores haereticorum* in which this *voluntas pertinax* is so palpable that we have no option but to describe and treat the persons in question as heretics are described in this way in allusion to definite passages of Scripture: *Fascinant alios ne obsequantur veritati; consilia ineunt de Christo e medio tollendo et interficiendis cultoribus eius sinceris; persequuntur Christum Jesum tum in ipso, tum in membris ipsius; prohibent annunciare verbum Dei; ineunt cogitationes et consilia de tollendis et medio praeconibus veritatis (mihi credite semper iunctus cum falso est dogmate caedis amor); laudant tempora quibus idololatriae dediti fuerunt et calamitates publicas adscribunt omissioni seu neglectui sui idololatriae, quaeruntur ab aliis negligi religionem, quam ipsi gravissime violant ac prope evertunt; veritatem et sermonem Christi accipiunt carnaliter, ludificantur, exagitant; verbum Dei pervertunt et alio sensu accipiunt quam dictum est; offenduntur et ad iram concitantur verbo Dei, commendant maiores et patres et se illorum discipulos ac sectatores esse gloriantur et interim Christum et doctrinam eius damnant et diabolo adscribunt (Syn. Theol. chr.,* 1609, p. 3527 f., 3536 f.).* Now it cannot be disputed that this kind of thing has often enough existed in the Church (or, rather, at once and *per se* outside the Church), and that it still exists to-day. And there could be no sense in trying to interpret the notion of heresy in a less stringent way than that suggested here. But this very understanding of heresy must be a warning against a careless use or arbitrary application of the term where it is not demanded or authorised by a decision of the Church itself. Even orthodoxy itself discriminated between the heresy which consciously and in spite of better information attacks the articles of the creed, betraying in such *mores* its evil will, and the not incorrigible error in subordinate phrases which only indirectly affect the substance of the faith. Thus Polan issued an express warning (p. 3528) that neither truth nor love nor any divine command justifies us in branding at once as a heretic an erring thinker of this kind. There is also a declaration of Pope Innocent XI (1679) which deserves a hearing in this connexion: *Tandem, ut ab iniuriosis contentionibus doctores seu scholastici aut alii quicunque in posterum se abstineant et ut paci et caritati consulatur, idem Sanctissimus in virtute sanctae oboedientiae eis praecipit ut tam in libris imprimendis ac manuscriptis, quam in thesibus, disputationibus ac praedicationibus caveant ab omni censura et nota, nec non a quibuscunque conviciis contra eas propositiones, quae adhuc inter catholicos hinc inde controvertuntur, donec a sancta sede, re cognita, super iisdem propositionibus iudicium proferatur (Denz.* No. 1216).

Dogmatics summons the teaching Church to listen again to the voice of Jesus Christ. Its business, therefore, is to issue a warning whenever it sees a threat to the obedience which Church proclamation must render. Its warning must be loud and clear. In face of possible aberrations it must show the threatened consequences and indicate the necessary decisions. And it must not allow itself to shrink from this task. But it does not have to judge, as it does not have to define articles of the faith. The most that can be said is that it may have to repeat the judgment and confession of the Church itself. Indeed, it may be constrained to repeat them according to its own insight and independent judgment.

2. THE DOGMATIC NORM

In its desire to summon the teaching Church to a fresh act of listening, dogmatics cannot speak down, as though to an inferior. The dogmatician can only place himself alongside the preacher and not over him. Basically, he can only do what the preacher does. That is, he can bring about the confrontation of the human word of Church proclamation with the divine Word of revelation in Holy Scripture only by himself appropriating this human word, not, of course, with the intention of contrasting it to the message of the listening Church—the special service of dogmatics in this respect is, as we shall see, a different one—but with the intention of examining its correctness and validity as serving the Word of God. The question which preaching must constantly bear in mind as the basic and controlling question laid upon it becomes in dogmatics the fundamental question and an end in itself. Dogmatics is contrasted with and distinct from preaching only in so far as by this shift of emphasis from outside to inside, from teaching to listening, it makes this basic and controlling question evident and urgent. It is specifically a summons to listen only in so far as, within the sphere of the teaching Church and itself sharing in its teaching, it assumes the office of the listening Church, and in that capacity consciously brings into the foreground and makes its special theme the necessary relation of teaching to listening. It is not in the position to confront the teaching Church with the Word of God itself and to explain and apply its judgment upon it. It can bring to bear only a human, relative judgment. And it can do this only by itself submitting to the judgment of the Word of God, thus giving an example to the teaching Church (and in this consists *in concreto* the summons to which we have already referred) of what it demands from it : namely, a thinking and speaking about God which is controlled and determined, assailed and disquietened, delimited and confined by the norm of the Word of God. As dogmatics itself teaches by listening, it reminds the teaching Church of the listening which is so necessary. It attempts to do justice to its formal task by allowing itself to assume this form. It works at Church proclamation in accordance with the law laid upon the Church, by working upon itself in accordance with the same law.

From this point of view it may be seen why Schleiermacher's system of doctrine is unsatisfying. It is unsatisfying because there is no shift of emphasis from teaching to listening. There is, therefore, no indirect application of the transcendent norm of all teaching. There is no work at Church proclamation according to the law laid upon the Church. There is only the teaching Church and the human word of its proclamation. This word is lifted into the sphere of reflexion, of dialectical systematisation and anthropological philosophy. But it is not a human word which is criticised and regulated from above. A criticism and control can, of course, be seen even in Schleiermacher's system of doctrine. But it is always immanent. It is a dialogue of the teaching Church with itself. It is not corrected by an address which is made to the Church as such. For Schleiermacher's dogmatician only does what the preacher does. He does not ask for an outside qualification of the Church for its work. Even when analysing in a scientific and methodical manner, he is not subject to any ultimate norm. He confines himself to the observable facts of Church proclamation. The dogmatician who is confined in this way to the phenomena of Church proclamation can have nothing decisive to say to the preacher. He can render him every kind of service in regard to his own understanding of himself, to the enrichment and deepening of what he already does, and to the illumination of the horizon within which he in any case finds himself ; but he cannot in the true sense instruct him or widen his horizon. He has nothing to say to him in regard to the basic and controlling question which should accompany the action of a Church preacher. In regard to this question he will lull him to sleep instead of awakening him, which is what he ought to do if dogmatics is an essentially independent and significant function.

The function of dogmatics is this. Within the teaching Church, and therefore within the sphere of the human word of Church proclamation, which is in itself always threatened and in need of a higher qualification and attestation, it has to be a demonstration and proof, a sign and witness of the presence and validity of the Word of God, in whose service alone the human word can receive its qualification and attestation, if it is to receive it at all. Dogmatics cannot desire to be anything but a witness to this transcendent point of view, just as preaching itself and Holy Scripture, and even, on its human side, the revelation of God in Jesus Christ, can only be a witness to it. The dogmatician, too, has the Word of God only in virtue of the freedom and sovereignty of the Word itself, and therefore in the hiddenness of his faith and obedience which are the gift of the Word. In dogmatics, too, the Word of God can become visible only as the divine is reflected in human being and action. Dogmatics, too, can only be what it ought to be through God's sovereign action. But, by God's sovereign grace, dogmatics can be this definite sign co-ordinate with Church proclamation ; and its created human character will be the exemplary determination of its form as human thinking and speaking of God which is entirely determined by the revelation attested in Holy Scripture. It is this orientation which distinguishes dogmatic from undogmatic thinking and speaking. The distinction is not between divine and human thinking and speaking. It is within the human sphere. On the one hand, we have a thinking and speaking which are conscious of the problem and promise of Church proclamation, and on the other, a thinking and speaking which are unaware of it and pay no attention to it. Or, again, on the one hand we have a thinking and speaking which are critical as they are required to be, and on the other hand a thinking and speaking which are naive as they are not allowed to be in this connexion. Man remains man and God remains God even in this service to the cause of Church proclamation. And even here in human being and action everything depends on the free all-powerful Yes of the divine blessing. Dogmatics as such can only remind us of the essential relation of the human word of Church proclamation to the divine Word ; it cannot bring about and produce it. Moreover, it can remind us only in human words. Precisely by reminding us of the revelation attested in Holy Scripture and of the Word of the Father, Son and Holy Ghost, it reminds us of the barrier which is also a gateway. How else can it remind us of God's Word? But, again: How else can it do so except by showing us that the gateway is also a barrier? The supremely critical but supremely positive task of dogmatics is to remind the preacher and the teaching Church as a whole of this gateway and barrier, and always of both together. It is to watch at this place. It is to say to the unauthorised that—not by itself but by the nature of the case—they are held up. It is to say to the authorised that they can pass, again not because dogmatics authorises, but the transcendent authority, of which dogmatics has to. remind us. It is loudly to proclaim the decision which has been made at this gateway and barrier, and will be made again and again. Dogmatics must remind Christian preaching of its Lord. It does so *in concreto*, aware that it too can perform only a human service, by trying itself to think and speak as we have to think and speak when we remember the Lord.

The dogmatic norm, i.e., the norm of which dogmatics must remind Church proclamation, and therefore itself first of all, as the objective possibility of pure doctrine, can be no other than the revelation attested in Holy Scripture as God's Word. We shall have to speak, therefore, of the theonomy, and only of the theonomy, of Church proclamation and therefore of dogmatics itself. But again we have to bear in mind that the theonomy established, recognised and effectual in the human sphere is not in any sense an empty abstraction, which cannot be grasped in practice, or can be grasped only arbitrarily or accidentally. On the contrary, where it is established, recognised and accepted, it has a definite, relative form. Therefore in the sphere of the human thinking and speaking of the teaching Church, it is not the direct and simple counterpart of an autonomy of man. In our final section we shall certainly have to think about a human autonomy in dogmatics which is the correlative of theonomy. This will correspond to the doctrine of freedom in the Church, in which we attempted to understand the Evangelical Scripture principle on its subjective side, but only secondarily, when we had first tried to understand it on its objective side, in the doctrine of authority in the Church. It is not, then, our business to speak of autonomy in dogmatics until we have first made it clear that the theonomy of dogmatics has as its primary counterpart a heteronomy. The " other law," to which Christian proclamation and therefore first and foremost dogmatics itself is subject, can only be the law of God. Therefore the heteronomy to which we refer necessarily implies the theonomy. All the same, the attestation of God's law, and therefore the successful indication of the theonomy, demands a recognition of the indicative, declaratory and symbolic form of another concrete law. We have to be able to describe the definitive form of dogmatics and of dogmatically informed thinking and speaking, not only outwardly by means of the ultimate Word, but also—for the sake of the ultimate Word—by means of penultimate words and therefore concretely in the form of a law which man can conceive and hear directly.

In order to determine this concrete law we must first of all look back to what we said in § 20, 2 concerning authority under the Word. In that section we recognised a relative, indirect and formal authority in the Church, founded upon and conditioned and limited by what is in the last resort the only compelling and deciding authority of the Word of God. But obviously this authority is also a concrete norm for Church proclamation and therefore for dogmatics, and must now be expressly interpreted and understood from this point of view. The reservations, under which alone it is possible and legitimate to speak in this connexion, belong to the essence of the matter at issue. We do not speak of an absolute heteronomy. We speak of the concrete form of the theonomy of Church proclamation and dogmatics. We do not set up a second authority alongside that of the Word of God. We look through and beyond all that is here called authority to the sole and exclusive authority of the Word of God. But we speak indefinitely, i.e., not at all, of dogmatics as the function of the listening Church, if from the only too obvious fear of misunderstanding and misuse we refuse to point to the concrete demands in which the one demand of obedience to God's Word issues in the sphere of human thinking and speaking : to the specific heteronomous forms of the theonomy in which dogmatics and Church proclamation must acknowledge and respect their norm.

I. The first concrete requirement which is made of dogmatics, and in obedience to which it has to be an example to all Church proclamation, is that its investigations, formulæ and demonstrations must have a biblical character. We do not mean by this the primary, general and fundamental fact which applies to every movement of Church life. We do not mean that it should come into existence and be formed only in the Church as the home of the revelation attested in Scripture, and only in the obedience of faith to the Word of God and not otherwise. All this is, of course, true of the work of the dogmatician. But as from the absolute authority of Holy Scripture as the Word of God there results the relative authority of the biblical Canon, so from the absolute requirement of the obedience of faith to the prophetic and apostolic witness there results the relative requirement of a basic mode of thinking and speaking which corresponds with this obedience of faith. This is what we have to describe and understand as the biblicism or biblical attitude of dogmatics.

We call it " biblical " because it has its prototype and exemplar in the attitude of the biblical witnesses themselves, because it consists in the regard for and imitation of this prototype, that is, in the institution of a kinship between the outlook, approach and method of the biblical writers and those of the Church preacher and therefore of the dogmatician. The teaching Church cannot listen afresh to the

Word of God except in a fresh adoption of this biblical attitude. It is, therefore, called to adopt this attitude *in concreto*, when it is called to listen again to the Word of God. Hence it follows that dogmatics must take up this attitude as an example for Church proclamation.

By the attitude of the biblical witnesses, we mean that orientation of their thinking and speaking which is still that of witnesses to the revelation of God even though they are conditioned by their historical and biographical situation, by their particular speech and outlook, by their concrete situation and intention. They are witnesses. But that means that they are not observers, reporters, dialecticians, partisans. No doubt they are all these other things too. No doubt they have not uttered a single sentence or syllable which does not also reveal them, to a greater or less extent, in these other attitudes. But cutting across all these attitudes, in the form and garments of them all, there is a certain fundamental attitude. This is the attitude of the witness. It is distinguished from the attitude of the interested spectator, or the narrating reporter, or the reflective dialectician, or the determined partisan, by the fact that when the witness speaks he is not answering a question which comes from himself, but one which the judge addresses to him. And his answer will be the more exact and reliable the more he ignores his own irrepressible questions in the shaping of his answer, and the more he allows it to be exclusively controlled by the realities which it is his duty to indicate and confirm. The attitude of the biblical witnesses is decided by the fact that, whatever else may rightly or wrongly be said about their other attitudes, they are in the position and are called to give information upon a question put to them from without. They are called by God in the face of all other men to be witnesses of His own action. They can and must attest, before all the world and so that every one may hear, that God has spoken and acted and how He has spoken and acted in Jesus Christ and to His people. Their starting-point is this speaking and acting of God in its determinate reality, and they think and speak before the face of the same God, who now as Judge asks of them nothing but the truth concerning this reality, concerning His own speaking and acting which has taken place once for all. They speak under this twofold presupposition, with the weight of it, and therefore with the unchecked flow of a headlong mountain stream. Of course, they also describe, narrate, reflect and argue. How can any witness speak without to some extent doing these things too ? But these things do not make him a witness. Nor did they make the prophets and apostles witnesses of God's revelation. What makes them its witnesses is the fact that they speak under this twofold presupposition : they believe and therefore speak. It is just this attitude which must be the standard for dogmatics as the model of Church proclamation. The requirement of this attitude, that is, of its imitation, is the primary and concrete principle of its form which we must always remember and respect. The dogmatician cannot be a witness to revelation in the same sense as the prophets and apostles, any more than the preacher. But for dogmatics as for Church proclamation everything depends on hearing the revelation attested by the prophets and apostles, as it is imparted to the Church and all the world in the form of testimony. What is to be heard here is the truth concerning the speaking and acting of God ; and again this truth is to be heard in the presence of God the Judge as they impart it to us. In what other manner can it be heard than in a manner appropriate to the character of the communication and therefore again in the attitude of witnesses—secondary witnesses who can only confirm and repeat, witnesses of the witness which the first witnesses have given, but still witnesses ? Again, the Church as a teaching Church is called to speak as a witness. As a hearing Church, therefore, what other attitude can it wish to assume than that of a witness ? Of course, in detail, dogmatic thinking and speaking is materially composed of disparate elements, to which may be attributed as such historical, psychological, political and philosophical characteristics— in short, characteristics other than those of witness. In themselves and as such they do actually have this other character. This other character is constituted by the fact that in dogmatics as a human activity of thinking and speaking the purely human attitude does, of course, always assert itself. Hence, instead of answering the question put to him, man answers such questions as he thinks he should put to himself. His thinking and speaking, instead of being controlled exclusively by the reality about which he must give information, is also controlled by his conception, his judgment and valuation of this reality. To this extent he becomes a witness whose credibility is obscured. It is impossible to remove from dogmatic thinking and speaking this subjective element, just as it is impossible to remove from it its human character. But it is certainly possible—and this possibility gives meaning to the demand for the biblical attitude—to have an awareness of this state of affairs, and as a result of this awareness to recognise and make room for a specific ranking within dogmatic thought and speech. What ought not to happen and what can be avoided is this : that those elements of which dogmatic thinking is undoubtedly composed should acquire the character and the role of independent presuppositions. In dogmatics the presupposition on which the attitude of the biblical witness was founded, that God has acted and spoken in a certain definite way, and that a true witness is to be given to this as in the presence of God, ought not to be set aside even for a single moment. In dogmatics it ought not to be made even for a single moment in a merely questioning, hypothetical or partial way. In dogmatics it ought not to be doubted even for a single moment that this presupposition takes precedence of all others. In dogmatics, it is no doubt possible and even necessary to think and speak historically, psychologically, politically and philosophically. But in dogmatics we cannot treat this kind of thinking and speaking with final seriousness. For from the sphere of these human questions and answers we cannot expect any decisions about the essential content of dogmatic thinking and speaking. We cannot even expect decisive standpoints for its formation. As can be seen, dogmatic thinking and speaking is humanly conditioned by these points of view. But it cannot be a type of thought which is essentially bound by any one of them. If it is to be true to itself, dogmatic scholarship especially must operate quite freely, in full accessibility to its object, and unreservedly at its disposal. In this sphere we cannot think and speak even for a single moment, except hypothetically, of *a priori* human ideas and conceptions, of history and experience, of a being and knowing which proceed from man upwards to God. Instead, we have to use freely the hypotheses which come to us from God, from the Word of God, and, because we are men and not God, from the Word as it is revealed to us by God, and, because we ourselves are not prophets and apostles, from the revealed Word as it comes to us in biblical testimony. Not for a single moment have we to think and speak as though God had not spoken and acted, as though the existence and work of God were one problem with others, and not the basis, and, whether we realise it or not, the solution of all other problems. God can never be for dogmatic thinking and speaking an object which can be affirmed apart from God. God can never be for dogmatic thinking and speaking a second term, if He is not already the first, and if He is not unashamedly and unreservedly recognised as the first.

The biblical attitude required of dogmatics can best be summarised in the answers to questions 94 and 95 of the *Heidelberg Catechism*:

What does the Lord require in the first commandment? That on pain of losing my soul's salvation and blessedness I should avoid and flee from all idolatry, magic, superstitious blessing, the invocation of saints or of other creatures, and should rightly confess the one true God, trust Him alone in all humility and patience, from Him alone await all good, and love, fear and honour Him with my whole heart: therefore that I rather surrender all created things than do the least thing contrary to His will.

What is idolatry? Instead of the one true God who has revealed Himself in His Word, or alongside Him, to invent or have some other thing in which man puts his trust.

It is to be noted that there is no question of excluding and silencing the criticism and scepticism which can arise from all these different points of view in relation to the content of the biblical testimony. Rather, it will have to be freely expressed in dogmatics, if only for the reason that the communication of the speaking and acting of God is only understandable against the background of the possible and in a sense even necessary attack and the objections which come from all these other sources. But in dogmatics, it will never be possible to express it from an abstract or an ostensibly final and secure point of view, and to that extent with decisive seriousness, but only as something already superseded by and contained in the reality attested by Scripture. Dogmatics can do full justice to the revolt of man with sincere sympathy for his distress. But the presupposition against which the revolt of man has to be viewed in dogmatics is that in the last resort man is wrong, because God alone is right. And in spite of all the sympathetic understanding, this presupposition must not be obscured or forgotten. It is to be noted further that there is no question of a systematic decision anticipating the detailed answers to individual questions as they occur. A prior decision of this kind is as utterly impossible as that the reality of God should be at the advance disposal of the dogmatician, or the preacher, or man in general (for example, in the form of a logical axiom). On the contrary, it has to be continually investigated and sought point by point, and it continually gives itself to be recognised point by point. A complacent dogmatism is nowhere more impossible than in dogmatics itself when rightly understood and practised. Everything in dogmatics is subject to questioning—except only that the dogmatician does not have to answer his own questions but those arising out of God's revelation. In dogmatics all questions and answers stand under a common denominator. All problems are bracketed together. They stand on a common ground, which dogmatics can never abandon without betraying itself, since it is as truly given as are the physical and biological phenomena of the natural sciences. Again, it is to be noted that when we speak of the biblical attitude required of dogmatics, we do not mean the assurance of faith which can neither be postulated nor established systematically. It is another matter that what is here called the biblical attitude cannot be attained, or can be attained only as a worthless travesty, apart from the assurance of faith. We are not speaking here of the assurance of faith as such, which the dogmatician, like any other Christian, can only believe and continually pray for as the gift of the Holy Ghost for his work. Nor are we speaking of any experience or feeling which may accompany such assurance of faith. We are speaking of a specific type of thinking which is not necessarily bound up with faith and the experience of faith, but which even on the basis of this faith we have to learn as a distinctive thing, although on this basis we can learn it with instruction and practice, just as we learn anything else.

For accustoming us to this form of thinking, and for facilitating our own impression by it and assimilation of it, the most serviceable thing will naturally be the reading and exegesis of Holy Scripture itself and also to some extent the example of other exegetes, preachers and dogmaticians. In fact, we can, without flippancy but rather in all seriousness, give everyone the advice to leave open for the time being the question of the assurance of faith, and to go to the school of Scripture and the Church to learn about this form of thinking, in the expectation that all other things will then be added.

Finally, it should be noted that the requirement of a biblical attitude in dogmatics is not interchangeable with the task of reproducing and explaining the text of the Bible. In theology, this is not the task of dogmatics but of exegesis. Biblical exegesis is the decisive presupposition and source of dogmatics. Indeed, we can and must go further and say that it is the task of dogmatics, not to leave the teaching Church to its own devices, but constantly to recall it to the work of biblical exegesis. But dogmatics in itself is not biblical exegesis. It is the examination, criticism and correction of the proclamation to which the teaching Church addresses itself on the basis of Holy Scripture, not merely by reproducing and explaining it, but also by applying and thus in some measure producing it. What is really demanded of dogmatics is that this examination, criticism and correction should be carried out with the same biblical attitude of thought and speech to which Church proclamation is called. Self-evidently, it will have to keep the text of the Bible continually and constantly in view in its content. Therefore, like theology in general, it will be continually and consistently occupied with its exegesis. Often enough, it will have to hark back to it directly, thus taking up again the immediate and detailed work of exegesis. Nevertheless this is not its special and peculiar function. Therefore it cannot be expected to put forward only such considerations or advance such arguments as may immediately be construed as the reproduction and explanation of the biblical text. Nor can it be expected to quote " proof-texts " for all its reflections and definitions in the sense of grounding and establishing them on definite biblical passages or by reference to specific biblical contexts.

Of course, this cannot mean that dogmatics does not remain continually and consistently responsible to the text of the Bible. It does not mean that it may develop in actual contradiction to the latter (even if only through negligence in view of the abundance of its material), nor does it mean that in a given instance it may not always and in all its considerations and arguments be called to order by the biblical text. What it does mean is this. Because dogmatics is not itself directly concerned with the biblical text but with the word of Church proclamation founded upon its testimony, it must not be expected and ought not to try to achieve what is really the business of a biblical theology of the Old and New Testaments. We make the point as a restriction upon the programme once assigned to dogmatics by J. T. Beck (and in a different way also by J. C. K. v. Hofmann). It is to be feared that in a dogmatics which itself tries to master the task of exegesis, or in an exegesis which itself tries to assume the functions of dogmatics, both theological tasks will in their own way necessarily suffer. The programme of a materially biblical dogmatics or of a dogmatic exegesis has its importance and value as a reminder of the necessary unity of theology which ought not to be left out of account for a single moment in either branch of study. But in this case—as opposed to the distinction between dogmatics and ethics which we have seen to be arbitrary and dubious—it will be necessary to pay attention to the difference in unity, and therefore to the distribution, although not, of course, the definitive separation of the two theological tasks.

Dogmatics must have the freedom to take up questions and concerns which cannot be answered directly either by individual scriptural phrases or by reference to specific biblical contexts of thought, and which cannot be those of exegesis, because they arise only in the

Church which listens to the voice of Scripture and teaches on this basis. It is natural, of course, that dogmatics will seize every possible opportunity to deal with these matters by direct reference back to Scripture. But it is not to be expected that such opportunities will always and everywhere exist. What has to be said is that dogmatics has no freedom to be an autonomous branch of Church theology in independence of the witness of Scripture. It cannot give its own witness from its own sources. In Church proclamation and the special questions and concerns of the teaching Church in every age, there can be no question of anything other than the repetition and confirmation of the biblical witness. Thus dogmatics has no freedom to decline to allow its thought to be formed by the prototype of the biblical witnesses. It has no freedom to become a historical or psychological, political or philosophical dogmatics. It may or may not be directly concerned in exegesis. It may or may not make actual textual references. But necessarily it takes the form of its thought from its submission to the biblical *Deus dixit*. And it can acquire this necessary form of thought only from confrontation with the biblical text. It cannot, therefore, escape perpetual sympathy with the other theological task—that of reproducing and explaining the biblical text. This is what we have to say about the biblical character of dogmatics.

2. To determine the second concrete formal characteristic of dogmatics and Church proclamation, we refer back to what we said in § 20[2] about the authority of the " fathers " and of dogma, and we define the resultant requirement as the requirement of a confessional attitude. In its concrete manifestation, utterance of the Word of God in the revelation attested in Scripture is conditioned for us by the voice of the teachers and doctrinal decisions which have established and moulded the listening Church of to-day, of which dogmatics is one of the functions. But if this is true, it necessarily has a definite effect on our understanding of the dogmatic norm to which this Church as a listening Church is subjected. Dogmatic thinking and speaking must be distinguished from undefined religious thinking and speaking, not only by its orientation to the Canon and text of the Bible, but also by a right connexion with the history which has moulded this Church and the confession which obtains in it. We have already said what is to be said generally concerning the responsibility of the Church with regard to its confession. All that remains is to draw some inferences which may be derived from these more general insights with regard to the norm of dogmatics as a function of the listening Church as opposed to the teaching Church. Even as regards its relation to the fathers and dogma, the position of dogmatic work in relation to what is ultimately the only normative revelation in Scripture is necessarily one that is relatively determined. That is to say, the dogmatician (or the preacher with whom he confers) necessarily has a relatively determined home in the life of the Church with its relatively determined

horizon. We say relatively determined, because obviously the home which is absolutely determined can be only the *una sancta catholica et apostolica*. We do not cease to believe in the existence of this *una sancta* even in the Church which is different from our own, and alien and perhaps even marked off as heretical. But it exists only where this belief is obedience and therefore where it is relatively determined. It exists only in the faith of this or that specific Church. Even dogmatics cannot escape this relative determination of faith.

It is, of course, a criticism, examination and correction of Church proclamation by reference to the sole standard of the Word of God. It remembers that the only existence of the Church is in its one Lord and Head Jesus Christ. Necessarily, therefore, it is strictly ecclesiastical. It is so in a universal sense. It is, therefore, ecumenical. We cannot think and speak dogmatically if we want to express and maintain the morphological peculiarity and uniqueness of our own Church as such, beside which there may be others to express and maintain. Nor can we think and speak dogmatically on the assumption that in another place we could do the same thing just as well and legitimately in another way. Properly speaking, there is no such thing as dogmatic tolerance. Nor, properly speaking, is there a Catholic, Lutheran or Reformed dogmatics in undisputed and even deliberate independence and co-ordination. Where dogmatics exists at all, it exists only with the will to be a Church dogmatics, a dogmatics of the ecumenical Church.

Wherever a different opinion has been advanced, it has always been necessary to go back to other claims and sources ; to the supposed guidance of God in history or the so-called harmony beyond ecclesiastical differences and contradictions. These are set alongside Holy Scripture, and the result is a basic surrender of the foundation of the Church. In a confessionalism which has this morphological basis and tendency, there lurks always at some point animistic heathenism with its awe and veneration of the spirits of field and wood and mountain. A dogmatics which thinks and speaks from this point of view may perhaps be able to judge with the eagerness and zeal of a collector of all sorts of rarities and curiosities, but it certainly cannot do so with the trustworthiness and compulsion which is needful in dogmatics if it is to perform its service to Church proclamation even in its own perhaps very small place within the Church. And this is to say nothing of the fact that beyond this place, even where it ought normally to be heard, it can awaken no more than a distant interest. The only dogmatics which can speak convincingly to the whole Church is one which is seriously aware of its responsibility towards the whole Church, so that it is not concerned with any idiosyncrasies and peculiarities, but with the one truth which is universally valid.

The nature of the task incumbent on dogmatics does not allow it to turn to any narrower sphere than that of the whole Christian Church. On the contrary, it demands that in the spirit and name of the one universal Christian Church it should address the one universal Christian Church. But this ecumenical approach and claim of a true dogmatics certainly must not be taken to mean that either positively or negatively the relative determinateness of faith can be neglected or denied. It cannot mean that dogmatics should withdraw from the visible listening Church, seeking its platform in an imagined unity of the so-called invisible Church transcending Church distinctions and divisions, and therefore expounding a universal Christian faith above and beyond the relatively determined faith of the various separated Churches. The faith artificially constructed and expounded from such a watch-tower can only be a faith of phantasy, for it can only be phantasy to try to stand upon such a watch-tower. The real Christian faith can be recognised, lived and expressed only in the relativity and determinateness of a specific place within the visible Church, which in its visibility is not uniform, and unfortunately not united, but differentiated within itself and very extensively divided. Therefore the place from which dogmatics, even ecumenical dogmatics, is to be pursued, can only be a specific place of this kind : specified by the experience through which the Church has here been founded and maintained ; specified by these fathers and this dogma ; specified as this place from which, without prejudice to faith in the invisible *una sancta*, but in obedience to the one Lord of the one Church, other places and the dogmatics pursued in them, are to be seen, understood and valued, not simply and neutrally as other and therefore interesting varieties of the same *genus*, but seriously in all their differentiation, perhaps in their strangeness, perhaps even in their heretical separatedness. It is as dogmatics takes itself and other dogmatics seriously in their relative determinateness, not taking its stand on the ethereal heights above Church differences and schisms, but right in their midst, in the midst of the divided, disunited Church, that it will obviously cleave more steadfastly to faith in the invisible *una sancta* and do more for the ecumenical Church, and even satisfy better the justifiable meaning of the idea of tolerance, than when it chooses the contrary part of phantasy.

Church dogmatics cannot, therefore, be at one and the same time Roman Catholic, Greek Orthodox, Neo-Protestant and Evangelical. It cannot be ecumenical by an attempted combination of them all. On the other hand, we cannot go on to say that dogmatics can choose between them and therefore be the first or second or third or fourth. There is no dogmatics which encompasses and unites all these four or more possibilities, nor are there four or more types of Church dogmatics between which we can safely choose. On the contrary, the danger of choosing between these apparently equal possibilities is so great that a false choice immediately implies that what is then chosen is not dogmatics at all, that is, Church dogmatics, but one of the possibilities of heretical gnosis excluded by the confession of the Church. There is only one choice, which means that there is no choice. Nor can we refuse to press further the necessary dogmatic intolerance. For when we say this, we do not mean that whatever may be our choice, we know that we are in the right and have a good conscience, and therefore we should not be deterred by the fact that others have chosen differently, but hold to the opinion that we have made the right and only choice, which is no choice. The confessional attitude of dogmatics does not really express the theonomy of Church proclamation if in the last analysis it is based on this individual absolutisation of our personal standpoint. Either the confessional attitude of dogmatics rests upon a compulsion by the Word of God which precludes the recognition of the rightness of any other choice, causing extreme uneasiness by the fact that different choices are made elsewhere, and implying a readiness to fight for the peace of the Church ; or it is a whim which might just as well be exchanged for what is at any rate the well-meaning if fanciful notion of a unified interconfessional dogmatics. We must be consistent here and confess that it is not possible for us suddenly to speak undogmatically about the confessional attitude of dogmatics, instead of standing ourselves within the confessional attitude. Negatively, the confessional point of view undeniably means this at least, that other confessional positions are excluded with a final seriousness, i.e., as heretical. Therefore we cannot concede that the compulsion may equally well be a compulsion towards the Roman Catholic, Greek Orthodox, Neo-Protestant or Evangelical positions. On the contrary, we can only say that the compulsion of the Word of God leads to one, the only possible, confessional position—that of the Evangelical Church. Church dogmatics is what it is only in the determination of the Evangelical confession. Church dogmatics is Evangelical dogmatics or it is not Church dogmatics. By " Evangelical dogmatics " is here to be understood the dogmatics of the one holy, universal and apostolic Church, as it was purified and founded anew by the reformers of the 16th century and by the confession which adopted their testimony, and as it hears the Word of God in this as the only possible and normative determination. Now, obviously, we cannot produce at once the evidence for this assertion. It can be produced only by Church dogmatics itself and as a whole. But it is already established even before this demonstration, the success of which cannot be guaranteed. When and where Jesus Christ finds in the Church the obedience of faith, when and where the Church may believe itself to be His, and therefore the true Church, because it is obedient to His Word, when and where the Church proves this obedience by confessing, and by confessing rightly, we have proof already, even before it is successfully or less successfully confirmed by Church dogmatics. This preliminary proof consists simply in the fact that when the Church is the true Church it is the Evangelical Church. How can Evangelical dogmatics take even a single step towards the criticism, examination and correction of Church proclamation if it tries to do so only in virtue of a fortuitous historical determination as Evangelical dogmatics, if, then, it does not regard the proof of that statement, not only as something which has still to be adduced, but as something which has already been adduced ?

How can its fathers and dogma be authoritative at all if it does not grant them an exclusive as well as a relative authority, if it does not have the faith and courage to contest as impossible every possibility of a choice of other fathers and other dogmas ? How can it be distinguished from other types of dogmatics, with what authority can it oppose them and therefore shoulder the responsibility for disunion and strife in the Church, if it is not a matter of fundamental antithesis, if it does not proceed from the obligatory presupposition that as an Evangelical dogmatics it is the dogmatics of the Church of Jesus Christ, and that in regard to proclamation it has to defend and represent with a view to the whole Church, not this or that non-obligatory view, but—of course by human estimation, but seriously human estimation—the one thing which is necessary ?

We obviously can and must speak of the *furor theologorum*, of theological quarrelling in an objectionable sense of the term, when the theological conflict does not have this ultimate necessity, but is at root only a matter of the peculiarities and predilections of individuals or whole groups or Church communities as such. Naturally enough, strife on such questions involves obstinacy and personal irritation. And we can easily see that the serious conflict between Church and heretical dogmatics does always carry with it an unfortunate distortion by all sorts of non-essential theological differences, and that it will probably become externally visible only in this distorted form. Therefore it is always a false kind of healing to try to remove the scandal in such a way that for the sake of peace the necessary dispute is patched up with the unnecessary. It is far more necessary, and far more salutary and serviceable to the cause of peace, not to suspend the essential conflict, but, paring away the non-essential factors, to resume it with all the more energy and seriousness. It is worth noting what is written on this point in the Formula of Concord (*Sol. Decl. de Antithesi, Bekenntnis-Schriften der evangelischen lutherischen Kirche*, 1930, 839, 23) : *Quare in hac etiam parte mentem nostram in vicem declaravimus et perspicue declaravimus, quod videlicet discrimen sit habendum inter non necessarias atque inutiles contentiones, quae plus destruunt quam aedificant, ne iis ecclesia perturbetur, et inter necessaria certamina, quando tales controversiae incidunt, ubi de articulis fidei aut praecipuis partibus Christianae doctrinae agitur ; tum enim ad veritatis defensionem necessario contraria et falsa doctrina est refutanda.* We meet a theological adversary in a manlier and more worthy way, the more it is recognised on both sides that in this clash ultimate things are at stake, not merely fortuitous inclinations and disinclinations, not merely things in which one side or the other could easily think differently, but is prevented only by the laziness or arrogance of the flesh. We may even go further. In a theological conflict, the opponents are still together in Christ and therefore still within the Church when it is clear that they are separated in Christ and that they contend, not about the respective rights of their Churches, or tendencies within their Churches, or only their own personal opinions, but about the right of the Church against heresy, which makes this dispute necessary. At this point we may refer expressly to the Roman Catholic *Vierteljahrsschrift für Kontroverstheologie*, published since 1932 by Robert Grosche under the title *Catholica*. For its contributors the presupposition of controversy is that Catholic theology is *the* theology of the Church, that the Evangelical opponent is therefore a heretic, and that as such he must be treated with real seriousness. Behind this presupposition of the Roman theologians who write in *Catholica* lies the further presupposition that they are dealing with an Evangelical theology which for its part is prepared to accept responsibility as the one theology of the one Church, and not merely to play the part of one theology of one Church. And from the contents of this very journal we can satisfy ourselves whether it is not the case that even on this very " intolerant " presupposition, with an attitude which is actually and not merely verbally confessional, it is still possible to conduct the controversy between Roman Catholicism and Protestantism in a way which is not merely worthy of the participants but of the matter which both sides confess to be indisputably at stake, and therefore in a way which is Christian in a unity even in disunity. Conversely, there is no question that in the shadow of an ecumenicism whose basic principle is that no Church should take itself or other Churches with final seriousness, the different wild beasts of an all too human egoism will, as occasion offers, bare and use their claws with all the greater abandon. It is only where adversaries are opposed with genuine dogmatic intolerance that there is the possibility of genuine and profitable discussion. For it is only there that one confession has something to say to the other.

Dogmatics, then, approaches its work with a confessional attitude in this sense. It does not admit the possibility that it could be anything else but Evangelical dogmatics. But this being the case, in answer to the more formal question, it will necessarily refuse to act or even to announce itself as " Evangelical dogmatics," or the " dogmatics of the Evangelical Church," or the like. It does not have to represent its Evangelical character as a specialised concern, but as the concern of the whole Church. Where other specialised concerns have a justifiable core, not recognised, perhaps, even by their exponents, this must be woven into its discussions and conclusions. If they have not, they are to be rejected. But either way they are not to be respected in their form as special concerns, but repressed in favour of the one concern of the Church. What consciously belongs only to the sect or to the provincial Church cannot as such belong to the Church. *In concreto* it may not be possible in any dogmatics to exclude its influence and savour. But it makes all the difference whether it is recognised and repressed as the human element clinging to what properly belongs to the Church, or whether it is admitted and authorised as a second principle side by side with it. This latter is what must not happen. Evangelical dogmatics must not try to be "Evangelical" in the sense of a specialised dogmatics. It will be better, therefore, if it is not proclaimed and propounded as such, but simply as " Church " dogmatics.

This is the occasion to come to a provisional understanding about the relation of dogmatics to a branch of theology whose nature and position in scholarship are much disputed : what is called " symbolics " or the study of confessions. Does this stand in a closer relation to dogmatics as a second or third department of so-called systematic theology ? Or does it constitute only a special section of Church history ? Or, as an extended study of the Church, does it form a branch of practical theology ? From the course of our argument the impossibility of at least one kind of symbolics is plain to see. Symbolics cannot take up an imaginary coign of vantage beyond all creeds from which Christianity can be normatively seen and understood and presented as a whole. It cannot go on to prove the special excellence of Evangelical Christianity, and then try to assign to Evangelical dogmatics its special part and function alongside all sorts of other types of dogmatics. It cannot, therefore, be independent or superior in relation to dogmatics, although itself in all probability subordinate to a general philosophy of religion (as with Schleiermacher and C. Stange). As understood in this sense, symbolics is an offshoot of the theology of the Enlightenment, and an acknowledgment of its existence and validity means the end of Church dogmatics at its very beginning. It is, of course, obvious that as an auxiliary to all theological disciplines Church history has also to give information about the genesis, substance and composition of confessions and confessional Churches. And it is a question of secondary importance whether this should fall within the framework of Church history generally, or whether it should constitute a special and subordinate historical or practical discipline. Again, alongside the possibility of such an unpretentiously factual and informative history or study of the confessions, there is the further and not unprofitable possibility of making the relationship and character of the various confessions as such the subject of a thoroughgoing investigation and exposition, thus associating them in some way with dogmatics. In contrast to the customary symbolics of systematic theology since the Enlightenment, a symbolics of this kind needs dogmatics, Evangelical dogmatics, as its presupposition. Its task is the comprehensive exposition of the faith of the Evangelical Church in its positive and negative aspects as the confession of the Church as a whole. Then and from this standpoint it has to survey the declarations and behaviour of Neo-Protestantism, which for good reasons has never gone so far as to make a confession. Then, after dealing with the special concerns of Neo-Protestantism, it can proceed to survey Roman Catholicism and, after working through its special concerns, and showing the Evangelical Church to be *the* Western Church, it can consider the Eastern Church. Maintaining the same principle of exclusion and arrangement established by the Evangelical confession, it can then go on to contrast the Christian faith and the non-Christian religions. In this survey it will have to give special consideration to Islam on account of its historical relation to the Old and New Testaments. But in this outer circle generally there is nothing that it can abstract and use. The Christian faith in its Evangelical form has to be opposed to all others with all the simplicity of a Gospel which is still missionary. It is the confession of truth as opposed to that of error and untruth. In the form of this type of subsidiary discipline symbolics could be a department of what is called systematic theology, or rather an auxiliary to dogmatics, and therefore a possible and legitimate theological enterprise. But if it cannot be conceived and executed in this way, we had better be content with an unpretentious historical study of the confessions.

The confessional attitude of dogmatics and Church proclamation means fidelity as required by the Word of God to the fathers and the confession of the Churches as the voice of those who were in the Church before us. The limit of this requirement lies in the nature of the case. The voice of the fathers and of the confession has no independent value and authority beside that of the Word of God. Its authority resides in the fact that it is the voice of secondary witnesses to this Word. Fidelity to them means obedience to the Word of God—an obedience formed and determined by our place in the Church and therefore by its previous experience and prior hearing of the Word. But in exercising fidelity to them, it is to the Word and not to them that we are giving obedience. The requisite fidelity to the fathers and the confession of the one, holy, catholic, apostolic and therefore Evangelical Church cannot mean that alongside the rule and standard given to the Church in Holy Scripture, we have to recognise the Reformers, and the Reformation confession, and the dogma of the Early Church as renewed and confirmed by them, as a second principle of the doctrine and life of the Church. There is no such second principle. But in virtue of the one principle there is our own specific direction into the Church, and we must abide by this unless we are forced to understand it differently as a result of further enlightenment by the same principle. The witnesses of our specific direction into the Church are witnesses to the previous experience of the Church, and the voice of the Church which existed before us. As such, they are the fathers and dogma. We truly acknowledge this direction when we understand that as hearers of the Word of God we are not emancipated individuals but both in dogmatics and in Church proclamation the hearing Church. As such, we do not think and speak from any freely chosen point of vantage, but in obedience to this direction into the confessional Church, and therefore in fidelity to the fathers and to dogma. The listening Church, of which dogmatics is a function, is the confessional Church. In placing ourselves in this position, we recognise that even the primary requirement of the " biblical attitude " cannot be a position taken up by the arbitrary will of the individual. It can only be the position of the Church itself, to which the Bible belongs, and which is called by the Bible to adopt the attitude of the witness. If the confessional attitude means, positively, fidelity towards a hearing of the Word of God incumbent upon us and determined for us by the example of the fathers and of dogma, negatively it must mean a reservation in regard to every other kind of supposed hearing of the same Word, which the fathers and dogma tell us is in some sense false, and also in regard to other supposed Churches, which again the fathers and dogma tell us are not churches in any sense which permits us to take over the responsibility for their supposed hearing. To be sure, all kinds of indications can and must force us to the conclusion that the Word of God does not leave itself unattested or without a witness in them. Therefore we cannot and must not deny that there is something of the Church in them. But we cannot allow that they are in fact the Church, because on the ground of what they teach we cannot regard them as the listening Church, that is, the Church which listens to the Word of God.

In this sense, and corresponding to our own direction into the Church, we have marked off the Evangelical Church as the Church of Jesus Christ from the three heresies : Neo-Protestantism, which at almost every point resembles the Evangelical Church in organisation and administration but is essentially alien to it in spirit ; Roman Catholicism ; and the Eastern Orthodox Churches. But even when Neo-Protestantism is strictly excluded as foreign to it, as in this discussion, it is obvious that the Evangelical Church is not a unity. At least three great forms are to be distinguished in it. And to some extent they have distinguished themselves with the same definiteness as if it were a question of an opposition between the Church and one of the heretical sects. These are the Lutheran, the Reformed and the Anglican branches of the Evangelical Church. Let us admit at once that when we speak of the Evangelical Church and therefore of the Church generally in this presentation of dogmatics we mean the Evangelical Reformed Church, in conformity with our own Church position, and the fathers and the dogma to which we owe loyalty in obedience to the Word of God until we are led by that same Word to something better. The localisation to which dogmatics must be content to submit is complete, and dogmatics cannot concretely understand itself as a function of the hearing Church if it tries to be neutral in regard to the question implied in the fact that Evangelical Church may mean the Lutheran or the Reformed or the Anglican Church, and if it does not occupy a specific position in regard to these possible and contrasting alternatives. The diversity between these branches is in any case too real and deep (indeed, the whole idea is excluded by our previous considerations) to allow or authorise us to stand on a watch-tower above and beyond at least the Evangelical confessions on the basis of an artificially constructed and designated union. Until the Evangelical Churches devise and complete a union in such a way that they can visibly present themselves as a new confession expressly superseding the old, it cannot be the business of dogmatics either to postulate a united Church or to construct a basis of union, even though to an individual or even to many individuals this may appear to be a not impossible theological task.

It is probably no accident that the attempts made in the 19th century to achieve a dogmatic basis of union between Lutheran and Reformed Churches, in the doctrinal systems of Schleiermacher, Marheineke, De Wette, C. J. Nitzsch, A. Schweizer, I. A. Dorner and A. E. Biedermann, were all undertaken more or less against the background of what were, from a theological and ecclesiastical point of view, most unjustifiable unions. In addition, they were conceived in terms of Neo-Protestant rather than Evangelical modes of thought and belief. One of the fundamental errors of Neo-Protestantism is to think that there is no such thing as what we here term the confessional attitude, at any rate within the Evangelical Church. On this view the individual theologian does not need to bother about the Church to which he belongs, but may choose, or, if need be, freely create his standpoint. This outlook provides a background against which the antithesis between the Evangelical Church and the non-Evangelical, and ultimately that between the Christian Church and religions in general, is seen as a matter for a choice and decision which are purely individual, and therefore not in the last resort necessary. If the individual theologian cannot choose, still less create, his standpoint in the Church, but only receive and therefore affirm it as it is assigned to him by the Word of God, until he is recalled from it by the same Word, this is just as true of his position with regard to antitheses within the Evangelical Church as it is of his attitude to the antitheses between the Evangelical Church and heresies or that which is outside the Church. For the time being, therefore, and within the limits appropriate to the case, he must regard himself as bound, and he cannot attempt anything for which he has no commission or authority from his Church's confession.

Our next step is simply to repeat and apply positively the characteristic features of dogmatics as Evangelical dogmatics. Even within the Evangelical Church we have only the one choice, which is no choice. A false choice jeopardises the whole character of dogmatics as Church dogmatics. We must take upon ourselves a necessary opposition to other types of Evangelical dogmatics. We cannot practise indifferently Anglican, Lutheran or Reformed dogmatics, but only Reformed dogmatics. For us, therefore, Church dogmatics is necessarily Reformed dogmatics. By this we mean the dogmatics of the particular Church which was purified and reconstituted by the work of Calvin and the confession which sealed his testimony. We mean the dogmatics of the Church which hears the Word of God in this determination imposed upon it and recognised and confessed by it to be the best. Again, the evidence for this preference cannot be adduced immediately, but only in the full range of dogmatics. And, again, prior to all proof, it will have to be taken as proven. Again, in the last resort it can only be a question of practising Church dogmatics in the form of Reformed dogmatics, that is, Evangelical and therefore ecumenical Church dogmatics, not the dogmatics of a particular branch of the Church distinguished by and proudly emphasising certain historical peculiarities. And, again, for this reason, Reformed dogmatics cannot be, nor can it wish to be called, " Reformed " but only Church dogmatics, or dogmatics pure and simple.

On the other hand, it is clear from our previous formulation, in which this has already been suggested, that the antithesis within the Evangelical Churches confronts us with a different situation from the antithesis to the non-Evangelical "churches." Here, too, of course, it is a question of tension, of an inevitable, exclusive choice and decision. But in this case it must take a different form. What we are going to say does not rest on individual opinion and historical or systematic judgment. It belongs to the attitude of Reformed confessionalism, which the Reformed confession and Reformed dogmatics have always adopted with Calvin himself. No matter what Lutherans or Anglicans may say on the same point, when it is a matter of the meaning and reach of confessionalism in the antithesis between the Evangelical Churches, our own attitude tells us that when we speak of the Lutheran, Reformed or Anglican Church, we are not speaking of three different Churches, but of the three present forms of one and the same Church— the Evangelical Church, the one holy, catholic and apostolic Church. As Reformed thinkers, it is impossible for us to say of the Anglican and Lutheran Church, as we do of the Roman Catholic Church, that in them also there is a Church ; we must say of them what in view of their doctrine may seem strange and difficult to approve, that in another form they are the one Church of Jesus Christ just as much as is the Reformed Church. The grounds of objection and division are not heresies but specific errors, specific theological notions, badly, misleadingly, erroneously and arbitrarily construed, of a type which may easily arise within the Reformed Confession itself without necessitating disruption. We do not take lightly these errors which separate us from the other Evangelical Churches. We take them so seriously that in view of them we hold fast to the testimony of the purer doctrine and therefore the special form of the Reformed Church and theology. We ask these other Churches whether they are not prepared to let go these errors and in agreement with us to make a better confession. But we cannot tell them, as we do the Roman and Neo-Protestant Churches, that we can believe ourselves one with them in the Church of Jesus Christ only when they have answered this question in a sense agreeable to us. What we feel is that, though their doctrine is imperilled by what we consider their errors, it does not exclude them from the one Church which is ours. We cannot say either of the Anglican or the Lutheran doctrine : *Anathema sit.* We may deplore it, reject it, attack it ; but as we see it, it is not essentially opposed to Reformed teaching, but only in debate with it. It over-emphasises and distorts certain elements integral to the faith of the Reformed Church and therefore of the Church as such, but it is still an alternative within the framework of the one Evangelical Church confession. We can tolerate it as an alternative. It need not be a cause of schism. Indeed, although we deplore and repudiate its specific expression, we recognise in it the common concern of the Church. And we shall not refuse to hear it, and if need be, we shall not decline to be called to order by it. Therefore we do not understand the antithesis between Reformed and other Evangelical dogmatics in the light of an antithesis between Churches which confront each other as Church and non-Church or anti-Church. We interpret it rather as the antithesis between various theological schools or movements within the same Church and its basically agreed confession. The concept of the Church does not in any case preclude this interpretation. It is not to be denied that, in general, diversity of doctrine such as arises within the Evangelical persuasion can mean a separation between Church and non-Church or anti-Church. But we cannot assert that this is always necessary *in concreto* and especially in regard to these particular Churches and their doctrines. Not every difference of doctrine need imply that. Unity in the Church is possible even on the assumption that there are differences of doctrine in it.

It should be noted that within all Churches, the Roman Catholic not excepted, there have always been and still are doctrinal divergences which can at least be compared in material importance and formal definition with those obtaining between Lutheran, Reformed and Anglican, but which have not been regarded as a necessary cause of schism. The Dominicans and Jesuits have sometimes clashed almost to the point of unchurching each other. In the more recent Reformed Church in Germany and elsewhere the heirs of Pietism on the one hand, and the pupils of H. F. Kohlbrügge on the other, have been, and still are, engaged in a conflict in which the most bitter charges and countercharges are bandied about ; and I betray no secret in alluding to the fundamental (and, if I may say so, mutual) aversion which exists between the "historical" Calvinism that follows in the footsteps of A. Kuyper and the Reformed theology represented here. The Anglican Church makes a rather dubious boast about its special mission and capacity to combine all and sundry under its roof, however opposed their standpoints. Even of Lutheranism, which has theoretically laid the greatest stress on the so-called *consensus de doctrina*, it cannot be said that in any century or decade of its existence it has been in a position (even in relation to the controversial article of the Lord's Supper) to manifest this consensus, and therefore Lutheran doctrine, with undisputed unanimity.

It is true that, rightly or wrongly, conflicts of theological schools and movements may lead, and often enough have led, to open schism. But again it is not clear why they should necessarily lead to it. It is not clear why there should not actually and historically be developments in opposing directions. It is not clear why certain Church schisms should not be regarded as belonging to the category of misunderstood theological differences, and why they should not increasingly be reduced to this position. The responsibility which one assumes in accepting such a view is obviously a large one, and it will have to be examined from time to time. But an equally grave responsibility is assumed, which it is equally necessary to examine, where it is thought that such a view should be excluded. Obviously, where it is thought that there is a place for this view, there must be no lapse into indifferentism. The existence of different theological schools or movements within the same Church presupposes their real unity over against all third parties, and therefore their unity in the confession of the Church itself and as such.

For the tensions within the Evangelical Churches, it is a presupposition that Lutheran, Reformed and Anglican theology are at one in that which divides them from the ancient heresies, from Roman theology and from Neo-Protestantism, that for all three schools this opposition and this unity is essential, and that in this opposition and unity they are not only determined and prepared to fight for the confession, but have in fact moved into position. Without this fundamental presupposition, the interpretation of the tension within the Evangelical Churches as a matter of schools and movements can only mean a betrayal of the Evangelical cause and therefore of the Church, and it can be nothing but an unmitigated evil. It was on this primary assumption that Calvin and the older Reformers adopted the basically irenical-polemical attitude to other Evangelical Churches and their doctrine which we are now adopting. They reckoned especially with a Lutheranism that was Evangelical in confession and based on the Scriptures. In view of this Evangelical basis, although they could not approve or connive at its deviations in the matter of eucharistic doctrine, Christology and the doctrine of election, they did not find in them definite heresy and therefore ground for schism. It was the great spiritual weakness of the unions of the 19th century that they did not rest on the strength but on the weakness of the common allegiance and the common confession, especially in outward appearance. In these circumstances, how could they signify any genuine inward unity ?

The existence of different theological schools and tendencies within one Church presupposes, on the other hand, that the points at issue

27

are not indifferent, superficial or superfluous. They are important, real and significant antitheses which it is worth while, because it is commanded, to raise ; and which must therefore be raised and decided in all seriousness. Purely individual differences originating in the personality of this or that theological leader, or differences due to the influence of secular movements influencing the Church from outside, are no proper basis for the formation of theological schools and tendencies. The danger of Church disunity inevitably implied in schools and tendencies formed in this way is far too great to allow the Church to declare every formation of this kind, perhaps in the name of freedom, permissible and legitimate. The only schools of thought which are permissible and legitimate in the Church are those in which the points at issue are obviously differences in the interpretation of the common faith which in its previous confessions the Church has recognised to be important, although it has not yet found in them their final solution. It is only in connexion with such issues that theological schools and tendencies can and ought to arise in the one Church. Their legitimacy will prove itself by the importance and necessity they acquire from this common confession and in the course of its interpretation. Again, indifference is precluded. It is required of the theological schools and tendencies existing in the one Church that they shall be aware of the issue involved, and that they shall not expound their own pet themes but necessary theses and antitheses arising from within the interpretation of the confession, and that they shall do so with real earnestness and vigour.

It is, therefore, a presupposition of the tensions within the Evangelical Churches that what presents or maintains itself legitimately as Lutheran, Reformed or Anglican theology must be able to show that it is not a question of personal, provincial or historical peculiarities or dogmatisms, perhaps masquerading under the honourable title of such Church differences, but, even in these divergences, of a recognisable common and necessary concern of the faith. It was in this sense that even on the common basis the 16th century Reformers and the later Reformed dogmaticians thought it necessary to offer a necessary protest against certain doctrines of the Lutheran Church. If in their differences with the Lutherans they never gave up this common basis, there was no lack of decisiveness in their protest. They, too, could do no other. Especially on German soil they worked for the victory of their doctrine with an energy very provoking to the Lutherans. They accomplished a good deal—we have only to think of Calvin's controversy with Joachim Westphal—in the way of a fine, and sometimes less fine, *furor theologicus*. Yet in it all they never denounced or attacked the Lutherans as heretics. To the best of my knowledge the reproach that the irenical attitude of the Reformed Church to confessional differences within the Evangelical Churches might have its ground in the weakness of their own position, or could issue in such weakness, was never actually brought against the Reformed school in the 16th and 17th centuries. The case was, of course, very different in this respect in the unions of the 19th century. Here the doubtful nature of the common basis was matched by that of the different interpretations, which inevitably acquired the character of oddities and dogmatisms that might equally well be ignored as disputed. As genuine antitheses between the schools and movements, the tensions within the Evangelical confession no longer played any part in these unions. The conflicts which dominated the scene were, first, that between rationalists and supranaturalists, and later, that between liberals, positivists and the movements mediating between them. This was an all the more thoroughly spurious and illegitimate quarrel because it was not really a question of differences in the interpretation of the common confession, but ultimately of differences within the common deviation from the confession.

If it is allowed that in the tensions within the Evangelical Churches we have to do with genuine theological tensions between schools and movements, this cannot finally mean a perpetuation of these tensions. They can be genuine only when they intend not to be or remain tensions. Therefore in the last analysis to assert them implies that they will finally be overcome. The existence of different schools and movements in the same Church means that the Church is engaged in the task of understanding better and taking more seriously than it has done the traditional confessions, which have brought out the points in dispute but have not so far succeeded in reconciling them. Obviously, the goal of this work must be the resolution of these tensions, the working out of a common interpretation of the confession, and therefore the drawing up of a new confession, not setting aside the old in the sense previously discussed, but superseding it. The existence of various theological schools and movements within the same Church, especially when by this is meant only the various Evangelical confessions, implies, therefore, a basic readiness to look beyond the various confessional " positions," not in unfaithfulness, but with the intention of a wholehearted fidelity, following the direction of the confessions and hearing above them what is in the last resort the only authoritative voice, that of Holy Scripture. But when we hear this voice we cannot be indefinitely content with doctrinal differences in the Church, for every difference of this kind has the character of a defect, and together they represent, not the gratifying wealth of the Church, but rather the evidence of its indecision and fragmentation, and therefore of its poverty. Where our own confessional position within the Evangelical Church is taken seriously, it means that we cannot be indifferent, but it also means that we none of us have the right or duty to entrench ourselves finally in our confessional position and to make the maintenance of it even a subsidiary aim of our will. On the contrary, the common faith and the commonly recognised authority of Holy Scripture require that different schools and movements should in all seriousness listen to one another, accepting teaching from the other side where the Word of God demands it, and on occasion surrendering their own position on the ground of a correction recommended by the other side. Without this readiness the conflict of these schools will inevitably sink to the level of futile squabbling. Where we are not defending the Church against heresy, i.e., where we remain within the limits of the Evangelical Church, we must obviously be sure of our own position, but we must also be quite open towards others.   If perhaps, even with such openness, the outcome is a repetition and affirmation of the contradiction, it must still be realised that it is only in this openness that the repetition and affirmation of the contradiction can be significant, profitable and obligatory.   This is not at all the case when the chief concern is not with the truth but with the perpetuation in principle of an individual tradition or peculiarity as such.   This kind of confessional attitude is quite wrong.

Again we may recall that in all this we have only described the attitude which Calvin and the older Reformed Church and theology did in fact adopt in the face of other Evangelical Churches.   In view of Calvin's eucharistic doctrine and other standard confessional writings of the Reformers, it cannot be doubted that the Reformed Churches did not adhere to the original Zwinglian conception of eucharistic doctrine.   On the contrary, they continually listened to Luther. We have only to remember how Calvin wrestled with Bullinger in the negotiation of the *Consensus Tigurinus* of 1549.   The Reformed school received as from Scripture that which in and through Luther they could allow to be from Scripture. And even later they remained true to this attitude, especially when they came into direct contact with Lutheranism in Germany.   We may even say that the eucharistic teaching and Christology of the Reformed theologians of the 16th and 17th centuries are wholly dominated by the attempt to understand the contribution of Luther and to incorporate it into the exposition of their own doctrine.   That this attempt was vain, that it was not considered satisfactory by the Lutherans, and appeared to them even as an enticement to idle compromises, is another matter which we need not judge here.   At any rate it may be said of the older Reformers that their conduct was not at all that of crabbed disputants who refused to give up under any circumstances a position they had once adopted.   As we have said already, they did not advocate unity at any price, but they held to their position not only with the proper resolution but also with the no less proper openness of mind.   In this their attitude may be said to have been exemplary, whatever we may think about the material questions in dispute or the attitude of the Lutherans to whom they were opposed. But it should be added that so far as the 19th century interconfessional conversations, both inside and outside the unions achieved, rested on the basis of a universal weakening in respect of the common confession, it showed itself in the fact that this openness of mind now became basically impossible on both sides. For the first time both sides now entrenched themselves in positions in which they could only stand firm once they had adopted them.   For the first time theology now proclaimed on the one hand a romantic fidelity to the fathers of the Church who were not regarded and valued as earlier witnesses to divine truth, but as additional witnesses to the historical existence of the Church of the present.   On the other hand, the discovery was made that, apart from the specific points of difference defined in 16th century confessions, on both sides a whole world of characteristic and contrasting features had to be brought into consideration.   With greater or lesser insight and success this difference in the internal and external structure of the whole doctrine and life of the two Churches was now related to the differences on the eucharist and election found in the confessional writings—presumably a better understanding of the fathers than they had of themselves !   The final result was a far greater interest in the general religious, intellectual and cultural differences than in the factors which had really separated the fathers.   Partly by historical romancing, partly, and even worse, by following certain secular and especially nationalistic moods and tendencies, a type of " Calvinism " and " Lutheranism " was conjured up which secretly at first, but later quite explicitly, was very different from anything that Calvin and Luther and the older Calvinists and Lutherans could ever have dreamt of (except perhaps in occasional nightmares !). These ecclesiastical forms were an expression of West European and Germanic "types." They were the manifestations of particular forms of piety determined by race, nation, speech and history, each with its own ethical emphasis and a co-related philosophical outlook. The seriousness of the earlier question about the truth of Scripture was now forgotten and it was supposed that in these types the principle of the confessional division could be seen with what appeared to be all the greater seriousness. The mutual open-mindedness required within the Evangelical Church was thus destroyed at its root. The antithesis between the Lutherans and the Reformed, as understood in the 16th and 17th centuries, did not have to be regarded as hopelessly futile, as the Reformers had shown by their attitude. But the antithesis of those types, the tension within the Evangelical Churches, as seen and understood by M. Schneckenburger, and later Max Weber and E. Troeltsch, R. Seeberg and O. Ritschl, and among the Reformed by E. Doumergue, and among the Lutherans by Werner Elert, could not be anything else but hopelessly futile. How can there be any open-mindedness when from the very outset it is only a question of confirming the fact that in the happy possession of a secular principle of interpretation man has deliberately closed his mind ? What can Lutheranism and Calvinism have to say to each other or receive from each other when their only understanding of themselves is as two miserable exponents of two miserable principles of outlook and interpretation, in which the ultimate antithesis is between the "German race" and the *esprit Latin* ? Where the Evangelical confessions are reduced to such principles, to such στοιχεῖα τοῦ κόσμου, their members can only harass and finally destroy one another. If the necessary openness is to be recovered in this relationship, and perhaps on both sides, the first requirement is a decision to renounce completely, not only a romantic and basically heathen ancestor worship, but especially the kind of morphologising which cannot be too severely condemned in this connexion, and to take up the dispute again where the genuine fathers left it off, as a dispute only about the interpretation of Scripture and the common confession of faith. When this is done the parties will again differ where they are also essentially together, and they can grow more deeply and closely united than was the case in the 16th and 17th centuries.

By the confessional attitude required of dogmatics, we understand that as a Church and therefore as an Evangelical dogmatics it will necessarily be opposed to all heretical dogmatics. Again, within the Evangelical Church, and in obedience to its specific tradition, it will necessarily be opposed to all non-Reformed dogmatics. This opposition will be seriously polemical, but it will also be irenical. It will be prepared to contradict. But it will also be prepared for contradiction, and open to the point of view of the opposite party. Its contradiction will be one in which it has not only to teach but to learn. It will betray itself and the Church if it ceases to oppose the heretical Church and its theology. It will again betray itself and the Church if to the non-Reformed Church and theology it does not offer opposition of the kind required from us by the Reformed school and movement. It is to be noted that, understood in this way, the confessionalism of dogmatics, like the biblicism we discussed earlier, does not denote a content of thought, but a form of thought, a principle of thought for dogmatic work. It cannot mean, then, that dogmatics has the task, or even the ancillary task, of expounding the general and particular

dogmas of the Church laid down in the confessions. It is another
thing that it will do this in a supplementary and implicit way, when,
in its testing of Church proclamation by God's Word it consults and
quotes the confessions as the normative commentary on it. But interpretation of the confessions or of the writings of Luther and Calvin
is just as little the special task of dogmatics as is biblical exegesis.
It cannot become merely a report on various doctrines of the fathers,
or have as its aim, even its subordinate aim, their rehabilitation. The
theology of the fathers and the confessions must be used as a pattern
only in proper subordination to the Word of God attested in Scripture.
It must never allow an appeal to them to replace the thinking for
which it is directly responsible to Scripture. It is not by referring to
the fathers and confessions and reproducing their doctrine, but only
by actually learning from them, that it maintains its confessional attitude. We can be confessional only κατὰ πνεῦμα. If we try to be so
κατὰ σάρκα, we shall not be so at all.

The conception of the confessional problem expressed here, especially in its
final formulation with regard to the tensions within the Evangelical Churches,
has its justification but also its limits in the fact that it is characteristic in the
first instance only of the Reformed Church—apart from some recent developments in the German Confessional Church. (I am thinking here of the writings
of Hans Asmussen : *Kirche Augsburgischer Konfession*, 1934, *Barmen !*, 1935,
Gottesgebot und Menschengebot, 1936, and of the decisions of the Old Prussian
confessional synod in Halle, May 1937.) Hence the question arises how far it
has successfully penetrated from the Reformed fathers and confessions into the
practice or even the theory of the Reformed Church generally. It should, of
course, be obligatory within the Reformed Church. This means that a Reformed
theology which tries to understand itself in any other way than that here set
forth, necessarily incurs the reproach of having abandoned the meaning and
framework of the Reformed creed and therefore of failing to satisfy its own
special Church tradition. For the members of other Evangelical Churches, the
argument can have only the character of an offer and a question—the question
whether they cannot and ought not to understand their own position in this
way too ? To put this question to them and expect a positive answer is a bold
undertaking, because merely to enter into this understanding of the formal
problem itself, quite apart from all detailed questions, requires from them a kind
of assent to the Reformed confession, and therefore a relativisation of their own
position, and a certain " Calvinisation." From our previous treatment of the
question we know how difficult this is for the Lutherans. In their case, Scripture
and the Lutheran confession have been so closely related from the start that
most Lutherans inevitably see in every confession deviating from the Lutheran,
and especially in the Reformed confession, not a possible but an impossible
diversity of doctrine, which will necessarily divide the Churches. The result
is to make very uncongenial to them any thought of reducing this diversity to
the status of a deplorable but tolerable difference between their own and another
theological school within the same Church. For our own part, we have to confess
that from our knowledge of the Lutheran position and its history, it seems almost
unfair to expect the Lutheran Church to adopt this Reformed view. And, of
course, it cannot be our business to try to anticipate the solution and answer
which will have to be discovered and offered by the Lutheran Church and
theology itself, after a new investigation of the material and formal meaning of
its position. We ought not to refrain from adding that in this matter as in

others we of the Reformed Church have the consciousness to which Calvin and
the older Calvinists occasionally gave expression ; that as the Reformed Church
we are the real, true and genuine Lutherans, that we claim and interpret as a
credal statement of the Reformed position a compendium of Lutheran doctrine
like the smaller or larger Catechism of Luther (with a few brackets and queries) ;
and that we certainly believe ourselves to interpret it in the sense of Luther
himself and therefore more authentically than happens in most Lutheran lecture-
rooms. In this sense, Heinrich Alting (*Exegesis Augustanae confessionis*, 1652,
p. 78) distinguished three *genera* of Lutherans. To the first belong those who,
Lutheri autoritate fascinati, teach the *corporalis praesentia Christi in coena, in
reliquis autem omnibus religionis capitibus sensum orthodoxum retinent.* A second
comprises all *qui non modo in doctrina de coena sed in plurimis quoque aliis articulis
contra scripturarum atque ipsius etiam Lutheri autoritatem, schismatis fovendi causa,
ab orthodoxis discedunt. Tertium eorum, qui reiectis Lutheri erroribus in omnibus
iis ipsi assentiuntur, quae ex Dei verbo contra Antichristum aliosque fanaticos magno
pioque zelo docuit. Atque hos pontificii quandoque per calumniam Lutheranos,
ipsi vero Lutherani Calvinianos sive Calvinistas vocant.* In this consciousness of
our own Lutheranism κατὰ πνεῦμα we have every reason to say that from the
point of view of the Lutheran Church it is right and necessary and hence possible
to give sympathetic consideration to a different, i.e., the Reformed view of the
confessional question. But that we have and justify this consciousness does not
alter the fact that there are " other " Lutherans who dispute our claim to this
consciousness. For them we cannot speak so long as we have to distinguish ourselves from them. Their decision in this question of form can only be their
own, and we can only wait for it. It may continue to be negative. After a
fresh technical inquiry into its doctrines of the eucharist and election, the initial
cause of disagreement, the Lutheran Church may come to the conclusion that
it must not only maintain its position materially—an aspect which stands outside the present discussion—but must also understand it formally to be a sufficient
cause of Church division. If this is the case, it will have to be accepted, though
again it cannot alter our attitude or cause us to retaliate. The Reformed suggestion to the other Evangelical Churches, to treat their differences as those of
theological schools and movements, must always remain open, whatever the
decision on the other side may be. This is not because of any rhapsodical love
of peace, but because it is integral to the Reformed position. Or rather, it is
integral to its understanding of the relation between Scripture and Church, which
in spite of every difference in doctrine sees the one, holy, catholic and apostolic
Church wherever Holy Scripture is recognised as the source and norm of all
doctrine, and therefore in the Lutheran Church. It cannot avoid doing this
without being false to its very nature. Lutheranism may define its own position
as it will. But it cannot expect us to withdraw this suggestion and the implied
query to other Evangelical Churches. It cannot expect us to cease agitating
about this division of the Churches which we refuse to recognise as complete,
and therefore to cease expecting from them at least a certain degree of Calvinisation. It has to respect this in us as the confessional attitude to which we are
obliged. Calvinism cannot live comfortably within its own bounds. It cannot
be preoccupied only with its own concerns. It cannot be self-satisfied. It cannot
leave Lutheranism comfortably alone as though it were another Church. If
anyone expects this of Calvinism, his idea of it is an imaginary product of wishful
thinking which the Reformed Church and its theology cannot possibly satisfy.

3. The third concrete requirement with regard to the norm to
which dogmatics must submit arises from the fact that, as it must
listen to Holy Scripture which is the basis of the Church, and to the
fathers and the confessions which have shaped the Church, so also it
must listen in a very definite way to the teaching Church of to-day.

Such a requirement we term the requirement of a Church attitude. What we understand by it is as follows : that in its testing of Church proclamation dogmatics must orientate itself to the actual situation in the light of which the message of the Church must be expressed, to its position and task in face of the special circumstances of contemporary society, i.e., to the Word of God as it is spoken by Him, and must be proclaimed by the Church in the present. Therefore along with the teaching Church it must throw itself into this contemporary situation, entering into the position and the task of the teaching Church in face of this situation, and seeking to listen attentively to the Word of God, as spoken to the present in the present. Seeing the problems, concerns, difficulties and hopes, which in this present hour claim and absorb the attention of Church administration (in the broadest sense), it must realise its absolute solidarity with the latter and think and speak from out of this absolute solidarity. To put it in the strictest terms, we must say that dogmatics must go with the teaching Church in the fellowship of prayer, out of the past, through the present and into the future ; with it, it must simply thank and praise God for the benefits of His revelation and atonement ; with it, it must do penance before God for all the failings of which the whole Church is constantly guilty in face of these benefits ; with it, it must pray for the Holy Spirit, which means for the possibility of a new and better and more decisive hearing and consequent proclamation of the Word. For this reason—and this is the essence of the " Church attitude " required of it—in all the babel of voices in the teaching Church, it must listen to that which is the voice of its prayer as the final meaning of all its speaking : not its speaking before men and to men, but its speaking on behalf of men before God and to God, the voice of its priestly intercession for men which forms the presupposition of its prophetic movement towards men. Dogmatics must try to find and study and take seriously the teaching Church in this its most essential function. It must allow its own thinking and speaking to be controlled by attentiveness to this most essential function of the teaching Church. When it does so, it will itself adopt a Church attitude. It will itself enter into this solidarity with the action, labour, struggles and sufferings of the Church of the present. What is required is that it should persist in this attitude, that its whole thinking and speaking should be a consequence and application of it.

We possess an ancient document of the Church which is very beautiful in its way and points in this direction. It is contained in a passage from the " *Indiculus* " *De gratia Dei* (Ch. 11) of Pope Celestine I (431) (*Denz.* No. 139). In it the liturgy of the Church is mentioned as a decisive source of Church doctrine : the *sacramenta obsecrationum sacerdotalium, quae, ab apostolis tradita, in toto mundo atque in omni ecclesia catholica uniformiter celebrantur, ut legem credendi lex statuat supplicandi. Cum enim sanctarum plebium praesules mandata sibimet legatione funguntur, apud divinam clementiam humani generis agunt causam et tota secum ecclesia congemiscente, postulant et praedicantur, ut infidelibus donetur fides, ut idololatrae ab impietatis suae liberentur erroribus, ut Iudaeis ablato cordis velamine lux veritatis appareat, ut haeretici catholicae fidei perceptione resipiscant, ut schismatici spiritum redivivae charitatis accipiant, ut lapsis poenitentiae remedia conferantur, ut denique catechumenis ad regenerationis sacramenta perductis coelestis misericordiae aula reseretur. . . . Quod adeo totum divini operis esse sentitur, ut haec efficienti Deo gratiarum semper actio laudisque confessio pro illuminatione talium vel correctione referatur.* Now in this exhortation we obviously find ourselves under the influence of Romish errors. According to the same document, the jurisdiction under which the liturgy stands consists in the decisions of the "apostolic chair," and by the liturgy itself is obviously meant, less the actual practice of Church prayer and intercession, than the traditional liturgical texts as such, as a piece of authoritative tradition. But the exhortation is correct and important in its essential meaning. Church doctrine must hold to the fact that within the Church the effectual *opus divinum* of prayer is taking place for unbelievers, idolaters, Jews, heretics, schismatics, the lapsed and the catechumens, and that the norm of this prayer must also be the norm of true belief and true proclamation.

We can better understand the requirement of a Church attitude if we indicate certain delimitations. A Church attitude precludes the possibility of a dogmatics which thinks and speaks, as it were, timelessly. It fails in its task if it interprets itself as a finely detached inquiry into the ontic and noetic suggestions opened up by the Bible and dogma and a presentation of them as such—as a Christian philosophy competing or co-operating with other philosophies. The Bible and dogma are not sources which can be exploited in the service of this type of inquiry and exposition. They are not concerned with relations but with events, not with things but with deeds, not with a being as such, but with its existence; or, rather, with relations, things and a being, only in so far as events, deeds and its existence are at stake. The Word of God did not found an academy but the Church. If, therefore, an academy is required to serve the Word of God, it can only be the academy of the Church, founded and maintained at a definite time and place by the existence of the Word of God. The question of the ultimate relations of God, man, and the world may be a legitimate issue. But dogmatics is another matter altogether. In and with the Church, whose business it is not so much to put these questions as to be responsible before God and man, its task is to give consideration and counsel how the Church may dutifully discharge this responsibility. It does not have to find in the Bible and dogma answers to questions which it has framed itself. It has to await instructions in accordance with which it may then formulate human questions too. It has to serve the reflection which the Church needs for its work, its struggle, its unavoidable temptations and sorrows. It is expressly an instrument of the *ecclesia militans*, in the conviction that the Church in time cannot be anything but an *ecclesia militans*, i.e., the Church of a specific time with its needs and hopes.

The Church attitude precludes further the possibility of a dogmatics which thinks and speaks æsthetically. It is true, of course, that the object with which it has to do has its characteristic and quite distinctive beauty which it would be unpardonable, because ungrateful, to overlook or to fail to find pleasing.   But the moment dogmatics even temporarily surrenders to and loses itself in the contemplation of this beauty as such, instead of letting itself be held by the object, this beauty becomes the beauty of an idol.   No doubt certain formal requirements of completeness, symmetry and balance can and must be satisfied, because they are requirements of the object itself.   But other requirements of this kind have their origin and justification only in the contemplating subject and its arbitrary fancy.   There are interesting but otiose problems, which stand in no essential connexion with the need and hope of the Church and which a dogmatics thinking and speaking from a Church attitude must recognise as such and therefore suppress or exclude.   There is a logical, historical, linguistic, even a juristic æsthetics, in contact with which dogmatics at once loses touch with its own object, and therefore becomes estranged from its proper task, if it does not allow this object to fix its limits and call it to order.   The business of dogmatics is simply to investigate that which edifies the Church in the strictest connotation of the term, i.e., the dominion of the Word of God which kills and makes alive.   Therefore it must not turn its attention and give itself to that which edifies in general (however sweet or bitter).   When it is orderly in this respect, and only then, it will be continually struck by the beauty of its object, and moved, willy-nilly, to genuine and grateful contemplation.

Again, a Church attitude excludes the possibility of a romantic dogmatics, a dogmatics which does not start honestly from the Church of the present day, but goes back more or less successfully to the past and critically or uncritically tries to think and speak from the standpoint of a past century of the Church.   Now it is implied in what we have defined as its confessional attitude that dogmatics has to think and speak in constant contact with the history of the Church, in the unity of the true Church of all time.   But this does not mean that it must pretend to be a primitive Christian dogmatics or one belonging to the 4th or 16th or 17th century, though if it did, in many respects it would no doubt be more imposing, profound and pious, more rich in content, than if it tried to be simply a modern dogmatics speaking in and to the Church of the present.   If we think we can meet the needs of the contemporary generation by retiring to the secure ground of a better epoch of the past, and engaging in a process of excavating and rehabilitating, we may obtain the specious results which can always be obtained when ghosts are conjured.   But we must add that the Church is not edified by magic of this kind, and that therefore dogmatics must divest itself of romantic as of every other form of magic.   The ghosts even of the true Church of the past may lead the Church astray and into temptation no less than the spirits of the present.

Finally, the Church attitude precludes the possibility of a secular dogmatics which goes to the opposite extreme and serves the spirits of every present. And we must add that these may be spirits of the Church and theology. The requisite modernity and actuality of dogmatics cannot consist in the fact that it speaks to any time, to any political, intellectual, social or ecclesiastical structure of the present, as though this can be the standard of Church proclamation. Nor can it consist in the fact that it becomes the mouthpiece and advocate of the cares, concerns and wishes which contemporary society, religious or secular, bears on its heart when faced by the Church's proclamation. And it certainly cannot consist in the fact that from its knowledge of the history of the Church, it has to produce a new revelation as the content of its proclamation. That is why we have to lay so decisive an emphasis on the fact that dogmatics must seek its norm in the most essential function of the Church itself, that it has to orientate itself to the prayer of the Church, that is, to the Church which speaks before God and to God and therefore on behalf of men. In the present and for the sake of the present, dogmatics will not inquire about the voices of the day, but about the voice of God for the day, and it will have to give expression to the anxieties, concerns and wishes which arise from this point, just as the preaching of the Church must also do. If dogmatics tries to do otherwise, if it tries to speak, not from the Church, but from the world to the Church, then at best it will only do for the Church what is in any case daily done for it by the world itself. It will again underline the fact that the Church is in the world and that there is enough of the world in the Church itself. It will not do its real work, which is to summon and direct the Church to reflection in the light of its own basis and nature. And in all probability it will then become a downright temptation to the Church. The Church attitude of dogmatics means that it must persist in its solidarity with the teaching Church, and that therefore it must prove the spirits of the time both inside and outside the Church. But it must not exceed its calling by becoming their witness. Its own testimony will always be the very different testimony, which the spirits of the time are not able to give, but which they must hear from the Church and therefore from dogmatics.

§ 24

DOGMATICS AS A FUNCTION OF THE TEACHING CHURCH

Dogmatics summons the listening Church to address itself anew to the task of teaching the Word of God in the revelation attested in Scripture. It can do this only as it accepts itself the position of the teaching Church and is therefore claimed by the Word of God as the object to which the teaching Church as such has devoted itself.

1. THE MATERIAL TASK OF DOGMATICS

The life of the Church is not exhaustively defined as the hearing of the Word of God. By reason of this hearing, the Church which hears the Word of God is called to teach. And if, broadly speaking, the task of dogmatics is to test Church doctrine, this very testing cannot be exhaustively defined as recalling the Church from teaching to hearing. Rather, it calls it back so as the better to call it forward. It calls the Church to hear so as to call it to teach. Thus in regard to Church proclamation, its task is not only critical and formal, but also positive and material. It must remind it not only of its norm but also of its object. In all this, there can be no question of a second concern distinct from the first. The one Church is both the hearing and the teaching Church. It can never be the one without the other. Therefore dogmatics cannot be the one without the other. It is both, not successively and alternately, but simultaneously and together. It can call back and call forward, not alternately, but in the one reminder that the Church has its being in Jesus Christ. It can exhort to hearing and teaching only as simultaneous and co-relative activities. Only as a unity, therefore, can it fulfil its critical and positive, its formal and material tasks. The object is not different from the norm, nor is the norm different from the object of Church proclamation. In both cases we are speaking of the Word of God in the revelation attested in Scripture, where norm and object are one and yet different, just as Law and Gospel are one and yet different. But, because they are not only one but distinct in their unity, the two facts must be consciously perceived and expressly emphasised: first, that the Word of God is both the norm and the object of Church proclamation; and second, that dogmatics must therefore summon to both hearing and teaching, and that it is itself, therefore, to be understood as a function of both the hearing and teaching Church.

In the previous section, our point of departure was the ambiguity of the phenomenon of Church proclamation. By this we understood the ever open question whether the message of the Christian preacher springs from the source from which it must always come if it is faithful to its nature and purpose, i.e., from the Word of God and not, like heretical preaching, from elsewhere. But there is another question which is always open in relation to Christian preaching, and therefore a second ambiguity about it : What does it really mean, in terms of its will and activity, that the Church hears the Word of God ? It is caught in the questionableness of all human activity, and therefore even in this activity and on this side it is certainly not exempt from questioning or in no need of warning. The Word of God, when it is heard, demands the service of the Church ; it demands to be proclaimed and made known ; and since it wills to be made known to men, it demands human speech, human tongues and human words. Because it demands genuine service, and wills to be proclaimed and made known in pure doctrine, the first requirement is that it should be continually heard. But it demands service. This demand does not alter the fact that under all circumstances it is to be taught and that therefore in the Church the passage must always be made from hearing to speaking. " I believe and therefore speak." Only when hearing produces this consequence has the Word of God been really heard. It must therefore be a subject of inquiry whether this consequence does in fact follow, and it must always be remembered that it ought to follow. In the human frailty of the Church, it is just as little a matter of course that it does actually follow as that when the Church speaks it really speaks from faith, and therefore from the hearing of the Word of God and not from any other source. The Word of God committed to the Church has not only an origin but also a *telos*. Therefore in its human fulfilment it not only has a necessary order but an equally necessary dynamic. And just as disloyalty and disobedience to it may issue in deviation from this order, so they may mean a shrinking from its dynamic. In itself, this shrinking is just as impossible as the deviation. By its very nature, it is impossible that the hearing of the Word of God should leave or render the Church indifferent, timid or passive, or that it should spare it or relieve it of the obligation of proclamation and put it in the position of a waiting spectator. It is intrinsically impossible that the hearing of the Word of God should not lead to activity on the part of the Church, or that this activity should be paralysed or broken off, just as it is impossible that the word of the divine justification of the sinner should be heard without leading at once to his complete and sustained sanctification. From the point of view of the Word of God as such, these things are quite impossible. But they are always possible from the point of view of its hearing, so far as this means the human hearing of the Church. This hearing may be necessary and demanded, but it is not secure from human sophistry, which can easily deduce from the command not to do what ought not to be done, permission not to do what ought to be done; or conversely, from the command to do what ought not to be left undone, permission to do what ought to be left undone; or from the command that the Church must teach, permission to teach arbitrarily. At present we are concerned with the other possibility: that from the command that the Church should hear, permission is deduced to listen without responsibility or action. The command to turn and retreat in order to break out and advance further can easily be used to justify the arrogated freedom of an indolence which refuses to take seriously the fact that the Word of God is given to man that he may go out into all the world and preach the Gospel to every creature. With the experience of judgment, which is unavoidable where the Word of God is heard afresh, excuse can be offered for the avoidance of the consecration, commission and duty which come upon men just as irresistibly whenever judgment has really taken place and been accepted. It can never be granted that a real hearing of the Word of God can ever take place without a renewed attempt to teach it, or with the consequence that the teaching of the Word of God can come to a standstill and cease. But there is every reason to allow that in its human frailty the hearing of the Word of God by the Church is constantly beset by the temptation of this omission or intermission, the temptation to become a hearing only in appearance and not in actuality, a hearing which ends in itself and in which a man becomes guilty of the same righteousness of works and the same idolatry as when his actions and speech are grounded elsewhere than in the hearing of the Word of God. The permission which human sophistry deduces is always permission for the righteousness of works and idolatry. It always tries to change the content of the divine command into the content of a self-chosen programme, and the service of God into the service of an ideal and idol of one's own making. The hearing of the Word of God can be made into this kind of programme, and what is heard as the Word into this kind of ideal and idol. Without changing their essential nature, human arrogance and self-will can very well put on the garment of a holy indolence and passivity, and the need to unmask them is just as great as when they assume the garment of a holy self-assertion and activity. Even if the Church itself tries to be only a hearing Church, an audience entertained but finally not involved, it ceases as such to be the Church. Its supposed enjoyment will definitely not be the enjoyment of hearing the Word of God. The notion and obligation of pure doctrine laid upon the Church does not imply only that the purity of doctrine should be tested and restored by renewed hearing of the Word of God, but also when this happens it involves a new attempt to teach it. What is the use of a purity of doctrine which is not the purity of a doctrine of the Word of God which is actually practised, and proclaimed? That this proclamation should take place, that its necessity should be realised, and that the requisite will, courage, resolution and joy, but also (in view and because of the judgment by which the hearing Church is always confronted) the requisite humility and trust should be really forthcoming—this is by no means a matter of course, considering that the sophistry of the natural man is always resilient at this point also. This act of proclamation can only come about because it is continually granted to the Church. For the Church is as definitely and constantly challenged to undertake this as to realise that it can only be legitimate when the purity of doctrine is seriously sought and the Word of God seriously heard.

There is good reason at this point to consider again the parable of the talents in Mt. 25[14f.]. The servant who receives his talent, only to do nothing with it but bury it and later produce it intact, is certainly not the heretical and heresy-propagating Church, which misuses its trust by exploiting it for its own selfish purposes and thus alienating it from the service of the Lord. But he is an unfaithful and wicked servant; indeed, in this parable he is the only one described as wicked, because he has not traded with his talent in the service and for the profit of his master. It is not only the thief, not only the heretical Church, or the Church which plays with heresy, which is guilty of rebellion against the Lord, who as the Lord is entitled to make such demands of and from His own. It is also and especially the type of servant who returns his deposit intact, the Church which, despite the purity of its doctrine, does not make proper use of it and therefore cannot be said to teach pure doctrine. No biblical, confessional or ecclesiastical attitude can justify its doctrine, if in this attitude it does not stride forward afresh and all the more to the activity of proclamation and to the multiplication of what it has received in this attitude.

From this angle, too, it is to be realised that the ambiguity of the phenomenon of Church proclamation is impossible and intolerable, being not only open to attack but actually attacked at its root by the fact that the Church of God has received His promise, that its concern is His concern, and that He Himself wills to speak and will speak His own Word in it. It has necessarily forgotten this promise if it tries to indulge in human sophistry in this second form, the form of an evasion of sanctification and the duty implied in it. Recollection of the actual promise will save it from this second trouble and set it on the right path. Therefore what the Church needs from this point of view too is simply that it should not cease to recollect this promise, but wait for it in faith, and in faith continually return to it.

By this true promise must be concretely understood the presence of Jesus Christ the Lord in the biblical testimony to His revelation. This in itself is the summons to renewed teaching, just as it is the summons to a renewed hearing of the Word of God. If, in view of this second ambiguity in Church proclamation, dogmatics has a mission to fulfil even to the hearing Church, basically this can consist only in answering this summons, and therefore again, from this side too, pointing to the presence of Jesus Christ. Here again its task will be a material task, because this summons, in so far as it is a positive summons to proclaim new doctrine, is grounded in the fact that the presence of Jesus Christ in His Church is not only the norm, but the specific theme or object to which the teaching Church is dedicated. For from His nature as this object it follows necessarily that He must be proclaimed. In His presence lies both the obligation and the inspiration to proclaim Him. And the dynamic, which the Church may neglect just as little as it may swerve from the norm He sets up, is the dynamic of this object.

The presence of Jesus Christ in the biblical testimony to His revelation signifies the operation of a definite law laid upon the Church only because and in so far as a quite specific happening takes place within it. The Word of God constitutes the norm which must constantly be borne in mind in all Church proclamation only because and in so far as it declares something quite specific and has a quite specific content. This specific event which has taken place in the person of Jesus Christ, this specific content of the Word of God, determines and characterises the law and the norm which are valid in the Church and which in its activity it must respect. But the primary requirement of this event and message, and therefore the theme given to the teaching Church, is simply that the Church should act. It should do so in respect for and within the framework of that law and norm. But at all costs it should act. That is to say, it should testify to this event and its content and speak to itself and to all the world about it. For in virtue of what takes place and what is contained, this event and content constitute a Gospel which wills to go forth, and which cannot be and cannot be understood except as a Gospel that does go forth. Because this is the case, the Church is obliged, encouraged and authorised to teach by the presence of Jesus Christ. In the presence of Jesus Christ it has no option but to teach, and therefore to do just what it is called to do. It is, then, the task of dogmatics to remind it that this is the case. It is the task of dogmatics to remind it that the Word of God is not the Word of God if it is not *viva vox*, a message that goes forth as directed by the Church. The object or theme given to the teaching Church, Jesus Christ, or, in other words, the divine Word, is the Lord of man, of every man. The whole desire of the Word of God is for this man. For him it is appointed. For his sake it has come into the world. It is there with a view to him. And for man everything depends upon his attitude towards it, that it should be the attitude demanded by the Word of God itself. The Word is nothing more nor less than the Creator of man, and therefore the Judge by whose sentence and verdict he does or does not exist. The same Word of God is also the Reconciler of man, through whose decision his existence, plunged into sin and guilt, is either preserved by justification and sanctification, or not preserved. The same Word is also the Redeemer of men, through whose work the ruined existence of man is either restored to its former splendour, or else not restored but abandoned to the curse that hangs over it, and therefore to nothingness. The attitude of man required by this Word of God is faith. The Word of God longs after man in order that he may believe and that believing he may live by the Word of God and be acquitted and sanctified, and finally saved. But that he may believe the Word of God, it must have come to him, he must have heard it, and therefore it must have been spoken to him. By himself he neither knows it, nor knows that it is his Lord and thus his Creator, Reconciler and Redeemer. By himself he certainly cannot say to himself what it has to say to him. By himself, therefore, he cannot believe, and therefore he cannot live, he cannot be acquitted and sanctified, he cannot be saved. The Word is therefore precipitated into this human vacuum with all the weight of the divine will and power of fulfilment—the Word of God which is entrusted to the Church, Jesus Christ the theme and object given to the teaching Church. It belongs, therefore, to the very nature of this object that it be proclaimed. It contains necessarily the dynamic of the *viva vox*, of a Gospel going forth inevitably and irresistibly. A message which can be passed over in silence, or which leaves to the Church the choice of delivering it or not, is not the Word of God. The Word of God exists and the human vacuum exists. This vacuum is revealed as such by the Word of God itself, so that it can no longer be overlooked. But the Church has the Word of God in virtue of the promise given to it. According to this promise the Church lives in the presence of Jesus Christ. Just because it is the bearer of the Word of God, and in face of this vacuum, it must always teach. That is, it must repeat in this vacuum what is said by this Word. The Word of God itself in virtue of its content, Jesus Christ Himself in virtue of what He is and does, constitutes the Church as the teaching Church. Thus the divine object is the foundation of the human subject of pure doctrine, that is, of the subjective possibility of pure doctrine as a human activity. The Church has actually only to remember the Word, Jesus Christ, and therefore the reality of the promise alive within it, to be called and geared to this activity. The call to *purity* of doctrine arises from the promise given to the Church as law and norm. The call to purity of *doctrine* arises from the promise as the object or theme given to the Church, in virtue of its very nature, and in virtue of what it has to say about man and to man concerning the gracious action of God for man. False teaching is forbidden by the norm, but silence is forbidden by the object. The promise cannot wait until the Church attains in sufficient measure the appropriate purity of doctrine demanded. It does demand this purity. It constitutes, therefore, a critical norm. It separates out all false teaching. But even so, it demands that the Church should teach in every time and place according to its existing constitution, however little it may have advanced towards purity, however far behind it may still be in this respect. On the one hand, therefore, it cannot claim any perfection which frees it from control by the promise. But on the other hand, it cannot claim any imperfection which frees it from the dynamic of the promise. There never is a time when the Church ought not to be concerned about its purity. But, again, there never is a time when this concern does not involve an equal concern that teaching be instituted and practised. The Law excludes the first and the Gospel excludes the second. The news which the Church has to proclaim is that in virtue of what has happened in Jesus Christ man can now live with God in faith and love and hope, on the ground of God's unfathomable and unmerited mercy. And this news is so urgent that in every time and place where the Church exists it must be proclaimed at once and in all circumstances. It is a contradiction of the content of this message if in view of the probable unworthiness even of its future achievements the Church tries to evade the demand for obedience, or if it is willing to obey only when it finds itself in a position to render this obedience worthily. According to the content of the message, the worthiness of human action can never be claimed as a right, nor can the unworthiness of human action ever be regarded as an obstacle to entering at once and in all circumstances into the fellowship which God offers man and therefore to discharging at once and in all circumstances the obedience which is enjoined.

But just at this point, by reason of the sophistry of the natural man, there is the continual temptation and danger that this obedience will be omitted because on this side, too, the phenomenon of Church proclamation is ambiguous. Here, then, the task of dogmatics is necessarily a material one. It has to call to the recollection and consciousness of the Church which hears the Word of God the content of what is heard when it hears this Word, so that in the dynamic of this content it will not only be the Church which hears, but the Church which hears and teaches. The aim is that it will be compelled to instant and constant obedience, quite irrespective of its present or future worthiness or unworthiness, wholly and utterly for the sake of the promise itself. It has not only to be prevented from becoming a heretical Church, but also from becoming a dead Church. Its duty has to press insistently upon it, jolting it out of all peace—even the peace of critical reflection—and compelling it to act. It has not to be guilty of neglecting its required responsibility because of fear of responsibility. For this reason the summons which dogmatics must address to the Church cannot and must not be confined to a formal requirement, to the bare proposition that the teaching Church must be content to be confronted by the Word of God and must shape itself accordingly. A postulate of this kind cannot and must not be left in the air. Even as the teaching Church, the Church is not a datum, the existence of which we can at once assume, which needs only to be purified and not reconstituted, which has not to be continually awakened and, especially and expressly in the human sphere, challenged not only to hear but also—for this is not a matter of course—to teach. The fact of Church proclamation is self-explanatory and certain in itself only from the point of view of the divine promise, not from the point of view of its human realisation. In the latter sphere there is constant ambiguity. Every day the Church needs to be newly aroused and newly sustained—sustained not merely with regard to the mode but also with regard to the substance of its teaching. The life of the Church as well as the formal constitution of its message is in danger. If its doctrine requires to be tested, this must be understood to mean that it requires to be positively confirmed and strengthened and invigorated and vivified. And if ultimately and decisively this can be expected only from the Word of God itself empowered by the Holy Spirit, dogmatics cannot refuse its service to the Word of God and the Church even from this angle. In the last resort, the purification which this testing involves is to be expected only from the Word of God itself. But this does not mean that the Church need not lay its hand to the plough in the work of dogmatics. It must do this here no less than elsewhere. Even the confirming and vivifying of doctrine, and the continually necessary reconstituting of the teaching Church, does not take place only by the fact that it finds in the Word of God its rule and touchstone, but, above and beyond that, in the fact that in the same Word of God it has its source, and is therefore empowered by the Word of God as well as ordered. And if in this respect, too, dogmatics has a particular service to render to the Word of God, it must clearly consist in pointing to the Word of God as the source of its teaching, in making the Word of God understood as the Word which, as and when it is heard, insists on proclamation and makes proclamation necessary, possible and actual—as the Word which founds and maintains not merely the formal content but also the life of Church doctrine. For the sake of fulfilling the Church's mission, it must make the gift of the Word understandable not only as task but also as gift. In pointing to it as the norm to which the whole Church and itself are subject, it must also display it so that it is revealed and speaks for itself as a gift. It must not only affirm the glory of the Word formally, but positively attest it as glory. In so doing, it must not betray in any way its essential nature and limits as dogmatics. It is still true that dogmatics is not preaching and that, as a scientific testing of Church doctrine, it is only an auxiliary to Church proclamation. But how can it fulfil this role if it views only from the outside the object which occupies and claims Church proclamation, holding it up to Church proclamation as the norm only as seen from the outside? How can it fulfil its role if it is not willing to enter right into the matter, understanding it as the Gospel which it is, and making it understandable as Gospel to the Church? Everything which Holy Scripture says against a supposed Word of God understood abstractly as a law applies automatically against a dogmatics interpreted and presented in this way. In the name of the freedom of the children of God we must protest against a dogmatics of this kind, and refuse the service which it ostensibly renders. It can be service in the Church and to the Law of God, and the necessary service to the Word of God, only when and in so far as it is service to the Gospel, and therefore its formal task is undertaken as a material one as well, that is, the unfolding and presenting of the content of the Word of God as something which awakens, confirms, strengthens, invigorates and vivifies the teaching of the Church. It will render this authoritative as a norm by expressing it as object. It will carry out the necessary criticism of all Church doctrine by addressing itself entirely to the matter which claims and occupies Church doctrine, explicitly or implicitly looking back from this point on the various more or less pure or impure forms of Church doctrine. Of itself, therefore, it will be impelled to pronounce over the whole range of the human work of Church teaching not only judgment but also the forgiveness of sins, which has to be declared even to the Church which teaches impurely, even to the heretical or heretically-minded Church, if judgment and repentance are really to be proclaimed to it. It will then be able to disclose, present and combat all the failings, errors and deviations of the Church as so many disloyalties to the truth primarily disclosed to it, thus dealing with them in connexion with the truth itself. This does not mean that it will minimise the Church's liability to error. It will not call the impure pure. It will not insinuate error into the true teaching of the Church. On the contrary, its concern will be to mark off the boundary between the Church and its doctrine on the one hand and error and falsehood on the other. The drawing of this dividing line will not be effected without positive implications, without a promise and invitation reaching beyond the limits demanded. The Law which slays can be made effective only on the basis and in the content of the Gospel which makes alive. For this reason and in this way dogmatics will be able to speak comfortably to the Church itself. Unfolding and presenting the Word of God, it will speak to the Church from no other standpoint than the Church's own being and essence. It will say to it only what it already is and has, because Jesus Christ is already present in it. It will confront it with the abundance of its own wealth. It will make clear to it in what quite unnecessary poverty and restriction it is moving, and how strong and rich it might immediately become. It will make the Church dear to itself. It will inspire it with new confidence and courage to become wholly itself. It will accomplish all this by causing the Word of God to be spoken again to it, not only by inviting it to hear the Word and adjust its life to it, but by doing its utmost to enable it to hear the Word, itself seeking to teach it as far as its capacity allows. And as it does so, although it will not compel, it will certainly urge the Church not only to hear, but to teach as it hears. The Church does not have to do this, but it ought to do it. For it is an honour and a joy, an inner necessity and a gracious privilege to serve and therefore to teach the Word of God. Indeed, it is the whole meaning of the Church's existence. Therefore the compulsion to proclaim the Gospel implies the incomparable freedom of the Church. It is not only disobedience and disloyalty, but folly and self-betrayal, not to make use of this freedom. For the Church can live only in the sphere of this freedom. Outside this sphere, it can only die. And when dogmatics has to call the Church to order, since this takes place only in the context of the unfolding and presenting of the Word, and in relation to its dynamic, it can only happen that the Church is compelled to realise that in all the weakness and ambiguity of its doctrine it is enfolded by the power and clarity of what God Himself will and actually does teach within it. Dogmatics cannot adequately reflect this power and clarity. But it can at least bring them to the notice of the Church as the transcendent by which the Church and its activity are relativised and judged, yet at the same time sustained, and of the presence of which they can avail themselves at any time if they only will.

2. THE DOGMATIC METHOD

We understand by dogmatic method the procedure which dogmatics must adopt if it is successfully to handle its material task, i.e., the unfolding and presentation of the content of the Word of God. In this respect, too, dogmatics can place itself only alongside and not above preaching. Essentially the dogmatician can do only what the preacher does : in obedience he must dare to say what he has heard, and to give out what he has received. With the intention and purpose of summoning the hearing Church to new exertions in teaching, dogmatics for its part adopts the attitude of the teaching Church, makes the task of teaching its very own, and attempts to offer an exemplary performance of this teaching task. It takes part in the proclaiming, just as, from the formal point of view, it takes part in the hearing of the Word of God. What in this connexion distinguishes it from preaching is a shift of emphasis. When the Church in general teaches, its meaning and purpose are mainly concerned with the reconstitution of a hearing Church. But this is impossible without a new invitation to teaching, to the service of witnessing, to the giving out of the received message by the congregation which hears it : just as it is impossible for the Church to teach without submitting the rightness and validity of its teaching to constant investigation and control. But when dogmatics teaches, on the material as well as on the formal side its most prominent and decisive question is one which, though unavoidable for the teaching Church in general, is kept in the background. On the material side, this question concerns the inciting and arousing of the Church to a fresh teaching of the Word of God. In this respect, the point of departure for dogmatics will naturally be the hearing Church which creates and receives from the Word of God as source. But just because the Church cannot remain at this point under the material constraint of the Word of God, because it is under constant pressure to declare what it has heard, because this compulsion signifies a call to the Church, and because one way in which dogmatics has to serve the Church is by voicing this call, in obedience dogmatics itself has to dare to take the step from hearing to speaking. This very step, the exemplary forging of the indispensable connexion between hearing and teaching, will become its special theme from this point of view. In taking this step, therefore, and as coming from the hearing Church, it assumes the attitude of the teaching Church. It does not do so in order to replace or even complete the teaching of the Church, or with the intention of introducing a second perhaps deeper, more learned, more exact, more comprehensive, type of Church preaching. It does not compete in any way with what the teaching Church in general has to do. What it does, it does for the sake of something which is never self-evident : the constitution of the teaching Church as such ; in order that the hearing Church may never forget or fail to become the teaching Church, and that in this second function it may never be dispirited, bewildered, joyless or inactive and therefore dead.

Of course, dogmatics is not in a position to bring the Word of God itself and as such before the hearing Church, and to set in motion its reviving power. It can do this as little as, on the formal side, it can set in motion the critical operation of the Word of God in regard to the teaching Church. The critical and the reviving power of the Word of God in the Church is the power of the Word of God itself and its power alone. In both aspects dogmatics can only serve this power. Thus it can attempt to revive only by human means. And even this cannot be done arbitrarily ; even these human means may not be self-chosen. But it can revive only by subjecting itself as readily and sincerely as it may to the reviving power of the Word of God. Its call to the listening Church is that it must never forget or fail to pass on to teaching and to proclaim the received Word of God. But *in concreto* this call necessarily consists in the fact that dogmatics sets an example to the listening Church and demands that it follow the example of human thinking and speaking nourished by the Word of God and really and essentially constituted by its content. It refuses to be silent itself, and in that way it testifies that it cannot be silent. It does not confine itself to establishing the Law or applying it as a norm to criticise teaching. It teaches as it hears, and in that way it shows that it can and must teach. In all this, it reminds the Church of the teaching function which is so essential a part of its very being. It tries to do justice in this way to its material task, being content to receive and appropriate its material, contents and themes from the Word of God, and in obedience daring to speak of them. It practises Church proclamation in a sense dictated by the Gospel given to the Church, in taking up the Gospel itself and attempting to proclaim it. Thus on this side too, within the sphere of the human word of Church proclamation which of itself is always jeopardised, it must be a demonstration and a token, a sign and a witness of the presence and the power of the Word of God, in whose service the word of man must continually receive not simply its qualification and authentication, but its very existence, if it is to exist at all. From this point of view, too, dogmatics, like preaching itself, cannot try to be anything more than what Holy Scripture and even the manhood of Jesus Christ are on the human side, namely, witness to God's Word. The dogmatician, then, has the power of the Word only by the free grace of the eternal Word of God itself, and therefore in the hiddenness of his faith and obedience, which justify him only in so far as they are given him by the Word of God itself. Seeing that in the material aspect of its task dogmatics unfolds and presents the content of the Word of God, the power of the Word of God, which it has to attest in this way, can only become visible in the light which is reflected from divine upon human being and doing. In dogmatics as such its operation can be only instrumental. Even in the material aspect, dogmatics is what it is either by the sovereign act of God or not at all. But dogmatics can and may and must continually return to the sovereign act of God on the basis of the promise given to the Church, just as preaching can and may and must return to it, and the biblical witnesses returned to it in their human action, and even the man Jesus, with exemplary significance for all human witness, returned to the sovereign act of God in His own existence, this continual recourse being the basis of His existence in the flesh as the Son of the Father. How can this recourse to God's grace be made without respecting its freedom ? How can it be made without fear ? But, again, how can it be made without the joy and confidence that overcome fear ? In the present connexion, how can it be made without the confidence that dogmatics, too, can and will be an effective sign, the ordained sign not only of the divine norm for Church proclamation, but also of divine power ? The work and structure of dogmatics are not of themselves divine, but human and creaturely. The nature of the sign is, then, that by way of example or pattern the work of dogmatics is wholly claimed by the object of Church doctrine, and that it is characterised as a type of human thinking and speaking occupied and filled with the revelation attested in Holy Scripture. The fact that they are claimed and occupied and filled in this way is what distinguishes dogmatic thinking and speaking from undogmatic. Again, this certainly does not mean the distinction of a divine from a human thinking and speaking but rather a distinction within the sphere of the human. Again, dogmatic thinking and speaking have to be differentiated from all other types by the fact that they have capitulated to this object, so that they take place in the confinement, but also, of course, in the freedom, of this object. At this point we must repeat and reverse the image used in § 23. In dogmatic work a type of thinking is expressed which is bound by its object, by the Word of the Father, the Son and the Holy Ghost in the revelation which Scripture attests. It reminds us, therefore, of the gate which is also a barrier. It is inevitably a criticism of the teaching Church in so far as the latter has forgotten the norm which prescribes a law for its activity. How else can it be a reminder of God's Word? But again, how can it really remind us of God's Word if it does not also remind us that the barrier is a gate as well, that a norm is fixed for the Church's teaching that it may take place rightly, not that it should not take place at all. It is only a work of man. But its emergence as a thinking and speaking occupied and filled with its object is a witness to the Church of something which is not self-evident but has need of witness, that the barrier is really a gate as well, and that if its action has to take place rightly, it is both necessary and possible that it should take place.

The dogmatic method is, then, the way necessarily taken by dogmatic work, as claimed by its object. Like the dogmatic norm, it must be identical with the revelation which Scripture attests as the Word of God, to the extent that this is not merely a norm but also a way : a specific integrated and ordered content. At the very deepest level, this content prescribes for dogmatics, as for Church proclamation, its way and its method. In its unfolding and presenting of the content of the Word of God, it has no option but to proceed in this way. The content of the Word of God itself must command, and dogmatics and Church proclamation must obey. Therefore the content of dogmatics can only be an exposition of the work and action of God as it takes place in His Word. We have seen that because the work of God takes place in the Word, it wills to be heard, and as it is heard, proclaimed. No work of man and therefore no dogmatics can accomplish this work of God. But in so far as this work is actualised in the Word of God, in so far as it is present to the Church in the biblically attested revelation of God in Jesus Christ, dogmatics can testify to it. This means, concretely, that it can describe and explain it in the light of its presence. This is the one task of Church proclamation. And for its inspiration, confirmation and stimulation, it is the exemplary task of dogmatics. The method of dogmatics will always be orderly when it is occupied with this task ; it will always be disorderly when it concerns itself with something other than this. Therefore from this point of view as well we have to speak, basically, of the theonomy and only of the theonomy of Church proclamation and dogmatics. We understand it now as the freedom and sovereignty of the divine work and action consummated in God's revealed Word, as the way which

God has taken, takes and will take with man in the person of Jesus Christ and through the operation of the Holy Spirit. The method of Church proclamation consists, and can only consist, in a treading of this way.

But what is the meaning of theonomy as established and effectually operative in the human sphere ? Without a relative concrete form, theonomy is an empty idea at the mercy of chance or arbitrariness. In this respect we can only repeat what we said in § 23. But our present concern is not with the formal but the material task of dogmatics. We are not investigating its norm but its method, and therefore the obedience which dogmatics must render to the work and action of God taking place in His Word, with a view to the fresh stimulation, confirmation and inspiration of a definite human activity in the Church, i.e., its proclamation, by the recalling of this work and the attestation of its power. In this case, then, it is not enough to refer to the heteronomy corresponding to the theonomy of dogmatics, to the relative and concrete form in which the Word of God encounters both Church proclamation and dogmatics as something other, as an alien law. If in regard to the material task of dogmatics there is a theonomy with its corresponding relative and concrete form, in this connexion—for it is now a question of the subjective possibility of pure doctrine— it must have the relative and concrete form of autonomy. Autonomy cannot be understood any more than heteronomy as in antithesis to theonomy, but only in correspondence and correlation with it. Nor, of course, can autonomy denote a contradiction to the heteronomy of dogmatics described in § 23. Both the autonomy and heteronomy of dogmatics describe as from below, and from the point of view of man himself, what from above and from the point of view of God is to be described as theonomy. Both together denote the necessary obedience of Church proclamation and therefore of dogmatics which accompanies it as a model. But just because this obedience is to be understood and described as strict and complete, it has to be described, not only formally and objectively from the standpoint of the norm, and therefore of heteronomy, but also positively and subjectively from the standpoint of the method, and therefore of autonomy. Like the obedience of the Church in general, the obedience of dogmatics is obviously not understood as real obedience if it is not understood as obedience given in freedom. A human action may be characterised as obedience to the Word of God by the fact that it stands under the alien law of the Word of God and that this law is also its own law. But this is true, of course, only if the two statements are made together. If the action is defined only from the one side or the other, from without or from within, it might equally well be described as an action of disobedience. If the theonomy of dogmatics is to be spoken of concretely and relatively, we must not speak merely of its autonomy, nor merely of its heteronomy, as though theonomy could be exhausted in one of these aspects. The autonomy of dogmatics denotes its obedience to the Word of God in so far as this obedience is the fully free decision belonging to the human subject of dogmatics, in so far as its theonomy has its concrete relative form in this free human decision. It is obviously only by this free human decision, and not in any other way, that it becomes linked and occupied and filled with the work and action of God taking place in the Word of God. What is the value to dogmatics of a biblical, confessional or Church attitude, if in this attitude it is not occupied with the work of God taking place in the Word ? The attitude required of dogmatics as its norm by the Word of God does not of itself guarantee that this will be the case. Let us suppose that the question of attitude can actually be isolated and settled in this way. Let us suppose that the obedience required in dogmatics and Church proclamation can be fulfilled by the adoption of this correct attitude. It can still happen that even in this attitude dogmatics fails to be in communion with the real work and operation of God which takes place in His Word. It can still try to unfold and present the content of the Word of God by an objective description and analysis of all the relevant features. It can, therefore, completely miss the real character of this content as a conversation, a process, a military action, an act of sovereignty. And in so doing, it will fail utterly in relation to the material side of its task. It is true, of course, that to make this mistake is in fact to fail to comply with its norm, and not to assume the attitude required. If it really occupies a biblical, confessional and Church position, how can it possibly overlook and miss the work of God which takes place in the Word of God ? But that it cannot do so does not result from the mere fact that it is subject to the requirement of this attitude. This state of affairs is not attained by a demand addressed to it. Its connexion with the central thing, with the object of Church doctrine, with the work and operation of God in His Word, certainly has its basis and explanation in its theonomy, but only in its autonomy, not in its heteronomy. The connexion is not made simply by subjecting dogmatic work to an objective law laid upon it from outside ; it is realised only if its obedience becomes a wholehearted and therefore a genuine obedience, that is, only if it makes the law of God its own and therefore appropriates it by a free act of decision on the part of the human subject of dogmatics. It is only in this decision that dogmatics comes to participate in the conversation, the process, the action, the act of sovereignty—in short, the work and operation of God which forms the real content of His Word. And how else but in this participation and decision can it truly report and unfold and present the real content of the Word of God ? In this decision, and only in this decision, it is set on its right path, and receives what we call its method. Everything naturally depends on whether this free decision of the human subject of dogmatics is not an arbitrary decision but a decision made in obedience, on whether therefore the autonomy of dogmatics is not really to be understood except (like its heteronomy) as a relative concrete form of its theonomy. It cannot be systematically presupposed that it is an autonomy which not only has nothing to do with arbitrariness, but by which all arbitrariness is automatically excluded. For it is the gift of grace and of the Holy Spirit which must come from God, so that man can take it into account only as a presupposition for which he must pray. But the same is true of the heteronomy of dogmatics as well as its autonomy. As the presupposition which God gives and for which man prays, it always has to be taken into account in Christian thinking and speaking. The reservations, under which alone this can be done, obviously apply in this case too. But every reservation which we have to make in this connexion is again a ratification of the promise given to the Church and therefore a permission of which man can and must make use. Therefore, on the view that God must give it and that man must pray for it, we understand the autonomy of dogmatics, too, as a relative concrete form of its theonomy, and the free decision of the human subject, not as arbitrariness but as obedience. It is the inner obedience in which our subjection to the Word does not mean only that we acknowledge it as the externally imposed norm of our thinking and speaking, but beyond this, that we accept the work and activity of God which takes place in the Word, allowing ourselves to be drawn into the sphere of its effective operation, that we therefore make our own the way which God Himself takes in His Word, adopting it as the way of our own thinking and speaking, and consequently of its method.

It has to be made clear, of course, that if as an act of obedience in this sense the decision about dogmatic method takes place in the free decision of the human subject of dogmatics, this means at once that it does not take place on the basis of an external law, and that it cannot of itself have the character of an external law. It certainly rests on the absolute requirement of obedience made by the Word of God itself. But it rests on a relative concrete demand only in so far as in obedience to God we have to address this requirement to our inmost selves—that is, not in heteronomy, but rather autonomy. This also means that we can propose and apply it to others as a witness to the absolute character of the demand for obedience of the Word of God, but not as a relative concrete demand which necessarily arises from the Word for them too. Because it is for us the necessary and only possible decision, we can represent it to all others as the decision which we have made in accordance with both knowledge and conscience. It will therefore carry with it what is, we hope, a serious challenge, a well-grounded suggestion and valuable counsel to which attention ought to be paid. But at bottom it can only be a challenge, a suggestion, a *consilium*, not an ultimately and absolutely binding command.

It is another matter if our decision does in fact acquire for others the force of a binding command, so that it now becomes for them too the necessary and only possible decision. What this means is that it has pleased God to ratify our decision as the right one, and to use it to declare His will to others. But although the decision as such may find a good deal of applause and approval and many followers, although it may even have the formal character of a decision of the community, it still cannot arrogate to itself the character of a command. Under no circumstances can it present itself to others as anything but a free decision which as such can only challenge others to make similar free decisions. The work and activity of God which takes place in His Word is concerned with man's free decision, and the free decision of man is concerned with the work of God which takes place in His Word (so that from both points of view we have to do with an encounter between God and man as between persons). This being the case, it is impossible for any human person to press his own understanding of the divine law upon others, as though the two things were identical. We shall have to elucidate and substantiate this later in our discussion of the concept and actuality of the divine commanding and commandments.

Now this means that in the concrete form in which it is made the decision with regard to dogmatic method, and therefore to the path that dogmatics has to tread in unfolding and presenting the contents of the Word of God, cannot possibly be based upon the arbitrary will of the human subject concerned, but solely upon his encounter with the work and activity of God. It must, therefore, be a decision made in obedience, and as such may claim to have for others the character of a challenge, a suggestion and a counsel. But, unlike the form and attitude in which it has to be made, it does not rest upon a demand laid upon it from outside, but upon the relative and concrete demand which the human subject must address to himself in full and free obedience to the Word of God, which he alone can address to himself, but which he cannot address to others as a demand. Basically, then, the decision in relation to dogmatic method is a free choice from within and a free offer from without. This does not mean that it will have to be examined any the less seriously, or be any the less seriously justified to others. If this is forgotten, or omitted, or undertaken lightly, if the decision is left to chance or to preference, if it is not made with a good understanding and conscience in self-surrender to the object of Church doctrine, and if it is not scrupulously justified in relation to others, it does not bode too well for its character as obedience. If dogmatics can be flippant with regard to the choice of its method, it is open to serious question whether, after all, in its most intimate personal character where its entire inward obedience is demanded, it does not finally rest upon arbitrariness, and how far under these circumstances, on the basis of the method it chooses and follows, it is really in a position to make an offer that can be taken seriously.

The principle : *methodus est arbitraria*, calls for discussion in this connexion. If it is true, it obviously cannot be taken to mean that the *arbiter* can sleep and dream, and then decide according to his fancy. He really must decide. He is not relieved of this duty of decision by any law imposed from outside. The requirement of a biblical or confessional and Church attitude does not anticipate the decision which method he must follow in dogmatics. He still has to decide in this biblical, confessional and Church attitude. This means that he has to decide after the most searching examination and consideration of the external law which he already knows, and even more searching inquiries into the inner law which he must discover for himself. In proportion as he neglects to do this, he sins against the object of Church doctrine and therefore against God, and the challenge, suggestion and counsel which his decision ought to mean for others will have no genuine reliability for them.

The freedom of dogmatic method is the freedom of obedience. This obedience will not be the obedience required, if it is not rendered freely, and if it does not leave freedom to others. Nor will the freedom be the freedom required, if it makes possible anything other than obedience, and does not therefore summon all others to render obedience in freedom.

If we approach the problem of dogmatic method with this insight, we already have our answer to the preliminary question, whether dogmatics has to unfold and present the content of the Word of God in the form of a system. As understood by all those who in philosophy and theology have attempted and created something of the kind, " system " means a structure of principles and their consequences, founded on the presupposition of a basic view of things, constructed with the help of various sources of knowledge and axioms, and self-contained and complete in itself. If dogmatic method consists in the development of this type of system, it will be the end both of the freedom in which its obedience is to be practised, and of the obedience in which it has to prove its freedom. At any rate, the presupposed basic view will necessarily have the character of a law. And what can its systematic development be but the exposition of this law ? If this view is really to be the basis for the development of this type of system, it must first be expounded definitively in the form of a concretely formulated first principle or a whole series of such first principles, and then the development of the system will consist in the analysis of these *a priori* principles. The subject of this dogmatic exercise will have to attend to this analysis and so in that way build up the system, thus being relieved of the duty of obedience in other respects. Will this be the obedience which corresponds to the Word of God ? The intrusion of the type of law by which alone a dogmatic system of this kind is possible will clearly contradict the objectivity required of dogmatics by the mere fact that in consequence the autonomy of dogmatic work will be eliminated and therefore the completeness of the obedience owed will be imperilled. It should be added that a dogmatic system is in any case an impracticable idea, because in it it is not the Word of God but the presupposed fundamental view of things that will become the object of dogmatics. And even at best a view of this kind can have only the form of a fundamental principle or theme or a construct of such themes or principles, derived more or less faithfully and skilfully from the Word of God. But *quo iure* can such a derivation take place ? *Quo iure* is it a theme (or themes) to be stated in this way ? *Quo iure* is it erected into a principle of exposition ? *Quo iure* does it step into the position which the Word of God ought to occupy ?

To what lengths this proceeding can go is best made clear by a few modern examples of dogmatic systems. C. E. Luthardt (*Komp. d. Dogm.*[4], 1873, p. 18) decrees that the material principle of dogmatics must be " communion with God in Christ which is grounded in justification by faith and in consequence manifests itself in righteousness of life." For J. Kaftan (*Dogm.*[3-4], 1901, p. 8) the essence of Christianity which dogmatics has to develop is to be found in the two ideas of the Kingdom of God and the atonement. F. Nitzsch (*Lehr. d. ev. Dogm.*[3] edit. by H. Stephan, 1912, p. 64) expresses the key-principle in the words: " Jesus Christ by the realisation of the Kingdom of God in humanity has become the everlasting Mediator of its salvation." R. Seeberg (*Chr. Dogm.* vol. 1, 1924, p. 161) defines Christianity as " the communion of man with God realised through Jesus Christ, and consisting in the Christian faith as the acceptance of the redeeming lordship of God and in love as surrender to God, and the Kingdom which is to be realised by Him." According to E. Troeltsch (*Glaubenslehre*, 1925, p. 71) the theme of Christianity is " the idea of raising human souls to God and redeeming and sanctifying them through communion with the living God, and of uniting them in God to a kingdom of persons arising from God and turned towards Him, and therefore inseparably bound together in religious love." All this may be more or less fine and useful, and it may even form a basis for detailed discussion. But by what right is it dared to make the systematic exposition of these assumptions the business of dogmatics ? And is it not almost comical to see how, after many authors had long enough boasted of their christocentric dogmatics, it occurred to someone to present his as theocentric, whereupon someone else preferred to be " staurocentric," and someone else again " hamartiocentric " ? What next ? From this point of view, perhaps an even less fortunate moment was the much earlier one when Cyril of Jerusalem began (*Cat. Intro.* 11) to compare Christian instruction to the " building of a house " (οἰκοδομή). But to be able to build a house in dogmatics, we have obviously first to lay the foundation (θεμέλιον), to which Cyril himself made specific reference. But was he really thinking of 1 Cor. 3[11] ?

It may clearly be seen that the very necessity of positing this basic view compromises seriously the intention and realisation of a dogmatic system. In dogmatic systems the presupposed basic view acquires inevitably the position and function which according to all our previous considerations can be ascribed only to the Word of God. But the Word of God may not be replaced even vicariously by any basic interpretation of the " essence of Christianity ", however pregnant, deep and well founded. The simple reason for this is that while its content is indeed the truth, it is the truth of the reality of the work and activity of God taking place within it. As such it is not to be condensed and summarised in any view, or idea, or principle. It can only be reported concretely, i.e., in relation to what is at any given time the most recent stage of the process or action or sovereign act of which it is the occurrence. And this report cannot be made the business and function of the object of dogmatics. In proportion as

the dignity and function of the object by which man finds himself surveyed, and which has complete freedom to control man whatever position he may adopt. If not, the object is not the Word of God and it cannot be said that what is thought and said is *sub ratione Dei*. If not, dogmatics cannot authentically summon the Church either to hear or to teach. If not, what happens under this heading will not be Church dogmatics at all in the strict sense of the expression. If, then, the autonomy in which it must take place is to consist in the recognition of its theonomy, the choice of dogmatic method can be made only with the intention of placing human thinking and speaking on the path of total surrender to the controlling power of its object—a path which for the sake of the one supreme presupposition is utterly without presuppositions in all other respects. But this means that from the human point of view the position which in a system is occupied by the fundamental principle of interpretation can only remain basically open in Church dogmatics, like the opening in the centre of a wheel. It cannot be occupied even hypothetically or provisionally by any *a priori* decisions. It is ready to receive those decisions with which the object will urgently confront human thinking and speaking. It is ready for new insights which no former store of knowledge can really confront on equal terms or finally withstand. Essentially dogmatic method consists in this openness to receive new truth, and only in this. It consists in unceasing and ready vigilance to see that the object is able to speak for itself, and that its effect on human thinking and speaking is not disturbed. It implies the confidence that these effects will come, and come with regal power, that the object can do this, and that what it can do it will actually do. Therefore it presupposes the operation of the object itself, to which is to be ascribed the awakening of this very confidence. It presupposes the reality of the promise given to the Church. In these presuppositions its supreme concern must essentially be not to be anxious, not to try to concern itself overmuch, especially in the form of a well-meant but prematurely intended occupation of that open position by a basic principle or view which first has to be purified. Dogmatic method consists essentially in the expectation that there will eventually be this purification and the consequent emergence of the essence of Christianity ; that no harm will be done to anything true and right which we might think we know, and announce and accept, as a basic principle for dogmatic work ; that it will be revealed and confirmed as true and right if only it does not try to prove itself prematurely, if only it is not too precipitately laid as a foundation, if only it is left to the confirmatory control of the object, if only it is not too soon withdrawn from the crucible in which it must be purified and refined by the effect of this object. In the last resort we may say that dogmatic method consists simply in this : that the work and activity of God in His Word are honoured and feared and loved (literally) above all things.

At this point it may be seen at once that in substance dogmatic method essentially coincides with what we have said about the dogmatic norm and especially its demand for a biblical attitude. Questions 94 and 95 of the *Heidelberg Catechism* may again be recalled. But this time we are not speaking of a command. We are speaking of what necessarily and automatically happens where the real free decision of the subject of dogmatics is determined by the real object of dogmatics. The content of this decision will then be that for the sake of the one supreme concern we will not busy ourselves with other concerns.

If, then, there is no *a priori* basic view in dogmatics, but, as its foundation and centre, only the Word of God which presupposes itself and proves itself by the power of its content, it is quite evident that there can be no dogmatic system. Rightly understood, it is the material principle of dogmatics itself which destroys at its root the very notion of a dogmatic system. Where there is no longer a secure platform for thinking and speaking, there is likewise no system. In dogmatics, laying the foundation means recollection that the foundation is already laid, and expectation that it will continually be laid. No system can be founded on this attitude of recollection and expectation. The laying of this foundation means the shaking of all and any systematic certainties that may arise. To be sure, it may in fact mean their eventual confirmation. But it can equally well mean their dissolution. And it certainly means that they are called in question. There is no point in dogmatic thinking and speaking if in it all systematic clarity and certainty is not challenged by the fact that the content of the Word of God is God's work and activity, and therefore God's free grace, which as such escapes our comprehension and control, upon which, reckoning with it in faith, we can only meditate, and for which we can only hope. It is not from an external attack of doubt or criticism, but from its own very concrete focal point and foundation, from the source of all Christian and therefore dogmatic certitude, that all its insights and first principles, the nexus of its axioms and inferences derive ; and even these statements are constantly questioned both as a whole and in detail, and their temporariness and incompleteness exposed. The focal point and foundation themselves determine that in dogmatics strictly speaking there are no comprehensive views, no final conclusions and results. There is only the investigation and teaching which take place in the act of dogmatic work and which, strictly speaking, must continually begin again at the beginning in every point. The best and most significant thing that is done in this matter is that again and again we are directed to look back to the centre and foundation of it all.

In this work—it cannot be otherwise in view of its object—we have to do with the question of truth. It is, therefore, inevitable that as a whole and in detail the aim must be definiteness and coherence, and it is to be hoped that the definiteness and sequence of the truth will actually be disclosed. But this being the case, is it not also inevitable that " something like a system " will assert itself more or less spontaneously in dogmatic work ? Why, then, should a " system " be so utterly abhorrent ? If it asserts itself spontaneously in this way, can it not be forgiven ? And if so, why should we be frightened away by a law forbidding systems ? May it not be that a " system " which asserts itself spontaneously (not as a system, but as a striving for definiteness and coherence) signifies obedience and is therefore a shadow of the truth ? It may well be so. But even in this case the danger is still there. The fact that unauthorised systematisation may be forgiven does not mean that the tendency to systematisation is authorised. Nor does the fact that even in the fatal form of an intrinsically unauthorised systematisation true obedience may finally be demonstrated and a shadow of the truth disclosed.

Concretely applied, all this means that the unfolding and presentation of the content of the Word of God must take place fundamentally in such a way that the Word of God is understood as the centre and foundation of dogmatics and of Church proclamation, like a circle whose periphery forms the starting-point for a limited number of lines which in dogmatics are to be drawn to a certain distance in all directions. The fundamental lack of principle in the dogmatic method is clear from the fact that it does not proceed from the centre but from the periphery of the circle or, metaphor apart, from the self-positing and self-authenticating Word of God. From this starting-point, it will draw only a limited number of lines, and even these only to a certain distance ; and it will refrain from drawing a second circle round the whole—or, metaphor apart, it will refrain from presenting the whole as a whole. The basis is given in the fact that the Word of God, which is the event of God's work and activity, does actually speak in all directions, and that therefore, like the periphery of a circle, something is said in all directions which can and must be heard and repeated. But because it has this basis, the repetition can lay no claims to completeness, either in the sense of attempting to draw the total number of theoretically possible lines from the centre or circumference of the circle, and thus saying all that it is theoretically possible to say as an account of the content of the Word of God ; or in the sense of attempting to extend these lines infinitely, and thus giving the account exhaustively in detail ; or again in the sense of attempting to draw an outer circle corresponding to the first (and therefore infinite), and thus trying to declare conclusively what the work and activity of God is and is not. The prohibition and the practical impossibility of doing all these things are obviously correlative. But it is important that we should recognise this practical impossibility as correlative with a prohibition, in order to understand the prohibition itself as the reverse side of the positive command that dogmatics and Church proclamation must not declare the Word of God so much as serve it, and that therefore they have to declare, and declare only, what is in fact revealed to us by the work and activity of God in His Word. When this is what dogmatics teaches, its teaching is pure and exemplary : and it is a summons to the whole Church to do, and to do only, what it may not leave undone. Dogmatic method is only genuinely method, and therefore a path, a plan, an order, a programme, it only goes to the heart of things, and is therefore different from a shoreless, rudderless cogitation and chattering, when it allows the starting-point for some of these lines and axioms to be prescribed for it by the object of Church proclamation, when it then goes on to draw them out under the sovereign control of the object itself and the guidance of what it has to say about itself, or, that is to say, when it goes on to understand and explain, speaking where it thinks it hears the object itself speak, silent where it thinks it silent, pushing on where the object guides, halting where it can only go forward under its own arbitrary self-guidance. The autonomy of dogmatics consists in the decision to be radical in this sense, and concretely to accept whatever basic tenets it may involve.

From a historical point of view, it may be said, therefore, that we have to dismiss the so-called " analytic " method which made its entry into Protestant theology at the beginning of the 17th century, and finally received expression in the doctrine of fundamental articles. We must return to the method of the *Loci*, the method of Melanchthon and also of Calvin, which was wrongly set aside as unscholarly by the more progressive of the contemporaries of J. Gerhard and A. Polanus. For this is the only truly scholarly method in dogmatics. The *Loci* of the older orthodoxy were in fact basic dogmatic tenets which did not pretend to proceed from a higher unity than that of the Word of God itself, or to express any higher syntheses than arise out of the Word of God, or to be rooted and held together in any higher system than that of the Word of God. When it was supposed that they were no longer enough it was not realised that the true basis of dogmatics and Church proclamation was in process of being lost. In dogmatics, too, the truth comes home inexorably : it cannot save its life by willing to do so ; it can save it only by losing it for the sake of the name which alone can and will rule in the Church and therefore in dogmatics too.

In accordance with what we have said, the concrete decision for individual tenets in the understanding and elucidation of which the dogmatic unfolding and presentation of the content of the Word of God must be carried out will involve both obedience and daring : obedience, because it can be inspired by the object alone ; daring, because in every attempt at dogmatic work our own free decision must come into play. As obedience it must consist in a well-founded decision, a proposition to be made in full responsibility ; as daring it cannot claim for itself the absolute necessity and binding force of the Word of God, but only that of a humanly grounded choice, a proposition made in human responsibility.

Now that we have clarified the sense both positively and critically, we turn to our final task, the exposition of the dogmatic method here to be followed.

In this matter, we must take as our starting-point the fact that the work and activity of God in His Word is identical with what we have described as the first form of the Word of God, namely, God's self-revelation. In revealing Himself to us, God has dealings with us. Church proclamation has to give an account of this, which is also the material task of dogmatics. But God's self-revelation, and therefore His work and dealings with us, is Jesus Christ as the positive relation which has now been once for all effected between God and man : God's gracious lordship over men. Because God's revelation stands in a definite victorious relationship to human darkness, and because God's gracious lordship consists in an overcoming of human rebellion and human need, revelation is in fact the same thing as atonement : the act of God in which He triumphantly transcends the human contradiction and thus turns the need of man to his salvation.

Should we not halt at this equation and continue thus : the Word of God which Church proclamation and dogmatics has to teach is the Word of atonement ? If anything else seems to present itself as a further content of the Word distinct from this, is it not really only a presupposition and consequence of this first thing, which is the one true and central theme of both Church proclamation and dogmatics ? Is it not merely a predicate behind this subject, a numerator to this denominator, or indeed a nought behind this one ? Is it not the case, then, that dogmatic method, the *omnia tractare sub ratione Dei*, should consist in unfolding and presenting the recognition of the atonement which has taken place in Jesus Christ ? Ought it not to be a Christology in this rather limited sense, a subordination and assimilation of all other insights to the account of this one happening on which they essentially depend ? The possibility seems very tempting and illuminating. Not only does the Reformation understanding of the Word of God seem to urge us in this direction ; the Bible itself seems to be only a single account of this event. We hesitate, no doubt, when we consider that the whole of the modern Protestant movement, from its beginning in the older orthodoxy, has actually taken this direction. But surely this fact alone does not prove that the right dogmatic method is to be sought along these lines ? Again, it is quite clear that if we do decide along these lines, we shall be committing ourselves irresistibly to the way of a system, or to the way towards a system. In atonement and its corresponding idea, we shall have attained one fundamental interpretation of revelation and of the content of the Word of God, one point of vantage from which everything else can be surveyed and ordered, from which everything else will necessarily appear and become a dependent whole consisting of statements and their implicates. But if this is the case, how far will the Word of God itself be exercising control over dogmatics and Church proclamation ? Where will be the vacant place at the centre of all Church teaching ? If, however, the Word of God itself really urges us along this path, pressing upon us this fundamental view and its accompanying system, it is certainly not for us to persist in this scruple and to try to follow some other way because of a systematic objection to systematisation. But it can be shown that the Word of God itself does not urge us along this path. On the contrary, although the course may seem very illuminating at a first glance, it actually restrains us from it. It is true enough that in the account which Church proclamation and dogmatics have to give of the work and activity of God their business is wholly with the work and activity of God in His Son Jesus Christ. It is in Him and Him alone that the Father is revealed. It is He and He alone whom the Holy Spirit reveals. Therefore dogmatics must actually be Christology and only Christology : but not Christology in this rather limited sense of the term ; not as if the revelation of the Father by the Son and of the Son by the Holy Spirit is in fact identical with the action of God in overcoming human rebellion and human need. It is incontestable that it is this too, even at its very centre. But it is not only this. It is this at its centre. But it is also more than this, and with such weighty authority and independence that although as more it is only to be understood together with this centre and with constant reference to it, it cannot be understood from this centre, as though the latter were a vantage point which the dogmatician himself could adopt, or as though it were given us as a fundamental principle of interpretation by means of which the whole could be understood, surveyed and ordered. Jesus Christ is given to us as the Word spoken by the Father. But it in no way follows that the atonement is singled out specially or *in abstracto*. The atonement is only one moment in the whole happening which is—and again we can only say, also—described in this way. Undeniably it forms the centre of this happening. Undeniably the Bible shows it to be the centre. And in the Reformation its positive meaning was recognised with new power. But we cannot isolate this moment. We cannot make it the centre of a system. If we do, we may give the other moments in this happening their proper value in the system constructed, but we shall still be guilty of a limitation of Christology itself which is not justified at any rate by its object.

But, above all, is it really possible to integrate the subject of this happening, God Himself, into a systematisation of it ? Have we been speaking of the real, divine reconciliation, when we have appraised God only as a factor within it ? The statement that God is God, that He is the Lord, does mean, of course, and at its very heart, that in victorious opposition to the opposition of man, and as a victorious helper in distress, God is his Reconciler. But the whole meaning of the statement is not comprised in this function. The statement is true of God's dealings in reconciliation. But it is at the same time independently true in itself. It is true of God's dealings in reconciliation, but not only of this. It is true of God's other dealings. It is to be recognised and understood as independently true in itself, because otherwise it is not recognised and understood as true also of God's dealings in reconciliation. In a faithful account of God's work and dealings, the truth that God is God must not be expressed only as a premise or implicate, or the commentary on a doctrine of the atonement. Certainly we must not lose sight even for a single moment of the truth of the atonement. But we must still express it as an independent affirmation, as a line which has to be drawn on its own account, and therefore in a special doctrine of God which is not subordinated to a doctrine of the atonement. Already, then, a dogmatics which is only a system of atonement seems to be excluded from this standpoint. As a doctrine of the atonement, at the very least it will have to be a doctrine of God as well. But, of course, we do just as little justice to the content of the Word of God if we try perhaps to reduce it to the doctrine of God itself, or to the doctrine of God's kingdom and lordship. In itself this, too, does perhaps appear to be quite illuminating and tempting. It will give us a dogmatics dominated perhaps by the concept of the freedom or sovereignty of God, of the *gloria Dei*, of predestination, of God's rule in His Word. All other divine truths, the truths of creation, atonement and redemption, will then appear and have to be valued as expositions of this fundamental truth, as the individual decrees and works of the *Deus Pantokrator*. It is certainly not easy to see why a powerful and impressive dogmatic system should not be built up on the basis of this fundamental principle. It could be very christological, and in it a legitimate and convincing appeal could be made to the Bible and the Reformers. But, again, it involves violence to the real content of God's Word. It is indeed undeniable that the Godhead of God is, in fact, the central truth in the biblical message. But that does not mean that this truth is, so to speak, placed in our hands as a key to all other truths, or that what is said to us in the Word of God raises us even momentarily to a position from which we can command all other truths. It is not the case that the absolutely dominating function of the concept of God in the biblical message authorises us to sketch out a metaphysic of the divine, in face of which all that God does according to this message appears and can be treated as a more or less necessary or contingent series of consequences. Who and what God is, His freedom, His sovereignty, and His glory cannot, of course, be merely the content of a premise or conclusion to the doctrine of the atonement, nor can it be merely provisionally, incidentally or consequentially included in the framework of an exposition of what takes place between the gracious God and sinful man. As the content of an independent primary affirmation, it is not an *a priori* to this happening or to any other acts of God. Basically it is to be understood, not before or above, but only in and with the recognition of the whole action of God—as Reconciler, but also as Creator and Redeemer. If, then, the doctrine of God cannot legitimately be subordinated or assimilated to these other elements of the doctrine of the truth of God, it may be very tempting to set it systematically above them, but the only genuine alternative is to set it alongside and co-ordinate it with them, taking care not to destroy their independence.

The same applies to the truth that God is Creator. Where else is it to be recognised but in God's reconciling action ? But is it exhausted in this action ? Can it be understood only as an unaccented beat or preface to the doctrine of the atonement ? Is it not, in fact, its supreme, independent presupposition ? Is man not a man before he is a sinner, and a pardoned sinner ? Must he not exist in order to be the object of atonement ? Must not God also be understood as His Creator before He can be understood as His Reconciler ? These questions are sufficiently serious to make it clear from this standpoint too that dogmatics cannot be a system of atonement. But now the relation between the two threatens to be reversed, and again in a most illuminating and inviting way. May it not be that we have here the basic plan of our knowledge of the content of the Word of God ? It is no accident that just at this point (from Aristotle to Heidegger) philosophy makes its bid with the challenge to interpret the whole action of God towards man in His Word as a series of modifications of the basic relationship between God and the creature, between self-existent and contingent, infinite and finite, absolute and relative being. Is the atonement anything more than the realisation and fulfilment of creation ? Is redemption anything more than its completion ? From this point of view, too, the proposal to systematise is genuinely tempting, and again it can easily appeal to the Bible and the Reformers, to say nothing of St. Augustine and St. Thomas. The doctrine of creation enables us to construct a concept of man and his destiny : it may be in cosmic terms or individual, in naturalistic or spiritual, in idealistic or existentialist, with or without regard to the I-Thou relation, with or without natural theology. The doctrine of creation will also give us a doctrine of law. The notion of law acquired in this way can then be presupposed as a dogmatic principle of interpretation. But then we can boldly declare that what the Bible says about atonement and redemption is simply a description of the fulfilment and consummation of this law of creation. Even God the Lord can then be dissolved in the comprehensive idea of the truth and necessity of this law in its consummation, and the action of God is simply the preservation and teleological striving of what He has created, or concretely the confirmation of human existence, however it may be understood. In particular, the idea of Jesus Christ dissolves into a concept of grace, completing the law of creation as variously interpreted. Is the truth that God is the Creator not great and powerful enough to permit and even to command this dissolution of all other truth in it as the one ultimate truth ? Why do we not decide to adopt a system of this kind, since in any case we cannot too highly commend it for moral and political usefulness ? We do not adopt it simply because, measured against the real content of the Word, it too—and especially—involves a flagrant act of violence. It is true that the truth of God in His Word is also the truth of God the Creator, and we have also to consider it as such. It is true that in the light of this truth we have to see and understand man, not merely as sinner and pardoned sinner, but, in order to realise what this means, as an existence created by God. And over and above this we have also to see and understand God as the Redeemer of man, and therefore man as called to a state of being on the far side of his conflict with God and his own conquest by the atonement. But the point is that in the relationship of Creator and creature neither God nor man is known to us in such a way as to put an *a priori* at our disposal on the basis of which we can apprehend the possibility and necessity of atonement and redemption, and from this infer the doctrine of atonement and of redemption, and then the doctrine of God, as well, as a premise and consequence. If atonement cannot be understood apart from creation, and if God is only to be known in creation *and* atonement, the converse is equally true that the person and nature of God the Creator, and the nature of human existence and its determining law, can be known materially and formally only in the atonement, in the incarnation, death and resurrection of Jesus Christ, in the new life, in justification and sanctification, in the sacrament and faith. And, again, the knowledge of God the Creator and the Reconciler is wholly dependent on the understanding of the divinity, freedom and sovereignty of God. If this is not independent truth, to be recognised as such, there can be no truth or knowledge of truth in relation to God the Creator. It is because there is this independent truth and knowledge of truth, which cannot be integrated into a system of creation, that there is also not a subordinate but an independent doctrine of God the Creator alongside the doctrine of God as such and alongside the doctrine of God the Reconciler.

And now it obviously remains to consider the final truth : God is the Redeemer. He who has made man and reconciled him to Himself, encounters him in His Word in order that He may be his entire future, fulfilling and consummating what is promised in His creative and reconciling work. Again, this has to be recognised in the action of God as Creator and Reconciler. It is only here that He meets us clearly as the God of everlasting faithfulness, who neither seeks us, nor allows Himself to be sought by us, without allowing us to find Him. But redemption does not simply dissolve into atonement. It is not a matter of course that a *regnum gloriae* follows the *regnum gratiae*. It is not a matter of course that God will also be our entire and perfect future. It is not a matter of course that Jesus Christ comes again and that in His Holy Spirit we may have here and now the pledge of His faithfulness and coming. Eschatology, then, cannot and must not be considered and treated merely as an appendix to the doctrine of the atonement. Jesus Christ in His New Testament totality can really be understood only as this Saviour who is to come. If He is not the One who comes, He is not the One who has already come. If the atonement which has taken place in Him is not understood in the future sense, it cannot be understood in the perfect tense, which means that it cannot be understood at all. Our regeneration, justification and sanctification, the Church and the sacrament, the whole existence and the whole work of Jesus Christ in the present are eschatological, i.e., they are actual only in the coming Redeemer. What can we have here in this present which we do not have in hope ? But when we have said this, we have to remember that here, too, a reversal is possible. A system can be constructed of which the central fact is that God's action is that of One who is not yet present, His kingdom is only future, the Church is distinctive only as contrasted with this coming kingdom, the life of the Church and believers is a mere expectation and hastening forward, the whole reality of the atonement is the precipitation of man into a state of longing which is never more than longing, and faith is a vacuum and nothing more. Viewed from an eschatological centre of this kind, creation recedes into the dim distance, perhaps in a very distorting light, with the fall and the present need in the forefront. From this point of view again, the doctrine of God inevitably acquires the character of a massive postulate. It is, of course, impossible to overlook the fact that God in His Word is also the coming Redeemer. And this fact can easily make a consistently eschatological systematisation of dogmatics appear a very illuminating and tempting possibility. It does not need to be proved that the Bible and especially the New Testament give plenty of encouragement to adopt this course. And if among the Reformers we find little or no inducement to an eschatologically centred dogmatics, we have to remember that their attitude to the last things was the weakest aspect of their doctrine, and the least worthy of imitation, so that we certainly cannot regard ourselves as bound by them. Why should we not actually adopt this course—perhaps by way of reaction to a powerful and dangerous systematisation of creation ? We certainly could, if obedience to the Word of God allowed arbitrary reactions of this kind. But aberrations on any side, and therefore on this side, obviously cannot be permitted if our concern is with a faithful account of the content of the Word of God. In the living Word the effected atonement does not evaporate into a longing for the coming redemption, nor the Church into the coming kingdom of God, nor faith into hope, nor recollection into expectation. Again, in the living Word creation does not withdraw into a dualistic distance or even contradiction. And in the living Word it is quite impossible that God, the subject of the whole process, should acquire the character of a postulate guaranteeing the initiation of the great future transformation. Gratitude and longing, patience and impatience, final peace and final disquietude, fidelity to the Church and a passionate desire for the new æon : these will not neutralise and blunt each other in a thinking and speaking that are controlled by the living Word of

God, nor, on the other hand, will they release each other in such a way that the one will express itself unrestrainedly to the exclusion of the other. In a co-existence that is to be neither resolved nor suspended, they will form the thinking and speaking appropriate to Christianity and to the Church. For this reason the doctrine of redemption cannot become the centre of a system. For this reason it must be accompanied by the doctrine of God, the doctrine of creation and the doctrine of atonement. It must not be subordinated or superordinated, but co-ordinated with them in a real union by reason of their common origin and end in the Word of God. It cannot be an *a priori* any more than they can. Along with them it can only be related to the *a priori* which by its very nature is not a principle that we can control, and never can be, but has instead all the qualities of a genuine *a priori*.

At all four points, the Word of God itself provides the basis of our knowledge, and similarly the coherence of the lines which we have to draw from these four points (with a hint, but only a hint, at infinity). At the centre, in the Word of God itself as the original point from which they diverge, they are one. But inevitably this point from which they proceed remains invisible. It cannot be the function of either Church proclamation or dogmatics to try to effect their union, or to use its own power or fancy to initiate it. The aim of initiating the unity of dogmatics is one which never has been and never will be accomplished except as one of the four given points throws the other three more or less into the shade, thus doing violence to the real content of the Word of God, not least in the particular point emphasised. If we keep these points separate and distinct and allow the lines that are to be drawn from them to retain their independence of each other, we are in no sense guilty of an arbitrary dismemberment of the one Word of God. That this is one in the *actus purissimus* of its actualisation by God, which is identical with the *actus purissimus* of the existence of the Trinity, is a truth which Church proclamation and dogmatics recognise when they renounce the attempt to usurp a kind of transcendent vantage point in the existence of God Himself. It is in this way, in differentiation, that the Word and the existence of God are revealed to us, that God grounds the knowledge of Himself, even the knowledge of Himself in His unity. This distinction and independence of the four *Loci* arises from the fact of the self-revelation of the one and triune God. If God Himself does not become entangled in contradictions by the fact that His *actus purissimus* in revelation is completed in time, if this act of condescension, so far from injuring His majesty, illuminates and authenticates it just where it most needs illumination and authentication, namely, in relation to His creature, if Church proclamation and dogmatics are really concerned to show how God really reveals Himself, that is, in time—which does not mean that He is untrue to Himself, but genuinely and altogether true—they for

29

their part do not need to fear that they are guilty of unreal distinctions and involved in contradictions if they follow closely the divine process of self-revelation. The disloyalty will be if they try to be wiser than God, creating an image of Him according to the measure of what we men call unity. So, then, we need not excuse and deplore as a necessary imperfection of human thinking and speaking the distinction and independence of the *Loci*: *De Deo, De creatione, De reconciliatione, De redemptione.* This determination of the method of dogmatics has as much or as little to do with the necessary limits of human creaturely knowledge as has the whole order in which faith and the knowledge of faith occur. If we accept the single presupposition that it has pleased God and still pleases Him to reveal Himself to man in His Word and to awaken him to faith in Him, then, in the fact that we hold to the way in which the process of revelation has actually taken place, we need not see an imperfection of our knowledge which we have to deplore and over the frontiers of which we have continually to peep and strain. The thing itself commits us to this order. How, then, can it be imperfect ? Obviously, only to the extent that we certainly never do keep to it as it intends. If in its essential character a course is prescribed to us by the matter in hand as the only one that is possible and legitimate, we cannot regard it merely as a concession to human weakness. We have to value it as a course which, in spite of human weakness, and in conflict with it, is perfect and right and good in virtue of its origin. And we have to adopt it wholeheartedly and with real confidence.

At this point we must not overlook an objection which may be raised from the opposite side, namely, our own presupposition that dogmatics should be systematically without presuppositions. The question arises whether behind the unfolding of the content of this Word of God in these four specific *Loci*, there is not implied a fundamental principle from which these four *Loci* may be systematically developed, viz., the dogma of the unity and trinity of God, which we have placed at the head of our doctrine of the Word as the revelation of God. In §§ 10–12 we thought it necessary to understand God in His revelation as Creator, Mediator and Redeemer in order to see as the foundation of this threefold division of His self-revealing action the fact that in Himself and to all eternity God is Father, Son and Holy Spirit. But this is itself the essential answer to the question. For we did not derive our differentiation of the *Loci* from the doctrine of the Trinity. We derived the doctrine of the Trinity itself from the same source as that from which is now derived the differentiation of the *Loci*, viz., the work and activity of God in His revelation. The content of the doctrine of the Trinity which the Church has formulated and dogmatics has to repeat and Church proclamation respect is not that God in His relation to man is Creator, Mediator and Redeemer, but that God in Himself is eternally God the Father, Son and Holy Spirit. The doctrine of the Trinity, opposing dangerous and destructive errors, affirms securely that even in this differentiation of God in His revelation—not merely in a hiddenness of God over and above His revelation, but because in His hiddenness, genuinely in His revelation too— we have to do with God Himself. It affirms securely that in the Father, the Son and the Holy Spirit, as they meet us in His revelation as Creator, Mediator and Redeemer, we have to do with the essence and the truth of the living God, not with mere appearances or emanations, not with demi-gods or deified creatures. The doctrine of the Trinity, like all other doctrines, is preceded by the fact of revelation itself and as such. The essence of this fact is that God confronts us as Creator, Mediator and Redeemer, that as such He speaks and deals with us, that He is therefore God and Lord in this threefold way. This being of God in His work and activity is not a dogma, or a basic view, or a controllable principle which can be used as such for the construction of a system. It is the actuality of the Word of God, freely preceding and underlying all views and dogmas. We attained our differentiation of the *Loci* by reference to this actuality and not to the doctrine of Trinity, although inevitably it both confirms the latter, and is itself confirmed by it, and safeguarded against misunderstandings. How can we affirm so definitely the interconnexion and yet also the independence of the doctrines of creation, atonement and redemption, if we are not instructed by the doctrine of the Trinity itself that the *opera trinitatis ad extra sunt indivisa*, and that the Father, Son and Holy Spirit as we recognise them in these *opera* are independent modes of the being of God Himself, and therefore irreducible to any higher unity? The organising and controlling centre of dogmatics is not, then, the doctrine of the Trinity, but it stands outside the series of *Loci* to which the doctrine of the Trinity belongs, as part of the doctrine of God. For we consider and treat the doctrine of God, which cannot be exhausted in the doctrine of the Trinity, as an independent *Locus* alongside the doctrines of creation, atonement and redemption. We have to do this because this Subject God Himself cannot be dissolved into His work and activity, but wills to be known and recognised as this Subject in this work and activity, if His work and activity is rightly to be seen and understood as His. In dogmatics it is impossible to speak only incidentally of the God who is Himself the Giver, the Giving and the Gift all in one. He cannot be treated as a mere appendage to His work and activity as such if this work and activity is rightly to be interpreted. Necessarily the insight already attained in the doctrine of the Trinity will be presupposed and applied in the doctrine of God. Yet it is not the doctrine of the Trinity in itself, but again the work and activity of God that even this doctrine can only attest, which also forms the source of the doctrine of God, or the other constituent elements which have to be expounded under this head. Since, then, the doctrine of God is a fourth point, not above but beside the three others, the impression can and must be destroyed that at every point we have to do with a system of trinitarian doctrine. In these circumstances it is almost superfluous to state and explain our inability to approve the course adopted by many modern dogmaticians (P. K. Marheineke, A. Schweizer, H. Martensen, T. Häring, M. Rade, cf. I, 1, p. 319), who with more or less inward justification and consistency have constructed their dogmatics according to a trinitarian plan.

There still remains the question of the order in which the four *Loci* mentioned are to be treated in dogmatics. We remember that in this whole matter we stand in the sphere of freedom as true obedience and obedience as true freedom. When there has to be a choice, a responsible choice, here again the decisive rule will be that the order must be both as unpretentious and also as meaningful as possible. Unpretentious, because we must be careful that the systematising which has been expelled may not re-enter at the back door by the choice of an order of treatment. Significant, because the choice of this or that particular order must have a didactic end. In itself every order can be possible, permissible and useful. And, of course, every order can also be pretentious, i.e., it can be selected and followed with the deliberate intention of systematising. But this is the very thing which must not happen. It must be avoided in every possible choice. From this point of view, it is therefore highly suspicious to wish to begin with creation, or atonement, or redemption, however possible and permissible and interesting all this may be. For it is just the particularly "interesting" thing which we ought not to seek and select. If one of these three is given precedence, the interesting thing may easily be to bring everything else into the framework of the possible and inviting system which, as we have seen, this doctrine suggests. On the other hand, to begin with the doctrine of God can easily arouse the suspicion that the characterisation of the subject of the divine work and activity involves the construction of a kind of key-position, whereas, if this doctrine forms the aim and end of the whole, gathering up the results of the three other parts, it will have a position which is unpretentious but at the same time significant. But the danger of systematising one of the other three, which will then have to be given the precedence, is greater than the danger of systematising the doctrine of God, because the really pressing temptations to make dogmatics the development of a basic view find far stronger weapons of attack in the various aspects of the concrete work and activity of God. There seems no reason why the doctrine of God itself should not stand very unpretentiously at the head. It can certainly do so meaningfully, more so didactically, than any other part. For after all, it is easier to speak about creation, atonement and redemption if there is an existing understanding concerning the One about whom it has all to be said, than it is if this decisive factor has continually to be provisionally supplied or anticipated. Our own decision, then, following the classical tradition of dogmatics, is to begin with the doctrine of God. Even in this position its content need not be an empty speculation nor its purpose a systematisation. Is there anything more unpretentious than the affirmation that God is God, which is what we shall have to discuss in this first section? And can anything be more meaningful and sensible than to begin with this beginning? When we begin in this way the dangers arising from the absolutising of each of the succeeding sections are to some extent warded off. To put the doctrine of God first in dogmatics necessarily exercises on everything that follows a calming and levelling effect. Excited and arbitrary action and reaction are restrained from the very outset. And the result is that after this beginning the treatment of the other sections can be continued in relative security. But having begun in this way, will it not be clearest and most unobjectionable to follow the, so to speak, natural pragmatic order which we have always so far observed in speaking of these three aspects of God's work and activity: creation, atonement and redemption? Here, too, then, we find ourselves in the footsteps of classical dogmatics, and it is obvious that this way is simply following the way of the creed, so that it is easy to clear ourselves of the suspicion of aiming at anything special or distinctive, and in the movement of thought along this way we can most safely use the teaching which each doctrine implies for all the others.

We conclude with a brief and hurried survey of the contents of dogmatics as it shapes itself on the presupposition of the decision taken.

1. In the doctrine of God we shall have to examine and expound the whole content of the Word, the whole work and activity of God in His Son Jesus Christ, from the standpoint of an investigation of the characteristic being and attributes of God as Subject. Our theme, then, will be the deity and sovereignty of God—not, of course, in abstraction from His activity, but the being of God Himself in the light of His activity. Four great complexes of questions and answers will engage our attention in this regard. First there is the question of the reality, the possibility and the actual realisation of a true knowledge of God founded upon revelation. Next, there is the question of the statements in which the content of this knowledge is to be expressed as a knowledge of the reality (of the " being " and " attributes ") of God. The third question concerns the unfolding of the Christian insight into the fundamental attitude of God to man as grounded in the freedom of God, and therefore the development of the doctrine of God's election of grace. The last question concerns the same fundamental relation of God to man as implying the exercise of a claim over man, and consisting in a divine command. At this point, in proper connexion with dogmatics, we shall have to lay the foundation of theological ethics as a doctrine of the knowledge and reality of the divine commandment.

2. The doctrine of creation is concerned with the understanding of the Word of God and therefore of God's Son Jesus Christ as the Word which concerns and confronts us in our very existence as men, because it is the Word of Him through whom our existence, and the existence of all that is not Himself, is created, maintained and controlled, because God's sovereignty, whatever else it may mean for us, always means primarily the absolute origin from which we come, no matter what may become of us, and what we may make of ourselves, as those who once were not, now are, and one day will be no more. Three great circles must be described here : first, God's being and activity as Creator in relation to His creature as such and to His creation in general ; then man, his insight as God's creature, his destiny as the focal point of creation, and the (lost) righteousness of his own decision, corresponding to his position in creation ; lastly—and here theological ethics begins—the absolute authority with which God claims and commands man, because His command is the command of our Creator, because we are claimed already by the very fact that we exist, and because this claim determines our existence, and therefore affects already our being and life as such.

3. With the doctrine of the atonement, we come to the real centre —not the systematic, but the actual centre—of dogmatics and Church proclamation. God the Mediator is the present, the absolute present, in which we find ourselves as hearers of God's Word. The atonement is the ratification and confirmation of the covenant into which God has entered with man by creation, and which cannot be destroyed by the faithlessness of man, but only the more clearly displayed by the faithfulness of God in face of that faithlessness. The Word of God and therefore God's Son Jesus Christ as the Word of atonement is the sovereignty of God asserting itself all the more emphatically and gloriously against the opposition of man. The Word of atonement comprehends man as fallen, but even more as upheld, as the enemy, but even more the beloved of God, as the rebel whom God never ceases to know as His servant, whom now for the first time He really calls His child with all the power of His regenerating Holy Spirit. Four great circles will concern us here. The first is the covenant between God and man which God ratifies and confirms ; it is only at this point, and therefore from the very outset in the light of the doctrine of grace, that we shall have to think of its corresponding shadow, and therefore develop the doctrine of sin. The second is the objective fact of the divine atonement in the person and work of the divine-human Mediator Jesus Christ. The third is man's subjective appropriation of the atonement by the presence of Jesus Christ in the Holy Spirit within the sphere of the Church, on the path marked out for man by the sacraments of baptism and the Lord's Supper, by his calling, justification, sanctification and perseverance. Finally, theological ethics must complete a second turn, the fact that man is claimed by the command of God, because it now encounters us as those who are placed under the judgment of God but also accepted by the grace of God, because it now comes to us as the Law of God, exposing and punishing our sin, but also healing and restoring us, because now in the Church our fellow-man becomes our neighbour and brother, who in his own need has for us the significance of a duty and an aid, declaring the commandment of God.

4. Lastly, in the doctrine of Redemption we must let the Word of God and God's Son Jesus Christ speak to us as the Word of Him who is not only the absolute origin as Creator but also the absolute end towards which we move. God the Redeemer is the First who is also the Last, whose kingdom comes as the kingdom of discord vanquished and destroyed, in the dawning of a new heaven and a new earth. Thus the Word of God as the Word of redemption comprehends man from the standpoint of the eternal, i.e., the completed and already consummated lordship of God. Man is shadowed by death as the destruction of all that he now is. But, because in Jesus Christ death has been swallowed up in victory, he is illuminated by His resurrection as the revelation of the life of God, the promise of resurrection and

eternal life towards which he, too, may now advance. Three circles
will have to be drawn here. The first is the life of man in hope in
which the objective content of faith, Jesus Christ, is present. The
second is the content of this faith as the content of the promise and
its future realisation. And the last—it is only in this eschatological
context that theological ethics can attain its goal—is the claim made
upon man by the command of God because according to the promise
we are heirs, expectant of eternal life in God's kingdom, because by
this command of God the consummation is held out, ascribed and
even appropriated, because we are inevitably summoned by God's
command not merely to live and bow before the Word, but, living and
bowing before His Word, to advance towards a genuine, qualitatively
and indeed infinitely better future.

These are the things which dogmatics has to say about the content
of the Word and therefore about the work and activity of God. God
is active in His Word ; therefore dogmatics must remain bound to
His Word, and can undertake only to give an account of that which
is revealed in the Word of God as the past, present and future activity
of God, of that which is an event in the Word, with all the force of
what occurred yesterday, occurs to-day and will occur to-morrow.
And God's Word is His Son Jesus Christ. Therefore in the most
comprehensive sense of the term dogmatics can and must be understood as Christology. In all four stages of its development it must
always remember that it can legitimately speak only of the God and
the work and activity of the God who is the revelation of the Father
in Jesus Christ by the Holy Spirit. This means that we know in
advance the origin and nature of all possible sources of error which
may come into operation in the course of our investigation and exposition. It means also that we know the rule, the observance of which
will enable us to avoid every possible error. But we know too that,
because all errors are necessarily errors at this one point, the decisive
corrective is not to be expected from a kind of human circumspection
or precision in the observance of this rule, but only from this same
point, namely, from the object of dogmatics itself. In this respect,
too, dogmatics must not try to adopt any other attitude than that, as
already shown, of the teaching Church, within which it has not only
a critical but also a positive task, that of calling the Church to bear
new witness to God's revelation. As it does this, and does it in such
a way as to be itself claimed by the object confronting the teaching
Church, it is itself exposed to the same danger as the Church. The
danger is even greater than that in which the rest of the teaching
Church stands, for dogmatics dares and must dare to comprehend and
present this object as a whole. Obviously, as we have seen, it is
particularly threatened at this point by the danger of systematisation ;
and systematisation means self-will, and self-will error. We are involved here in a relative movement away from exegesis. And even a

relative movement away from exegesis is dangerous. But it is not made arbitrarily. We know that it is necessary because for Church proclamation itself the purpose of exegesis is address, and the significance of *explicatio* is *applicatio*. Is it not necessarily the case that Church proclamation itself makes an even greater movement away from exegesis? But the danger which Church proclamation thereby incurs does not constitute a prohibition. It must have the courage to incur this danger. It must cherish the hope not to stumble. This being the case, dogmatics cannot be prohibited from effecting the transitional step from *explicatio* to *applicatio* and therefore venturing to comprehend and express the object as a whole. In that it effects this mediating step from exegesis to address and application, and as a reminder of the wholeness of the object of Church proclamation, dogmatics is the call to the Church to venture what must be ventured, what, in view of the promise given to the Church, ought not to remain unventured. But the danger remains, and it is a particular danger to dogmatics. Therefore it must not be forgotten. What we have to remember is that the autonomy of dogmatic thinking and speaking cannot be a primary but only a secondary autonomy. It can be only a function of the theonomy which alone founds and maintains, justifies and sanctifies both the Church and dogmatics. The autonomy of dogmatic thinking, in which we must venture to decide for a particular dogmatic method as we have now done, implies, denotes and signifies (like its heteronomy, of which we spoke in the last section) the autonomy of the Holy Spirit. It is we who think and speak. And in dogmatics we ought to—no, must speak, just as in Church proclamation, too, it is man who is summoned, authorised and empowered to exercise his own thinking and speaking by the grace of God. But not even for a moment can we forget that, when and in so far as we do think and speak the truth in Church proclamation and dogmatics, it is God Himself and alone who, using man as His servant, and without incurring any obligation to him, has actually thought *His* thoughts and spoken *His* word. It is only in this modesty that we do think and speak the truth. And this modesty includes the realisation that in God's light we are shown to be darkness, in God's judgment we are exposed as liars, and that we shall think and speak the truth always against our own selves.

The Church dogmatician, like the Church preacher, will always have to say of himself what Ignatius of Antioch once wrote of himself: ᾿Εὰν γὰρ σιωπήσητε ἀπ᾽ ἐμοῦ, ἐγὼ λόγος θεοῦ. ᾿Εὰν δὲ ἐρασθῆτε τῆς σαρκός μου, πάλιν ἔσομαι φωνή (*Ad Rom.* 2¹). In this modesty, which combines the greatest courage and the greatest humility, the greatest awe and the greatest joy, the relationship of the dogmatician and the preacher to their object may be summed up in the words of the Psalmist (Ps. 103¹): "Bless the Lord, O my soul: and all that is within me, bless his holy name."

INDEXES

I. SCRIPTURE REFERENCES

II. NAMES

III. SUBJECTS

901

Church (*continued*)—
visible, 219 f., 226.
Word of God, 214 f., 644, 666, 710, 801.
work of man, as, 213, 347, 690, 807, 845 f., 850 f.
and world, 112, 335, 422, 501 f., 663, 685, 759.
cf. Church Proclamation, Confession, Holy Scripture (Canon), Word of God (three forms).
v. Calvinism, Catholicism, Dogmatics, Holy Spirit, Jesus Christ, Lutheranism, Neo-Protestantism, Revelation, Witness.
Church Proclamation, 162, 229 f., 249, 305, 422 f., 490, 500, 591, 650, 711, 743 ff., 769, 777, 884.
as act of God, 751, 884.
attack on, 753.
Christ as its object, 744, 800, 844, 848.
differences in teaching, 803 ff., 835.
Holy Scripture, 457 ff., 551 ff.
man as its object, 206 ff., 235 ff., 247 f., 293 f., 362 ff., 367, 402 ff., 486.
mission, 771, 883.
office, 760.
orthodoxy ?, 765.
promise, 766, 768, 781, 804, 806, 847, 849, 867.
pure doctrine, 758 ff., 803 ff., 849.
task of, 844.
as word of man, 740 ff., 758, 776, 798.
cf. Church.
v. Dogmatics, Word of God.
Confession, 620 ff.
attack on, 642 f.
authority, 173 f., 625 ff., 634, 640, 647 ff.
churchliness, 622 ff.
content, 641.
criticism, 655.
decision, 629 ff. (*damnamus*).
faith, 624 f., 646 f.
Holy Scripture, 622 f., 624 f., 636, 639, 642, 649.
humanity, 625 ff.
legitimation, 647 f.
limitation, 625 ff.
new, 659 f.
obedience, 635.
occasion of, 628.
origin, 637.
publicity, 639 ff.
relevance, 663 f.
revelation, 657.
text of, 656.
Confessional Churches, Evangelical, 163 f., 168 ff., 604, 609, 632, 831 ff.

Confessional Churches (*continued*)—
Calvinisation ?, 838 f.
tension, 168 ff., 831 ff.
union, 830.
Conscience, 570, 661, 697, 703, 710.
Conversion, 706, 709.
Council, 658.
Creation, 162, 379, 688 f., 872 f.
atonement, 187 f.
preservation, 688 f.
revelation, 37, 43, 162.

Decision, v. Faith.
Docetism, 17 f., 147 f., 163–164, 266, 375, 510, 520, 525.
Dogma, v. Confession.
Dogmatics, 123, 743, 766 ff., 804 ff., 808 f., 824 f., 827.
attitude of, biblical, 816 ff.
confessional, 822 ff., 864.
Church, 839 ff.
autonomy, 857 ff., 866, 884.
and the Church, 770 f., 775 ff., 797, 799 ff., 806 ff., 839 ff.
Christology, 122 f., 871, 882.
content, 366, 881 ff.
v. Atonement, God, Creation, Redemption.
dangers of, 860 ff., 882 ff.
end, 800.
and ethics, 239, 782 ff., 881 ff.
faith, 809, 823, 855, 868.
heteronomy, 815, 857 ff.
material of, 779 f.
method, 853 ff.
freedom of, 861.
norm of, 812 ff.
prayer, 776, 840, 843.
and Church proclamation, 770 f., 775 ff., 798 f., 812 f., 852, 854.
prolegomena, 3, 124, 870 f.
relevance of, 843.
results ?, 769.
scholastic ?, 772
system ?, 861 ff.
task, 766 ff., 775 ff., 781 ff., 804 ff., 808 f.
theonomy, 815, 857 ff., 866.
unity, 877.
cf. Church, Confession, Proclamation.
v. Holy Scripture, Neo-Protestantism, Witness.

Ebionitism, 19 f., 136, 163, 375, 526.
Election, 102, 209 ff., 225, 348, 378, 881.
Enlightenment, 4 ff., 290 f., 291, 292, 560, 785, 828.
Eschatology, v. Redemption.
Eternity, 47 ff.
Ethics, v. Dogmatics.

PRINTED IN GREAT BRITAIN BY
MORRISON AND GIBB LIMITED
LONDON AND EDINBURGH